Cisco ASA
All-in-One Firewall, IPS, Anti-X, and VPN Adaptive Security Appliance, Second Edition

Jazib Frahim, CCIE No. 5459
Omar Santos

Cisco Press
800 East 96th Street
Indianapolis, IN 46240

Cisco ASA: All-in-One Firewall, IPS, Anti-X, and VPN Adaptive Security Appliance, Second Edition

Jazib Frahim, Omar Santos

Published by:
Cisco Press
800 East 96th Street
Indianapolis, IN 46240 USA

Printed in the United States of America

First Printing December 2009

Library of Congress Cataloging-in-Publication data is on file.

ISBN-13: 978-1-58705-819-6

ISBN-10: 1-58705-819-7

Warning and Disclaimer

This book is designed to provide information about Cisco ASA. Every effort has been made to make this book as complete and as accurate as possible, but no warranty or fitness is implied.

The information is provided on an "as is" basis. The authors, Cisco Press, and Cisco Systems, Inc., shall have neither liability nor responsibility to any person or entity with respect to any loss or damages arising from the information contained in this book or from the use of the discs or programs that may accompany it.

The opinions expressed in this book belong to the author and are not necessarily those of Cisco Systems, Inc.

Trademark Acknowledgments

All terms mentioned in this book that are known to be trademarks or service marks have been appropriately capitalized. Cisco Press or Cisco Systems, Inc., cannot attest to the accuracy of this information. Use of a term in this book should not be regarded as affecting the validity of any trademark or service mark.

Corporate and Government Sales

The publisher offers excellent discounts on this book when ordered in quantity for bulk purchases or special sales, which may include electronic versions and/or custom covers and content particular to your business, training goals, marketing focus, and branding interests. For more information, please contact: **U.S. Corporate and Government Sales**
1-800-382-3419
corpsales@pearsontechgroup.com

For sales outside the United States please contact:
International Sales
international@pearsoned.com

Feedback Information

At Cisco Press, our goal is to create in-depth technical books of the highest quality and value. Each book is crafted with care and precision, undergoing rigorous development that involves the unique expertise of members from the professional technical community.

Readers' feedback is a natural continuation of this process. If you have any comments regarding how we could improve the quality of this book, or otherwise alter it to better suit your needs, you can contact us through email at feedback@ciscopress.com. Please make sure to include the book title and ISBN in your message.

We greatly appreciate your assistance.

Publisher: Paul Boger

Associate Publisher: Dave Dusthimer

Executive Editor: Brett Bartow

Managing Editor: Patrick Kanouse

Project Editor: Seth Kerney

Book and Cover Designer: Louisa Adair

Composition: Mark Shirar

Business Operation Manager, Cisco Press: Anand Sundaram

Manager Global Certification: Erik Ullanderson

Technical Editors: Randy Ivener, Jay Johnston

Development Editors: Kimberley Debus, Dayna Isley

Copy Editor: Margo Catts

Editorial Assistant: Vanessa Evans

Indexer: Ken Johnson

Proofreaders: Water Crest Publishing, Inc., Apostrophe Editing Services

---

Americas Headquarters
Cisco Systems, Inc.
San Jose, CA

Asia Pacific Headquarters
Cisco Systems (USA) Pte. Ltd.
Singapore

Europe Headquarters
Cisco Systems International BV
Amsterdam, The Netherlands

Cisco has more than 200 offices worldwide. Addresses, phone numbers, and fax numbers are listed on the Cisco Website at **www.cisco.com/go/offices.**

About the Authors

Jazib Frahim, CCIE No. 5459, has been with Cisco Systems for more than ten years. With a bachelor's degree in computer engineering from Illinois Institute of Technology, he started out as a TAC engineer in the LAN Switching team. He then moved to the TAC Security team, where he acted as a technical leader for the security products. He led a team of 20 engineers in resolving complicated security and VPN technologies. He is currently working as a technical leader in the Worldwide Security Services Practice of Advanced Services for Network Security. He is responsible for guiding customers in the design and implementation of their networks with a focus on network security. He holds two CCIEs, one in routing and switching and the other in security. He has written numerous Cisco online technical documents and has been an active member on the Cisco online forum NetPro. He has presented at Networkers on multiple occasions and has taught many on-site and online courses to Cisco customers, partners, and employees.

While working for Cisco, he pursued his master of business administration (MBA) degree from North Carolina State University.

He is also an author of the following Cisco Press books:

- *Cisco ASA: All-in-One Firewall, IPS, and VPN Adaptive Security Appliance*
- *Cisco Network Admission Control, Volume II: NAC Deployment and Troubleshooting*
- *SSL Remote Access VPNs*

Omar Santos is an incident manager at Cisco's Product Security Incident Response Team (PSIRT). Omar has designed, implemented, and supported numerous secure networks for Fortune 500 companies and the U.S. government, including the United States Marine Corps (USMC) and the U.S. Department of Defense (DoD). He is also the author of many Cisco online technical documents and configuration guidelines. Prior to his current role, he was a technical leader within the World Wide Security Practice and Cisco's Technical Assistance Center (TAC), where he taught, led, and mentored many engineers within both organizations.

Omar has also delivered numerous technical presentations to Cisco customers and partners; as well as executive presentations to CEOs, CIOs, and CSOs of many organizations. He is also the author of the following Cisco Press books:

- *Cisco ASA: All-in-One Firewall, IPS, and VPN Adaptive Security Appliance*
- *Cisco Network Admission Control, Volume II: NAC Deployment and Troubleshooting*
- *End-to-End Network Security: Defense-in-Depth*

About the Technical Reviewers

Randy Ivener, CCIE No. 10722, is a security engineer in the Cisco Security Research and Operations team. He is a CISSP and PMI PMP. He has spent many years as a network security consultant helping companies understand and secure their networks. Randy has presented security topics at industry events including Blackhat and Cisco Networkers. Before becoming immersed in information security, he spent time in software development and as a training instructor. Randy graduated from the U.S. Naval Academy and holds an MBA.

Jay Johnston, CCIE No. 17663, is a security specialist in the Cisco TAC center located in Research Triangle Park, North Carolina. His networking career began in 2002 when he joined Cisco as a co-op while attending North Carolina State University. After graduating with a bachelors of computer science in 2004, he joined Cisco full time as a TAC Engineer. He obtained his Security CCIE in 2007. He enjoys working for Cisco, especially the constant technical challenges that working with customers in the TAC provides.

Dedications

Jazib Frahim: I would like to dedicate this book to my lovely wife, Sadaf, who has patiently put up with me during the writing process.

I would also like to dedicate this book to my parents, Frahim and Perveen, who support and encourage me in all my endeavors.

Finally, I would like to thank my siblings, including my brother Shazib and sisters Erum and Sana, sister-in-law Asiya, my cute nephew Shayan, and my adorable nieces Shiza and Alisha. Thank you for your patience and understanding during the development of this book.

Omar Santos: I would like to dedicate this book to my lovely wife, Jeannette, and my two beautiful children, Hannah and Derek, who have inspired and supported me throughout the development of this book.

I also dedicate this book to my parents, Jose and Generosa. Without their knowledge, wisdom, and guidance, I would not have the goals that I strive to achieve today.

Acknowledgments

We would like to thank the technical editors, Randy Ivener and Jay Johnston, for their time and technical expertise. They verified our work and corrected us in all the major and minor mistakes that were hard to find. Special thanks go to Aun Raza for reviewing many chapters prior to final editing.

We would like to thank the Cisco Press team, especially Brett Bartow, Dayna Isley, Kimberley Debus, and Andrew Cupp for their patience, guidance, and consideration. Their efforts are greatly appreciated.

Many thanks to our Cisco management team, including David Philips, Ken Cavanagh, and Jean Reese for their continuous support. They highly encouraged us throughout this project.

Kudos to the Cisco ASA product development team for delivering such a great product. Their support is also greatly appreciated during the development of this book.

Finally, we would like to acknowledge the Cisco TAC. Some of the best and brightest minds in the networking industry work there, supporting our Cisco customers often under very stressful conditions and working miracles daily. They are truly unsung heroes, and we are all honored to have had the privilege of working side by side with them in the trenches of the TAC.

Contents at a Glance

Contents

Part II: Firewall Technology

Icons Used in This Book

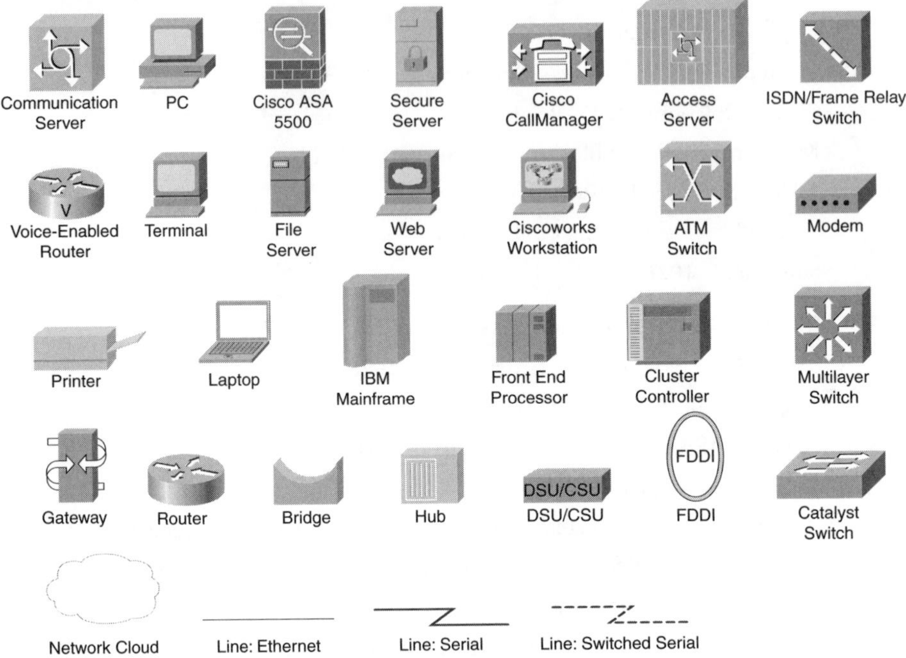

Command Syntax Conventions

The conventions used to present command syntax in this book are the same conventions used in the IOS Command Reference. The Command Reference describes these conventions as follows:

- **Boldface** indicates commands and keywords that are entered literally as shown. In actual configuration examples and output (not general command syntax), boldface indicates commands that are manually input by the user (such as a **show** command).
- *Italic* indicates arguments for which you supply actual values.
- Vertical bars (|) separate alternative, mutually exclusive elements.
- Square brackets ([ ]) indicate an optional element.
- Braces ({ }) indicate a required choice.
- Braces within brackets ([{ }]) indicate a required choice within an optional element.

Introduction

Network security has always been a challenge for many organizations that cannot deploy separate devices to provide firewall, intrusion prevention, and virtual private network (VPN) services. The Cisco ASA is a high-performance, multifunction security appliance that offers firewall, IPS, network antivirus, and VPN services. The Cisco ASA delivers these features through improved network integration, resiliency, and scalability.

This book is an insider's guide to planning, implementing, configuring, and troubleshooting the Cisco Adaptive Security Appliances. It delivers expert guidance from senior Cisco network security consulting engineers. It demonstrates how adaptive identification and mitigation services on the Cisco ASA provide a sophisticated network security solution to small, medium, and large organizations. This book brings together expert guidance for virtually every challenge you will face—from building basic network security policies to advanced VPN and IPS implementations.

Who Should Read This Book?

This book serves as a guide for any network professional who manages network security or installs and configures firewalls, VPN devices, or intrusion detection/prevention systems. It encompasses topics from an introductory level to advanced topics on security and VPNs. The requirements of the reader include a basic knowledge of TCP/IP and networking.

How This Book Is Organized

This book has five parts, which provide a Cisco ASA product introduction and then focus on firewall features, intrusion prevention, content security, and VPNs. Each part includes many sample configurations, accompanied by in-depth analyses of design scenarios. Your learning is further enhanced by a discussion of a set of debugs included in each technology. Groundbreaking features, such as SSL VPN and virtual and Layer 2 firewalls, are discussed extensively.

The core chapters, Chapters 2 through 12, cover the following topics:

- Part I, "Product Overview," includes the following chapters:
  - Chapter 1, "Introduction to Security Technologies"—This chapter provides an overview of different technologies that are supported by the Cisco ASA and widely used by today's network security professionals.
  - Chapter 2, "Cisco ASA Product and Solution Overview"—This chapter describes how the Cisco ASA incorporates features from each of these products, integrating comprehensive firewall, intrusion detection and prevention, and VPN technologies in a cost-effective, single-box format. Additionally, it provides a hardware overview of the Cisco ASA, including detailed technical specifications and installation guidelines. It also covers an overview of the Adaptive Inspection and Prevention Security Services Module (AIP-SSM) and Content Security and Control Security Services Module (CSC-SSM).

- Chapter 3, "Initial Setup and System Maintenance"—A comprehensive list of initial setup tasks and system maintenance procedures is included in this chapter. These tasks and procedures are intended to be used by network professionals who will be installing, configuring, and managing the Cisco ASA.

- Part II, "Firewall Technology," includes the following chapters:
  - Chapter 4, "Controlling Network Access"—The Cisco ASA can protect one or more networks from intruders. Connections between these networks can be carefully controlled by advanced firewall capabilities, enabling you to ensure that all traffic from and to the protected networks passes only through the firewall based on the organization's security policy. This chapter shows you how to implement your organization's security policy, using the features the Cisco ASA provides.
  - Chapter 5, "IP Routing"—This chapter covers the different routing capabilities of the Cisco ASA.
  - Chapter 6, "Authentication, Authorization, and Accounting (AAA)"—The Cisco ASA supports a wide range of AAA features. This chapter provides guidelines on how to configure AAA services by defining a list of authentication methods applied to various implementations.
  - Chapter 7, "Application Inspection"—The Cisco ASA stateful application inspection helps to secure the use of applications and services in your network. This chapter describes how to use and configure application inspection.
  - Chapter 8, "Virtualization"—The Cisco ASA virtual firewall feature introduces the concept of operating multiple instances of firewalls (contexts) within the same hardware platform. This chapter shows how to configure and troubleshoot each of these security contexts.
  - Chapter 9, "Transparent Firewalls"—This chapter introduces the transparent (Layer 2) firewall model within the Cisco ASA. It explains how users can configure the Cisco ASA in transparent single mode and multiple mode while accommodating their security needs.
  - Chapter 10, "Failover and Redundancy"—This chapter discusses the different redundancy and failover mechanisms that the Cisco ASA provides. It includes not only the overview and configuration, but also detailed troubleshooting procedures.
  - Chapter 11, "Quality of Service"—QoS is a network feature that lets you give priority to certain types of traffic. This chapter covers how to configure and troubleshoot QoS in the Cisco ASA.

- Part III, "Intrusion Prevention System (IPS) Solutions," includes the following chapters:
  - Chapter 12, "Configuring and Troubleshooting Intrusion Prevention System (IPS)"—Intrusion detection and prevention systems provide a level of protection beyond the firewall by securing the network against internal and external

attacks and threats. This chapter describes the integration of Intrusion Prevention System (IPS) features within the Cisco ASA and expert guidance on how to configure the AIP-SSM IPS software. Troubleshooting scenarios are also included to enhance learning.

- Chapter 13, "Tuning and Monitoring IPS"—This chapter covers the IPS tuning process, as well as best practices on how to monitor IPS events.

- Part IV, "Content Security," includes the following chapters:
  - Chapter 14, "Configuring Cisco Content Security and Control Security Services Module"—The Content Security and Control Security Services Module (CSC-SSM) is used to detect and take action on viruses, worms, Trojans, and other security threats. It supports the inspection of SMTP, POP3, HTTP, and FTP network traffic. This chapter provides configuration and troubleshooting guidelines to successfully deploy the CSC-SSM within your organization.
  - Chapter 15, "Monitoring and Troubleshooting the Cisco Content Security and Control Security Services Module"—This chapter provides best practices and methodologies used while monitoring the CSC-SSM and troubleshooting any problems you may encounter.
- Part V, "Virtual Private Network (VPN) Solutions," includes the following chapters:
  - Chapter 16, "Site-to-Site IPSec VPNs"—The Cisco ASA supports IPSec VPN features that enable you to connect networks in different geographic locations. This chapter provides configuration and troubleshooting guidelines to successfully deploy site-to-site IPSec VPNs.
  - Chapter 17, "IPSec Remote-Access VPNs"—This chapter discusses two IPSec remote-access VPN solutions (Cisco IPSec and L2TP over IPSec) that are supported on the Cisco ASA. A large number of sample configurations and troubleshooting scenarios are provided.
  - Chapter 18, "Public Key Infrastructure (PKI)"—This chapter starts by introducing PKI concepts. It then covers the configuration and troubleshooting of PKI in the Cisco ASA.
  - Chapter 19, "Clientless Remote-Access SSL VPNs"—This chapter provides details about the Clientless SSL VPN functionality in Cisco ASA. This chapter covers the Cisco Secure Desktop (CSD) solution in detail and also discusses the Host Scan feature that is used to collect posture information about end-workstations. The dynamic access policy (DAP) feature, its usage, and detailed configuration examples are also provided. To reinforce learning, many different deployment scenarios are presented along with their configurations.
  - Chapter 20, "Client-Based Remote-Access SSL VPNs"— This chapter provides details about the AnyConnect SSL VPN functionality in Cisco ASA.

Chapter 1

Introduction to Security Technologies

This chapter covers the following topics:

- Firewalls
- Intrusion Detection Systems (IDS) and Intrusion Prevention Systems (IPS)
- Monitoring and troubleshooting

The cost of reported computer and network security breaches at enterprises, schools, and government organizations has risen dramatically during the last several years. Both hints and detailed instructions for creating exploits to break into networks and computer systems are becoming more easily available on the Internet, consequently requiring network security professionals to carefully analyze what techniques they deploy to mitigate these risks.

Security threats vary from distributed denial-of-service (DDoS) attacks to viruses, worms, Trojan horses, and theft of information. These threats can easily destroy or corrupt vital data, requiring difficult and expensive remediation tasks to restore business continuity.

This chapter introduces the essentials of network security technologies and provides the necessary foundation for technologies involved in the Cisco Adaptive Security Appliances (ASA) security features and solutions.

Firewalls

A detailed understanding of how firewalls and their related technologies work is extremely important for all network security professionals. This knowledge helps you to configure and manage the security of your networks accurately and effectively. The word *firewall* commonly describes systems or devices that are placed between a trusted and an untrusted network.

Several network firewall solutions offer user and application policy enforcement that provides protection for different types of security threats. They often provide logging capabilities that enable the security administrators to identify, investigate, validate, and mitigate such threats.

Additionally, several software applications can run on a system to protect only that host. These types of applications are known as *personal firewalls.* This section includes an overview of network and personal firewalls and their related technologies.

Network Firewalls

Network-based firewalls provide key features used for perimeter security. The primary task of a network firewall is to deny or permit traffic that attempts to enter the network based on explicit preconfigured policies and rules. The processes used to allow or block traffic may include the following:

- Simple packet-filtering techniques
- Multifaceted application proxies
- Stateful inspection systems
- Network address translation

Packet-Filtering Techniques

The purpose of packet filters is simply to control access to specific network segments by defining which traffic can pass through them. They usually inspect incoming traffic at the transport layer of the Open System Interconnection (OSI) model. For example, packet filters can analyze Transmission Control Protocol (TCP) or User Datagram Protocol (UDP) packets and judge them against a set of predetermined rules called access control lists (ACLs). They inspect the following elements within a packet:

- Source address
- Destination address
- Source port
- Destination port
- Protocol

Note Packet filters do not commonly inspect additional Layer 3 and Layer 4 fields such as sequence numbers, TCP control flags, and TCP acknowledgement (ACK) fields.

Various packet-filtering firewalls can also inspect packet header information to find out whether the packet is from a new or an existing connection. Simple packet-filtering firewalls have several limitations and weaknesses:

- Their ACLs or rules can be relatively large and difficult to manage.

- They can be deceived into permitting unauthorized access of spoofed packets. Attackers can orchestrate a packet with an IP address that is authorized by the ACL.
- Numerous applications can build multiple connections on arbitrarily negotiated ports. This makes it difficult to determine which ports will be selected and used until after the connection is completed. Examples of this type of application are multimedia applications such as RealAudio, QuickTime, and other streaming audio and video applications. Packet filters do not understand the underlying upper-layer protocols used by this type of application, and providing support for this type of application is difficult because the ACLs need to be manually configured in packet-filtering firewalls.

Application Proxies

Application proxies, or proxy servers, are devices that operate as intermediary agents on behalf of clients that are on a private or protected network. Clients on the protected network send connection requests to the application proxy to transfer data to the unprotected network or the Internet. Consequently, the application proxy sends the request on behalf of the internal client. The majority of proxy firewalls work at the application layer of the OSI model. Most proxy firewalls can cache information to accelerate their transactions. This is a great tool for networks that have numerous servers that experience high usage. Additionally, proxy firewalls can protect against some web-server specific attacks; however, in most cases, they do not provide any protection against the web application itself. Another disadvantage of application proxies is their inability to scale. This makes them difficult to deploy in large environments.

Network Address Translation

Several Layer 3 devices can provide Network Address Translation (NAT) services. The Layer 3 device translates the internal host's private (or local) IP addresses to a publicly routable (or global) address. NAT is often used by firewalls; however, other devices such as routers and wireless access points provide support for NAT. By using NAT, the firewall hides the internal private addresses from the unprotected network, and exposes only its own address or public range. This enables a network professional to use any IP address space as the internal network. A best practice is to use the address spaces that are reserved for private use (see RFC 1918, "Address Allocation for Private Internets"). Table 1-1 lists the private address ranges specified in RFC 1918.

Table 1-1 *RFC 1918 Private Address Ranges*

Network Address Range	Network/Mask
10.0.0.0–10.255.255.255	10.0.0.0/8
172.16.0.0–172.31.255.255	172.16.0.0/12
192.168.0.0–192.168.255.255	192.168.0.0/16

It is important to think about the different private address spaces when you plan your network (for example, the number of hosts and subnets that can be configured). Careful planning and preparation leads to substantial time savings if changes are encountered down the road.

Tip The whitepaper titled "A Security-Oriented Approach to IP Addressing" provides numerous tips on planning and preparing your network IP address scheme. This whitepaper is posted at the following link:

http://www.cisco.com/web/about/security/intelligence/security-for-ip-addr.html

Port Address Translation

Normally, firewalls perform a technique called Port Address Translation (PAT). This feature is a subset of the NAT feature that allows many devices on the internal protected network to share one IP address by inspecting the Layer 4 information on the packet. This address is usually the firewall's public address; however, it can be configured to any other available public IP address. Figure 1-1 shows how PAT works.

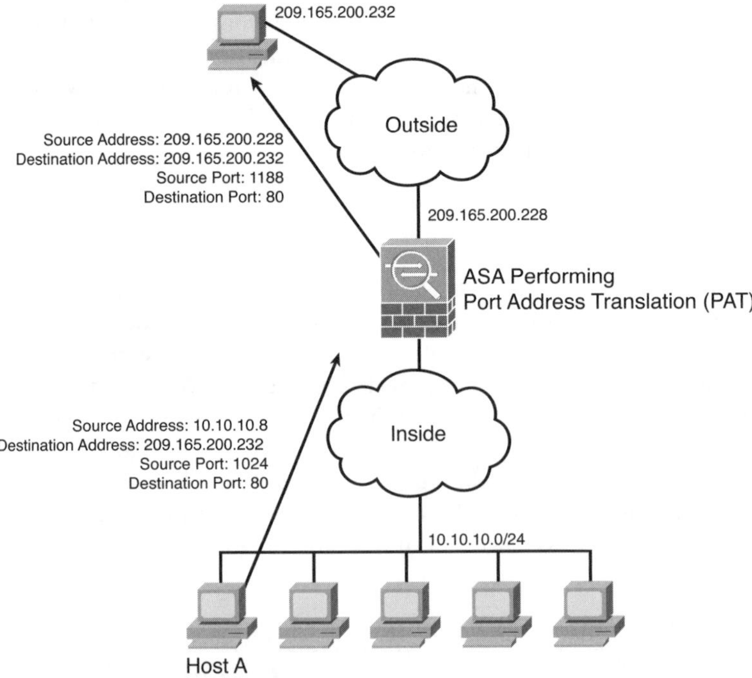

Figure 1-1 *PAT Example*

As illustrated in Figure 1-1, several hosts on a protected network labeled "inside" are configured with an address from the network 10.10.10.0 with a 24-bit subnet mask. The ASA is performing PAT for the internal hosts and translating the 10.10.10.x addresses into its own address (209.165.200.228). In this example, Host A sends a TCP port 80 packet to the web server located in the "outside" unprotected network. The ASA translates the request from the original 10.10.10.8 IP address of Host A to its own address. It does this by randomly selecting a different Layer 4 source port when forwarding the request to the web server. The TCP source port is modified from 1024 to 1188 in this example.

Static Translation

A different methodology is used when hosts in the unprotected network need to initiate a new connection to specific hosts behind the NAT device. You do so by creating a static one-to-one mapping of the public (global) IP address to the address of the internal (local) protected device. For example, static NAT can be configured when a web server resides on the internal network and has a private IP address but needs to be contacted by hosts located in the unprotected network or the Internet. Figure 1-2 demonstrates how static translation works.

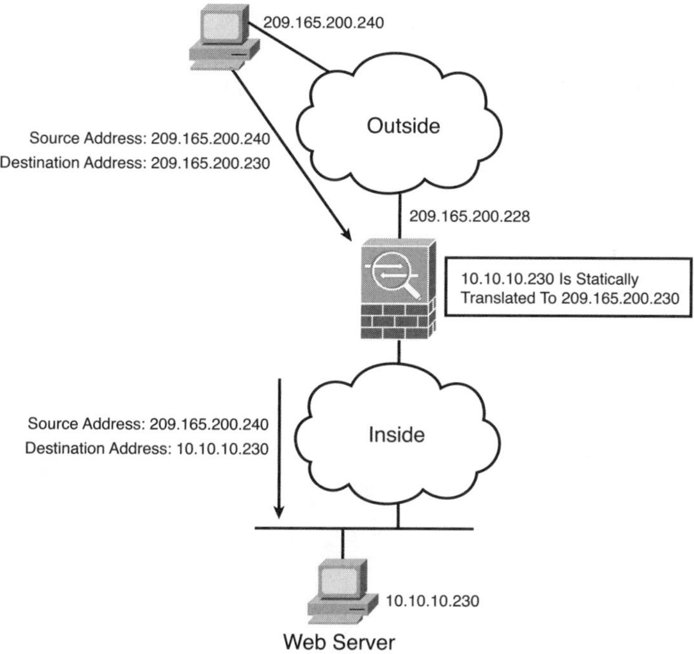

Figure 1-2 *Example of Static Translation*

In Figure 1-2, the web server address (10.10.10.230) is statically translated to an address in the outside network (209.165.200.230, in this case). This allows the outside host to initiate a connection to the web server by directing the traffic to 209.165.200.230. The device performing NAT then translates and sends the request to the web server on the inside network.

Address translation is not limited to firewalls. Nowadays, all sorts of lower-end network devices such as simple small office, home office (SOHO) routers and wireless access points can perform different NAT techniques.

Stateful Inspection Firewalls

Stateful inspection firewalls provide enhanced benefits when compared to simple packet-filtering firewalls. They track every packet passing through their interfaces by assuring that they are valid, established connections. They examine not only the packet header contents, but also the application layer information within the payload. This is done because the packet's payload is examined; subsequently, different rules can be created on the firewall to permit or deny traffic based on specific payload patterns. A stateful firewall monitors the state of the connection and maintains a database with this information, usually called the *state table*. The state of the connection details whether such a connection has been established, closed, reset, or is being negotiated. These mechanisms offer protection for different types of network attacks.

Firewalls can be configured to separate multiple network segments (or zones), usually called *demilitarized zones* (DMZ). These zones provide security to the systems that reside within them with different security levels and policies between them. DMZs can have several purposes; for example, they can serve as segments on which a web server farm resides or as extranet connections to a business partner. Figure 1-3 shows a firewall (a Cisco ASA in this case) with two DMZs.

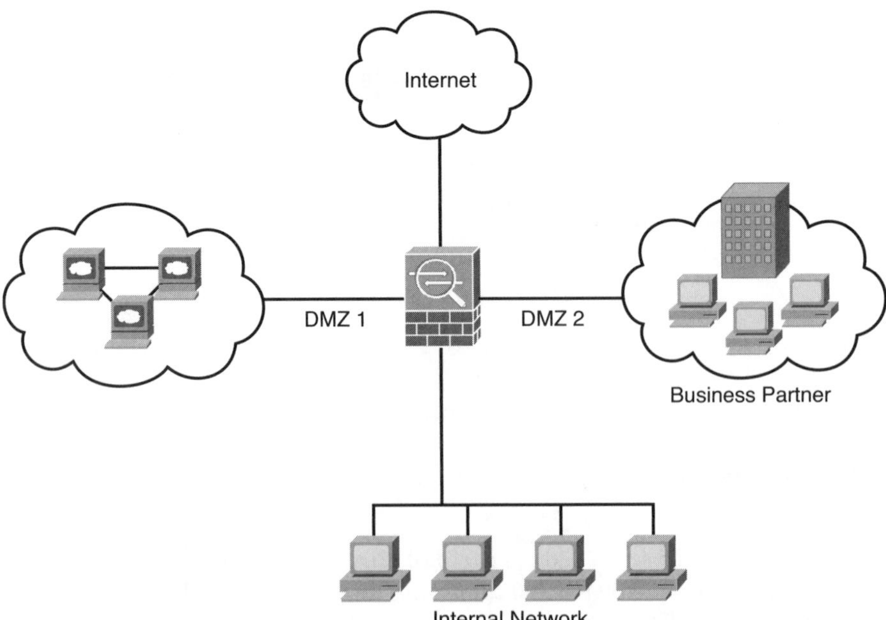

Figure 1-3 *Firewall DMZ Configurations*

DMZs minimize the exposure of devices and clients on your internal network by allowing only recognized and managed services on those hosts to be accessible from the Internet.

In Figure 1-3, *DMZ 1* hosts web servers that are accessible by internal and Internet hosts. The Cisco ASA controls access from an extranet business partner connection on *DMZ 2.*

Note In large organizations, you can deploy multiple firewalls in different segments and DMZs.

Deep Packet Inspection

Several applications require special handling of data packets when they pass through firewalls. These include applications and protocols that embed IP addressing information in the data payload of the packet or open secondary channels on dynamically assigned ports. Sophisticated firewalls and security appliances such as the Cisco ASA, Cisco PIX firewall, and Cisco IOS firewall offer application inspection mechanisms to handle the embedded addressing information to allow the previously mentioned applications and protocols to work. Using application inspection, these security appliances can identify the dynamic port assignments and allow data exchange on these ports during a specific connection.

With deep packet inspection, firewalls can look at specific Layer 7 payloads to protect against security threats. For example, you can configure a Cisco ASA or a Cisco PIX firewall running version 7.0 or later to not allow peer-to-peer (P2P) applications to be transferred over the HTTP protocol. You can also configure these devices to deny specific FTP commands, HTTP content types, and other application protocols.

Note The Cisco ASA and Cisco PIX firewall running version 7.0 or later provide a Modular Policy Framework (MPF) that offers a consistent and flexible way to configure application inspection and other features to specific traffic flows in a manner similar to the Cisco IOS Software Modular quality of service (QoS) command-line interface (CLI).

Personal Firewalls

Personal firewalls are popular software applications that you can install on end-user machines or servers to protect them from external security threats and intrusions. The term *personal firewall* typically applies to basic software that can control Layer 3 and Layer 4 access to client machines. Today, sophisticated software is available that not only provides basic personal firewall features but also protects the system based on the behavior of the applications installed on such systems. An example of this type of software is the Cisco Security Agent (CSA), which provides several features that offer more robust security than a traditional personal firewall, such as host intrusion prevention and protection against spyware, viruses, worms, Trojans, and other types of malware.

Intrusion Detection Systems (IDS) and Intrusion Prevention Systems (IPS)

Intrusion detection systems (IDS) are devices that detect (in promiscuous mode) attempts from an attacker to gain unauthorized access to a network or a host, to create performance degradation, or to steal information. They also detect distributed denial of service (DDoS) attacks, worms, and virus outbreaks. Figure 1-4 shows how an IDS device is configured to promiscuously detect security threats.

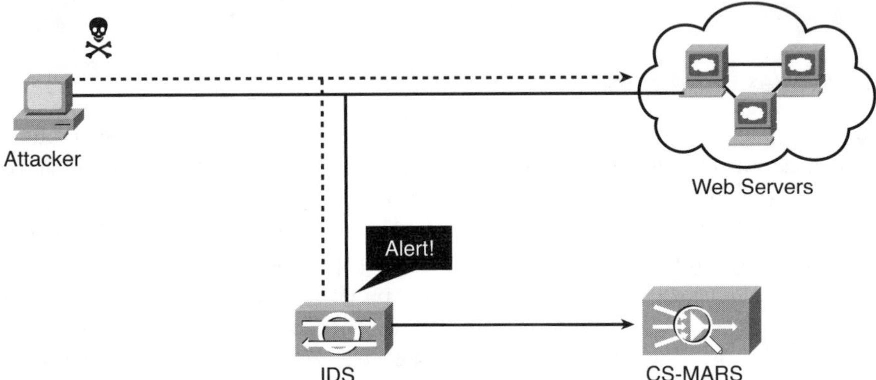

Figure 1-4 *IDS Example*

In Figure 1-4, an attacker sends a malicious packet to a web server. The IDS device analyzes the packet and sends an alert to a monitoring system (CS-MARS in this example). The malicious packet still successfully arrives at the web server.

Intrusion prevention system (IPS) devices, on the other hand, are capable of detecting all these security threats; however, they are also able to drop malicious packets inline.

Figure 1-5 shows how an IPS device is placed inline and drops the noncompliant packet while sending an alert to the monitoring system.

Two different types of IPS exist:

- Network-based (NIPS)
- Host-based (HIPS)

Note Examples of NIPSs are the Cisco IPS 4200 sensors, the Catalyst 6500 IPS Module, and the Cisco ASA with the Advanced Inspection and Prevention Security Services Module (AIP-SSM). An example of a host-based IPS is the Cisco Security Agent (CSA).

The Cisco ASA 5500 Series IPS Solution provides intrusion prevention, firewall, and VPN in a single, easy-to-deploy platform. Intrusion prevention services enhance firewall protection by looking deeper into the flows to provide protection against threats and vulnerabilities. Detailed IPS configuration and troubleshooting methodologies are included in Chapter 12. Additionally, Chapter 13 includes information on tuning and monitoring IPS.

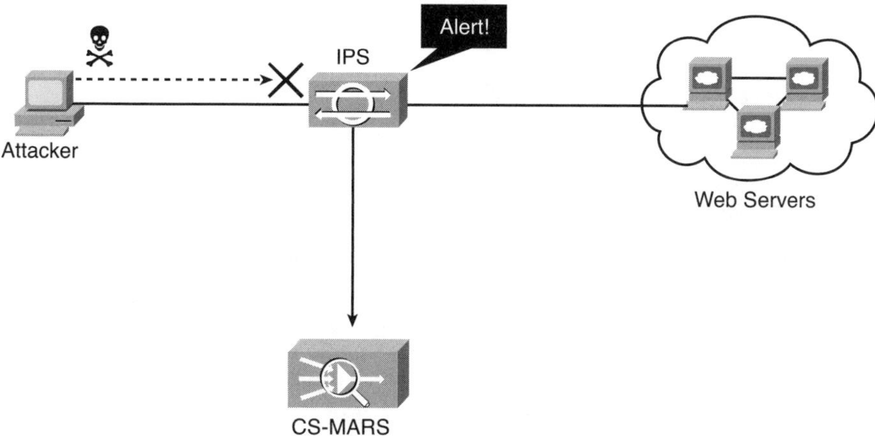

Figure 1-5 *IPS Example*

Network-based IDS and IPS use several detection methodologies, such as the following:

- Pattern matching and stateful pattern-matching recognition
- Protocol analysis
- Heuristic-based analysis
- Anomaly-based analysis

Pattern Matching and Stateful Pattern-Matching Recognition

Pattern matching is a methodology in which the intrusion detection device searches for a fixed sequence of bytes within the packets traversing the network. Generally, the pattern is aligned with a packet that is related to a specific service or, in particular, associated with a source and destination port. This approach reduces the amount of inspection made on every packet. However, it is limited to services and protocols that are associated with well defined ports. Protocols that do not use any Layer 4 port information are not categorized. Examples of these protocols are Encapsulated Security Payload (ESP), Authentication Header (AH), and Generic Routing Encapsulation (GRE) protocol.

This tactic uses the concept of signatures. A *signature* is a set of conditions that point out some type of intrusion occurrence. For example, if a specific TCP packet has a destination port of 1234 and its payload contains the string **ff11ff22**, an alert is triggered to detect that string.

Alternatively, the signature could include an explicit starting point and endpoint for inspection within the specific packet.

The benefits of the plain pattern-matching technique include the following:

- Direct correlation of an exploit
- Trigger alerts on the pattern specified
- Can be applied across different services and protocols

One of the main disadvantages is that pattern matching can lead to a considerably high rate of false positives. *False positives* are alerts that do not represent a genuine malicious activity. In contrast, any alterations to the attack can lead to overlooked events of real attacks, which are normally referred as *false negatives*.

To address some of these limitations, a more refined method was created. This methodology is called *stateful pattern-matching recognition*. This process dictates that systems performing this type of signature analysis must consider the chronological order of packets in a TCP stream. In particular, they should judge and maintain a stateful inspection of such packets and flows.

The advantages of stateful pattern-matching recognition include the following:

- It has the capability to directly correlate a specific exploit within a given pattern.
- Supports all non-encrypted IP protocols.

Systems that perform stateful pattern matching keep track of the arrival order of non-encrypted packets and handle matching patterns across packet boundaries.

However, stateful pattern-matching recognition shares some of the same restrictions of the simple pattern-matching methodology, which was discussed previously, including an uncertain rate of false positives and a possibility of some false negatives. Additionally, stateful pattern-matching consumes more resources in the IPS device because it requires more memory and CPU processing.

Protocol Analysis

Protocol analysis (or protocol decode-base signatures) is often referred to as the extension to stateful pattern recognition. A Network Intrusion Detection System (NIDS) accomplishes protocol analysis by decoding all protocol or client-server conversations. The NIDS identifies the elements of the protocol and analyzes them while looking for an infringement. Some intrusion detection systems look at explicit protocol fields within the inspected packets. Others require more sophisticated techniques, such as examination of the length of a field within the protocol or the number of arguments. For example, in SMTP, the device may look at specific commands and fields such as HELO, MAIL, RCPT, DATA, RSET, NOOP, and QUIT. This technique diminishes the possibility of encountering false positives if the protocol being analyzed is properly defined and enforced. On the other hand, the system can generate numerous false positives if the protocol definition is ambiguous or tolerates flexibility in its implementation.

Heuristic-Based Analysis

A different approach to network intrusion detection is to perform heuristic-based analysis. Heuristic scanning uses algorithmic logic from statistical analysis of the traffic passing through the network. Its tasks are CPU and resource intensive, so it is an important consideration while planning your deployment. Heuristic-based algorithms may require fine tuning to adapt to network traffic and minimize the possibility of false positives. For example, a system signature can generate an alarm if a range of ports is scanned on a particular host or network. The signature can also be orchestrated to restrict itself from specific types of packets (for example, TCP SYN packets). Heuristic-based signatures call for more tuning and modification to better respond to their distinctive network environment.

Anomaly-Based Analysis

A different practice keeps track of network traffic that diverges from "normal" behavioral patterns. This practice is called *anomaly-based analysis.* The limitation is that what is considered to be normal must be defined. Systems and applications whose behavior can be easily considered as normal could be classified as heuristic-based systems.

However, sometimes it is challenging to classify a specific behavior as normal or abnormal based on different factors. These factors include negotiated protocols and ports, specific application changes, and changes in the architecture of the network.

A variation of this type of analysis is *profile-based detection.* This allows systems to orchestrate their alarms on alterations in the way that other systems or end users interrelate on the network.

Another kind of anomaly-based detection is *protocol-based detection.* This scheme is related to, but not to be confused with, the protocol-decode method. The protocol-based detection technique depends on well-defined protocols, as opposed to the protocol-decode method, which classifies as an anomaly any unpredicted value or configuration within a field in the respective protocol. For example, a buffer overflow can be detected when specific strings are detected within the payload of the inspected IP packets.

> **Note** A buffer overflow occurs when a program attempts to store more data in a temporary storage area within memory (buffer) than it was designed to hold. This might cause the data to incorrectly overflow into an adjacent area of memory. An attacker may craft specific data inserted into the adjacent buffer. Subsequently, when the corrupted data is read, the target computer executes new instructions and malicious commands.

Traditional IDS and IPS provide excellent application layer attack-detection capabilities. However, they do have a weakness: They cannot detect DDoS attacks where the attacker uses valid packets. IDS and IPS devices are optimized for signature-based application layer attack detection. Another weakness is that these systems utilize specific signatures to identify malicious patterns, yet if a new threat appears on the network before a signature is created to identify the traffic, this could lead to false negatives. An attack for which there is no signature is called a *zero-day attack*.

Although some IPS devices do offer anomaly-based capabilities, which are required to detect such attacks, they require extensive manual tuning and have a major risk of generating false positives.

Tip Cisco IPS Software Version 6.x and later support more sophisticated anomaly detection techniques. More information can be obtained at http://www.cisco.com/go/ips.

You can use more elaborate anomaly-based detection systems to mitigate DDoS attacks and zero-day outbreaks. Typically, an anomaly detection system monitors network traffic and alerts or reacts to any sudden increase in traffic and any other anomalies. Cisco delivers a complete DDoS protection solution based on the principles of detection, diversion, verification, and forwarding to help ensure total protection. Examples of sophisticated anomaly detection systems are the Cisco Traffic Anomaly Detectors and the Cisco Guard DDoS Mitigation Appliances.

You can also use NetFlow as an anomaly detection tool. NetFlow is a Cisco proprietary protocol that provides detailed reporting and monitoring of IP traffic flows through a network device, such as a router, switch, or the Cisco ASA.

Note Refer to the Cisco feature navigator to find out in what Cisco IOS image NetFlow is supported. You can access this tool at http://tools.cisco.com/ITDIT/CFN/jsp/index.jsp.

Netflow support was introduced in the Cisco ASA in software version 8.2.

NetFlow uses a UDP-based protocol to periodically report on flows seen by the Cisco IOS device. A flow consists of session setup, data transfer, and session teardown. You can also integrate NetFlow with Cisco Secure Monitoring and Response System (CS-MARS). When NetFlow is integrated with CS-MARS, you can use statistical profiling, which can pinpoint day-zero attacks such as worm outbreaks, to take advantage of anomaly detection.

Virtual Private Networks

Organizations deploy VPNs to provide data integrity, authentication, and data encryption to assure confidentiality of the packets sent over an unprotected network or the Internet. VPNs are designed to avoid the cost of unnecessary leased lines.

Many different protocols are used for VPN implementations, including

- Point-to-Point Tunneling Protocol (PPTP)
- Layer 2 Forwarding (L2F) Protocol
- Layer 2 Tunneling Protocol (L2TP)
- Generic Routing Encapsulation (GRE) Protocol
- Multiprotocol Label Switching (MPLS) VPN
- Internet Protocol Security (IPsec)
- Secure Socket Layer (SSL)

Note L2F, L2TP, GRE, and MPLS VPNs do not provide data integrity, authentication, and data encryption. On the other hand, you can combine L2TP, GRE, and MPLS with IPsec to provide these benefits. Many organizations use IPsec as their preferred protocol because it supports all three of these features.

VPN implementations can be categorized into two distinct groups:

- **Site-to-site VPNs**—Enable organizations to establish VPN tunnels between two or more network infrastructure devices in different sites so that they can communicate over a shared medium such as the Internet. Many organizations use IPsec, GRE, and MPLS VPN as site-to-site VPN protocols.
- **Remote-access VPNs**—Enable users to work from remote locations such as their homes, hotels, and other premises as if they were directly connected to their corporate network.

Note Typically, site-to-site VPN tunnels are terminated between two or more network infrastructure devices, as opposed to remote access VPN where the tunnels are formed by a VPN head-end device a end-user workstation or hardware VPN client.

Figure 1-6 illustrates a site-to-site IPsec tunnel between two sites (corporate headquarters and a branch office).

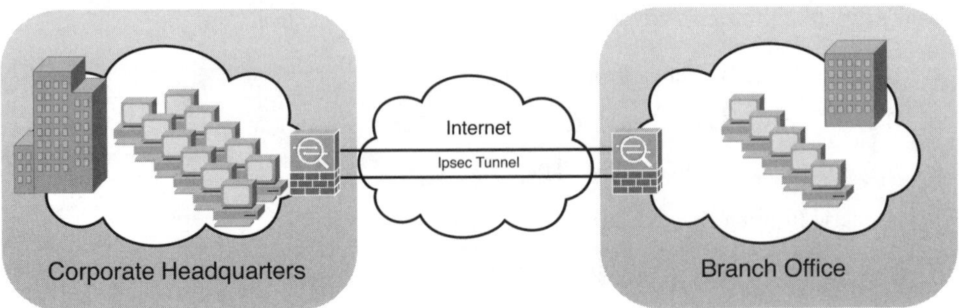

Figure 1-6 *Site-to-Site VPN Example*

Figure 1-7 shows an example of remote access VPN. In this example, a telecommuter uses IPSec VPN while a remote user from a hotel uses SSL VPN to connect to the corporate headquarters.

Technical Overview of IPSec

IPsec uses the Internet Key Exchange (IKE) Protocol to negotiate and establish secured site-to-site or remote access VPN tunnels. IKE is a framework provided by the Internet Security Association and Key Management Protocol (ISAKMP) and parts of two other key management protocols, namely Oakley and Secure Key Exchange Mechanism (SKEME).

Note IKE is defined in RFC 2409, "The Internet Key Exchange."

ISAKMP has two phases. Phase 1 is used to create a secure bidirectional communication channel between the IPsec peers. This channel is known as the ISAKMP Security Association (SA). Phase 2 is used to negotiate the IPsec SAs.

Phase 1

Within Phase 1 negotiation, several attributes are exchanged, including the following:

- Encryption algorithms
- Hashing algorithms
- Diffie-Hellman groups
- Authentication method
- Vendor-specific attributes

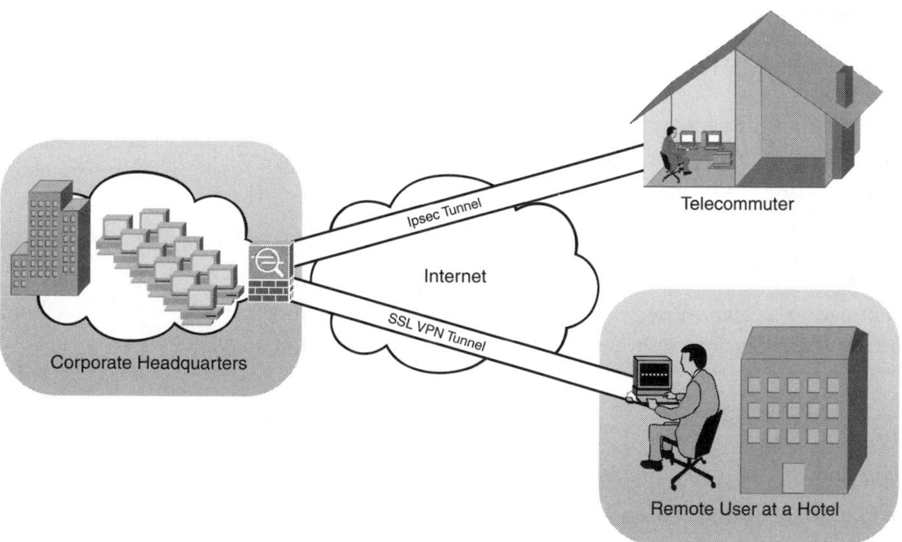

Figure 1-7 *Remote Access VPN Example*

The following are the typical encryption algorithms:

- Data Encryption Standard (DES): 64 bits long
- Triple DES (3DES): 168 bits long
- Advanced Encryption Standard (AES): 128 bits long
- AES 192: 192 bits long
- AES 256: 256 bits long

Hashing algorithms include these:

- Secure Hash Algorithm (SHA)
- Message digest algorithm 5 (MD5)

The common authentication methods are preshared keys (where peers use a shared secret to authenticate each other) and digital certificates with the use of Public Key Infrastructure (PKI).

> **Note** Typically, small and medium-sized organizations use preshared keys as their authentication mechanism. Several large organizations use digital certificates for scalability, for centralized management, and for the use of additional security mechanisms.

You can establish a Phase 1 SA in main mode or aggressive mode.

In main mode, the IPsec peers complete a six-packet exchange in three round trips to negotiate the ISAKMP SA, whereas aggressive mode completes the SA negotiation in three packet exchanges. Main mode provides identity protection if preshared keys are used. Aggressive mode provides identity protection only if digital certificates are used.

> **Note** Cisco products that support IPsec typically use main mode for site-to-site tunnels and aggressive mode for remote-access VPN tunnels. This is the default behavior when preshared keys are used as the authentication method.

Figure 1-8 illustrates the six-packet exchange in main mode negotiation.

In Figure 1-8, two Cisco ASAs are configured to terminate a site-to-site VPN tunnel between them. The Cisco ASA labeled as ASA-1 is the initiator, and ASA-2 is the responder. The following are the steps illustrated in Figure 1-8.

Step 1. ASA-1 (the initiator) has two ISAKMP proposals configured. In the first packet, ASA-1 sends its configured proposals to ASA-2.

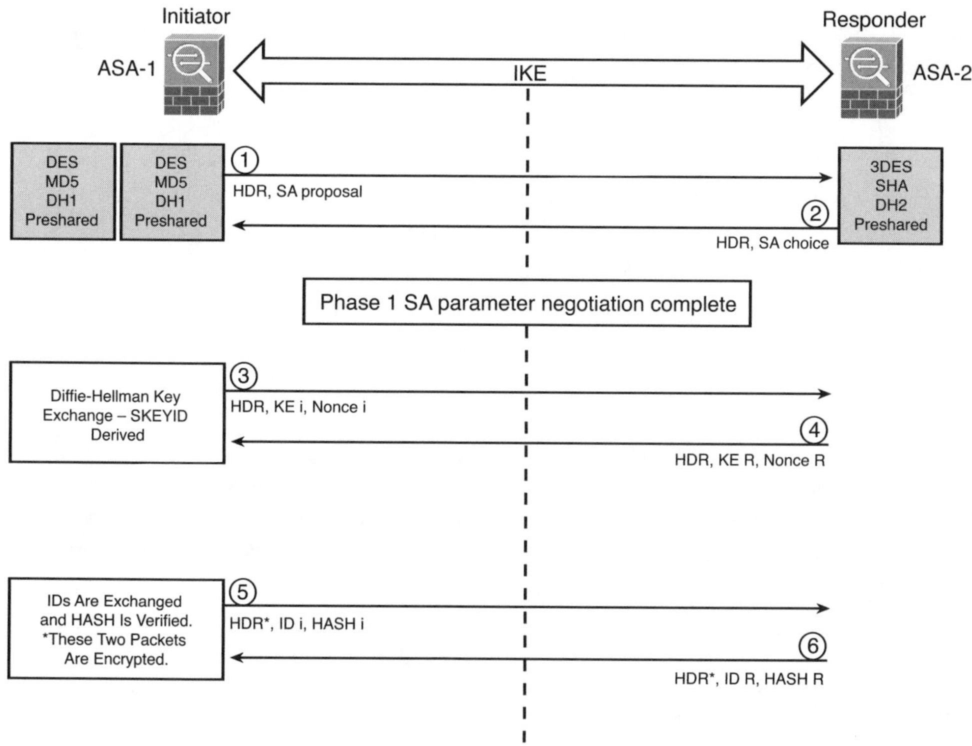

Figure 1-8 *IKE Negotiation*

Step 2. ASA-2 evaluates the received proposal. Because it has a proposal that matches the offer of the initiator, ASA-2 sends the accepted proposal back to ASA-1 in the second packet.

Step 3. Diffie-Hellman exchange and calculation is started. Diffie-Hellman is a key agreement protocol that enables two users or devices to authenticate each other's pre-shared keys without actually sending the keys over the unsecured medium. ASA-1 sends the Key Exchange (KE) payload and a randomly generated value called a *nonce*.

Step 4. ASA-2 receives the information and reverses the equation, using the proposed Diffie-Hellman group/exchange to generate the SKEYID. The SKEYID is a string derived from secret material that is known only to the active participants in the exchange.

Step 5. ASA-1 sends its identity information. The fifth packet is encrypted with the keying material derived from the SKEYID. The asterisk in Figure 1-8 is used to illustrate that this packet is encrypted.

Step 6. ASA-2 validates the identity of ASA-1, and ASA-2 sends its own identity information to ASA-1. This packet is also encrypted.

Note IKE uses UDP port 500 for communication. UDP port 500 is used to send all the packets described in the previous steps.

Phase 2

Phase 2 is used to negotiate the IPsec SAs. This phase is also known as quick mode. The ISAKMP SA protects the IPsec SAs because all payloads are encrypted except the ISAKMP header.

A single IPSec SA negotiation always creates two security associations—one inbound and one outbound. Each SA is assigned a unique security parameter index (SPI) value—one by the initiator and the other by the responder.

Tip The security protocols (AH or ESP) are Layer 3 protocols and do not have Layer 4 port information. If an IPSec peer is behind a PAT device, the ESP or AH packets are typically dropped. To work around this, many vendors, including Cisco Systems, use a feature called IPSec pass-thru. The PAT device that is IPSec pass-thru capable builds the Layer 4 translation table by looking at the SPI values on the packets.

Many industry vendors, including Cisco Systems, implement another new feature called NAT Traversal (NAT-T). With NAT-T, the VPN peers dynamically discover whether an address translation device exists between them. If they detect a NAT/PAT device, they use UDP port 4500 to encapsulate the data packets, subsequently allowing the NAT device to successfully translate and forward the packets.

Another interesting point is that if the VPN router needs to connect multiple networks over the tunnel, it needs to negotiate twice as many IPSec SAs. Remember, each IPSec SA is unidirectional, so if three local subnets need to go over the VPN tunnel to talk to the remote network, then six IPSec SAs are negotiated. IPSec can use quick mode to negotiate these multiple Phase 2 SAs, using the single pre-established ISAKMP SA. The number of IPSec SAs can be reduced, however, if source and/or destination networks are summarized.

Many different IPSec attributes are negotiated in quick mode, as shown in Table 1-3.

In addition to generating the keying material, quick mode also negotiates identity information. The Phase 2 identity information specifies what network, protocol, and/or port number to encrypt. Hence, the identities can vary anywhere from an entire network to a single host address, allowing a specific protocol and port.

Figure 1-9 illustrates the Phase 2 negotiation between the two routers that just completed Phase 1.

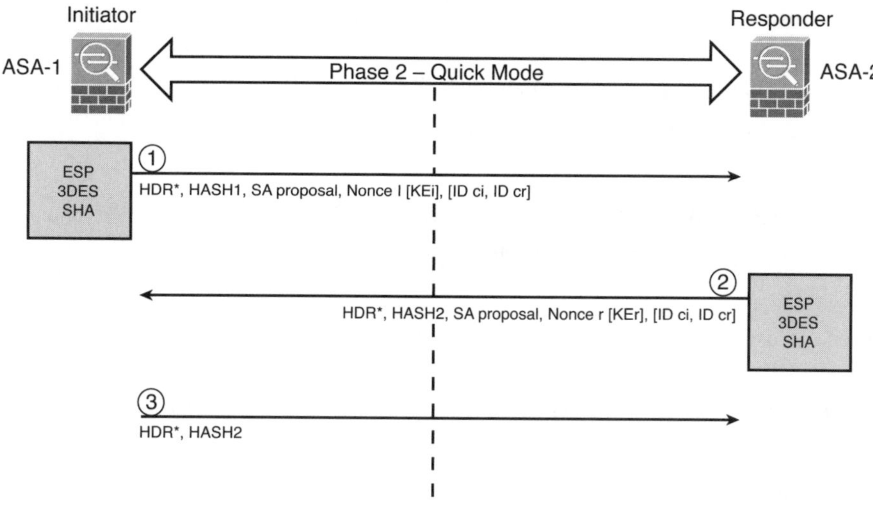

Figure 1-9 *IPsec Phase 2 Negotiation*

The following are the steps illustrated in Figure 1-9.

Step 1. ASA-1 sends the identity information, IPsec SA proposal, nonce payload, and (optional) Key Exchange (KE) payload if Perfect Forward Secrecy (PFS) is used. PFS is used to provide additional Diffie-Hellman calculations.

Step 2. ASA-2 evaluates the received proposal against its configured proposal and sends the accepted proposal back to ASA-1, along with its identity information, nonce payload, and the optional KE payload.

Step 3. ASA-1 evaluates the ASA-2 proposal and sends a confirmation that the IPsec SAs have been successfully negotiated. This starts the data encryption process.

Table 1-3 *IPSec Attributes*

Attribute	Possible Values
Encryption	None, DES, 3DES, AES128, AES192, AES256
Hashing	MD5, SHA, or null
Identity information	Network, Protocol, Port number
Lifetime	120–2,147,483,647 seconds 10–2,147,483,647 kilobytes
Mode	Tunnel or transport
Perfect Forward Secrecy (PFS) group	None, 1, 2, or 5

IPsec uses two different protocols to encapsulate the data over a VPN tunnel:

- Encapsulation Security Payload (ESP): IP Protocol 50
- Authentication Header (AH): IP Protocol 51

Note ESP is defined in RFC 4303, "IP Encapsulating Security Payload (ESP)," and AH is defined in RFC 4305, "IP Authentication Header."

IPsec can use two modes with either AH or ESP:

- **Transport mode**—Protects upper-layer protocols, such as User Datagram Protocol (UDP) and TCP
- **Tunnel mode**—Protects the entire IP packet

Transport mode is used to encrypt and authenticate the data packets between the peers. A typical example of this is the use of GRE over an IPsec tunnel. Tunnel mode is used to encrypt and authenticate the IP packets when they are originated by the hosts connected behind the Virtual Private Network (VPN) device. Tunnel mode adds an additional IP header to the packet, as illustrated in Figure 1-10.

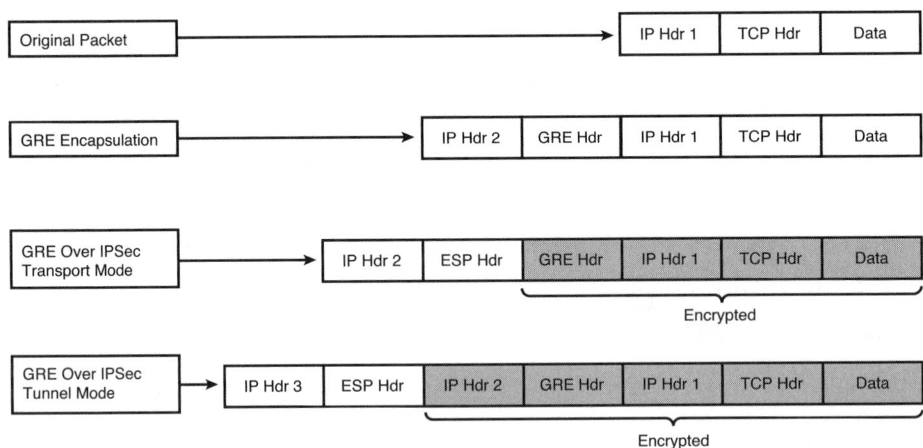

Figure 1-10 *Transport vs. Tunnel Mode*

Figure 1-10 demonstrates the major difference between transport and tunnel mode. It includes an example of an IP packet encapsulated in GRE and the difference when it is encrypted in transport mode and tunnel mode. As demonstrated in Figure 1-10, tunnel mode increases the overall size of the packet in comparison to transport mode.

Note Tunnel mode is the default mode in Cisco IPsec devices.

SSL VPNs

SSL-based VPNs leverage the SSL protocol. SSL, also referred to as Transport Layer Security (TLS), is a matured protocol that has been in existence since the early 1990s. The Internet Engineering Task Force (IETF) created TLS to consolidate the different SSL vendor versions into a common and open standard.

One of the most popular features of SSL VPN is the capability to launch a browser such as Microsoft Internet Explorer and Firefox and simply connect to the address of the VPN device, as opposed to running a separate VPN client program to establish an IPSec VPN connection. In most implementations, a clientless solution is possible. Users can access corporate intranet sites, portals, and email from almost anywhere (even from an airport kiosk). Because most people allow SSL (TCP port 443) over their firewalls, it is unnecessary to open additional ports.

The most successful application running on top of SSL is HTTP because of the huge popularity of the World Wide Web. All the most popular web browsers in use today support HTTPS (HTTP over SSL/TLS). This ubiquity, if used in remote access VPNs, provides some appealing properties:

- **Secure communication using cryptographic algorithms**—It offers confidentiality, integrity, and authentication.
- **Ubiquity**—The ubiquity of SSL/TLS makes it possible for VPN users to remotely access corporate resources from anywhere, using any PC, without having to preinstall a remote access VPN client.
- **Low management cost**—The clientless access makes this type of remote access VPN free of deployment costs and free of maintenance problems at the end-user side. This is a huge benefit for the IT management personnel, who would otherwise spend considerable resources to deploy and maintain their remote access VPN solutions.
- **Effective operation with a firewall and NAT**—SSL VPN operates on the same port as HTTPS (TCP/443). Most Internet firewalls, proxy servers, and NAT devices have been configured to correctly handle TCP/443 traffic. Subsequently, there is no need for any special consideration to transport SSL VPN traffic over the networks. This has been viewed as a significant advantage over native IPsec VPN, which operates over IP protocol 50 (ESP) or 51 (AH), which in many cases needs special configuration on the firewall or NAT devices to let them pass through.

As SSL VPN evolves to fulfill another important requirement of remote access VPN, namely the requirement of supporting any application, some of these properties are no longer true, depending on which SSL VPN technology the VPN users choose. But overall, these properties are the main drivers for the popularity of SSL VPN in recent years and are heavily marketed by SSL VPN vendors as the main reasons for IPsec replacement.

Today's SSL VPN technology uses SSL/TLS as secure transport and employs a heterogeneous collection of remote access technologies such as reverse proxy, tunneling, and terminal services to provide users with different types of access methods that fit different environments. Subsequent chapters examine some commonly used SSL VPN technologies, such as

- Reverse proxy technology
- Port-forwarding technology
- SSL VPN tunnel client
- Integrated terminal services

HTTPS provides secure web communication between a browser and a web server that supports the HTTPS protocol. SSL VPN extends this model to allow VPN users to access corporate internal web applications and other corporate application servers that might or might not support HTTPS, or even HTTP. SSL VPN does this by using several techniques that are collectively called reverse proxy technology.

A *reverse proxy* is a proxy server that resides in front of the application servers, normally web servers, and functions as an entry point for Internet users who want to access the corporate internal web application resources. To the external clients, a reverse proxy server appears to be the true web server. Upon receiving the user's web request, a reverse proxy relays the user request to the internal web server to fetch the content on behalf of the users and relays the web content to the user with or without additional modifications to the data being presented to the user.

Many web server implementations support reverse proxy. One example is the mod_proxy module in Apache. With so many implementations, you might wonder why you need an SSL VPN solution to have this functionality. The answer is that SSL VPN offers much more functionality than traditional reverse proxy technologies:

- SSL VPN can transform complicated web and some non-web applications that simple reverse proxy servers cannot handle. The content transformation process is sometimes called *webification*. For example, SSL VPN solutions enable users to access Windows or UNIX file systems. The SSL VPN gateway needs to be able to communicate with internal Windows or UNIX servers and webify the file access in a web browser–presentable format for the VPN users.
- SSL VPN supports a wide range of business applications. For applications that cannot be webified, SSL VPN can use other resource access methods to support them. For users who demand ultimate access, SSL VPN can provide network-layer access to directly connect a remote system to the corporate network, in the same manner as an IPsec VPN.
- SSL VPN provides a true remote access VPN package, including user authentication, resource access privilege management, logging and accounting, endpoint security, and user experience.

The reverse proxy mode in SSL VPN is also known as clientless web access or clientless access because it does not require any client-side applications to be installed on the client machine.

Note Configuration and troubleshooting of clientless remote access SSL VPN is covered in Chapter 19. Configuration and troubleshooting of client-based remote access SSL VPN is covered in Chapter 20.

Summary

Network security is a science that needs to be put into practice carefully. There are many different techniques at the disposal of a network administrator to prevent attackers from gaining access to private networks and computer systems. This chapter provides an overview of the different technologies, principles, and protocols related to the integrated features of Cisco ASA. An overview of different firewall technologies and implementations was covered in the beginning of the chapter, followed by the introduction of IDS and IPS solutions. At the end, a technical overview of site-to-site and remote access VPN technologies was discussed in detail.

Chapter 2

Cisco ASA Product and Solution Overview

This chapter covers the following topics:

- Cisco ASA 5505 hardware overview
- Cisco ASA 5510 hardware overview
- Cisco ASA 5520 hardware overview
- Cisco ASA 5540 hardware overview
- Cisco ASA 5550 hardware overview
- Cisco ASA 5580-20 hardware overview
- Cisco ASA 5580-40 hardware overview
- Cisco ASA AIP-SSM module overview
- Cisco ASA CSC-SSM module overview
- Deployment examples

The Cisco ASA 5500 Series Adaptive Security Appliances integrate firewall, IPS, and VPN capabilities, providing an all-in-one solution for your network. Incorporating all these solutions into Cisco ASA secures the network without the need for extra overlay equipment or network alterations. This is something that many Cisco customers and network professionals have requested in a security product.

There are several Cisco ASA 5500 Series models. These include

- Cisco ASA 5505
- Cisco ASA 5510
- Cisco ASA 5520
- Cisco ASA 5540

- Cisco ASA 5550
- Cisco ASA 5580-20
- Cisco ASA 5580-40

This chapter provides an overview of the Cisco ASA 5500 Series Adaptive Security Appliance hardware, including performance and technical specifications. It also provides an overview of the Adaptive Inspection and Prevention Security Services Module (AIP-SSM), which is required for IPS features. Additionally, it introduces the Content Security and Control Security Services Module (CSC-SSM), designed to provide antivirus, anti-spyware, file blocking, anti-spam, anti-phishing, URL blocking/filtering, and content filtering. This chapter also discusses the Cisco ASA 4-Port Gigabit Ethernet Security Services Module (4GE SSM) that extends the number of physical interfaces in an appliance.

Cisco ASA 5505 Model

The Cisco ASA 5505 Adaptive Security Appliance is designed for small business, branch office, and telecommuting environments. Despite its small size, it provides firewall, SSL and IPsec VPN, and numerous networking services expected on a bigger appliance. Figure 2-1 shows the front view of the Cisco ASA 5505.

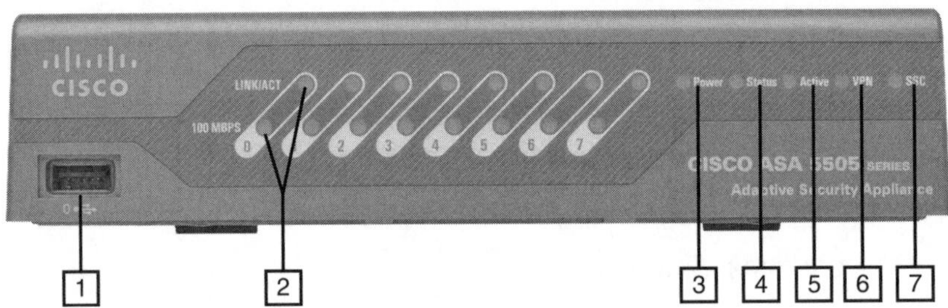

Figure 2-1 *Cisco ASA 5505 Front View*

The front panel has the following components:

Step 1. **USB Port**—Reserved for future use.

Step 2. **Speed and Link Activity LEDs**—The Cisco ASA 5505 has a speed indicator LED and a separate link activity indicator LED for each of its eight ports. When the speed indicator LED is not lit it indicates that network traffic is flowing at 10 Megabits per second (Mbps). When the speed indicator LED is green it indicates that network traffic is flowing at 100 Mbps. When the link activity LED is solid green it indicates that the physical network link has been established; when flashing it indicates that there is network activity.

Step 3. **Power LED**—Solid green indicates that the appliance is powered on.

Step 4. Status LED—Flashing green indicates that the system is booting and power-up tests are running. Solid green indicates that the system tests passed and the system is operational. Amber solid indicates that the system tests failed.

Step 5. Active—Green indicates that this Cisco ASA is active when configured for failover.

Step 6. VPN—Solid green indicates that one or more VPN tunnels are active.

Step 7. Security Services Card (SSC) LED—Solid green indicates that an SSC card is present in the SSC slot. Reserved for future use.

The Cisco ASA 5505 features a flexible 8-port 10/100 Fast Ethernet switch, whose ports can be dynamically grouped to create up to three separate VLANs for home, business, and Internet traffic for improved network segmentation and security. The Cisco ASA 5505 provides two Power over Ethernet (PoE) ports, enabling simplified deployment of Cisco IP phones with zero-touch secure voice over IP (VoIP) capabilities, and deployment of external wireless access points for extended network mobility. Figure 2-2 illustrates the back panel of the ASA 5505.

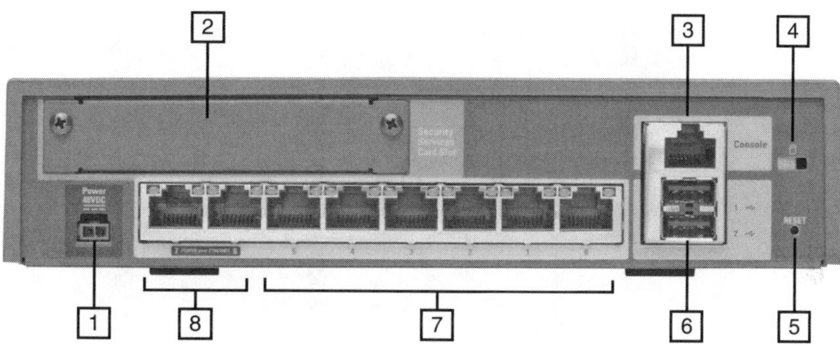

Figure 2-2 *Cisco ASA 5505 Back Panel*

The real panel has the following components:

Step 1. Power connector.

Step 2. SSC slot—Reserved for future use.

Step 3. Serial console port—The RJ-45 console port enables you to physically connect to the appliance to access its command-line interface (CLI) for initial configuration.

Step 4. Lock device—Used to physically lock the Cisco ASA.

Step 5. Reset button—Reserved for future use.

Step 6. Two USB version 2.0 ports—Reserved for future use.

Step 7. Ethernet switch ports 0 thru 5—10/100 Fast Ethernet switch ports.

Step 8. **Ethernet switch ports 6 and 7**—10/100 Fast Ethernet switch ports with Power over Ethernet (PoE).

You can install a Security Plus upgrade license, enabling the Cisco ASA 5505 to scale to support a higher connection capacity and a higher number of IPsec VPN users, add full DMZ support, and integrate into switched network environments through VLAN trunking support. Furthermore, this upgrade license maximizes business continuity by enabling support for redundant ISP connections and stateless Active/Standby high-availability services. This makes the Cisco ASA 5505 a great solution for small businesses and branch offices. Figure 2-3 illustrates how a Cisco ASA 5505 is deployed at a small branch office.

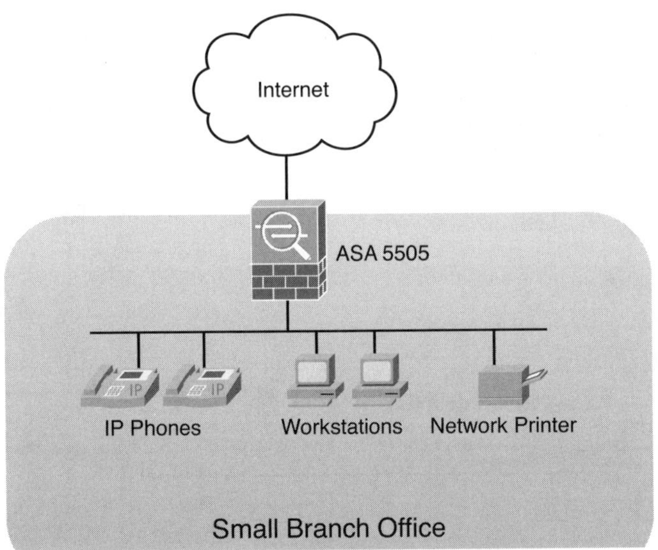

Figure 2-3 *Cisco ASA 5505 Small Branch Office Deployment*

In the example illustrated in Figure 2-3, several workstations, a network printer, and IP phones are protected by the Cisco ASA 5505. The IP phones are connected to the Fast Ethernet switch ports 6 and 7 (which provide power to the phones).

Figure 2-4 shows how a Cisco ASA 5505 is deployed at a small business with two different protected network segments.

The inside network (vlan 10) has several workstations, the DMZ (vlan 20) has two web servers, and the outside interface faces towards the Internet.

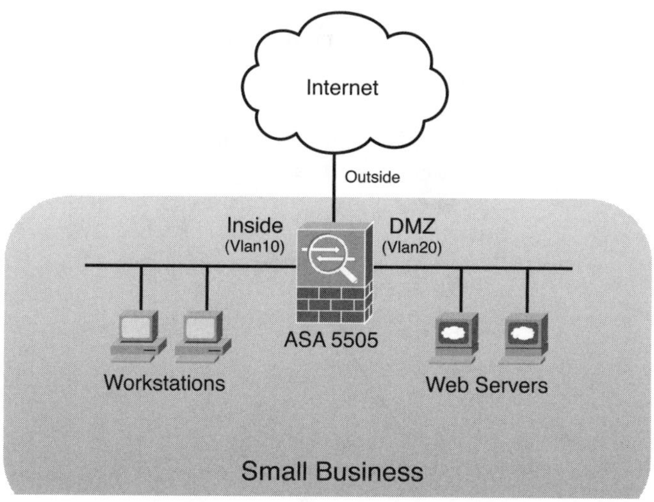

Figure 2-4 *Cisco ASA 5505 Small Business Deployment with Separate Protected Networks*

Note Configuration information on how to control network access and create different interfaces with separate security levels is covered in Chapter 4, "Controlling Network Access."

Figure 2-5 shows how a Cisco ASA 5505 can be used by telecommuters and home users to connect to a centralized location via VPN.

In Figure 2-5, telecommuters are protected by a Cisco ASA 5505 on each respective location. The Cisco ASA 5505s connect to the Corporate Headquarters via IPsec VPN tunnels.

Note Configuration and troubleshooting of remote access VPN tunnels is covered in Chapter 17, "IPSec Remote Access VPNs."

Cisco ASA 5510 Model

The Cisco ASA 5510 model is designed to deliver advanced security services for small- and medium-sized businesses and enterprise branch offices. This model provides advanced firewall and VPN capabilities and has optional Anti-X (Adaptive Threat Defense) and IPS services that use the Cisco AIP-SSM-10 module.

Figure 2-6 shows a front view of the Cisco ASA 5510 model.

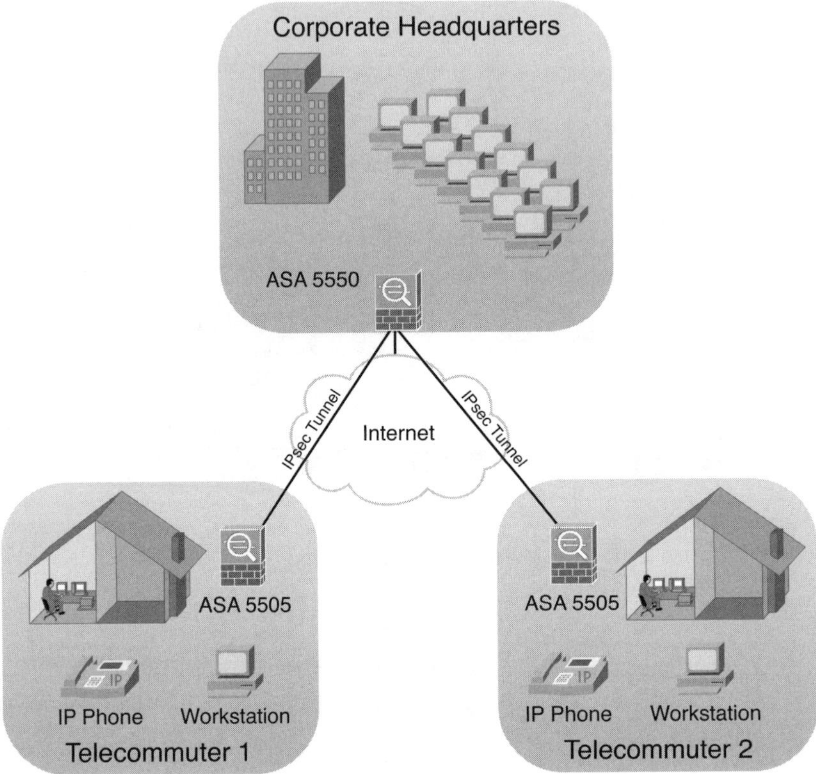

Figure 2-5 *Cisco ASA 5505 for Telecommuters*

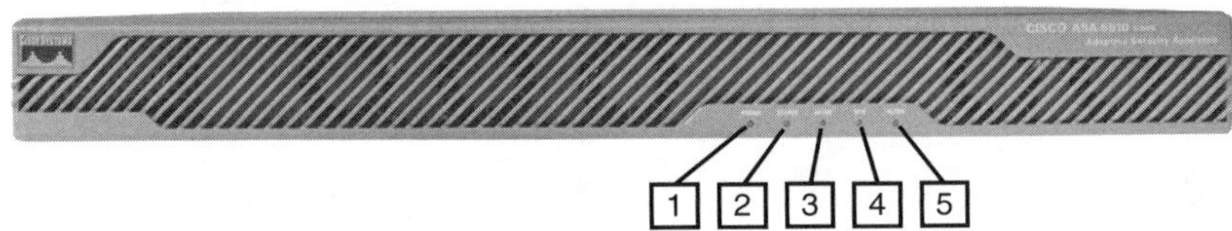

Figure 2-6 *Cisco ASA 5510 Front View*

The front panel has the following five LEDs:

Step 1. Power—Solid green indicates that the appliance is powered on.

Step 2. Status—Flashing green indicates that the system is booting and power-up tests are running. Solid green indicates that the system tests passed and the system is operational. Amber solid indicates that the system tests failed.

Step 3. Active—Green indicates that this Cisco ASA is active when configured for failover.

Step 4. VPN—Solid green indicates that one or more VPN tunnels are active.

Step 5. **Flash**—Flashing green indicates that the Flash memory card is being accessed.

The Cisco ASA 5510, 5520, 5540, and 5550 offer a one-rack unit (1RU) design. They also have an expansion slot for security-services modules. Figure 2-7 shows a back view of the Cisco ASA 5510 model.

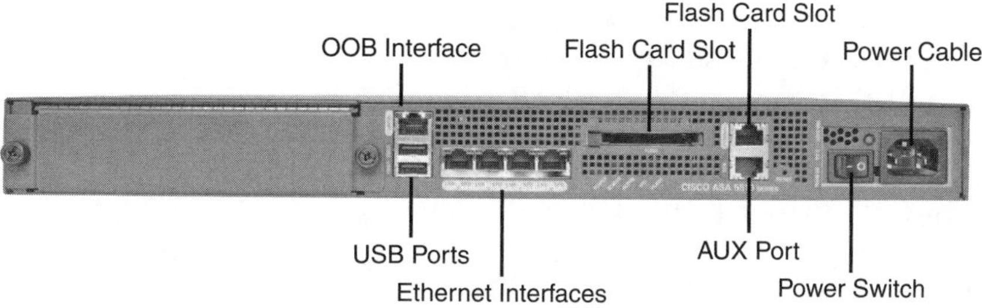

Figure 2-7 *Cisco ASA 5510 Back View*

The Power, Status, Active, VPN, and Flash LEDs are also present on the back of the Cisco ASA 5510. The Cisco ASA 5510 includes five integrated 10/100 Fast Ethernet network interfaces. Three of these five Fast Ethernet ports are enabled by default (0 to 2). The fifth interface is reserved for out-of-band (OOB) management. Starting with Cisco ASA software version 7.2(2) and 8.0(3) respectively, restriction on the OOB port is removed. Therefore, you can use all five Fast Ethernet interfaces for the through traffic and apply security services.

Note The OOB Ethernet port restriction is removed since versions 7.2(2) and 8.0(3); however, it is highly recommended that you use this port solely for OOB management.

Each Fast Ethernet port has an activity LED and a link LED:

- The activity LED shows that data is passing on the network to which the port is attached.
- The link LED shows that the port is operational.

The Cisco ASA 5510 Security Plus license enables Cisco ASA 5510 to provide VLAN support on switched networks (up to 100 VLANs). The Security Plus upgrade license also upgrades two of the interfaces to Gigabit Ethernet, allows up to five virtual firewalls, and provides a greater number of concurrent virtual private network (VPN) connections for remote users and site-to-site connections.

Similar to the Cisco PIX firewalls, Cisco ASA requires a unique license key to enable certain features. This license key is a 40-digit hexadecimal number represented in five tuples (set of fixed-length data types). The security appliance allows an administrator to enter the license key by using the **activation-key** command.

The output of the **show version** command includes information about the license installed on the Cisco ASA. The following is an example of the output:

```
ciscoasa# show version
Cisco Adaptive Security Appliance Software Version 8.0(4)
Device Manager Version 6.1(5)
Compiled on Tue 17-Apr-08 05:47 by builders
System image file is "disk0:/asa804-k8.bin"
Config file at boot was "startup-config"
ciscoasa up 48 days 23 hours
Hardware:   ASA5510-K8, 256 MB RAM, CPU Pentium 4 Celeron 1600 MHz
Internal ATA Compact Flash, 64MB
Slot 1: ATA Compact Flash, 256MB
BIOS Flash AT49LW080 @ 0xffe00000, 1024KB
Encryption hardware device : Cisco ASA-55x0 on-board accelerator (revision 0x0)
                             Boot microcode   : CN1000-MC-BOOT-2.00
                             SSL/IKE microcode: CNLite-MC-SSLm-PLUS-2.01
                             IPSec microcode  : CNlite-MC-IPSECm-MAIN-2.04
0: Ext: Ethernet0/0         : address is 0018.7317.ccce, irq 9
1: Ext: Ethernet0/1         : address is 0018.7317.cccf, irq 9
2: Ext: Ethernet0/2         : address is 0018.7317.ccd0, irq 9
3: Ext: Ethernet0/3         : address is 0018.7317.ccd1, irq 9
4: Ext: Management0/0       : address is 0018.7317.ccd2, irq 11
5: Int: Not used            : irq 11
6: Int: Not used            : irq 5
Licensed features for this platform:
Maximum Physical Interfaces  : Unlimited
Maximum VLANs                : 100
Inside Hosts                 : Unlimited
Failover                     : Active/Active
VPN-DES                      : Enabled
VPN-3DES-AES                 : Enabled
Security Contexts            : 5
GTP/GPRS                     : Disabled
VPN Peers                    : 250
WebVPN Peers                 : 250
Advanced Endpoint Assessment : Enabled
This platform has an ASA 5510 Security Plus license.
Serial Number: JMX10999999
Running Activation Key: 0x1d2d507c 0xb4540465 0xf0509560 0x98e00ce8 0x87372783
Configuration register is 0x1
Configuration last modified by enable_15 at 18:19:35.101 UTC Fri Nov 28 2008
```

The highlighted lines show the license (features) enabled on the Cisco ASA version.

Alternatively, you can use the **show activation-key** command, as shown in the following example:

```
ciscoasa# show activation-key
Serial Number:  JMX10999999
Running Activation Key: 0x1d2d507c 0xb4540465 0xf0509560 0x98e00ce8 0x87372783
Licensed features for this platform:
Maximum Physical Interfaces  : Unlimited
Maximum VLANs                : 100
Inside Hosts                 : Unlimited
Failover                     : Active/Active
VPN-DES                      : Enabled
VPN-3DES-AES                 : Enabled
Security Contexts            : 5
GTP/GPRS                     : Disabled
VPN Peers                    : 250
WebVPN Peers                 : 250
Advanced Endpoint Assessment : Enabled
This platform has an ASA 5510 Security Plus license.
The flash activation key is the SAME as the running key.
ciscoasa#
```

Note Information on how to install the activation key and other system maintenance guidance is covered in Chapter 3, "Initial Setup and System Maintenance."

The RJ-45 console port enables you to physically connect to the appliance to access its command-line interface (CLI) for initial configuration. The AUX (auxiliary) port enables you to connect an external modem for OOB management. The Flash card slot enables you to use an external Flash card to save system images and configuration files.

Two USB ports in the back of all Cisco ASA models are designed for future features. The Reset button is reserved for future use.

Table 2-1 lists the capabilities of the Cisco ASA 5510 appliance, as well as performance and connection limit numbers.

Note Performance numbers vary depending on the packet size and other applications running on the appliance. For more detailed information, go to http://www.cisco.com/go/asa.

Table 2-1 *Cisco ASA 5510 Model Capabilities*

Description	Without Security Plus License	With Security Plus License
Firewall throughput	Up to 300 Mbps	Up to 300 Mbps
3DES/AES IPSec VPN throughput	Up to 170 Mbps	Up to 170 Mbps
Maximum firewall connections	50,000	130,000
IPSec VPN peers	250	250
WebVPN peers	2	250
Interfaces	Five Fast Ethernet ports for security services (including one OOB management port)	Two Gigabit Ethernet ports and three Fast Ethernet ports for security services
Virtual interfaces (VLANs)	50	100
High availability	—	Active/Active and Active/Standby

Cisco ASA 5520 Model

Cisco ASA 5520 provides security services for medium-sized enterprises. The Cisco ASA 5520 and 5540 models are similar to the Cisco ASA 5510 model. All three models are all 1RUs, and the external chassis layouts are similar with the exception of the interfaces. The Cisco ASA 5520 has four Gigabit Ethernet (10/100/1000) copper-based RJ-45 ports instead. They also include a Fast Ethernet port for OOB management.

Figure 2-8 illustrates the front view of the Cisco ASA 5520 model.

Figure 2-8 *Cisco ASA 5520 Front View*

The front panel of the Cisco ASA 5520 has the same five LEDs that are present in the Cisco ASA 5510.

The back view of ASA 5520 is identical to that of ASA 5510, except that the Cisco ASA 5520 has four Gigabit Ethernet (10/100/1000) ports, whereas the Cisco ASA 5510 has four Fast Ethernet ports.

With the installation of a VPN Plus upgrade license, Cisco ASA 5520 can terminate up to 750 IPsec or WebVPN tunnels. Beginning with Cisco ASA software version 7.1, SSL VPN (Web VPN) capability requires a license. The Cisco ASA supports 2 SSL VPN connections by default for evaluation and remote management purposes.

Table 2-2 lists the capabilities of the Cisco ASA 5520 appliance and its performance and connection limit numbers.

> **Note** Performance numbers vary depending on the packet size and other applications running on the appliance.
>
> For more information about licensing, go to http://www.cisco.com/go/asa.

Table 2-2 *Cisco ASA 5520 Model Capabilities*

Description	Performance
Firewall throughput	Up to 450 Mbps
3DES/AES IPSec VPN throughput	Up to 225 Mbps
Maximum firewall connections	280,000
IPSec VPN peers	Up to 750 (depending on license)
WebVPN peers	Up to 750 (depending on license)
Interfaces	Four Gigabit Ethernet ports for security services and one Fast Ethernet port for OOB management
Virtual interfaces (VLANs)	150
High availability	Active/Active and Active/Standby
VPN scalability	VPN clustering and load balancing
Threat mitigation throughput (IPS, firewall, and Anti-X)	225 (with Adaptive Inspection and Prevention Security Services Module (AIP-SSM) 10
375 (with AIP-SSM 20)	450 (with AIP-SSM 40)
Security contexts	Up to 20

Cisco ASA 5540 Model

The Cisco ASA 5540 appliances provide security services to medium-sized enterprises. The Cisco ASA 5540 model supports a higher number of security contexts (50) to provide more flexibility and compartmentalized control of security policies. It also provides support for up to 10 appliances in a VPN cluster, supporting a maximum of 50,000 IPSec VPN peers per cluster (25,000 for WebVPN).

Cisco ASA 5540 is also a 1RU device. The external front and back layouts of the Cisco ASA 5540 appliance are identical to those of the Cisco ASA 5510 and 5520 appliances. Table 2-3 lists the capabilities of the Cisco ASA 5540 appliance and its performance and connection limit numbers.

Beginning with Cisco ASA software version 7.1, SSL VPN (Web VPN) capability requires a license. The Cisco ASA supports 2 SSL VPN connections by default for evaluation and remote management purposes.

Cisco ASA 5550 Model

The Cisco ASA 5550 appliances provide high-availability security services for large enterprise and service-provider networks in a 1RU form-factor. This model provides gigabit connectivity in the form of both Ethernet and fiber-based interfaces.

Table 2-3 *Cisco ASA 5540 Model Capabilities*

Description	Performance
Firewall throughput	Up to 650 Gbps
3DES/AES IPSec VPN throughput	Up to 325 Mbps
Connections	400,000
IPSec VPN peers	5000
SSL VPN peers	2500
Interfaces	Four Gigabit Ethernet ports for security services and one Fast Ethernet port for OOB management
Virtual interfaces (VLANs)	200
High availability	Active/Active and Active/Standby
VPN scalability	VPN clustering and load balancing
Threat mitigation throughput (IPS, firewall, and Anti-X)	500 (wth AIP SSM-20) 650 (with AIP SSM-40)
Security contexts	Up to 50

The external front layout of the Cisco ASA 5550 appliance is identical to that of the Cisco ASA 5510, 5520, and 5540 appliances. The Cisco ASA 5550 appliances have two internal buses providing copper Gigabit Ethernet and fiber Gigabit Ethernet connectivity:

- Slot 0 corresponds to B and has four embedded copper Gigabit Ethernet ports.
- Slot 1 corresponds to Bus 1 and has four embedded copper Gigabit Ethernet ports and four embedded Small Form-Factor Pluggable (SFP) interfaces that support fiber Gigabit Ethernet connectivity.

Tip To maximize traffic throughput, configure the Cisco ASA 5550 so that traffic is distributed equally between the two buses in the device. In other words, configure and lay out the network interfaces so that all traffic connections flow through both Bus 0 (Slot 0) and Bus 1 (Slot 1), entering through one bus and exiting through the other.

Figure 2-9 illustrates the rear view of the Cisco ASA 5550.

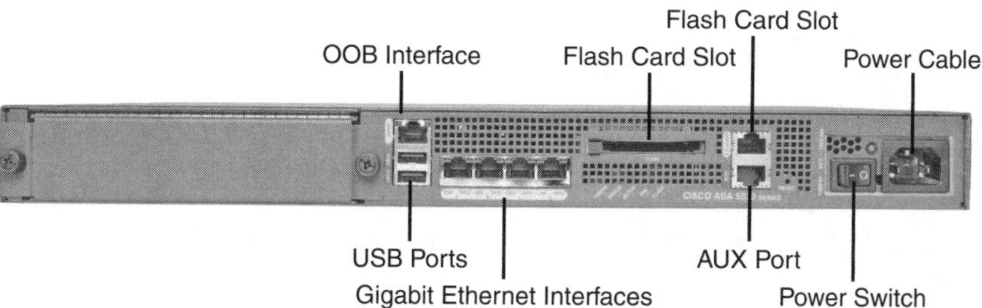

Figure 2-9 *Cisco ASA 5550 Rear View*

Slot 1 has four copper Ethernet ports and four fiber Ethernet ports; however, you can use only four Slot 1 ports at a time. For instance, you could use two Slot 1 copper ports and two fiber ports, but you cannot use fiber ports if you are already using all four Slot 1 copper ports.

Table 2-4 lists the capabilities of the Cisco ASA 5550 and its performance and connection limit numbers.

Beginning with Cisco ASA software version 7.1, SSL VPN (Web VPN) capability requires a license. The Cisco ASA supports two SSL VPN connections by default for evaluation and remote management purposes.

Table 2-4 *Cisco ASA 5550 Model Capabilities*

Description	Performance
Firewall throughput	Up to 1.2 Gbps
3DES/AES IPSec VPN throughput	Up to 425 Mbps
Connections	650,000
IPSec VPN peers	5000
SSL VPN peers	5000
Interfaces	Eight Gigabit Ethernet ports for security services and one Fast Ethernet port for OOB management
Virtual interfaces (VLANs)	250
High availability	Active/Active and Active/Standby
VPN scalability	VPN clustering and load balancing
Threat mitigation throughput (IPS, firewall, and Anti-X)	Not available
Security contexts	Up to 50

Cisco ASA 5580-20 and 5580-40 Models

The Cisco ASA 5580 series adaptive security appliances are available in two models:

- Cisco ASA 5580-20
- Cisco ASA 5580-40

Because of their high performance, these models are typically deployed in the datacenters of large corporations or at the edge of very demanding networks. The Cisco ASA 5580 series adaptive security appliances introduce new capabilities such as highly scalable logging, system environmental monitoring, VPN remote access user limits, and 10-Gigabit Ethernet interfaces.

The ASA 5580-20 and the ASA 5580-40 supports 50 security contexts and up to 100 VLAN interfaces (250 VLAN interfaces will be supported in a future release) and 1 Gigabit of IPSec VPN 3DES performance. They support up to 24 Gigabit data ports or up to 12 10-Gigabit data ports, as well as two additional Gigabit ports for management. Optional redundant, hot-swappable power capabilities are available, as well as hot-swappable cooling fans in case of a fan failure.

Cisco ASA 5580-20

The Cisco ASA 5580-20 can scale to up to 5 Gigabits per second of TCP traffic (UDP performance is even greater). It delivers greater than 90,000 TCP connections per second and supports up to 1 million connections.

Figure 2-10 illustrates the front view of the Cisco ASA 5580 series. Both the Cisco ASA 5580-20 and the 5580-40 have the same physical design.

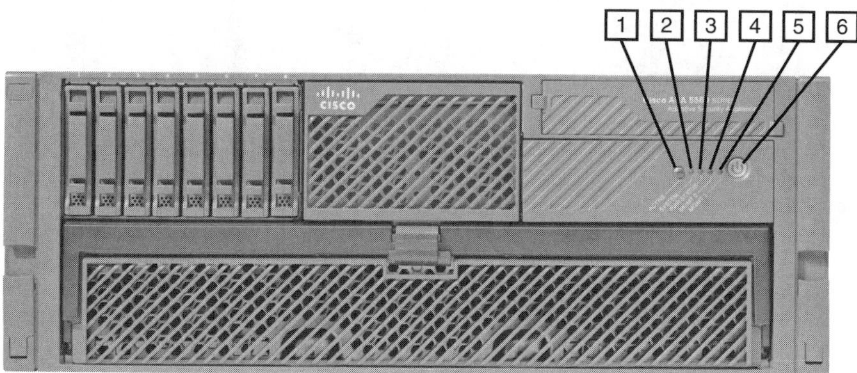

Figure 2-10 *Cisco ASA 5580 Front View*

The following are the components illustrated in Figure 2-10:

Step 1. **Active LED**—Indicates the active and standby failover status. When the system is active the LED is on. When the system is in standby status the LED is off.

Step 2. **System LED**—Shows internal system health. Green indicates that the system is powered on under normal operation. Flashing amber indicates that the system health is degraded. Flashing red indicates that the system health is critical.

Step 3. **Power status LED**—Shows power supply status. Green indicates that the power supply is on. Flashing amber indicates that the power supply health is degraded. Flashing red indicates that the power supply health is critical.

Step 4. **Management 0/0 interface LED**—Green indicates that the interface is connected to the network. Flashing green indicates that there is network activity. The LED is off when there is no network connection.

Step 5. **Management 0/1 interface LED**—Green indicates that the interface is connected to the network. Flashing green indicates that there is network activity. The LED is off when there is no network connection.

Step 6. **Power switch and indicator**—Turns power on and off. Amber means that the system has power and is in standby mode. Green indicates that the system has power and it is turned on.

Figure 2-11 illustrates the back view of the Cisco ASA 5580 series security appliances.

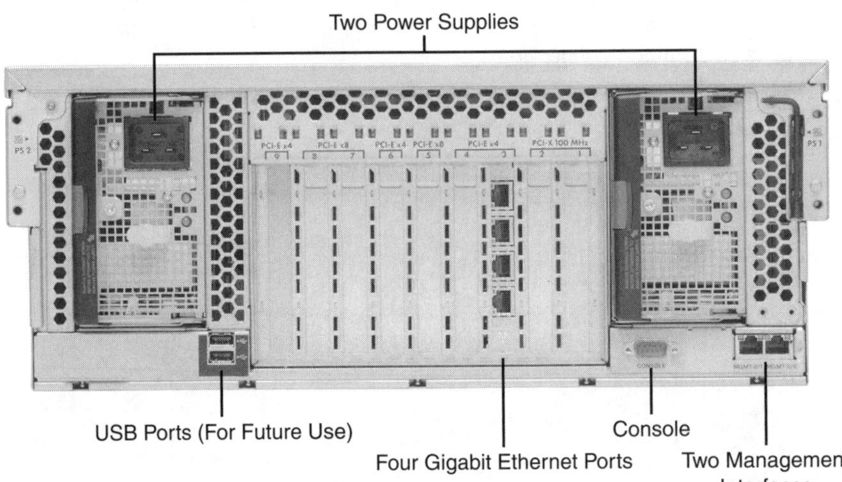

Figure 2-11 *Cisco ASA 5580 Back View*

Table 2-5 lists the capabilities of the Cisco ASA 5580-20 and its performance and connection limit numbers.

Note Performance numbers vary depending on the packet size and other applications running on the appliance. For more detailed information go to www.cisco.com/go/asa.

Cisco ASA 5580-40

The Cisco ASA 5580-40 can scale to up to 10 Gigabits per second of TCP traffic and similar to ASA 5580-20 the UDP performance will be even greater. Additionally, it can process up to 150,000 TCP connections per second and up to 2 million connections in total.

Note The Cisco ASA 5580-20 and the 5580-40 have the same physical design.

Table 2-6 lists the capabilities of the Cisco ASA 5580-40 and its performance and connection limit numbers.

Table 2-5 *Cisco ASA 5580-20 Model Capabilities*

Description	Performance
Firewall throughput	Up to 5 Gbps (real-world HTTP) and 10 Gbps (jumbo frames)
3DES/AES IPSec VPN throughput	Up to 1 Gbps
Connections	1,000,000
IPSec VPN peers	10,000
SSL VPN peers	10,000
Interfaces	Two Gigabit Ethernet management interfaces. Four Gigabit Ethernet (with ASA5580-4GE-CU) Four Gigabit Ethernet SR LC (with ASA5580-4GE-FI) Two 10-Gigabit Ethernet SR LC (with ASA5580-2X10GE-SR)
Virtual interfaces (VLANs)	250 (starting in 8.1(2) the limit was increased from 100 to 250)
High availability	Active/Active and Active/Standby
VPN scalability	VPN clustering and load balancing
Threat mitigation throughput (IPS, firewall, and Anti-X)	Not available
Security contexts	Up to 50

Cisco ASA AIP-SSM Module

The following are the three Adaptive Inspection and Prevention Security Services Module (AIP-SSM) models, which provide support for IPS services delivered by Cisco IPS software:

- AIP-SSM-10—Supported only on the Cisco ASA 5510 and 5520 appliances.
- AIP-SSM-20—Supported only on the Cisco ASA 5510, 5520, and 5540 appliances.
- AIP-SSM-40—Supported only on the Cisco ASA 5520 and 5540 appliances.

Table 2-6 *Cisco ASA 5580-40 Model Capabilities*

Description	Performance
Firewall throughput	Up to 10 Gbps (real-world HTTP) and 20 Gbps (jumbo frames)
3DES/AES IPSec VPN throughput	Up to 1 Gbps
Connections	2,000,000
IPSec VPN peers	10,000
SSL VPN peers	10,000
Interfaces	Two Gigabit Ethernet management interfaces Four Gigabit Ethernet (with ASA5580-4GE-CU) Four Gigabit Ethernet SR LC (with ASA5580-4GE-FI) Two 10-Gigabit Ethernet SR LC (with ASA5580-2X10GE-SR)
Virtual interfaces (VLANs)	250 (starting in 8.1(2) the limit was increased from 100 to 250)
High availability	Active/Active and Active/Standby
VPN scalability	VPN clustering and load balancing
Threat mitigation throughput (IPS, firewall, and Anti-X)	Not available
Security contexts	Up to 50

Note The Cisco ASA 5550 and 5580 series do not support the AIP-SSM modules.

All the Cisco AIP-SSM modules have the same physical characteristics. Figure 2-12 shows the Cisco AIP-SSM-20 module.

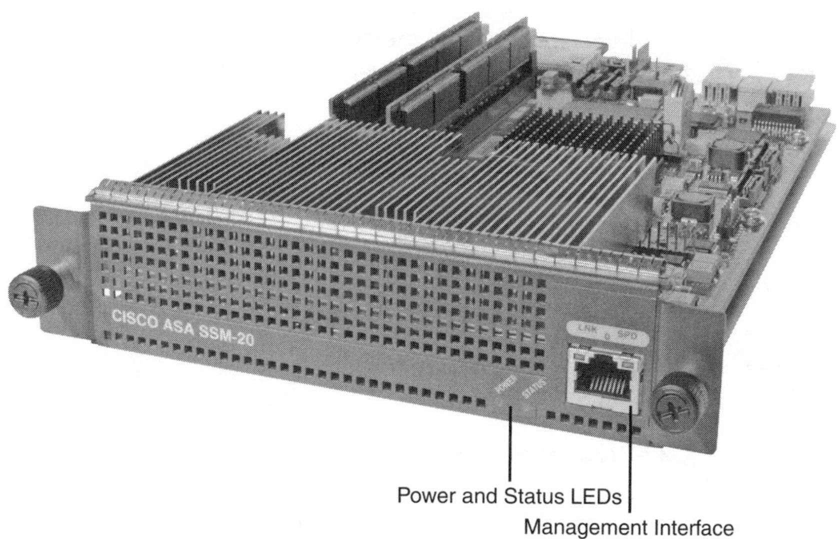

Figure 2-12 *Cisco ASA AIP-SSM-20*

Cisco ASA AIP-SSM-10

The Cisco ASA AIP-SSM-10 concurrent threat mitigation throughput can scale to up to 150 Mbps with the Cisco ASA 5510 and up to 225 Mbps with the Cisco ASA 5520. It comes with 1 Gigabyte (GB) of Random Access Memory (RAM) and 256 Megabyte (MB) of flash memory.

Cisco ASA AIP-SSM-20

The Cisco ASA AIP-SSM-20 concurrent threat mitigation throughput can scale to up to 300 Mbps with the Cisco ASA 5510, up to 375 Mbps with the Cisco ASA 5520, and up to 500 Mbps with the Cisco ASA 5540. It comes with 2 GB of RAM and 256 MB of flash memory.

Cisco ASA AIP-SSM-40

The Cisco ASA AIP-SSM-40 concurrent threat mitigation throughput can scale to up to 450 Mbps with the Cisco ASA 5520 and up to 650 Mbps with the Cisco ASA 5540. It comes with 4 GB of RAM and 2 GB of flash memory.

Note Configuration and troubleshooting of the Cisco ASA AIP-SSM modules is covered in Chapter 12, "Configuring and Troubleshooting Intrusion Prevention System (IPS)."

Cisco ASA Gigabit Ethernet Modules

There are several Gigabit Ethernet expansion modules for the Cisco ASA appliances. The Cisco ASA 5510, 5520, 5540, and 5550 support the Cisco ASA 4-Port Gigabit Ethernet Security Services Module (4GE-SSM).

Note The Cisco ASA 5550 is already equipped with this module.

The Cisco ASA 5580-20 and 5580-40 support the following modules:

- 4-Port Gigabit Ethernet Copper PCI Express Card
- 2-Port 10 Gigabit Ethernet Fiber PCI Express Card
- 4-Port Gigabit Ethernet Fiber PCI Express Card

Cisco ASA 4GE-SSM

The Cisco ASA 4GE-SSM has four 10/100/1000 RJ-45 ports and four Small Form-Factor Pluggable (SFP) ports to support both copper and optical connections. You can choose copper or fiber connectivity for each of the four ports, providing flexibility for data center, campus, or enterprise edge connectivity (with a maximum of four ports in service concurrently). It expands the Cisco ASA 5510 with a Security Plus license to three Fast Ethernet and six Gigabit Ethernet ports. Similarly, it expands the Cisco ASA 5520 and 5540 appliances to eight Gigabit Ethernet ports and one Fast Ethernet management port. Figure 2-13 illustrates the Cisco ASA 4GE-SSM.

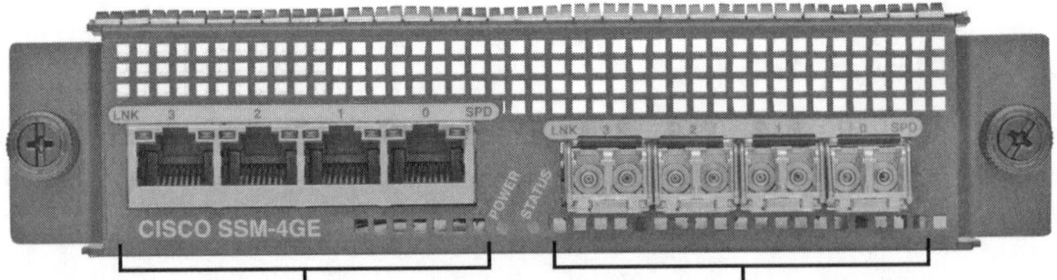

Figure 2-13 *Cisco ASA 4GE-SSM*

Cisco ASA 5580 Expansion Cards

The Cisco ASA 5580 4-Port Gigabit Ethernet Copper PCI Express card provides four 10/100/1000BASE-T interfaces, which allow up to 24 total Gigabit Ethernet interfaces in a fully populated chassis. Figure 2-14 shows the 4-Port Gigabit Ethernet Copper PCI Express Card.

The Cisco ASA 5580 4-Port Gigabit Ethernet Fiber PCI Express card provides four 1000BASE-SX (fiber) interfaces, expanding to up to 24 total Gigabit Ethernet fiber interfaces in a fully populated chassis.

Figure 2-14 *4-Port Gigabit Ethernet Copper PCI Express Card*

Note The 4-Port Gigabit Ethernet Fiber PCI Express card ports require a multi-mode fiber cable with an LC connector to connect to the SX interface of the chassis.

Figure 2-15 shows the 4-Port Gigabit Ethernet Fiber PCI Express card.

The Cisco ASA 5580 2-Port 10-Gigabit Ethernet Fiber PCI Express card provides two 1000BASE-SX (fiber) interfaces, expanding to up to 12 total 10-Gigabit Ethernet fiber interfaces in a fully populated chassis.

Note The 2-Port 10-Gigabit Ethernet Fiber PCI Express card ports require a multi-mode fiber cable with an LC connector to connect to the SX interface of the chassis.

Figure 2-16 shows the 2-Port Gigabit Ethernet Fiber PCI Express card.

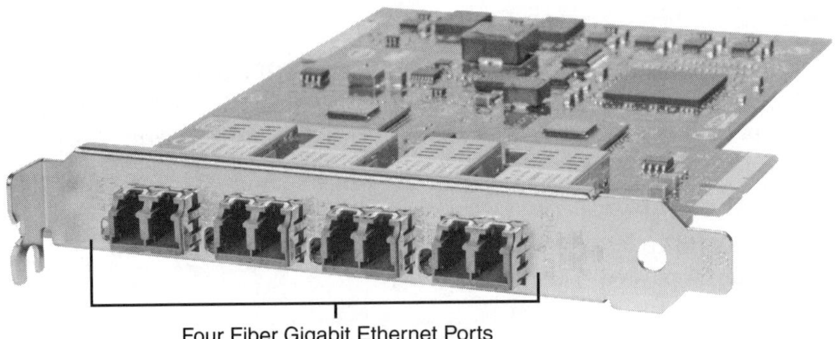

Figure 2-15 *4-Port Gigabit Ethernet Fiber PCI Express Card*

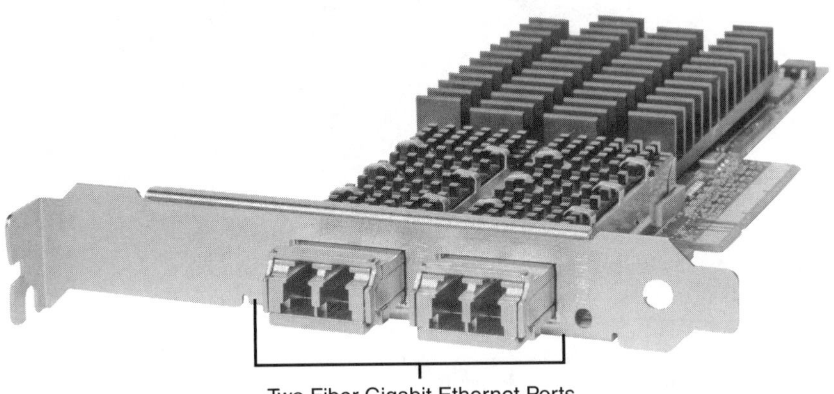

Figure 2-16 *2-Port Gigabit Ethernet Fiber PCI Express Card*

Cisco ASA CSC-SSM Module

The Cisco ASA CSC-SSM module provides an all-in-one content management solution for detection and stoppage of viruses, worms, Trojans, and other threats in SMTP, POP3, HTTP, and FTP network traffic. It runs Trend Micro InterScan software.

> **Note** The Cisco ASA CSC-SSM cannot scan traffic using the HTTPS protocol because this traffic is encrypted.

Additionally, the Cisco ASA CSC-SSM can block compressed or very large files that exceed specified parameters. There are two different licenses for this module: the base license and the security plus. If you have purchased the plus level of the CSC SSM license, in addition to the previously mentioned features you can also accomplish the following:

- Decrease the amount of spam in your email traffic.
- Protect against phishing fraud.
- Set up content filters to allow or prohibit email traffic containing key words or phrases.
- Block URLs according to predefined filters that you allow or disallow, such as adult or mature content, games, chat or instant messaging, gambling sites, or URLs that are known to have hidden or malicious purposes.

The Cisco ASA CSC-SSM provides virus protection, spyware blocking, spam detection, or content filtering in a single, easy-to-maintain solution.

The Cisco ASA CSC-SSM is available in two models:

- **Cisco ASA CSC-SSM-10**—Supported on the Cisco ASA 5510, 5520, and 5540.
- **Cisco ASA CSC-SSM-20**—Supported on the Cisco ASA 5510, 5520, and 5540.

> **Note** The main difference between the CSC-SSM-10 and CSC-SSM-20 is the amount of RAM memory and the processor speed.

The Cisco ASA CSC-SSM modules have the same physical characteristics as the Cisco ASA AIP-SSM modules (as previously illustrated in Figure 2-16).

> **Note** Configuration and troubleshooting of the Cisco ASA CSC-SSM modules is covered in Chapter 12.

Summary

This chapter provided a hardware overview of all Cisco ASA 5500 Series appliances and additional modules. It provided information about the broad range of firewall, VPN, application inspection, IPS, and Anti-X services they offer to small, medium, and large enterprises. In-depth technical information for each feature and capability is provided in subsequent chapters.

Chapter 3

Initial Setup and System Maintenance

This chapter covers the following topics:

- Accessing the Cisco ASA appliances
- Managing licenses
- Initial setup
- IP version 6
- Setting up the system clock
- Configuration management
- Remote system management
- System maintenance
- System monitoring

Cisco Adaptive Security Appliance (ASA) can be set up in a number of ways to adapt to any network topology. However, proper planning is essential for successful implementations of the security features that Cisco ASA offers. This chapter guides you through the initial configuration of the security appliance and shows ways to monitor the system's health and status.

Accessing the Cisco ASA Appliances

Cisco ASA provides two types of user interfaces:

- **Command-line interface (CLI)**—The CLI provides non-graphical access to the Cisco ASA. The CLI can be accessed from a console, Telnet, or Secure Shell (SSH) session. Telnet and SSH are discussed later in the chapter, under "Remote System Management."

- **Graphical user interface (GUI) via ASDM**—Cisco Adaptive Security Device Manager (ASDM) provides an easy-to-navigate and simple graphical interface to set up and manage the different features that Cisco Adaptive Security Appliance (ASA) provides. It is bundled with a variety of administration and monitoring tools to check the health of the appliance and the traffic traversing through it. ASDM access requires IP connectivity between the ASDM client and the security appliance. If you have a new security appliance, you can assign the initial IP address via the CLI and then establish a GUI ASDM connection.

Establishing a Console Connection

A new security appliance, by default, has no configuration and thus it does not have IP addresses assigned to any of its interfaces. To access the CLI, you need a successful connection to the console port of the security appliance. The console port is a serial asynchronous port with the settings listed in Table 3-1.

You can connect the console port on the security appliance to a serial port on a PC by using a flat rolled console cable, with a DB9 serial adapter on one end and a RJ-45 port on the other. The DB9 side of the cable goes to the serial port of a PC, and the RJ-45 end of the cable goes to the console port of the security appliance, as illustrated in Figure 3-1.

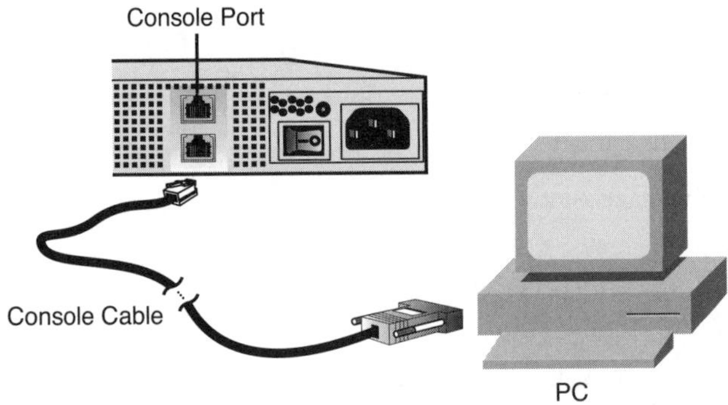

Figure 3-1 *Console Port Connectivity from a Computer*

After connecting the console cable to the security appliance and the computer, launch terminal-emulation software, such as HyperTerminal or TeraTerm, to send and receive output. You can launch HyperTerminal by navigating to **Start > Programs > Accessories > Communications > HyperTerminal** on a Windows-based PC. The initial configuration window of HyperTerminal is shown in Figure 3-2. In the Connection Description dialog box, enter a connection name to identify this session as a unique connection. A connection name of **Console Connection to the Cisco ASA** is specified in Figure 3-2. You can choose an icon to associate with the connection entry. After filling out the connection name and selecting an icon, click **OK** to proceed.

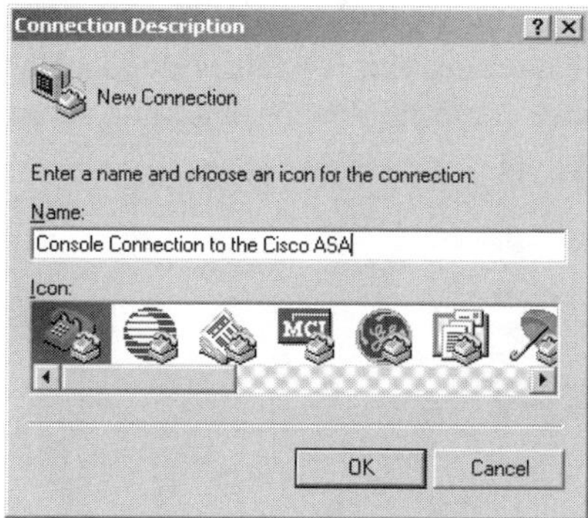

Figure 3-2 *Initial Configuration of HyperTerminal*

Specify the connection type in the Connect To window. Because the console port uses an asynchronous serial connection, the HyperTerminal setting must use a COM port. As illustrated in Figure 3-3, COM3 is being set up for the serial connection to the security appliance. After you are finished, click **OK** to proceed to the next configuration window.

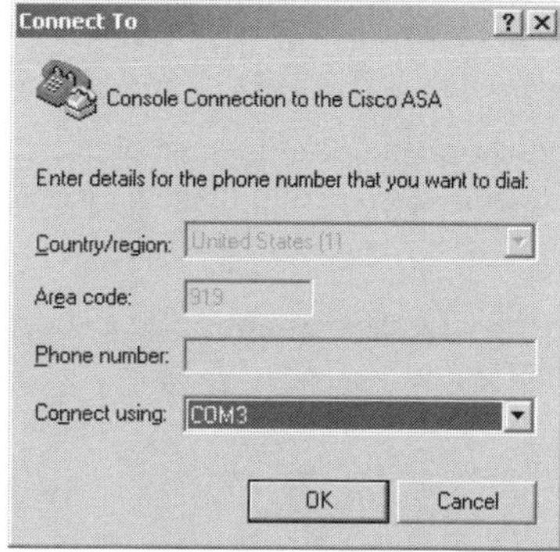

Figure 3-3 *Setting HyperTerminal Connection Type*

Table 3-1 *Console Port Settings*

Parameters	Value
Baud rate	9600
Data bits	8
Parity	None
Stop bits	1
Flow control	Hardware

The last window is used to configure port properties, such as the baud rate and flow control. Figure 3-4 shows HyperTerminal set up with the values listed in Table 3-1. After configuring the port settings, click **OK** to complete the configuration setup.

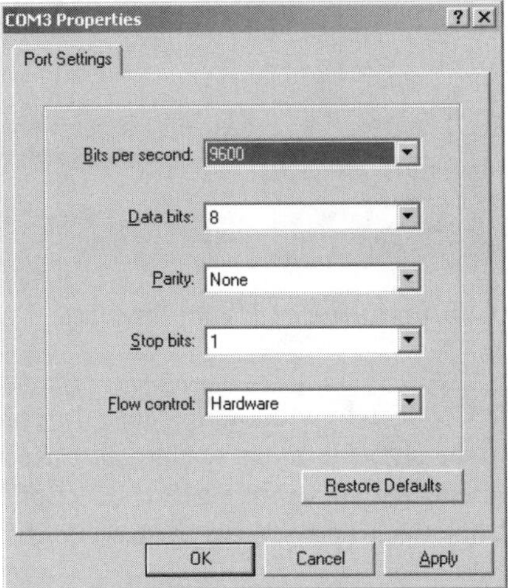

Figure 3-4 *Setting HyperTerminal Port Specification*

The HyperTerminal application is ready to transmit and receive data from the security appliance. If you press **Enter** a couple of times, you should see a **ciscoasa>** prompt in the HyperTerminal window.

The next section describes how to use the CLI after establishing a successful console connection.

Command-Line Interface

After a successful console connection, the security appliance is ready to accept your commands. The Cisco ASA contains a command set structure similar to that of a Cisco IOS router and offers the following access modes:

- User mode, also known as user access mode
- Privileged mode
- Configuration mode
- Sub-configuration mode
- ROMMON mode

User mode, shown as the hostname with a **>** sign, is the first mode of access available when you log in to the security appliance. This mode offers a limited set of commands that are useful in obtaining basic information about the security appliance. One of the important commands in this mode is **enable**, which prompts a user to specify a password to log in to privileged mode.

Privileged mode, shown as the hostname with a # sign, gives full access to a user after a successful logon. This mode also allows execution of all the commands that are available in user mode. The security appliance offers a rich set of monitoring and troubleshooting commands to check the health of different processes and features in the security appliance. One of the important commands in this mode is **configure terminal**, which places a user in configuration mode.

Note The security appliance enables you to restrict the commands a user can run by implementing command authorization. This is covered in Chapter 6, "Authentication, Authorization, and Accounting (AAA) Services."

Configuration mode, displayed as the host name with a **(config)#** prompt, allows a user to enable or disable a feature, set up security and networking components, and tweak the default parameters. This mode not only enables the user to configure the security appliance, but also allows the use of all the commands that are available in the user and privileged modes. A user may enter into the sub-configuration mode of different features from this mode.

Sub-configuration mode, displayed as the hostname with a **(config-*xx*)#** prompt, lets a user configure specific networking or security features on the security appliance. The *xx* is replaced by the process/feature keyword that is being configured on the security appliance. For example, if a user is setting up specific parameters on an interface, the prompt changes to **(config-if)#**. Sub-configuration mode enables the user to execute all the configuration mode commands as well as the user and privileged mode commands.

In Example 3-1, a user logs in to privileged mode from user access mode by typing the **enable** command. The security appliance prompts a user to specify a password to gain privileged mode access. If the security appliance has the default configuration, it uses a null (no) password to grant access. After logging in to privileged mode, the user types **configure terminal** to access configuration mode. The user enters into interface sub-configuration mode by typing the **interface GigabitEthernet0/0** command. To go back to the previous mode, the user can enter **exit** or **quit**, as shown in Example 3-1.

Example 3-1 *Accessing the Privileged and Configuration Modes*

```
ciscoasa> enable
Password: <cr>
ciscoasa# configure terminal
ciscoasa(config)# interface GigabitEthernet0/0
ciscoasa(config-if)# exit
ciscoasa(config)# exit
ciscoasa#
```

Tip In the preceding example, the administrator of the security appliance typed **exit** twice to return to the privileged mode prompt. Optionally, you can type **end** to return to privileged mode from any configuration mode.

Like a Cisco IOS router, the security appliance also allows you to press the Tab key to complete a partial command. For example, to enter a **show** command, type **sho** and press the Tab key. The security appliance displays the complete **show** command on the screen.

The security appliance allows you to abbreviate commands and keywords to the number of characters that identify a distinct abbreviation. For example, you can abbreviate the **enable** command as **en**.

All the supported options and arguments of a command are displayed when you type **?** after the command. For example, you can type **show ?** to see all the options that are supported under the **show** command.

The security appliance also provides a brief description and command syntax when you type **help** followed by the command. For example, when you type **help reload**, the security appliance shows the command syntax for **reload**, a description, and the supported arguments.

The security appliance uses *ROMMON mode* (*Read-Only-Memory Monitor mode*) when it does not find a bootable image or when an administrator forces it to enter into that mode. In ROMMON mode, you can use a TFTP server to load a system image into the security appliance. ROMMON mode is also used to recover the system password, discussed later in this chapter under "Image Recovery Using ROMMON."

Managing Licenses

As mentioned in Chapter 2, "Cisco ASA Product and Solution Overview," the security appliance controls the security and networking features through the use of a license key. You can obtain the information of the currently installed license key by issuing the **show version** command. This command also displays other system information, such as:

- The current version and the location of the system image
- The ASDM version, if installed
- The security appliance uptime
- The security appliance hardware model number, including the memory and flash information
- The physical interface and the associated IRQs (Interrupt Requests)
- The current features that are active on the security appliance
- The license information

- The security appliance's serial number
- Configuration register setting
- Information about last configuration modification

Example 3-2 shows the output of **show version**, which has a VPN Plus–based license key installed.

Example 3-2 *Output of show version*

```
Chicago> show version
Cisco Adaptive Security Appliance Software Version 8.2(1)
Device Manager Version 6.2(1)

Compiled on Tue 05-May-09 22:45 by builders
System image file is "disk0:/asa821-k8.bin"
Config file at boot was "startup-config"

Chicago up 31 days 4 hours

Hardware:   ASA5520, 512 MB RAM, CPU Pentium 4 Celeron 2000 MHz
Internal ATA Compact Flash, 64MB
BIOS Flash M50FW016 @ 0xffe00000, 2048KB

Encryption hardware device : Cisco ASA-55x0 on-board accelerator (revision 0x0)
                              Boot microcode   : &#x263B;CN1000-MC-BOOT-2.00
                              SSL/IKE microcode: ♥CNLite-MC-SSLm-PLUS-2.03
                             IPSec microcode   : &#x263A;CNlite-MC-IPSECm-MAIN-2.04
 0: Ext: GigabitEthernet0/0  : address is 000f.f775.4b54, irq 9
 1: Ext: GigabitEthernet0/1  : address is 000f.f775.4b55, irq 9
 2: Ext: GigabitEthernet0/2  : address is 000f.f775.4b56, irq 9
 3: Ext: GigabitEthernet0/3  : address is 000f.f775.4b57, irq 9
 4: Ext: Management0/0       : address is 000f.f775.4b53, irq 11
 5: Int: Internal-Data0/0    : address is 0000.0001.0002, irq 11
 6: Int: Internal-Control0/0 : address is 0000.0001.0001, irq 5

Licensed features for this platform:
Maximum Physical Interfaces  : Unlimited
Maximum VLANs                : 150
Inside Hosts                 : Unlimited
Failover                     : Active/Active
VPN-DES                      : Enabled
VPN-3DES-AES                 : Enabled
Security Contexts            : 10
GTP/GPRS                     : Enabled
```

```
SSL VPN Peers                 : 2
Total VPN Peers               : 750
Shared License                : Disabled
AnyConnect for Mobile         : Disabled
AnyConnect for Linksys phone  : Disabled
AnyConnect Essentials         : Disabled
Advanced Endpoint Assessment  : Disabled
UC Phone Proxy Sessions       : 2
Total UC Proxy Sessions       : 2
Botnet Traffic Filter         : Disabled

This platform has an ASA 5520 VPN Plus license.

Serial Number: JAB00000001
Running Activation Key: 0x00000001 0x00000001 0x00000001 0x00000001 0x00000001
Configuration register is 0x1
Configuration last modified by cisco at 20:45:09.870 UTC Mon Jul 20 2009
```

In Example 3-2, the security appliance is running a system image of 8.2(1) with the ASDM image of 6.2(1). The hardware model is ASA5520, running the Plus license. The serial number and the license activation key are masked to protect this system's identity. The configuration register is set to 0x1, which instructs the security appliance to load the image from flash. The configuration register is discussed later in the "Password Recovery Process" section.

You can change the installed license key by using the **activation-key** command followed by the five-tuple key, as shown in Example 3-3. After the new activation key is entered, the security appliance shows the features set activated by the new license key. In this example, a VPN premium license key is installed.

Example 3-3 *Changing the Activation Key*

```
Chicago# activation-key 0x11223344 0x55667788 0x9900aabb 0xccddeeff 0x01234567

Licensed features for this platform:
Maximum Physical Interfaces : Unlimited
Maximum VLANs               : 100
Inside Hosts                : Unlimited
Failover                    : Active/Active
VPN-DES                     : Enabled
VPN-3DES-AES                : Enabled
Security Contexts           : 50
GTP/GPRS                    : Disabled
VPN Peers                   : 5000
This machine has a VPN Premium license.
```

```
Both running and flash activation keys were updated with the requested key.
```

Note Feature-specific activation keys are discussed in their respective chapters. For example, Chapter 19 discusses the license model for SSL VPN tunnels.

Initial Setup

If you are setting up a new security appliance, it must be configured from the CLI first. You cannot use ASDM until the security appliance is configured with the appropriate IP addresses and it has IP connectivity to ASDM client machine.

Initial Setup via CLI

When the security appliance is booted with no configuration, it offers a setup menu that enables you to configure the initial parameters such as the device name and the IP address. You can choose to go through the initial setup menu for quick configuration.

In Example 3-4, a security appliance prompts users to specify whether they wish to go through the interactive menu to preconfigure the device. If a user types **no**, the interactive menu is not shown and the security appliance shows the **ciscoasa>** prompt. If a user types **yes**, the default option, the security appliance walks the user through the configuration of ten parameters. The security appliance shows the default values in brackets ([]) before prompting the user to accept or change them. To accept the default input, press Enter. After going through the initial setup menu, the security appliance displays the summary of the new configuration before prompting the user to accept or reject it.

Example 3-4 *Initial Setup Menu*

```
Pre-configure Firewall now through interactive prompts [yes]? yes
Firewall Mode [Routed]:
Enable password [<use current password>]: C1$c0123
Allow password recovery [yes]?
Clock (UTC):
  Year [2009]:
  Month [Jul]: Nov
  Day [21]:
  Time [01:08:57]: 21:27:00
Inside IP address: 192.168.10.1
Inside network mask: 255.255.255.0
Host name: Chicago
Domain name: securemeinc.com
IP address of host running Device Manager: 192.168.10.77
```

```
The following configuration will be used:
Enable password: cisco123
Allow password recovery: yes
Clock (UTC): 21:27:00 Nov 21 2009
Firewall Mode: Routed
Inside IP address: 192.168.10.1
Inside network mask: 255.255.255.0
Host name: Chicago
Domain name: securemeinc.com
IP address of host running Device Manager: 192.168.10.77

Use this configuration and write to flash? yes
INFO: Security level for "inside" set to 100 by default.
WARNING: http server is not yet enabled to allow ASDM access.
Cryptochecksum: e15ea3e4 a499e6cf e84f5b82 1994bde0

1809 bytes copied in 3.490 secs (621 bytes/sec)
Type help or '?' for a list of available commands.
Chicago>
```

Table 3-2 lists all the parameters that can be configured in the initial setup menu. It also provides a brief description of each parameter, along with the default and configured values.

You can define the initial parameters and features by using either the CLI commands or the ASDM. They are discussed throughout this chapter. The next section discusses how to configure a device name from the ASDM.

Tip You can rerun the interactive setup process by using the **setup** command in configuration mode.

Initial Setup of ASDM

Before you can access the ASDM graphical console, you must install the ASDM software image on the local flash of the security appliance. The ASDM console can manage a local security appliance only. Therefore, if you need to manage multiple security appliances, the ASDM software must be installed on all the Cisco ASAs. However, a single workstation can launch multiple instances of ASDM clients to manage the different appliances. Optionally, you can leverage Cisco Security Manager (CSM) to configure multiple appliances simultaneously.

Table 3-2 *Initial Setup Parameters and Their Values*

Parameter	Description	Default Value	Configured Value
Enable password	Specifies the enable password	None	**C1$c0123**
Firewall mode	Sets up the security appliance as a Layer 2 (Transparent) or Layer 3 (Routed) firewall	Routed	**Routed**
Inside IP address	Specifies the IP address on the inside interface	None	**192.168.10.1**
Inside subnet mask	Specifies the subnet mask on the inside interface	None	**255.255.255.0**
Host name	Sets the hostname on the device	ciscoasa	**Chicago**
Domain name	Sets the domain name on the device	None	**securemeinc.com**
IP address of host running Device Manager	Specifies the IP address of the host machine responsible for managing the Cisco ASA	None	**192.168.10.77**
Clock	Sets up the current time on the Cisco ASA	varies	**9:27 PM November 21st 2009**
Save configuration	Prompts the user if configuration needs to be saved	Yes	**Yes**
Allow password recovery	Prompts the user if password recovery is allowed	Yes	**Yes**

Note This book focuses on setting up Cisco ASA through ASDM and the CLI. Configuring ASA through CSM is beyond the scope of this book.

Uploading ASDM

You can use the **dir** command to determine whether the ASDM software is installed. If the security appliance does not have the ASDM software, your first step is to upload the image from an external file server, using the one of the supported protocols. The appliance needs to be set up for basic configuration, such as the interface names, security levels, IP addresses, and proper routes, discussed later in this chapter. After setting up basic information, use the **copy** command to transfer the image file, as shown in Example 3-5, where an ASDM file, named **asdm-621.bin**, is being copied from a TFTP server located at

192.168.10.10. Verify the content of the local flash after the file is successfully uploaded. Copying images is discussed later in this chapter.

Example 3-5 *Uploading the ASDM Image to the Local Flash*

```
Chicago# copy tftp flash
Address or name of remote host []? 192.168.10.10
Source filename []? asdm-621.bin
Destination filename [asdm-621.bin]? asdm-621.bin

Accessing tftp://192.168.10.10/asdm-621.bin...!!!!!!!!!!!!!!!!!!!!!!!!!!!!!!!!!!!
! Output omitted for brevity.
!!!!!!!!!!!!!!!!!!!!!!!!!!!!!!!!!!!!!!!!!
Writing file disk0:/asdm-621.bin...
!!!!!!!!!!!!!!!!!!!!!!!!!!!!!!!!!!!!!!!!!!!!!!!!!!!!!!!!!!!!!!!!!!!!!!!!!!!!!!!!!!
! Output omitted for brevity.
!!!!!!!!!!!!!!!!!!!!!!!!!!!!!!!!!!!!!!!!!!!!!!!!!!!!!!!!!!!!!!!!!!!!!!!!!!!!!!!
6889764 bytes copied in 161.420 secs (36500 bytes/sec)
Chicago# dir
Directory of disk0:/
1260    -rw-   14524416     16:47:34 May 13 2009   asa821-k8.bin
2511    -rw-   6889764      17:38:14 May 13 2009   asdm-621.bin

62881792 bytes total (46723072 bytes free)
```

Setting Up the Appliance

When the ASDM file is accessed, the Cisco ASA loads the first ASDM image that it finds from the local flash. If multiple ASDM images exist in the flash, use the **asdm image** command and specify the location of the ASDM image you want to load. This ensures that the appliance always loads the specified image when ASDM is launched. In Example 3-6, the appliance is set up to use **asdm-621.bin** as the ASDM image file.

Example 3-6 *Specifying the ASDM Location*

```
Chicago(config)# asdm image disk0:/asdm-621.bin
```

The security appliance uses the Secure Socket Layer (SSL) protocol to communicate with the client. Consequently, the security appliance acts as a web server to process the requests from the clients. You must enable the web server on the appliance by using the **http server enable** command.

The security appliance discards the incoming requests until the ASDM client's IP address is in the trusted network to access the HTTP engine. In Example 3-7, the administrator enables the HTTP engine and sets up the appliance to trust the **192.168.10.0/24** network connected toward the **inside** interface.

Example 3-7 *Enabling the HTTP Server*

```
Chicago(config)# http server enable
Chicago(config)# http 192.168.10.0 255.255.255.0 inside
```

Note The SSL VPN implementation on the appliance also requires you to run the HTTP server on the appliance. Starting from version 8.0, you can set up the security appliance to terminate both the SSL VPN as well as the ASDM sessions on the same interface, using the default port of 443. Use https://<ASAipaddress>/admin to access the GUI for admin and management purposes. This is discussed in Chapter 19.

Accessing ASDM

ASDM's interface can be accessed from any workstation whose IP address is in the trusted network list. Before you establish the secure connection to the appliance, verify that IP connectivity exists between the workstation and the Cisco ASA.

To establish an SSL connection, launch a browser and point the URL to the appliance's IP address. In Figure 3-5, the administrator accesses ASDM by entering **https://192.168.10.1/admin** as the URL. The URL is redirected to https://192.168.10.1/admin/public/index.html.

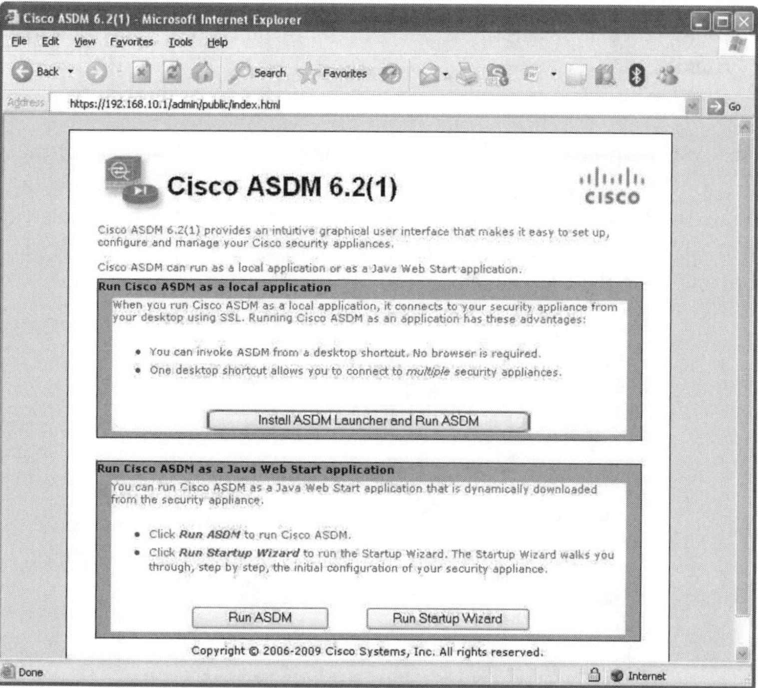

Figure 3-5 *Accessing the ASDM URL*

Note ASDM requires Sun Java plug-in 1.4(2), 1.5.0, or 6.0 installed on the web browser. The supported operating systems include Microsoft Windows Vista, 2003 Server, XP, 2000 Service Pack 4, Macintosh OS X, Red Hat Desktop, and Enterprise version 4.

The new security appliance presents its self-signed certificate to the workstation so that a secure connection can be established. If the certificate is accepted, the security appliance prompts the user to present authentication credentials. If the ASDM authentication or enable password is not set up, there is no default username or password. If enable password is defined, there is no default username and you must use enable password as the login password. If user authentication is enabled on the security appliance through use of the **aaa authentication http console** command, then those login credentials must be provided. After a successful user authentication, the appliance presents two ways to launch ASDM:

- **Run ASDM as Java web start application**—The security appliance launches ASDM in the client's browser as a Java applet. This option is not feasible if a firewall that filters out Java applets exists between the client and the security appliance.
- **Run ASDM as a local application**—The security appliance offers a setup utility called asdm-launcher.msi, which can be saved to the workstation's local hard drive.

Note ASDM as a local application feature is currently supported on Windows-based operating systems.

When the ASDM application is launched, it prompts for the IP address of the security appliance to which you are trying to connect, as well as the user authentication credentials. Figure 3-6 illustrates this, where an SSL connection is being made to an appliance located at 192.168.10.1. If you have an enable password configured, specify it under Password and leave the Username blank to log in to ASDM.

Figure 3-6 *Launching ASDM*

Note If you are running version 8.2(1) on the security appliance, make sure that you use version 6.2(1) of ASDM. For more information about ASDM, consult http://www.cisco.com/go/asdm.

If the user authentication is successful, ASDM checks the current version of the installer application and downloads a new copy if necessary. It loads the current configuration from the security appliance and displays it in the GUI, as shown in Figure 3-7.

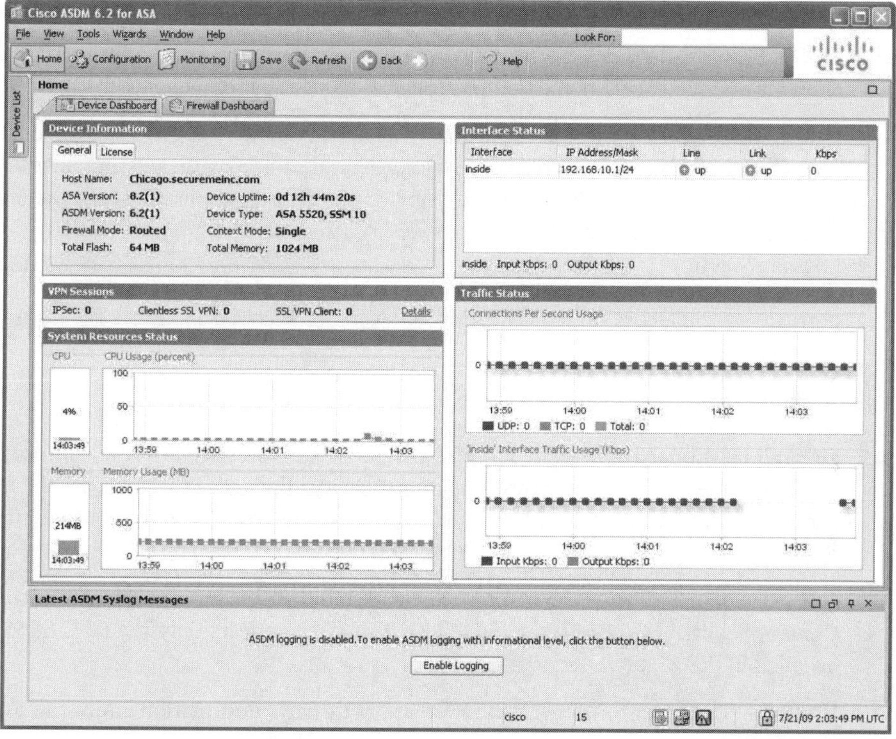

Figure 3-7 *Initial ASDM Screen*

Tip ASDM logs debug and error messages into a file to troubleshoot any application-related issues. The name of the file is asdm-log-[timestamp].txt, and it is located at *user_home_directory*\.asdm\log. For example, C:\Documents and Settings\user\.asdm\log.

ASDM divides the initial screen, also known as the Home screen, into the following six sections:

- **Device Information—**Displays the hardware and software information of the security appliance, such as the current version of operating system and the device type. If the License tab is selected, ASDM shows the features that are enabled on the security appliance.

- **VPN Sessions—**Displays the number of active IPSec, clientless, and AnyConnect SSL VPN tunnels
- **System Resources Status—** Provides the current status of CPU and memory usage on the appliance.
- **Interface Status—**Displays the interface name and the assigned IP address. It also shows the link information of the currently configured interfaces and the rate of traffic passing through them.
- **Traffic Status—**Provides information about the number of active TCP and UDP connections and the traffic rate passing through the outside interface.
- **Latest ASDM Syslog Messages—**Shows the latest ASDM syslog messages that are generated by the security appliance. Syslogging is disabled by default and needs to be enabled for log monitoring. When enabled, the security appliance sends the messages to the ASDM client. This is discussed later in the chapter, in the "System Logging" section.

The statistics on the Home screen are refreshed every 10 seconds and show the information for the last 5 minutes.

ASDM shows three additional tabs on the home screen. They include

- **Firewall Dashboard Tab—**The Firewall Dashboard tab presents statistical information about the traffic passing through your security appliance. This includes the number of connections, NAT translations, dropped packets, attacks, and top usage statistics.
- **Content Security Tab—**The Content Security tab displays information about the Content Security and Control (CSC) SSM. This pane appears only if a CSC SSM is installed in the adaptive security appliance.
- **IPS Tab—**The Intrusion Prevention System tab displays information about the IPS module, if present.

Functional Screens of ASDM

In addition to the Home screen, the ASDM interface comes with the following two functional screens:

- Configuration screen
- Monitoring screen

Configuration Screen

The Configuration screen is useful when the new or existing configuration needs to be modified. On the left side, it contains five to six features icons, depending on the hardware setup of the appliance, as shown in Figure 3-8.

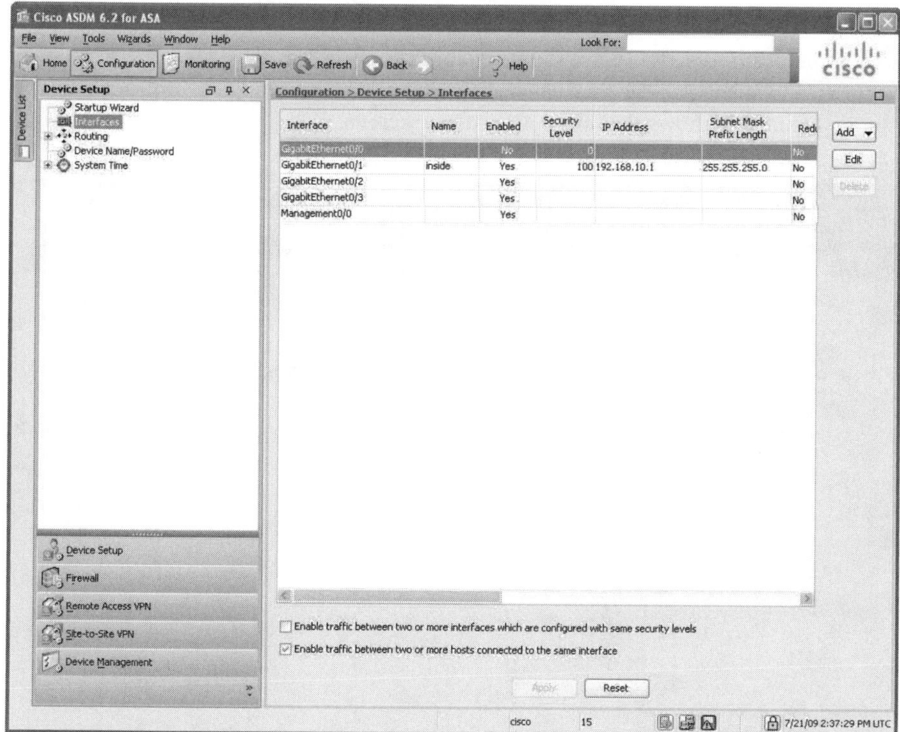

Figure 3-8 *Configuration Screen*

The Feature icons of the Configuration screen are as follows:

- **Device Setup**—Configures interfaces and sub-interfaces on the security appliance. This panel is discussed in the section "Configuring an Interface," later in the chapter.
- **Firewall**—Helpful in creating security policies to filter and to translate packets traversing through the appliance. Also enables you to define Failover, QoS, AAA, certificates, and many other firewall-related features.
- **Remote Access VPN**—Sets up the remote access VPN connections such as IPSec, L2TP over IPSec, Clientless SSL VPN, and AnyConnect tunnels.
- **Site-to-site VPN**—Sets up the site-to-site VPN tunnels.
- **IPS**—Sets up policies for the SSM card to monitor and drop unauthorized packets. This icon is not visible if an SSM card is not present.
- **Device Management**—Here, the basic device features can be set up. Most of these features are discussed later in this chapter. Helpful in setting up the basic software features, such as system logging and failover.

Monitoring Screen

The Monitoring screen displays statistics about the hardware and software features of the security appliance. ASDM provides real-time graphs to monitor the appliance's health and status. Figure 3-9 shows the initial Monitoring screen.

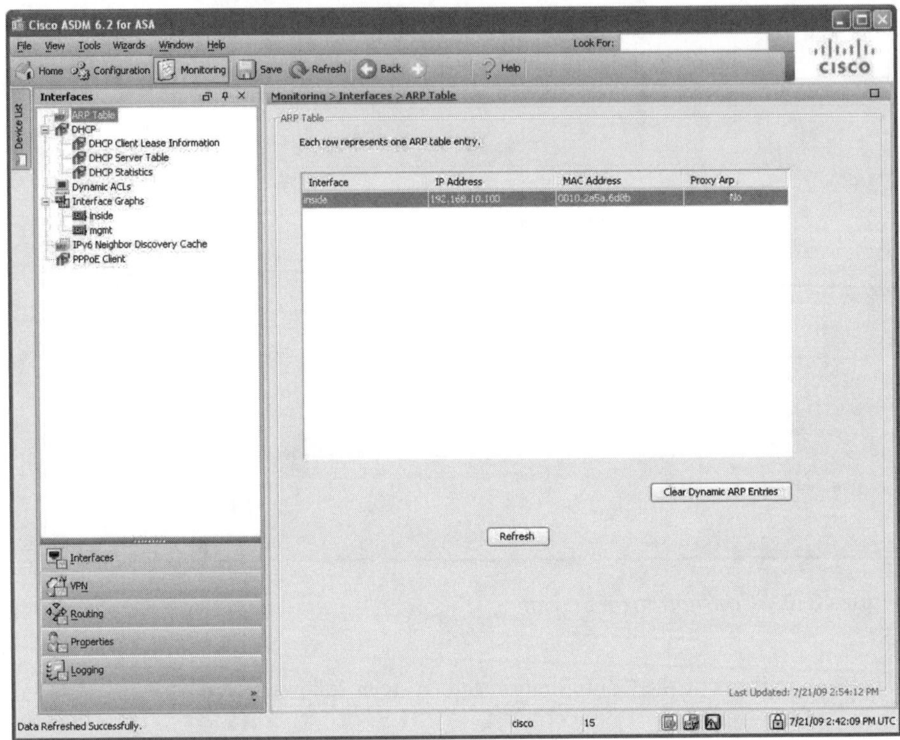

Figure 3-9 *Monitoring Screen*

Similar to the Configuration screen, the Monitoring screen also displays five or six icons, depending on whether or not you have the SSM module installed.

The Features icons of the Monitoring screen are described below:

- **Interfaces**—Monitors interfaces and sub-interfaces by maintaining ARP, DHCP, and dynamic ACLs tables. It also provides a graphical representation of interface utilization and packet throughput.
- **VPN**—Monitors the active VPN connections on the security appliance. It provides graphs and statistical analysis of the site-to-site, IPSec, and SSL VPN–based remote-access tunnels.
- **IPS**—Provides statistical information for the packets going through the IPS engine. This icon is not present if the IPS module is not installed.

- **Routing**—Displays the current routing table and provides information on EIGRP and OSPF neighbors.
- **Properties**—Monitors active administrative sessions such as Telnet, SSH, and ASDM. It also provides graphical information about CPU, memory, and blocks utilization. Provides graphical information about the active translations and UDP/TCP connections. It provides graphical information of the IP audit, WCCP, CRL, and DNS Cache features
- **Logging**—Displays log messages as live events. It also shows log messages from the buffer space.
- **Trend Micro Content Security**—ASDM enables you to monitor the CSC SSM statistics, as well as CSC SSM-related features such as types of threats detected by the module, live event logs for real-time monitoring, and resource utilization graphs.

Note If you use ASDM as the primary mode of configuring a security appliance, it is highly recommended that you enable the Preview Command Before Sending Them to the Device option in ASDM. This way, before the commands are pushed to the ASA, ASDM shows them to you for verification. You can enable this feature on ASDM under **Tools > Preferences** and selecting **Preview commands before sending them to the device.**

Device Setup

After you have connectivity to the security appliance, either via CLI or ASDM, you are ready to start configuring the device. This section guides you to configure the security appliance for basic setup.

Setting Up Device Name and Passwords

The default device name—also known as the hostname—of a security appliance is **ciscoasa**. It is highly recommended that you set a unique device name to identify the security appliance on the network. Additionally, networking devices usually belong to a network domain. A domain name appends the unqualified hostnames with the configured domain name. For example, if the security appliance tries to reach a host, **secweb**, by its hostname and the configured domain name on the security appliance is **securemeinc.com**, then the fully qualified domain name (FQDN) will be **secweb.securemeinc.com**.

In a new security appliance, you can configure the Telnet and enable password. The Telnet password is used to authenticate remote sessions either via the Telnet or SSH protocol, discussed later in this chapter. By default, the Telnet password is **cisco**. For the SSH sessions, the default username is **pix**. The enable password, on the other hand, gives you access to the privileged exec mode if you are on the user mode. The enable password is also used for ASDM user authentication. There is no enable password by default.

Note If you have user authentication configured for Telnet and/or SSH access, the security appliance does not use the Telnet/enable passwords for those sessions.

To configure the hostname, domain name, and the Telnet/enable passwords via ASDM, navigate to **Configuration > Device Setup > Device Name/Password** and specify the new settings. As shown in Figure 3-10, the hostname is **Chicago** and the domain name is **securemeinc.com.** If you want to configure a new Telnet and/or enable password, select the appropriate change the Telnet and/or enable password option and specify the current and the new passwords. In Figure 3-10, both passwords are set to **C1$c0123** (masked).

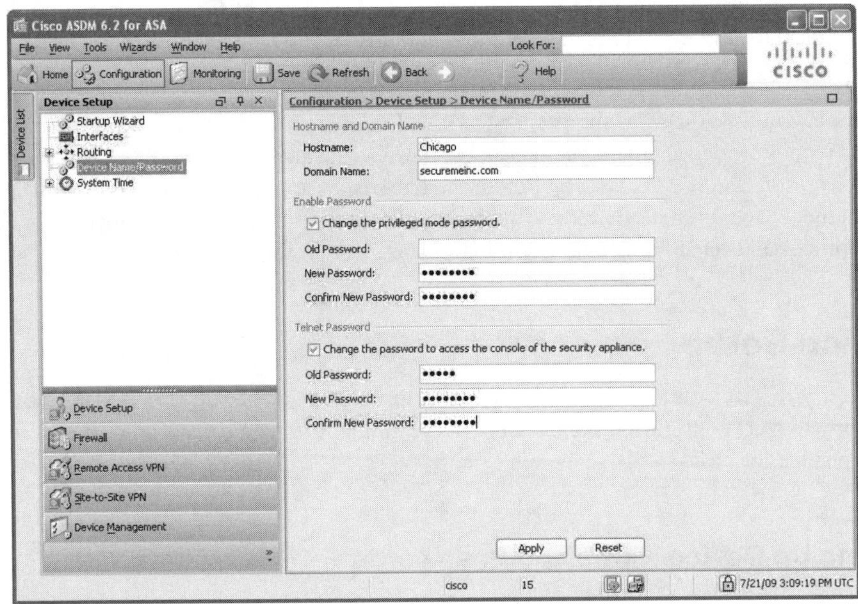

Figure 3-10 *Configuring Hostname, Domain Name, and Local Passwords*

If you prefer to use the CLI, Example 3-8 shows the identical configuration of Figure 3-10. The hostname is changed using the **hostname** command, the domain name is changed using the **domain-name** command, and the Telnet and enable passwords are changed using the **passwd** and **enable password** commands, respectively.

Example 3-8 *Setting Up the Hostname, Domain Name, and Passwords*

```
ciscoasa# configure terminal
ciscoasa(config)# hostname Chicago
Chicago(config)# domain-name securemeinc.com
Chicago(config)# passwd C1$c0123
Chicago(config)# enable password C1$c0123
```

Tip If you view the configuration after adding the passwords, the security appliance displays the encrypted passwords as follows:

Chicago# **show running-config | include pass**

enable password 9jNfZuG3TC5tCVH0 encrypted

passwd 2KFQnbNIdI.2KYOU encrypted

Configuring an Interface

Cisco ASA 5500 appliances come with a number of Fast-Ethernet, Gigabit-Ethernet and Ten Gigabit-Ethernet interfaces. They also include one management interface (Management0/0) in all one-rack unit (1RU) models and two management interfaces (Management0/0 and Management0/1) in ASA5580s. Additionally, you can create one or more sub-interfaces off each physical interface. The Fast-Ethernet, Gigabit-Ethernet, and Ten Gigabit-Ethernet interfaces are used to route traffic from one interface to another based on the configured policies, whereas the management interface is designed to establish out-of-band connections.

Configuring Data-Passing Interface

Cisco ASA protects the internal network from external threats. Each interface is assigned a name to designate its role on the network. The most secure network is typically labeled as the *inside* network, whereas the least secure network is tagged as the *outside* network. For semi-trusted networks, you can define them as demilitarized zones (DMZs) or any logical interface name. You must use the interface name to set up the configuration features that are linked to an interface.

Note If you go through the initial setup and configure an IP address and a subnet mask, the security appliance designates the GigabitEthernet0/1 interface as the inside interface on the Cisco ASA 5520, 5540, and 5550, and it designates Ethernet0/1 as the inside interface on the Cisco ASA 5510. By default, all these interfaces are shut down, meaning no traffic can pass through them.

The security appliance also uses the concept of assigning security levels to the interfaces. The higher the security level, the more secure an interface is. Consequently, the security level is used to reflect the level of trust of this interface with respect to the level of trust of another interface on the Cisco ASA. The security level can be between 0 and 100. Therefore, the most secure network is placed behind the interface with a security level of 100, whereas the least secure network is placed behind an interface with a security level of 0. A DMZ interface can be assigned a security level between 0 and 100.

The Cisco ASA enables you to assign the same security level to more than one interface. If communication is required between the hosts on interfaces at the same security level, use the global configuration **same-security-traffic permit inter-interface** command.

Additionally, if an interface is not assigned a security level, it does not respond back at the network layer.

> **Note** When an interface is configured with a **nameif** command, the security appliance automatically assigns a preconfigured security level. If an interface is configured with the **inside** name, the security appliance assigns a security level of 100. For all the other interface names, the security appliance sets the security level to 0.

The most important parameter under the interface configuration is the assignment of an IP address. This is required if an interface is to be used to pass traffic in the Layer 3 firewall, also known as *routed mode*. An address can be either statically or dynamically assigned. For a static IP address, configure an IP address and its respective subnet mask.

The security appliance also supports interface address assignment through a Dynamic Host Configuration Protocol (DHCP) server and via PPPoE. Assigning an address via DHCP is a preferred method if an ISP dynamically allocates an IP address to the outside interface. You can also inform the security appliance to use the DHCP server's specified default gateway as the default route if the "Obtain default route using DHCP" option is enabled on ASDM.

> **Note** If a security appliance is deployed in transparent mode, as discussed in Chapter 9, "Transparent Firewalls," the IP address is configured in global configuration mode.

To configure a physical interface on a security appliance via ASDM, navigate to **Configuration > Device Setup > Interfaces**, select an interface, and click the **Edit** button. As shown in Figure 3-11, the physical GigabitEthernet0/0 interface is configured as the **outside** interface with a security level of **0**. The static IP address is **209.165.200.225** with a mask of **255.255.255.224**. The **Enable Interface** box is checked to activate the interface.

In Example 3-9, the administrator enables the **GigabitEthernet0/0** interface as the **outside** interface and assigns a security level of **0**. The IP address is **209.165.200.225** with a mask of **255.255.255.224**.

Example 3-9 *Enabling an Interface*

```
Chicago# configure terminal
Chicago(config)# Interface GigabitEthernet0/0
Chicago(config-if)# no shutdown
Chicago(config-if)# nameif outside
Chicago(config-if)# security-level 0
Chicago(config-if)# ip address  209.165.200.225 255.255.255.224
```

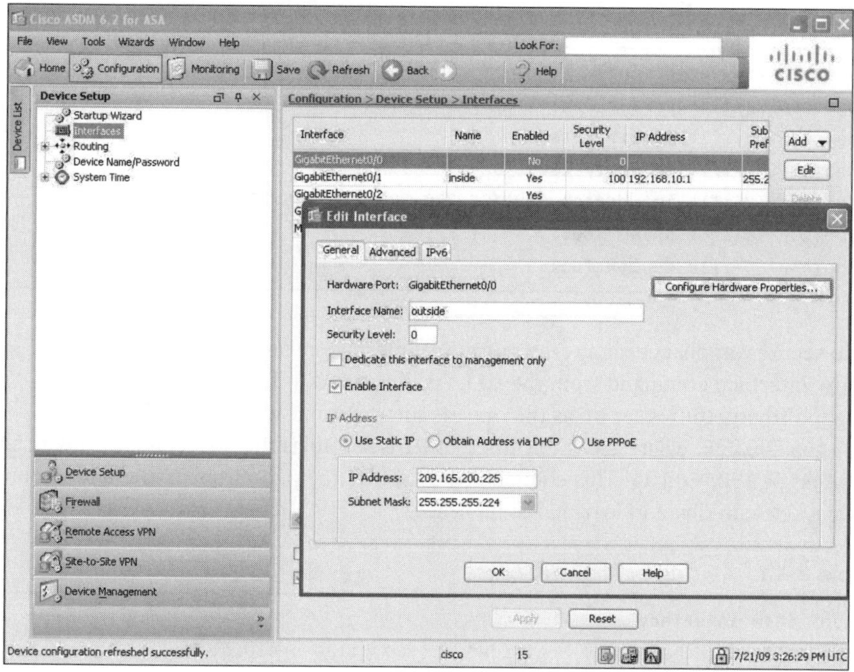

Figure 3-11 *Configuring a Physical Interface with an IP Address*

ASDM enables you to configure speed, duplex, and media-type on an interface if you click an interface's **Configure Hardware Properties**. By default, the speed and duplex are set to auto and can be changed to avoid link negotiations. If the speed and duplex settings do not match the speed and duplex settings on the other end of the Ethernet connection, you see packet loss, which results in performance degradation. The media-type is either RJ45 for copper-based interfaces or SFP for fiber-based interfaces. RJ45 is the default media-type.

> **Tip** The Ethernet-based interfaces on the Cisco ASA 5500 series use the auto-MDI/MDIX (media-dependent interface/media-dependent interface crossover) feature, which does not require a crossover cable when connecting interfaces of two similar types. They perform an internal crossover when a straight network cable connects two similar interfaces. This feature works only when both the speed and duplex parameters are set to auto-negotiate.

As demonstrated in Example 3-10, the outside interface is set up with a connection speed of 1000 Mbps, using full-duplex mode.

Example 3-10 *Configuring Speed and Duplex on an Interface*

```
Chicago# configure terminal
Chicago(config)# interface GigabitEthernet0/0
Chicago(config-if)# nameif outside
Chicago(config-if)# security-level 0
Chicago(config-if)# ip address 209.165.200.225 255.255.255.224
Chicago(config-if)# speed 1000
Chicago(config-if)# duplex full
```

The security appliance shows the output of interface-related statistics when you issue the **show interface** command from the CLI. As illustrated in Example 3-11, GigabitEthernet0/0 is set up as the outside interface and has an IP address of 209.165.200.225, whereas GigabitEthernet0/1 is set up as the inside interface with an IP address of 192.168.10.1. This command also shows the packet rate and the total number of packets entering and leaving the interface.

Example 3-11 *Output of* **show** *interface*

```
Chicago# show interface
Interface GigabitEthernet0/0 "outside", is up, line protocol is up
  Hardware is i82546GB rev03, BW 1000 Mbps, DLY 10 usec
        Auto-Duplex(Full-duplex), Auto-Speed(1000 Mbps)
        MAC address 000f.f775.4b53, MTU 1500
        IP address 209.165.200.225, subnet mask 255.255.255.224
        70068 packets input, 24068922 bytes, 0 no buffer
        Received 61712 broadcasts, 0 runts, 0 giants
        0 input errors, 0 CRC, 0 frame, 0 overrun, 0 ignored, 0 abort
        0 L2 decode drops
        13535 packets output, 7196865 bytes, 0 underruns
        0 output errors, 0 collisions, 0 interface resets
        0 babbles, 0 late collisions, 0 deferred
        0 lost carrier, 0 no carrier
        input queue (curr/max packets): hardware (0/1) software (0/11)
        output queue (curr/max packets): hardware (0/19) software (0/1)
  Traffic Statistics for "outside":
        70081 packets input, 23044675 bytes
        13540 packets output, 6992176 bytes
        49550 packets dropped
      1 minute input rate 1 pkts/sec,  362 bytes/sec
      1 minute output rate 0 pkts/sec,  362 bytes/sec
      1 minute drop rate, 0 pkts/sec
      5 minute input rate 1 pkts/sec,  342 bytes/sec
      5 minute output rate 0 pkts/sec,  362 bytes/sec
      5 minute drop rate, 0 pkts/sec
Interface GigabitEthernet0/1 "inside", is up, line protocol is up
```

```
Hardware is i82546GB rev03, BW 1000 Mbps, DLY 10 usec
        Auto-Duplex(Full-duplex), Auto-Speed(1000 Mbps)
        MAC address 000f.f775.4b55, MTU 1500
        IP address 192.168.10.1, subnet mask 255.255.255.0
        1447094 packets input, 152644956 bytes, 0 no buffer
        Received 1203884 broadcasts, 0 runts, 0 giants
        0 input errors, 0 CRC, 0 frame, 0 overrun, 0 ignored, 0 abort
        20425 L2 decode drops
        332526 packets output, 151244141 bytes, 0 underruns
        0 output errors, 0 collisions, 0 interface resets
        0 babbles, 0 late collisions, 0 deferred
        0 lost carrier, 0 no carrier
        input queue (curr/max packets): hardware (0/1) software (0/14)
        output queue (curr/max packets): hardware (0/26) software (0/1)
Traffic Statistics for "inside":
        777980 packets input, 80481496 bytes
        151736 packets output, 85309705 bytes
        395607 packets dropped
      1 minute input rate 0 pkts/sec,  58 bytes/sec
      1 minute output rate 0 pkts/sec,  0 bytes/sec
      1 minute drop rate, 0 pkts/sec
      5 minute input rate 0 pkts/sec,  66 bytes/sec
      5 minute output rate 0 pkts/sec,  0 bytes/sec
      5 minute drop rate, 0 pkts/sec
```

Configuring a Subinterface

Cisco ASA has a limited number of Ethernet-based interfaces, depending on the platform you are using. However, you can divide a physical interface into multiple logical interfaces to increase the total number of interfaces. You do so by tagging each subinterface with a unique virtual LAN (VLAN) ID, which keeps the network traffic separate from other VLANs using the same physical interface. The security appliance uses the IEEE-specified 802.1Q trunking to connect the physical interface to an 802.1Q-enabled device.

The number of VLANs (subinterfaces) can range from 3 to 250 depending on the security appliance model and the license key used, as shown in Table 3-3. VLAN ID must be between 1 and 4094, whereas the subinterface must be an integer between 1 and 4,294,967,295. Although the subinterface number and the VLAN ID do not have to match, it is a good practice to use the same number for ease of management.

To create subinterfaces via ASDM, you can go to **Configuration > Device Setup > Interfaces**, select a physical interface, and click the **Add** button. As shown in Figure 3-12, the administrator is creating a sub-interface from a physical GigabitEthernet0/0 interface. The sub-interface number is 300 and it is linked to VLAN 300. A static IP address of 192.168.20.1/24 is configured for this sub-interface.

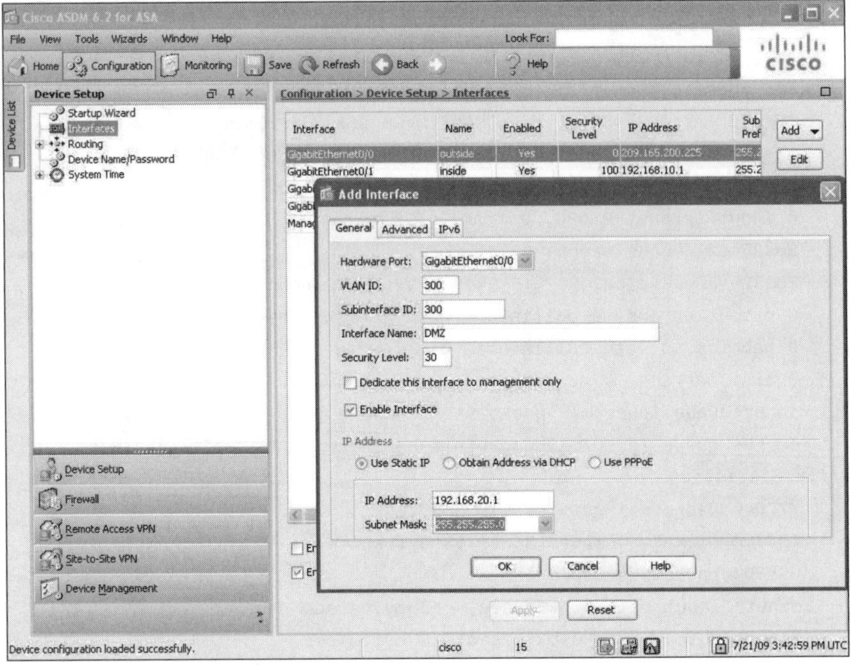

Figure 3-12 *Configuring a Subinterface*

Example 3-12 demonstrates how to create a subinterface **300** off **GigabitEthernet0/0.** It is linked to **VLAN 300** and configured with an IP address of **192.168.20.1/24.**

Table 3-3 *Supported Subinterfaces on the Security Appliances*

Appliance Model	License Feature	Maximum Number of VLANs
ASA5505	Base	3
ASA5505	Security Plus	20
ASA5510	Base	50
ASA5510	Security Plus	100
ASA5520	Base	150
ASA5540	Base	200
ASA5550	Base	250
ASA5580-20	Base	250
ASA5580-40	Base	250

Example 3-12 *Creating a Subinterface*

```
Chicago# configure terminal
Chicago(config)# interface GigabitEthernet0/0.300
Chicago(config-if)# vlan 300
Chicago(config-if)# no shutdown
Chicago(config-if)# nameif DMZ
Chicago(config-if)# security-level 30
Chicago(config-if)# ip address  192.168.20.1 255.255.255.0
```

Note If the main physical interface is shut down, all the associated subinterfaces are disabled as well.

Even if you create subinterfaces, a security appliance can still pass untagged traffic over the physical interface if an interface name (**nameif**), a security-level, and an IP address are configured.

Configuring a Management Interface

All Cisco 1 RU security appliances have one built-in Management0/0 port, whereas the 5580 appliances have two built-in Management0/0 and Management0/1 interfaces. These interfaces are designed to pass management-related traffic only. The management interface blocks all the traffic that is trying to pass through it, and permits only traffic destined to the security appliance. This ensures that the management traffic is separate from the data traffic on an appliance. Any Gigabit Ethernet or Fast Ethernet interface can act as a dedicated management interface when **Dedicate this interface for management only** option is configured within ASDM or the **management-only** command is issued from the CLI. Some general characteristics about management interfaces include the following:

- Routing protocols such as RIP and OSPF are supported on a management interface.
- A subinterface can also act as a management interface if configured to do so.
- Multiple management interfaces are supported on an appliance.
- Traffic through the security appliance is dropped on a management interface and a **syslog** message is generated to log this event.
- VPN tunnels for remote management are allowed to terminate on a management interface.

As shown in Example 3-13, the **Management0/0** interface is set up as a **management-only** interface with an IP address of **172.18.82.64/24** and a security level of **100**.

Example 3-13 *Configuring a Management-Only Interface*

```
Chicago# configure terminal
```

```
Chicago(config)# interface Management0/0
 Chicago(config-if)# management-only
Chicago(config-if)# ip address 172.18.82.64 255.255.255.0
Chicago(config-if)# security-level 100
```

You can change this default behavior of Management0/0 interface so that it can start passing through-traffic if you use the **no management-only** interface command.

DHCP Services

Cisco ASA can act as a DHCP server to distribute IP addresses to the end machines that are running DHCP client services. This feature is particularly important if you have a small branch office that does not own a dedicated DHCP server. To configure the DHCP server via ASDM, go to **Configuration > Device Management > DHCP > DHCP Server** and select the interface where you want to enable the DHCP services. ASDM opens a new window where you can define the following attributes:

- **Enable DHCP Server**—The first thing in setting up the DHCP server is to enable it on the selected interface by selecting the Enable DHCP Server check box.
- **DHCP Address Pool**—You must define a pool of addresses that can be assigned to a DHCP client. Specify a start and an end address for the DHCP pool. The network addresses need to be on the same network as the address assigned to the interface.
- **Optional Parameters**—Cisco ASA enables you to set up a number of useful DHCP parameters such as the WINS and DNS addresses, domain-name, lease length, and the ping timeouts. The DHCP server sends the WINS, DNS, and domain name when an address is offered to a DHCP client. The client computers do not need to be manually set up for these addresses. If the ping timeout is configured, the security appliance sends two ICMP request packets to the address it is about to assign, before it allocates the IP address to a DHCP client. It waits for 50 milliseconds to receive an ICMP response. If a response is received, the security appliance assumes that the address is being used and thus does not assign it. If a response is not received, the security appliance allocates the IP address until the DHCP lease expires. After the lease expires, the DHCP client is expected to return the assigned IP address. You can change the default lease time setting of 3600 seconds by specifying a value in the Lease Length box.
- **Enable Auto-Configuration from Interface**—In many network implementations, the security appliance acts as a DHCP client on one interface and a DHCP server on another. This is usually the case when the security appliance gets an IP address from the ISP's DHCP server on its outside interface. At the same time, it acts as a DHCP server to assign addresses to the DHCP clients connected on the inside networks. In this network scenario, the security appliance can pass the DNS, WINS, and domain-name information to the DHCP clients after it receives those attributes from a DHCP server that resides on its interface acting as a DHCP client. You enable this feature by

selecting the Enable Auto-Configuration from Interface box and specifying a DHCP client–enabled interface such as the outside.

- **Advanced**—The security appliance enables you to assign DHCP option codes ranging from 0 to 255. These DHCP option codes are defined in RFC 2132 and can be set up on the security appliance if you click the **Advanced** option. For example, the DHCP option code **66** (TFTP server) is assigned to the DHCP clients with a TFTP server address. This DHCP option code is typically used by the Cisco IP Phones to retrieve their configuration from the TFTP server.

In Figure 3-13, a DHCP server is enabled on the inside interface with a pool of addresses that starts at **192.168.10.100** and ends at **192.168.10.200**. The optional parameters are configured where the DNS address of **192.168.10.10**, WINS address of **192.168.10.20**, and a domain name of **securemeinc.com** are sent to the DHCP clients. The ICMP ping timeout is set to **20 milliseconds** and the lease time of **86400 seconds** (1 day) is defined. The DHCP auto-configuration is not enabled.

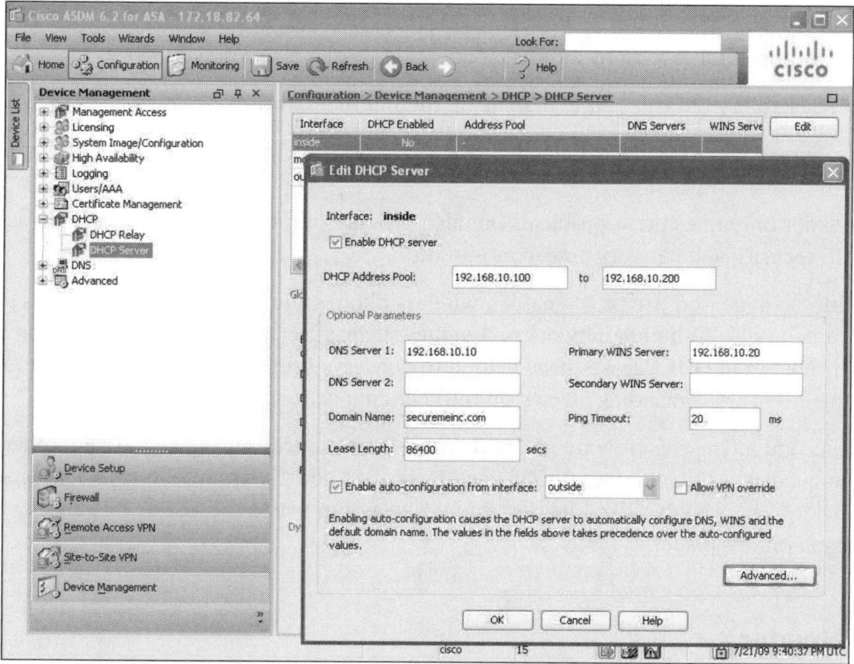

Figure 3-13 *Configuring DHCP Service on the Security Appliance*

Example 3-14 shows that DHCP service is enabled for the inside interface with the address range from **192.168.10.100** to **192.168.10.200**. The assigned DNS and WINS addresses are **192.168.10.10** and **192.168.10.20** respectively. A DHCP option code **66** (TFTP server) is assigned to the DHCP clients, with a TFTP server address of **192.168.10.10**.

Example 3-14 *Configuring DHCP Service on the Inside Interface*

```
Chicago# configure terminal
Chicago(config)# dhcpd address 192.168.10.100-192.168.10.200 inside
Chicago(config)# dhcpd enable inside
Chicago(config)# dhcpd dns 192.168.10.10  interface inside
Chicago(config)# dhcpd wins 192.168.10.20  interface inside
Chicago(config)# dhcpd lease 86400 interface inside
Chicago(config)# dhcpd ping_timeout 20 interface inside
Chicago(config)# dhcpd option 66 ip 192.168.10.10
Chicago(config)# dhcpd domain securemeinc.com interface inside
```

IP Version 6

IP version 6 (IPv6) is a relatively new IP protocol developed to fix the shortcomings of the current IPv4 implementations. When IPv4 was standardized in 1981, the current challenges were not anticipated. The challenges include

- Exponential growth of Internet usage
- Scalability of large routing tables on the Internet backbone routers.
- Supportability of real-time data delivery

IPv6 not only fixes these problems but also provides improvements to IPv4 in areas such as IP security and network auto-configuration.

With the increased use of IP-enabled wireless phones and PDAs, the IPv4 address space is running out. Although network techniques such as Network Address Translation (NAT) and short-term DHCP leases have helped to conserve these addresses, more and more home users are demanding always-on Internet connections.

To accommodate the growing global demand for IP addresses, the new IPv6 implementation quadruples the number of bits used in an IPv4 address-from 32 bits to 128 bits. It provides 2^{128} routable IP addresses, enough to assign over a thousand IP addresses per person on this planet.

IPv6 Header

IPv6 specifications, defined in RFC 2460, describe an IPv6 header, as shown in Figure 3-14.

Table 3-4 lists and describes the fields in an IPv6 header.

In the case of IPv4, an IP address is represented in four octets, separated by dots (.). To accommodate a 128-bit IPv6 address, the address is divided into eight blocks of 16 bits each, separated by colons (:). Consequently, this representation is referred to as *colon-hexadecimal notation.*

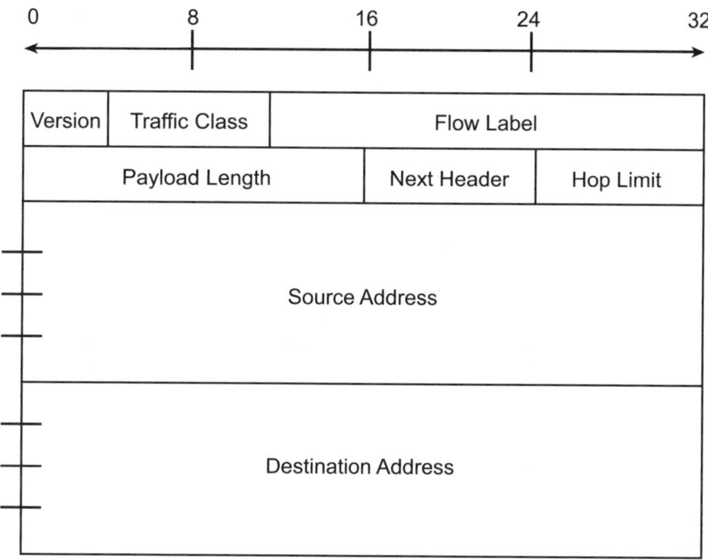

Figure 3-14 *IPv6 Header*

The following are a few examples of IPv6 addresses:

FEDC:BA98:0001:3210:FEDC:BA98:0001:3210
1080:0000:0000:0000:0008:0800:200C:417A
0000:0000:0000:0000:0000:0000:0000:0001

Table 3-4 *IPv6 Header Fields*

Field	Description
Version	A 4-bit Internet Protocol version number = 6
Traffic Class	An 8-bit field that enables the source to specify a desired delivery priority of its packets relative to other packets
Flow Label	A 20-bit field that may be set to request special handling of the packets by the IPv6-based router
Payload Length	A 16-bit integer that specifies the length of the data payload
Next Header	An 8-bit field that identifies the type of header following the IPv6 header
Hop Limit	An 8-bit integer that is decremented by 1 whenever the packet passes through a network node
Source Address	A 128-bit address to identify the packet's source
Destination Address	A 128-bit address to identify the packet's destination

In an IPv6 address, it is not required to write the leading zeros in the individual block, as in an IPv4 address. Thus the preceding addresses can be rewritten as follows:

FEDC:BA98:1:3210:FEDC:BA98:1:3210

1080:0:0:0:8:800:200C:417A

0:0:0:0:0:0:0:1

As you can see from the preceding addresses, an IPv6 address may have long strings of zero bits. For ease of representation, an IPv6 address with long sequences of zeros can be compressed and replaced with ::. This notation, also known as *double colon*, can compress contiguous blocks of zeros. However, the :: notation can appear only once in an address, to avoid confusion on how many zeros should go to which instance of ::. The preceding addresses, with zero compression, can be written as follows:

FEDC:BA98:1:3210:FEDC:BA98:1:3210

1080::8:800:200C:417A

::1

Configuring IPv6

The security appliance supports a number of IPv6 features, which include IP address assignment, packet filtering, basic routing using static routes, neighbor discovery, limited remote-access VPNs, and IPv6-supported application inspections such as FTP, HTTP, and SMTP. This section discusses IP address assignment, whereas packet filtering and basic routing using static routes are discussed in Chapter 4 and Chapter 5 respectively. In version 8.2(1) or higher, the security appliance supports the intrusion prevention system (IPS) and transparent firewall features.

IP Address Assignment

The security appliance supports simultaneous IPv4 and IPv6 addresses on an interface. You can configure an IPv6 address on an interface by navigating to **Configuration > Device Setup > Interfaces**, selecting an interface, clicking the **Edit** button, and then selecting the **IPv6** tab, as shown in Figure 3-15.

The security appliance supports four types of interface address assignments:

- Global Unicast address
- Site-local address
- Link-local address
- Auto-configuration address

Note For detailed information about these types, consult RFC 4291.

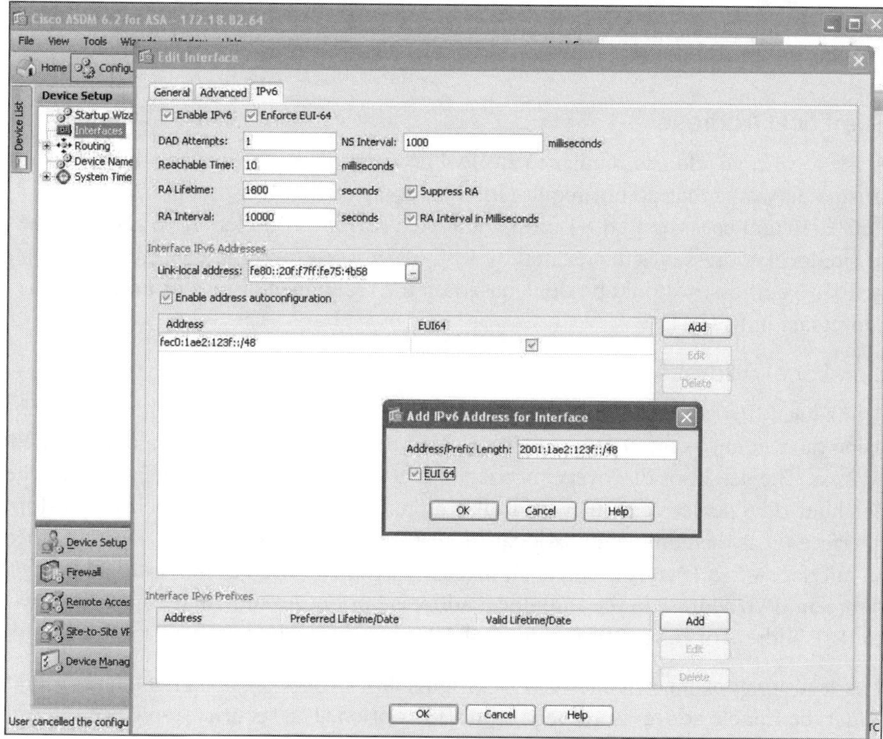

Figure 3-15 *IPv6 Address Assignment*

Global Unicast Address

A global unicast IPv6 address, similar to an IPv4 public routable address, is used for Internet connectivity. It uses a prefix of 2000::/3 and requires a 64-bit interface identifier in the extended universal identifier 64 (EUI-64) format.

Each physical interface has an embedded 48-bit MAC address that specifies a unique link-layer address. You can derive the EUI-64 format interface ID from the interface MAC address by using the following rules:

- Insert FFFE between the upper and the lower 24 bits. For example, if the interface's MAC address is 000F.F775.4B57, the modified address will be 000F.F7FF.FE75.4B57.
- Change the 7th bit in the leftmost byte to 1. For example, if the 64-bit address is 000F.F7FF.FE75.4B57 (derived in the previous step), after the 7th bit is changed the new address becomes 020F.F7FF.FE75.4B57. This new address is in the EUI-64 format.

The earlier Figure 3-15 shows how to set up a global unicast IPv6 address of **2001:1ae2:123f** with a mask of **/48** followed by the **EUI-64** format identifier to make up the full 128-bit address.

Note You can set up multiple IPv6 addresses on an interface.

Site-Local Address

A site-local IPv6 address, similar to an IPv4 private address, is used for the hosts on the trusted networks that do not require Internet connectivity. It uses a prefix range of FEC0::/10 and uses the EUI-64 format interface ID for a complete IPv6 address. The use of site-local addresses is deprecated by RFC 3879. Therefore, the configuration of a private IPv6 addresses should be done based on the recommendations of unique local addressing in RFC 4193.

Link-Local Address

A link-local IPv6 address allows IPv6-enabled hosts to communicate with each other by using the neighbor discovery protocol without needing to configure a global or site-local address. The neighbor discovery protocol provides a messaging channel on which the neighbor IPv6 devices can interact. It uses a prefix of FE80::/10 and the EUI-64–format interface ID as the complete link-local address. The link-local address is auto-assigned to an interface when IPv6 is enabled. To manually assign a different link-local address, configure an IPv6 address in the **Link-local address** option. As shown in Figure 3-15, where an IPv6 address of **fe80::20f:f7ff:fe75:4b58** is being assigned.

The security appliance enables you to assign a link-local address on the interface if you select the **Enable addresss autoconfiguration** option. The security appliance listens for the Router Advertisement (RA) messages to determine the prefix and generates an IPv6 address by using the EUI-64–format interface ID.

Example 3-15 shows complete IPv6 interface configuration on the **outside** interface, where a global address of **2001:1ae2:123f::/48** and a link-local address of fe80::20f:f7ff:fe75:4b58 are configured.

Example 3-15 *Assigning IPv6 Addresses*

```
Chicago(config)# interface GigabitEthernet0/0
Chicago(config-if)# ipv6 enable
Chicago(config-if)# ipv6 address 2001:1ae2:123f::/48 eui-64
Chicago(config-if)# ipv6 address fe80::20f:f7ff:fe75:4b58 link-local
Chicago(config-if)# ipv6 enforce-eui64 outside
```

Note The current implementation of IPv6 on the security appliances does not support anycast addresses.

Optional IPv6 Parameters

The security appliance supports a number of IPv6 optional parameters that are configured under the IPv6 tab of an interface, as shown earlier in Figure 3-15. These parameters are discussed in the following sections.

Neighbor Solicitation Messages

These messages are sent to perform duplicate address detection. By default, the security appliance sends one duplicate address detection message on an IPv6-enabled interface. The security appliance sends Neighbor Solicitation messages only when it needs to do neighbor discovery. You can change this behavior by specifying a new value under the DAD Attempts option. If you specify a value of 0, the security appliance disables duplicate address detection on the interface.

If you configure an interface to send out more than one duplicate address detection message, you can also specify the interval at which the neighbor solicitation messages are sent out. The security appliance sends out one message every second. You can change this behavior by specifying a new value under the NS Interval option.

Neighbor Reachable Time

The neighbor reachable time is the amount of time, in milliseconds, that a remote IPv6 node is considered reachable. The security appliance can detect the unavailable neighbors in an IPv6 network by using the neighbor reachable time. If you define short reachable times, the security appliance can quickly detect unavailable neighbors. However, it adds bandwidth and processing overhead on the IPv6-enabled devices, and thus configuring short reachable time is not recommended in a typical IPV6 network. You can change this behavior by specifying a new value under the Reachable Time option. The default value of 0 indicates that the reachable time is sent as undetermined. It is up to the receiving devices to set and track the reachable time value.

Router Advertisement Transmission Interval

A security appliance can send router advertisements to an all-nodes multicast address so that neighboring devices can dynamically learn a default router address. The security appliance includes the router lifetime value to indicate its usefulness as the default router on the network. You can change the router lifetime from its default interval time of 1800 seconds by specifying a new value under the RA Lifetime box.

Router advertisement messages use ICMPv6 Type 134 and are periodically sent out to all the IPv6-enabled interfaces. If you would rather change the router advertisement interval from its default value of 200 seconds to something different, specify a new value in the RA Interval box. The transmission interval must be less than or equal to the IPv6 router advertisement lifetime.

Lastly, you can configure the security appliance to suppress router advertisement messages so that the security appliance does not provide its IPv6 prefix on an interface, such as an untrusted interface. You can do that by enabling the Suppress RA option.

Example 3-16 shows the **GigabitEthernet0/0** is set up for a neighbor solicitation messages interval of **2000 milliseconds**, a neighbor reachable time of **10 milliseconds**, and a router lifetime value of **10000 milliseconds**. The security appliance is also set up to suppress router advertisement messages on the interface.

Example 3-16 *Setting Up Optional IPv6 Parameters*

```
Chicago(config)# interface GigabitEthernet0/0
Chicago(config-if)# ipv6 nd ns-interval 2000
Chicago(config-if)# ipv6 nd reachable-time 10
Chicago(config-if)# ipv6 nd ra-interval msec 10000
Chicago(config-if)# ipv6 nd suppress-ra
```

Setting Up the System Clock

One of the most important tasks when setting up the security appliance is to verify that the clock settings are accurate. The security appliances can use the system clock to timestamp the syslog messages before sending them, as discussed in the "Enabling Logging" section. The system clock is also checked when the VPN tunnels, using PKI, are being negotiated to verify the validity of the certificate presented by the VPN peer. The security appliance supports two methods to adjust the system clock:

- Manual clock adjustment
- Automatic clock adjustment using the Network Time Protocol

Manual Clock Adjustment

Similar to a Cisco IOS router, the security appliance allows the use of the **clock set** command to adjust the system clock. After setting the clock, the security appliance updates the system BIOS, powered by a battery on the motherboard. Consequently, if the security appliance is rebooted, the time setting does not need to be reconfigured. To manually adjust the system clock using ASDM, navigate to **Configuration > Device Setup > System Time > Clock** and specify a time zone, date, and the current time.

Time Zone

Cisco ASA supports displaying the system time in the correct time zone. It maintains the system clock in Universal Time, Coordinated (UTC), but shows it in the configured time zone. As shown in Figure 3-16, the configured time zone is Eastern Standard Time (EST), which is 5 hours behind UTC time. The security appliance automatically displays the system clock in the correct daylight savings time (DST).

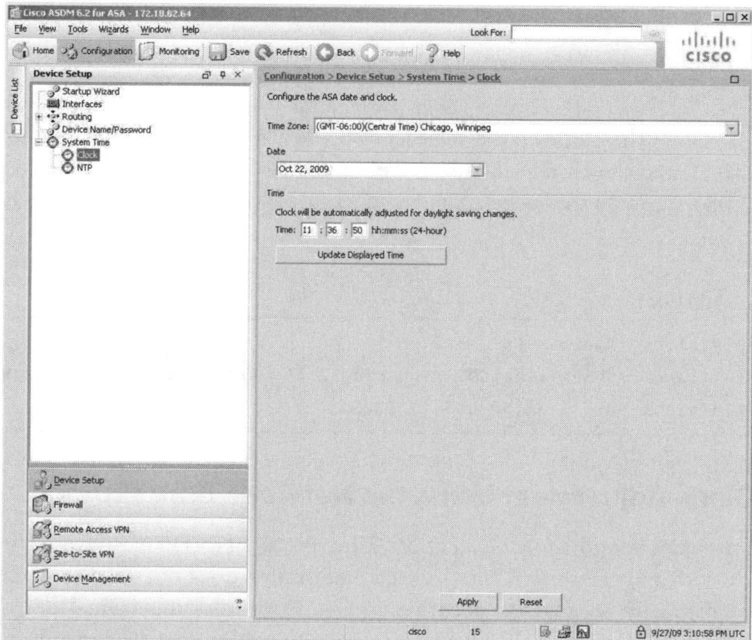

Figure 3-16 *Adjusting System Clock Manually*

Note Even though the ASDM automatically adjusts the system clock for DST, you can manually override the DST setting using one of the two formats:

- Using specific date and time settings
- Using recurring date and time settings

The command syntax for both formats is as follows:

```
clock summer-time zone date {day month | month day} year hh:mm {day month |
month day} year hh:mm [offset]
clock summer-time zone recurring [week weekday month hh:mm week weekday month
hh:mm] [offset]
```

For example, you can set a policy to always start DST at 5 a.m. on the first Sunday of April and end it at 5 a.m. on the last Sunday of October, as follows:

```
Chicago(config)# clock summer-time CDT recurring 1 Sun Apr 5:00 last Sun Oct
5:00
```

Date

Cisco ASDM presents a drop-down calendar where you can select the current date. The calendar year is a four-digit number ranging between 1993 and 2035. In Figure 3-16, the current date is October 22, 2009.

Time

Cisco ASDM allows you to specify time in hours, minutes, and seconds, using the 24-hour time format.

Example 3-17 shows the clock on the security appliance is updated to use the current time of **11:36:50** and the current date of **October 22, 2009**. The current time zone is **CST**, where DST starts on the second Sunday in March and ends on the first Sunday in November.

Example 3-17 *Setting the System Clock and Time Zone*

```
Chicago(config)# clock timezone CST -6 0
Chicago(config)# clock summer-time CDT recurring 2 Sun Mar 2:00 1 Sun Nov 2:00 60
Chicago(config)# clock set 11:36:50 OCT 22 2009
```

Automatic Clock Adjustment Using the Network Time Protocol

Cisco ASA provides support for the Network Time Protocol (NTP) to synchronize the system clock with an NTP server. The device administrator does not need to update the system clock manually because the security appliance overrides the manual clock setting when it synchronizes the time with the NTP server. Setting up an NTP server is important when an organization uses certificates (PKI) to authenticate users and devices on the network.

To set up NTP, navigate to **Configuration > Device Setup > System Time > NTP > Add** and specify the attributes discussed in Table 3-5.

Figure 3-17 illustrates two NTP servers located on the inside interface. The server at **192.168.10.16** is a trusted and preferred server, whereas the server at **192.168.10.15** is the secondary NTP server. Both servers use an authentication key of **919919**. They require an MD5 authentication key of **cisco123** to successfully authenticate the security appliance.

Example 3-18 shows the equivalent configuration of Figure 3-17 via the CLI.

Example 3-18 *Configuration of NTP Server*

```
Chicago(config)# ntp trusted-key 919919
Chicago(config)# ntp server 192.168.10.15 key 919919 source inside
Chicago(config)# ntp server 192.168.10.16 key 919919 source inside prefer
Chicago(config)# ntp authenticate
Chicago(config)# ntp authentication-key 919919 md5 cisco123
```

To verify whether the system clock is synchronized with the NTP server, use the **show ntp status** command, as shown in Example 3-19.

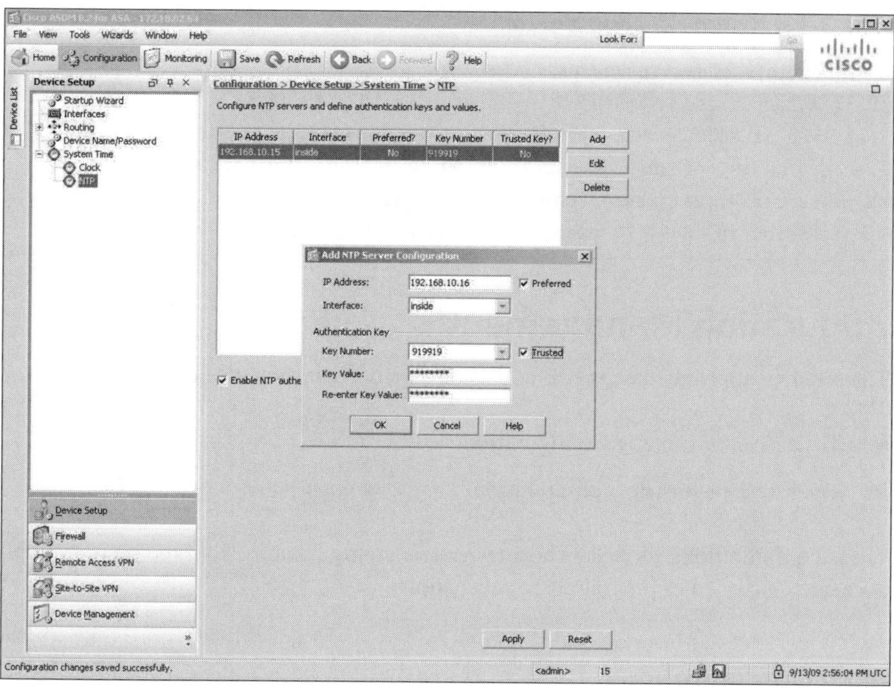

Figure 3-17 *Adjusting System Clock Automatically via NTP*

Table 3-5 *NTP Arguments and Description*

Syntax	Syntax Description
IP Address	Specify the actual IP address of the NTP server.
Preferred	If multiple NTP servers are specified, the security appliance chooses the NTP server that is preferred. NTP uses an algorithm to determine which server is the most accurate and synchronizes to that one. If servers are of similar accuracy, then the preferred server is used. However, if a server is significantly more accurate than the preferred one, the security appliance uses the more accurate one. That is, the security appliance uses a more accurate server over a less accurate server that is preferred.
Interface	Specify the name of the interface that sources the packets to the NTP server.
Key Number	Specify the authentication key number, between 1 and 4,294,967,295.
Key Value	Specify the actual key, up to 35 characters, used for MD5 authentication
trusted-key	Keyword to specify an authentication key for all the configured NTP servers. Sets this key as a trusted key. You must select this box for authentication to work.
Authenticate	Keyword to enable NTP authentication.

Example 3-19 *Output of show ntp status*

```
Chicago(config)# show ntp status
Clock is synchronized, stratum 9, reference is 192.168.10.16
nominal freq is 99.9984 Hz, actual freq is 99.9984 Hz, precision is 2**6
reference time is ce8b80ac.a44d8c73 (21:09:00.641 EDT Thu Oct 22 2009)
clock offset is 4.1201 msec, root delay is 1.92 msec
root dispersion is 15894.78 msec, peer dispersion is 15890.63 msec
```

Configuration Management

The security appliance keeps two copies of the configuration in the system:

- The active, or running, configuration
- The saved, or startup, configuration

These configurations, as well as how to remove configurations from the security appliance, are discussed in the following subsections.

Running Configuration

The running configuration is the actual configuration that the security appliance loads in its memory. When the security appliance boots up, it copies the saved configuration in its memory and then uses it to function as configured. Use the **show running-config** or **write terminal** command to display the current configuration that the security appliance is using. These are the most important commands to verify that the security appliance is configured properly. The running configuration is not saved in nonvolatile RAM (NVRAM) until the security appliance is instructed to store it there.

Example 3-20 shows the current configuration on an appliance via the CLI. As you can see, the configuration file can be fairly large and complex, depending on the number of features configured on the security appliance. The configuration file displays the current version of the system image and then the rest of the configuration parameters. If you prefer to see the same configuration via ASDM, click **File > Show Running Configuration in New Window**. ASDM launches a new default browser window to show the running configuration.

Example 3-20 *Output of show running-config*

```
Chicago# show running-config
: Saved
:
ASA Version 8.2(1)
!
hostname Chicago
domain-name securemeinc.com
```

```
enable password 9jNfZuG3TC5tCVH0 encrypted
passwd 2KFQnbNIdI.2KYOU encrypted
names
!
interface GigabitEthernet0/0
 nameif outside
 security-level 0
 ip address 209.165.200.225 255.255.255.224
!
interface GigabitEthernet0/1
 nameif inside
 security-level 100
 ip address 192.168.10.1 255.255.255.0
!
<some output removed for brevity>
!
interface Management0/0
 nameif mgmt
 security-level 100
 ip address 172.18.82.64 255.255.255.0
 management-only
!
ftp mode passive
pager lines 24
mtu outside 1500
mtu inside 1500
mtu mgmt 1500
asdm image disk0:/asdm-621.bin
timeout xlate 3:00:00
timeout conn 1:00:00 half-closed 0:10:00 udp 0:02:00 icmp 0:00:02
timeout sunrpc 0:10:00 h323 0:05:00 h225 1:00:00 mgcp 0:05:00 mgcp-pat 0:05:00
timeout sip 0:30:00 sip_media 0:02:00 sip-invite 0:03:00 sip-disconnect 0:02:00
timeout sip-provisional-media 0:02:00 uauth 0:05:00 absolute
timeout tcp-proxy-reassembly 0:01:00
http server enable
http 0.0.0.0 0.0.0.0 mgmt
no snmp-server location
no snmp-server contact
snmp-server enable traps snmp authentication linkup linkdown coldstart
Telnet timeout 5
console timeout 0
policy-map global_policy
 class inspection_default
  inspect dns preset_dns_map
```

```
  inspect ftp
  inspect h323 h225
  inspect h323 ras
  inspect rsh
  inspect rtsp
  inspect esmtp
  inspect sqlnet
  inspect skinny
  inspect sunrpc
  inspect xdmcp
  inspect sip
  inspect netbios
  inspect tftp
!
service-policy global_policy global
prompt hostname context
Cryptochecksum:b1161684d23e24b33e29fe4e8b1a2b09
: end
```

Cisco ASA allows you to display specific parts of the configuration by using **show running-config**, followed by the name of the command you are interested in checking. As shown in Example 3-21, the **show running-config ?** command shows all possible keywords you can use, and the **show running-config interface gigabitEthernet0/0** command shows the running configuration of the GigabitEthernet0/0 interface.

Example 3-21 *Partial Output of show running-config*

```
Chicago# show running-config ?
  aaa                         Show aaa configuration information
  aaa-server                  Show aaa-server configuration information
  access-group                Show access group(s)
  access-list                 Show configured access control elements
  alias                       Show configured overlapping addresses with dual NAT
  all                         Current operating configuration including defaults
  arp                         Show configured arp entries, arp timeout
  asdm                        Show ASDM configuration
! Output omitted for brevity
Chicago# show running-config interface GigabitEthernet0/0
!
interface GigabitEthernet0/0
 nameif outside
 security-level 0
 ip address 209.165.200.225 255.255.255.224
```

Tip The **show running-config** command does not display all security appliance commands set to their default values. Use **show running-config all** to display the entire running configuration.

The Cisco ASA operating system enables you to enhance the search capabilities when a **show** command is executed, by using **| grep** at the end of the command. Alternatively, **| include** displays the output when the exact phrase matches a **show** command. You can also use **| exclude** command to exclude lines that match a particular phrase. In Example 3-22, the administrator is only interested in looking at the IP addresses set up on the security appliance and their respective subnet masks in the running configuration.

Example 3-22 *Selective Output of* **show running-config**

```
Chicago# show running-config | include ip address
 ip address 209.165.200.225 255.255.255.224
 ip address 192.168.10.1 255.255.255.0
 no ip address
 no ip address
 ip address 172.18.82.64 255.255.255.0
```

The security appliance can also display the selective output of a **show** command when the **| begin** option is used. In this case, the security appliance displays the output beginning from a specific keyword. As shown in Example 3-23, the administrator is interested in looking at the running configuration beginning from the physical interfaces. Use the **show running-config | begin interface** command to do this.

Example 3-23 *Output of* **show running-config** *Beginning from the Interface Configuration*

```
Chicago# show running-config | begin interface
interface GigabitEthernet0/0
 nameif outside
 security-level 0
 ip address 209.165.200.225 255.255.255.224
!
interface GigabitEthernet0/1
 nameif inside
 security-level 100
 ip address 192.168.10.1 255.255.255.0
!
interface GigabitEthernet0/2
 shutdown
 no nameif
 no security-level
```

```
 no ip address
! Output omitted for brevity
```

Startup Configuration

During the bootup process, the security appliance uses the saved configuration as the running configuration. This saved configuration is known as the *startup configuration*. You can view the startup configuration by using the **show startup-config** or **show configuration** command, as shown in Example 3-24.

Example 3-24 *Output of* **show startup-config**

```
Chicago# show startup-config
: Saved
: Written by cisco at 21:13:44.064 CDT Fri Oct 22 2009
!
ASA Version 8.2(1)
!
hostname Chicago
domain-name securemeinc.com
enable password 9jNfZuG3TC5tCVH0 encrypted
passwd 2KFQnbNIdI.2KYOU encrypted
names
!
interface GigabitEthernet0/0
 nameif outside
 security-level 0
 ip address 209.165.200.225 255.255.255.224
!
interface GigabitEthernet0/1
 nameif inside
 security-level 100
 ip address 192.168.10.1 255.255.255.0
! Output omitted for brevity
```

The output of **show running-config** and **show startup-config** may or may not be identical, depending on whether the two configurations were synced. Use the **copy running-config startup-config** or **write memory** command to copy the active configuration into NVRAM, as shown in Example 3-25.

Example 3-25 *Output of* **copy running-config startup-config**

```
Chicago# copy running-config startup-config
Source filename [running-config]?
```

```
Cryptochecksum: 28b8d710 e2eaeda0 bc98a262 2bf3247a
3205 bytes copied in 3.230 secs (1068 bytes/sec)
```

Using ASDM, save the running-configuration as startup-configuration by clicking **File > Save Running Configuration to Flash.**

Removing the Device Configuration

If you use ASDM, you can remove any configured feature by selecting that feature and deleting it or changing the values to their defaults. For example, if you created a subinterface on the Gigabit-Ethernet0/0, you can remove that subinterface by selecting it and then clicking the **Delete** button.

Using the CLI, you can remove a configured command from the configuration by using the **no** form of the command. This undoes the command that was previously entered into the configuration. In Example 3-26, the security appliance is set up for ISAKMP processing on the outside interface. It is being disabled with the **no isakmp enable outside** command.

Example 3-26 *Disabling ISAKMP Processing on the Outside Interface*

```
Chicago(config)# isakmp enable outside
Chicago(config)# no isakmp enable outside
```

The security appliance can also remove the current configuration for a specific feature if the **clear configure** command is used. If the security appliance is set up with an ISAKMP policy 10 for Phase 1 IPsec negotiations, the **clear configure isakmp** command removes all the **isakmp** commands from the running configuration. This is demonstrated in Example 3-27.

Note The use of **no** in a command removes a single line, whereas **clear configure** removes the parts of the configuration for a feature.

Example 3-27 *Clearing All ISAKMP Commands from the Running Configuration*

```
Chicago(config)# show running-config | include
isakmp
crypto isakmp enable outside
crypto isakmp policy 10

Chicago(config)# clear configure isakmp
Chicago(config)# show running-config | include
isakmp
```

The preceding example not only cleared the ISAKMP policy, but also removed the **crypto isakmp enable outside** command from the running configuration. Use the **clear configure crypto isakmp policy** command to remove only the ISAKMP policy from the active configuration.

Unlike a Cisco IOS router, the Cisco ASA can clear the running configuration without going through the reboot process. This is helpful in a scenario where the security appliance needs to be put in the default configuration. Use the **clear configure all** command to clear the running configuration, as shown in Example 3-28.

Example 3-28 *Clearing the Running Configuration*

```
Chicago(config)# clear configure all
ciscoasa(config)#
```

Warning The use of **clear configure all** command disconnects your connection if your connection to the security appliance uses a remote-management protocol such as SSH. Make sure that you are connected to the ASA via console before you issue this command.

With ASDM, you can also clear the entire configuration of a security appliance by clicking **File > Reset Device to the Factory Default Configuration**. ASDM prompts you to configure an IP address on the management interface. You can reestablish your ASDM connection to this IP address.

The security appliance can also erase the startup configuration from NVRAM if the **write erase** command is issued from privileged mode, as shown in Example 3-29.

Example 3-29 *Clearing the Startup Configuration*

```
Chicago# write erase
Chicago#
```

Tip Cisco ASDM allows you to back up the configuration, certificates, XML files, SSL VPN customized files, and CSD/AnyConnect images. You can restore them in a different security appliance if you are configuring both appliances identically. Navigate to **Tools > Backup Configuration** to start the backup process.

Remote System Management

You do not have to be physically connected to the console port of the security appliance to access the CLI. The security appliance supports three remote-management protocols:

- Telnet
- Secure Shell (SSH)

- ASDM (GUI)

As mentioned earlier, we discuss ASDM throughout this book. The other remote system management protocols are discussed next.

Telnet

Cisco ASA comes with a Telnet server that enables users to manage it remotely via the CLI. The default behavior of the security appliance is to deny Telnet access from all clients unless they are explicitly permitted.

> **Note** The communication between a client and the security appliance is not encrypted; therefore, it is highly recommended to use SSH rather than Telnet for remote device management.

You may choose to enable Telnet on all interfaces. However, the security appliance does not allow clear-text Telnet communication on the outside interface unless the session is protected by an IPSec tunnel. The security appliance requires a user to establish an IPSec tunnel to the outside interface to encrypt the traffic destined to the security appliance. After the tunnel is successfully negotiated, the user can start a Telnet session to the outside interface.

When a Telnet client tries to connect, the security appliance verifies the following two conditions:

- The client's IP address falls in the allowed address space.
- The interface that is receiving the request is allowed to accept requests from the client's address space.

If either one of the conditions is not valid, the security appliance simply drops the request and generates a syslog message for this incident. Syslogs are discussed later in this chapter.

An external authentication server, such as CiscoSecure Access Control Server (ACS), can be used to authenticate the Telnet sessions. Consult Chapter 6, "Authentication, Authorization, and Accounting (AAA) Services" for more information.

You can configure the security appliance to accept Telnet sessions on an interface by navigating to **Configuration > Device Management > Management Access > ASDM/HTTPS/Telnet/SSH** and clicking **Add**. ASDM prompts you to select the following:

- Interface name from which the Telnet clients will be coming.
- IP Address of the hosts or a network address that is allowed to connect to the selected interface.

- Mask of the allowed IP or subnet address.

In Figure 3-18, the management network, **172.18.82.0/24**, is allowed to establish Telnet sessions to the security appliance's **mgmt** interface.

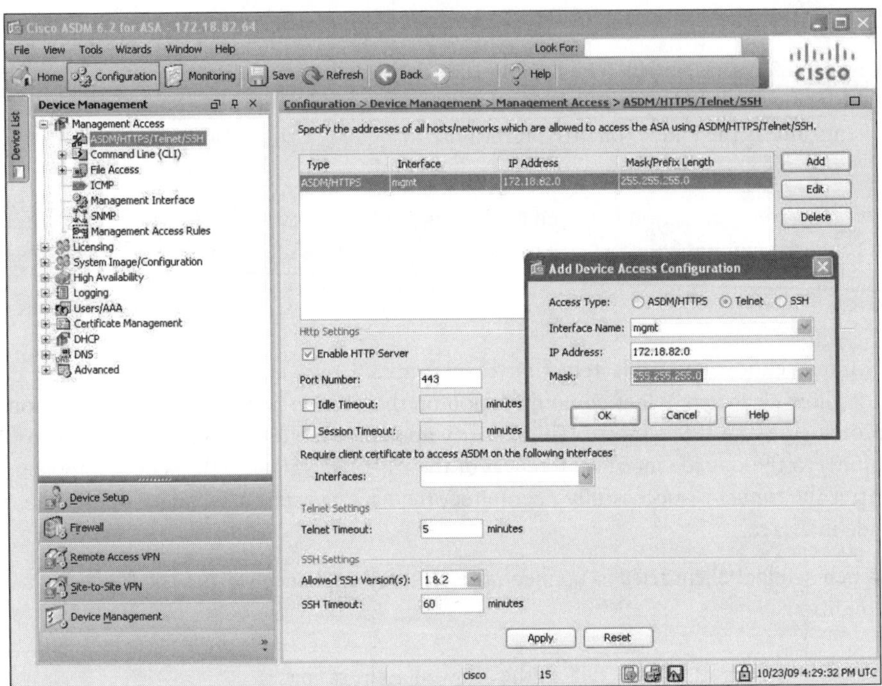

Figure 3-18 *Telnet Services for the Management Network*

Example 3-30 shows the relevant configuration for this setup. If the Telnet connection is idle, the security appliance is set up to time it out after 5 minutes, which is the default timeout.

Example 3-30 *Configuration of Telnet Access on the Management Interface*

```
Chicago# configure terminal
Chicago(config)# Telnet 172.18.82.0 255.255.255.0 mgmt
Chicago(config)# Telnet timeout 5
```

If a user is allowed to connect, the security appliance goes through the user authentication phase and prompts the user for login credentials. The default Telnet password to gain user access mode is **cisco**. Consult the "Setting Up Device Name and Passwords" section earlier in the chapter to learn how to change the Telnet password.

> **Note** It is highly recommended that you change the default password of the security appliance to avoid unauthorized access.

If the authentication is successful, the security appliance grants user access–mode CLI to the authenticated user. You can monitor the active Telnet sessions by going to **Monitoring > Properties > Device Access > ASDM/HTTPS/Telnet/SSH Sessions.** This displays the Telnet connection ID along with the client's IP address. You can use the connection ID to clear out a session if you believe that it should not be established. You do so by selecting the user and clicking the **disconnect** button.

In Figure 3-19, the security appliance has assigned a connection ID of 0 to a Telnet client 172.18.82.77. An ASDM session is also established from the same client IP address.

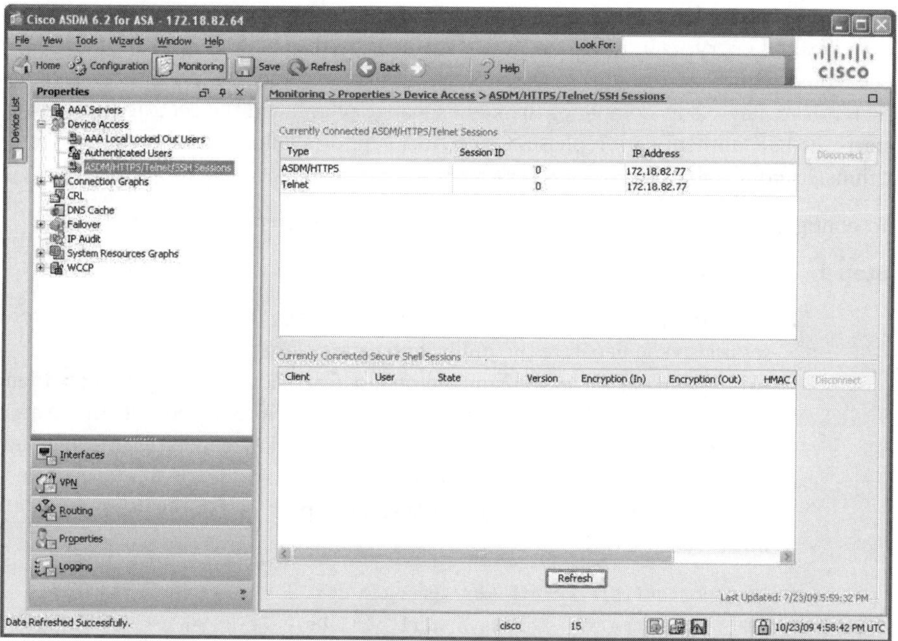

Figure 3-19 *Monitoring Remote Management Sessions*

Example 3-31 shows the relevant configuration for this setup. A Telnet session is built from 172.18.82.77. This connection is being disconnected by use of the **kill** command.

Example 3-31 *Monitoring and Clearing Active Telnet Sessions*

```
Chicago# configure terminal
Chicago# who
        0: 172.18.82.77
```

```
Chicago# kill 0
Chicago# who
Chicago#
```

Secure Shell (SSH)

SSH is the recommended way to connect to the security appliance for remote management because the data packets are encrypted by industry-standard algorithms such as 3DES and AES. The SSH implementation on the security appliance supports both version 1 and 2.

Before the SSH client and the Cisco ASA SSH server encrypt data, they go through an exchange of RSA security keys. These keys are used to ensure that an unauthorized user cannot look at the packet content. When a client tries to connect, the security appliance presents its public keys to the client. After receiving the keys, the client generates a random key and encrypts it, using the public key sent by the security appliance. These encrypted client keys are sent to the security appliance, which decodes them using its own private keys. This completes the key exchange phase, and the security appliance starts the user authentication phase. Cisco ASA supports a number of security algorithms, listed in Table 3-6.

To configure SSH on the security appliance, follow these steps:

Step 1. Generate the RSA keys.

The SSH daemon on the security appliance uses the RSA keys to encrypt the sessions. You generate the public and private key pair by going to **Configuration > Device Management > Certificate Management > Identity Certificates > Add > Add a New Identity Certificate** and selecting **New** for Key Pair. Alternatively, you can use the **crypto** key generate rsa command from the CLI as shown in the following output. For detailed information about generating the RSA keys, consult Chapter 18, "Public Key Infrastructure (PKI)."

```
Chicago(config)# crypto key generate rsa
INFO: The name for the keys will be: <Default-RSA-Key>
Keypair generation process begin. Please wait...
```

Table 3-6 *Security Algorithms Supported by Cisco ASA*

Attributes	Supported Algorithm
Data encryption	3DES and AES
Packet integrity	MD5 and SHA
Authentication method	RSA public keys
Key exchange	Diffie-Hellman group 1

You can change the default modulus size, 1024 bits, to 512, 768, or 2048 bits. After the keys have been generated, you can view the public keys by using the **show crypto key mypubkey rsa** command:

```
Chicago(config)# show crypto key mypubkey rsa
Key pair was generated at: 22:41:07 UTC Aug 21 2009
Key name: <Default-RSA-Key>
 Usage: General Purpose Key
 Modulus Size (bits): 1024
 Key Data:
  30819f30 0d06092a 864886f7 0d010101 05000381 8d003081 89028181
00b85a0c
  7af04bc1 028c072e 4be49fad 29e7c8e2 9b1341cc e6ace229 2556b310
66a12627
  05166501 30ca3360 e32307d7 31d2f839 7a36005e 0656cc36 4fa23aa5
7d9a3f09
  fd5b35b2 cdf1b393 8e4ba10f 0752f2ec c29915cf f058945a 4ac11cd6
d46c72d7
  a45766e1 851d1093 e1cd4a93 f222631f 6c51a55f e9ef229a 4481f719
55020301 0001
```

Step 2. Enable SSH on an interface.

You can configure the security appliance to accept SSH sessions on an interface by navigating to **Configuration > Device Management > Management Access > ASDM/HTTPS/Telnet/SSH** and clicking **Add.** ASDM prompts you to select an interface name and specify the IP address/mask, similar to what was covered in the Telnet section. As shown in the following example, the security appliance is configured to accept SSH sessions from the **mgmt** network, **172.18.82.0/24**:

```
Chicago(config)# ssh 172.18.82.0 255.255.255.0 mgmt
```

Note Unlike Telnet, Cisco ASA enables you to terminate SSH sessions on the outside interface. SSH sessions are already encrypted and do not require an IPSec tunnel.

After a client negotiates the security parameters, the security appliance prompts the user for authentication credentials. If the authentication is successful, the user is put into user access mode.

Note If AAA settings or local user accounts are not used, the default username is **pix** and the password is **cisco.**

Step 3. Restrict the SSH version.

The security appliance can restrict a user to use either SSH version 1 (SSHv1) or SSH version 2 (SSHv2) when a connection is made. By default, the security appliance accepts both versions. SSHv2 is the recommended version because of its strong authentication and encryption capabilities. However, the security appliance does not provide support for the following SSHv2 features:

- X11 forwarding
- Port forwarding
- Secure File Transfer Protocol (SFTP) support
- Kerberos and AFS ticket passing
- Data compression

In ASDM, select the SSH version from the **Allowed SSH Version(s)** drop-down menu, as shown in Figure 3-18. To set a specific SSH version via CLI, use the **ssh version** command, followed by the actual version of the shell.

> **Note** The security appliance must have the 3DES-AES feature set in the license to support SSHv2 sessions.

Step 4. Modify the idle timeout (optional).

Similar to the Telnet timeout, you can fine-tune the idle timeout value between 1 and 60 minutes. If the organizational security policy does not allow long idle connections, the idle timeout value can be changed to a lower value, such as 3 minutes, from its default value of 5 minutes.

Step 5. Monitor the SSH sessions.

As with Telnet sessions, you can monitor the SSH session by going to **Monitoring > Properties > Device Access > ASDM/HTTPS/Telnet/SSH Sessions**. This displays useful information such as the username, IP address of the client, encryption and hashing used, the current state of the connection, and the SSH version that is used. You can also use the **show ssh session** command from the CLI to get similar information.

If you like to manually disconnect an active SSH session, click the **Disconnect** button. CLI admins can issue the **ssh disconnect** command followed by the session ID number.

Step 6. Enable secure copy (SCP).

You can use the SCP file transfer protocol to move files to the network device securely. It functions similarly to FTP but with the added advantage of data encryption. The security appliance can act as an SCP server to allow SSHv2 clients to copy files in Flash. SCP can be enabled by navigating to **Configuration > Device Management > Management Access > File Access**

> Secure Copy (SCP) Server and selecting **Enable Secure Copy Server**. If you prefer to use the CLI, use the **ssh scopy enable** command as follows:

```
Chicago(config)# ssh scopy enable
```

Note The SSH client must be SCP capable to be able to transfer files.

System Maintenance

This section explains how to manage and install a different system image file on the Cisco ASA and ways to recover a device with no operating system. This section also discusses how to recover authentication passwords if they are lost.

Software Installation

Cisco ASA supports upgrading a system image file to flash via both the Cisco ASDM and the Cisco ASA CLI.

In case the security appliance does not have a bootable image, this section also discusses steps to upload the image from ROMMON.

Image Upgrade via the Cisco ASDM

ASDM can upload either an ASA or an ASDM image to the Cisco ASA flash with the HTTPS protocol if you click **Tools > Software Updates**. ASDM gives you two options:

- Upload a file from the local computer to the local flash of Cisco ASA.
- Check Cisco's website for the latest version of the ASA bootable image.

In most cases, you want to download a bootable image from Cisco.com to your local workstation. Many enterprises want to test an ASA image in their lab environment first to make sure that the new image fits their requirements.

If you choose **Upgrade Software from Local Computer**, select whether you want to upload an ASDM or an ASA image, and then specify the path to the image file on the local drive. For ease of use, you can also click **Browse Local Files** and select the file by browsing the local hard-drive file structure. Specify the destination location on the Cisco ASA flash and then click **Upload Image** to initiate the file transfer process, as shown in Figure 3-20.

If the system Flash contains more than one system image, the security Cisco ASA boots off from the first image it finds in Flash. If the image you want to boot is not the first one on the disk, you should set the boot order to load the desired binary image file. Navigate to **Configuration > Device Administration > System Image/Configuration > Boot Image/Configuration > Add > Browse Flash** and select the image from which you want

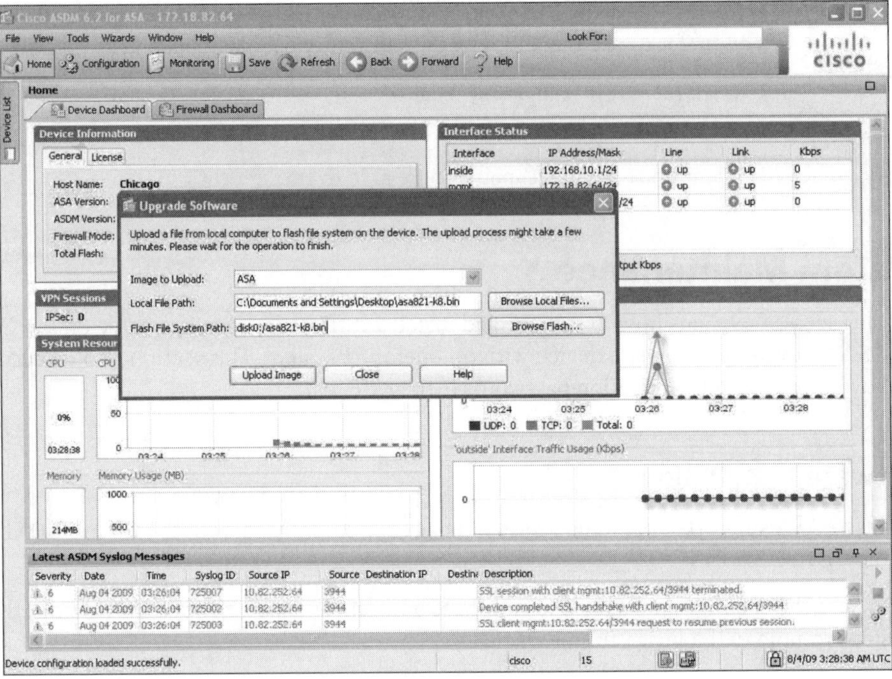

Figure 3-20 *Upgrading Image Through ASDM*

to boot. If you have selected multiple images to boot from, you can change the priority of a particular image by clicking the **Move Up** and **Move Down** buttons.

After a new image has been uploaded, you must reboot the appliance to load the new image. You do so by clicking **Tools > System Reload.** Cisco ASDM prompts to ask whether you want to save the running configuration in the NVRAM and whether you want to reload now or schedule a time to reboot later.

Image Upgrade via the Cisco ASA CLI

The security appliance supports a number of file server types, including TFTP, HTTP(s), and FTP, to download a system image into flash (disk0). The image upgrade process uses the **copy** command followed by the name of the file transfer type. The **copy** command copies the specified files from the source location or URL to the destination location (flash). The destination location of the system image is the local file system. The security appliance has an internal storage disk, referred to as disk0: or flash. Additionally, an external storage device, referred to as disk1:, can be used to save system images.

You can also use the **noconfirm** option to notify the security appliance to accept the parameters without prompting the user for confirmation. This is useful if customized scripts are used to upload system images.

Example 3-32 illustrates how to configure the security appliance to download an image file, called **asa821-k8.bin**, from a TFTP server located at **192.168.10.250**. The security appliance initiates the download process and stores the image file as **asa821-k8.bin.**

Example 3-32 *Copying a System Image from a TFTP Server to the Local Flash*

```
Chicago# copy tftp: flash:
Address or name of remote host []? 192.168.10.250
Source filename []?asa821-k8.bin
Destination filename [asa821-k8.bin]? asa821-k8.bin

Accessing tftp://192.168.10.250/asa821-k8.bin...!!!!!!!!!!!!!!!!!!!!!!!!!!!!!!!
! Output omitted for brevity
Writing file disk0: asa821-k8.bin...
!!!!!!!!!!!!!!!!!!!!!!!!!!!!!!!!!!!!!!!!!!!!!!!!!!!!!!!!!!!!!!!!!!!!!!!!!!!!!!!
! Output omitted for brevity
5124096 bytes copied in 151.370 secs (33934 bytes/sec)
```

Example 3-33 illustrates how to configure the security appliance to download an image file, called **asa821-k8.bin**, from an FTP server located at **192.168.10.251**. The username is **Cisco** and the password is **cisco123**.

Example 3-33 *Copying a System Image from a FTP Server to the Local Flash*

```
Chicago(config)# copy ftp://Cisco:cisco123@192.168.10.251/asa821-k8.bin flash
Address or name of remote host [192.168.10.251]?
Source username [Cisco]?
Source password [cisco123]?
Source filename [asa821-k8.bin]?
Destination filename [asa821-k8.bin]?
Accessing ftp://Cisco:cisco123@192.168.10.251/asa821-k8.bin...!
Writing file disk0:/asa821-k8.bin...
!!!!!!!!!!!!!!!!!!!!!!!!!!!!!!!!!!!!!!!!!!!!!!!!!!!!!!!!!!!!!!!1
! Output omitted for brevity
5124096 bytes copied in 151.370 secs (33934 bytes/sec)
```

You can verify that the downloaded image file was successfully saved in flash by typing the **dir** command, as demonstrated in Example 3-34.

Example 3-34 *Output of the* **dir flash** *Command*

```
Chicago# dir
Directory of disk0:/
6       -rw-  5124096      05:37:16 May 6 2009  asa821-k8.bin
10      -rw-  5919340      04:29:18 May 5 2009  asdm-621.bin
```

As mentioned earlier, the security appliance allows multiple system image files to reside in flash. If rebooted, the security appliance loads the first available system image. You can modify this default behavior by using the **boot system** command to ensure that the newly uploaded image file is used for bootup. This is shown in Example 3-35, where the security appliance is set up to boot from **asa821-k8.bin**.

Example 3-35 *Setting the Boot Parameter*

```
Chicago(config)# boot system disk0:/asa821-k8.bin
Chicago(config# exit
```

After configuring the Cisco ASA to boot a specific image upon bootup, the running configuration needs to be saved to NVRAM, as shown in Example 3-36.

Example 3-36 *Copy Running-Config to NVRAM*

```
Chicago# copy running-config startup-config
```

To reboot the security appliance, you can use the **reload** command, as shown in Example 3-37. The security appliance shuts down all the processes and reloads itself. Based on the boot system parameters, it loads the asa821-k8.bin image.

Example 3-37 *Reloading the Security Appliance*

```
Chicago# reload
Proceed with reload? [confirm] <cr>
***
*** —- START GRACEFUL SHUTDOWN —-
Shutting down isakmp
Shutting down File system
! Output omitted for brevity

Loading disk0:/asa821-k8.bin... Booting...
##########################################################################
! Output omitted for brevity
Type help or '?' for a list of available commands.
Chicago>
```

Note Before you reload the security appliance, schedule a maintenance window to avoid disrupting production traffic.

The last step in verifying that the security appliance is running the desired version of code is to issue the **show version** command, as shown in Example 3-38.

Example 3-38 *Output of* show version

```
Chicago# show version | include Version
Cisco ASA Software Version 8.2(1)
Device Manager Version 6.2(1)
```

Image Recovery Using ROMMON

The security appliance provides a way to recover the system image in case the file is lost or gets corrupted and the security appliance ends up in ROMMON mode. If the security appliance is actively running an image file, you can upload a new image in flash by using the guidelines described previously in the "Software Installation" section. However, if an image file is not present and the security appliance is reloaded, ROMMON mode can be invoked to upload an image using the TFTP protocol. You must complete this process through the CLI.

Before an image can be uploaded, verify that the TFTP server hosts the file in the root directory and that network connectivity exists between the security appliance and the TFTP server. Assign an IP address to the security appliance by using the **address** command, and configure a TFTP server by using the **server** command. You can map the configured IP address to an interface by using the **interface** command followed by the physical interface name. The **file** command can be used to set the name of the system image file. Example 3-39 assigns an IP address of **192.168.10.1** to the **GigabitEthernet0/1** interface. The TFTP server is **192.168.10.250** and the name of the system image file is **asa821-k8.bin.**

Example 3-39 *Setting Up TFTP Parameters*

```
rommon #0> address 192.168.10.1
rommon #1> server 192.168.10.250
rommon #2> interface GigabitEthernet0/1
GigabitEthernet0/1
MAC Address: 000f.f775.4b54
rommon #3> file asa821-k8.bin
```

Note If the security appliance and the TFTP server reside on different IP subnets, then you must define a default gateway on the security appliance by using the **gateway** command:

```
rommon #2> gateway 192.168.10.100
```

To verify whether all the attributes are properly configured, use the **set** command, as shown in Example 3-40. Start the TFTP process by issuing the **tftpdnld** command.

Example 3-40 *Verifying the TFTP Parameters*

```
rommon #4> set
ROMMON Variable Settings:
  ADDRESS=192.168.10.1
  SERVER=192.168.10.250
  PORT=GigabitEthernet0/1
  VLAN=untagged
  IMAGE=asa821-k8.bin
  CONFIG=

rommon #5> tftpdnld
tftp asa821-k8.bin@192.168.10.250
!!!!!!!!!!!!!!!!!!!!!!!!!!!!!!!!!!!!!!!!!!!!!!!!!!!!!!!!!!!!!!!!!!!!!!!!
```

Note The security appliance downloads the system image file in memory and boots up the device. However, the downloaded system image is not stored in Flash. Follow the guidelines described previously in the section "Image Upgrade via the Cisco ASA CLI" to upload the image in the system flash.

Password Recovery Process

The password recovery process on a security appliance is used when the system password is either locked out due to configured authentication parameters or lost. This process for Cisco ASA is similar to the password recovery process for an IOS router, which uses ROMMON mode to recover. You should schedule a maintenance window in which to recover the system passwords, because this process will require you to reboot the security appliance. Use the following steps for password recovery:

Step 1. Establish a console connection.

This process requires you to have physical access to the security appliance, for security reasons. This is to ensure that remote or unauthorized users cannot reset passwords. Consequently, a console connection to the security appliance is required. Consult the "Establishing a Console Connection" section earlier in the chapter.

Step 2. Reload the security appliance.

You start the password recovery process by turning the security appliance off and then turning it back on. This is necessary when you do not have the password to reboot the appliance from the CLI.

Step 3. Break into ROMMON.

When the security appliance starts to reboot, the startup messages are displayed on the console. Press the Esc (Escape) key after Use BREAK or ESC to interrupt boot is shown. This takes you into ROMMON mode, as follows:

```
Evaluating BIOS Options ...
Launch BIOS Extension to setup ROMMON
Cisco Systems ROMMON Version (1.0(10)0) #0: Fri Mar 25 23:02:10 PST
2005
Platform ASA5520
GigabitEthernet0/0
Link is UP
MAC Address: 000f.f775.4b54

Use ? for help.
rommon #0>
```

Step 4. Set the ROMMON configuration register.

ROMMON mode includes the **confreg** command, which sets the configuration register responsible for changing the security appliance boot behavior. It can be used to specify how an appliance should boot (ROMMON, NetBoot, and Flash boot) or if it should ignore the default configuration during bootup. When the **confreg** command is entered, the security appliance displays the current configuration register value and prompts the user for several options. Record the current configuration register value and press **y** to enter interactive mode:

The security appliance prompts the user for new values to be assigned to the configuration register. Select all the default values until the system prompts the user to disable system configuration. Enter **y** as shown in the following configuration:

```
rommon #0> confreg
Current Configuration Register: 0x00000001
Configuration Summary:
boot default image from Flash
Do you wish to change this configuration? y/n [n]: y
enable boot to ROMMON prompt? y/n [n]:
enable TFTP netboot? y/n [n]:
enable Flash boot? y/n [n]:
select specific Flash image index? y/n [n]:
disable system configuration? y/n [n]: y
go to ROMMON prompt if netboot fails? y/n [n]:
enable passing NVRAM file specs in auto-boot mode? y/n [n]:
disable display of BREAK or ESC key prompt during auto-boot? y/n [n]:
Current Configuration Register: 0x00000040
```

```
Configuration Summary:
  boot ROMMON
  ignore system configuration
Update Config Register (0x40) in NVRAM...
```

Step 5. Boot up the security appliance.

After setting up the configuration register to ignore the configuration file, boot the security appliance by using the **boot** command:

```
rommon #1> boot
Launching BootLoader...
Boot configuration file contains 1 entry.
Searching / for images to boot.
Loading /asa821-k8.bin... Booting...
```

Step 6. Access privileged mode.

The security appliance loads the default configuration, which does not use an enable password to access privileged mode. After the security appliance shows the default **ciscoasa** prompt, type the **enable** command to gain privileged mode access:

```
ciscoasa>
ciscoasa> enable
Password:<cr>
ciscoasa#
```

Step 7. Load the saved configuration.

After you have privileged mode access to the security appliance CLI, load the saved configuration from NVRAM. You do so by using the **copy** command, which copies the startup-config file to the running-config as follows:

```
ciscoasa# copy startup-config running-config
Destination filename [running-config]?<cr>
Cryptochecksum(unchanged): 3a3748e9 43700f38 7712cc11 2c6de52b
1104 bytes copied in 0.60 secs
```

Step 8. Reset the passwords.

After loading the saved configuration, change the login, enable, and user passwords. The login password is used to get user mode access, and the enable password is used to gain privileged-mode access. In the following example, login and enable passwords are changed to **C1$c0123**:

```
Chicago# config terminal
Chicago(config)# passwd C1$c0123
Chicago(config)# enable password C1$c0123
```

If the security appliance is using local user authentication, the user passwords can also be changed, as shown here for user **cisco**:

```
Chicago(config)# username cisco password C1$c0123
```

Step 9. Restore the original configuration register value.

To ensure that the security appliance does not ignore the saved configuration in the next reboot, you must change the configuration register value to reflect this. Restore the original configuration register value of 0x1 by using the **config-register** configuration-mode command:

```
Chicago(config)# config-register 0x1
```

Step 10. Save the current configuration into NVRAM.

Make sure that the newly specified passwords are stored in the saved NVRAM configuration. You do so by using the **copy** command to copy the running-config file in NVRAM as the startup-config, as follows:

```
Chicago(config)# copy running-config startup-config
Source filename [running-config]?
Cryptochecksum: 6167413a 17ad1a46 b961fb7b 5b68dd2b
1104 bytes copied in 3.270 secs (368 bytes/sec)
```

Note The **write memory** command copies the running-config file into NVRAM as start-up-config.

Disabling the Password Recovery Process

Cisco ASA can disable the password recovery process discussed in the previous section to enhance device security. This ensures that even if an unauthorized user gets access to the console port, that user should not be able to compromise the device or configuration settings. Use the **no service password-recovery** command to disable password recovery from configuration mode, as shown in Example 3-41. The security appliance displays a warning message saying that the only way to do password recovery is by erasing all files in flash and then downloading a new image and a configuration file from an external server such as TFTP. With this option, access to ROMMON mode is disabled to protect the system from unauthorized users.

Example 3-41 *Disabling the Password Recovery Process*

```
Chicago(config)# no service password-recovery
WARNING: Executing "no service password-recovery" has disabled the
password recovery mechanism and disabled access to ROMMON.  The only
means of recovering from lost or forgotten passwords will be for ROMMON
to erase all file systems including configuration files and images.
You should make a backup of your configuration and have a mechanism to
restore images from the ROMMON command line.
```

You can also disable the password recovery process by going through the initial setup as demonstrated in Example 3-42. The security appliance prompts users to reconfirm whether they really want to disable the password recovery process after displaying a warning that specifies the consequences of this option.

Example 3-42 *Disabling Password Recovery Using Initial Setup*

```
Pre-configure Firewall now through interactive prompts [yes]?
! Output omitted for brevity
Allow password recovery [yes]? no
WARNING: entering 'no' will disable password recovery and disable access
to ROMMON CLI. The only means of recovering from lost or forgotten passwords
will be for ROMMON to erase all file systems including configuration files
and images.
If entering 'no' you should make a backup of your configuration and have a
mechanism to restore images from the ROMMON command line...
Allow password recovery [yes]?no
Clock (UTC):
! Output omitted for brevity
```

If you have forgotten the security appliance password and the password recovery process is disabled, the only way to recover out of this state is to erase all system files (including the software image and the configuration file). Make sure that the configuration and system image files are stored in an external server with IP connectivity to the security appliance. Use the following procedure to recover system passwords when password recovery is disabled:

Step 1. Establish a console connection.

This process requires you to have physical access to the security appliance, for security reasons. This is to ensure that remote or unauthorized users cannot reset passwords. Consequently, a console connection to the security appliance is required. Consult the "Establishing a Console Connection" section earlier in the chapter.

Step 2. Reload the security appliance.

You start the password recovery process by turning off the security appliance and then turning it back on.

Step 3. Break into ROMMON.

When the security appliance starts to reboot, the startup messages are displayed on the console. Press the **Esc** (Escape) key after Use BREAK or ESC to Interrupt Boot is shown. This displays a warning message saying that all files will be erased from flash if access to ROMMON is made. The following example illustrates this process:

```
Evaluating BIOS Options ...
Launch BIOS Extension to setup ROMMON
Cisco Systems ROMMON Version (1.0(3)0) #0: Mon Aug  9 14:51:06 MDT
2004
  Platform ASA5540-K8
Management0/0
Ethernet auto negotiation timed out.

WARNING:  Password recovery and ROMMON command line access has been
disabled by your security policy.  Choosing YES below will cause ALL
configurations, passwords, images, and files systems to be erased.
ROMMON command line access will be re-enabled, and a new image must be
downloaded via ROMMON.

Erase all file systems? y/n [n]:
```

Step 4. Erase system files from flash.

Before the security appliance allows a user to get access to ROMMON mode, it issues a prompt to erase all file systems. Press **yes** to start the process of erasing all system files. After all files have been erased, the security appliance enables the password recovery process and grants access to ROMMON mode.

```
Erase all file systems? y/n [n]: yes
Permanently erase Disk0: and Disk1:? y/n [n]: y
Erasing Disk0:
..........................................................
! Output omitted for brevity
Disk1: is not present.
Enabling password recovery...
rommon #0>
```

Step 5. Upload a system image.

When access to ROMMON mode is available, go through the image upgrade process discussed earlier in this chapter. The following example shows a system image, asa821-k8.bin, being uploaded from a TFTP server, 192.168.10.250:

```
rommon #0> address=192.168.10.1
rommon #1> server=192.168.10.250
rommon #3> interface GigabitEthernet0/1
GigabitEthernet0/1
```

```
MAC Address: 000f.f775.4b54
rommon #4> file asa821-k8.bin
rommon #5> tftpdnld
tftp asa821-k8.bin@192.168.10.250
!!!!!!!!!!!!!!!!!!!!!!!!!!!!!!!!!!!!!!!!!!!!!!!!!!!!!!!!!!!!!!!!!!!!!!
!!!!!!!!!
```

Note The security appliance downloads the system image file in memory and boots up the device. However, the downloaded system image is not stored in flash.

Step 6. Upload a configuration file.

The security appliance loads a default configuration file without an interface configured. To upload a configuration file, the interface closest to the external file server must be set up to upload the saved file. In the following example, GigabitEthernet 0/1 is set up to upload a configuration file called **Chicago.conf** from a TFTP server located at **192.168.10.250** toward the **inside** interface:

```
ciscoasa> enable
Password:<cr>
ciscoasa# configure terminal
ciscoasa(config)# interface GigabitEthernet0/1
ciscoasa(config-if)# ip address 192.168.10.1 255.255.255.0
ciscoasa(config-if)# nameif inside
INFO: Security level for "inside" set to 100 by default.
ciscoasa(config-if)# no shutdown
ciscoasa(config)# copy tftp: running-config
Address or name of remote host []? 192.168.10.250
Source filename []? Chicago.conf
Destination filename [running-config]?
Accessing tftp://192.168.10.250/Chicago.conf...!
!
Cryptochecksum(unchanged): 1c9855a1 2cca93c7 a9691450 9bab6e92
1246 bytes copied in 0.90 secs
Chicago#
```

Step 7. Reset the passwords.

After uploading the saved configuration, change the login, enable, and user passwords. The login password is used to get user-mode access, and enable password is used to gain privileged mode access. In the following example, login and enable passwords are changed to **C1$c0123**:

```
Chicago# config terminal
```

```
Chicago(config)# passwd C1$c0123
Chicago(config)# enable password C1$c0123
```

If the security appliance is using local user authentication, the user passwords can also be changed, as follows:

```
Chicago# config terminal
Chicago(config)# username cisco password C1$c0123
```

Step 8. Save the current configuration into NVRAM.

Make sure that the newly specified passwords are stored in the saved NVRAM configuration. Do so by using the **copy** command to copy the running-config file in NVRAM as the startup-config:

```
Chicago(config)# copy running-config startup-config
Source filename [running-config]? <cr>
```

Load ASA image to Flash.

Finally, load the image from the TFTP server to the local flash. Follow the guidelines discussed under the "Image Upgrade via the Cisco ASA CLI" section earlier in this chapter.

System Monitoring

The security appliance generates system and debug messages when an event occurs. These messages can be logged to the local buffer or to an external server, depending on an organization's security policies. This section discusses how to enable event logging and Simple Network Management Protocol (SNMP) polling, which can be used to check the security appliance's status.

System Logging

System logging is a process by which the Cisco ASA generates an event for any significant occurrence that affects the system, such as network problems, error conditions, and threshold breaches. These messages can either be stored locally on the system buffer or be transferred to external servers. You can use these logs for event correlations to detect network anomalies or you can use them for monitoring and troubleshooting purposes.

The security appliance assigns a message ID to each event it generates. As of version 8.2, these message IDs range from 101001 to 741006 and contain a brief description of the event. The security appliance also associates each message ID to a severity level ranging from 0 to 7. The lower the severity level number is, the more critical the message is. Table 3-7 lists the severity levels, along with the associated keyword and a brief description.

Table 3-7 *Severity Levels and Their Descriptions*

Severity Level	Level Keyword	Level Description
0	emergencies	Event used to indicate that the system is unusable
1	alerts	Message used to specify that an immediate action is needed, such as when a power failure on the standby failover appliance has occurred
2	critical	Message used to identify a critical condition, such as spoofed attacks
3	errors	Event used for error messages such as memory allocation failures
4	warnings	Event used to inform about the warning messages, such as exceeding certain thresholds
5	notifications	Message used to identify a normal but significant condition, such as when a user logs in
6	informational	Event used to classify informational messages, such as the creation of IKE security associations
7	debugging	Event used to indicate low-level debug messages, such as the acknowledgement of VPN hello requests

Each severity level not only displays the events for that level but also shows the messages from the lower severity levels. For example, if logging is enabled for debugging (level 7), the security appliance also logs levels 0 through 6 events.

Note For a complete list of all the severity messages, please consult the *System Log Messages* Guide located at www.cisco.com/go/asa under "Troubleshoot and Alerts."

The next subsection discusses how to enable system logging (syslog) on the security appliance to log relevant events.

Enabling Logging

To enable logging of system events through ASDM, go to **Configuration > Device Management > Logging > Logging Setup** and select the **Enable Logging** option. This option enables the security appliance to send logs to all the terminals and devices set up to receive the syslog messages.

The security appliance does not send debug messages as logs, such as **debug icmp trace**, to a syslog server unless you explicitly turn it on using the **Send debug messages as syslogs** option. For UDP-based syslogs, the security appliance allows logging of messages in the Cisco EMBLEM format. Many Cisco devices, including the Cisco IOS routers and CiscoWorks management server, use this format for syslogging. Figure 3-21 illustrates that syslogging is globally enabled, with debugs being sent as syslogs to an external server in the EMBLEM format.

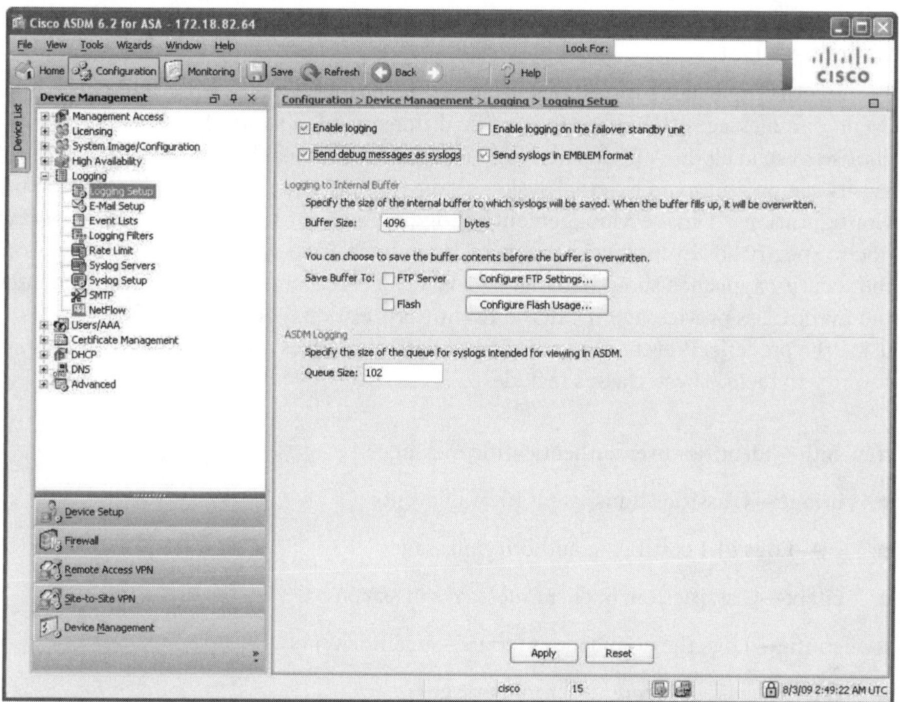

Figure 3-21 *Enabling Syslog via ASDM*

Example 3-43 shows the equivalent configuration in the CLI format.

Example 3-43 *Enabling Syslog*

```
Chicago# configure terminal
Chicago(config)# logging enable
Chicago(config)# logging debug-trace
Chicago(config)# logging emblem
```

After the logging is enabled, ensure that the messages are timestamped before they are sent. This is extremely important because in case of a security incident, you want to use the logs generated by the security appliance to back trace. Navigate to **Configuration > Device Management > Logging > Syslog Setup** and select the **Include timestamp in syslog** option. If you prefer to use the CLI, use the **logging timestamp** command, as shown in Example 3-44.

Example 3-4 *Enabling Syslog Timestamps*

```
Chicago(config)# logging timestamp
```

Defining Event List

The security appliance's robust operating system enables you to define and choose the events and messages to be sent to specific different syslog stores. For example, you can choose to send all the VPN-related log messages to the local buffer, whereas all the other events can be sent to an external syslog server. You do so by defining a logging list under **Configuration > Device Management > Logging > Event Lists > Add.** ASDM prompts you to specify an "Event List" name, which can be used to specify the level of messages the security appliance should be logging. You can add events to this list based on either the Event Class or Message ID. In the Event Class option, you can classify messages using the predefined event classes to log specific processes and then assign appropriate severity to them. These classes include

- **auth**—Identifies user authentication messages
- **bridge**—Classifies transparent firewall events
- **ca**—Logs PKI certificate authority messages
- **citrix**—Classifies citrix client messages in sslvpn
- **config**—Logs the command interface–specific events
- **csd**—Classifies secure desktop messages
- **dap**—Logs dynamic access policies messages
- **eap**—Identifies EAP messages in NAC implementations
- **eapoudp**—Logs EAPoUDP messages in NAC implementations
- **eigrp**—Classifies EIGRP routing events
- **email**—Logs WebVPN email proxy messages
- **ha**—Logs failover events
- **ids**—Classifies the intrusion detection system events
- **ip**—Identifies IP stack messages
- **ipaa**—Identifies IP address assignment messages
- **nac**—Logs NAC messages in NAC implementations
- **nacpolicy**—Logs NAC policy messages in NAC
- **nacsettings**—Classifies NAC setting messages
- **np**—Logs network processor events
- **ospf**—Classifies OSPF routing events

- **rip**—Logs RIP routing messages
- **rm**—Identifies resource manager events
- **session**—Identifies user session–specific messages
- **snmp**—Classifies SNMP-specific events
- **ssl**—Logs SSL-specific events
- **svc**—Classifies AnyConnect client messages
- **sys**—Logs system-specific events
- **vm**—Classifies VLAN mapping messages
- **vpdn**—Classifies L2TP session messages
- **vpn**—Classifies the IKE- and IPSec-related messages
- **vpnc**—Identifies the VPN client–specific events
- **vpnfo**—Logs VPN failover messages
- **vpnlb**—Logs VPN load-balancing events
- **webfo**—Logs WebVPN failover messages
- **webvpn**—Logs WebVPN-related messages

Note The default severity level for a logging list is 3 (errors).

In Figure 3-22, a logging list called **IPSec_Critical** is set up to group all the **vpn** (IKE and IPSec) messages. The selected severity level is **critical**, which also includes level 0 and level 1 events.

Example 3-45 shows the equivalent configuration of Figure 3-22.

Example 3-45 *Setting Up a Logging List*

```
Chicago# configure terminal
Chicago(config)# logging list IPSec_Critical level Critical class vpn
```

Logging Types

Cisco ASA supports the following types of logging capabilities:

- Console logging
- Terminal logging
- ASDM logging
- Email logging

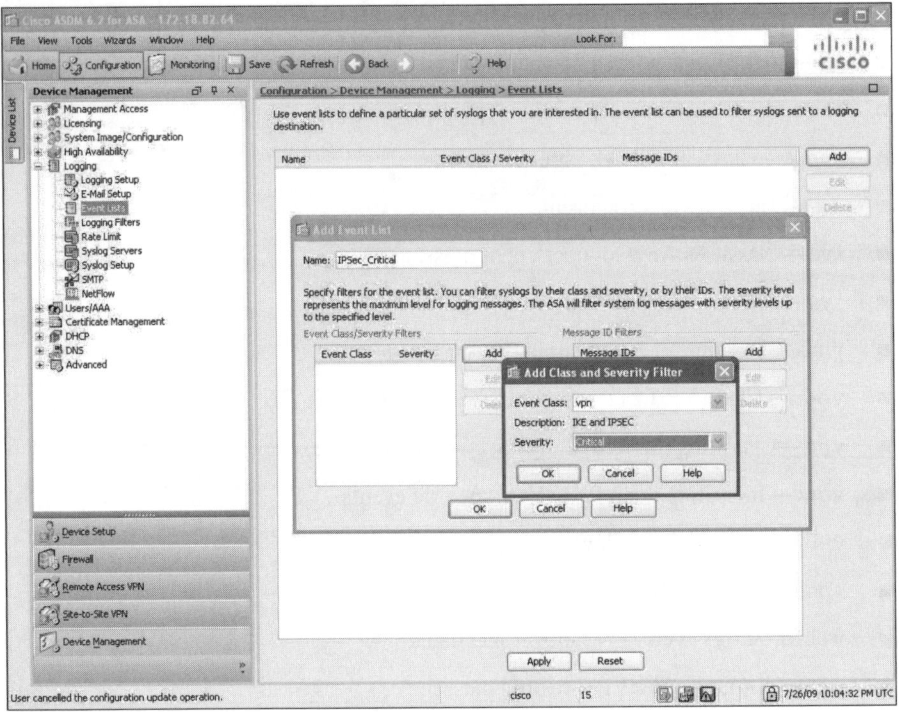

Figure 3-22 *Defining Event Class for Logging via ASDM*

- External syslog server logging
- External SNMP server logging
- Buffered logging

The followings sections describe each logging type in detail.

Console Logging

Console logging enables the security appliance to send syslog messages to the console serial port. This method is useful for viewing specific live events during troubleshooting.

> **Caution** Enable console logging with caution; the serial port is only 9600 bits per second, and the syslog messages can easily overwhelm the port.
>
> If the port is already overwhelmed, access the security appliance from an alternate method, such as SSH or Telnet, and lower the console-logging severity.

Terminal Logging

Terminal logging sends syslog messages to a remote terminal monitor such as a Telnet or a SSH session. This method is also useful for viewing live events during troubleshooting. It is recommended that you define an event class for terminal logging so that your session does not get overwhelmed with the logs.

ASDM Logging

You can enable the security appliance to send logs to Cisco ASDM. This feature is extremely useful if you use ASDM as the configuration and monitoring platform. You can specify the number of messages that can exist in the ASDM buffer. By default, ASDM shows 100 messages in the ASDM logging window.

Email Logging

The security appliance supports sending log messages directly to individual email addresses. This feature is extremely useful when you are interested in getting immediate notification when the security appliance generates a specific log message. When an interesting event occurs, the security appliance contacts the specified email server and sends an email message to the e-mail recipient from a preconfigured e-mail account.

Syslog Server Logging

Cisco ASA supports sending the event logs to one or multiple external syslog servers. Messages can be stored for use in anomaly detection or event correlation. The security appliance allows the use of both TCP and UDP protocols to communicate with a syslog server. You must define an external server to send the logs to it, as discussed later in the "Defining a Syslog Server" section.

Cisco ASA also supports sending the event logs to one or multiple external SNMP servers. Messages are sent as SNMP traps for anomaly detection or event correlation. This is discussed in detail under the SNMP section.

Buffered Logging

The security appliance allocates 4096 bytes of memory to store log messages in its buffer. This is the preferred method to troubleshoot an issue because it does not overwhelm the console or the terminal ports. If you are troubleshooting an issue that needs to store more messages than it can store, increase the buffer size up to 16,384 bytes.

Note The allocated memory is a circular buffer; consequently, the security appliance does not run out of memory as the older events get over-written by newer events.

In Figure 3-23, the logging level for the syslog server is set up for debugging. The figure also illustrates that the logging level for SNMP trap is an event list called **FailoverCommunication**, internal buffered logging is set to **debug**, email logging is set to the **FailoverCommunication** event list, Telnet and SSH sessions logging is set to the **IPSec_Critical** event list, syslogging is set to **debug**, and ASDM logging is set to the

Informational level. The email and syslog server parameters are configured later in this chapter.

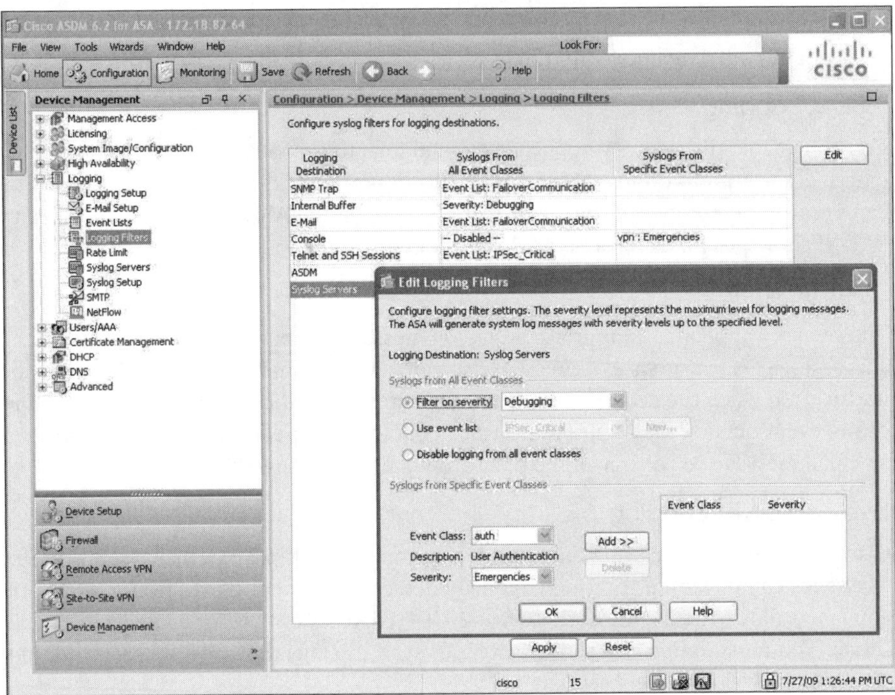

Figure 3-23 *Forwarding Syslogs to Multiple Stores*

Example 3-46 shows the equivalent configuration of Figure 3-23.

Example 3-46 *Setting Up a Logging List*

```
Chicago# configure terminal
Chicago(config)# logging list IPSec_Critical level critical class vpn
Chicago(config)# logging list FailoverCommunication message 105005
Chicago(config)# logging monitor IPSec_Critical
Chicago(config)# logging buffered debugging
Chicago(config)# logging trap debugging
Chicago(config)# logging history FailoverCommunication
Chicago(config)# logging asdm informational
Chicago(config)# logging mail FailoverCommunication
Chicago(config)# logging class vpn console emergencies
```

You can view the buffered logs by using the **show logging** command, as demonstrated in Example 3-47. This shows all different types of logging supported on the security appliance and indicates whether they are enabled or disabled. Additionally, it provides the number of messages logged on each of the configured logging types with the logging severity. Each syslog message starts with **%ASA**, to indicate that a Cisco security appliance generated the message, followed by the logging level, the unique message ID, and then a brief string to describe the log message.

Example 3-47 *Output of* **show logging**

```
Chicago# show logging
Syslog logging: enabled
    Facility: 20
    Timestamp logging: enabled
    Standby logging: disabled
    Debug-trace logging: enabled
    Console logging:  class vpn, 0 messages logged
    Monitor logging: list IPSec_Critical, 0 messages logged
    Buffer logging: level debugging, 113923 messages logged
    Trap logging: level debugging, facility 20, 194382 messages logged
    History logging: list FailoverCommunication, 18 messages logged
    Device ID: disabled
    Mail logging: list FailoverCommunication, 0 messages logged
    ASDM logging: level informational, 6487 messages logged
<167>:Aug 30 14:27:53 UTC: %ASA-session-7-710005: UDP request discarded from
172.18.82.99/137 to mgmt:172.18.82.255/137
<167>:Aug 30 14:27:54 UTC: %ASA-session-7-710005: UDP request discarded from
172.18.82.99/137 to mgmt:172.18.82.255/137! Output omitted for brevity
```

Defining a Syslog Server

You must define an external UDP- or TCP-based syslog server before the Cisco ASA can send logs to it. To define a syslog server, navigate to **Configuration > Device Management > Logging > Syslog Servers > Add.** ASDM prompts you to specify an interface where the syslog server resides, the IP address of the server, a selection of UDP or TCP port and the respective port numbers, and whether you want to send the log in the Cisco EMBLEM format to UDP-based syslog servers.

For TCP-based syslog servers, the security appliance

- Enables you to create a secure TLS connection so that the messages can be encrypted.
- Drops all new connections if the session to the syslog server cannot be established.

To enable secure communication between the security appliance and the TCP-based syslog server, select the **Enable secure logging using SSL/TLS (TCP only)** option. To allow new connections to be established if the TCP-based syslog server is down, enable the **Allow user traffic to pass when TCP syslog server is down** global option, which is configured in the "Syslog Servers" window.

In Figure 3-24, two syslog servers to which log messages are to be sent are defined. The first server collects the logs, using UDP and in the Cisco EMBLEM format, and the other server uses TCP port 1470 to accept the syslog messages. The security appliance sends all logging level 7 and below messages to these servers. The security appliance is configured to establish secure connection with the TCP-based syslog server. If the syslog server is not enabled, the security appliance continues to establish new connections.

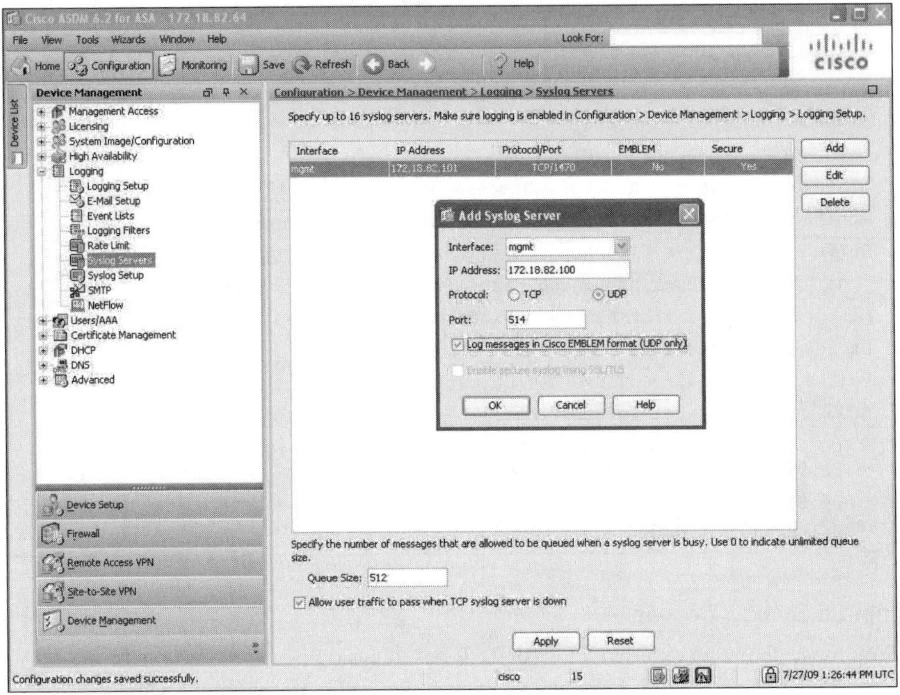

Figure 3-24 *Defining Syslog Servers*

Example 3-48 shows the equivalent configuration of Figure 3-24.

Example 3-48 *Setting Up Syslog Servers*

```
Chicago# configure terminal
Chicago(config)# logging host mgmt 172.18.82.100 format emblem
Chicago(config)# logging host mgmt 172.18.82.101 6/1470 secure
Chicago(config)# logging trap debugging
Chicago(config)# logging permit-hostdown
```

Defining an Email Server

The security appliance enables you to send sensitive log messages via an email. This is extremely useful if you are monitoring a specific event or a group of events and want to get alerted right away when it occurs. To define a new SMTP server, navigate to

Configuration > Device Management > Logging > SMTP and specify the IP address of the primary and optionally the secondary SMTP server. Additionally, you must specify the source and destination email addresses. You can define them by choosing **Configuration > Device Management > Logging > E-Mail Setup.** The source address is used to generate the log messages, whereas the destination email address is where the messages are sent.

In Example 3-49, a logging list called **FO_Cable** is set up with a message ID of **101002** to classify the failover cable issues. This logging list is linked to send email messages from **Chicago@securemeinc.com** to **admin@securemeinc.com**, using **192.168.10.50** as the primary email server and **192.168.10.51** as the secondary email server.

Example 3-49 *Configuration of Email Logging*

```
Chicago(config)# logging list FO_Cable message 101002
Chicago(config)# logging mail FO_Cable
Chicago(config)# logging from-address Chicago@securemeinc.com
Chicago(config)# logging recipient-address admin@securemeinc.com level errors
Chicago(config)# smtp-server 192.168.10.50 192.168.10.51
```

Storing Logs Internally and Externally

The ASA enables you to save the buffered log messages as files to the local flash or to an FTP server for future analysis. The security appliance supports two methods to save buffered logs:

- Flash logging
- FTP logging

Flash Logging

Using the flash logging method, you can save the log messages located in the buffer space to the local flash (disk0: or disk1:). The security appliance creates a file in the /syslog directory of flash, using the default name of LOG-*YYYY-MM-DD-HHMMSS*.TXT, where *YYYY* stands for year, the first *MM* for month, *DD* for days, *HH* for hours, the second *MM* for minutes, and *SS* for seconds. Navigate to **Configuration > Device Management > Logging > Logging Setup** and enable the **Save Buffer to Flash** check box. If you click the **Configure Flash Usage**, you can specify the following options:

- **Maximum Flash to Be Used by Logging**—The maximum space the security appliance can use to store the buffered logs in flash.
- **Minimum Free Space to Be Preserved**—The minimum space in kilobytes that the security appliance should maintain to ensure that there is room left in flash for other administrative tasks.

Note The Cisco ASA uses the local clock settings to add the timestamp. Consult the "Setting Up the System Clock" section earlier in this chapter.

Example 3-50 shows that the security appliance is allocating 2 MB of space to save logs in flash and the minimum free space in flash should be 4 MB.

Example 3-50 *Automatic Saving of Logs in Flash*

```
Chicago# configure terminal
Chicago(config)# logging flash-bufferwrap
Chicago(config)# logging flash-maximum-allocation 2000
Chicago(config)# logging flash-minimum-free 4000
```

Tip The Cisco ASA also enables you to manually save the buffered logs to the local flash if you issue the **logging savelog** command. You can check the flash directory by using the **dir /recursive** command. The **/recursive** option shows the complete file structure of the Flash by displaying all files even if they are located in sub-directories.

FTP Logging

The security appliance can transfer the buffer logs to an FTP server to conserve disk space. You enable this by navigating to **Configuration > Device Management > Logging > Logging Setup** and enabling the **Save Buffer to FTP Server** check box. You must click **Configure FTP Settings**, then the **Enable FTP Client** check box and specify the IP address, username, and password.

In Example 3-51, an appliance is set up to send log files to an FTP server, located at **192.168.10.150**. The username to log in to the FTP server is **cisco** with a password of **C1$c0123**. The logs will be stored in the root directory (.) of the FTP server for that user.

Example 3-51 *Automatic Saving of Logs in the FTP Server*

```
Chicago# configure terminal
Chicago(config)# logging ftp-bufferwrap
Chicago(config)# logging ftp-server 192.168.10.150 . cisco C1$c0123
```

Syslog Message ID Tuning

The security appliance sends all log messages to the logging devices, internal and external. However, if you are not interested in logging a particular message, you can suppress it by navigating to **Configuration > Device Management > Logging > Syslog Setup**, selecting the message ID, clicking **Edit** and selecting the **Disable Messages** check box. You can also achieve the same result with the CLI by issuing the **no logging message** command followed by the message ID number, as shown in Example 3-52, where message ID 101001 is disabled.

Example 3-52 *Disabling a Message ID*

```
Chicago# configure terminal
Chicago(config)# no logging message 101001
```

Even though the debug-level syslogs provide extensive information about the traffic and device health, many enterprises do not want to enable syslogs at that level. They choose to enable logging at information or notification level and then move the appropriate debug-level message to a lower level. You can change a message's logging level by navigating to **Configuration > Device Management > Logging > Syslog Setup**, selecting the message ID, clicking **Edit**, and selecting the appropriate level under **Logging Level.**

NetFlow Secure Event Logging (NSEL)

Cisco security appliance supports using the NetFlow architecture to send syslogs, if you are using version 8.2(1) or higher. If you are using ASA 5580s, you can also enable this feature in the 8.1(1) version of the software. Sending logs via syslog is considered inefficient because

- Syslog sends logs in the ASCII text format, which produces logs that are verbose and lengthy.
- Syslog generates a single UDP packet for each log messages, which results in a large number of small packets.
- Generating lots of text-based syslogs adds considerable load on the security appliance.

Using NetFlow as a means to send syslogs can greatly enhance performance. The security appliance generates log information in binary, which can be parsed easily and sends multiple records in a single flow packet.

Note You must have a NetFlow collector in your network that can parse the flow of information the security appliance sends. CS-MARS running version 6.0 can read and parse NetFlow v 9 information. To learn more about NetFlow version 9, consult RFC 3954.

Cisco ASA uses NetFlow version 9, which leverages the template-based approach as a flow export mechanism. The NetFlow template defines the structure of the NetFlow record being exported. The NetFlow implementation exports records when a significant event in the life of a flow, such as creation and teardown, occurs. The security appliance also exports information about flows that are allowed or denied by access control lists (ACLs). ACLs are discussed in Chapter 4.

Note Cisco ASA does not support information for the flows denied by an ethertype ACL.

You cannot display the NetFlow packets on a terminal session, unlike what you can do with a Cisco IOS router, where you can view the NetFlow data via a terminal session. Additionally, the security appliance exports the flow information periodically to a collector. This is also different from the typical NetFlow version 9, such as on a Cisco IOS router, where the flows are exported in a single packet when a number of flows are collected.

When you are exporting logs via NetFlow, you do not want to send the same logs via syslog to avoid duplication of packets. The security appliance allows you to disable all syslogs messages that generate the same information as NetFlow. This way, you do not have to manually disable individual syslogs in the ASA configuration. The security appliance disables 106015, 106023, 106100, 302013, 302014, 302015, 302016, 302017, 302018, 302020, 302021, 313001, 313008, and 710003 syslog messages.

The configuration of NSEL can be broken into two steps:

Step 1: Defining a NetFlow Collector

Using ASDM, you can define a NetFlow collector by navigating to **Configuration > Device Management > Logging > NetFlow > Add** under "Collectors". You can specify the IP address, the UDP port that your collector uses for NetFlow packets, and the interface where the collector resides.

You can optionally configure a delay in sending the flow creation event. This option is useful if you have a large number of created connections so that the appliance can package them up into fewer export packets. If the flow is torn down before the configured delay, only the flow teardown event is dispatched and the flow creation event is not sent. You configure this by selecting the **Delay transmission of flow creation events for short-lived flows** check box.

The security appliance sends the template record to your NetFlow collector, by default, every 30 minutes. You can change the frequency when the template record is sent, in minutes, under the **Template Timeout Rate** option box. The default timeout value of 30 minutes works in most cases.

Figure 3-25 illustrates that a new NetFlow collector is being added. It is located toward the **mgmt** interface at **172.18.82.81** and listens on UDP port **2055**. The **Disable redundant syslog messages** check box is also enabled to avoid duplication of syslog messages.

Example 3-53 shows the equivalent configuration of Figure 3-25.

Example 3-53 *Configuring NetFlow via CLI*

```
Chicago# configure terminal
Chicago(config)# no logging message 106015
Chicago(config)# no logging message 106023
```

```
Chicago(config)# no logging message 106100
Chicago(config)# no logging message 302013
Chicago(config)# no logging message 302014
Chicago(config)# no logging message 302015
Chicago(config)# no logging message 302016
Chicago(config)# no logging message 302017
Chicago(config)# no logging message 302018
Chicago(config)# no logging message 302020
Chicago(config)# no logging message 302021
Chicago(config)# no logging message 313001
Chicago(config)# no logging message 313008
Chicago(config)# no logging message 710003
Chicago(config)# flow-export destination mgmt 172.18.82.81 2055
```

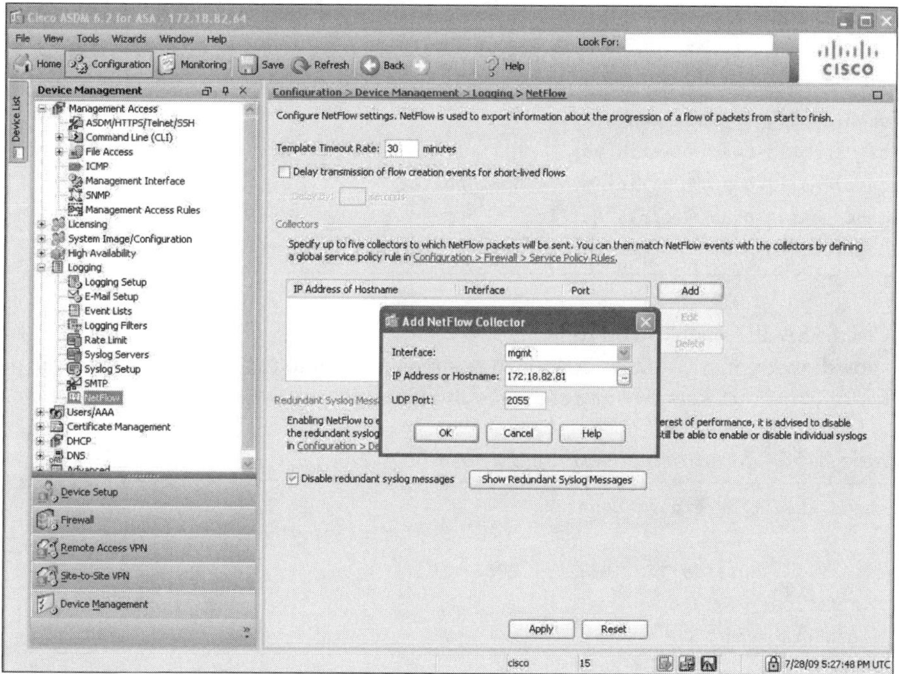

Figure 3-25 *Defining NetFlow Collector*

Step 2: Defining a NetFlow Export Policy

The security appliance does not send NetFlow to an external collector until you classify the traffic type it should be monitoring to generate the NetFlow events. For example, if you want it to monitor all traffic for NetFlow exports, specify a global policy that analyzes all traffic. NetFlow export policy is constructed via the modular policy framework

(MPF), discussed in Chapter 7 and 11. Follow these steps to successfully configure an export policy:

Step 1. Navigate to **Configuration > Firewall > Service Policy Rules**, select **inspection_default** policy, and then click **Add > Insert After.** ASDM launches a Service Policy Rule Wizard where you can select **Global—applies to all interfaces.** Click **Next.**

Step 2. Under **Traffic Match Criteria**, specify a traffic class name of **NetFlow.** Select **Any Traffic** as the Traffic Match Criteria and click **Next.**

Step 3. Under **Rule Action**, click the **NetFlow** tab and click **Add.** A new window opens where you can specify Flow Event Type. Select **All** and enable the **Send** check box next to the collector's IP address. This collector was defined under the preceding "Defining a NetFlow Collector" section. Click **OK** and then **Finish** to complete defining a NetFlow export policy.

If you prefer to use the CLI, you can define an identical policy as shown in Example 3-54.

Example 3-54 *Defining an NetFlow Export Policy*

```
Chicago(config)# class-map NetFlow
Chicago(config-cmap)# match any
Chicago(config-cmap)# policy-map global_policy
Chicago(config-pmap)# class NetFlow
Chicago(config-pmap-c)# flow-export event-type all destination 172.18.82.81
```

Cisco ASA also enables you to monitor the status of the NetFlow exports if you use the **show flow-export counters** command as shown in Example 3-55. It shows you the number of export packets sent and statistics about any potential export issues.

Example 3-55 *Monitoring NetFlow Exports*

```
Chicago# show flow-export counters

 destination: outside 172.18.82.81 2055
   Statistics:
     packets sent                                              100
   Errors:
     block allocation failure                                 0
     invalid interface                                        0
     template send failure                                    0
```

Simple Network Management Protocol (SNMP)

SNMP is an application layer protocol that was developed to monitor the health of network devices. It has become a de facto standard because of its simple protocol design. A successful SNMP implementation requires a management station, also known as the *manager*, and at least one agent, such as the Cisco ASA. The network management station, such as CiscoWorks, monitors the agents by collecting the device and network information and presenting it in a GUI. The agents, on the other hand, respond to the manager's request for information. If an important event occurs, the agents can also initiate a connection to the manager to send the message.

The SNMP implementation uses the following five message types, known as *protocol data units* (PDUs), for the communication between the management station and the agent:

- GET
- GET-NEXT
- GET-RESPONSE
- SET
- TRAP

The network manager uses the Management Information Base (MIB) to initiate the GET and GET-NEXT messages and request specific information. The agent replies with a GET-RESPONSE, which provides the requested information, if available. In a case where the requested information is not available, the agent sends an error detailing why the request cannot be processed.

The network manager uses the SET message type to change or add values in the configuration rather than retrieve the information. The agent replies with a GET-RESPONSE message to indicate whether the change was successful. The TRAP messages are agent-initiated to inform the network manager about an event, such as a link failure, so that an immediate action can be taken. Figure 3-26 illustrates the PDU communication between a security appliance, as an agent, and a CiscoWorks server, as a management server.

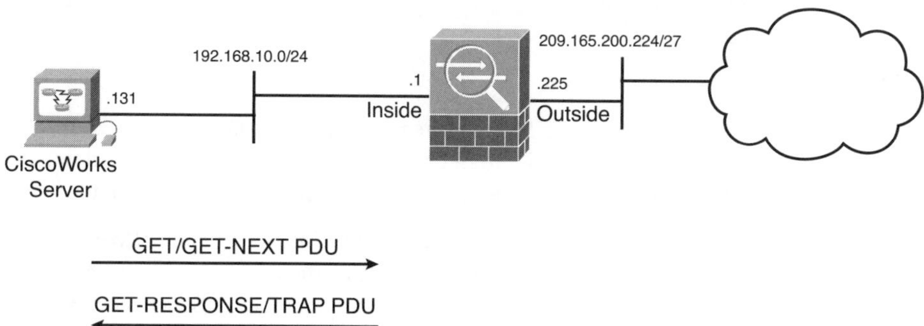

Figure 3-26 *SNMP Communication Between the Cisco ASA and CiscoWorks*

Note The security appliance does not allow SET PDUs, for device-security reasons. Consequently, you cannot use SNMP to modify the configuration of the security appliance.

Configuring SNMP

The security appliance must be configured before a network management server can initiate a connection. Configure SNMP on a security appliance through ASDM by navigating to **Configuration > Device Management > Management Access > SNMP** and following these steps:

Step 1. Configure a global community string.

A community string acts as a password when the management server tries to connect to the security appliance to get information. It is used to validate the communication messages between the devices. In ASDM, specify a global community string under "Community String (Default)". If you prefer to use the CLI, set a global community string by using the **snmp-server community** command.

Step 2. Set device information.

Specify the location of the security appliance so that the SNMP server knows where the device is physically located. The security appliance enables you to set up contact information for an individual who is responsible for it. In ASDM, specify the device information, such as the Contact and ASA Locations options. If you prefer to use the CLI, use the **snmp-server location** and **snmp-server contact** commands.

Step 3. Modify SNMP Polling ports.

The Cisco ASA can be configured to listen on a nondefault port for SNMP polls. To use a port other than UDP 161, specify it under the "Listening Port" option. If using the CLI, use the **snmp-server listen-port** command, followed by a port number.

Step 4. Define an SNMP server.

You must specify an SNMP management server before the ASA can listen for polls or send SNMP traps. To define a new SNMP server, click **Add** under SNMP Management Stations and specify the following information:

- **Interface Name**—The name of the interface where the SNMP server resides. In most cases, it is the inside or the management interface. If you select an interface other than the inside interface, ASDM generates a warning that you should consider about using an inside interface for security reasons. However, using a management interface is as secure if you have a dedicated management network.

- **IP address**—The actual IP address of the SNMP server. The IP address must reside toward the interface selected
- **UDP Port**—The security appliance uses UDP port 162 when it needs to send SNMP traps to the management server. If the SNMP server listens on a different port, you can change the UDP port on the security appliance by specifying a port under the "UDP Port" option.
- **SNMP Version**—The security appliance supports SNMP versions 1, 2c, and 3. Version 2c overcomes the deficiencies and problems associated with version 1. It uses the administrative framework of version 1 but enhances protocol operations by increasing security capabilities. SNMPv3 adds many security and remote configuration enhancements such as *message integrity* (to ensure that a packet has not been tampered with in transit), *authentication* (to verify that the message is from a valid source), and *encryption* (to prevent snooping by an unauthorized source). If you select SNMP version 3, you must define a username. If you select SNMP version 1 or 2c, ASA enables you to specify a host-specific SNMP community string.
- **Server Poll/Trap Specification**—The security appliance allows an SNMP server to poll information from the security appliance. It also sends event traps when unusual incidents occur. You can optionally restrict the security appliance to allow either SNMP polls only or traps only. In most implementations, an SNMP server is designed to poll as well as receive traps from the network devices.

Step 5. Configure SNMP traps.

The security appliance sends limited SNMP traps by default; however, you can configure it to send all supported traps or a superset of all traps. Do so by clicking the Configure Traps icon and selecting the following trap types:

- **Standard event traps**—These traps include interface link up/link down, authentication, and device cold start.
- **IPSec event traps**—These include IPSec tunnel start and stop traps.
- **Remote-access traps**—The security appliance generates a trap when remote-access sessions reach the session threshold limit.
- **Entity traps**—These traps are sent when changes are made to the device, such as configuration modification or insertion/removal of hardware modules into or from the chassis.
- **Syslog traps**—The security appliance sends syslog messages as SNMP traps to the management station.

> **Note** To set up traps for syslog messages, you must determine what severity of syslog messages need to be forwarded to the management server. This was discussed earlier in the "Logging Types" section.

In Figure 3-27 a new SNMP server is being added. The IP address of the server is **172.18.82.90** and it is located toward the **mgmt** interface. The server is configured to use SNMP **version 3**, which requires you to configure a username. The configured user name is **cisco**.

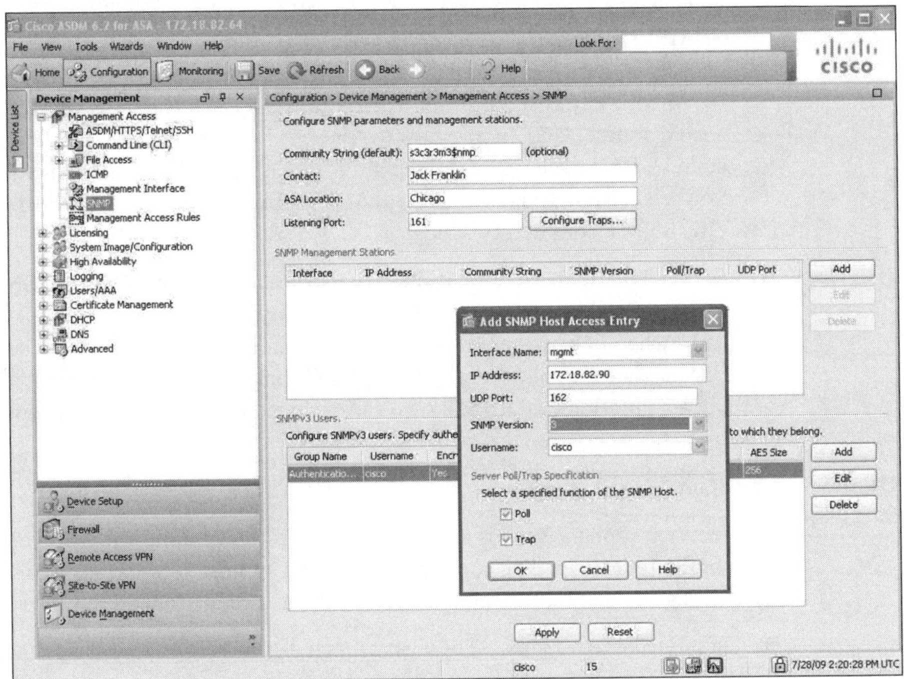

Figure 3-27 *SNMP Server Definition*

Example 3-56 shows equivalent configuration of Figure 3-27.

Example 3-56 *Automatic Saving of Logs in the FTP Server*

```
Chicago# configure terminal
Chicago(config)# snmp-server group Authentication&Encryption v3 priv
Chicago(config)# snmp-server user cisco Authentication&Encryption v3 encrypt auth
MD5 00:55:99 priv AES 256 00:55:99
Chicago(config)# snmp-server community s3c3r3m3$nmp
Chicago(config)# snmp-server location Chicago
Chicago(config)# snmp-server contact Jack Franklin
```

```
Chicago(config)# snmp-server host mgmt 172.18.82.90 version 3 cisco
Chicago(config)# logging history debugging
Chicago(config)# snmp-server enable traps syslog
```

SNMP Monitoring

The **show snmp-server statistics** command is useful for checking the statistics of the SNMP engine. It displays not only the total SNMP packets received and transmitted but also any bad or illegal packets handled by the security appliance. Example 3-57 displays the output of this command, where the security appliance received 12 GET requests and replied to all of them as GET-RESPONSE.

Example 3-57 *Output of* show snmp-server statistics

```
Chicago# show snmp-server statistics
12 SNMP packets input
    0 Bad SNMP version errors
    0 Unknown community name
    0 Illegal operation for community name supplied
    0 Encoding errors
    36 Number of requested variables
    0 Number of altered variables
    12 Get-request PDUs
    0 Get-next PDUs
    0 Get-bulk PDUs
    0 Set-request PDUs (Not supported)
12 SNMP packets output
    0 Too big errors (Maximum packet size 512)
    0 No such name errors
    0 Bad values errors
    0 General errors
    12 Get-response PDUs
    0 SNMP trap PDUs
```

Device Monitoring and Troubleshooting

Cisco ASA is loaded with a number of **show** and **debug** commands to monitor the health of the device and troubleshoot any network- or device-level issues.

CPU and Memory Monitoring

The **show cpu usage** command indicates current CPU utilization. It displays an approximation of load over 5, 60, and 300 seconds. Example 3-58 shows that the 5-second utilization is 2 percent, whereas the 1-minute and 5-minute utilizations are 1 percent.

Example 3-58 *Output of* **show cpu usage**

```
Chicago(config)# show cpu usage
CPU utilization for 5 seconds = 2%; 1 minute: 1%; 5 minutes: 1%
```

The security appliance can display memory usage through the **show memory** command. It shows a summary of the available and allocated memory in bytes and as a percentage. In Example 3-59, the free memory on the security appliance is 849,120,760 bytes (~810 MB), and the allocated or used memory is 224,621,064 bytes (~214 MB). The total memory on the security appliance is 1024 MB.

Example 3-59 *Output of* **show memory**

```
Chicago# show memory
Free memory:        849120760 bytes (79%)
Used memory:        224621064 bytes (21%)
-------.           ---------
Total memory:      1073741824 bytes (100%)
```

> **Note** Using the **show memory detail** command output with **show memory binsize** enables you to check the number of bytes allocated to a given size memory chunk. These commands should be used under a TAC engineer's supervision if advanced memory troubleshooting needs to be done.

The security appliance can display the system buffer utilization if the **show block** command is executed. When the security appliance boots up, the operating system carves out memory to create the maximum number of blocks for different block sizes. The maximum number of blocks does not change, except for the 256- and 1550-size blocks. For these blocks, the security appliance can dynamically create more blocks if necessary. The security appliance allocates a block from the pool when it needs to use it, and returns it when it is done using it.

There are eleven different sizes of buffer blocks, and each buffer type is responsible for handling specific packets. Table 3-8 shows the buffer block sizes and provides a brief description on where they are used.

When you run the **show block** command, the security appliance displays the following counters:

- MAX—Indicates the maximum number of blocks available for a specific block size.
- LOW—Indicates the lowest numbers of blocks available at one point since the last reboot or the last time the counters were cleared by the **clear block** command. A low count of 0 indicates that the security appliance had run out of buffer space for a particular block at some point since the last reboot or the last time the counters were cleared.
- CNT—Displays the currently available blocks for each block size

Table 3-8 *Buffer Sizes*

Buffer Block Size	Description
0	Used by dubp blocks.
4	Used to duplicate existing blocks in applications such as DNS, ISAKMP, URL filtering, uauth, TFTP, H323, and TCP modules.
80	Used by the TCP intercept feature to generate an ACK packet. It is also used by the failover for hello messages.
256	Used by the stateful failover, syslog, and some TCP modules.
1550	Used to buffer Ethernet packets when they are processed by the security appliance.
2048	Used to send control updates.
2560	Used to buffer IKE messages.
4096	Used by the QoS metrics engine.
8192	Used by the QoS metrics engine.
16384	Used only for the 64-bit, 66-MHz Livengood Gigabit Ethernet cards (i82543).
65536	Used by the QoS metrics engine.

In Example 3-60, the security appliance has allocated 300 blocks for the 4-byte block size, and it is currently using one block. The LOW counter is set to 299 because the security appliance had allocated only one block of it since the last reboot.

Example 3-60 *Output of* **show block**

```
Chicago# show block
  SIZE    MAX    LOW    CNT
     0    700    700    700
     4    300    299    299
    80   1089   1078   1089
   256   3100   3093   3100
  1550  10396  10078  10137
  2048   3100   3081   3100
  2560   2052   2052   2052
  4096    100    100    100
  8192    100    100    100
 16384    152    152    152
 65536     16     16     16
```

Using ASDM, you can monitor the health of a security appliance by navigating to **Monitoring > Properties > System Resources Graphs** and selecting a graph for Block use, CPU utilization and memory use and availability.

Troubleshooting Device Issues

Cisco ASA provides a number of troubleshooting and diagnostic commands for troubleshooting traffic as well as device-related issues.

Troubleshooting Packet Issues

In any firewall deployment, administrators spend most of their time defining new policies and troubleshooting packet flow issues. The following sections discuss three scenarios to show how the security appliance assists in troubleshooting those issues.

Tracing Packet Flow

To learn which processes are being applied to a packet flow, use the packet tracer feature. Using this feature, describe how a packet should be structured based on the IP protocol, source and destination IP addresses, and source and destination ports. The security appliance provides information when that packet goes through different processes such as the access-control lists (ACLs), routing, and address translation (NAT). Each process inspects the packet individually and decides whether it needs to allow or deny that packet.

Use this feature by choosing **Tools > Packet Tracer** and specifying the interface from which the packet should be coming, the IP protocol, and the source and destination IP addresses and ports. As illustrated in Figure 3-28, the administrator is tracing a TCP packet sourced toward the **inside** interface from **192.168.10.50** and destined to **209.165.200.229** on source port **1024** and destination port **80**. Each process checks the packet and allows it, the end result is successful, and that packet is allowed to pass through the security appliance.

Example 3-61 shows the CLI equivalent of Figure 3-28.

Example 3-61 *Tracing Packet Through the CLI*

```
Chicago# packet-tracer input inside tcp 192.168.10.50 1024 209.165.200.229 80
```

Capturing Packets

One of the most robust features in the security appliance for troubleshooting traffic-related problems is the packet capture feature. When packet capture is turned on, the security appliance sniffs interesting traffic and stores it in the buffer. This is important if you want to confirm that traffic from a particular host or network is reaching the interfaces. You can use an ACL to identify the type of traffic and bind it to an interface by using the **capture** command. The captured packets can be viewed either locally on the security appliance or on an external device such as Wireshark if you export the information in the pcap format.

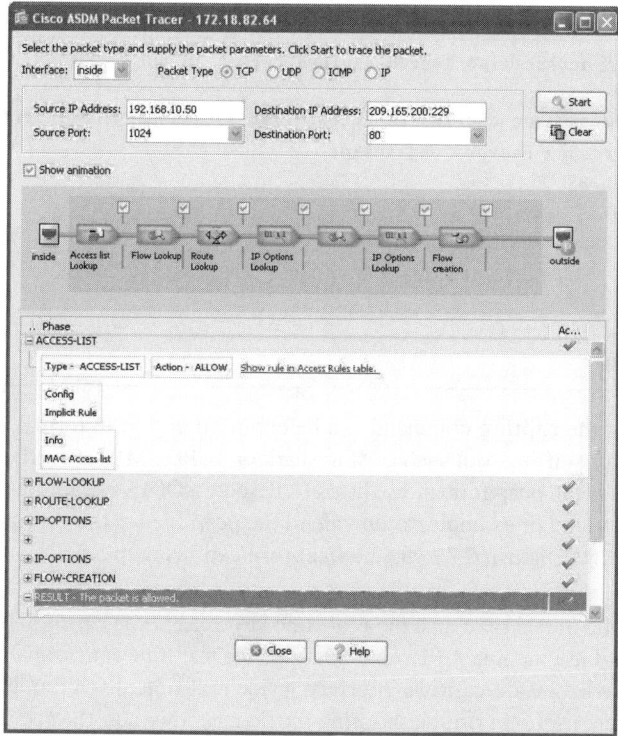

Figure 3-28 *Tracing Packets Through the Security Appliance*

In Example 3-61, an ACL, called **inside-capture**, is set up to identify packets sourced from **209.165.202.130** and destined for **209.165.200.230**. The security appliance is using this ACL to capture the identified traffic on the **inside** interface, using a capture list named **cap-inside**.

To view the captured packets, use the **show capture** command, followed by the name of the capture list. In Example 3-62, the security appliance captured 15 packets that matched the ACL on the inside interface. The highlighted entry shows that it is a TCP SYN (shown as "S" after the destination port) packet sourced from 209.165.202.130 with a source port of 11084 and it is destined for 209.165.200.230 on destination port 23. The TCP window size is 4128, and the Maximum Segment Size (MSS) is set to 536 bytes.

Note When the capture command is enabled, the security appliance allocates memory right away. The default memory allocation is 512 KB. The security appliance can overwrite content when the allocated memory is full by removing the oldest entry first. The capture command has minimal CPU impact and therefore it is one of the most important troubleshooting tools available in Cisco ASA.

Example 3-62 *Packet Capturing*

```
Chicago(config)# access-list inside-capture permit ip host 209.165.202.130 host
209.165.200.230
Chicago(config)# capture cap-inside access-list inside-capture interface inside
Chicago(config)# show capture cap-inside
15 packets captured
1: 02:12:47.142189 209.165.202.130.11084 > 209.165.200.230.23: S
433720059:433720059(0) win 4128 <mss 536>
   2: 02:12:47.163489 209.165.202.130.11084 > 209.165.200.230.23: . ack
1033049551 win 4128
!Output omitted for brevity
15 packets shown
```

The output of the **capture** command can be exported into pcap format, which can be imported into a sniffing tool such as Wireshark or TCPDUMP for further analysis. To download the file in pcap format, use https://<IPAddressOfASA>/capture/<CaptureName>/pcap in a browser. For example, to download the pcap file for the capture defined in Example 3-62, use **https://172.18.82.64/capture/cap-inside/pcap.**

Tip To see traffic in real time, use the **real-time** keyword in the capture. For example, the capture command in Example 3-61 can be defined for real-time traffic analysis as **capture out-inside access-list inside-capture interface inside real-time.** Even though real-time capturing is extremely useful in troubleshooting traffic-related issues, the security appliance displays up to only 1000 packets in case of excessive traffic load.

Monitoring Dropped Packets

The security appliance, being a firewall, drops packets if they do not adhere to an enterprise's security policy. These drops could be related to the **deny** statements in the ACLs, illegitimate VPN packets, a malformed TCP segment, or a packet with invalid header information. In some cases, you will want to get the statistical information about the packets or connections dropped by the security appliance within its accelerated security path (ASP). Use the **show asp drop** command as shown in Example 3-63, which shows that over 57,000 packets were dropped because of the **deny** statement in the ACLs.

Example 3-63 *Output of show asp drop*

```
Chicago# show asp drop

Frame drop:
  Flow is denied by configured rule (acl-drop)                          57455
  First TCP packet not SYN (tcp-not-syn)                                  295
  Interface is down (interface-down)                                        3

Last clearing: Never
```

Note For a complete list of **asp drop** reasons, refer to the command reference guide for the security appliance.

You can see that the security appliance has dropped over 57,000 packets because they were denied by the ACLs. About 300 packets were dropped because the adaptive security appliance received a non-SYN packet as the first packet of a connection. This usually occurs when the client and server believe that a connection was opened but the firewall has already closed that session. Finally, the security appliance dropped three packets when the interface was shut down.

Note The security appliance enables you to capture on a specific drop type or all **asp drop** types through the **capture** command, as follows:

```
Chicago# capture AspCapture type asp-drop ?
  acl-drop                                        Flow is denied by configured rule
  all                                             All packet drop reasons
  bad-crypto                                      Bad crypto return in packet
<output removed for brevity>
```

Troubleshooting CPU Issues

If you are monitoring your CPU utilization and it is constantly running high, you can activate the CPU profiling feature on the security appliance by using the **cpu profile activate** command. You can also allocate memory for storing a specific number of samples, which can vary from 1 to 100,000, with the default being 1000. The more memory you allocate to this process, the better the accuracy for CPU profiling. After CPU profiling is activated, use the **show cpu profile** output to view the output. Unfortunately, you have to send the output of this **show** command to a TAC engineer for analysis.

Summary

This chapter introduced the different CLI modes and discussed the initial configuration of the Cisco ASA. It presented a brief overview of the networking technologies, such as IPv6, DHCP, NTP, and SNMP, and provided examples of how to set them up. Telnet and SSH were discussed as the remote-management protocols. This chapter also assisted in system maintenance features such as image upgrade and password recovery methods. The last section discussed the security appliance monitoring capabilities, such as system logging, SNMP, and a set of **show** commands to check the device's status and health.

Chapter 4

Controlling Network Access

This chapter covers the following topics:

- Packet filtering
- Configuring traffic filtering
- Advanced ACL features
- Content and URL filtering
- Deployment scenarios using access control lists
- Monitoring network access control
- Address translation
- DNS doctoring
- Monitoring address translations

Cisco Adaptive Security Appliances (ASA) can act as a network firewall and can help protect one or more networks from intruders and attackers. You can control and monitor connections between these networks by using the robust features that Cisco ASA offers. You can ensure that all traffic from the protected networks to the unprotected networks (and vice versa) passes through the firewall based on the organization's security policies. This chapter focuses on the features available for packet filtering, their implications, and their implementations.

Packet Filtering

The Cisco ASA can protect the inside network, the demilitarized zones (DMZs), and the outside network by inspecting all traffic that passes through it. You can specify policies and rules that identify what traffic should be permitted into or out of an interface. The security appliance uses an access control list to drop unwanted or unknown traffic when it attempts to enter the firewall. The *access control list* (ACL) is a collection of security rules or policies that allows or denies packets after looking at the packet headers and other attributes. Each permit or deny statement in the ACL is referred to as an *access control entry* (ACE). These ACEs can classify packets by inspecting Layer 2 through Layer 4 headers for a number of parameters, including the following:

- Layer 2 protocol information such as EtherTypes
- Layer 3 protocol information such as ICMP, TCP, or UDP
- Layer 3 header information such as source and destination IP addresses
- Layer 4 header information such as source and destination TCP or UDP ports

After an ACL has been properly configured, you can apply it to an interface to filter traffic. The security appliance can filter packets in both the inbound and outbound direction on an interface. When an inbound ACL is applied to an interface, the security appliance analyzes packets against the ACEs after receiving them. If a packet is permitted by the ACL, the firewall continues to process the packet and eventually passes the packet out the egress interface.

Note The big difference between a router ACL and an appliance ACL is that only the first packet of a flow is subjected by an ACL in the security appliance. After that the connection is built, and subsequent packets matching that connection are not checked by the ACL.

If a packet is denied by the ACL, the security appliance discards the packet and generates a syslog message indicating that such an event has occurred. In Figure 4-1, the security appliance administrator has applied to the outside interface an inbound ACL that permits only HTTP traffic destined for 209.165.202.131. All other traffic is dropped at the outside interface by the security appliance.

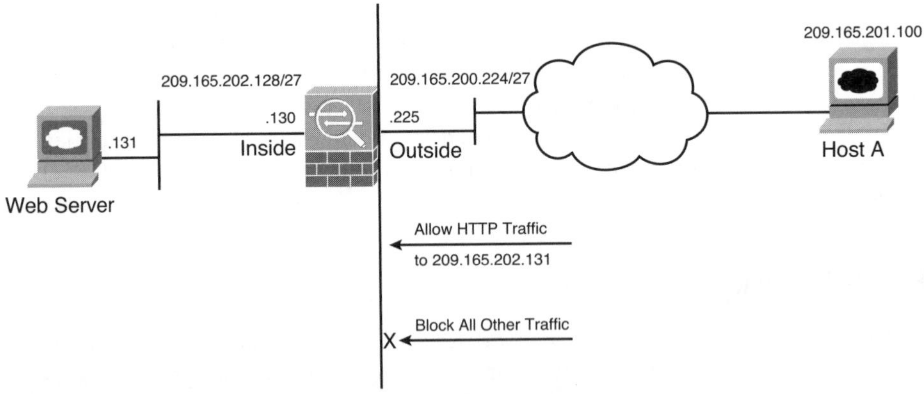

Figure 4-1 *Inbound Packet Filtering*

If an outbound ACL is applied on an interface, the security appliance processes the packets by sending them through the different processes (NAT, QoS, and VPN) and then applies the configured ACEs before transmitting the packets out on the wire. The security appliance transmits the packets only if they are allowed to go out by the outbound ACL on that interface. If the packets are denied by any one of the ACEs, the security appliance discards the packets and generates a syslog message indicating that such an event has occurred. In Figure 4-2, the security appliance administrator has applied to the inside interface an outbound ACL that permits only HTTP traffic destined for 209.165.202.131. All other traffic gets dropped at the interface by the security appliance.

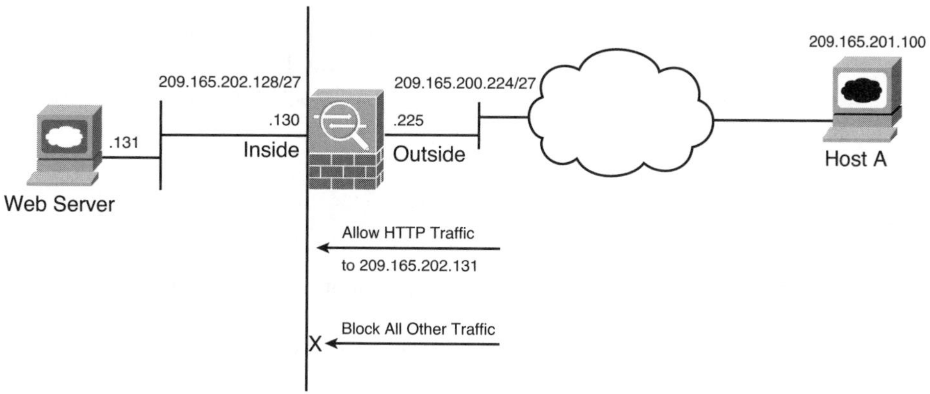

Figure 4-2 *Outbound Packet Filtering*

Following are the some of the important characteristics of an ACL:

- When a new ACE is added to an existing ACL, it is appended to the end of the ACL.
- When a packet enters the security appliance, the ACEs are evaluated in sequential order. Hence, the order of an ACE is critical. For example, if you have an ACE that allows all IP traffic to pass through, and then you create another ACE to block all IP traffic, then the packets will never be evaluated against the second ACE because all packets will match the first ACE entry.
- There is an implicit deny at the end of all ACLs. If a packet is not matched against a configured ACE, then it is dropped and a syslog with message ID of 106023 is generated.
- By default, you do not need to define an ACE to permit traffic from a high security–level interface to a low security–level interface. However, if you want to restrict traffic flows from a high security–level interface to a low security–level interface, you can define an ACL. If you configure an ACL to a high security–level interface to a low security–level interface, it disables the implicit permit from that interface. All traffic is now subject to the entries defined in that ACL.

- An ACL must explicitly permit traffic traversing the security appliance from a lower to a higher security–level interface of the firewall. The ACL must be applied to the lower security–level interface.
- The ACLs (Extended or IPv6) must be applied to an interface to filter traffic that is passing through the security appliance.
- You can bind one extended and one Ethertype ACL in each direction of an interface at the same time.
- You can apply the same ACL to multiple interfaces. However, it is not considered to be a good security practice.
- You can use ACLs to control traffic through the security appliance as well as to control traffic to the security appliance. The ACLs controlling traffic to the appliance are applied differently than ACLs filtering traffic through the appliance, discussed in the "To-The-Box-Traffic Filtering" section.
- When TCP or UDP traffic flows through the security appliance, the return traffic is automatically allowed to pass through because they are considered established and bi-directional connections.
- Other protocols such as ICMP are considered unidirectional connections and thus you need to allow ACL entries in both directions. There is an exception for the ICMP traffic when you enable the ICMP inspection engine, discussed in Chapter 7 "Application Inspection."

Types of ACLs

The security appliance supports five different types of ACLs to provide a flexible and scalable solution to filter unauthorized packets into the network:

- Standard ACLs
- Extended ACLs
- IPv6 ACLs
- EtherType ACLs
- Webtype ACLs

Standard ACLs

Standard ACLs are used to identify packets based on their destination IP addresses. These ACLs can be used in scenarios such as split tunneling for the remote-access VPN tunnels (discussed in Chapter 17, "IPSec Remote Access VPNs") and route redistribution within route maps (discussed in Chapter 5, "IP Routing"). These ACLs, however, cannot be applied to an interface for filtering traffic. A standard ACL can be used only if the security appliance is running in routed mode. In routed mode, the Cisco ASA routes packets from one subnet to another subnet by acting as an extra Layer 3 hop in the network.

Extended ACLs

Extended ACLs, the most commonly deployed ACLs, can classify packets based on the following attributes:

- Source and destination IP addresses
- Layer 3 protocols
- Source and/or destination TCP and UDP ports
- Destination ICMP type for ICMP packets

An extended ACL can be used for interface packet filtering, QoS packet classification, packet identification for NAT and VPN encryption, and a number of other features listed shortly in the "Comparing ACL Features" section. These ACLs can be set up on the security appliance in the routed and the transparent mode.

Note Transparent Firewall mode is discussed in Chapter 9.

IPv6 ACLs

An IPv6 ACL functions similarly to an extended ACL. However, it identifies only IPv6 traffic passing through a security appliance.

EtherType ACLs

EtherType ACLs can be used to filter IP- and non-IP-based traffic by checking the Ethernet type code field in the Layer 2 header. IP-based traffic uses an Ethernet type code value of 0x800, whereas Novell IPX uses 0x8137 or 0x8138, depending on the Netware version.

An EtherType ACL can be configured only if the security appliance is running in transparent mode, as covered in Chapter 9, "Transparent Firewalls."

Like all ACLs, the EtherType ACL has an implicit deny at the end of it. However, this implicit deny does not affect the IP traffic passing through the security appliance. As a result, you can apply both EtherType and extended ACLs to each direction of an interface. If you configure an explicit deny at the end of an EtherType ACL, it blocks IP traffic even if an extended ACL is defined to pass those packets.

Webtype ACLs

A Webtype ACL allows security appliance administrators to restrict traffic coming through the SSL VPN tunnels (discussed in Chapter 19). In cases where a Webtype ACL is defined but there is no match for a packet, the default behavior is to drop the packet because of implicit deny. On the other hand, if no ACL is defined, the security appliance allows traffic to pass through it.

Comparing ACL Features

Table 4-1 compares the various types of ACLs, and specifies whether they can be used in conjunction with supported features on the security appliance.

Table 4-1 *ASA Features and Types of ACLs*

Feature	Standard	Extended	IPv6	EtherType	WebVPN
Layer 2 packet filtering	No	No	No	Yes	No
Layer 3 packet filtering	No	Yes	Yes	No	Yes
Packet capture	No	Yes	Yes	Yes	No
AAA	No	Yes	Yes	No	No
Time range	No	Yes	Yes	No	Yes
Object grouping	No	Yes	Yes	No	No
NAT exemption	No	Yes	No	No	No
PIM	Yes	No	No	No	No
Application layer inspection	No	Yes	No	No	No
IPS inspection	No	Yes	No	No	No
VPN encryption	No	Yes	No	No	Yes[1]
Remarks	Yes	Yes	Yes	Yes	Yes
Line numbers	No	Yes	Yes	No	No
ACL logging	No	Yes	Yes	No	Yes
QoS	Yes	Yes	No	No	No
Policy NAT	No	Yes	No	No	No
OSPF route-map	Yes	Yes	No	No	No

[1]Only WebVPN encrypted traffic.

Configuring Traffic Filtering

Access-control lists on a security appliance can be used to not only filter out packets passing through the appliance but also to filter out packets destined to the appliance. This section discusses ways to set up the appliance for packet filtering.

- Thru-traffic filtering via CLI
- Thru-traffic filtering via ASDM
- To-the-box-traffic filtering
- IPv6 traffic filtering (optional)

Note Throughout this chapter, we show you configuration examples through ASDM as well as the command-line interface (CLI).

Thru-Traffic Filtering via CLI

Thru-traffic filtering refers to traffic that is passing through the security appliances from one interface to another interface. The configuration to filter packets through the CLI in a security appliance is completed in two steps: Set up an ACL and apply that ACL to an interface.

Step 1: Set Up an ACL

As mentioned earlier, an access-control list is a collection of access-control entries. When new connections try to pass through the security appliance, they are subjected to the ACL configured on the interfaces. The packets are either allowed or dropped based on the configured action on each ACE. An ACE can be as simple as permitting all IP traffic from one network to another, to as complicated as permitting or denying traffic originating from a unique source IP address on a particular port destined for a specific port on the destination address in a specific time period. You define an ACE by using the **access-list** command. You can define an extended ACL, an IPv6 ACL, or an EtherType ACL for filtering through the box traffic. The command syntax to define an extended ACE is as follows:

```
access-list id [line line-num][extended] {deny | permit}{protocol | object-group
protocol_obj_grp_id {source_addr source_mask} | interface src_interface_name |
object-group network_obj_grp_id | host src_host_addr [operator port [port] |
object-group service_obj_grp_id]   {destination_addr destination_mask} | interface
dst_interface_name | object-group network_obj_grp_id | host dst_host_addr [operator
port [port] | object-group service_obj_grp_id]} [log [[disable | default] | level]
[interval secs] [time_range name]] [inactive]
access-list id [line line-num] remark text
access-list alert-interval secs
access-list deny-flow-max flow_num
```

Table 4-2 lists and defines the arguments used in an ACE.

Table 4-2 *ACE Syntax and Description*

Syntax	Description
access-list	Keyword used to create an ACL.
id	Name or number of an ACL.
extended	Optional argument, used to specify an extended IP ACL.
line *line-num*	Optional argument, used to specify the line number at which to insert an ACE.
deny	Discards the packet if it matches the configured conditions.
permit	Allows the packet if it matches the configured conditions.
protocol	Name or number of an IP protocol such as TCP, UDP, 112. To allow or deny all IP traffic, use "ip" as protocol.
object-group[1]	Grouping of different objects in a list.
protocol_obj_grp_id[1]	An object name containing the list of protocols to be filtered.
source_addr	Network or host address from which the packet is being sent.
source_mask	Network mask applied to *source_addr*. ASA does not accept a source mask if you use the *host* keyword.
network_obj_grp_id[1]	An object name containing the list of networks to be filtered.
interface	A keyword used to specify an interface address when traffic is sourced or destined to an appliance's interface.
src_interface_name	Specifies the interface address as the source address.
host	A keyword used to specify a single IP address for traffic filtering.
src_host_addr	Specifies the source IP address to be filtered.
operator	An optional keyword used to compare the source or destination ports. Possible operands include **lt** for less than, **gt** for greater than, **eq** for equal, **neq** for not equal, and **range** for an inclusive range.
port	Name or number of TCP or UDP port to be filtered.
service_obj_grp_id[1]	An object name containing the list of services to be filtered.
destination_addr	Network or host address to which the packet is sent.
destination_mask	Network mask applied to *destination_addr*. ASA does not accept a source mask if you use the *host* keyword.
dst_interface_name	Specifies the interface address as the destination address.

Table 4-2 *ACE Syntax and Description*

Syntax	Description
dst_host_addr	Specifies the destination IP address to be filtered.
log	Generates a syslog message 106100 if a packet matches the ACE. If you do not have the **log** keyword in an ACE, ASA generates a syslog message 106023 for the packets that are denied by ASA.
level	Specifies the logging level, 0 through 7, where: 0 = emergencies 1 = alerts 2 = critical 3 = errors 4 = warnings 5 = notifications 6 = informational (default) 7 = debugging
disable	Does not send syslog message if packets hit the configured ACE.
default	Uses the default behavior, which generates a syslog 106023 message whenever packet matches a deny in the ACE.
interval	A keyword to specify the time interval to generate the subsequent new syslog messages.
secs	The actual time interval in seconds. The default time interval is 300 seconds.
Time-range[1]	A keyword to specify the time-range name.
name	A predefined time-range name.
inactive	Keyword to disable an ACE.
remark	Keyword to specify remarks on an ACL. This is useful for auditing and reference purposes.
text	Actual text, up to 100 characters, to be added as remarks.
alert-interval	Keyword to specify the number of seconds to generate a 106101 syslog message when the maximum number of deny flows is reached.
deny-flow-max	Keyword to limit the maximum number of concurrent deny flows allowed. The ASA tracks the denied flows in its cache. With this option, if a denial-of-service attack is directed through the firewall, causing a large number of flows to be denied and tracked, you can protect the ASA resources by limiting the denied flows.

Table 4-2 *ACE Syntax and Description*

Syntax	Description
flow_num	Actual number of deny flows that can be created. This can be between 1 and 4096 (the default).

[1]These options are discussed in the "Object Grouping" section, later in this chapter.

> **Note** The security appliance ignores the log option if an ACL is used with a feature other than interface traffic filtering.

The access-control list arguments may appear complicated at first but are fairly simple when you start implementing them in a lab or production environment. They not only give you full control over how you want to inspect traffic, but also provide you full logging capabilities in case you want to analyze traffic flow later. In Figure 4-3, SecureMe (the fictional company used in examples throughout this book) hosts a web server and an email server at its location in Chicago. One web server (209.165.202.131) allows traffic on port 80 (HTTP), whereas the email server (209.165.202.132) allows traffic on port 25 (SMTP). The security appliance allows only two client hosts—209.165.201.1 and 209.165.201.2—to initiate the traffic. All other traffic passing through the security appliance will be dropped and logged.

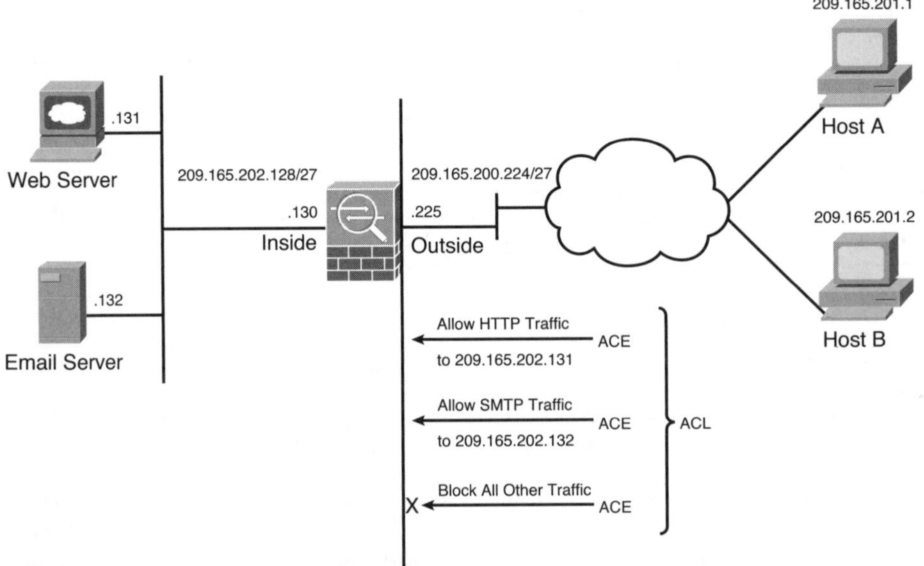

Figure 4-3 *SecureMe Traffic Filtering*

Example 4-1 shows the related configuration. An extended ACL called **outside_access_in** is set up with four ACEs. The first two ACEs allow HTTP traffic destined for

209.165.202.131 from the two client machines, whereas the last two ACEs allow SMTP access to 209.165.202.132 from both machines. Adding remarks to an ACL is recommended because it helps others to recognize its function. The system administrator has added **This is the interface ACL to block inbound traffic except HTTP and SMTP** as the remark on this ACL.

Example 4-1 *Configuration of an Extended ACL*

```
Chicago# configure terminal
Chicago(config)# access-list outside_access_in remark This is the interface ACL to
block inbound traffic except HTTP and SMTP
Chicago(config)# access-list outside_access_in extended permit tcp host
209.165.201.1 host 209.165.202.131 eq http
Chicago(config)# access-list outside_access_in extended permit tcp host
209.165.201.2 host 209.165.202.131 eq http
Chicago(config)# access-list outside_access_in extended permit tcp host
209.165.201.1 host 209.165.202.132 eq smtp
Chicago(config)# access-list outside_access_in extended permit tcp host
209.165.201.2 host 209.165.202.132 eq smtp
Chicago(config)# access-list outside_access_in extended deny ip any any log
```

Chapter 3, "Initial Setup and System Maintenance," discussed the concept of assigning security levels to an interface. As mentioned earlier in this chapter, the security appliance does not block the return TCP or UDP traffic on the lower-security interface if the traffic is originated from a host on the higher-security interface and vice-versa. For other connectionless protocols, such as GRE or ESP, you must permit the return traffic in the ACL applied on that interface. For the ICMP, you can either allow the return traffic in the ACL or enable ICMP inspection (discussed in Chapter 7, "Application Inspection").

The security appliance software enables you to stop processing an ACE temporarily without removing the entry from the configuration. This is helpful if you are troubleshooting a connection issue through the security appliance and want to disable the entry. You do so by adding the **inactive** keyword at the end of the ACE.

> **Note** In version 8.0 or higher, you can rename an ACL by using the **access-list** *<ACL-Name>* **rename** command.

Step 2: Apply an ACL to an Interface

After configuring an ACL to identify traffic allowed or denied by the security appliance, the next step is to apply the ACL to an interface in either the inbound or the outbound direction. Apply the ACL by using the **access-group** command, followed by the name of the ACL, as shown in the following syntax:

```
access-group access-list {in | out} interface interface_name [per-user-override |
control-plane]
```

Table 4-3 lists and defines the arguments used in the **access-group** command.

Table 4-3 **access-group** *Command Definition*

Syntax	Description
access-group	Keyword used to apply an ACL to an interface.
access-list	The name of the actual ACL to be applied to an interface.
in	The ACL will filter inbound packets.
out	The ACL will filter outbound packets.
interface	Keyword to specify the interface to which to apply the ACL.
interface_name	The name of the interface to which to apply an ACL.
per-user-override	Option that allows downloadable ACLs to override the entries on the interface ACL. Downloadable ACLs are discussed later in this chapter.
control-plane	Keyword to specify whether the applied ACL analyzes traffic destined to ASA for management purposes.

In Example 4-2, an ACL called **outside_access_in** is applied to the **outside** interface in the **inbound** direction.

Example 4-2 *Applying an ACL on the Outside Interface*

```
Chicago# configure terminal
Chicago(config)# access-group outside_access_in in interface outside
```

Note You can apply only one extended ACL in each direction of an interface. That means you can apply an inbound and an outbound extended ACL simultaneously on an interface.

Additionally, you can apply an extended and an IPv6 ACL in the same direction if the security appliance is set up to be in routed mode. In transparent mode, you can apply an extended and an etherType ACL in the same direction.

Thru-Traffic Filtering via ASDM

Now that you understand how ACLs are deployed in a security appliance via the CLI, setting it up via ASDM is even simpler. Simply log into ASDM as discussed in Chapter 3 and define an ACL and its associated ACEs by navigating to **Configuration > Firewall > Access Rules,** selecting the pull-down **Add** list and clicking **Add Access Rule**. ASDM opens up a new window where you can specify the following attributes:

- **Interface—**Select the name of the interface where you want to apply the access-control list. In a security appliance, traffic must be allowed from a low security–level interface to a high security–level interface and you can optionally filter traffic from high security–level interface to low security–level interface.

- **Action**—Select the action, either permit or deny, for the traffic matching this ACE. If you select permit, traffic is allowed to enter or exit an interface. If you choose deny, traffic is dropped by the security appliance.
- **Source**—Specify the source host IP, network, or object-group. The source information is any entity that originates traffic. For example, if a web client sends traffic to a web server, specify the IP address of the client as the source address.
- **Destination**—Specify the destination host IP, network, or object-group. The destination information is any entity that receives traffic. For example, if a web client sends traffic to a web server, specify the IP address of the server as the destination address.
- **Service**—Specify the destination service name such as TCP, UDP, SMTP, HTTP. For example, if a web client sends traffic to a web server, specify HTTP as the service. If you want all IP traffic to pass from specific source and destination addresses, specify IP as the service name. It can also be a protocol number such as 47 (for GRE) or 112 (for VRRP).
- **Description**—Specify a description, applied as a remark statement, for this access control entry. This optional argument is useful for auditing and reference purposes. You can specify up to 100 characters as the description of an access rule.
- **Enable Logging**—Specify whether you want the security appliance to generate a syslog message (106100) if a packet matches the ACE. If you do not have this option enabled, ASA generates a syslog message (106023) for packets that are denied by the firewall. If this option is enabled, you can specify a logging level, 0 through 7, where logging level 6 (informational) is the default. By default, permitted packets are not logged and if the logging argument is added, the security appliance generates a syslog only at the configured logging interval time and rate.

The following options are located under the More Options pull-down:

- **Enable Rule**—Select this option if you want the access rule to be operational. This is the default behavior and if you do not check this box, the access rule is inactive and does not process any traffic.
- **Traffic Direction**—Specify whether you want the firewall to apply the ACE in the inbound or outbound direction on the selected interface. When you define a new access rule, the default behavior is to inspect traffic in the inbound direction. If you would rather analyze traffic when it leaves a firewall interface, select **Out** as traffic direction.
- **Source Service**—Specify the source service name such as TCP, UDP, SMTP, or HTTP. If this option is not specified, then by default all source ports are allowed.

- **Logging Interval**—Specify the time interval, in seconds, after which the subsequent syslog messages are generated. The default time interval is 300 seconds. This option is grayed out until you select a logging level other than the default.
- **Time Range**—Specify a time-range name for this ACE. Time-based ACLs are discussed later in this chapter.

Tip If you enter an address without the subnet mask, ASDM considers that to be a host address even if the address ends with a 0.

Note ASDM defined an ACL name using *InterfaceName_access_Direction* as the standard format. For example, if you define an ACL to be applied to the outside interface in the inbound direction, then the ACL name is *outside_access_in*.

As shown earlier in Figure 4-3, SecureMe hosts a web server and an email server located at 209.165.202.131 and 209.165.202.132 respectively. However, only two client hosts—209.165.201.1 and 209.165.201.2—are allowed to initiate traffic. All other traffic initiated from the outside interface is dropped and logged. Figure 4-4 shows the related configuration where three ACE entries have already been configured. The administrator is adding the fourth ACE entry to allow the traffic from 209.165.201.2 to 209.165.202.131 on service TCP/SMTP. This rule is active and logging is enabled to generate syslog messages whenever there is a hit on the ACE. Traffic will be inspected in the inbound direction on the outside interface.

Tip For the well-known ports such as HTTP, SMTP, DNS, FTP, you do not need to specify TCP or UDP protocols in the service box. For example, if you want to specify SMTP as the service, you do not need to type **tcp/smtp**. You can simply type **smtp** in the service box.

To-The-Box-Traffic Filtering

To-the-box-traffic filtering, also known as management access rule, applies to traffic that terminates on the security appliances. This feature was introduced in version 8.0 of the code to filter traffic destined to the control plane of the security appliance. Some management-specific protocols such as SSH and Telnet have their own control list, where you can specify what hosts and networks are allowed to connect to the security appliance. However, they do not provide full protection from other types of traffic such as IPsec. Before you implement management access rules, consult these guidelines:

- Traffic filtering requires you to configure an ACL and then apply the ACL to the appropriate interface, using the **control-plane** keyword at the end.

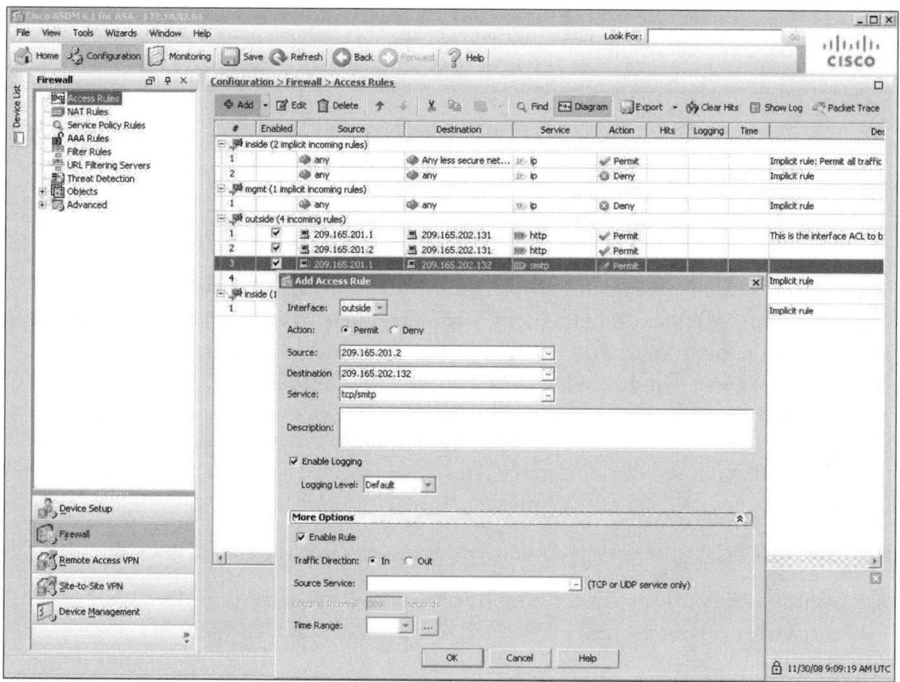

Figure 4-4 *Defining an ACE on ASDM*

- The ACL cannot be applied to an interface designated as a **management-only** interface.
- Management-specific protocols provide their own control-plane protection and have higher precedence than a to-the-box traffic filtering ACL. For example, if you allow a host to establish an SSH session (by defining its IP address in the **ssh** command) and then block its IP address in the management access rule, the host can establish an SSH session to the security appliance.

If you want to use the CLI to define a policy, use the **control-plane** keyword at the end of the **access-group** command. This declares that it is a management access rule to block traffic destined to the security appliance. In Example 4-3, a control-plane ACL called **outside_access_in_1** is configured to block all IP traffic destined to the security appliance. This ACL is then applied to the outside interface in the inbound direction using the **control-plane** keywordcommand

Example 4-3 *Defining a Management Access Rule Through CLI*

```
Chicago# configure terminal
Chicago(config)# access-list outside_access_in_1 remark Block all Management
Traffic on Outside Interface
```

```
Chicago(config)# access-list outside_access_in_1 extended deny ip any any
Chicago(config)# access-group outside_access_in_1 in interface outside control-plane
```

Note The management access rule can be applied only for incoming traffic. Therefore, the ACL can be applied only by using the **in** keyword of the **access-group** command.

Want to set up an identical to-the-box traffic ACL through ASDM? Navigate to **Configuration > Device Management > Management Access > Management Access Rules**, click the pull-down **Add** list, and then select **Add Management Access Rule.** ASDM opens a new window where you can specify the following attributes:

- **Interface**—Select the interface where you want to allow or block the to-the-box traffic. You cannot select an interface already designated as the management-only interface.
- **Action**—Select the action, either permit or deny, for the traffic matching this rule.
- **Source**—Specify the source host IP, network, or object-group. The source is any entity that originates traffic destined to the interface of the security appliance.
- **Service**—Specify the destination service name, such as TCP, UDP, SMTP, or HTTP, that you want to allow or deny.
- **Description**—Specify a description of up to 100 characters that are useful for auditing and reference purposes.
- **Enable Logging**—Enable this option if you want the security appliance to generate a syslog message (106100) if a packet matches the control-plane ACE. You can include the appropriate logging level, discussed earlier in the chapter.
- **Enable Rule**—Select this option to make this ACE operational.
- **Source Service**—You can be more specific in defining the ACE by specifying the source service name (either TCP or UDP).
- **Logging Interval**—Specify the time interval to generate the subsequent new syslog messages in seconds.
- **Time Range**—Specify a time-range name for this ACE. Time-based ACLs are discussed later in this chapter.

As shown in Figure 4-5, a management access rule is defined to block all IP traffic that originates from the outside interface and is destined to the security appliance. A description of **Block All Management Traffic on Outside Interface** is added as a best practice.

Note Using ASDM, you can move an ACE up or down by selecting an ACE and then clicking the up or down arrow.

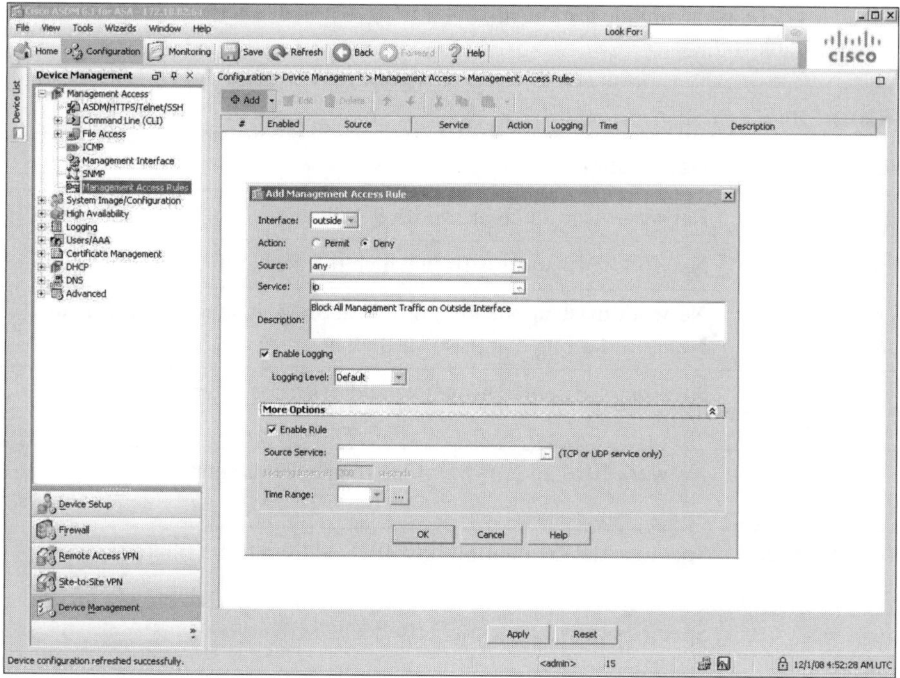

Figure 4-5 *Defining a Management Access Rule through ASDM*

Set Up an IPv6 ACL (Optional)

If you use IPv6 traffic in your network, you can optionally configure an IPv6 ACL to control the traffic passing through the security appliance.

As discussed previously in the "Types of ACLs" section, the security appliance supports filtering IPv6 traffic that is passing through interfaces. You define an IPv6 ACL by using the **ipv6 access-list** command, followed by the name of the ACL. Like an extended ACL, the IPv6 ACL uses similar command options, as shown in the following syntax:

```
ipv6 access-list id [line line-num] {deny | permit} {protocol | object-group
protocol_obj_grp_id} {source-ipv6-prefix/prefix-length | any | host source-ipv6-
address | object-group network_obj_grp_id} [operator {port [port] | object-group
service_obj_grp_id}] {destination-ipv6-prefix/prefix-length | any | host
destination-ipv6-address | object-group network_obj_grp_id}  [log [[level]
[interval secs] | disable |  default]]
```

```
ipv6 access-list id [line line-num] {deny | permit} icmp6 {source-ipv6-
prefix/prefix- length | any | host source-ipv6-address | object-group
network_obj_grp_id}   {destination-ipv6-prefix/prefix-length | any | host
destination-ipv6-address |  object-group network_obj_grp_id} [icmp_type | object-
group icmp_type_obj_grp_id]   [log [[level] [interval secs] | disable | default]]
```

```
ipv6 access-list id [line line-num] remark text
```

Table 4-4 defines the unique arguments of an IPv6 ACE that are different from the ones listed in Table 4-2.

Table 4-4 *IPv6 ACE Definition*

Attributes	Description
ipv6	Keyword used to create an IPv6 ACL.
source-ipv6-prefix	Network IPv6 address from which the packet is being sent.
prefix-length	Network mask applied to an IPv6 address. It specifies how many higher-order bits comprise an IPv6 network address.
source-ipv6-address	Specifies the source host IPv6 address to be filtered.
destination-ipv6-prefix	Network IPv6 address to which the packet is sent.
destination-ipv6-address	Specifies the destination host IPv6 address to be filtered.
icmp6	Specifies that the protocol used is ICMPv6.

Note IPv6 ACLs are supported only in Cisco ASDM 6.2. If you use an earlier version of code, you must create IPv6 ACLs through the CLI.

In Example 4-4, an ACL called **inbound-ipv6-traffic-on-outside** consists of two ACEs. The first ACE denies traffic from an IPv6 source **fedc:ba98:1:3210:fedc:ba98:1:3210** if it is destined for a mail server (TCP port 25) located at **1080::8:800:200c:417a.** The second ACE permits all mail traffic from the **fedc:ba98:1:3210::/64** network if it is destined to **1080::8:800:200c:417a.** The ACL is applied to the **outside** interface in the **inbound** direction.

Example 4-4 *Configuring and Applying an IPv6 ACL on the Outside Interface*

```
Chicago(config)# ipv6 access-list inbound-ipv6-traffic-on-outside permit tcp host
fedc:ba98:1:3210:fedc:ba98:1:3210 host 1080::8:800:200c:417a eq smtp
Chicago(config)# ipv6 access-list inbound-ipv6-traffic-on-outside permit tcp
fedc:ba98:1:3210::/64 host 1080::8:800:200c:417a eq smtp
Chicago(config)# access-group inbound-ipv6-traffic-on-outside in interface outside
```

Advanced ACL Features

Cisco ASA provides many advanced packet-filtering features to suit any network environments. These features include

- Object grouping
- Standard ACLs
- Time-based ACLs
- Downloadable ACLs

Object Grouping

Object grouping is a way to group similar items together to reduce the number of ACEs. Without object grouping, the configuration on the security appliance may contain thousands of lines of ACEs, which can become hard to manage. The security appliance follows the multiplication factor rule when ACEs are defined. For example, if three outside hosts need to access two internal servers running HTTP and SMTP services, the security appliance will have 12 host-based ACEs, calculated as follows:

Number of ACEs = (2 internal servers) × (3 outside hosts) × (2 services) = 12

If you use object grouping, you can reduce the number of ACEs to just a single entry. Object grouping can cluster network objects such as internal servers into one group and outside hosts into another. The security appliance can also combine both TCP services into a service object group. All these groups can be linked to each other in one ACE.

Note Although the number of viewable ACEs is reduced when object groups are used, the actual number of ACEs is not. Use the show access-list command to display the expanded ACEs in the ACL.

The security appliance supports nesting an object group into another one. This hierarchical grouping can further reduce the number of configured ACEs in Cisco ASA.

Object Types

The security appliance supports four different types of objects that can group similar items or services. They include

- Protocol
- Network
- Service
- ICMP type

Protocol

A protocol-based object group combines IP protocols (such as TCP, UDP, and ICMP) into one object. For example, if you want to group both TCP and UDP services of DNS, you can create an object group and add TCP and UDP protocols into that group.

> **Caution** When the protocol-based object group is used, all the protocols are expanded into different ACEs. It is therefore easy to permit unintended traffic if object groups are applied too liberally.

Network

A network-based object group specifies a list of IP host, subnet, or network addresses. Defining a network-based object group is very similar to defining a protocol-based object group.

Service

A service-based object group is used to cluster the TCP and/or UDP services together. By using the service-based object group, you can group TCP, UDP, or TCP and UDP ports into an object.

In versions 8.0 or higher, the security appliance enables you to create a service object group that can contain a mix of TCP services, UDP services, ICMP-type services, and any protocol such as ESP, GRE, and TCP, to name a few. This removes the need for a specific ICMP-type object group and a protocol object group. For example, you can create a service object group, called ProtocolServices, that can have HTTP, DNS, ICMP echo, and GRE protocols as its members.

ICMP-Type

The ICMP protocol uses unique types to send control messages, as documented in RFC 792. Using the ICMP-type object group, you can group the necessary types required to meet an organization's security needs. For example, you can create an object group called **echo** to group echo and echo-reply. These two ICMP types are used when a user issues the **ping** command.

> **Tip** For more information about ICMP Type Numbers, visit http://www.iana.org/assignments/icmp-parameters.

Configuration of Object Types

If you prefer to use the CLI, you can configure object groups by using the **object-group** command followed by the object type. The complete command syntax is:

```
object-group {{protocol | network | icmp-type} grp_id | service grp_id {tcp | udp |
tcp-udp}}
```

Table 4-5 lists and defines the arguments used in the **object-group** command.

Table 4-5 object-group *Command Description*

Syntax	Description
object-group	Keyword used to define an object group.
protocol	Keyword to specify Layer 3 IP protocols such as TCP, UDP, ICMP, GRE, and IGMP.
network	Keyword to specify the host, subnet, or network addresses.
icmp-type	Keyword to specify ICMP types such as echo, echo-reply, and traceroute.
grp_id	Name that identifies the object group. This name can be linked to an ACE or to another object group.
service	Keyword to specify the Layer 4 services for TCP and UDP protocols.
tcp	Keyword to group TCP services such as HTTP, FTP, Telnet, and SMTP.
udp	Keyword to group UDP services such as DNS, TFTP, and ISAKMP.
tcp-udp	Keyword to group services that uses both TCP and UDP protocols such as DNS and Kerberos.

For example, if you want to set up a protocol-based object group, use the **object-group protocol** command followed by the name of the object group. As shown in Example 4-5, the **protocol-object** command is used to set up an object group called **TCP_UDP** to group the TCP and UDP protocols. The security appliance enables you to add a description under an object group. In this example, the description **Grouping of TCP and UDP protocols** identifies this group.

Example 4-5 *Configuration of Protocol-Based Object Group*

```
Chicago(config)# object-group protocol TCP_UDP
Chicago(config-protocol)# description Grouping of TCP and UDP protocols
Chicago(config-protocol)# protocol-object tcp
Chicago(config-protocol)# protocol-object udp
```

As mentioned earlier, an object group can be nested into another object group. You do so by using the **group-object** command. In Example 4-6, another protocol-based object group called **IP_Protocols** is set up to include GRE as the IP protocol. This object group also contains the **TCP_UDP** object group, defined in the preceding example. The description **nested object group to include GRE, TCP and UDP** is added to this group.

Example 4-6 *Nesting of Protocol-Based Object Groups*

```
Chicago(config)# object-group protocol IP_Protocols
```

```
Chicago(config-protocol)# description nested object group to include GRE, TCP and
UDP
Chicago(config-protocol)# protocol-object gre
Chicago(config-protocol)# group-object TCP_UDP
```

Defining an object group via ASDM is even simpler. Navigate to **Configuration > Firewall > Objects > Service Groups > Add** and select **Protocol Group** from the drop-down menu. ASDM opens a new window where you can specify a group name and an optional description. You can also select the desired protocol from an existing/predefined protocol list. You can even add a new IP protocol if it is not in the predefined protocol list. As illustrated in Figure 4-6, a new protocol-based object group called **TCP-UDP** is added with a description of **Group TCP and UDP Protocols.** From the Existing Service/Service Groups list, both **TCP** and **UDP** protocols are added to the Members in Group list. Click **OK** when you are finished.

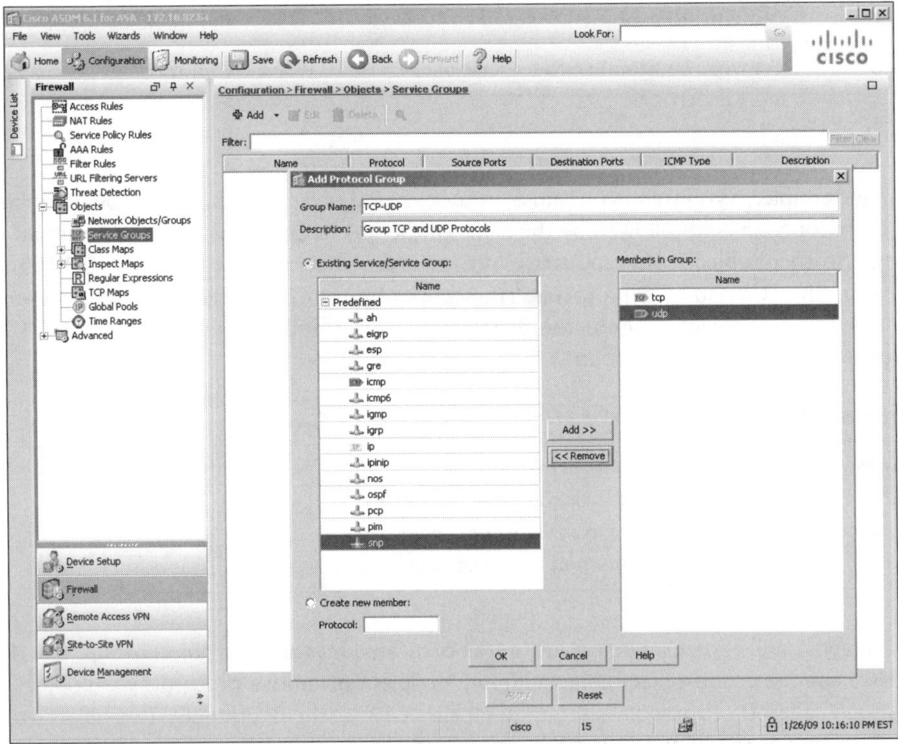

Figure 4-6 *Defining a Protocol-Based Object Group Through ASDM*

If you want to set up a services-based object group, use the **object-group service** command, followed by the name of the object group. As shown in Example 4-7, the **service-object** command is used to set up an object group called **All-Services** to group the

HTTP, DNS, ICMP echo, and GRE protocols. The security appliance enables you to add a description under an object group. In this example, the description **Grouping of All Services** identifies this group.

Example 4-7 *Configuration of Server-Based Object Group*

```
Chicago(config)# object-group service All-Servicess
Chicago(config-service)# description Grouping of All Services
Chicago(config-service)# service-object gre
Chicago(config-service)# service-object icmp echo
Chicago(config-service)# service-object tcp eq http
Chicago(config-service)# service-object udp eq domain
```

Want to define a service object group via ASDM? Navigate to **Configuration > Firewall > Objects > Service Groups > Add** and select **Service Group** from the drop-down menu. ASDM opens a new window where you can specify a service group name and an optional description. You can also select the desired protocols, TCP, UDP, and/or ICMP services from an existing/predefined protocol list. You can even add a new protocol or service if it is not in the predefined list. In Figure 4-7, a new service-based object group called **All-Services** is added with a description of **Grouping of All Services.** From the Existing Service/Service Groups list, select **HTTP** and move it to the Members in Group list. Similarly, select **domain, GRE,** and ICMP **echo** to the Members in Group list. Click **OK** when you are finished.

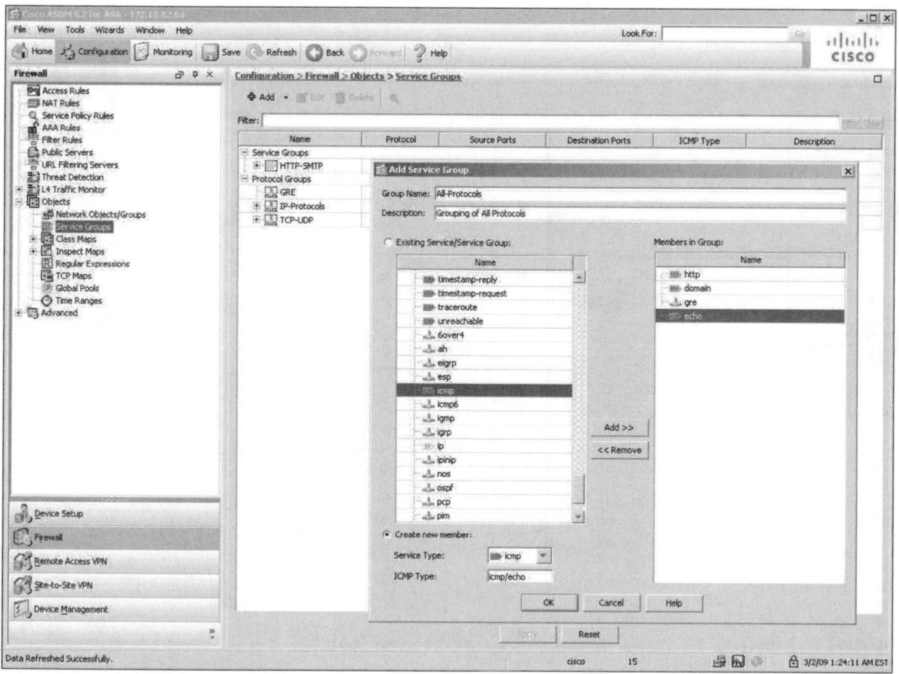

Figure 4-7 *Defining a Service-Based Object Group Through ASDM*

Object Grouping and ACLs

After object groups have been set up, you can use them in an ACL. The command syntax to define an ACE using **object-group** is

```
access-list id line line-num] [extended][ {deny | permit} object-group
protocol_obj_grp_id object-group network_obj_grp_id object-group
service_obj_grp_id] object-group network_obj_grp_id object-group
service_obj_grp_id] [log level] [interval secs] [[disable | default] | [time-range
time_range_ID]] | [inactive]
```

Table 4-6 defines the arguments used in an object group ACE that are different from the ones in Table 4-2.

In Figure 4-8, the inside network has two servers, both running HTTP and SMTP services. If two hosts on the outside network try to access those servers, then eight ACEs should be configured to allow the hosts to communicate with each other. By using object group parameters in the ACE, you can reduce the viewable number of ACEs to one.

Example 4-8 shows the corresponding ACE using the object groups. A protocol-based object group called **TCP** is set up with the TCP protocol. The two network object groups configured are **Internal-Servers** and **Internet-Hosts.** The **Internal-Servers** object group specifies the IP addresses of the servers that are on the inside network, whereas **Internet-Hosts** is configured with the IP addresses of the hosts that are allowed to access the internal servers. A service-based object group called **HTTP-SMTP** is set up to group the

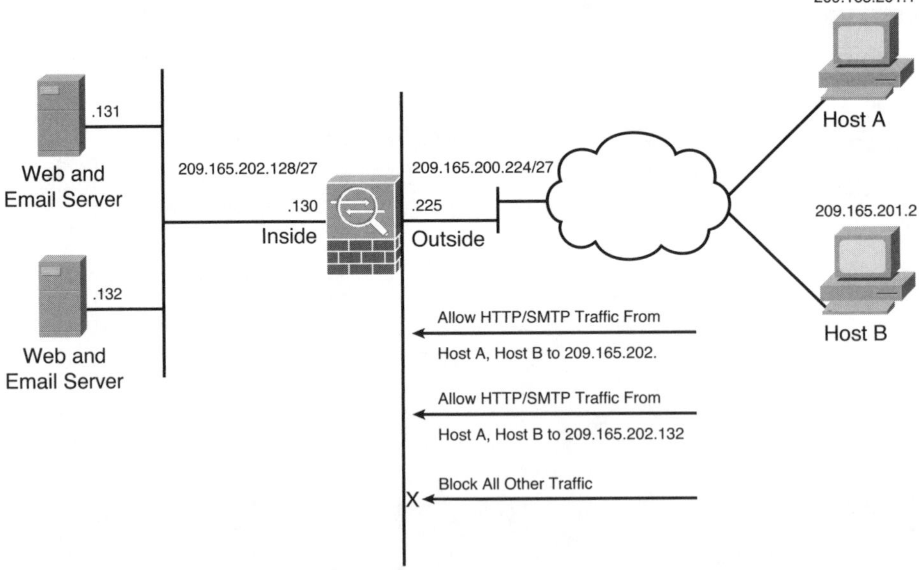

Figure 4-8 *Inbound Packet Filtering Using Object Groups*

Table 4-6 *ACE Definition Using* object-group

Syntax	Description
object-group	Grouping of different objects in a list.
protocol_obj_grp_id	An object name containing the list of protocols to be filtered.
network_obj_grp_id	An object name containing the list of networks to be filtered.
service_obj_grp_id	An object name containing the list of services to be filtered.

HTTP and SMTP services. An ACL, named **outside_access_in**, is used to link all the configured object groups together.

Example 4-8 *Configuration of an ACE Using Object Groups*

```
Chicago(config)# object-group protocol TCP
Chicago(config-protocol)# protocol-object tcp
Chicago(config-protocol)# object-group network Internal-Servers
Chicago(config-network)# network-object host 209.165.202.131
Chicago(config-network)# network-object host 209.165.202.132
Chicago(config-network)# object-group network Internet-Hosts
Chicago(config-network)# network-object host 209.165.201.1
Chicago(config-network)# network-object host 209.165.201.2
Chicago(config-network)# object-group service HTTP-SMTP tcp
Chicago(config-service)# port-object eq smtp
Chicago(config-service)# port-object eq www
Chicago(config-service)# exit
Chicago(config)# access-list outside_access_in extended permit object-group TCP
object-group Internet-Hosts object-group Internal-Servers object-group HTTP-SMTP
```

After configuring the ACL, you can bind it to an interface for traffic filtering, as shown in Example 4-9. The ACL **outside_access_in** is applied to the **outside** interface in the **inbound** direction.

Example 4-9 *Applying an ACL on the Outside Interface*

```
Chicago(config)# access-group outside_access_in in interface outside
```

Note The security appliance enables you to use any mix of object group and non–object group parameters to set up an ACE. You can choose to use TCP as the protocol and an object group for source and destination IP addresses and subnet masks. An example of this is shown under the "Deployment Scenarios for Traffic Filtering" section later in this chapter.

To define an ACL with object groups through ASDM, simply navigate to **Configuration > Firewall > Access Rules**, select the pull-down **Add** list and click **Add Access Rule.** ASDM opens a new window where you can select the preconfigured object groups in the source and destination services and addresses. As shown in Figure 4-9, an ACL is being configured for the outside interface that allows traffic from the **Internet-Hosts** object group to the **Internal-Servers** object group on the **HTTP-SMTP** service object group.

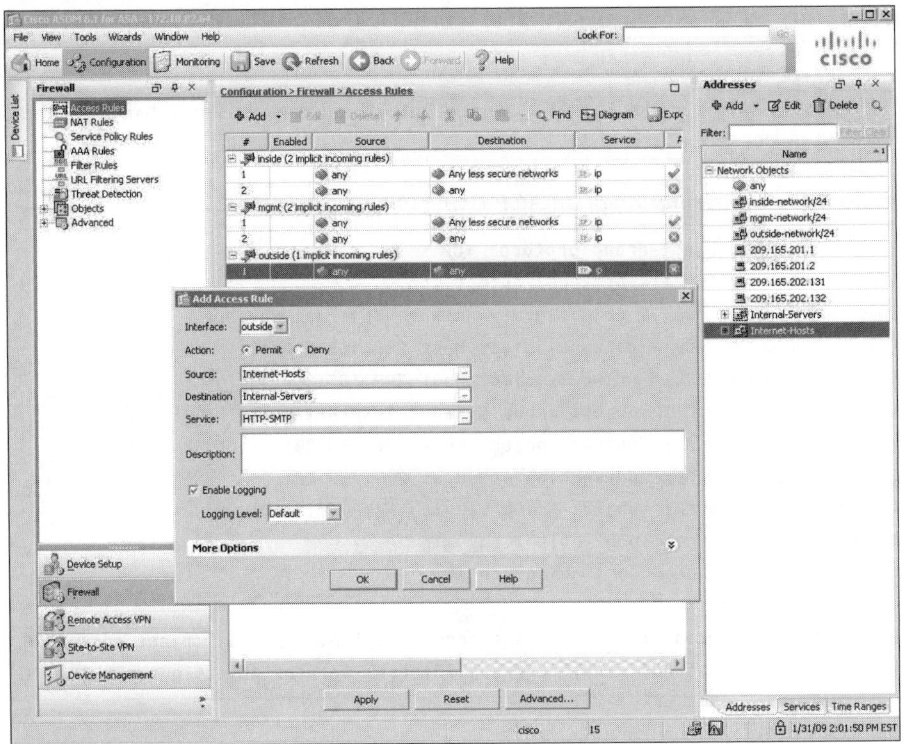

Figure 4-9 *ACL Definition Using Object Groups*

Standard ACLs

As mentioned earlier in this chapter, standard ACLs are used when the source network in the traffic is not important. These ACLs are used by processes, such as OSPF and VPN tunnels, to identify traffic based on the destination IP addresses.

You define standard ACLs by using the **access-list** command and the **standard** keyword after the ACL name. The command syntax to define a standard ACE is

```
access-list id standard [line line-num]{deny | permit} {any | host ip_address |
ip_address subnet_mask}
```

In Example 4-10, the security appliance identifies traffic destined for host **192.168.10.100** and network **192.168.20.0** and denies all other traffic explicitly. The ACL name is **Dest-Net.**

Example 4-10 *Configuration of a Standard ACL*

```
Chicago(config)# access-list Dest_Net standard permit host 192.168.10.100
Chicago(config)# access-list Dest_Net standard permit 192.168.20.0 255.255.255.0
Chicago(config)# access-list Dest_Net standard deny any
```

After a standard ACL is defined, it must be applied to a process for implementation. In Example 4-11, a route map called **OSPFMAP** is set up to use the standard ACL configured in the previous example. Route maps are discussed in Chapter 5, "IP Routing."

Example 4-11 *Route Map Using a Standard ACL*

```
Chicago(config)# route-map OSPFMAP permit 10
Chicago(config-route-map)# match ip address Dest_Net
```

If you prefer to use ASDM to define a standard ACL, browse to **Configuration > Firewall > Advanced > Standard ACL > Add > Add ACL**. ASDM opens a new window where you can specify an ACL name. Click **OK** to add this ACL in the system. After the ACL is defined, you must add access-control entries (ACE). Click **Add > Add ACE** and specify the destination network that you want to permit or deny. In Figure 4-10, an ACL called **Dest-Net** is added with two ACEs. The first ACE permits traffic destined to **192.168.10.100**, whereas the second ACE allows traffic destined to **192.168.20.0/24** network.

Time-Based ACLs

The security appliance can apply the ACLs based on the time interval to allow or deny network access. These rules, commonly referred as *time-based ACLs,* can prevent users from accessing the network services when the packets arrive outside the preconfigured time intervals. The ASA relies on the system's clock when time-based ACLs are evaluated. Consequently, it is important to ensure that the system clock is accurate, and thus the use of Network Time Protocol (NTP) is highly recommended. You can use the time-based ACLs with the extended, IPv6, and Webtype ACLs.

Note The time-based ACLs apply only to new connections and therefore the existing connections are not affected when the time-based ACLs become activate.

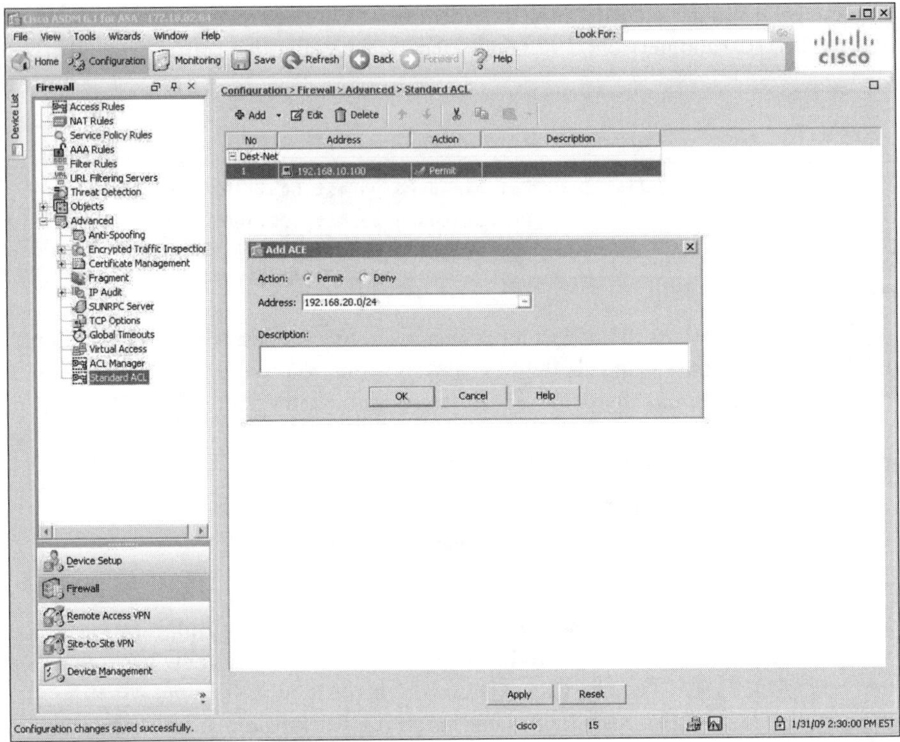

Figure 4-10 *Standard ACL Definition*

The security appliances enable you to specify two different types of time restrictions:

- **Absolute**—Using the *absolute* function, you can specify the values based on a start and/or an end time. This function is useful in cases where a company hires consultants for a period of time and wants to restrict access when they leave. In this case, you can set an absolute time and specify the start and the end time. After the time period expires, the consultants cannot pass traffic through the security appliance. The start and end times are optional. If no start time is provided, the security appliance assumes that the ACL needs to be applied right away. If no end time is configured, the security appliance applies the ACL indefinitely. Additionally, only one instance of the absolute parameter is allowed to be set up in a given time range.
- **Periodic**—Using the *periodic* function, you can specify the values based on the recurring events. The security appliance provides many easy-to-configure parameters to suit an environment. Time-based ACLs using this option are useful when an enterprise wants to allow user access during the normal business hours on the weekdays and wishes to deny access over the weekends. Cisco ASA enables you to configure multiple instances of the periodic parameter.

Note The start and end times use the same format as the **clock set** command when configuring time and date values in the absolute function.

If both absolute and periodic parameters are configured in a time range, the absolute time parameters are evaluated first, before the periodic time value.

In periodic time ranges, you can configure a day-of-the-week such as **Monday**, specify the keyword **weekdays** for a work-week from Monday to Friday, or specify the keyword **weekend** for Saturday and Sunday. The security appliance can further the restrictions on the users by setting the optional 24-hour format hh:mm time specifications.

You can set up the time-based ACLs by using the **time-range** command, followed by the name of this entity. In Example 4-12, the administrator has created a time-range policy called **consultant_hours** for a new consultant whose start time/date is 8:00 a.m. on June 1, 2009, and end time/date is 5:00 p.m. on December 31, 2009. The administrator has created another time-range policy called **business_hours** for the regular employees who work from 8:00 a.m. to 5:00 p.m. on weekdays and from 8:00 a.m. to 12:00 p.m. on Saturdays.

Example 4-12 *Time-Range Configuration*

```
Chicago(config)# time-range consultant_hours
Chicago(config-time-range)# absolute start 08:00 01 June 2009 end 17:00 31
December 2009
Chicago(config)# time-range business_hours
Chicago(config-time-range)# periodic weekdays 8:00 to 17:00
Chicago(config-time-range)# periodic Saturday 8:00 to 12:00
```

Using ASDM, configure time-range policies under **Configuration > Firewall > Objects > Time Ranges > Add.** ASDM opens a new window where you can specify a time-range policy name and define the absolute and/or periodic attributes. As shown in Figure 4-11, the administrator has defined a policy in ASDM similar to the policy in Example 4-12.

After a time-range entry has been set up, the next step is to link it to the ACL by using the **time-range** keyword, as illustrated in Example 4-13, in which the administrator allows outside users access to an internal web server, **209.165.202.131**, during business hours (8:00 a.m. to 5:00 p.m. Monday through Friday, and 8:00 a.m. to 12:00 p.m. Saturday). If the outside users try to access the servers outside this time window, the security appliance drops the packets and generates a syslog message logging this event. The ACL name is **inside_server** and the time-range name is **business_hours**. The ACL is applied to the **outside** interface in the **inbound** direction.

Example 4-13 *Configuration of a Time-Based ACL*

```
Chicago(config)# access-list inside_server extended permit tcp any host
209.165.202.131 eq 80 time-range business_hours
Chicago(config)# access-group inside_server in interface outside
```

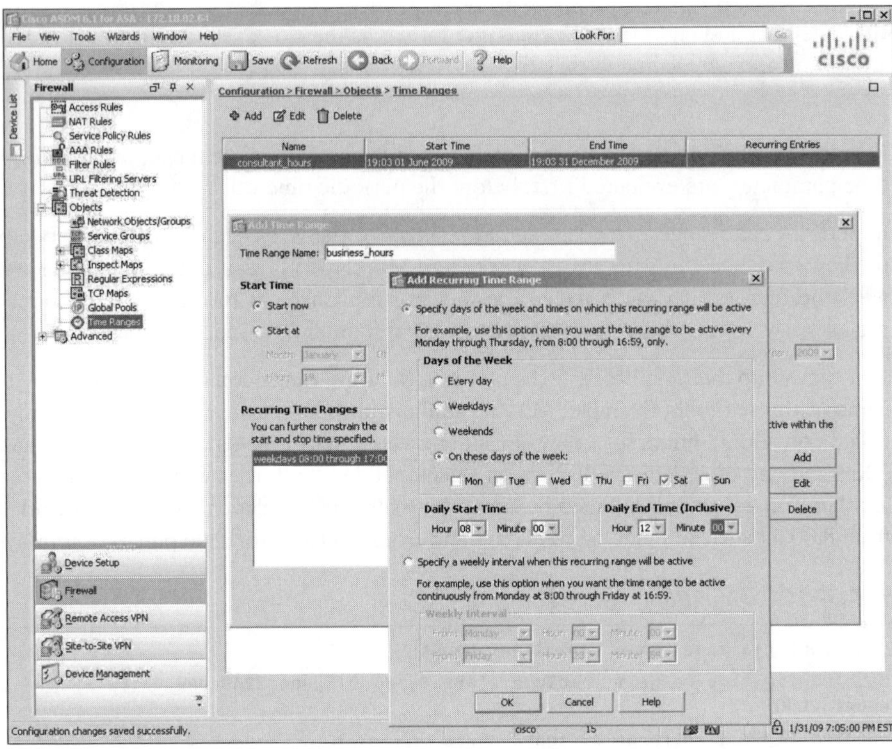

Figure 4-11 *Definition of Time Range Policy in ASDM*

Using ASDM, you can link the time-range policy to an ACL by editing or adding a new access rule. In Figure 4-12, a previously defined time-range policy, business_hours, is linked to an access rule that allows any source to send HTTP traffic to an inside server located at 209.165.202.131.

Downloadable ACLs

The security appliance can dynamically download the ACLs from an external authentication server such as RADIUS or TACACS. This feature is discussed in Chapter 6, "Authentication, Authorization, and Accounting (AAA) Services." When a user needs to access a service on the outside, the following sequence of events occurs, as illustrated in Figure 4-13:

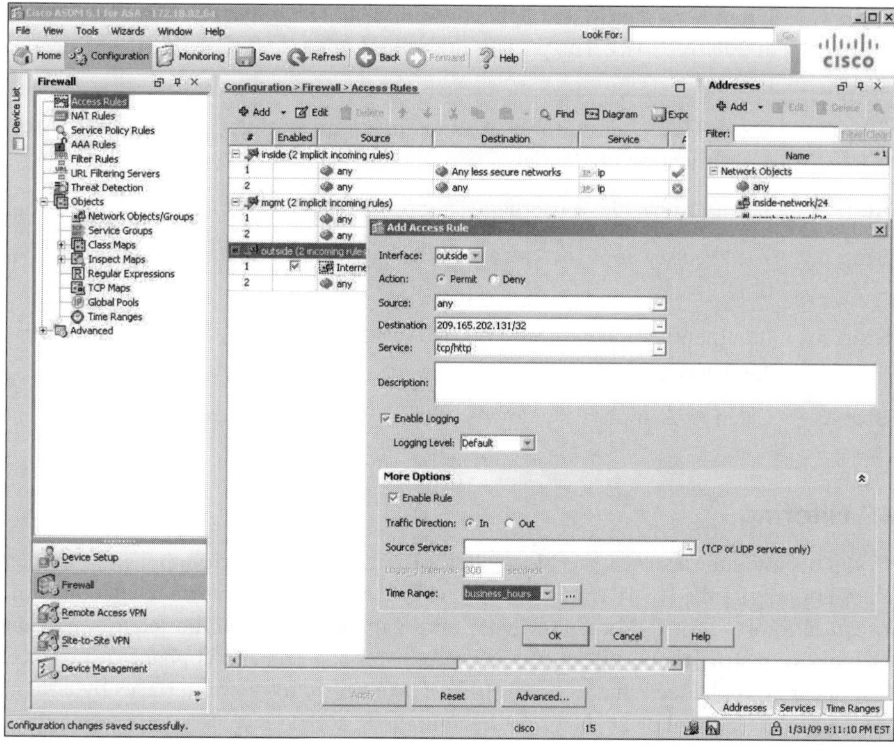

Figure 4-12 *Mapping a Time-Range Policy to an ACL in ASDM*

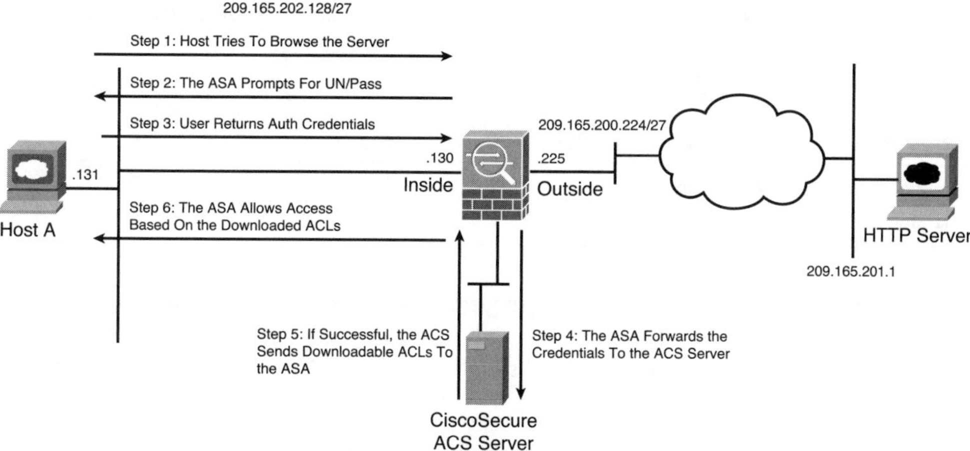

Figure 4-13 *Downloadable ACLs*

Step 1. User opens a browser application and tries to navigate to a web server located at 209.165.201.1. The packets are routed to Cisco ASA to reach the destination web server.

Step 2. Cisco ASA is set up for user authentication and thus prompts the user for authentication credentials.

Step 3. The user provides a username and password.

Step 4. The security appliance forwards the username and password to an authentication server.

Step 5. If authentication is successful, the server returns the ACLs to the security appliance.

Step 6. Cisco ASA applies the downloadable ACLs to the user.

ICMP Filtering

If you deploy interface ACLs to block all ICMP traffic, the security appliance, by default, does not restrict the ICMP traffic that is destined to its own interface. Depending on an organization's security policy, an ICMP policy can be defined on the security appliance to block or restrict the ICMP traffic that terminates at a security appliance's interface. The security appliances enable you to filter ICMP traffic to their interfaces by either deploying the control plane ACLs or defining the ICMP policy.

If you use the CLI, you can define an ICMP policy by using the **icmp** command, followed by an action (**permit** or **deny**), source network, ICMP type, and the interface where you want to apply this policy. As shown in Example 4-14, an ICMP policy is applied to the **outside** interface to block the ICMP echo packets sourced from any IP address. The second **icmp** statement permits all other ICMP types that are destined for the security appliance's IP address.

Example 4-14 *Defining an ICMP Policy*

```
Chicago(config)# icmp deny any echo outside
Chicago(config)# icmp permit any outside
```

The ICMP commands are processed in sequential order, with an implicit deny at the end of the list. If an ICMP packet is not matched against a specific entry in the ICMP list, the packet is dropped. If there is no ICMP list defined, all ICMP packets are allowed to be terminated on the security appliance.

Prefer to use ASDM? Navigate to **Configuration > Device Management > Management Access > ICMP > Add** and specify an ICMP policy.

Content and URL Filtering

Traditionally, firewalls filter data packets by analyzing Layer 3 and/or Layer 4 header information. Cisco ASA can enhance this functionality by inspecting the content information in many Layer 7 protocols such as HTTP, HTTPS, and FTP. Based on an organization's security policy, the security appliance can either pass or drop the packets if they contain content not allowed in the network. Cisco ASA supports two types of application layer filtering, namely content filtering and URL filtering.

> **Note** Cisco ASA also allows filtering and analyzing data traffic via application inspection, discussed in Chapter 7.

Content Filtering

Enabling Java or ActiveX in the production environment can cause naive users to download malicious executables that can cause loss of files and corruption in the user environment. A security network professional can disable Java and ActiveX processing in the browser, but this is not a very scalable solution. The other option is to use a network device such as Cisco ASA to remove the malicious content from the packets. Using the local content-filtering feature, the security appliance can inspect the HTTP header and filter out ActiveX and Java applets when the packets try to traverse from non-trusted hosts.

Cisco ASA can differentiate between friendly applets and untrusted applets. If a trusted website sends Java or ActiveX applets, the security appliance can forward them to the host requesting the connection. If the applets are sent from untrusted web servers, the security appliance can modify the content and remove the applets from the packets. This way, end users are not making decisions regarding which applet to accept or refuse. They can download any applets without being extra cautious.

As shown in Figure 4-14, SecureMe wants to filter both ActiveX and Java from the data packets. After completing TCP negotiations, the web client sends an HTTP request to the web server. If Java/ActiveX is embedded in the packets, the security appliance removes them before sending them to the client.

ActiveX Filtering

As mentioned in the preceding section, ActiveX can cause potential problems on the network devices if malicious ActiveX code is downloaded on the end-host devices. The **<OBJECT ID>** and **</OBJECT> HTML** tags are used to insert ActiveX code into the web page. The security appliance searches for these tags for traffic that originated on a preconfigured port. If the security appliance finds these tags, it replaces them with the comment tags **<!—** and **—>**. When the browser receives the HTTP packets with **<!—** and **—>**, it ignores the actual content by assuming that the content is the author's comments.

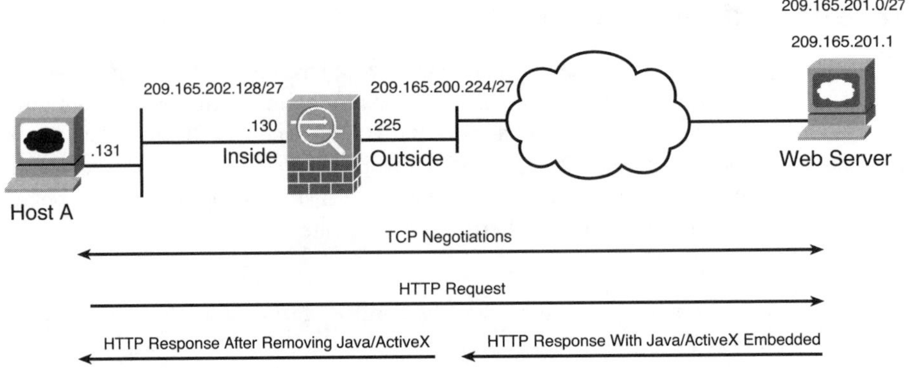

Figure 4-14 *ActiveX-Based Content Filtering*

> **Note** The security appliance cannot comment out the HTML tags if they are split across multiple network packets.

Java Filtering

For Java-based content filtering, the security appliance looks for **<applet>** and **</applet>** tags in the HTML data packets. Without Java filtering, the client browser tries to execute the code specified in **<applet>**, which begins with a 4-byte header, **ca fe ba be**. Therefore, to block Java applets, the security appliance searches for the **<applet>** and **</applet>** tags and replaces them with the comment tags, **<!—** and **—>**. Additionally, it blocks the applets if it sees the **ca fe ba be** string embedded in the packet.

Configuring Content Filtering

You set up local content filtering on the security appliance by using the **filter** command, followed by the content name to be removed. The following shows the complete command syntax:

```
filter activex|java port[-port] except local_ip local_mask foreign_ip
foreign_mask
```

Table 4-7 describes the arguments used in the **filter** command.

In Example 4-15, the security administrator of an appliance in Chicago has set up a content-filtering policy to remove ActiveX objects from the HTTP packets (TCP port 80). The policy will be enforced if packets originate from the inside subnet 209.165.202.128/27 and destined for the external subnet 209.165.201.0/27. If traffic originates from or is destined for a different host, the security appliance will not filter ActiveX content.

Table 4-7 *Syntax Description for* **filter java** *and* **filter activex** *Commands*

Syntax	Description
filter	Keyword used to enable content filtering.
activex	Keyword to enable ActiveX filtering.
java	Keyword to enable Java filtering.
except	Define an exception to a previously defined filter.
port[-*port*]	TCP port number(s) for the security appliance to inspect HTTP packets. This can be either a single port or a range of ports. Typically, it is TCP port 80.
local_ip	Host IP or subnet address of the inside hosts where the connection originated.
local_mask	Subnet mask of the local host IP or subnet address.
foreign_ip	Host IP or subnet address of the outside servers to which the connection is made.
foreign_mask	Subnet mask of the outside host IP or subnet address.

Example 4-15 *ActiveX Content Filtering*

```
Chicago(config)# filter activex 80 209.165.202.128 255.255.255.224 209.165.201.0
255.255.255.224
```

In Example 4-16, the security appliance is set up to filter Java applets from the TCP packets received on TCP port 8080. The Java applets are removed if packets originate from the inside subnet **209.165.202.128/27** and are destined for external subnet **209.165.201.0/27**.

Example 4-16 *Java Content Filtering*

```
Chicago(config)# filter java 8080 209.165.202.128 255.255.255.224 209.165.201.0
255.255.255.224
```

Define a filter for ActiveX and Java by navigating to **Configuration > Firewall > Filter Rules > Add** and selecting either **Add Filter ActiveX Rule** or **Add Filter Java Rule**. ASDM opens a new window where you can specify the attributes discussed in Table 4-7. Figure 4-15 shows that a filter is defined to remove Java applets from the packets if they are sourced from **209.165.202.128/27** and destined to **209.165.201.0/27** on TCP port **8080**.

URL Filtering

Traditionally, corporations monitor and control user Internet access by filtering questionable content. This prevents users from accessing sites that are deemed inappropriate based on the organization's security policies. Additionally, employees do not waste network

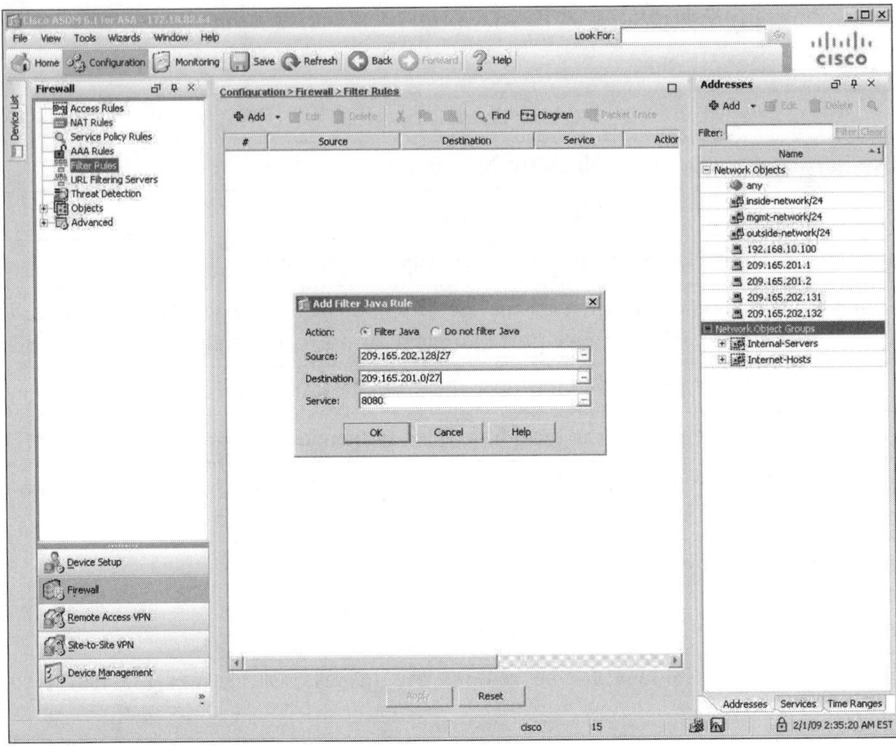

Figure 4-15 *Defining Java-Based Content Filtering via ASDM*

resources by sending traffic to the blocked Internet sites, which results in lower bandwidth usage and increased employee productivity. Cisco ASA can delegate packet-filtering responsibilities to an external server, such as Secure Computing SmartFilter (acquired by McAfee) or Websense. The URL-filtering process follows this sequence of events, shown in Figure 4-16.

Step 1. A web client (Host A) opens a browser application for Server 1.

Step 2. The security appliance forwards to the filtering server the URLs that the inside hosts try to reach. At the same time, the security appliance also forwards the original request to the external content server (Server 1).

Step 3. The filtering server analyzes the URLs and sends a permit or deny message back to the security appliance.

Step 4. The web server sends a reply destined for Host A.

Step 5. If the filtering server allows the connection, the security appliance forwards the response packet from the content server to the client. If the filtering server denies the connection, the security appliance drops the response packet from the content server and sends a message indicating a failed connection.

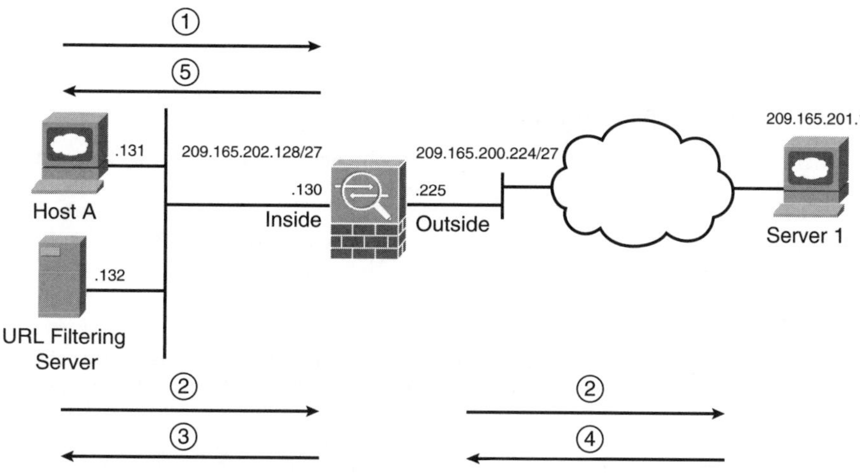

1
5
Host A
.131
209.165.202.128/27
.130
Inside
209.165.200.224/27
.225
Outside
209.165.201.1
Server 1
.132
URL Filtering Server
2
3
2
4
Step 1: Host Tries To Browse the Server
Step 2: Request Is Sent To the Filtering Server and To the Web Server
Step 3: Server Analyzes Request and Sends a Response
Step 4: Web Server Sends a Response To the Original Request
Step 5: If Allowed, the Response Is Sent To the Client

Figure 4-16 *URL Filtering*

Both Websense and SmartFilter are external servers that can filter HTTP, HTTPS, and FTP requests from the client machines based on many attributes, including destination hostname, destination IP address, and URL. These servers can organize a list of Internet URLs into different categories and sub-categorizes, including MP3, gambling, shopping, and adult content, for the ease of management.

> **Note** For more information about Websense and its features, visit http://www.websense.com.
>
> Secure Computing was acquired by McAfee. Visit http://www.mcafee.com for more information.

Configuring URL Filtering

Configure URL filtering as follows:

Step 1. Define a filtering server.

Step 2. Configure HTTP, HTTPS, and FTP filtering.

Step 3. Buffer server responses (optional).

Step 4. Enable long URL support (optional).

Step 5. Cache server responses (optional).

These steps are described in more detail in the following sections.

Step 1: Defining a Filtering Server

You define an external filtering server by using the **url-server** command. The complete command syntax to specify a Websense server is

```
url-server (if_name) vendor websense host local_ip [timeout <seconds>] [protocol
TCP|UDP] [connections num_conns] [version 1|4]
```

To define a SmartFilter server, the command syntax is

```
url-server [<(if_name)>] vendor {smartfilter | n2h2} host <local_ip> [port
<number>] [timeout <seconds>] [protocol TCP|UDP] [connections num_conns]]
```

> **Note** Users may experience longer access times if the response from the filtering server is slow or delayed. This may happen if the filtering server is located at a remote location and the WAN link is slow.
>
> Additionally, if the URL server cannot keep up with the number of requests being sent to it you may experience slow response times as well.

Table 4-8 lists and describes the arguments used in the **url-server** command.

The **url-server** command does not verify whether a Websense or SmartFilter server is reachable from the security appliance. You can specify up to 16 filtering servers for redundancy. If the security appliance is not able to reach the first server in the list, it tries the second server from the list, and so on. Additionally, Cisco ASA does not allow for both SmartFilter and Websense servers to be defined at the same time. One must be deleted before the other is set up.

> **Note** If the security appliance is virtualized (as discussed in Chapter 8) you can define up to four filtering servers per context.

In Example 4-17, the administrator defines a **Websense** server located on the **inside** interface. The IP address of the server is **209.165.202.132**, using TCP protocol version **4** with the default timeout value of **30** seconds.

Example 4-17 *URL Filtering Using Websense*

```
Chicago(config)# url-server (inside) vendor websense host 209.165.202.132 timeout
30 protocol TCP version 4
```

Table 4-8 url-server *Command Syntax and Description*

Syntax	Description
url-server	Keyword used to enable URL filtering.
if_name	Specifies the interface toward the URL filtering server.
vendor	Keyword used to identify the vendors.
websense	Keyword to specify Websense as the URL-filtering server.
host	Keyword used to specify a host address for the filtering server.
local_ip	Specifies the IP address of the filtering server.
timeout	Keyword to specify the maximum idle timeout before the security appliance switches over to the next URL-filtering server.
seconds	The actual idle timeout in seconds. The default is 5 seconds.
protocol	Keyword to specify the protocol to be used for communication. The default is TCP.
TCP	Keyword to specify the TCP protocol to be used.
UDP	Keyword to specify the UDP protocol to be used.
version	Keyword to specify the version of protocol to be used when Websense server is set up as the filtering server.
1	Specifies version 1 for TCP protocol communication. This is the default.
4	Specifies version 4 for TCP or UDP protocol communication.
smartfilter	Keyword to specify SmartFilter as the URL-filtering server.
port	Keyword to specify the port number for the security appliance to communicate with the SmartFilter server.
number	The actual port number for SmartFilter server. The default is port 4005.
connections	Keyword to limit the maximum number of connections permitted to a URL-filtering server.
num_cons	Specifies the maximum number of connections permitted.

Note The security appliance does not allow multiple SmartFilter URL servers to use different port numbers.

If you would rather use ASDM to define a URL server, follow **Configuration > Firewall > URL Filtering Servers** and select either the Websense or SmartFilter server. Click **Add** to specify the network parameters for the filtering server. Figure 4-17 illustrates a Websense server located at **209.165.202.132** and using TCP protocol version **4**.

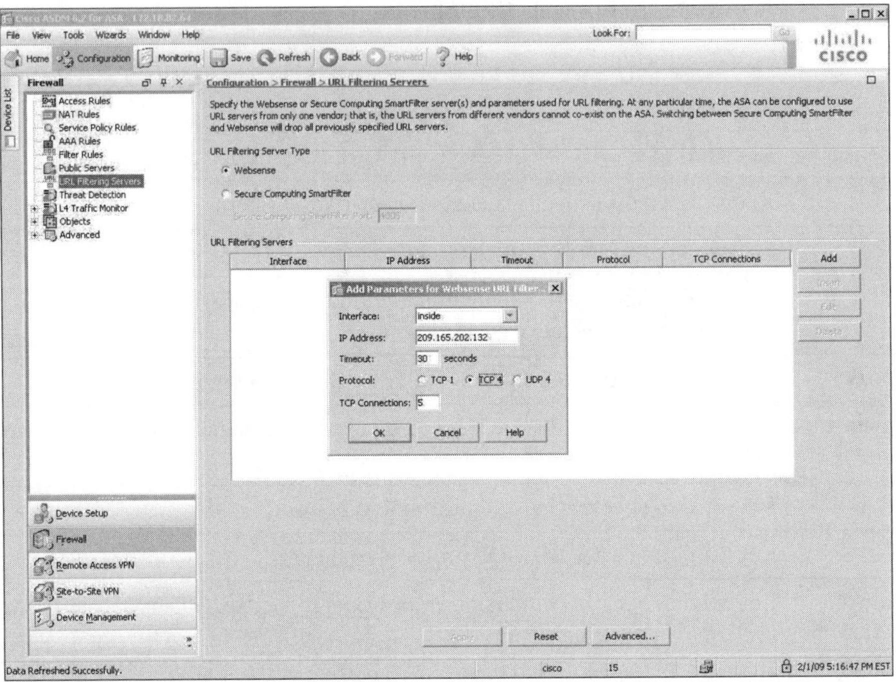

Figure 4-17 *Defining a Websense Server Through ASDM*

Step 2: Configuring HTTP, HTTPS, and FTP Filtering

After identifying the URL server, the security appliance can forward the HTTP, HTTPS, and FTP requests to the appropriate filtering servers. If the filtering server allows the connection, the security appliance forwards the response from the web and/or FTP server to the client host. If the filtering server denies the connection, the security appliance server drops the response and takes one of the following actions:

- It redirects the HTTP or HTTPS connection to a blocked page. The URL of the blocked page is returned by the filtering server.
- It returns a "code 550: Requested file is prohibited by URL filtering policy" error message to the FTP client.

The command syntax to enable HTTP filtering is

```
filter url port[-port]| except <local_IP> <local_mask> <foreign_IP> <foreign_mask>
[allow] [proxy-block] [longurl-truncate] [longurl-deny] [cgi-truncate]
```

Table 4-9 **filter** *Command Syntax and Description*

Syntax	Description
filter	Keyword used to enable content filtering.
url	Keyword to enable HTTP filtering.
port[*-port*]	TCP port number(s) for URL filtering. The security appliance inspects packets on this port(s). This can be either a single port or a range of ports.
local_ip	IP/subnet address of the inside hosts where the connection originated.
local_mask	Subnet mask of the local IP/subnet address.
foreign_ip	IP/subnet address of the outside servers to which the connection is made.
foreign_mask	Subnet mask of the outside IP/subnet address.
except	Defines an exception to a previously defined filter.
allow	Allows the response from the content server if the filtering server is not available.
proxy-block	Denies requests going to the HTTP proxy server.
longurl-truncate	Truncates URLs that are longer than the maximum allowed length before sending the request to the filtering server. It sends the hostname or the IP address to the filtering server.
longurl-deny	Denies outbound connection if the URLs are longer than the maximum allowed length.
cgi-truncate	Truncates long CGI URLs before sending the request to the filtering server, to save memory resources and improve firewall performance. It truncates the URL when a question mark (?) is detected and removes all characters after the ?.
https	Keyword to enable HTTPS filtering.
ftp	Keyword to enable FTP filtering.
interact-block	Denies interactive FTP sessions that do not provide the entire directory path.

The command syntax to enable HTTPS filtering is

```
filter https port[-port] | except <local_IP> <local_mask> <foreign_IP>
<foreign_mask> [allow]
```

The command syntax to enable FT filtering is

```
filter ftp port[-port] | except <local_IP> <local_mask> <foreign_IP>
<foreign_mask> [allow][interact-block]
```

Table 4-9 describes the arguments used in the **filter** command for URL filtering.

In case a URL-filtering server is not available, the security appliance drops the response from the content (HTTP or FTP) server. You can change this default behavior by specifying the **allow** keyword at the end of the **filter** command.

In Example 4-18, a security appliance is set up to filter HTTP, HTTPS, and FTP packets if the connections originate from **209.165.202.128/27** and are destined for any outside network (represented as **0.0.0.0 0.0.0.0**). If the URL server is not available, the inside hosts are allowed to connect to the content servers. For the HTTP packets, the security appliance truncates CGI scripts and the long URLs. For the FTP connections, the security appliance restricts users from changing directories without specifying the complete directory path..

Example 4-18 *Filtering of HTTP, HTTPS, and FTP Packet Content*

```
Chicago(config)# filter url 80 209.165.202.128 255.255.255.224 0.0.0.0 0.0.0.0
allow longurl-truncate cgi-truncate
Chicago(config)# filter https 443 209.165.202.128 255.255.255.224 0.0.0.0 0.0.0.0
allow
Chicago(config)# filter ftp 21 209.165.202.128 255.255.255.224 0.0.0.0 0.0.0.0
allow interact-block
```

To define an HTTP, HTTPS, or FTP filter, go to **Configuration > Firewall > Filter Rules > Add** and select an appropriate filter rule (HTTP, HTTPS, or FTP) from the drop-down menu. In Figure 4-18, a HTTP filter rule is being added to check with the filtering server whether the connections originate from **209.165.202.128/27** and are destined for **any** outside network on port **80**.

Step 3: Buffering Server Responses (Optional)

Using the URL-filtering feature, the security appliance sends a client's request to the outside content (HTTP or FTP) server and simultaneously makes a URL lookup request to the filtering server. If the content server's reply arrives prior to the URL-filtering server's response, the security appliance drops the packet. You can change this default behavior by buffering the response packets from the content server until a reply is received from the filtering server. The command to enable packet buffering is **url-block block** followed by the number of blocks to be buffered. In Example 4-19, the security appliance is set up to buffer up to 128 1550-byte blocks in the HTTP response.

Example 4-19 *Buffering of Server Responses*

```
Chicago(config)# url-block block 128
```

You can configure the security appliance to buffer response packets on the ASDM if you navigate to **Configuration > Firewall > URL Filtering Servers > Advanced**, select the **Enable Buffering** option, and specify a buffer size, as shown in Figure 4-19.

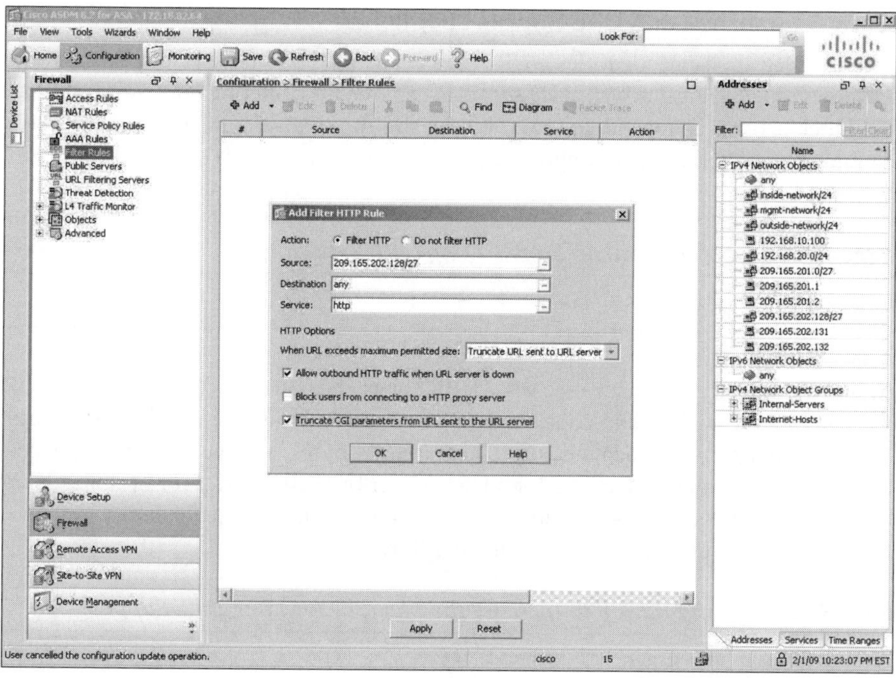

Figure 4-18 *Defining an HTTP Filter Rule via ASDM*

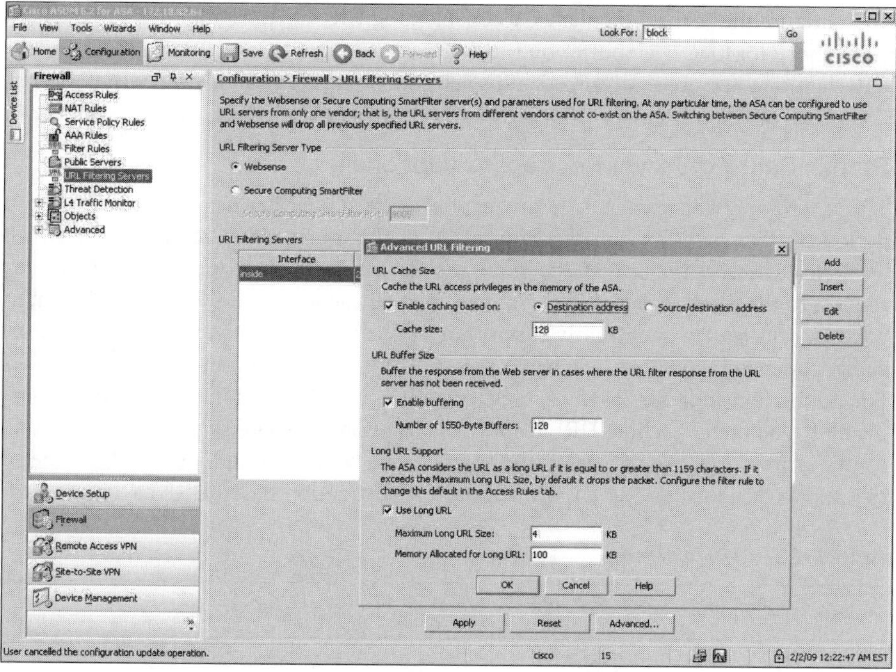

Figure 4-19 *Buffering of Server Responses via ASDM*

Step 4: Enabling Long URL Support (Optional)

The security appliance identifies a URL greater than 1159 bytes as a long URL. You can change this behavior if a Websense server is deployed for filtering purposes by using the **url-block url-size** command, followed by the size of the maximum long URL in kilobytes. In Example 4-20, the security appliance is set up to change the HTTP long URL size from 2 KB to 4 KB.

Example 4-20 *Configuration to Enable Long URL Support*

```
Chicago(config)# url-block url-size 4
```

When the security appliance receives a URL longer than 1024 bytes, it breaks the URL into multiple IP packets and copies the TCP payload and the content of the URL into the buffer memory chunk. Each memory chunk is 1024 bytes, and the security appliance allocates another memory chunk for a URL longer than 1024 bytes for optimized memory management. Example 4-21 shows how to increase the allocated memory available for long URL support and packet buffering to 100 KB.

Example 4-21 *Configuration to Increase the Memory for Long URL Support*

```
Chicago(config)# url-block url-mempool 100
```

To configure the security appliance to enable long URL support and increase the allocated memory for long URL buffer on the ASDM, navigate to Configuration > Firewall > URL Filtering Servers > Advanced and select Use Long URL, and specify the Maximum Long URL Size and Memory Allocated for Long URL, as previously shown in Figure 4-19.

Step 5: Caching Server Responses (Optional)

The security appliance can cache the responses from the filtering servers for a certain period of time, based on the destination and/or the source IP addresses. This way, when a user tries to access the same URL again, the security appliance does not forward the request to the filtering server but consults its local cache before allowing or denying the packets. This feature is currently supported by Websense filtering servers. Use the **url-cache** command to enable caching of server responses followed by the addressing policy. For destination address–based caching, use **dst** as the keyword in the **url-cache** command. If you prefer caching URL responses based on the source and destination addresses of a connection, use **src_dst** with the **url-cache** command. In Example 4-22, the security appliance allocates 128 KB of memory for destination-based URL caching.

Example 4-22 *URL Caching*

```
Chicago(config)# url-cache dst 128
```

To enable this feature within ASDM, navigate to **Configuration > Firewall > URL Filtering Servers > Advanced**, select the **Enable caching based** on option, and choose whether you want to enable destination-based or source/destination-based caching. Specify the memory you want to allocate for caching server responses. This was illustrated previously in Figure 4-19.

Deployment Scenarios for Traffic Filtering

Traffic filtering is the core functionality of any network or personal firewall. However, Cisco ASA integrates this core functionality with novel features to provide a scalable packet identification and filtering mechanism that can be used in almost any environment. Although ACLs can be deployed in many different ways, we examine two primary design scenarios to further your understanding of ACL deployment, namely using ACLs to filter inbound traffic and enabling content filtering using Websense.

Note These design scenarios are discussed here to reinforce learning and thus should be used for reference only.

Using ACLs to Filter Inbound Traffic

In this first scenario, SecureMe hosts three web servers, two email servers, and a DNS server at its Chicago office. All these servers are located on the DMZ network 209.165.201.0/27, as shown in Figure 4-20.

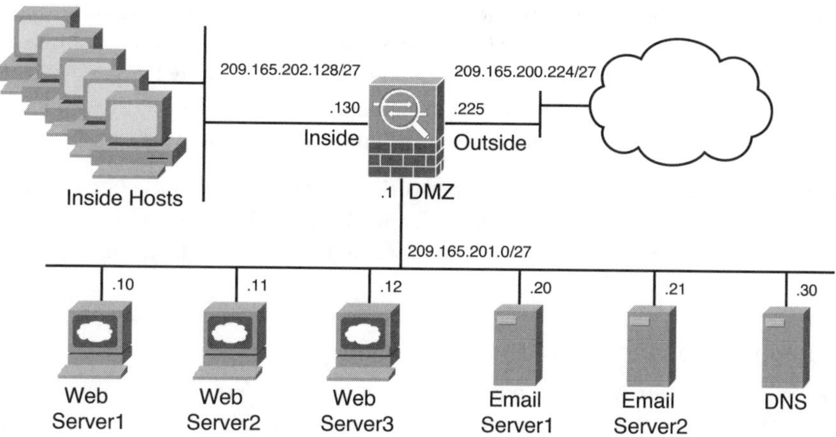

Figure 4-20 *SecureMe ASA in Chicago, Using ACLs*

Table 4-10 lists all the servers and their corresponding IP addresses.

Table 4-10 *Server Address Assignments*

Server	IP Address
Web Server1	209.165.201.10
Web Server2	209.165.201.11
Web Server3	209.165.201.12
Email Server1	209.165.201.20
Email Server2	209.165.201.21
DNS	209.165.201.30

SecureMe wants to provide Internet connectivity for all inside trusted users. However, inside hosts are allowed to access only Web Server1 and DNS server on the DMZ network. Internet users can access all servers in the DMZ network on their respective TCP and UDP ports, but they should not be able to send any traffic to the inside network. All traffic dropped by the access lists should be logged.

To achieve these requirements, the administrator has configured two object groups: DMZWebServers to group all the HTTP servers and DMZEmailServers to group both email servers. Both network groups are bound to the ACL to allow DNS, HTTP, and SMTP traffic only. All other traffic gets denied and logged by the security appliance. This ACL is applied on the outside interface in the inbound direction.

To limit the inside traffic to the DMZ network, the administrator has configured an access rule to allow the trusted hosts on the inside network to access Web Server1 and DNS. The ACL is applied to the inside interface in the inbound direction.

Configuration Steps with ASDM

The configuration for ASDM as outlined here assumes that you have IP connectivity from the ASDM client to the management IP address (172.18.82.64) of the security appliance.

Step 1. Navigate to **Configuration > Firewall > Objects > Network Objects/Groups**, click **Add > Network Object Groups** and specify **DMZWebServers** as the **Group Name**. Choose **Create New Network Object Member**, specify **209.165.201.10** under IP address with a Netmask of **255.255.255.255**, and click **Add>>**. Similarly, add **209.165.201.11** and **209.165.201.12** as object group members. Click **OK** to create the object group.

Step 2. Navigate to **Configuration > Firewall > Objects > Network Objects/Groups**, click **Add > Network Object Groups**, and specify **DMZEmailServers** as the **Group Name** Choose **Create New Network Object Member**, specify **209.165.201.20** under IP address with a Netmask of **255.255.255.255**, and click **Add>>**. Similarly, add **209.165.201.21** as an object group member. Click **OK** to create the object group.

Step 3. Navigate to **Configuration > Firewall > Access Rules > Add > Add Access Rules** and specify the following attributes:

- Interface: **outside**
- Action: **Permit**
- Source: **any**
- Destination: **DMZWebServers**
- Service: **tcp/http**. Click **OK** when you are finished.

Step 4. Navigate to **Configuration > Firewall > Access Rules > Add > Add Access Rules** and specify the following attributes:

- Interface: **outside**
- Action: **Permit**
- Source: **any**
- Destination: **DMZEmailServers**
- Service: **tcp/smtp**. Click **OK** when you are finished.

Step 5. Navigate to **Configuration > Firewall > Access Rules > Add > Add Access Rules** and specify the following attributes:

- Interface: **outside**
- Action: **Permit**
- Source: **any**
- Destination: **209.165.201.30/32**
- Service: **udp/domain**. Click **OK** when you are finished.

Step 6. Navigate to **Configuration > Firewall > Access Rules > Add > Add Access Rules** and specify the following attributes:

- Interface: **outside**
- Action: **Deny**
- Source: **any**
- Destination: **any**

- Service: **IP**
- Enable Logging: **Checked.** Click **OK** when you are finished.

Step 7. Navigate to **Configuration > Firewall > Access Rules > Add > Add Access Rules** and specify the following attributes:

- Interface: **inside**
- Action: **Permit**
- Source: **any**
- Destination: **209.165.201.10/32**
- Service: **tcp/http.** Click **OK** when you are finished.

Step 8. Navigate to **Configuration > Firewall > Access Rules > Add > Add Access Rules** and specify the following attributes:

- Interface: **inside**
- Action: **Permit**
- Source: **any**
- Destination: **209.165.201.30/32**
- Service: **udp/domain.** Click **OK** when you are finished.

Step 9. Navigate to **Configuration > Firewall > Access Rules > Add > Add Access Rules** and specify the following attributes:

- Interface: **inside**
- Action: **Deny**
- Source: **any**
- Destination: **DMZWebServers**
- Service: **ip.** Click **OK** when you are finished.

Step 10. Navigate to **Configuration > Firewall > Access Rules > Add > Add Access Rules** and specify the following attributes:

- Interface: **inside**
- Action: **Deny**
- Source: **any**
- Destination: **DMZEmailServers**
- Service: **ip.** Click **OK** when you are finished.

Step 11. Navigate to **Configuration > Firewall > Access Rules > Add > Add Access Rules** and specify the following attributes:

- Interface: **inside**
- Action: **Permit**
- Source: **any**
- Destination: **any**
- Service: **IP**. Click **OK** when you are finished.

Configuration Steps with CLI

Example 4-23 shows the relevant configuration of the ASA in Chicago. Some configuration output has been removed for brevity.

Example 4-23 *ASA's Full Configuration Using Inbound and Outbound ACLs*

```
Chicago# show running
! GigabitEthernet0/0 interface set as outside
interface GigabitEthernet0/0
 nameif outside
 security-level 0
 ip address 209.165.200.225 255.255.255.224
! GigabitEthernet0/1 interface set as inside
interface GigabitEthernet0/1
 nameif inside
 security-level 100
 ip address 209.165.202.129 255.255.255.224
! GigabitEthernet0/2 interface set as DMZ
interface GigabitEthernet0/2
 nameif DMZ
 security-level 50
ip address 209.165.201.1 255.255.255.224
! Network Object-group to group the web-servers
object-group network DMZWebServers
 network-object host 209.165.201.10
 network-object host 209.165.201.11
 network-object host 209.165.201.12
! Network Object-group to group the Email-servers
object-group network DMZEmailServers
 network-object host 209.165.201.20
 network-object host 209.165.201.21
! Access-list to filter inbound traffic on the outside interface
access-list outside_access_in extended permit tcp any object-group DMZWebServers
eq www
```

```
access-list outside_access_in extended permit tcp any object-group
DMZEmailServers eq smtp
access-list outside_access_in extended permit udp any host 209.165.201.30 eq domain
access-list outside_access_in extended deny ip any any log
! Access-list to filter outbound traffic on the inside interface
access-list inside_access_in extended permit tcp any host 209.165.201.10 eq www
access-list inside_access_in extended permit udp any host 209.165.201.30 eq domain
access-list inside_access_in extended deny ip any object-group DMZWebServers
access-list inside_access_in extended deny ip any object-group DMZEmailServers
access-list inside_access_in extended permit ip any any
! Access-list bound to the outside interface in the inbound direction
access-group outside_access_in in interface outside
! Access-list bound to the inside interface in the inbound direction
access-group inside_access_in in interface inside
```

Using Websense to Enable Content Filtering

In this scenario, SecureMe wants to enable content filtering for its users to ensure that they do not access certain questionable URLs such as pornographic and gaming sites. The administrator has set up a Websense server to filter out the URLs if the packets are destined for these Internet sites, using the HTTP, HTTPS, or FTP protocols. The administrator does not want to overload the filtering server by sending the duplicate request for the same source and destination addresses. SecureMe's policy allows users to go through the security appliance if the filtering server is unavailable. Additionally, if the reply from the content server arrives before the response is received from the filtering server, SecureMe wants the security appliance to buffer the reply rather than drop it.

To meet the company's goals, the administrator has specified a Websense server as a URL-filtering device in the network that is located on the DMZ interface at 209.165.201.50, as illustrated in Figure 4-21. To avoid overloading the filtering server, the maximum simultaneous limit is set to 15, and the server's responses are cached because 100 KB of memory space has been allocated. The security appliance is set up to buffer replies from the remote content servers if they are received before the websense reply. It is set up to store up to 128 packets.

Configuration Steps with ASDM

The ASDM configuration steps as outlined here assume that you have IP connectivity from the ASDM client to the management IP address (172.18.82.64) of the security appliance.

Step 1. Navigate to **Configuration > Firewall > URL Filtering Servers** and select **Websense.** Under **URL Filtering Servers**, click **Add** and specify the following attributes:

- Interface: **DMZ**

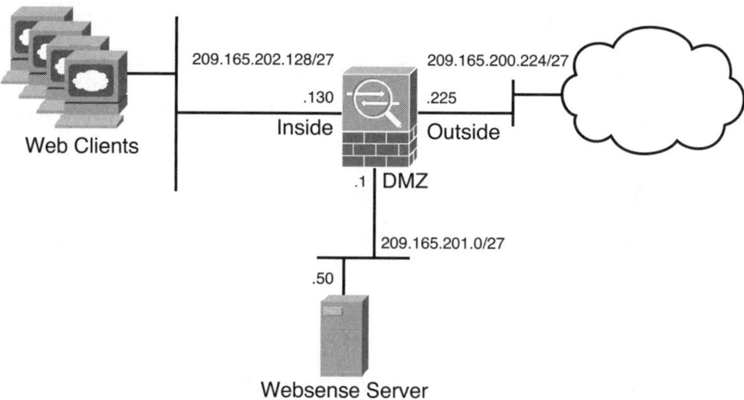

Figure 4-21 *SecureMe Network Using Content Filtering*

- IP Address: **209.165.201.50**
- Protocol: **TCP 4**
- Connections: **15**

Step 2. Navigate to **Configuration > Firewall > URL Filtering Servers > Advanced** and specify the following attributes:

- Enable caching based on: **Source/destination address**
- Cache Size: **100**
- Enable Buffering: **Checked**
- Number of 1550-Byte Buffers: **128**

Step 3. Navigate to **Configuration > Firewall > Filter Rules > Add > Add HTTP Filter Rule** and specify the following attributes:

- Action: **Filter HTTP**
- Source: **209.165.202.128/27**
- Destination: **any**
- Service: **http**
- Allow outbound HTTP traffic when URL server is down: **Checked**

Step 4. Navigate to **Configuration > Firewall > Filter Rules > Add > Add HTTPS Filter Rule** and specify the following attributes:

- Action: **Filter HTTPS**
- Source: **209.165.202.128/27**
- Destination: **any**

- Service: **https**
- Allow outbound HTTPS traffic when URL server is down: **Checked**

Step 5. Navigate to **Configuration > Firewall > Filter Rules > Add > Add FTP Filter Rule** and specify the following attributes:

- Action: **Filter FTP**
- Source: **209.165.202.128/27**
- Destination: **any**
- Service: **ftp**
- Allow outbound FTP traffic when URL server is down: **Checked**

Example 4-24 shows the complete configuration for Cisco ASA used in this deployment. Some configuration output is removed for brevity.

Example 4-24 *ASA's Full Configuration Using a URL-Filtering Server*

```
Chicago# show running
! GigabitEthernet0/0 interface set as outside
interface GigabitEthernet0/0
 nameif outside
 security-level 0
 ip address 209.165.200.225 255.255.255.224
! GigabitEthernet0/1 interface set as inside
interface GigabitEthernet0/1
 nameif inside
 security-level 100
 ip address 209.165.202.130 255.255.255.224
! GigabitEthernet0/2 interface set as DMZ
interface GigabitEthernet0/2
 nameif dmz
 security-level 50
 ip address 209.165.201.1 255.255.255.224
! Definition of a URL Filtering Server
url-server (dmz) vendor websense host 209.165.201.50 timeout 30 protocol TCP ver-
sion 4 connections 15
! Cache server's responses by allocating 100 KB of memory space
url-cache src_dst 100
! Content filtering of HTTP, HTTPS and FTP traffic
filter url http 209.165.202.128 255.255.255.224 0.0.0.0 0.0.0.0 allow
filter https 443 209.165.202.128 255.255.255.224 0.0.0.0 0.0.0.0 allow
filter ftp 21 209.165.202.128  255.255.255.224 0.0.0.0 0.0.0.0 allow
! buffer replies from the remote content server and to store up to 128 packets
url-block block 128
```

Monitoring Network Access Control

The **show** commands provided by Cisco ASA are extremely useful both in checking the health and status of the hardware and in isolating network-related issues. The necessary **show** commands to manage network access control are discussed in the following two sections.

Monitoring ACLs

Cisco ASA provides the **show access-list** command to determine whether the packets are passing through the configured ACLs. When a packet is matched against an ACE, the security appliance increments the **hitcnt** (hit count) counter by one. This is useful if you want to know what ACEs are heavily used in your network.. Example 4-25 shows the output of an ACL called **outside_access_in.** If object groups are used and the **show access-list outside_access_in** command is executed, Cisco ASA expands and displays all the ACEs that are otherwise grouped into protocols, networks, and services. As shown in this example, the security appliance processed 1009 packets in the sixth ACE where the packets were denied and logged by the ACE.

Example 4-25 *Output of* show access-list outside_access_in

```
Chicago(config)# show running-config access-list outside_access_in
access-list outside_access_in extended permit tcp any object-group DMZWebServers
eq www
access-list outside_access_in extended permit tcp any object-group
DMZEmailServers eq smtp
access-list outside_access_in extended deny ip any any log
Chicago(config)# exit
Chicago(config)# show access-list outside_access_in
access-list outside_access_in; 6 elements; name hash: 0xb96d481d
access-list outside_access_in line 1 extended permit tcp any object-group
DMZWebServers eq www 0x15369b29
access-list outside_access_in line 1 extended permit tcp any host 209.165.201.10
eq www (hitcnt=9) 0x2bb79574
access-list outside_access_in line 1 extended permit tcp any host 209.165.201.11
eq www (hitcnt=100) 0xf1219a41
access-list outside_access_in line 1 extended permit tcp any host 209.165.201.12
eq www (hitcnt=24) 0x6fea99cb
access-list outside_access_in line 2 extended permit tcp any object-group
DMZEmailServers eq smtp 0xe22d55da
access-list outside_access_in line 2 extended permit tcp any host 209.165.201.20
eq smtp (hitcnt=3) 0x5000ae48
access-list outside_access_in line 2 extended permit tcp any host 209.165.201.21
eq smtp (hitcnt=199) 0x4dbaed00
access-list outside_access_in line 3 extended deny ip any any log informational
interval 300 (hitcnt=1009) 0xecd4916b
```

Tip The security appliance assigns a unique hash to each:

- ACL such as 0xb96d481d is assigned to ACL **outside_access_in.**
- Object-group ACE such as 0x15369b29 is assigned to the DMZWebServers entry.
- Expanded object-group entry such as 0x2bb79574 is assigned to the ACE used for 209.165.201.10.

If you are interested to see hit counts for a specific ACE entry and you know its associated hash, you can use the **show access-list | include** followed by the hash number.

To reset the hit-count counters, you can issue the **clear access-list** *<ACL_name>* **counters** command, as shown in Example 4-26, in which the counters for the **outside_access_in** ACL are being cleared.

Example 4-27 *Resetting Hit-Count Counters with* **clear access-list counters**

```
Chicago(config)# clear access-list outside_access_in counters
```

If you are using ASDM, you can monitor the ACL usage by going to **Configuration > Firewall > Access Rules** and monitoring the **Hits** column next to each ACL entry. Unlike the **show access-list** command, where it expands each ACL entry, the hit count information via ASDM shows only packets matching the ACL entries with object-groups as shown in Figure 4-22. ASDM also shows the top 10 ACL entries of an access control list. Want to reset the ACL hit counts? Click the **Clear Hits** option.

If a UDP, TCP, or ICMP packet is allowed to pass through the security appliance, a connection entry is created, which can be shown by using the **show conn** command, as displayed in Example 4-27.

Example 4-27 *Output of* **show conn**

```
Chicago# show conn
3 in use, 17 most used
UDP outside 209.165.201.10:53 inside 209.165.202.130:53376 idle 0:00:01 flags -
TCP outside 209.165.201.10:23 inside 209.165.202.130:11080 idle 0:00:02 bytes 108
flags UIO
ICMP outside 209.165.201.10:0 inside 209.165.202.130:15467 idle 0:00:00 bytes 72
```

The first column of the connection entry displays the protocol used, followed by **outside** and an IP address to indicate the IP address of the outside host and then **inside** and an IP address to display the inside hosts' IP addresses. It also shows the source and destination Layer 4 ports. The security appliance shows the idle timer per connection in hours, minutes, and seconds. The most important information to look at is the flags counter, which

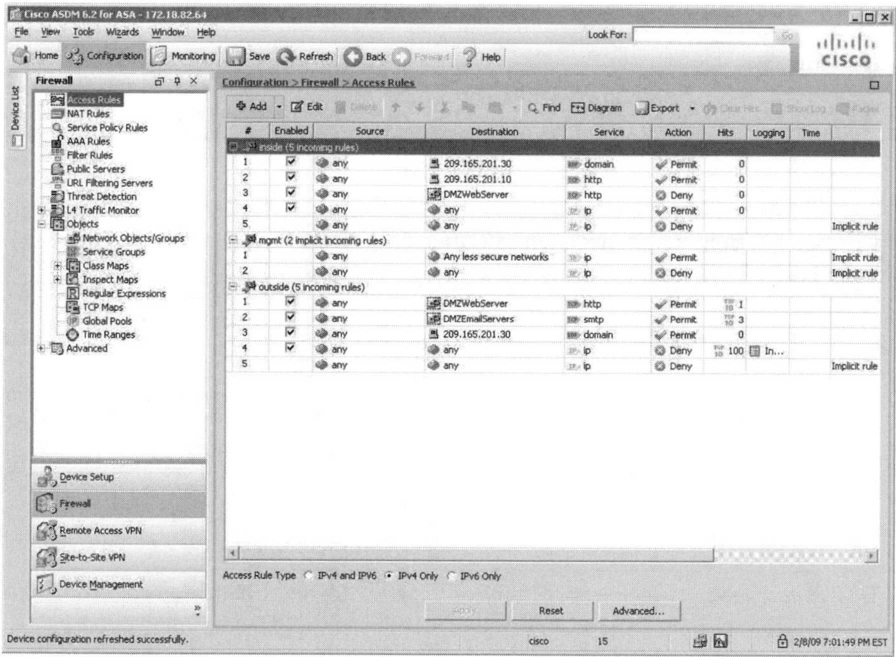

Figure 4-22 *Viewing ACL Hit Counts via ASDM*

has the information about the current state of the connection. Table 4-11 lists and describes all the flags. The highlighted TCP entry, in Example 4-28, has flags set to **UIO** to indicate that the connection is up and is passing traffic in both inbound and outbound directions.

Cisco ASA can act as a sniffer to gather information about the packets passing through the interfaces. This is important if you want to confirm that traffic from a particular host or network is reaching the interfaces. You can use an ACL to identify the type of traffic and bind it to an interface by using the **capture** command.

In Example 4-28, an ACL, called **inside-capture**, is set up to identify packets sourced from **209.165.202.130** and destined for **209.165.200.230**. The security appliance is using this ACL to capture the identified traffic on the **inside** interface, using a capture list named **cap-inside**.

To view the captured packets, use the **show capture** command followed by the name of the capture list. In Example 4-28, the security appliance captured 15 packets that matched the ACL on the inside interface. The highlighted entry shows that it is a TCP SYN (shown as "S" after the destination port) packet sourced from 209.165.202.130 with a source port of 11084 and it is destined for 209.165.200.230 on destination port 23. The TCP window size is 4128, whereas the Maximum Segment Size (MSS) is set to 536 bytes.

Table 4-11 *Description of Flags in the* **show conn** *Command Output*

Flag	Description	Flag	Description
a	Awaiting outside ACK to SYN	A	Awaiting inside ACK to SYN
b	TCP state bypass (this flag was added in version 8.2)	B	Initial SYN from outside
C	Computer Telephony Interface Quick Buffer Encoding (CTIQBE) media connection	D	DNS
d	Dump	E	Outside back connection
F	Outside FIN	f	Inside FIN
G	Connection is part of a group	g	Media Gateway Control Protocol (MGCP) connection
H	H.323 packet	h	H.225 packet
I	Inbound data	i	Incomplete TCP or UDP connection
K	GTP t3-response	k	Skinny Client Control Protocol (SCCP) media connection
m	SIP media connection	M	SMTP data
O	Outbound data	P	Inside back connection
p	Replicated (unused)	q	SQL*NET data
r	Inside acknowledged FIN	R	Outside acknowledged FIN for TCP connection or UDP RPC
s	Awaiting outside SYN	S	Awaiting inside SYN
t	SIP transient connection	T	SIP connection
U	Up	V	VPN orphan
W	WAAS	X	Inspected by a services module such as a CSC SSM

Note When the **capture** command is enabled, the security appliance allocates memory right away. The default memory allocation is 512 KB. The security appliance can overwrite content when the allocated memory is full by removing the oldest entry first. The **capture** command has minimal CPU impact and therefore it is one of the most important troubleshooting tools available in Cisco ASA.

Example 4-28 *Packet Capturing*

```
Chicago(config)# access-list inside-capture permit ip host 209.165.202.130 host
209.165.200.230
Chicago(config)# capture cap-inside access-list inside-capture interface inside
Chicago(config)# show capture cap-inside
15 packets captured
1: 02:12:47.142189 209.165.202.130.11084 > 209.165.200.230.23: S
433720059:433720059(0) win 4128 <mss 536>
   2: 02:12:47.163489 209.165.202.130.11084 > 209.165.200.230.23: . ack
1033049551 win 4128
!Output omitted for brevity
15 packets shown
```

The output of the **capture** command can be exported into pcap format, which can be imported into a sniffing tool such as Wireshark or TCPDUMP for further analysis. To download the file in pcap format, use **https://<IPAddressOfASA>/capture/<CaptureName>/pcap** in a browser. For example, to download the pcap file for the capture defined in Example 4-28, use **https://172.18.82.64/capture/cap-inside/pcap.**

Tip If you want to see traffic in real time, you can use the **real-time** keyword in the capture. For example, the **capture** command in Example 4-29 can be defined for real-time traffic analysis as **capture out-inside access-list inside-capture interface inside real-time.** Even though real-time capturing is extremely useful in troubleshooting traffic-related issues, the security appliance displays up to only 1000 packets in case of excessive traffic load.

If the security appliance is dropping packets but you are not sure of the reason, look at the asp (accelerated security path) drop counter by issuing the **show asp drop** command, as shown in Example 4-29.

Example 4-29 *Output of* show asp drop

```
Chicago# show asp drop
Frame drop:
  Flow is denied by configured rule (acl-drop)                        1087795
  First TCP packet not SYN (tcp-not-syn)                                  618
  Interface is down (interface-down)                                        3
Last clearing: Never
```

You can see that the security appliance has dropped over a million packets because they were denied by the ACLs. Over 600 packets were dropped because the adaptive security appliance received a non-SYN packet as the first packet of a connection. This usually occurs when the client and server believe that a connection was opened but the firewall has already closed that session. Finally, the security appliance dropped three packets when the interface's link was down.

Note The security appliance allows you to capture on a specific drop type or on all ASP drop types through the **capture** command, as follows:

```
Chicago# capture AspCapture type asp-drop ?

  acl-drop                                         Flow is denied by configured rule
  all                                              All packet drop reasons
  bad-crypto                                       Bad crypto return in packet
<output removed for brevity>
```

Monitoring Content Filtering

If the security appliance is set up to filter traffic by inspecting URLs, you can view the packet-filtering statistics to ensure that any non-allowed traffic is denied. Use the **show url-server statistics** command to check how many packets have been allowed and dropped based on the responses from the URL server (such as Websense). In Example 4-30, the security appliance has denied 9000 URL (HTTP) attempts because of restricted or blocked content, whereas it has allowed 161,302 requests. The status of the Websense server is up, which indicates that there is a bidirectional communication channel between the server and the security appliance.

Example 4-30 *Output of* **show url-server statistics**

```
Chicago# show url-server statistics
URL Server Statistics:
----------
Vendor                               websense
URLs total/allowed/denied          170302/161302/9000
HTTPSs total/allowed/denied        1765/876/889
FTPs total/allowed/denied          10/8/2
URL Server Status:
--------
209.165.201.50               UP
URL Packets Sent and Received Stats:
------------------.
Message                        Sent     Received
STATUS_REQUEST                496908   482321
LOOKUP_REQUEST                170694   170603
LOG_REQUEST                   0         NA
------------------.
```

If URL caching is enabled, as in the case of the deployment scenario, you can collect statistics such as allocated memory for this purpose. In Example 4-31, the security appliance shows that the total maximum number of cached URLs is 171, the total number of active URLs in the cache is 100, the total lookups it performed is 456, and the number of packets that matched the cached URLs is 306.

Example 4-31 *Output of* show url-cache statistics

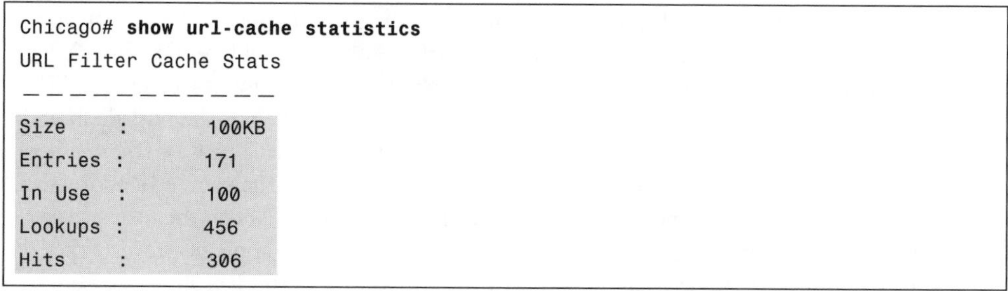

```
Chicago# show url-cache statistics
URL Filter Cache Stats
----------------------
Size     :    100KB
Entries  :    171
In Use   :    100
Lookups  :    456
Hits     :    306
```

Understanding Address Translation

Cisco ASA, being a security device, can mask the network address on the trusted side from the untrusted networks. This technique, commonly referred to as *address translation,* allows an organization to hide the internal addressing scheme from the outside by displaying a different IP address space. Address translation is useful in the following network deployments:

- You use a private addressing scheme internally and want to assign global routable addresses to those hosts.
- You change to a service provider that requires you to modify your addressing scheme. Rather than redesigning the entire IP infrastructure, you implement translation on the border appliance.
- For security reasons, you do not want to advertise the internal addressing scheme to the outside hosts.
- You have multiple internal networks that require Internet connectivity through the security appliance, but only one global address (or a few) is available for translation.
- You have overlapping networks in your organization and you want to provide connectivity between the two without modifying the existing addressing scheme.

Cisco ASA supports two types of address translation, namely *Network Address Translation* (NAT) and *Port Address Translation* (PAT).

The following sections discuss the two address translation types, packet flow sequence, security protection in address translation, NAT and security levels, configuration steps, ways to bypass address translation, and address translation order of operation.

Network Address Translation

Network Address Translation (NAT) defines a one-to-one address mapping when a packet passes through the security appliance and matches criteria for translation. The security appliance either assigns a static IP address (static NAT) or allocates an address from a pool of addresses (dynamic NAT).

Cisco ASA can translate an internal address to a global address when packets are destined for the public network. With this method, also known as *inside NAT*, the security appliance converts the global address of the return traffic to the original internal address. Inside NAT is used when traffic originates from a higher-security interface, such as the inside interface, and is destined for a lower-security interface, such as the outside interface. In Figure 4-23, a host on the internal network, 192.168.10.10, sends traffic to a host on the outside network, 209.165.201.1. The Cisco ASA converts the source IP address to 209.165.200.226 while keeping the destination IP address intact. When the web server responds to the global IP address, 209.165.200.226, the security appliance reverts the global IP address to the original internal real IP address of 192.168.10.10.

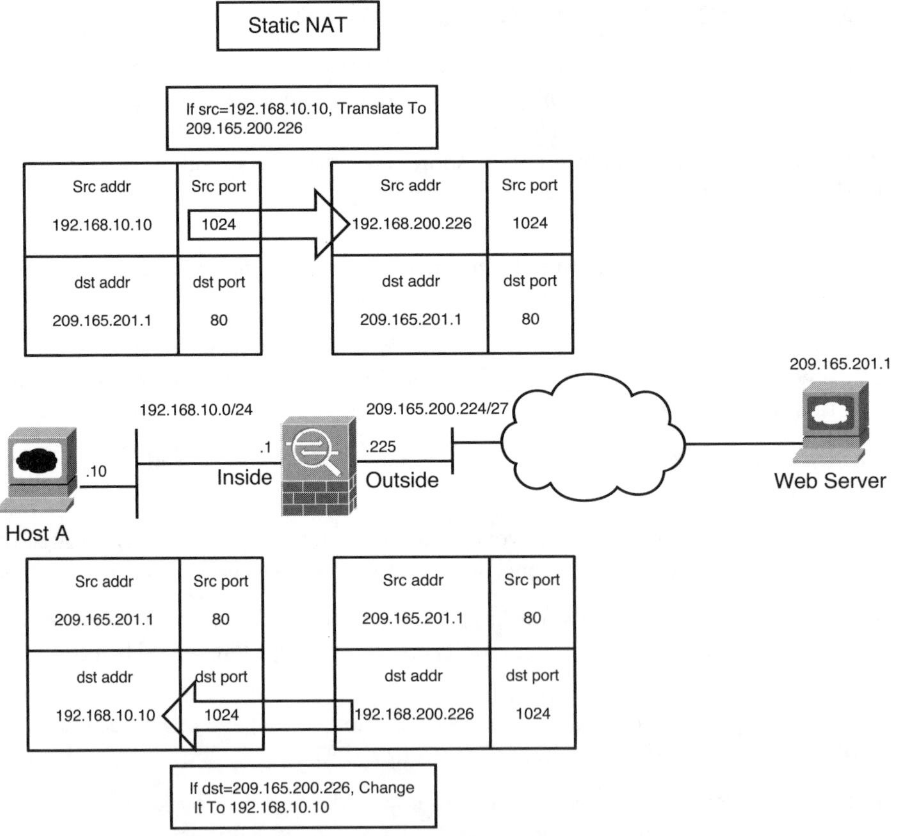

Figure 4-23 *Inside Network Address Translation*

Optionally, the hosts on the lower-security interface can be translated when traffic is destined for a host on the higher-security interface. This method, known as *outside NAT*, is useful when you want a host on the outside network to appear as one of the internal IP addresses. In Figure 4-24, a host on the outside network, 209.165.201.1, sends traffic to a host on the inside network, 192.168.10.10, by using its global IP address as the destination address. Cisco ASA converts the source IP address to 192.168.10.100 while changing the destination IP address to 192.168.10.10. Because both the source and destination IP addresses are changing, this is also *Bidirectional NAT.*

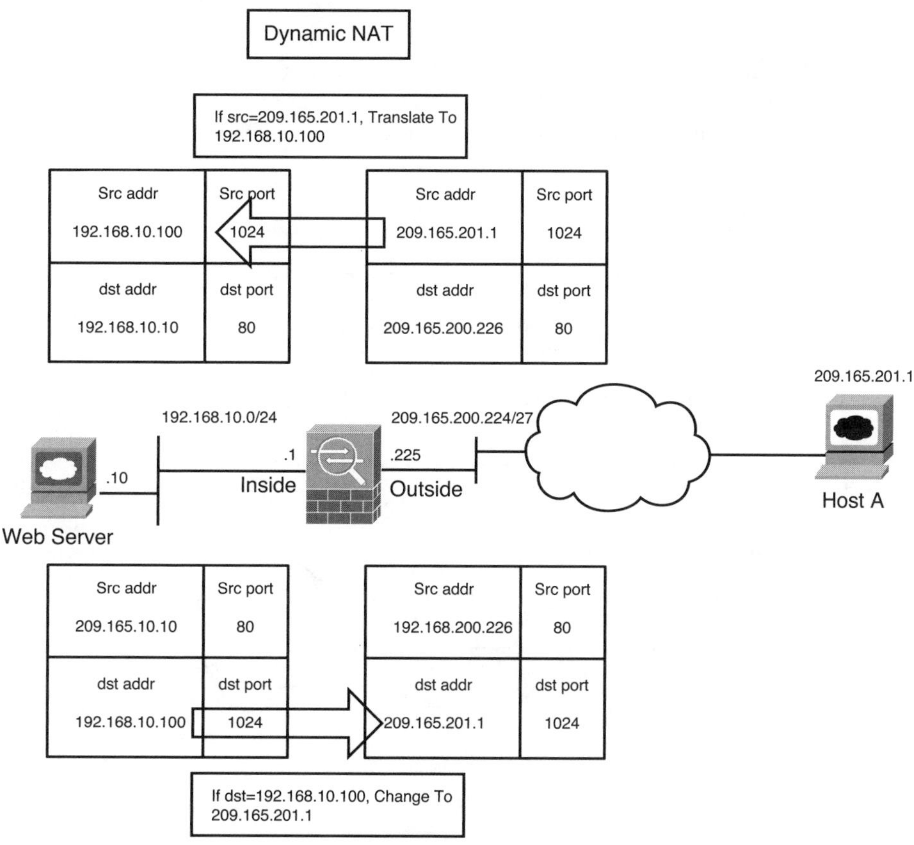

Figure 4-24 *Outside Network Address Translation*

Note If the packets are denied by the interface ACLs, the security appliance does not build the corresponding address translation table entry.

Port Address Translation

Port Address Translation (PAT) defines a many-to-one address mapping when a packet passes through the security appliance and matches criteria for translation. The security appliance creates the translation table by looking at the Layer 4 information in the header to distinguish between the inside hosts using the same global IP address.

Figure 4-25 illustrates an appliance set up for PAT for the inside network of 192.168.10.0/24. However, only one global address is available for translation. If two inside hosts, 192.168.10.10 and 192.168.10.20, require connectivity to an outside host, 209.165.201.1, the security appliance builds the translation table by evaluating the Layer 4 header information. In this case, because both inside hosts have the same source port number, the security appliance assigns a random source port number to keep both entries unique from each other. This way, when the response from the web server returns to the security appliance, the security appliance knows to which inside host to forward the packets.

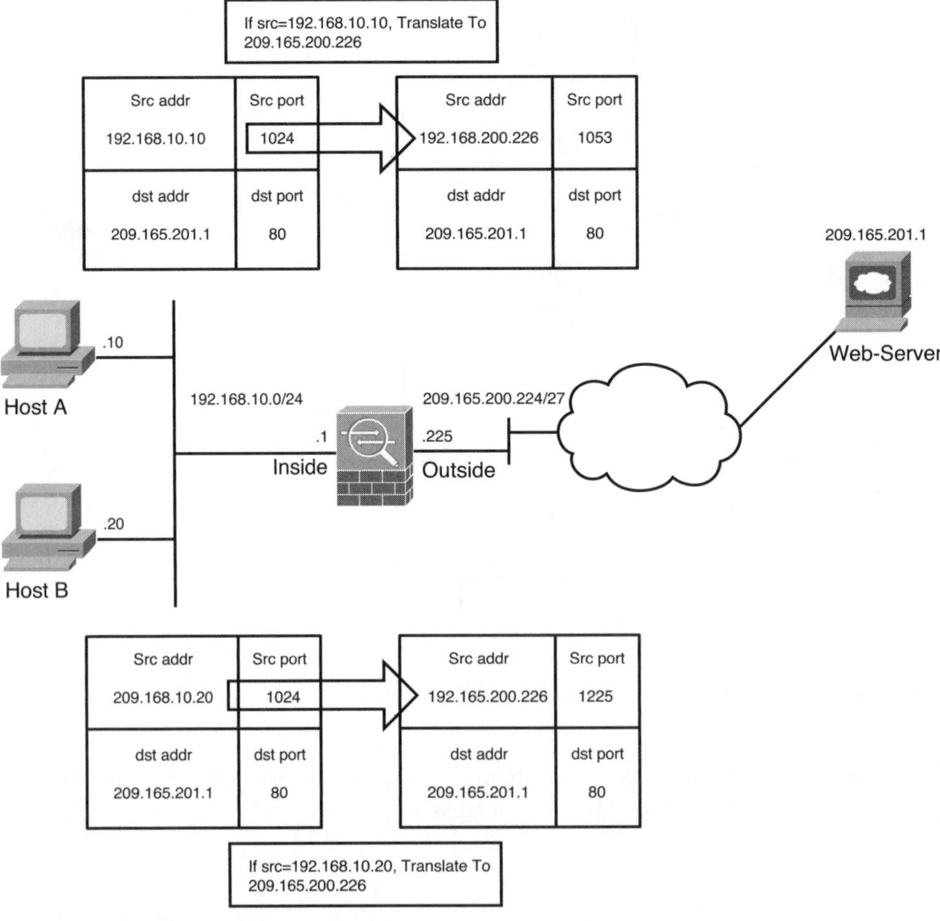

Figure 4-25 *Port Address Translation*

Address Translation and Interface Security Levels

By default, Cisco ASA does not require an address translation policy to be created when the inside machines (host toward the higher security–level interface) need to access the hosts on the outside network (resources toward the lower security–level interface). However, if a packet matches a NAT/PAT policy, the security appliance translates the address. If packets do not match a policy, they are sent out without being translated.

Some organizations mandate that a translation policy be defined before hosts can send traffic through their firewalls. To meet that requirement, you can enable the **nat-control** feature on the security appliance. If implemented, any traffic trying to pass through the security appliance without an address translation policy is dropped. Even if you do not want to translate an address but the **nat-control** feature is turned on, you must define a policy to bypasss address translation. Table 4-12 discusses the NAT behavior with or with the **nat-control** feature when traffic is originated from different security-level interfaces.

Table 4-12 *Security Levels and NAT-Control Feature*

Traffic Direction	NAT Control Disabled	NAT Control Enabled
From low security–level interface to high security–level interface Or, From high security–level interface to low security–level interface	No address translation policy is required for translating the inside IP addresses. If traffic matches a policy, address is translated based on the configured policy.	Address translation policy is required for translating the inside IP addresses. If traffic does not match a policy, address is dropped by ASA and a log message of 305005 is generated.
Between same security–level interfaces[1]	No address translation policy is required. If traffic matches a policy, address is translated based on the configured policy.	No address translation policy is required. If traffic matches a policy, address is translated based on the configured policy.

[1]Assuming that you allow communication between interfaces with the same security level. You need the **same-security-traffic permit inter-interface** command to achieve this.

As mentioned in Table 4-12, address translation is not required when traffic passes between the same security–level interfaces, even if the NAT-control feature is enabled. However, if you define a dynamic NAT/PAT policy with the NAT-control feature enabled, then the security appliance performs address translation for the traffic passing between the same security-level interfaces.

Note If NAT rules are defined on the same security interfaces, then the security appliance does not support any voice over IP (VoIP) inspection engines such as Skinny, SIP, and H.323. Traffic flows from one of the same security interfaces to a different security–level interface are still inspected even if NAT rules are defined.

Packet Flow Sequence

When a packet passes through an appliance configured for address translation, the following sequence of events occurs:

Step 1. The packet arrives at the ingress interface from the end host.

Step 2. The security appliance checks to see whether the packet is a part of an existing connection. If it matches an existing connection, the processing function skips to step 4. If the packet is not a part of an existing connection, and that packet is the first packet in a flow (for example, a SYN packet for TCP), the packet is evaluated against the inbound ACL applied on the ingress interface.

Step 3. If the packet is allowed in, the security appliance first checks to see whether a translation with a global IP matching the destination of the packet exists on the interface where the packet is received. A quick route lookup is done only to determine egress interface. If there is a match, the packet is "virtually forwarded" to the interface of the translated address, skipping the global routing table check. If there is no translation matching the destination IP of the packet on that ingress interface, proceed to step 4.

Step 4. If address translation is enabled and the packet matches the translation criteria, the security appliance creates a translation for the host.

Step 5. On the egress interface, the security appliance consults the routing table to ensure only routes pointing to the egress interface are eligible.

Step 6. The security appliance creates a stateful connection entry for the TCP and UDP packets. The security appliance can, optionally, create a stateful connection entry for ICMP traffic if ICMP inspection is turned on.

Step 7. On the egress interface, packet is transmitted on the physical interface.

Security Protection Mechanisms Within Address Translation

Address translation not only masquerades the original IP address; it also provides protection against TCP connection hijacking for hosts with weak SYN implementation. When a packet enters the higher-security interface and is destined for a lower-security interface during the TCP three-way handshake, the security appliance randomizes the original sequence numbers used by the hosts. This process is illustrated in Figure 4-26. When the host 192.168.10.10 sends a TCP SYN HTTP packet to host 209.165.201.1 with an Initial Sequence Number (ISN) of "12345678", the Cisco ASA changes the source IP address to 209.165.200.226 and also modifies the ISN to a randomly generated value of "a1b2e3c4".

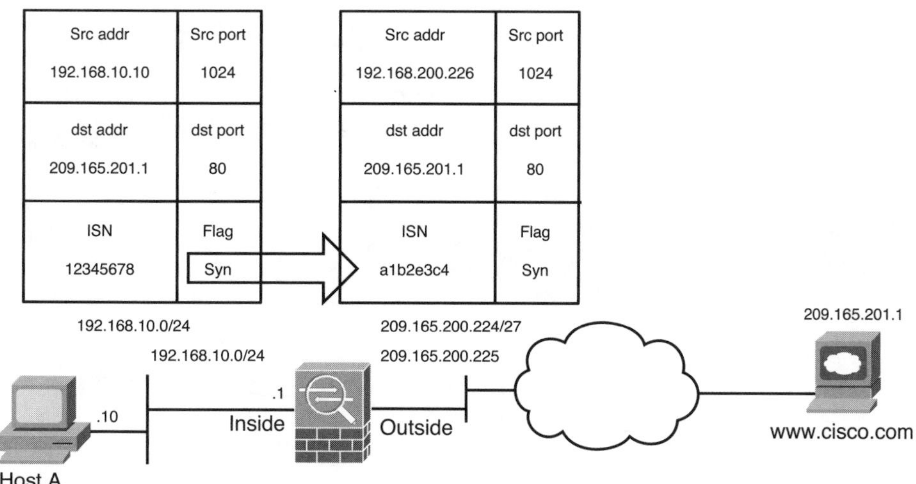

Figure 4-26 *Randomization of ISN*

In some deployment scenarios, such as BGP peering with MD5 authentication, it is recommended to turn off the randomization of TCP packets. When two routers establish BGP peering with each other, the TCP header and data payload are 128-bit hashed, using the BGP password. When the sequence number is changed, the peering router fails to authenticate the packets because of the mismatched hash. For more information about BGP MD5 authentication, consult RFC 2385.

Cisco ASA also provides protection against certain types of denial of service (DoS) attacks. By using the embryonic and maximum connection limit, the security appliance can restrict the establishment of new connections to the inside servers. An embryonic connection is a half-opened connection from the client to the server during the TCP three-way handshake. When the number of embryonic connections hits the maximum allowed limit, Cisco ASA starts intercepting the SYN packets from the client to the servers. This process of intercepting the TCP packets is known as *TCP interception*. It is illustrated in Figure 4-27 and consists of the following seven steps:

Step 1. The client sends a TCP SYN packet destined for the server.

Step 2. The security appliance responds with an ACK on behalf of the server.

Step 3. The client (if legitimate) acknowledges the receipt of the previous packet; the security appliance marks the connection as valid.

Step 4. The security appliance sends a TCP SYN packet destined to the server.

Step 5. The server responds with an ACK to the security appliance.

Step 6. The security appliance acknowledges the receipt of the previous packet and joins both connections transparently without any user interception.

Step 7. The client and the server pass data traffic.

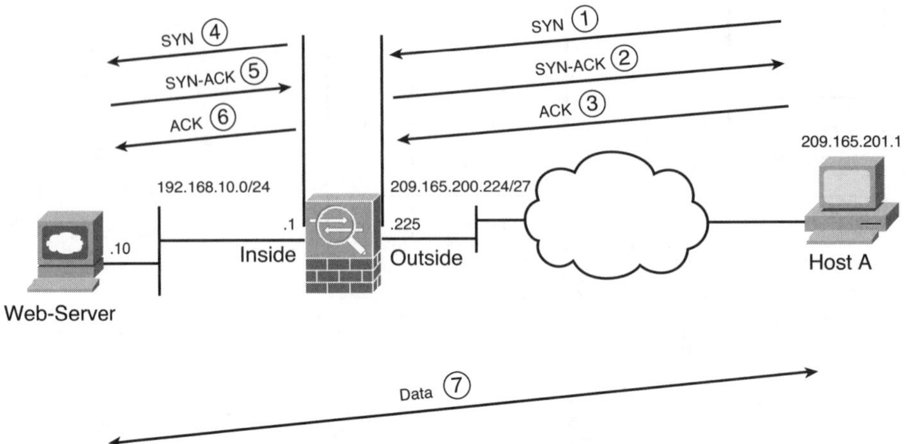

Figure 4-27 *TCP Interception*

Note The TCP intercept feature is enhanced in version 8.0 of the security appliance, where you can now use modular policy framework (MPF) to set connection limits. MPF is discussed in Chapter 7 and then in Chapter 11. An example, shown here, illustrates MPF being used to set the maximum connection limit to **1500** and the embryonic connection limit to **2000** for all traffic traversing the **outside** interface.

```
Chicago(config)# class-map TCPIntercept
Chicago(config-cmap)# match any
Chicago(config-cmap)# policy-map TCPInterceptPolicy
Chicago(config-pmap)# class TCPIntercept
Chicago(config-pmap-c)# set connection conn-max 1500 embryonic-conn-max 2000
Chicago(config-pmap-c)# service-policy TCPInterceptPolicy interface outside
```

The security appliance can also protect network resources from an unexpected increase in the number of connections by setting maximum limits. This is applicable for both TCP- and UDP-based connections.

Configuring Address Translation

Cisco ASA supports the following five types of address translation, each of which is configured uniquely:

- Static NAT
- Dynamic NAT

- Static PAT
- Dynamic PAT
- Policy NAT/PAT

Static NAT

Static NAT defines a fixed translation of an inside host or subnet address to a global routable address or subnet. The security appliance uses the one-to-one methodology by assigning one global IP address to one inside IP address. Thus, if 100 hosts residing on the inside network require address translation, the security appliance should be configured for 100 global IP addresses. Additionally, the inside hosts are assigned the same IP address whenever the security appliance translates the packets going through it. This is a recommended solution in scenarios in which an organization provides services such as email, web, DNS, and FTP for outside users. Using static NAT, the servers use the same global IP address for all the inbound and outbound connections.

Define a static entry via ASDM by navigating to **Configuration > Firewall > NAT Rules > Add > Add Static NAT Rule**. A new window opens where you can specify the following attributes:

- **Original Interface**—Specify the interface where the real host or network exists. It is the higher-security interface (such as inside or DMZ) if inside NAT is used or the lower-security interface (such as outside) if outside NAT is implemented. In Figure 4-24, the original host (192.168.10.10) is connected toward the inside interface. If you want to translate its IP address, select **inside** from the drop-down menu.
- **Original Source**—Specify the real or pre-translated IP address of the source whose IP address you want to change. Referring back to Figure 4-24, specify **192.168.10.10** as the original source address.
- **Translated Interface**—Select the interface name that owns a host's translated IP address. It is the lower-security interface (such as outside) if inside NAT is used or the higher-security interface if outside NAT is implemented.
- **Translated Use IP Address**—Specify translated or NAT'ed IP address of host. Referring back to Figure 4-24, specify **209.165.200.226** as the translated source address.

In Figure 4-28, a static entry is being created to translate an inside host, **192.168.10.10**, to **209.165.200.226**. The maximum TCP and UDP simultaneous connection limits are set to **1000**, and the embryonic connections are restricted to **100** before the security appliance initiates the TCP intercept mode. The sequence numbers are also randomized. These parameters are defined in the Connection Settings pull-down menu.

If you prefer to use the CLI, the corresponding configuration of Figure 4-28 is shown in Example 4-32.

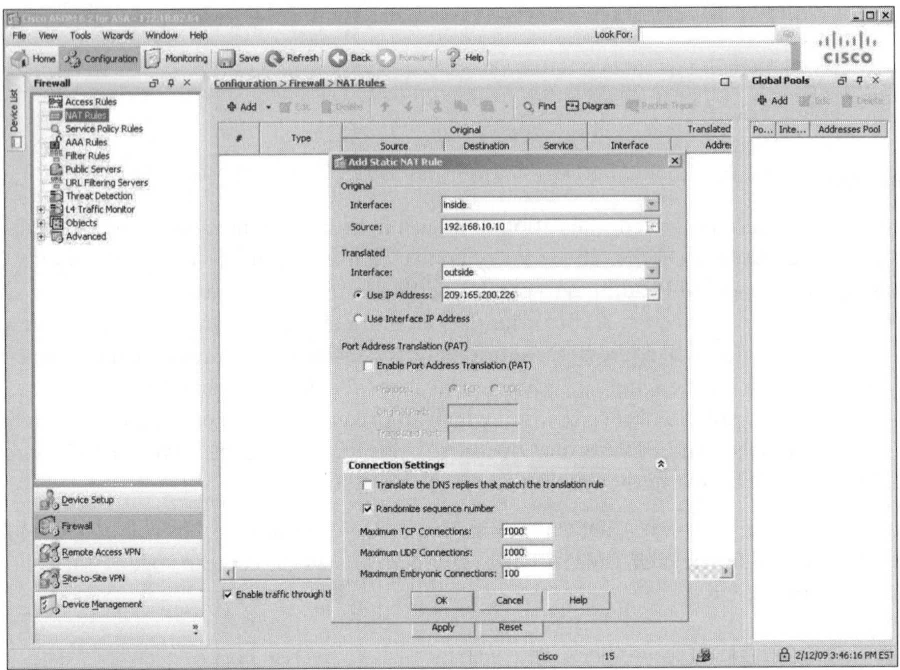

Figure 4-28 *Inside Static NAT*

Example 4-32 *Inside NAT*

```
Chicago(config)# static (inside,outside) 209.165.200.226 192.168.10.10 netmask
255.255.255.255 tcp 1000 100 udp 1000
```

To add a network-based static translation, specify the valid subnets in the **static** command. As shown in Example 4-34, the security appliance is configured to translate the **192.168.10.0/29** subnet to **209.165.200.232/29**. Any host that falls in this range of IP addresses will be assigned an IP address from the 209.165.200.232/29 subnet.

Example 4-33 also illustrates how to set up an outside NAT static entry. An outside host, 209.165.201.1, is translated to an inside address, 192.168.10.100, before the packets enter the inside network.

Example 4-33 *Network-Based Inside Static NAT and Outside Static NAT*

```
Chicago(config)# static (inside,outside) 209.165.200.232 192.168.10.0 netmask
255.255.255.248
Chicago(config)# static (outside,inside) 192.168.10.100 209.165.201.1 netmask
255.255.255.255
```

> **Note** The security appliance does not support outside NAT or PAT if the Cisco CallManager server reside on the inside network and the IP phones connect from the outside network.

Dynamic Network Address Translation

Dynamic NAT assigns a random IP address from a preconfigured pool of global IP addresses. The security appliance uses a one-to-one methodology by allocating one global IP address to an inside IP address. Hence, if 100 hosts reside on the inside network, then you have at least 100 addresses in the pool of addresses. This is a recommended solution in scenarios in which an organization uses protocols that don't contain Layer 4 information, such as Generic Routing Encapsulation (GRE), Reliable Datagram Protocol (RDP), and Data Delivery Protocol (DDP). After the security appliance has built a dynamic NAT for an inside host, any outside machine can connect to the assigned translated address, assuming that the security appliance allows the inbound connection, as discussed in the "Monitoring Network Access Control" section earlier in this chapter.

Configuration of dynamic NAT is a two-step process:

- Defining a global pool
- Mapping the global pool to real addresses

Define a Global Pool

You must define a pool of translated addresses that you want the pre-NAT hosts to use. You can define a pool of addresses by navigating to **Configuration > Firewall > NAT Rules** and clicking **Add** under "Global Pools", located as a tab to the far right. ASDM opens a new window where you can specify the following attributes:

- **Interface**—Select the interface name that owns a host's translated IP address. It is the lower-security interface, such as outside, if inside NAT is used.
- **Pool ID**—This is a positive number between 1 and 65,535 that is linked to the Dynamic NAT statements so that an address can be allocated from the respective global pool.
- **Starting IP Address**—Specify a start address to be assigned to the pre-NAT hosts. Because these entries are dynamically created, the security appliance assigns these addresses in round-robin fashion by assigning this address from the pool first.
- **Ending IP Address**—Specify the last address in the range. After the security appliance assigns the last address to a host, it cannot create additional dynamic NAT translations until a previously allocated address is freed up.
- **Netmask**—Specify a mask for the translated addresses in the range. This attribute is optional because a default mask of the appropriate address class is used if you don't specify a value.

Note Pool ID with a value of 0 (zero) is used to bypass address translation. This option is discussed later in the chapter, in the "Bypassing Address Translation" section.

In Figure 4-29, an administrator wishes to dynamically assign global addresses from a pool of IP addresses ranging from **209.165.200.230** to **209.165.200.237**. The assigned pool ID is **1** and this pool of addresses resides toward the **outside** interface.

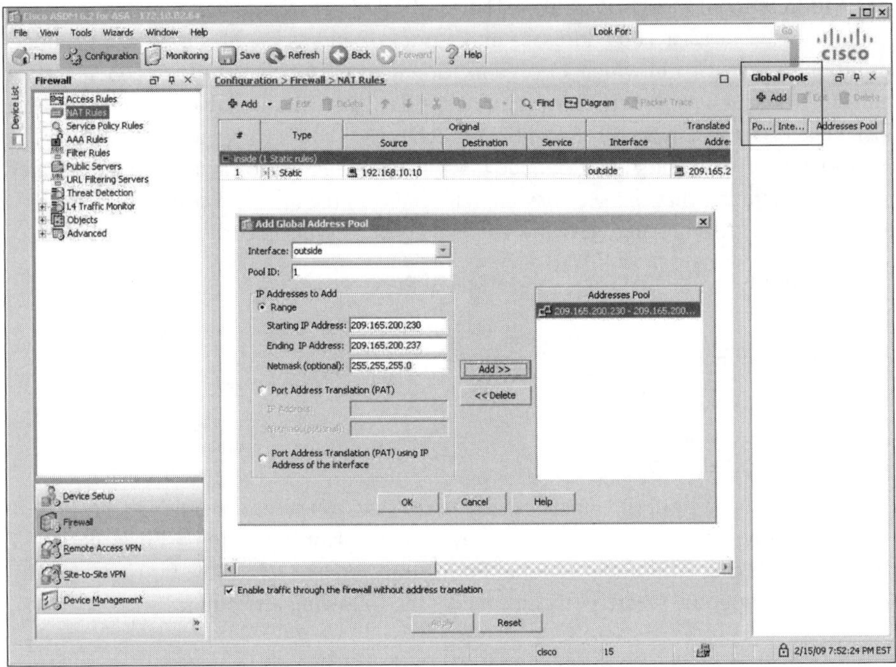

Figure 4-29 *Defining a Global Pool of Addresses*

The CLI equivalent of Figure 4-29 is shown in Example 4-34.

Example 4-34 *Configuration of Global NAT Pool*

```
Chicago(config)# global (outside) 1 209.165.200.230-209.165.200.237 netmask
255.255.255.0
```

Note When address translation is turned on, the security appliance does proxy ARP for the configured translated addresses. Proxy ARP is a process in which the security appliance answers ARP requests on behalf of other addresses.

Map the Global Pool to Real Addresses

After defining the global address pool, the next step is to identify the original host or network address that you want to translate. This network entity is then mapped to the global pool, defined in the previous step, so that a real address can be translated to one of the addresses in the pool. Browse to **Configuration > Firewall > NAT Rules > Add > Add Dynamic NAT Rule** to add the pre-NAT addresses and select a previously defined pool. As illustrated in Figure 4-30, the **inside** subnet of **192.168.10.0/24** is defined as the pre-NAT entity. Under translated global pools, the pool ID of **1** is selected for dynamic NAT.

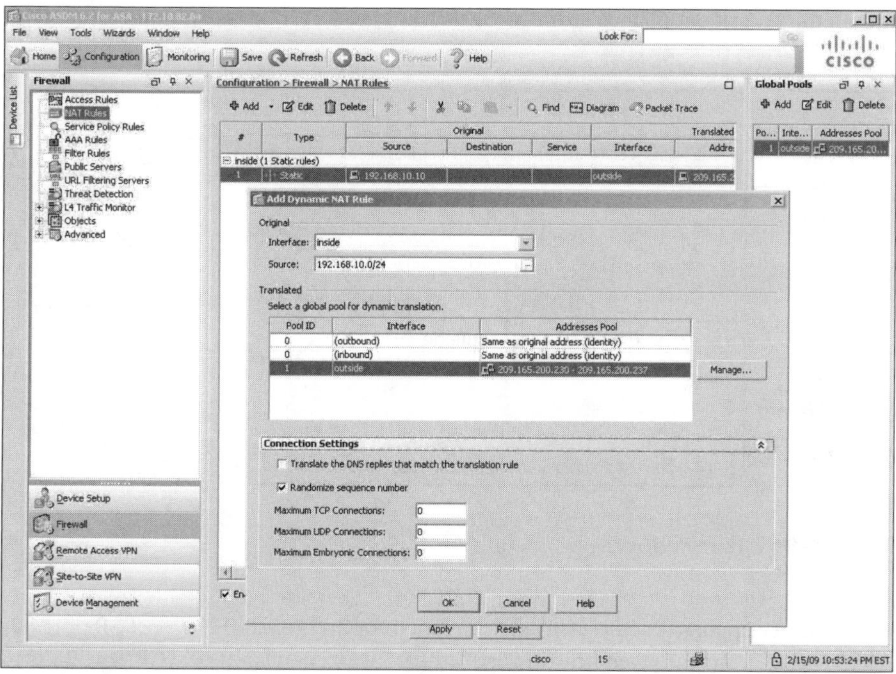

Figure 4-30 *Mapping the Global Pool to Pre-NAT Addresses*

The CLI equivalent of Figure 4-30 is shown in Example 4-35.

Example 4-35 *Configuration of Global NAT Pool*

```
Chicago(config)# nat (inside) 1 192.168.10.0 255.255.255.0
```

Note If you want to define an outside dynamic NAT entry via the CLI, you must add the outside keyword in the **nat** statement after specifying the subnet mask. The **outside** keyword is used only when translating the source of a packet as it moves from a lower to higher security–level interface.

ASDM automatically sends the **outside** keyword command when you define an outside dynamic NAT entry via ASDM. You do not have to manually select any options to set this attribute.

Static Port Address Translation

port redirection, is useful when the security appliance needs to statically map multiple inside servers to one global IP address. Port redirection is applied to traffic when it passes through the security appliance from a lower-security interface to a higher-security interface. The outside hosts connect to the global IP address on a specific TCP or UDP port, which the security appliance redirects to the internal server, as shown in Figure 4-31.

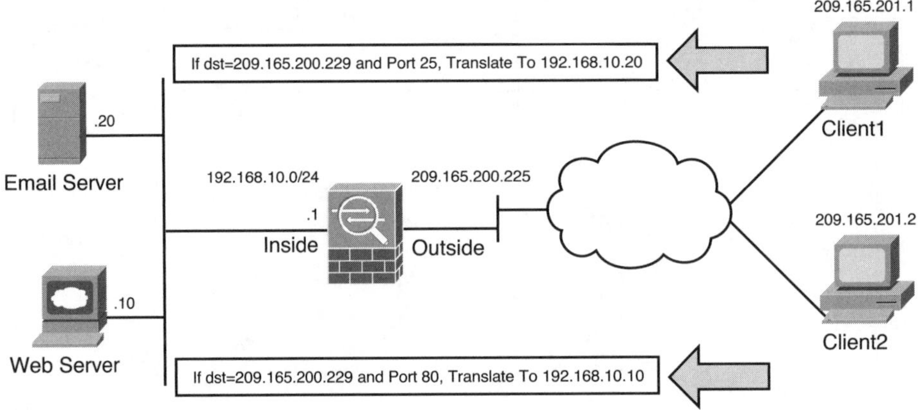

Figure 4-31 *Port Redirection*

The security appliance redirects traffic destined for 209.165.200.229 on TCP port 80 to 192.168.10.10. Similarly, any traffic destined for 209.165.200.229 on TCP port 25 is redirected to 192.168.10.20.

The security appliance allows the use of either a dedicated IP address or the global interface's IP address for port redirection.

When port redirection is set up to use the public interface's IP address, the security appliance uses the same address for

- Address translation for the traffic traversing through the security appliance.
- Traffic destined for the security appliance.

Configuring a static port address translation is similar to defining a static NAT entry. Navigate to **Configuration > Firewall > NAT Rules > Add Static NAT Rule** and specify the real and translated address in the ASDM window. Select the **Enable Port Address Translation (PAT)** option and specify the following attributes:

- **Protocol**—Select the **tcp** and **udp** options in protocols to specify which protocol to consider for address translation.
- **Original Port**—This is the port that the original host is using for its services. For example, if a web server resides on the inside network and uses the default TCP port 80 for web services, then specify 80 as the original port.
- **Translated Port**—This is the port that the outside users connect to when they need to access the original server. For example, if a web server resides on the inside network and uses the default TCP port 80 for web services, but you want the outside users to connect to TCP port 8080 when they need to connect to this server, then specify 8080 as the translated port.

As illustrated in Figure 4-32, a static PAT entry has been defined for an internal web-server located at **192.168.10.10**. The web clients on the public network will connect to the server using the translated address of **209.165.200.229** on TCP port **80**.

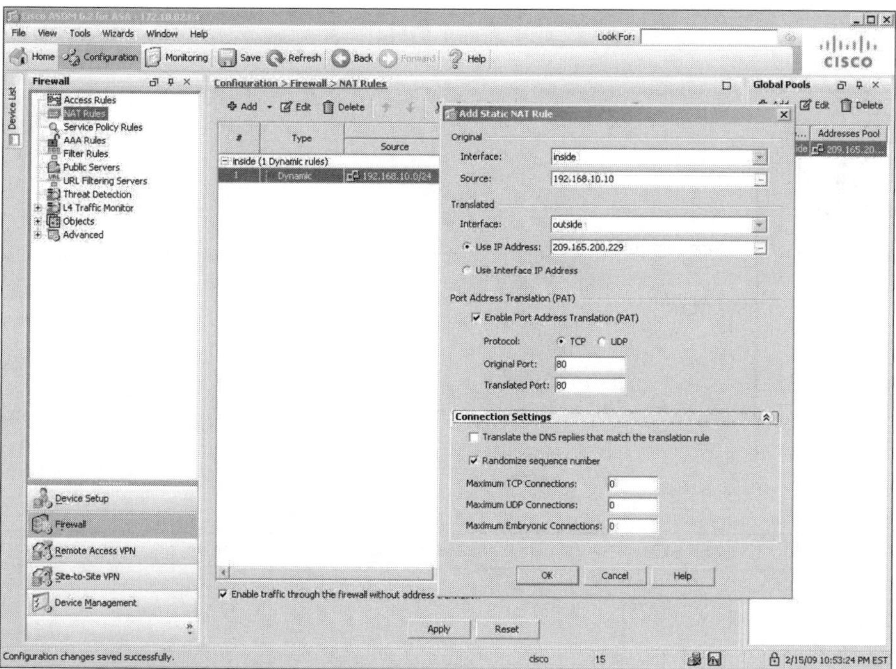

Figure 4-32 *Static PAT*

Example 4-36 shows the CLI equivalent output of the configuration steps discussed in Figure 4-32.

Example 4-36 *Configuration of Static PAT*

```
Chicago(config)# static (inside,outside) tcp 209.165.200.229 80 192.168.10.10 80
netmask 255.255.255.255
```

Dynamic Port Address Translation

Using dynamic PAT, the security appliance builds the address translation table by looking at the Layer 3 and Layer 4 header information. It is the most commonly deployed scenario because multiple inside machines can get outside connectivity through one global IP address. In dynamic PAT, the security appliance uses the source IP addresses, the source ports, and the IP protocol information (TCP or UDP) to translate an inside host. As with static PAT, you have the option of using either a dedicated public address or the IP address of an interface for translations. As shown in Figure 4-33, two inside machines are accessing an external web server, using the IP address of the outside interface.

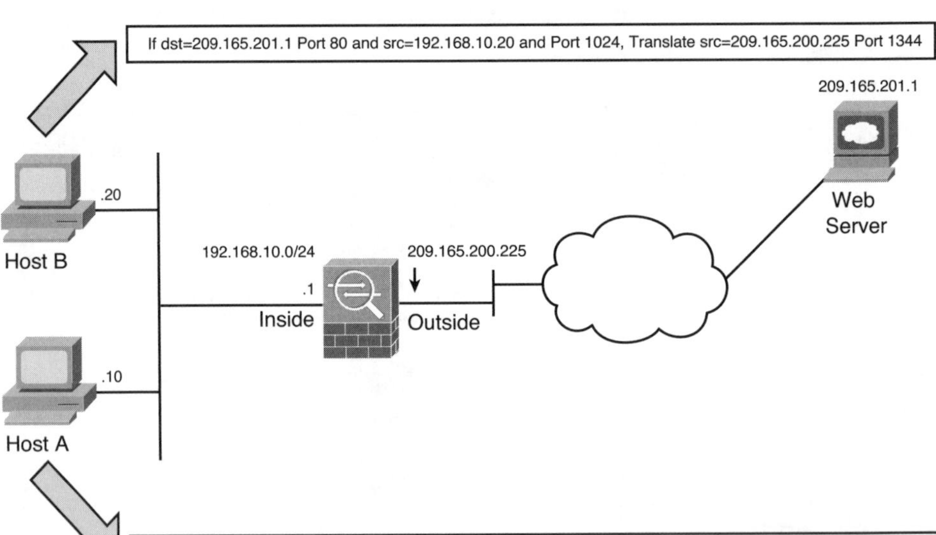

Figure 4-33 *Dynamic PAT*

> **Note** The security appliances randomize the source ports based on an enhancement included in version 8.0(4), 8.1(2), and 8.2(1)

The security appliance supports up to 65,535 PAT translations using a single address. The PAT addresses time out every 30 seconds of inactivity to accommodate as many hosts as possible. The PAT address timeout if non-configurable.

The configuration of dynamic PAT is also a two-step process, similar to setting up a dynamic NAT entry:

- Defining a global PAT entry
- Mapping global pool to real addresses

Define a Global PAT Entry

You must define a public address that you want the inside machines to use for translation. You can define a public address by navigating to **Configuration > Firewall > NAT Rules**, clicking **Add** under "Global Pools" and then selecting either "Port Address Translation (PAT)" or "Port Address Translation (PAT) using IP address of the interface". With the "Port Address Translation (PAT)" option, you can assign a dedicated address to be used by the inside hosts when they need to access resources on the public network. However, the "Port Address Translation (PAT) using IP address of the interface" option uses the IP address of the selected interface for translating inside hosts. Both options analyze the Layer 4 header information within the data packets for creating new translations.

Figure 4-34 illustrates that an administrator is modifying a previously defined global pool. The Pool ID is **1** and already has a range of public addresses from **209.165.200.230** to **209.165.200.237**. The administrator had selected Port **Address Translation (PAT) using IP address of the interface** as the second entry in the pool.

> **Note** If both dynamic NAT and dynamic PAT are set up using the same Pool ID (or NAT-ID if you are using the CLI), then the security appliance tries to allocate addresses from the pool of addresses first. When all the addresses have been allocated, the security appliance starts using dynamic PAT.

Map Global PAT Entry to Real Addresses

After defining the global PAT entry, you must identify the original host or network address that you want to translate, similar to what you do with dynamic NAT. Example 4-37 shows a security appliance set up to translate the inside network, **192.168.10.0/24**, by allocating addresses from the **209.1658.200.230-209.165.200.237** range. It is also using the IP address on the **outside** interface, 209.165.200.225.

Example 4-37 *Configuration of Dynamic PAT*

```
Chicago(config)# nat (inside) 1 192.168.10.0 255.255.255.0
Chicago(config)# global (outside) 1 209.165.200.230-209.165.200.237 netmask
255.255.255.0
Chicago(config)# global (outside) 1 interface
INFO: outside interface address added to PAT pool
```

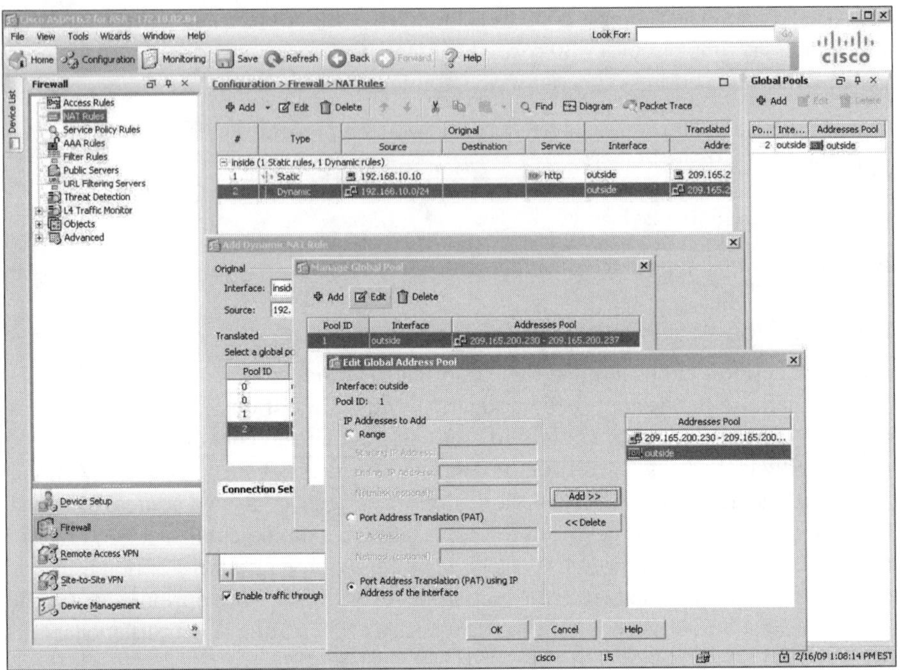

Figure 4-34 *Defining a Global PAT Entry*

Policy NAT/PAT

Policy NAT/PAT translates the IP address of the packets passing through the security appliance only if those packets match a defined criterion or policy. You define the policy by identifying interesting traffic through the use of ACLs. If traffic matches against the defined entries in the ACL, then the original source or destination address can be translated to a different address. As illustrated in Figure 4-35, an administrator has defined a policy to translate the source IP address to 209.165.200.226 if the packets originate from 192.168.10.10 and are destined for 209.165.201.1. Similarly, if the packets are sourced from 192.168.10.10 and destined for a different address, say 209.165.201.2, the security appliance changes the source IP address to 209.165.200.227.

With ASDM, you can set up Policy NAT/PAT for both static and dynamic address translations by navigating to **Configuration > Firewall > NAT Rules > Add** and then selecting either **Add Static Policy NAT Rule** or **Add Dynamic Policy NAT Rule**, respectively. In Figure 4-36 a static policy NAT is being set up to translate the source address from **192.168.10.10** to **209.165.200.226** if the destination address is **209.165.201.1**.

Example 4-38 shows the configuration of static policy NAT where two ACLs are defined to identify the traffic coming from **192.168.10.10** and destined for **209.165.201.1** and **209.165.201.2**. The ACLs are then mapped to the static commands to change the source address to **209.165.200.226** if the destination is **209.165.201.1** and change the source address to **209.165.200.227** if the destination is **209.165.201.2**

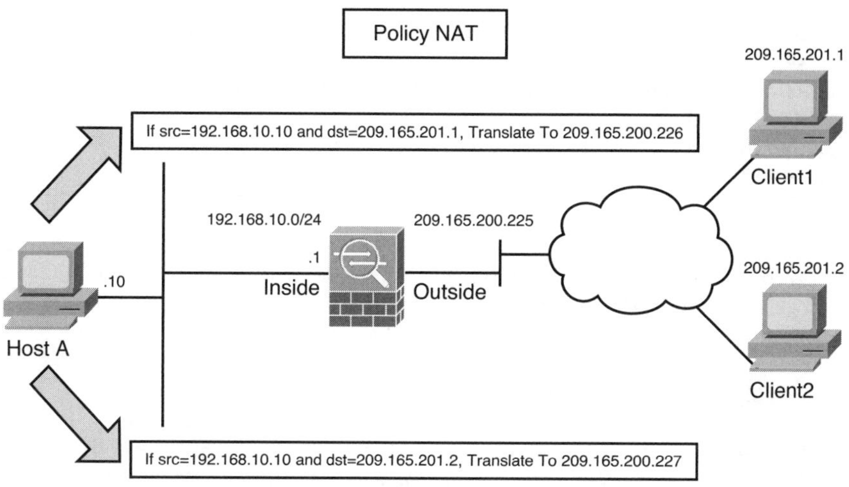

Figure 4-35 *Policy-Based Network Address Translation*

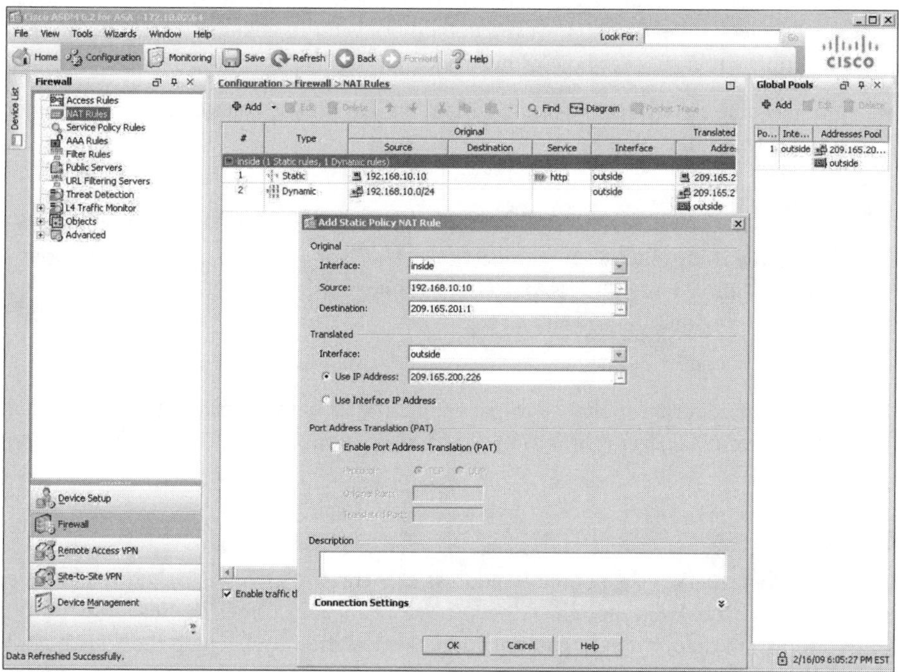

Figure 4-36 *Policy-Based Static NAT*

Example 4-38 *Configuration of Static Policy NAT*

```
Chicago(config)# access-list inside_nat_static_1 permit ip host 192.168.10.10 host
209.165.201.1
```

```
Chicago(config)# access-list inside_nat_static_2 permit ip host 192.168.10.10 host
209.165.201.2
Chicago(config)# static (inside,outside) 209.165.200.226 access-list
inside_nat_static_1
Chicago(config)# static (inside,outside) 209.165.200.227 access-list
inside_nat_static_2
```

Note If host-based static policy NAT entries are defined, the access list should contain only a single source IP address to maintain a one-to-one mapping.

Bypassing Address Translation

In many scenarios you want to bypass address translation so that the security appliance does not change the source or the destination address. You may want to bypass address translation if

- You already have address translation defined for the inside network so that hosts can get internet connectivity. However, you do not want to change their addresses if they send traffic to a specific host or network.
- You have the NAT-control feature turned on, but you do not want to translate hosts on a DMZ or any other interface.

Note Using ASDM, you can enable the NAT-control feature by deselecting the "Enable traffic through the firewall without address translation" option. This option can be found under **Configuration > Firewall > NAT Rules**, as shown in Figure 4-37. With the CLI, you use the **nat-control** command to enable the NAT-control feature.

If you want the security appliance to pass some traffic without translating it, you can use Identity NAT or NAT Exemption to bypass address translation.

Identity NAT

Identity NAT preserves the source IP address as it traverses from a higher to a lower security–level interface. Even though the security appliance translates the real address to the same address, in theory it is bypassing address translation by keeping the source address intact. For example, if you want your inside network to keep the same source address when it sends traffic through the security appliances, you can use identity NAT. With identity NAT, hosts located on the other interfaces such as DMZ or outside cannot initiate traffic unless an entry already exists in the translation table.

If you use ASDM, you can define identity NAT by browsing to **Configuration > Firewall > NAT Rules > Add > Add Dynamic NAT Rule** and then mapping the specified network

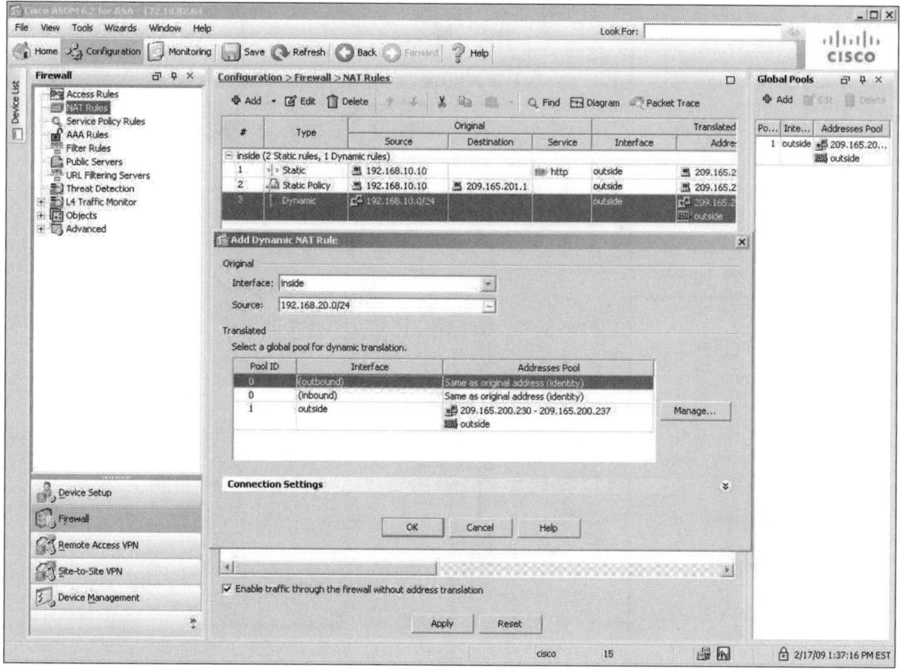

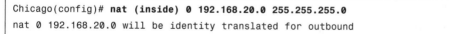

Figure 4-37 *Identity NAT*

to a pool with an ID of "0". In Figure 4-37 an inside network of **192.168.20.0/24** is defined to bypass address translation for all outbound traffic.

When you use the CLI, you enable identity NAT by using the **nat 0** command followed by the host or subnet address to be bypassed for address translation, as shown in Example 4-39. The security appliance does not translate the outbound connections from the inside network, **192.168.20.0/24**.

Example 4-39 *NAT Bypass Using Identity NAT*

```
Chicago(config)# nat (inside) 0 192.168.20.0 255.255.255.0
nat 0 192.168.20.0 will be identity translated for outbound
```

NAT Exemption

NAT exemption bypasses address translation for the network entities identified by an ACL. NAT exemption allows both inside and outside hosts to initiate traffic without their source addresses being translated. In Figure 4-38, a security appliance uses dynamic PAT to translate the inside network to its outside interface. However, the administrator does not want to change the addresses when the two email servers send packets to each other.

To accomplish this task via ASDM, navigate to **Configuration > Firewall > NAT Rules > Add > Add NAT Exempt Rule** and specify the following attributes:

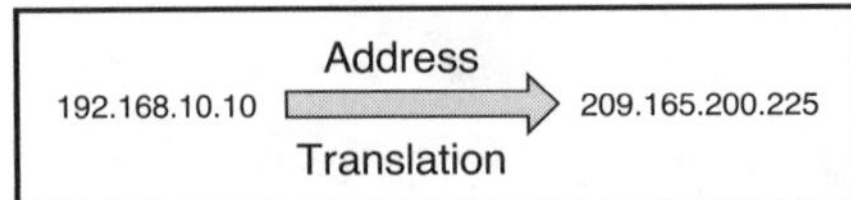

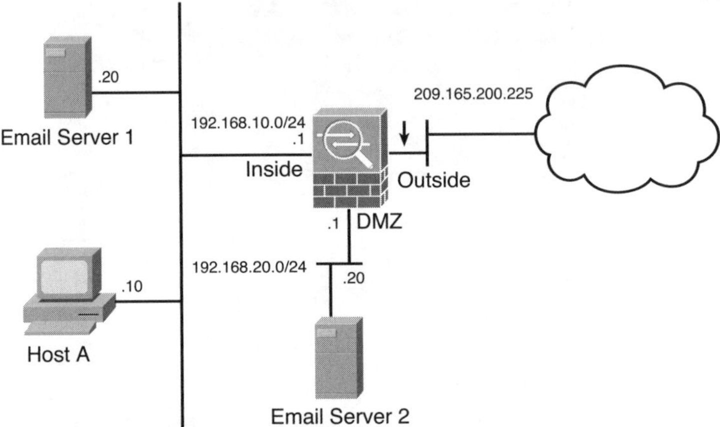

Figure 4-38 *NAT Exemption*

- **Action**—Select **Exempt** if you want to bypass address translation for the traffic matching the rest of the attributes. If you have already defined exceptions for a network and you would rather that a few hosts not be exempted by NAT, you can define another rule and select the **Do Not Exempt** option for those hosts.
- **Interface**—Choose the interface where the hosts with real addresses are connected and need to be exempted by the address translation process. For example, select the inside interface if one of the email servers resides toward that interface.
- **Source**—Specify the source address of the network entity that you want to exempt from NAT.
- **Destination**—Specify the destination address of the network entity that you want to exempt from NAT.
- **NAT Exempt Direction**—Specify the direction of the NAT exemption policy. By default, the "NAT Exempt outbound traffic ..." option is selected which exempts traffic from a higher-security interface to lower-security interface. If you choose the "NAT Exempt inbound traffic..." option then traffic from a lower-security interface to a higher-security interface is exempt.

Note The security appliance processes NAT exemption rules before identity NAT rules.

As shown in Figure 4-39, a NAT exempt policy is defined for traffic flowing from **192.168.10.20** to **192.168.20.20**.

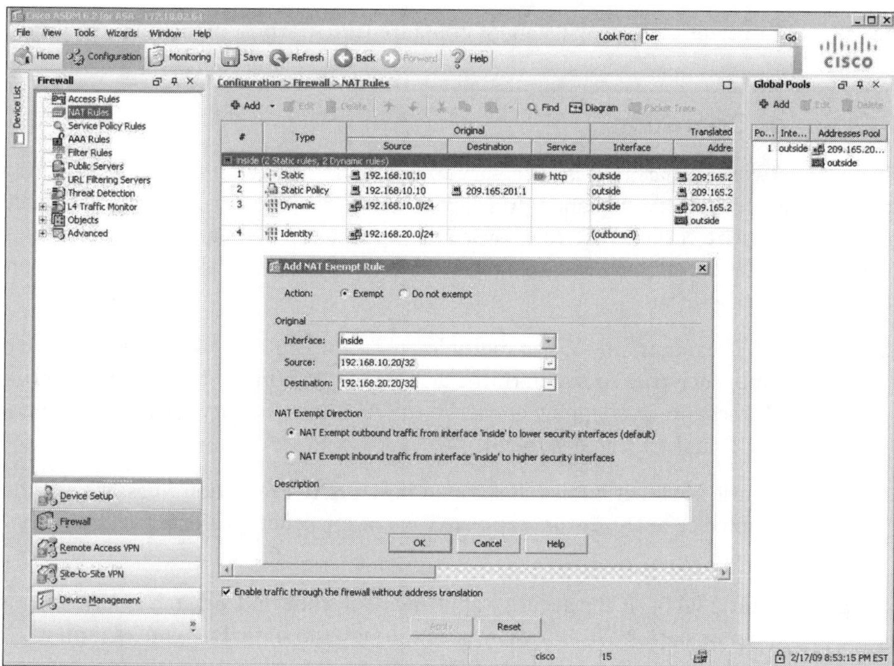

Figure 4-39 *NAT Exempt Policy Definition*

Using CLI, you must define an ACL first to identify interesting traffic and then apply that ACL to the **nat 0** statement, as shown in Example 4-40. An ACL called **EmailServers** identifies the two email servers and then it is linked to the **nat 0** statement bound to the inside interface. All other traffic from the inside 192.168.10.0/24 network is translated to the outside interface's IP address.

Example 4-40 *NAT Bypass Using NAT Exemption*

```
Chicago(config)# access-list EmailServers extended permit ip host 192.168.10.20
host 192.168.20.20
Chicago(config)# nat (inside) 0 access-list EmailServers
Chicago(config)# nat (inside) 1 192.168.10.0 255.255.255.0
Chicago(config)# global (outside) 1 interface
```

The main difference between identity NAT and NAT exemption is that with identity NAT, the inside hosts must first send traffic outbound, building the identity translation, before outside hosts can respond to that host, whereas with NAT exemption, traffic can be initiated by the hosts on either side of the security appliance. NAT exemption is a preferred method to bypass traffic when it is flowing over a VPN tunnel. This will be discussed in Chapter 16, "Site-to-Site IPSec VPNs," and Chapter 17, "IPSec Remote Access VPNs."

> **Note** In NAT exemption, the ACL cannot contain TCP/UDP port numbers.

NAT Order of Operation

In many network scenarios, it is necessary to configure different types of address translation on a single security appliance. To adapt to those scenarios, the security appliance needs to prioritize certain NAT rules over others to make sure that it knows what to do if there is a conflict. You must maintain the order of these rules as listed below to ensure they are properly set up:

Step 1. **NAT exemption**—When multiple NAT types/rules are set up, the security appliance tries to match traffic against the ACL in the NAT exemption rules. If there are overlapping entries in the ACL, the security appliance analyzes the ACEs until a match is found.

Step 2. **Static NAT**—If no match is found in the NAT exemption rules, the security appliance analyzes the static NAT entries in sequential order to determine a match.

Step 3. **Static PAT**—If the security appliance does not find a match in NAT exemption or static NAT entries, it goes through the static PAT entries until it locates a match.

Step 4. **Policy NAT/PAT**—The security appliance evaluates the policy NAT entries if it is still not able to find a match on the packet flow.

Step 5. **Identity NAT**—The security appliance tries to find a match using the identity NAT statement.

Step 6. **Dynamic NAT**—If the security appliance fails to find a match using the first five rules, it checks to see whether the packets need to be translated using dynamic NAT.

Step 7. **Dynamic PAT**—The packets are checked against the dynamic PAT rules as the last resort, if all the previously mentioned rules fail.

If the security appliance does not find an exact match by using all the rules and policies, and if the **nat-control** feature is enabled, it drops the packet and generates a syslog message (305005) indicating such an event has occurred.

> **Tip** When multiple NAT types are configured on a security appliance, ASDM displays the order of NAT operation under **Configuration > Firewall > NAT Rules** and under the "#" column.

Integrating ACLs and NAT

Cisco ASA integrates the two core features, ACLs and NAT, to provide a complete security framework. This way, the real IP address of an inside host is hidden from the host on the less trusted networks while appropriate traffic filtering policies are applied. In Figure 4-40, both features are implemented on a security appliance.

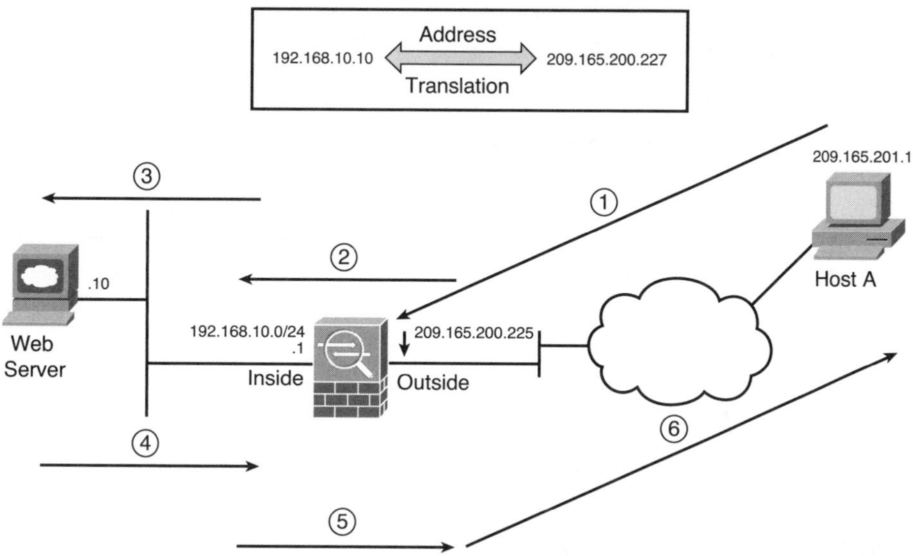

Figure 4-40 *ACL and NAT*

A host on the public network (209.165.201.1) establishes a new connection by sending a packet to an inside web server. The security appliance handles the packet in the following sequence:

Step 1. The packet arrives at the outside interface of the security appliance with a source address of 209.165.201.1 and a destination address of 209.165.200.227. Cisco ASA checks the inbound ACL to make sure that it is allowed in.

Step 2. If the packet is permitted to pass through, the security appliance sends the packet to the NAT engine to determine whether the addresses need to be translated. The destination address is changed to 192.168.10.10.

Step 3. The security appliance creates a connection entry and forwards the packet to the egress (inside) interface after evaluating it against the outbound ACL on the inside interface.

Step 4. The web server replies to Host A, using its source IP address of 192.168.10.10.

Step 5. The packet is forwarded to the NAT engine, which changes the source IP address to 209.165.200.227.

Step 6. The security appliance sends the packet to Host A.

You can use ASDM to define a NAT and an ACL to allow traffic from the web clients on the outside to communicate with the web server on the inside network. Follow these steps:

Step 1. Navigate to **Configuration > Firewall > Access Rules > Add** and select **Add Access Rule.** Configure the following Access Rule:

- Interface: **Outside**
- Action: **Permit**
- Source: **any**
- Destination: **209.165.200.227**
- Service: **http**. Click **OK** when you are finished.

Step 2. Navigate to **Configuration > Firewall > NAT Rules > Add** and select **Add Static NAT Rule**. Configure the following policy for the Static NAT Rule:

- Original Interface: **inside**
- Source: **192.168.10.10**
- Translated Interface: **outside**
- Source: **209.165.200.227**. Click **OK** when you are finished.

Using the CLI, a static NAT entry translates the original IP of the web server from **192.168.10.10** to **209.165.200.227**. An ACL named **inbound_traffic_on_outside** then allows any outside host to establish an HTTP connection to the web server, using its translated address. The ACL is then applied to the **outside** interface to filter the inbound packets, as shown in Example 4-41.

Example 4-41 *Configuration of NAT and Interface ACLs*

```
Chicago(config)# static (inside,outside) 209.165.200.227 192.168.10.10 netmask
255.255.255.255
Chicago(config)# access-list inbound_traffic_on_outside permit tcp any host
209.165.200.227 eq http
Chicago(config)# access-group inbound_traffic_on_outside in interface outside
```

Note Address translation was not supported in transparent mode until the 8.0 version of code. In the pre-8.0 versions, the nat and static commands were solely used to set embryonic and connection limits in transparent mode.

DNS Doctoring

In many network deployments, the DNS servers and DNS clients are set up for address translation but they are located on different subnets through the security appliance,. This is illustrated in Figure 4-41. The web server (www.securemeinc.com) and the web clients are located toward the inside network, whereas the DNS server is on the outside network. The real IP address of the web server is 192.168.10.10 and the translated public address is 209.265.200.227.

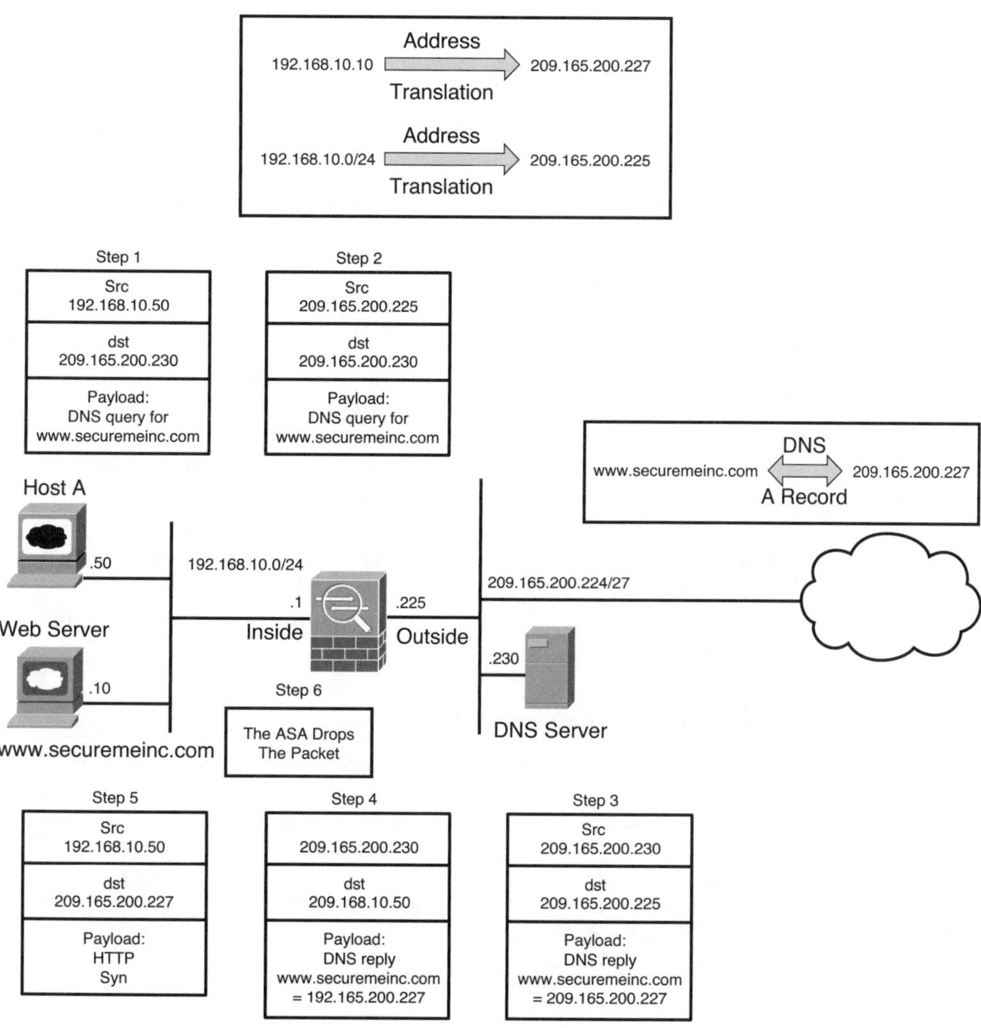

Figure 4-41 *DNS and NAT Without DNS Doctoring*

The problem arises when a web client (Host A) tries to access the web server using servers's hostname. In this scenario, the following sequence of events occurs:

Step 1. Host A sends a request to the DNS server, inquiring about the IP address of the web server.

Step 2. The source IP address is translated to 209.165.200.225, using dynamic PAT or any other form of address translation.

Step 3. The DNS server replies with the translated IP address of the web server (209.165.200.227) as a type A DNS record.

Step 4. The security appliance translates the destination IP address to 192.168.10.50 (Host A's IP address).

Step 5. The client, not knowing that the web server is on the same subnet, tries to connect to the public IP address.

Step 6. The security appliance drops the packets because the server resides on the inside interface and the packets are destined for the public IP address.

The DNS doctoring feature of Cisco ASA inspects the data payload of the DNS replies and changes the type A DNS record (IP address sent by the DNS server) to an address specified in the NAT configuration. In Figure 4-42, the security appliance modifies the IP address in the payload from 209.165.200.227 to 192.168.10.10 (Step 4) before forwarding the DNS reply to the client. The client uses this address to connect to the web server.

Using ASDM, you can enable the DNS doctoring feature by selecting the **Translate the DNS replies that match the translation rule** option when you try to add a NAT entry as shown earlier in Figure 4-28. If you prefer to use the CLI, you can add the **dns** keyword to the **static** and/or **nat** commands that are translating the real IP address of the server. In Example 4-42, a static NAT entry is set up to translate a real IP address from 192.168.10.20 to a global IP address, 209.165.200.227. The **dns** keyword is specified to enable DNS doctoring for this server.

Example 4-42 *Configuration of DNS Doctoring*

```
Chicago(config)# static (inside,outside) 209.165.200.227 192.168.10.20 netmask
255.255.255.255 dns
```

> **Note** The security appliance also supports DNS doctoring through use of the alias command. However, the recommended method is to use DNS doctoring with static and nat commands because the alias command will be deprecated in the future.

DNS doctoring can also be set up for the outside NAT connections. This is useful in deployments where the DNS server and the content (such as web or email) server reside on the outside network and the clients are located on the inside network, as shown in Figure 4-43.

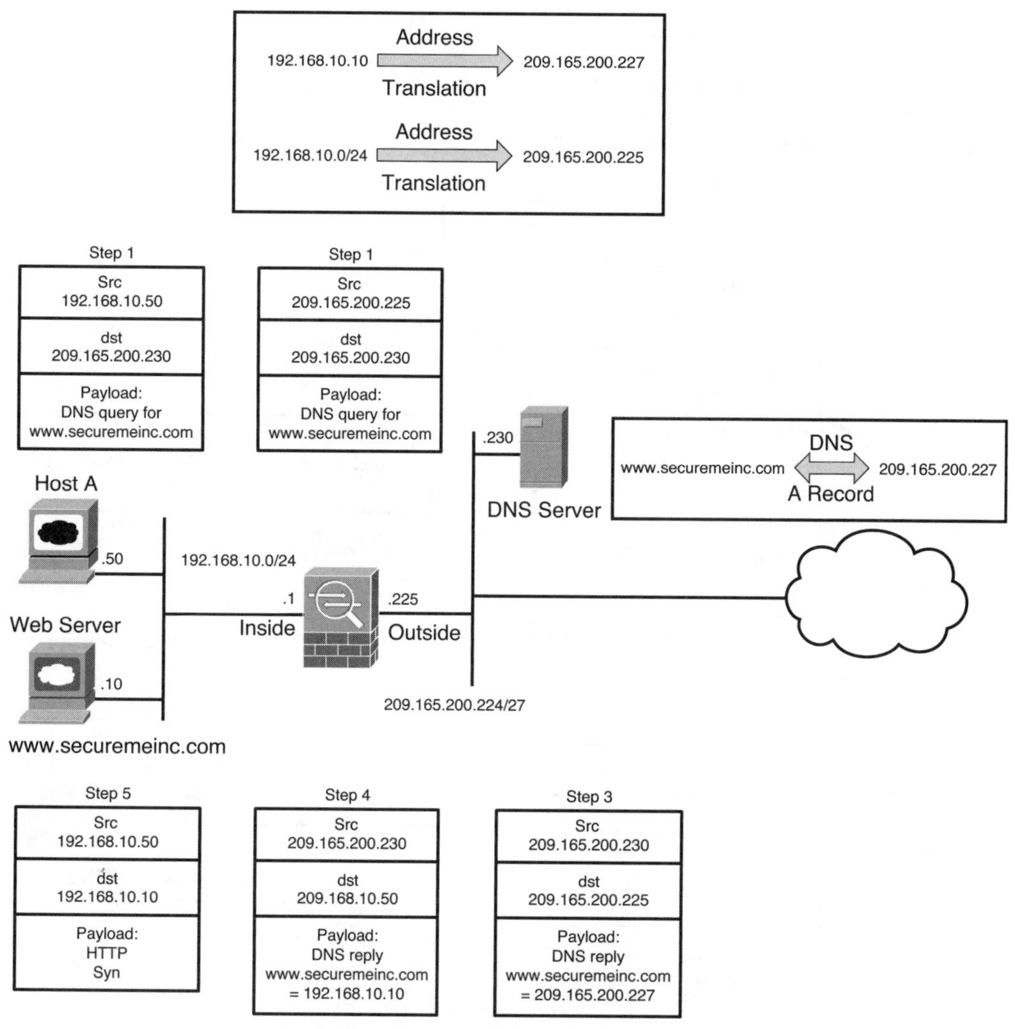

Figure 4-42 *DNS and NAT with DNS Doctoring*

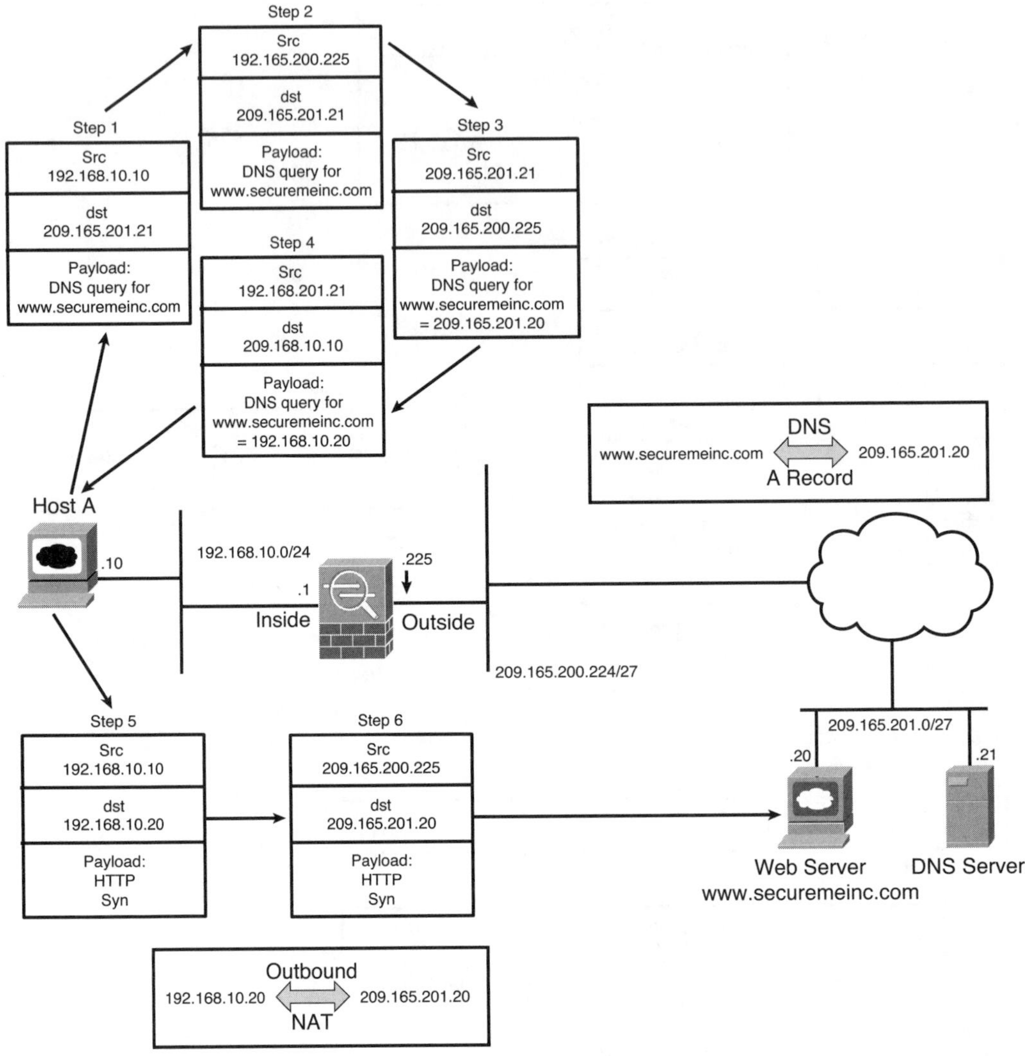

Figure 4-43 *DNS Doctoring for Outside NAT*

The following sequence of events takes place when a host on the inside network connects to a web server on the outside network:

Step 1. Host A sends a DNS query to the server to resolve www.securemeinc.com.

Step 2. The security appliance translates the source IP address to 209.165.200.225 before forwarding the packet to the DNS server.

Step 3. The DNS server replies with the IP address of the web server, 209.165.201.20, in the data payload.

Step 4. The security appliance changes the embedded IP address to 192.168.10.20 before it forwards the reply to Host A.

Step 5. The client sends a TCP SYN packet to connect to the web server, using 192.168.10.20 as the destination IP address.

Step 6. As the packet passes through, the security appliance changes the destination IP address to 209.165.201.20. The packet gets routed to the Internet before it reaches the web server.

Example 4-43 shows the respective configuration of the security appliance to enable DNS doctoring for outside NAT.

Example 4-43 *Configuration of DNS Doctoring for Outside NAT*

```
Chicago(config)# static (outside,inside) 192.168.10.20 209.165.201.20 netmask
255.255.255.255 dns
```

Monitoring Address Translations

Cisco ASA provides a rich set of **show** commands to monitor and troubleshoot issues related to address translation. The most important monitoring command is **show xlate**, which displays the real (local) address and the mapped (global) IP address assigned to a host. In Example 4-44, the security appliance is translating an inside host located at 192.168.10.10 to 209.165.200.225, using PAT. Cisco ASA changes the source port number from 11085 (local) to 1024 (global) before forwarding the packet to the egress interface. The security appliance also shows the maximum number of simultaneous translations (10) it has performed since the last reboot and the current active translations (1).

Example 4-44 *Output of* show xlate

```
Chicago(config)# show xlate
1 in use, 10 most used
PAT Global 209.165.200.225(1024) Local 192.168.10.10(11085)
```

Tip You can add the debug option at the end of show xlate to display the interfaces to which the translations are bound, along with the connection flags and idle times.

You can use a single command, **show local-host**, to display connection and translation statistics, as shown in Example 4-45. It displays the network states of each host on the local network. The TCP and UDP flow count counters display the active sessions going through the security appliance from that particular host.

Example 4-45 *Output of* **show local-host**

```
Chicago# show local-host
Interface inside: 1 active, 1 maximum active, 0 denied
local host: <192.168.10.10>,
    TCP flow count/limit = 1/unlimited
    TCP embryonic count to (from) host = 0 (0)
    TCP intercept watermark = unlimited
    UDP flow count/limit = 0/unlimited

  Xlate:
    PAT Global 209.165.200.225(1024) Local 192.168.10.10(11085)

  Conn:
    TCP outside 209.165.200.240:23 inside 192.168.10.10:11085 idle 0:00:13 bytes
87 flags UIO
```

Note The show local-host all command can be used to see both the connections made to and from the security appliance and the connections made through the security appliance.

Summary

This chapter explained the features available to protect the critical network resources by using two important features: network access control and network address translation. This chapter demonstrated how a security appliance can be configured for both features via the CLI as well as ASDM. Other features such as content filtering and DNS doctoring were discussed to exhibit the robustness of Cisco ASA. This chapter also discussed a number of **show** commands to monitor and troubleshoot these features.

Chapter 5

IP Routing

This chapter covers the following topics:

- Configuring static routes
- Configuring and troubleshooting RIP
- Configuring and troubleshooting OSPF
- Configuring and troubleshooting EIGRP
- Configuring and troubleshooting IP multicast routing

Network devices use a routing decision to identify which interface and gateway should be used to forward packets for a specific destination. To make this decision, they use dynamic routing protocols or static entries configured on such devices. This chapter covers the different routing capabilities of Cisco ASA. Cisco ASA supports the following routing mechanisms and protocols:

- Static routes
- Routing Information Protocol (RIP)
- Open Shortest Path First (OSPF)
- Enhanced Interior Gateway Routing Protocol (EIGRP)

This chapter also covers the Cisco ASA IP multicast routing capabilities.

Configuring Static Routes

Deployment and configuration of static routes is appropriate when the Cisco ASAs cannot dynamically build a route to a specific destination. This may be because the device to which the Cisco ASA is forwarding the packets might not support any dynamic routing protocols. Another example when static routes are appropriate is when the network topology is small and uncomplicated. Static routes are easy to configure. However, they do not scale well in large environments. Dynamic routing protocols, such as RIP, OSPF or EIGRP, must be considered if the network is fairly large and complex.

It is strongly recommended that you have a complete understanding of your network topology before configuring routing in your Cisco ASA. A best practice is to have a network topology diagram on hand to refer to when configuring your Cisco ASA.

Figure 5-1 shows a simple static route topology that includes a Cisco ASA with two interfaces configured (outside and inside).

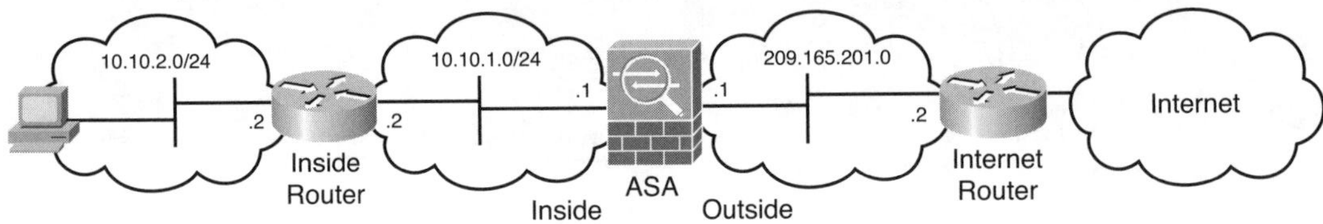

Figure 5-1 *Basic IP Routing Configuration Using Static Routes*

The goal in this example is to configure a static default route for the Cisco ASA to be able to forward packets to the Internet through the Internet router. Additionally, the Cisco ASA must be configured with a static route on the inside interface to be able to reach the 10.10.2.0/24 network.

To complete these tasks with the Cisco Adaptive Security Device Manager (ASDM), complete the following steps:

Step 1. Launch ASDM and login to the Cisco ASA.

Step 2. Navigate to **Configuration > Device Setup > Routing > Static Routes.**

Step 3. Click on **Add.**

Step 4. The dialog box illustrated in Figure 5-2 is shown. First add a default route to the *Internet Router* (209.165.201.2), as shown in Figure 5-2.

Step 5. Select the **outside** interface under the **Interface** field.

Step 6. Enter **0.0.0.0** in the **IP Address** field.

Step 7. Enter **0.0.0.0** in the **Netmask** field.

Step 8. The IP address of the Internet Router is 209.165.201.2. Enter **209.165.201.2** in the Gateway IP field.

Step 9. Leave all other options with their default values and Click **Ok.**

Note The Metric field specifies the administrative distance of the route. The default is 1 if a metric is not specified. The Tunneled option classifies the route as the default tunnel gateway used for VPN traffic. This option is covered in more detail in Chapter 17. One

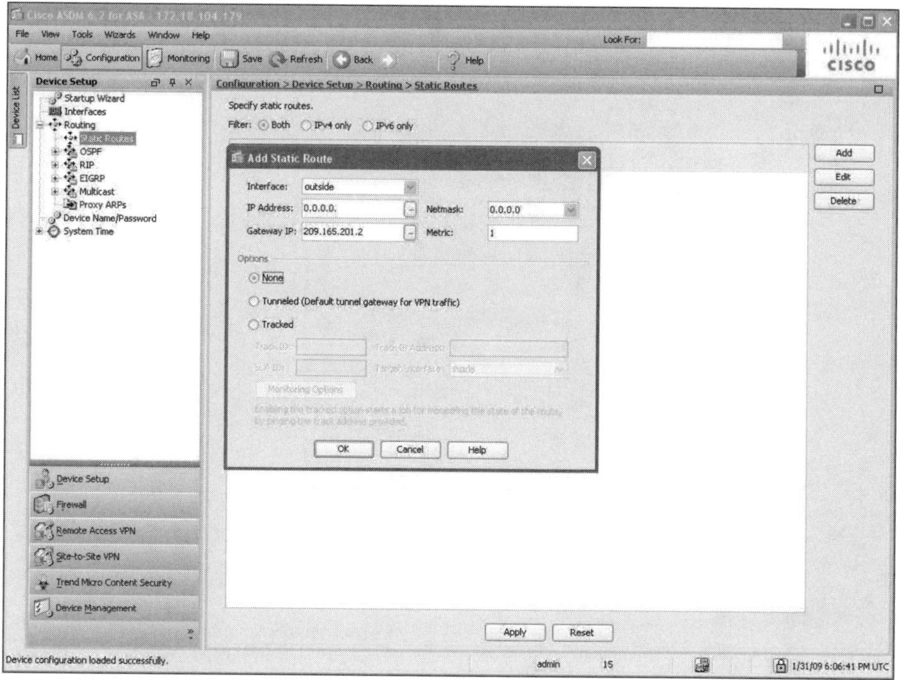

Figure 5-2 *Adding a Default Route in ASDM*

important note to remember is that this option is used only for a default route. You can configure only one tunneled route per device. The Tracked option is discussed later in this chapter.

Step 10. Add a static route so the Cisco ASA can reach the 10.10.2.0/24 network. To do this, navigate to **Configuration > Device Setup > Routing Static Routes** and click on **Add** to add a new static route, as shown on Figure 5-3.

Step 11. Select the **inside** interface under the **Interface** field.

Step 12. Enter **10.10.2.0** in the **IP Address** field.

Step 13. Enter **255.255.255.0** in the **Netmask** field.

Step 14. The IP address of the inside router is 10.10.1.2. Enter **10.10.1.2** in the **Gateway IP** field.

Step 15. Leave all other options with their default values and click **OK**.

Step 16. Click **Apply** to apply the changes to the configuration.

Step 17. Click **Save** to save the configuration on the Cisco ASA.

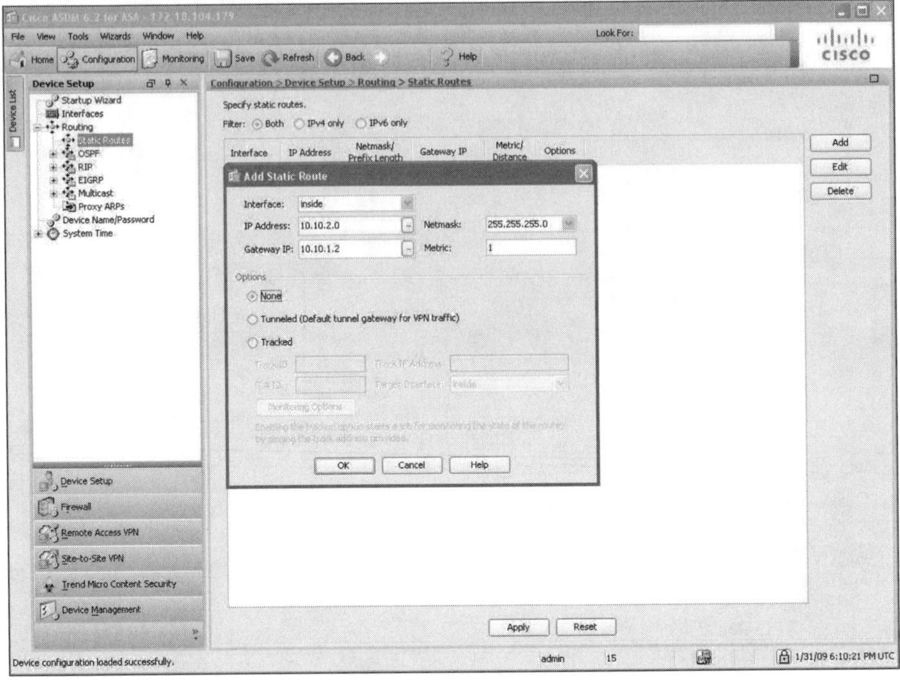

Figure 5-3 *Adding a Static Route in ASDM*

Alternatively, you can use the command-line interface (CLI) **route** command to add a static route. The following example shows how the default route is added on the Cisco ASA:

```
route outside 0.0.0.0 0.0.0.0 209.165.201.2 1
```

You configure static routes by using the **route** command, as shown in the following syntax:

```
route interface network netmask gateway metric [tunneled]
```

Table 5-1 details the options available within the **route** command.

A new feature was added in Cisco ASA software version 7.2(1) to allow for monitoring of the availability of a static route and installing a backup route if the primary route should fail. The following section provides more details about the tracking option.

Static Route Monitoring

Initially, there was no mechanism for determining whether a route was "up" or "down" on the Cisco ASA. Static routes stayed in the routing table even if the next hop gateway became unavailable, and they were removed from the routing table only if the corresponding interface went down. The ability to track the availability of a static route and installing a backup route was added in Cisco ASA software version 7.2(1).

Table 5-1 route *Command Options*

Option	Description
Interface	The specific interface name for which the route will apply. It must match the interface name configured by the **nameif** command under the specific interface configuration section.
network	The address of the remote network or host. If configuring a default route, use 0.0.0.0 or just 0.
netmask	The subnet mask of the remote network. If configuring a default route, use 0.0.0.0 or just 0 as the subnet mask.
gateway	The gateway to which the ASA will forward the packets.
metric	(optional) administrative distance for this route. The metric can be any value from 1 to 255. The default is 1.
tunneled	This option is used to configure a tunnel default gateway. This option can be used only with default gateways.
Track *number*	Optionally used to track a static route. The track number value ranges from 1 to 500.

The security appliance does this by associating a static route with a monitoring target that you define. It uses ICMP echo requests to monitor the target. If an echo reply is not received within a specified time period, the object is considered down and the associated route is removed from the routing table. A previously configured backup route is used in place of the removed route.

Note The route monitoring feature is supported only in single-context routed mode.

The network topology illustrated in Figure 5-4 shows a Cisco ASA configured with three interfaces (inside, outside, and DMZ). The goal in this example is to configure the route monitoring feature to track the default route to the Internet service provider (ISP) number 1 connection. If the connection to ISP number 1 fails, the Cisco ASA should use the connection to ISP number 2 in the DMZ interface.

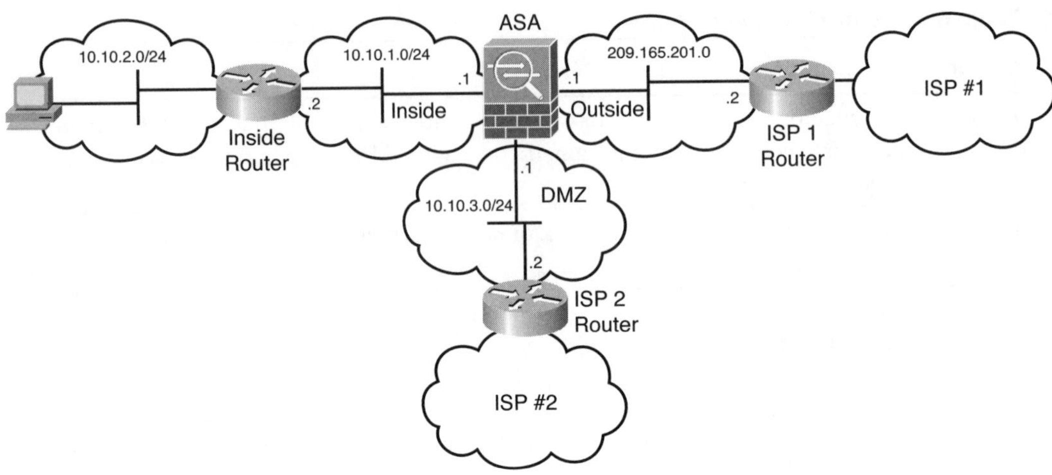

Figure 5-4 *Route Monitoring Example*

In ASDM, configure route monitoring as follows:

Step 1. Navigate to **Configuration > Device Setup > Routing > Static Routes.** Click on **Add** to add a new static route or **Edit** to edit an existing route.

Step 2. The dialog box illustrated in Figure 5-5 is displayed. In this example, the default route is edited. To enable route monitoring, select the Tracked option, as shown in Figure 5-5.

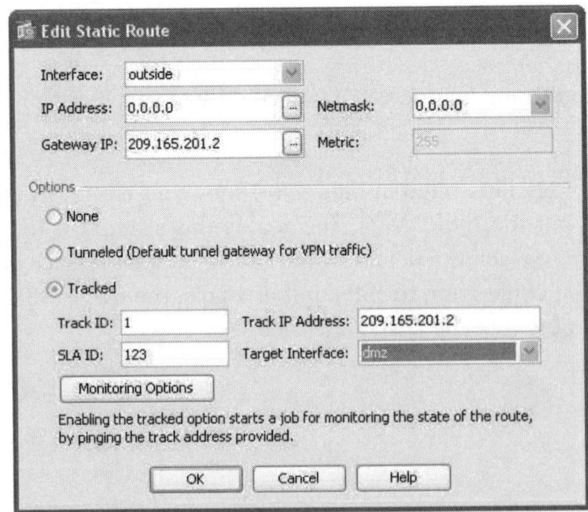

Figure 5-5 *Configuring Route Monitoring in ASDM*

Step 3. The **Track ID** is a unique identifier for the route tracking process. The number **1** is entered in this example.

Step 4. The **Track IP Address** defines the target host being tracked. Usually, the IP address of the next-hop gateway for the route is defined here; however, this could be any host in the network off the interface where this route is configured. In this example, an upstream IP address residing in ISP 1 network (**209.165.201.2**) is entered.

Step 5. The **SLA ID** is a unique identifier for the SLA monitoring process. The SLA process is used to monitor the availability of the IP address defined under the **Track IP Address** option. This allows the Cisco ASA to use a pre-configured backup route. In this example the value entered is **123**.

Step 6. The **Target Interface** is the interface where the selected host resides. In this example the **outside** interface is selected.

(Optional) You can customize several optional monitoring options. To customize these options click the **Monitor Options** button. The Route Monitoring Options dialog box shown in Figure 5-6 is displayed.

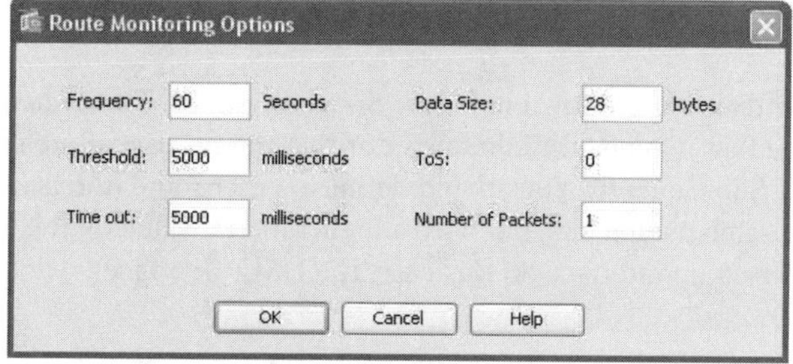

Figure 5-6 *Route Monitoring Options in ASDM*

Step 7. You can specify how often the Cisco ASA should check that the tracking target is reachable by using the **Frequency** field. The default value of 60 seconds is used in this example; however, you can configure this value from 1 to 604,800 seconds.

Step 8. The **Threshold** field enables you to specify a lifetime (in milliseconds) for this route. The default value is used in this example (5000 milliseconds).

Step 9. The **Timeout** field enables you to specify the amount of time the Cisco ASA waits for a response from the tracked host. The default value is used in this example (5000 milliseconds); however, valid values are from 0 to 604,800,000 milliseconds.

Note An important point to remember is that the threshold value cannot be more than the timeout value so that the tracking doesn't time out before the threshold lifetime expires.

Step 10. The Cisco ASA uses Internet Control Message Protocol (ICMP) echo request packets to verify that the tracked host is alive. The **Data Size** field specifies the size of data payload to use in such ICMP echo request packets. The default value of **28** bytes is used in this example; however, the value can be any number from 0 to 16384.

Step 11. The **ToS** field enables you to specify a value for the type of service (ToS) byte in the IP header of the echo request. The default value of **0** is used in this example; however, you can specify any number from 0 to 255.

Step 12. You can specify the number of ICMP echo requests to be sent for each test by using the **Number of Packets** field. The default value is used in this example (1 packet); however, this can be any number from 1 to 100. Be aware that specifying several packets per test may have a direct impact on network performance.

Step 13. Click **OK** on the Route Monitoring Options dialog box.

Step 14. Click **OK** on the Edit Static Route box.

Step 15. The dialog box shown in Figure 5-7 is displayed. This is an informational message that reminds the administrator that the primary route is set up for tracking. Subsequently, you should define another route (the backup route) with the same parameters, but with a higher metric value on the interface chosen as the backup interface (in this case, the DMZ interface).

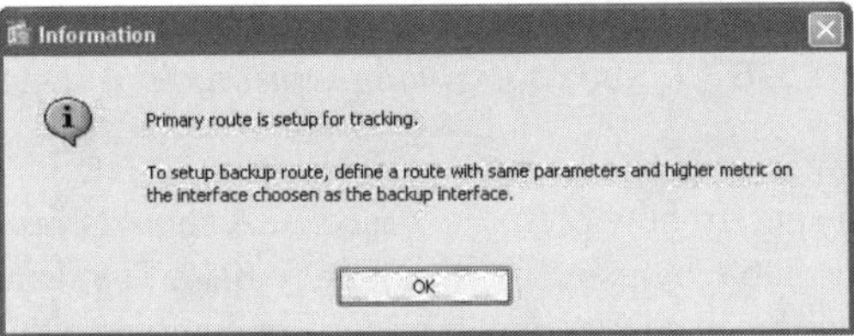

Figure 5-7 *Route Monitoring Alert Message*

Example 5-1 shows the CLI commands sent to the Cisco ASA from ASDM.

Example 5-1 *Static Routing Commands Sent by ASDM*

```
! The following are the three static routes that were
! previously configured. The track option is used on the first default route.
route outside 0.0.0.0 0.0.0.0 209.165.201.2 255 track 1
route dmz 0.0.0.0 0.0.0.0 10.10.3.2 5
```

```
route inside 10.10.2.0 255.255.255.0 10.10.1.2 1
!
! The sla monitor command is shown with the 123 identifier.
! The ICMP protocol is used to test the ISP 1 router.
! If this route fails the default route on the dmz is used.
sla monitor 123
 type echo protocol ipIcmpEcho 209.165.201.2 interface dmz
sla monitor schedule 123 life forever start-time now
!
! The track command is used with 1 as the identifier. The sla (123) is associated
to this command.
track 1 rtr 123 reachability
```

Displaying the Routing Table

To display the Cisco ASA's routing table in ASDM, navigate to **Monitoring > Routing > Routes.** Alternatively, in the CLI you can use the **show route** command in the Cisco ASA's routing table and verify the configuration. Example 5-2 shows the output of the **show route** command after the previously mentioned static route statements have been configured.

Example 5-2 *Displaying the Routing Table via the CLI*

```
NewYork# show route
Codes: C - connected, S - static, I - IGRP, R - RIP, M - mobile, B - BGP
       D - EIGRP, EX - EIGRP external, O - OSPF, IA - OSPF inter area
       N1 - OSPF NSSA external type 1, N2 - OSPF NSSA external type 2
       E1 - OSPF external type 1, E2 - OSPF external type 2, E - EGP
       i - IS-IS, L1 - IS-IS level-1, L2 - IS-IS level-2, ia - IS-IS inter area
       * - candidate default, U - per-user static route, o - ODR
       P - periodic downloaded static route
Gateway of last resort is 10.10.3.2 to network 0.0.0.0
C     172.18.104.128 255.255.255.192 is directly connected, management
C     209.165.201.0 255.255.255.224 is directly connected, outside
C     10.10.1.0 255.255.255.0 is directly connected, inside
S     10.10.2.0 255.255.255.0 [1/0] via 10.10.1.2, inside
C     10.10.3.0 255.255.255.0 is directly connected, dmz
S*    0.0.0.0 0.0.0.0 [5/0] via 209.165.201.2, outside
```

The letter S by each route statement indicates that it is a statically configured route entry. The letter C indicates that it is a directly connected route. The first number in the brackets is the administrative distance of the information source; the second number is the metric for the route. Administrative distance is the feature used by routing devices to select the best path when there are two or more different routes to the same destination from two different routing protocols.

Tip The **show route** command is useful when troubleshooting any routing problems. It provides not only the gateway's IP address for each route entry, but also the interface that is connected to that gateway.

The **show route** command can be used with an interface name to display only the routes going out of the specified interface.

Static routes do not provide a scalable solution for medium and large networks. To achieve better scalability use dynamic routing protocols. The Cisco ASA supports RIP, OSPF, and EIGRP. The following sections discuss these dynamic routing protocols in more detail.

Note Dynamic routing protocols are not supported when the security Cisco ASA is running in multi-context mode. Cisco ASA has the ability to create multiple security contexts (virtual firewalls), as covered in Chapter 8, "Virtualization."

RIP

RIP is a fairly old Interior Gateway Protocol (IGP), but it is still deployed in many networks. It is typically used in small and homogeneous networks. RIP is a distance-vector routing protocol, and it is defined in RFC 1058, "Routing Information Protocol." Its second version is defined in RFC 2453, "RIP Version 2."

RIP uses broadcast or multicast packets—depending on the version—to communicate with its neighbors and exchange routing information. It uses the hop-count methodology to calculate its metric. *Hop count* is the number of routing devices that the packets forwarded by a router or a Cisco ASA (in this case) will traverse. RIP has a limit of 15 hops. A route to a network that is directly connected to the Cisco ASA has a metric of 0. A route with a metric reaching or exceeding 16 is considered unreachable. Two versions of the RIP routing protocol are available (Cisco ASA supports both versions):

- **RIP version 1 (RIPv1)**—Does not support classless interdomain routing (CIDR) and variable-length subnet masks (VLSMs). VLSMs enable routing protocols to define different subnet masks for the same major network. For example, 10.0.0.0 is a Class A network. Its mask is 255.0.0.0. VLSM makes it possible to divide this network into smaller segments (i.e., 10.1.1.0/24, 10.1.2.0/24, etc.). Because RIPv1 does not support VLSM, no subnet mask information is present in its routing updates. RIP uses various techniques, such as holddowns, count-to-infinity, split horizon, and poison reverse, to prevent loops.
- **RIP version 2 (RIPv2)**—Supports CIDR and VLSMs. RIPv2 also converges faster than its predecessor. It also supports peer or neighbor authentication (plain-text or MD5 authentication), which provides additional security. RIPv2 uses multicast for communication between peers, in contrast to RIPv1, which uses broadcast.

Configuring RIP

The configuration of the Cisco ASA is simple, but somewhat limited. Figure 5-8 illustrates the first example topology.

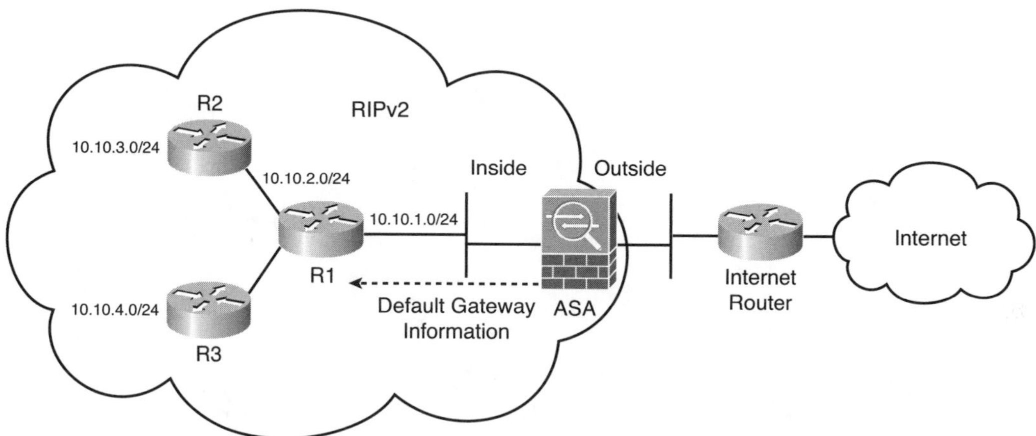

Figure 5-8 *Basic RIP Configuration*

In the example shown in Figure 5-8, the Cisco ASA is connected to a router (R1) running RIPv2. This router is learning routes from two other routers (R2 and R3). Subsequently, routes to all these networks are being advertised by the router connected to the Cisco ASA. The Cisco ASA is also injecting a default route to the inside router.

To configure RIP using ASDM, complete the following steps:

Step 1. Navigate to **Configuration > Device Setup > Routing > RIP > Setup** and click **Enable RIP** routing, as shown in Figure 5-9. When you enable RIP, it is enabled on all interfaces. When you select this check box, the other fields on this page are also available.

Step 2. To enable automatic route summarization, click on **Enable RIP Routing.** This option is enabled by default when you enable RIP in ASDM.

Note You cannot disable automatic summarization for RIP Version 1.

Step 3. To specify the RIP version used by the Cisco ASA, check **Enable RIP Version** then select **Version 1** or **Version 2.** In this example, RIP version 2 is used. This setting can be also configured on a per-interface basis in the ASDM **Interface** configuration section.

Step 4. In this example, the Cisco ASA should generate a route advertisement, so the internal routers use the Cisco ASA as their default gateway. Check the **Enable**

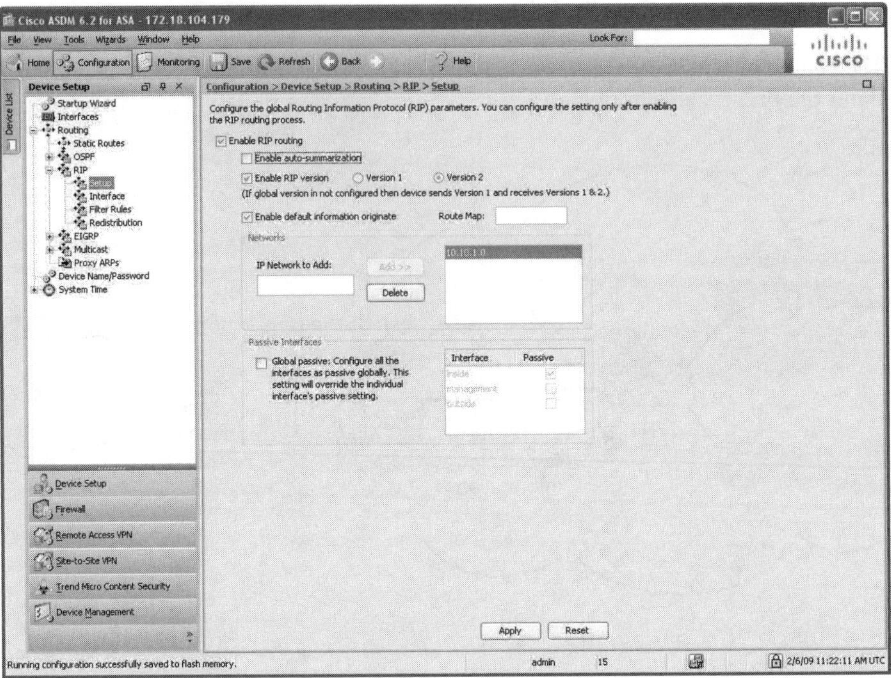

Figure 5-9 *Enabling RIP in ASDM*

Default Information Originate check box to generate a default route into the RIP routing process.

Step 5. Define the network(s) for the RIP routing process under the **IP Network to Add** section. The network number specified must not contain any subnet information. There is no limit to the number of networks you can add to the RIP configuration. RIP routing updates are sent and received through only those interfaces on the networks you define in this section. In this example the **10.10.1.0** network is used.

Step 6. You can configure the Cisco ASA to listen for RIP routing broadcasts globally on all interfaces and use that information to populate the routing tables, but to not broadcast routing updates with the **Global Passive** option under the **Passive Interfaces** section. In this example, only the inside interface is selected as a passive RIP interface, using the options under the **Passive Interfaces** table.

Step 7. Click **Apply** to apply the configuration changes in ASDM.

Step 8. Click **Save** to send the configuration to the Cisco ASA.

Example 5-3 shows the CLI commands configured in the Cisco ASA by ASDM.

Example 5-3 *RIP CLI commands*

```
router rip
 network 10.0.0.0
 passive-interface inside
 default-information originate
 version 2
 no auto-summary
```

The **rip** command enables RIP on the Cisco ASA. The networks specified for the RIP routing process are defined by the **network** command. Note that in this example the ASA has configured 10.10.1.0; however, the Cisco ASA CLI automatically summarizes this network to 10.0.0.0.

With the **passive-interface** command, the Cisco ASA interface listens for RIP routing packets and uses that information to update its routing table, but it does not advertise any routing updates through the specified interface.

The desired result is for the Cisco ASA to learn the internal routes and advertise default route information. To do this, the **default-information originate** command is used. The **version** command specifies what RIP version is used. RIP version 2 is used in this example.

> **Note** Use the **no router rip** command to remove all the RIP-related commands from the Cisco ASA.

Example 5-4 shows the output of the **show route** command after learning the routes from R1.

Example 5-4 *Output of the* **show route** *Command After Learning RIP Routes*

```
NewYork# show route
Codes: C - connected, S - static, I - IGRP, R - RIP, M - mobile, B - BGP
       D - EIGRP, EX - EIGRP external, O - OSPF, IA - OSPF inter area
       N1 - OSPF NSSA external type 1, N2 - OSPF NSSA external type 2
       E1 - OSPF external type 1, E2 - OSPF external type 2, E - EGP
       i - IS-IS, L1 - IS-IS level-1, L2 - IS-IS level-2, ia - IS-IS inter area
       * - candidate default, U - per-user static route, o - ODR
       P - periodic downloaded static route
Gateway of last resort is 209.165.201.2 to network 0.0.0.0
C    172.18.104.128 255.255.255.192 is directly connected, management
C    209.165.201.0 255.255.255.224 is directly connected, outside
C    10.10.1.0 255.255.255.0 is directly connected, inside
R    10.10.2.0 255.255.255.0 [120/1] via 10.10.1.2, 0:00:15, inside
R    10.10.3.0 255.255.255.0 [120/1] via 10.10.1.2, 0:00:15, inside
R    10.10.4.0 255.255.255.0 [120/1] via 10.10.1.2, 0:00:13, inside
S*   0.0.0.0 0.0.0.0 [255/0] via 209.165.201.2, outside
```

RIP Authentication

RIPv1 does not support authentication. Cisco ASA supports two modes of RIPv2 authentication: plain-text authentication and Message Digest 5 (MD5) authentication.

> **Tip** A best practice is to use MD5 instead of plain-text authentication because MD5 authentication provides a higher level of security.

RIP authentication using MD5 is added in Figure 5-10.

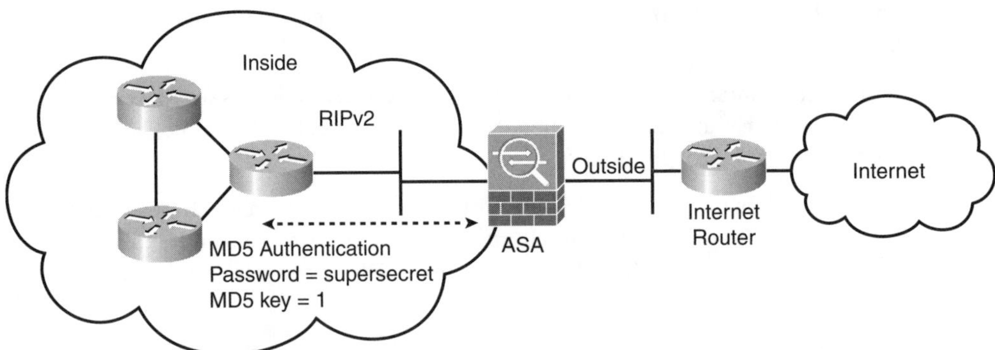

Figure 5-10 *MD5 RIP Authentication Example*

To enable RIP authentication using MD5, complete the following steps:

Step 1. Log in to ASDM and navigate to **Configuration > Device Setup > Routing > RIP > Interface.**

Step 2. Select the interface where RIP is enabled and click on **Edit**, as shown in Figure 5-11. In this example, the **inside** interface is used.

Step 3. The **Edit RIP Interface Entry** dialog box is shown, as illustrated in Figure 5-11.

Step 4. (Optional) Check the **Override Global Send Version** check box to select the RIP version sent by the interface. In this example, RIP version 2 is used. You can disable this option to restore the global setting.

Step 5. Check the **Enable Authentication** check box to enable RIP authentication.

Step 6. Enter the key to be used for RIP authentication under the **Key** field. In this example the key **supersecretkey** is used. This key can contain up to 16 characters.

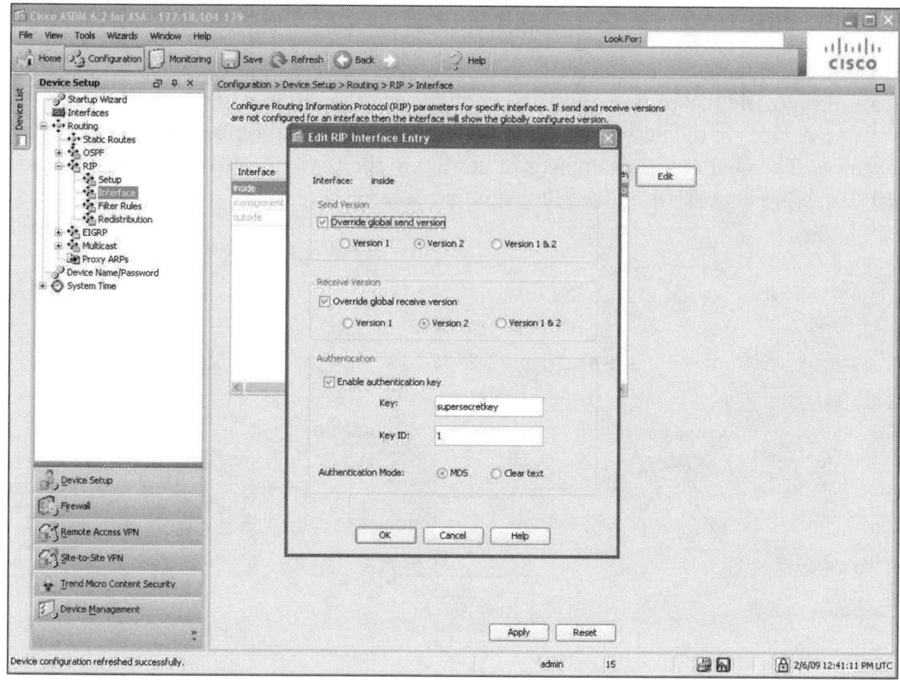

Figure 5-11 *Enabling MD5 RIP Authentication in ASDM*

Step 7. Enter the Key ID used by the RIP authentication process. In this example the key ID value of **1** is used. The valid values are from 0 to 255.

Step 8. Under the Authentication Mode select MD5.

Step 9. Click **Apply** to apply the configuration changes in ASDM.

Step 10. Click **Save** to save the configuration on the Cisco ASA.

Example 5-5 shows the commands sent by ASDM to the Cisco ASA.

Example 5-5 *Output of the* **show route** *Command After Learning RIP Routes*

```
interface GigabitEthernet0/1
 nameif inside
!- RIP is enabled on the inside interface
!- RIP send and receive version is configured for version 2
 rip send version 2
 rip receive version 2
!- RIP authentication mode is set to MD5
 rip authentication mode md5
!- RIP authentication key in the CLI is shown as <removed> by the Cisco ASA for
security purposes.
 rip authentication key <removed> key_id 1
```

RIP Route Filtering

The Cisco ASA can be configured to prevent other routers on the local network from learning specific RIP routes. Similarly, it can be configured to filter routes from other routing devices in the network. Figure 5-12 illustrates the topology used for the next example. The goal in this example is to configure the Cisco ASA to filter the route for the 10.10.4.0/24 network from the RIP neighbor router (R1).

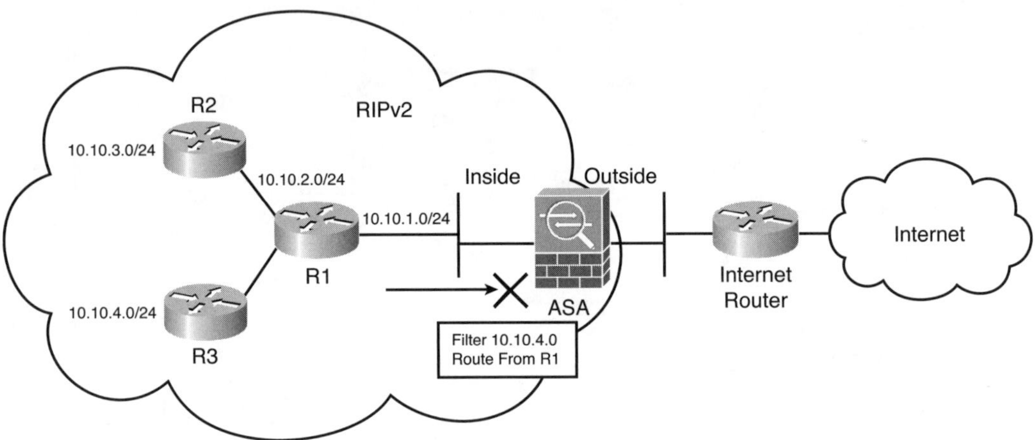

Figure 5-12 *Filtering RIP Routes*

To configure the Cisco ASA to filter the route for the 10.10.4.0/24 network from R1, complete the following steps:

Step 1. Log in to ASDM and navigate to **Configuration > Device Setup > Routing > RIP > Filter Rules.**

Step 2. Click on **Add** to create a new filter rule.

Step 3. The dialog box shown in Figure 5-13 is displayed.

Step 4. Select **in** under the **Direction** field to filter incoming RIP updates from another routing device (in this case R1). To prevent other routing devices from learning one or more RIP routes, you can suppress routes from being advertised in routing updates by selecting **out** in the **Direction** field. However, in this example the goal is to filter incoming routes from R1.

Step 5. Select the interface where the routes will be filtered. In this example R1 resides in the **inside** interface.

Step 6. Click on **Add** to add the filter rule. The **Network Rule** dialog box shown in Figure 5-14 is displayed.

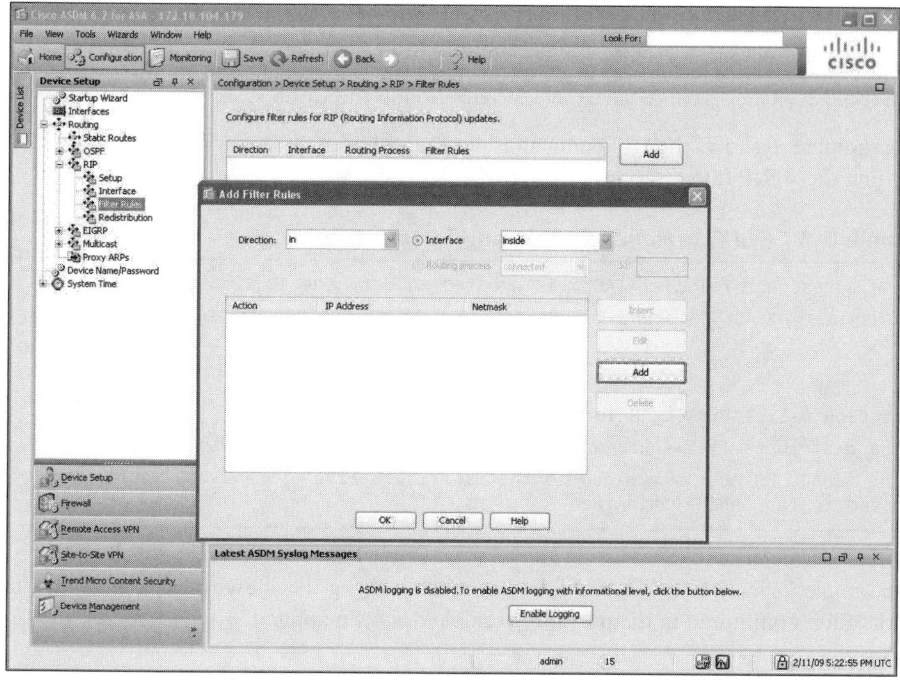

Figure 5-13 *RIP Filtering Rules in ASDM*

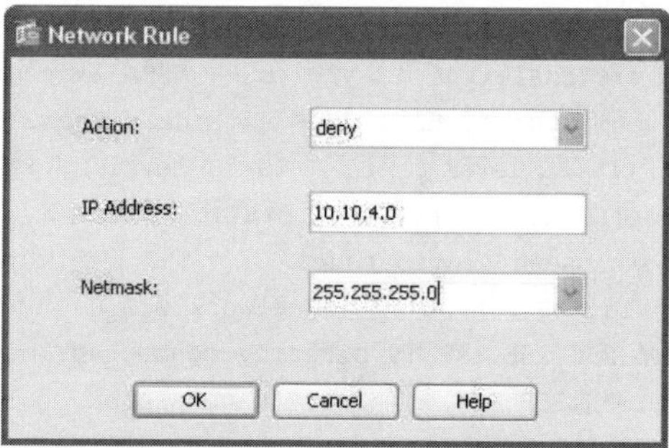

Figure 5-14 *Network Rule Dialog Box*

Step 7. Select **Deny** under the Action field to deny a specific network or IP address.

Step 8. The goal is to filter the incoming route advertisement for the 10.10.4.0/24 network. Enter **10.10.4.0** under the **IP Address** field, as shown in Figure 5-14.

Step 9. The 10.10.4.0 is a 24 bit network. Enter **255.255.255.0** in the **Netmask** field, as shown in Figure 5-14.

Step 10. Click **OK** to add the new rule in the **Network Rule** dialog box.

Step 11. Click **OK** to add the new filter in the **Add Filter Rules** dialog box.

Step 12. Click **Apply** to apply the configuration changes in ASDM and add them to the Cisco ASA's running-configuration.

Step 13. Click **Save** to save the configuration in the Cisco ASA.

Example 5-6 shows the CLI commands configured in the Cisco ASA by ASDM when creating these RIP filtering rules.

Example 5-6 *CLI Commands for Filtering Incoming RIP Routes*

```
!- An access control list (ACL) is created to deny the 10.10.4.0
access-list ripACL_FR standard deny 10.10.4.0 255.255.255.0
!
router rip
 distribute-list ripACL_FR in interface inside
! The distribute-list subcommand is used to create the filtering rule.
! The ripACL_FR ACL is applied to the distribute-list command and configured
inbound to the inside interface.
```

Example 5-7 shows the Cisco ASA routing table, using the **show route** command, after the filter configured in the previous example has been applied.

Example 5-7 *Routing Table After Application of Route Filtering Rules*

```
NewYork# show route
Codes: C - connected, S - static, I - IGRP, R - RIP, M - mobile, B - BGP
       D - EIGRP, EX - EIGRP external, O - OSPF, IA - OSPF inter area
       N1 - OSPF NSSA external type 1, N2 - OSPF NSSA external type 2
       E1 - OSPF external type 1, E2 - OSPF external type 2, E - EGP
       i - IS-IS, L1 - IS-IS level-1, L2 - IS-IS level-2, ia - IS-IS inter area
       * - candidate default, U - per-user static route, o - ODR
       P - periodic downloaded static route
Gateway of last resort is 209.165.201.2 to network 0.0.0.0
C     172.18.104.128 255.255.255.192 is directly connected, management
C     209.165.201.0 255.255.255.224 is directly connected, outside
C     10.10.1.0 255.255.255.0 is directly connected, inside
R     10.10.2.0 255.255.255.0 [120/1] via 10.10.1.2, 0:01:24, inside
R     10.10.3.0 255.255.255.0 [120/1] via 10.10.1.2, 0:01:24, inside
S*    0.0.0.0 0.0.0.0 [255/0] via 209.165.201.2, outside
```

As you see in Example 5-7, the route to the 10.10.4.0/24 network is no longer shown.

Configuring RIP Redistribution

The Cisco ASA can be configured to redistribute routes from other routing processes into RIP. Complete the following steps to configure RIP redistribution using ASDM.

Step 1. Log in to ASDM and navigate to **Configuration > Device Setup > Routing > RIP > Redistribution.**

Step 2. Select the routing protocol being redistributed into the RIP routing process under the **Protocol** section. You can select from the following protocols:

- **Static**—Used to redistribute static routes.
- **Connected**—Used to redistribute directly connected networks.
- **OSPF**—Used to redistribute routes learned by a specific OSPF routing process.
- **EIGRP**—Used to redistribute routes learned by a specific EIGRP routing process.

Step 3. Enter the metric type and value under the **Metric** section. This is the RIP metric being applied to the redistributed routes. The metric in this example is set to the number **10**.

Step 4. (Optional) You can configure route maps to specify with more granularity which routes from the specified routing process are redistributed into RIP.

Step 5. Click **OK** on the **Add Redistribution** dialog box.

Step 6. Click **Apply** to apply the configuration changes in ASDM and add them to the Cisco ASA's running-configuration.

Step 7. Click on **Save** to save the configuration in the Cisco ASA.

Alternatively, you can configure RIP redistribution with the **redistribute** RIP subcommand. The following example shows the options for the **redistribute** command.

```
NewYork(config)# router rip
NewYork(config-router)# redistribute ?
router mode commands/options:
  connected  Connected
  eigrp      Enhanced Interior Gateway Routing Protocol (EIGRP)
  ospf       Open Shortest Path First (OSPF)
  rip        Routing Information Protocol (RIP)
static     Static routes
```

Troubleshooting RIP

This section includes several commands and techniques that you can use while troubleshooting different issues that may arise throughout your deployment of RIP. A number of scenarios are provided to exemplify these troubleshooting techniques.

Scenario 1: RIP Version Mismatch

Using the same network topology illustrated in Figure 5-12, the internal router was intentionally configured with the incorrect RIP version. The Cisco ASA was configured with RIP version 2 on the inside interface (as previously shown) and the internal router was configured with RIP version 1. The output of the **show route** command does not display any routes learned via RIP. Example 5-7 shows the output of this command.

Example 5-8 *Output of* **show route** *Command Missing RIP Routes*

```
NewYork# show route
Codes: C - connected, S - static, I - IGRP, R - RIP, M - mobile, B - BGP
       D - EIGRP, EX - EIGRP external, O - OSPF, IA - OSPF inter area
       N1 - OSPF NSSA external type 1, N2 - OSPF NSSA external type 2
       E1 - OSPF external type 1, E2 - OSPF external type 2, E - EGP
       i - IS-IS, L1 - IS-IS level-1, L2 - IS-IS level-2, ia - IS-IS inter area
       * - candidate default, U - per-user static route, o - ODR
       P - periodic downloaded static route
Gateway of last resort is 209.165.201.2 to network 0.0.0.0
C     172.18.104.128 255.255.255.192 is directly connected, management
C     209.165.201.0 255.255.255.224 is directly connected, outside
C     10.10.1.0 255.255.255.0 is directly connected, inside
S*    0.0.0.0 0.0.0.0 [255/0] via 209.165.201.2, outside
```

The debug command **debug rip events** is used as a troubleshooting tool for this problem, as demonstrated in Example 5-9.

Example 5-9 *Output of* **debug rip events** *Showing Incorrect RIP Version During Negotiation*

```
NewYork# debug rip events
RIP event debugging is on
NewYork#
RIP: ignored v1 packet from 10.10.1.2 (illegal version)
```

In the highlighted line, the Cisco ASA displays an error message indicating that the router (10.10.1.2) is sending the incorrect RIP version (v1). The solution to this problem is to configure RIP version 2 on the internal router. Example 5-10 shows the output of the **debug rip events** messages when the correct information is received from the inside router.

Example 5-10 *Output of* **debug rip events** *Showing Correct RIP Version During Negotiation*

```
RIP: received v2 update from 10.10.1.2 on inside
     10.10.2.0 255.255.255.0 via 0.0.0.0 in 1 hops
     10.10.3.0 255.255.255.0 via 0.0.0.0 in 1 hops
```

```
    10.10.4.0 255.255.255.0 via 0.0.0.0 in 1 hops
RIP: Update contains 3 routes
```

Notice that the Cisco ASA receives a RIP version 2 (v2) update from the router (10.10.1.2) on the inside interface. Additionally, the routes learned are also displayed.

Scenario 2: RIP Authentication Mismatch

The topology shown in Figure 5-12 is also used in this example. The internal router and the Cisco ASA were configured to perform RIP authentication using MD5. The MD5 password was configured incorrectly in the inside router (R1). Example 5-11 shows the output of **debug rip events** on the Cisco ASA, which shows that there is a problem with MD5 authentication.

Example 5-11 *Output of* **debug rip events** *Showing Invalid Authentication During Negotiation*

```
RIP: ignored v2 packet from 10.10.1.2 (invalid authentication)
```

This message also appears if the incorrect authentication method or mode is selected.

Scenario 3: Multicast or Broadcast Packets Blocked

RIPv1 uses broadcast packets and RIPv2 uses multicast packets. If broadcast or multicast packets (respectively) are blocked, the Cisco ASA will never be able to successfully establish a RIP neighbor relationship with its peers. The **debug rip events** command is also useful to troubleshoot this problem. Example 5-12 shows the output of **debug rip events** while RIPv2 multicast packets were being blocked.

Example 5-12 *Output of* **debug rip events** *While Multicast Packets Are Being Dropped or Blocked*

```
RIP: sending v2 update to 224.0.0.9 via inside (10.10.1.1)
RIP: build update entries
        0.0.0.0 0.0.0.0 via 0.0.0.0, metric 1, tag 0
RIP: Update contains 1 routes
RIP: Update queued
RIP: Update sent via inside rip-len:32
```

As you can see from this example, the Cisco ASA is sending the RIPv2 packets to the address 224.0.0.9 without receiving anything back from its peers. You will also see this behavior when RIP is not enabled on any other routing device on that segment.

Tip You can also ping the multicast address of 224.0.0.9 to verify that packets are not blocked. The Cisco ASA does not respond to pings destined to the 224.0.0.9 address, as opposed to Cisco IOS routers.

OSPF

The OSPF routing protocol was drafted by the IGP Working Group of the Internet Engineering Task Force (IETF). It was developed because RIP was not able to scale for large, heterogeneous networks. The OSPF specification is defined in RFC 2328, "OSPF Version 2." It is based on the Shortest Path First (SPF) algorithm (usually referred to as the Dijkstra algorithm after its author).

OSPF is a link-state routing protocol. It sends information about attached interfaces, metrics used, and other variables to its peers or neighbors. This information is called link-state advertisements (LSAs). They are sent to all the peers within a specific hierarchical area.

OSPF operates in hierarchies of separate autonomous systems. These autonomous systems can be divided into groups of contiguous networks called *areas*. Routers that are part of more than one area are referred to as *Area Border Routers* (ABRs). Figure 5-15 illustrates an example of this concept.

As shown in Figure 5-15, more than one OSPF area can be joined together by an ABR. On the other hand, an OSPF backbone, OSPF area 0, must be present to propagate routing information to all other areas. The Cisco ASA can be configured to act as an ABR. It then can provide not only connectivity, but also security while performing type 3 LSA filtering. Type 3 LSAs refer to summary links and are sent by ABRs to advertise destinations outside an area. The OSPF ABR type 3 LSA filtering feature gives the user improved control of route distribution between OSPF areas. This feature also provides the capability of hiding the private networks by using Network Address Translation (NAT) without advertising them.

Figure 5-16 provides an example of how the Cisco ASA can be configured as an ABR and provide LSA type 3 filtering.

Note If the Cisco ASA is configured as an Autonomous System Boundary Router (ASBR), it propagates Type 5 LSAs for the entire autonomous system, including areas in private and public networks. Type 5 LSAs provide external routes to the autonomous system. This is not a recommended security practice because this causes all private networks to be externally advertised.

The **ospf database-filter all out** command can be used to filter out all outgoing LSAs to an OSPF interface during synchronization and flooding.

The following section provides different sample configurations explaining all the OSPF features supported by Cisco ASA.

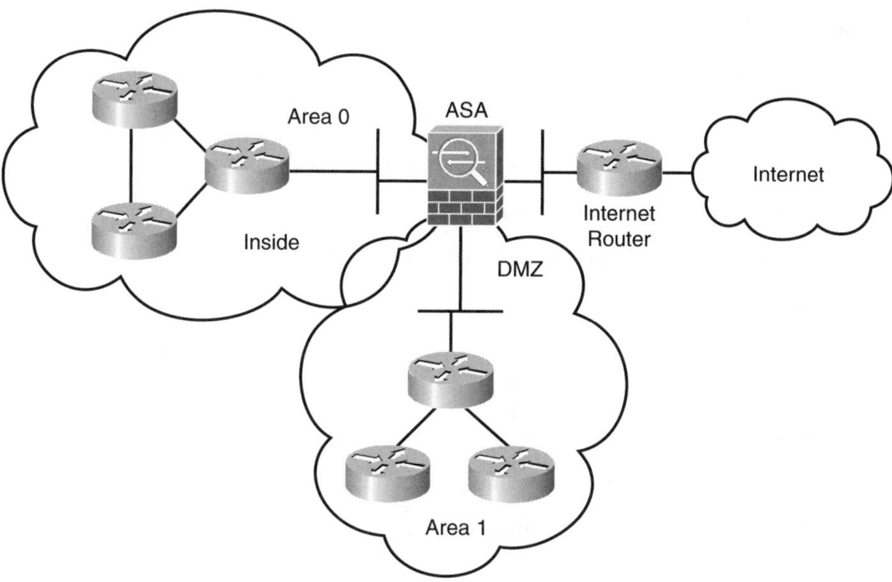

Figure 5-15 *Areas in OSPF*

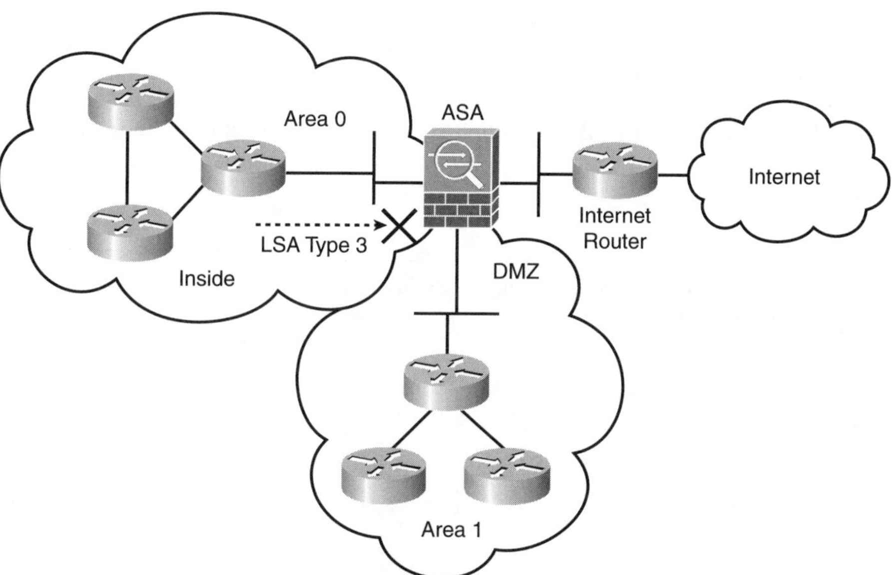

Figure 5-16 *Cisco ASA LSA Type 3 Filtering*

Configuring OSPF

Cisco ASA supports several OSPF features and capabilities. The following summarizes the Cisco ASA OSPF support:

- Intra-area, inter-area, and external (Type 1 and Type 2) routes
- Support to act as a designated router (DR)
- Support to act as a backup designated router (BDR)
- Support to act as an ABR
- Support to act as an ASBR, with route redistribution between OSPF processes including OSPF, static, and connected routes
- Virtual links
- OSPF authentication (both clear-text and MD5 authentication)
- Stub areas and not-so-stubby areas (NSSAs)
- LSA flooding
- ABR type 3 LSA filtering
- OSPF **neighbor** command and dynamic routing over VPN
- Load balancing between a maximum of three peers on a single interface, using equal-cost multipath (ECMP) routes

The following sections provide configuration examples for most of these features.

Enabling OSPF

The topology illustrated in Figure 5-17 is used in this example. It includes a Cisco ASA connected to a router named R1 on its inside interface. This router is also connected to two other routers (R2 and R3).

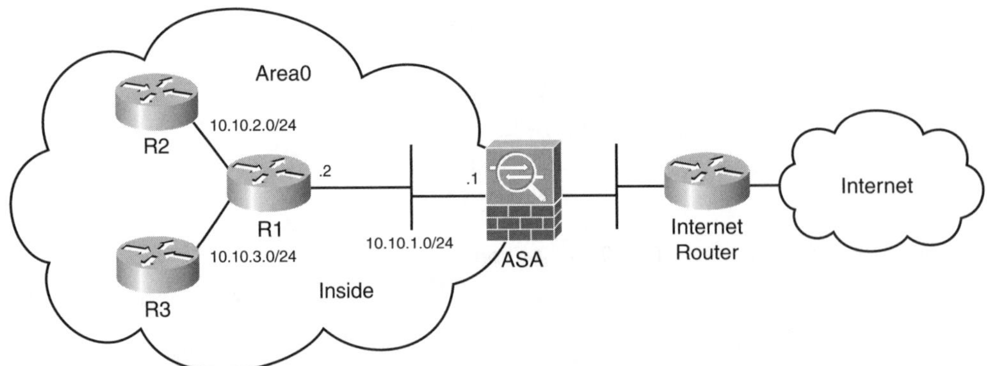

Figure 5-17 *Basic OSPF Configuration*

In this first example, the Cisco ASA, R1, R2, and R3 are all configured in area 0.

To initially configure OSPF, perform these tasks:

Step 1. Log in to ASDM and navigate to **Configuration > Device Setup > Routing > OSPF > Setup.**

Step 2. The Cisco ASA supports up to only two OSPF process instances on its configuration. Each OSPF process has its own associated areas and networks. To enable an OSPF process select **Enable this OSPF Process** for one of the two available processes as shown in Figure 5-18. In this example the **OSPF Process 1** is used.

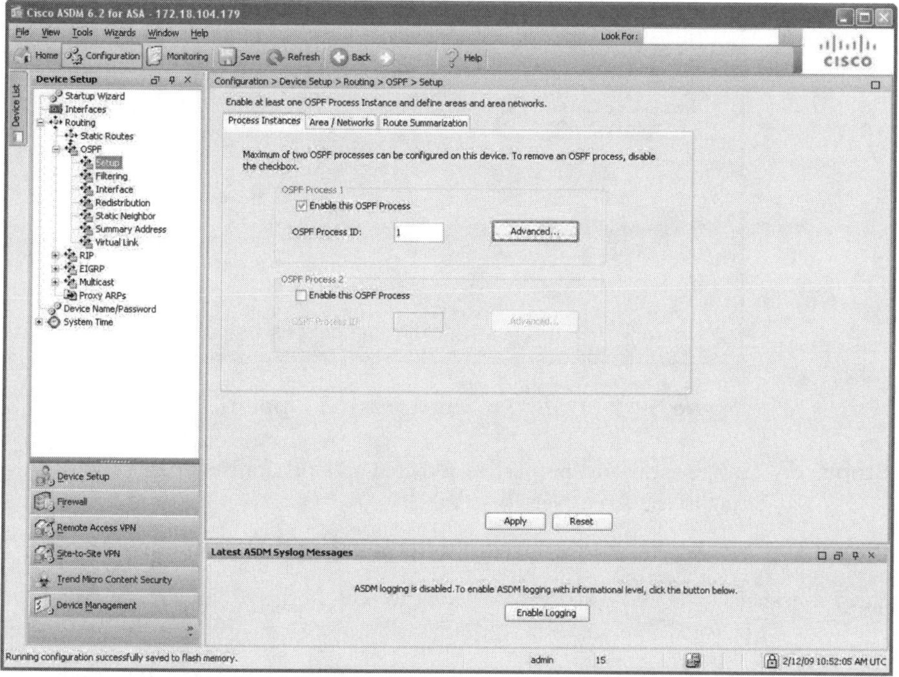

Figure 5-18 *Enabling an OSPF Process*

Step 3. Under the **OSPF Process ID** field enter a unique numeric identifier for the respective OSPF process. In this example the process ID is the number **1**. The Cisco ASA uses this process ID internally and does not need to match the OSPF process ID on any other routing device. You can select any value from 1 to 65535.

Step 4. (Optional) You can click on the **Advanced** button to configure additional OSPF parameters such as the Router ID, Adjacency Changes, Administrative Route Distances, Timers, and Default Information Originate settings. The **Edit OSPF Process Advanced Properties** dialog box shown in Figure 5-19 is displayed. Figure 5-19 shows the default options. In this example, the default values are configured for simplicity.

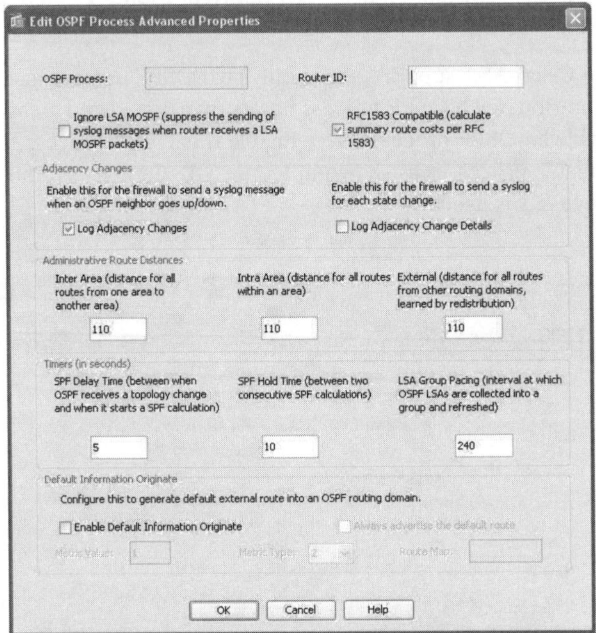

Figure 5-19 *OSPF Process Advanced Properties*

Step 5. Configure the area properties and area network for the OSPF process by navigating to the **Area/Networks** tab.

Step 6. Click **Add** to add the specific networks. The screen is shown in Figure 5-20.

Step 7. Select the OSPF Process you want to edit. In this example, the OSPF process 1 is used.

Step 8. Enter the area ID in the Area ID field. In this example Area 0 is used; however, area values range from 0 to 4294967295. You can also enter the area ID using an IP address.

Step 9. There are three different area types:

- **Normal** makes the area a standard OSPF area. This is the default option when an area is initially created and the one used in this example.
- **Stub** makes the area a stub area. Stub areas stop AS External LSAs (type 5 LSAs) from being flooded into the stub area. When you create a stub area, the **Summary** check box is available. You can prevent summary LSAs (type 3 and 4) from being flooded into the area by not selecting the **Summary** check box.

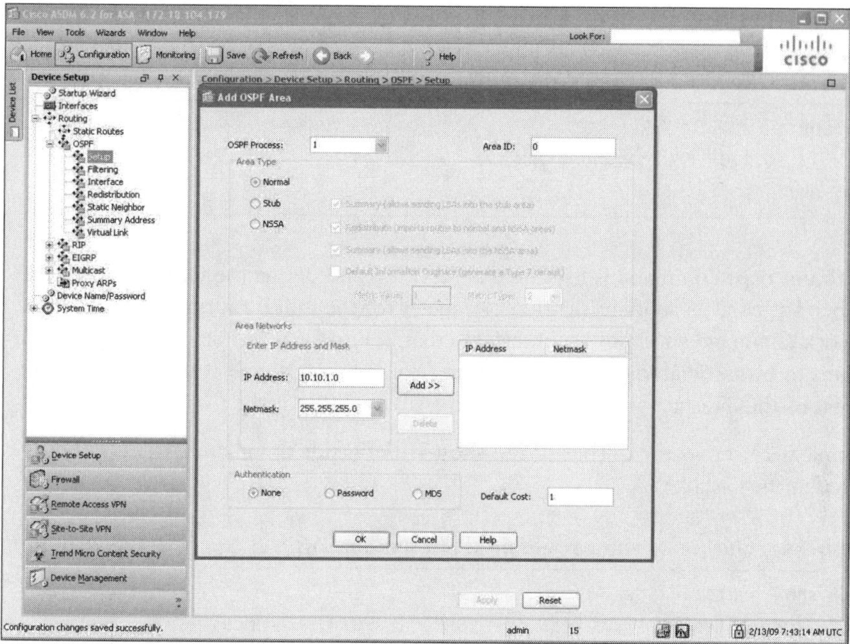

Figure 5-20 *Enabling an OSPF Process*

- **NSSA** makes the area a not-so-stubby area. NSSA areas accept type 7 LSAs. As with stub area configuration, you can uncheck the **Summary** check box to stop summary LSAs from being flooded into the area. Route redistribution can also be disabled if you don't select the **Redistribute** check box and do enable **Default Information Originate.**

  The **Default Information Originate** option enables the Cisco ASA to generate a type 7 default into the NSSA. This option is disabled by default. You can also specify the OSPF metric value for the default route (in the range from 0 to 16777214). The default value is 1. The **Metric Type** option is used to specify the OSPF metric type for the default route. You can select the number 1 for type 1; or 2 for type 2. If **Default Information Originate** is configured the default value is 2.

Step 10. Define the networks in the area by entering the IP address and Mask of the networks under the **Area Networks** section. In this example the 10.10.1.0/24 network is added.

Step 11. Click on the **Add** button to add the network defined in the **Enter IP Address** and **Netmask** sections to the area. These networks appear in the **Area Networks** table.

> **Note** This screen also enables you to configure OSPF authentication. OSPF authentication is covered later in this chapter.

Example 5-13 shows the CLI commands generated by ASDM and sent to the Cisco ASA.

Example 5-13 *Basic CLI OSPF Configuration*

```
router ospf 1
 network 10.10.1.0 255.255.255.0 area 0
 log-adj-changes
```

The **router ospf** command is used to enable OSPF and define the OSPF process. The number **1** is used as an identification parameter for the OSPF routing process. The **network** command specifies the interfaces that will run OSPF. Furthermore, it specifies the area to be associated with that interface. You can use the network address or the address of the interface where you want to enable OSPF.

Example 5-14 shows the output of the **show route inside** command after OSPF was configured in the Cisco ASA.

Example 5-14 *Output of* **show route inside** *Command After Basic OSPF Configuration*

```
NewYork# show route inside
Codes: C - connected, S - static, I - IGRP, R - RIP, M - mobile, B - BGP
       D - EIGRP, EX - EIGRP external, O - OSPF, IA - OSPF inter area
       N1 - OSPF NSSA external type 1, N2 - OSPF NSSA external type 2
       E1 - OSPF external type 1, E2 - OSPF external type 2, E - EGP
       i - IS-IS, L1 - IS-IS level-1, L2 - IS-IS level-2, ia - IS-IS inter area
       * - candidate default, U - per-user static route, o - ODR
       P - periodic downloaded static route
Gateway of last resort is 209.165.201.2 to network 0.0.0.0
C     10.10.1.0 255.255.255.0 is directly connected, inside
O     10.10.3.0 255.255.255.0 [110/11] via 10.10.1.2, 0:28:15, inside
O     10.10.2.0 255.255.255.0 [110/11] via 10.10.1.2, 0:28:15, inside
```

Note The output of **show route inside** has two routes learned via OSPF on the inside interface of Cisco ASA. The first number in the brackets is the administrative distance of the information source. The second number is the metric for the route.

The **show ospf** command can be used to display the general information about the OSPF routing processes. Example 5-15 shows the output of the **show ospf** command in the Cisco ASA.

Example 5-15 *Output of* **show ospf** *Command After Basic OSPF Configuration*

```
NewYork# show ospf
 Routing Process "ospf 1" with ID 209.165.201.1 and Domain ID 0.0.0.1
 Supports only single TOS(TOS0) routes
```

```
Does not support opaque LSA
SPF schedule delay 5 secs, Hold time between two SPFs 10 secs
Minimum LSA interval 5 secs. Minimum LSA arrival 1 secs
Number of external LSA 0. Checksum Sum 0x      0
Number of opaque AS LSA 0. Checksum Sum 0x      0
Number of DCbitless external and opaque AS LSA 0
Number of DoNotAge external and opaque AS LSA 0
Number of areas in this router is 1. 1 normal 0 stub 0 nssa
External flood list length 0
   Area BACKBONE(0)
       Number of interfaces in this area is 1
       Area has no authentication
       SPF algorithm executed 2 times
       Area ranges are
       Number of LSA 3. Checksum Sum 0x 15b1f
       Number of opaque link LSA 0. Checksum Sum 0x      0
       Number of DCbitless LSA 0
       Number of indication LSA 0
       Number of DoNotAge LSA 0
       Flood list length 0
```

The highlighted lines in Example 5-15 show the OSPF process information and show that area 0 is associated to this process and active in only one interface (the inside interface in this case).

OSPF Virtual Links

All areas must talk to area 0 (the backbone area). It's likely that this will not always be possible. However, in OSPF, virtual links can be configured to connect an area through a non-backbone area. They can also be used to connect two parts of a segmented backbone through non-backbone areas.

Figure 5-21 illustrates the topology of the network used in the following example. The Cisco ASA is configured with a virtual link to a router located on a DMZ interface.

To configure a virtual link on the Cisco ASA, complete the following steps:

Step 1. Log in to ASDM and navigate to **Configuration > Device Setup > Routing > OSPF > Virtual Link.**

Step 2. Click Add to add a new virtual link.

Step 3. The dialog box shown in Figure 5-22 is displayed.

Step 4. Select the **OSPF Process** associated with the virtual link. In this example, the OSPF process **1** is selected.

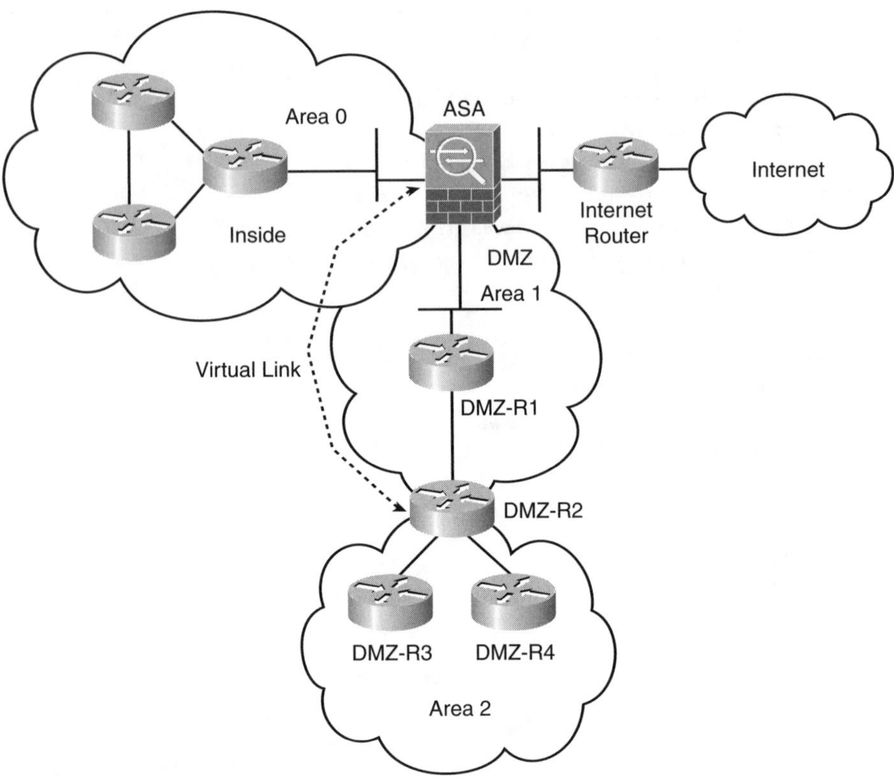

Figure 5-21 *Virtual Link Example*

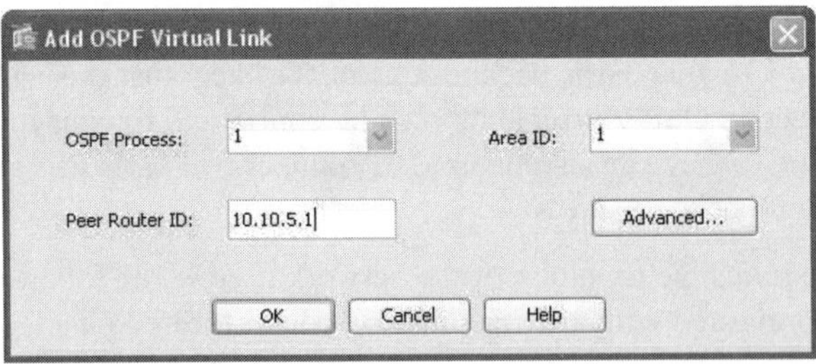

Figure 5-22 *Configuring Virtual Links in ASDM*

Step 5. Select the area shared by the neighbor OSPF devices, under the **Area ID** pull-down menu. Please note that NSSA or Stub areas cannot be associated with a virtual link. In this example, area **1** is selected.

Step 6. Enter the router ID of the virtual link neighbor under the **Peer Router ID** field. The virtual link peer is the router with the ID of 10.10.5.1 (DMZ-R2).

Note You can click on the **Advanced** button to configure more OSPF properties for the virtual link in this area. These properties include authentication and packet interval settings. This example uses all default values for these properties.

At first, the virtual link is down because the Cisco ASA does not know how to reach the router labeled DMZ-R2. All the LSAs in area 1 need to be flooded, and the shortest path first (SPF) algorithm must run within area 1 for the Cisco ASA to successfully reach DMZ-R2 through area 1. In this example, area 1 is the transit area. After the Cisco ASA reaches DMZ-R2, the router and the Cisco ASA try to form an adjacency across the virtual link. After the Cisco ASA and the DMZ-R2 router become adjacent on the virtual link, DMZ-R2 becomes an ABR because it now has a link in area 0. Consequently, a summary LSA for the networks in area 0 and area 1 is created.

Example 5-16 shows the CLI command sent by ASDM to the Cisco ASA to create the virtual link to the DMZ-R2 router.

Example 5-16 *OSPF Virtual Link CLI Configuration*

```
router ospf 1
 network 10.10.1.0 255.255.255.0 area 0
 network 10.10.4.0 255.255.255.0 area 1
 area 1 virtual-link 10.10.5.1
```

The highlighted line in Example 5-16 shows how the **area 1 virtual-link** command is used to create the virtual link to 10.10.5.1.

The **show ospf virtual-links** command can be used to display statistical information about an OSPF virtual link. The output of the **show ospf virtual-links** is included in Example 5-17.

Example 5-17 *Output of the* **show ospf virtual-links** *Command*

```
New York# show ospf virtual-links
Virtual Link dmz to router 10.10.5.1 is up
  Run as demand circuit
  DoNotAge LSA allowed.
  Transit area 1, via interface dmz, Cost of using 10
  Transmit Delay is 1 sec, State UP,
  Timer intervals configured, Hello 10, Dead 40, Wait 40, Retransmit
```

The highlighted lines in Example 5-17 show that the virtual link to the DMZ-R2 router (10.10.5.1) is **up**.

Configuring OSPF Authentication

Cisco ASA supports both plain-text and MD5 OSPF authentication. MD5 authentication is recommended because it is more secure than plain-text authentication. When configuring authentication, an entire area must be configured with the same type of authentication. For example, if area 1 is configured for MD5 authentication, all devices running OSPF must run MD5 authentication. Figure 5-23 includes an example of a Cisco ASA performing MD5 authentication on its inside interface. All routers and the Cisco ASA reside in area 0, and they must use the same authentication type and shared secret (password) to learn routes from each other.

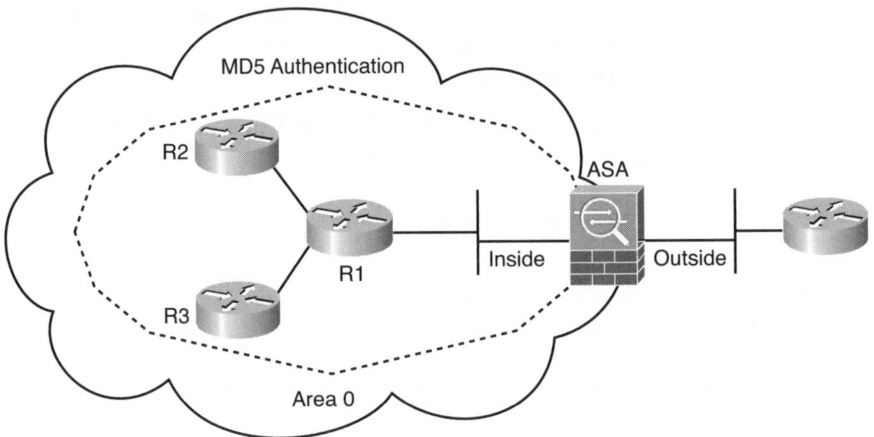

Figure 5-23 *OSPF MD5 Authentication Example*

Complete the following steps to configure OSPF MD5 authentication using ASDM:

Step 1. Log in to ASDM and navigate to **Configuration > Device Setup > Routing > OSPF > Setup**.

Step 2. Click on the **Area / Networks** tab and select the **OSPF Process** where MD5 authentication is to be enabled. In this example, OSPF process **1** is selected.

Step 3. Click on **Edit** to edit the OSPF process settings. The dialog box shown in Figure 5-24 is displayed.

Step 4. Select **MD5** under the **Authentication** section.

Step 5. Click **OK**.

Step 6. Click **Apply** to apply the OSPF process changes.

Step 7. Navigate to **Configuration > Device Setup > Routing > OSPF > Interface**.

Step 8. Select the interface where OSPF MD5 authentication is to be enabled and click **Edit**. In this example, OSPF MD5 authentication is enabled in the **inside** interface.

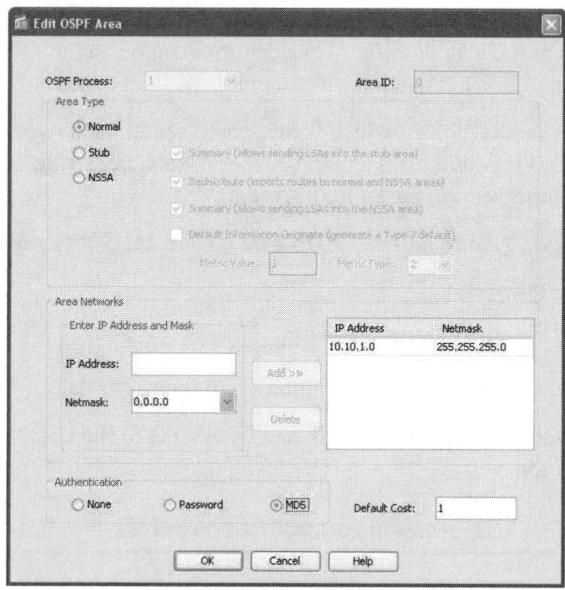

Figure 5-24 *Configuring OSPF MD5 Authentication in ASDM*

Step 9. The dialog box shown in Figure 5-25 is displayed. Click on **MD5 authentication** under the **Authentication** section.

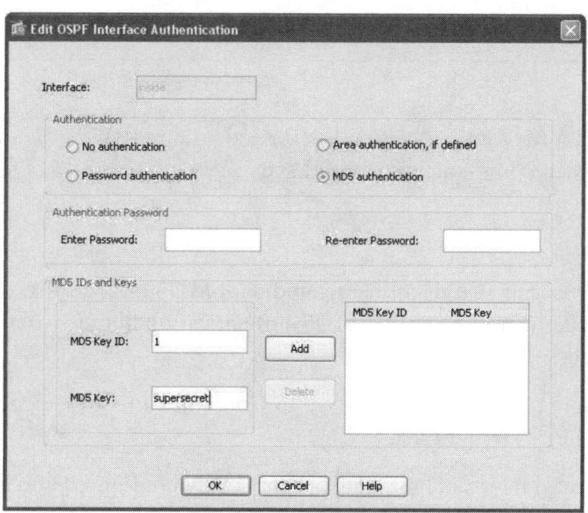

Figure 5-25 *OSPF Interface Authentication Settings*

Step 10. Enter the MD5 Key ID under the **MD5 IDs and Keys** section. The MD5 Key ID is numerical identifier. This identifier can be any number from 1 to 255. The number **1** is used in this example.

Step 11. Enter the MD5 Key, which is the shared secret used by the Cisco ASA and the OSPF peer. This is an alphanumeric character string of up to 16 bytes. The key **supersecret** is used in this example.

Step 12. Click on **Add** to add the **MD5 Key ID** and **MD5 Key** settings.

Step 13. Click **OK**.

Step 14. Click **Apply** to apply the configuration changes.

Step 15. Click **Save** to save the configuration in the Cisco ASA.

Example 5-18 shows the CLI commands sent by ASDM to the Cisco ASA to enable OSPF MD5 authentication.

Example 5-18 *OSPF MD5 Authentication CLI Commands*

```
router ospf 1
 area 0 authentication message-digest
! MD5 authentication  is enabled for area 0
!
interface GigabitEthernet0/1
 nameif inside
! OSPF MD5 authentication is enabled under the inside interface
! The MD5 Key ID is 1 and the shared secret is supersecret.
 ospf message-digest-key 1 md5 supersecret
 ospf authentication message-digest
```

Tip Although plain-text authentication is less secure than MD5 authentication, it is sometimes used when communicating with Layer 3 devices that do not support MD5 authentication.

OSPF virtual links can also be authenticated with MD5 or plain-text authentication. The following steps show how to enable MD5 authentication in the virtual link configuration previously discussed:

Step 1. Log in to ASDM and navigate to **Configuration > Device Setup > Routing > OSPF > Virtual Link.**

Step 2. Select the virtual link that was previously configured and click on **Edit**.

Step 3. Click on **Advanced** to configure the advanced OSPF virtual link properties. The dialog box shown in Figure 5-26 is displayed.

Step 4. Select MD5 authentication under the Authentication section.

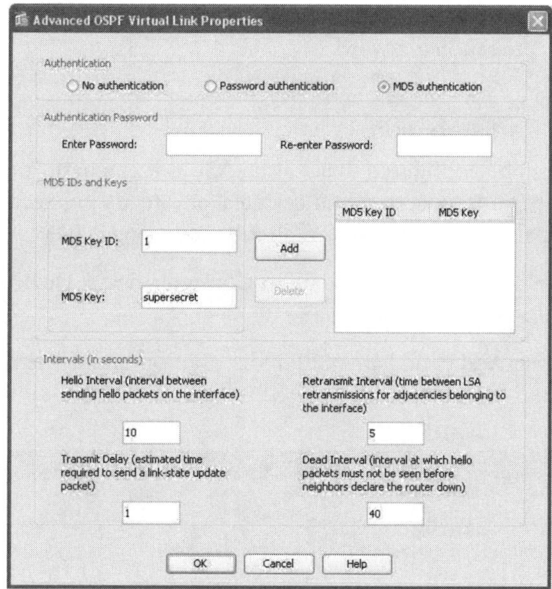

Figure 5-26 *Virtual Link Authentication*

Step 5. Enter the MD5 Key ID and MD5 Key under the **MD5 IDs and Keys** section. In this example, the MD5 Key ID is the number **1** and the MD5 Key is **supersecret.**

Step 6. Click **Add** to add the MD5 Key ID and the MD5 Key to the table on the right.

Step 7. Click **OK** on the **Advanced OSPF Virtual Link Properties** dialog box.

Step 8. Click **OK** on the **Edit OSPF Virtual Link** dialog box.

Step 9. Click **Apply** to apply the configuration changes in ASDM and add them to the Cisco ASA's running-configuration.

Step 10. Click on **Save** to save the configuration in the Cisco ASA.

Example 5-19 shows the CLI commands sent by ASDM to the Cisco ASA to enable OSPF Virtual Link MD5 authentication.

Example 5-19 *OSPF Virtual Link MD5 Authentication CLI Commands*

```
router ospf 1
 area 0 virtual-link 10.10.5.1 authentication message-digest
 area 0 virtual-link 10.10.5.1 message-digest-key 1 md5 supersecret
```

The first highlighted line in Example 5-19 shows how MD5 (**message-digest**) authentication is enabled in the virtual link to **10.10.5.1.** The second highlighted line shows how the

MD5 key ID **1** is added with the **message-digest-key** keyword, as well as the MD5 key (**supersecret**) with the **md5** keyword.

Configuring OSPF Redistribution

The Cisco ASA can be configured to act as an ASBR. It can perform route redistribution between different OSPF processes, static routes, or directly connected subnets. Complete the following steps to configure OSPF redistribution using ASDM.

Step 1. Log in to ASDM and navigate to **Configuration > Device Setup > Routing > OSPF > Redistribution.**

Step 2. Click on **Add** to add an OSPF redistribution Entry. The dialog box shown in Figure 5-27 is displayed.

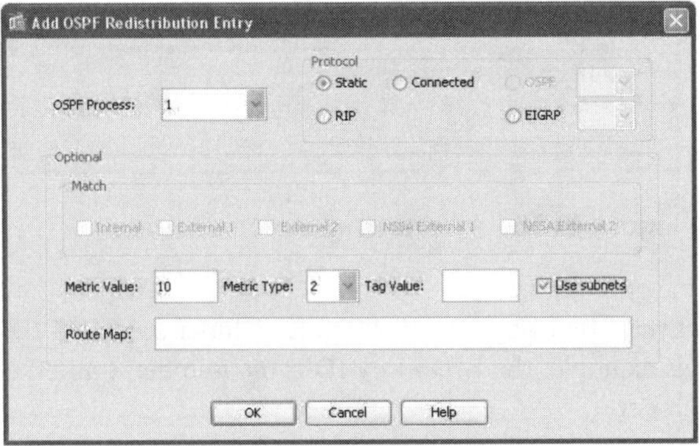

Figure 5-27 *OSPF Redistribution Entry*

Step 3. Select the OSPF process where redistribution will be configured. **OSPF Process 1** is used in this example.

Step 4. Select the protocol to be redistributed under the **Protocol** section. This example shows how to redistribute all the static routes into OSPF.

Step 5. Enter the metric that is used for the redistribute routes under the Metric Value field. This column is blank for redistribution entries if the default metric is used. In this example, the metric value entered is **10**.

Step 6. Select the metric type under the **Metric Type** pull-down menu. One (1) specifies that the route is a Type 1 external route; the number (2) specifies that the metric is a Type 2 external route. Type 2 routes are selected in this example.

Step 7. (Optional) You can configure a 32-bit decimal tag under the **Tag Value** field. This is an identifier used on each external route. This value is not used by the Cisco ASA itself; however, it may be used by other routing devices to communicate information between ASBRs. You can configure this tag with any value from 0 to 4294967295.

Step 8. (Optional) You can configure route maps to specify with more granularity which routes from the specified routing process are redistributed into RIP.

Step 9. Click **OK** on the Add OSPF Redistribution Entry dialog box.

Step 10. Click **Apply** to apply the configuration changes.

Step 11. Click on **Save** to save the configuration in the Cisco ASA.

Example 5-20 shows the CLI commands sent by ASDM to the Cisco ASA to enable OSPF Virtual Link MD5 authentication.

Example 5-20 *OSPF Virtual Link MD5 Authentication CLI Commands*

```
router ospf 1
 redistribute static metric 10 subnets
```

Static routes are redistributed into OSPF as shown in the highlighted line. The **redistribute static** command is used to enable OSPF redistribution for static routes. In this example, the static routes are redistributed with a metric value of 10.

Tip Use the **subnets** attribute to allow the Cisco ASA to consider any configured subnets. This is commonly used when other routing protocols are being redistributed into OSPF. Only classful routes are redistributed if you do not specify the **subnets** attribute.

Stub Areas and NSSAs

An ASBR advertises external routes throughout the OSPF autonomous system. However, in some situations, there is no need to advertise external routes into an area to reduce the size of the OSPF database. A *stub area* is an area that does not allow the advertisements of external routes. In stub areas, a default summary route is injected along with information about networks that belong to other areas within the same OSPF network.

To use ASDM to configure an area as a stub area, complete the following steps:

Step 1. Log in to ASDM and navigate to **Configuration > Device Setup > Routing > OSPF > Setup.**

Step 2. Select the **Area / Networks** tab.

Step 3. Click on **Add** to add an area or **Edit** to edit an area.

Step 4. Under the **Area Type** section select **Stub.**

Step 5. Click **OK.**

Step 6. Click **Apply** to apply the configuration changes.

Step 7. Click on **Save** to save the configuration in the Cisco ASA.

Alternatively, you can use the CLI **stub** option with the **area** OSPF subcommand to configure this feature in the Cisco ASA. The following is the command syntax:

```
area area-id stub [no-summary]
```

Tip Use the **no-summary** attribute if you do not want to send summary LSAs into the stub area.

If an area is configured as a stub, all the routers within the area must also be configured as stub routers. Otherwise, the neighbor relationship will not be established.

The OSPF NSSA feature is defined in RFC 3101 as "The OSPF Not-So-Stubby Area (NSSA) Option." Redistribution of routes into an NSSA generates a special type of LSA known as LSA type 7. This type only exists in NSSAs.

To use ASDM to configure an area as an NSSA, complete the following steps:

Step 1. Log in to ASDM and navigate to **Configuration > Device Setup > Routing > OSPF > Setup.**

Step 2. Select the **Area / Networks** tab.

Step 3. Click on **Add** to add an area or **Edit** to edit an area.

Step 4. Under the **Area Type** section select **NSSA.**

Step 5. Click **OK.**

Step 6. Click **Apply** to apply the configuration changes.

Step 7. Click on **Save** to save the configuration in the Cisco ASA.

In the CLI, you can use the **nssa** option with the **area** OSPF subcommand to configure this feature in the Cisco ASA. The following is the command syntax:

```
area area-id nssa [no-redistribution][default-information-originate [metric
metric]    [metric-type 1|2]][no-summary]
```

OSPF Type 3 LSA Filtering

The Cisco ASA supports OSPF Type 3 LSA filtering. Follow these steps to use ASDM to configure OSPF Type 3 LSA filtering:

Step 1. Log in to ASDM and navigate to **Configuration > Device Setup > Routing > OSPF > Filtering.**

Step 2. Click on **Add** to add OSPF filtering rules. The dialog box shown in Figure 5-28 is displayed.

Step 3. Select the **OSPF Process** to be associated with the filter entry; in this example the OSPF process **1** is selected.

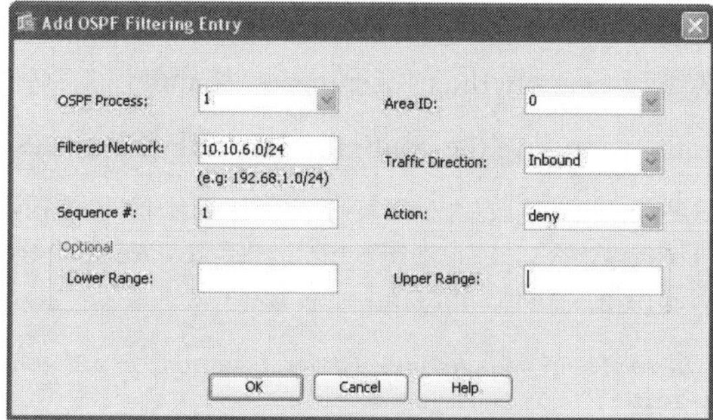

Figure 5-28 *OSPF Filtering Entry*

Step 4. Select the **Area ID** to be associated with the filter entry. In this example, area **0** is selected.

Step 5. Enter the network address and subnet mask bit to be filtered in the **Filtered Network** field. In this example the network 10.10.6.0/24 is filtered.

Step 6. Select the direction on how the filter is applied, using the **Traffic Direction** pull-down menu. The **Inbound** direction is used in this example; with this configuration the Cisco ASA filter entry applies to LSAs coming into area 0.

> **Note** You can also select **Outbound** to filter LSAs coming out of an OSPF area.

Step 7. Enter the sequence number to be used for the filter entry under the **Sequence #** field. In this example, the sequence number used is the number **1**. This sequence number is used if multiple filters are configured on the Cisco ASA; the filter with the lowest sequence number is applied first.

The Cisco ASA begins the search at the top of the prefix list. After a match or deny occurs, the Cisco ASA does not need to go through the rest of the prefix list.

> **Note** For efficiency, you may want to put the most common matches or denials near the top of the list.

Step 8. Select the **Action** to be applied to this filter. In this example, the **deny** action is selected to deny any route advertisements for the 10.10.6.0/24 network.

Step 9. (Optional) You can specify the minimum prefix length to be matched with an OSPF filter in the **Lower Range** field. In this example, this field is left blank.

Step 10. (Optional) You can specify the maximum prefix length to be matched with an OSPF filter in the **Upper Range** field. In this example, this field is left blank.

Step 11. Click **OK**.

Step 12. Click **Apply** to apply the configuration changes.

Step 13. Click on **Save** to save the configuration in the Cisco ASA.

To filter Type 3 LSAs in the Cisco ASA via the CLI, use the **prefix-list** command. After it is configured, the Cisco ASA can control which prefixes are sent from one area to another. The syntax of the **prefix-list** command is as follows:

```
prefix-list list-name [seq seq-value] {deny | permit prefix/length} [ge min-value]   [le max-value]
```

Table 5-2 lists all the options of the **prefix-list** command.

Table 5-2 prefix-list *Command Options*

Option	Description
list-name	Name of the prefix list.
seq *seq-value*	The **seq** keyword specifies the sequence number for the prefix list entry. The *sec-value* is used to specify the value of the sequence number.
deny	Denies access for a matching condition.
permit	Permits access for a matching condition.
prefix/length	The network number and length (in bits) of the network mask.
ge	Applies the *ge (greater or equal) value* to the range specified.
min-value	Specifies the lesser value of a range (the "from" portion of the range description); the range is 0 to 32.
le	Applies the *le (less or equal) value* to the range specified.
max-value	Specifies the greater value of a range (the "to" portion of the range description); the range is 0 to 32.

Tip You can enter a description (up to 225 characters) for each prefix list by using the **prefix-list** *list-name* **description** command.

OSPF **neighbor** Command and Dynamic Routing over VPN

OSPF Hello messages are sent over multicast by default. However, IPSec does not support multicast over a VPN tunnel. Consequently, OSPF adjacency using multicast cannot be established over IPSec VPN tunnels. Cisco ASA provides a solution to this problem by supporting the configuration of statically defined neighbors. When you configure a statically defined neighbor, the Cisco ASA communicates with its peers using unicast packets. This enables the OSPF messages to be successfully encrypted and sent over the VPN tunnel.

The OSPF neighbors can be defined only on nonbroadcast media. Because the underlying physical media is Ethernet (broadcast), the media type must be changed to nonbroadcast under the interface configuration. This would override the default physical broadcast media type.

To configure a static OSPF neighbor using ASDM, complete the following steps:

Step 1. Log in to ASDM and navigate to **Configuration > Device Setup > Routing > OSPF > Static Neighbor.**

Step 2. Click on **Add** to add a new neighbor.

Step 3. Select the **OSPF Process** to be used for this entry.

Step 4. Enter the neighbor IP address under the **Neighbor** field.

Step 5. Select the interface where the neighbor resides in the **Interface** pull-down menu.

Step 6. Click **OK.**

Step 7. Click **Apply** to apply the configuration changes.

Step 8. Click on **Save** to save the configuration in the Cisco ASA.

Alternatively, you can use the **neighbor** command to specify an OSPF neighbor.

Example 5-21 demonstrates how to use the **neighbor** command for an IPSec peer located at 209.165.201.2.

Example 5-21 *OSPF Static Neighbors*

```
New York(config)# router ospf 1
New York(config-router)# neighbor 209.165.201.2  interface outside
INFO: Neighbor command will take effect only after OSPF is enabled
and network-type is configured on the interface
```

Notice the warning message in Example 5-21. The command does not take effect until the network type is changed to **nonbroadcast** under the interface. Use the **ospf network point-to-point non-broadcast** interface command to accomplish this. Example 5-22 demonstrates this command.

Example 5-22 *Changing the Default Physical Media Type to Nonbroadcast*

```
New York(config-router)# interface GigabitEthernet0/0
New York(config-if)# ospf network point-to-point non-broadcast
```

Additionally, OSPF expects neighbors to belong to the same subnet. The subnet requirement is overlooked for point-to-point links. Because the IPSec site-to-site VPN tunnels are considered a point-to-point connection, the previous command provides the solution to this problem. Only one neighbor can be configured on a point-to-point link.

Note After an interface is declared to be a point-to-point nonbroadcast link, it cannot form adjacencies unless neighbors are configured explicitly.

If OSPF is configured to run over a site-to-site IPSec tunnel, then that same interface cannot form an OSPF neighbor with the directly connected router.

Note The following are several key points to take in consideration when configuring OSPF over a VPN tunnel:

- When configuring OSPF, only one neighbor can be defined for each interface. Additionally, you must configure a static route pointing to the IPsec peer.
- An OSPF adjacency cannot be established unless static neighbors are configured.
- If OSPF over a VPN connection is running on a given interface, you cannot run any other OSPF instance or neighbor on the same interface.
- It is recommended to bind the crypto-map to the interface before configuring the OSPF neighbor. This is done to make sure that the OSPF updates are sent over the VPN tunnel.

On IPSec site-to-site and remote-access VPN configurations, you can optionally use reverse route injection (RRI). RRI is a feature on the Cisco ASA that provides a solution for topologies that require encrypted traffic to be diverted to the Cisco ASA and all other traffic to be sent to a separate router. In other words, RRI eliminates the need to manually define static routes on internal routers or hosts to be able to send traffic to remote site-to-site connections or remote-access VPN connections. RRI is not required if the Cisco ASA is used as the default gateway and all traffic passes through it to get into and out of the network.

Note RRI is covered in detail in Chapter 16, "Site-to-Site IPSec VPNs," and Chapter 17, "IPSec Remote-Access VPNs."

There are several advantages to running OSPF over an IPSec VPN tunnel instead of using RRI. One of the major advantages is that when RRI is used, the routes to the remote networks or hosts are always advertised to the internal network, regardless of whether or not the VPN tunnel is operational. When using OSPF over an IPSec site-to-site tunnel, the routes to the remote networks or hosts are advertised only if the VPN tunnel is operational.

Troubleshooting OSPF

This section includes many mechanisms and techniques that are used to troubleshoot OSPF problems, such as several **show** and **debug** commands.

Useful Troubleshooting Commands

A commonly used command is **show ospf** [*process-id*]. It displays general information about OSPF routing-process IDs. The *process-ID* option displays information for a specific OSPF routing process. Example 5-23 shows the output of this command.

Example 5-23 *Output of the* **show ospf [process-id]** *Command*

```
NewYork# show ospf 1
 Routing Process "ospf 1" with ID 192.168.10.1 and Domain ID 0.0.0.1
 Supports only single TOS(TOS0) routes
 Does not support opaque LSA
 SPF schedule delay 5 secs, Hold time between two SPFs 10 secs
 Minimum LSA interval 5 secs. Minimum LSA arrival 1 secs
 Number of external LSA 0. Checksum Sum 0x      0
 Number of opaque AS LSA 0. Checksum Sum 0x      0
 Number of DCbitless external and opaque AS LSA 0
 Number of DoNotAge external and opaque AS LSA 0
 Number of areas in this router is 1. 1 normal 0 stub 0 nssa
 External flood list length 0
    Area BACKBONE(0)
        Number of interfaces in this area is 1
        Area has no authentication
        SPF algorithm executed 5 times
        Area ranges are
        Number of LSA 3. Checksum Sum 0x 1da9c
        Number of opaque link LSA 0. Checksum Sum 0x      0
        Number of DCbitless LSA 0
        Number of indication LSA 0
        Number of DoNotAge LSA 0
        Flood list length 0
```

As demonstrated in Example 5-23, the **show ospf** command gives you details about the OSPF configuration, LSA information, OSPF router ID, and number of areas configured in the Cisco ASA.

To display OSPF-related interface information, use the **show ospf interface** command. Example 5-24 includes the output of this command for the inside interface.

Example 5-24 *Output of the* **show ospf interface** *Command*

```
NewYork# show ospf interface inside
inside is up, line protocol is up
  Internet Address 192.168.10.1 mask 255.255.255.0, Area 0
  Process ID 1, Router ID 192.168.10.1, Network Type BROADCAST, Cost: 10
  Transmit Delay is 1 sec, State BDR, Priority 1
```

```
Designated Router (ID) 192.168.10.2, Interface address 192.168.10.2
Backup Designated router (ID) 192.168.10.1, Interface address 192.168.10.1
Timer intervals configured, Hello 10, Dead 40, Wait 40, Retransmit 5
  Hello due in 0:00:00
Index 1/1, flood queue length 0
Next 0x0(0)/0x0(0)
Last flood scan length is 1, maximum is 1
Last flood scan time is 0 msec, maximum is 0 msec
Neighbor Count is 1, Adjacent neighbor count is 1
  Adjacent with neighbor 192.168.10.2  (Designated Router)
Suppress hello for 0 neighbor(s)
```

The output of the **show ospf interface** command shows not only information about the OSPF communication on that specific interface, but also other information, such as the network type, cost, designated router information, and so on.

To display OSPF neighbor information, use the **show ospf neighbor** command. The following is the command syntax:

show ospf neighbor [*interface-name*] [*neighbor-id*] [**detail**]

To show neighbor information on a per-interface basis, use the *interface-name* argument. Use the *neighbor-id* option to display information about a specific neighbor, and use the **detail** option to display detailed neighbor information. The *interface-name* and *neighbor-id* options are mutually exclusive. Example 5-25 shows the output of the **show ospf neighbor** command.

Example 5-25 *Output of the* **show ospf neighbor** *Command*

```
NewYork# show ospf neighbor
Neighbor ID     Pri   State           Dead Time   Address         Interface
192.168.10.2      1    FULL/DR         0:00:34     192.168.10.2      inside
```

When OSPF adjacency is formed, the Cisco ASA goes through several state changes before it becomes fully adjacent with its neighbor. The information that these states represent is crucial when troubleshooting OSPF problems in the Cisco ASA. These states are as follows:

- **Down**—The first OSPF neighbor state. It means that no Hello packets have been received from this neighbor, but Hello packets can still be sent to the neighbor in this state.
- **Attempt**—Only valid for manually configured neighbors in a non-broadcast multiaccess (NBMA) environment. In Attempt state, the Cisco ASA sends unicast Hello packets every poll interval to the neighbor, if it has not received any Hello packets within the dead interval.

- **Init**—Specifies that the Cisco ASA has received a Hello packet from its neighbor, but the receiving router's ID was not included in the Hello packet. When the Cisco ASA or any router running OSPF receives a Hello packet from a neighbor, the neighbor's router ID is received in the Hello packet..
- **2Way**—Designates that bidirectional communication has been established between the Cisco ASA and its neighbor.
- **Exstart**—The Cisco ASA is exchanging information to select who will be the DR and BDR (master-slave relationship) and chooses the initial sequence number for adjacency formation. The device with the higher router ID becomes the master and starts the exchange and, as such, is the only device that can increment the sequence number.
- **Exchange**—Indicates the exchange of database descriptor (DBD) packets. Database descriptors contain LSA headers only and describe the contents of the entire link-state database used to determine whether new or more current link-state information is available.
- **Loading**—The Cisco ASA is doing the actual exchange of link-state information with its neighbor.
- **Full**—The Cisco ASA and its neighbor are fully adjacent with each other. All the router and network LSAs are exchanged and the routing databases are fully synchronized.

Example 5-26 shows the output of the **show ospf neighbor** command with the **detail** option. The neighbor in this example is a router with IP address 192.168.10.2. In this example, you can see that the OSPF state is Full and that there were six state changes. Additionally, you can see that the neighbor has been up for 26 minutes and 21 seconds.

Example 5-26 *Output of the* **show ospf neighbor** detail *Command*

```
NewYork# show ospf neighbor inside 192.168.10.2 detail
 Neighbor 192.168.10.2, interface address 192.168.10.2
    In the area 0 via interface inside
    Neighbor priority is 1, State is FULL, 6 state changes
    DR is 192.168.10.2 BDR is 192.168.10.1
    Options is 0x2
    Dead timer due in 0:00:31
    Neighbor is up for 00:26:21
    Index 1/1, retransmission queue length 0, number of retransmission 1
    First 0x0(0)/0x0(0) Next 0x0(0)/0x0(0)
    Last retransmission scan length is 1, maximum is 1
    Last retransmission scan time is 0 msec, maximum is 0 msec
```

Use the **show ospf database** command to display information related to the Cisco ASA OSPF database. The command displays information about the different OSPF LSAs. It displays detailed information about the neighbor router and the state of the neighbor relationship. Example 5-27 shows the output of the **show ospf database** command.

Example 5-27 *Output of the* **show ospf database** *Command*

```
NewYork# show ospf database
       OSPF Router with ID (192.168.10.1) (Process ID 1)
                Router Link States (Area 0)
Link ID         ADV Router      Age         Seq#       Checksum Link count
192.168.10.1     192.168.10.1     1943        0x80000005 0x99dd 1
192.168.10.2     192.168.10.2     20          0x80000003 0xa1d2 1
                Net Link States (Area 0)
Link ID         ADV Router      Age         Seq#       Checksum
192.168.10.2     192.168.10.2     1944        0x80000001 0xa2e6
                Type-5 AS External Link States
Link ID         ADV Router      Age         Seq#       Checksum Tag
192.168.20.0      192.168.10.2     19          0x80000001 0xfa25 0
192.168.13.0      192.168.10.2     19          0x80000001 0x8293 0
192.168.10.0     192.168.10.2     19          0x80000001 0xa72c 0
```

As demonstrated in Example 5-27, several external routes are learned from router 192.168.10.2. The 192.168.10.2 neighbor is advertising two routes for networks 192.168.20.0/24 and 192.168.13.0/24. Example 5-28 shows the output of the **show route** command for this example. The **O** by the route statement indicates that the route is learned via OSPF, and the **E2** indicates that it is an external type 2 route.

Example 5-28 *Output of the* **show route** *Command*

```
NewYork# show route
S     0.0.0.0 0.0.0.0 [1/0] via 209.165.200.226, outside
C     209.165.200.224 255.255.255.224 is directly connected, outside
C     192.168.10.0 255.255.255.0 is directly connected, inside
O E2 192.168.20.0 255.255.255.0 [110/10] via 192.168.10.2, 0:00:04, inside
O E2 192.168.13.0 255.255.255.0 [110/10] via 192.168.10.2, 0:00:04, inside
```

Tip Make sure that the exact subnet mask is configured on the interfaces that are running OSPF between the Cisco ASA and its neighbor. A subnet mismatch creates a discrepancy in the OSPF database that prevents routes from being installed in the routing tables. Furthermore, the maximum transmission unit (MTU) size must also match between peers.

Table 5-3 lists some of the common reasons why OSPF neighbors have problems forming an adjacency and suggests the **show** commands that you can use to troubleshoot the problem.

The **debug ospf** command is extremely useful for troubleshooting OSPF problems. However, turn on debug commands only if any of the **show** commands discussed cannot help you solve the problem. Table 5-4 lists all the options of the **debug ospf** command.

Table 5-3 *OSPF Common Problems and Useful* **show** *Commands*

Problem	Command
OSPF is not enabled on an interface where it is needed.	**show ospf interface**
OSPF **Hello** or **dead timer interval** values are mismatched.	**show ospf interface**
OSPF network-type mismatch on the adjoining interfaces.	**show ospf interface**
OSPF area type is stub on one neighbor, but the adjoining neighbor in the same area is not configured for stub.	**show ospf interface**
OSPF neighbors have duplicate router IDs.	**show ospf**
OSPF Hellos are not processed because of a lack of resources, such as high CPU utilization or not enough memory.	**show memory** **show cpu usage**
Neighbor information is incorrect.	**show ospf neighbor**
An underlying layer problem is preventing OSPF Hellos from being received.	**show ospf neighbor** **show ospf interface** **show interface**

Table 5-4 **debug ospf** *Options*

Option	Description
adj	Outputs information about adjacency process transactions
database-timer	Outputs database timer information
events	Outputs OSPF transaction event information
flood	Includes OSPF flooding information
lsa-generation	Outputs OSPF LSA generation information
packet	Outputs detailed OSPF packet information
retransmission	Provides information about retransmissions during OSPF transactions
spf external	Outputs SPF information external to local area
spf internal	Outputs SPF information within a given area
spf intra	Outputs SPF intra-area information

Tip If the **debug ospf** command is entered without any options, all options are enabled by default. This may not be appropriate for busy OSPF networks.

Example 5-29 shows the output of the **debug ospf events** command during a new adjacency. The first highlighted line shows that a two-way communication has been started to the router 192.168.10.2 on the inside interface and the state is 2WAY. The second highlighted line shows that non-broadcast (NBR) negotiation has been completed and the Cisco ASA is classified as the slave. The third and fourth highlighted lines indicate that the exchange has been completed and that the state is now FULL.

Example 5-29 *Output of the* **debug ospf events** *Command*

```
OSPF: Rcv DBD from 192.168.10.2 on inside seq 0x167f opt 0x2 flag 0x7 len 32  mtu
1500 state INIT
OSPF: 2 Way Communication to 192.168.10.2 on inside, state 2WAY
OSPF: Neighbor change Event on interface inside
OSPF: DR/BDR election on inside
OSPF: Elect BDR 192.168.10.2
OSPF: Elect DR 192.168.10.1
        DR: 192.168.10.1 (Id)   BDR: 192.168.10.2 (Id)
OSPF: Send DBD to 192.168.10.2 on inside seq 0x7c1 opt 0x2 flag 0x7 len 32
OSPF: NBR Negotiation Done. We are the SLAVE
OSPF: Send DBD to 192.168.10.2 on inside seq 0x167f opt 0x2 flag 0x2 len 132
OSPF: Rcv DBD from 192.168.10.2 on inside seq 0x1680 opt 0x2 flag 0x3 len 152
mtu 1500 state EXCHANGE
OSPF: Send DBD to 192.168.10.2 on inside seq 0x1680 opt 0x2 flag 0x0 len 32
OSPF: Rcv hello from 192.168.10.2 area 0 from inside 192.168.10.2
OSPF: Neighbor change Event on interface inside
OSPF: DR/BDR election on inside
OSPF: Elect BDR 192.168.10.2
OSPF: Elect DR 192.168.10.1
        DR: 192.168.10.1 (Id)   BDR: 192.168.10.2 (Id)
OSPF: End of hello processing
OSPF: Rcv DBD from 192.168.10.2 on inside seq 0x1681 opt 0x2 flag 0x1 len 32  mtu
1500 state EXCHANGE
OSPF: Exchange Done with 192.168.10.2 on inside
OSPF: Synchronized with 192.168.10.2 on inside, state FULL
OSPF: Send DBD to 192.168.10.2 on inside seq 0x1681 opt 0x2 flag 0x0 len 32
OSPF: service_maxage: Trying to delete MAXAGE LSA
OSPF: Rcv hello from 192.168.10.2 area 0 from inside 192.168.10.2
OSPF: End of hello processing
```

Mismatched Areas

Example 5-30 shows the output of the **debug ospf events** command during an OSPF transaction where the Cisco ASA was configured with area 0 and the adjacent router was configured with area 1. Consequently, the mismatch area message is displayed in the debug output.

Example 5-30 *Mismatched OSPF Areas*

```
OSPF: Rcv pkt from 192.168.10.2, inside, area 0.0.0.0
      mismatch area 0.0.0.1 in the header
```

OSPF Authentication Mismatch

In the next example, the Cisco ASA was configured to perform OSPF authentication. OSPF authentication was not enabled on the neighbor router. Example 5-31 shows the output of the **debug ospf event** command.

Example 5-31 *Mismatched OSPF Authentication Parameters*

```
NewYork# debug ospf event
OSPF: Rcv pkt from 192.168.10.2, inside : Mismatch Authentication type. Input
packet specified type 0, we use type 1

NewYork#
```

Troubleshooting Virtual Link Problems

To display parameters and the current state of OSPF virtual links configured in the Cisco ASA, use the **show ospf virtual-links** command. Example 5-32 shows the output of the **show ospf virtual-links** command while the state of the virtual link to router 192.168.10.2 is down.

Example 5-32 *Output of the* **show ospf virtual-links** *Command During a Configuration Mismatch in the Neighbor Router*

```
NewYork# show ospf virtual-links
Virtual Link dmz to router 192.168.3.1 is down
  Run as demand circuit
  DoNotAge LSA allowed.
  Transit area 1, via interface dmz, Cost of using 10
  Transmit Delay is 1 sec, State DOWN,
  Timer intervals configured, Hello 10, Dead 40, Wait 40, Retransmit 5
```

The problem is a configuration error on the Cisco ASA's neighbor router. The administrator notices, by looking at the running configuration with the **show running-config** command, that the router does not have the Cisco ASA's IP address in its configuration.

EIGRP

EIGRP is an enhanced version of the Interior Gateway Protocol (IGRP), which is a distance vector routing protocol. The distance vector routing technology defines that each router does not need to know all the router/link relationships for the entire network because each router advertises destinations with a corresponding distance. Each router, hearing the information, adjusts the distance and propagates it to neighboring routers. The same distance vector technology found in IGRP is also used in EIGRP. However, one of the major differences is the enhanced convergence properties and operating efficiency.

EIGRP uses the Diffusing Update Algorithm (DUAL). This algorithm is used to calculate route options while maintaining loop-freedom at every instant.

EIGRP has four basic components:

- **Neighbor Discovery/Recovery**—This is the process that routers use to dynamically learn of other routing devices within the adjacent network, and when they become unreachable or inoperative.
- **Reliable Transport Protocol**—Guarantees the ordered delivery of EIGRP packets to all neighbors.
- **DUAL Finite State Machine**—This is what does all route computations. It tracks all routes advertised by all neighbors. The distance information, known as a metric, is used to calculate the best (loop free) path.
- **Protocol Dependent Modules**—Responsible for network layer, protocol-specific requirements (i.e., packet encapsulation).

Configuring EIGRP

The following sections cover the configuration of EIGRP in the Cisco ASA.

Enabling EIGRP

The first step is to configure basic EIGRP on the Cisco ASA. The topology illustrated in Figure 5-29 is used for the following examples. The goal is to configure the Cisco ASA to learn routes from the inside router (R1) via EIGRP.

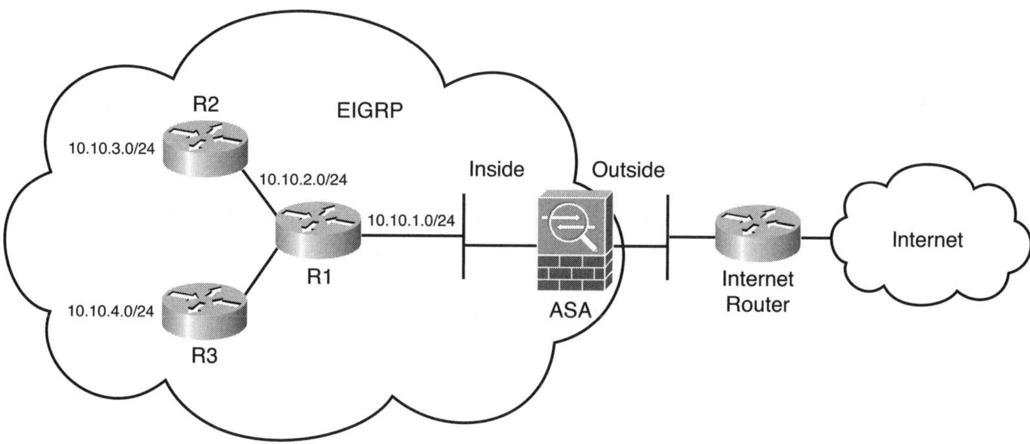

Figure 5-29 *EIGRP Example Topology*

Complete the following steps to enable EIGRP in the Cisco ASA using ASDM:

Step 1. Log in to ASDM and navigate to **Configuration > Device Setup > Routing > EIGRP > Setup**. The screen shown in Figure 5-30 is displayed.

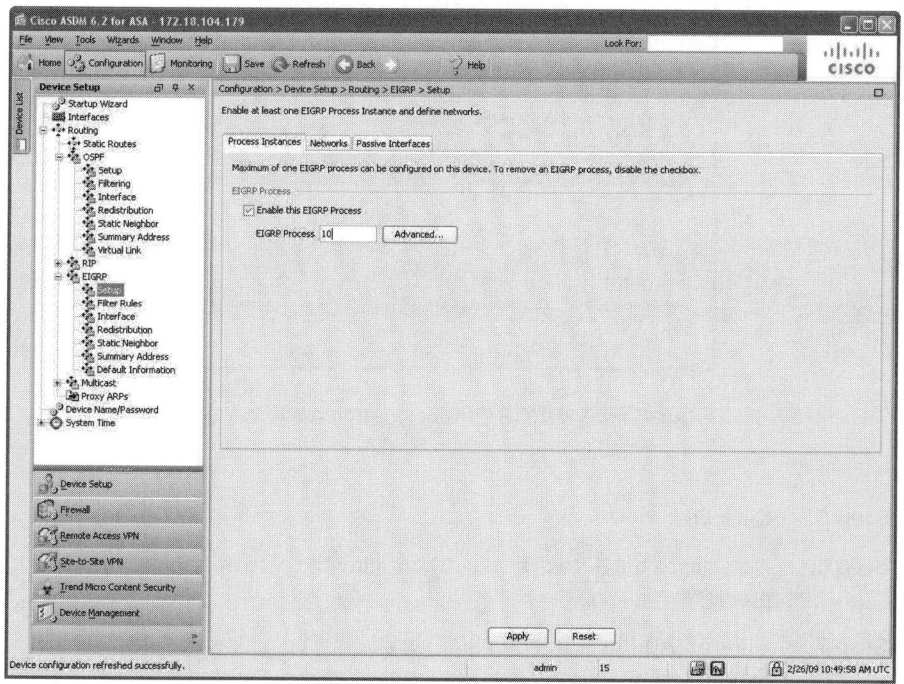

Figure 5-30 *Enabling EIGRP*

Step 2. To enable EIGRP, select **Enable this EIGRP Process** under the **EIGRP Process** section.

Step 3. Enter the EIGRP autonomous system (AS) number under the **EIGRP Process** field. The number **10** is used in this example. This number must match in all EIGRP neighbors. The AS number can be any value from 1 to 65535.

Step 4. (Optional) You can click on the **Advanced** button to configure EIGRP advanced properties, such as automatic route summarization, router ID, metric parameters, stub configuration, administrative distance, and others. The **Edit EIGRP Process Advanced Properties** dialog box shown in Figure 5-31 is displayed. In this example, automatic summarization is disabled; all other default values are used.

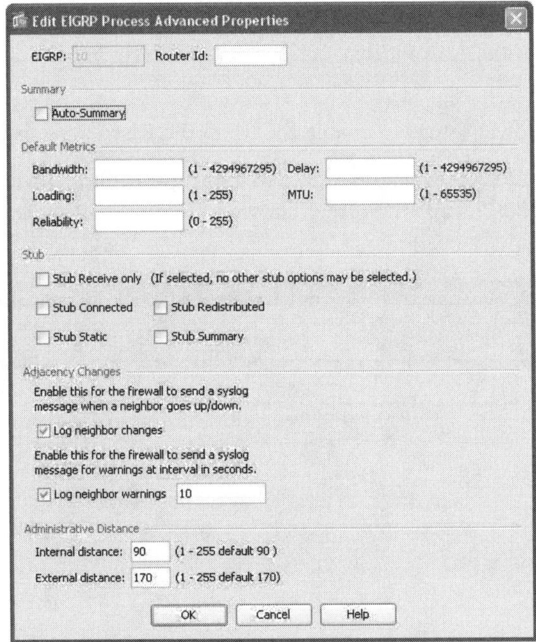

Figure 5-31 *EIGRP Process Advanced Properties*

Step 5. Click **OK**.

Step 6. Navigate to the **Networks** tab to configure the networks for the EIGRP process.

Step 7. Click on **Add** to add the EIGRP networks. The dialog box displayed in Figure 5-32.

Step 8. In this example, the inside network **10.10.1.0** with netmask **255.255.255.0** is used.

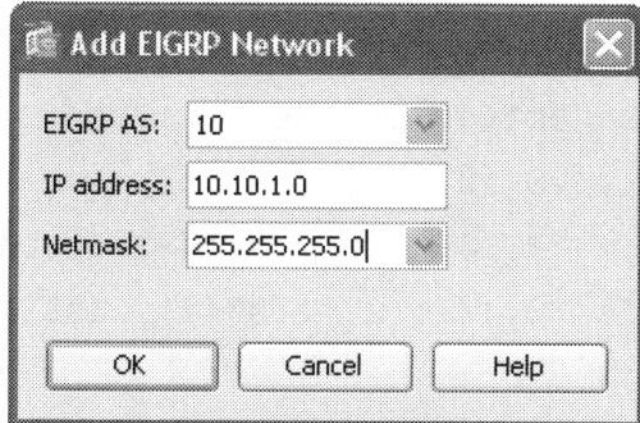

Figure 5-32 *Adding Networks to the EIGRP Process*

Step 9. Click **OK**.

> **Note** The **Passive Interface** tab enables you to configure specific interfaces as passive interfaces. A passive interface does not send or receive routing updates. In this example, no passive interfaces are configured.

Step 10. Click **Apply** to apply the configuration changes.

Step 11. Click on **Save** to save the configuration in the Cisco ASA.

Alternatively, you can use the CLI to configure EIGRP. Example 5-33 shows the CLI commands sent by ASDM to the Cisco ASA.

Example 5-33 *Enabling EIGRP via the CLI*

```
router eigrp 10
 no auto-summary
 network 10.10.1.0 255.255.255.0
```

Use the **router eigrp 10** command to enable EIGRP, using the AS number 10. The **no auto-summary** command disables automatic route summarization. The **network** command is used to configure all networks for the EIGRP process.

Example 5-34 shows the output of the **show route inside** command after the EIGRP routes have been learned from R1.

Example 5-34 *Output of* show route inside *Command Showing EIGRP Routes*

```
NewYork# show route inside
Codes: C - connected, S - static, I - IGRP, R - RIP, M - mobile, B - BGP
       D - EIGRP, EX - EIGRP external, O - OSPF, IA - OSPF inter area
       N1 - OSPF NSSA external type 1, N2 - OSPF NSSA external type 2
       E1 - OSPF external type 1, E2 - OSPF external type 2, E - EGP
       i - IS-IS, L1 - IS-IS level-1, L2 - IS-IS level-2, ia - IS-IS inter area
       * - candidate default, U - per-user static route, o - ODR
       P - periodic downloaded static route
```

```
Gateway of last resort is 209.165.201.2 to network 0.0.0.0
C     10.10.1.0 255.255.255.0 is directly connected, inside
D     10.10.2.0 255.255.255.0 [90/130816] via 10.10.1.2, 0:01:47, inside
D     10.10.3.0 255.255.255.0 [90/130816] via 10.10.1.2, 0:01:43, inside
D     10.10.4.0 255.255.255.0 [90/130816] via 10.10.1.2, 0:00:21, inside
```

In this example, three routes are learned for the internal networks via R1 (10.10.1.2). The letter **D** indicates that these routes are learned via EIGRP.

Configuring Route Filtering for EIGRP

The Cisco ASA supports EIGRP route filtering. You can filter routes learned via EIGRP or prevent specific routes from being advertised to EIGRP neighbors. The goal in the following example is to configure the Cisco ASA to filter the route to the network 10.10.4.0/24 learned from R1. To achieve this goal complete the following steps:

Step 1. Log in to ASDM and navigate to **Configuration > Device Setup > Routing > EIGRP > Filter Rules.**

Step 2. Click on **Add** to add a filter rule. The dialog box shown in Figure 5-33 is displayed.

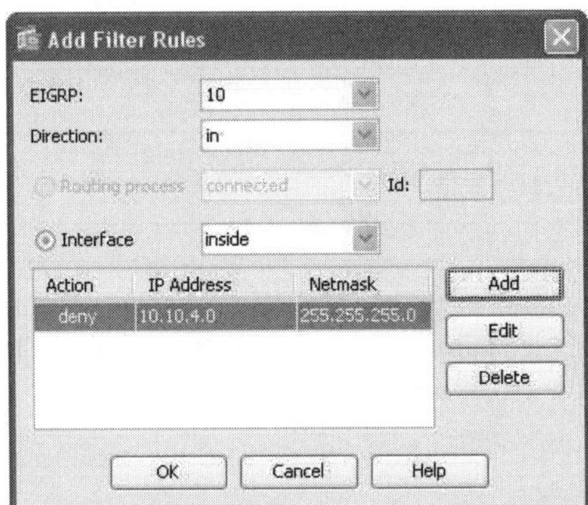

Figure 5-33 *Adding EIGRP Filter Rules*

Step 3. Select the respective EIGRP AS from the pull-down menu. In this example, the EIGRP AS number **10** is used.

Step 4. Select the direction on how the filter is to be applied. In this example, the filter is applied inbound (**in**).

Step 5. Select the interface where the filter is to be applied. In this example, the **inside** interface is selected.

Step 6. Click on **Add** to enter the routes/networks to be allowed or denied. In this example, the action is set to deny incoming route advertisements for the 10.10.4.0/24 network.

Step 7. Click **OK**.

Step 8. Click **Apply** to apply the configuration changes.

Step 9. Click on **Save** to save the configuration in the Cisco ASA.

Example 5-35 shows the CLI commands sent by ASDM to the Cisco ASA for EIGRP route filtering.

Example 5-35 *Configuring EIGRP Route Filtering via the CLI*

```
access-list eigrpACL_FR standard deny 10.10.4.0 255.255.255.0
access-list eigrpACL_FR standard permit any
router eigrp 10
 distribute-list eigrpACL_FR in interface inside
```

In Example 5-35, a standard ACL (eigrpACL_FR) is configured to deny the 10.10.4.0 network. This ACL is then applied inbound to the **distribute-list** command in the **inside** interface.

EIGRP Authentication

The Cisco ASA supports EIGRP authentication using MD5 hashing. Complete the following steps to enable EIGRP MD5 authentication:

Step 1. Log in to ASDM and navigate to **Configuration > Device Setup > Routing > EIGRP > Interface.**

Step 2. Select the interface where EIGRP MD5 authentication is to be enabled and click on Edit. The **Edit EIGRP Interface Entry** dialog box shown in Figure 5-34 is displayed.

Step 3. Under the **Authentication** section, select **Enable MD5 Authentication.**

Step 4. Enter the key (password) to be used under the **Key** field. The key **supersecret** is used in this example.

Step 5. Enter the key identifier under the **Key ID** field. The **Key ID 1** is used in this example.

Step 6. Click **OK**.

Step 7. Click **Apply** to apply the configuration changes.

Step 8. Click on **Save** to save the configuration in the Cisco ASA.

Example 5-36 shows the CLI commands sent by ASDM to the Cisco ASA to enable EIGRP MD5 authentication.

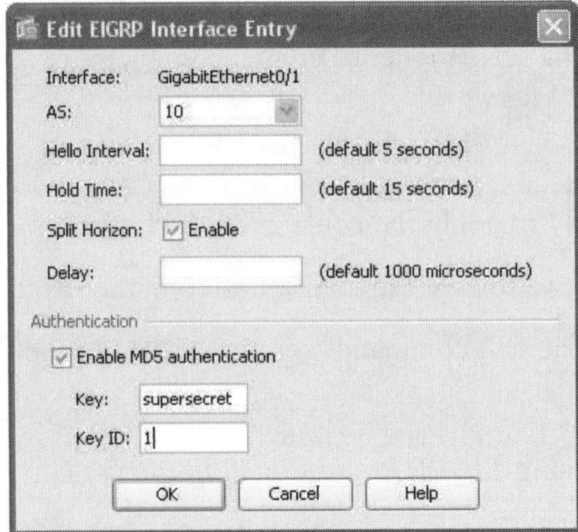

Figure 5-34 *Edit EIGRP Interface Entry Dialog Box*

Example 5-36 *Configuring EIGRP MD5 Authentication Using the CLI*

```
interface GigabitEthernet0/1
 authentication key eigrp 10 supersecret key-id 1
 authentication mode eigrp 10 md5
```

EIGRP authentication is enabled under the inside interface (**GigabitEthernet0/1**). The first highlighted line defines the key **supersecret** and key ID **1** for the EIGRP AS number **10**. The second highlighted line enables MD5 authentication. The authentication key is removed and labeled as **<removed>** when you view the configuration, using the **show running-config** or **show configuration** commands.

Defining Static EIGRP Neighbors

The Cisco ASA supports statically defined EIGRP neighbors. Typically, EIGRP neighbors are dynamically discovered; however, on point-to-point, non-broadcast networks, you must statically define the neighbors.

Configure a static neighbor in the Cisco ASA by completing the following steps:

Step 1. Log in to ASDM and navigate to **Configuration > Device Setup > Routing > EIGRP > Static Neighbor.**

Step 2. Click on **Add** to add a new EIGRP static neighbor.

Step 3. Enter the EIGRP neighbor IP address in the **Add EIGRP Neighbor Entry** dialog box.

Step 4. Click **OK**.

Step 5. Click **Apply** to apply the configuration changes.

Step 6. Click on **Save** to save the configuration in the Cisco ASA.

Alternatively, in the CLI you can use the **neighbor** command, as shown in Example 5-37.

Example 5-37 *Configuring a Static EIGRP Neighbor*

```
router eigrp 10
 neighbor 10.10.1.2 interface inside
```

In Example 5-37 the neighbor **10.10.1.2** is statically defined.

Route Summarization in EIGRP

The Cisco ASA supports EIGRP route summarization. This is used to manually define summary addresses if you want to create summary addresses that do not occur at a network number boundary. In other words, if any specific routes are in the routing table, EIGRP advertises the summary address out the specified interface with a metric equal to the minimum of all the more specific routes.

EIGRP route summarization is configured on the Cisco ASA when automatic route summarization is disabled. Summary addresses are configured in the Cisco ASA on a per-interface basis.

Complete the following steps to create a summary address:

Step 1. Log in to ASDM and navigate to **Configuration > Device Setup > Routing > EIGRP > Summary Address.**

Step 2. Click on **Add** to add a summary address entry. The dialog box shown in Figure 5-35 is displayed.

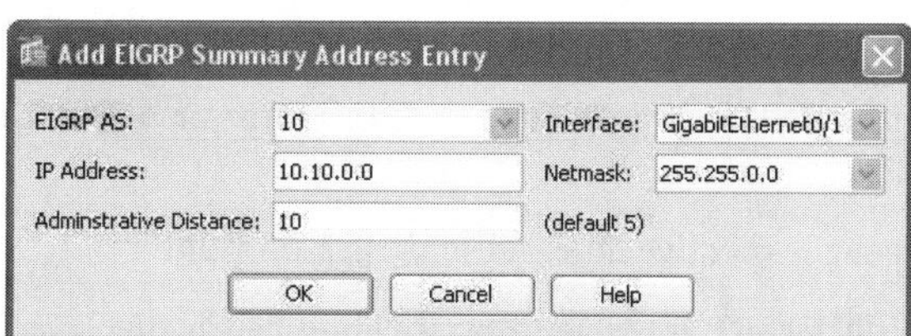

Figure 5-35 *Add EIGRP Summary Address Entry Dialog Box*

Step 3. Select the **EIGRP AS** where summarization is applied. The EIGRP AS used in this example is **10**.

Step 4. Enter the **IP Address** and the **Netmask** of the summary address. In this example, the **10.10.0.0** network address and **255.255.0.0** netmask are used. Subsequently, the 10.10.1.0/24, 10.10.2.0/24, 10.10.3.0/24, and 10.10.4.0/24 networks will be summarized as **10.10.0.0/16.**

Step 5. Enter the **Administrative distance** used for this summary address. In this example, the administrative distance used is **10**. The default is 5.

Step 6. Click **OK**.

Step 7. Click **Apply** to apply the configuration changes.

Step 8. Click on **Save** to save the configuration in the Cisco ASA.

Alternatively, you can use the **summary-address** interface subcommand to configure summarization under a specific interface. Example 5-38 shows the CLI commands sent by ASDM to the Cisco ASA.

Example 5-38 *Configuring an EIGRP Summary Address*

```
interface GigabitEthernet0/1
  summary-address eigrp 10 10.10.0.0 255.255.0.0 10
```

In this example, the **summary-address** interface subcommand defines the summary address **10.10.0.0** with netmask **255.255.0.0** applied to the EIGRP AS number **10**. The administrative distance is set to **10** at the end of the command.

Split Horizon

The Cisco ASA supports split horizon. Split horizon is enabled on all interfaces by default. When you configure split horizon, EIGRP update and query packets are not sent for destinations for which the specified interface is the next hop. This is used to minimize the potential of routing loops.

In some cases, for instance in nonbroadcast networks, split horizon may not be necessary and may need to be disabled. You can disable split horizon with ASDM by completing the following steps:

Step 1. Log in to ASDM and navigate to **Configuration > Device Setup > Routing > EIGRP > Interface.**

Step 2. Select the respective interface and click on **Edit.**

Step 3. The **Edit EIGRP Interface Entry** dialog box is displayed. This dialog box was illustrated earlier in Figure 5-34. Uncheck the **Enable** box in the **Split Horizon** field.

Step 4. Click **OK**.

Step 5. Click **Apply** to apply the configuration changes.

Step 6. Click on **Save** to save the configuration in the Cisco ASA.

Alternatively, you can use the **no split-horizon eigrp <as number>** interface subcommand to disable split horizon on a specific interface.

Route Redistribution in EIGRP

As with RIP and OSPF, in EIGRP you can redistribute routes from other routing protocols. To configure route redistribution in ASDM, complete the following steps:

Step 1. Log in to ASDM and navigate to **Configuration > Device Setup > Routing > EIGRP > Redistribution.**

Step 2. Click on **Add** to add an EIGRP redistribution entry. The dialog box shown in Figure 5-36 is displayed.

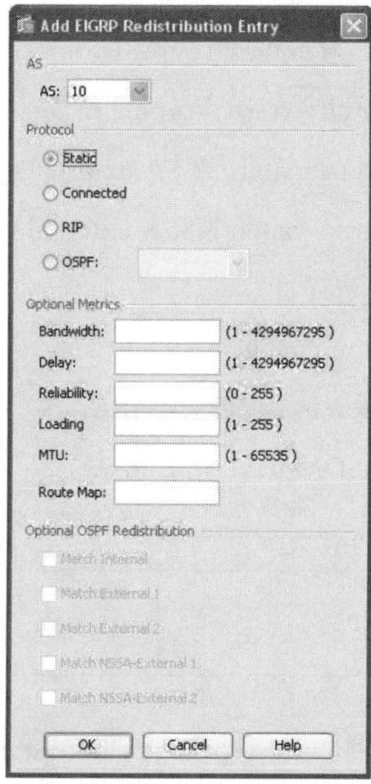

Figure 5-36 *Add EIGRP Redistribution Entry Dialog Box*

Step 3. Select the **AS** number where route redistribution will be applied. In this example, the EIGRP AS number **10** is selected.

Step 4. Select the **Protocol** to be redistributed into EIGRP. In this example, static routes are redistributed into EIGRP. The **Static** option is selected.

Step 5. You can configure several optional metrics and OSPF redistribution parameters. In this example, the defaults are used. However, the following are all the supported advanced options:

- **Bandwidth**—Used to specify the EIGRP bandwidth metric in Kilobits per second.
- **Delay**—Used to specify the EIGRP delay metric, in 10-microsecond units.
- **Reliability**—Used to specify the EIGRP reliability metric.

- **Loading**—Used to specify the EIGRP loading bandwidth metric.
- **MTU**—Used to specify the minimum MTU of the path.
- **Route Map**—Used to granularly define which routes are redistributed into the EIGRP.

You can also (optionally) specify which OSPF routes are redistributed into the EIGRP routing process by selecting any of the following options under the **Optional OSPF Redistribution** section:

- **Match Internal**—Used for internal OSPF routes.
- **Match External 1**—Used to match external type 1 routes.
- **Match External 2**—Used to match external type 2 routes.
- **Match NSSA-External 1**—Used to match NSSA external type 1 routes.
- **Match NSSA-External 2**—Used to match NSSA external type 2 routes.

Step 6. Click **OK**.

Step 7. Click **Apply** to apply the configuration changes.

Step 8. Click on **Save** to save the configuration in the Cisco ASA.

Example 5-39 includes the commands sent by ASDM to the Cisco ASA.

Example 5-39 *Redistributing Static Routes into EIGRP*

```
router eigrp 10
 redistribute static
```

In this example, the **redistribute static** command is used to redistribute static routes into the EIGRP process.

You can use the **redistribute connected** command to redistribute connected routes into the EIGRP routing process, as shown below:

```
redistribute connected [metric bandwidth delay reliability loading mtu] [route-map map_name]
```

To redistribute routes from an OSPF routing process into the EIGRP routing process, use the **redistribute ospf** command as follows:

```
redistribute ospf pid [match {internal | external [1 | 2] | nssa-external [1 | 2]}]
[metric bandwidth delay reliability loading mtu] [route-map map_name]
```

To redistribute routes from a RIP routing process into the EIGRP routing process, use the **redistribute rip** command as follows:

```
redistribute rip [metric bandwidth delay reliability load mtu] [route-map
map_name]
```

Tip The **default-metric** command in the EIGRP router configuration can be used to specify default metric values to be used for all routes redistributed into EIGRP. On the other hand, you must specify the EIGRP metric values in the preceding **redistribute** commands if the **default-metric** command is not used.

Controlling Default Information

When EIGRP is enabled, default routes are sent and accepted in the Cisco ASA by default, which is a configurable behavior. To configure a set of rules for controlling the sending and receiving of default route information in EIGRP updates, complete the following steps:

Step 1. Log in to ASDM and navigate to **Configuration > Device Setup > Routing > EIGRP > Default Information.**

Step 2. You can have one **in** and one **out** rule for each EIGRP routing process. However, only one process is currently supported. In this example, the goal is to deny any default route to be learned by the EIGRP process. Select the direction of the filter rule that reads **in** and click on **Edit**. The **Edit Default Information** dialog box is displayed.

Step 3. Select the EIGRP process.

Step 4. Make sure that the **Direction** is set to **in**.

Step 5. Click on **Add** to add the new rule. The **Network Rule** dialog box is displayed.

Step 6. Select **deny** from the Action pull down menu.

Step 7. Enter **0.0.0.0** in the **IP address** field.

Step 8. Enter **0.0.0.0** in the **Netmask** field.

Step 9. Click **OK** in the **Network Rule** dialog box.

Step 10. Click **OK** in the **Add Default Information** dialog box.

Step 11. Click **OK**.

Step 12. Click **Apply** to apply the configuration changes.

Step 13. Click on **Save** to save the configuration in the Cisco ASA.

Example 5-40 shows the CLI commands sent by ASDM to the Cisco ASA.

Example 5-40 *Default Information Filtering in EIGRP*

```
access-list eigrpACL_DI standard deny any
router eigrp 10
 default-information in eigrpACL_DI
```

In Example 5-40 a standard ACL named **eigrpACL_DI** is configured denying **any**. Then the **default-information** router subcommand is used with the **in** keyword to deny the default routes inbound. The **eigrpACL_DI** ACL name is entered at the end of the **default-information** command.

Troubleshooting EIGRP

This section covers detailed information for troubleshooting problems in EIGRP.

Useful Troubleshooting Commands

The **show eigrp topology** command can be used to display the EIGRP topology in the Cisco ASA. Example 5-41 shows the output of this command.

Example 5-41 *Displaying the EIGRP Topology*

```
NewYork# show eigrp topology
EIGRP-IPv4 Topology Table for AS(10)/ID(209.165.201.1)
Codes: P - Passive, A - Active, U - Update, Q - Query, R - Reply,
       r - reply Status, s - sia Status
P 10.10.1.0 255.255.255.0, 1 successors, FD is 2816
        via Connected, GigabitEthernet0/1
P 10.10.2.0 255.255.255.0, 1 successors, FD is 130816
        via 10.10.1.2 (130816/128256), GigabitEthernet0/1
P 10.10.3.0 255.255.255.0, 1 successors, FD is 130816
        via 10.10.1.2 (130816/128256), GigabitEthernet0/1
P 10.10.4.0 255.255.255.0, 1 successors, FD is 130816
        via 10.10.1.2 (130816/128256), GigabitEthernet0/1
```

In Example 5-41, the three routes learned from 10.10.1.2 are displayed.

Tip By default only routes from feasible successors are displayed. However, you can use the **all-links** keyword to display all routes, including those that are not feasible successors.

The **show eigrp neighbors** command provides the details of current EIGRP neighbors. Example 5-42 shows the output of this command.

Example 5-42 *Output of* **show eigrp neighbors** *Command*

```
NewYork# show eigrp neighbors
EIGRP-IPv4 neighbors for process 10
H   Address                 Interface         Hold Uptime   SRTT   RTO  Q   Seq
                                              (sec)         (ms)       Cnt Num
0   10.10.1.2               Gi0/1              12  00:03:06 1     200   0   6
```

In Example 5-42 the inside router (10.10.1.2) is displayed. You can also see the interface where the neighbor resides (Gi0/1 in this example). You can also see the Hold timer, which is the length of time (in seconds) that the Cisco ASA waits to receive a hello packet from the neighbor routing device before declaring it down.

Note If the Hold timer value reaches 0, the Cisco ASA marks the neighbor unreachable (down).

The Uptime value is the elapsed time since the Cisco ASA first heard from this neighbor. This is displayed in hours:minutes:seconds.

The smooth round-trip time (SRTT) is the number of milliseconds required for an EIGRP packet to be sent to this neighbor and for the Cisco ASA to receive a reply.

Retransmission timeout (RTO) is the amount of time the Cisco ASA waits before resending a hello packet to a neighbor. The Q Cnt is the number of EIGRP packets that are in queue to be sent by the Cisco ASA. The Seq Num is the sequence number of the last EIGRP packet received from the neighbor.

The **show eigrp events** command displays the EIGRP event log. This output is limited to 500 events. New events are added to the bottom of the output and old events are removed from the top of the output. Example 5-43 shows the output of the **show eigrp events** command.

Example 5-43 *Output of* **show eigrp events** *Command*

```
NewYork#  show eigrp events
Event information for AS 10:    1 18:53:31.353 Change queue emptied, entries: 3
   2 18:53:31.353 Metric set: 10.10.4.0 255.255.255.0 130816
   3 18:53:31.353 Update reason, delay: new if 4294967295
   4 18:53:31.353 Update sent, RD: 10.10.4.0 255.255.255.0 4294967295
   5 18:53:31.353 Update reason, delay: metric chg 4294967295
   6 18:53:31.353 Update sent, RD: 10.10.4.0 255.255.255.0 4294967295
   7 18:53:31.353 Route install: 10.10.4.0 255.255.255.0 10.10.1.2
   8 18:53:31.353 Find FS: 10.10.4.0 255.255.255.0 4294967295
   9 18:53:31.353 Rcv update met/succmet: 130816 128256
```

In Example 5-43, updates are sent and received from the neighbor router. In this example the route to the network 10.10.4.0/24 is received and installed in the routing table.

Tip You can use the **clear eigrp events** command to clear the EIGRP event log. Neighbor changes, neighbor warning, and DUAL FSM messages are logged by default in the Cisco ASA. However, you can disable neighbor change event logging by using the **no eigrp log-neighbor-changes** command. You can disable neighbor warning event logging by using the

no eigrp log-neighbor-warnings command under the **router eigrp** process. On the other hand, you cannot disable the logging of DUAL FSM events.

Use the **show eigrp interfaces** command to display the interfaces where EIGRP is enabled. Example 5-44 shows the output of the **show eigrp interfaces** command.

Example 5-44 *Output of* **show eigrp interfaces** *Command*

```
NewYork# show eigrp interfaces
EIGRP-IPv4 interfaces for process 10
                        Xmit Queue   Mean   Pacing Time   Multicast    Pending
Interface        Peers  Un/Reliable  SRTT   Un/Reliable   Flow Timer   Routes
inside             1        0/0         1       0/1           50            0
```

In this example EIGRP is enabled only on the inside interface and it currently has one peer.

Use the **show eigrp traffic** command to display EIGRP traffic statistics. Example 5-45 shows the output of the **show eigrp traffic** command.

Example 5-45 *Output of* **show eigrp traffic** *Command*

```
NewYork# show eigrp traffic
EIGRP-IPv4 Traffic Statistics for AS 10
  Hellos sent/received: 5976/467
  Updates sent/received: 3/8
  Queries sent/received: 0/0
  Replies sent/received: 0/0
  Acks sent/received: 6/0
  Input queue high water mark 1, 0 drops
  SIA-Queries sent/received: 0/0
  SIA-Replies sent/received: 0/0
  Hello Process ID: 253
  PDM Process ID: 252
```

As shown in Example 5-45, the **show eigrp traffic** command displays the number of EIGRP packets sent and received in the Cisco ASA. These packets include hellos, updates, queries, replies, acknowledgements, and other statistical information.

The **debug eigrp fsm** command is one of the most useful debug commands used to troubleshoot EIGRP problems. Example 5-46 shows the output of the **debug eigrp fsm** command during normal operations.

Example 5-46 *Output of* **debug eigrp fsm** *Command During Normal Operations*

```
NewYork# debug eigrp fsm
```

```
EIGRP FSM Events/Actions debugging is on
DUAL: rcvupdate: 10.10.2.0 255.255.255.0 via 10.10.1.2 metric 130816/128256 on
topoid 0
DUAL: Find FS for dest 10.10.2.0 255.255.255.0. FD is 4294967295, RD is 4294967295
on topoid 0 found
EIGRP-IPv4(Default-IP-Routing-Table:10): route installed for 10.10.2.0  ()
DUAL: RT installed 10.10.2.0 255.255.255.0 via 10.10.1.2
DUAL: Send update about 10.10.2.0 255.255.255.0.  Reason: metric chg on topoid 0
DUAL: Send update about 10.10.2.0 255.255.255.0.  Reason: new if on topoid 0
DUAL: dest(10.10.3.0 255.255.255.0) not active
DUAL: rcvupdate: 10.10.3.0 255.255.255.0 via 10.10.1.2 metric 130816/128256 on
topoid 0
DUAL: Find FS for dest 10.10.3.0 255.255.255.0. FD is 4294967295, RD is 4294967295
on topoid 0 found
EIGRP-IPv4(Default-IP-Routing-Table:10): route installed for 10.10.3.0  ()
DUAL: RT installed 10.10.3.0 255.255.255.0 via 10.10.1.2
DUAL: Send update about 10.10.3.0 255.255.255.0.  Reason: metric chg on topoid 0
DUAL: Send update about 10.10.3.0 255.255.255.0.  Reason: new if on topoid 0
DUAL: dest(10.10.4.0 255.255.255.0) not active
DUAL: rcvupdate: 10.10.4.0 255.255.255.0 via 10.10.1.2 metric 130816/128256 on
topoid 0
DUAL: Find FS for dest 10.10.4.0 255.255.255.0. FD is 4294967295, RD is 4294967295
on topoid 0 found
EIGRP-IPv4(Default-IP-Routing-Table:10): route installed for 10.10.4.0  ()
DUAL: RT installed 10.10.4.0 255.255.255.0 via 10.10.1.2
DUAL: Send update about 10.10.4.0 255.255.255.0.  Reason: metric chg on topoid 0
DUAL: Send update about 10.10.4.0 255.255.255.0.  Reason: new if on topoid 0
```

In Example 5-46, the updates are received from the EIGRP neighbor 10.10.1.2 and the routes received are installed on the routing table.

Stability and failure in the EIGRP neighbor relationship are some of the most common issues. The following are some of the reasons why EIGRP neighbors may fail (flap):

- Underlying link flaps.
- Misconfigured hello and hold intervals.
- Loss of hello packets.
- Existence of unidirectional links.
- Route goes stuck-in-active. When a router enters the stuck-in-active state, the neighbors from which the reply was expected are reinitialized, and the router goes active on all routes learned from those neighbors and is able to process all routing updates.
- Provision of insufficient bandwidth for the EIGRP process and improperly set bandwidth statements.

- One-way multicast traffic.
- Routes that are stuck in active.
- Query storms.
- Authentication problems.

The following sections cover different common scenarios encountered while troubleshooting EIGRP issues.

Scenario 1: Link Failures

When an interface goes down, EIGRP takes down the neighbors that are reachable through that interface and flushes all routes learned through that neighbor. The **debug eigrp fsm** command is very useful while troubleshooting these kinds of problems. In the following example the link between the Cisco ASA and the inside router (10.10.1.2) failed. Example 5-47 shows the output of the **debug iegrp fsm** when the link went down.

Example 5-47 *Output of* **debug eigrp fsm** *Command During a Link Failure*

```
NewYork# debug eigrp fsm
EIGRP FSM Events/Actions debugging is on
NewYork# IGRP2: linkdown: start - 10.10.1.2 via GigabitEthernet0/1
DUAL: Destination 10.10.1.0 255.255.255.0 for topoid 0
DUAL: Destination 10.10.2.0 255.255.255.0 for topoid 0
DUAL: Find FS for dest 10.10.2.0 255.255.255.0. FD is 130816, RD is 130816 on
topoid 0
DUAL:    10.10.1.2 metric 4294967295/4294967295
 not found Dmin is 4294967295
DUAL: Peer total 0 stub 0 template 0 for topoid 0
DUAL: Dest 10.10.2.0 255.255.255.0 (No peers) not entering active state for topoid
0.DUAL: Removing dest 10.10.2.0 255.255.255.0, nexthop 10.10.1.2
DUAL: No routes.  Flushing dest 10.10.2.0 255.255.255.0
DUAL: Destination 10.10.3.0 255.255.255.0 for topoid 0
DUAL: Find FS for dest 10.10.3.0 255.255.255.0. FD is 130816, RD is 130816 on
topoid 0
DUAL:    10.10.1.2 metric 4294967295/4294967295
 not found Dmin is 4294967295
DUAL: Peer total 0 stub 0 template 0 for topoid 0
DUAL: Dest 10.10.3.0 255.255.255.0 (No peers) not entering active state for topoid
0.DUAL: Removing dest 10.10.3.0 255.255.255.0, nexthop 10.10.1.2
DUAL: No routes.  Flushing dest 10.10.3.0 255.255.255.0
DUAL: Destination 10.10.4.0 255.255.255.0 for topoid 0
DUAL: Find FS for dest 10.10.4.0 255.255.255.0. FD is 130816, RD is 130816 on
topoid 0
DUAL:    10.10.1.2 metric 4294967295/4294967295
 not found Dmin is 4294967295
```

```
DUAL: Peer total 0 stub 0 template 0 for topoid 0
DUAL: Dest 10.10.4.0 255.255.255.0 (No peers) not entering active state for topoid
0.DUAL: Removing dest 10.10.4.0 255.255.255.0, nexthop 10.10.1.2
DUAL: No routes.  Flushing dest 10.10.4.0 255.255.255.0
DUAL: linkdown: finish
```

In Example 5-47, the Cisco ASA detected that the link was down and removed all the entries for the routes learned from the neighbor (10.10.1.2).

Scenario 2: Misconfigured Hello and Hold Intervals

In the Cisco ASA and Cisco IOS routers, the EIGRP hold interval can be set independently of the hello interval. This is done with the **hold-time eigrp** interface subcommand. If you set a hold interval smaller than the hello interval, it results in the neighbors flapping continuously. Therefore, it is recommended that the hold time be at least three times the hello interval.

In the following example the hold interval was set to 2 seconds on the neighbor router (10.10.1.2). Example 5-48 shows the output of the **debug eigrp fsm** while the neighbor relationship between the Cisco ASA and the inside router was flapping continuously.

Example 5-45 *Output of* **debug eigrp fsm** *Command While Neighbors Are Flapping*

```
DUAL: rcvupdate: 10.10.2.0 255.255.255.0 via 10.10.1.2 metric 130816/128256 on
topoid 0
DUAL: Find FS for dest 10.10.2.0 255.255.255.0. FD is 4294967295, RD is 4294967295
on topoid 0 found
EIGRP-IPv4(Default-IP-Routing-Table:10): route installed for 10.10.2.0  ()
DUAL: RT installed 10.10.2.0 255.255.255.0 via 10.10.1.2
DUAL: Send update about 10.10.2.0 255.255.255.0.  Reason: metric chg on topoid 0
DUAL: Send update about 10.10.2.0 255.255.255.0.  Reason: new if on topoid 0
DUAL: dest(10.10.3.0 255.255.255.0) not active
DUAL: rcvupdate: 10.10.3.0 255.255.255.0 via 10.10.1.2 metric 130816/128256 on
topoid 0
DUAL: Find FS for dest 10.10.3.0 255.255.255.0. FD is 4294967295, RD is 4294967295
on topoid 0 found
EIGRP-IPv4(Default-IP-Routing-Table:10): route installed for 10.10.3.0  ()
DUAL: RT installed 10.10.3.0 255.255.255.0 via 10.10.1.2
DUAL: Send update about 10.10.3.0 255.255.255.0.  Reason: metric chg on topoid 0
DUAL: Send update about 10.10.3.0 255.255.255.0.  Reason: new if on topoid 0
DUAL: dest(10.10.4.0 255.255.255.0) not active
DUAL: rcvupdate: 10.10.4.0 255.255.255.0 via 10.10.1.2 metric 130816/128256 on
topoid 0
DUAL: Find FS for dest 10.10.4.0 255.255.255.0. FD is 4294967295, RD is 4294967295
on topoid 0 found
EIGRP-IPv4(Default-IP-Routing-Table:10): route installed for 10.10.4.0  ()
DUAL: RT installed 10.10.4.0 255.255.255.0 via 10.10.1.2
```

```
DUAL: Send update about 10.10.4.0 255.255.255.0.  Reason: metric chg on topoid 0
DUAL: Send update about 10.10.4.0 255.255.255.0.  Reason: new if on topoid 0
IGRP2: linkdown: start - 10.10.1.2 via GigabitEthernet0/1
DUAL: Destination 10.10.1.0 255.255.255.0 for topoid 0
DUAL: Destination 10.10.2.0 255.255.255.0 for topoid 0
DUAL: Find FS for dest 10.10.2.0 255.255.255.0. FD is 130816, RD is 130816 on
topoid 0
DUAL:    10.10.1.2 metric 4294967295/4294967295
 not found Dmin is 4294967295
DUAL: Peer total 0 stub 0 template 0 for topoid 0
DUAL: Dest 10.10.2.0 255.255.255.0 (No peers) not entering active state for topoid
0.DUAL: Removing dest 10.10.2.0 255.255.255.0, nexthop 10.10.1.2
DUAL: No routes.  Flushing dest 10.10.2.0 255.255.255.0
DUAL: Destination 10.10.3.0 255.255.255.0 for topoid 0
DUAL: Find FS for dest 10.10.3.0 255.255.255.0. FD is 130816, RD is 130816 on
topoid 0
DUAL:    10.10.1.2 metric 4294967295/4294967295
 not found Dmin is 4294967295
DUAL: Peer total 0 stub 0 template 0 for topoid 0
DUAL: Dest 10.10.3.0 255.255.255.0 (No peers) not entering active state for topoid
0.DUAL: Removing dest 10.10.3.0 255.255.255.0, nexthop 10.10.1.2
DUAL: No routes.  Flushing dest 10.10.3.0 255.255.255.0
DUAL: Destination 10.10.4.0 255.255.255.0 for topoid 0
DUAL: Find FS for dest 10.10.4.0 255.255.255.0. FD is 130816, RD is 130816 on
topoid 0
DUAL:    10.10.1.2 metric 4294967295/4294967295
 not found Dmin is 4294967295
DUAL: Peer total 0 stub 0 template 0 for topoid 0
DUAL: Dest 10.10.4.0 255.255.255.0 (No peers) not entering active state for topoid
0.DUAL: Removing dest 10.10.4.0 255.255.255.0, nexthop 10.10.1.2
DUAL: No routes.  Flushing dest 10.10.4.0 255.255.255.0
DUAL: linkdown: finish
DUAL: dest(10.10.2.0 255.255.255.0) not active
DUAL: rcvupdate: 10.10.2.0 255.255.255.0 via 10.10.1.2 metric 130816/128256 on
topoid 0
DUAL: Find FS for dest 10.10.2.0 255.255.255.0. FD is 4294967295, RD is 4294967295
on topoid 0 found
EIGRP-IPv4(Default-IP-Routing-Table:10): route installed for 10.10.2.0  ()
DUAL: RT installed 10.10.2.0 255.255.255.0 via 10.10.1.2
DUAL: Send update about 10.10.2.0 255.255.255.0.  Reason: metric chg on topoid 0
DUAL: Send update about 10.10.2.0 255.255.255.0.  Reason: new if on topoid 0
DUAL: dest(10.10.3.0 255.255.255.0) not active
DUAL: rcvupdate: 10.10.3.0 255.255.255.0 via 10.10.1.2 metric 130816/128256 on
topoid 0
...
<output truncated>
```

The output of Example 5-48 is truncated; however, you can see the neighbor relationship between the Cisco ASA and the inside router flapping continuously. Routes first are learned and then removed.

The output of the **show eigrp events** command also displays the neighbor relationship flapping. One of the advantages of the **show eigrp events** is that it includes a timestamp at the beginning of each log entry. Example 5-49 includes the output of the **show eigrp events** command while the neighbors were flapping.

Example 5-49 *Output of* **show eigrp events** *Command While Neighbors Are Flapping*

```
NewYork# show eigrp events
Event information for AS 10:    1 15:55:59.882 Change queue emptied, entries: 3
   2 15:55:59.882 Metric set: 10.10.4.0 255.255.255.0 130816
   3 15:55:59.882 Update reason, delay: new if 4294967295
   4 15:55:59.882 Update sent, RD: 10.10.4.0 255.255.255.0 4294967295
   5 15:55:59.882 Update reason, delay: metric chg 4294967295
   6 15:55:59.882 Update sent, RD: 10.10.4.0 255.255.255.0 4294967295
   7 15:55:59.882 Route install: 10.10.4.0 255.255.255.0 10.10.1.2
   8 15:55:59.882 Find FS: 10.10.4.0 255.255.255.0 4294967295
   9 15:55:59.882 Rcv update met/succmet: 130816 128256
  10 15:55:59.882 Rcv update dest/nh: 10.10.4.0 255.255.255.0 10.10.1.2
  11 15:55:59.882 Metric set: 10.10.4.0 255.255.255.0 4294967295
  12 15:55:59.882 Metric set: 10.10.3.0 255.255.255.0 130816
  13 15:55:59.882 Update reason, delay: new if 4294967295
  14 15:55:59.882 Update sent, RD: 10.10.3.0 255.255.255.0 4294967295
  15 15:55:59.882 Update reason, delay: metric chg 4294967295
  16 15:55:59.882 Update sent, RD: 10.10.3.0 255.255.255.0 4294967295
  17 15:55:59.882 Route install: 10.10.3.0 255.255.255.0 10.10.1.2
  18 15:55:59.882 Find FS: 10.10.3.0 255.255.255.0 4294967295
  19 15:55:59.882 Rcv update met/succmet: 130816 128256
  20 15:55:59.882 Rcv update dest/nh: 10.10.3.0 255.255.255.0 10.10.1.2
  21 15:55:59.882 Metric set: 10.10.3.0 255.255.255.0 4294967295
  22 15:55:59.882 Metric set: 10.10.2.0 255.255.255.0 130816
  23 15:55:59.882 Update reason, delay: new if 4294967295
  24 15:55:59.882 Update sent, RD: 10.10.2.0 255.255.255.0 4294967295
  25 15:55:59.882 Update reason, delay: metric chg 4294967295
  26 15:55:59.882 Update sent, RD: 10.10.2.0 255.255.255.0 4294967295
  27 15:55:59.882 Route install: 10.10.2.0 255.255.255.0 10.10.1.2
  28 15:55:59.882 Find FS: 10.10.2.0 255.255.255.0 4294967295
  29 15:55:59.882 Rcv update met/succmet: 130816 128256
  30 15:55:59.882 Rcv update dest/nh: 10.10.2.0 255.255.255.0 10.10.1.2
  31 15:55:59.882 Metric set: 10.10.2.0 255.255.255.0 4294967295
  32 15:55:59.882 Rcv peer INIT: 10.10.1.2 GigabitEthernet0/1
  33 15:55:57.572 NDB delete: 10.10.4.0 255.255.255.0 1
  34 15:55:57.572 Poison squashed: 10.10.4.0 255.255.255.0 rt gone
```

```
  35 15:55:57.572 RDB delete: 10.10.4.0 255.255.255.0 10.10.1.2
  36 15:55:57.572 Not active net/1=SH: 10.10.4.0 255.255.255.0 0
  37 15:55:57.572 FC not sat Dmin/met: 4294967295 130816
  38 15:55:57.572 Find FS: 10.10.4.0 255.255.255.0 130816
  39 15:55:57.572 NDB delete: 10.10.3.0 255.255.255.0 1
  40 15:55:57.572 Poison squashed: 10.10.3.0 255.255.255.0 rt gone
  41 15:55:57.572 RDB delete: 10.10.3.0 255.255.255.0 10.10.1.2
  42 15:55:57.572 Not active net/1=SH: 10.10.3.0 255.255.255.0 0
  43 15:55:57.572 FC not sat Dmin/met: 4294967295 130816
  44 15:55:57.572 Find FS: 10.10.3.0 255.255.255.0 130816
  45 15:55:57.572 NDB delete: 10.10.2.0 255.255.255.0 1
  46 15:55:57.572 Poison squashed: 10.10.2.0 255.255.255.0 rt gone
  47 15:55:57.572 RDB delete: 10.10.2.0 255.255.255.0 10.10.1.2
48 15:55:57.572 Not active net/1=SH: 10.10.2.0 255.255.255.0 0
```

The output shown in Example 5-49 is truncated; however, you can see the number of times the neighbor relationship flapped. Note the events in the highlighted lines are repeated within the command output.

Scenario 3: Misconfigured Authentication Parameters

In the following sample scenario, authentication was configured in the Cisco ASA, but it was not configured in the inside router (10.10.1.2). The **debug eigrp fsm** is not useful for authentication problems. The **debug eigrp packets** can be used to show the transactions between the Cisco ASA and the inside router. Example 5-50 shows the output of the **debug eigrp packets**.

Example 5-50 *Output of* **debug eigrp packets** *Command During EIGRP Authentication Failures*

```
NewYork# debug eigrp packets
EIGRP Packets debugging is on
    (UPDATE, REQUEST, QUERY, REPLY, HELLO, PROBE, ACK, STUB, SIAQUERY, SIAREPLY)
EIGRP: Sending HELLO on GigabitEthernet0/1
  AS 655362, Flags 0x0, Seq 0/0 interfaceQ 255/254 iidbQ un/rely 0/0
EIGRP: GigabitEthernet0/1: ignored packet from 10.10.1.2, opcode = 5 (missing
authentication)
```

In Example 5-50, you can see the Cisco ASA sending an EIGRP hello packet on the interface GigabitEthernet0/1 and then ignoring a packet received from 10.10.1.2 because it was not an authenticated packet (missing authentication).

Note The output of the **debug eigrp packets** command was modified in Cisco ASA software version 8.0(3). Please refer to the product release notes posted at http://www.cisco.com/en/US/docs/security/asa/asa80/release/notes/arn804n.html.

IP Multicast

IP multicast provides the capability to transmit information to multiple devices in the network by efficiently utilizing bandwidth. Several video and audio applications use IP multicast as their method of communication. Additionally, some of the routing protocols covered earlier use multicast. These routing protocols include OSPF, EIGRP, and RIP version 2. Many other applications, such as database replication software and emergency alert systems, also use IP multicast.

Traditionally, a multicast device communicates with a group of receivers by using an associated Layer 3 Class D address. The lowest bit of the first byte of the Ethernet multicast destination addresses must be a 1, which allows the device to differentiate between multicast and unicast packets.

Multicast has a mechanism that tells the network about what hosts are members of a specific group. This technique prevents unnecessary flooding. The Internet Group Multicast Protocol (IGMP) is the protocol used to prevent unnecessary flooding. IGMP version 2 is defined in RFC 2236 and IGMP version 3 is defined by RFC 3376. The Cisco ASA can operate in two different multicast modes: IGMP stub mode and PIM sparse mode.

IGMP Stub Mode

To join a specific multicast group, a host sends an IGMP report or join message to the routing device. The routing device sends query messages to discover which devices are still associated to a specific group. The host sends a response to the router query if it wants to continue to be a member of the specific group. If the router does not receive a response, it prunes the group list. This minimizes unnecessary transmissions.

The Cisco ASA can be configured as an IGMP proxy. When configured as an IGMP proxy, the Cisco ASA forwards only IGMP messages from the downstream hosts. Additionally, it can send multicast transmissions from upstream routers. It can also be configured to statically join a multicast group.

PIM Sparse Mode

In IP multicast routing, the network must be able to assemble packet distribution trees that identify a unique forwarding path between the source and each subnet containing members of the multicast group. One of the key objectives in the creation of distribution trees is to allow at least one copy of each packet to be forwarded to each branch of the tree. Several IP multicast protocols exist, but the most commonly used is Protocol Independent Multicast (PIM).

There are two different flavors of PIM routing protocols:

- **Dense mode (PIM-DM)**—Routers running DM routing protocols are required to forward multicast traffic to each group by assembling distribution trees. They do so by flooding the entire network even if the receivers do not request such updates. Subsequently, they prune all the paths that do not have any receivers. Dense mode is not widely used or recommended.
- **Sparse mode (PIM-SM)**—The SM protocols require that each router participating in the PIM domain be explicitly configured with a rendezvous point, which controls group membership and is initially the root of the distribution tree. SM IP multicast routing protocols start with an empty distribution tree and add only devices that specifically request to join the distribution.

Cisco ASA supports PIM-SM as the multicast routing protocol. It can use unicast routing information base (RIB) or multicast-capable RIB (MRIB) to route multicast packets. PIM-SM assembles unidirectional shared trees rooted at a rendezvous point (RP) per multicast group. Additionally, it can create shortest-path trees (SPTs) per each source.

Configuring Multicast Routing

This section includes the necessary steps to configure multicast routing with ASDM and the CLI.

Enabling Multicast Routing

The first step to configure IP multicast routing on the Cisco ASA is to enable it. To enable multicast routing using ASDM, navigate to **Configuration > Device Setup > Routing > Multicast** and check the **Enable Multicast Routing** check box.

Alternatively, you can enable multicast routing via the CLI by invoking the **multicast-routing** command in global configuration mode. To disable IP multicast routing, use the **no multicast-routing** command.

> **Note** The **multicast-routing** command enables IGMP on all interfaces by default. To disable IGMP on a specific interface, use the **no igmp subinterface** command.
>
> The **multicast-routing** command enables PIM on all interfaces by default. If configured globally, use the **no pim interface** command to disable PIM on a specific interface.

Statically Assigning an IGMP Group

You can configure the Cisco ASA to statically join a specific multicast group. Complete the following steps to statically join a specific multicast group with ASDM.

Step 1. Log in to ASDM and navigate to **Configuration > Device Setup > Routing > Multicast > IGMP > Join Group**.

Step 2. Click on **Add** to add an IGMP join group.

Step 3. Select the interface where the multicast group address is to be configured.

Step 4. Enter the multicast group address under the **Multicast Group Address** field. In this example the **239.0.10.1** multicast group address is used.

Step 5. Click **OK**.

Step 6. Click **Apply** to apply the configuration changes.

Step 7. Click on **Save** to save the configuration in the Cisco ASA.

You can also accomplish this via the CLI by using the **igmp static-group** command in interface configuration mode. Example 5-51 shows how to statically assign an IGMP group in the Cisco ASA.

Example 5-51 *Statically Assigning an IGMP Group*

```
interface GigabitEthernet0/1
 igmp static-group 239.0.10.1
 igmp forward-interface
```

In Example 5-51, the statically configured group in interface GigabitEthernet0/1 is 239.0.10.1. The **igmp static-group** command only adds the interface to the multicast group. This is different from the **join-group** command. The **join-group** command adds the configured interface to the outgoing interface list (OIL), also sending an IGMP report for the configured group via such interface.

Limiting IGMP States

The IGMP State Limit feature provides protection against DoS attacks when attackers use IGMP packets. Complete the following steps to configure the IGMP State Limit (group limit) to limit the number of hosts allowed to join the multicast group on a per-interface basis.

Step 1. Log in to ASDM and navigate to **Configuration > Device Setup > Routing > Multicast > IGMP > Protocol.**

Step 2. Select the interface where the group limit will be configured and click **Edit**.

Step 3. Configure the group limit under the **Group Limit** field. In this example the limit is set to 100 states.

Step 4. Click **OK**.

Step 5. Click **Apply** to apply the configuration changes.

Step 6. Click on **Save** to save the configuration in the Cisco ASA.

Alternatively, you can use the **igmp limit** command in interface configuration mode to limit the number of hosts allowed to join the multicast group on a per-interface basis. Example 5-52 shows how to configure this feature.

Example 5-52 *Limiting IGMP States*

```
interface GigabitEthernet0/1
 igmp limit 100
```

In Example 5-52, the limit is set to 100 hosts. The maximum number of IGMP states allowed on an interface is 500 and it is the default value.

IGMP Query Timeout

In the Cisco ASA, you can configure the timeout period before the Cisco ASA takes over as the multicast query router for the configured interface. The Cisco ASA waits for any query messages to be received on the configured interface. If a query message is not received within the timeout period, the Cisco ASA takes over as the multicast query routing device. You can configure the IGMP query timeout in ASDM by also navigating to **Configuration > Device Setup > Routing > Multicast > IGMP > Protocol** and editing the interface IGMP parameters.

To do this via the CLI, use the **igmp query-timeout** command in interface configuration mode. The range is from 60 to 300 seconds. The default is 255 seconds. Example 5-53 shows how to configure this feature with the query timeout value of 100 seconds.

Example 5-53 *IGMP Query Timeout*

```
interface GigabitEthernet0/1
 igmp query-timeout 100
```

Defining the IGMP Version

Cisco ASA supports IGMP versions 1 and 2. IGMP version 2 is the default. To specify the version you want in ASDM, navigate to **Configuration > Device Setup > Routing > Multicast > IGMP > Protocol** and edit the interface IGMP parameters. In the CLI use the **igmp version** interface subcommand. Example 5-54 demonstrates how to specify IGMP version 1 on the GigabitEthernet0/1 interface.

Example 5-54 *Defining the IGMP Version*

```
interface GigabitEthernet0/1
 igmp version 1
```

Enabling PIM

Complete the following steps to enable PIM under a specific interface when using ASDM:

Step 1. Log in to ASDM and navigate to **Configuration > Device Setup > Routing > Multicast > PIM > Protocol.**

Step 2. Select the interface where PIM is to be enabled and click **Edit.**

Step 3. Check the **Enable PIM** option.

Step 4. Click **OK.**

Step 5. Click **Apply** to apply the configuration changes.

Step 6. Click on **Save** to save the configuration in the Cisco ASA.

The same screen in ASDM enables you to configure the PIM designated router (DR) priority, hello interval, and join-prune intervals.

Note PIM is enabled by default when multicast routing is enabled.

PIM elects a designated router (DR), which is similar to the mechanism in OSPF. Via the CLI you can use the **pim dr-priority** command in interface configuration mode to set the priority for which a router is elected as the DR. The following is the command syntax:

```
pim dr-priority value
```

The priority value can range from 1 to 4,294,967,295, and the default is 1. The highest value is the priority in the DR election process.

The Cisco ASA sends PIM hello messages to the neighbor routers. To configure the frequency of PIM hello messages, use the **pim hello-interval** command in interface configuration mode. The following is the command syntax:

```
pim hello-interval seconds
```

The number of seconds that the router waits before sending a hello message can vary from 1 to 3600 seconds. The default is 30 seconds. Example 5-55 demonstrates all the PIM subcommand options.

Example 5-55 *Customizing PIM Values at the Interface Level*

```
interface GigabitEthernet0/1
 pim hello-interval 100
 pim dr-priority 5
 pim join-prune-interval 120
```

In Example 5-55, the PIM hello interval is set to 100 seconds, the DR priority to 5, and the PIM join and prune interval to 120 seconds on interface GigabitEthernet0/1.

Configuring Rendezvous Points

Rendezvous points (RPs) are used as a temporary way to connect a multicast receiver to an existing shared multicast tree. RPs are required only when PIM stub mode is enabled. To configure an RP in ASDM, complete the following steps:

Step 1. Log in to ASDM and navigate to **Configuration > Device Setup > Routing > Multicast > PIM > Rendezvous Points.**

Step 2. If your RP is a Cisco IOS router, check the **Generate IOS Compatible Register Messages** check box.

Step 3. Click **Add** to add the RP.

Step 4. Enter the IP address of the RP under the **Rendezvous Point IP Address** field.

Step 5. PIM can be configured in bidirectional mode. When configured in bidirectional mode, if the Cisco ASA receives a multicast packet and has no directly connected members or PIM neighbors present, it sends a Prune message back to the source. You configure bidirectional mode by checking the **Use Bi-directional Forwarding** check box. If you want the specified multicast groups to operate in sparse mode, you must uncheck this box.

Step 6. If the RP is associated with all multicast groups on the interface, select the **Use this RP for All Multicast Groups** option. This is the default option and it is the one used in this example. However, you can also specify the multicast groups to be used by the RP. To do this, select the **Use this RP for the Multicast Groups as Specified Below** option and define the specific groups.

Step 7. Click **OK.**

Step 8. Click **Apply** to apply the configuration changes.

Step 9. Click on **Save** to save the configuration in the Cisco ASA.

If using the CLI, you can use the **pim rp-address** command to configure the address of a PIM RP for a particular group. Example 5-56 demonstrates how to configure a PIM RP for a particular group.

Example 5-56 *Configuring a PIM RP*

```
New York# configure terminal
New York(config)# pim rp-address 10.10.1.2 bidir
```

In Example 5-56, a PIM RP with IP address 10.10.1.2 is configured. The **bidir** keyword indicates that the specified multicast groups operate in bidirectional mode. If the command is configured without this option, the specified groups operate in PIM sparse mode.

Note You can, optionally, configure an ACL defining the groups that should map to the given RP. If no ACL is specified, the RP is used for all available groups.

Filtering PIM Neighbors

Specific multicast sources can be filtered when the Cisco ASA is acting as an RP. This can be used as a security mechanism to allow only trusted sources to register with the RP. Complete the following steps to define the multicast sources from which the Cisco ASA will accept PIM register messages:

Step 1. Log in to ASDM and navigate to **Configuration > Device Setup > Routing > Multicast > PIM > Neighbor Filter.**

Step 2. Click **Add** to add a filter entry.

Step 3. Select the interface name where the filter is to be applied.

Step 4. Select the action (permit or deny) to be taken. In this example, we allow only the **10.10.1.2** router to register.

Step 5. Enter the IP address of the device(s) to filter. In this example, the **10.10.1.2** address is used.

Step 6. Enter the **Netmask** of the host or subnet. In this example **255.255.255.255** is used.

Step 7. Click **OK.**

Step 8. Click **Apply** to apply the configuration changes.

Step 9. Click on **Save** to save the configuration in the Cisco ASA.

Example 5-57 shows the commands sent by ASDM to the Cisco ASA.

Example 5-57 *Filtering PIM Neighbors*

```
access-list inside_multicast standard permit host 10.10.1.2
interface GigabitEthernet0/1
 pim neighbor-filter inside_multicast
```

A standard ACL named **inside_multicast** is configured to define what hosts or networks are to be filtered. In this example, **10.10.1.2** is the only host allowed to register to the Cisco ASA. The ACL is then applied to the **pim neighbor-filter** interface subcommand, as shown in Example 5-53.

Configuring a Static Multicast Route

You can configure a static multicast route entry with ASDM by navigating to **Configuration > Device Setup > Routing > Multicast > MRoute.** Alternatively, you can use the **mroute** CLI command. The following is the command syntax:

```
mroute src mask [in-interface-name] [dense out-interface-name] [distance]
```

Table 5-4 lists and explains all the available options for the **mroute** command.

Table 5-4 **mroute** *Command Options*

Option	Description
src	IP address of the multicast source.
mask	Subnet mask of the multicast source.
in-interface-name	Incoming interface name for the multicast route.
out-interface-name	Outgoing interface name for the multicast route.
[**distance**] (optional)	Defines whether a unicast route or a static multicast route should be used for the Reverse Path Forwarding (RPF) lookup. The lower the distance, the higher the preference. A static multicast route takes precedence if it has the same distance as the unicast route. The default distance is 0.
[ip address]	Starting in Cisco ASA software version 7.2, the optional argument **ip address** can be configured to define the IP address of the next-hop router adjacent to the interface for the **mroute**.

Troubleshooting IP Multicast Routing

This section includes detailed information on several commands and mechanisms that are useful while troubleshooting IP multicast routing problems in the Cisco ASA.

> **Note** One of the most common interoperability issues between the Cisco ASA and older Cisco IOS router versions is that the register messages were generated differently. The Cisco ASA and newer versions of Cisco IOS generate PIM RFC–compliant registers. To generate registers that are compatible with older versions of Cisco IOS, use the **pim old-register-checksum** command.

Useful show Commands

The following **show** commands help you to monitor and view the current multicast (PIM or IGMP) configuration information:

- **show pim df**—Shows bidirectional PIM designated forwarder (DF) information
- **show pim group-map**—Displays PIM group-to-protocol mapping information
- **show pim interface**—Displays PIM interface information
- **show pim join-prune statistic**—Shows PIM join/prune information

- **show pim neighbor**—Displays PIM neighbor information
- **show pim range-list**—Shows PIM range-list information
- **show pim topology**—Displays the PIM topology table information
- **show pim traffic**—Displays PIM traffic counters
- **show pim tunnel**—Lists information about the PIM tunnel interfaces
- **show igmp groups**—Displays group membership information
- **show igmp interface**—Provides interface IGMP information
- **show igmp traffic**—Displays traffic counters
- **show mroute**—Displays the contents of the multicast routing table
- **show mfib**—Displays the details of the multicast forwarding information base (MFIB)

  ```
  show mroute source-address group-address [summary] [count] [pruned]
  ```

  To display the active multicast streams, use the **show mroute** [*group*] **active** [*kbps*] syntax of this command. The active multicast streams whose data rate is greater or equal to the specified value in Kbps are displayed. The default Kbps is 4. The **show mroute** command (without any additional arguments) can also be used.
- **show mroute summary**–Displays a summary of the multicast routing table

Useful debug Commands

The following commands are crucial for debugging IP multicast routing problems:

- **debug pim**—Enables debugging for PIM events
- **debug pim neighbor**—Enables debugging of PIM neighbor events
- **debug pim group** *group*—Enables PIM protocol activity debugging for only the matching group
- **debug pim interface** *interface*—Enables debugging of PIM protocol activity for only the specified interface
- **debug pim df-election**—Enables debugging of PIM DF election exchange messages
- **debug mrib route** [*group*]—Enables debugging of MRIB routing activity
- **debug mrib client**—Enables debugging of MRIB client management activity
- **debug mrib io**—Enables debugging of MRIB I/O events
- **debug mrib table**—Enables debugging of MRIB table management activity

Take into consideration the amount of traffic that is passing through the Cisco ASA and other features enabled within your network before enabling any of the previously mentioned **debug** commands. For example, if the Hot Standby Router Protocol (HSRP) feature is enabled in an upstream router, PIM messages may be dropped and not shown within the previous debug commands.

Summary

This chapter covered the different routing protocols supported by Cisco ASA. Configuration examples included information on how to add a static route and configure dynamic routing protocols such as RIP, OSPF, and EIGRP, using ASDM and the CLI. Detailed sample configurations were provided, as well as tips on how to troubleshoot common problems when deploying these dynamic routing protocols.

Cisco ASA also supports IP multicast routing protocols. IGMP versions 1 and 2 are supported, as well as PIM-SM. PIM-SM allows Cisco ASA to have direct participation in the creation of a multicast tree. This technique enhances the multicast support for IGMP forwarding and provides an alternative to multicast transparent-mode operations. At the end of the chapter, deployment scenarios were added to enhance the level of learning.

Chapter 6

Authentication, Authorization, and Accounting (AAA)

This chapter covers the following topics:

- AAA protocols and services supported by Cisco ASA
- Defining an authentication server
- Authenticating administrative sessions
- Configuring authorization
- Configuring downloadable ACLs
- Configuring accounting
- Troubleshooting AAA

This chapter provides a detailed explanation of the configuration and troubleshooting of authentication, authorization, and accounting (AAA) network security services that Cisco ASA supports. AAA offers different solutions that provide access control to network devices. The following services are included within its modular architectural framework:

- **Authentication**—The process of validating users based on their identity and predetermined credentials, such as passwords and other mechanisms like digital certificates.
- **Authorization**—The method by which a network device assembles a set of attributes that regulates what tasks the user is authorized to perform. These attributes are measured against a user database. The results are returned to the network device to determine the user's qualifications and restrictions. This database can be located locally on Cisco ASA or it can be hosted on a RADIUS or Terminal Access Controller Access-Control System Plus (TACACS+) server.
- **Accounting**—The process of gathering and sending user information to an AAA server used to track login times (when the user logged in and logged off) and the services that users access. This information can be used for billing, auditing, and reporting purposes.

AAA Protocols and Services Supported by Cisco ASA

Cisco ASA can be configured to maintain a local user database or to use an external server for authentication. The following are the AAA authentication underlying protocols and servers that are supported as external database repositories:

- RADIUS
- TACACS+
- RSA SecurID (SDI)
- Windows NT
- Kerberos
- Lightweight Directory Access Protocol (LDAP)

Table 6-1 shows the different methods and the functionality that each protocol supports.

Table 6-1 *AAA Support Matrix*

Method	Authentication	Authorization	Accounting
Internal server	Yes	Yes	No
RADIUS	Yes	Yes	Yes
TACACS+	Yes	Yes	Yes
SDI	Yes	No	No
Windows NT	Yes	No	No
Kerberos	Yes	No	No
LDAP	No	Yes	No

Using an external authentication server in medium and large deployments is recommended, for better scalability and easier management.

Cisco ASA supports the authentication methods listed in Table 6-1 with the following services:

- Virtual private network (VPN) user authentication
- Administrative session authentication
- Firewall session authentication (cut-through proxy)

Table 6-2 outlines the support for the authentication methods in correlation to the specific services.

Table 6-2 *Authentication Support Services*

Service	Local	RADIUS	TACACS+	SDI	Windows NT	Kerberos
VPN users	Yes	Yes	Yes	Yes	Yes	Yes
Administration	Yes	Yes	Yes	No	No	No
Firewall sessions	Yes	Yes	Yes	No	No	No

Cisco ASA VPN user authentication support is similar to the support provided on the Cisco VPN 3000 Series Concentrator.

As previously mentioned, the authorization mechanism assembles a set of attributes that describes what the user is allowed to do within the network or service. Cisco ASA supports local and external authorization, depending on the service used. Table 6-3 shows the authorization support matrix.

Table 6-3 *Authorization Support*

Service	Local	RADIUS	TACACS+	SDI	NT	Kerberos	LDAP
VPN users	Yes	Yes	No	No	No	No	Yes
Administration	Yes	No	Yes	No	No	No	No
Firewall sessions	No	No	Yes	No	No	No	No

Note Local authorization for administrative sessions can be used only for command authorization.

Cisco ASA does not support RADIUS command authorization for administrative sessions because of limitations in the RADIUS protocol.

Accounting is supported by RADIUS and TACACS+ servers only. Table 6-4 shows the Cisco ASA accounting support matrix.

Table 6-4 *Accounting Support*

Service	Local	RADIUS	TACACS+	SDI	NT	Kerberos	LDAP
VPN users	No	Yes	Yes	No	No	No	No
Administration	No	Yes	Yes	No	No	No	No
Firewall sessions	No	Yes	Yes	No	No	No	No

The following subsections introduce each of the authentication protocols and servers that Cisco ASA supports.

RADIUS

RADIUS is a widely implemented authentication standard protocol that is defined in RFC 2865, "Remote Authentication Dial-In User Service (RADIUS)." RADIUS operates in a client/server model. A RADIUS client is usually referred to as a *network access server* (NAS). A NAS is responsible for passing user information to the RADIUS server. Cisco ASA acts as a NAS and authenticates users based on the RADIUS server's response.

Note Cisco ASA supports several RADIUS servers, including the following:

- CiscoSecure ACS for NT
- CiscoSecure ACS for UNIX
- Cisco Access Registrar
- Livingston
- Merit
- Funk Steel Belted
- Microsoft Internet Authentication Server

These are some of the most commonly deployed RADIUS server vendors. Support and testing with other servers is a continuous effort between vendors.

The RADIUS server receives user authentication requests and subsequently returns configuration information required for the client (in this case, the Cisco ASA) to support the specific service to the user. The RADIUS server does this by sending Internet Engineering Task Force (IETF) or vendor-specific attributes. (RADIUS authentication attributes are defined in RFC 2865.) Figure 6-1 illustrates how this process works.

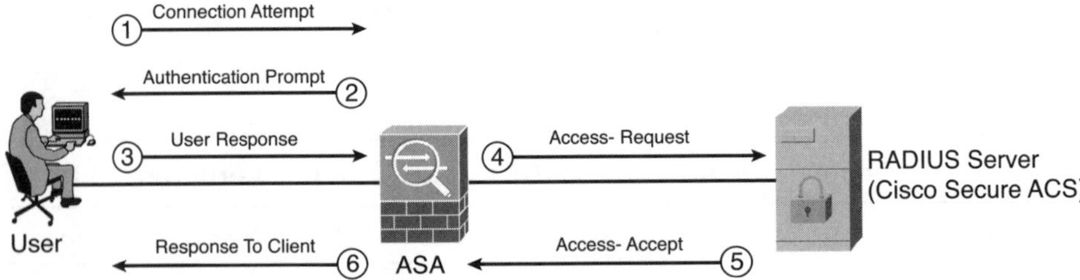

Figure 6-1 *Basic RADIUS Authentication Process*

In this example, a Cisco ASA acts as a NAS and the RADIUS server is a Cisco Secure Access Control Server (ACS). The following sequence of events is shown in Figure 6-1:

Step 1. A user attempts to connect to the Cisco ASA (i.e., administration, VPN, or cut-through proxy).

Step 2. The Cisco ASA prompts the user, requesting a username and password. The user sends his or her credentials to the Cisco ASA.

Step 3. The Cisco ASA sends the authentication request (Access-Request) to the RADIUS server.

Step 4. The RADIUS server sends an Access-Accept message (if the user is successfully authenticated) or an Access-Reject (if the user is not successfully authenticated).

Step 5. The Cisco ASA responds to the user and allows access to the specific service.

The RADIUS server can also send IETF or vendor-specific attributes to the Cisco ASA, depending on the implementation and services used. These attributes can contain information such as an IP address to assign the client and authorization information. RADIUS servers combine authentication and authorization phases into a single request-and-response communication cycle. The Cisco ASA authenticates itself to the RADIUS server by using a preconfigured shared secret. For security reasons, this shared secret is never sent over the network.

Note Passwords are sent as encrypted messages from the Cisco ASA to the RADIUS server. This is useful to protect this critical information from an intruder. The Cisco ASA hashes the password, using the shared secret that is defined on the Cisco ASA and the RADIUS server.

The RADIUS servers can also proxy authentication requests to other RADIUS servers or other types of authentication servers. Figure 6-2 illustrates this methodology.

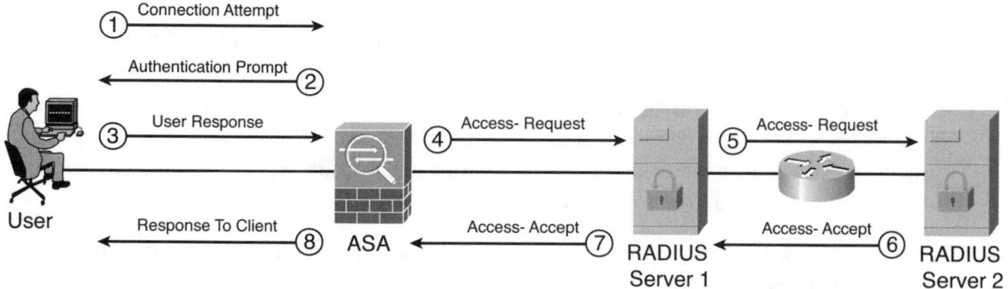

Figure 6-2 *RADIUS Server Acting as Proxy to Other Authentication Servers*

In Figure 6-2, RADIUS Server 1 acts as a proxy to RADIUS Server 2. It sends the authentication request from the Cisco ASA to RADIUS Server 2 and proxies the response back to the ASA.

TACACS+

TACACS+ is an AAA security protocol that provides centralized validation of users who are attempting to gain access to NASs. The TACACS+ protocol offers support for separate and modular AAA facilities. The TACACS+ protocol's primary goal is to supply complete AAA support for managing multiple network devices.

TACACS+ uses port 49 for communication and allows vendors to use either User Datagram Protocol (UDP) or TCP encoding. Cisco ASA uses the TCP version for its TACACS+ implementation.

The TACACS+ authentication concept is similar to RADIUS. The NAS sends an authentication request to the TACACS+ server (daemon). The server ultimately sends any of the following messages back to the NAS:

- ACCEPT—User has been successfully authenticated and the requested service is allowed. If authorization is required, the authorization process begins at this point.
- REJECT—User authentication is denied. The user may be prompted to retry authentication, depending on the TACACS+ server and NAS.
- ERROR—A certain error takes place during authentication. This can be experienced because of network connectivity problems or a configuration error.
- CONTINUE—User is prompted to provide further authentication information.

After the authentication process is complete, if authorization is required the TACACS+ server proceeds with the authorization phase. The user must first successfully be authenticated before proceeding to TACACS+ authorization.

RSA SecurID

RSA SecurID (SDI) is a solution provided by RSA Security. The RSA ACE/Server is the administrative component of the SDI solution. It enables the use of one-time passwords (OTPs). Cisco ASA supports SDI authentication natively only for VPN user authentication. However, if it is using an authentication server, such as CiscoSecure ACS for Windows NT, the server can use external authentication to an SDI server and proxy the authentication request for all other services supported by Cisco ASA. Cisco ASA and SDI use UDP port 5500 for communication.

The SDI solution uses small physical devices called *tokens* that provide users with an OTP that changes every 60 seconds. These OTPs are generated when a user enters a personal identification number and are synchronized with the server to provide the authentication service. The SDI server can be configured to require the user to enter a new PIN when trying to authenticate. This process is called *New PIN mode*, which Cisco ASA supports. Figure 6-3 demonstrates how this solution works when a user attempts to connect to the Cisco ASA using the Cisco VPN Client software.

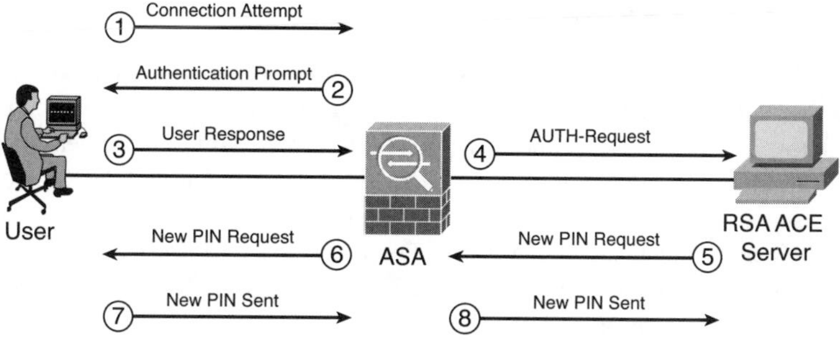

Figure 6-3 *SDI Authentication Using New PIN Mode*

The purpose of New PIN mode is to allow the user to change its PIN for authentication. The following sequence of events occurs when using SDI authentication with the New PIN mode feature, as shown in Figure 6-3:

Step 1. The user attempts to establish a VPN connection with the Cisco VPN client and negotiates IKE Phase 1. (Complete information about IKE and IPSec negotiations is provided in Chapter 1, "Introduction to Security Technologies.")

Step 2. The Cisco ASA prompts the user for authentication via X-Auth (extended authentication). The user provides a username and passcode. (X-Auth is also covered in Chapter 17, "IPSec Remote Access VPNs.")

Step 3. The Cisco ASA forwards the authentication request to the SDI server.

Step 4. If New PIN mode is enabled, the SDI server authenticates the user and requests a new PIN to be used during the next authentication session for that user.

Step 5. The Cisco ASA prompts the user for a new PIN.

Step 6. User enters new PIN.

Step 7. The Cisco ASA sends the new PIN information to the SDI server.

Note You can find more information about the RSA SDI server at http://www.rsasecurity.com.

Microsoft Windows NT

Cisco ASA supports Windows NT native authentication only for VPN remote-access connections. It communicates with the Windows NT server via TCP port 139. Similarly to SDI, you can use a RADIUS/TACACS+ server, such as CiscoSecure ACS, to proxy authentication to Windows NT for other services supported by Cisco ASA.

Active Directory and Kerberos

Cisco ASA can authenticate VPN users via an external Windows Active Directory, which uses Kerberos for authentication. Kerberos is an authentication protocol created by the Massachusetts Institute of Technology (MIT) that provides mutual authentication used by many vendors and applications. It can also communicate with a UNIX/Linux-based Kerberos server. Support for this authentication method is available for VPN clients only. Cisco ASA communicates with the Active Directory and/or a Kerberos server via UDP port 88. Configuration and troubleshooting of remote access VPN tunnels are covered in Chapter 16, "Site-to-Site IPSec VPNs."

Lightweight Directory Access Protocol

Cisco ASA supports LDAP authorization for remote-access VPN connections only. The LDAP protocol is defined in RFC 3377, "Lightweight Directory Access Protocol (v3)," and RFC 3771, "The Lightweight Directory Access Protocol (LDAP) Intermediate Response Message." LDAP provides authorization services when given access to a user database within a Directory Information Tree (DIT). This tree contains entities called *entries*, which consist of one or more attribute values called *distinguished names* (DNs). The DN values must be unique within the DIT.

> **Note** Cisco ASA communicates with an LDAP server over TCP port 389. LDAP provides only authorization services. Consequently, a separate protocol is required for authentication services.

HTTP Form Protocol

The Cisco ASA supports single sign-on (SSO) authentication of WebVPN users, using the HTTP Form protocol. The SSO feature is designed to allow WebVPN users to enter a username and password only once while accessing WebVPN services and any web servers behind the Cisco ASA.

> **Note** The Cisco ASA acts as a proxy for the user to the authenticating server. The Cisco ASA keeps a cookie and uses it to authenticate the user to any other protected web servers. The SSO feature is covered in more detail in Chapter 19, "Clientless Remote Access SSL VPN."

Defining an Authentication Server

Before configuring an authentication server on Cisco ASA, you must specify AAA server groups. A server group defines the attributes of one or more AAA servers. This information includes the AAA protocol used, IP address of the AAA servers, and other related information. Complete the following steps to accomplish this using ASDM:

Step 1. Log in to ASDM and navigate to **Configuration > Device Management > Users/AAA > AAA Server Groups > AAA Server Groups.**

Step 2. By default the LOCAL Server group is present in the configuration. To add a AAA server group click on **Add.**

Step 3. The screen illustrated in Figure 6-4 is shown. Enter a server group name under the **Server Group** field, as illustrated in Figure 6-4. The AAA server group name used in this example is **my-radius-group.**

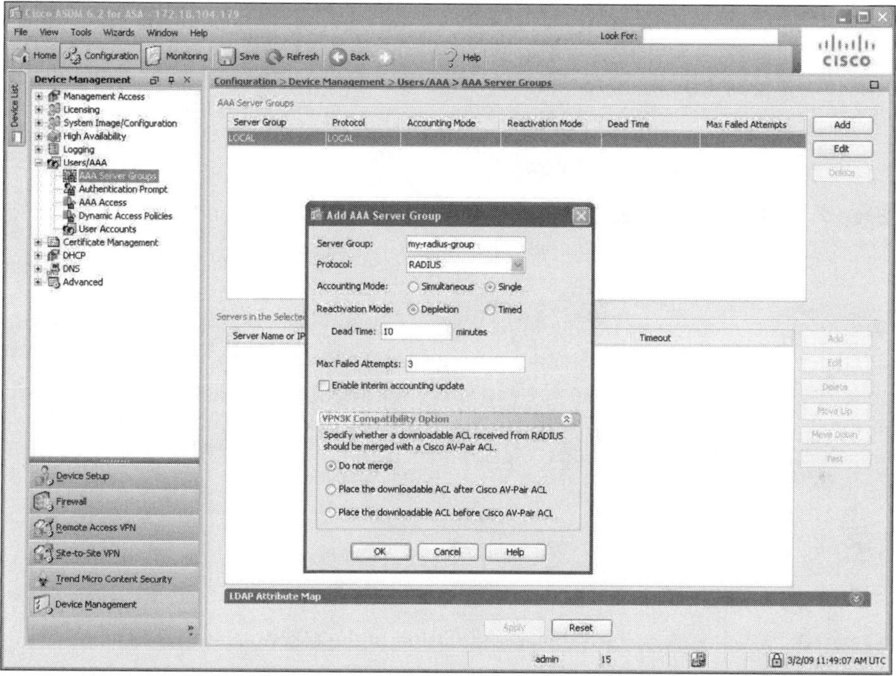

Figure 6-4 *Add AAA Server Group Dialog Box*

Step 4. Select the AAA protocol to be used from the **Protocol** drop-down list. RADIUS is used in this example; however, you can choose from any of the following server types:

- RADIUS
- TACACS+
- SDI
- NT Domain
- Kerberos
- LDAP
- HTTP Form

Step 5. Several of the parameters in this dialog box depend on the authentication protocol that is used. In this example all the other fields are left with default values. The **Accounting Mode** field has two options: **Simultaneous** and **Single.** When single mode is selected, the Cisco ASA sends accounting data to only one accounting server. To send accounting data to all servers in the group select **Simultaneous.**

Step 6. **Depletion** is selected in the **Reactivation Mode** field. The reactivation mode is used to control the behavior when AAA servers fail. When depletion mode is selected in the Cisco ASA, failed servers are reactivated only after all the servers in the group are inactive. If this option is selected you must add a time interval in the **Dead Time** field. In this example, the default value is configured (**10** minutes).

Alternatively, you can select Timed mode where failed servers are reactivated after 30 seconds of down time.

Step 7. The **Max Failed Attempts** is used to limit the maximum number of failed authentication attempts. The default is 3 attempts.

> **Note** The Cisco ASA supports downloadable access control lists (ACLs). This is discussed later in this chapter in the "Configuring Downloadable ACLs" section. To be compatible with the Cisco VPN 3000, you can specify whether a downloadable ACL received from the RADIUS server should be merged with a Cisco AV-Pair ACL, as shown in Figure 6-4 under the **VPN3k Compatibility Option** section.

Step 8. Click **OK.**

Step 9. Click **Apply** to apply the configuration changes.

Step 10. Click **Save** to save the configuration in the Cisco ASA.

Complete the following steps to add the AAA server to the AAA server group that was previously configured:

Step 1. Log in to ASDM and navigate to **Configuration > Device Management > Users/AAA > AAA Server Groups > AAA Server Groups.**

Step 2. Click on **Add** under the Servers in the Selected Group (while selecting the group called **my-radius-group.** The dialog box shown in Figure 6-5 is displayed.

Step 3. As you see in Figure 6-5, the **Server Group my-radius-group** is already prepopulated in the screen. Select the interface where the RADIUS server resides, using the **Interface Name** pull-down menu. In this example, the RADIUS server is reachable through the **management** interface.

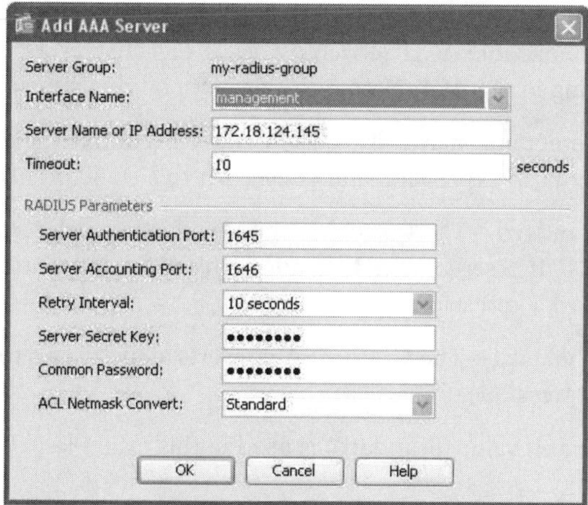

Figure 6-5 *Add AAA Server Dialog Box*

Step 4. Enter the AAA server name or IP address under the **Server Name or IP Address** field. In this example, the RADIUS server's IP address is **172.18.124.145**.

Step 5. Specify the amount of time (in seconds) that the Cisco ASA waits before timing out the authentication session under the **Timeout** field. The default value of **10** seconds is used in this example.

Step 6. You can specify the port used by the Cisco ASA to communicate to the RADIUS server for authentication purposes. In this example, the default RADIUS authentication port **1645** is entered under the **Server Authentication Port** field.

Step 7. Similarly, you can specify the port used by the Cisco ASA to communicate to the RADIUS server for accounting. In this example, the default RADIUS accounting port **1646** is entered under the **Server Accounting Port** field.

Step 8. The **Retry Interval** is the amount of time the Cisco ASA waits to retry an authentication attempt, in case the RADIUS server does not respond. The default value of **10** seconds is used in this example.

Step 9. Enter the secret key used by the Cisco ASA and the RADIUS server to authenticate each other under the **Server Secret Key** field. This can be a string of up to 64 characters.

Step 10. Enter a case-sensitive password that is common among users who access this RADIUS authorization server via the Cisco ASA under the **Common Password** field. If you do not use a common password, the user's username is used as the password when accessing the RADIUS authorization server.

Step 11. You can optionally specify how the Cisco ASA will handle netmasks received in downloadable ACLs (covered later in this chapter) by selecting any of the following in the **ACL Netmask Convert** pull down menu:

- **Detect automatically**—The Cisco ASA automatically detects a wildcard netmask expression and converts it to a standard netmask.
- **Standard**—The Cisco ASA honors the netmask received from the RADIUS server and does not perform any translation from wildcard netmask expressions.
- **Wildcard**—The Cisco ASA converts all netmasks to standard netmask expressions.

The default value (**Standard**) is used in this example.

Step 12. Click **OK**.

Step 13. Click **Apply** to apply the configuration changes.

Step 14. Click **Save** to save the configuration in the Cisco ASA.

If you are using the command line interface (CLI) to configure the Cisco ASA, specify AAA server groups with the **aaa-server** command. The syntax of the **aaa-server** command to specify a new AAA server group and the respective protocol is as follows:

```
aaa-server server-tag protocol server-protocol
```

The **server-tag** keyword is the server group name that is referenced by the other AAA command, and **server-protocol** is the name of the supported AAA protocol. Example 6-1 shows the different authentication protocols that can be defined within a AAA server group.

Example 6-1 *AAA Server Group Authentication Protocols*

```
New York(config)# aaa-server my-radius-group protocol ?
  kerberos  Protocol Kerberos
  ldap      Protocol LDAP
  nt        Protocol NT
  radius    Protocol RADIUS
  sdi       Protocol SDI
  tacacs+   Protocol TACACS+
```

In Example 6-1, the AAA server group tag is named **my-radius-group**. After defining the AAA server group with the respective authentication protocol, you are shown the (**config-aaa-server**) prompt. Example 6-2 shows the commands that are used to accomplish the same tasks that were previously demonstrated for ASDM.

Example 6-2 *Configuring the AAA Server Using the CLI*

```
NewYork(config)# aaa-server my-radius-group protocol radius
NewYork(config-aaa-server-group)# aaa-server my-radius-group (management) host
172.18.124.145
NewYork(config-aaa-server-host)#  key myprivatekey
NewYork(config-aaa-server-host)#  radius-common-pw mycommonpassword
```

In Example 6-2, the AAA server group my-radius-group is defined to process authentication requests using the RADIUS protocol. In the second line the RADIUS server (**172.18.124.145**) is defined, as well as the interface (**management**) where the RADIUS server resides. The key used for authentication is **myprivatekey**. The RADIUS common password is set to **mycommonpassword.**

Note Accounting mode options are available only if you are configuring an AAA server group for RADIUS or TACACS+.

You can also use the **max-failed-attempts** subcommand, which specifies the maximum allowed number of communication failures for any server in the AAA server group before that server is disabled or deactivated. The maximum number of failures can be configured in a range from 1 to 5.

Cisco ASA supports two different AAA server reactivation policies or modes:

- **Timed mode**—The failed or deactivated servers are reactivated after 30 seconds of downtime.
- **Depletion mode**—The failed or deactivated servers remain inactive until all other servers within the configured group are inactive.

To view statistics about all AAA servers defined for a specific protocol, use the following command:

show aaa-server protocol *server-protocol*

Example 6-3 includes the output of this command for the RADIUS protocol.

Example 6-3 *Output of the* **show aaa-server protocol** *Command*

```
New York# show aaa-server protocol radius
Server Group:     mygroup
Server Protocol: radius
Server Address:  172.18.124.145
Server port:      1645(authentication), 1646(accounting)
Server status:   ACTIVE, Last transaction at unknown
Number of pending requests                0
Average round trip time                   0ms
```

```
Number of authentication requests       55
Number of authorization requests        13
Number of accounting requests           45
Number of retransmissions               0
Number of accepts                        54
Number of rejects                        1
Number of challenges                     54
Number of malformed responses           0
Number of bad authenticators            0
Number of timeouts                       0
Number of unrecognized responses        0
```

Several counters can be helpful when troubleshooting AAA-related problems. For instance, you can compare the number of authentication requests versus the number of authentication rejects and accepts. Additionally, you should pay attention to any malformed authentication requests, unrecognized responses, or timeouts to determine whether there is a communication problem with the AAA server.

To show the configuration of a specific AAA server, use the following command:

show running-config aaa-server [*server-group* [(*if_name*) **host** *ip_address*]]

To show statistics about a specific AAA server, use the following command:

show aaa-server [*server-tag* [**host** *hostname*]]

Example 6-4 includes the output of this command for server 172.18.124.145.

Example 6-4 *Output of the* show aaa-server *Command for a Specific Host*

```
New York# show aaa-server mygroup host 172.18.124.145
Server Group:     my-radius-group
Server Protocol: radius
Server Address:   172.18.124.145
Server port:      1645(authentication), 1646(accounting)
Server status:    ACTIVE, Last transaction at unknown
Number of pending requests              0
Average round trip time                  0ms
Number of authentication requests       55
Number of authorization requests        13
Number of accounting requests           45
Number of retransmissions               0
Number of accepts                        54
Number of rejects                        1
Number of challenges                     54
Number of malformed responses           0
Number of bad authenticators            0
```

```
Number of timeouts                    0
Number of unrecognized responses      0
```

To clear the AAA server statistics for a specific server, use this command:

```
clear aaa-server statistics [tag [host hostname]]
```

To clear the AAA server statistics for all servers providing services for a specific protocol, use this command:

```
clear aaa-server statistics protocol server-protocol
```

To erase a specific AAA server group from the configuration, use this command:

```
clear configure aaa-server [server-tag]
```

Configuring Authentication of Administrative Sessions

Cisco ASA supports authentication of administrative sessions by using a local user database, a RADIUS server, or a TACACS+ server. An administrator can connect to the Cisco ASA via

- Telnet
- Secure Shell (SSH)
- Serial console connection
- Cisco ASA Device Manager (ASDM)

If connecting via Telnet or SSH, the user can retry authentication three times in case of user error. After the third time, the authentication session and connection to the Cisco ASA are closed. Authentication sessions via the console prompt the user continuously until the correct username and password are entered.

Before you start the configuration, you must decide which user database you will use (local or external AAA server). If you are using an external AAA server, configure the AAA server group and host as covered in the previous section. You can use the **aaa authentication** command to require authentication verification when accessing Cisco ASA for administration. The following sections teach you how to configure external authentication for each type of connection.

Authenticating Telnet Connections

You can enable Telnet access to the Cisco ASA to any internal interface or to the outside if an IPSec connection is established. (Telnet sessions are allowed to the outside interface only over an IPSec connection.) To configure authentication for Telnet connections to the Cisco ASA using ASDM, complete the following steps:

Step 1. Log in to ASDM and navigate to **Configuration > Device Management > Users/AAA > AAA Access > Authentication**. The screen illustrated in Figure 6-6 is displayed.

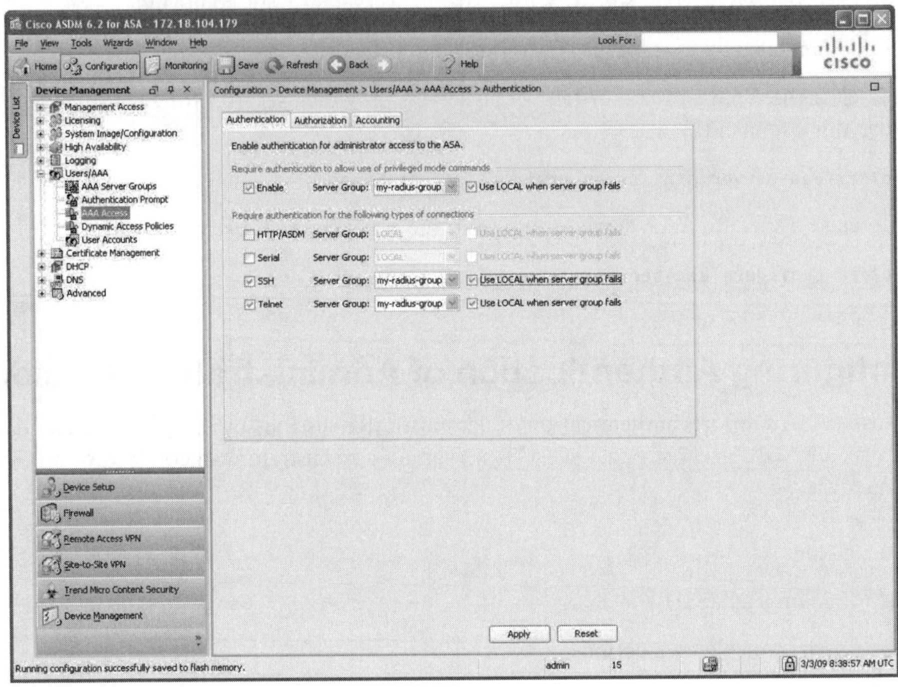

Figure 6-6 *Using ASDM to Configure Authentication for Telnet Connections*

Step 2. Select **Telnet** under the **Require Authentication for the Following Types of Connections** section.

Step 3. In this example, the RADIUS server previously configured in the AAA server group is used for authentication. Select the server group (**my-radius-group**) from the **Server Group** pull-down menu.

Step 4. If you would like to fall back to the local user database in case the RADIUS server fails, select **Use LOCAL when Server Group Fails**, as shown in Figure 6-6.

Step 5. Click **OK**.

Step 6. Click **Apply** to apply the configuration changes.

Step 7. Click **Save** to save the configuration in the Cisco ASA.

You can also authenticate any users before they use the **enable** command via the CLI. To accomplish this task, complete the following steps:

Step 1. Log in to ASDM and navigate to **Configuration > Device Management > Users/AAA > AAA Access > Authentication.**

Step 2. Select the **Enable** check box under the **Require Authentication to Allow Use of Privilege Mode Commands** section, as shown in Figure 6-6.

Step 3. In this example, the RADIUS server is used for authentication. Select the server group **my-radius-group** from the **Server Group** drop-down list.

Step 4. To allow the Cisco ASA to use the local database as a fallback method, select the **Use LOCAL when Server Group Fails** check box.

Step 5. Click **OK**.

Step 6. Click **Apply** to apply the configuration changes.

Step 7. Click **Save** to save the configuration in the Cisco ASA.

Example 6-5 shows the CLI commands sent by ASDM to the Cisco ASA.

Example 6-5 *Using the CLI to Configure Authentication for Telnet Connections*

```
aaa authentication enable console my-radius-group LOCAL
aaa authentication telnet console my-radius-group LOCAL
telnet 0.0.0.0 0.0.0.0 inside
```

In Example 6-5, the **aaa authentication enable console** command is set to require authentication before any user can enter into enable mode. The **my-radius-group** AAA server group name is applied to this command. The keyword **LOCAL** is used to enable fallback to the local database if the configured authentication server is unavailable.

The second line in Example 6-5 enables authentication for Telnet connections by using the **my-radius-group** AAA server group, as well as the **LOCAL** keyword to enable fallback to the local database.

> **Note** Do not confuse the keyword **console** with the serial console on the Cisco ASA. This keyword is used to force the Cisco ASA to require AAA authentication for any client trying to connect to it via Telnet, serial console, HTTP, or SSH. Telnet is used in Example 6-9.

Authenticating SSH Connections

The steps for using ASDM to configure authentication for SSH administrative sessions to the Cisco ASA are very similar to the ones discussed in the previous section. Complete the following steps to configure authentication for SSH connections to the Cisco ASA:

Step 1. Log in to ASDM and navigate to **Configuration > Device Management > Users/AAA > AAA Access > Authentication.** The same screen illustrated in Figure 6-6 is displayed.

Step 2. Select **SSH** under the **Require Authentication for the Following Types of Connections** section.

Step 3. In this example, the RADIUS server previously configured in the AAA server group (**my-radius-group**) is used for authentication.

Step 4. If you would like to fall back to the local user database in case the RADIUS server fails, select **Use LOCAL when Server Group Fails**, as shown in Figure 6-6.

Step 5. Click **OK.**

Step 6. Click **Apply** to apply the configuration changes.

Step 7. Click **Save** to save the configuration in the Cisco ASA.

To enable SSH on Cisco ASA via the CLI, you first configure a hostname and domain name before generating the RSA key pair used by SSH. Example 6-6 shows how to generate the RSA key pair and enable SSH version 2 connections from any systems on the inside interface.

Example 6-6 *Generating RSA Key Pair and Enabling SSH Version 2*

```
New York# configure terminal
New York(config)# hostname ASA
New York(config)# domain-name cisco.com
New York(config)# crypto key generate rsa modulus 2048
INFO: The name for the keys will be: ASA.cisco.com
Keypair generation process begin.
New York(config)# ssh 0.0.0.0 0.0.0.0 inside
New York(config)# ssh version 2
```

After the RSA key pair has been generated and SSH has been enabled, complete your AAA server group and host configuration. In this example, the **my-radius-group** AAA server group is used in the **aaa authentication ssh console** command to enable SSH authentication, as shown in Example 6-7.

Example 6-7 *Configuring SSH Authentication to a TACACS+ Server*

```
New York(config)# aaa authentication ssh console my-radius-group LOCAL
```

The **LOCAL** keyword is used in Example 6-7 to enable fallback to the local database. Make sure to issue the **write memory** command to save the configuration after the RSA keypair is generated.

Authenticating Serial Console Connections

Complete the following steps to configure authentication for serial console connections to the Cisco ASA, using ASDM:

Step 1. Log in to ASDM and navigate to **Configuration > Device Management > Users/AAA > AAA Access > Authentication.**

Step 2. Select **Serial** under the **Require Authentication for the Following Types of Connections** section.

Step 3. In this example, the RADIUS server previously configured in the AAA server group (**my-radius-group**) is used for authentication.

Step 4. If you would like to fall back to the local user database in case the RADIUS server fails, select **Use LOCAL when Server Group Fails.**

Step 5. Click **OK.**

Step 6. Click **Apply** to apply the configuration changes.

Step 7. Click **Save** to save the configuration in the Cisco ASA.

To configure authentication of serial console connections, use the **aaa authentication serial console** command. Be aware that you can get locked out of the Cisco ASA easily with any misconfiguration. Example 6-8 demonstrates how to configure serial console authentication, using the AAA server group previously configured.

Example 6-8 *Configuring Serial Console Authentication*

```
New York(config)# aaa authentication serial console my-radius-group LOCAL
```

Note Establishing two separate sessions to the Cisco ASA is always recommended when configuring AAA authentication. The purpose of this procedure is to avoid getting locked out of the CLI. Open one session using a Telnet or SSH connection and connect to the serial console of the Cisco ASA. One of the sessions can be disconnected after the configuration is verified and tested. If the administrator is locked out of the security appliance, follow the password recovery procedure discussed in Chapter 3, "System Maintenance."

Authenticating Cisco ASDM Connections

Complete the following steps to configure authentication for ASDM administrative connections to the Cisco ASA using ASDM:

Step 1. Log in to ASDM and navigate to **Configuration > Device Management > Users/AAA > AAA Access > Authentication.**

Step 2. Select **HTTP/ASDM** under the **Require Authentication for the Following Types of Connections** section.

Step 3. In this example, the RADIUS server previously configured in the AAA server group (**my-radius-group**) is used for authentication.

Step 4. If you would like to fall back to the local user database in case the RADIUS server fails, select **Use LOCAL when Server Group Fails.**

Step 5. Click **OK**.

Step 6. Click **Apply** to apply the configuration changes.

Step 7. Click **Save** to save the configuration in the Cisco ASA.

Alternatively, the **aaa authentication http console** CLI command can be configured to require authentication for Cisco ASDM users. Example 6-9 demonstrates how to configure ASDM authentication, using the AAA server group previously configured.

Example 6-9 *Configuring HTTP Authentication for ASDM Users*

```
New York(config)# aaa authentication http console my-radius-group LOCAL
```

If this command is not configured, Cisco ASDM users can gain access to the ASA by entering only the enable password, and no username, at the authentication prompt.

Authenticating Firewall Sessions (Cut-Through Proxy Feature)

Cisco ASA firewall session authentication is similar to the cut-through proxy feature on the Cisco Secure PIX Firewall. The firewall cut-through proxy requires the user to authenticate before passing any traffic through the Cisco ASA. A common deployment is to authenticate users before accessing a web server behind the Cisco ASA. Figure 6-7 illustrates how firewall session authentication works.

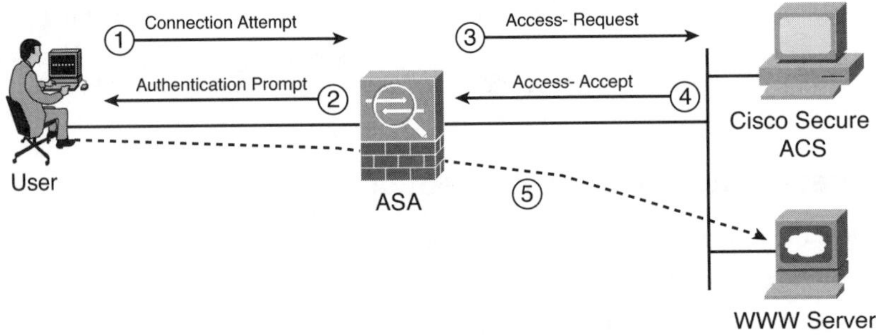

Figure 6-7 *Cut-Through Proxy Feature Example*

The following are the steps represented in Figure 6-7:

Step 1. The user on the outside of the Cisco ASA attempts to create an HTTP connection to the web server behind the ASA.

Step 2. The Cisco ASA prompts the user for authentication.

Step 3. The Cisco ASA receives the authentication information from the user and sends an AUTH Request to the CiscoSecure ACS server.

Step 4. The server authenticates the user and sends an AUTH Accept message to the Cisco ASA.

Step 5. The Cisco ASA allows the user to access the web server.

Complete the following steps to enable network access authentication via the cut-through proxy feature, using ASDM.

Step 1. Log in to ASDM and navigate to **Configuration > Firewall > AAA Rules.**

Step 2. Click on **Add** and select **Add Authentication Rule.** The dialog box illustrated in Figure 6-8 is displayed.

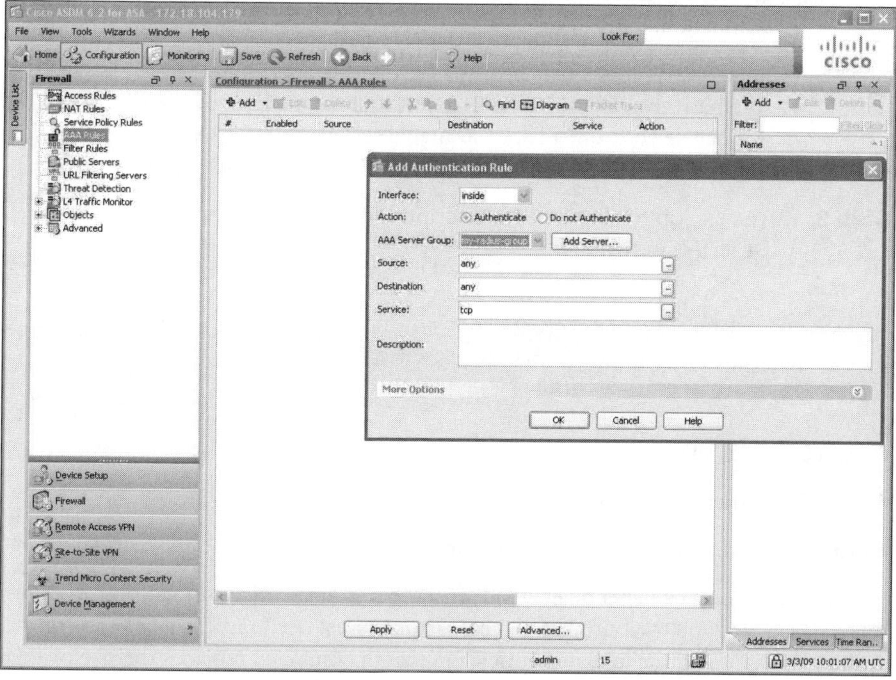

Figure 6-8 *Adding an Authentication Rule via ASDM*

Step 3. Select the interface where the authentication rule will be applied from the **Interface** pull-down menu. The **inside** interface is selected in this example.

Step 4. Select **Authenticate** in the **Action** field to require user authentication.

Step 5. Select the AAA server group (**my-radius-group**) from the **AAA Server Group** pull-down menu.

Note You can add a AAA server to the server group by clicking the **Add Server** button. In this example, the preconfigured AAA server is used.

Step 6. You must specify a source and a destination for traffic that will require authentication. Enter the source IP address, network address, or the any keyword in the **Source** field. Alternatively, you can click the ellipsis (...) to select an address that has already been configured in ASDM. In this example, the **any** keyword is entered to require authentication for any source from the inside interface.

Step 7. Enter the destination IP address, network address, or the **any** keyword in the **Destination** field. Alternatively, you can click the ellipsis (...) to select an address that has already being configured in ASDM. In this example, the **any** keyword is entered to require authentication when a host tries to reach any destination.

Step 8. Enter an IP service name for the destination service in the **Service** field. Alternatively, click the ellipsis (...) button to open a separate dialog box where you can select from a list of available services. In this example, authentication is required for any host trying to access any TCP-based applications.

Step 9. You can optionally enter a description for the authentication rule in the **Description** field.

Note You can click on More Options to specify a source service for TCP or UDP applications or set a time range within which this rule is to be applied.

Step 10. Click OK.

Step 11. Click **Apply** to apply the configuration changes.

Step 12. Click **Save** to save the configuration in the Cisco ASA.

Cut-through proxy can also be enabled with the **aaa authentication match** CLI command. It enables you to configure an access control list (ACL) to classify what traffic is authenticated. Using the **aaa authentication match** command replaces the use of the **include** and **exclude** options and it is now the preferred method to configure authentication through the Cisco ASA appliance. The following is the command syntax:

```
aaa authentication match acl interface server-tag
```

The *acl* keyword refers to the name or number of the ACL configured to define what traffic is authenticated. The *interface* keyword defines the interface that receives the connection request. The *server-tag* is the AAA server group defined by the **aaa-server** command.

Example 6-10 shows the commands sent by ASDM to the Cisco ASA to enable cut-through proxy.

Example 6-10 *Configuring Cut-Through Proxy Using the CLI*

```
access-list inside_authentication extended permit tcp any any
aaa authentication match inside_authentication inside my-radius-group
```

In Example 6-10, an ACL named **inside_authentication** is configured to **permit** (or match) TCP traffic from **any** source to **any** destination. This ACL is then applied to the **aaa authentication match** command. The **inside** keyword specifies that this rule is applied to the inside interface. The AAA server group named **my-radius-group** is associated to the end of the command.

You can also add exceptions to not authenticate certain users based on IP address. Figure 6-9 illustrates an example of how the **aaa authentication match** command works. SecureMe, Inc., has two users in the 10.10.1.0/24 network who need to access the web server in the 10.10.2.0/24 network. The Cisco ASA is configured to authenticate all users in the 10.10.1.0 network; however, User2 is allowed to connect to the web server without being authenticated.

The following are the steps represented in Figure 6-9:

Step 1. User1 attempts to access the web server (10.10.2.88).

Step 2. The Cisco ASA prompts the user to authenticate.

Step 3. User1 replies with his credentials.

Step 4. The Cisco ASA sends the authentication request (Access-Request) to the CiscoSecure ACS RADIUS server (172.18.124.141).

Step 5. The CiscoSecure ACS server sends back its reply (Access-Accept) to the Cisco ASA.

Step 6. User1 is able to access the web server.

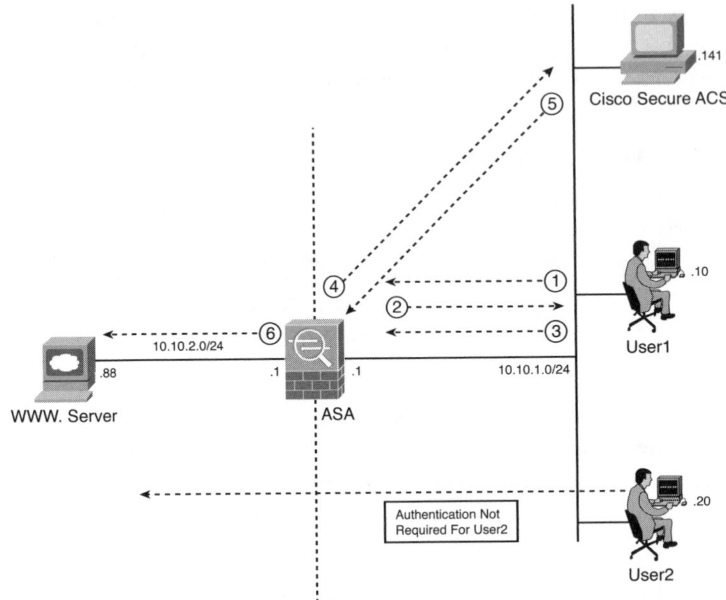

Figure 6-9 *Firewall Session Authentication Exceptions*

User2 can access the web server without being required to authenticate.

The commands to achieve this configuration are included in Example 6-11.

Example 6-11 *Configuring Firewall Session Authentication Exceptions*

```
!An ACL is configured to require authentication of all traffic except for User2
(10.10.1.20)
access-list 150 extended permit ip any any
access-list 150 extended deny ip host 172.18.124.20 any
!
!The aaa authentication match command is configured with the corresponding ACL.
aaa authentication match 150 inside my-radius-group
```

Cisco ASA is capable of excluding authentication for devices by using their MAC addresses. This feature is practical when bypassing authentication for devices such as printers and IP phones. Create a MAC address list by using the **mac-list** command. Subsequently, use the **aaa mac-exempt** command to bypass authentication for the specified MAC addresses on the list. Example 6-12 demonstrates how to configure the Cisco ASA to achieve this functionality.

Example 6-12 *Configuring Authentication Exceptions by Using MAC Address Lists*

```
mac-list MACLIST permit 0003.470d.61aa ffff.ffff.ffff
mac-list MACLIST permit 0003.470d.61bb ffff.ffff.ffff
aaa mac-exempt match MAC
```

In Example 6-12, a MAC list named MACLIST is defined with two host MAC addresses and is associated with the **aaa mac-except** command.

> **Note** Only one MAC list can be associated with **aaa mac-exempt.**
> Both authentication and authorization are bypassed if this feature is turned on.

Authentication Timeouts

Authentication timeouts specify how long the Cisco ASA should wait before requiring the user to reauthenticate after a period of inactivity or absolute duration. Customize authentication timeouts in ASDM by navigating to **Configuration > Firewall > Advanced > Global Timeouts** and editing the **Authentication inactivity** timeout field. Alternatively, you can configure authentication timeouts via the CLI by using the **timeout uauth** command. The following is the command syntax:

```
timeout uauth hh:mm:ss [absolute | inactivity]
```

The inactivity timer begins after a user connection becomes idle. The absolute timer runs continuously. If you use the inactivity and absolute timeouts at the same time, the absolute timeout duration should be longer than the inactivity timeout. If you set the timeouts the opposite way, the inactivity timeout does not work because the absolute timeout always expires sooner.

> **Note** It is recommended to configure the **absolute timeout** command value for at least 2 minutes. Never configure the **timeout uauth** duration to 0, particularly when using passive FTP, because the authentication session then never times out.

Additionally, you can use the **clear uauth** command to delete all cached credentials and make all users reauthenticate when attempting to create a new connection through the Cisco ASA. You can append a username at the end of the command to make a specific user reauthenticate. For example, use **clear uauth joe** to force a user called "joe" to reauthenticate.

Customizing Authentication Prompts

Cisco ASA enables you to customize the authentication prompts by navigating to the **Configuration > Device Management > Users/AAA > Authentication Prompt** in ASDM and entering an authentication prompt under the **Prompt** section. Similarly, the **auth-prompt** command can be used in the CLI to customize the authentication prompt. This customization is available only for Telnet, HTTP, or FTP authentication. The following is the usage and syntax of this command:

```
auth-prompt [prompt | accept | reject] prompt text
```

Table 6-5 lists all the options of the **auth-prompt** command.

Table 6-5 auth-prompt *Command Options*

Option	Description
prompt text	The actual text that will be printed at challenge, accept, or reject time.
prompt	Specifies that text following this keyword is printed as the authentication prompt.
accept	The text following this keyword is printed at authentication acceptance time.
reject	The text following this keyword is printed at authentication rejection time.

Note The **accept** and **reject** options apply only for Telnet connections.

Configuring Authorization

Cisco ASA supports authorization services over TACACS+ for firewall cut-through proxy sessions. It also supports authorization services over TACACS+ and its internal user database for administrative sessions. RADIUS-downloadable ACLs are also supported by Cisco ASA. Command access is authorized by privilege level only when authorization is done against the local database.

Additionally, authorization over RADIUS, LDAP, and internal user databases is available for VPN user connections. This is used for **mode-config** attributes for remote-access VPN clients. Information about **mode-config** and its attributes is provided in Chapter 17.

Complete the following steps to configure authorization with ASDM:

Step 1. Log in to ASDM and navigate to **Configuration > Firewall > AAA Rules.**

Step 2. Click on **Add** and select **Add Authorization Rule.** The dialog box shown in Figure 6-10 is displayed.

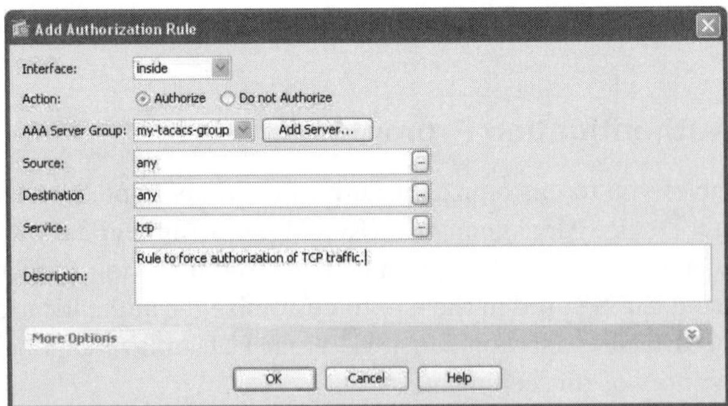

Figure 6-10 *Add Authorization Rule Dialog Box*

Step 3. Select the interface where the authentication rule will be applied from the **Interface** pull-down menu. The **inside** interface is selected in this example.

Step 4. Select **Authorize** in the **Action** field to require user authentication.

Step 5. Select the AAA server group (**my-tacacs-group**) from the **AAA Server Group** pull-down menu.

Note You can add a AAA server to the server group by clicking the **Add Server** button. In this example, the preconfigured AAA server is used. The TACACS+ server was previously added to the configuration via navigation to **Configuration > Device Management > Users/AAA > AAA Server Groups.**

Step 6. You must specify a source and a destination for traffic that will require authorization. Enter the source IP address, network address, or the any keyword in the **Source** field. Alternatively, you can click the ellipsis (...) to select an address that has already being configured in ASDM. In this example the **any** keyword is entered to require authentication for any source from the inside interface.

Step 7. Enter the destination IP address, network address, or the any keyword in the **Destination** field. Alternatively, you can click the ellipsis (...) to select an address that has already been configured in ASDM. In this example, the **any** keyword is entered to require authorization when a host tries to reach any destination

Step 8. Enter an IP service name for the destination service in the **Service** field. Alternatively, click the ellipsis (...) button to open a separate dialog box where you can select from a list of available services. In this example, authentication is required for any host trying to access any TCP-based applications.

Step 9. You can optionally enter a description for the authentication rule in the **Description** field.

Note You can click on More Options to specify a source service for TCP or UDP applications or set a time range within which this rule is to be applied.

Step 10. Click OK.

Step 11. Click **Apply** to apply the configuration changes.

Step 12. Click **Save** to save the configuration in the Cisco ASA.

Alternatively, in the CLI, the **aaa authorization match** command enables authorization for firewall cut-through proxy and administrative sessions. The following is the syntax for this command to enable authorization for firewall cut-through proxy sessions:

```
aaa authorization match access_list_name if_name server_tag
```

The *access_list_name* option specifies the ACL name used to categorize which traffic requires authorization.

Command Authorization

You enable command authorization in ASDM by following these steps:

Step 1. Log in to ASDM and navigate to **Configuration > Device Management > Users/AAA > AAA Access > Authorization.**

Step 2. Click on **Enable** to enable authorization.

Step 3. Select the AAA server group under the **Server Group** pull-down menu.

> **Note** TACACS+ server commands can be configured as a shared profile component, for a group, or for individual users. If you enable TACACS+ command authorization, and a user enters a command at the CLI, the Cisco ASA sends the command and username to the TACACS+ server to determine whether the command is authorized.

Step 4. Optionally, you can select the **Use LOCAL when Server Group Fails** check box as a fallback method in case the TACACS+ server is unreachable.

Step 5. To perform authorization for exec shell access, click on **Enable** under the **Perform Authorization for Exec Shell Access** section. You can specify whether authorization is performed by using the remote server parameters or the local authentication server.

Step 6. Click **Apply** to apply the configuration changes.

Step 7. Click **Save** to save the configuration in the Cisco ASA.

To configure command authorization via the CLI, use the following command:

```
aaa authorization command {LOCAL | tacacs_server_tag [LOCAL]}
```

The server tag **LOCAL** defines local command authorization. It can also be used as a fallback method in case the TACACS+ server is unreachable.

When using authorization, the following attributes are passed to the TACACS+ server in the attribute payload of the authorization request message:

- **cmd**—The command string to be authorized (used for authorization for administrative sessions only)

- **cmd-arg**—The command arguments to be sent (used for authorization for administrative sessions only)
- **service**—The type of service for which authorization is requested

The following attributes may be received from a TACACS+ server in an authorization response message:

- **idletime**—Idle timeout value for firewall cut-through proxy sessions
- **timeout**—Absolute timeout value for firewall cut-through proxy sessions
- **acl**—The identifier of an ACL to be applied to a specific user

Configuring Downloadable ACLs

Cisco ASA provides support for a per-user ACL authorization by enabling you to download an ACL from a RADIUS or TACACS+ server. This feature allows you to push an ACL to the Cisco ASA from a CiscoSecure ACS server. The downloadable ACL works in combination with the ACLs configured in the ASA. The user traffic needs to be permitted by both ACLs for it to flow through the ASA. However, the **per-user-override** option can be configured at the end of the **access-group** command to bypass this requirement. The following is an example of applying the **per-user-override** option on an **access-group** command applied to the inside interface:

```
access-group 100 in interface inside per-user-override
```

In ASDM, configure this by navigating to **Configuration > Firewall > Access Rules** and clicking on the **Advanced** button. The **Access Rules Advanced Options** dialog box is displayed, enabling you to select the **Per User Override** option on each access list entry.

All downloadable ACLs are applied to the interface from which the user is authenticated.

Figure 6-11 and the steps following illustrate an example of how downloadable ACLs work.

Step 1. A user initiates a web connection to Cisco.com. The Cisco ASA is configured to perform authentication (cut-through proxy) and prompts the user for authentication credentials.

Step 2. The user replies with his credentials.

Step 3. The Cisco ASA sends the RADIUS authentication request (Access-Accept) to the CiscoSecure ACS server.

Step 4. The CiscoSecure ACS server authenticates the user and sends a RADIUS response (Access-Accept), including an ACL name associated with the user.

Step 5. The Cisco ASA verifies whether it has an ACL named the same as the one downloaded from the CiscoSecure ACS server. There is no need to download a new ACL if an ACL is identified with the same name.

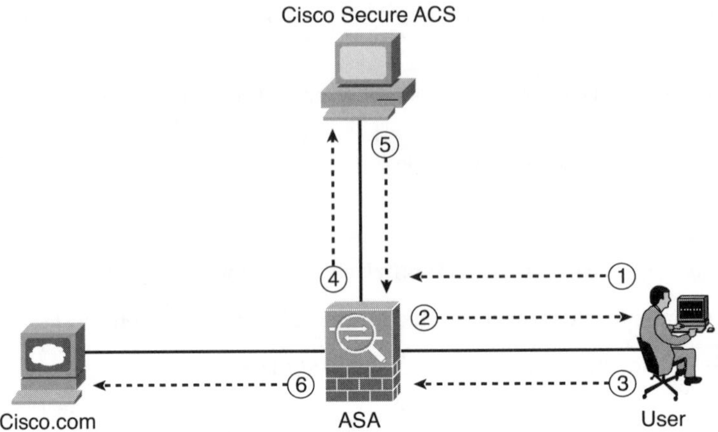

Figure 6-11 *Downloadable ACL Example*

You can configure downloadable ACLs in CiscoSecure ACS in a few different ways:

- Configure a Shared Profile Component (SPC), including both the ACL name and the actual ACL. This enables you to apply the ACL to any number of users within CiscoSecure ACS.
- Configure each ACL entry within a specific user profile.
- Configure the ACLs to be applied to a specific group.

These options are supported with Cisco ASA to better fit your security policies.

Configuring Accounting

To configure accounting on the Cisco ASA via ASDM, complete the following steps. The goal in the following example is to enable accounting for all IP traffic sourced from the 10.10.1.0/24 network and destined to the 10.10.2.0/24 network.

Step 1. Log in to ASDM and navigate to **Configuration > Firewall > AAA Rules**.

Step 2. Click on **Add** and select **Add Accounting Rule**.

Step 3. Select the interface where the accounting rule is to be applied. In this example, the **inside** interface is used.

Step 4. Under **Action**, select **Account** to enable accounting.

Step 5. Select the AAA server group from the **AAA Server Group** pull-down menu. In this example, the previously configured AAA server group called **my-radius-group** is used.

Step 6. You can configure the source and destination to define specific traffic traversing the Cisco ASA that is to be used for accounting. Configure the specific source IP address or network under the **Source** field. By default the **any** keyword is displayed to enable accounting for all sources. In this example, the source network **10.10.1.0/24** is used.

Step 7. Configure the specific destination IP address or network under the **Destination** field. By default, the **any** keyword is displayed to enable accounting for all sources. In this example, the destination network **10.10.2.0/24** is used.

Step 8. Select the specific service or protocol in the Service field. In this example, the **ip** keyword is used to enable accounting for all IP traffic sourced from the 10.10.1.0/24 network and destined to the 10.10.2.0/24 network.

Step 9. Optionally, you can enter a description for this accounting rule in the **Description** field.

Step 10. Click **Apply** to apply the configuration changes.

Step 11. Click **Save** to save the configuration in the Cisco ASA.

To enable accounting via the CLI use the **aaa accounting** command:

```
aaa accounting match access_list_name if_name server_tag
```

Example 6-13 demonstrates how to configure accounting on the Cisco ASA via the CLI.

Example 6-13 *Enabling Accounting by Using an ACL to Define Interesting Traffic*

```
New York(config)# access-list 100 permit ip 10.10.1.0 255.255.255.0 10.10.2.0
255.255.255.0
New York(config)# aaa accounting match 100 inside my-radius-group
```

In Example 6-13, an ACL is configured to enable accounting for all connections initiated from 10.10.1.0/24 to 10.10.2.0/24. The ACL is then applied to the **aaa accounting match** command. A previously defined AAA server group named **my-radius-group** is used with this command.

You can also use the **aaa accounting include | exclude** command options, as demonstrated for the **aaa authentication** command. The **aaa accounting match** command makes the **include** and **exclude** options obsolete.

RADIUS Accounting

Table 6-6 lists all the RADIUS accounting messages supported by Cisco ASA.

The **accounting-on** message marks the start of accounting services. Subsequently, to mark the end of accounting services, use the **accounting-off** message. The **start** and **stop accounting records** messages are used to label when a user started a connection to a specific service. These sessions are labeled with their own accounting session IDs.

Table 6-6 *RADIUS Accounting Messages Supported in the Cisco ASA*

Attribute	Applicable Messages
acct-authentic	on, off, start, stop
acct-delay-time	on, off, start, stop
acct-status-type	on, off, start, stop
acct-session-id	start, stop
nas-ip-address	on, off, start, stop
nas-port	on, off, start, stop
user-name	on, off, start, stop
class	start, stop
service type	start, stop
framed-protocol	start, stop
framed-ip-address	start, stop
tunnel-client-endpoint	start, stop
acct-session-time	stop
acct-input-packets	stop
acct-output-packets	stop
acct-input-octets	stop
acct-output-octets	stop
acct-terminate-cause	stop
login-ip-host	on, off, start, stop
login-port	on, off, start, stop
Cisco AV pair (used to send source addr/port and dest addr/port)	on, off, start, stop
isakmp-initiator-ip	on, off, start, stop
isakmp-phase1-id	on, off, start, stop
isakmp-group-id	on, off, start, stop
acct-input-gigawords	stop
acct-output-gigawords	stop

TACACS+ Accounting

Table 6-7 lists all the TACACS+ accounting messages that Cisco ASA supports.

Table 6-7 *TACACS+ Accounting Messages Supported by Cisco ASA*

Attribute	Applicable Messages
username (fixed field)	start, stop
port (NAS) (fixed field)	start, stop
remote_address (fixed field)	start, stop
task_id	start, stop
foreign_IP	start, stop
local_IP	start, stop
cmd	start, stop
elapsed_time	stop
bytes_in	stop
bytes_out	stop

Cisco ASA also enables you to configure command accounting, depending on the user's privilege level. Use the following command to enable this feature:

aaa accounting command {**privilege** *level*} *tacacs_server_tag*

Example 6-14 demonstrates how to configure command accounting on the Cisco ASA, depending on the user's privilege level.

Example 6-14 *Enabling Command Accounting*

```
New York(config)# aaa accounting command privilege 15 my-tacacs-group
```

In Example 6-14, the **accounting** command is enabled for users that execute a **privilege level 15** command.

Alternatively, you can configure command accounting via ASDM by navigating to **Configuration > Device Management > Users/AAA > AAA Access > Accounting** and selecting **Enable** under the **Require Command Accounting for ASA** section.

Troubleshooting Administrative Connections to Cisco ASA

You can authenticate administrative connections by using RADIUS, TACACS+, or the Cisco ASA local user database. The following **debug** commands are available to troubleshoot AAA problems when you are trying to connect to the Cisco ASA for administration:

- **debug aaa**—Provides information about the authentication, authorization, or accounting messages generated and received by the Cisco ASA.
- **debug radius**—To troubleshoot RADIUS transactions, use this command, which has several options:
  - **all**—Enables all debug options
  - **decode**—Shows decoded RADIUS transaction messages
  - **session**—Provides information about all RADIUS sessions
  - **user**—Enables you to capture RADIUS transaction information for a specific user connection
- **debug tacacs**—To troubleshoot TACACS+ transactions, use this command with either of the following options:
  - **session**—Provides detailed information about all TACACS+ transactions
  - **user**—Allows you to capture TACACS+ transaction information for a specific user connection

If you enter **debug tacacs** without any options, the **debug** command is enabled with the **session** option by default. Example 6-15 includes the output of **debug tacacs** during a successful Telnet authentication.

Example 6-15 *Output of* **debug tacacs** *During a Successful Telnet Authentication*

```
New York# debug tacacs
 mk_pkt - type: 0x1, session_id: 4
 user: user1
 Tacacs packet sent
Sending TACACS Start message. Session id: 4, seq no:1
Received TACACS packet. Session id:4  seq no:2
tacp_procpkt_authen: GETPASS
Authen Message: Password:
mk_pkt - type: 0x1, session_id: 4
mkpkt_continue - response: ***
 Tacacs packet sent
Sending TACACS Continue message. Session id: 4, seq no:3
Received TACACS packet. Session id:4  seq no:4
tacp_procpkt_authen: PASS
TACACS Session finished. Session id: 4, seq no: 3
```

In Example 6-15, User1 connected to the Cisco ASA via Telnet. The Cisco ASA was configured to perform authentication via an external TACACS+ server. The first highlighted line shows that User1 attempted a connection to the Cisco ASA. The second highlighted line shows the ASA requesting the user's password. The user information is sent to the TACACS+ server and is finally authenticated. The third highlighted line shows that the authentication was successful. Example 6-16 includes the output of **debug tacacs** during an authentication failure. In this example, the incorrect password was entered by the user and the TACACS+ server failed its authentication.

Example 6-16 *Output of* **debug tacacs** *During a Failed Authentication Because of Wrong Password*

```
New York# debug tacacs
 mk_pkt - type: 0x1, session_id: 5
 user: user1
 Tacacs packet sent
Sending TACACS Start message. Session id: 5, seq no:1
Received TACACS packet. Session id:5  seq no:2
tacp_procpkt_authen: GETPASS
Authen Message: Password:
mk_pkt - type: 0x1, session_id: 5
mkpkt_continue - response: ***
 Tacacs packet sent
Sending TACACS Continue message. Session id: 5, seq no:3
Received TACACS packet. Session id:5  seq no:4
tacp_procpkt_authen: FAIL
TACACS Session finished. Session id: 5, seq no: 3
The highlighted line in Example 6-22 shows the authentication FAIL message.
```

In Example 6-17, the TACACS+ server was offline or unreachable.

Example 6-17 *Output of* **debug tacacs** *While TACACS+ Server Is Unreachable*

```
New York# debug tacacs
mk_pkt - type: 0x1, session_id: 6
 user: user1
 Tacacs packet sent
Sending TACACS Start message. Session id: 6, seq no:1
Received TACACS packet. Session id:6  seq no:2
TACACS Request Timed out. Session id: 6, seq no:1
TACACS Session finished. Session id: 6, seq no: 1
mk_pkt - type: 0x1, session_id: 6
```

```
user: user1
 Tacacs packet sent
Sending TACACS Start message. Session id: 6, seq no:1
Received TACACS packet. Session id:6  seq no:2
TACACS Request Timed out. Session id: 6, seq no:1
TACACS Session finished. Session id: 6, seq no: 1
mk_pkt - type: 0x1, session_id: 6
 user: user1
 Tacacs packet sent
Sending TACACS Start message. Session id: 6, seq no:1
Received TACACS packet. Session id:6  seq no:2
TACACS Request Timed out. Session id: 6, seq no:1
TACACS Session finished. Session id: 6, seq no: 1
aaa server host machine not responding
```

The highlighted lines show how the Cisco ASA attempts to communicate with the TACACS+ server three times and finally finishes all authentication transactions. The **show aaa-server** command is useful while troubleshooting and monitoring authentication transactions. Example 6-18 includes the output of the **show aaa-server** command for all TACACS+ transactions.

Example 6-18 *Monitoring and Troubleshooting TACACS+ Transactions with the* **show aaa-server** *Command*

```
New York# show aaa-server protocol tacacs+
Server Group:     mygroup
Server Protocol: tacacs+
Server Address:  172.18.124.145
Server port:      49
Server status:   ACTIVE, Last transaction at 21:05:43 UTC Fri March 20 2009
Number of pending requests              0
Average round trip time                 43ms
Number of authentication requests      4
Number of authorization requests       0
Number of accounting requests           0
Number of retransmissions               0
Number of accepts                        3
Number of rejects                        1
Number of challenges                     4
Number of malformed responses           0
Number of bad authenticators            0
Number of timeouts                       0
Number of unrecognized responses        0
```

In Example 6-18, the Cisco ASA processed a total of four authentication requests. Three of those requests were successfully authenticated and one was rejected by the TACACS+ server.

Troubleshooting Firewall Sessions (Cut-Through Proxy)

The techniques to troubleshoot cut-through proxy sessions on Cisco ASA are similar to those mentioned in the previous section. Additionally, the **show uauth** command can be used to display information about authenticated users and current transactions. Example 6-19 shows the output of this command.

Example 6-19 *Output of the* **show uauth** *Command*

```
New York# show uauth
                             Current     Most Seen
Authenticated Users           0           0
Authen In Progress            1           3
```

In Example 6-19, a total of three concurrent authentication requests were processed by the Cisco ASA. One is currently being processed.

Summary

Cisco ASA supports several AAA solutions for different services. It ensures the enforcement of assigned policies by allowing you to control who can log in to the Cisco ASA or in to the network. Additionally, it controls what each user is allowed to do. It can also record security audit information by using accounting services. This chapter covered how Cisco ASA can use authentication services to control pass-through access by requiring valid user credentials. It also demonstrated how Cisco ASA is configured to authenticate administrative sessions from Telnet, SSH, serial console, and ASDM.

This chapter demonstrated how authorization can enforce per-user access control after authentication is done. It guided you through configuring the Cisco ASA appliance to authorize management and administrative commands and network access.

The Cisco ASA accounting services track traffic that passes through the security appliance, enabling you to have a record of user activity. This chapter also demonstrated how you can enable accounting to track and audit user activity.

Chapter 7

Application Inspection

This chapter covers the following topics:

- Enabling Application Inspection
- Selective Inspection
- Computer Telephony Interface Quick Buffer Encoding Inspection
- Distributed Computing Environment Remote Procedure Calls (DCERPC) Inspection
- Domain Name System Inspection
- Extended Simple Mail Transfer Protocol Inspection
- File Transfer Protocol Inspection
- General Packet Radio Service Tunneling Protocol Inspection
- H.323 Inspection
- Unified Communications Advanced Support Inspection HTTP Inspection
- ICMP Inspection
- ILS Inspection
- Instant Messenger (IM) Inspection
- IPSec pass-through Inspection
- MGCP Inspection
- NetBIOS Inspection PPTP Inspection
- Sun RPC Inspection
- RSH Inspection
- RTSP Inspection

- SIP Inspection Skinny (SCCP) Inspection
- SNMP Inspection
- SQL*Net Inspection
- TFTP Inspection
- WAAS Inspection
- XDMCP Inspection

The Cisco ASA mechanisms used for stateful application inspection enforce the secure use of applications and services in your network. The stateful inspection engine keeps information about each connection traversing through the security appliance's interfaces and makes sure they are valid. Stateful application inspection examines not only the packet header, but also the contents of the packet up through the application layer.

Several applications require special handling of data packets when they pass through the Layer 3 devices. These include applications and protocols that embed IP addressing information in the data payload of the packet or open secondary channels on dynamically assigned ports. The Cisco ASA application inspection mechanisms recognize the embedded addressing information, which allows Network Address Translation (NAT) to work and update any other fields or checksums.

Using application inspection, the Cisco ASA can identify the dynamic port assignments and allow data exchange on these ports during a specific connection. The application inspection capabilities are similar to the traditional fixup protocol functionality on the Cisco PIX firewalls. However, the Cisco ASA software dramatically enhances the capabilities of application inspection.

The following are all the applications and protocols supported by Cisco ASA:

- Computer Telephony Interface Quick Buffer Encoding (CTIQBE)
- Distributed Computing Environment Remote Procedure Calls (DCERPC)
- Domain Name Server (DNS) over UDP
- Extended Simple Mail Transfer Protocol (ESMTP)
- File Transfer Protocol (FTP)
- General Packet Radio Service Tunneling Protocol (GTP)
- H.323
- Hypertext Transfer Protocol (HTTP)
- Internet Control Message Protocol (ICMP) and ICMP Error
- Integrated Library System (ILS) protocol
- Instant Messenger (IM)
- IPSec pass-through

- Media Gateway Control Protocol (MGCP)
- Multi-chassis Multilink PPP (MMP)
- NetBIOS
- Point to Point Tunneling Protocol (PPTP)
- Remote Shell (RSH)
- Real-Time Streaming Protocol (RTSP)
- Session Initiation Protocol (SIP)
- Skinny Call Control Protocol (SCCP)
- Simple Network Management Protocol (SNMP)
- SQL*Net
- SUNRPC
- Trivial File Transfer Protocol (TFTP)
- Wide Area Application Services (WAAS)
- X Display Manager Control Protocol (XDMCP)

The following sections include thorough information on how to enable application inspection and details about these applications and protocols.

Note Certain protocol inspection requires a separate license. An example is GTP. More licensing information can be found at http://www.cisco.com/go/asa.

Enabling Application Inspection

Cisco ASA provides a Modular Policy Framework (MPF) to provide application security or to perform quality of service (QoS) functions. MPF provides a consistent and flexible way to configure the Cisco ASA application inspection and other features in a manner similar to that used for the Cisco IOS Software Modular QoS CLI.

Note Chapter 11, "Quality of Service," covers the QoS functionality in detail.

As a general rule, the provisioning of inspection policies requires the following steps:

Step 1. Configuring traffic classes to identify interesting traffic.

Step 2. Associating actions to each traffic class to create service policies.

Step 3. Activating the service policies on an interface or globally.

You can complete these policy provisioning steps by using these three main commands of the MPF:

- **class-map**—Classifies the traffic that will be inspected. Various types of match criteria in a class map can be used to classify traffic. The primary criterion is the use of an access control list (ACL). Example 7-1 demonstrates this.
- **policy-map**—Configures security or QoS policies. A policy consists of a **class** command and its associated actions. Additionally, a policy map can contain multiple policies.
- **service-policy**—Activates a policy map globally (on all interfaces) or on a targeted interface.

Example 7-1 *Matching Specific Traffic Using an ACL*

```
NewYork(config)# access-list tftptraffic permit udp any any eq 69
NewYork(config)# class-map TFTPclass
NewYork(config-cmap)# match access-list tftptraffic
NewYork(config-cmap)# exit
NewYork(config)# policy-map tftppolicy
NewYork(config-pmap)# class TFTPclass
NewYork(config-pmap-c)# inspect tftp
NewYork(config-pmap-c)# exit
NewYork(config-pmap)# exit
NewYork(config)# service-policy tftppolicy global
```

In Example 7-1, an ACL named **tftptraffic** is configured to identify all UDP traffic. This ACL is then applied to a class map named **TFTPclass.**

A policy map named **tftppolicy** is configured that has the class map **TFTPclass** mapped to it. The policy map is set up to inspect all TFTP traffic from the UDP packets that are being classified in the class map. Finally, the service policy is applied globally.

The security appliance contains a default class map named **inspection_default** and a policy map named **tftppolicy.** Example 7-2 shows the default class map and policy map in the Cisco ASA.

Example 7-2 *Default Class and Policy Maps*

```
class-map inspection_default
 match default-inspection-traffic
!
!
policy-map global_policy
 class inspection_default
  inspect dns preset_dns_map
```

```
  inspect ftp
  inspect h323 h225
  inspect h323 ras
  inspect netbios
  inspect rsh
  inspect rtsp
  inspect skinny
  inspect esmtp
  inspect sqlnet
  inspect sunrpc
  inspect tftp
  inspect sip
  inspect xdmcp
!
service-policy global_policy global
```

If using the Cisco ASDM, navigate to **Configuration > Firewall > Service Policy Rules** to edit or create a new service policy for application inspection. Steps on how to configure each application inspection parameter are shown later in this chapter.

Selective Inspection

As previously mentioned, the **match** command enables you to specify what traffic the Cisco ASA inspection engine is to process. It can be used in conjunction with an ACL to determine what traffic is to be inspected. Example 7-3 shows all the supported options for traffic classification in a class map named **UDPclass.**

Example 7-3 *Supported Traffic Classification Options*

```
NewYork(config)# class-map UDPclass
NewYork(config-cmap)# match ?
mpf-class-map mode commands/options:
  access-list                 Match an Access List
  any                          Match any packet
  default-inspection-traffic  Match default inspection traffic:
                                 ctiqbe——tcp—2748      dns———-udp—53
                                 ftp———-tcp—21         gtp———-udp—2123,3386
                                 h323-h225-tcp—1720    h323-ras—udp—1718-1719
                                 http———tcp—80         icmp———icmp
                                 ils———-tcp—389        mgcp———udp—2427,2727
                                 netbios—-udp—137-138  rpc———-udp—111
                                 rsh———-tcp—514        rtsp———tcp—554
                                 sip———-tcp—5060       sip———-udp—5060
```

```
                              skinny——tcp—2000      smtp———tcp—25
                              sqlnet——tcp—1521      tftp———udp—69
                              xdmcp——-udp—177
  dscp                        Match IP DSCP (DiffServ CodePoints)
  flow                        Flow based Policy
  port                        Match TCP/UDP port(s)
  precedence                  Match IP precedence
  rtp                         Match RTP port numbers
  tunnel-group                Match a Tunnel Group
```

Table 7-1 lists briefly describes all the options supported by the **match** command.

Table 7-1 match *Subcommand Options*

Option	Description
access-list	Specifies an ACL used to match or classify the traffic to be inspected.
any	Any IP traffic.
default-inspec-tion-traffic	The default entry for inspection of the supported protocols. This match applies only to the **inspect** command. It cannot be associated with any action commands but **inspect**.
dscp	Matches based on IP DSCP (DiffServ CodePoints).
flow	Used for flow-based policy.
port	Used to match TCP and/or UDP ports.
precedence	Matches based on IP Precedence value represented by the TOS byte in the IP header. The precedence value can be in a range from 0 to 7.
rtp	Matches Real Time Protocol (RTP) port numbers.
tunnel-group	Matches VPN traffic of a specific tunnel group.

If using ASDM, you can configure traffic classification by navigating to **Configuration > Firewall > Service Policy Rules** and clicking on **Edit** to edit a service policy. The **Edit Service Policy Rule** dialog box shown in Figure 7-1 is displayed.

In this figure you can see the corresponding options for traffic classification on ASDM.

To display statistics on the traffic being inspected on the Cisco ASA, use the **show service-policy** command. Example 7-4 shows the output of this command.

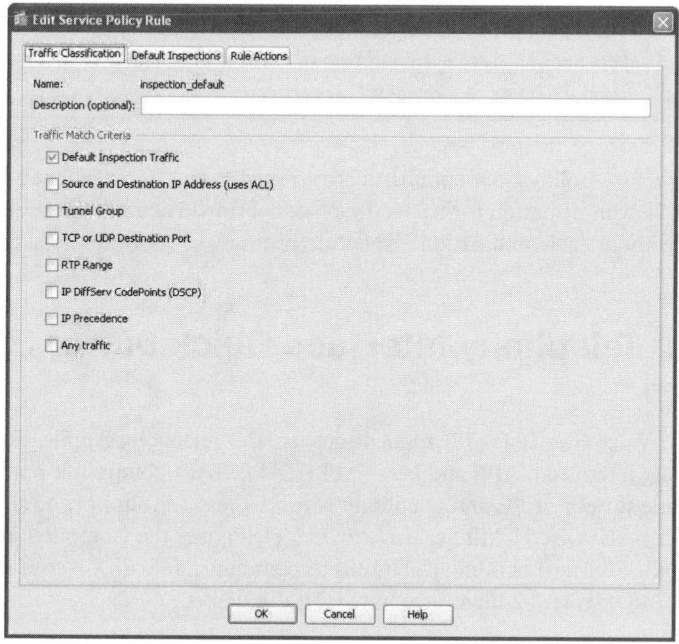

Figure 7-1 *Service Policy Traffic Classification*

Example 7-4 *Output of* show service-policy *Command*

```
NewYork(config)# show service-policy
Global policy:
  Service-policy: global_policy
    Class-map: inspection_default
      Inspect: dns preset_dns_map, packet 0, drop 0, reset-drop 0
      Inspect: ftp, packet 24, drop 0, reset-drop 0
      Inspect: h323 h225 _default_h323_map, packet 0, drop 0, reset-drop 0
               tcp-proxy: bytes in buffer 0, bytes dropped 0
      Inspect: h323 ras _default_h323_map, packet 0, drop 0, reset-drop 0
      Inspect: netbios, packet 43, drop 0, reset-drop 0
      Inspect: rsh, packet 0, drop 0, reset-drop 0
      Inspect: rtsp, packet 0, drop 0, reset-drop 0
               tcp-proxy: bytes in buffer 0, bytes dropped 0
      Inspect: skinny , packet 0, drop 0, reset-drop 0
               tcp-proxy: bytes in buffer 0, bytes dropped 0
      Inspect: esmtp _default_esmtp_map, packet 155, drop 0, reset-drop 0
      Inspect: sqlnet, packet 0, drop 0, reset-drop 0
               tcp-proxy: bytes in buffer 0, bytes dropped 0
      Inspect: sunrpc, packet 0, drop 0, reset-drop 0
               tcp-proxy: bytes in buffer 0, bytes dropped 0
      Inspect: tftp, packet 0, drop 0, reset-drop 0
```

```
    Inspect: sip , packet 0, drop 0, reset-drop 0
             tcp-proxy: bytes in buffer 0, bytes dropped 0
    Inspect: xdmcp, packet 0, drop 0, reset-drop 0
```

The **show service-policy flow** command is also very useful because it can be used to display traffic flow information for a specific protocol flow. The following sections include information about each application inspection protocol supported on Cisco ASA.

Computer Telephony Interface Quick Buffer Encoding Inspection

Some Cisco Voice over IP (VoIP) applications use the Telephony Application Programming Interface (TAPI) and Java TAPI (JTAPI). TAPI-compatible applications can run on a wide variety of PC and telephony hardware and can support a variety of network services. The Cisco TAPI Service Provider (TSP) uses the Computer Telephony Interface Quick Buffer Encoding (CTIQBE) to communicate with Cisco CallManager on TCP port 2748. Figure 7-2 illustrates how CTIQBE works.

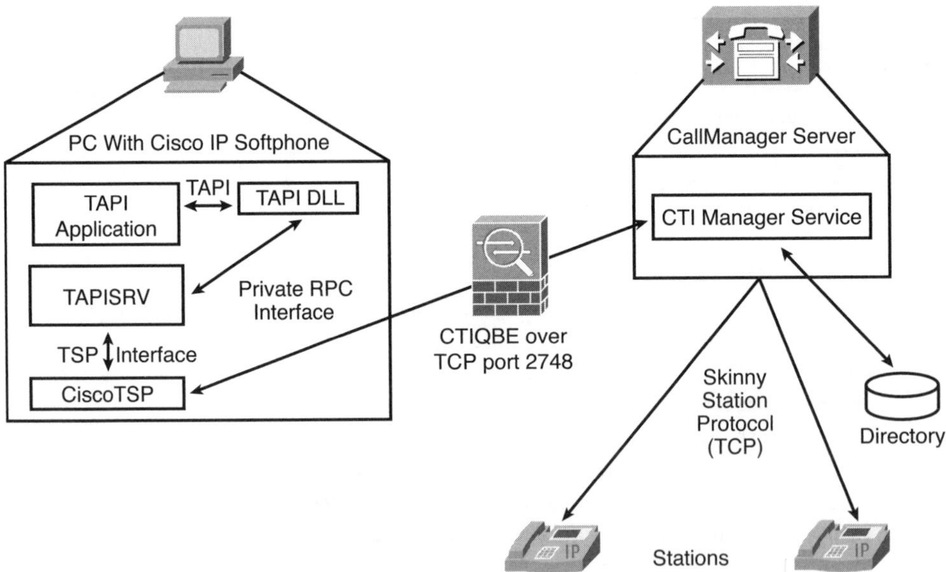

Figure 7-2 *Explanation of CTIQBE*

In Figure 7-2, a PC with Cisco IP SoftPhone communicates with a Cisco CallManager. CTIQBE inspection is not enabled by default.

Complete the following steps to enable CTIQBE inspection via ASDM:

Step 1. Log in to ASDM and navigate to **Configuration > Firewall > Service Policy Rules.**

Step 2. Click on **Edit** to edit a service policy. The **Edit Service Policy Rule** dialog box shown in Figure 7-3 is displayed.

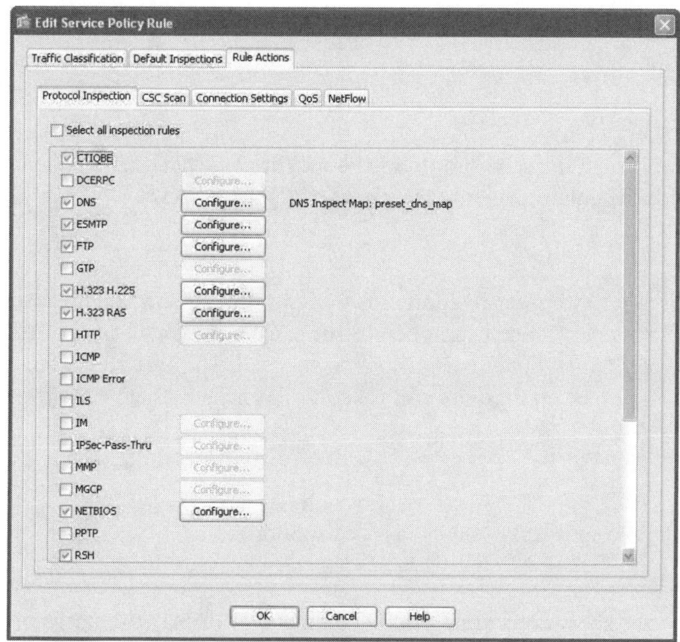

Figure 7-3 *Enabling CTIQBE Inspection*

Step 3. Click on the **Rule Actions** tab.

Step 4. Select **CTIQBE.**

Step 5. Click **OK.**

Step 6. Click **Apply** to apply the configuration changes.

Step 7. Click **Save** to save the configuration in the Cisco ASA.

> **Note** The **Edit Service Policy Rule** dialog box can be used to enable or disable any other application inspection protocols.

If configuring the Cisco ASA via the CLI, use the **inspect ctiqbe** command to enable CTIQBE inspection, as shown in Example 7-5.

Example 7-5 *Enabling CTIQBE Inspection*

```
NewYork# configure terminal
NewYork(config)# policy-map global_policy
NewYork(config-pmap)# class inspection_default
NewYork(config-pmap-c)# inspect ctiqbe
```

Note CTIQBE application inspection is not supported if the **alias** command is present in the configuration.

Tip CTIQBE calls fail if two Cisco IP SoftPhones are registered with different Cisco CallManagers connected to different interfaces of the Cisco ASA.

Tip If the Cisco CallManager IP address is to be translated and you are also using PAT, TCP port 2748 must be statically mapped to the same port as that of the PAT (interface) address for Cisco IP SoftPhone registrations to succeed. The CTIQBE listening port (TCP 2748) is fixed and is not configurable on Cisco CallManager, Cisco IP SoftPhone, or Cisco TSP.

Note Stateful failover of CTIQBE calls is not supported.

You can use the **show conn state ctiqbe** command to display the status of CTIQBE connections. The C flag represents the media connections allocated by the CTIQBE inspection engine. Example 7-6 includes the output of the **show conn state ctiqbe** command.

Example 7-6 *Output of the* **show conn state ctiqbe** *Command*

```
NewYork# show conn state ctiqbe
5 in use, 11 most used
```

Distributed Computing Environment Remote Procedure Calls (DCERPC)

DCERPC is a protocol that allows programmers to write distributed software without having to worry about the underlying network code. It is widely used by Microsoft distributed client and server applications. The Cisco ASA allows the appropriate port number and network address and also applies NAT, if needed, for the secondary connection. DCERPC inspect maps inspect for native TCP communication between the EPM and client on well-known TCP port 135.

To enable DCERPC inspection with ASDM, navigate to **Configuration > Firewall > Service Policy Rules** and edit the respective service policy. Then select **DCERPC** under the Rule Actions in the **Edit Service Policy Rule** dialog box shown in Figure 7-3.

If configuring the Cisco ASA via the CLI, use the **inspect dcerpc** command to enable DCERPC inspection, as shown in Example 7-7.

Example 7-7 *Enabling DCERPC Inspection*

```
NewYork# configure terminal
NewYork(config)# policy-map global_policy
NewYork(config-pmap)# class inspection_default
NewYork(config-pmap-c)# inspect dcerpc
```

Domain Name System

Domain Name System (DNS) implementations require application inspection so that DNS queries don't have to rely on the generic UDP handling based on activity timeouts. As a security mechanism, the UDP connections associated with DNS queries and responses are torn down as soon as a reply to a DNS query has been received in the Cisco ASA. This is similar to the old DNS Guard feature in Cisco PIX Firewall.

Cisco ASA DNS inspection provides the following benefits:

- Guarantees that the ID of the DNS reply matches the ID of the DNS query.
- Allows the translation of DNS packets through the use of NAT.
- Reassembles the DNS packet to verify its length. The Cisco ASA allows DNS packets of up to 65,535 bytes. When necessary, reassembly is done to verify that the packet length is less than the maximum length specified by the user. The packet is dropped if it is not compliant.

To enable DNS inspection via ASDM, select **DNS** under the **Edit Service Policy Rule** dialog box previously shown in Figure 7-3. You can also configure several optional parameters for this DNS inspection by clicking on the **Configure** button. The **Select DNS Inspect Map** is displayed. To configure a new DNS inspect map, click on **Add**. The dialog box shown in Figure 7-4 is displayed.

To configure the protocol conformance settings for DNS, select the Protocol Conformance tab, as shown in Figure 7-4. The following options are available:

- **Enable DNS Guard Function**—This option enables the Cisco ASA to do a DNS query-and-response mismatch check, using the identification field within the header of the DNS packet.
- **Enable NAT Re-write Function**—The Cisco ASA performs IP address translation in the A record of the DNS response.

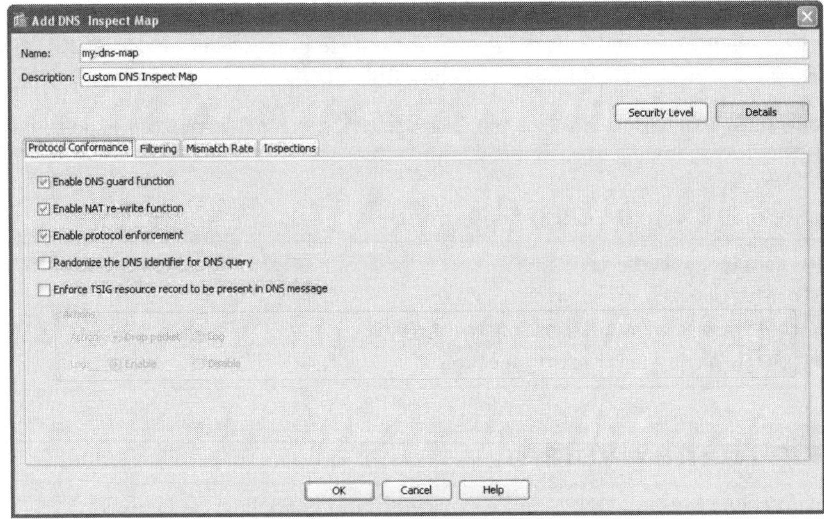

Figure 7-4 *Adding a DNS Inspect Map*

- **Enable Protocol Enforcement**—The Cisco ASA performs a DNS message-format check, including the following:
  - Domain name
  - Label length
  - Compression
  - Looped pointer check
- **Randomize the DNS Identifier for DNS Query**—Select this to randomize the DNS identifier in the DNS query message.
- **Enforce TSIG Resource Record to Be Present in DNS Message**—The Cisco ASA enforces that a TSIG resource record be present in DNS transactions. The Cisco ASA can either drop the packet or log associated messages, depending on what you configure in the **Actions** section.

The Filtering tab enables you to configure the filtering settings for DNS, as shown in Figure 7-5.

Under the **Global Settings** section you can enable the Cisco ASA to drop packets that exceed specified maximum length (globally). You can specify the maximum packet length (in bytes) under the **Maximum Packet Length** field.

The **Server Settings** section enables you to configure server specific parameters. The **Client Settings** section enables you to configure client-specific parameters. The following options are available for both:

- Drop packets that exceed specified maximum length
- Drop packets sent to server that exceed length indicated by the Resource Record (RR)

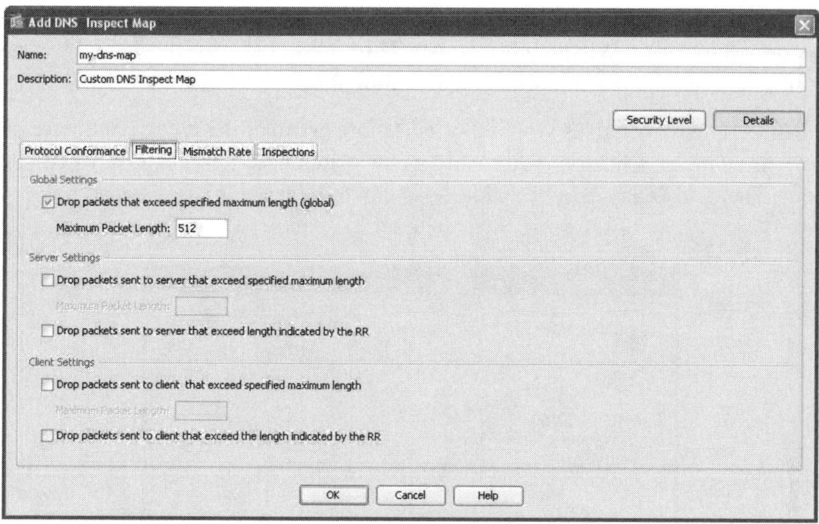

Figure 7-5 *DNS Inspect Map Filtering Tab*

The Mismatch Rate tab enables you configure the ID mismatch rate for DNS, as shown in Figure 7-6.

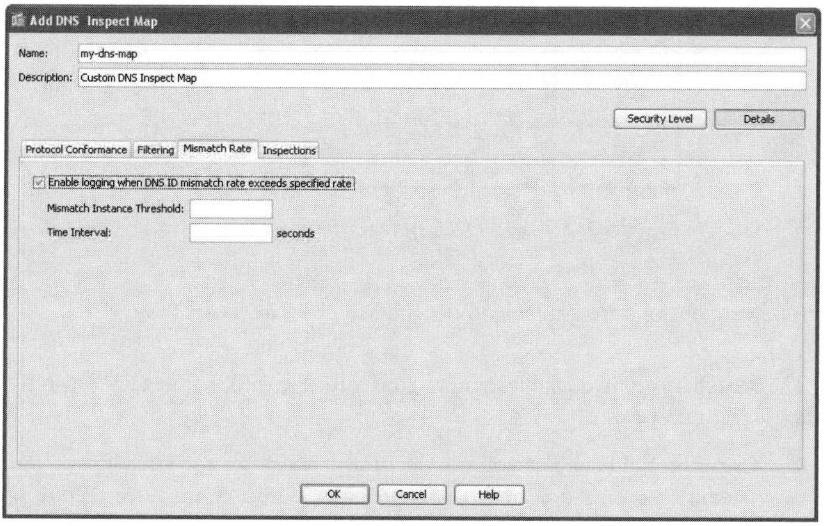

Figure 7-6 *DNS Inspect Map Mismatch Rate Tab*

Click the **Enable Logging when DNS ID Mismatch Rate Exceeds Specified Rate** to enable logging on the Cisco ASA when excessive instances of DNS identifier mismatches are received. You can specify the maximum number of mismatch instances before logging is performed under the **Mismatch Instance Threshold** field. Use the **Time Interval** field to configure the time period (in seconds) to monitor.

The **Inspections** tab enables you add or edit more granular matching parameters and actions to be taken. Click on **Add** to add a new matching criteria or **Edit** to edit an existing one. The **Add DNS Inspect** dialog box shown in Figure 7-7 is displayed.

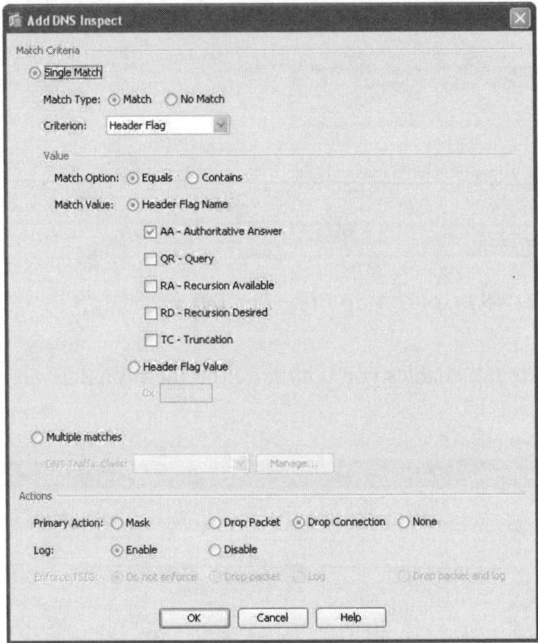

Figure 7-7 *Add DNS Inspect Dialog Box*

The following options are available under the **Match Criteria** section:

- The **Match Type** field enables you to configure a positive or negative match based on a specific criterion.
- The **Criterion** field enables you to select the criterion of the DNS inspection. You can match based on the header flag, type, class, question, resource record, or based on a domain name.
- The **Value** section enables you to configure the value to match in the DNS inspection.
- Similarly, you can also configure multiple matches under the **Multiple matches** field.

The **Action** section enables you to configure the action to be taken by the Cisco ASA if the match condition is met.

The primary action can be configured to mask, drop the offending packet, drop the connection, or take no action. Logging can also be enabled. Additionally, when TSIG enforcement is enabled, you can drop the packet, enable logging, or do both.

If you are using the CLI, use the **inspect dns** command. Example 7-8 includes the CLI commands for the parameters configured via ASDM in the previous examples.

Example 7-8 *Enabling DNS Inspection*

```
policy-map type inspect dns my-dns-map
 description Custom DNS Inspect Map
 parameters
  message-length maximum 512
 match header-flag eq AA
  drop-connection log
policy-map global_policy
 class inspection_default
    inspect dns my-dns-map
```

Extended Simple Mail Transfer Protocol

Cisco ASA Extended SMTP (ESMTP) inspection enhances the traditional SMTP inspection provided by Cisco PIX Firewall version 6.x or earlier. It provides protection against SMTP-based attacks by restricting the types of SMTP commands that can pass through the Cisco ASA. The following are the supported ESMTP commands:

- AUTH
- DATA
- EHLO
- ETRN
- HELO
- HELP
- MAIL
- NOOP
- QUIT
- RCPT
- RSET
- SAML
- SEND
- SOML
- VRFY

If an illegal command is found in an ESMTP or SMTP packet, it is modified and forwarded. This causes a negative server reply, forcing the client to issue a valid command. Figure 7-8 shows an example in which a user is trying to send **TURN**, which is an unsupported illegal command. The Cisco ASA modifies it and makes the receiver reply with an SMTP error return code of 500 (command not recognized) and tears down the connection.

Note The Cisco ASA replaces the illegal command characters with X's, as illustrated in Figure 7-8.

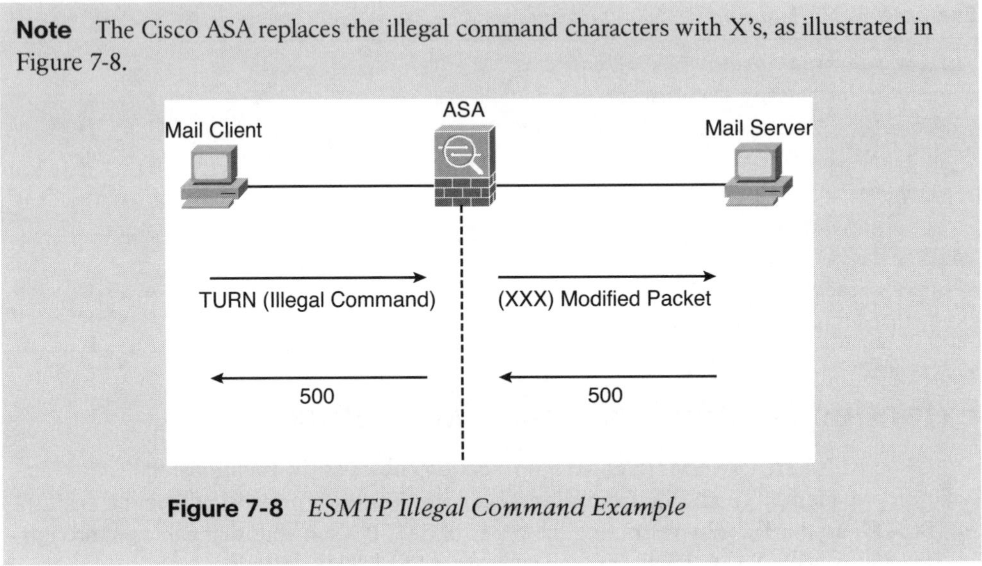

Figure 7-8 *ESMTP Illegal Command Example*

The Cisco ASA may perform deeper parameter inspection for packets containing legal commands. This type of inspection is required for SMTP and ESMTP extensions. Deeper parameter inspection is used to inspect the following SMTP and ESMTP extensions:

- Message Size Declaration (SIZE)
- Remote Queue Processing Declaration (ETRN)
- Binary MIME (BINARYMIME)
- Command Pipelining (PIPELINING)
- Authentication (AUTH)
- Delivery Status Notification (DSN)

To enable ESMTP inspection via ASDM, navigate to **Configuration > Firewall > Service Policy Rules > Edit Service Policy Rule** and select **ESMTP** under the **Edit Service Policy Rule** dialog box (previously shown in Figure 7-3). You can also configure several optional parameters for this ESMTP inspection by clicking on the **Configure** button. The **Select ESMTP Inspect Map** dialog box is displayed.

To configure a new ESMTP inspect map, click on **Add.** The **Add ESMTP Inspect Map** dialog box shown in Figure 7-9 is displayed.

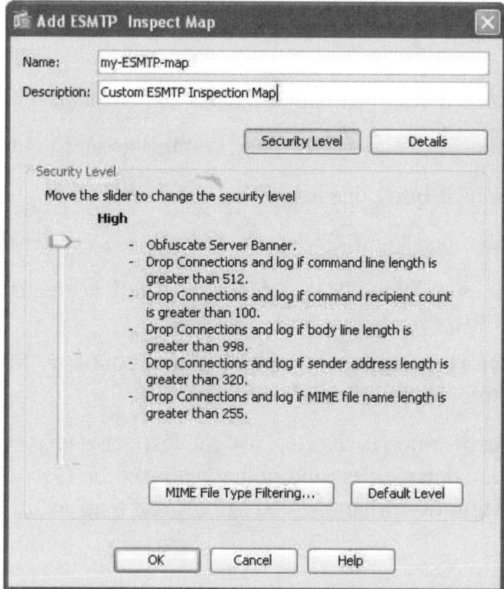

Figure 7-9 *Adding an ESMTP Inspect Map*

There are three different security levels: high, medium, or low. **Low** is the default and includes the following checks and actions:

- Log if command line length is greater than 512
- Log if command recipient count is greater than 100
- Log if body line length is greater than 1000
- Log if sender address length is greater than 320
- Log if MIME file name length is greater than 255

When you select **Medium** for the security level, the following checks and actions are performed:

- Obfuscate Server Banner
- Drop Connections if command line length is greater than 512
- Drop Connections if command recipient count is greater than 100
- Drop Connections if body line length is greater than 1000
- Drop Connections if sender address length is greater than 320

- Drop Connections if MIME file name length is greater than 255

When you select **High** for the security level the following checks and actions are performed:

- Obfuscate Server Banner
- Drop Connections if command line length is greater than 512
- Drop Connections if command recipient count is greater than 100
- Drop Connections if body line length is greater than 1000
- Drop Connections and log if sender address length is greater than 320
- Drop Connections and log if MIME file name length is greater than 255

The **MIME File Type Filtering** button enables you to configure MIME file type filters that can be defined by custom regular expressions.

To enable ESMTP inspection via the CLI, use the **inspect esmtp** command. This command is enabled in the default class and policy maps on the Cisco ASA. Example 7-9 shows the CLI configuration when the ESTMP inspect map security level was set to **High** in ASDM.

Example 7-9 *Enabling ESMTP Inspection via the CLI*

```
policy-map type inspect esmtp my-ESMTP-map
 description Custom ESMTP Inspection Map
 parameters
 match sender-address length gt 320
  drop-connection log
 match MIME filename length gt 255
  drop-connection log
 match cmd line length gt 512
  drop-connection log
 match cmd RCPT count gt 100
  drop-connection log
 match body line length gt 998
  drop-connection log
policy-map global_policy
 class inspection_default
  inspect esmtp my-ESMTP-map
```

File Transfer Protocol

Cisco ASA FTP application inspection examines the FTP sessions to provide the following features:

- Enhanced security while creating dynamic secondary data connections for FTP transfers
- Enforcement of FTP command-response sequence
- Generation an audit trail for FTP sessions
- Translation of embedded IP address

To enable FTP inspection via ASDM, navigate to **Configuration > Firewall > Service Policy Rules > Edit Service Policy Rule** and select **FTP** under the **Edit Service Policy Rule** dialog box. You can also configure several optional parameters for this FTP inspection by clicking the **Configure** button. The **Select FTP Inspect Map** dialog box is displayed.

To configure FTP inspection via the CLI, use the **inspect ftp** command to enable FTP inspection. The **strict** keyword (optional) enables the Cisco ASA to prevent client systems from sending embedded commands in FTP requests:

```
inspect ftp [strict] ftp-map-name
```

ftp-map-name is the name of an FTP map used to define FTP request commands to be denied. Example 7-10 demonstrates how to use the **inspect ftp strict** command in conjunction with an FTP map, called **myftpmap**, to deny several FTP commands.

Example 7-10 *Denying Specific FTP Commands*

```
ftp-map myftpmap
 deny-request-cmd cdup rnfr rnto stor stou
!
class-map inspection_default
 match default-inspection-traffic
!
policy-map asa_global_fw_policy
 class inspection_default
  inspect ftp strict myftpmap
```

> **Note** The **strict** option may break FTP sessions from clients that do not comply with the RFC standards; however, it provides more security features.

When the **strict** option is enabled, the following anomalous activities in FTP commands and replies are denied:

- The total number of commas in the **PORT** and **PASV** reply commands is checked. If they are not 5, the **PORT** command is considered to be truncated and the connection is closed.
- The Cisco ASA inspects all FTP commands to see whether they end with **<CR><LF>** characters, as specified by the RFC 959, "FTP Protocol." The connection is closed if these are not present.
- The **PORT** command is always expected to be sent from the FTP client. If the **PORT** command is sent from the server, the connection is dropped.
- The **PASV** reply command is always expected to be sent from the server. If the **PASV** command is sent from the client, the connection is dropped.
- The Cisco ASA checks the negotiated dynamic port value in the passive FTP mode. The port should not be in the range from 1 to 1024. These are reserved for well-known protocols. The connection is closed if the negotiated port is within this range.
- The security appliance checks the number of characters included after the port numbers in the **PORT** and **PASV** reply commands. The maximum number of characters must be eight. The Cisco ASA closes the TCP connection if the number of characters exceeds eight.

The FTP map **request-command deny** subcommand is used to deny specific FTP commands on the Cisco ASA. Table 7-2 lists all the **request-command deny** subcommand options that can be restricted under an FTP map.

Table 7-2 *List of FTP Commands Available for Restriction*

Option	Description
all	Denies all supported FTP commands
appe	Denies the ability to append to a file
cdup	Denies a user's request to change to a parent directory of current directory (i.e., **cd ../**)
help	Restricts the user to access the help information from the FTP server
retr	Denies the retrieval of a file from the FTP server
rnfr	Denies the user permission to rename from a filename
rnto	Denies the user permission to rename to a specific filename
site	Denies the user permission to specify server-specific commands
stor	Denies the user permission to store a file
stou	Denies the user permission to store a file with a unique name

The **SYST FTP** command allows a system to ask for information about the server's operating system. The server accepts this request with code 215 and sends the requested information. The Cisco ASA replaces the FTP server response to the **SYST** command with an **X** for each character sent, to prevent FTP clients from seeing the FTP server system–type information. You can use the **no mask-syst-reply** subcommand in FTP map configuration mode to disable this default behavior, as shown in Example 7-11.

Example 7-11 mask-syst-reply *Subcommand*

```
ftp-map myftpmap
 no mask-syst-reply
```

General Packet Radio Service Tunneling Protocol

The General Packet Radio Service (GPRS) is a new carrier service for Global System for Mobile Communication (GSM) that enhances and simplifies wireless access to packet data networks. GPRS architecture uses a radio-packet technique to transfer user data packets in an efficient way between GSM mobile stations and external data networks.

The GPRS Tunneling Protocol (GTP) enables multiprotocol packets to be tunneled through a GPRS backbone.

Figure 7-10 illustrates a basic representation of the GPRS architecture.

This figure shows a mobile station (MS) logically connected to an SGSN. The SGSN provides data services to the MS. The SGSN is logically connected to a GGSN via GTP. If the GTP tunnel connection is over the same Public Land Mobile Network (PLMN), the interface connecting the tunnel is called the Gn interface. Connections between two different PLMNs are known as the *Gp interfaces*. The GGSN acts as a gateway to external networks such as the Internet or the corporate network via the Gi interface. In other words, the interface between a GGSN and an SGSN is called Gn, whereas the interface between the GGSN and an external data network is called Gi. GTP encapsulates data from the mobile station and controls the establishment, movement, and deletion of tunnels between SGSN and GGSN in roaming scenarios.

There are two versions of GTP:

- GTPv0
- GTPv1

GTPv0

In GTPv0, the GPRS mobile stations are connected to a SGSN without knowing GTP. A Packet Data Protocol (PDP) context is identified by the tunnel identifier (TID), which is a combination of the International Mobile Subscriber Identity (IMSI) and Network Service

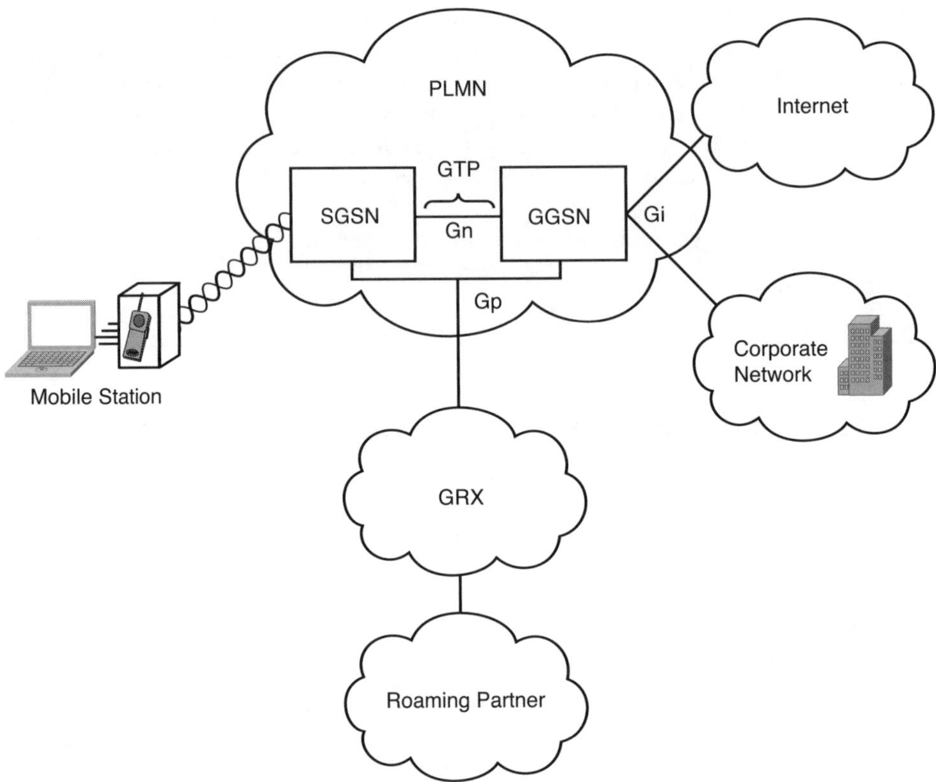

Figure 7-10 *GPRS Architecture Example*

Access Point Identifier (NSAPI). The mobile stations can have up to 15 NSAPIs each. This allows the mobile stations to create multiple PDP contexts with different NSAPIs. These NSAPIs are based on application requirements for different QoS levels.

The common transport protocol for signaling messages for GTPv0 and v1 is UDP. GTPv0 can allow the use of TCP for the transport protocol data units (TPDUs). The Cisco ASA supports only UDP. The UDP destination port for requests is port 3386.

Figure 7-11 illustrates call flow and the signaling messages involved for GTPv0.

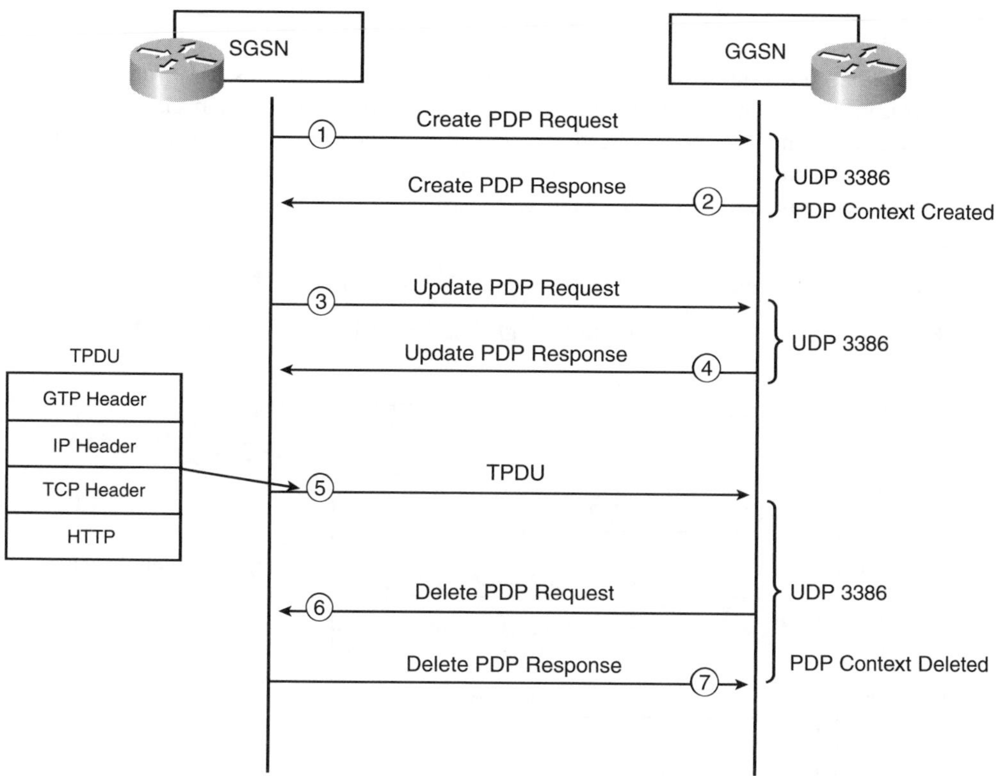

Figure 7-11 *GTPv0 Call Flow*

The following is the sequence of events in the call flow shown in Figure 7-11:

Step 1. The SGSN sends a **create PDP** request to the GGSN.

Step 2. The PDP context is created and the GGSN sends a PDP response back to the SGSN.

Step 3. The SGSN sends an **update PDP** request message to the GGSN.

Step 4. The GGSN replies back.

Step 5. TPDUs are sent by the SGSN. (Figure 7-4, shown previously, shows a sample of the TPDU as seen by the Cisco ASA inspection engine.)

Step 6. The SGSN sends a request to delete the PDP context.

Step 7. The PDP context is deleted and the GGSN sends its deletion response.

GTPv1

GTPv1 supports primary and secondary contexts for mobile stations. The primary context is identified with an IP address. Secondary contexts are created that share the IP address and other parameters already associated with the primary context. The advantage of this technique is that the mobile station is able to initiate a connection to a context with different QoS requirements, while also sharing the IP address obtained for the primary context.

GTPv1 uses UDP port 2123 for requests and UDP port 2152 for data transfer.

Figure 7-12 illustrates call flow and the signaling messages involved for GTPv1.

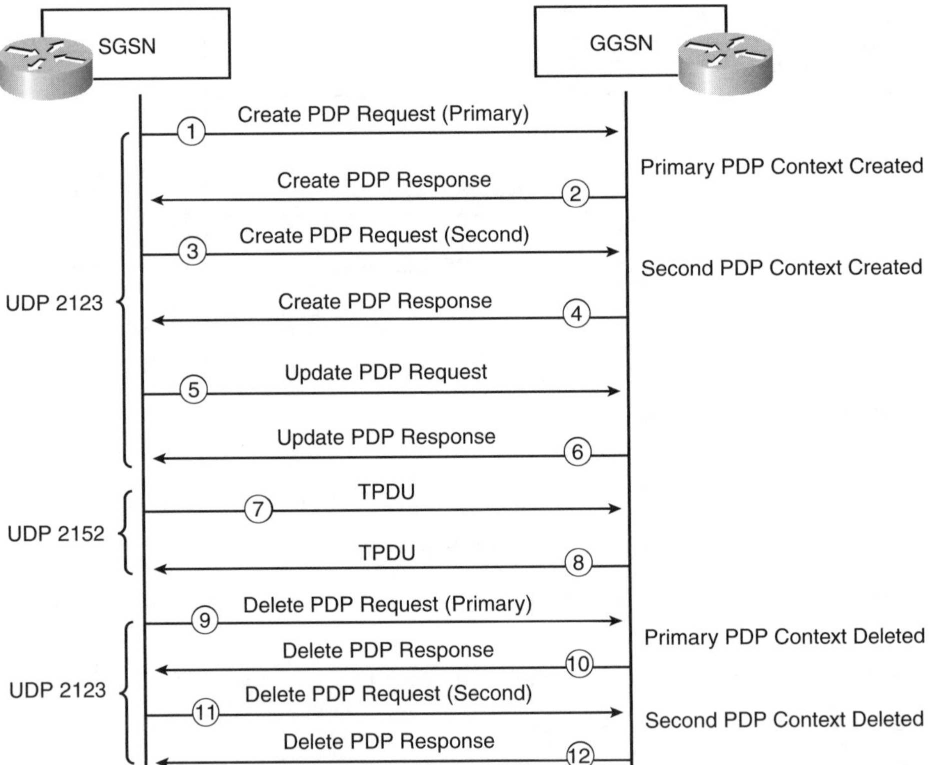

Figure 7-12 *GTPv1 Call Flow*

The following is the sequence of events in the call flow shown in Figure 7-12:

Step 1. The SGSN sends a **PDP context create** request for the primary PDP context.

Step 2. The primary context is created and the GGSN sends its response.

Step 3. The SGSN sends a **PDP context create** request for the second PDP context.

Step 4. The second context is created and the GGSN sends its response.

Step 5. The SGSN sends a **PDP update** request to the GGSN.

Step 6. The GGSN replies back with a **PDP update** response.

Step 7. TPDU (data packets) are sent to the GGSN.

Step 8. TPDU (data packets) are sent to the SGSN.

Step 9. The SGSN sends a request to delete the primary PDP context.

Step 10. The primary PDP context is deleted and the GGSN sends its response.

Step 11. The SGSN sends a request to delete the second PDP context.

Step 12. The second PDP context is deleted and the GGSN sends its response.

Figure 7-13 illustrates the Cisco ASA positioned between GPRS networks.

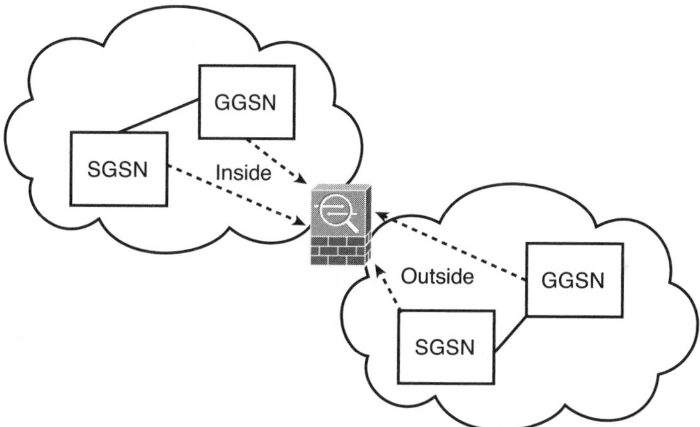

Figure 7-13 *Cisco ASA in GPRS Network*

In Figure 7-13, the Cisco ASA is positioned between two GPRS PLMNs. This exemplifies how a mobile station may move from its home PLMN (HPLMN) to a visited PLMN (VPLMN) and communication will still be possible through the Cisco ASA. The Cisco ASA inspects all traffic between the respective SGSNs and GGSNs.

Configuring GTP Inspection

To enable GTP inspection via ASDM, navigate to **Configuration > Firewall > Service Policy Rules > Edit Service Policy Rule** and select **GTP** under the **Edit Service Policy Rule** dialog box. You can also configure several optional parameters for this GTP inspection by clicking on the **Configure** button. The **Select GTP Inspect Map** dialog box is displayed.

There is only one security level setting for GTP inspection (low) and the following parameters are set:

- Do not Permit Errors
- Maximum Number of Tunnels: 500
- GSN timeout: 00:30:00
- Pdp-Context timeout: 00:30:00
- Request timeout: 00:01:00
- Signaling timeout: 00:30:00
- Tunnel timeout: 01:00:00
- T3-response timeout: 00:00:20
- Drop and log unknown message IDs

To configure IMSI prefix filters, click on the **MSI Prefix Filtering** button. The **IMSI Prefix Filtering** dialog box enables you to configure the IMSI prefix to allow within GTP requests. The following options are available:

- **Mobile Country Code**—Non-zero, three-digit value identifying the mobile country code.
- **Mobile Network Code**—Two- or three-digit value identifying the network code.

The **Add** and **Delete** buttons enable you to add or delete the specified country code and network code to the **IMSI Prefix** table.

To enable GTP inspection, use the **inspect gtp** command. You can also associate a GTP map to create a more customizable configuration. This provides granular control of various GTP parameters and filtering options.

> **Note** GTP inspection is not supported with NAT or PAT. GTP inspection requires a special license from Cisco. For more information about licensing go to Cisco's website at www.cisco.com/go/nac.

You can create a GTP map by using the **gtp-map** command, followed by the name of the map. Example 7-12 demonstrates how the Cisco ASA is configured with a GTP map, called **mygtpmap**, to enforce different restrictions.

Example 7-12 *GTP Inspection Example*

```
gtp-map mygtpmap
 tunnel-limit 1000
```

```
 request-queue 500
class-map inspection_default
 match default-inspection-traffic
policy-map asa_global_fw_policy
 class inspection_default
  inspect gtp mygtpmap
```

In Example 7-12, the Cisco ASA allows a maximum of only 1000 GTP tunnels and allows a maximum of only 500 requests to be queued. The GTP map is mapped to the default policy map under the default inspection class.

Table 7-3 lists all the subcommands available to configure under a GTP map.

Table 7-3 *GTP Map Subcommands*

Subcommand	Description
description	Used to enter a brief description of the GTP map.
drop	Used to drop messages based on three different keywords: apn—The APN to be dropped after this keyword message—The message ID to be dropped version—Used to specify the version to be dropped
mcc	Used to specify a three-digit mobile country code. Values can be from 000 to 999. Country codes with one or two digits are prepended with zeros.
message-length	Used to specify the minimum and maximum message length.
permit	Used to enable the Cisco ASA to allow packets with errors.
request-queue	Used to specify the maximum requests allowed on the queue.
timeout	Used to configure the idle timeout for the following: • GSN (GPRS Support Node) • PDP (Packet Data Protocol) contexts • Requests • Signaling connections • Tunnels
tunnel-limit	Used to configure the maximum tunnels allowed.

H.323

The H.323 standard stipulates the components, protocols, and procedures that provide multimedia communication services (audio, video, and data) over IP-based networks. H.323 is defined in RFC 3508. Four kinds of H.323 components provide point-to-point and point-to-multipoint multimedia communication services:

- **Terminals**—Endpoints on the network that provide real-time two-way communications, such as Cisco IP Phones.
- **Gateways**—Provide translation between circuit-switched networks and packet-based networks, enabling the endpoints to communicate.
- **Gatekeepers**—Responsible for call control and routing services to H.323 endpoints, system management, and some security policies.
- **Multipoint control units (MCUs)**—Maintain all the audio, video, data, and control streams between all the participants in the conference.

Figure 7-14 shows a basic network topology that illustrates the components of an H.323 network.

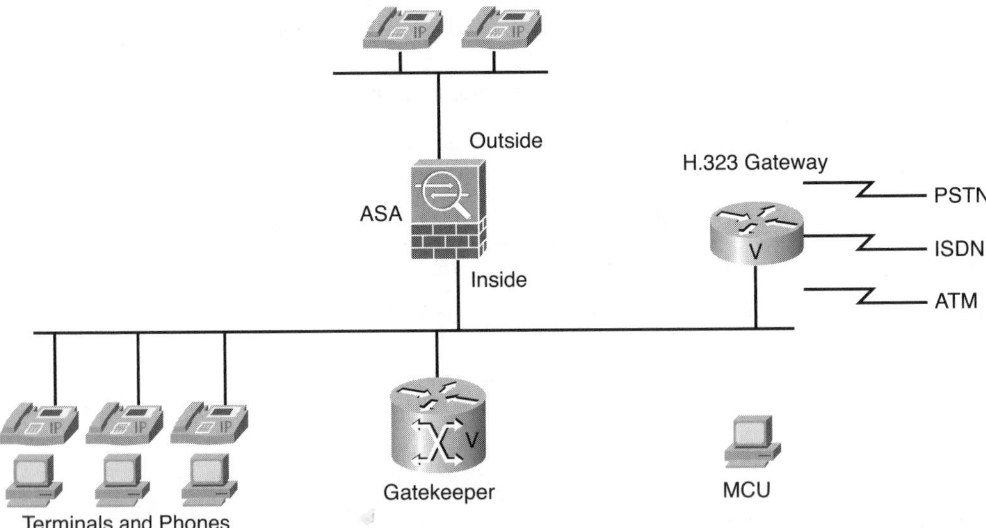

Figure 7-14 *H.323 Network Components*

H.323 Protocol Suite

The following are the main H.323 components illustrated in Figure 7-15:

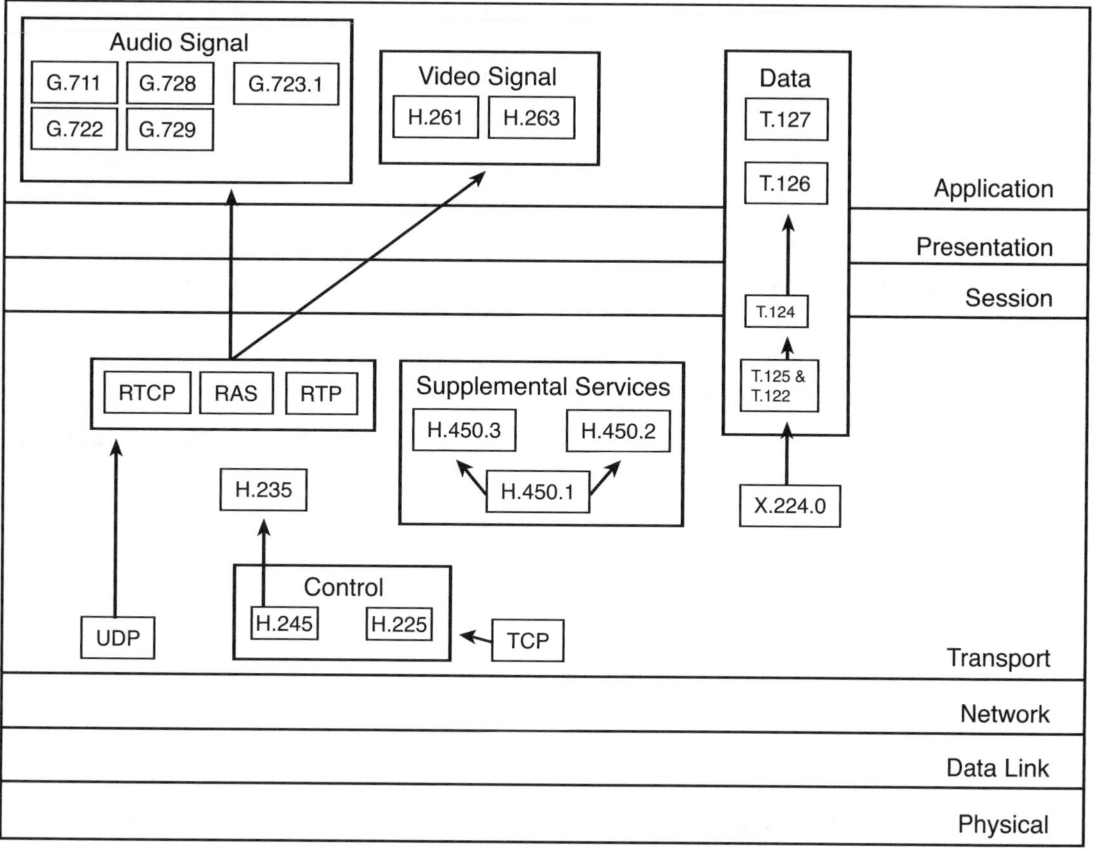

Figure 7-15 *H.323 Protocols*

- The G.7xx components are audio codecs.
- The H.26x components are video codecs. The standard is H.261.
- Audio and video components sit on top of the Real-Time Transport Protocol (RTP).
- The T.12*x* protocols are used in real-time exchange of data. One example is an online whiteboard application.

In Figure 7-15, the protocols are illustrated in relation to the respective OSI layers.

The H.323 suite of protocols may use up to two TCP connections and four to six UDP connections:

- RTP uses the Real-Time Transport Control Protocol (RTCP) to control and synchronize streaming audio and video. It allows the application to adapt the flow to specific network conditions.

- Terminals and gatekeepers use the Registration, Admission, and Status (RAS) Protocol to exchange information about call registrations, admissions, and terminations. This protocol communicates over UDP.

Note The FastConnect H.323 feature uses only one TCP connection, and RAS uses UDP requests and responses for registration, admissions, and status.

- H.225 is a protocol used to establish connections between two terminals. It runs over TCP.
- H.245 is a protocol used between two terminals to exchange control messages. These messages include flow control and channel management commands.
- Clients may request a Q.931 call setup over TCP port 1720 to H.323 servers. During the call setup process, the H.323 terminal provides the TCP port number for the client to use for an H.245 connection.

Note The initial packet is transmitted over UDP if H.323 gatekeepers are used.

- The Cisco ASA can monitor the Q.931 TCP connection to determine the H.245 port number. It dynamically allocates the H.245 connection based on the inspection of the H.225 messages if FastConnect is not used.
- The terminals negotiate the port numbers to be used for subsequent UDP streams within each H.245 message. The Cisco ASA also monitors the H.245 messages to know about these ports and to create the necessary connections.

RTP uses the negotiated port number; however, RTCP uses the next higher port number.

The following are the key TCP and UDP ports in H.323 inspection:

- **Gatekeeper discovery**—UDP port 1718
- **RAS**—UDP port 1719
- **Control port**—TCP port 1720

H.323 Version Compatibility

Cisco ASA is compatible with H.323 versions 1, 2, 3, and 4.

Note The H.323 inspection support must not be confused with the Cisco Unified Communications (UC) advanced support. Cisco UC advanced support is covered in detail later in this chapter in the "Unified Communications Advanced Support" section.

Figure 7-16 and Figure 7-17 show a major difference between older versions of H.323 and H.323v3 and higher.

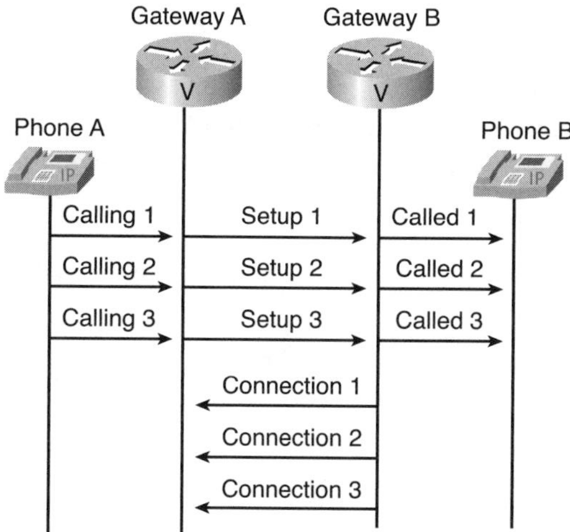

Figure 7-16 *Call Setup Pre H.323v3*

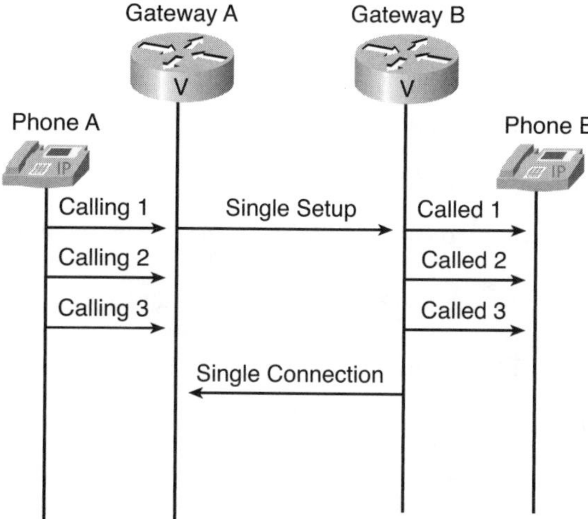

Figure 7-17 *H.323v3 Call Setup Features*

H.323v3 and higher supports multiple calls on one signaling connection. It accomplishes this by examining the call reference value (CRV) within the Q.931 message, as shown in Figure 7-10. This results in reduced call setup and clearing times.

Enabling H.323 Inspection

To enable H.323 inspection via ASDM for H.225, navigate to **Configuration > Firewall > Service Policy Rules > Edit Service Policy Rule** and select **H.323 H.225** under the **Edit Service Policy Rule** dialog box. You can also configure several optional parameters for this H.323 H.225 inspection by clicking on the **Configure** button. The **Select H.232 Inspect Map** dialog box is displayed. Click on **Add** to add a new inspection map or use the default H.323 inspection map parameters. When adding a new H.323 inspection map, you can configure three different security levels (low, medium, or high).

The low is the default and supports the following checks and actions:

- State Checking H.225 disabled
- State Checking RAS disabled
- Call Party Number disabled
- Call Duration Limit disabled
- RTP Conformance not enforced

The medium security level supports the following checks and actions:

- State Checking H.225 enabled
- State Checking RAS enabled
- Call Party Number disabled
- Call Duration Limit disabled
- RTP Conformance enforced
- Does not limit payload to audio or video, based on the signaling exchange

The high security level supports the following checks and actions:

- State Checking H.225 enabled
- State Checking RAS enabled
- Call Party Number enabled
- Call Duration Limit 1:00:00
- RTP Conformance enforced
- It adds support to limit payload to audio or video, based on the signaling exchange

The **Phone Number Filtering** button enables you to configure the settings for a phone number filter.

You can configure additional settings for H.323 application inspection maps by clicking on the **Details** button.

The **State Checking** tab enables you to configure state checking parameters for the H.323 inspection map. The following options are available:

- **Check State Transition of H.225 Messages**—Used to enforce H.323 state checking on H.225 messages.
- **Check State Transition of RAS Messages**—Used to enforce H.323 state checking on RAS messages.

The **Call Attributes** tab is where you configure call attribute parameters for the H.323 inspection map.

The following options are available:

- **Enforce Call Duration Limit**—Used in combination with the Call Duration Limit field.
- **Enforce Presence of Calling and Called Party Numbers**—Used to enforce the presence of "calling" and "called" party numbers.

The Tunneling and Protocol Conformance tab is where you configure tunneling and protocol conformance parameters for the H.323 inspection map. The following options are available:

- **Check for H.245 Tunneling**—Enables you to check for H.245 tunneling and to drop a connection or perform logging.
- **Check RTP Packets for Protocol Conformance**—Used to check RTP/RTCP packets on the pinholes for protocol conformance. This can be used in combination with the **Limit Payload to Audio or Video, Based on the Signaling Exchange** option to enforce the payload type to be audio or video based on the signaling exchange.

The **HSI Group Parameters** tab enables you to configure an HSI group. In the **Inspections** tab you add or edit advanced matching parameters for H.323 inspection, using regular expressions.

To enable H.323 inspection for H.225, use the **inspect h323 h225** command. For RAS, use the **inspect h323 ras** command. Example 7-13 shows both commands.

Example 7-13 *H.323 Inspection Commands*

```
policy-map global_policy
 class inspection_default
  inspect h323 h225
  inspect h323 ras
```

Example 7-14 shows the commands sent by ASDM to the Cisco ASA in the previous examples.

Example 7-14 *H.323 Inspection Commands Sent by ASDM*

```
policy-map type inspect h323 my-h323-map
 description Custom H.232 Inspect Map
 parameters
  state-checking h225
  state-checking ras
policy-map global_policy
 class inspection_default
  inspect h323 ras
  inspect h323 h225 my-h323-map
```

The Cisco ASA can translate the necessary embedded IP addresses in the H.225 and H.245 packets. It also can translate H.323 connections. It uses an ASN.1 decoder to decode the H.323 Packet Encoding Rules (PER) encoded messages. The Cisco ASA also dynamically allocates the negotiated H.245, RTP, and RTCP sessions.

Additionally, the Cisco ASA analyzes the TPDU Packet (TPKT) header to define the length of the H.323 messages. In H.323, Q.931 messages are exchanged over a TCP stream demarcated by TPKT encapsulations. It maintains a data structure for each connection that also contains the TPKT length for the H.323 messages to be received.

Note Cisco ASA supports segmented TPKT messages.

Direct Call Signaling and Gatekeeper Routed Control Signaling

Two control-signaling methods are defined in the ITU-T H.323 recommendation:

- Direct Call Signaling (DCS)
- Gatekeeper Routed Control Signaling (GKRCS)

Cisco ASA supports both methods. The Cisco ASA inspects DSC and GKRCS to ensure that the negotiation messages and correct fields are transferred between the respective devices. GKRCS inspection is done when H.323 inspection is enabled in the Cisco ASA. No additional configuration is needed.

Note The Cisco ASA must see the calling endpoint address within the initial H.225 setup information to allow the respective connection.

T.38

T.38 is the protocol used with Fax over IP (FoIP). This protocol is part of the ITU-T H.323 VoIP architecture. Cisco ASA supports inspection of this protocol. Because T.38 is a part of the H.323 protocol, inspection will be done if H.323 inspection is enabled on the Cisco ASA. No additional configuration is needed.

Unified Communications Advanced Support

The Cisco ASA provides advanced support for Cisco Unified Communications (UC) solutions. This advanced support includes the following solutions:

- Phone Proxy
- TLS Proxy
- Mobility Proxy
- Presence Federation Proxy

Phone Proxy

The Cisco ASA phone proxy feature provides secure remote access for Cisco encrypted endpoints (SRTP/TLS), and VLAN traversal for Cisco SoftPhones. This feature was designed to increase scalability in large deployments without a need of a large and complex VPN remote access hardware deployment.

Note The Cisco ASA phone proxy was designed to replace the Cisco Unified Phone Proxy. For information about the differences between the TLS proxy and phone proxy go to http://www.cisco.com/go/secureuc.

The phone proxy feature has several limitations:

- It is not supported in multiple-context or transparent mode.
- Packets from phones connecting to the phone proxy over a VPN tunnel cannot be inspected.
- It does not support IP phones sending Real-Time Control Protocol (RTCP) packets.
- It does not support end-users resetting their device name in CIPC environments.
- It does not support IP phones sending SCCP video messages using Cisco VT Advantage because SCCP video messages do not support SRTP keys.
- For mixed and non-mixed mode clusters, the phone proxy does not support the Cisco Unified Call Manager using TFTP to send encrypted configuration files to IP phones through the adaptive security appliance.
- When the phone proxy is configured for a mixed-mode cluster and multiple IP phones are behind one NAT device and registering through the phone proxy, all the SIP and SCCP IP phones must be configured as authenticated or encrypted, or all as non-secure on the Unified Call Manager.

- When used with Cisco Unified Communications Manager Express (CUCME), Directory Services does not work on remote IP phones that register with Cisco UME through the Cisco ASA. This limitation occurs because the Cisco ASA requires HTTPS.
- When used with UCME, the phone proxy does not support remote IP phones configured with MTP and G729 codec option for media. G729 is supported by the Cisco ASA; on the other hand, this configuration results in one-way audio when both IP phones used in the call are remote.

Complete the following steps to configure the phone proxy feature using ASDM.

Step 1. Log in to ASDM and navigate to **Configuration > Firewall > Advanced > Encrypted Traffic Inspection > Phone Proxy**. The screen shown in Figure 7-18 is displayed.

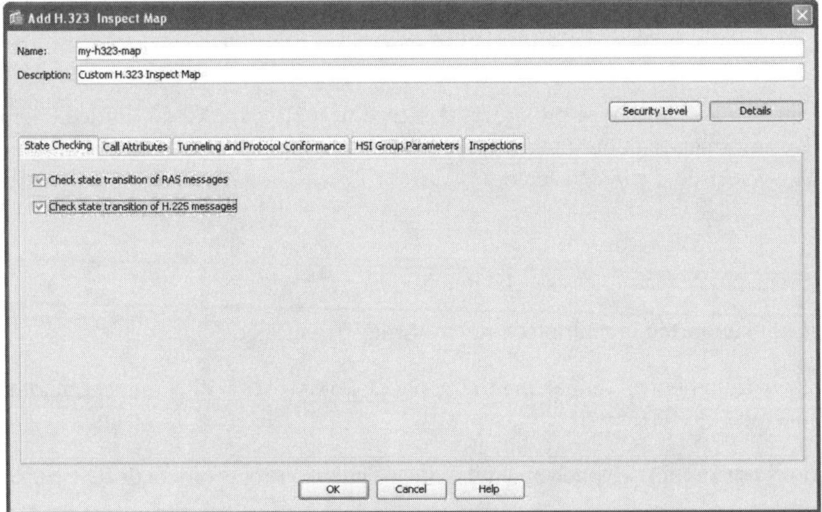

Figure 7-18 *Configuring Phone Proxy Using ASDM*

Step 2. Select **Enable Phone Proxy** to enable phone proxy support.

Step 3. The Cisco ASA must have a media termination address (MTA) instance, according to the following criteria:

- One media termination instance must be configured for each phone proxy on the Cisco ASA. Multiple media termination instances are not supported.
- A global media-termination address can be configured for all interfaces; alternatively, a media-termination address can be configured for different

interfaces. A global media-termination address and media-termination addresses cannot be configured for each interface at the same time.

- If you configure a media termination address for multiple interfaces, you must configure an address on each interface that the security appliance uses when communicating with IP phones.
- The IP address on an interface cannot be the same address as that interface on the security appliance.
- The IP addresses cannot overlap with existing static NAT pools or NAT rules.
- The IP addresses cannot be the same as the CUCM or TFTP server IP address.
- When IP phones are behind a router or gateway, you must add routes to the media termination address on the Cisco ASA interface with which the IP phones communicate so that the phone can reach the media termination address.

Step 4. At least one TFTP server must be configured on a trusted network for the Call Manager cluster. Add a TFTP server under the **TFTP Server Settings** section. In this example the TFTP server is 172.18.108.26 and it resides on the inside interface. The default TFTP port (UDP port 69) is also used.

Step 5. Click the **Click Here to Generate Certificate Trust List File** option to create a Certificate Trust List (CTL) file that is required by the Phone Proxy. This enables you to create trustpoints and generate certificates for each entity in the network (CUCM, CUCM and TFTP, TFTP server, CAPF) that the IP phones must trust. The certificates are used in creating the CTL file. Trustpoints must be created for each CUCM (primary and secondary) and TFTP server in the network. The trustpoints need to be in the CTL file for the phones to trust the CUCM.

Note An internal trustpoint is created and used by the phone proxy to sign the TFTP files. The trustpoint is named **_internal_PP_ctl-instance_filename.**

After you click the **Click Here to Generate Certificate Trust List File** option, the screen shown in Figure 7-19 is displayed. There you can add the specific record entry used for the CTL file. Additionally, you can select the trustpoint to be used for the respective certificate. In this example, the **ASDM_Trustpoint0** is used. Optionally, you can define a domain name to be used by the CTL. In this example **securemeinc.com** is used.

Step 6. Click the **Use the Certificate Trust List File Generated by the CTL Instance** option to use the respective CTL file.

Step 7. The CUCM cluster mode can be configured to Non-secure or Mixed. **Mixed** mode is used in this example.

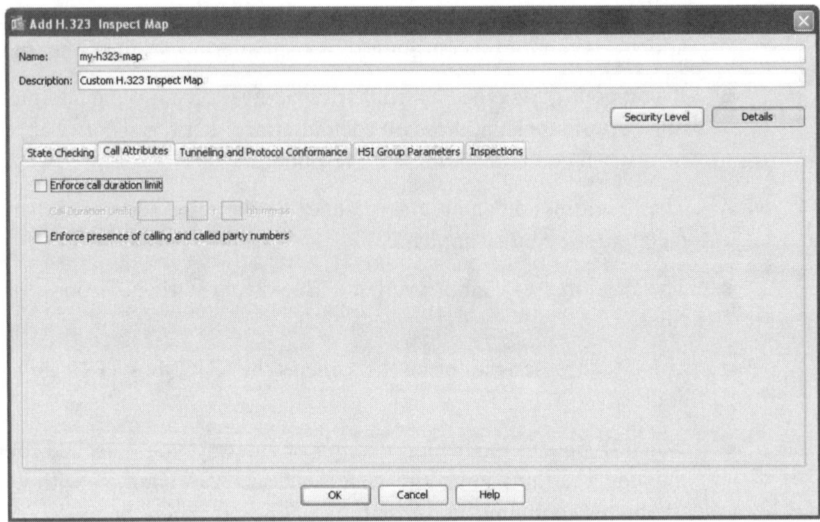

Figure 7-19 *Generating the CTL File*

Step 8. Configure the idle timeout after which the secure-phone entry is removed from the Phone Proxy database. The default value of 5 minutes is used in this example.

Step 9. (Optional) To preserve Call Manager configuration on the IP phones, check the **Preserve the Call Manager's Configuration on the Phone** option. When this option is not enabled, the following service settings are disabled on the IP phones:

- PC Port
- Gratuitous ARP
- Voice VLAN access
- Web Access
- Span to PC Port

Step 10. (Optional) To force Cisco IP Communicator (CIPC) SoftPhones to operate in authenticated mode when CIPC SoftPhones are deployed in a voice and data VLAN scenario, check the **Enable CIPC Security Mode Authentication** check box.

Step 11. (Optional) To configure an HTTP proxy for the Phone Proxy feature that is written into the IP phone's configuration file under the **<proxyServerURL>** tag, check the **Configure a HTTP-Proxy Which Would Be Written into the Phone's Config File so that the Phone URLs Are Directed for Services on the Phone** check box. Enter the IP address and the listening port of the HTTP proxy.

Step 12. Click **Apply** to apply the configuration changes.

Step 13. Click **Save** to save the configuration in the Cisco ASA.

Example 7-15 shows the commands sent by ASDM to the Cisco ASA for the previous configuration example.

Example 7-15 *Phone Proxy Commands Sent by ASDM*

```
crypto ca trustpoint ASDM_TrustPoint0
 enrollment self
 subject-name CN=NewYork
 crl configure
crypto ca trustpoint _internal_asdm_CTL_File_SAST_0
 enrollment self
 fqdn none
 subject-name cn="_internal_asdm_CTL_File_SAST_0";ou="STG";o="Cisco Inc"
 keypair _internal_asdm_CTL_File_SAST_0
 crl configure
crypto ca trustpoint _internal_asdm_CTL_File_SAST_1
 enrollment self
 fqdn none
 subject-name cn="_internal_asdm_CTL_File_SAST_1";ou="STG";o="Cisco Inc"
 keypair _internal_asdm_CTL_File_SAST_1
 crl configure
crypto ca trustpoint _internal_PP_asdm_CTL_File
 enrollment self
 fqdn none
 subject-name cn="_internal_PP_asdm_CTL_File";ou="STG";o="Cisco Inc"
 keypair _internal_PP_asdm_CTL_File
 crl configure
crypto ca certificate chain ASDM_TrustPoint0
 certificate 3a70634a
    308201cb 30820134 a0030201 0202043a 70634a30 0d06092a 864886f7 0d010104
    0500302a 3110300e 06035504 0313074e 6577596f 726b3116 30140609 2a864886
<output truncated>
  quit
crypto ca certificate chain _internal_asdm_CTL_File_SAST_0
 certificate c070634a
    3082020d 30820176 a0030201 020204c0 70634a30 0d06092a 864886f7 0d010104
    0500304b 31123010 06035504 0a130943 6973636f 20496e63 310c300a 06035504
<output truncated>
  quit
crypto ca certificate chain _internal_asdm_CTL_File_SAST_1
 certificate c170634a
    3082020d 30820176 a0030201 020204c1 70634a30 0d06092a 864886f7 0d010104
```

```
    0500304b 31123010 06035504 0a130943 6973636f 20496e63 310c300a 06035504
    0b130353 54473127 30250603 55040314 1e5f696e 7465726e 616c5f61 73646d5f
    43544c5f 46696c65 5f534153 545f3130 1e170d30 39303731 39313931 3531335a
    170d3139 30373137 31393135 31335a30 4b311230 10060355 040a1309 43697363
<output truncated>
  quit
crypto ca certificate chain _internal_PP_asdm_CTL_File
 certificate c270634a
    30820205 3082016e a0030201 020204c2 70634a30 0d06092a 864886f7 0d010104
    05003047 31123010 06035504 0a130943 6973636f 20496e63 310c300a 06035504
<output truncated>
  quit
!
ctl-file asdm_CTL_File
 record-entry cucm-tftp trustpoint ASDM_TrustPoint0 address 172.18.108.26 domain-
name securemeinc.com
 no shutdown
!
phone-proxy asdm_phone-proxy
 tftp-server address 172.18.108.26 interface inside
 cluster-mode mixed
 ctl-file asdm_CTL_File
```

TLS Proxy

The TLS Proxy feature is used for decryption and inspection of Cisco Unified Communications encrypted signaling. This feature enables the Cisco ASA to intercept and decrypt encrypted signaling from Cisco-encrypted endpoints to the CUCM, while also applying the threat protection and access control. This feature is also often used to ensure confidentiality by re-encrypting the traffic onto the CUCM servers. TLS Proxy is never configured on its own; it is always used in conjunction with other features, such as Phone Proxy and Mobility Proxy.

Complete the following steps to configure the TLS Proxy feature, using ASDM:

Step 1. Log in to ASDM and navigate to **Configuration > Firewall > Advanced > Encrypted Traffic Inspection > TLS Proxy.**

Step 2. Click on **Add** to add a new TLS Proxy instance. The TLS Proxy wizard screen is displayed.

Step 3. Enter a name for the TLS Proxy instance and click on Next. In this example, the name used is **my-tls-proxy.**

Step 4. Specify the server proxy certificate from the **Server Proxy Certificate** pull-down menu.

Step 5. Click **Install TLS Server's Certificate** to install the TLS server certificate in Cisco ASA's trust store. This is used to authenticate the TLS server during TLS handshake between the TLS proxy and the TLS server.

Step 6. Check the **Enable Client Authentication During TLS Proxy Handshake** check box so that the Cisco ASA sends a certificate and authenticates the TLS client during TLS handshake.

Step 7. Click **Next.**

Step 8. (Optional) Check the **Specify the Proxy Certificate for the TLS Client** check box to specify a client proxy certificate to use for the TLS Proxy.

Step 9. (Optional) Click the **Specify the Internal Certificate Authority to Sign the Local Dynamic Certificate for Phones** check box to specify an LDC Issuer to use for the TLS Proxy.

Step 10. In the **Security Algorithms** area, specify the available and active algorithms to be announced or matched during the TLS handshake (i.e., des-sha1, 3des-sha1, aes128-sha1, aes256-sha1, and null-sha1).

Step 11. Click **Next.**

Step 12. Click **Finish.**

Step 13. Click **Apply** to apply the configuration changes.

Step 14. Click **Save** to save the configuration in the Cisco ASA.

Example 7-16 shows the commands sent by ASDM to the Cisco ASA for the previous configuration example.

Example 7-16 *TLS Proxy Commands Sent by ASDM*

```
tls-proxy my-tls-proxy
 server trust-point ASDM_TrustPoint0
```

Mobility Proxy

The Mobility Proxy feature is designed to provide secure connectivity between Cisco Unified Mobility Advantage server and Cisco Unified Mobile Communicator clients. The Cisco ASA can act as a proxy, terminating and re-originating the TLS signaling between the CUMC and CUMA. Mobility Proxy is enabled for the Cisco UMA Mobile Multiplexing Protocol (MMP) by the MMP inspection feature on the Cisco ASA.

To enable MMP inspection via ASDM, navigate to **Configuration > Firewall > Service Policy Rules > Edit Service Policy Rule** and select **MMP** under the **Edit Service Policy Rule** dialog box. You can also configure several optional parameters for this MMP inspection by clicking on the **Configure** button. The **Configure TLS Proxy** dialog box is displayed. Select the TLS proxy name from the TLS Proxy Name pull-down menu. The previously configured TLS proxy (my-tls-proxy) is used in this example.

To configure FTP inspection via the CLI, use the **inspect mmp** command to enable FTP inspection. Example 7-17 shows the commands sent by ASDM to the Cisco ASA for the previous configuration example.

Example 7-17 *MMP Inspection Commands Sent by ASDM*

```
policy-map global_policy
 class inspection_default
  inspect mmp tls-proxy my-tls-proxy
```

Presence Federation Proxy

The Presence Federation Proxy feature in the Cisco ASA provides secure connectivity between Cisco Unified Presence servers and Cisco or Microsoft Presence servers. The Cisco ASA terminates the TLS connectivity between these servers, and can inspect and apply policies for the SIP communications between the servers.

The configuration of the Presence Federation Proxy feature is the same as the TLS Proxy configuration.

HTTP

The Cisco ASA HTTP inspection engine checks whether an HTTP transaction is compliant with RFC 2616 by checking the HTTP request message. The following are the predefined HTTP commands:

- OPTIONS
- GET
- HEAD
- POST
- PUT
- DELETE
- TRACE
- CONNECT

The Cisco ASA checks for these HTTP commands; if the message does not have any of these, the Cisco ASA verifies that it is an HTTP extension method/command (such as **MOVE, COPY, EDIT**). A syslog message is generated if both checks fail and the packet can be dropped. The Cisco ASA also has the capability to detect double-encoding attacks. This method, known as HTTP de-obfuscation, is one where an HTTP message is encoded by the normalization of encoded characters to ASCII-equivalent characters (sometimes also referred to as ASCII normalization). In a double-encoding attack, the attacker sends an encoded HTTP URI request that has been through two rounds of encoding. Traditionally, firewalls and intrusion detection devices detect the first round of encoding and normalize it. Therefore the attack still evades the firewall or IDS. The Cisco ASA HTTP inspection engine is able to detect double encoding and prevent this from happening.

The Cisco ASA also provides a feature to filter HTTP messages based on keywords. This is useful when looking for specific applications running over HTTP, such as online instant messenger (IM) applications, music sharing applications, and so on.

Enabling HTTP Inspection

To enable HTTP inspection via ASDM, navigate to **Configuration > Firewall > Service Policy Rules > Edit Service Policy Rule** and select **HTTP** under the **Edit Service Policy Rule** dialog box. You can also configure several optional parameters for this HTTP inspection by clicking on the **Configure** button. The **Select HTTP Inspect Map** dialog box is displayed. To create a HTTP inspect map for fine control over inspection, click on **Add**.

You can configure three different security levels (low, medium, or high). Low is the default. The following checks and actions are active when the security level is set to low:

- Protocol violation action: Drop connection
- URI filtering (if configured)
- Advanced inspections (if configured)

> **Note** Dropping of connections for unsafe methods and the dropping of connections for requests with non-ASCII headers are disabled when the security level is set to low.

The following checks and actions are active when the security level is set to medium:

- Protocol violation action: Drop connection
- Drop connections for unsafe methods: Allow only **GET**, **HEAD**, and **POST**
- URI filtering (if configured)
- Advanced inspections (if configured)

> **Note** Dropping of connections for requests with non-ASCII headers is disabled when the security level is set to medium.

The following checks and actions are active when the security level is set to high:

- Protocol violation action: Drop connection and log
- Drop connections for unsafe methods: Allow only **GET** and **HEAD**

- Drop connections for requests with non-ASCII headers
- URI filtering (if configured)
- Advanced inspections (if configured)

The **URI Filtering** button enables you configure the settings for an URI filter with the use of regular expressions.

If you are configuring the Cisco ASA via the CLI, use the **inspect http** command to enable HTTP inspection. You can also enable enhanced HTTP inspection by creating an HTTP map and associating it to the **inspect http** command. To create an HTTP map, use the **http-map** command, as shown in Example 7-18.

Example 7-18 *HTTP Inspection Using an HTTP Map*

```
http-map myhttpmap
 request-method rfc default action allow
 request-method ext move action reset
 request-method ext copy action reset
policy-map asa_global_fw_policy
 class inspection_default
 inspect http myhttpmap
```

In Example 7-18, an HTTP map named **myhttpmap** is configured. Request method inspection is enabled to allow all default RFC-compliant methods. The two extension methods, **move** and **copy**, are not allowed. If these two extensions are detected, the HTTP connection is reset. The following HTTP extensions are supported by the Cisco ASA:

- copy
- edit
- getattribute
- getattributenames
- getproperties
- index
- lock
- mkdir
- move
- revadd
- revlabel

- revlog
- revnum
- save
- setattribute
- startrev
- stoprev
- unedit
- unlock

Several enhanced HTTP inspection options can be configured under the **http-map** subcommands. When you configure an HTTP map, you are placed into the **http-map** prompt. The following subcommands are available to configure the necessary rules for enhanced HTTP inspection:

- strict-http
- content-length
- content-type-verification
- max-header-length
- max-uri-length
- port-misuse
- request-method
- transfer-encoding

strict-http

The **strict-http** command changes the default action taken when noncompliant HTTP traffic is detected. The following is the subcommand syntax:

```
strict-http action {allow | reset | drop} [log]
```

Table 7-4 describes the **strict-http** command options.

Table 7-4 strict-http *Command Options*

Option	Description
allow	Allows the message to be transferred through the Cisco ASA.
reset	Causes Cisco ASA to send a TCP-RST (reset) message to the client and/or server.
drop	Drops the packet and closes the connection.
log	Generates a syslog message.

The **strict-http** command is enabled by default. The default action is to log and send a TCP reset.

content-length

The **content-length** command limits the HTTP traffic allowed through the Cisco ASA, based on the content length of the HTTP message body. The following is the command syntax:

```
content-length {min bytes max bytes} action {allow | reset | drop} [log]
```

Table 7-5 describes the **content-length** command options.

Table 7-5 content-length *Command Options*

Option	Description
min	Minimum content length allowed, in bytes. The range is from 0 to 65,535 bytes.
max	Maximum content length allowed, in bytes. The range is from 0 to 50,000,000 bytes.
bytes	The length, in bytes.
allow	Allows the message to be transferred through the Cisco ASA.
reset	Causes Cisco ASA to send a TCP-RST (reset) message to client and/or server.
drop	Drops the packet and closes the connection.
log	Generates a syslog message.

content-type-verification

When a web browser receives a document via HTTP, it must determine the document's encoding (sometimes referred to as *charset*). The browser must know this to display non-ASCII characters correctly. The **content-type-verification** command limits the content types in HTTP messages transferred through the Cisco ASA. The Cisco ASA verifies that the header content-type value is in the internal list of supported content types. Additionally, it checks that the header content type matches the actual content in the data or entity body portion of the message. Here are the currently supported HTTP content types:

- Text/HTML
- Application/ Microsoft Word
- Application/octet-stream
- Application/x-zip

The following is the **content-type-verification** command syntax:

```
content-type-verification [match-req-rsp] action {allow | reset | drop} [log]
```

The **match-req-rsp** keyword enables the Cisco ASA to verify that the **content-type** field in the HTTP response matches the **accept** field in the corresponding HTTP request message.

max-header-length

The **max-header-length** command limits the HTTP header length on traffic that passes through the Cisco ASA. Messages with a header length less than or equal to the configured value are allowed; otherwise, the configured action is taken. The following is the command syntax:

```
max-header-length {request bytes response bytes} action {allow | reset | drop} [log]
```

Table 7-6 describes the **max-header-length** command options.

Table 7-6 max-header-length *Command Options*

Option	Description
request	Used to specify the length of the request message header.
response	Used to specify the length of the response message header.
bytes	The length, in bytes. The range is 1 to 65,535.
allow	Allows the message to be transferred through the Cisco ASA.
reset	Causes Cisco ASA to send a TCP-RST (reset) message to client and/or server.
drop	Drops the packet and closes the connection.
log	Generates a syslog message.

max-uri-length

The **max-uri-length** command limits the length of the Universal Resource Identifier (URI) in a request message. The command syntax is as follows:

```
max-uri-length bytes action {allow | reset | drop} [log]
```

Table 7-7 describes the **max-uri-length** command options.

Table 7-7 max-uri-length *Command Options*

Option	Description
bytes	The length, in bytes. The range is 1 to 65,535.
allow	Allows the message to be transferred through the Cisco ASA.
reset	Causes Cisco ASA to send a TCP-RST (reset) message to client and/or server.
drop	Drops the packet and closes the connection.
log	Generates a syslog message.

port-misuse

The **port-misuse** command restricts applications, such as instant messengers, that use HTTP as a transport protocol. The following is the command syntax:

```
port-misuse {default | im | p2p | tunneling} action {allow | reset | drop} [log]
```

Table 7-8 describes the **port-misuse** command options.

> **Note** The **port-misuse** command is disabled by default.

Table 7-8 port-misuse *Command Options*

Option	Description
default	Allows inspection for all supported applications.
im	Enables IM application inspection (Yahoo Messenger).
p2p	Peer-to-peer application inspection. Applications include Kazaa and Gnutella.
tunneling	Enables tunneling application inspection. The following applications are inspected: • HTTPort/HTTHost • GNU Httptunnel • GotoMyPC • Firethru • Http-tunnel.com
allow	Allows the message to be transferred through the Cisco ASA.
reset	Causes Cisco ASA to send a TCP-RST (reset) message to client and/or server.
drop	Drops the packet and closes the connection.
log	Generates a syslog message.

request-method

The **request-method** command configures a specific action for each of the supported HTTP request methods. The following is the command syntax:

```
request-method  rfc rfc_method action {allow | reset | drop} [log]
request-method  ext ext_method action {allow | reset | drop} [log]
```

Table 7-9 describes the **request-method** command options.

> **Note** The **request-method** command is disabled by default.

Table 7-9 request-method *Command Options*

Option	Description
rfc	Used to specify methods defined in RFC 2616, "Hypertext Transfer Protocol".
ext	Used to specify extended methods.
rfc_method	The RFC 2616 supported methods are as follows: • **connect** • **default** • **delete** • **get** • **head** • **options** • **post** • **put** • **trace**
ext_method	The extended methods are as follows: • **copy** • **default** • **edit** • **getattribute** • **getattribute** • **getproperties** • **index** • **lock** • **mkdir** • **move** • **revadd** • **revlabel** • **revlog** • **revnum** • **save** • **setattribute** • **startrev** • **stoprev** • **unedit** • **unlock**
allow	Allows the message to be transferred through the Cisco ASA.

Table 7-9 request-method *Command Options*

Option	Description
reset	Causes Cisco ASA to send a TCP-RST (reset) message to client and/or server.
drop	Drops the packet and closes the connection.
log	Generates a syslog message.

transfer-encoding type

The **transfer-encoding type** command configures a specific action for each of the supported HTTP transfer-encoding types passing through the Cisco ASA. The following is the command syntax:

```
transfer-encoding type encoding_types action {allow | reset | drop} [log]
```

Table 7-10 describes the **transfer-encoding type** command options.

Table 7-10 transfer-encoding type *Command Options*

Option	Description
encoding_types	Used to specify the encoding type. The following encoding types are supported: default—The default action. Enables all supported HTTP transfer-encoding types. chunked—Message body is transferred in chunks. compress—UNIX file compression. deflate—Supports ZLIB format, as specified in RFC 1950, and deflate compression, defined in RFC 1951. gzip—GNU zip, as specified in RFC 1952. identity—Used as default encoding (no transfer encoding is done).
action	Action taken when a violation occurs.
allow	Allows the message to be transferred through the Cisco ASA.
reset	Causes Cisco ASA to send a TCP-RST (reset) message to client and/or server.
drop	Drops the packet and closes the connection.
log	Generates a syslog message.

ICMP

Cisco ASA supports stateful inspection of Internet Control Message Protocol (ICMP) packets. To enable inspection of ICMP packets, use the **inspect icmp** command.

Additionally, Cisco ASA can translate ICMP error messages. It translates intermediate hops that send ICMP error messages based on the NAT configuration. Cisco ASA does this by overwriting the packet with the translated IP addresses.

Note The **traceroute** command (which can be known as **tracert** on Microsoft Windows, **trace** or **traceroute** on Cisco IOS Software, or **traceroute** on UNIX) can be used to troubleshoot connectivity problems. The Cisco ASA blocks **traceroute** messages by default, and information about devices behind the Cisco ASA is not displayed in the output of the **traceroute** command. ICMP inspection is often used to allow **traceroute** messages.

Cisco ASA also has the capability to inspect ICMP error messages. ICMP error messages always contain the full IP header, including options, of the IP packet that failed and the first eight bytes of the IP data field. Cisco ASA makes sure that this information is present and that it is correct.

To enable ICMP inspection via ASDM, navigate to **Configuration > Firewall > Service Policy Rules > Edit Service Policy Rule** and select **ICMP** under the **Edit Service Policy Rule** dialog box. To enable ICMP error inspection via ASDM, navigate to the same location and select **ICMP Error** under the **Edit Service Policy Rule** dialog box.

To enable inspection of ICMP error messages via the CLI, use the **inspect icmp error** command. If this command is disabled, Cisco ASA does not translate any ICMP error messages generated by intermediate devices.

ILS

Cisco ASA supports inspection for the Internet Locator Service (ILS) protocol. ILS is based on the Lightweight Directory Access Protocol (LDAP) specification. Numerous applications use ILS for directory services, including the following:

- Microsoft NetMeeting
- Microsoft SiteServer
- Microsoft Active Directory

To enable ILS inspection via ASDM, navigate to **Configuration > Firewall > Service Policy Rules > Edit Service Policy Rule** and select **ILS** under the **Edit Service Policy Rule** dialog box.

To enable ILS inspection via the CLI, use the **inspect ils** command. This command is disabled by default.

The Cisco ASA ILS inspection engine provides support for the following:

- Decoding of the LDAP REQUEST/RESPONSE PDUs using the BER decode functions
- Parsing the LDAP packet
- Extracting the IP addresses
- Translating IP addresses as necessary (PAT is not supported)
- Encoding the PDU with translated addresses using BER encode functions
- Copying the newly encoded PDU back to the TCP packet
- Performing incremental TCP checksum and sequence number adjustment

Instant Messenger (IM)

The Cisco ASA supports IM inspection to protect against information leakage, propagation of worms, and other threats to the corporate network. Yahoo! and MSN Messenger protocols are supported.

To enable IM inspection via ASDM, navigate to **Configuration > Firewall > Service Policy Rules > Edit Service Policy Rule** and select **IM** under the **Edit Service Policy Rule** dialog box. You can also configure several optional parameters for this IM inspection by clicking on the **Configure** button. The **Select IM Inspect Map** dialog box is displayed. To create an IM inspect map for fine control over inspection, click on **Add**.

You can configure the match criterion and value for the IM inspect map within the **Add IM Inspect** dialog box shown in Figure 7-20.

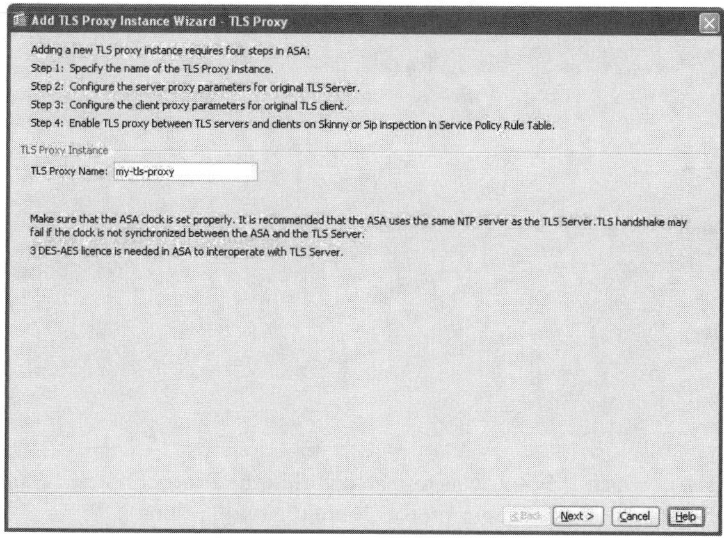

Figure 7-20 Add IM Inspect *Dialog Box*

To specify that the IM inspect has only one match statement, select the **Single Match** button. The **Match Type** is used define whether traffic should match or not match the values. The Criterion pull-down menu enables you to configure the specific criterion of IM traffic to match. The following options are available:

- Protocol
- Service
- Source IP Address
- Destination IP Address
- Version
- Client Login Name
- Client Peer Login Name
- Filename

Note You can allow or restrict the use of several IM services by using the Service criterion. The supported services include the following:

- Chat
- Conference
- File Transfer
- Games
- Voice Chat (not available for Yahoo! IM)
- Web Cam

You can select which IM protocols to match within the **Protocol** section. **Yahoo! Messenger** and **MSN Messenger** protocols are the two options.

You can also specify multiple matches for the IM inspection by selecting the **Multiple Matches** field. Click on **Manage** to add, edit, or delete IM Class Maps.

The **Actions** section enables you to configure the Cisco ASA to drop connection, reset, or enable logging when traffic matches the previously configured parameters.

To enable IM inspection via the CLI, use the **inspect im** command. This command is disabled by default. Example 7-19 shows the command sent by ASDM to the Cisco ASA for the previously configured parameters.

Example 7-19 *IM Inspection CLI Configuration*

```
policy-map type inspect im my-im-map
 description IM Inspection Custom Map
 parameters
 match protocol msn-im yahoo-im
  drop-connection log
policy-map global_policy
 class inspection_default
  inspect im my-im-map
```

IPSec Pass-Through

The Cisco ASA supports IPSec pass-through, which is used to open pinholes for Encapsulating Security Payload (ESP) protocol traffic. When IPSec pass-through is enabled, all ESP data flows are allowed when a forward flow exists. There is no limit on the maximum number of connections that can be allowed. IPSec pass-through supports only the ESP protocol; it does not support the Authentication Header (AH) protocol. When IPSec pass-through is configured, ESP traffic does not need to be explicitly permitted by the use of ACLs; only Internet Key Exchange (IKE) traffic (UDP port 500) between the IPSec peers needs to be allowed.

To enable IPSec pass-through inspection via ASDM, navigate to **Configuration > Firewall > Service Policy Rules > Edit Service Policy Rule** and select **IPSec Pass-Through** under the **Edit Service Policy Rule** dialog box. You can also configure several optional parameters for this IPSec pass-through inspection by clicking on the **Configure** button. The **Select IPSec Pass-Through Inspect Map** dialog box is displayed. To create an IPSec pass-through inspect map for fine control over inspection, click on **Add.**

There are two different security levels (high and low). **Low** is the default and includes the following checks and actions:

- Maximum ESP flows per client: Unlimited.
- ESP idle timeout: 00:10:00.
- Maximum AH flows per client: Unlimited.
- AH idle timeout: 00:10:00.

When the security level is set to High the following checks and actions are enabled:

- Maximum ESP flows per client: 10.
- ESP idle timeout: 00:00:30.
- Maximum AH flows per client: 10.
- AH idle timeout: 00:00:30.

To enable IPSec pass-through inspection via the CLI, use the **inspect ipsec-pass-thru** command. Example 7-20 shows the CLI commands sent by ASDM when the security level is set to High.

Example 7-20 *IPSec Pass-Through Inspection CLI Configuration*

```
policy-map type inspect ipsec-pass-thru my-ipsec-passthru-map
 description Custom IPSec passthru inspection map
 parameters
  esp per-client-max 10 timeout 0:00:30
  ah per-client-max 10 timeout 0:00:30
```

```
policy-map global_policy
 class inspection_default
  inspect ipsec-pass-thru my-ipsec-passthru-map
```

MGCP

The Media Gateway Control Protocol (MGCP) is the IETF standard for multimedia conferencing over IP. It offers a mechanism for controlling media gateways by providing conversion between the audio signals carried on telephone circuits and data packets carried over IP networks.

MGCP messages are ASCII based and are transmitted over UDP. This protocol is defined in RFC 3661. There are eight types of MGCP commands:

- **CreateConnection**
- **ModifyConnection**
- **DeleteConnection**
- **NotificationRequest**
- **Notify**
- **AuditEndpoint**
- **AuditConnection**
- **RestartInProgress**

Each command requires a reply. The first four commands are sent by the call agent to the gateway. The **Notify** command is sent by the gateway to the call agent. In some cases the gateway may also send a **DeleteConnection** command to tear down a connection to the call agent. The **RestartInProgress** command is used in the registration process of the MGCP gateway. The **AuditEndpoint** and the **AuditConnection** commands are sent by the call agent to the gateway.

The Cisco ASA performs the following tasks for MGCP inspection:

- Inspects all messages exchanged between the call agents and the media gateways
- Dynamically creates RTP and RTCP connections
- Supports and inspects retransmitted commands and responses
- Dynamically adapts to allow a command response to arrive from any of the call agents

A call agent is a device that provides call-processing functions, feature logic, and gateway control in an IP telephony system. An MGCP gateway handles the translation between audio signals and the IP packet network. In the MGCP configurations that Cisco IOS supports, the gateway can be a Cisco router, access server, or cable modem, and the call agent can be a server from Cisco (Cisco PGW or Cisco BTS Softswitches) or from a third-party vendor.

To enable MGCP inspection via ASDM, navigate to **Configuration > Firewall > Service Policy Rules > Edit Service Policy Rule** and select **MGCP** under the **Edit Service Policy Rule** dialog box. You can also configure several optional parameters for this MGCP inspection by clicking on the **Configure** button. The **Select MGCP Inspect Map** dialog box is displayed. To create an MGCP inspect map for fine control over inspection, click on **Add.**

The **Command Queue** tab enables you to configure the permitted queue size (1 to 2,147,483,647) for MGCP commands. The **Gateways and Call Agents** tab enables you to configure groups of gateways and call agents. Click on **Add** to add a new group of gateways and call agents for MGCP inspection. The **Group ID** identifies the ID of the call agent group. This group is used to associate one or more call agents with one or more MGCP media gateways. The **Gateways** field enables you to configure the IP address of the media gateway that is controlled by the associated call agent. The **Call Agents** field enables you to configure the IP address of a call agent that controls the MGCP media gateways in the call agent group.

To enable MGCP inspection via the CLI, use the **inspect mgcp** command. Create an MGCP map using the **mgcp-map** command to enable enhanced MGCP inspection. Example 7-21 demonstrates how to create an MGCP map for enhanced MGCP inspection.

Example 7-21 *Enhanced MGCP Inspection*

```
mgcp-map mymgcpmap
 call-agent 10.10.10.133 876
 command-queue 500
 gateway 192.168.11.23 876
policy-map asa_global_fw_policy
 class inspection_default
inspect mgcp mymgcpmap
```

In Example 7-21, an MGCP map named **mymgcpmap** is configured. The **call-agent** command specifies a group of call agents that can manage one or more gateways. A call agent with IP address **10.10.10.133** and group ID **876** is configured.

Note The group ID option can be any number between 0 and 2,147,483,647. Call agents with the same group ID belong to the same group. They may belong to more than one specific group.

The Cisco ASA can limit the maximum number of MGCP commands that will be queued waiting for a response to 500. The range of allowed values for the **command-queue limit** option is 1 to 2,147,483,647.

A gateway with IP address 192.168.11.23 in group 876 is also configured. This is used to specify which call agents are managing a particular gateway.

NetBIOS

NetBIOS was originally developed by IBM and Sytek as an API for client software to access LAN resources. NetBIOS has become the basis for many other networking applications. NetBIOS names are used to identify resources (e.g., workstations, servers, printers) on a network. Applications use these names to start and end sessions. NetBIOS names can consist of up to 16 alphanumeric characters. Clients advertise their names to the network. This is called the NetBIOS registration process and it is completed as follows:

Step 1. The client broadcasts itself and its NetBIOS information when it boots up.

Step 2. If there is another machine on the network that already has the broadcasted name, that NetBIOS client issues its own broadcast to advertise that the name is in use. Subsequently, the client that is trying to register stops all attempts to register that specific name.

Step 3. The client finishes the registration process if there is no other machine with the same name on the network.

Cisco ASA supports NetBIOS by performing NAT of the packets for NetBIOS Name Server (NBNS) UDP port 137 and NetBIOS Datagram Service (NBDS) UDP port 138.

To enable NetBIOS inspection via ASDM, navigate to **Configuration > Firewall > Service Policy Rules > Edit Service Policy Rule** and select **NetBIOS** under the **Edit Service Policy Rule** dialog box.

To enable NetBIOS inspection on the Cisco ASA, use the **ip inspect netbios** command.

PPTP

The Point-to-Point Tunneling Protocol (PPTP) is typically used for VPN solutions. (It is defined in RFC 2637.) Traditionally, the PPTP session negotiation is done over TCP port 1723 and the data traverses over the generic routing encapsulation (GRE) protocol (IP protocol 47). GRE does not have any Layer 4 port information. Consequently, it cannot be port address translated (PATed). PAT is performed for the modified version of GRE (RFC 2637) only when negotiated over the PPTP TCP control channel. PAT is not supported for the unmodified version of GRE (RFC 1701 and RFC 1702).

The Cisco ASA inspects PPTP protocol packets and dynamically creates the necessary GRE connections and translations to permit PPTP traffic. GRE traffic does not need to be explicitly permitted in the ASA when PPTP inspection is enabled.

Note Cisco ASA supports only PPTP version 1.

To enable PPTP inspection via ASDM, navigate to **Configuration > Firewall > Service Policy Rules > Edit Service Policy Rule** and select **PPTP** under the **Edit Service Policy Rule** dialog box.

Use the **inspect pptp** command to enable PPTP inspection via the CLI.

Sun RPC

The Sun Remote Procedure Call (RPC) is a protocol used by the Network File System (NFS) and Network Information Service (NIS). NIS clients attempt to communicate with their administratively configured NIS server through RPC portmapper requests immediately after bootup. The RPC portmapper service converts RPC program numbers into TCP/UDP ports. The RPC server tells portmapper what port number it is listening to and what RPC program numbers it will use. The client first contacts portmapper on the server machine to determine the port number to which RPC packets should be sent. The default RPC portmapper port is 111.

Cisco ASA Sun RPC inspection provides the following:

- Bidirectional inspection of Sun RPC packets
- Support of Sun RPC over TCP and UDP
- Support of Portmapper v2 and RPCBind v3 and v4
- Support of DUMP procedure used by the client to query the server for all the supported services
- NAT and PAT support

To enable Sun RPC inspection via ASDM, navigate to **Configuration > Firewall > Service Policy Rules > Edit Service Policy Rule** and select **SUNRPC** under the **Edit Service Policy Rule** dialog box.

To enable Sun RPC inspection via the CLI, use the **inspect sunrpc** command. Use the Sun RPC services table to control Sun RPC traffic through the adaptive security appliance based on established Sun RPC sessions. To create entries in the Sun RPC services table, use the **sunrpc-server** command in global configuration mode.

RSH

Remote Shell (RSH) is a management protocol used by numerous UNIX systems. It uses TCP port 514. The client and server negotiate the TCP port number to be used by the client for the STDERR (standard error) output stream.

Cisco ASA supports NAT of the negotiated port number with RSH inspection.

To enable RSH inspection via ASDM, navigate to **Configuration > Firewall > Service Policy Rules > Edit Service Policy Rule** and select **RSH** under the **Edit Service Policy Rule** dialog box.

To enable this RSH inspection via the CLI, use the **inspect rsh** command.

RTSP

The Real-Time Streaming Protocol (RTSP) is a multimedia streaming protocol that many vendors use. Cisco ASA supports inspection for this protocol in compliance with RFC 2326. The following are some of the applications that use RTSP:

- RealAudio
- Apple QuickTime
- RealPlayer
- Cisco IP/TV

Most RTSP applications use TCP port 554. On some rare occasions, UDP is used in the control channel.

The commonly used TCP control channel negotiates the data channels used to transmit audio and video. This is negotiated based on the transport mode specified on the client.

The following are the supported Real Data Transport (RDT) protocol transports:

- rtp/avp
- rtp/avp/udp
- x-real-rdt
- x-real-rdt/udp
- x-pn-tng/udp

To enable RTSP inspection via ASDM, navigate to **Configuration > Firewall > Service Policy Rules > Edit Service Policy Rule** and select **RTSP** under the **Edit Service Policy Rule** dialog box.

Use the **inspect rtsp** command to enable RTSP inspection via the CLI.

SIP

The Session Initiation Protocol (SIP) is a signaling protocol used in multimedia conferencing applications, IP telephony, instant messaging, and some event-notification features on several applications. This protocol is defined in RFC 3261. SIP signaling is sent over UDP or TCP port 5060. The media streams are dynamically allocated. Figure 7-21 illustrates the basics of an SIP call flow between two SIP calling entities and gateways, respectively.

The Cisco ASA is able to inspect any NAT SIP transactions successfully.

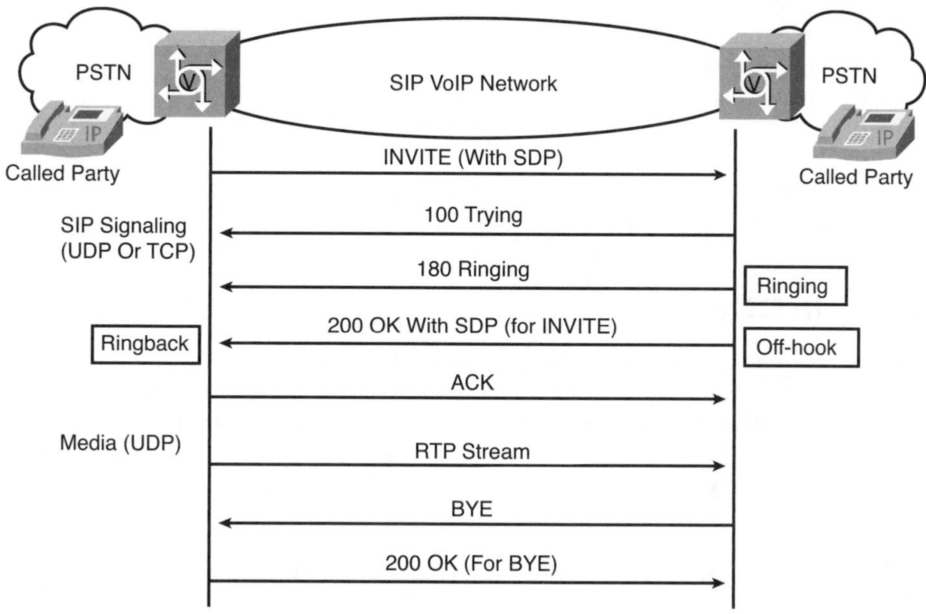

Figure 7-21 *SIP Call Flow*

To enable SIP inspection via ASDM, navigate to **Configuration > Firewall > Service Policy Rules > Edit Service Policy Rule** and select **SIP** under the **Edit Service Policy Rule** dialog box.

To enable SIP inspection via the CLI, use the **inspect sip** command. You can see SIP connection statistics by using the **show conn state sip** command. The **show service-policy** command provides you with SIP inspection statistics.

SIP is also used by IM applications. The details on SIP extensions for instant messaging are defined in RFC 3428. Instant messengers use MESSAGE/INFO requests and 202 Accept responses when users chat with each other. The MESSAGE/INFO requests are sent after registration and subscription transactions are completed. For example, two users may have their IM application connected at any time, but not talk to each other for a long period of time. The Cisco ASA SIP inspection engine maintains this information for a set period of time according to the configured SIP timeout value.

To configure the idle timeout after which an SIP control connection will be closed, use the **timeout sip** command. The default timeout value is 30 minutes. Use the **timeout sip_media** command to configure the idle timeout after which an SIP media connection will be closed. The default is two minutes.

Example 7-22 shows how the Cisco ASA is configured with a SIP timeout of one hour.

Example 7-22 *SIP Timeout Example*

```
NewYork(config)# timeout sip 1:00:00
NewYork(config)# timeout sip_media 0:30:00
```

Note The SIP media timeout value must be configured at least five minutes longer than the subscription duration **(timeout sip)**.

Skinny (SCCP)

Skinny is a protocol used in VoIP applications. (Skinny is another name for the Simple Client Control Protocol [SCCP].) Cisco IP Phones, Cisco CallManager, and Cisco CallManager Express use this protocol. Figure 7-22 demonstrates the registration and communication process between a Cisco IP Phone and all the respective components such as Cisco CallManager.

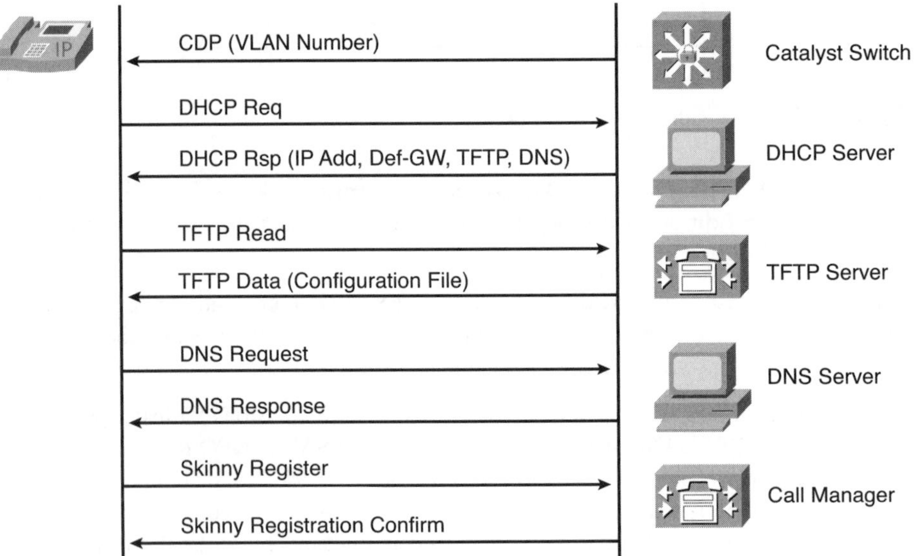

Figure 7-22 *Cisco IP Phone Registration and Communication Flow*

In Figure 7-22, the Cisco IP Phone is assigned to a specific VLAN. After that, it sends a request to the DHCP server to get an IP address, DNS server address, and TFTP server name or address. It also gets a default gateway address if you have set these options in the DHCP server.

Note If a TFTP server name is not included in the DHCP reply, the Cisco IP Phone uses the default server name.

The Cisco IP Phone obtains its configuration from the TFTP server. It resolves the Cisco CallManager name via DNS and starts the Skinny registration process.

To enable Skinny inspection via ASDM, navigate to **Configuration > Firewall > Service Policy Rules > Edit Service Policy Rule** and select **SCCP (Skinny)** under the **Edit Service Policy Rule** dialog box.

To configure Skinny inspection via the CLI, use the **inspect skinny** command. This command is enabled by default.

Note Cisco ASA does not support fragmented Skinny messages.

As previously discussed, Cisco IP phones download their configuration information from a TFTP server. This information includes the name or IP address of the Cisco CallManager server to which they need to connect. You must use an ACL to open UDP port 69 when the Cisco IP Phones are on a lower-security interface compared to the TFTP server. Enabling TFTP inspection with the **inspect tftp** command may be necessary to allow the secondary data connection initiated by the Cisco CallManager. If the Cisco IP Phones are on a lower-security interface compared to the Cisco CallManager, create a static NAT entry for the Cisco CallManager.

Note Instructions on how to create ACLs and static NAT entries are covered in Chapter 4, "Controlling Network Access."

SNMP

The Simple Network Management Protocol (SNMP) manages and monitors networking devices. Cisco ASA SNMP inspection enables packet traffic monitoring between network devices. The Cisco ASA can be configured to deny traffic based on the SNMP packet version. Early versions of SNMP are less secure. Denying SNMPv1 traffic may be required by your security policy. You do so by configuring an SNMP map with the **snmp-map** command and then associating it to the **inspect snmp** command via the CLI, as shown in Example 7-23.

Example 7-23 *SNMP Inspection*

```
snmp-map mysnmpmap
 deny version 1
policy-map global_policy
 class inspection_default
  inspect snmp mysnmpmap
```

In Example 7-23, the Cisco ASA is set up for an SNMP map, called **mysnmpmap**, which denies any SNMPv1 packets. The following are the **deny version** subcommand options:

- **1** = SNMP version 1
- **2** = SNMP version 2 (party based)
- **2c** = SNMP version 2c (community based)
- **3** = SNMP version 3

To enable SNMP inspection via ASDM, navigate to **Configuration > Firewall > Service Policy Rules > Edit Service Policy Rule** and select **SNMP** under the **Edit Service Policy Rule** dialog box. Click on **Configure** to configure the specific SNMP version(s) that are to be denied.

The **Add SNMP Map** dialog box is displayed, and it enables you to create a new SNMP map for controlling SNMP application inspection.

The following are the available SNMP version options:

- SNMP version 1
- SNMP version 2 (party based)
- SNMP version 2c (community based
- SNMP version 3

SQL*Net

Cisco ASA provides support for Oracle SQL*Net protocol inspection. It supports both versions 1 and 2. Cisco ASA is able to perform NAT and look in the packets for all embedded ports to allow the necessary communication for SQL*Net. SQL*Net inspection supports only the Transparent Network Substrate (TNS) Oracle SQL*Net format; it does not support the Tabular Data Stream (TDS) format.

To enable SQL*Net inspection via ASDM, navigate to **Configuration > Firewall > Service Policy Rules > Edit Service Policy Rule** and select **SQLNET** under the **Edit Service Policy Rule** dialog box.

To enable SQL*Net inspection via the CLI, use the **inspect sqlnet** command.

TFTP

The Trivial File Transfer Protocol (TFTP) allows systems to read and write files between them in a client/server relationship. One of the advantages of TFTP application inspection is that the Cisco ASA can prevent a host from opening invalid connections. Additionally, the Cisco ASA enforces the creation of a secondary channel initiated from the server. This restriction prevents the TFTP client from creating the secondary connection because the TFTP inspection uses ephemeral ports that cannot be guessed by an attacker.

To enable TFTP inspection via ASDM, navigate to **Configuration > Firewall > Service Policy Rules > Edit Service Policy Rule** and select **TFTP** under the **Edit Service Policy Rule** dialog box.

Use the **inspect tftp** command to enable TFTP inspection on the Cisco ASA via the CLI.

WAAS

The Cisco ASA supports application inspection for Wide Area Application Services (WAAS). When WAAS inspection is enabled, the Cisco ASA automatically detects WAAS connections and allows the optimized TCP traffic to enter the protected network.

To enable WAAS inspection via ASDM, navigate to **Configuration > Firewall > Service Policy Rules > Edit Service Policy Rule** and select **WAAS** under the **Edit Service Policy Rule** dialog box.

To enable WAAS application inspection via the CLI, use the **inspect waas** command.

XDMCP

The X Display Manager Control Protocol (XDMCP) is a protocol that many UNIX systems use to remotely execute and view applications.

> **Tip** Using XDMCP is inherently insecure; therefore, most of the UNIX distributions shipped have XDMCP turned off by default. Use XDMCP only in a trusted network.

XDMCP uses UDP port 177 to negotiate X sessions using a TCP port. The X manager communicates with the X server over TCP port 6000 + *n* (*n* = negotiated port).

To enable XDMCP inspection via ASDM, navigate to **Configuration > Firewall > Service Policy Rules > Edit Service Policy Rule** and select **XDMCP** under the **Edit Service Policy Rule** dialog box.

To enable XDMCP inspection via the CLI, use the **inspect xdmcp** command.

Summary

This chapter described how to use and configure application inspection on Cisco ASA. It demonstrated how the application inspection features ensure the secure use of applications and services. Details on the protocols that require special application inspection were covered in detail.

Chapter 8

Virtualization

This chapter covers the following topics:

- Architectural overview
- Configuration of security contexts
- Deployment scenarios
- Monitoring and troubleshooting

The virtual firewall methodology enables a physical firewall to be partitioned into multiple standalone firewalls. Each standalone firewall acts and behaves as an independent entity with its own configuration, interfaces, security policies, routing table, and administrators. In Cisco ASA, these virtual firewalls are also known as *security contexts*.

The following are some example scenarios in which security contexts are useful in network deployments:

- You act as a service provider and you want to provide firewall services to customers. However, you do not want to purchase additional physical firewalls for each customer.
- You manage an educational institution and you want to segregate student networks from faculty networks for improved security while using one physical security appliance.
- You administer a large enterprise with different departmental groups, and each department wants to implement its own security policies.
- You have overlapping networks in your organization and you want to provide firewall services to all those networks without changing the addressing scheme.
- You currently manage many physical firewalls and you want to integrate security policies from all firewalls into one physical firewall.

- You manage a data center environment and you want to provide end-to-end virtualization to reduce operational costs and increase efficiency.

In Figure 8-1, SecureMe, our fictional enterprise headquartered in Chicago, has a Cisco ASA providing firewall services to two of its customers. To implement a cost-effective solution, SecureMe has configured two virtual firewalls in the security appliance: "Bears" and "Cubs" for two customers. Each customer can manage and administer his or her own security context without interfering with the other context. On the other hand, the security appliance administrator (the administrator responsible for managing the entire firewall) can manage both contexts—the admin context and the system execution space—which are discussed in the next section.

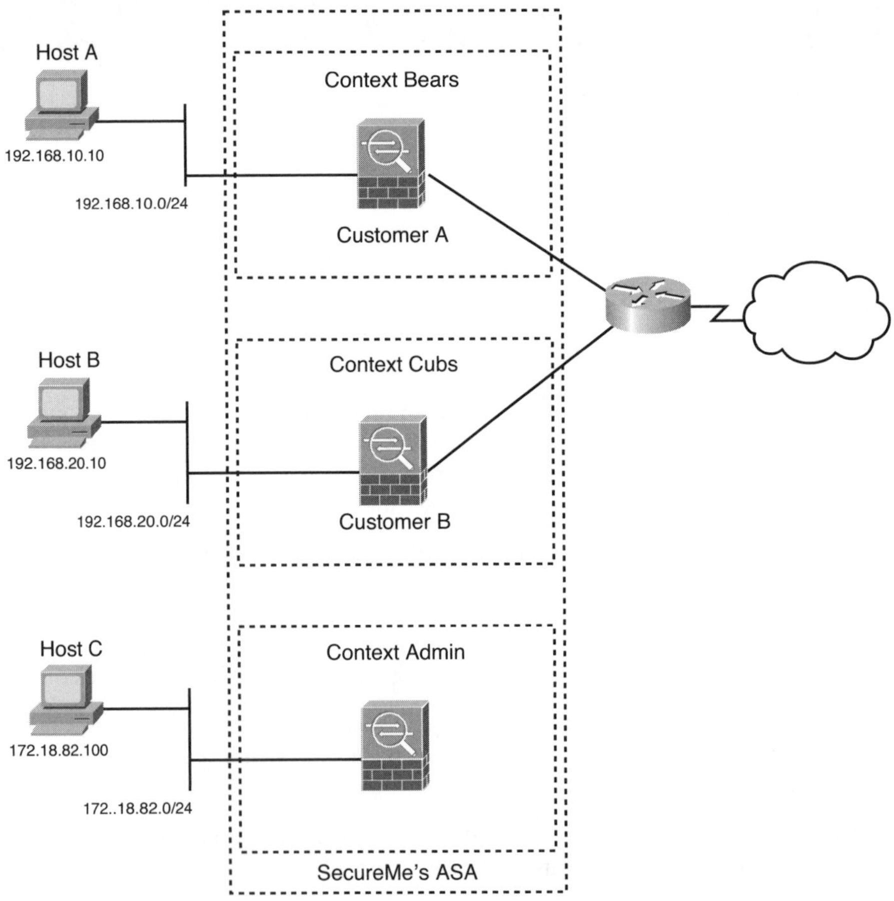

Figure 8-1 *Security Contexts in Cisco ASA*

In this figure, each horizontal dotted box represents a security context that has a Cisco ASA inspecting and protecting the packets flowing through it, and the vertical box represents the physical Cisco security appliance with multiple security contexts.

Note The virtual firewall feature is supported on Cisco ASA 5510 through Cisco ASA 5580. It is currently not supported on Cisco ASA 5505. Additionally, it is not supported on Cisco ASA 5510 if you have the base license loaded.

At the time of writing, the latest released version of the Cisco ASA code is 8.2(1).

Architectural Overview

In a virtual firewall environment, the Cisco security appliance can be divided into three types:

- A system execution space
- An admin context
- One or more user contexts (also known as Customer Contexts)

All contexts must be configured correctly for proper function. Even though the contexts are independent virtual firewalls, there are cases when one virtual firewall can affect the functionality and performance of another.

System Execution Space

Unlike other contexts, the system execution space does not have any Layer 2 or Layer 3 interfaces or any network settings. Rather, it is mainly used to define the attributes and settings of other security contexts. The three important settings configured for each context in the system execution space are

- Context name
- Location of context's startup configuration, also known as a configlet
- Interface allocation

Additionally, many optional features, such as interface, failover, and boot parameters, can be configured within the system execution space. Table 8-1 lists the important features that can be set up within the system execution space.

The system execution space configuration resides in the nonvolatile random-access memory (NVRAM) area of the security appliance, whereas the configurations for security contexts are stored either in local Flash memory or on a network storage server, using one of the following protocols:

- TFTP
- FTP
- HTTPS
- HTTP

Table 8-1 *Options Available in the System Execution Space*

Feature	Description
Interfaces	Sets up physical interfaces for speed and duplex. Interfaces can be enabled or disabled.
Banner	Specifies a login or session banner when users connect to the security appliance.
Boot	Specifies boot parameters to load proper image.
Activation key	Enables or disables security appliance features via the activation key.
Resource management	Assigns resource allocation to different security contexts.
File management	Adds or deletes the security context configurations that are stored locally on the security appliance.
Firewall mode	Configures single- or multiple-mode firewall in the system execution space.
Transparent mode	Configures routed- or transparent-mode firewall in the system execution space. Transparent firewalls are discussed in Chapter 9.
Failover	Sets the failover parameters to accommodate multiple physical security appliances. Failover is discussed in Chapter 10.
NTP	Configures Network Time Protocol–specific parameters in the security appliance.
mac-address	Enables you to auto-generate unique MAC addresses for each context
Prompt	Enables you to configure how the session prompt is displayed to a user.

The system execution space designates one of the security contexts as the admin context, which is responsible for providing network access when the system needs to contact resources.

Admin Context

The admin context provides connectivity to the network resources such as the AAA or syslog server. It is recommended that you assign the management interface(s) of the security appliance to the admin context. You must assign IP addresses to the allocated interfaces as you would with any other context. The security appliance uses the configured IP addresses to retrieve configurations for other contexts if those configurations are stores on a network share, or to provide remote management of the device through SSH or Telnet. A system administrator with access to the admin context can switch into the other contexts to manage them. The security appliance also uses the admin context to send the syslog messages that relate to the physical system.

The admin context must be created before you define other contexts. Additionally, it must reside on the local disk. You can designate a new admin context at any time by using the **admin-context** command, which is discussed in the "Configuration of Security Contexts" section of this chapter.

When a Cisco ASA is converted from single mode to multi-mode, the network-related configuration of the single-mode security appliance is saved as the admin context. The security appliance, by default, names this context as **admin.**

Note Changing the name of the admin context from **admin** is not recommended.

The admin context configuration is similar to a user context. Aside from its relationship to the system execution space, it can be used as a regular context. However, using it as a regular context is not recommended because of its system significance.

User Context

Each user or customer context acts as a virtual firewall with its own configuration that contains almost all the options that are available in a standalone firewall. A virtual firewall supports a number of features that are available in a standalone firewall such as IPS functionality, routing tables, firewall features, and management. Table 8-2 lists the differences between a security appliance running in single mode and an appliance running in multiple mode.

The maximum number of configurable user contexts depends on the installed activation key. To find out how many user contexts are allowed on a security appliance, look at the security context information in show version, as shown in Example 8-1. In this example, the security appliance can have up to 20 user contexts.

Example 8-1 *Verifying the Number of Security Contexts*

```
Chicago# show version ¦ include Security Contexts
Security Contexts            : 20
```

To determine the supported number of contexts in a security appliance through ASDM, navigate to **Home**, click the **License** tab in the "Device Information" section and look at the "Security Contexts" option.

Note The number of available contexts does not include the admin context because of its significance to the system execution space.

Table 8-2 *Contrasting Single- and Multiple-Mode Firewalls*

Features	Single Mode	Multiple Mode
Interface	All physical interfaces are available for use.	Only allocated interfaces are available in the contexts.
File management	Enables an administrator to copy system images and configurations.	Restricts a context administrator to manage the context configurations only. A device administrator can copy images and maintain configuration.
Firewall management	Enables a system administrator to fully manage the security appliance.	Enables a system administrator to fully manage the security appliance. Also enables a context administrator to manage the assigned context.
Addressing scheme	Does not allow overlapping networks in the device configuration.	Allows overlapping networks in the contexts.
Routing protocols	Supports RIP, EIGRP, and OSPF as the dynamic routing protocols.	Does not allow any dynamic routing protocols.
Licensing	There are no security contexts in single mode; therefore, no license is needed to turn on the security contexts.	Needs a license to activate more than two security contexts. The default license includes two customer contexts and an admin context.
Resource allocation	The security appliance uses all the available resources.	The security appliance, by default, shares the system resources between the contexts. You can use the resource allocation feature to dedicate different hardware resources to each context.
Failover	Does not allow Active/Active failover. Failover is discussed in Chapter 10.	Allows Active/Active failover for redundancy and load balancing.
Quality of service	Supports QoS.	Does not support QoS.
Multicast	Supports multicast using PIM-SM.	Does not support multicast.
Threat detection	Supports threat detection against scanning attacks.	Does not support threat detection.
IPSec VPN	Supports remote access and site-to-site IPSec VPN tunnels.	Does not support IPSec VPNs.
SSL VPN	Supports SSL VPN tunnels.	Does not support SSL VPNs.

Table 8-3 shows the maximum number of security contexts and the maximum number of supported VLANs on each of the Cisco ASA devices.

Table 8-3 *Contrasting Single- and Multiple-Mode Firewalls*

Devices	Maximum Number of Security Contexts	Number of Supported VLANs
5505	0 (Not Supported)	20[1]
5510	5[2]	100[3]
5520	20	150
5540	50	200
5550	50	250
5580-20	50	250[4]
5580-40	50	250[4]

[1] You need the Security Plus license to activate 20 VLAN support. With the base security license, VLAN trunking is disabled.

[2] You need the Security Plus license to activate security contexts. With the base security license, security contexts are not allowed.

[3] You need the Security Plus license to activate 100 VLAN support. With the base security license, only 50 VLANs were supported.

[4] You need to use 8.1(2) or higher versions of code to get 250 VLAN support. In pre-8.1(2) versions of code, only 100 VLANs were supported.

Packet Classification

When packets traverse through the security appliance in multiple-context mode, they are classified and forwarded to the correct context. One of the benefits of using virtualization is the sharing of resources such as the physical interfaces between the security contexts.

This brings up the question of how Cisco ASA classifies packets when they are received by the firewall and to which security context the security appliance should forward those packets. Cisco Systems provides a solution to this issue through the use of a packet classifier, which classifies packets at the ingress interface. The security appliance applies one of the packet classifying criteria to identify to which security context to forward the packet. After packets are sent to a security context, they are processed based on the security policies configured in that context.

Packet Classification Criteria

Cisco ASA uses a number of criteria to classify packets before they are forwarded to the correct security context. Depending on how you want to implement a security appliance, the packet classifying criteria is different. You can deploy the security contexts in either a shared interface environment or a non-shared interface environment.

Criteria for Non-Shared Interfaces

If all contexts in the Cisco ASA use unique physical or logical sub-interfaces, the packet classification becomes easier because the security appliance classifies these packets based on the source interface. As illustrated in Figure 8-2, when the packet is sourced from 192.168.10.10, the classifier assigns the packet to context Bears because the packet was received on G0/0, which is a part of the Bears security context.

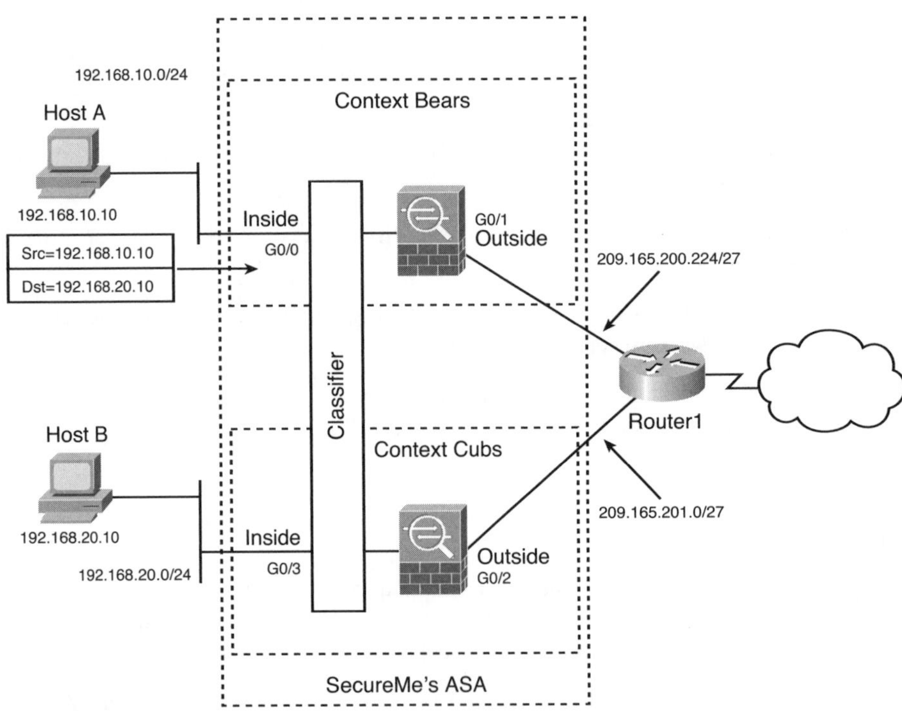

Figure 8-2 *Packet Classification Using Source Interface*

Criteria for Shared Interfaces

The security appliance enables you to share one or more interfaces between the security contexts. In this deployment model, the security appliance can use either a destination IP address or a unique MAC address on the security appliance to classify the packet to the correct context.

Destination IP Address: If you are sharing an interface between multiple security contexts, then by default the interface uses the same MAC address across all virtual firewalls. With this approach, the ingress packets on the physical interface, regardless of the security context, have the same MAC address. When the packet is received by the security appliance for a particular security context, the classifier does not know to which security context to send the packets.

To address this challenge, the classifier uses the packet's destination IP address to identify which security context should receive packets in a shared environment. However, the firewall cannot classify traffic based on the routing table of the contexts because multimode allows for overlapping networks, and the routing table might be the same for two contexts. The classifier relies strictly on the network address translation (NAT) table of each security context to learn about the subnets located behind each security context. This is illustrated in Figure 8-3.

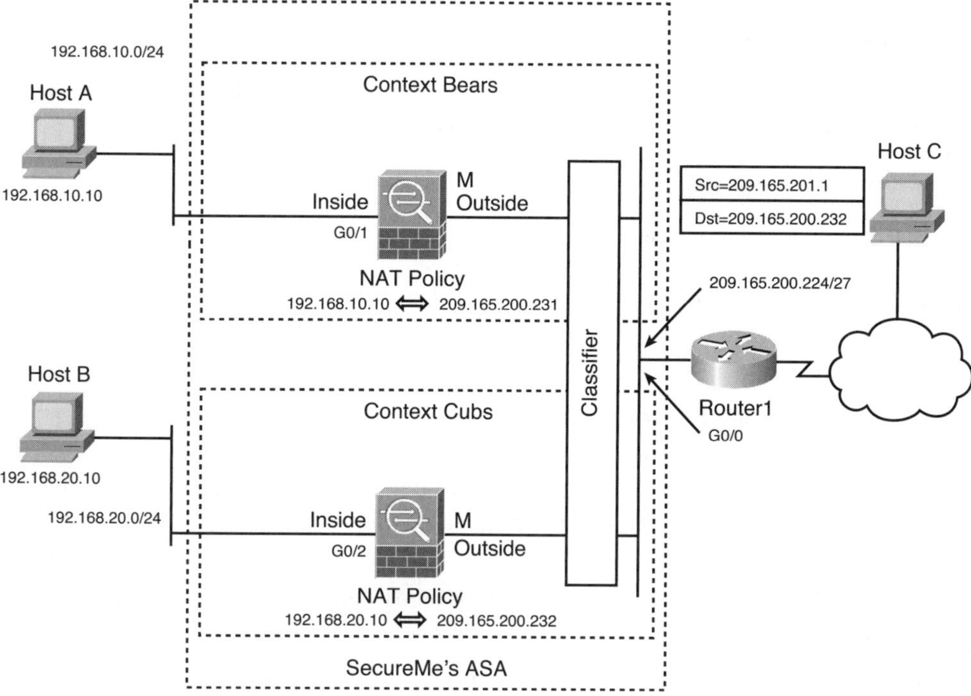

Figure 8-3 *Packet Classification Using Destination IP*

Note The classifier can use both static NAT and dynamic NAT to classify packets. If the traffic is initiated from an outside shared interface, then you have to define static NAT. However, if the traffic is initiated from an inside non-shared interface to a host toward a shared interface, then you can define static and dynamic NAT for that traffic.

Unique MAC Address: In a shared interface environment, the preferred method for packet classifier is to use unique MAC addresses. This is also a required option if you do not want to define NAT entries for the subnets behind each security context. You can either:

- Manually define a unique MAC address
- Automatically generate a system MAC address for each security context

This way each security context has a unique MAC address and the next-hop router (toward the shared interface) should be able to identify to which context to send the packets when packets need to pass through the security appliance. You can use the **mac-address auto** command to auto-generate unique MAC addresses for each shared interface in a context.

Packet Flow in Multiple Mode

In multiple mode, the two contexts pass traffic to one another as though there were separate physical appliances. The security contexts can talk to each other in two ways:

- Without a shared interface
- With a shared interface

Depending on what mode you use, the packet flow is different, as discussed in the following subsections.

Forwarding Without a Shared Interface

As Figure 8-4 illustrates, SecureMe's ASA has four interfaces: Two belong to the Bears context and the remaining two are assigned to Cubs. The outside interface of both contexts is connected to Router1, which is responsible for routing packets from one context to another.

If NAT and packet filtering are set up on the security appliance, then the following sequence of events takes place when Host A sends an ICMP ping packet to Host B:

Step 1. Host A sends an ICMP ping packet with a source address of 192.168.10.10 and a destination address of 192.168.20.10. Because the security appliance is not using a shared interface, the classifier assigns the packet coming in on G0/0 interface to the Bears context for further processing.

Step 2. The packet is inspected by the inbound ACL and, if allowed, forwarded to the firewall engines such as address translation or application inspection for further processing. Before the security appliance forwards the packet to Router1, it is inspected by the outbound ACL to ensure that it is allowed to leave. The packet is physically transmitted on interface G0/1.

Step 3. Router1 checks the destination IP address in the routing table and sends the packet to the G0/2 interface of the security appliance.

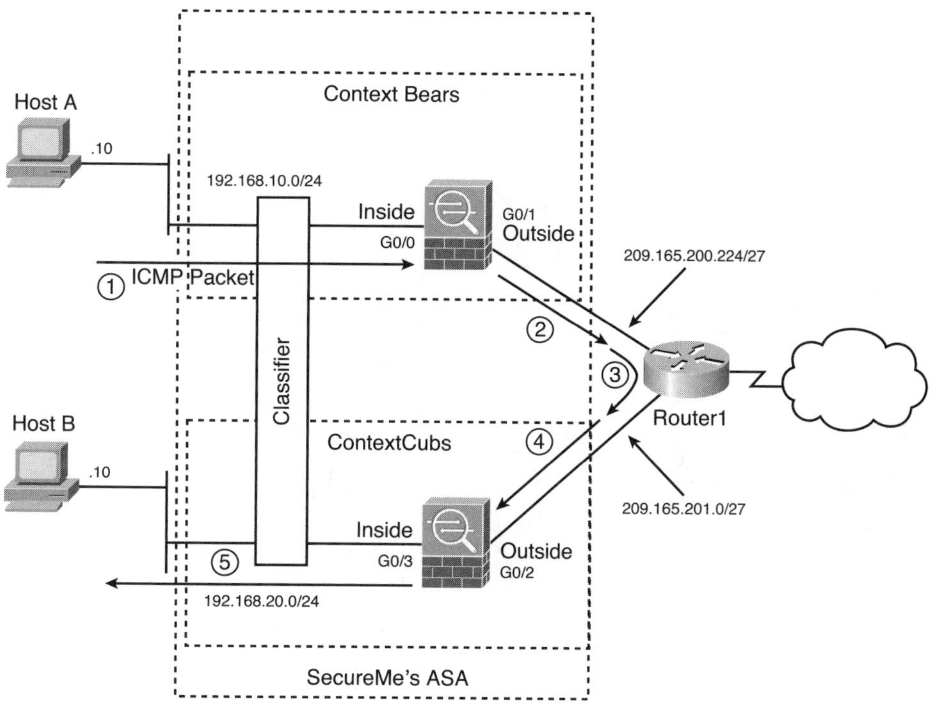

Figure 8-4 *Security Contexts Without a Shared Interface*

Step 4. The classifier sends the packet to the Cubs context for further processing on its outside interface. It is inspected by the inbound ACL and if it is allowed in, the packet goes through the different firewall engines to ensure it adheres to the security policies.

Step 5. The security context forwards the packet to Host B after verifying that the outbound ACL on the inside interface does not deny it. The packet is physically transmitted on interface G0/3.

Forwarding with a Shared Interface

Figure 8-5 illustrates another network topology, where SecureMe uses a shared outside LAN interface (G0/1). This model is deployed by many service providers to provide Internet connectivity to their end customers through a shared outside interface. With this design, SecureMe can conserve the address space and the allocated interfaces. In this deployment scenario, Router1 is connected to the same shared interface of G0/1 to provide access to the Internet for the hosts sitting behind each security context.

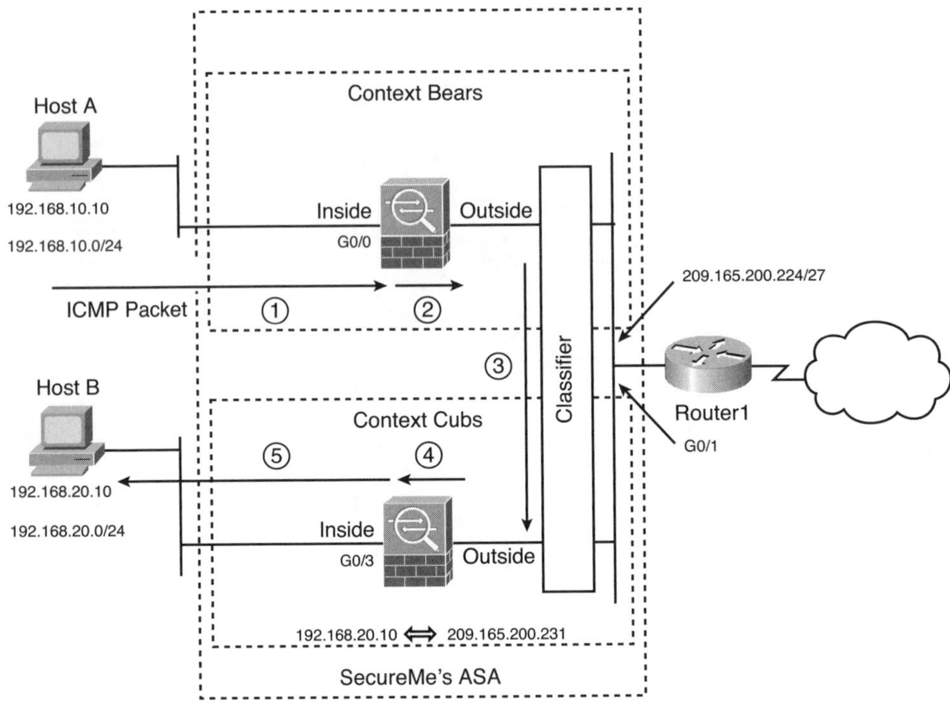

Figure 8-5 *Security Contexts with a Shared Interface*

> **Note** In a shared environment, the classifier prefers static NAT statements over the statically defined routes. Look at Figure 8-5, for example. If traffic is sourced from 192.168.10.10 and destined to 209.165.200.231 (which is translated to 192.168.20.10 on Cubs) and a static route is defined on the Bears security context to forward traffic to Router1, then the classifier prefers the static translation on Cubs despite a static route on Bears.

Using the previous example, when Host A sends an ICMP ping packet to Host B, the following steps are taken for successful communication, assuming that the shared interfaces are not using unique MAC addresses:

Step 1. Host A sends an ICMP ping packet with a source address of 192.168.10.10 and a destination address of 209.165.200.231. The classifier receives packet on G0/0 and forwards it to the inside interface of Bears for more processing.

Step 2. The packet is inspected by the inbound ACL on the inside interface of the Bears context and, if allowed, forwarded to the firewall engines such as address translation or application inspection for further processing. The packet is then inspected by the outbound ACL to ensure that it is allowed to leave.

Step 3. The packet passes through the classifier, which looks at the destination IP address and forwards it to the outside interface of the Cubs security context because 209.165.200.231 is owned by Cubs.

Note Because the security contexts reside on a physical security appliance, the packet never leaves the physical ASA device when it moves between the outside interfaces of the two contexts.

Step 5. The Cubs context applies security policies after receiving the packet on the outside interface. The packet is inspected by the inbound ACL and if allowed in, the NAT engine translates the destination address to 192.168.20.10 from 209.165.200.231.

Note If you are not using a unique MAC address for each shared security context interface, you must use address translation as discussed earlier.

Step 6. The Cubs context forwards the packet to Host B after verifying that the outbound ACL on the inside interface does not deny it.

Note If your network design uses two shared interfaces and you allow traffic to communicate between the shared contexts, you must use a unique MAC address for each shared interface in the context.

Configuration of Security Contexts

The configuration of a security context can be broken down into eight steps:

Step 1. Enable multiple security contexts globally.

Step 2. Set up the system execution space.

Step 3. Allocate the interfaces.

Step 4. Specify a configuration URL.

Step 5. Configure an admin context.

Step 6. Configure a user context.

Step 7. Manage the security contexts (optional).

Step 8. Resource Management (optional)

Refer to Figure 8-4 throughout this section to visualize how to configure a virtual firewall.

Step 1: Enable Multiple Security Contexts Globally

The conversion process from single- to multiple-context mode must be done through the CLI. You can start the conversion process either through a Telnet/SSH connection or through a console connection. It is best practice to do the conversion through the console connection because if you lose the network access you can still connect to the security appliance. You enable the security context by using the mode multiple command, as shown in Example 8-2. When this command is executed, the security appliance prompts the system administrator to verify mode conversion before proceeding further. This initiates the reboot process to complete the conversion.

Note If your Cisco ASA is already in production, please schedule a maintenance window to go through the conversion process because it requires you to reboot your security appliance.

Example 8-2 *Enabling Security Contexts*

```
Chicago# configure terminal
Chicago(config)# mode ?
configure mode commands/options:
  multiple   Multiple mode; mode with security contexts
  noconfirm  Do not prompt for confirmation
  single     Single mode; mode without security contexts
Chicago(config)# mode multiple
WARNING: This command will change the behavior of the device
WARNING: This command will initiate a Reboot
Proceed with change mode? [confirm]
Convert the system configuration? [confirm]
!
The old running configuration file will be written to flash
The admin context configuration will be written to flash
The new running configuration file was written to flash
Security context mode: multiple
***
*** —- SHUTDOWN NOW —-
***
*** Message to all terminals:
***
***   change mode

Rebooting....
Booting system, please wait...
! Output omitted for brevity.
INFO: Admin context is required to get the interfaces

Creating context 'admin'... Done. (1)
*** Output from config line 26, "admin-context admin"

*** Output from config line 30, "  config-url flash:/admi..."
```

```
INFO: Context admin was created with URL disk0:/admin.cfg
INFO: Admin context will take some time to come up .... please wait.
Chicago>
```

When multiple-mode conversion is initiated, the security appliance prompts the administrator to convert the current running configuration into the system execution space and admin context. The appliance stores the system execution space in NVRAM and saves the admin context in the local Flash memory as admin.cfg. During conversion, it copies all the network-related information in the admin.cfg file, whereas all the device-related system information is stored in the NVRAM space.

Tip The security appliance saves the running configuration of the single-mode firewall as old_running.cfg in the Flash memory during the conversion process.

After the appliance comes online, you can use show mode to verify whether it is running in multiple mode. Example 8-3 shows the output of show mode.

Example 8-3 *Verifying Virtual Firewall Mode*

```
Chicago# show mode
Security context mode: multiple
```

Note If you do not have a license for multiple security contexts, the system key still enables you configure two user contexts, in addition to one admin context. Refer to Chapter 3, "Initial Setup and System Maintenance," for more information about licensing.

To convert the device back to single mode, you have to copy the saved old_running.cfg as the startup configuration. After that, you need to switch the security appliance to single mode. Both steps are shown in Example 8-4.

Example 8-4 *Reverting to Single-Mode Firewall*

```
Chicago# copy disk0:/old_running.cfg startup-config
Source filename [old_running.cfg]?
Copy in progress...C
1465 bytes copied in 0.250 secs
Chicago# configure terminal
Chicago(config)# mode single
WARNING: This command will change the behavior of the device
WARNING: This command will initiate a Reboot
Proceed with change mode? [confirm]
```

```
Security context mode: single
***
*** —- SHUTDOWN NOW —-
***
*** Message to all terminals:
***
***   change mode
Rebooting....
Booting system, please wait...
! Output omitted for brevity.
admin-context admin
 ^
ERROR: % Invalid input detected at '^' marker.
*** Output from config line 26, "admin-context admin"
```

Step 2: Set Up the System Execution Space

As mentioned earlier, the system execution space is created as soon as multiple mode is enabled. To access the system execution space, do any one of the following:

- Access the security appliance via the console or the auxiliary port.
- Log in to the admin context using SSH or Telnet, and then switch to the system execution space.
- Access the security appliance through ASDM, using the IP address of an interface in the admin context. Configuring a security appliance via ASDM for multi-mode requires that you have a preconfigured admin context and that the IP connectivity exists between the ASDM client and the IP address of the admin context. (The admin context was discussed earlier under the "Architectural Overview" section.) After you are logged in, navigate to **Home > System > Connect** icon under the device list pane, as shown in Figure 8-6.

If you are logged in to the admin context through the command-line interface, use the change to system command to get access to the system execution space. Example 8-5 demonstrates how to log in to the system from the admin context.

If you are in a security context, the host name contains a /. The text before the / is the hostname of the security appliance, whereas the text after is the name of the security context. If the hostname does not contain a /, you are in the system execution space.

Example 8-5 *Switching to System Execution Space*

```
Chicago/admin# changeto system
Chicago#
```

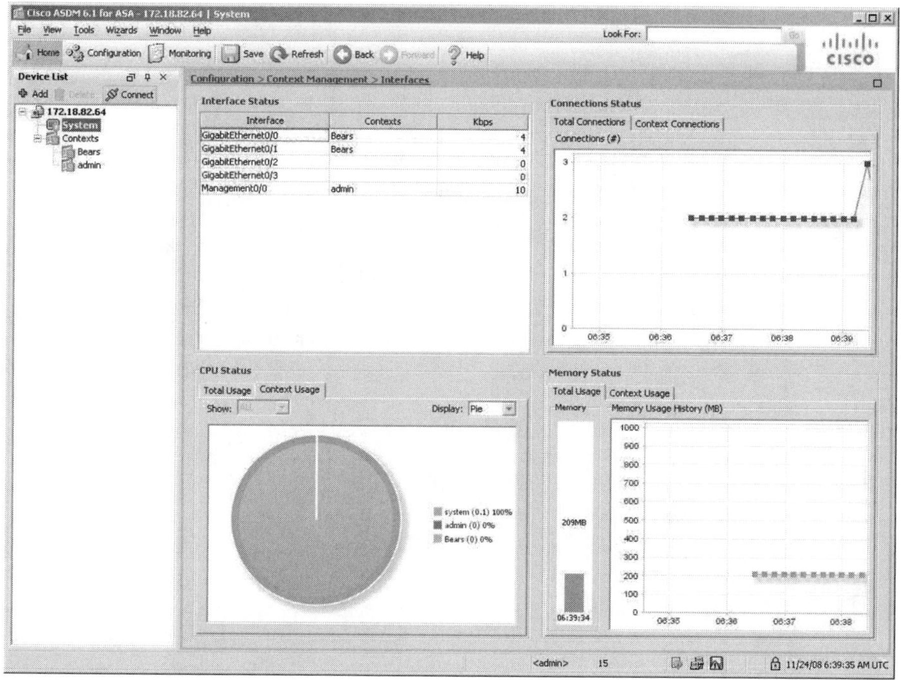

Figure 8-6 *System Execution Space in ASDM*

The purpose of system execution space is to define and maintain the admin and user contexts on the appliance.

If you manage the security appliances through the ASDM, navigate to **Configuration > System > Connect > Context Management > Security Contexts > Add.** If using the CLI, you can add a context by using the context command, followed by the name of the context under the configuration mode.

As shown in Figure 8-7, a new security context, called **Cubs**, is being added. After you specify a security context name, you can define a number of configuration parameters. They include

- Interface Allocation (Mandatory)
- Configuration URL (Mandatory)
- Description (Optional)
- Resource Assignment (Optional)
- Failover Group (Optional)

If you use the CLI to manage Cisco ASA, you can add Cubs security context in the Chicago ASA, as shown in Example 8-6. The security context name is case sensitive, so

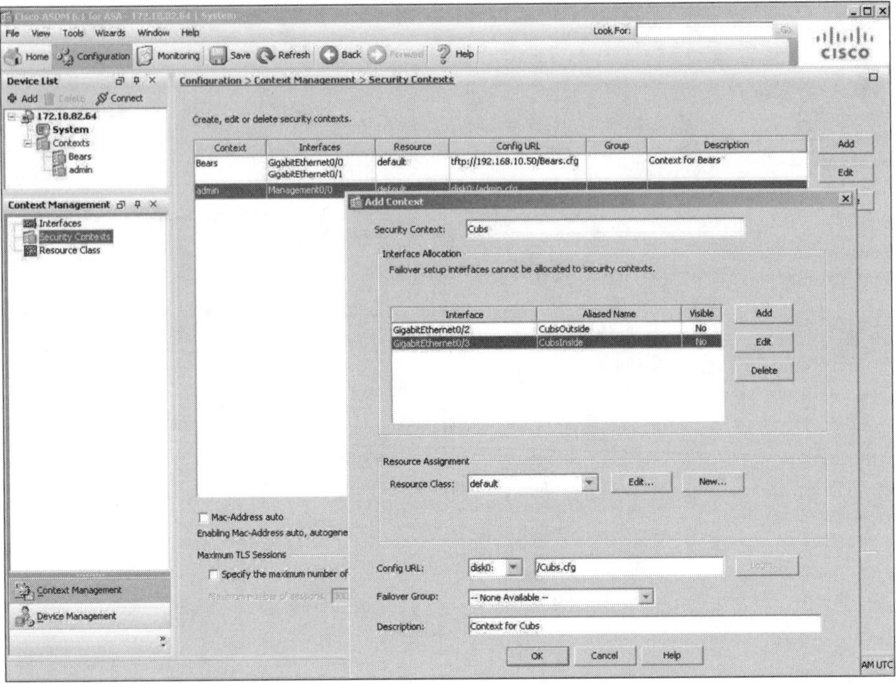

Figure 8-7 *Adding a New Security Context Through ASDM*

double-check it when adding the contexts. The appliance takes you into the context sub-configuration mode (config-ctx) to configure the necessary parameters.

Example 8-6 *Adding User Contexts in System Execution Space*

```
Chicago# configure terminal
Chicago(config)# context Cubs
Creating context 'Cubs'.. Done. (2)
Chicago(config-ctx)# exit
```

> **Note** Even if you create a new context, the security appliance does not allow you to log in to the newly created context until it is initialized, as discussed in "Specify a Configuration URL" later in this chapter.

The Cisco appliance enables you to add a description to the configured contexts. It is recommended that you add a description under each context for references purposes. As shown in Figure 8-7, a description of "Context for Cubs" is defined. If you prefer to use the ASA CLI, you can add context description as shown in Example 8-7.

Example 8-7 *Configuring a Description on the Security Context*

```
Chicago# configure terminal
Chicago(config)# context Cubs
Chicago(config-ctx)# description Context for Cubs
```

Caution If you issue the clear configure all command from the system configuration, the Cisco ASA removes all security contexts from the device. However, the configlets are not deleted and can be referenced later if you need to rebuild a context. The saved configuration will then be loaded into that context's running configuration.

Step 3: Allocate Interfaces

After creating the context, the next step is to allocate interfaces to each of the security contexts. You can assign either a physical interface or a sub-interface to a security context. Using ASDM, you can allocate one or multiple interfaces to a context in the **Interface Allocation** section by clicking **Add**. You can assign an interface when you define a new context or when you edit an existing one.

The security appliance, by default, displays the allocated interface as the interface ID in the context. If you want to display the name for an interface instead of the interface ID, you can specify an alias for that interface. This is extremely useful when you do not want the context administrator to find out which physical interface is being used as the inside or the outside interface.

Using the CLI, you can assign interfaces to a context by entering into the context sub-configuration mode and using the allocate-interface command

As shown in Figure 8-7, a new security context called **Cubs** is being added. The administrator has allocated **GigabitEthernet0/2** and **GigabitEthernet0/3** to this security context and has used **CubsOutside** and **CubsInside** respectively as interface aliases. Example 8-8 shows how a security appliance can be configured to achieve the same results through the command-line interface.

Example 8-8 *Allocating Interfaces to a User Context*

```
Chicago(config)# context Cubs
Chicago(config-ctx)# allocate-interface GigabitEthernet0/2 CubsOutside invisible
Chicago(config-ctx)# allocate-interface GigabitEthernet0/3 CubsInside invisible
```

Note If the appliance is converted from a single- to multiple-mode firewall, it allocates all the non-shut-down interfaces to the admin context. It is highly recommended that you use the admin context only for management purposes. Reallocate the interfaces to the proper contexts as desired.

Step 4: Specify a Configuration URL

The configuration URL, sometimes referred to as Config URL, specifies the location of the startup configuration for each context. The configured contexts (either admin or customer) are not active unless there is a configuration URL. The supported storage locations include the local disk and a network drive that uses the HTTP, HTTPS, FTP, or TFTP protocol. After a configuration URL is specified, Cisco ASA tries to retrieve the configuration from that location. If it does not find the configuration file, the Cisco security appliance creates a configuration file with the default settings.

An administrator can choose to specify different external servers as the configuration URL location for the security contexts. As shown in Figure 8-7, the Chicago ASA has an admin and a user context, Bears, already defined. The system administrator has decided to use the following:

- A TFTP server, 192.168.10.50, to store the Bears configuration
- The local disk for the admin context configuration

By default, these configuration files are saved in the root directory of the network protocol used by the context. For example, if the root directory of a TFTP server is C:\TFTP\files, the configuration URL, using the TFTP protocol, saves the configuration file at that location. The security appliance saves the configuration of these security contexts when either **write memory** or **copy running-config startup-config** is issued from within the security context. The security appliance also saves the configuration files of all security contexts when **write memory all** is issued from the system execution space.

In Figure 8-7, a new security context, called **Cubs**, is being added. While adding the new security context, the administrator has decided to save the startup configuration file in the local disk as **Cubs.cfg.** The config URL for the newly defined security context, using the CLI, is as shown in Example 8-9. After a configuration URL is added, you are ready to configure that virtual firewall by changing into it the context.

Example 8-9 *Defining Config URL*

```
Chicago(config)# context Cubs
Chicago(config-ctx)# config-url disk0:/Cubs.cfg
Chicago# exit
Chicago# changeto context Cubs
Chicago/Cubs#
```

Note If you use the FTP protocol, you must specify a username and a password to save and retrieve the configuration file. For example, if the FTP server is located at **192.168.10.50** and the username is **cisco** with a password of **c1$c0123**, then the config URL should be defined as config-url ftp://cisco:c1$c0123@192.168.10.50/Bears.cfg.

When the configuration URL is changed, the appliance merges a context's running configuration with the new configuration specified in the URL. This may add unnecessary commands and may cause system instability. If you do not want to merge the two configurations, you can follow these guidelines:

Step 1. Log in to the security context whose URL is to be changed, and clear the running configuration.

Step 2. Log in to the system execution space and enter into the context configuration mode.

Step 3. Specify the new configuration URL that you want to use.

Note You cannot change the location of the configuration URL from within a context. You have to be in the system execution space to accomplish this.

As soon as the new URL is entered, the appliance loads the new configuration immediately in the running configuration.

Step 5: Configure an Admin Context

Cisco ASA creates an admin context automatically, if you convert it from single to multiple mode and you answer **Yes** to **Convert the System Configuration?**. The admin context is treated as any other user context in the security appliance. To manage an admin context, or any other user context, navigate to **Configuration > Context > Admin (or a user context) > Connect**, as shown in Figure 8-8.

Using the CLI, you can log in to the admin context by typing the **changeto context** command, followed by the name of the context. As shown in Example 8-10, an administrator logs in to the admin context called admin from the system context.

Example 8-10 *Changing to an Admin Context*

```
Chicago# changeto context admin
Chicago/admin#
```

If you would rather designate a different context as the admin context, use the following command in the system execution space:

admin-context *context_name*

where *context_name* is the name of the context you want to designate as the admin context. Before a context is declared to be an admin context, it must meet two requirements:

- The context must be predefined and have a config-url.
- The config-url must point to a file in the local disk.

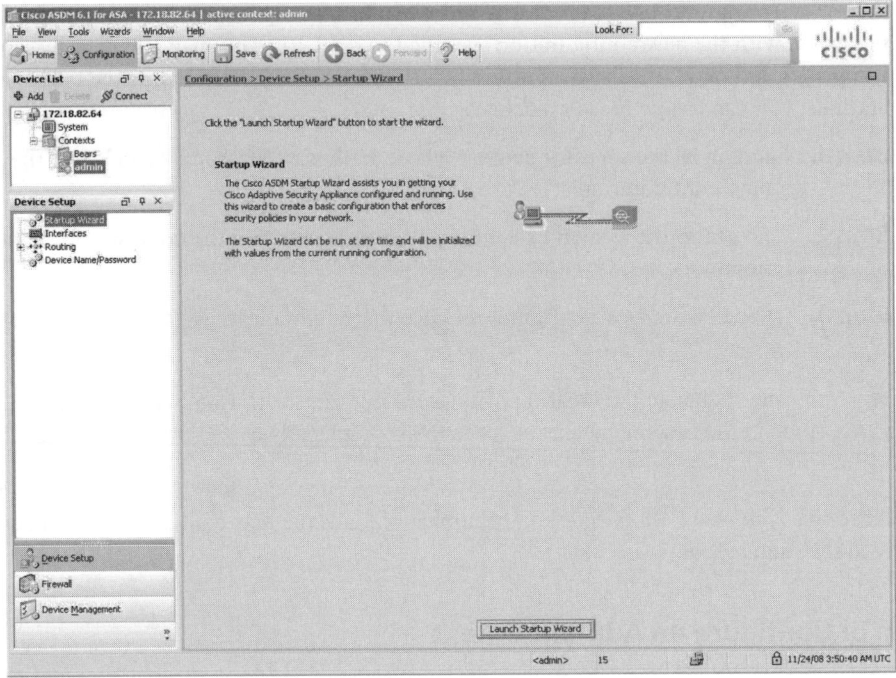

Figure 8-8 *Connecting to the Admin Context*

> **Note** The current version of Cisco ASDM does not allow you to designate a different context as the admin context. However, you can do that through the CLI by using the **admin-context** command.

Example 8-11 shows how to designate Bears as the admin context in a security appliance. Because Bears used a TFTP server to store the startup configuration, the administrator is modifying it to use the local disk0: before setting up the **admin-context** command.

Example 8-11 *Setting Up an Admin Context*

```
Chicago(config)# context Bears
Chicago(config-ctx)# config-url disk0:/Bears.cfg
Chicago(config-ctx)# exit
Chicago(config)# admin-context Bears
```

Not sure which context is set up as the admin context? Use one of the following three methods from the system execution space to find out:

- **show running-config | include admin-context**
- **show admin-context**

- **show context**, and look for the context name with an asterisk (*)

In Example 8-12, the highlighted entries indicate that Bears is currently set as the admin context.

Example 8-12 *Verifying the Admin Context*

```
Chicago# show running-config | include admin-context
admin-context Bears
Chicago# show admin-context
Admin: Bears disk0/:Bears.cfg
Chicago# show context
Context Name    Interfaces              URL
 admin           Management0/0           disk0:/admin.cfg
*Bears           GigabitEthernet0/0,    disk0:/Bears.cfg
                  GigabitEthernet0/1
 Cubs            GigabitEthernet0/2,     disk0:/Cubs.cfg
                  GigabitEthernet0/3
```

Step 6: Configure a User Context

Any context that is not designated as the admin context is referred to as a *user context*. As mentioned earlier in this chapter, a user context is configured similarly to a standalone firewall, with a few exceptions that are listed earlier in this chapter. You can log in to a user context through ASDM by navigating to **Configuration > Contexts > <user context name>** and then clicking the **Connect** button. As shown in Figure 8-9, an administrator is connected to the Cubs context.

If you prefer to use CLI, you can use the **changeto** command, followed by the name of the context. The command prompt displays the name of that context, as shown in Example 8-13.

Example 8-13 *Changing to a User Context*

```
Chicago# changeto context Cubs
Chicago/Cubs#
```

After logging in to the user context, you can configure all the supported firewall-related options.

Note The security appliance can save the configuration of all security contexts if **write memory all** is executed from the system execution space. This is useful if the security appliance needs to be reloaded and you want to save configurations of all contexts from the system execution space.

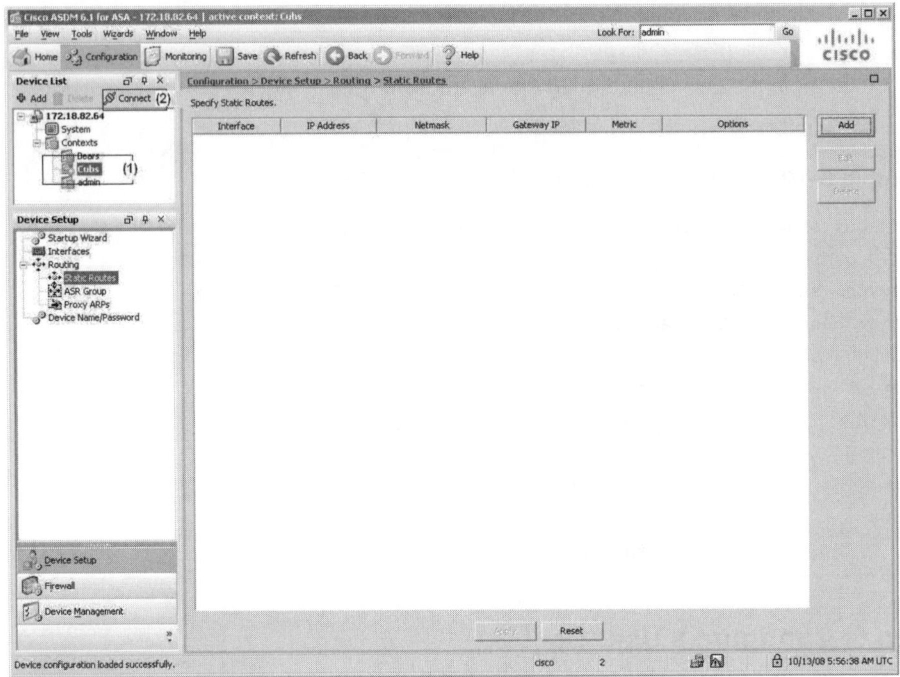

Figure 8-9 *Connecting to a User Context*

Step 7: Manage the Security Contexts (Optional)

Cisco ASA provides many ways to manage and optimize system resources. For example, if a context name is mistyped, or if it needs to be deleted, you can remove it by navigating to **Configuration > System > Connect > Security Contexts**, selecting the context, and then clicking the **Delete** button. The earlier Figure 8-7 shows the Delete button to remove security contexts from the appliance.

You can also type no context followed by the name of that context to remove a context from the CLI. In Example 8-14, the administrator of the Chicago ASA does not want to use Cubs as a user context anymore; instead, the administrator wants to remove it from the system configuration. By deleting any unused security context, you do not waste security contexts, which are restricted by the system license. Additionally, the system does not have to allocate CPU and memory resources to maintain the unused contexts.

Example 8-14 *Removing a Security Context*

```
Chicago(config)# no context Cubs
WARNING: Removing context 'Cubs'
Proceed with removing the context? [confirm]
Removing context 'Cubs' (3)... Done
```

In a situation where all contexts need to be removed, you can use the clear configure context command, as shown in Example 8-15.

Example 8-15 *Removing All Security Contexts*

```
Chicago(config)# clear configure context
```

Caution The clear configure context command also removes the designated admin context. If you are remotely logged in to the appliance over a Telnet or a SSH session, you will lose connectivity to the security appliance.

Step 8: Resource Management (Optional)

In a virtualized environment, all security contexts share the same hardware resources, such as the memory, CPU, throughput, and bandwidth. If you do not control the usage of these resources, it is quite possible that one context can exhaust all physical resources of the firewall, and other contexts cannot get their fair share. In the Cisco security appliances, you can manage the usage of the security contexts by limiting the use of physical resources per security context. For example, you can define two different levels of services, such as Gold and Silver, and then assign an appropriate level of service to each context. Security contexts that are subscribed to the Gold service can receive the guaranteed bandwidth, connections per second, total connections, etc., that are assigned to that service level. Similarly, customers that subscribe to the Silver service can be limited to the guarantees that come with that service level.

By default the security appliances do not impose any restrictions and all virtual firewalls have full unlimited access to the hardware resources. However, if you want to restrict security contexts to limit hardware utilization, you can use the resource management functionality in the security appliance. For example, many service providers provide a tiered array of services at different price points.

Using the resource management functionality of the security appliances, you can modify the attributes shown in Table 8-4.

The maximum system and context values for most of the resources are different. For example, the maximum context value for concurrent ASDM sessions is 5, whereas the maximum system value for concurrent ASDM sessions is 32. That means up to 5 admins are allowed to log in to a particular context, and up to 32 admins can log in to the security appliance at a given time.

You can set either an absolute value or a percent value to resources that are associated with the management sessions of the security appliances. They include ASDM, Telnet, and SSH session to Cisco ASA. If an absolute value is defined for a resource, then the connections that exceed that limit are denied. Similarly, if you define a percent value to a resource, the security appliance determines the maximum value based on the capabilities of the hardware device. For example, if you assign a 10 percent connection limit to a security context on Cisco ASA 5520, then the security appliance allows up to 28,000 connections to pass through within that context.

Table 8-4 *Resource Management Attributes and Definition*

Resource	Description
Xlates	Number of concurrent address translations
Conns	Number of concurrent UDP or TCP connections
Hosts	Number of concurrent hosts that are allowed to connect
Inspect rate	Number of application inspections per second
Conn rate	Number of connections per second
Syslog rate	Number of system log messages per second
ASDM	Number of concurrent ASDM management sessions
SSH	Number of concurrent SSH management sessions
Telnet	Number of concurrent Telnet management sessions
MAC addresses	Number of total MAC addresses that are allowed in transparent mode; transparent mode is covered in Chapter 9

Note It is possible to oversubscribe the security appliance by allocating more than 100 percent of a resource across different security contexts. For example, if you allocate a 10 percent connection limit to a class and assign the class to 30 security contexts, then you have technically allocated 300 percent of the total system resources. In this case, each context will receive less than 10 percent of the total connection limit.

Configuration of resource management on a security appliance is a two-step process:

Step 1. Defining a resource class

Step 2. Mapping resource class to a context

Step 1: Define a Resource Member Class

Apply the system resource limitations to a member class that can be defined under **Configuration > System > Connect > Context Management > Resource Class** by clicking **Add**. ASDM prompts you to assign a name to this new member class. Assign appropriate resource limitations to the attributes under the count-limited resources and the rate-limited resources. If you do not define a value to a resource in the member class, the resource inherits its value from the default class. For example, if you do not assign a value to the Telnet resource, then the class inherits the value of 5 from the default class.

As illustrated in Figure 8-10, a member class called **Silver** is configured with the following resource limits:

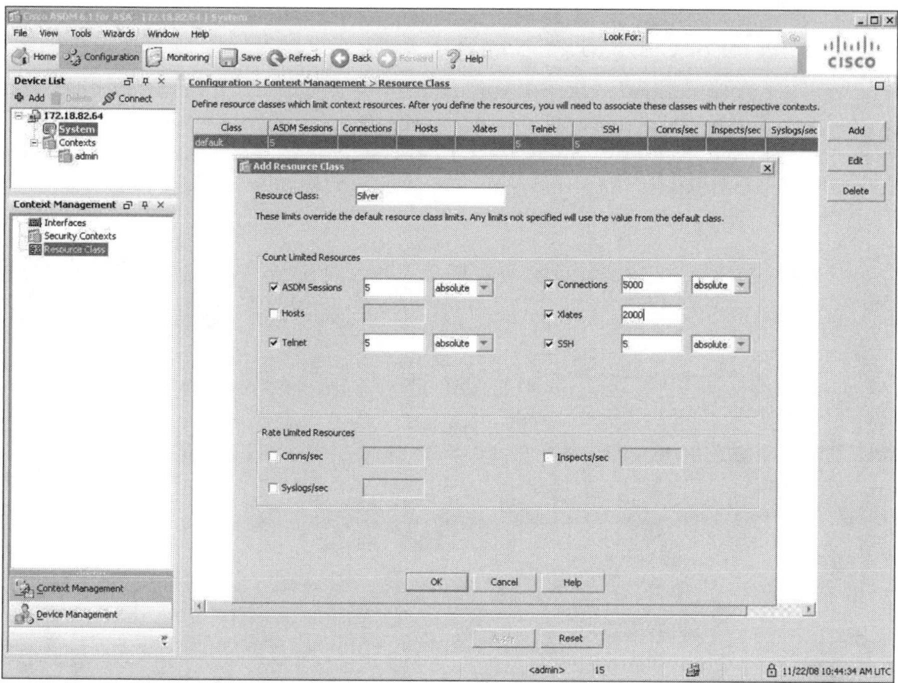

Figure 8-10 *Defining Resource Limits in a Member Class*

- ASDM Sessions = 5
- Telnet Sessions = 5
- SSH Sessions = 5
- Total Connection Limit = 5000
- Total Translations Allowed = 2000

If you prefer to use CLI, you can use the **class** command, followed by the name of the member class. The security appliance puts you in the class sub-configuration menu. You can use the **limit-resource** commands to define the limits, as shown in Example 8-16.

Example 8-16 *Resource Allocation for a Member Class*

```
Chicago(conf)# class Silver
Chicago(config-class)# limit-resource xlates 2000
Chicago(config-class)# limit-resource asdm 5
Chicago(config-class)# limit-resource conns 5000
```

```
Chicago(config-class)# limit-resource ssh 5
Chicago(config-class)# limit-resource telnet 5
```

Step 2: Map Member Class to a Context

The member class, defined in Step 1, is then mapped to a context. Choose **Configuration > System > Connect > Security Context**, select the context you want to assign the member class, and click **Edit**. Under **Resource Assignment**, select the appropriate class from the **Resource Class** drop-down menu and click **OK** when you are finished.

Note If you do not assign a member class to a context, then the context belongs to the default class and uses all resource limits that are defined in the default class.

As shown in Figure 8-11, a member class of **Silver** is mapped to **Bears** context.

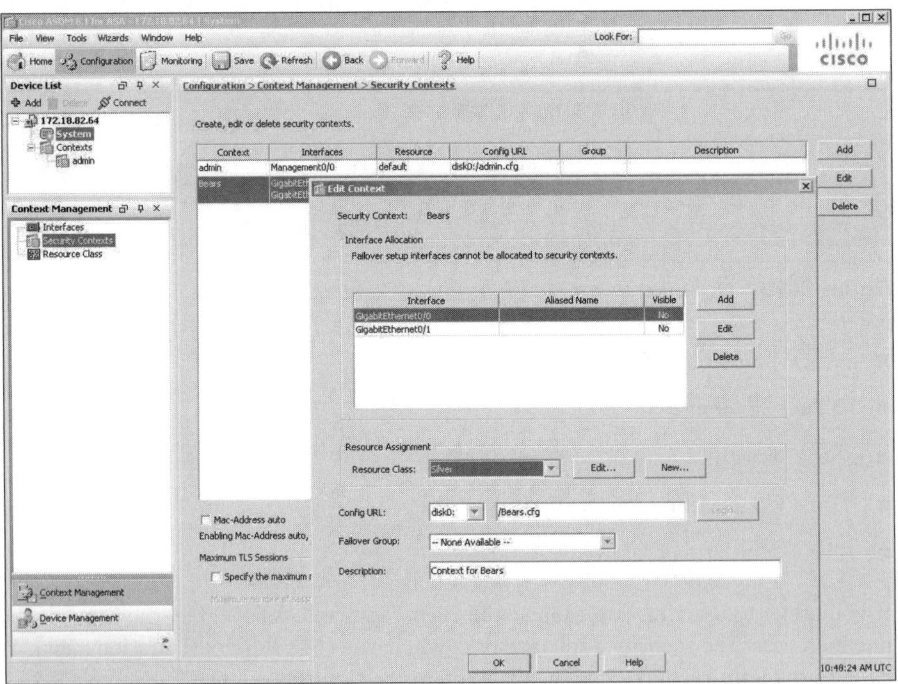

Figure 8-11 *Mapping of a Member Class to a Context*

If you prefer the CLI, use the **member** command followed by the name of the member class in the context definition. As shown in Example 8-17, a member class of **Silver** is linked to **Bears.**

Example 8-17 *Member Class to Context Mapping*

```
Chicago(config)# context Bears
Chicago(config-ctx)# member Silver
```

Deployment Scenarios

The virtual firewall solution is useful in deployments where multiple firewalls are needed to protect traffic to and from the trusted networks. Although virtual firewalls can be deployed in many ways, for ease of understanding, we will cover two design scenarios:

- Virtual firewalls that use non-shared interfaces
- Virtual firewalls that use a shared interface

Note The design scenarios discussed in this section are used solely to reinforce learning. They should be used for reference purposes only.

Virtual Firewalls That Use Non-Shared Interfaces

SecureMe has an office in Chicago that provides firewall services to two small companies, Cubs and Bears. SecureMe's office is located in the same building as the offices of these companies. Cubs and Bears have specific requirements that SecureMe is obliged to meet. However, the appliance in Chicago has two active physical interfaces, and as a result, SecureMe wants to create sub-interfaces to accommodate these customers. To conserve public addresses on the outside interfaces, the administrator uses a subnet mask of 255.255.255.248. Figure 8-12 shows SecureMe's new topology that will be set up in Chicago.

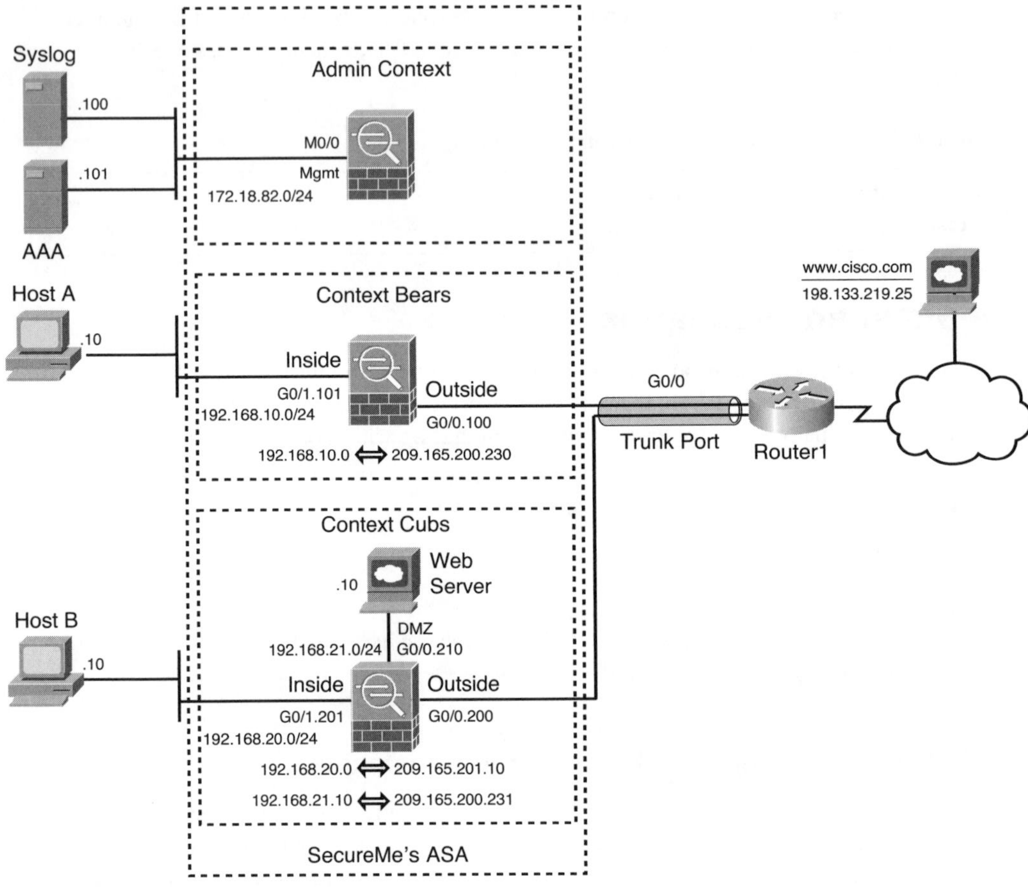

Figure 8-12 *SecureMe's Chicago Multi-Context Mode Topology*

The security requirements for SecureMe, along with Cubs and Bears, are as follows:

SecureMe security requirements:

- Allow SSH sessions from the management network of 172.18.82.0/24. Use an AAA server located at 172.18.82.101.
- Log all the system-generated messages to a syslog server located at 172.18.82.100.

Bears security requirements:

- Allow hosts on the 192.168.10.0/24 subnet to access host 198.133.219.25 (www.cisco.com) on HTTP only. All other traffic should be blocked.
- The source IP address should be translated to 209.165.200.225, using interface PAT.
- Block and log all inbound traffic on the outside interface.

Cubs security requirements:

- All hosts on 192.168.20.0/24 should be able to access the Internet.
- The source IP address should be translated to 209.165.201.10 using PAT.
- Allow HTTP clients from the Internet to access Cub's web server (192.168.21.10) on the DMZ network. This address should appear as 209.165.201.11 for the Internet users.
- Deny and log all other inbound traffic on the outside interface.

Configuration Steps with ASDM

The configuration through ASDM assumes that you have IP connectivity from the ASDM client to the management IP address of the security appliance. The management IP address is 172.18.82.64 and it is allocated to the admin context.

Configuration of System Execution Space

Step 1. Navigate to **Configuration > System > Context Management > Interfaces**, click **Add > Interfaces**, and select **GigabitEthernet0/0** under the hardware port. Specify **100** under both "VLAN ID" and "Subinterface ID". Add a description of **Bears Outside Interface** and then click **OK** to add this subinterface.

Step 2. Navigate to **Configuration > System > Context Management > Interfaces**, click **Add > Interfaces**, and select **GigabitEthernet0/0** under the hardware port. Specify **200** under both "VLAN ID" and "Subinterface ID". Add a description of **Cubs Outside Interface** and then click **OK** to add this subinterface.

Step 3. Navigate to **Configuration > System > Context Management > Interfaces**, click **Add > Interfaces**, and select **GigabitEthernet0/0** under the hardware port. Specify **210** under both "VLAN ID" and "Subinterface ID". Add a description of **Cubs DMZ Interface** and then click **OK** to add this subinterface.

Step 4. Navigate to **Configuration > System > Context Management > Interfaces, click Add > Interfaces**, and select **GigabitEthernet0/1** under the hardware port. Specify **101** under both "VLAN ID" and "Subinterface ID". Add a description of **Bears Inside Interface** and then click **OK** to add this subinterface.

Step 5. Navigate to **Configuration > System > Context Management > Interfaces, click Add > Interfaces** and select **GigabitEthernet0/1** under the hardware port. Specify **201** under both "VLAN ID" and "Subinterface ID". Add a description of **Cubs Inside Interface** and then click **OK** to add this subinterface.

Step 6. Navigate to **Configuration > System > Connect > Context Management > Security Contexts**, click **Add**, and specify **Bears** as the context name in

Security Context. Configure the following interface allocations by clicking **Add** under **Interface Allocation**, then

- Select **GigabitEthernet0/0** from the **Physical Interface** drop-down menu. Select **100** from the Sub Interface range drop-down menu and click **OK.**
- Select **GigabitEthernet0/1** from the **Physical Interface** drop-down menu. Select **101** from the Sub Interface Range drop-down menu and click **OK.**

Step 7. Under **Config URL**, select **disk0:** and then define the configuration filename as **/Bears.cfg.** Finally, under "Description", specify **Bears Context** and click **OK** when you are finished.

Step 8. Navigate to **Configuration > System > Connect > Context Management > Security Contexts**, click **Add**, and specify **Cubs** as the context name in **Security Context.** Configure the following interface allocations by clicking **Add** under **Interface Allocation**, then

- Select **GigabitEthernet0/0** from the **Physical Interface** drop-down menu. Select **200** from the Sub Interface Range drop-down menu and click **OK.**
- Select **GigabitEthernet0/0** from the **Physical Interface** drop-down menu. Select **210** from the Sub Interface Range drop-down menu and click **OK.**
- Select **GigabitEthernet0/1** from the **Physical Interface** drop-down menu. Select **201** from the Sub Interface range drop-down menu and click **OK.**

Step 9. Under **Config URL**, select **disk0:** and then define the configuration filename as **/Cubs.cfg.** Finally, under "Description", specify **Cubs Context** and click **OK** when you are finished.

Configuration of Admin Context

Step 1. Navigate to **Configuration > Context > admin > Connect> Device Management > Logging > Logging Setup** and select the **Enable Logging** option.

Step 2. Navigate to **Configuration > Context > admin > Connect> Device Management > Logging > Syslog Server** and click **Add.** Specify the following under

- Interface: **mgmt**
- IP Address: **172.18.82.100**
- Protocol: **UDP;** Port: **514.** Click **OK** when you are finished.

Step 3. Navigate to **Configuration > Context > admin > Connect> Device Management > Logging > Syslog Setup.** Select **Include timestamps in syslogs** to add timestamps when syslogs are generated.

Step 4. Navigate to **Configuration > Context > admin > Connect > Device Management > Logging > Logging Filters**, select **Syslog Servers** and click **Edit.** Under "Filter on Severity", choose **Informational** from the drop-down menu.

Step 5. Navigate to **Configuration > Context > admin > Connect> Device Management > Management Access > ASDM/HTTPS/Telnet/SSH** and click **Add.** Select **SSH** radio button and configure the following attributes:

- Interface Name: **mgmt**
- IP Address: **172.18.82.0**; Mask: **255.255.255.0.** Click **OK** when you are finished.

Step 6. Navigate to **Configuration > Context > admin > Connect> Device Management > Users/AAA > AAA Server Groups** and select **Add** under the "AAA Server Groups" option. Configure the following attributes:

- Server Group: **RADIUS**
- Protocol: **RADIUS**
- Leave other options as Default. Click **OK** when you are finished.

Step 7. Navigate to **Configuration > Context > admin > Connect> Device Management > Users/AAA > AAA Server Groups.** Click **RADIUS** under "AAA Server Group" and then select **Add** under the "Servers in the Selected Group" option. Configure the following attributes:

- Interface Name: **mgmt**
- Server Name or IP Address: **172.18.82.101**
- Server Secret Key: **C1$c0123**
- Leave other options as Default. Click **OK** when you are finished.

Step 8. Navigate to **Configuration > Context > admin > Connect> Device Management > Users/AAA > AAA Access > Authentication.** Enable **SSH** and select **RADIUS** from the "Server Group" drop-down menu. Click **Apply** when you are finished.

Configuration of Bears Context

Step 1. Navigate to **Configuration > Contexts > Bears > Connect > Device Setup > Interfaces.** Select the **GigabitEthernet0/0.100** interface, click **Edit**, and specify the following attributes:

- Interface Name: **outside**
- Security Level: **0**
- IP Address: **Use Static IP of 209.165.200.225**
- Subnet Mask: **255.255.255.224.** Click **OK** when you are finished.

Step 2. Navigate to **Configuration > Contexts > Bears > Connect > Device Setup > Interfaces.** Select the **GigabitEthernet0/1.101** interface, click **Edit**, and specify the following attributes:

- Interface Name: **inside**
- Security Level: **100**
- IP Address: **Use Static IP of 192.168.10.1**
- Subnet Mask: **255.255.255.0.** Click **OK** when you are finished.

Step 3. Navigate to **Configuration > Contexts > Bears > Connect > Firewall > Access Rules > Add** and select **Add Access Rule.** Configure the following Access Rule:

- Interface: **Inside**
- Action: **Permit**
- Source: **192.168.10.0/24**
- Destination: **198.133.219.25/32**
- Service: **http**
- Enable Logging: **Not Checked.** Click **OK** when you are finished.

Step 4. Navigate to **Configuration > Contexts > Bears > Connect > Firewall > Access Rules > Add** and select **Add Access Rule.** Configure the following Access Rule:

- Interface: **Outside**
- Action: **Deny**
- Source: **any**
- Destination: **any**
- Service: **ip**
- Enable Logging: **Checked.** Click **OK** when you are finished.

Step 5. Navigate to **Configuration > Contexts > Bears > Connect > Firewall > NAT Rules > Add** and select **Add Dynamic NAT Rule.** Under the "Translated" section, click **Manage > Add** and configure the following policy for the Global Address Pool:

- Interface: **outside**
- Pool ID: **1**
- IP Address to Add: **Port Address Translation (PAT),** using the IP address of the interface. Click **Add>>** and then **OK** when you are finished.

Step 6. Configure the following NAT Access Rule under the Original section:

- Interface: **inside**
- Source: **192.168.10.0/24**
- Translated Global Pool ID: **1**. Click **OK** when you are finished.
- Select the **Enable Traffic Through the Firewall Without Address Translation** option.

Configuration of Cubs Context

Step 1. Navigate to **Configuration > Contexts > Cubs > Connect > Device Setup > Interfaces.** Select the **GigabitEthernet0/0.200** interface, click **Edit**, and specify the following attributes:

- Interface Name: **outside**
- Security Level: **0**
- IP Address: **Use Static IP of 209.165.201.1**
- Subnet Mask: **255.255.255.224**. Click **OK** when you are finished.

Step 2. Navigate to **Configuration > Contexts > Cubs > Connect > Device Setup > Interfaces.** Select the **GigabitEthernet0/1.201** interface, click **Edit**, and specify the following attributes:

- Interface Name: **inside**
- Security Level: **100**
- IP Address: **Use Static IP of 192.168.20.1**
- Subnet Mask: **255.255.255.0.** Click **OK** when you are finished.

Step 3. Navigate to **Configuration > Contexts > Cubs > Connect > Device Setup > Interfaces.** Select the **GigabitEthernet0/0.210** interface, click **Edit**, and specify the following attributes:

- Interface Name: **dmz**
- Security Level: **50**
- IP Address: **Use Static IP of 192.168.21.1**
- Subnet Mask: **255.255.255.0**. Click **OK** when you are finished.

Step 4. Navigate to **Configuration > Contexts > Cubs > Connect > Firewall > Access Rules > Add** and select **Add Access Rule.** Configure the following Access Rule:

- Interface: **outside**
- Action: **Permit**
- Source: **any**

- Destination: **209.165.201.11**
- Service: **http**. Click **OK** when you are finished.

Step 5. Navigate to **Configuration > Contexts > Cubs > Connect > Firewall > Access Rules > Add** and select **Add Access Rule.** Configure the following Access Rule:

- Interface: **outside**
- Action: **Deny**
- Source: **any**
- Destination: **any**
- Service: **ip**
- Enable Logging: **Checked.** Click **OK** when you are finished.

Step 6. Navigate to **Configuration > Contexts > Cubs > Connect > Firewall > NAT Rules > Add** and select **Add Dynamic NAT Rule....** Under the **Translated** section, click **Manage > Add** and configure the following policy for the Global Address Pool:

- Interface: **outside**
- Pool ID: **1**
- IP Address to Add: **Port Address Translation (PAT)**
- IP Address: **209.165.201.10**
- Netmask (optional): **255.255.255.255**. Select **Add>>** to move the configured address under "Addresses Pool". Click **OK** when you are finished.

Step 7. Configure the following NAT Access Rule under the **Original** section:

- Interface: **inside**
- Source: **192.168.20.0/24**
- Translated Global Pool ID: **1**. Click **OK** when you are finished.

Step 8. Navigate to **Configuration > Contexts > Cubs > Connect > Firewall > NAT Rules > Add** and select **Add Static NAT Rule.** Configure the following policy for the Static NAT Rule:

- Original Interface: **dmz**
- Source: **192.168.21.10**
- Translated Interface: **outside**
- Source: **209.165.201.11**. Click **OK** when you are finished.
- Select the **Enable traffic through the firewall without address translation** option.

Configuration Steps with CLI

Example 8-18 shows the relevant configuration to achieve the goals just listed. Some of the unrelated CLI commands have been removed for brevity.

Example 8-18 *ASA's Relevant Configuration with Multiple Security Contexts*

```
System Execution Space
Chicago# show run
ASA Version 8.2(1) <system>
!
hostname Chicago
! Main GigabitEthernet0/0 interface
interface GigabitEthernet0/0
! Sub-interface assigned to the Bears context as the outside interface. A VLAN ID
is  assigned to the interface
interface GigabitEthernet0/0.100
 description Bears Outside Interface
 vlan 100
! Sub-interface assigned to the Cubs context as the outside interface. A VLAN ID
is  assigned to the interface
interface GigabitEthernet0/0.200
 description Bears Outside Interface
 vlan 200
! Sub-interface assigned to the Cubs context as the DMZ interface. A VLAN ID is
assigned to the interface
interface GigabitEthernet0/0.210
 description Cubs DMZ Interface
 vlan 210
! Main GigabitEthernet0/1 interface
interface GigabitEthernet0/1
! Sub-interface assigned to the Bears context as the inside interface. A VLAN ID
is  assigned to the interface
interface GigabitEthernet0/1.101
 description Bears Inside Interface
 vlan 101
! Sub-interface assigned to the Cubs context as the inside interface. A VLAN ID
is assigned to the interface
interface GigabitEthernet0/1.201
description Cubs Inside Interface
 vlan 201
! Main Management0/0 interface
interface Management0/0
```

```
! context named "admin" is the designated Admin context
admin-context admin
! "admin" context definition along with the allocated interfaces.
context admin
  description admin Context
  allocate-interface Management0/0
  config-url disk0:/admin.cfg
! "Bears" context definition along with the allocated interfaces.
context Bears
  description Bears Context
  allocate-interface GigabitEthernet0/0.100
  allocate-interface GigabitEthernet0/1.101
  config-url disk0:/Bears.cfg
! "Cubs" context definition along with the allocated interfaces.
context Cubs
  description Cubs Context
  allocate-interface GigabitEthernet0/0.200
  allocate-interface GigabitEthernet0/0.210
  allocate-interface GigabitEthernet0/1.201
  config-url disk0:/Cubs.cfg
Admin Context
Chicago/admin# show running
ASA Version 8.2(1) <context>
!
hostname admin
!Management interface of the admin context with security level set to 100
interface Management0/0
 nameif mgmt
 security-level 100
 ip address 172.18.82.64 255.255.255.0
 management-only
!
!configuration of a syslog server with timestamped logging level set to informa-
tional
logging enable
logging timestamp
logging trap informational
logging host mgmt 172.18.82.100
!
!configuration of a AAA server using RADIUS for authentication
aaa-server RADIUS protocol radius
aaa-server RADIUS (mgmt) host 172.18.82.101
key C1$c0123
!setting up SSH authentication
```

```
aaa authentication ssh console RADIUS
!SSH to the admin context is allowed from the mgmt interface
ssh 172.18.82.0 255.255.255.0 mgmt
Bears Context
Chicago/Bears# show running
ASA Version 8.2(1) <context>
!
hostname Bears
!Outside interface of the Bears context with security level set to 0
interface GigabitEthernet0/0.100
 nameif outside
 security-level 0
 ip address 209.165.200.225 255.255.255.224
! outside interface of the Bears context with security level set to 100
interface GigabitEthernet0/1.101
 nameif inside
 security-level 100
 ip address 192.168.10.1 255.255.255.0
!
! Access-list configuration to permit web traffic initiated from the inside net-
work to 198.133.219.25
access-list inside_access_in extended permit tcp 192.168.10.0 255.255.255.0 host
198.133.219.25 eq www
! Access-list configuration to deny all internet originated traffic.
access-list outside_access_in extended deny ip any any log
! NAT configuration to allow inside hosts to get Internet connectivity
global (outside) 1 interface
nat (inside) 1 192.168.10.0 255.255.255.0
! The access-list is applied to the inside interface.
access-group inside_access_in in interface inside
! The access-list is applied to the outside interface.
access-group outside_access_in in interface outside
! Default route
route outside 0.0.0.0 0.0.0.0 209.165.200.226 1
Cubs Context
Chicago/Cubs# show running
ASA Version 8.2(1) <context>
!
hostname Cubs
!Outside interface of the Cubs context with security level set to 0
interface GigabitEthernet0/0.200
 nameif outside
 security-level 0
 ip address 209.165.201.1 255.255.255.224
!DMZ interface of the Cubs context with security level set to 50
```

```
interface GigabitEthernet0/0.210
 nameif dmz
 security-level 50
 ip address 192.168.21.1 255.255.255.0
!Inside interface of the Cubs context with security level set to 100
interface GigabitEthernet0/1.201
nameif inside
 security-level 100
 ip address 192.168.20.1 255.255.255.0
!
!Access-list configuration to allow web traffic.
access-list outside_access_in extended permit tcp any host 209.165.201.11 eq www
access-list outside_access_in extended deny ip any any log
!NAT configuration to allow inside hosts to get Internet connectivity
nat (inside) 1 192.168.20.0 255.255.255.0
global (outside) 1 209.165.201.10 netmask 255.255.255.255
!Static address translation for the Web-Server
static (dmz,outside) 209.165.201.11 192.168.21.10 netmask 255.255.255.255
! The access-list is applied to the outside interface.
access-group outside_access_in in interface outside
! Default route
route outside 0.0.0.0 0.0.0.0 209.165.201.2 1
```

Virtual Firewalls That Use a Shared Interface

SecureMe, acting as an internet service provider, has started providing managed firewall services to its end customers. Two of SecureMe's customers, Dodgers and Lakers, have unique requirements with one thing in common: They want hosts on their private network to access the Internet. SecureMe wants to conserve their routable public space and prefers to use a shared outside segment to achieve this goal. Because the security appliance has limited active physical interfaces, SecureMe wants to create sub-interfaces for the inside networks to accommodate these customers.

Additionally, SecureMe wants to implement resource management to ensure that they can sell different classes of services to their end customers. Dodgers will be restricted to have up to 1000 connections per second, whereas Lakers will not be restricted to any classes.

Figure 8-13 shows SecureMe's proposed topology.

The security requirements for SecureMe, along with Dodgers and Lakers, are as follows:

SecureMe Security Requirements:

- The SecureMe global policy restricts access of the security appliance to valid and authorized users on the AAA server. Use an AAA server located at 172.18.82.101 with a shared key of C1$c0123.

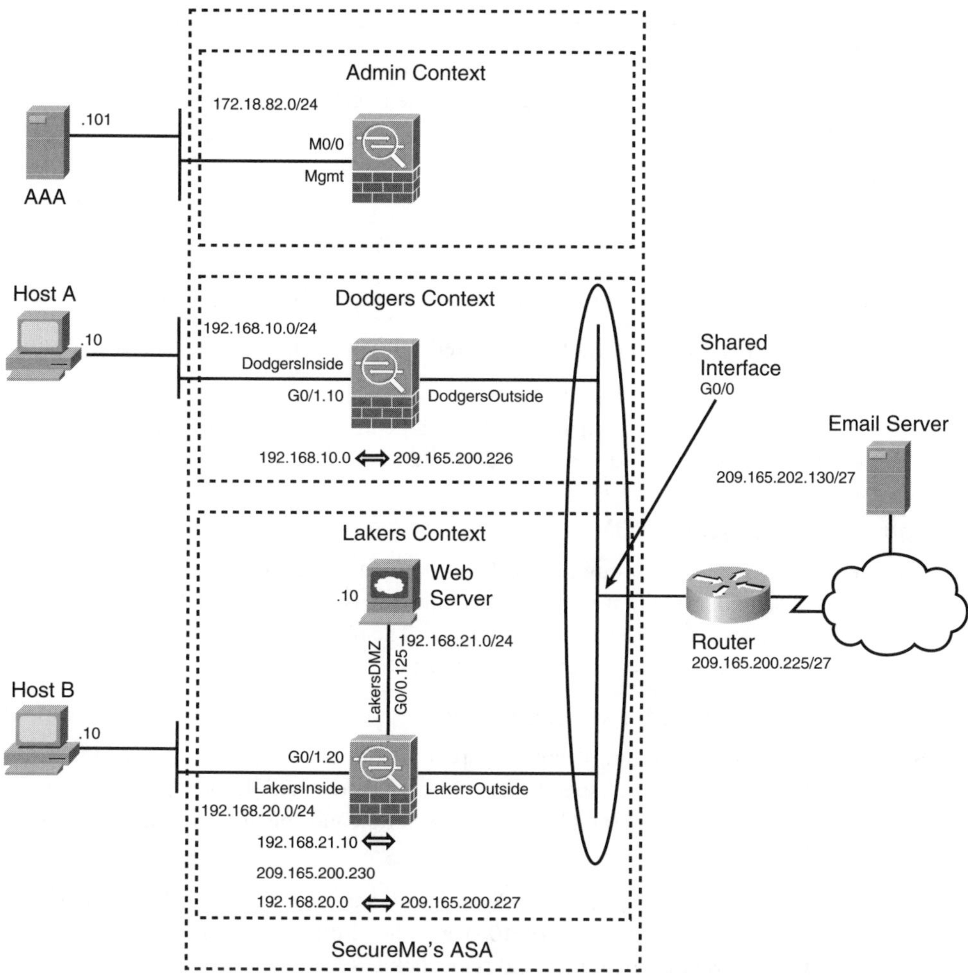

Figure 8-13 *SecureMe's Multi-Context Mode Using Shared Interfaces*

- SecureMe does not have many public addresses available, so it is using interface PAT for address translation in all contexts.
- SecureMe does not want the administrators of the individual security contexts to be able to determine the interface assignment for their contexts.
- Only SSH and ASDM are allowed for device and context management.

Dodgers Security Requirements:

- The hosts in the Dodgers context are allowed to access a web server in the Lakers context. The original IP address of the server is 192.168.21.10.

- The hosts are allowed to check their email messages. The IP of the email server is 209.165.202.130.
- Translate private IP addresses using the outside interface's IP address (209.165.200.226).
- Block and log all inbound traffic.

Lakers Security Requirements:

- The host in the Lakers context can freely access any resources on the Internet.
- The source IP address should be translated to the outside interface address through PAT.
- Block and log all inbound traffic on the outside interface, except for the traffic coming from the Dodgers inside network destined to the web server.

Configuration Steps with ASDM

The relevant configuration through ASDM is discussed in the following sections. These configuration steps assume that you have IP connectivity from the ASDM client to the management IP address of the security appliance. The management IP address is 172.18.82.64 and it is allocated to the admin context.

Configuration of System Execution Space

Step 1. Navigate to **Configuration > System > Connect > Context Management > Resource Class** and specify a resource class of **Gold.** Under "Rate Limited Resources", select the **Conns/sec** check box and specify **1000** as the value. Click **OK.**

Step 2. Navigate to **Configuration > System > Connect > Context Management > Interfaces > GigabitEthernet0/0** and click **Edit.** Add a description of **Outside Shared Interface** and then click **OK.**

Step 3. Navigate to **Configuration > System > Connect > Context Management > Interfaces**, click **Add > Interfaces** and select **GigabitEthernet0/1** under the hardware port. Specify **10** under both "VLAN ID" and "Subinterface ID". Add a description of **Dodgers Inside Interface** and then click **OK** to add this subinterface.

Step 4. Navigate to **Configuration > System > Interfaces, click Add > Interfaces** and select **GigabitEthernet0/1** under the hardware port. Specify **20** under both "VLAN ID" and "Subinterface ID". Add a description of **Lakers Inside Interface** and then click **OK** to add this subinterface.

Step 5. Navigate to **Configuration > System > Interfaces, click Add > Interfaces** and select **GigabitEthernet0/1** under the hardware port. Specify **25** under both "VLAN ID" and "Subinterface ID". Add a description of **Lakers DMZ Interface** and then click **OK** to add this subinterface.

Step 6. Navigate to **Configuration > System > Connect > Context Management > Security Contexts**, click **Add**, and specify **Dodgers** as the context name in **Security Context**. Configure the following interface allocations by clicking **Add**, then

- Select **GigabitEthernet0/0** from the "Physical Interface" drop-down menu. Enable **Used Aliased Name in Context** and specify **DodgersOutside** as the interface name. Click **OK**.
- Select **GigabitEthernet0/1** from the "Physical Interface" drop-down menu. Select **10** from the Sub Interface Range drop-down menu and enable **Used Aliased Name in Context**. Specify **DodgersInside** as the interface name and click **OK**.

Step 7. Under **Resource Assignment**, select **Gold** from the drop-down menu. To specify a **Config URL**, select **disk0:** and then define the configuration filename as **/Dodgers.cfg**. Finally, under Description, type **Dodgers Context** and click OK.

Step 8. Navigate to **Configuration > System > Connect > Context Management > Security Contexts**, click **Add**, and specify **Lakers** as the context name in **Security Context**. Configure the following interface allocations by clicking **Add**, then

- Select **GigabitEthernet0/0** from the "Physical Interface" drop-down menu. Enable **Used Aliased Name in Context** and specify **LakersOutside** as the interface name. Click **OK**.
- Select **GigabitEthernet0/1** from the "Physical Interface" drop-down menu. Select **20** from the Sub Interface Range drop-down menu and enable **Used Aliased Name in Context**. Specify **LakersInside** as the interface name and click **OK**.
- Select **GigabitEthernet0/1** from the "Physical Interface" drop-down menu. Select **25** from the Sub Interface range drop-down menu and enable **Used Aliased Name in Context**. Specify **LakersDMZ** as the interface name and click **OK**.

Step 9. Under **Config URL**, select **disk0:** and then define the configuration filename as **/Lakers.cfg**. Finally, under Description, specify **Lakers Context** and click OK.

Step 10. Navigate to **Configuration > System > Connect > Context Management > Security Contexts** and enable **MAC-Address Auto** so that the security appliance can auto-generate a unique MAC address for each shared interface in a context.

Configuration of Admin Context

Step 1. Navigate to **Configuration > Context > admin > Connect> Device Management > Management Access > ASDM/HTTPS/Telnet/SSH** and click **Add.** Select the **ASDM/HTTPS** radio button and configure the following attributes:

- Interface Name: **mgmt**
- IP Address: **172.18.82.0**; Mask: **255.255.255.0.** Click **OK** when you are finished.

Step 2. Navigate to **Configuration > Context > admin > Connect> Device Management > Management Access > ASDM/HTTPS/Telnet/SSH** and click **Add.** Select the **SSH** radio button and configure the following attributes:

- Interface Name: **mgmt**
- IP Address: **172.18.82.0**; Mask: **255.255.255.0.** Click **OK.**

Step 3. Navigate to **Configuration > Context > admin > Connect> Device Management > Users/AAA > AAA Server Groups** and select **Add** under the "AAA Server Groups" option. Configure the following attributes:

- Server Group: **RADIUS**
- Protocol: **RADIUS**

Step 4. Leave other options as Default. Click **OK.** Navigate to **Configuration > Context > admin > Connect> Device Management > Users/AAA > AAA Server Groups.** Click **RADIUS** under "AAA Server Group" and then select **Add** under the "Servers in the Selected Group" option. Configure the following attributes:

- Interface Name: **mgmt**
- Server Name or IP Address: **172.18.82.101**
- Server Secret Key: **C1$c0123**
- Leave other options as Default. Click **OK.**

Step 5. Navigate to **Configuration > Context > admin > Connect> Device Management > Users/AAA > AAA Access > Authentication.** Enable SSH and HTTP/ASDM and select **RADIUS** from the "Server Group" drop-down menu for both options. Click **Apply.**

Configuration of Dodgers Context

Step 1. Navigate to **Configuration > Contexts > Dodgers > Connect > Device Setup > Interfaces.** Select the **DodgersOutside** interface, click **Edit,** and specify the following attributes:

- Interface Name: **outside**

- Security Level: **0**
- IP Address: **Use Static IP of 209.165.200.226**
- Subnet Mask: **255.255.255.224.** Click **OK.**

Step 2. Navigate to **Configuration > Contexts > Dodgers > Connect > Device Setup > Interfaces.** Select the **DodgersInside** interface, click **Edit**, and specify the following attributes:

- Interface Name: **inside**
- Security Level: **100**
- IP Address: **Use Static IP of 192.168.10.1**

Subnet Mask: 255.255.255.0. Click **OK.**

Step 3. Navigate to **Configuration > Contexts > Dodgers > Connect > Firewall > Access Rules > Add** and select **Add Access Rule.** Configure the following Access Rule:

- Interface: **inside**
- Action: **Permit**
- Source: **192.168.10.0/24**
- Destination: **209.165.202.130/32**
- Service: **smtp**
- Enable Logging: **Checked.** Click **OK.**

Step 4. Navigate to **Configuration > Contexts > Dodgers > Connect > Firewall > Access Rules > Add** and select **Add Access Rule.** Configure the following Access Rule:

- Interface: **inside**
- Action: **Permit**
- Source: **192.168.10.0/24**
- Destination: **209.165.200.230/32**
- Service: **http**
- Enable Logging: **Checked.** Click **OK.**

Step 5. Navigate to **Configuration > Contexts > Dodgers > Connect > Firewall > Access Rules > Add** and select **Add Access Rule.** Configure the following Access Rule:

- Interface: **Outside**
- Action: **Deny**

- Source: **any**
- Destination: **any**
- Service: **ip**
- Enable Logging: **Checked.** Click **OK.**

Step 6. Navigate to **Configuration > Contexts > Dodgers > Connect > Firewall > NAT Rules > Add** and select **Add Dynamic NAT Rule.** Under the **Translated** section, click **Manage > Add** and configure the following policy for the Global Address Pool:

- Interface: **outside**
- Pool ID: **1**
- IP Address to Add: **Port Address Translation (PAT),** using the IP address of the interface. Click **Add>>** and then **OK.**

Step 7. Configure the following NAT Access Rule under the **Original** section:

- Interface: **inside**
- Source: **192.168.10.0/24**
- Translated Global Pool ID: **1.** Click **OK.**
- Select the **Enable Traffic Through the Firewall Without Address Translation** option.

Configuration of Lakers Context

Step 1. Navigate to **Configuration > Contexts > Lakers > Connect > Device Setup > Interfaces.** Select the **LakersOutside** interface, click **Edit,** and specify the following attributes:

- Interface Name: **outside**
- Security Level: **0**
- IP Address: **Use Static IP of 209.165.200.227**
- Subnet Mask: **255.255.255.224.** Click **OK.**

Step 2. Navigate to **Configuration > Contexts > Lakers > Connect > Device Setup > Interfaces.** Select the **LakersInside** interface, click **Edit,** and specify the following attributes:

- Interface Name: **inside**
- Security Level: **100**
- IP Address: **Use Static IP of 192.168.20.1**
- Subnet Mask: **255.255.255.0.** Click **OK.**

Step 3. Navigate to **Configuration > Contexts > Lakers > Connect > Device Setup > Interfaces**. Select the **LakersDMZ** interface, click **Edit**, and specify the following attributes:

- Interface Name: **dmz**
- Security Level: **50**
- IP Address: **Use Static IP of 192.168.21.1**
- Subnet Mask: **255.255.255.0**. Click **OK**.

Step 4. Navigate to **Configuration > Contexts > Lakers > Connect > Firewall > Access Rules > Add** and select **Add Access Rule**. Configure the following Access Rule:

- Interface: **outside**
- Action: **Permit**
- Source: **209.165.200.226**
- Destination: **209.165.200.230**
- Service: **http**
- Enable Logging: **Checked**. Click **OK**.

Step 5. Navigate to **Configuration > Contexts > Lakers > Connect > Firewall > Access Rules > Add** and select **Add Access Rule**. Configure the following Access Rule:

- Interface: **outside**
- Action: **Deny**
- Source: **any**
- Destination: **any**
- Service: **ip**
- Enable Logging: Checked. Click **OK**.

Step 6. Navigate to **Configuration > Contexts > Lakers > Connect > Firewall > NAT Rules > Add** and select **Add Dynamic NAT Rule**. Under the **Translated** section, click **Manage > Add** and configure the following policy for the Global Address Pool:

- Interface: **outside**
- Pool ID: **1**
- IP Address to Add: **Port Address Translation (PAT)**, using IP address of the interface. Click **Add>>** and then **OK**.

Step 7. Configure the following NAT Access Rule under the **Original** section:

- Interface: **inside**
- Source: **192.168.20.0/24**
- Translated Global Pool ID: **1**. Click **OK.**

Step 8. Navigate to **Configuration > Contexts > Lakers > Connect > Firewall > NAT Rules > Add** and select **Add Static NAT Rule.** Configure the following policy for the Static NAT Rule:

- Original Interface: **dmz**
- Source: **192.168.21.10**
- Translated Interface: **outside**
- Source: **209.165.200.230**. Click **OK.**
- Select the **Enable Traffic Through the Firewall Without Address Translation** option.

Configuration Steps Using CLI

Example 8-19 shows the relevant configuration to achieve the goals just listed. Some of the unrelated CLI commands have been removed for brevity.

Example 8-19 *ASA's Relevant Configuration with Multiple Security Contexts*

```
System Execution Space
LA-ASA# show running
ASA Version 8.2(1) <system>
hostname LA-ASA
!
mac-address auto
!
! Management0/0 interface
interface Management0/0
description Management Interface
!
! Main GigabitEthernet0/0 interface used as the shared outside interface
interface GigabitEthernet0/0
description Outside Shared Interface
!
! Main GigabitEthernet0/1 interface
interface GigabitEthernet0/1

! Sub-interface assigned to Dodgers as the inside interface. A VLAN ID is
assigned to the interface
```

```
interface GigabitEthernet0/1.10
 description Dodgers Inside Interface
 vlan 10

! Sub-interface assigned to Lakers as the inside interface. A VLAN ID is assigned
to the interface
interface GigabitEthernet0/1.20
 description Lakers Inside Interface
 vlan 20
!
! Sub-interface assigned to Laker as the dmz interface. A VLAN ID is assigned to
the  interface
interface GigabitEthernet0/1.25
 description Lakers DMZ Interface
 vlan 25
!
class Gold
  limit-resource rate Conns 1000

! context named "admin" is the designated Admin context
admin-context admin
! "admin" context definition along with the allocated interfaces.
context admin
  allocate-interface Management0/0
  config-url disk0:/admin.cfg
!
! "Dodgers" context definition along with the allocated interfaces.
context Dodgers
  description Dodgers Context
  member Gold
  allocate-interface GigabitEthernet0/0 DodgersOutside
  allocate-interface GigabitEthernet0/1.10 DodgersInside
  config-url disk0:/Dodgers.cfg
!
! "Lakers" context definition along with the allocated interfaces.
context Lakers
  description Lakers Context
  allocate-interface GigabitEthernet0/0 LakersOutisde
  allocate-interface GigabitEthernet0/1.20 LakersInside
  allocate-interface GigabitEthernet0/1.25 LakersDMZ
  config-url disk0:/Lakers.cfg
Admin Context

LA-ASA/admin# show running
ASA Version 8.2(1) <system>
hostname LA-ASA
```

```
! Management interface of the admin context with security level set to 100
interface Management0/0
 nameif mgmt
 security-level 100
 ip address 172.18.82.64 255.255.255.0
 management-only

! RADIUS server with an IP address of 172.18.82.101
aaa-server RADIUS protocol radius
aaa-server RADIUS (mgmt) host 172.18.82.101
 key C1$c0123

! AAA authentication for SSH and HTTP sessions
aaa authentication ssh console RADIUS
aaa authentication http console RADIUS

! HTTP Server for ASDM
http server enable
http 172.18.82.0 255.255.255.0 mgmt

! SSH sessions to be accepted from 172.18.82.0/24
ssh 172.18.82.0 255.255.255.0 mgmt
<output removed for brevity>
```

Dodgers Context

```
LA-ASA/Dodgers# show run
ASA Version 8.2(1) <system>
hostname Dodgers

!outside interface of the Dodgers context with security level set to 0
interface DodgersOutside
 nameif outside
 security-level 0
 ip address 209.165.200.226 255.255.255.224
!
!inside interface of the Dodgers context with security level set to 100
interface DodgersInside
 nameif inside
 security-level 100
 ip address 192.168.10.1 255.255.255.0
! <output removed for brevity>
!Access-list configuration to allow email and web traffic. The access-list is
applied to the inside interface.
```

```
access-list inside_access_in extended permit tcp 192.168.10.0 255.255.255.0 host
209.165.202.130 eq smtp log
access-list inside_access_in extended permit tcp 192.168.10.0 255.255.255.0 host
209.165.200.230 eq www log
!Access-list configuration to deny all packets. The access-list is applied to the
outside interface.
access-list outside_access_in extended deny ip any any log

! <output removed for brevity>
global (outside) 1 interface
nat (inside) 1 192.168.10.0 255.255.255.0
access-group inside_access_in in interface inside
access-group outside_access_in in interface outside

! Default Route
route outside 0.0.0.0 0.0.0.0 209.165.200.225 1
```

Lakers Context

```
LA-ASA/Lakers# show running
ASA Version 8.2(1) <system>
hostname Lakers

!outside interface of the Lakers context with security level set to 0
interface LakersOutside
 nameif outside
 security-level 0
ip address 209.165.200.227 255.255.255.224
!
!inside interface of the Lakers context with security level set to 100
interface LakersInside
 nameif inside
 security-level 100
 ip address 192.168.20.1 255.255.255.0
!
!dmz interface of the Lakers context with security level set to 50
interface LakersDMZ
 nameif dmz
 security-level 50
 ip address 192.168.21.1 255.255.255.0
!
<output removed for brevity>
!Access-list configuration to allow incoming web request. The access-list is
applied to the outside interface.
access-list outside_access_in extended permit tcp host 209.165.200.226 host
209.165.200.230 eq www
```

```
access-list outside_access_in extended deny ip any any log
access-group outside_access_in in interface outside
<output removed for brevity>
!Address translation policies.
global (outside) 1 interface
nat (inside) 1 192.168.20.0 255.255.255.0
static (dmz,outside) 209.165.200.230 192.168.21.10 netmask 255.255.255.255
!Default Route
route outside 0.0.0.0 0.0.0.0 209.165.200.225 1
```

Monitoring and Troubleshooting the Security Contexts

Cisco ASA provides show and debug commands that are useful to check the health of the appliance or to isolate a problem. The necessary show and debug commands that are used to manage multiple security contexts in the appliance are discussed here.

Monitoring

After the system is converted to multiple contexts, the first thing to verify is that the system is using the new mode by using the show mode command, as shown in Example 8-20.

Example 8-20 *Output of show mode*

```
Chicago# show mode
Security context mode: multiple
```

After you verify that the system is running in multiple mode, configure the necessary contexts and assign the appropriate interfaces. A good way to check whether the interfaces have been correctly assigned to the proper context is to use the show context command. It lists all the configured contexts, the allocated interfaces, and the configuration URL. Example 8-21 shows the output of **show context** in the Chicago ASA, after an administrator logs into the system execution space.

Example 8-21 *Output of show context in the System Execution Space*

```
Chicago# show context
Context Name    Class     Interfaces                   URL
*admin                     Management0/0                disk0:/admin.cfg
 Bears                     GigabitEthernet0/0.100,     disk0:/Bears.cfg
                            GigabitEthernet0/1.101
 Cubs                      GigabitEthernet0/0.200,     disk0:/Cubs.cfg
                            GigabitEthernet0/0.201,
                            GigabitEthernet0/0.210
Total active Security Contexts: 3
```

The asterisk (*) next to admin indicates that this is an admin context. Another way to find out which context is designated as the admin context is to use the show admin-context command, as illustrated in Example 8-22.

Example 8-22 *Output of show admin-context in the System Execution Space*

```
Chicago# show admin-context
Admin: admin disk0:/admin.cfg
```

A context administrator can view the context settings from within his security context. In Example 8-23, the administrator of the Cubs context is verifying the allocated interfaces and the configuration URL.

Example 8-23 *Output of show context from a Security Context*

```
Chicago/Cubs# show context
Context Name      Class      Interfaces              URL
Cubs                      GigabitEthernet0/0.200,     disk0:/Cubs.cfg
                          GigabitEthernet0/0.201,
                          GigabitEthernet0/0.210
```

Cisco ASA allows monitoring of CPU usage per security context. This is useful to determine which context is utilizing the most CPU cycles. Use the show cpu usage context all command to check the CPU utilization on each of the configured security contexts. In Example 8-24, the total system CPU utilization is 9.5 percent averaged over 5 seconds, 9.2 percent averaged over 1 minute, and 9.3 percent averaged over 5 minutes. The Cubs security context is using the most CPU cycles, averaging 5 percent over 5 seconds, 1 minute, and 5 minutes.

Example 8-24 *Output of show cpu usage context all from the System Execution Space*

```
Chicago# show cpu usage context all
5 sec  1 min  5 min  Context Name
9.5%   9.2%   9.3%   system
0.3%   0.0%   0.1%   admin
5.0%   5.0%   5.0%   Bears
4.2%   4.2%   4.2%   Cubs
```

Troubleshooting

For troubleshooting purposes, Cisco ASA includes a number of important debug and syslog messages to help you isolate the issue. Below are four troubleshooting scenarios related to security contexts.

Security Contexts Are Not Added

When adding new contexts, the Cisco security appliance displays a message that the new security contexts creation failed, as shown in Example 8-25.

Example 8-25 *Security Context Creation Failure*

```
Chicago(config)# context  WhiteSox
Creating context 'WhiteSox'...
Cannot create context 'WhiteSox': limit of 10 contexts exceeded
ERROR: Creation for context 'WhiteSox' failed
```

The Cisco ASA appliance complains about exceeding the maximum number of security contexts allowed in this device. To verify the maximum number of allowed security contexts, use the show version command, as shown in Example 8-26.

Example 8-26 *Verifying the Maximum Number of Security Contexts*

```
Chicago# show version | include Security Contexts
Security Contexts            : 10
```

Depending on the security appliance model number, the administrator can add the maximum allowed security context number. Refer to Chapter 3, "Initial Setup and System Maintenance," for more information about the allowed number of security contexts in a Cisco ASA.

Security Contexts Are Not Saved on the Local Disk

If the security context configuration files are stored locally on the disk butthe appliance is having trouble either retrieving or saving them, you can enable debug disk to gather information.

In Example 8-27, debug disk file, file-verbose, and filesystem are enabled with a log level of 255. In this example, the administrator saves the running configuration into the Flash file system. The highlighted entries show that the appliance opens the running configuration file from the disk and writes the new contents. If Flash is corrupt, the administrator sees failed attempts to read or write files. These messages are analyzed by the Cisco Technical Assistance (TAC) engineers.

Example 8-27 *Output of debug disk*

```
Chicago# debug disk file 255
Chicago# debug disk file-verbose 255
Chicago# debug disk filesystem 255
Chicago# write memory
Building IFS: Opening: file system:/running-config, flags 1, mode 0
IFS: Opened: file system:/running-config as fd 0
IFS: Fioctl: fd 0, fn 5, arg 370e7e0
configuration...
IFS: Read: fd 1, bytes 147456
IFS: Read: fd 1, bytes 146664
IFS: disk0:/.private/startup-config 100% chance ascii text
<Output removed for brevity>
1047 IFS: Close: fd 0
bytes copied in 4.40 secs (261 bytes/sec)IFS: Write: fd 0, bytes 1
```

Security Contexts Are Not Saved on the FTP Server

If the security appliance is having issues when saving and retrieving configuration files from an FTP server, use the debug ftp client command to isolate the issue. In Example 8-28, the appliance is being configured to use an FTP server. The debug shows that the user password is incorrect in the configuration URL.

Example 8-28 *Output of debug ftp client*

```
Chicago(config)# debug ftp client
Chicago# context Cubs
Chicago(config-ctx)# config-url ftp://cisco:cisco123@172.18.82.101/Cubs.cfg
IFS: Opening: file ftp://cisco:cisco123@172.18.82.101/Cubs.cfg, flags 1, mode 0
IFS: Opened: file ftp://cisco:cisco123@172.18.82.101/Cubs.cfg as fd 0
IFS: Fioctl: fd 0, fn 5, arg 279bc64
Loading Cubs.cfg
FTP: 220 Please enter your user name.
FTP: —-> USER cisco
FTP: 331 User name okay, Need password.
FTP: —-> PASS *
FTP: 530 Password not accepted.
FTP: —-> QUIT
FTP: 221 Goodbye. Control connection closed.
IFS: Close: fd 0
```

User Having Connectivity Issues When Shared Security Contexts Are Used

As shown earlier in Figure 8-12, when Host A in the Bears context is not able to reach Host B in the Cubs context, the administrator can take the following steps to isolate the issue:

Step 1. Ping the IP address of the inside interface of Bears from Host A. If successful, move to Step 2; otherwise, check to see whether there is a control-plane ACL that is blocking the packets. Also verify that physical connectivity exists between the host and the inside interface.

Step 2. Ping the IP address of the outside interface of Cubs from Host A. If successful, move to Step 3; otherwise, check the outbound ACL and NAT configuration on the Bears context. Additionally, verify that the control-plane ACL on Cubs allows ICMP traffic from Host A.

Step 3. Because this topology uses a shared interface, check the NAT configuration on the Cubs context. Ping from Host A to Host B and verify that the outbound ACL on inside interface of Cubs does not block the ICMP packets.

Step 4. If Host A is still not able to communicate with Host B, follow Step 1 through Step 3 again, except this time work backwards and ping from Host B to Host A. You can use the **show asp drop** command and look for any potential packet drops. Additionally, log in to the admin context and make sure that syslogs are enabled. Look for any potential logs indicating an issue.

Summary

Multiple-context mode is a robust feature that provides a cost-effective firewall solution by integrating multiple firewalls into one physical appliance. Each security context has its own interfaces, security policies, and routing tables. The packets that traverse through the security contexts are classified based on the source interface, the destination IP address, or the unique MAC-address. This chapter discussed the configuration steps and provided deployment scenarios to help you understand this concept better. For troubleshooting purposes, the chapter introduced the relevant show and **debug** commands and walked you through isolating the issues related to security contexts.

Chapter 9

Transparent Firewalls

This chapter covers the following topics:

- Architectural overview
- Restrictions within transparent firewalls
- Configuration of transparent firewalls
- Deployment scenarios
- Monitoring and troubleshooting

Traditionally, network firewalls have been deployed to filter traffic passing through them. These firewalls usually examine the upper-layer headers (Layer 3 or above) and occasionally the data payload in the packets. The packets are then either allowed or dropped based on the configured access control lists (ACLs). These firewalls, commonly referred as routed firewalls, segregate protected networks from unprotected ones by acting as an extra hop in the network design. They route packets from one IP subnet to another subnet by using the Layer 3 routing table. In most cases, these firewalls translate addresses to protect the original IP addressing scheme used in the network.

Figure 9-1 illustrates a routed firewall protecting the inside network and translating the source address of Host A from 192.168.1.2 to 209.165.201.2 for the traffic destined to www.cisco.com.

Routed firewalls do not provide a way to filter packets that traverse from one host to another in the same LAN segment. The Layer 3 firewalls require a new network segment to be created when they are inserted into a network, which requires quite a bit of planning, network downtime, and reconfiguration of network devices. To avoid these issues, stealth or transparent firewalls have been developed to provide LAN-based protection. An administrator can place a transparent firewall between the LAN and the next-hop Layer 3 device (a router) without having to readdress the network devices.

By using transparent firewalls, administrators can optionally inspect Layer 2 traffic and filter disallowed traffic.

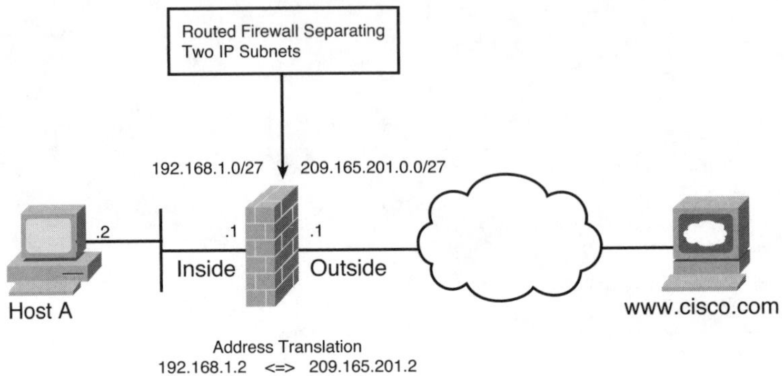

Figure 9-1 *Routed Firewall*

Figure 9-2 shows SecureMe's network running a transparent firewall. SecureMe wants to inspect all traffic before it hits the default gateway. When the host 192.168.1.2 sends traffic destined to www.cisco.com, the firewall makes sure that the packets are allowed before passing them to the default gateway, 192.168.1.1. In this case, the default gateway router is responsible for translating the 192.168.1.0/27 subnet to 209.165.201.0/27 to achieve the Internet connectivity.

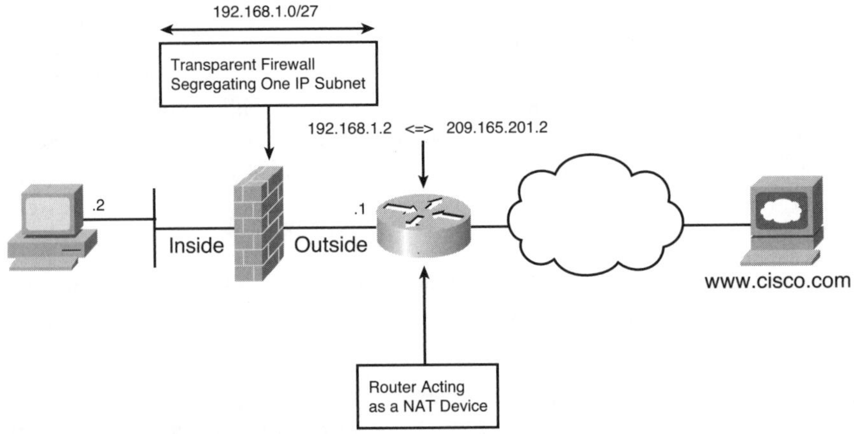

Figure 9-2 *Transparent Firewall*

Table 9-1 summarizes major differences between routed and transparent firewalls.

Table 9-1 *Contrasting Routed and Transparent Firewalls*

Features	Routed Firewall	Transparent Firewall
Interface	Can use all available interfaces, which can be further subdivided.	Supports only two interfaces.
Single-mode addressing	IP address assignment at the interface level.	IP address assignment at the global level, which is solely used for management purposes.
Multimode addressing	Unique IP address assignment at the interface level.	A unique IP address for each context for management purposes.
IPv6 addressing	IPv6 is supported.	IPv6 is supported in version 8.2(1) or higher.
Routing protocols	Supports RIP, EIGRP, and OSPF as the dynamic routing protocols.	Does not participate in routing protocols but can still pass routing protocol traffic through it. You can define static routes for the traffic originated by the ASA.
Non-IP traffic	Does not allow passing non-IP traffic.	Allows IP and non-IP traffic to pass through it.
Network topology	Adds an extra hop on the network if you set up routed interfaces.	Does not add an extra hop; thus, no need to readdress network addressing.
NAT[1]	Supports both static and dynamic NAT/PAT. Also supports interface PAT.	Supports both static and dynamic NAT/PAT. Does not support interface PAT.
Quality of service	Supports QoS.	Does not support QoS.
Multicast	Supports multicast using PIM-SM.	Does not participate in multicast. However, it allows passing multicast traffic through the use of the ACLs.
Inspection	Inspects Layer 3 and higher packet headers.	Inspects Layer 2 and higher packet headers.
Dynamic DNS	Supports Dynamic DNS.	No Dynamic DNS support.
DHCP Relay	Supports DHCP relay.	Does not support DHCP relay. However, it supports DHCP server functionality.
Unicast reverse path forwarding	Supports uRPF.	Does not support uRPF.

Table 9-1 *Contrasting Routed and Transparent Firewalls*

Features	Routed Firewall	Transparent Firewall
IPSec VPN[2]	Supports remote access and site-to-site tunnels.	Supports site-to-site VPN only for management purposes.
SSL VPN	Supports SSL VPN tunnels.	Does not support SSL VPNs.

[1]Transparent firewalls and limitations related to NAT are discussed under the "Transparent Firewalls and NAT" section.

[2]Transparent firewalls and limitations related to VPN are discussed under the "Transparent Firewalls and VPNs" section.

Architectural Overview

As discussed in Chapter 8, "Virtualization," Cisco ASA can be deployed in either single or multiple mode. A transparent firewall can coexist with these modes to provide a great deal of flexibility for network deployments. This section discusses these modes for transparent firewall in detail.

Single-Mode Transparent Firewalls

In a single-mode transparent firewall (SMTF), the security appliance acts as a secured bridge that switches traffic from one interface to another. You do not configure IP addresses on either the inside or the outside interface. Rather, you must specify a global IP address that is primarily used for management purposes—Telnet and Secure Shell (SSH). The transparent firewall also uses the management IP address when it needs to source packets such as ARP requests and Syslog messages.

This is the simplest form of configuration because it does not require configuration of security contexts, dynamic routing protocols, or interface specific addresses. The configuration only requires you to define the ACLs, inspection rules, and optionally NAT policies to determine what traffic is allowed. The next section talks about how a packet flows through an SMTF.

> **Note** You must define static routes for certain inspection engines such as voice to function properly.

Packet Flow in an SMTF

Figure 9-3 shows SecureMe's office in Chicago, where the company has recently installed a Cisco ASA firewall in transparent mode. The network administrator in Chicago is curious to know how traffic traverses through the security appliance so that he can implement network security efficiently. Therefore, he is monitoring the traffic sourced from Host A that is destined to www.cisco.com.

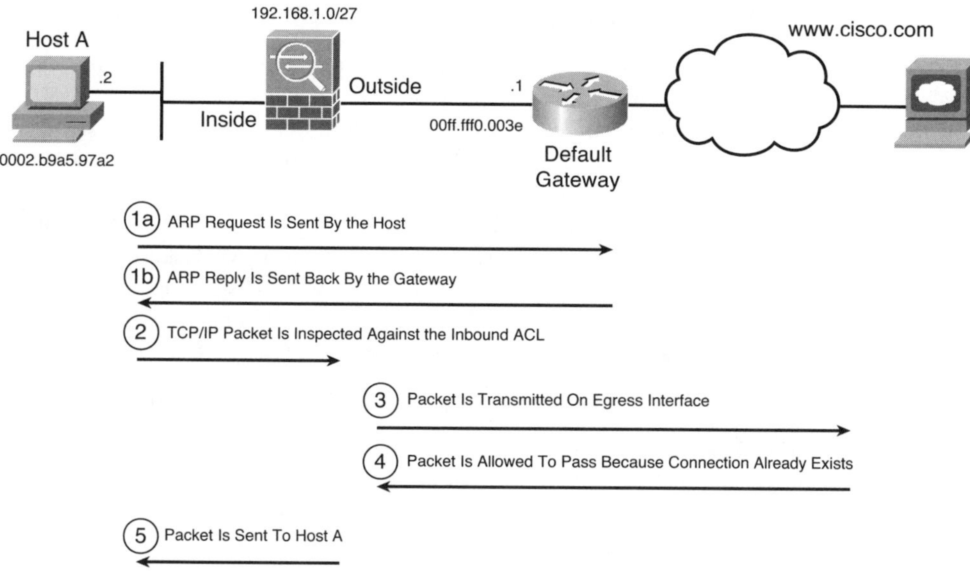

Figure 9-3 *Packet Flow in an SMTF*

For a successful connection, Cisco ASA follows these steps:

Step 1. **ARP resolution**—Because the Cisco website is located in a different subnet from Host A's network, Host A needs to perform Address Resolution Protocol (ARP) to determine its default gateway, 192.168.1.1. For the ARP process through an ASA, there are four possible cases:

Case 1: Host A and ASA do not have the gateway's MAC address.

For ARP resolution, Host A sends out an ARP broadcast request, shown as Step 1a. The ASA, after receiving this broadcast, performs two operations:

- It populates the Layer 2 forwarding (L2F) table with the source MAC address of Host A and the originating interface (inside) information.
- It forwards the broadcast ARP packet out the outside interface.

Upon receipt of this ARP request, the default gateway replies with a unicast ARP response packet, shown as Step 1b. The security appliance, once again, does two things:

- It inserts the MAC address of the default gateway router into its L2F table, along with the interface information on which the default gateway is located.
- It forwards the response packet to Host A.

Case 2: Host A has the gateway's MAC address but ASA does not.

If, for some reason, the Cisco ASA does not learn the MAC address of the default gateway (either it aged out or someone manually cleared it), it goes through the process of learning the destination MAC address. Hence, when Host A sends a packet to its default gateway, Cisco ASA drops the packet and generates an ICMP request packet with TTL (time to live) set to 1. The security appliance drops the packet because it does not yet know where the destination host lives. In the ICMP request, the destination MAC address is set to the default gateway, learned from the packet sent by Host A. The security appliance sends the packet on the outside interface. If a response is received on an interface, the security appliance updates its L2F table accordingly.

Case 3: Host A does not have the gateway's MAC address, but ASA does.

When Host A needs to resolve a gateway's MAC address, it sends out an ARP broadcast. The Cisco ASA treats this case similarly to Case 1. If there is a discrepancy between what the Cisco ASA learns and what is already in the L2F table, the ASA updates its table with the new information.

Case 4: Host A and ASA have MAC address resolution.

If both devices know about the MAC address of the default gateway, they do not need to update either the ARP or the L2F table. As such, they do not participate in any address resolution process.

Note For non-IP traffic, such as an Internetwork Packet Exchange (IPX) packet, there is no concept of ARP or ICMP to resolve destination MAC addresses. In this case, when the ASA receives a non-IP packet and does not find an entry in its L2F table, it drops the packet and does not participate in resolution.

Step 2. **ACL checking**—As soon as Host A knows about the MAC address of its default gateway, it sends out a SYN packet to the web server to initiate a three-way TCP handshake. When the packet enters the inside interface of the security appliance, the packet is checked for uauth (user authentication) and an inbound ACL. If the packet is allowed in, it is then forwarded to the bridging engine, where the L2F table is used to determine the correct outbound interface (outside interface, in this case). The packet is then checked against the outbound interface ACL. If allowed, the inspection rules and TCP checks are applied and a connection entry is created.

Step 3. **Egress packet transmission**—After the packet has been bridged to the outside interface, it is forwarded to the interface drivers for transmission.

Step 4. The web server replies with a SYN-ACK, the ASA allows the packet to pass because the connection had already been created.

Step 5. The packet is bridged to Host A and both devices (Host A and the web server) complete the TCP three-way handshake and initiate data transmission.

As you can see from this packet flow, the appliance applies security policies regardless of the firewall mode.

Multimode Transparent Firewalls

In a multimode transparent firewall (MMTF), Cisco ASA acts in a similar fashion to how it acts in single mode, with two major exceptions:

- Packets are handled in different contexts. Because each context acts and behaves as an independent entity, you must configure an IP address in each context for administration and management purposes.
- An interface cannot be shared between multiple contexts.

Packet Flow in an MMTF

Figure 9-4 illustrates SecureMe's topology for its Chicago office. SecureMe has recently acquired a small startup company (Site 2) in the same office building and is now responsible for providing the network services to the office. The new company currently uses an IP subnet of 192.168.2.0/27, and SecureMe wants to transparently add a firewall to inspect the Internet traffic. When Host B sends traffic to www.cisco.com, the following steps occur in an MMTF:

Step 1. **ARP resolution and classification**—The process to resolve the default gateway's IP address is the same as discussed in the previous section. Host B sends a broadcast if it does not know the MAC address of its gateway. The security appliance receives that packet on its GigabitEthernet0/3(G0/3) interface. Because G0/3 is allocated to the Site 2 context, the classifier forwards it to the appropriate context. Cisco ASA bridges this request to its outside interface. Because the default gateway (192.168.2.1/27) is also on the same context, it sends a unicast reply to Host B. The appliance updates its L2F table after the reply packet traverses through it.

Step 2. **ACL checking**—After the MAC address is known, Host B sends out the first packet to initiate the TCP three-way handshake. When the packet enters the inside interface of the security appliance, it is forwarded to the bridging engine where the L2F table is used to determine the correct outbound interface (outside interface, in this case). The packet is then checked against the outbound interface ACL. If allowed, the inspection rules and TCP checks are applied and a connection entry is created.

Step 3. **Egress packet transmission**—After packet has been bridged to the outside interface, it is forwarded to the interface drivers for transmission to the next-hop router located in the same context. The packet is then routed out to the Cisco website.

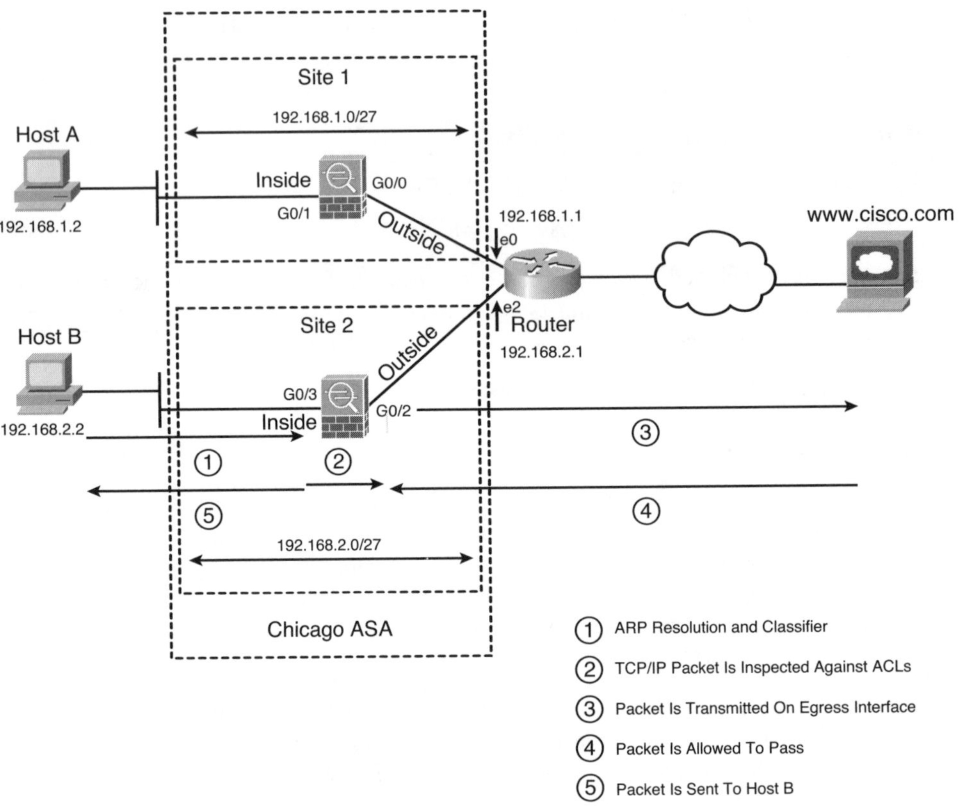

Figure 9-4 *Packet Flow in an MMTF*

Step 4. The web server sends a reply packet back to Host B. The router sends traffic to G0/2 interface of Cisco ASA. The classifier analyzes the traffic and sends it to Site2 context, which owns G0/2. The traffic is then inspected for an existing connection entry within that context.

Step 5. Because a connection entry already exists, the security appliance forwards the packet to Host B.

Restrictions Within Transparent Firewalls

As mentioned earlier, a transparent firewall behaves differently from a traditional routed firewall. The following section discusses some of the major features of a security appliance and their restrictions within a transparent firewall environment.

Transparent Firewalls and VPNs

When Cisco ASA is set up in transparent mode, the following limitations and restrictions apply to configuring the IPSec tunnels on it:

- The appliance can terminate the IPSec tunnels for management purposes only. That means you cannot establish an IPSec tunnel to pass traffic through a Cisco ASA.
- An IPSec tunnel is allowed only if the appliance is running in single mode. Multimode transparent firewalls and IPSec VPNs are not supported.
- SSL and IPSec remote-access VPNs are not supported. You can configure only one site-to-site IPSec tunnel, which needs to be set up in answer-only mode to respond to a tunnel request. The answer-only mode is discussed in Chapter 16, "Site-to-Site IPSec VPNs."
- Cisco ASA does not affect the IPSec tunnels going through it. You may still set up ACLs to block IPSec traffic passing through the ASA.
- Because routing protocols are not supported in transparent mode, reverse route injection (RRI) is also not supported.
- The IPSec tunnel uses the management IP address to terminate the connection. The IPSec tunnel could be terminated on either interface—inside or outside.
- Load balancing, stateful failover, QoS, and NAT over the VPN tunnel are not supported in IPSec VPN implementations.
- NAT Traversal (NAT-T) and public key infrastructure (PKI) are fully supported in transparent mode for the management tunnel.

Note Configuration of IPSec tunnels is outside the scope of this chapter. Refer to Chapter 16, "Site-to-Site IPSec VPNs," for more information about the site-to-site tunnels in the security appliance.

Transparent Firewalls and NAT

In the Pre-7.2(1) releases of the Cisco ASA software, address translation was not supported in transparent firewalls. Consequently, a NAT or a PAT device was needed to translate RFC 1918 addresses from the inside network as discussed in Figure 9-2. A need for NAT functionality was recognized in many deployments where a NAT/PAT device could not be added in the network topologies. Cisco enhanced the transparent firewall functionality by adding static NAT in version 7.2(1) and Dynamic NAT in version 8.0(2).

When Cisco ASA is set up in transparent mode, the following limitations and restrictions apply to configuring address translation:

- When the translated address is in the same subnet/network as the global IP address, the appliance replies to ARP requests for the translated address.
- Interface PAT (static or dynamic) is not supported because there is no IP address on the physical interface of the security appliance.
- The use of the **alias** command is not supported in transparent firewall mode.
- If the translated address is not on the same network as the global IP address of the security appliance, you must add a static route on the upstream router (router that resides toward the outside interface of the appliance) for the translated address or network. The next-hop IP address of the static route should point to a downstream router (a router that resides behind the inside interface of the firewall).
- You must define static routes on the security appliance if the original IP address/network is one or multiple hops away from the appliance. The security appliance does a route lookup rather than a MAC address lookup when address translation is in use.
- NAT exemption and NAT control functionality are fully supported in transparent firewall mode.
- If a host on one side of the firewall ARPs for a host on the other side of the firewall, and the original IP address of the initiating host is translated to an address on the same network, then the security appliance does not perform ARP inspection. This means that the original IP address may be exposed to the outside network.

Figure 9-5 shows a network topology where a Cisco security appliance is set up in multi-transparent mode and using overlapping IP addresses. The outside interface of each context is connected to a Cisco 7600 router set up for virtual routing and forwarding (VRF). There is a limitation on Cisco 7600 router where they do not support NAT per VRF. In this case, using NAT on the transparent firewalls is a must if you do not want to place an additional router for translations.

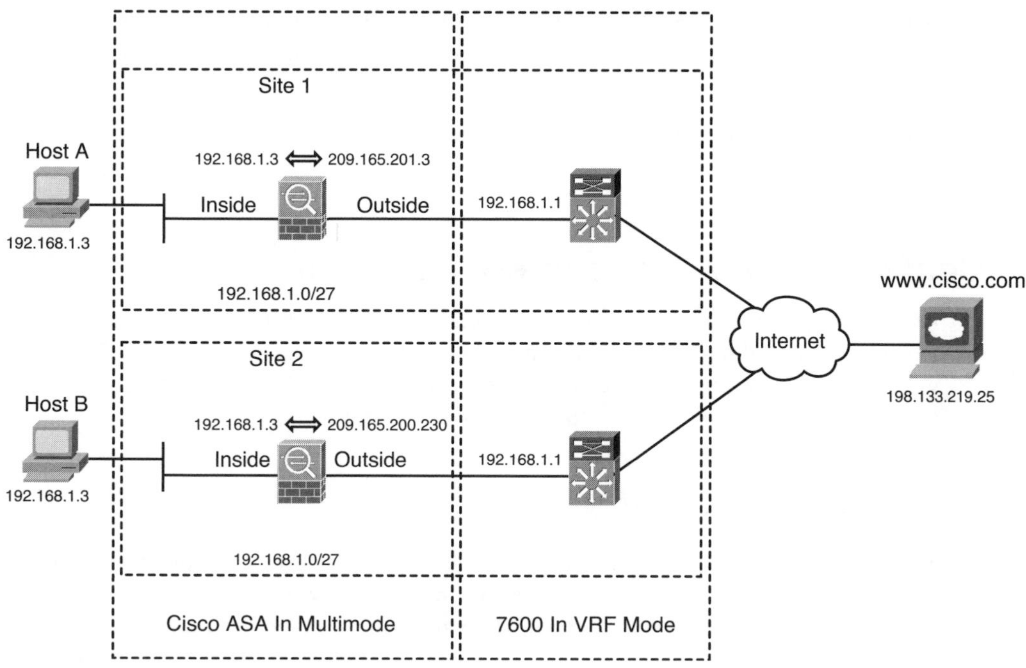

Figure 9-5 *Transparent Firewalls with NAT*

When host A sends traffic to 198.133.219.25 (www.cisco.com), the following steps occur in transparent mode:

Step 1. Host A ARPs for its default gateway (192.168.1.1), which is assigned to one of the interfaces on Cisco 7600 router. The interface is placed in Site1 VRF.

Step 2. After resolving the ARP for 192.168.1.1, host A sends a TCP syn packet to 198.133.219.25. It uses its default gateway's MAC address as the destination MAC address.

Step 3. Packets are intercepted by the security appliance, which applies appropriate ACL and traffic inspection policies. Source IP address is changed from 192.168.1.3 to 209.165.201.3.

Step 4. The security appliance forwards traffic to 192.168.1.1, which eventually routes traffic out to the Internet to 198.133.219.25.

Step 5. The web server (www.cisco.com) sends TCP SYN-ACK back to 209.165.201.3, which is routed to the VRF for Site1.

Step 6. A static route for 209.165.201.3 on Site1 VRF sends traffic through the security appliance.

Step 7. The security appliance inspects the inbound traffic on the outside interface and translates the destination address from 209.165.201.3 to 192.168.1.3.

Step 8. The security appliance ARPs for 192.168.1.3 (if it aged out or it was manually cleared) and upon receiving a response, forwards traffic to host A, using its MAC address.

Step 9. Host A and the web server complete TCP three-way handshake and pass data traffic.

Configuration of Transparent Firewalls

Implementing a transparent firewall increases design flexibility and network scalability. However, you need to consider some limitations before you implement a transparent firewall. This section discusses the configuration guidelines and configuration steps for a successful implementation of transparent firewalls in a network.

Configuration Guidelines

The following guidelines are useful if you are introducing a new Cisco ASA firewall into an environment where renumbering an existing network is not possible. They are also relevant if you are inspecting non-IP traffic through the firewall for improved security.

- Setting the Cisco ASA to either routed or transparent mode is a global feature. Thus, if you use multiple contexts and you set the ASA to transparent mode, all security contexts use transparent mode to forward traffic between the interfaces.
- Switching from routed to transparent mode or vice versa clears the running configuration. Save active configurations prior to making this change.
- There is no support for dynamic routing protocols such as RIP, OSPF or EIGRP in either SMTFs or MMTFs. All OSPF-, RIP-, and EIGRP-related commands are disabled.
- NAT in transparent mode is supported with a few restrictions. Please consult the "Transparent Firewalls and NAT" section earlier in this chapter.
- The static and NAT commands can also be used to specify the embryonic and maximum connection limit. You can also use them to disable TCP sequence number randomization. Additionally, you can use the **set connection** commands through modular policy framework (MPF).
- Currently, only two interfaces—inside and outside—are used to pass traffic through the Cisco ASA transparent firewall, running it either in SMTF or MMTF. These interfaces use different security levels.
- If a dedicated management interface is used, it can be on a different Layer 3 subnet.
- Cisco ASA transparent firewall is implemented to inspect and filter out traffic traversing a subnet. This requires both inside and outside interfaces to be on the same Layer 3 subnet. The global IP address must belong to the same subnet as the directly connected interfaces. In an MMTF, interfaces cannot be shared between the

contexts. Unique interfaces (either physical or logical) are required to segregate traffic between the security contexts.

- For traffic filtering, Layer 3 or EtherType ACLs can be used to allow IP or non-IP traffic to pass through the ASA.
- Static routes are required for some application inspections to work correctly, in particular voice protocols.

Configuration Steps

The following steps can be taken to configure Cisco ASA for transparent firewalls:

Step 1. Enable transparent firewalls.

Step 2. Set up interfaces.

Step 3. Configure an IP address.

Step 4. Set up routes.

Step 5. Configure interface ACLs.

Step 6. Configure NAT (optional).

Step 7. Add static L2F table entries (optional).

Step 8. Enable ARP inspection (optional).

Step 9. Modify L2F table parameters (optional).

Step 1: Enable Transparent Firewalls

You can change the default routed mode to transparent mode by using the **firewall transparent** command, as shown in Example 9-1. You can start the conversion process either through a Telnet/SSH connection or through a console connection. It is highly recommended by Cisco Systems to initiate the switchover through the console connection. After a switchover, you will lose network connectivity and will not be able to access the security appliance through Telnet or SSH.

Example 9-1 *Enabling Transparent Firewalls*

```
Chicago# configure terminal
Chicago(config)# firewall transparent
ciscoasa(config)#
```

Note At the moment, you cannot change the firewall behavior through ASDM.

After switching modes, Cisco ASA clears the running configuration because most of the routed mode commands are not compatible in transparent mode. As you can see in

Example 9-1, the security appliance clears the running configuration and displays the default prompt of **ciscoasa**. You do not need to reboot the security appliance after you switch firewall modes.

If you want to revert to routed mode, use the **no firewall transparent** command as illustrated in Example 9-2. It is highly recommended that you save the transparent firewall configuration before you switch mode from transparent to routed. The running configuration is saved as transparent.cfg in disk0.

Example 9-2 *Enabling Routed Firewalls*

```
Chicago# copy running-config disk0:/transparent.cfg
Source filename [running-config]?
Destination filename [transparent.cfg]?
Cryptochecksum: 8b13d308 7f3d6971 7e6805e8 9551f8f5
2165 bytes copied in 3.320 secs (721 bytes/sec)
Chicago# configure terminal
Chicago(config)# no firewall transparent
```

To determine the firewall mode your security appliance is using, use the **show firewall** command as illustrated in Example 9-3.

Example 9-3 *Verifying Firewalls Mode*

```
Chicago# show firewall
Firewall mode: Transparent
```

Step 2: Set Up Interfaces

After you turn on the transparent firewall on the security appliance, you can define the inside and outside interfaces. You do so by assigning a name and a security level on an interface. Example 9-4 shows how to define an inside interface with security level 100, and an outside interface with security level 0. By default, all interfaces are in the shutdown state, which you can enable by using the **no shutdown** command.

> **Note** You cannot use ASDM until the interfaces are ready to pass traffic and the global/management IP address is configured on the security appliance.

Example 9-4 *Setting Up Interfaces*

```
Chicago(config)# interface GigabitEthernet0/0
Chicago(config-if)# no shutdown
Chicago(config-if)# nameif outside
INFO: Security level for "outside" set to 0 by default.
Chicago(config-if)# security-level 0
```

```
Chicago(config-if)# exit
Chicago(config)# interface GigabitEthernet0/1
Chicago(config-if)# no shutdown
Chicago(config-if)# nameif inside
INFO: Security level for "inside" set to 100 by default.
Chicago(config-if)# security-level 100
```

Transparent firewall mode on the security appliance allows only two interfaces to pass through traffic. However, you can set up a dedicated management interface, which can be either a physical interface or a subinterface, as a third interface. This interface must be set up for the **management-only** command.

Note If the security appliance is configured to accept ASDM client connections and the IP connectivity exists between the client and the ASA, you can navigate to **Configuration > Device Setup > Interface** and modify the interfaces accordingly.

Step 3: Configure an IP Address

Unlike routed mode, the ASA in transparent mode does not allow you to configure IP addresses on the physical or sub-interfaces. Rather, an IP address is assigned in global configuration mode that is used exclusively for management purposes, such as SSH, Telnet, ASDM, SNMP traps and polling, AAA, and ARP resolution.

Example 9-5 shows how to configure an IP address of **192.168.1.10** with a 27-bit mask on the ASA running in transparent mode.

Example 9-5 *Assigning an IP Address*

```
Chicago(config)# ip address 192.168.1.10 255.255.255.224
```

Note In an MMTF, an IP address must be configured for each context.

The transparent mode allows you to assign an IP address to a management interface under the interface sub-configuration mode. As shown in Example 9-6, an IP address of **172.18.82.64/24** is configured for the **Management0/0** interface, whereas the global IP address of the transparent mode firewall is **192.168.1.10/27**. The security level on the management interface is set to **100** because it is a secure interface.

Example 9-6 *Assigning a Management IP Address*

```
Chicago# configure terminal
Chicago(config)# interface Management0/0
Chicago(config-if)#  nameif mgmt
```

```
Chicago(config-if)# security-level 100
Chicago(config-if)#  ip address 172.18.82.64 255.255.255.0
Chicago(config-if)# no shutdown
Chicago(config-if)# exit
Chicago(config)# ip address 192.168.1.10 255.255.255.224
```

If ASDM connectivity exists between the client and the security appliance, you can use ASDM to edit or assign a global management IP address on the security appliance. Navigate to **Configuration > Device Management > Management Access >** **Management IP Address** and specify the **Global IP Address** under **Management IP Address.** Select the appropriate subnet mask under the **Subnet Mask** drop-down menu.

Note Configuring an IP address from ASDM is useful if you have the security appliance in multimode so that you can change contexts and assign global addresses for each context.

Step 4: Set Up Routes

If you are not using a dedicated management interface, the default gateway of the transparent firewall is typically the downstream router toward the inside interface. The security appliance sends traffic to the default gateway for the networks that it does not know about. If you are using a dedicated management interface, the default gateway is typically the router that resides toward the management interface. Example 9-7 shows how to set up a default gateway if a dedicated management interface is used.

Example 9-7 *Setting Up a Default Gateway Toward the Management Interface*

```
Chicago# configure terminal
Chicago(config)# route mgmt 0.0.0.0 0.0.0.0 172.18.82.1
```

Figure 9-6 shows a network topology where a transparent firewall is bridging traffic between the inside and the outside interfaces. A Cisco router (Router1) connects the internal network to the Internet, whereas Router2 provides connectivity to another internal network of 192.168.2.0. A syslog server residing at 192.168.2.100 is configured to accept messages from the security appliance.

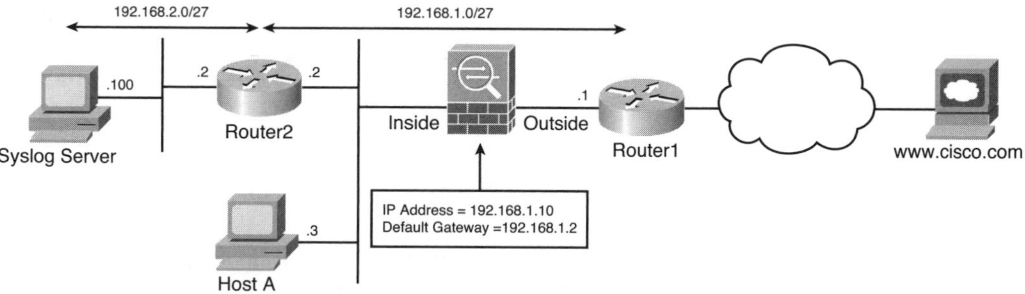

Figure 9-6 *Default Gateway Towards Inside Interface*

> **Note** Static routes are required for some application inspections to work correctly—voice protocols, in particular.

Example 9-8 shows how to set up a default gateway, which is the router located toward the inside interface.

Example 9-8 *Setting Up a Default Gateway Toward the Inside Interface*

```
Chicago# configure terminal
Chicago(config)# route inside 0.0.0.0 0.0.0.0 192.168.1.2
```

> **Note** After assigning an IP address, setting up the appropriate default gateway and configuring the ASDM-specific commands, you can use ASDM to configure the other transparent-specific features such as the Interface ACLs and NAT policies. Simply point the ASDM launcher to the management IP address if you use a dedicated management interface, or to the global IP address if you do not have a dedicated management interface. See Deployment Scenario "SMTF Deployment" for the commands used to set up the appliance for basic ASDM connectivity.

Step 5: Configure Interface ACLs

As discussed in Chapter 4, "Controlling Network Access," extended ACLs can filter out IP packets by looking at various headers. EtherType-based ACLs can be used to filter IP- and non-IP-based traffic. Because the EtherType ACLs can be used to analyze a frame at Layer 2, they behave differently from a typical extended ACL. Consult the following guidelines when using the ACLs in your environment:

- **CDP Packets**—The security appliance does not allow Cisco Discovery Protocol (CDP) packets to traverse through it, even if you allow them.

- **ARP Packets—**In its default behavior, the security appliance does not restrict ARP packets to pass through it in either direction. You can use an EtherType ACL to block ARP traffic. All other packets, such as DHCP, RIP, OSPF, EIGRP, BGP, BPDU, multicast, and MPLS packets, can be controlled by the EtherType ACL entries.

> **Note** The security appliance classifies DHCP (UDP ports 67 and 68), EIGRP (Protocol 88), OSPF (Protocol 89), Multicast streams (Varying UDP ports), and RIP (UDP port 520) as special types. They are considered connectionless traffic types and an extended access list must be applied to both interfaces for successful communication.

- BPDUs—Cisco ASA does not forward bridge protocol data units (BPDUs) to prevent bridging loops. However, they can be allowed to pass through the security appliance if permitted by an EtherType ACL. This is a must if your security appliances are set up in the failover mode to avoid bridging loops. Additionally, because a transparent firewall uses different VLANs on the inside and on the outside interface, the trunk BPDUs payload is modified with the outgoing VLAN.
- **Interaction with Extended ACLs—**Like all ACLs, the EtherType ACL has an implicit deny at the end of it. However, this implicit deny does not affect the IP traffic passing through the security appliance. As a result, you can apply both EtherType and extended ACLs to each direction of an interface. If you configure an explicit deny at the end of an EtherType ACL, it may block IP traffic even if an extended ACL is defined to pass the IP packets.
- **MPLS—**If you want to pass MPLS traffic through the security appliance, make sure that you manually specify the router-id for the TDP and LDP sessions. The router-id must be the IP address of the router interface that is connected to the security appliance.

You can define an EtherType ACL by using the following command syntax:

```
access-list id ethertype {deny | permit} {ether-value | bpdu | ipx | mpls-unicast |
mpls-multicast | any}
```

where *ether-value* is a 2-byte value specified in the Layer 2 datagram under the EtherType code field. For IP-based traffic, the EtherType code value is 0x800. Novell IPX uses 0x8137-8138 or 0xAAAA, depending on the NetWare version.

> **Note** Cisco ASA supports only Ethernet II frames. The IEEE 802.3 frames contain a length field instead of an EtherType code field and are not filtered by the EtherType ACLs. The only exception is the BPDU frames, which are SNAP encapsulated and can still be controlled by an EtherType ACL.
>
> A list of commonly used EtherType (Ethernet Type) codes is available on the following Cisco.com page:
>
> http://www.cisco.com/univercd/cc/td/doc/product/software/ios100/rpcr/35177.htm

Figure 9-7 shows an IPX packet captured using Wireshark, a sniffing tool. As you can see, the Ethernet type of the IPX frame is 0x8137.

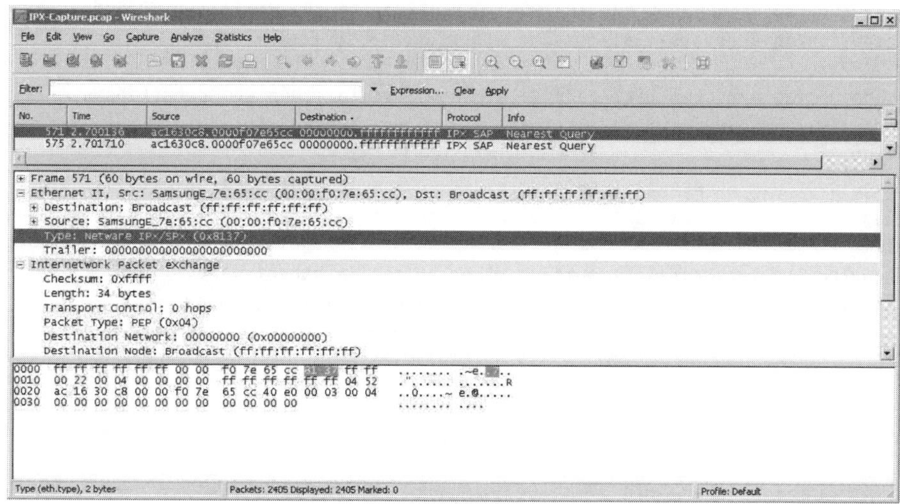

Figure 9-7 *Sniffer Trace Showing an IPX Frame*

You can define an EtherType ACL through ASDM by navigating to **Configuration > Firewall > Ethertype Rules**, and then clicking the pull-down **Add** list and selecting **Add Ethertype Rule**. A new window pops up where you can define an entry for the EtherType ACL. In Figure 9-8, an entry is defined to allow IPX traffic to pass through the inside interface.

> **Note** Because the non-IP packets do not create sessions, the security appliance must be configured for ACLs on both interfaces.

Example 9-9 shows the output if you want to configure an EtherType ACL through the CLI. The EtherType ACL allows IPX and BPDU traffic to pass through, and it blocks all other traffic, including IP frames. The ACL is applied to the **inside** and **outside** interface to analyze inbound traffic.

Example 9-9 *Configuring an EtherType ACL*

```
Chicago(config)# access-list inside_ether_access_in remark Allow Inbound BPDUs on
Inside
Chicago(config)# access-list inside_ether_access_in ethertype permit bpdu
Chicago(config)# access-list inside_ether_access_in remark Allow Inbound IPX on
Inside
Chicago(config)# access-list inside_ether_access_in ethertype permit ipx
```

```
Chicago(config)# access-list inside_ether_access_in remark Explicit Deny for all
traffic
Chicago(config)# access-list inside_ether_access_in ethertype deny any
Chicago(config)# access-group inside_ether_access_in in  interface inside
Chicago(config)# access-list outside_ether_access_in remark Allow Inbound BPDUs
on Outside
Chicago(config)# access-list outside_ether_access_in ethertype permit bpdu
Chicago(config)# access-list outside_ether_access_in remark Allow Inbound IPX on
Outside
Chicago(config)# access-list outside_ether_access_in ethertype permit ipx
Chicago(config)# access-list outside_ether_access_in remark Explicit Deny for all
traffic
Chicago(config)# access-list outside_ether_access_in ethertype deny any
Chicago(config)# access-group outside_ether_access_in in  interface outside
```

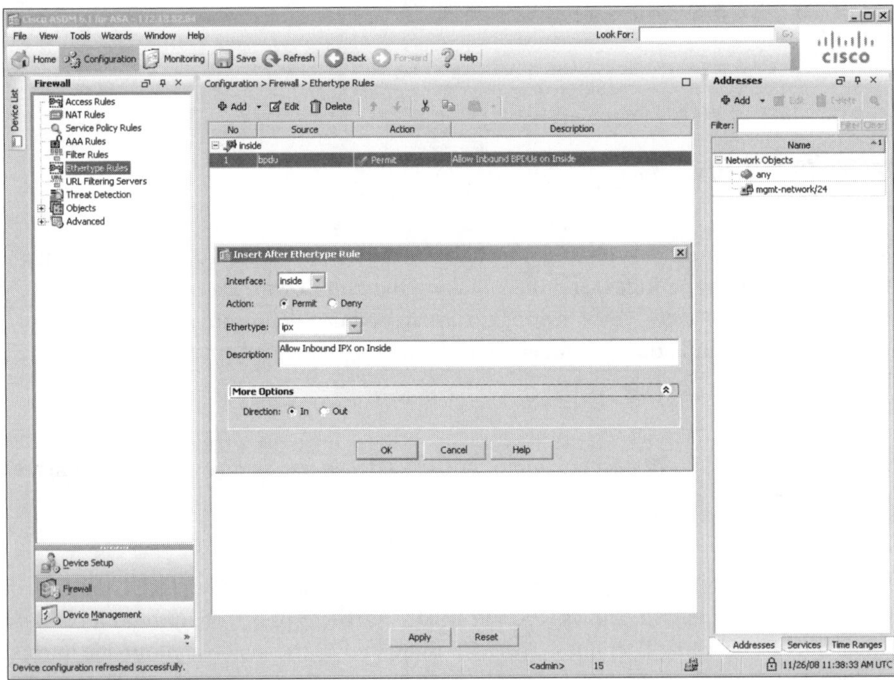

Figure 9-8 *Configuration of an EtherType ACL through ASDM*

Caution If you want to add more than one remark statement in an EtherType ACL, make sure that your appliance is not susceptible to CSCsw18184. This issue is fixed in 8.2(1) version of code. To learn more about it, please visit the following URL and specify the above mentioned ID:

http://tools.cisco.com/Support/BugToolKit/action.do?hdnAction=searchBugs

Step 6: Configure NAT (Optional)

If you want the security appliance to do address translation for the traffic flowing through the transparent firewall, you can navigate to **Configuration > Firewall > NAT Rules** and click **Add** to define an appropriate NAT policy. As shown in Figure 9-9, a static NAT policy is defined to translate the internal host **192.168.1.3** to **209.165.201.3**.

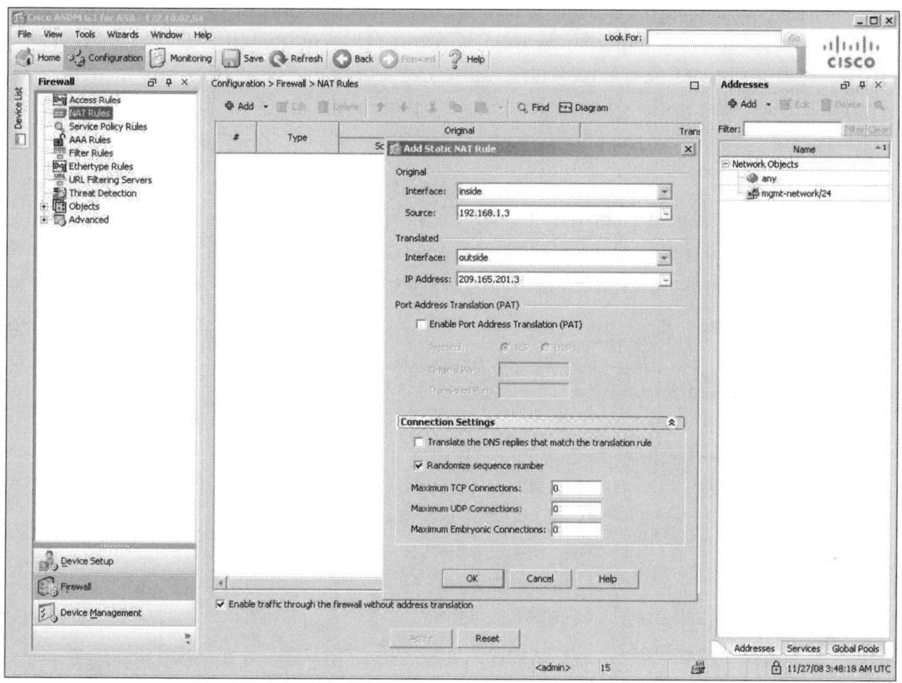

Figure 9-9 *Configuration of Static NAT Policy*

Example 9-10 shows the output if you want to configure the same NAT policy through the CLI.

Example 9-10 *Configuring a Static NAT Translation*

```
Chicago(config)# static (inside,outside) 209.165.201.3 192.168.1.3 netmask
255.255.255.255
```

> **Note** The upstream router (router that resides toward the outside interface of the security appliance) may need a static route for 209.165.201.3. The next-hop IP address for the route should be a Layer 3 address on the inside network as follows:
>
> **ip route 209.165.201.3 255.255.255.255 192.168.1.2**

If you do not have a router that resides toward the inside interface, then the next-hop IP address should be the original IP of the end host (192.168.1.3).

Step 7: Add Static L2F Table Entries (Optional)

As mentioned earlier in this chapter, the L2F entries are learned dynamically when the IP packets traverse through the appliance. You can view the output of the L2F table (or MAC-address table) by using **show mac-address-table**, as shown in Example 9-11. However, you can define a host-based static L2F entry to associate a host's MAC address to an interface. The security appliance stops learning the MAC address and does not allow dynamic port binding (MAC-address to interface) for that particular host.

Example 9-11 shows the output of **show mac-address-table** where the dynamically learned mac-addresses are shown. It also shows the interface name where those hosts reside. A static L2F entry is added for a router so that the ASA does not have to time out the entry and go through the learning process again.

Example 9-11 *Static L2F Entry*

```
Chicago# show mac-address-table
interface                     mac  address            type      Age(min)
-----------------------------------------------------------------
inside                       0019.0746.d400           dynamic     4
inside                       0016.36ca.1aaa           dynamic     1
inside                       000c.29b5.ca36           dynamic     5
inside                       0015.1738.ebd9           dynamic     5
mgmt                         00c0.9f7f.452b           dynamic     3
Chicago# configure terminal
Chicago(config)# mac-address-table static outside 0000.0c07.ac00
```

Using ASDM, you can navigate to **Configuration > Device Management > Advanced > Bridging > MAC Address Table.**

Note If a static ARP entry is configured, the appliance also adds the corresponding static L2F table entry.

Step 8: Enable ARP Inspection (Optional)

Cisco ASA, deployed in transparent mode, provides a way to prevent attacks related to ARP spoofing. This feature, called *ARP inspection*, examines all ARP packets (reply and gratuitous ARPs) before forwarding them. The security appliance compares the MAC address, IP address, and the source interface of the ARP packets to the static entries in the ARP table. This ensures that a rogue device cannot intercept packets by sending ARP responses with an incorrect MAC address.

ARP inspection is disabled by default, but can be configured to either flood the packet to other interfaces (through use of the **flood** keyword) or drop the packet and generate a syslog (through use of **no-flood**). It can be enabled per interface. When the Cisco ASA receives an ARP packet, it checks the static ARP table for a match and takes one of the following actions:

- If the MAC address matches and it finds a correct static ARP entry, it forwards the packet through the security appliance.
- If the MAC address matches against a static ARP entry but a mismatch either on the IP address or the interface is detected, then the appliance drops the packet and generates a syslog message.
- If the MAC address is not found in the static ARP table and the flood option is enabled, the appliance forwards the packet to the interface opposite the interface where the packet is received.
- If the MAC address is not found in the static ARP table and the **no-flood** option is enabled, the appliance drops the packet and generates a syslog message. By default, the security appliance floods the packet and you must enable the **no-flood** option to change this behavior.

The command syntax to enable ARP inspection is

```
arp-inspection interface_name enable [flood | no-flood]
```

Figure 9-10 illustrates how to turn on ARP inspection on the outside interface with **no-flood.** With this option enabled, the security appliance drops all packets from a host if it does not have a correct static ARP entry defined. Therefore, the security appliance needs to know the ARP entries of all the hosts that reside on that interface. This enhances the firewall's security because all unknown hosts are denied access to pass traffic through the security appliance.

Prefer to use the CLI to enable ARP inspection on the outside interface? Use the **arp-inspection** command as shown in Example 9-12.

Example 9-12 *Enabling ARP Inspection*

```
Chicago(config)# arp-inspection outside enable no-flood
```

As you can see, the ARP inspection functionality relies heavily on the static ARP entries. You can define a static ARP entry by navigating to **Configuration > Device Management > Advanced > ARP > ARP Static Table** and clicking the **Add** option. You can specify the following attributes:

- **Interface**—Select the interface where the host resides. For example, if you want to define a static ARP entry for the upstream router, select the outside interface from the drop-down list.

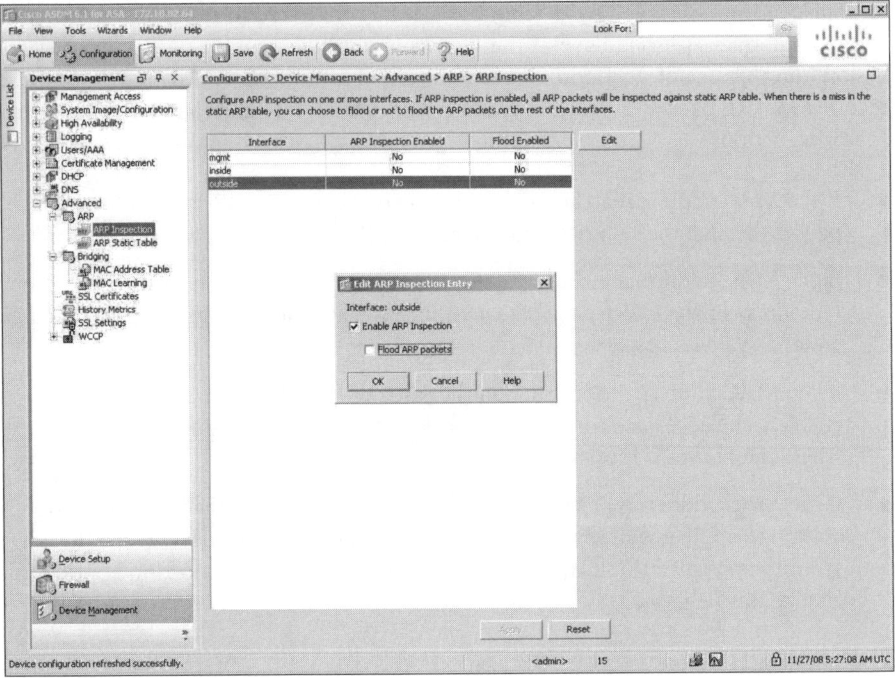

Figure 9-10 *Enabling ARP Inspection on Outside Interface*

- **IP Address**—Specify the IP address of the host whose ARP entry is being defined.
- **MAC Address**—Specify the MAC address of the host whose ARP entry is being defined. The MAC address should be in 0000.0000.0000 format.
- **Proxy ARP**—In transparent mode, the security appliance does not utilize the proxy ARP feature even if it is enabled.

In Figure 9-11, a static ARP entry is being added for the outside router with an IP address of **192.168.1.1**. The MAC address of the router is **0000.0c07.ac00**.

To define a static ARP entry, you can use the **arp** command followed by the name of the interface and the IP and the MAC addresses of a host. Example 9-13 shows the output of a static ARP entry for the host located at **192.168.1.1** and whose MAC address is **0000.0c07.ac00**.

Example 9-13 *Defining a Static ARP Entry via CLI*

```
Chicago(config)# arp outside 192.168.1.1 0000.0c07.ac00
```

Note To set ARP inspection back to the default on all interfaces, use **clear configure arp-inspection.**

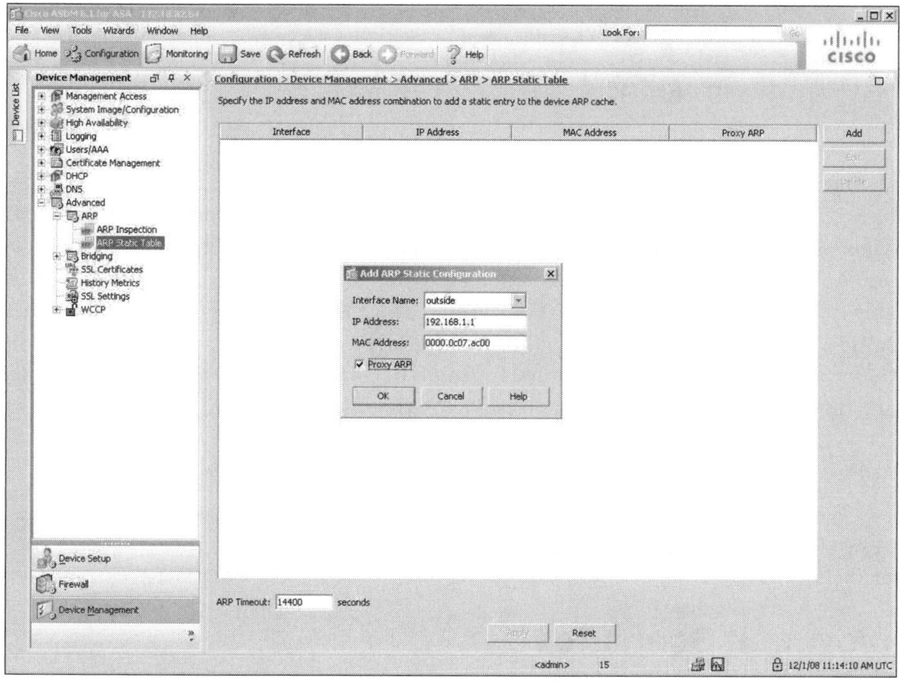

Figure 9-11 *Defining Static ARP Entry*

Step 8: Modify L2F Table Parameters (Optional)

Cisco ASA has the flexibility to suit different network architectures. For example, the default L2F table aging time can be changed from 5 minutes to a maximum of 12 hours. This way, dynamically learned entries for a specified host will not be aged out so frequently. Using ASDM, navigate to **Configuration > Device Management > Advanced > Bridging > MAC Address Table** and specify timeout in minutes under the "Dynamic Entry Timeout" option. If you want to use the CLI, Example 9-14 illustrates how the L2F aging time can be modified from 5 minutes to 60 minutes.

Example 9-14 *L2F Table Aging Time*

```
Chicago(config)# mac-address-table aging-time 60
```

Caution In some deployment scenarios, because of the way traffic passes through the transparent firewall, sometimes entries age out on the transparent firewall, causing potential outages. For example, imagine a host is on the inside of the firewall, and the default gateway of the host resides on the outside, yet an ICMP redirect is sent by the default gateway to the host telling it to go to a next-hop gateway living on the inside of the firewall to get to the destination. The result is that after the first SYN packet is sent through the firewall, the subsequent packets don't pass through the firewall. So the transparent firewall MAC entry might age out after 5 minutes. Then, at minute 10, the host sends a new packet to the default gateway, but by then the packet is dropped because of the missing MAC entry on the firewall.

If your security policy does not allow the ASA to learn the L2F table dynamically on an interface, you can disable the learning process by navigating to **Configuration > Device Management > Advanced > Bridging > MAC Learning** and selecting the interface where you want to disable dynamic MAC address learning. You can also use the **mac-learn disable** command. After you disable the learning process on an interface, you need to add static MAC address entries for the hosts toward that interface. Example 9-15 shows how to define a static MAC address entry for **0000.0c07.ac00** toward the **outside** interface and how to turn off MAC address learning on that interface.

Example 9-15 *Defining an L2F Table and Disabling MAC Learning*

```
Chicago(config)# mac-address-table static outside 0000.0c07.ac00
Chicago(config)# mac-learn outside disable
```

Deployment Scenarios

The robust transparent firewall solution can be deployed in different ways, including the following two design scenarios, discussed in this section:

- SMTF deployment
- MMTF deployment using security contexts

Note The design scenarios discussed in this section are used solely to reinforce learning. They should be used for reference purposes only.

SMTF Deployment

SecureMe has a remote location in New York that uses IP and IPX as the Layer 3 protocols. SecureMe wants to seamlessly deploy an ASA in transparent firewall mode so that it does not have to modify the existing network addresses. Figure 9-12 shows SecureMe's new topology in New York after introducing the security appliance. The private IP network behind Router1 is 10.10.1.0/24, and the private IPX network is AB0198CA. The private IP network behind Router2 is 10.10.3.0/24, and the private IPX network is AB0198CC.

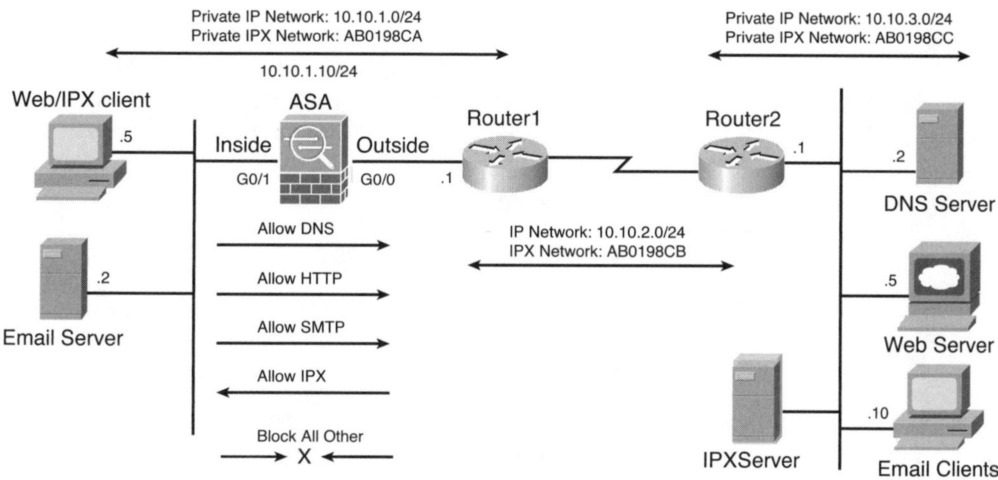

Figure 9-12 *SecureMe's New York Network Topology*

Additionally, SecureMe wants to achieve the following goals:

- Allow DNS traffic to query the DNS server.
- Allow HTTP clients to talk to the web server.
- Allow access to an email server from the remote client.
- Allow IPX traffic to pass through.
- Protect the email server from TCP SYN attacks by setting the embryonic connections to 200 and maximum connections to 300.
- Deny all other traffic.
- Set up a dedicated management interface and log all the informational system-generated messages to a syslog server located at 172.18.82.100.

SecureMe has defined two types of ACLs:

- **EtherType ACL**—Allows IPX traffic to pass through the security appliance. The IPX packets are connectionless and therefore the ACL must be applied to the inside and outside interface of the appliance.
- **Extended ACLs**—Two extended ACLs are defined: inside and outside. The inside ACL allows inbound DNS and HTTP traffic and block everything else. This ACL is applied to the inside interface. The outside ACL allows SMTP traffic from the email clients to the email server. This ACL is applied on the outside interface in the inbound direction.

Note Before you launch ASDM to configure this deployment scenario, make sure that the security appliance is configured with the following minimum commands. This assumes that the management IP address of the security appliance is 172.18.82.64 with a default gateway of 172.18.82.1. Additionally, this assumes that you will be managing the security appliance from the 172.18.82.0 subnet.

```
ciscoasa(config)# firewall transparent
ciscoasa(config)# hostname NewYork
NewYork(config)# interface Management0/0
NewYork(config-if)# no shut
NewYork(config-if)# nameif mgmt
INFO: Security level for "mgmt" set to 0 by default.
NewYork(config-if)# security-level 100
NewYork(config-if)# ip address 172.18.82.64 255.255.255.0
NewYork(config-if)# route mgmt 0.0.0.0 0.0.0.0 172.18.82.1
NewYork(config)# http server enable
NewYork(config)# http 172.18.82.0 255.255.255.0 mgmt
NewYork(config)# asdm image disk0:/asdm-621.bin
```

Configuration Steps Using ASDM

The relevant configuration to achieve the listed goals is described in the following steps:

Step 1. Navigate to **Configuration > Device Setup > Interfaces**, select **GigabitEthernet0/0**, click **Edit**, and configure the following attributes:

- Interface Name: **outside**
- Security Level: **0**
- Enable Interface: **Checked**
- Description: **Outside Interface in Transparent mode**

Step 2. Navigate to **Configuration > Device Setup > Interfaces**, select **GigabitEthernet0/1**, click **Edit**, and configure the following attributes:

- Interface Name: **inside**
- Security Level: **100**
- Enable Interface: **Checked**
- Description: **Inside Interface in Transparent Mode**

Step 3. Navigate to **Configuration > Device Management > Management Access > Management IP Address** and configure the following parameters:

- Management IP Address: **10.10.1.10**
- Subnet Mask: **255.255.255.0**

Step 4. Navigate to **Configuration > Firewall > Ethertype Rules**, click the pull-down **Add** list, and select **Add Ethertype Rule.** Configure the following Access Rule:

- Interface: **inside**
- Action: **Permit**
- Ethertype: **ipx**
- Direction: **in**
- Description: **To forward IPX packets**

Step 5. Navigate to **Configuration > Firewall > Ethertype Rules**, click the pull-down **Add** list, and select **Add Ethertype Rule.** Configure the following Access Rule:

- Interface: **outside**
- Action: **Permit**
- Ethertype: **ipx**
- Direction: **in**
- Description: **To forward IPX packets**

Step 6. Navigate to **Configuration > Firewall > Access Rules**, click the pull-down **Add** list, and select **Add Access Rule.** Configure the following Access Rule:

- Interface: **inside**
- Action: **Permit**
- Source: **10.10.1.0/24**
- Destination: **10.10.3.2/32**
- Service: **udp/domain**
- Description: **To Allow DNS Packets**
- Direction: **in**
- Enable Rule: **Checked.** Click **OK** when you are finished.

Step 7. Navigate to **Configuration > Firewall > Access Rules**, click the pull-down **Add** list, and select **Add Access Rule.** Configure the following Access Rule:

- Interface: **inside**
- Action: **Permit**

- Source: **10.10.1.0/24**
- Destination: **10.10.3.5/32**
- Service: **http**
- Description: **To Allow HTTP Packets**
- Direction: **in**
- Enable Rule: **Checked.** Click **OK** when you are finished.

Step 8. Navigate to **Configuration > Firewall > Access Rules**, click the pull-down **Add** list, and select **Add Access Rule.** Configure the following Access Rule:

- Interface: **outside**
- Action: **Permit**
- Source: **10.10.3.0/24**
- Destination: **10.10.1.2/32**
- Service: **smtp**
- Description: **To Allow Email Packets**
- Direction: **in**
- Enable Rule: **Checked.** Click **OK** when you are finished.

Step 9. Navigate to **Configuration > Firewall > NAT Rules > Add** and select **Add Static NAT Rule.** Configure the following policy for the Static NAT Rule:

- Original Interface: **inside**
- Source: **10.10.1.2**
- Translated Interface: **outside**
- Source: **10.10.1.2.** Click **Connection Settings.**
- Randomize Sequence Numbers: **Checked**
- Maximum TCP Connections: **300**
- Maximum Embryonic Connection: **200.** Click **OK** when you are finished.

Step 10. Navigate to **Configuration > Device Management > Logging > Logging Setup** and select the **Enable Logging** option.

Step 11. Navigate to **Configuration > Device Management > Logging > Syslog Server** and click **Add.** Specify the following under

- Interface: **mgmt**
- IP Address: **172.18.82.100**

- Protocol: **UDP**; Port: **514**. Click **OK** when you are finished.

Step 12. Navigate to **Configuration > Device Management > Logging > Syslog Setup.** Check **Include Timestamps in Syslogs** to add timestamps when syslogs are generated.

Step 13. Navigate to **Configuration > Device Management > Logging > Logging Filters**, select **Syslog Servers**, and click **Edit.** Under "Filter on Severity", choose **Informational** from the drop-down menu.

Configuration Steps using CLI

Example 9-16 shows the relevant configuration to achieve the above-mentioned goals. Some commands have been removed for brevity.

Example 9-16 *ASA Relevant Configuration to Allow IP Traffic*

```
NewYork# show running
ASA Version 8.2(1)
! transparent firewall mode is enabled
firewall transparent
hostname NewYork
! outside interface
Interface GigabitEthernet0/0
 description Outside Interface in Transparent Mode
 nameif outside
 security-level 0
! inside interface
Interface GigabitEthernet0/1
 description Inside Interface in Transparent Mode
 nameif inside
 security-level 100
! Management interface
interface Management0/0
nameif mgmt
 security-level 100
 ip address 172.18.82.64 255.255.255.0
 management-only
! EtherType Access-list entry to pass IPX traffic for inside and outside inter-
faces.
access-list inside_ether_access_in remark To forward IPX packets
access-list inside_ether_access_in ethertype permit ipx
access-list outside_ether_access_in remark To forward IPX packets
access-list outside_ether_access_in ethertype permit ipx
! Extended Access-list entry to pass DNS, HTTP traffic.
access-list inside_access_in remark To Allow DNS Packets
```

```
access-list inside_access_in extended permit udp 10.10.1.0 255.255.255.0 host
10.10.3.2 eq domain
access-list inside_access_in remark To Allow HTTP Packets
access-list inside_access_in extended permit tcp 10.10.1.0 255.255.255.0 host
10.10.3.5 eq www
! Extended Access-list entry to pass Email traffic.
access-list outside_access_in remark To Allow Email Packets
access-list outside_access_in extended permit tcp 10.10.3.0 255.255.255.0 host
10.10.1.2 eq smtp
! Extended Access-list is applied to the inside interface of the ASA
access-group inside_access_in in interface inside
! EtherType Access-list is applied to the inside interface of the ASA
access-group inside_ether_access_in in  interface inside
! Extended Access-list is applied to the outside interface of the ASA
access-group outside_access_in in interface outside
! EtherType Access-list is applied to the outside interface of the ASA
access-group outside_ether_access_in in  interface outside

! Static command is used to specify the maximum and embryonic connection limit
static (inside,outside) 10.10.1.2 10.10.1.2 netmask 255.255.255.255 tcp 300 200
! Syslogging to an external server
logging enable
logging trap Informational
logging timestamp
logging host mgmt 172.18.82.100
! Global IP address
ip address 10.10.1.10 255.255.255.0
! Default gateway. It is used by ASA for the traffic originating from it
route mgmt 0.0.0.0 0.0.0.0 172.18.82.1 1
! HTTP Server to accept ASDM connections from the management network
http server enable
http 172.18.82.0 255.255.255.0 mgmt
<some output removed for brevity>
```

MMTF Deployment with Security Contexts

SecureMe plans to provide firewall services to two different enterprises at its Chicago office. These organizations not only use different Layer 3 protocols, but also have unique sets of requirements that SecureMe needs to account for. Figure 9-13 shows SecureMe's new topology in Chicago to provide these services.

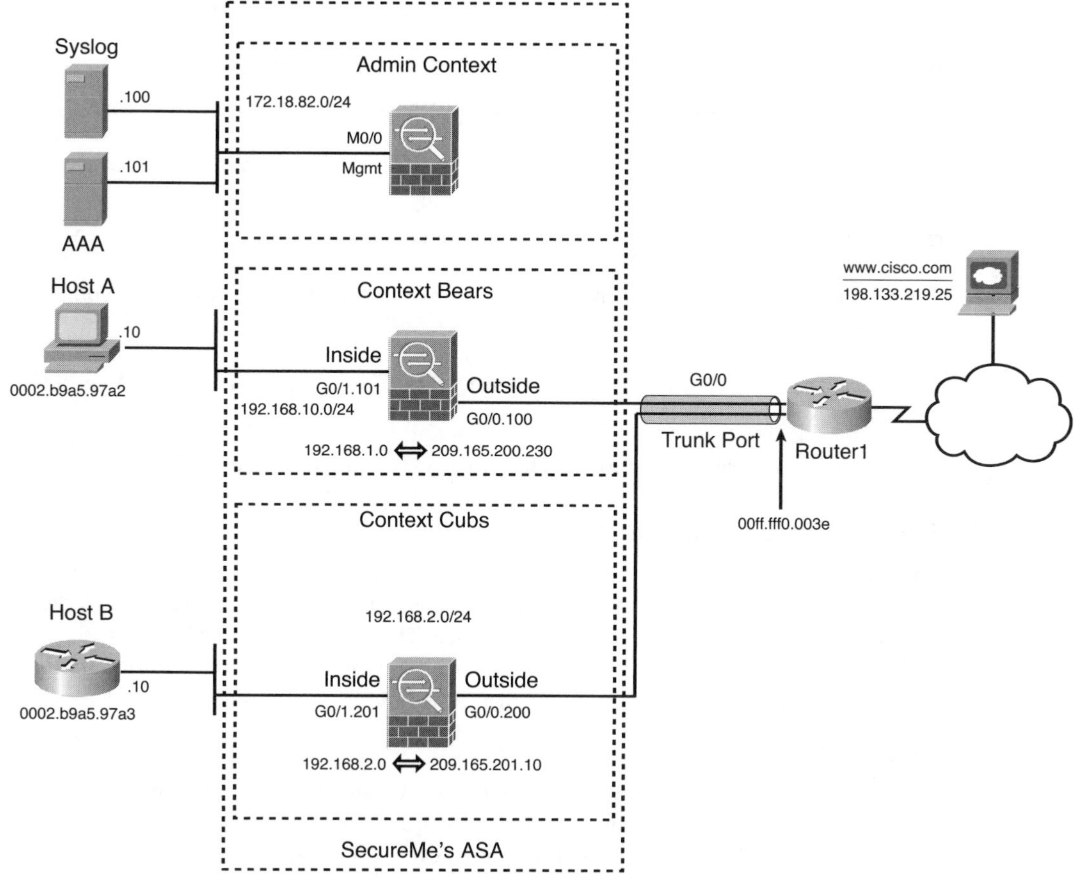

Figure 9-13 *SecureMe Chicago's Multimode Topology*

Cubs and Bears have specific requirements that SecureMe is obliged to meet. However, the security appliance has two active physical interfaces and, as a result, SecureMe wants to create sub-interfaces to accommodate these customers.

Bears

- Allow all BPDUs to pass.
- Provide Internet access by enabling address translation for the inside network.
- Deny all other traffic.
- Set L2F table timeout of 20 minutes.

Cubs

- Allow Enhanced Interior Gateway Routing Protocol (EIGRP) updates to pass.

- Allow Virtual Router Redundancy Protocol (VRRP) updates to pass.
- Deny and log all other inbound traffic on the outside interface.
- Provide Internet access by enabling address translation for the inside network.
- Add a static L2F entry for a Router on outside interface. The MAC address is 00ff.fff0.003e.
- Deny learning dynamic MAC address on the outside interface.

The system execution space has been set up to allocate interfaces to customers' contexts. An admin context is configured to do the following:

- Use an AAA server for SSH user authentication. The IP address of the AAA server is 172.18.82.101.
- Log all the system-generated messages to a syslog server located at 172.18.82.100.

Configuration Steps Using ASDM

The relevant configuration through ASDM is discussed in the following sections. These configuration steps assume that you have IP connectivity from the ASDM client to the management IP address of the security appliance. The management IP address is 172.18.82.64 and it is allocated to the admin context. Consult the initial security appliance configuration for ASDM under the SMTF deployment scenario.

Configuration of System Execution Space

Step 1. Navigate to **Configuration > System > Connect > Context Management > Interfaces**, select **GigabitEthernet0/0**, and click **Edit**. Make sure that the **Enable Interface** option is checked. Click **OK** when you are finished.

Step 2. Navigate to **Configuration > System > Connect > Context Management > Interfaces**, select **GigabitEthernet0/1**, and click **Edit**. Make sure that the **Enable Interface** option is checked. Click **OK** when you are finished.

Step 3. Navigate to **Configuration > System > Connect > Context Management > Interfaces**, click **Add > Interfaces**, and select **GigabitEthernet0/0** under the hardware port. Specify **100** under both "VLAN ID" and "Subinterface ID". Add a description of **Bears Outside Interface** and then click **OK** to add this subinterface.

Step 4. Navigate to **Configuration > System > Connect > Context Management > Interfaces**, click **Add > Interfaces**, and select **GigabitEthernet0/**0 under the hardware port. Specify **200** under both "VLAN ID" and "Subinterface ID". Add a description of **Cubs Outside Interface** and then click **OK** to add this subinterface.

Step 5. Navigate to **Configuration > System > Connect > Context Management > Interfaces**, click **Add > Interfaces**, and select **GigabitEthernet0/1** under the hardware port. Specify **101** under both "VLAN ID" and "Subinterface ID".

Add a description of **Bears Inside Interface** and then click **OK** to add this subinterface.

Step 6. Navigate to **Configuration > System > Connect> Context Management > Interfaces**, click **Add > Interfaces**, and select **GigabitEthernet0/1** under the hardware port. Specify **201** under both "VLAN ID" and "Subinterface ID". Add a description of **Cubs Inside Interface** and then click **OK** to add this subinterface.

Step 7. Navigate to **Configuration > System > Connect > Context Management > Security Contexts**, click **Add** and specify **Bears** as the context name in Security Context. To configure the following interface allocations, click **Add** and

- Select **GigabitEthernet0/0** from the "Physical Interface" drop-down menu. Select **100** from the "Sub Interface Range" drop-down menu, and click OK.
- Select **GigabitEthernet0/1** from the "Physical Interface" drop-down menu. Select **101** from the "Sub Interface Range" drop-down menu and click **OK.**

Step 8. Under **Config URL**, select **disk0:** and then define the configuration filename as **Bears.cfg.** Finally, under Description, specify **Bears Context** and click **OK** when you are finished.

Step 9. Navigate to **Configuration > System > Connect > Context Management > Security Contexts**, click **Add**, and specify **Cubs** as the context name in Security Context. To configure the following interface allocations, click **Add** and

- Select **GigabitEthernet0/0** from the "Physical Interface" drop-down menu. Select **200** from the "Sub Interface Range" drop-down menu, and click **OK.**
- Select **GigabitEthernet0/1** from the "Physical Interface" drop-down menu. Select **201** from the "Sub Interface Range" drop-down menu and click **OK.**

Step 10. Under **Config URL**, select **disk0:** and then define the configuration filename as **Cubs.cfg.** Finally, under Description, specify **Cubs Context** and click **OK** when you are finished.

Configuration of Admin Context

Step 1. Navigate to **Configuration > Context > admin > Connect > Device Management > Logging > Logging Setup** and check the **Enable Logging** option.

Step 2. Navigate to **Configuration > Context > admin > Connect > Device Management > Logging > Syslog Server** and click **Add.** Specify the following under

- Interface: **mgmt**
- IP Address: **172.18.82.100**
- Protocol: **UDP**; Port: **514**. Click **OK** when you are finished.

Step 3. Navigate to **Configuration > Context > admin > Connect > Device Management > Logging > Syslog Setup**. Check **Include Timestamps in Syslogs** to add timestamps when syslogs are generated.

Step 4. Navigate to **Configuration > Context > admin > Connect > Device Management > Logging > Logging Filters**, select **Syslog Servers** and click **Edit**. Under "Filter on Severity", choose **Informational** from the drop-down menu.

Step 5. Navigate to **Configuration > Context > admin > Connect> Device Management > Management Access > ASDM/HTTPS/Telnet/SSH** and click **Add**. Select the **SSH** radio button and configure the following attributes:

- Interface Name: **mgmt**
- IP Address: **172.18.82.0**; Mask: **255.255.255.0**. Click **OK** when you are finished.

Step 6. Navigate to **Configuration > Context > admin > Connect > Device Management > Users/AAA > AAA Server Groups** and select **Add** under the "AAA Server Groups" option. Configure the following attributes:

- Server Group: **RADIUS**
- Protocol: **RADIUS**
- Leave other options as Default. Click **OK** when you are finished.

Step 7. Navigate to **Configuration > Context > admin > Connect> Device Management > Users/AAA > AAA Server Groups.** Click **RADIUS** under "AAA Server Group" and then select **Add** under the "Servers in the Selected Group" option. Configure the following attributes:

- Interface Name: **mgmt**
- Server Name or IP Address: **172.18.82.101**
- Server Secret Key: **Cisco123**
- Leave other options as Default. Click **OK** when you are finished.

Step 8. Navigate to **Configuration > Context > admin > Connect > Device Management > Users/AAA > AAA Access > Authentication.** Enable **SSH** and select **RADIUS** from the "Server Group" drop-down menu. Click **Apply** when you are finished.

Configuration of Bears Context

Step 1. Navigate to **Configuration > Contexts > Bears > Connect > Device Setup > Interfaces.** Select the **GigabitEthernet0/0.100** interface, click **Edit**, and specify the following attributes:

- Interface Name: **outside**
- Security Level: **0**
- Description: **Bears Outside Interface.** Click **OK** when you are finished.

Step 2. Navigate to **Configuration > Contexts > Bears > Connect > Device Setup > Interfaces.** Select the **GigabitEthernet0/1.101** interface, click **Edit**, and specify the following attributes:

- Interface Name: **inside**
- Security Level: **100**
- Description: **Bears Inside Interface.** Click **OK** when you are finished.

Step 3. Navigate to **Configuration > Contexts > Bears > Connect > Device Management > Management Access > Management IP Address** and configure the following parameters:

- Management IP Address: **192.168.1.10**
- Subnet Mask: **255.255.255.0**

Step 4. Navigate to **Configuration > Contexts > Bears > Connect > Firewall > Ethertype Rules > Add** and configure the following Access Rule:

- Interface: **Inside**
- Action: **Permit**
- Ethertype: **bpdu**
- Direction: **in.** Click **OK.**

Step 5. Navigate to **Configuration > Contexts > Bears > Connect > Firewall > Ethertype Rules > Add** and configure the following Access Rule:

- Interface: **Outside**
- Action: **Permit**
- Ethertype: **bpdu**
- Direction: **in.** Click **OK.**

Step 6. Navigate to **Configuration > Contexts > Bears > Connect > Firewall > NAT Rules > Add** and select **Add Dynamic NAT Rule.** Under the **Translated** section, click **Manage > Add** and configure the following policy for the Global Address Pool:

- Interface: **outside**
- Pool ID: **1**

- IP Address to Add: **Select Port Address Translation (PAT)** and specify **209.165.200.230** with a Netmask of **255.255.255.255**. Click **Add>>** and then **OK** when you are finished.

Step 7. Configure the following NAT Access Rule under the **Original** section:

- Interface: **inside**
- Source: **192.168.1.0/24**
- Translated Global Pool ID: **1**. Click **OK** when you are finished.

Step 8. Navigate to **Configuration > Contexts > Bears > Connect > Device Management > Advanced > Bridging > MAC Address Table** and specify **20** under "Dynamic Entry Timeout."

Configuration of Cubs Context

Step 1. Navigate to **Configuration > Contexts > Cubs > Connect > Device Setup > Interfaces.** Select the **GigabitEthernet0/0.200** interface, click **Edit**, and specify the following attributes:

- Interface Name: **outside**
- Security Level: **0**
- Description: **Cubs Outside Interface**. Click **OK** when you are finished.

Step 2. Navigate to **Configuration > Contexts > Cubs > Connect > Device Setup > Interfaces.** Select the **GigabitEthernet0/1.201** interface, click **Edit**, and specify the following attributes:

- Interface Name: **inside**
- Security Level: **100**
- Description: **Cubs Inside Interface**. Click **OK** when you are finished.

Step 3. Navigate to **Configuration > Contexts > Cubs > Connect > Device Management > Management Access > Management IP Address** and configure the following parameters:

- Management IP Address: **192.168.2.10**
- Subnet Mask: **255.255.255.0**

Step 4. Navigate to **Configuration > Contexts > Cubs > Connect > Firewall > Access Rules > Add** and select **Add Access Rule**. Configure the following Access Rule:

- Interface: **outside**
- Action: **Permit**
- Source: **any**
- Destination: **any**

- Service: **eigrp**
- Description: **To Allow EIGRP Packets**
- Direction: **in**
- Enable Rule: **Checked.** Click **OK** when you are finished.

Step 5. Navigate to **Configuration > Contexts > Cubs > Connect > Firewall > Access Rules > Add** and select **Add Access Rule.** Configure the following Access Rule:

- Interface: **outside**
- Action: **Permit**
- Source: **any**
- Destination: **any**
- Service: **112**
- Description: **To Allow VRRP Packets**
- Direction: **in**
- Enable Rule: **Checked.** Click **OK** when you are finished.

Step 6. Navigate to **Configuration > Contexts > Cubs > Connect > Firewall > Access Rules > Add** and select **Add Access Rule**. Configure the following Access Rule:

- Interface: **outside**
- Action: **Deny**
- Source: **any**
- Destination: **any**
- Service: **ip**
- Description: **Deny all Packets**
- Direction: **in**
- Enable Rule: **Checked.** Click **OK** when you are finished.

Step 7. Navigate to **Configuration > Contexts > Cubs > Connect > Firewall > NAT Rules > Add** and select **Add Dynamic NAT Rule.** Under the **Translated** section, click **Manage > Add** and configure the following policy for the Global Address Pool:

- Interface: **outside**
- Pool ID: **1**
- IP Address to Add: **Select Port Address Translation** (**PAT**) and specify **209.165.201.10** with a Netmask of **255.255.255.255**. Click **Add>>** and then **OK** when you are finished.

Step 8. Configure the following NAT Access Rule under the **Original** section:

- Interface: **inside**
- Source: **192.168.2.0/24**
- Translated Global Pool ID: **1**. Click **OK** when you are finished.

Step 9. Navigate to **Configuration > Contexts > Cubs > Connect > Device Management > Advanced > Bridging > MAC Address Table**, click **Add** and specify the following:

- Interface Name: **outside**
- MAC Address: **00ff.fff0.003e**

Step 10. Navigate to **Configuration > Contexts > Cubs > Connect > Device Management > Advanced > Bridging > MAC Learning**, select the **outside** interface, and then click **Disable.**

Configuration Steps Using CLI

Example 9-17 shows the relevant configuration to achieve the listed goals. Some commands have been removed for brevity.

Example 9-17 *ASA's Relevant Configuration with Multiple Security Contexts*

```
System Execution Space
Chicago# show running
ASA Version 8.2(1) <system>
! Enable Transparent Firewall Globally
firewall transparent
hostname Chicago
! Main GigabitEthernet0/0 interface
interface GigabitEthernet0/0
! Sub-interface assigned to the Bears context as the outside interface. A VLAN ID
is assigned to the interface
interface GigabitEthernet0/0.100
 description Bears Outside Interface
 vlan 100
! Sub-interface assigned to the Cubs context as the outside interface. A VLAN ID
is assigned to the interface
interface GigabitEthernet0/0.200
 description Cubs Outside Interface
 vlan 200
! Main GigabitEthernet0/1 interface
```

```
interface GigabitEthernet0/1
! Sub-interface assigned to the Bears context as the inside interface. A VLAN ID
is assigned to the interface
interface GigabitEthernet0/1.101
 description Bears Inside Interface
 vlan 101
! Sub-interface assigned to the Cubs context as the inside interface. A VLAN ID
is assigned to the interface
interface GigabitEthernet0/1.201
description Cubs Inside Interface
 vlan 201
! Main Management0/0 interface
interface Management0/0
! context named "admin" is the designated Admin context
admin-context admin
! "admin" context definition along with the allocated interfaces.
context admin
  allocate-interface Management0/0
  config-url disk0:/admin.cfg
! "Bears" context definition along with the allocated interfaces.
context Bears
  description Bears Context
  allocate-interface GigabitEthernet0/0.100
  allocate-interface GigabitEthernet0/1.101
  config-url disk0:/Bears.cfg
! "Cubs" context definition along with the allocated interfaces.
context Cubs
  description Cubs Context
  allocate-interface GigabitEthernet0/0.200
  allocate-interface GigabitEthernet0/1.201
  config-url disk0:/Cubs.cfg
<Some Output Removed For Brevity>

Admin Context

Chicago/admin(config)# show running
: Saved
:
ASA Version 8.2(1) <context>
! transparent firewall mode is enabled
firewall transparent
hostname Chicago
!
! Management interface of the admin context with security level set to 100
interface Management0/0
 nameif mgmt
```

```
 security-level 100
ip address 172.18.82.64 255.255.255.0
 management-only
! configuration of a syslog server with logging level set to informational with
timestamp
logging enable
logging timestamp
logging trap informational
logging host mgmt 172.18.82.100
! Default route towards mgmt interface
route mgmt 0.0.0.0 0.0.0.0 172.18.82.1 1
! configuration of a AAA server using RADIUS for authentication
aaa-server RADIUS protocol radius
aaa-server RADIUS (mgmt) host 172.18.82.101
 key Cisco123
! SSH using RADIUS for authentication
aaa authentication ssh console RADIUS
ssh 172.18.82.0 255.255.255.0 mgmt
! HTTP Server for ASDM
http server enable
http 172.18.82.0 255.255.255.0 mgmt
<Some Output Removed For Brevity>
```

Bears Context

```
Chicago/Bears(config)# show running
: Saved
:
ASA Version 8.2(1) <context>
! transparent firewall mode is enabled
firewall transparent
hostname Bears

!outside interface of the Bears context with security level set to 0
interface GigabitEthernet0/0.100
 description Bears Outside Interface
 nameif outside
 security-level 0

!inside interface of the Bears context with security level set to 100
interface GigabitEthernet0/1.101
 description Bears Inside Interface
 nameif inside
 security-level 100

! Access-list entry to allow BPDU traffic on inside
access-list inside_ether_access_in remark To forward BPDU packets
access-list inside_ether_access_in ethertype permit bpdu
```

```
! Access-list entry to allow BPDU traffic on outside
access-list outside_ether_access_in remark To forward BPDU packets
access-list outside_ether_access_in ethertype permit bpdu


! Global IP address
ip address 192.168.1.10 255.255.255.0

! NAT policy to translate inside network to 209.165.200.230
global (outside) 1 209.165.200.230 netmask 255.255.255.255
nat (inside) 1 192.168.1.0 255.255.255.0
! Access-list is applied to the inside interface
access-group inside_ether_access_in in interface inside
! Access-list is applied to the outside interface
access-group outside_ether_access_in in interface outside

! L2F timeout is set to 20 minutes
mac-address-table aging-time 20
!
<Some Output Removed For Brevity>
```

Cubs Context

```
Chicago/Cubs(config)# show running
: Saved
:
ASA Version 8.2(1) <context>
! transparent firewall mode is enabled
firewall transparent
hostname Cubs

!outside interface of the Cubs context with security level set to 0
interface GigabitEthernet0/0.200
 description Cubs Outside Interface
 nameif outside
 security-level 0

!inside interface of the Cubs context with security level set to 100
interface GigabitEthernet0/1.201
 description Cubs Inside Interface
 nameif inside
 security-level 100

! Access-list entry to only allow EIGRP and VRRP traffic on the outside interface
access-list outside_access_in remark Allow EIGRP to pass through
access-list outside_access_in extended permit eigrp any any
access-list outside_access_in remark To Allow VRRP
```

```
access-list outside_access_in extended permit 112 any any
access-list outside_access_in extended deny ip any any

! Global IP address
ip address 192.168.2.10 255.255.255.0
!NAT Configuration to translate 192.168.2.0 to 209.165.201.10
global (outside) 1 209.165.201.10 netmask 255.255.255.255
nat (inside) 1 192.168.2.0 255.255.255.0

! Access-list is applied to the outside interface
access-group outside_access_in in interface outside

! Static L2F entry of outside router as dynamic learning is not allowed
mac-address-table static outside 00ff.fff0.003e

! learning MAC address on the outside interface is not allowed
mac-learn outside disable
<Some Output Removed For Brevity>
```

Monitoring and Troubleshooting the Transparent Firewalls

Cisco ASA provides **show** commands to ensure that the transparent firewall is working as expected. In the event of a problem, you can enable relevant debugs (which are discussed later in this section).

Monitoring

If transparent firewall mode is configured, first verify that the system is recognizing this mode. Achieve this by using the **show firewall** command, as shown in Example 9-18.

Example 9-18 *Output of* show firewall

```
Chicago# show firewall
Firewall mode: Transparent
```

Second, confirm that the system is running in the configured single or multiple mode, as shown in Example 9-19.

Example 9-19 *Output of* show mode

```
Chicago# show mode
Security context mode: multiple
```

After you have verified that the system is switching packets in the correct mode, monitor the status of the L2F table, as demonstrated in Example 9-20. By using **show mac-address-table**, verify the entries in the bridge table if they look accurate, including static and dynamic entries. Four dynamic L2F entries are learned on the outside interface. There is also a static L2F entry pointing to the outside interface with no aging time.

Example 9-20 *Checking the L2F Table*

```
Chicago# show mac-address-table
interface          mac address      type    Age(min)
------------------------------------------------------
outside          00d0.c0d2.8030      dynamic   1
outside          0040.8c5c.0e92      dynamic   4
outside          000b.cdf0.8e39      dynamic   4
outside          000e.8315.0bff      dynamic   2
outside          00ff.fff0.003e      static
```

The **show arp-inspection** command displays whether ARP inspection is enabled or disabled on all interfaces. Example 9-21 shows that ARP inspection is enabled on the **outside** interface with the **no-flood** option if a miss occurs on the static ARP table. ARP inspection is disabled on the inside interface.

Example 9-21 *Checking the Interfaces for ARP Inspection*

```
Chicago # show arp-inspection
interface                        arp-inspection                        miss
------------------------------------------------------------------------------.
inside                           disable                                -
outside                          enable          no-flood
```

If everything looks good yet traffic is still not flowing, verify the hit counts on the configured interface ACL. Example 9-22 shows 10 hit counts for IPX traffic.

Example 9-22 *Monitoring ACLs*

```
Chicago# show access-list
access-list inside ethertype permit ipx (hitcount=10)
access-list inside ethertype permit bpdu (hitcount=0)
access-list inside ethertype deny any (hitcount=0)
```

For TCP-, UDP-, and, optionally, ICMP-based traffic passing through the security appliance, you can use the **show conn** command and verify the connection status. As shown in Example 9-23, a connection is established from 10.10.1.10 to a Telnet server located at 10.10.1.1.

Example 9-23 *Output of* show conn

```
Chicago# show conn
1 in use, 1 most used
TCP outside 10.10.1.1:23 inside 10.10.1.10:11018 idle 0:00:02 bytes 90 flags UIO
```

Troubleshooting

For troubleshooting purposes, Cisco ASA includes a number of important debug and syslog messages to help isolate issues in the transparent mode firewall. This section discusses three scenarios to help you gain the troubleshooting skills when the firewalls are deployed in transparent mode:

- **Hosts are not able to communicate**—As shown in Figure 9-12, when the web client is not able to communicate with the web server located at 10.10.3.5, the administrator can take the following steps to isolate the issue:

  Step 1. Ping the IP address of the transparent firewall from the web client to ensure that the connectivity exists between the client and the transparent firewall. If successful, move to Step 2; otherwise, check the cable and VLAN assignments if a switch is placed between the host and the transparent firewall. Additionally, check the L2F table on the appliance by using the **show mac-address-table** command to ensure that the host is being learned on the correct interface. If the MAC address is not learned, you can enable **debug mac-address-table**, which is used to view L2F table updates. The appliance uses this table to forward a packet out to an interface. This is shown in Example 9-24, where the security appliance adds a MAC address of 0003.a088.da86 in the table on the inside interface.

Example 9-24 *Debugging the L2F Table Entries*

```
Chicago# debug mac-address-table
add_l2fwd_entry: Going to add MAC 0003.a088.da86.
add_l2fwd_entry: Added MAC 0003.a088.da86 into bridge table thru inside.
add_l2fwd_entry: Sending LU to add MAC 0003.a088.da86.
set_l2: Found MAC entry 0003.a088.da86 on inside.
```

  Step 2. Ping the IP address of the gateway router (10.10.1.1) from the web client, assuming that you allow ICMP traffic to pass through the firewall. If successful, move to Step 3. If unsuccessful, check the inbound ACL and outbound ACL on the security appliance. If the ACLs look properly configured, enable **debug arp-inspection** to determine whether the ARP requests are being forwarded and inspected through the transparent firewall. Example 9-25 shows the output of **debug arp-inspection**, where the appliance is forwarding the ARP requests from 10.10.1.5 destined to 10.10.1.1 located on the outside interface.

Example 9-25 *Output of debug arp-inspection*

```
Chicago# debug arp-inspection
arp_in_forward: Forwarding arp request from 10.10.1.5 to 10.10.1.1 smac
0003.a088.da86
learn_and_forward_arp_request: Forwarding arp request to outside
```

Step 3. Ping the remote gateway (10.10.3.1) from the web client. If it fails, check the inbound ACL and outbound ACL on the router for the ICMP traffic. If it works, make sure that the ACLs allow TCP and UDP connections necessary for browsing the website. Ports such as UDP 53 for DNS resolution and TCP 80 for web browsing should be opened.

- **Traffic capture on the ASA**—One of the most commonly used troubleshooting tools is the capture command, discussed in Chapter 3 and Chapter 4. If you are isolating the communication problem between the web client and server, then define an ACL with the interesting traffic (IP addresses of the client and server). Link this ACL to the capture command on the inside and outside interface. View the captured packets by issuing the show capture command, followed by the name of the capture. As shown in Example 9-26, two captures, cap-inside and cap-outside, are defined. The show capture cap-inside shows five packets that were exchanged between the 10.10.1.5 and 10.10.3.5 addresses.

Example 9-26 Output of **capture** Command

```
Chicago(config)# access-list capture permit ip host 10.10.1.5 host 10.10.3.5
Chicago(config)# access-list capture permit ip host 10.10.3.5 host 10.10.1.5
Chicago(config)# capture cap-inside access-list capture interface inside
Chicago(config)# capture cap-outside access-list capture interface outside
Chicago(config)# show capture cap-inside

5 packets captured

1: 03:43:09.965663 10.10.1.5.29307 > 10.10.3.5.80: S 4212401036:4212401036(0) win
4128 <mss 1460>
2: 03:43:09.965755 10.10.3.5.80 > 10.10.1.5.29307: S 496621581:496621581(0) ack
4212401037 win 8192 <mss 1380>
```

```
3: 03:43:09.966319 10.10.1.5.29307 > 10.10.3.5.80: . ack 496621582 win 4128
4: 03:43:09.967235 10.10.3.5.80 > 10.10.1.5.29307: P 496621582:496621602(20) ack
4212401037 win 8192
5: 03:43:09.967937 10.10.1.5.29307 > 10.10.3.5.80: P 4212401037:4212401057(20) ack
496621602 win 4108
5 packets shown
```

- **Moved host is not able to communicate**—If a host is moved from an outside interface to the inside interface, or vice versa, and is not able to communicate after the move, check to ensure that a static L2F entry does not point to the old interface. Additionally, **debug l2-indication** can be enabled to verify the processing of Layer 2 indications such as miss, learn, host move, and refresh of IP packets. Example 9-26 shows the output of **debug l2-indication** when a static entry is defined for a MAC address **00e0.b06a.412c** toward the outside interface and the host is moved toward the inside interface. The Cisco ASA indicates a host move to the inside interface from the outside interface.

Example 9-26 Output of **debug l2-indication**

```
Chicago# debug l2-indication
debug l2-indication  enabled at level 1
f1_tf_process_l2_hostmove:HOST MOVE: Host move indication cur_ifc outside, new_ifc
inside mac address: 00e0.b06a.412c
HOST MOVE: cur_vStackNum 0, new_vStackNum 1
HOST MOVE: Host move indication for static entry 00e0.b06a.412c
f1_tf_process_l2_hostmove:HOST MOVE: Host move indication cur_ifc outside, new_ifc
inside mac address: 00e0.b06a.412c
f1_tf_process_l2_hostmove:HOST MOVE: cur_vStackNum 0, new_vStackNum 1
f1_tf_process_l2_hostmove:HOST MOVE: Host move indication for static entry
00e0.b06a.412c
```

If the security appliance dynamically learns the MAC address of a host on a particular interface and the host is moved to another interface, you can remove the dynamic entries associated with an interface by using **clear mac-address-table** followed by the name of the interface.

As shown in Example 9-28, the administrator wants to clear the L2F entries associated with the outside interface.

Example 9-28 Clearing the L2F Table Associated with the Outside Interface

```
Chicago# clear mac-address-table outside
```

Additionally, you can remove all dynamic entries in the entire table by issuing the **clear mac-address-table** command.

- **General syslogging**—The ASA includes four syslog messages to assist in preventing either MAC spoofing or ARP inspection issues. The ASA logs an L2F message when
    - A host is moved from one interface to another. This is known as *host move*. You will see a message with an ID of 412001.
    - The ASA detects MAC spoofing in the L2F table. MAC spoofing is similar to host move, but the original MAC address was statically mapped to an interface. You will see a message with an ID of 322001.
    - The L2F table gets completely full. You will see a message with an ID of 412002.
    - The ARP packets are dropped because they fail the ARP inspection check. You will see a message with an ID of 322003.

Summary

The transparent firewall feature is designed for security professionals who do not want to change existing address schemes, but still require a firewall to inspect all packets leaving a subnet. Cisco ASA integrates features like security contexts with the transparent firewall and, therefore, presents a complete solution to fit any design scenario. This chapter covered the architectural overview of the transparent firewall and provided detailed configuration guides to suit any network deployments. This chapter also provided two deployment scenarios to enforce learning and to show the robustness of this feature. Extensive **show** and **debug** commands were discussed to assist a network administrator in troubleshooting complicated transparent firewall deployments.

Chapter 10

Failover and Redundancy

This chapter covers the following topics:

- Architectural overview
- Failover configuration
- Deployment scenarios
- Monitoring and troubleshooting

With more organizations moving toward e-commerce, dependence on both LANs and WANs has increased drastically. They cannot afford to lose connectivity with their core servers in the network infrastructure. This connectivity loss could cause multimillion-dollar revenue losses per minute. Consequently, organizations want to deploy and maintain reliable network devices to ensure nonstop availability and nearly 100 percent uptime. They do so by implementing layers of redundant devices to prevent interruption should any network component fail.

Because Cisco is fully committed to provide a resilient infrastructure to its customer base, Cisco ASA provides many valuable failover features to suit your environment. For failover to work, you must have two Cisco ASA devices connected to each other, using a dedicated network connection. The appliances have to be identical in terms of hardware model, number of interfaces, and the software license. Thus, if one of the appliances fails to perform its duties, the other appliance takes over and seamlessly starts passing traffic.

Architectural Overview

When two identical Cisco ASAs are set up in failover, one of the appliances, the *active appliance*, is responsible for creating the state and translation tables, transferring the data packets, and monitoring the other unit. The other security appliance, the *standby appliance*, is responsible for monitoring the status of the active unit. The active and standby appliances are connected through a dedicated network link to send failover-related messages to each other. This connection, known as a *failover control link*, is established over a dedicated failover LAN interface. When a failure occurs on the active appliance, the standby takes over the active role and starts forwarding traffic. This newly active appliance also takes over the IP and MAC addresses that were used by the previous appliance. After the failed unit recovers, it assumes the standby role.

The failover control link provides a medium over which the two security appliances can communicate and update one another about:

- The unit state (whether active or standby)
- Network link status
- Hello or keepalive messages (which are sent on all interfaces)
- MAC address exchange
- Configuration replication from active to standby

Figure 10-1 shows two Cisco ASA devices connected to each other through the GigabitEthernet interfaces. The GigabitEthernet0/2 interface is used as the failover link, shown as the dotted line.

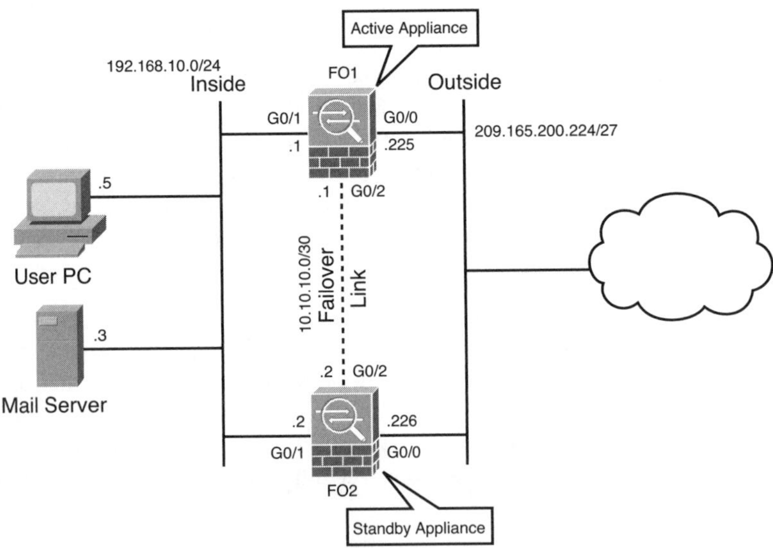

Figure 10-1 *Failover Setup Between Two ASAs*

Conditions that Trigger Failover

For failover to occur, any one of the following conditions has to be met:

- **An administrator manually has switched over from active to standby**—This happens when either **no failover active** is issued on the active unit or **failover active** is issued on the standby unit.
- **The active appliance has lost power or crashed due to hardware/software defects.**
- **A standby appliance has stopped receiving hello (or keepalive) packets on the failover control interface**—In this condition, if the standby unit does not receive three consecutive hello packets, it sends additional testing packets to the remaining data-passing interfaces. If it still does not receive a response from the active unit, it assumes that a failure has occurred and takes over the role of the active appliance.
- **The failover control interface link is down**—In this scenario, the security appliance sends additional testing packets to the remaining interfaces to determine whether the peer's control interface is also down. If the peer's control interface is also down then failover does not occur and the failed interface is marked as "Failed." However, if the peer's control interface is not down, then failover occurs because the standby is deemed healthier then the current active appliance.
- **The link state of a data-passing interface is down**—In this condition, the appliance marks the interface as failed and initiates the failover process. Additionally, if the standby appliance does not receive the hello packets for two consecutive polling periods on an interface, the appliance goes through a series of additional tests on the interface to determine the root cause of the problem. These tests are discussed in detail in the following section.

Note When using the Active/Active failover and the **preempt** command, discussed later in the "Active/Active Failover" section, the failover group might change which firewall is active for a context based upon whether the preferred physical unit is online and healthy.

Failover Interface Tests

To ensure that a failure is properly detected on monitored interfaces before initiating a failover, the security appliance goes through four different interface tests. These tests are discussed in the order in which they are checked:

- **Link up/down test**—The security appliance determines the status of its network interface card (NIC) by doing the link up/down test, which finds out whether one of the ports on the security appliance is not plugged into an operational network. In this case, the security appliance marks the interface as failed and initiates the failover process. Some examples of this failover include hardware port failure, unplugged cable of an interface, and a failure on the hub or switch to which the interfaces are connected. If the interface passes the link up/down test, the security appliance moves to the network activity test.

- **Network activity test—**In this test, the security appliance counts all received packets for up to 5 seconds. If the security appliance receives any packet during this time interval, it stops this test and marks the interface operational. If no traffic is received, the test is inconclusive, so the security appliance proceeds to the next test.
- **ARP test—**In the ARP test, the security appliance reads its ARP table for the last ten acquired entries. It sends an ARP request to those machines one at a time, and then counts packets for up to 5 seconds. If it receives traffic during this time window, it marks the interface as operational. If it does not receive a response from the host, it moves to the next host and sends an ARP request, and so on. At the end of the list, if the security appliance does not receive any traffic, it moves on to the ping test.
- **Broadcast ping test—**In this test, the security appliance sends out a broadcast ping request and then counts all received packets for up to 5 seconds. If it receives any packets during this time window, the security appliance declares this interface operational and stops the test. If the appliance does not receive any traffic, it marks the interface as failed and initiates failover.

Note Although the network activity, ARP, and broadcast ping tests are time consuming, they do help avoid unnecessary failover on the security appliance. Even when an interface is going through these tests, the security appliance forwards traffic on the remaining interfaces.

If both active and standby interfaces fail all tests, then both interfaces go into the "unknown state." The interfaces with the unknown state do not count toward the monitored interface failover limit. Interface monitoring is discussed in the "Monitoring Failover Interfaces" section.

Stateful Failover

When a connection is established through the active appliance, Cisco ASA updates its connection table. A connection entry includes the source and destination IP addresses, protocol used, current state of the connection, the interface to which it is tied, and the number of bytes transferred. Depending on the failover configuration, the security appliance takes one of the following actions:

- **Stateless failover—**The security appliance maintains the connection table but does not replicate entries to the standby appliance.
- **Stateful failover—**The security appliance maintains the connection table and replicates it to the standby appliance.

In a stateless failover, the active appliance is not responsible for sending the state table updates to the standby appliance. When the standby unit becomes active (whether by detecting a failure or by manually switching over), it has to build all the connection entries from scratch. This causes all the stateful traffic, such as TCP, to get disrupted.

In a stateful failover, the active appliance sends an update to the standby unit whenever there is a change in the state table. In this mode, the active appliance sends stateful updates over a dedicated link to the standby unit. When the standby unit becomes active, it does not need to build any connection entries because all the entries already exist in its database. This dedicated connection is known as the *stateful link*.

> **Note** You can use the same physical interface for both failover control and stateful link updates. However, it is not recommended if your appliances generate a lot of state updates. Additionally, it is recommended that you use the fastest interface as the stateful link and that the latency for the link should be less than 10 milliseconds to avoid performance degradation.

Table 10-1 lists the entries and the types of traffic that are replicated to the standby appliance in the stateful failover.

> **Note** The security appliances replicate IPSec states only if stateful failover is used in Active/Standby. Any form of VPN is not supported in multimode firewall, and Active/Active failover works only in multimode.

Hardware and Software Requirements

For failover to work properly, the following specifications must be identical:

- **Product or model number of the appliance**—For example, both appliances must be Cisco ASA 5520. You cannot use an ASA 5520 and an ASA 5540 in failover.
- **Amount of RAM**—You cannot use 512 MB of RAM in one appliance and 1024 MB in the other one.
- **Number of interfaces**—Both appliances must have the same number of physical interfaces. For example, if you plan to deploy ASA5580s in your network in failover, then you cannot have mismatched interfaces on the two security appliances. Additionally, interfaces must be of the same type. You cannot use copper-based interfaces on one of them and fiber-based interfaces on the other.
- **External Module**—If you have a security module such as SSM-IPS, then both appliances must have it.
- **Activation key with the same features**—The activation key must have the same features, such as the failover mode, encryption level, and number of VPN peers.

Table 10-1 *Types of Traffic and Stateful Replication*

Type of Traffic	Stateful Replication
HTTP connection	Yes, if enabled
TCP connection	Yes
UDP connection	Yes
Xlate	Yes
IKE/IPSec SA	Yes
ARP table	Yes
Layer 2 table, in transparent mode	Yes
GTP PDP table	Yes
SIP sessions	Yes
SSL VPN sessions	Yes[1]
Uauth cache	No
URL filtering cache	No
TCP intercept	No
SNMP firewall MIB	No
Routing table	No
State information for Security Services Modules (SSM)	No
Phone proxy sessions	No
IPv6 session information	No

[1]SSL VPN sessions are replicated to standby firewall with the exceptions of Smart Tunnels, Port Forwarding, Plugins, Java Applets, or IPv6 clientless/AnyConnect sessions. Additionally, Citrix authentication sessions are not replicated and users must reauthenticate themselves after a failover.

Note The software version does not have to be the same on the security appliances when failover is configured. This is called zero-downtime software upgrade, covered later in this chapter.

Before setting up security appliances for failover, verify that they have a valid license to run failover. After you verify the activation key, you can proceed with failover configuration.

Additionally, it is recommended that you use the same size of Flash memory on both appliances.

Types of Failover

Cisco ASA supports two different types of failover: device-level failover and interface-level failover.

Device-Level Failover

In device-level failover, if the active appliance starts experiencing issues such as hardware failure, the standby device can change its role and become the active device in the network. In the initial device-level failover configuration, you designate one device as *primary* and the other one as *secondary*. If both devices are powered on at the same time, then the primary appliance becomes active while the secondary appliance assumes the standby role. If the primary/active device experiences issues and a failover occurs, then the secondary appliance becomes active. When the primary appliance recovers, it keeps itself in the standby role until a failover occurs on the secondary/active appliance.

Cisco ASA supports two different types of device-level failover:

- Active/Standby failover
- Active/Active failover

Note Device-level failover supports up to two physical security appliances.

Active/Standby Failover

Active/Standby failover is identical to the failover scenario described earlier in the chapter where the active unit is responsible for passing the traffic and the standby appliance monitors the status of the active appliance. Both appliances send hello messages to monitor the status of one another.

Note Cisco 5505 security appliances support Active/Standby stateless failover only if a Security Plus license is purchased. You cannot use failover on an ASA 5505 if it is used as an EasyVPN client. EasyVPN client functionality is discussed in Chapter 17, "IPSec Remote-Access VPNs."

In Active/Standby failover, the Cisco ASAs go through the following election process. They assume roles based on their designated status, whether primary or secondary.

Step 1. When both appliances are up and running, one of them assumes the active role while the other appliance assumes the standby role.

Step 2. If both devices boot up simultaneously, the primary appliance takes over the active appliance role, and the secondary appliances goes into the standby state. The primary uses the active IP address and its MAC-address as the Layer 3 and Layer 2 addresses respectively. If failover occurs, the secondary firewall keeps using the IP address and primary's MAC address as the active addresses.

Step 3. If one of the security appliances boots up and detects an active failover unit, it goes into the standby state regardless of its primary or secondary designation.

Step 4. If one of the security appliances boots up and does not detect an active failover unit, it goes in the active state regardless of its primary or secondary designation.

Step 5. In case both appliances become active, the secondary changes its state to standby as soon as it discovers another active primary firewall, while the primary remains active.

Step 6. In case both appliances become standby, the primary changes its state to active, while the secondary remains standby after they detect each other's state.

Active/Active Failover

Active/Active failover is a feature in which both appliances, while monitoring the status of their peers, actively pass traffic. The appliances in Active/Active failover mode can be deployed only in multimode, discussed in Chapter 8, "Virtualization." Figure 10-2 shows a network topology where two appliances are set up in stateful multimode Active/Active failover. The primary appliance is named FO1 and the secondary appliance is named FO2. The appliances are set up for two customer contexts: Cubs and Bears. In this deployment, the Cubs security context is active on FO1 and standby on FO2. However, the Bears security context is active on FO2 and standby on FO1. If FO1 fails, the standby security context on FO2 for Cubs becomes active and takes over the IP and MAC addresses of FO1. As a result, both security contexts will be active on FO2.

If stateful failover is turned on, the device failover is completely transparent to the end hosts because the firewalls replicate state and connection tables. When the security appliances are deployed in Active/Active mode, both the Primary and Secondary firewalls pass traffic and thus the firewall resources are efficiently utilized. If one of the appliances fails, the active firewall passes all traffic; it is therefore recommended that you do not oversubscribe the failover pair.

A key point to remember is that the failover in the Cisco ASA is per failover redundancy group (discussed in the section, "Failover Configuration") as opposed to per-context failover. The Cisco ASA's failover is currently limited to only two failover redundancy groups.

Note If you are sharing an interface between multiple contexts, all those contexts need to be in the same failover redundancy group.

In Active/Active failover, it is possible that packets can leave from one active unit and can return to the other active unit. Cisco ASA implements a feature known as *asymmetric routing* to guide packets back to the context from which they originated. This feature is discussed in the following section.

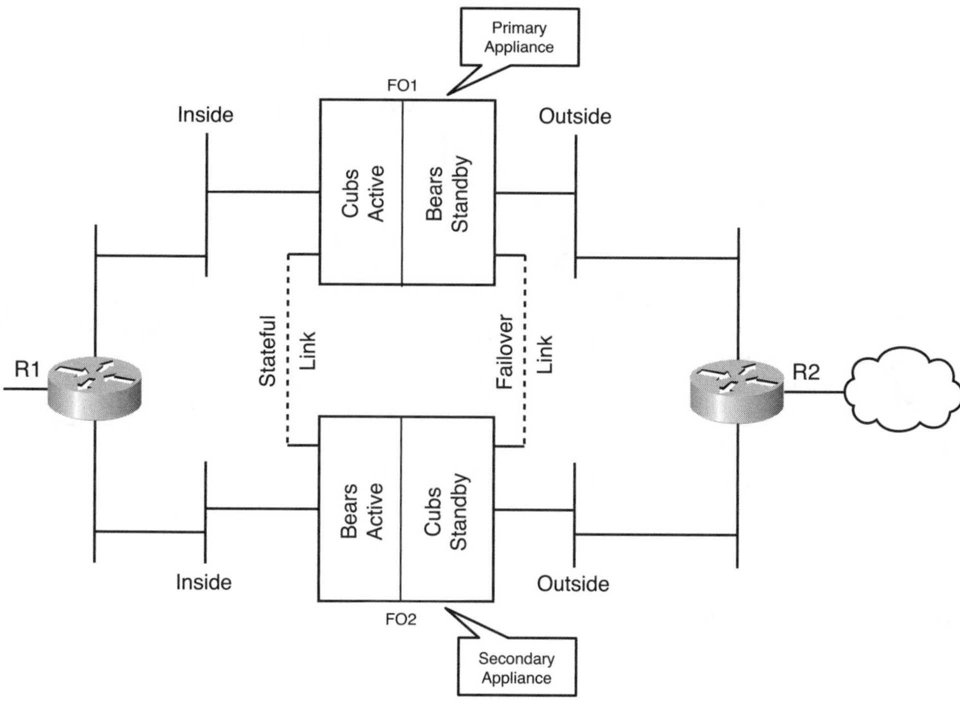

Figure 10-2 *Appliances in Active/Active Multiple Mode*

Active/Active Failover and Asymmetric Routing

Many enterprise customers use multiple ISPs to get connectivity to the Internet or to their remote locations. Depending on their implementation, these enterprises can use these ISPs to either load-balance traffic or back each other up in the event of a failure.

Figure 10-3 depicts two appliances connected to two different ISPs and running in Active/Active failover with multiple contexts. Context Cubs is active on FO1, whereas context Bears is active on FO2. The problem arises when both ISPs are load-balancing the traffic out to the cloud and both appliances are in Active/Active mode. If Host A, sitting behind context Cubs, sends out a TCP SYN packet to Host B, the packet can leave the active appliance (FO1). However, there is no guarantee that the SYN-ACK, the reply from the server, will be routed back through the same unit. If the SYN-ACK packet lands on the other active appliance (FO2), FO2 drops the packet because it does not have the connection table entry for the original SYN packet.

Note The asymmetric routing feature is supported only in multimode. Asymmetric routing is not supported if the appliances use shared interfaces.

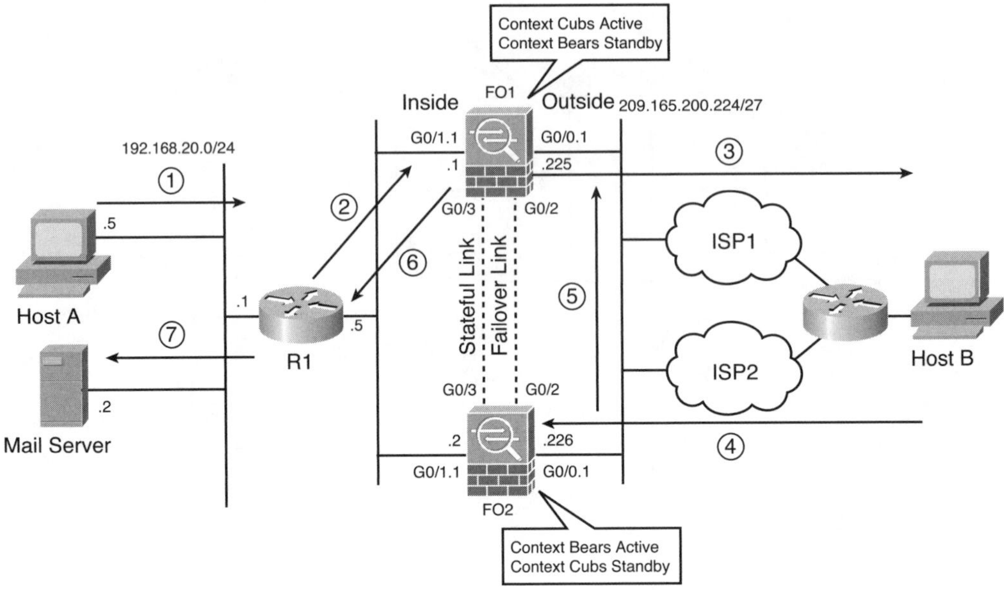

Figure 10-3 *Asymmetric Routing*

If the asymmetric routing functionality is enabled, the appliances restore asymmetric routed packets to the correct interface. FO1 will replicate the connection table entry for the SYN packet to FO2 over the stateful failover link. Thus, when the active context on FO2 (Bears) receives the SYN-ACK packet, it will forward the packet to FO1 because it belongs to context Cubs, which is active on FO1. Figure 10-4 depicts all the steps when Host A communicates with Host B.

Step 1. Host A sends the SYN packet to its gateway router.

Step 2. The gateway router consults its routing table and forwards the SYN packet to FO1, because it belongs to context Cubs.

Step 3. FO1 looks at the routing table and forwards the SYN packet out to the Internet through ISP1.

Step 4. Host B sends SYN-ACK, which gets routed to FO2 through ISP2.

Step 5. FO2 receives the packet on context Bears (as it is active) but it does not have an active connection. It checks other interfaces that are in the same asymmetric routing group for the corresponding connection. In this case, it detects an active connection from FO1 for context Cubs. Therefore, it forwards the packet to FO1 via the outside interface by rewriting the Layer 2 information. It will continue to forward packets until the connection is terminated on FO1.

Step 6. FO1 forwards the packet to its next-hop router (R1).

Step 7. R1 forwards the packet to Host A, after checking the routing table.

Note As a race condition, if the SYN-ACK packet arrives at FO2 before FO2 has the chance to process the state update message from FO1, then FO2 will drop the SYN-ACK packet. You can remedy this problem by using a high-bandwidth link as the stateful failover interface.

Interface-Level Failover

In traditional failover scenarios, when a data-passing interface fails, the firewall starts the process of failing over to the standby device. Consequently, some of the traffic gets disrupted during a device failover, even if stateful failover is enabled. Some examples of traffic disruption with device-level failover include

- All incomplete TCP sessions have to be reinitiated.
- Routing updates (for OSPF, RIP and EIGRP) have to be relearned as new adjacencies have to be established.
- Most inspection engines' states will need to be re-created because they are not synchronized to the failover peer unit.

Cisco security appliances can provide an additional layer of redundancy by grouping two physical interfaces into a logical interface. This way if one of the physical interfaces fails, the security appliance activates the standby interface of that group, rather than activating a device failover. The interface-level switchover takes less than 500ms, which is faster than the device-level failover.

In interface-level redundancy, only one physical interface is active at a time while the other interface is in standby. When the active interface fails, the standby interface starts passing traffic to avoid device-level failover. When both physical interfaces of the redundant logical interface fail, the security appliance triggers the device-level failover, assuming it is configured and enabled.

Note You must use version 8.0 or higher to use the interface-level redundancy feature.

Redundant Interface Guidelines

Before you enable a redundant interface, follow these guidelines:

- Any physical interface can be added as a member to a redundant interface except the management interface (M0/0 or M0/1).
- You can define up to eight redundant interfaces.
- You do not configure any network-related command, such as the IP address, **nameif**, or security level on the physical interface. They are configured on the logical redundant interface. If you have the **nameif** command configured on a physical interface,

you must remove it first before the interface can be part of the redundant interface. All the other network commands are cleared from a physical interface as soon as it is assigned to a redundant interface.

- You can define parameters such as speed, duplex, shutdown, and description under a physical interface.
- Link status for the physical interfaces is monitored by default as soon as you configure the **nameif** command on the redundant interface. If the link status on the active interface fails but the link status is up on the standby interface, then the security appliance triggers switch to the standby interface.
- The standby interface drops all inbound packets and does not send any outbound packets.
- Interface statistics on the redundant interface are the summation of the active and standby interfaces. As soon as a physical interface becomes a member of the redundant interface, its interface statistics are cleared.
- The redundant interface uses the MAC address of the first member physical interface, unless you are manually assigning a unique virtual MAC address on the redundant interface. In case of an interface switchover, the redundant interface keeps the same MAC address. If the first member is removed from the group, then the redundant interface changes its MAC address to the other member's address, assuming that no virtual MAC address is configured.

In Figure 10-4, GigabitEthernet0/0 (G0/0) and GigabitEthernet0/1 (G0/1) are grouped together as the Redundant1 logical interface. G0/0 on the active firewall is physically connected to switch 1, whereas G0/1 is connected to switch 2. Similarly, G0/0 on the standby firewall is physically connected to switch 2, whereas G0/1 is connected to switch 1. If one of the physical interfaces fails to pass traffic, the standby interface within the redundant interface starts passing traffic.

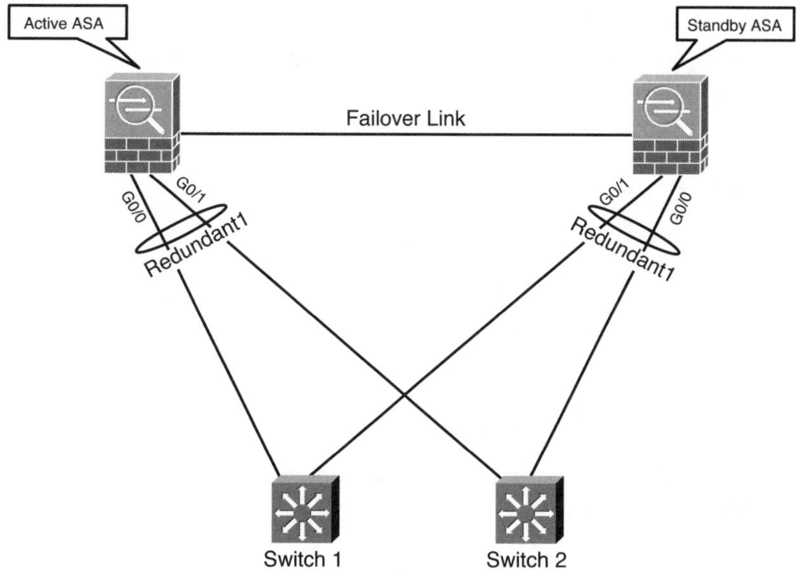

Figure 10-4 *Redundant Interfaces*

You can use a redundant interface for any type of interface, such as

- Data interfaces
- Management interface
- Failover control link interface
- Stateful link interface

> **Note** The physical interfaces in the redundant interface must both be of the same physical type.
>
> The redundant interfaces can be configured with or without device-level failover.

Failover Configuration

As mentioned in the previous section, the Cisco ASA supports two types of redundancy: device-level redundancy and interface-level redundancy. Configuration for these redundancy types is discussed in the next subsection.

Device-Level Redundancy Configuration

As discussed earlier, you can have two types of device-level failover: Active/Standby and Active/Active. The configuration steps are discussed in the next subsections.

Active/Standby Failover Configuration

The configuration of the Active/Standby failover feature in the Cisco ASA is broken down into seven steps:

Step 1. Select the failover link.

Step 2. Assign failover IP addresses.

Step 3. Set the failover key (optional).

Step 4. Designate the primary appliance.

Step 5. Enable the stateful failover (optional).

Step 6. Enable failover globally.

Step 7. Configure failover on the secondary appliance.

Figure 10-1 is used throughout this section to demonstrate how to configure Active/Standby failover functionality on the Cisco ASA.

> **Note** Before configuring the failover, verify that the secondary appliance is turned off. This way, you are not going to have two active firewalls in the network.
>
> Also verify that the license on the security appliances is identical and supports failover.

Using ASDM, you can configure device failover by browsing to **Configuration > Device Management > High Availability > Failover** and selecting the **Setup** tab. Figure 10-5 illustrates how to configure ASDM for Active/Standby failover.

Step 1: Select the Failover Link

Decide which interface will be used to send failover control messages. With ASDM, the failover control link interface is selected under the **LAN Failover** interface drop-down menu. As shown in Figure 10-5, **GigabitEthernet0/2** is selected as the failover control link interface and assigned a logical name of **FOCtrlIntf**.

Use the **failover lan interface** command followed by the interface name to configure the failover link via the CLI. Example 10-1 shows that the appliances are using **GigabitEthernet0/2** as the failover control interface. In this example, the LAN interface is given a name of **FOCtrlIntf**. However, you can specify any name for this interface.

Example 10-1 *Assigning an Interface for LAN-Based Failover*

```
FO1(config)# failover lan interface FOCtrlIntf GigabitEthernet0/2
```

> **Note** If an interface already has the **nameif** statement configured, the security appliance displays an error stating that the interface is already in use. For example:
>
> FO1(config)# **failover lan interface FOCtrlIntf GigabitEthernet0/2**
>
> Interface already in use

To fix this issue, issue the **no nameif** command under that interface.

You can use the management interface as the failover link by issuing the **clear config interface management0/0** command. This removes the **management-only** parameter, which then allows the interface to be configured as the failover link.

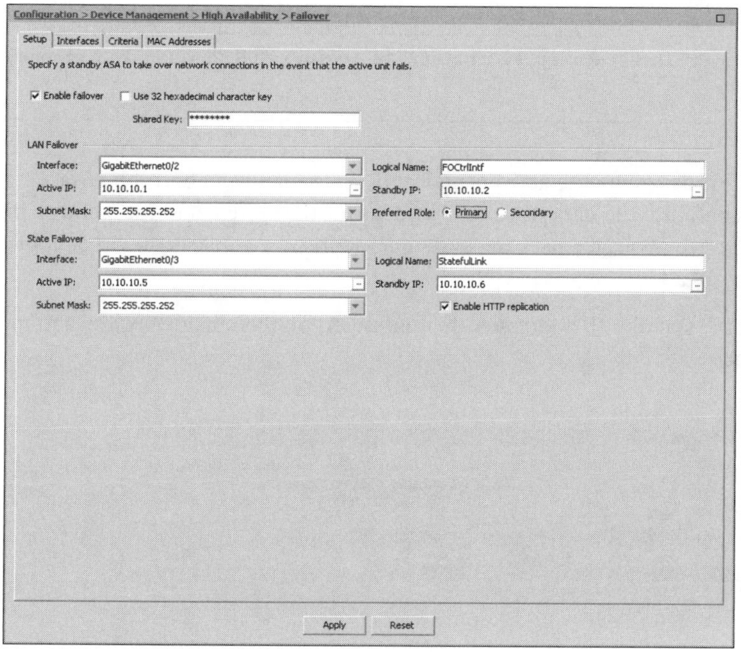

Figure 10-5 *Active/Standby Configuration Through ASDM*

After the **failover lan interface** command is configured, the appliance adds a description of **LAN Failover Interface** under the failover interface configuration, as shown in Example 10-2.

Example 10-2 *Description Under the Failover Interface Configuration*

```
FO1# show running | begin interface GigabitEthernet0/2
interface GigabitEthernet0/2 description LAN Failover Interface
```

Step 2: Assign Failover IP Addresses

For two security appliances to communicate, the designated failover control interface should be configured with two IP addresses: The first address is used by the active appliance, and the second IP address is owned by the standby appliance. The active unit uses its address to synchronize the running configuration with the standby and to send and receive hello messages.

As shown in Figure 10-5, the active IP address is **10.10.10.1** and the standby IP address **10.10.10.2**. The configured subnet mask is **255.255.255.252.**

Example 10-3 shows how to configure the IP addresses on the failover control interface, using the CLI.

Example 10-3 *Configuring LAN Interface for Failover IP Addresses*

```
FO1(config)# failover interface ip FOCtrlIntf 10.10.10.1 255.255.255.252 standby
10.10.10.2
```

After selecting and assigning the active/standby IP on the failover control interface, the next step is to configure the data-passing interfaces for the system and the standby IP addresses. The active appliance uses the system IP addresses, whereas the other appliance uses the standby IP addresses.

In Figure 10-6, the standby IP addresses are configured on the outside, inside, and management interfaces.

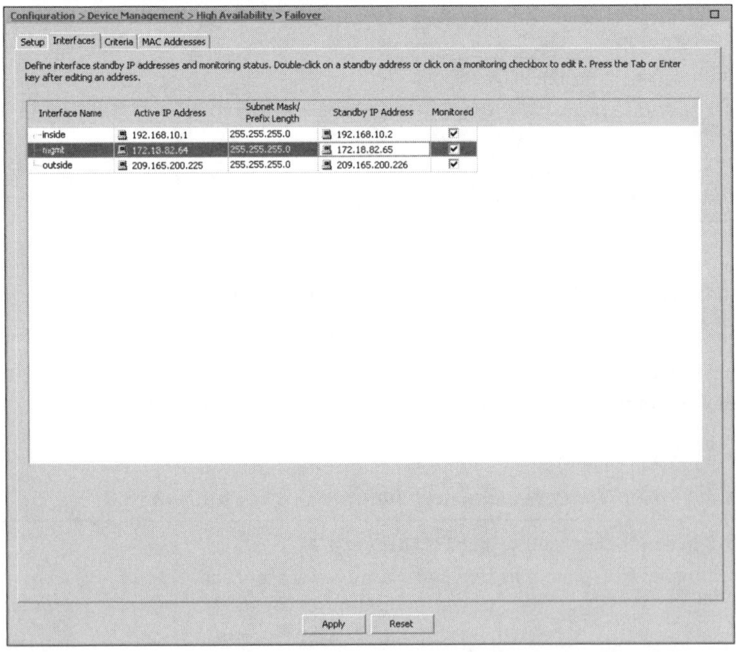

Figure 10-6 *Standby IP Address Configuration Through ASDM*

Example 10-4 shows that the FO1 appliance is using 209.165.200.225, 192.168.10.1, and 172.18.82.64 as the system IP addresses and 209.165.200.226, 192.168.10.2 and 172.18.82.65 as the failover IP addresses on the outside, inside, and management (mgmt) interfaces, respectively.

Example 10-4 *Configuring Interface and Failover IP Addresses*

```
F01(config)# interface GigabitEthernet0/0
F01(config-if)# nameif outside
F01(config-if)# security-level 0
F01(config-if)# ip address 209.165.200.225 255.255.255.224 standby 209.165.200.226
F01(config-if)# exit
F01(config)# interface GigabitEthernet0/1
F01(config-if)# nameif inside
F01(config-if)# security-level 100
F01(config-if)# ip address 192.168.10.1 255.255.255.0 standby 192.168.10.2
F01(config-if)# exit
F01(config)# interface Management0/0
F01(config-if)# nameif mgmt
F01(config-if)# security-level 100
F01(config-if)# ip address 172.18.82.64 255.255.255.0 standby 172.18.82.65
```

Note If you are not sure whether you are on the active or the standby firewall and want to send commands to the correct unit, you can use the **failover exec** command, introduced in 8.0(2). For example, if you are logged in to the standby appliance and want to change the hostname on the active appliance to ChicagoASA, issue the following command:

```
failover exec active hostname ChicagoASA
```

The **failover exec** commands are sent over the failover link. It is important that you use a failover key to encrypt traffic, discussed next.

Step 3: Set the Failover Key (Optional)

To secure the failover control messages that are sent between the Cisco ASA appliances, an administrator can optionally specify a shared secret key. It is highly recommended that you specify the shared secret to encrypt and authenticate the failover messages if they are susceptible to interception by unauthorized users. If a failover key is not used, the active appliance sends all information in clear text, including the UDP/TCP states, the user credentials, and the VPN-related information.

Using ASDM, the failover key can be defined under the Shared Key option. Figure 10-5 shows a secret key of **cisco123** (obfuscated) is configured to secure the communication between the two devices. Example 10-5 illustrates how to configure a failover shared secret key of **cisco123** using the CLI. After you enter the key, it is obfuscated if you view the configuration.

Example 10-5 *Configuring Shared Secret Key*

```
FO1(config)# failover key cisco123
```

The failover key uses DES or AES, depending on the installed license. It also uses MD5 as the hash to authenticate the message. Therefore, it is important that both appliances use the same cipher license key.

Step 4: Designate the Primary Appliance

The two security appliances send failover control messages through a network cable that has identical ends. Unlike a Cisco PIX Firewall, in which the serial failover cable decides which firewall becomes primary, it is impossible to designate a Cisco ASA as primary based on the Ethernet cable. To resolve the problem of which device should act as primary or secondary, you must designate the primary and secondary status through software configuration.

In ASDM, select the preferred role as either primary or secondary. As illustrated earlier in Figure 10-5, the security appliance is designated as primary. If you prefer to user the CLI, use the **failover lan unit** command, followed by its role. In Example 10-6, FO1 is designated as the primary failover appliance.

Example 10-6 *Designating a Primary Appliance*

```
FO1(config)# failover lan unit primary
```

Step 5: Enable the Stateful Failover (Optional)

As discussed earlier, the stateful failover feature in the Cisco appliances replicates the state and translation tables from the active unit to the standby unit. In the event of a failure, the standby unit becomes active and begins passing traffic so that data flows are not disrupted. The stateful failover feature requires a network connection between the two units to replicate the connection state information. The appliances can use either a dedicated or the failover control interface to replicate the updates. You can use the failover LAN interface if the stateful updates do not oversubscribe the interface bandwidth. Set up a different interface for stateful failover if you are concerned about possibly oversubscribing the failover control interface.

If you want to set up a stateful link via ASDM, select the physical interface to be used to send stateful packets and specify the active/standby addresses under the **Stateful Failover** section. As shown in Figure 10-5, **GigabitEthernet0/3** is used for stateful failover. The logical name is defined as **StatefulLink** and is configured with **10.10.10.5** as the active and **10.10.10.6** as the standby IP address with a mask of **255.255.255.252**.

Define the stateful interface in the CLI by using the **failover link** command followed by the name of the interface. Example 10-7 shows **GigabitEthernet0/3** is used as the stateful interface, **10.10.10.5** as the active address, and **10.10.10.6** as the standby IP address. The administrator uses **StatefulLink** as the interface name.

Example 10-7 *Configuring Stateful Failover*

```
F01(config)# failover link StatefulLink GigabitEthernet0/3
F01(config)# failover interface ip StatefulLink 10.10.10.5 255.255.255.252 standby
  10.10.10.6
```

Note If you want to use the failover control interface as the stateful link, use the failover link command without the physical interface reference, as follows:

```
F01(config)# failover link StatefulLink
```

The stateful failover does not replicate HTTP-based connections. HTTP connections usually have a short lifetime and therefore are not replicated by default. Additionally, they add considerable load on the security appliance if the amount of HTTP traffic is large in comparison to other traffic. If you want to replicate the HTTP connections to the standby appliance, check the **Enable HTTP Replication** option in ASDM. You can use **failover replication http** command via CLI, as illustrated in Example 10-8.

Example 10-8 *Configuring HTTP Replication*

```
F01(config)# failover replication http
```

Note Like the **failover lan interface** command, the appliance adds a description under the stateful link interface and clears any configuration on that interface.

Step 6: Enable Failover Globally

The last step in configuring failover on the primary appliance is to enable failover globally. Select the **Enable Failover** option in ASDM as shown in Figure 10-5. If you prefer to use the CLI, use the **failover** command as shown in Example 10-9.

Example 10-9 *Enabling Failover Globally*

```
F01(config)# failover
```

Note If you turn off failover on the active appliance by using the **no failover** command, the standby appliance goes in the pseudo-failover state.

Step 7: Configure Failover on the Secondary Appliance

In the Cisco failover feature, there is no need to manually configure the secondary appliance. Instead, you just need to configure some basic information about failover. After that, the primary/active appliance starts synchronizing its configuration. The bootstrap configuration includes the following six configuration parameters:

- Enabling the failover control interface
- Failover designation as secondary
- Failover link interface
- Same failover interface IP addresses
- Same failover shared key
- Failover enable

Example 10-10 shows the bootstrap configuration of the secondary appliance needed in LAN-based failover.

Example 10-10 *Bootstrap Configuration of the Secondary Appliance*

```
interface gi0/2
no shutdown
failover lan unit secondary
failover lan interface FOCtrlIntf GigabitEthernet0/2
failover key cisco123
failover interface ip FOCtrlIntf 10.10.10.1 255.255.255.252 standby 10.10.10.2
failover
```

Note After failover is enabled on both appliances, their running configuration is identical except for the **failover lan unit** command.

Active/Active Failover Configuration

The configuration of the Active/Active failover feature in the Cisco ASA is broken down into 11 steps:

Step 1. Select the failover link.

Step 2. Assign failover interface IP addresses.

Step 3. Set the failover key (optional).

Step 4. Designate the primary appliance.

Step 5. Enable the stateful failover (optional).

Step 6. Set up failover groups.

Step 7. Assign failover-group membership.

Step 8. Assign interface IP addresses.

Step 9. Set up asymmetric routing (optional).

Step 10. Enable failover globally.

Step 11. Configure failover on the secondary appliance.

Figure 10-2 is used throughout this section to demonstrate how to configure Active/Active failover functionality on the Cisco ASA.

Using ASDM, you can configure device failover by browsing to **Configuration > System Context > Device Management > High Availability > Failover** and selecting the **Setup** tab. Figure 10-7 is used throughout this section to illustrate how to configure ASDM for Active/Active failover.

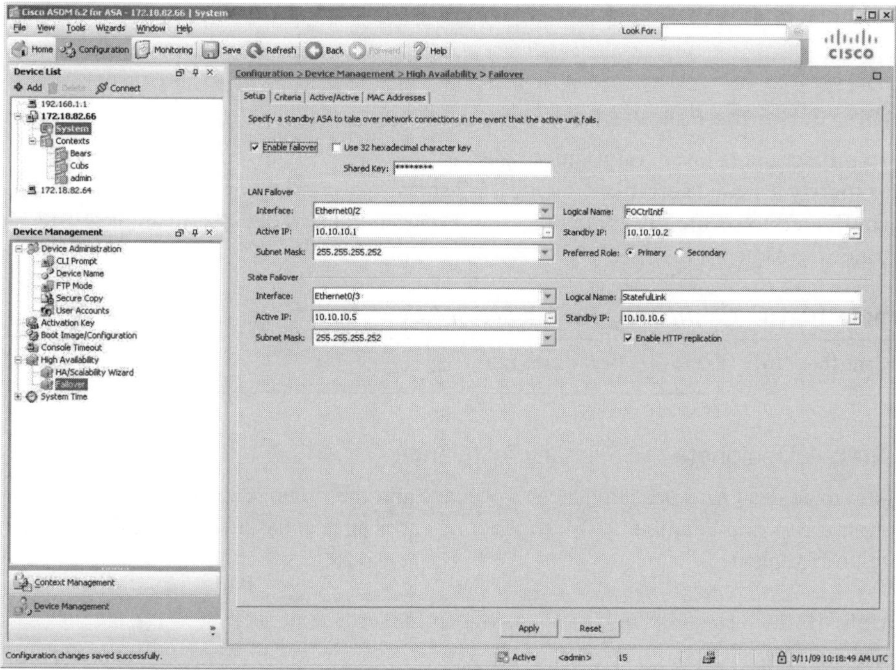

Figure 10-7 *Active/Active Configuration Through ASDM*

Step 1: Select the Failover Link

Decide which interface will be used to send failover control messages. The failover control link interface in ASDM is selected under the **LAN Failover** interface drop-down menu. As shown in Figure 10-7, **GigabitEthernet0/2** is selected as the failover control link interface and assigned a logical name of **FOCtrlIntf**.

Example 10-11 illustrates how to configure **GigabitEthernet0/2** as the LAN failover interface in the appliance when you're using the CLI. In this example, the LAN interface is given a name of **FOCtrlIntf**.

Example 10-11 *Assigning an Interface for LAN-based Failover*

```
Chicago(config)# failover lan interface FOCtrlIntf GigabitEthernet0/2
```

Step 2: Assign Failover Interface IP Addresses

After selecting the failover control interface, configure the active/standby IP addresses. As shown in Figure 10-7 and Example 10-12, the active IP address is **10.10.10.1** and the standby IP address is **10.10.10.2**. The configured subnet mask is **255.255.255.252**.

Example 10-12 *Configuring LAN Interface for Failover IP Addresses*

```
Chicago(config)# failover interface ip FOCtrlIntf 10.10.10.1 255.255.255.252
standby 10.10.10.2
```

Step 3: Set the Failover Key

To protect the failover control messages sent between two Cisco ASAs, you can optionally specify a shared secret key. Figure 10-7 shows a secret key of **cisco123** (obfuscated) is configured to secure the communication between the two devices. Example 10-13 illustrates the same via the CLI.

Example 10-13 *Configuring Shared Secret Key*

```
Chicago(config)# failover key cisco123
```

Step 4: Designate the Primary Appliance

You must designate one appliance as primary and the other as secondary. As illustrated in Figure 10-7 and Example 10-14, the security appliance is designated as the **primary** failover appliance.

Example 10-14 *Designating a Primary Appliance*

```
Chicago(config)# failover lan unit primary
```

Step 5: Enable the Stateful Failover

To implement Active/Active failover, the appliances use a stateful failover link to send continuous connection table updates. The asymmetric routing also heavily depends on the stateful failover link. To define a stateful link via ASDM, select the physical interface to be used to send stateful packets and specify the active/standby addresses under the **Stateful Failover** section. As shown in Figure 10-7 and Example 10-15,

GigabitEthernet0/3 is used for stateful failover. The logical name is defined as **StatefulLink** and is configured with **10.10.10.5** as the active and **10.10.10.6** as the standby IP address with a mask of **255.255.255.252**.

Example 10-15 *Configuring Stateful Failover*

```
Chicago(config)# failover link StatefulLink GigabitEthernet0/3
Chicago(config)# failover interface ip StatefulLink 10.10.10.5 255.255.255.252
  standby 10.10.10.6
```

Step 6: Set Up Failover Groups

As mentioned earlier, the Active/Active failover is available only if you have multiple security contexts configured on a security appliance. Let us say you have two security contexts configured on the security appliance: Bears and Cubs. An administrator can designate the first security appliance to be active for the Bears context while backing up Cubs. Similarly, the other security appliance can act as an active unit for Cubs while backing up Bears. This Active/Active failover is achieved by using the **failover group** command via the CLI:

```
failover group group#
```

Example 10-16 shows all the options that can be defined within a failover group. The appliance is configured to use failover with a group ID of 1. This group ID is later used to link the failover group to a context.

Example 10-16 *Failover Group Submenu Options*

```
Chicago(config-fover-group)# ?

Failover User Group configuration mode:
  help                  Help for user Failover Group configuration commands
  interface-policy      Set the policy for failover due to interface failures
  mac                   Specify the virtual mac address for a physical interface
  no                    Remove user failover group configuration
  polltime              Configure failover interface polling interval
  preempt               Allow preemption of lower priority active unit
  primary               Primary unit has higher priority
  replication           Configure the replication option
  secondary             Secondary unit has higher priority
  <cr>
```

> **Note** You can configure only a group ID of 1 or 2 in the current implementation. If you are using more than two contexts, then you must assign each context to one of the failover groups.

The **interface-policy**, **polltime**, and **mac** parameters are discussed extensively in the upcoming section, "Optional Failover Commands."

The **preempt** option instructs the security appliance to immediately become the active unit for that group if it has a higher priority. This typically occurs when a security appliance goes through the reboot process. The priority is determined when the group is configured with the **primary** or the **secondary** options. **Primary** means that this unit has a higher priority and should be the active appliance for the group. **Secondary**, on the other hand, assigns a lower priority and prefers the other unit to act as an active device for that group.

The **replication** option is useful if you want the active appliance to send updates about the HTTP state and connection entries to the standby appliance.

Note You must enable HTTP inspection to allow the HTTP traffic to work in the Active/Active setup with asymmetric routing.

To define a failover group with ASDM, navigate to **Configuration > System > Connect > Device Management > High Availability > Failover > Active/Active** tab and click **Add.** If you don't have a previously defined failover group, then the very first group is defined as failover group 1. In Figure 10-8, a new group (group 1) is being added. This group is set up to act as a **primary** and to preempt the failover state in case it is rebooted. However, it waits 15 seconds before initializing the preempt process. After 15 seconds of the last failover occurrence, the failover Group 1 becomes active. Additionally, when it is acting as the active device, it sends updates regarding the HTTP connections to the other appliance.

Example 10-17 shows the Chicago FO1 appliance is configured for two failover groups. Group 1 is set up to act as a primary failover device (the default option of a group) and to preempt the failover state after 15 seconds. Group 2, on the other hand, is set up to be in secondary mode. It also tries to preempt the state after it completes the boot sequence.

Note The admin context is always a part of failover group 1. If you don't explicitly map a context to a failover group, then it is automatically assigned to group 1.

Example 10-17 *Configuring Failover Groups*

```
Chicago(config)# failover group 1
Chicago(config-fover-group)# preempt 15
Chicago(config-fover-group)# replication http
Chicago(config-fover-group)# failover group 2
Chicago(config-fover-group)# secondary
Chicago(config-fover-group)# preempt 15
Chicago(config-fover-group)# replication http
```

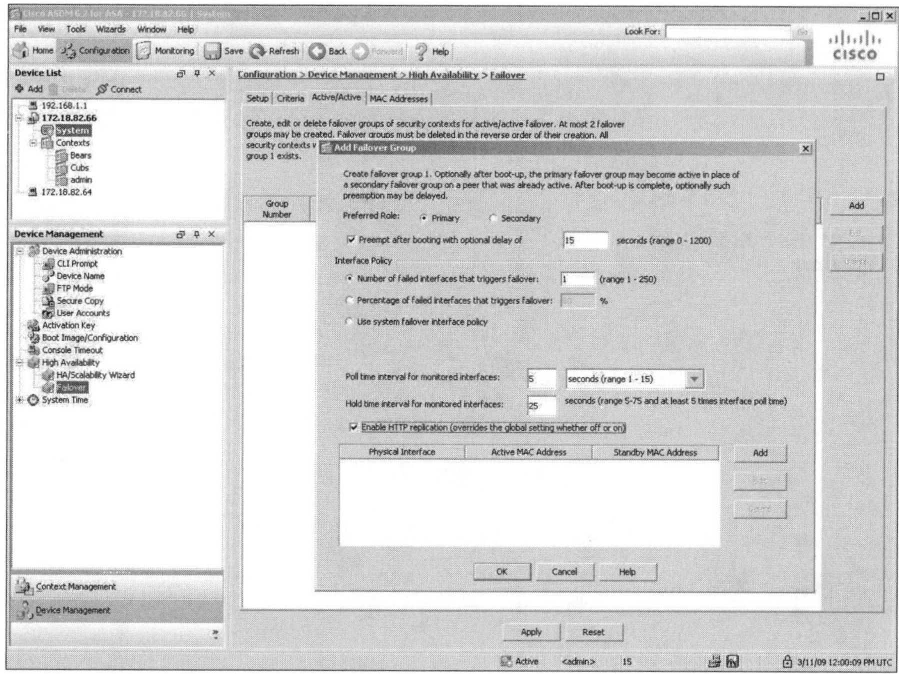

Figure 10-8 *Failover Group Configuration Through ASDM*

> **Note** The **http replication** command in the failover group overrides the global **http replication** command.

Step 7: Assign Failover Group Membership

After setting up the failover groups, map these groups to the appropriate security contexts. In Figure 10-4, the administrator wants to designate FO1 as the active appliance for Cubs and standby for Bears, and wants to designate FO2 as the active appliance for Bears and standby for Cubs. Figure 10-9 illustrates that failover group 1 is mapped to the Bears context.

Example 10-18 illustrates how you achieve assignment of the failover group to a context by using the **join-failover-group** command. Context Cubs is a part of failover group 1, whereas context Bears is a member of failover group 2.

Example 10-18 *Failover Group Assignment*

```
Chicago(config)# context Cubs
Chicago(config-ctx)#  join-failover-group 1
Chicago(config-ctx)# context Bears
Chicago(config-ctx)# join-failover-group 2
```

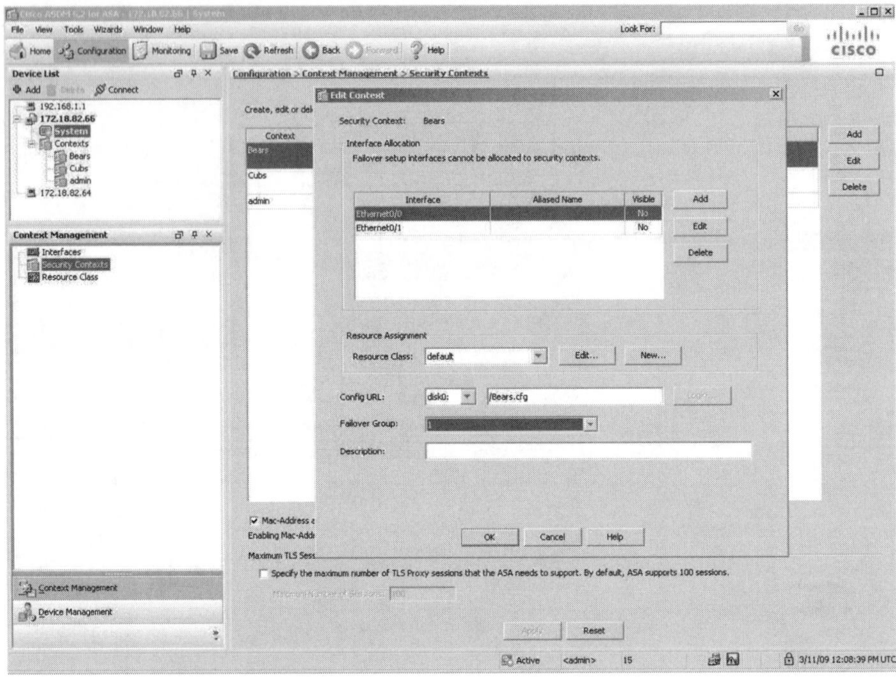

Figure 10-9 *Failover Group Assignment Through ASDM*

With this configuration, Cubs context is active on the FO1 device, and the Bears context is active on FO2.

Step 8: Assign Interface IP Addresses

For all the interfaces, except the failover link and stateful link interface, the system and standby IP addresses are configured in the security contexts. As shown in Figure 10-10, Bears is configured to use **209.165.200.225** and **209.165.200.226** as the system and standby IP addresses, respectively, on the outside interface. It is also configured to use **192.168.10.1** and **192.168.10.2** as the system and standby IP address, respectively, on the inside interface.

Example 10-19 presents the equivalent configuration of Figure 10-10 in the CLI format.

Example 10-19 *Configuration of System and Standby IP Addresses*

```
Chicago(config)# change context Bears
Chicago/Bears(config)# interface GigabitEthernet0/0.1
Chicago/Bears(config-if)# ip address 209.165.200.225 255.255.255.224 Standby
  209.165.200.226
Chicago/Bears(config-if)# interface GigabitEthernet0/1.1
Chicago/Bears(config-if)# ip address 192.168.10.1 255.255.255.0 standby
  192.168.10.2
```

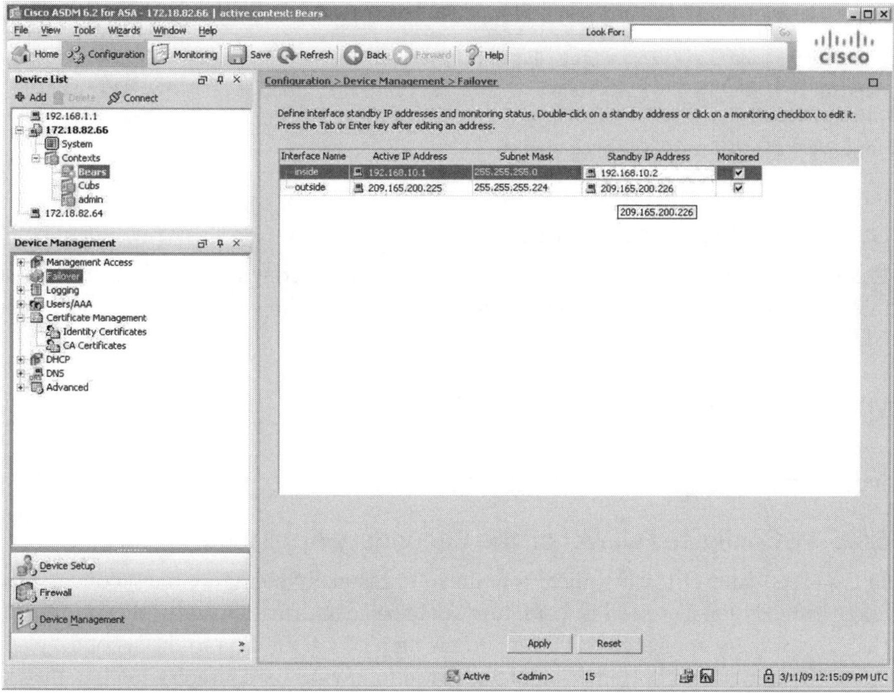

Figure 10-10 *Interface Address Assignment Through ASDM*

Step 9: Set Up Asymmetric Routing (Optional)

As discussed earlier, Cisco ASA enables you to set up asymmetric routing to ensure that return traffic can be forwarded to the active device in the Active/Active deployment. When it is enabled on an interface and the incoming traffic reaches a context that is active on the other security appliance and does not have the associated flow, the security appliance

- Reclassifies the incoming traffic to another interface of the same **asr-group** after determining the flow.
- Forwards the packet to the active unit for further processing.

To enable asymmetric routing via ASDM, browse to **Configuration > <Context Name> > Connect > Device Setup > Routing > ASR Group** and select an asr group on the interface. In most implementations, it is the outside interface.

Use the **asr-group** interface command to enable asymmetric routing on the security appliances via the CLI. In Example 10-20, the GigabitEthernet0/0.1 interface is configured for asymmetric routing and it belongs to **asr-group 1.**

Example 10-20 *Configuring Asymmetric Routing*

```
Chicago/Bears(config)# interface GigabitEthernet0/0.1
Chicago/Bears(config-if)# ip address 209.165.200.225 255.255.255.224 standby
209.165.200.226
Chicago/Bears(config-if)# asr-group 1
```

Step 10: Enable Failover Globally

Enable failover globally on the primary appliance by selecting the **Enable Failover** option in ASDM as shown in Figure 10-7. Example 10-21 shows how to enable failover on the Chicago appliance.

Example 10-21 *Enabling Failover Globally*

```
Chicago(config)# failover
```

Step 11: Configure Failover on the Secondary Appliance

In the Cisco failover feature, there is no need to manually configure the secondary appliance. Instead, you just need to configure some basic information about the failover. After that, the primary appliance starts synchronizing its configuration to the secondary appliance. The bootstrap configuration includes the following six configuration parameters:

- Enabling the failover control interface
- Failover designation as Secondary
- Failover link interface
- Same failover interface IP address
- Failover shared key (optional)
- Failover enable

ASDM Failover Wizard Configuration

The easiest way to define a failover between two devices is by following the HA/Failover wizard. Launch the failover wizard by navigating to **Configuration > Device Management > High Availability > HA/Scalability Wizard**, or clicking **Wizards** in the toolbar and then selecting **High Availability and Scalability Wizard.**

ASDM launches the failover wizard with the option to choose a Failover Configuration Type. You can define one of the following failover types:

- Active/Active Failover
- Active/Standby Failover
- VPN Cluster Load balancing

Note VPN Cluster load balancing is discussed in Chapter 17.

Following are the steps for defining an Active/Active failover connection with the wizard. Configuration of Active/Standby failover via ASDM wizard is very similar.

Step 1. Select the Configure Active/Active Failover radio button.

To define an **Active/Active failover**, your ASDM must have connectivity to both failover devices. After you select Active/Active failover, click **Next** to go to Step 2.

Step 2. Specify peer information.

ASDM prompts you to specify the IP address of the secondary security appliance so that it can conduct all the checks and appropriate failover tests before it configures Active/Active failover. Click **Next** after all tests have passed.

Step 3. Select the failover group.

If you have two customer contexts (Bears and Cubs), then specify failover **group 1** to Bears and failover **group 2** to Cubs. Click **Next** to proceed to the next step.

Step 4. Specify the failover attributes.

Next, ASDM prompts you to specify the interface you want to use as a failover link control interface. Select GigabitEthernet0/3 as the **LAN Failover** and assign **FOCtrlIntf** as its logical name. Define the primary failover interface IP address as **10.10.10.1** and the standby address as **10.10.10.2**. Specify the subnet mask of **255.255.255.252** and the shared key as **cisco123** (obfuscated). Click **Next** when you are finished.

Step 5. Specify the stateful link attributes

If you also want to use the failover link interface as the stateful link interface, select **Use the LAN Link as the State Link**. If you would rather use a different physical interface for stateful failover, select **Configure Separate Stateful Failover Interface** and select an unused interface from the drop-down menu. Also specify the active and standby IP addresses for the stateful link interface.

Step 6. Define standby addresses.

In this next step, ASDM shows all the predefined contexts, the allocated interfaces, and their assigned system IP addresses. You must define the standby IP address to each interface to complete the Active/Active configuration.

Step 7. Verify failover configuration.

ASDM shows the summary of the failover configuration. If everything looks accurate, click **Finish**. ASDM pushes the failover commands to the primary firewall first and then to the secondary firewall.

Interface Level Redundancy Configuration

ASDM enables you to define a redundant interface for both single-mode and multiple-mode firewalls.

Interface-Level Redundancy in Single-Mode Firewall

You can configure interface-level redundancy through ASDM by navigating to **Configuration > Device Setup > Interfaces > Add > Redundant Interface**. ASDM opens a new window where you can bind up to two physical interfaces to a redundant logical interface. As illustrated in Figure 10-11, a redundant interface with an ID of 1 is being defined. The administrator has grouped **GigabitEthernet0/2** and **GigabitEthernet0/3** as the primary and secondary member interfaces. The interface name (**nameif**) is **EmailDMZ** and the security level of **50** is defined. A static IP address of **192.168.20.1** with a mask of **255.255.255.0** is also configured.

Example 10-22 presents the equivalent configuration of Figure 10-11 in the CLI format.

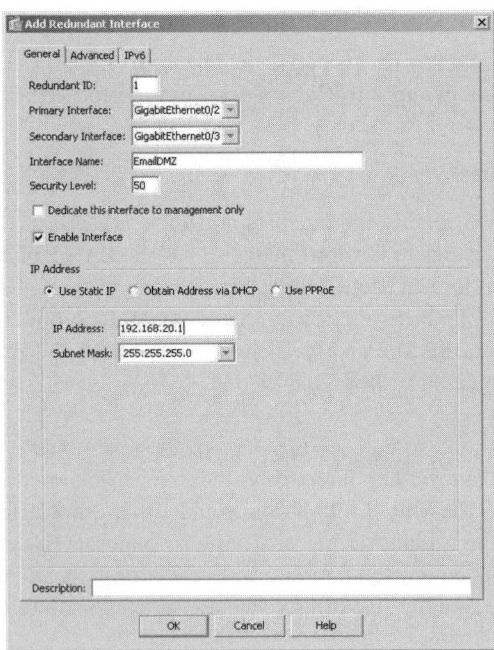

Figure 10-11 *Redundant Interface Definition Through ASDM*

Example 10-22 *Defining a Redundant Interface*

```
Chicago(config)# interface Redundant1
Chicago(config-if)# member-interface GigabitEthernet0/2
Chicago(config-if)# member-interface GigabitEthernet0/3
Chicago(config-if)# nameif EmailDMZ
Chicago(config-if)# security-level 50
Chicago(config-if)# ip address 192.168.20.1 255.255.255.0
```

Interface-Level Redundancy in Multiple-Mode Firewall

In a multiple-mode firewall, define a redundant interface by navigating to **Configuration > System > Connect > Device Setup > Interfaces > Add > Redundant Interface.** ASDM opens a new window where you can bind up to two physical interfaces to a redundant logical interface and add an interface description. ASDM does not allow you to configure any other attribute such as the interface name or a security level. In Example 10-23, the administrator has grouped **GigabitEthernet0/2** and **GigabitEthernet0/3** as the primary and secondary member interfaces under **interface Redundant1**.

Example 10-23 *Defining a Redundant Interface in Multimode firewall*

```
Chicago(config)# interface Redundant1
Chicago(config-if)# member-interface GigabitEthernet0/2
Chicago(config-if)# member-interface GigabitEthernet0/3
```

After a redundant interface has been configured in a multimode firewall, you can either allocate that interface to a security context or you can create subinterfaces and then allocate those subinterfaces to a security context. As shown in Example 10-24, a sub-interface has been defined with a VLAN ID of **100**. It is then assigned to a security context called **Bears**.

Example 10-24 *Defining a Redundant Subinterface in Multimode Firewall*

```
Chicago(config)# interface redundant1
Chicago(config-if)# member-interface GigabitEthernet0/2
Chicago(config-if)# member-interface GigabitEthernet0/3
Chicago(config-if)# interface redundant1.100
Chicago(config-subif)# vlan 100
Chicago(config-subif)# description Outside Interface for Bears
Chicago(config-subif)# exit
Chicago(config)# context Bears
Chicago(config-ctx)# allocate-interface redundant1.100
```

Optional Failover Commands

The security appliance allows you to optionally tweak many default failover parameters to optimize device redundancy in your network. These parameters include

- Specifying failover MAC addresses
- Configuring interface policy
- Managing failover timers
- Monitoring failover interfaces

Specifying Failover MAC Addresses

In Active/Standby failover, the active device uses the primary unit's MAC addresses. In the event of a failover, the secondary appliance becomes active and takes over the primary unit's MAC addresses, whereas the active device (now standby) takes over the standby unit's MAC addresses. After the standby appliance becomes active, it sends out a gratuitous ARP on the network. A *gratuitous ARP* is an ARP request that the appliance sends out on the Ethernet networks with the source and destination IP addresses of the active IP addresses. The destination MAC address is the Ethernet broadcast address, ffff.ffff.ffff. All devices on the Ethernet segment process this broadcast frame and update their ARP table with this information. Using gratuitous ARP, the Layer 2 devices, including bridges and switches, also update the Content Addressable Memory (CAM) table with the MAC address and the updated switch port information.

When a secondary appliance boots up before the primary appliance, it uses its physical MAC addresses as active Layer 2 addresses. However, when the primary appliance boots up, the secondary swaps the MAC addresses and uses the primary appliance's physical MAC addresses as active. Therefore, the use of a virtual MAC address is recommended to avoid network disruptions. With the virtual MAC address, the appliances do not need to swap the MAC address.

Specifying MAC Addresses in Active/Standby Failover

A MAC address can be assigned at multiple locations on the security appliances. If multiple virtual MAC addresses are defined in an Active/Standby failover deployment, then the security appliances can follow a priority list:

Step 1. Use of a virtual active and standby MAC address at the physical, logical or subinterface.

Step 2. Use of **failover mac address** command in the global configuration mode.

Step 3. Use of an interface's burned-in MAC addresses, if no virtual mac address is defined.

Using ASDM, assign a virtual MAC address to an interface by navigating to **Configuration > Device Management > High Availability > Failover > MAC addresses** tab and clicking **Add**, if you have an Active/Standby firewall. ASDM prompts you to select an interface whose mac address you want to change and then assign an active and a standby MAC address. As shown in Figure 10-12, the primary active appliance is being configured to use **0000.1111.2222** as the active MAC address and **0000.1111.2223** as the standby MAC address on the **GigabitEthernet0/2** interface on an Active/Standby firewall.

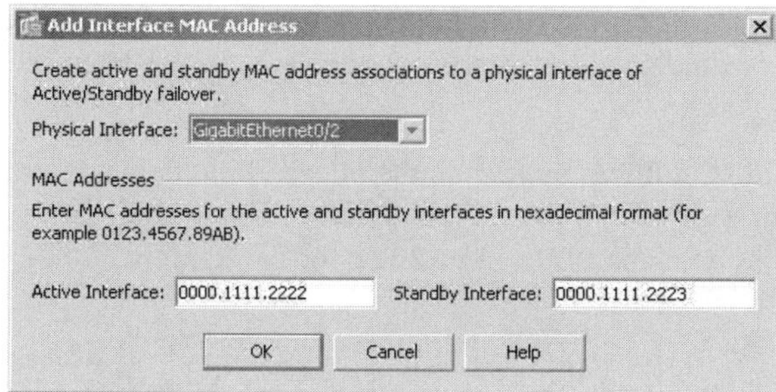

Figure 10-12 *Assigning Virtual MAC Addresses Through ASDM*

In Example 10-25, the administrator assigns **0000.1111.2222** as the active MAC address and **0000.1111.2223** as the standby MAC address on the **GigabitEthernet0/2** interface via the CLI on an Active/Standby firewall.

Example 10-25 *Defining System and Standby MAC Addresses for Active/Standby*

```
Chicago(config)# failover mac address GigabitEthernet0/2 0000.1111.2222
0000.1111.2223
```

Specifying MAC Addresses in Active/Active Failover

As mentioned earlier, a MAC address can be assigned at multiple locations on the security appliances. If multiple virtual MAC addresses are defined in an Active/Active failover deployment, then the security appliances can follow a priority list as follows:

Step 1. Use of a virtual active and standby MAC address at the physical, logical or subinterface

Step 2. Use of **mac address** command in the failover group configuration mode.

Step 3. Use of the **mac address auto** command in the system execution space. This auto-generates the virtual active and standby addresses. Consult Chapter 8 for more information about the **mac address auto** command.

Step 4. If no virtual mac address is defined, the security appliance uses the physical interface MAC address.

In Active/Active failover, you can assign unique virtual MAC addresses to each interface under each security context. You can change the MAC address from its default by navigating to **Configuration > {Security Context} > Connect > Device Setup > Interfaces > {Interface} > Edit > Advanced** tab and specifying the active and standby MAC address to that interface.

Using the CLI, assign a unique MAC address by issuing the **mac address** command to an interface in a specific context. In Example 10-26, the MAC address is changed to 0000.1111.2222 for the active system and 0000.1111.2223 for the standby system GigabitEthernet0/0.100 in the Bears context.

Example 10-26 *Assigning System and Standby MAC Addresses for Active/Active*

```
Chicago(config)# change context Bears
Chicago(config-ctx)# interface GigabitEthernet0/0.100
Chicago(config-int)# mac address 0000.1111.2222 standby 0000.1111.2223
```

Note In Active/Active setup, the failover **mac address** command has no effect if issued in the global configuration menu.

```
Chicago(config)# failover mac address GigabitEthernet0/0 0000.1111.2222
  0000.1111.2223
```

WARNING: command has no effect for active/active failover

Configuring Interface Policy

The appliance monitors the status of all the interfaces. If one of the interfaces fails to respond, failover occurs and the standby appliance takes over the connections. However, if you prefer the system to fail over when two or more interfaces fail to respond, then you can modify this default behavior by changing the interface failover policy. If you use ASDM, navigate to **Configuration > Device Management > High Availability > Failover > Criteria** tab and specify the number of monitored interfaces that must fail before triggering a failover under "Interface Policy." As illustrated in Figure 10-13, the interface policy is changed to **2**.

Using the CLI, you can use the **failover interface-policy** command for Active/Standby failover, as shown in Example 10-27, to change the interface policy from 1 to 2.

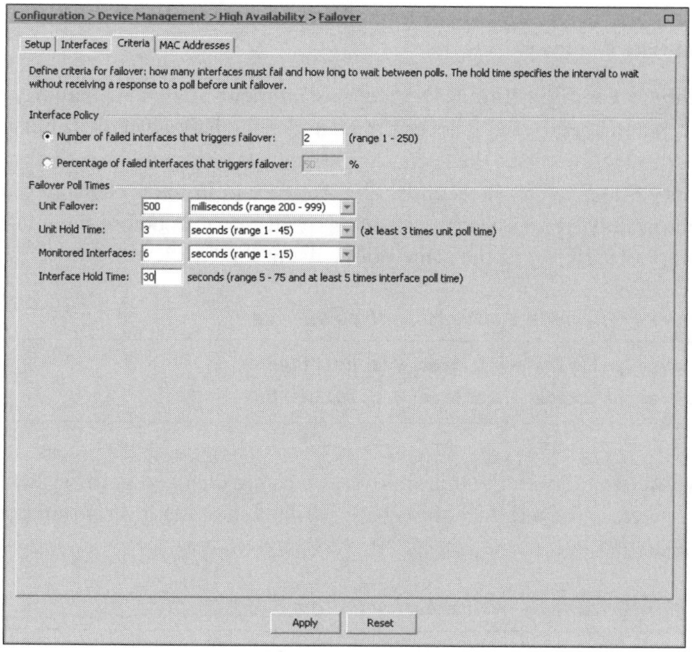

Figure 10-13 *Changing Interface Policy Through ASDM*

Example 10-27 failover interface-policy *Command in Active/Standby Failover*

```
Chicago(config)# failover interface-policy 2
```

In the Active/Active failover, the interface policy is applied under the Failover Group Sub-configuration menu.

Managing Failover Timers

The Cisco ASAs, by default, send periodic keepalive (hello) packets to check the status of the peer failover unit. If the standby appliance does not receive acknowledgments for the keepalive packet it sends out, it initiates a failover only if it deems itself healthier than the current active. The appliances support two types of failover hello messages:

- **Unit**—Sent every second to monitor the status of the failover control interface
- **Interface**—Sent every 15 seconds to monitor the health of the physical interfaces

You can, however, change this default behavior to send keepalive (hello) packets based on custom timeouts. For example, you can send keepalive packets every 500 milliseconds for 3 seconds (hold-time timer) to monitor the status of the failover interface. The security appliances send out hello packets to the failover mate every 500 milliseconds. If the unit interface hold-time is reached (which is 3 seconds) and no response has been heard, the failover process is initiated. The results of the interface test dictate whether the secondary appliance needs to initiate a failover.

Using ASDM, navigate to **Configuration > Device Management > High Availability > Failover > Criteria** tab and specify the failover timers under the **Failover Poll Times** section. As shown earlier in Figure 10-13, the security appliance is configured to send keepalive packets every 500 msec for 3 seconds. The interface polltime is changed to 6 seconds so that hello packets are sent every 6 seconds for 30 seconds before the interface test is initiated. Example 10-28 shows the same policy using the CLI.

Example 10-28 *Failover Polltime in Active/Standby Failover*

```
Chicago(config)# failover polltime unit msec 500 holdtime 3
Chicago(config)# failover polltime interface 6 holdtime 30
```

If you use the Active/Active failover, the unit failover timers are changed in the system configuration menu, whereas the interface timers are changed in the failover group policy, as shown in Example 10-29.

Example 10-29 *Failover Polltime in Active/Active Failover*

```
Chicago(config)# failover polltime unit msec 500 holdtime 3
Chicago(config)# failover group 1
Chicago(config-fover-group)# polltime interface 6 holdtime 30
```

Monitoring Failover Interfaces

When an appliance is configured for failover, whether Active/Standby or Active/Active, it monitors the status of all the main physical interfaces that have a **nameif** and an IP address configured. If you do not want the failover process to monitor a particular interface, such as a dummy or test interface, for example, you can disable monitoring for that interface.

Interface monitoring is disabled, by default, on all the subinterfaces until you explicitly enable it. For example, if you have subinterfaces defined in an Active/Active scenario, and those interfaces are allocated to specific security contexts, then the security appliance does not send keepalive packets on those subinterfaces. If you want instead to enable failover monitoring on those subinterfaces, you must enable interface monitoring on those interfaces.

Under ASDM, you can enable or disable interface monitoring by navigating to following locations:

- **Configuration > Device Management > High Availability > Failover > Interfaces** tab, if using single-mode firewall
- **Configuration > {Context Name} > Connect > Device Management > Failover**, if using multiple-mode firewall

Using the CLI, you can use the **no monitor-interface** command to disable interface monitoring and **monitor-interface** to enable monitoring on that interface. Example 10-30 illustrates how to enable failover monitoring on the **EmailDMZ** interface.

Example 10-30 *Enabling Failover Interface Monitoring*

```
Chicago(config)# change context Bears
Chicago/Bears(config)# monitor-interface EmailDMZ
```

Zero-Downtime Software Upgrade

Certain firewalls are not compatible when they are deployed in failover and are running different software versions. The Cisco security appliance allows you to run failover even if the appliances are running different versions of images. This is useful when the security appliances need to be upgraded to a newer maintenance release without any service disruption. Follow these steps to complete the image-upgrade process without any network outage:

> **Note** Stateful failover is mandatory for a zero-downtime software upgrade.

Step 1. Upload the new image to both security appliances.

You can use any of the supported transfer methods to upload the new maintenance image to both security appliances. In the following example, the administrator uploads the 8.2(2) system image from a TFTP server located at 172.18.108.26 to the system flash:

```
Chicago(config)# copy tftp disk0:
Address or name of remote host []? 172.18.108.26
Source filename []? asa822-k8.bin
Destination filename [asa822-k8.bin]?
Accessing tftp://172.18.108.26/asa822-
k8.bin...!!!!!!!!!!!!!!!!!!!!!!!!!!!!!!!!
<snip>
Writing file disk0:/asa822-k8.bin...
!!!!!!!!!!!!!!!!!!!!!!!!!!!!!!!!!!!!!!!!!!!!!!!!!!!!!!!!!!!!
<snip>
16275456 bytes copied in 58.630 secs (88346 bytes/sec)
Chicago(config)#
```

After the image is uploaded, use the **show flash** command to verify whether the image resides in the disk:

```
Chicago# show flash | include asa822-k8.bin
17 16275456      Oct 04 2009 07:13:46 asa822-k8.bin
```

Note The zero-downtime software upgrade process can be used to upgrade the maintenance image on the security appliances, such as from 8.2(1) to 8.2(3). You can also upgrade from a minor release to the next minor release, such as from 8.1(1) to 8.2(1). Additionally, you can also upgrade from the last major release to the first version of the next major release, such as from 8.1(2) to 8.2(1). The failover is disabled if the security appliances run any other release that does not meet the criteria. That means you cannot run 7.0(2) on one security appliance and 8.2(1) on the other.

Step 2. Set boot parameters.

After an image is uploaded, log in to the active appliance and set the system boot parameters to instruct the security appliance to load the newly uploaded image on the next reboot. Here, the administrator configures the active security appliance to load the asa822-k8.bin image on the next reboot:

```
Chicago(config)# boot system disk0:/asa822-k8.bin
Chicago(config)# write mem
```

Note The commands entered on the active security appliance are synchronized with the standby unit.

Step 3. Reboot the standby appliance.

After the new image is uploaded, log in to the standby security appliance and check failover status by using the **show failover** command. Verify that the security appliance is in the standby state. Here, the secondary security appliance is in standby mode:

```
Chicago# show failover
Failover On
Failover unit Secondary
Failover LAN Interface: FOCtrlIntf GigabitEthernet0/2 (up)
Unit Poll frequency 500 milliseconds, holdtime 3 seconds
Interface Poll frequency 6 seconds, holdtime 30 seconds
Interface Policy 2
Monitored Interfaces 2 of 250 maximum
Last Failover at: 09:00:37 UTC Jul 13 2009
        This host: Secondary - Standby Ready
                Active time: 71475 (sec)
```

Use the **reload** command to reboot the standby security appliance:

```
Chicago# reload
Proceed with reload? [confirm]
***
*** —- START GRACEFUL SHUTDOWN —-
```

```
Shutting down isakmp
Shutting down File system
```

Step 4. Force failover.

After the standby appliance comes online, check the version of the system image. If it is running the newly uploaded image, wait for five minutes so that the connections are replicated and then force the failover so that the standby security appliance becomes active and takes over the connections. Issue the **failover active** command to switch failover, as follows:

```
Chicago# show version
Cisco Adaptive Security Appliance Software Version 8.2(2)
<snip>
Chicago# failover active
        Switching to Active
```

Step 5. Reboot the standby appliance.

Reboot the standby appliance (which was active before forced failover) so that it can also load the updated image. Use the **reload** command on the standby appliance to initiate the reboot process.

Step 6. Force failover (optional).

After the standby firewall comes online, you can optionally issue the **failover active** command to switch the failover state.

Note If the standby security appliance is set up with the **preempt** option in Active/Active mode, it automatically becomes active after coming online.

Deployment Scenarios

The failover feature is useful in deployments where redundancy is required to ensure near 100 percent uptime of the network devices. Although the failover feature can be deployed in many ways, we cover only two design scenarios for ease of understanding:

- Active/Standby failover in single mode
- Active/Active failover in multiple security contexts

Note The design scenarios discussed in this section should be used solely to reinforce learning. They should be used only for reference purposes.

Active/Standby Failover in Single Mode

In the first deployment scenario, SecureMe, Inc., is looking to implement failover at its Chicago location. It has purchased two Cisco ASA 5580 appliances for this purpose. The company requires implementation of the stateful failover feature to ensure that all the active connections (excluding the HTTP connections) are replicated to the standby unit in case there is a failure on the primary unit. SecureMe requires the standby appliance to become active if the primary appliance does not acknowledge the keepalive packets for three seconds. Additionally, SecureMe wants to implement interface redundancy for all its interfaces, including inside, outside, failover control, and stateful link. Figure 10-14 illustrates a proposed design for Active/Standby failover.

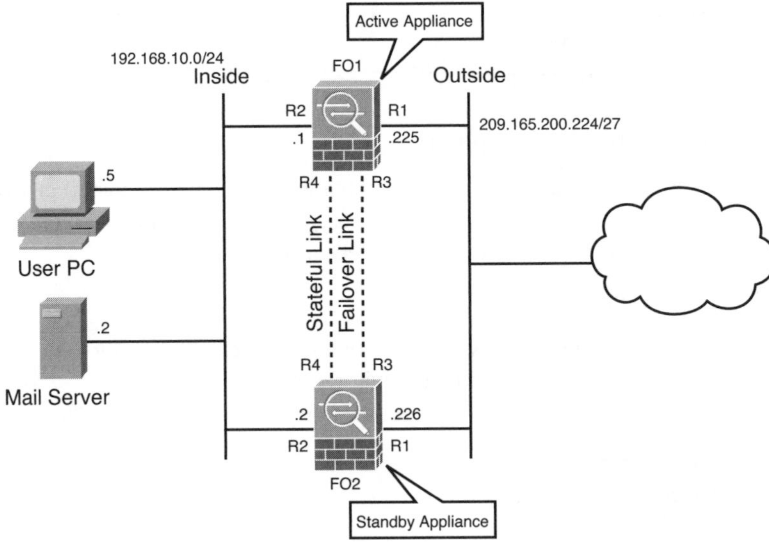

Figure 10-14 *Deployment Scenario Using Active/Standby Failover*

Configuration Steps Through ASDM

The relevant configuration through ASDM is discussed here. These configuration steps assume that you have IP connectivity from the ASDM client to the management IP address of the security appliances. The management IP address of the primary security appliance is 172.18.82.64 and the IP address of the secondary security appliance is 172.18.82.65. The connection and translation tables are constantly replicated to the secondary appliance over a dedicated stateful link interface.

Step 1. Navigate to **Configuration > Device Setup > Interfaces > Add** and click the **Redundant Interfaces.** Configure the following parameters:

- Redundant ID: **1**
- Primary Interface: **GigabitEthernet3/0**
- Secondary Interface: **GigabitEthernet4/0**

- Interface Name: **outside**
- Security Level: **0**
- IP Address: **209.165.200.225**
- Subnet Mask: **255.255.255.248**
- Leave all other options to default. Click **OK** and **Apply** when you are finished.

Step 2. Navigate to **Configuration > Device Setup > Interfaces > Add** and click the **Redundant Interfaces.** Configure the following parameters:

- Redundant ID: **2**
- Primary Interface: **GigabitEthernet3/1**
- Secondary Interface: **GigabitEthernet4/1**
- Interface Name: **inside**
- Security Level: **100**
- IP Address: **192.168.10.1**
- Subnet Mask: **255.255.255.0**
- Leave all other options to default. Click **OK** and **Apply** when you are finished.

Step 3. Navigate to **Configuration > Device Setup > Interfaces > Add** and click the **Redundant Interfaces.** Configure the following parameters:

- Redundant ID: **3**
- Primary Interface: **GigabitEthernet3/2**
- Secondary Interface: **GigabitEthernet4/2**
- Leave all other options to default. Click **OK** and **Apply** when you are finished.

Step 4. Navigate to **Configuration > Device Setup > Interfaces > Add** and click the **Redundant Interfaces.** Configure the following parameters:

- Redundant ID: **4**
- Primary Interface: **GigabitEthernet3/3**
- Secondary Interface: **GigabitEthernet4/3**
- Leave all other options to default. Click **OK** and **Apply** when you are finished.

Step 5. Navigate to **Configuration > Device Management > High Availability > Failover** and click the **Setup** tab. Configure the following parameters:

- Enable Failover box: **Checked**
- Shared Key: **cisco123**
- LAN Failover Interface: **Redundant3**
- LAN Failover Logical Name: **FOCtrlIntf**
- LAN Failover Active IP: **10.10.10.1**
- LAN Failover Standby IP: **10.10.10.2**
- LAN Failover Active IP: **255.255.255.252**
- Preferred Role: **Primary**
- State Failover Interface: **Redundant4**
- State Failover Logical Name: **StatefulLink**
- State Failover Active IP: **10.10.10.5**
- State Failover Standby IP: **10.10.10.6**
- State Failover Active IP: **255.255.255.252**
- Enable HTTP Replication: **Not checked.**

Step 6. Navigate to **Configuration > Device Management > High Availability > Failover** and click the **Interfaces** tab. Configure the following parameters:

- Inside Interface Standby IP Address: **192.168.10.2**
- Outside Interface Standby IP Address: **209.165.200.226**

Step 7. Navigate to **Configuration > Device Management > High Availability > Failover** and click the **Criteria** tab. Configure the following parameters:

- Failover Poll Times Unit Failover: **500 milliseconds**
- Failover Poll Times Unit Hold Time: **3 seconds**
- Leave all other options to default. Click **Apply** when you are finished. ASDM prompts you to specify the IP address of the secondary appliance so that it can configure the necessary commands.

Configuration Steps Through CLI

Example 10-31 shows the relevant configuration of the primary appliance and the bootstrap configuration of the secondary appliance. The primary appliance, being the active unit, synchronizes the entire running configuration to the secondary appliance.

Example 10-31 *Cisco ASA Configuration Using Active/Standby Failover*

```
Configuration of Primary Appliance
Chicago# show running
<snip>
! The system IP address on outside is 209.165.200.225. The Standby IP address is
209.165.200.226
interface Redundant1
 member-interface GigabitEthernet3/0
 member-interface GigabitEthernet4/0
 nameif outside
 security-level 0
 ip address 209.165.200.225 255.255.255.224 standby 209.165.200.226
! The system IP address on inside is 192.168.10.1. The Standby IP address is
192.168.10.2
interface Redundant2
 member-interface GigabitEthernet3/1
 member-interface GigabitEthernet4/1
 nameif inside
 security-level 100
 ip address 192.168.10.1 255.255.255.0 standby 192.168.10.2
! Interface used as a failover control interface
interface Redundant3
 description LAN Failover Interface
 member-interface GigabitEthernet3/2
 member-interface GigabitEthernet4/2
! Interface used as a Stateful link
interface Redundant4
 description  STATE Failover Interface
 member-interface GigabitEthernet3/3
 member-interface GigabitEthernet4/3
! Failover is enabled and the unit is acting as a Primary device
failover
failover lan unit primary
! Failover control interface is Redundant3
failover lan interface FOCtrlIntf Redundant3
! Appliances will send periodic hellos every 500 milliseconds, and initiate a
failover if hellos are not acknowledged for 3 seconds
failover polltime unit msec 500 holdtime 3
! Failover key to encrypt the control messages. This keys will be X'ed out in the
configuration
failover key cisco123
! Stateful interface is Redundant4
failover link StatefulLink Redundant4
! IP address assignment on the failover control interface
failover interface ip FOCtrlIntf 10.10.10.1 255.255.255.252 standby 10.10.10.2
! IP address assignment on the stateful failover interface
```

```
failover interface ip statefulLink 10.10.10.5 255.255.255.252 standby 10.10.10.6

Configuration of Secondary Appliance
! Failover Link Redundant Interface
interface Redundant3
 member-interface GigabitEthernet3/2
 member-interface GigabitEthernet4/2
! The unit is acting as a Secondary device
failover lan unit secondary
! Failover control interface is Redundant3
failover lan interface FOCtrlIntf Redundant3
! Failover key to encrypt the control messages. This keys will be X'ed out in the
configuration
failover key cisco123
! IP address assignment on the failover control interface
failover interface ip FOCtrlIntf 10.10.10.1 255.255.255.252 standby 10.10.10.2
! Failover is enabled
Failover
```

Active/Active Failover in Multiple Security Contexts

SecureMe's managed services group is currently using a Cisco ASA 5540 appliance as the Internet gateway for its customers, Bears and Cubs. SecureMe's management is looking to implement an Active/Active failover solution where it can make Bears active on one appliance and Cubs on the other. It has purchased another Cisco ASA 5540 appliance to implement this solution. The primary appliance is to act as an active unit for Bears, the other appliance is to act as an active unit for Cubs, and both are to back up each other in the event of a failure. Figure 10-15 illustrates a proposed design to meet these requirements.

When both appliances are active and passing traffic, the administrator also wants these devices to send connection and translation table updates to one another, using the failover control interface.

Configuration Steps Through ASDM

The relevant configuration through ASDM is discussed here. These configuration steps assume that you have IP connectivity from the ASDM client to the management IP address of the security appliances. The management IP address of the primary security appliance is 172.18.82.66 and the IP address of the secondary security appliance is 172.18.82.67.

Step 1. Navigate to **Configuration > System > Connect > Device Management > High Availability > Failover** and click the **Setup** tab. Configure the following parameters:

- Enable Failover box: **Checked**

- Shared Key: **cisco123**
- LAN Failover Interface: **GigabitEthernet0/2**
- LAN Failover Logical Name: **FOCtrlIntf**
- LAN Failover Active IP: **10.10.10.1**
- LAN Failover Standby IP: **10.10.10.2**
- LAN Failover Active IP: **255.255.255.252**
- Preferred Role: **Primary**
- State Failover Interface: **GigabitEthernet0/2**
- Enable HTTP Replication: **Not checked.**

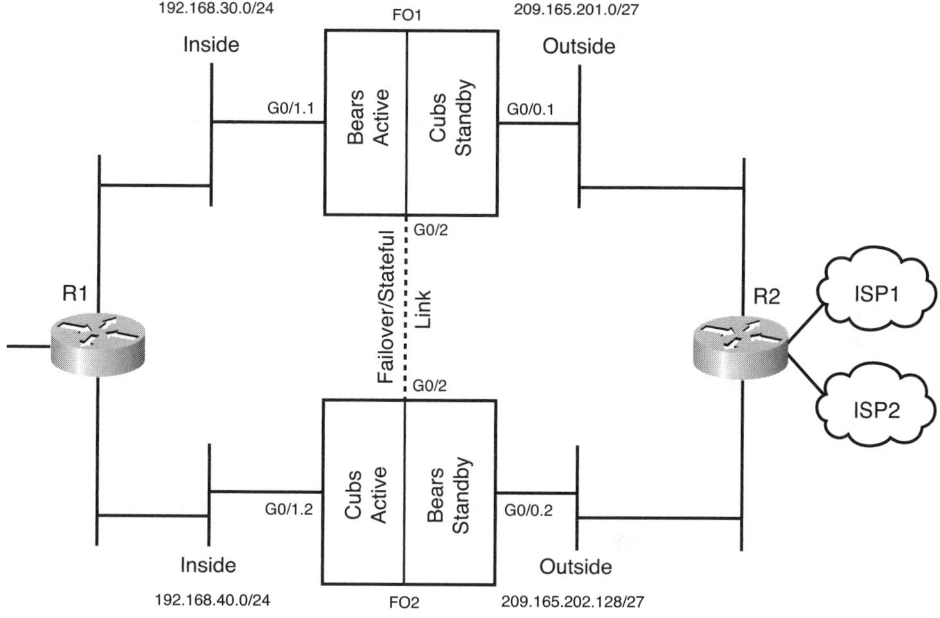

Figure 10-15 *Deployment Scenario Using Active/Active Failover*

Step 2. Navigate to **Configuration > System > Connect > Device Management > High Availability > Failover**, click the **Active/Active** tab, and then **Add.** Configure the following parameters:

- Preferred Role: **Primary**
- Preempt after booting with optional delay of: **15 seconds**
- Enable HTTP Replication: **Checked**, select **OK.**

Step 3. Navigate to **Configuration > System > Connect > Device Management > High Availability > Failover**, click the **Active/Active** tab and then **Add.** Configure the following parameters:

- Preferred Role: **Secondary**
- Preempt after booting with optional delay of: **15 seconds**
- Enable HTTP Replication: **Checked.** Click **OK** and then **Apply** when you are finished. ASDM prompts you to specify the IP address of the secondary appliance so that it can configure the necessary commands.

Step 4. Navigate to **Configuration > System > Connect > Context Management > Security Contexts**, select **Bears** and then click **Edit.** Under Failover Group, select **1.**

Step 5. Navigate to **Configuration > System > Connect > Context Management > Security Contexts**, select **Cubs**, and then click **Edit.** Under Failover Group, select **2** and **Apply.**

Step 6. Navigate to **Configuration > Bears > Connect > Device Management > High Availability > Failover** and specify the standby IP addresses to all interfaces. Additionally, select the **Monitored** option under all interfaces.

Step 7. Navigate to **Configuration > Bears > Connect > Device Setup > ASR Routing > ASR Group** and select **ASR group 1** for the outside interface.

Step 8. Navigate to **Configuration > Cubs > Connect > Device Management > High Availability > Failover** and specify the standby IP addresses to all interfaces. Additionally, select the **Monitored** option under all interfaces.

Step 9. Navigate to **Configuration > Cubs > Connect > Device Setup > ASR Routing > ASR Group** and select **ASR group 1** for the outside interface.

Step 10. Navigate to **Configuration > admin > Connect > Device Management > High Availability > Failover** and specify the standby IP addresses to all interfaces.

Configuration Steps Through CLI

Example 10-32 shows relevant configuration of the primary appliance and the bootstrap configuration of the secondary appliance. The primary appliance synchronizes the entire running configuration to the secondary appliance. The administrator has implemented the asymmetric routing feature to avoid routing issues if packets arrive on the other active appliance.

Example 10-32 *Cisco ASA Configuration Using Active/Active Failover in Multiple Security Contexts*

```
Configuration of Primary Appliance System Execution Space
```

```
! Subinterface assigned to the Bears context as the outside interface. VLAN ID of
  10 is assigned
interface GigabitEthernet0/0.10
 vlan 10
! Subinterface assigned to the Cubs context as the outside interface. VLAN ID of
  20 is assigned
interface GigabitEthernet0/0.20
 vlan 20
! Sub-interface assigned to the Bears context as the inside interface. VLAN ID of
  11 is assigned
interface GigabitEthernet0/1.11
 vlan 11
! Sub-interface assigned to the Cubs context as the inside interface. VLAN ID of
  21 is assigned
interface GigabitEthernet0/1.21
 vlan 21
! Interface used as a Failover control and Stateful link
interface GigabitEthernet0/2
 description LAN/STATE Failover Interface
<snip>
! Failover is enabled and the unit is acting as a Primary device
failover
failover lan unit primary
! Failover control interface is GigabitEthernet0/2
failover lan interface FOCtrlIntf GigabitEthernet0/2
! Failover key to encrypt the control messages
failover key cisco123
! IP address assignment on the failover control interface
failover interface ip FOCtrlIntf 10.10.10.1 255.255.255.252 standby 10.10.10.2
! Failover link interface is GigabitEthernet0/2
failover link FOCtrlIntf GigabitEthernet0/2
! Failover group configuration. Group 1 is primary and group 2 is secondary
failover group 1
  preempt 15
failover group 2
  secondary
  preempt 15
! Admin Context
admin-context admin
context admin
  allocate-interface Management0/0
  config-url disk0:/admin.cfg
! Context Assignment with the failover group ID
context Bears
  allocate-interface GigabitEthernet0/0.10
```

```
  allocate-interface GigabitEthernet0/1.11
  config-url disk0:/Bears.cfg
  join-failover-group 1
! Context Assignment with the failover group ID
context Cubs
  allocate-interface GigabitEthernet0/0.20
  allocate-interface GigabitEthernet0/1.21
  config-url disk0:/Cubs.cfg
  join-failover-group 2

Configuration of Primary Appliance's Bears Context
!outside interface with system IP address of 209.165.201.1 and Standby IP address
  of 209.165.201.2. The asr-group ID is 1
interface GigabitEthernet0/0.10
 nameif outside
 security-level 0
 ip address 209.165.201.1 255.255.255.224 standby 209.165.201.2
 asr-group 1
!inside interface with system IP address of 192.168.30.1 and Standby IP address of
  192.168.30.2.
interface GigabitEthernet0/1.11
 nameif inside
 security-level 100
 ip address 192.168.30.1 255.255.255.0 standby 192.168.30.2
<snip>
! interfaces to be monitored for failover
monitor-interface inside
monitor-interface outside

Configuration of Primary Appliance's Cubs Context
!outside interface with system IP address of 209.165.202.129 and Standby IP
  address of 209.165.202.130. The asr-group ID is 1
interface GigabitEthernet0/0.20
 nameif outside
 security-level 0
 ip address 209.165.202.129 255.255.255.224 standby 209.165.202.130
 asr-group 1
!inside interface with system IP address of 192.168.40.1 and Standby IP address of
  192.168.40.2.
interface GigabitEthernet0/1.21
 nameif inside
 security-level 100
 ip address 192.168.40.1 255.255.255.0 standby 192.168.40.2
<snip>
```

```
! interfaces to be monitored for failover
monitor-interface inside
monitor-interface outside
<snip>
```

Monitoring and Troubleshooting Failovers

The Cisco ASA has a rich set of **show** and **debug** commands that are useful to monitor the status of the standby appliance. These commands are particularly important in isolating a problem if something behaves unexpectedly. The necessary **show** and **debug** commands that are used to manage Active/Standby and Active/Active failover in the appliance are discussed in this section. Deployment Scenario 1 is used for references in this section.

Monitoring

After the primary appliance is configured for failover, verify that the appliance recognizes failover as enabled. You can check the status of an appliance's failover by using the **show failover** command, as shown in Example 10-33.

Example 10-33 *Output of* **show failover** *to Check Whether Failover Is Enabled*

```
Chicago(config)# show failover
Failover On
Failover unit Primary
Failover LAN Interface: FOCtrlIntf GigabitEthernet0/2 (up)
Unit Poll frequency 500 milliseconds, holdtime 3 seconds<snip>
```

After the secondary appliance is configured for bootstrap configuration, the primary appliance synchronizes the running configuration to the secondary appliance, as shown in Example 10-34.

Example 10-34 *Configuration Replication*

```
Beginning configuration replication: Sending to mate.
End Configuration Replication to mate
```

The secondary appliance loads the running configuration and becomes standby to monitor the status of the primary appliance. In Example 10-35, the secondary appliance is in standby with its current IP addresses set as the standby addresses.

Example 10-35 *Output of* **show ip**

```
Chicago# show ip
```

```
System IP Addresses:
Interface              Name            IP address        Subnet mask       Method
GigabitEthernet0/0 outside             209.165.200.225   255.255.255.224   CONFIG
GigabitEthernet0/1 inside              192.168.10.1      255.255.255.0     CONFIG
GigabitEthernet0/2 FOCtrlIntf          10.10.10.1        255.255.255.252   CONFIG
GigabitEthernet0/3 statefullink        10.10.10.5        255.255.255.252   CONFIG
Current IP Addresses:
Interface              Name            IP address        Subnet mask       Method
GigabitEthernet0/0 outside             209.165.200.226   255.255.255.224   CONFIG
GigabitEthernet0/1 inside              192.168.10.2      255.255.255.0     CONFIG
GigabitEthernet0/2 FOCtrlIntf          10.10.10.2        255.255.255.252   CONFIG
GigabitEthernet0/3 statefullink        10.10.10.6        255.255.255.252   CONFIG
```

You can check the failover or standby IP addresses by using the **show failover** command. If stateful failover is set up, **show failover** also displays the stateful failover statistics, along with the number of updates it has received and transmitted. Example 10-36 shows the output of **show failover** with the system and standby IP addresses and information about stateful failover.

Example 10-36 *Output of* **show failover** *in Active/Standby Deployment*

```
Chicago# show failover
Failover On
Failover unit Secondary
Failover LAN Interface: FOCtrlIntf GigabitEthernet0/2 (up)
Unit Poll frequency 500 milliseconds, holdtime 3 seconds
Interface Poll frequency 3 seconds
Interface Policy 1
Monitored Interfaces 2 of 250 maximum
Last Failover at: 16:50:50 UTC Jul 13 2009
          This host: Secondary - Standby Ready
                    Active time: 4903 (sec)
                    slot 0: ASA5520 hw/sw rev (1.0/8.2(1)5) status (Up Sys)
                    slot 1: ASA-SSM-10 hw/sw rev (1.0/5.0(2)S152.0) status (Up)
                    Interface outside (209.165.200.226): Normal
                    Interface inside (192.168.10.2): Normal
          Other host: Primary - Active
                    Active time: 26492 (sec)
                    slot 0: ASA5520 hw/sw rev (1.0/8.2(1)5) status (Up Sys)
                    slot 1: ASA-SSM-10 hw/sw rev (1.0/5.0(2)S152.0) status (Up)
                    Interface outside (209.165.200.225): Normal
                    Interface inside (192.168.10.1): Normal

Stateful Failover Logical Update Statistics
```

```
        Link : statefullink GigabitEthernet0/3 (up)
        Stateful Obj     xmit         xerr         rcv          rerr
        General          7509         0            23239        0
        sys cmd          4009         0            4009         0
        up time          0            0            0            0
        RPC services     0            0            0            0
        TCP conn         55001        0            43023        0
        UDP conn         3300         0            3205         0
        ARP tbl          3500         0            19230        0
        Xlate_Timeout    0            0            0            0
        VPN IKE upd      14           0            13           0
        VPN IPSEC upd    30           0            28           0
        VPN CTCP upd     0            0            0            0
        VPN SDI upd      0            0            0            0
        VPN DHCP upd     0            0            0            0
        Logical Update Queue Information
                         Cur       Max       Total
        Recv Q:          0         2         110826
        Xmit Q:          0         1         12417
```

Note The **xerr** and **rerr** are transmit and receive errors that occur when the appliances send stateful information to each other. Stateful failover is enacted as a best effort and there will be times when errors increment because of congestion and other reasons.

In the Active/Active failover, the failover can be verified either from the system execution space or from the security context. The failover information from the security context displays the current status of the context, along with the system and current IP addresses. It also displays the stateful failover statistics, as shown in Example 10-37.

Example 10-37 *Output of* **show failover** *in Active/Active Deployment*

```
Chicago/SecureMe# show failover
Failover On
Last Failover at: 11:34:19 UTC Oct 1 2009
        This context: Active
                Active time: 155887 (sec)
                Interface outside (209.165.200.225): Normal
                Interface inside (192.168.10.1): Normal
        Peer context: Standby Ready
                Active time: 0 (sec)
                Interface outside (209.165.200.226): Normal
                Interface inside (192.168.10.2): Normal
```

```
Stateful Failover Logical Update Statistics
        Status: Configured.
        Stateful Obj     xmit         xerr        rcv         rerr
        RPC services     0            0           0           0
        TCP conn         40           0           0           0
        UDP conn         1984         0           18          0
<snip>
```

If failover occurs and you do not know why it occurred, issue the **show failover state** command, as shown in Example 10-38. The security appliance provides you a reason, such as interface failure, that caused failover to occur.

Example 10-38 *Output of* **show failover state**

```
Chicago# show failover state

              State          Last Failure Reason      Date/Time
This host  -  Primary
              Active         None
Other host -  Secondary
              Failed         Ifc Failure               14:48:45 EDT Jun 17 2009
 ====Configuration State===
       Sync Done
====Communication State===
       Mac set
```

Troubleshooting

If the failover is properly set up, but the security appliances are not synchronizing the configuration, verify the status of security appliances. If the status of the other security appliance is failed, as shown in Example 10-39, the failover is not operational.

Example 10-39 *Failover Failure*

```
Chicago(config)# show failover | include host
  This host:     Primary
         Other host: Secondary - Failed
```

To resolve this issue, check the following settings:

- The failover cable is physically connected between the security appliances. If they are connected via a Layer 2 switch, ensure that both failover control interfaces belong to the same VLAN.
- Failover is enabled on both security appliances.

- Failover configuration is valid on both security appliances.

The security appliance supports a number of **debug** commands for troubleshooting purposes. Use the **debug fo** commands as shown in Example 10-40 to enable the failover debug messages.

> **Caution** The **failover debug** commands produce a lot of output. Do not enable these debugs without consulting a TAC engineer.

Example 10-40 *Available Failover Debugs*

```
Chicago(config)# debug fo ?

exec mode commands/options:
  cable          Failover LAN status
  cmd-exec       Failover EXEC command execution
  fail           Failover internal exception
  fmsg           Failover message
  ifc            Network interface status trace
  open           Failover device open
  rx             Failover Message receive
  rxdmp          Failover recv message dump (serial console only)
  rxip           IP network failover packet recv
  switch         Failover Switching status
  sync           Failover config/command replication
  tx             Failover Message xmit
  txdmp          Failover xmit message dump (serial console only)
  txip           IP network failover packet xmit
  verify         Failover message verify
```

To troubleshoot issues related to failover timing, use the **debug fo rxip** and **debug fo txip** commands to determine whether the packets are being exchanged according to the configured polltimes. As illustrated in Example 10-41, the FHELLO (failover hello) packets are received on all the configured interfaces.

Example 10-41 *Output of* **debug fo rxip** *and* **debug fo txip**

```
Chicago# debug fo rxip
Chicago# debug fo txip
fover_ip: fover_ip(): ifc 3 got Fover Msg 10.10.10.2 -> 10.10.10.1
fover_ip: fover_ip(): ifc 1 209.165.200.226 -> 209.165.200.225
fover_ip: fover_ip(): ifc 1 got FHELLO
fover_ip: fover_ip(): ifc 2 192.168.10.2 -> 192.168.10.1
fover_ip: fover_ip(): ifc 2 got FHELLO
```

It is recommended that you enable logging of failover messages to either an internal buffer or an external syslog server to avoid overwhelming the console or remote administrative session. In Example 10-42, the administrator sets up buffer logging for the failover (ha) logging class, represented as **fo_logging**, with a logging buffer size of 20,000 bytes.

Example 10-42 *Enable Failover Logging*

```
Chicago(config)#  logging enable
Chicago(config)#  logging list fo_logging level debugging class ha
Chicago(config)#  logging buffer-size 20000
Chicago(config)#  logging buffered fo_logging
Chicago(config)#  logging class ha buffered debugging
```

After enabling failover logging, the administrator can use the **show logging** command. In Example 10-43, the primary security appliance is changing its role from active to standby. The failover was initiated by the secondary appliance. The physical interfaces change their state from waiting to normal.

Example 10-43 *Output of* show logging

```
Chicago# show logging
Syslog logging: enabled
     Facility: 20
     Timestamp logging: enabled
<snip>
     Buffer logging: list test, class ha, 19073 messages logged
<snip>
Oct 1 2009 11:36:39: %ASA-1-104002: (Primary) Switching to STNDBY - Other
  unit want me Standby
Oct 1 2009 11:36:40: %ASA-1-105003: (Primary) Monitoring on interface outside
  waiting
Oct 1 2009 11:36:40: %ASA-1-105003: (Primary) Monitoring on interface inside
  waiting
Oct 1 2009 11:36:42: %ASA-6-210022: LU missed 317 updates
Oct 1 2009 11:36:52: %ASA-1-105004: (Primary) Monitoring on interface outside
  ormal
Oct 1 2009 11:36:52: %ASA-1-105004: (Primary) Monitoring on interface inside normal
```

If the standby firewall determines that the replication of configuration from the active appliance is incomplete or the active appliance has partial configuration, it goes through a reboot process. This is necessary so that the standby device with the partial configuration does not become an active device in case of a failure on the current active device. Example 10-44 shows the error message you will see on the console connection of the standby device when it is about to reboot. After it completes the reboot process, the active device sends the complete configuration to the standby device.

Example 10-44 *Standby Firewall Rebooting Due to Partial Configuration*

```
******REPLICATION OF CONFIGURATION FROM ACTIVE TO STANDBY UNIT IS INCOMPLETE, TO
PREVENT THE STANDBY UNIT TAKING OVER AS ACTIVE WITH A PARTIAL CONFIGURATION, THE
STANDBY UNIT WILL NOW REBOOT*******
```

Summary

The failover feature in the Cisco security appliance is designed to allow network administrators to achieve near 100 percent uptime for their network devices. The robust appliance operating system allows administrators to have two appliances in the active state to pass traffic. It also allows the appliances to support asymmetric routing to load-balance traffic across multiple service providers. This chapter covered extensive **show** and **debug** commands to assist in troubleshooting simple and complicated failover deployments.

Chapter 11

Quality of Service

This chapter covers the following topics:

- Architectural overview
- Configuration of quality of service
- Deployment scenarios
- Monitoring quality of service

In a standard IP network, all packets are processed identically, based on best effort. The network devices usually ignore the importance or criticality of the data that is passing through the network. This creates problems in deployments where time-sensitive traffic, such as voice and video packets, is delayed or dropped because the network devices do not prioritize it over other traffic. The feature of prioritizing some traffic over other traffic is known as *quality of service (QoS)*.

Imagine a long-distance phone call that involved a satellite connection. If the conversation is interrupted with brief, but perceptible, gaps at odd intervals, you cannot tolerate long latency times. Using QoS, you can prioritize the VoIP traffic to prevent against bandwidth hogging and protect time-sensitive traffic.

QoS is useful in almost any network deployment, including the following:

- You run voice, video, and data traffic on the same network. Because voice and video streams are time sensitive and do not tolerate network delays, QoS policies must be implemented to ensure traffic prioritization.
- You run data applications such as time-sensitive databases that require traffic prioritization if there is congestion on the network.
- You want to prioritize management traffic, such as Telnet or SSH, so that you do not lose access to the network devices if there is an outbreak of a new virus in the local network.

- You are a service provider and want to offer different classes of service (CoS) to your customers, based on their needs.
- You have virtual private networks (VPNs) deployed and you want to prioritize or rate-limit traffic going over the VPN tunnel.

Note QoS is useful in policing, shaping, and prioritizing packets only when there is congestion in the network. For end-to-end QoS, all network devices along the path should be QoS-capable.

Many different types of QoS mechanisms are available in the Cisco devices, such as the following:

- Traffic policing
- Traffic prioritization
- Traffic shaping
- Traffic marking

Table 11-1 displays QoS compatibility on the security appliance when other features, such as a transparent firewall, are implemented.

Table 11-1 *Support of QoS with Other Features*

Feature	Support Under QoS
TOS byte preservation	Yes
Packet prioritization	Yes
Packet policing	Yes
Packet shaping	Yes
Packet marking	No
Class-based weighted fair queuing (CBWFQ)	No
QoS for the IPSec VPN tunnels	Yes
QoS for the AnyConnect VPN tunnels	No
Support in Security contexts (Virtualization)	No
Support in transparent firewall	No
Routed firewall	Yes

QoS Types

Cisco ASA supports three types of QoS:

- Traffic prioritization
- Traffic policing
- Traffic shaping

You configure all these methods by using the robust Modular Policy Framework (MPF), discussed briefly in Chapter 7, "Application Inspection."

Traffic Prioritization

Traffic prioritization, also known as *class of service (CoS)* or *low-latency queue (LLQ)*, is used to give important network traffic precedence over normal or unimportant network traffic. It assigns to traffic different priority levels or classes, such as high, medium, and low. The lower the packet's importance, the lower its priority, and thus the greater its chances of getting dropped in case of network congestion.

In the current implementation of Cisco ASA, two classes of traffic prioritization are supported: priority QoS and nonpriority QoS. With priority QoS packets are prioritized over regular traffic, whereas with nonpriority QoS packets are processed by the rate limiter, discussed in the next section.

When traffic is classified as priority, it gets express-forwarded without passing through the rate limiter. The traffic is then flagged to take the priority queue at the egress interface level.

To ensure priority forwarding of traffic at the interface, the security appliance looks at the flag for the priority queue and sends the packet for immediate transmission unless the transmit ring is congested. In that case, traffic is queued to the high-priority queue. As soon as the transmit ring has room available, the security appliance services the priority queue and transmits the packet.

Note Traffic prioritization and traffic policing are the two mutually exclusive methods for setting up QoS. You cannot prioritize some traffic and simultaneously police it in same class map configuration, discussed later in this chapter under "Configuring Quality of Service." If you try to configure traffic policing while priority is configured, you receive the following error message:

```
ERROR: Must deconfigure priority in this class before issuing this command
```

Traffic Policing

Traffic policing, also known as *traffic rate-limiting*, allows you to control the maximum rate of traffic eligible to pass through an interface. Traffic that falls within the configured parameters is allowed to pass, whereas traffic that exceeds the limit is dropped.

In Cisco ASA, if traffic is not classified as "priority," as discussed in the preceding "Traffic Prioritization" section, it is processed through the rate limiter. The security appliance tags the packet for rate-limiting and sends the packet to the QoS engine for processing. The packet passes through the rate limiter, which determines whether the packet conforms to the configured rate. If it does not, then the packet can be forwarded for additional processing or can be dropped based on the policies. If it conforms to the configured rate, the packet is flagged to take the nonpriority queue. Figure 11-1 illustrates how a packet is processed in the security appliance when it passes through the QoS engine.

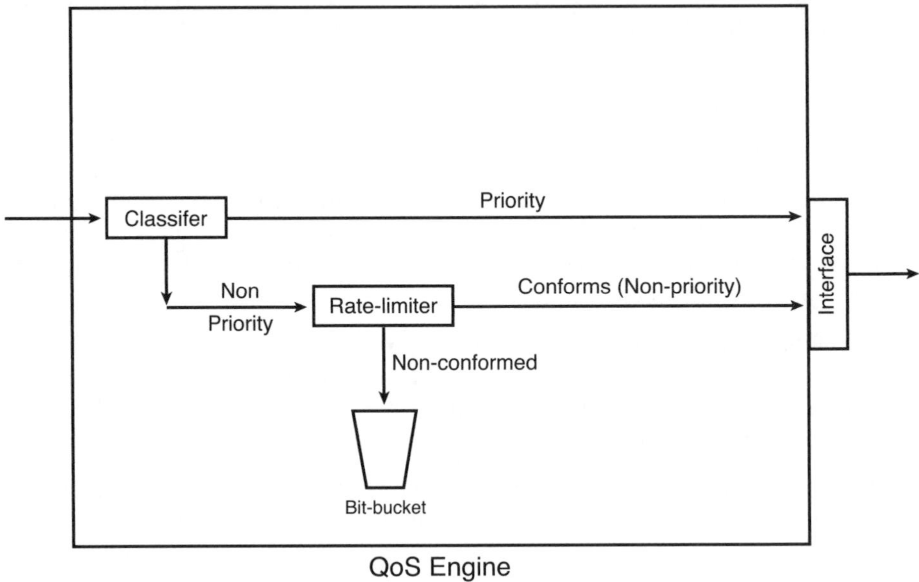

Figure 11-1 *Packet Flow Through the QoS Engine*

When traffic leaves the QoS engine, it is forwarded to the egress interface for physical transmission. The security appliance implements another level of QoS processing at the interface to guarantee traffic with a non-priority flag gets proper handling. Packet processing at the interface depends on the depth of the queue and the conditions of the transmit ring. The transmit ring is the buffer space used by the security appliance to hold packets before transmitting them at the driver level. If the ring is congested, the packet is queued. If the transmit ring has room, the non-prioritized packet is sent immediately after ensuring that the priority queue is empty. If the priority queue has traffic to send, the transmit ring services it first.

With QoS rate limiting, the security appliance implements a tail drop mechanism when a packet does not conform to the configured profile. The tail drop mechanism drops the packets at the end of the queue if the queue is already full. Cisco ASA logs this event through syslog locally in the buffer or to an external server.

Traffic Shaping

Traffic shaping is a mechanism that enables you to control the rate of traffic through the security appliance. This is extremely useful in scenarios where you have congested WAN links and you are sending more traffic through the security appliance than your WAN link can support. For example, if you have a 5510 with a 100 Mbps interface with an upstream Internet gateway with a 10 Mbps uplink, then you can define traffic shaping policies on the security appliance so that the excessive packets can be queued up for transmission over time at the configured rate. If the queue is full, packets are tail-dropped.

Traffic shaping is implemented when a packet is about to be transmitted on an outbound interface. This includes shaping both through-the-box and from-the-box traffic. With traffic shaping, you cannot

- Shape traffic in any traffic selection class, other than the default class. This is discussed later in the chapter under the "Configuring Quality of Service" section.
- Shape traffic on multiple VLAN interfaces defined under a physical interface. Traffic shaping is allowed only on the physical interface or, in the case of a Cisco ASA 5505, on a VLAN interface.
- Shape traffic on a 5580 security appliance.

In the current implementation, Cisco ASA enables you to configure limited hierarchical QoS policies. This allows you to shape traffic on an interface and within the shaped traffic, you can prioritize specific traffic such as VoIP. The hierarchical QoS policy support allows you to shape traffic only at the top level and then provide priority queuing at the next level. With this implementation, you cannot

- Prioritize traffic and then shape it.
- Police traffic and then shape it.
- Shape traffic and then police it.

Using the hierarchical QoS policy, the prioritized packets are always queued at the head of the shaped traffic and therefore prioritized packets are transmitted ahead of any other traffic. Similarly, the prioritized packets are never dropped from the shaped queue unless the sustained rate of the prioritized traffic exceeds the shaped traffic rate.

Additionally, Cisco ASA does not allow you to shape specific traffic flows. For example, you cannot shape the outbound SSH traffic on the outside interface to 1 Mbps.

> **Note** Certain critical keep-alive packets such as EIGRP Hello packets are never dropped even if they are not prioritized in the shaped traffic.

QoS Architecture

The following sections examine packet flow sequence and packet classification in the security appliance when QoS is applied on an interface.

Packet Flow Sequence

When a packet passes through a security appliance configured for QoS, the following sequence of events occurs, as illustrated in Figure 11-2:

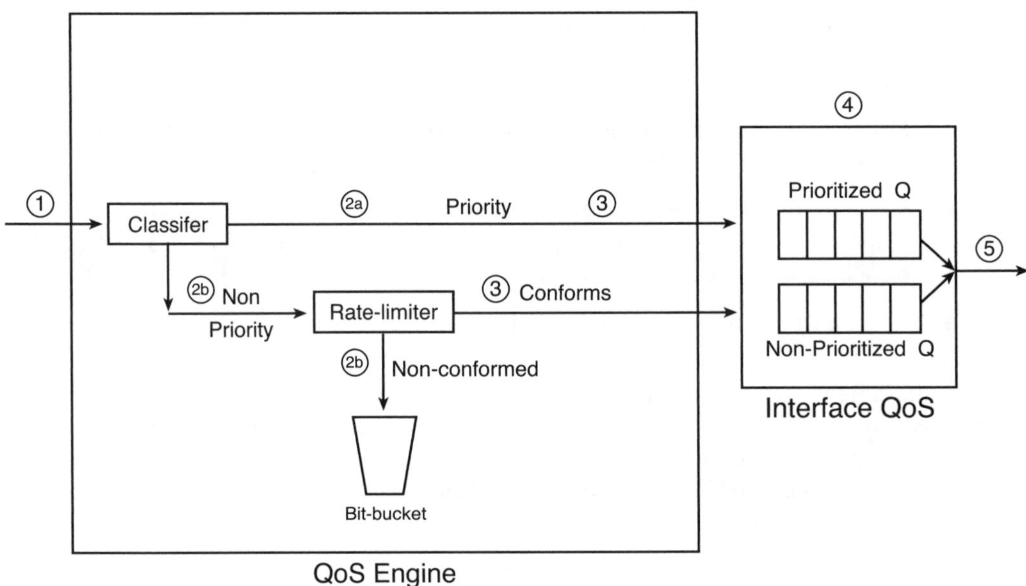

Figure 11-2 *Packet Flow Through the Security Appliance*

Step 1. The packet arrives at the ingress interface. If it is the first packet of the flow, the security appliance attempts to route the packet out to the proper interface and creates a flow for the subsequent packets. The flow contains the rules and actions associated with the packets.

Step 2. Based on the QoS rules, the security appliance takes one of the following actions:

- If the packet matches the priority queue, it is directed to the prioritized queue for express handling. For the priority queue, there is no rate limiting on the packets.
- If rate limiting is configured on the security appliance, the packet is checked to see whether a flow for QoS is already established. If there is

none, a flow is created based on the source and destination IP address, source and destination ports, IP protocol, and the interfaces forwarding the packets. The security appliance checks that it conforms to the configured rate-limiting parameters. If traffic matches a rate-limiting policy but exceeds the threshold, the security appliance drops the packet. If traffic does not match a rate-limiting policy and a default class is defined with traffic shaping, the security appliance shapes traffic based on the configured parameters and buffer burst traffic in the queue.

Step 3. At this point, the QoS flow is up and the packet is forwarded to the egress interface for physical transmission.

Step 4. The egress interface has two allocated queues for QoS. One is used for the prioritized traffic and the other is used for the non-prioritized traffic. If traffic is rate-limited and there are packets to be sent in the prioritized queue, the security appliance services the prioritized queue first and then processes the rate-limited queue.

Step 5. The security appliance transmits the packet over the physical interface.

Packet Classification

Packet classification is a way to identify packets on which QoS policies need to be applied. This can range from simple functions such as IP precedence and DSCP fields to complicated methods such as complex access lists. The following subsections discuss the supported packet-classification methods.

IP Precedence Field

IP packets contain a type of service (TOS) byte, which is used to indicate the priority in which the packets should be processed. In the TOS byte, the leftmost three bits set the IP precedence, as shown in Figure 11-3. The network devices use the next four bits, known as the TOS bits, to determine how a packet should be handled by looking at delay (D), throughput (T), reliability (R), and cost (C). However, these bits are not currently used in the IP network infrastructures. The last bit in the TOS byte is typically referred as MBZ (abbreviation for "must be zero"). This bit is not used, either.

Table 11-2 lists all the IP precedence bits along with their IP precedence names as defined in RFC 791.

IP DSCP Field

Differentiated Services Code Point (DSCP) is intended to replace the definitions of the IP TOS byte. DSCP field takes the same space within the IP header as the IP TOS byte. It uses the six most significant bits for packet classification. The two least significant bits are currently unused, as shown in Figure 11-4. By using the six bits in DSCP, you can classify up to 64 streams of packets.

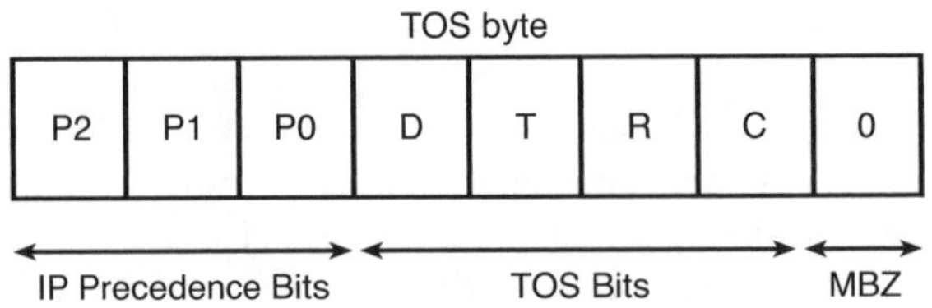

IP Header

<table>
<tr><td>Version</td><td>IHL</td><td>TOS</td><td colspan="2">Total Length</td></tr>
<tr><td colspan="3">Identification</td><td>Flags</td><td>Fragmentation Offset</td></tr>
<tr><td colspan="2">Time to Live</td><td>Protocol</td><td colspan="2">Header Checksum</td></tr>
<tr><td colspan="5">Source IP Address</td></tr>
<tr><td colspan="5">Destination IP Address</td></tr>
<tr><td colspan="5">Options and Padding</td></tr>
<tr><td colspan="5">Data</td></tr>
</table>

Figure 11-3 *TOS Byte Displaying IP Precedence Bits*

DSCP provides backward compatibility to IP precedence. Table 11-3 lists the IP precedence values with the corresponding DSCP values.

Table 11-2 *IP Precedence Bits and IP Precedence Names*

Precedence Value	Precedence Bit	Precedence Name
0	000	Routine
1	001	Priority
2	010	Immediate
3	011	Flash
4	100	Flash Override
5	101	Critical
6	110	Internetwork Control
7	111	Network Control

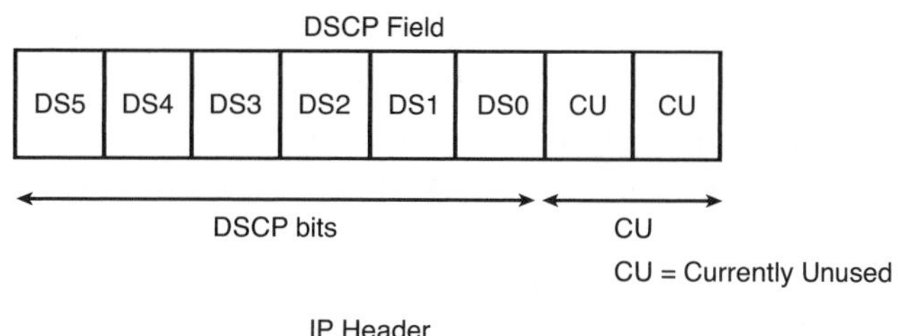

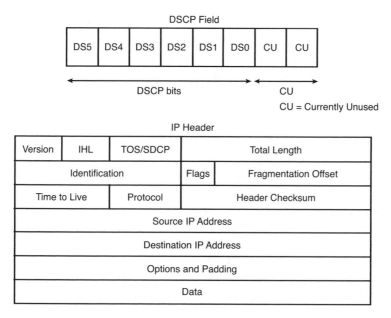

Figure 11-4 *DSCP Field*

As shown in Table 11-3, DSCP offers fine granularity to packet identification by using the additional three bits. The Internet Engineering Task Force (IETF) has divided the DSCP bits into four service concepts:

- Default DCSP, defined as 000 000, offers best-effort packet switching through the network devices.
- Class selector provides backward-compatibility bits, shown in Table 11-3. All the DSCP bits shown in the table belong to this service.

Table 11-3 *Correlation of IP Precedence Bits to DSCP Bits*

Precedence Value	Precedence Bit	DSCP Bit
0	000	000 000
1	001	001 000
2	010	010 000
3	011	011 000
4	100	100 000
5	101	101 000
6	110	110 000
7	111	111 000

- Expedited Forwarding (EF) per-hop behavior (PHB), with the DSCP bit of 101 110, defines the premium service for the IP packets.
- Assured Forwarding (AF) PHB, with four different classes and three different class levels, defines a total of 12 code points for packet classification.

Example 11-1 lists the well known DSCP bits supported by Cisco ASA.

Example 11-1 *Available DSCP Options in Class Maps*

```
Chicago(config-cmap)# match dscp ?
  <0-63>    Differentiated services codepoint value
  af11      Match packets with AF11 dscp (001010)
  af12      Match packets with AF12 dscp (001100)
  af13      Match packets with AF13 dscp (001110)
  af21      Match packets with AF21 dscp (010010)
  af22      Match packets with AF22 dscp (010100)
  af23      Match packets with AF23 dscp (010110)
  af31      Match packets with AF31 dscp (011010)
  af32      Match packets with AF32 dscp (011100)
  af33      Match packets with AF33 dscp (011110)
  af41      Match packets with AF41 dscp (100010)
  af42      Match packets with AF42 dscp (100100)
  af43      Match packets with AF43 dscp (100110)
  cs1       Match packets with CS1(precedence 1) dscp (001000)
  cs2       Match packets with CS2(precedence 2) dscp (010000)
  cs3       Match packets with CS3(precedence 3) dscp (011000)
  cs4       Match packets with CS4(precedence 4) dscp (100000)
  cs5       Match packets with CS5(precedence 5) dscp (101000)
  cs6       Match packets with CS6(precedence 6) dscp (110000)
  cs7       Match packets with CS7(precedence 7) dscp (111000)
  default   Match packets with default dscp (000000)
  ef        Match packets with EF dscp (101110)
```

Note The QoS implementation in Cisco ASA observes and honors the DSCP and IP precedence bits in the packet. For the IPSec VPN tunnels, the security appliance preserves the TOS byte from the inner header to the outer header. By doing so, the security appliance and the devices along the VPN tunnel can correctly prioritize traffic.

IP Access Control List

Access control lists (ACLs) are the most commonly used form of packet classification. They can identify traffic based on many Layer 3 as well as Layer 4 headers of the packet. Please consult Chapter 4, "Controlling Network Access," for more information about ACL.

IP Flow

Classification based on IP flow is usually based on information found in the following five tuples:

- Destination IP address
- Source IP address
- Destination port
- Source port
- IP protocol field

In Cisco ASA, flow-based classification is done based on the destination IP address. That means that if the traffic is destined to an IP address, an IP flow is created and the appropriate policies are applied to it.

VPN Tunnel Group

Cisco ASA can also classify packets destined to an IPSec tunnel. When a packet is received by the security appliance and matches a particular tunnel group (whether site-to-site or remote-access), the security appliance applies the configured QoS policies before transmitting the packet.

> **Note** The security appliance allows only one **match** command in the class map. However, you can have two **match** commands when setting up QoS for the VPN tunnels. Use the **match tunnel-group** *<tunnel-group-name>* command in the class map first before specifying a second qualifying **match** statement in the class map. Currently, **match flow ip destination-address** is the only supported second **match** command.

QoS and VPN Tunnels

Cisco ASA supports full QoS implementation on both the site-to-site and remote-access VPN tunnels. For the best-effort method, the site-to-site QoS implementation rate-limits traffic for the entire tunnel. This means that all hosts within the tunnel share the same bandwidth. However, for the remote-access VPN tunnels, the QoS implementation rate-limits traffic per remote-access peer. This means that each VPN tunnel within a remote-access group gets the configured data throughput.

> **Note** Even though there is a static ACL for each site-to-site tunnel, the QoS rules are not inserted into the database until there is an active VPN tunnel. This ensures that the security appliance does not allocate bandwidth for the IPSec security associations (SAs) that are not being used.

When both QoS and VPN engines are set up on the security appliance, the following events can occur during device configuration:

- **New QoS policy is set up for existing tunnels**—If a QoS policy is applied to an interface with an active VPN tunnel, the security appliance invokes the IPSec engine to apply the appropriate QoS parameters to the IPSec SAs.
- **Tunnel goes down for QoS-enabled group**—When a VPN tunnel goes down (whether a user deletes the connection or the administrator clears the established SA), the security appliance invokes the QoS process to delete the appropriate QoS parameters for that particular IPSec SA.
- **QoS policy is removed for the group**—When the VPN commands are removed from the QoS configuration, the security appliance invokes the QoS engine to clear up relevant parameters. The security appliance also makes sure not to call the QoS engine for the future VPN tunnels.

Configuring Quality of Service

The QoS configuration on Cisco ASA can be achieved in the following two ways:

- QoS configuration via ASDM
- QoS configuration via CLI

In Figure 11-5, SecureMe, a fictional company, has Cisco ASA set up to classify traffic sourced from the 192.168.10.0/24 subnet and destined to the mail server, 209.165.201.1. The administrator of the security appliance also prefers to identify the Voice over IP (VoIP) traffic passing through the security appliance.

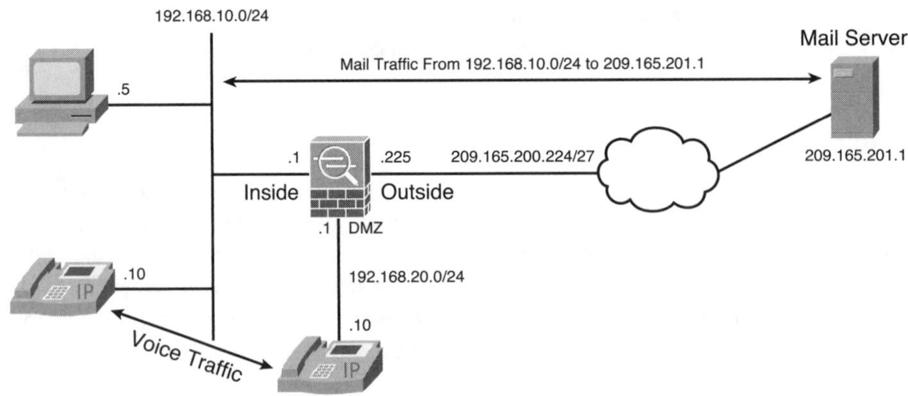

Figure 11-5 *Packet Classification in an Appliance*

QoS Configuration via ASDM

After you are logged in to the security appliance via ASDM, you must tune the priority queue in case you want to prioritize traffic. After a priority queue is defined, you can create a new QoS policy.

To create a QoS policy, follow the steps described in the following sections.

Step 1: Tune Priority Queue

When the QoS engine has processed the packets, they are queued to the interface for transmission on the wire. The security appliance implements the priority queue at the interface to ensure that prioritized packets are preferred over nonprioritized packets. If the priority queuing is not enabled on an interface, you cannot configure packet prioritization. If you do not want to prioritize traffic, you do not have to configure priority queue.

You can define the transmit ring and the depth of the priority queues to minimize the delay for the high-priority packets. The transmit ring specifies the number of packets allowed into the interface driver's transmit queue. The depth of the priority queues specifies the maximum number of packets that can be queued up to a priority queue before packets start getting dropped.

The queue's upper limit and the transmission ring are dynamically determined at run time. The main factor is the amount of memory available on the device to support the queues. When both queues are full and the QoS engine is forwarding more traffic than the queues can handle, the security appliance simply drops the received data. Moreover, it processes the transmit ring first before servicing the priority queues.

Note Cisco 5580 security appliances do not support priority queue on the 10-Gigabit Ethernet interfaces.

You can tune a priority queue for an interface by navigating to **Configuration > Device Management > Advanced > Priority Queue**. In Figure 11-6, the administrator of the security appliance has fine-tuned the priority queue parameters on the outside interface. The transmit-ring limit is changed to hold up to 200 packets in the queue, whereas the high- and low-priority queue depth is set up to hold 2000 packets. This allows the priority queue to be processed efficiently with minimum latency caused by the transmit ring.

Step 2: Define a Service Policy

After tuning the priority queue, you can create a new QoS policy by navigating to **Configuration > Firewall > Service Policy Rules**, selecting the pull-down **Add** list, and clicking **Add Service Policy Rule**. ASDM opens up a new window and prompts you to select whether you want to create an interface or a global policy.

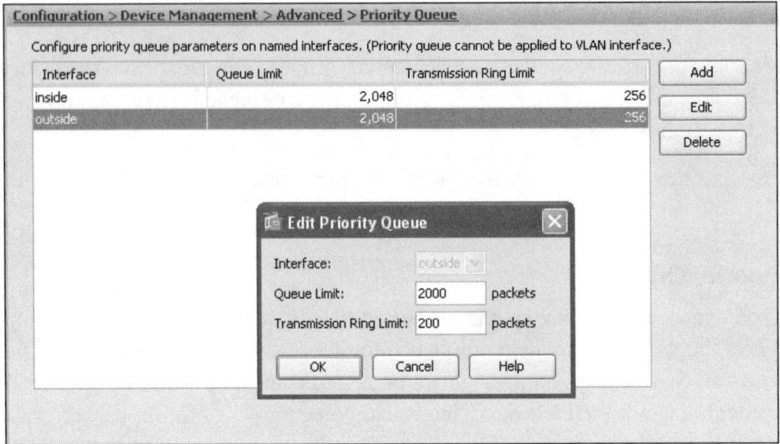

Figure 11-6 *Priority Queue for the Outside Interface*

- **Interface—**If you want to create a QoS policy for a specific interface, select the Interface option. Interface policies takes precedence over global policies, as discussed in Chapter 7. An interface specific policy is useful if, for example, you want to prioritize all VPN traffic on the outside interface. In this case, you want to apply the QoS policies on the outside interface. You can define all types of QoS policies (traffic prioritization, traffic shaping, and traffic policing) to an interface-based service policy.
- **Global–Applies to All Interfaces—**If you would rather apply a QoS policy on all interfaces, select the **Global–Applies to All Interfaces** option. A global policy is useful if, for example, you want to prioritize all VoIP traffic on all interfaces. In this case, you want to apply the QoS policies globally on the Cisco ASA. You cannot define a traffic-shaping policy to the global policy.

In Figure 11-7, a new service policy, called **Traffic-Map-Outside**, is applied on the **outside** interface. A description of **Service Policy for Outside Interface** is also added to this policy.

Step 3: Specify a Traffic Selection Criteria

In the next step, you identify packets to which you want to apply the QoS policies. In the security appliance, there are many ways to classify traffic. However, the use of an ACL is the most robust method available for selecting a specific traffic type. You can specify the Layer 3 and Layer 4 information in the packets when ACLs are used. The security appliance can also match based on the DSCP and IP precedence bits in the IP header.

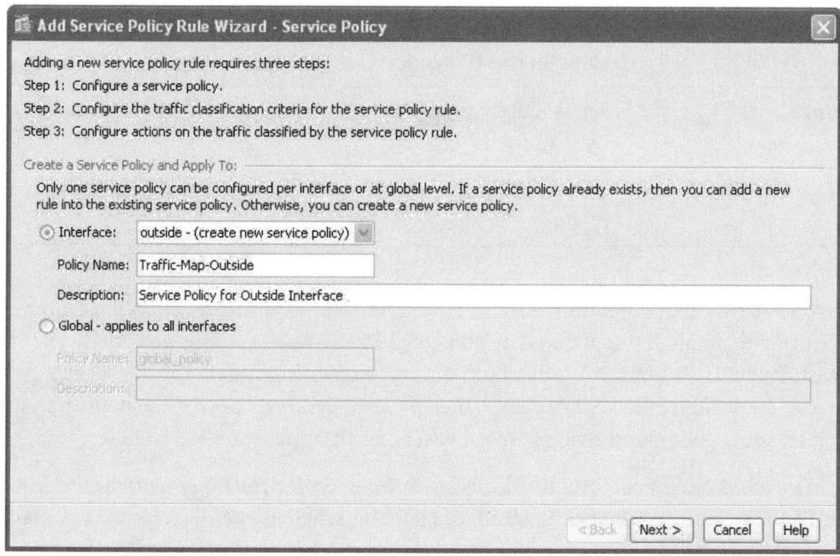

Figure 11-7 *Defining a New Service Policy*

Table 11-4 defines all the methods available for traffic selection criteria.

Table 11-4 *Available Traffic Selection Criteria*

Feature	Description
default-inspection-traffic	This option is used by the inspection engines, discussed in Chapter 7.
Source and Destination IP Addresses (uses ACL)	Packet classification is done based on an ACL. The ACL can have source and destination addresses and can optionally contain Layer 4 port information.
Tunnel Group	Packet classification is done based on the tunnel group. This is used for site-to-site and remote-access IPSec tunnels.
TCP or UDP Destination Port	Packets are classified based on the TCP or UDP destination ports for any source or destination address.
RTP Range	Using RTP (real-time protocol) as the keyword, packets are matched based on the RTP stream on the even-numbered UDP port number. The even-numbered ports act as a starting point for a range of UDP ports to identify the RTP streams.

IP DiffServ CodePoints (DSCP)	Packet classification is done based on the IETF-defined DSCP value in the IP header.
IP Precedence	The security appliance classifies packets based on the TOS byte in the IP header.
Any Traffic	The Any Traffic option is used to classify all packets flowing through the security appliance.

Figure 11-8 shows that a new traffic selection criterion is defined as **mail-class.** Our goal is to identify the mail server located at 209.165.201.1. To achieve this goal, ACL (Source and Destination IP Addresses) is used to identity interesting traffic for the service policy. When you click **Next**, the security appliance prompts you to specify the source and destination IP address of the traffic to which you want to apply the QoS policies.

In the next window, specify the IP addresses to be used for traffic classification. In Figure 11-9, the source network is **192.168.10.0/24**, whereas the destination is a mail server located at **209.165.201.1**. The destination service is **tcp/smtp**, and a description of **ACL to identify outbound mail traffic** is also added. Click **Next** when you are finished.

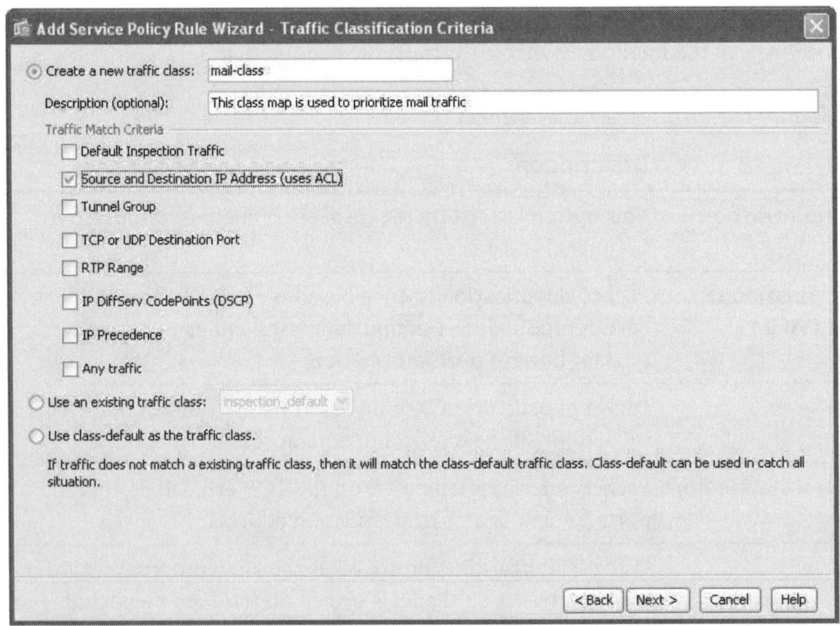

Figure 11-8 *Selecting a Traffic Criteria*

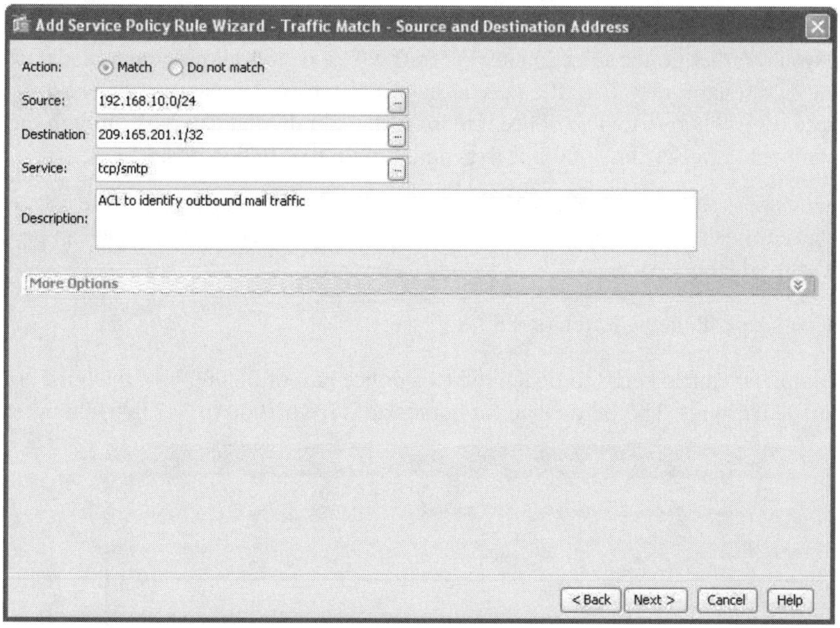

Figure 11-9 *Defining Traffic Criteria*

In addition to the traffic selection criteria, the security appliance has a default class that can be used in catch all situations. Any traffic that is not explicitly matched by the selection criteria can be caught by this default class. You can apply appropriate actions (traffic prioritization, shaping, or policing) to the default class. Traffic shaping can be applied only to a default class. To enable the default class for QoS policies, select "Use class-default as the traffic class."

Step4: Apply an Action Rule

In the final step, the security appliance prompts you to apply a QoS action for your identified traffic. As mentioned earlier in the chapter, you have three options:

- Traffic prioritization
- Traffic policing
- Traffic shaping

Traffic Prioritization

As mentioned earlier in the chapter, you can prioritize specific traffic through the LLQ while all other traffic goes to the best-effort queue on an interface. After you have identified traffic that you want to prioritize, discussed in Step 2, you can click the QoS tab and then select the **Enable priority for this flow** option, as shown in Figure 11-10.

Traffic Policing

If you would rather police some interesting traffic, Cisco ASA allows you to use traffic policing to rate-limit that. If traffic falls in the police rate and burst size, the security appliance transmits traffic. The police rate is the actual rate that can pass through the QoS engine. It ranges from 8000 bps (bits per second) to 2 billion bps.

The burst size is the amount of instantaneous burst that the security appliance can send at any given time without applying the exceed action. The following formula can be used to configure the burst size:

Burst size = (Policing Rate) [ts] 1.5 / 8

For example, if traffic needs to be limited to a police rate of 56,000 bps, the burst size will be 10,500 bytes. The valid range for burst size is from 1000 to 512,000,000 bytes.

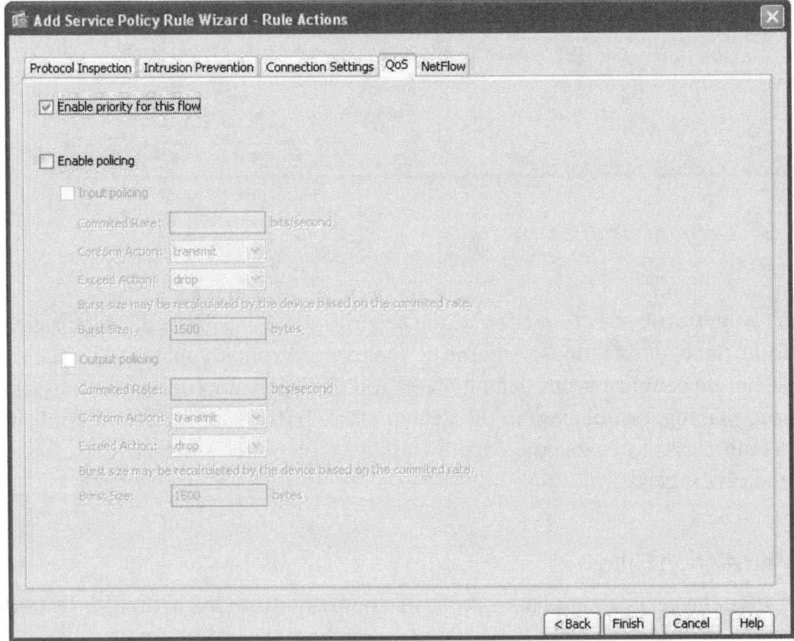

Figure 11-10 *Enabling Traffic Priority*

Note The policing rate is in bits per second, whereas the burst size is in bytes.

In Figure 11-11, the security appliance is configured to rate-limit the identified traffic to **56000 bits/second** in the **outbound** direction, with a burst size of **10,500 bytes.** If traffic falls within this range, the security appliance transmits it as it conforms to the configured policy. Otherwise, traffic that exceeds these rates is dropped.

The default **conform** action is to transmit traffic, whereas the default **exceed** action is to drop it.

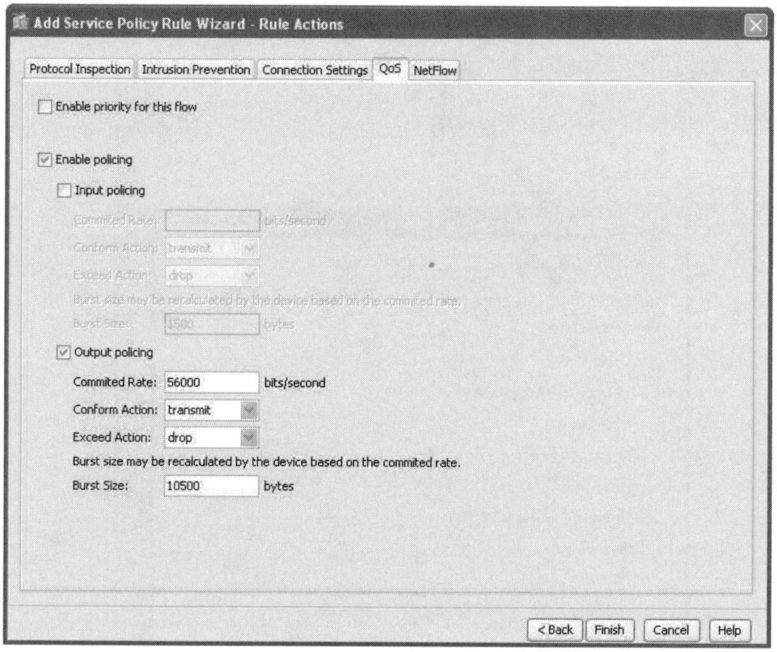

Figure 11-11 *Enabling Traffic Policing*

Traffic Shaping

As discussed earlier in the chapter, you can only configure the traffic shaping policies within a default traffic class. The security appliance enables you to specify the average rate of shaped traffic over a period of time. For example, if your WAN link speed is 2 Mbps, you can specify the average rate of shaped traffic to be 2 Mbps also.

The security appliance, optionally, enables you to specify the average size of burst that can be transmitted in a time interval. The following formula can be used to calculate the time interval:

Time interval (t) = (average burst size) / (average rate of shaped traffic)

The effect of the burst size and the time interval can be best explained by an example. If, for example, you want to shape traffic at 2 Mbps on a 100 Mbps interface and specify 500 Kbps as the burst size, the time interval is 250 msecs. What that means is, every 250 msecs the security appliance sends 500 Kbps traffic. Because the outbound interface is a 100 Mbps interface, it can send 500 Kbps traffic in the first 5 msec and then the link is idle for the remaining 245 msecs until the next time interval. If the time interval is too large, delay-sensitive traffic such as voice or video can be severely impacted.

In Figure 11-12, the security appliance is configured to shape traffic at **2 Mbps** with an average burst size of **16 Kbps** so that the time interval is 8 msecs.

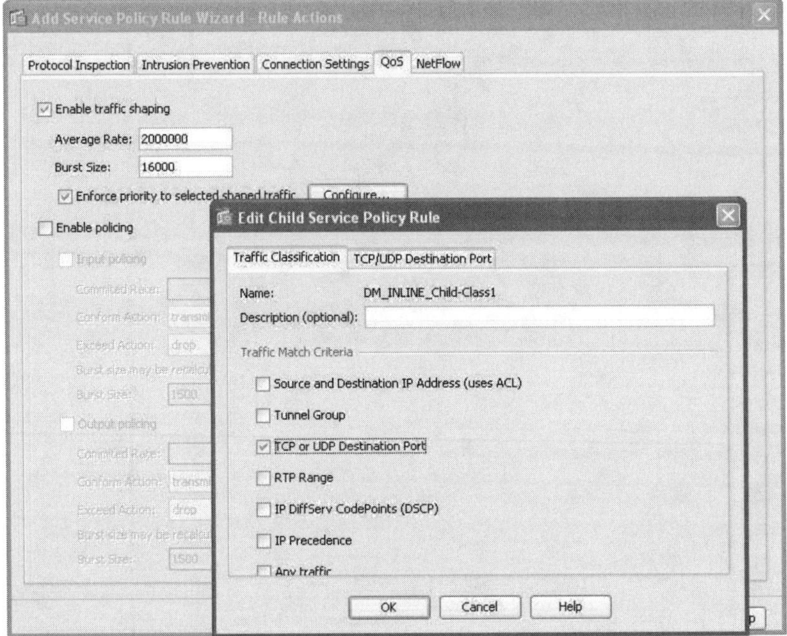

Figure 11-12 *Enabling Traffic Shaping*

As mentioned earlier in the chapter, the security appliance supports concurrent interface shaping and priority queuing on an interface by using the hierarchical QoS policies. You can shape traffic on an interface and then prioritize specific data packets within the shaped traffic. In Figure 11-12, the security appliance is configured to prioritize some data based TCP and UDP ports within the shaped traffic.

Note The security appliance does not permit you to prioritize some data within the shaped traffic if you are prioritizing traffic in a different traffic selection class and both of them belong to the same service policy.

QoS Configuration via CLI

Like the QoS configuration via ASDM, the QoS configuration via the CLI can be broken into the following four steps:

Step 1. Tune the priority queue.

Step 2. Set up a class map.

Step 3. Configure a policy map.

Step 4. Apply the policy map on the interface.

Step 1: Tune the Priority Queue

Configure the priority queue on an interface by using the **priority-queue** command, followed by the name of the interface. In Example 11-2, the administrator of the security appliance has fine-tuned the priority queue parameters on the **outside** interface. The transmit-ring limit is changed to hold up to **200** packets in the queue, whereas the high- and low-priority queue depth is set up to hold **2000** packets. This enables the priority queue to be processed efficiently with minimum latency caused by the transmit ring.

Example 11-2 *Configuration of Priority Queue*

```
Chicago(config)# priority-queue outside
Chicago(priority-queue)# tx-ring-limit 200
Chicago(priority-queue)# queue-limit 2000
```

> **Note** On Cisco ASA Model 5505, when you configure **priority-queue** on one interface, it overwrites the same values on all other interfaces as well.

Step 2: Set Up a Class Map

A traffic class identifies packets on which you want to apply the QoS policies. This is similar to the traffic selection criteria you define via ASDM. You create a traffic class by using the **class-map** command, followed by the name of the class. You do packet classification by using the **match** statements along with the appropriate option, described earlier in Table 11-4.

> **Note** You cannot configure multiple **match** statements under one class map, with one exception: One additional **match** statement is allowed when you have **match tunnel-group** or **default-inspect-traffic** commands configured in a class map.

Example 11-3 shows how to configure a class map for identifying mail and VoIP packets. An ACL named **mail-traffic** is configured to specify the source and destination IP addresses and the TCP destination port 25 (SMTP). This ACL is mapped to a class map called **mail-class.** One additional class map, **voip-class**, is set up to identify VoIP packets. VoIP uses DSCP values **af31** and **ef** for voice signaling and RTP streams, respectively.

Example 11-3 *Class Maps to Identify Mail and VoIP Traffic*

```
Chicago(config)# access-list mail-traffic extended permit tcp 192.168.10.0
  255.255.255.0 host 209.165.201.1 eq smtp
Chicago(config)# class-map mail-class
Chicago(config-cmap)# match access-list mail-traffic
Chicago(config-cmap)# exit
Chicago(config)# class-map voip-class
Chicago(config-cmap)# match dscp af31 ef
```

Note If you configure two classes with overlapping traffic and then apply policies to rate-limit traffic, the security appliance applies the most stringent traffic policy.

The security appliance can also match traffic destined to go over a tunnel. By using the **match tunnel-group** command, you can identify packets if they match against a VPN connection. In Example 11-4, the administrator has configured a class map called **tunnel-class** to identify traffic destined to go over a VPN group called **SecureMeGroup**. The administrator also uses destination-based IP flow to match traffic.

Note The use of **match flow ip destination-address** along with **tunnel-group** is mandatory if the VPN traffic needs to be rate-limited. You do not need to use **match flow ip destination-address** if the VPN traffic needs to be prioritized.

Example 11-4 *Class Maps to Identify Tunnel Traffic*

```
Chicago(config)# class-map tunnel-class
Chicago(config-cmap)# match flow ip destination-address
Chicago(config-cmap)# match tunnel-group SecureMeGroup
```

Note If you configure two classes with overlapping traffic, and apply priority to one class and rate limiting to the other class, the security appliance matches traffic to the priority queue and does not apply the rate-limited policies.

Step 3: Configure a Policy Map

The configured class maps are bound to a policy map that defines the action to be applied on the identified traffic. Apply the priority, rate-limit, or shaping QoS functions under the **policy-map** sub-configuration mode. Example 11-5 shows a policy map called **Traffic-Map-Outside** configured to apply actions to the class maps, defined in the previous step. The class map, such as **mail-class**, **voip-class**, and/or **tunnel-class**, is linked to the policy map by the **class** command.

Example 11-5 *Configuration of Policy Maps in the Security Appliance*

```
Chicago(config)# policy-map Traffic-Map-Outside
Chicago(config-pmap)# class voip-class
```

After mapping the class and the policy maps, Cisco ASA needs to be configured for an action that can be applied to the identified traffic. In Example 11-6, the security appliance is configured to prioritize VoIP traffic by the **priority** statement.

Example 11-6 *Traffic Prioritization for the VoIP Traffic*

```
Chicago(config)# policy-map Traffic-Map-Outside
Chicago(config-pmap)# class voip-traffic
Chicago(config-pmap-c)# priority
```

In Example 11-7, the security appliance is configured to rate-limit the tunnel traffic to 56 Kbps, with a burst size of 10,500 bytes. If traffic falls within this range, the security appliance transmits it because it conforms to the configured policy. Otherwise, traffic that exceeds these rates is dropped.

Example 11-7 *Rate-Limiting of Tunnel Traffic*

```
Chicago(config)# policy-map Traffic-Map-Outside
Chicago(config-pmap)# class tunnel-class
Chicago(config-pmap-c)# police 56000 10500 conform-action transmit exceed-action
drop
```

The security appliance also has a default class configured to match all the remaining traffic. This class can be used for shaping traffic at an average rate. In Example 11-8, a default traffic class is configured to shape traffic at 2 Mbps with 16 Kbps as the average burst size. Within this class, another policy-map called **DM_INLINE_Child-Policy3** is defined to prioritize SMTP traffic.

Example 11-8 *Traffic Shaping and Hierarchical Traffic Priority*

```
Chicago(config)# class-map DM_INLINE_Child-Class3
Chicago(config-cmap)# match port tcp eq smtp
Chicago(config-cmap)# policy-map DM_INLINE_Child-Policy3
Chicago(config-pmap)# class DM_INLINE_Child-Class3
Chicago(config-pmap-c)#  priority
Chicago(config-pmap-c)#  policy-map traffic-map
Chicago(config-pmap)#  class class-default
Chicago(config-pmap-c)#  shape average 2000000 16000
Chicago(config-pmap-c)#  service-policy DM_INLINE_Child-Policy3
```

Step 4: Apply the Policy Map on the Interface

The next step in completing the QoS configuration is the association of the policy map to an interface. You do so by using the **service-policy** command along with the policy name and the interface on which the policy needs to be applied. Example 11-9 demonstrates how to apply a policy map called **Traffic-Map-Outside** to the outside interface.

Example 11-9 *Applying QoS on the Outside Interface*

```
Chicago(config)# service-policy Traffic-Map-Outside interface outside
```

Cisco ASA supports policing, shaping, and prioritizing traffic in the outbound direction. However, traffic policing is also supported in the inbound direction. That means that if the service policy is applied to the outside interface in the inbound direction, then the classified packets can be inspected in the ingress direction.

Note An interface-based QoS policy takes precedence over a global QoS policy. The global QoS policy is applied to all the interfaces.

QoS Deployment Scenarios

The QoS solution is extremely useful when organizations run into network congestion, or when they want to prioritize some network traffic over other traffic. Although this important feature can be deployed in many ways, this section covers two design scenarios for the ease of understanding:

- QoS for VoIP traffic
- QoS for the remote-access VPN tunnels

Note The design scenarios discussed in this section should be used solely to enforce learning. They should be used for reference purposes only.

QoS for VoIP Traffic

SecureMe's information technology (IT) group is responsible for providing network services to its internal users. The IT group hosts an email server and uses Cisco IP Phones for telecommunications. SecureMe management has some specific requirements that the IT group is obliged to meet:

- Internal clients should have full Internet web access. They should get bandwidth based on best effort and should be restricted to 56 Kbps.
- For VoIP calls, there should not be any network-related delays.

- Internet email users should not be allowed to fully utilize the bandwidth when they use POP3 to download their email. They should be restricted to have up to 56 Kbps bandwidth. Additionally, users should be restricted to 56 Kbps when they upload their email via SMTP.
- All the system-generated syslog messages should be logged to a server.

Figure 11-13 shows the SecureMe topology that will be used to meet the network requirements.

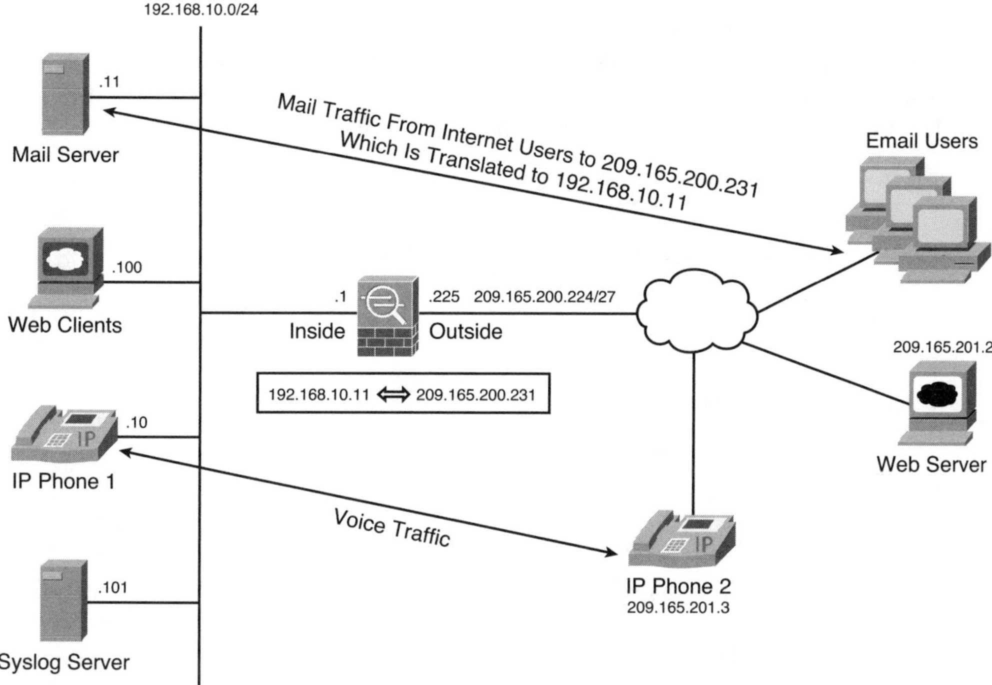

Figure 11-13 *SecureMe's VoIP and Email QoS Policy*

The administrator has put together the following to meet the requirements:

- The administrator has set up four class maps to identify traffic.
- A class map called **mail-pop3** is configured to classify all the packet sources from the mail server to the email users when users download their emails with POP3.
- The second class map, called **mail-smtp**, identifies SMTP traffic from the email users to the email server when they upload their emails. The email server is translated to 209.165.200.231.
- The third class map, called **web**, classifies the web traffic destined to the Internet. The internal hosts are translated to the public interface's IP address.

- The last class map, **VoIP**, identifies VoIP traffic.
- The **mail-pop3** and **mail-smtp** are linked to a policy map called **InsideQoSPolicy**, whereas the **web** and **VoIP** classes are mapped to a policy map called **OutsideQoSPolicy**.

The **OutsideQoSPolicy** policy map is applied to the outside interface, and the **InsideQoSPolicy** policy map is applied to the inside interface.

Configuration Steps Through ASDM

The relevant configuration through ASDM is discussed here. These configuration steps assume that you have IP connectivity from the ASDM client to the management IP address of the security appliance. The management IP address is 172.18.82.64.

Step 1. Navigate to **Configuration > Device Management > Advanced > Priority Queue**. Click **Add** and specify the following attributes:

- Interface: **outside**
- Queue Limit: **2000** packets
- Transmission ring Limit: **200**

Step 2. Click **Add** again and specify the following attributes:

- Interface: **inside**
- Queue Limit: **2000** packets
- Transmission ring Limit: **200**

Step 3. Navigate to **Configuration > Firewall > Service Policy Rules**, select the pull-down **Add** list, and click **Add Service Policy Rules**. Configure the following Service Policy Rule:

- Interface: **inside–(create new service policy)**
- Policy Name: **InsideQoSPolicy**
- Description: **Policy for Mail on Inside Interface**. Click **Next** when you are finished.

Step 4. Under **Traffic Selection Criteria**, specify a traffic class name of **mail-smtp**. Select **source and destination IP addresses (uses ACL)** as the "Traffic Match Criteria" and click **Next**. Configure the ACL using the following information:

- Action: **Match**
- Source: **any**
- Destination: **192.168.10.11/32**
- Service: **tcp/smtp**

Step 5. Under **Rule Action**, click the **QoS** tab and select the **Enable Policing** option. Specify the following information:

- Output policing: **Checked**
- Committed Rate: **56000** bits/second
- Confirm Action: **transmit**
- Exceed Acton: **drop**
- Burst Size: **10500** bytes. Click **Finish** when you are finished.

Step 6. Navigate to **Configuration > Firewall > Service Policy Rules** and select the previously defined policy map. Click the pull-down **Add** list and then select **Insert After**. Configure the following Service Policy Rule:

- Interface: **Inside–InsideQoSPolicy**

Step 7. Under "Traffic Selection Criteria," specify a traffic class name of **mail-pop3**. Select **Source and Destination IP Addresses (Uses ACL)** as the **Traffic Match Criteria** and click **Next**. Configure the ACL, using the following information:

- Action: **Match**
- Source: **192.168.10.11/32**
- Destination: **any**
- Service: **tcp**
- More Options -> Source Service: **tcp/pop3**. Click **Next**.

Step 8. Under "Rule Action," click the **QoS** tab and select the **Enable Policing** option. Specify the following information:

- Input policing: **Checked**
- Committed Rate: **56000** bits/second
- Confirm Action: **transmit**
- Exceed Acton: **drop**
- Burst Size: **10500** bytes. Click **Finish** when you are finished.

Step 9. Navigate to **Configuration > Firewall > Service Policy Rules**, select the pull-down **Add** list, and click **Add Service Policy Rules**. Configure the following Service Policy Rule:

- Interface: **outside–(create new service policy)**
- Policy Name: **OutsideQoSPolicy**
- Description: **Policy for Web, VoIP Traffic on Outside Interface**. Click **Next** when you are finished.

Step 10. Under "Traffic Selection Criteria," specify a traffic class name of **web.** Select **Source and Destination IP Addresses (Uses ACL)** as the **Traffic Match Criteria** and click **Next.** Configure the ACL, using the following information:

- Action: **Match**
- Source: **209.165.200.225**
- Destination: **any**
- Service: **tcp/http**

Step 11. Under "Rule Action," click the **QoS** tab and select the **Enable Policing** option. Specify the following information:

- Output policing: **Checked**
- Committed Rate: **56000** bits/second
- Confirm Action: **transmit**
- Exceed Acton: **drop**
- Burst Size: **10500** bytes. Click **Finish** when you are finished.

Step 12. Navigate to **Configuration > Firewall > Service Policy Rules** and select the previously defined policy map. Click the pull-down **Add** list and then select **Insert After.** Configure the following Service Policy Rule:

- Interface: **Inside–OutsideQoSPolicy**

Step 13. Under "Traffic Selection Criteria," specify a traffic class name of **VoIP.** Select **IP DiffServ CodePoints (DSCP)** as the Traffic Match Criteria and click **Next.** Add **af31** and **ef** to the "Match on DSCP" list. Click **Next.**

Step 14. Under "Rule Action," click the **QoS** tab and select the **Enable priority for this flow** option. Click **Finish** to complete the setup.

Step 15. Navigate to **Configuration > Device Management > Logging > Logging Setup** and select the **Enable Logging** option.

Step 16. Navigate to **Configuration > Device Management > Logging > Syslog Server** and click **Add.** Specify the following:

- Interface: **inside**
- IP Address: **192.168.10.101**
- Protocol: **UDP;** Port: **514.** Click **OK** when you are finished.

Step 17. Navigate to **Configuration > Device Management > Logging > Logging Filters**, select **Syslog Servers** and click **Edit.** Under "Filter on Severity," choose **Informational** from the drop-down menu.

Configuration Steps Through CLI

Example 11-10 shows the relevant configuration of SecureMe's ASA to achieve the previously listed requirements.

Example 11-10 *ASA's Full Configuration Showing QoS for VoIP, Mail and Web*

```
SecureMe# show running
ASA Version 8.2(1)
! ip address on the outside interface
interface GigabitEthernet0/0
 nameif outside
 security-level 0
 ip address 209.165.200.225 255.255.255.224
! ip address on the inside interface
interface GigabitEthernet0/1
 nameif inside
 security-level 100
 ip address 192.168.10.1 255.255.255.0
!
hostname SecureMe
!Access-list to classify Mail-traffic. SecureMe uses SMTP to upload emails
access-list mail-smtp-acl extended permit tcp any host 192.168.10.11 eq smtp
!Access-list to classify Mail-traffic. SecureMe uses POP3 to download emails
access-list mail-pop3-acl extended permit tcp host 192.168.10.11 eq pop3 any
!Access-list to classify Web-traffic to the internet.
access-list web-acl extended permit tcp host 209.165.200.225 any eq http
!Syslog Server information to log the dropped packets.
logging enable
logging trap informational
logging host inside 192.168.10.101
!NAT configuration to allow inside hosts to get Internet connectivity
global (outside) 1 interface
nat (inside) 1 192.168.10.0 255.255.255.0
!Static address translation for the Mail-Server
static (inside,outside) 209.165.200.231 192.168.10.11 netmask 255.255.255.255
!
route outside 0.0.0.0 0.0.0.0 209.165.200.230 1
!Class-map to classify Mail traffic in the inbound direction
class-map mail-smtp
 match access-list mail-smtp-acl
class-map mail-pop3
 match access-list mail-pop3-acl
!Class-map to classify Web traffic in the outbound direction
class-map web
 match access-list web-acl
```

```
!Class-maps to classify VoIP traffic
class-map VoIP
 match dscp 26 46
! Policy-map to define rules applied on traffic-class
policy-map OutsideQoSPolicy
 description Policy for Web, VoIP traffic on Outside Interface
! Web-mail is rate-limited to 56 Kbps
  class web
    police output 56000 10500 conform-action transmit exceed-action drop
! VoIP signal is prioritized
  class VoIP
    priority
policy-map InsideQoSPolicy
  description Policy for Mail on Inside Interface
! POP ans SMTP mail is rate-limited to 56 Kbps
  class mail-smtp
    police output 56000 10500 conform-action transmit exceed-action drop
  class mail-pop
    police input 56000 10500 conform-action transmit exceed-action drop
! Default Inspection Policies
policy-map global_policy
 class inspection_default
  inspect ctiqbe
  inspect http
<snip>
  inspect icmp
! Global Policy - applied for traffic inspection
service-policy global_policy global
! QoS policy is applied to the outside interface
service-policy OutsideQoSPolicy interface outside
! QoS policy is applied to the inside interface
service-policy InsideQoSPolicy interface inside
! Priority Queue is setup on the inside and outside interface for QoS efficiency
priority-queue inside
 tx-ring-limit 200
 queue-limit 2000
priority-queue outside
 tx-ring-limit 200
 queue-limit 2000
```

QoS for the Remote-Access VPN Tunnels

Figure 11-14 shows network topology for SecureMe's London's office. It has a Cisco ASA that it uses to provide VPN services for remote users. These users use the security appliance to connect to a file server to access their home directories. SecureMe does not want its broadband VPN users to fully utilize the bandwidth for its office. Therefore, it is interested in using QoS for the VPN tunnels to restrict the users to 256 Kbps. SecureMe also hosts a web server at this location. However, it prefers to prioritize the web traffic from the server to the Internet-based web clients.

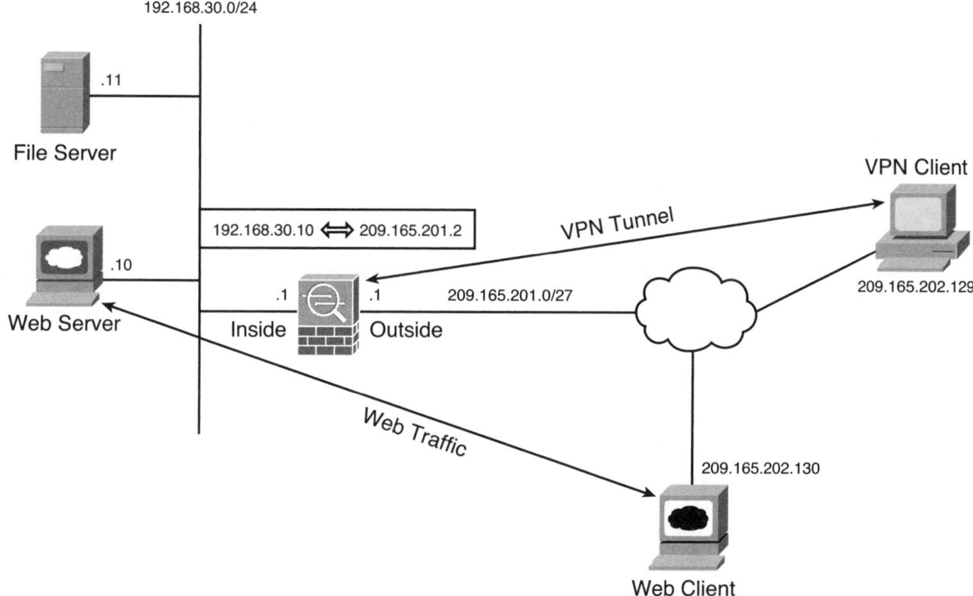

Figure 11-14 *SecureMe Network Using QoS for VPN Tunnels*

> **Note** Refer to Chapter 17, "IPSec Remote-Access VPNs," for detailed VPN configuration examples.

Configuration Steps Through ASDM

The relevant configuration through ASDM is discussed here. These configuration steps assume that you have IP connectivity from the ASDM client to the management IP address of the security appliance. The management IP address is 172.18.82.64.

Step 1. Navigate to **Configuration > Device Management > Advanced > Priority Queue**. Click **Add** and specify the following attributes:

- Interface: **outside**

- Queue Limit: **2000** packets
- Transmission ring Limit: **200**

Step 2. Navigate to **Configuration > Firewall > Service Policy Rules**, select the pull-down **Add** list, and click **Add Service Policy Rules.** Configure the following Service Policy Rule:

- Interface: **Outside–(Create New Service Policy)**
- Policy Name: **OutsideQoSPolicy**
- Description: **Policy for VPN and Web on Outside Interface.** Click **Next** when you are finished.

Step 3. Under "Traffic Selection Criteria," specify a traffic class name of **web-traffic.** Select source and destination IP addresses (uses ACL) as the **Traffic Match Criteria** and click **Next.** Configure the ACL using the following information:

- Action: **Match**
- Source: **209.165.201.2**
- Destination: **any**
- Service: **tcp**
- More Options > Source Service: **tcp/http.** Click **Next.**

Step 4. Under "Rule Action," click the **QoS** tab and select the **Enable Priority for this Flow** option. Click **Finish** when you are finished.

Step 5. Navigate to **Configuration > Firewall > Service Policy Rules** and select the previously defined policy map. Click the pull-down **Add** list and select **Insert After.** Configure the following Service Policy Rule:

- Interface: **inside–OutsideQoSPolicy**

Step 6. Under "Traffic Selection Criteria," specify a traffic class name of **VPNQoSClass.** Select **Tunnel Group** as the Traffic Match Criteria and click **Next.** Select the tunnel group **SecureMeIPSec** to apply the QoS policies. Also select the **Match Flow Destination IP Address** option.

Step 7. Under "Rule Action," click the **QoS** tab and select the **Enable Policing** option. Specify the following information:

- Input policing: **Checked**
- Committed Rate: **256000** bits/second
- Confirm Action: **transmit**
- Exceed Acton: **drop**
- Burst Size: **48000** bytes. Click **Finish** when you are finished.

Configuration Steps Through CLI

Example 11-11 shows the running configuration of the security appliance in London. A class map called **VPNQoSClass** is configured to match all the packets destined to the VPN group called **SecureMeGroup.** To prioritize Internet users' access to the web server, another class map called **web-traffic** is set up. The traffic is matched against an ACL that is configured to identify TCP port 80 packets. Both these classes are linked to a policy map called **OutsideQoSPolicy**, where the VPN traffic is rate-limited to 256 Kbps for normal traffic with a burst rate of 48000 bytes. The security appliance is also configured to prioritize web traffic passing through it. The policy is then applied to the outside interface.

Example 11-11 *Full Configuration of the ASA in Chicago Using QoS*

```
London# show running
! ip address on the outside interface
interface GigabitEthernet0/0
 nameif outside
 security-level 0
 ip address 209.165.201.1 255.255.255.224
! ip address on the inside interface
interface GigabitEthernet0/1
 nameif inside
 security-level 100
 ip address 192.168.30.1 255.255.255.0
!
hostname London
!ACL to classify Web-traffic
access-list web-traffic extended permit tcp host 209.165.201.2 eq http any
!ACL to bypass address translation for the traffic destined to the VPN clients
access-list nonat extended permit ip 192.168.30.0 255.255.255.0 192.168.50.0
  255.255.255.0
!NAT 0 to bypass traffic identified in ACL nonat
nat (inside) 0 access-list nonat
!Static address translation for the web server
static (inside,outside) 209.165.201.2 192.168.30.10 netmask 255.255.255.255
! Local pool of addresses to be assigned to the VPN clients
ip local pool vpnpool 192.168.50.1-192.168.50.199
! Transform set to specify encryption and hashing algorithm
! Crypto map configuration
crypto ipsec transform-set myset esp-aes-256 esp-sha-hmac
crypto dynamic-map dynmap 10 set transform-set myset
crypto map IPSec_map 10 ipsec-isakmp dynamic dynmap
crypto map IPSec_map interface outside
! isakmp configuration
isakmp enable outside
```

```
isakmp policy 10 authentication pre-share
isakmp policy 10 encryption aes-256
isakmp policy 10 hash sha
isakmp policy 10 group 2
isakmp policy 10 lifetime 86400
! Remote Access tunnel-group configuration
tunnel-group SecureMeIPSec type ipsec-ra
tunnel-group SecureMeIPSec general-attributes
 address-pool vpnpool
tunnel-group SecureMeIPSec ipsec-attributes
 pre-shared-key *
! Class-map to classify VPN packets
class-map VPNQoSClass
  match tunnel-group SecureMeIPSec
  match flow ip destination-address
!Class-map to classify Web traffic
class-map web-traffic
  match access-list web-traffic
! Policy-map to define rules applied on traffic-class
policy-map OutsideQoSPolicy
  description Policy for VPN and Web on Outside Interface
  class web-traffic
    priority
  class VPNQoSClass
    police output 256000 48000 conform-action transmit exceed-action drop
! Inspection Policies
policy-map global_policy
 class inspection_default
  inspect ctiqbe
  inspect http
<snip>
  inspect icmp
! Global Policy - applied for traffic inspection
service-policy global_policy global
! Priority Queue is setup on the outside interface for QoS efficiency
priority-queue outside
  tx-ring-limit 200
  queue-limit 2000
! QoS policy is applied to the outside interface
service-policy OutsideQoSPolicy interface outside
```

Monitoring QoS

Cisco ASA includes a set of **show** commands to check the health of the security appliance and to ensure guaranteed QoS through the security appliance. These commands are also helpful in isolating any configuration-related issues. Most of the QoS-related commands start with **show service-policy**, as shown in Example 11-12.

Example 11-12 *Options Available in the* **show service policy** *Command*

```
Chicago# show service-policy ?
csc         Show status/statistics of Content Security and Control policy
flow        Show all policies that are enabled on a flow
global      show status/statistics of the global policy
inspect     Show status/statistics of 'inspect' policy
interface   show status/statistics of an interface policy
ips         Show status/statistics of 'ips' policy
police      Show status/statistics of 'police' policy
priority    Show status/statistics of 'priority' policy
set         Show status/statistics of 'set' policy
shape       Show status/statistics of 'shape' policy
|           Output modifiers
<cr>
```

The **show service-policy interface** command displays the QoS interface policy name of the class map, along with the configured policies within each class. In Example 11-13, two class maps are configured: **VPNQoSClass** and **web-traffic**. The VPNQoSClass class is configured to rate-limit the traffic to 256,000 bps with burst size of 48,000 bytes. The security appliance dropped 6 packets because they exceeded the rate-limiting policies, and transmitted 128 packets. On the other hand, the **web-traffic** class, being the priority class, transmitted 250 packets.

Example 11-13 *Output of* **show service-policy interface outside** *Command*

```
Chicago# show service-policy interface outside
Interface outside:
  Service-policy: OutsideQoSPolicy
    Class-map: web-traffic
      Priority:
        Interface outside: aggregate drop 0, aggregate transmit 250
    Class-map: VPNQoSClass
      Output police Interface outside:
        cir 256000 bps, bc 48000 bytes
        conformed 128 packets, 137472 bytes; actions:  transmit
        exceeded 6 packets, 6444 bytes; actions:  drop
        conformed 0 bps, exceed 0 bps
    Class-map: class-default
```

The robust CLI of the security appliance enables you to monitor the depth of interface priority queues. As shown in Example 11-14, **show priority-queue statistics** displays the queue statistics of the inside and outside interfaces. There are two queue types for each interface: one for the priority traffic (LLQ) and the other for best-effort (BE) traffic. The outside interface best-effort queue transmitted 84,792 packets and dropped 1056. The priority queue, shown as LLQ, forwarded 6589 packet and dropped none. The inside interface transmitted 44902 packets on the best-effort queue.

Example 11-14 *Output of* show priority-queue *Command*

```
Chicago# show priority-queue statistics
Priority-Queue Statistics interface outside
Queue Type         = BE
Packets Dropped    = 1056
Packets Transmit   = 84792
Packets Enqueued   = 0
Current Q Length   = 0
Max Q Length       = 0

Queue Type         = LLQ
Packets Dropped    = 0
Packets Transmit   = 6589
Packets Enqueued   = 0
Current Q Length   = 0
Max Q Length       = 0

Priority-Queue Statistics interface inside
Queue Type         = BE
Packets Dropped    = 0
Packets Transmit   = 44902
Packets Enqueued   = 0
Current Q Length   = 0
Max Q Length       = 0

Queue Type         = LLQ
Packets Dropped    = 0
Packets Transmit   = 0
Packets Enqueued   = 0
Current Q Length   = 0
Max Q Length       = 0
Chicago#
```

Summary

QoS is a robust feature that provides network professionals a means to prioritize time-sensitive and critical data over regular traffic. The three modes—traffic prioritization, traffic shaping, and traffic policing—can be deployed in Cisco ASA to guarantee that important traffic goes through during network congestion. Cisco ASA enables you to fine-tune the QoS engine by setting the transmit ring and priority queue depths to control data delay. This chapter also showed you how to monitor traffic statistics, such as the number of packets matching the priority and best-effort QoS policies.

Chapter 12

Configuring and Troubleshooting Intrusion Prevention System (IPS)

This chapter covers the following topics:

- Overview of the Adaptive Inspection Prevention Security Services Module (AIP-SSM) and Adaptive Inspection Prevention Security Services Card (AIP-SSC)
- AIP-SSM and AIP-SSC management
- Cisco IPS software architecture
- Configuring the AIP-SSM
- AIP-SSM maintenance
- Advanced features and configuration
- Cisco ASA Botnet detection

Cisco ASA integrates firewall capabilities with sophisticated intrusion prevention features that provide a deep-packet inspection solution. Cisco Intrusion Prevention System (CIPS) integration makes it possible to effectively mitigate a wide range of network attacks without compromising Cisco ASA's performance.

This chapter covers Cisco ASA IPS integration, providing several deployment examples and considerations. Additionally, it covers the configuration and troubleshooting of the Adaptive Inspection Prevention Security Service Module (AIP-SSM).

Overview of the Adaptive Inspection Prevention Security Services Module (AIP-SSM) and Adaptive Inspection Prevention Security Services Card (AIP-SSC)

CiscoASA supports the Adaptive Inspection Prevention Security Service Module (AIP-SSM), running Cisco Intrusion Prevention System (CIPS) software version 5.0 or later.

One of the major features of CIPS is its capability to process and analyze traffic inline. This qualifies Cisco ASA to be classified as an IPS. The system image file is similar to the ones that run on the Cisco IPS 4200 Series sensors, Cisco IDS Services Module-2 (IDSM-2) for Cisco Catalyst 6500, and Cisco IDS Network Module for Cisco IOS routers.

There are four different AIP-SSM modules:

- AIP-SSC-5—Only supported on the Cisco ASA 5505.
- AIP-SSM-10—Supported on the Cisco ASA 5510 and 5520.
- AIP-SSM-20—Supported on the Cisco ASA 5520 and 5540.
- AIP-SSM-40—Supported on the Cisco ASA 5520 and 5540.

AIP-SSM and AIP-SSC Management

You can manage the AIP-SSM from its management interface port by using Telnet, SSH, or Cisco Adaptive Security Device Manager (ASDM). You can also manage it from the ASA's backplane by using the **session** command:

```
session module-number
```

The *module-number* is the slot number in the Cisco ASA. Because there is only one available slot, the module number is always 1. Example 12-1 demonstrates how to open a command session to the AIP-SSM module. The AIP-SSM module prompts the user for authentication credentials.

Example 12-1 session *Command*

```
NewYork# session 1
Opening command session with slot 1.
Connected to slot 1. Escape character sequence is 'CTRL-^X'.
login: cisco
Password:
```

After the user session is connected to the AIP-SSM, the configuration steps are the same as for any other system running CIPS 5.0 or later software. You can use the **show module** command in the Cisco ASA to see high-level information about the installed AIP-SSM module (see Example 12-2).

Example 12-2 *Output of* show module *Command*

```
NewYork# show module
Mod Card Type                                    Model              Serial No.
--- -------------------------------------------- ------------------ -----------
  0 ASA 5520 Adaptive Security Appliance         ASA5520            P0000000227
  1 ASA 5500 Series Security Services Module-10  ASA-SSM-10         01234567890
```

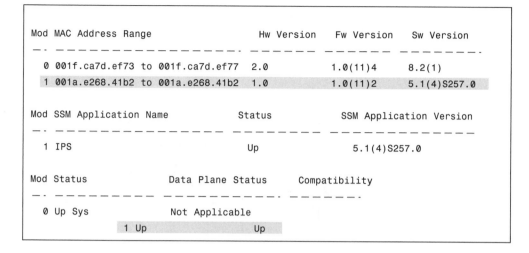

```
Mod MAC Address Range                 Hw Version   Fw Version    Sw Version
--- --------------------------------- ------------ ------------ ---------------
  0 001f.ca7d.ef73 to 001f.ca7d.ef77  2.0          1.0(11)4     8.2(1)
  1 001a.e268.41b2 to 001a.e268.41b2  1.0          1.0(11)2     5.1(4)S257.0

Mod SSM Application Name           Status           SSM Application Version
--- ------------------------------ ---------------- --------------------------
  1 IPS                            Up               5.1(4)S257.0

Mod Status             Data Plane Status     Compatibility
--- ------------------ --------------------- -------------
  0 Up Sys             Not Applicable
  1 Up                 Up
```

The first highlighted line shows the card type. In this case, the New York ASA 5540 is running an AIP-SSM-20 with serial number 01234567890. The second highlighted line shows the MAC address of the card and the software version it is running. The third highlighted line shows the status of the module, **Up**, meaning it is operational.

Inline Versus Promiscuous Mode

Cisco ASA supports both inline and promiscuous IPS modes. When configured as an inline IPS, the AIP-SSM module can drop malicious packets, generate alarms, or reset a connection, allowing the ASA to respond immediately to security threats and protect the network. Inline IPS configuration forces all traffic to be directed to the AIP-SSM. The ASA does not forward any traffic out to the network without the AIP-SSM first inspecting it.

Figure 12-1 shows the traffic flow when the Cisco ASA is configured in inline IPS mode.

The following is the sequence of events illustrated in Figure 12-1:

Step 1. The Cisco ASA receives an IP packet from the Internet.

Step 2. Because the Cisco ASA is configured in inline IPS mode, it forwards the packet to the AIP-SSM for analysis, assuming that the configured security policies allow this traffic into the protected network. If an ACL is configured in the Cisco ASA to deny this traffic, the packet is never sent to the AIP-SSM.

Step 3. The AIP-SSM analyzes the packet and, if it determines that the packet is not malicious, forwards the packet back to the Cisco ASA.

Step 4. The Cisco ASA forwards the packet to its final destination (the protected host).

When the Cisco ASA is configured in promiscuous IPS mode, the ASA forwards a copy of the packet to the AIP-SSM for inspection; however, the packet makes it to the internal

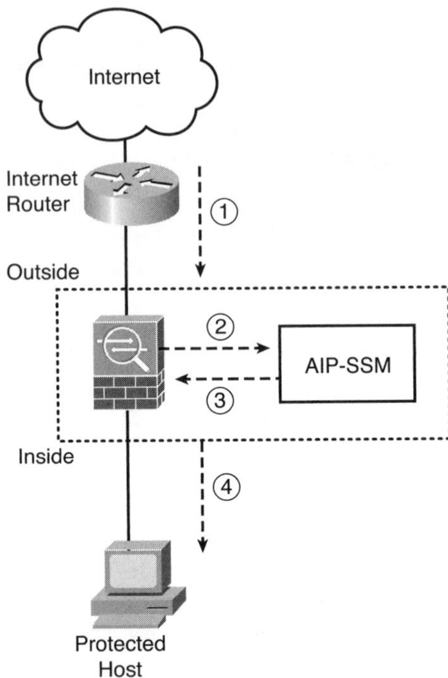

Figure 12-1 *Traffic Flow of Inline IPS Mode*

network, depending on the configured security policies. Figure 12-2 shows the traffic flow when the Cisco ASA is configured in promiscuous IPS mode.

The following is the sequence of events illustrated in Figure 12-2:

Step 1. The Cisco ASA receives an IP packet from the Internet.

Step 2. Because the Cisco ASA is configured in promiscuous IPS mode, it forwards a copy of the packet to the AIP-SSM for analysis. The Cisco ASA forwards the packet to its final destination (the protected host), assuming that the configured security policies allow this traffic into the protected network. If an ACL is configured in the Cisco ASA to deny this traffic, the packet is never sent to the AIP-SSM.

Step 3. The AIP-SSM analyzes the copy of the packet and, if it determines that the packet is malicious, it can alert the administrator, or take any configured action. The configuration of specific IPS security policies and the respective actions are covered later in this chapter in the "Advanced Features and Configuration" section.

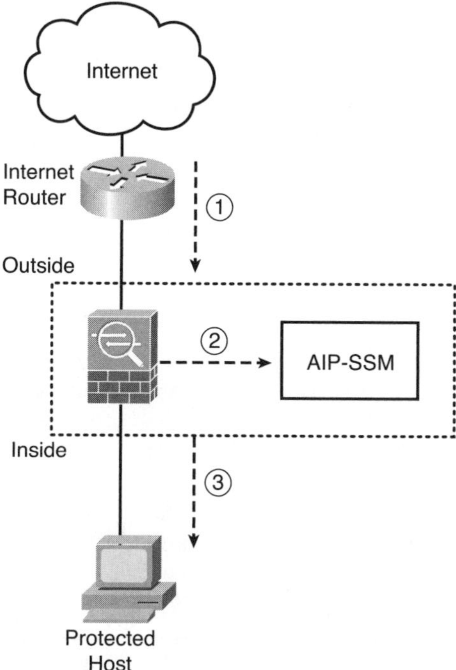

Figure 12-2 *Traffic Flow of Promiscuous IPS Mode*

Cisco IPS Software Architecture

The CIPS software uses the Security Device Event Exchange (SDEE) protocol. SDEE is a standardized IPS communication protocol developed by Cisco for the IDS Consortium at the International Computer Security Association (ICSA). Remote applications such as Adaptive Security Device Manager (ASDM), IPS Device Manager (IDM), Intrusion Prevention System Management Console (IPSMC), and Cisco Security Monitoring, Analysis and Response System (CS-MARS) can retrieve events from the sensor through this protocol.

The major components of CIPS software include the following:

- MainApp
- SensorApp
- Attack Response Controller (formerly known as the Network Access Controller (NAC))
- AuthenticationApp
- cipsWebserver

- Logger
- EventStore
- Transactional Services for Security Device Event Exchange (SDEE)
- NotificationApp
- InterfaceApp
- CLI

Figure 12-3 illustrates the main components of CIPS in correlation with the AIP-SSM.

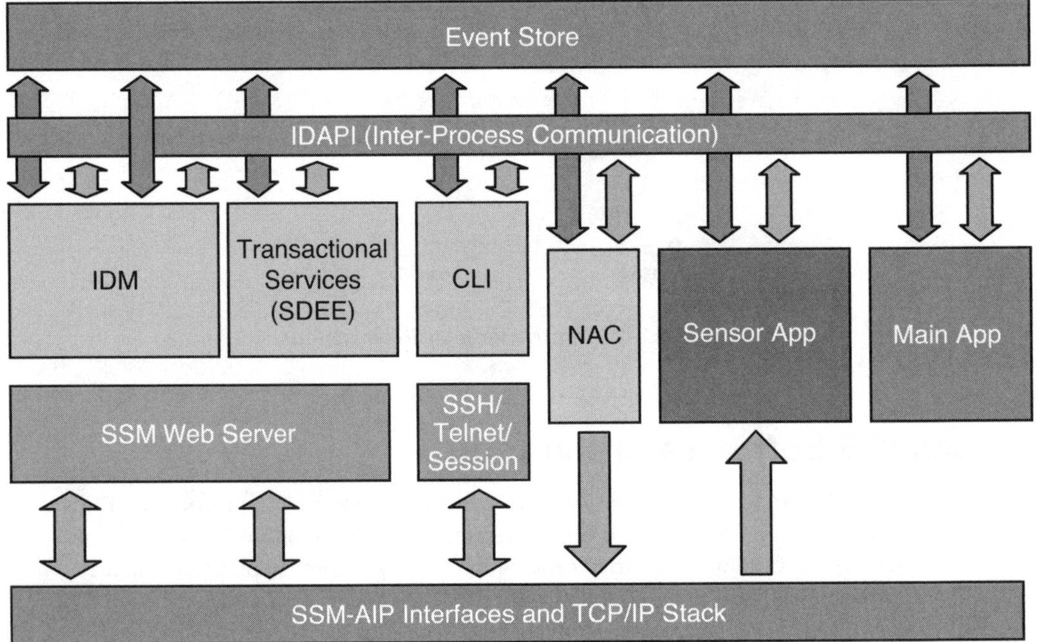

Figure 12-3 *CIPS Software Architecture Overview*

MainApp

MainApp is responsible for several critical tasks in the AIP-SSM (as well as all other platforms that support CIPS software). These tasks include the following:

- Initializing all CIPS components and applications
- Scheduling, downloading, and installing software updates
- Configuring communication parameters
- Managing the system clock

- Gathering system statistics and software version information
- Cleanly shutting down/restarting all CIPS services

MainApp is initialized by the CIPS operating system and starts the CIPS applications in the following sequence:

Step 1. Reads and validates dynamic and static configurations.

Step 2. Synchronizes dynamic configuration data to system files.

Step 3. Creates EventStore and the Intrusion Detection Application Programming Interface (IDAPI) shared components.

Step 4. Initializes status event subsystem.

Step 5. Launches IPS applications as stated in the static configuration.

Step 6. Waits until an initialization status event from each application is sent.

Step 7. Generates an error event identifying all applications that did not start, if all status events are not received within 60 seconds.

Step 8. Listens for control transaction requests and processes them accordingly.

MainApp controls the CIPS software installation and upgrades. It also controls network communication parameters, such as the following:

- AIP-SSM hostname
- IP addressing and default gateway configuration for the AIP-SSM command and control interface
- Network access control list

MainApp manages the system clock (whether NTP is configured or not) and collects system statistics.

SensorApp

SensorApp is the application responsible for the analysis of network traffic, examining it for any malicious content. The packets flow through it from the Gigabit Ethernet network interface on the AIP-SSM, which is directly connected to the Cisco ASA backplane.

If the Cisco ASA AIP-SSM configuration is set for promiscuous mode, the packets are discarded after processing by SensorApp. If configured for inline operation, the packets are either forwarded back to the Cisco ASA or dropped according to the defined policy.

SensorApp has two modules crucial for the operation of the AIP-SSM or any other device running CIPS:

- Analysis Engine

- Alarm Channel

The Virtual Sensor is the Analysis Engine Configuration Module, which handles the AIP-SSM configuration. This module interprets the configuration and maps it into internal configuration objects. Figure 12-4 illustrates both of these modules.

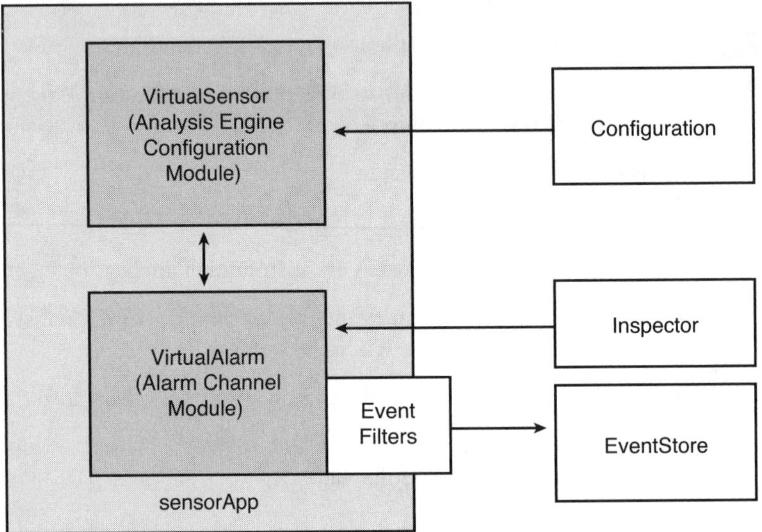

Figure 12-4 *SensorApp Virtual Sensor and Virtual Alarm*

In CIPS, a new protocol is introduced, called the Intrusion Detection Configuration (IDCONF) protocol. IDCONF provides clean, consistent, and accurate signature definitions. This replaces the old IDIOM framework in previous versions. It supports multiple layers of parameters to ensure that a signature is defined in terms that are understandable and valid for the inspection engines. The Virtual Alarm is the alarm channel module, which is responsible for processing all signature events generated by the traffic inspector engine. The primary function of the Alarm Channel Module is to generate alarms for each event as it is passed. Event or alarm filters may be configured and are processed by the alarm channel module, as illustrated in Figure 12-4.

Attack Response Controller

The Attack Response Controller is the application responsible for communicating with the Cisco ASA or any other supported device while shunning (blocking) connections if the AIP-SSM is configured in promiscuous mode.

One of the functions of the Attack Response Controller is to forward shunning information to other IPS devices on the network to collectively control network access devices. IPS sensing devices that perform this operation are referred to as master blocking sensors.

AuthenticationApp

AuthenticationApp, as its name suggests, is the process that controls user authentication on the AIP-SSM or any other device running Cisco IPS 5.x and later software. Additionally, it administers all the user accounts, privileges, Secure Shell (SSH) keys, and digital certificates, while also controlling what authentication method is used.

As illustrated in Figure 12-5, AuthenticationApp controls authentication when the user connects via Telnet, SSH, a session through ASA, ASDM, IDM, or IDSMC.

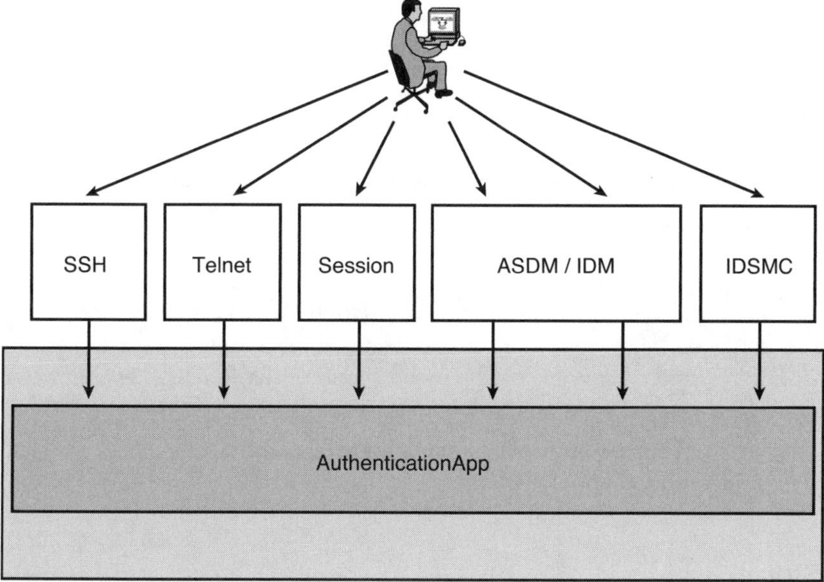

Figure 12-5 *AuthenticationApp Architecture*

cipsWebserver

The CIPS web server (cipsWebserver) within AIP-SSM provides configuration support for IDM and provides support for SDEE transactions, such as the following:

- Reporting security events
- Receiving IDCONF transactions
- Processing IP logs

ASDM is hosted and controlled by the Cisco ASA; however, it launches IDM, which uses SDEE to communicate with the AIP-SSM hosted by the CIPS web server. The CIPS web server supports HTTP 1.0 and 1.1 running Secure Sockets Layer (SSL)/Transport Layer Security (TLS).

Logger

The AIP-SSM logs alert, error, status, and debug messages, as well as IP logs. These messages and IP logs are accessible through the CLI and SDEE clients such as IDM, Cisco Security Manager (CSM), and CS-MARS. Logger sends log messages with the following five levels of severity:

- Debug
- Timing
- Warning
- Error
- Fatal

These messages are written to the following file on AIP-SSM module:

/usr/cids/idsRoot/log/main.log.

Note To access this file, you must be logged in with the service account. Instructions on how to create the service account are discussed later in this chapter, in the "User Administration" section. These messages are mostly used by Cisco TAC engineers for troubleshooting purposes.

Messages that are generated at warning level or above are converted into evErrors and inserted into the Event Store.

EventStore

All IPS events are stored in the EventStore with a time stamp and a unique ascending identifier. Additionally, CIPS internal applications write log, status, and error events into the EventStore.

Note IPS alerts are written only by the SensorApp application.

The EventStore is designed to store CIPS events in a circular fashion. In other words, when it reaches the configured size, the oldest events are overwritten by new events and log messages.

Note In CIPS code, the EventStore is reduced to 30 MB from 4 GB in earlier code.

CtlTransSource

SDEE and HTTP remote-control transactions are handled by an internal application called CtlTransSource (formerly known as TransactionSource). It handles all TLS communications with external management servers and monitoring systems. CtlTransSource performs basic authentication to remote management applications and monitoring systems. When an application attempts a remote-control transaction, IDAPI redirects the transaction to CtlTransSource.

Configuring the AIP-SSM

You can configure the AIP-SSM by using the command line interface (CLI) or ASDM. The following sections introduce the CIPS CLI and then cover step-by-step instructions on how to configure the AIP-SSM.

Introduction to the CIPS CLI

The CIPS CLI provides a user interface for all direct connections to the AIP-SSM (e.g., Telnet, SSH, and session from the ASA). This section covers

- How to log in to the AIP-SSM via the CLI
- CLI command modes
- Initial AIP-SSM configuration

Logging In to the AIP-SSM via the CLI

You can connect to the AIP-SSM CLI via the ASA backplane by using the **session** command, or by initiating an SSH or Telnet connection via the external management Ethernet port.

The default username is **cisco** and the default password is **cisco**. The user is forced to change his password after the first login. Example 12-3 shows the user **cisco** successfully logging in to the AIP-SSM CLI via the ASA backplane, using the **session** command.

Example 12-3 *Logging In to the CLI*

```
NewYork# session 1
Opening command session with slot 1.
Connected to slot 1. Escape character sequence is 'CTRL-^X'.
login: cisco
Password: <password>
Last login: Fri Aug  7 12:53:12 from 127.0.1.1
***NOTICE***
This product contains cryptographic features and is subject to United States
```

```
and local country laws governing import, export, transfer and use. Delivery
of Cisco cryptographic products does not imply third-party authority to import,
export, distribute or use encryption. Importers, exporters, distributors, and
users are responsible for compliance with U.S. and local country laws. By using
this product you agree to comply with applicable laws and regulations. If you
are unable to comply with U.S. and local laws, return this product immediately.
A summary of U.S. laws governing Cisco cryptographic products may be found at:
http://www.cisco.com/wwl/export/crypto/tool/stqrg.html
If you require further assistance please contact us by sending email to
export@cisco.com.
NewYorkSSM#
```

Note There are four major user account roles that determine which operations a user is allowed to perform. They are covered later in this chapter under "User Administration."

CLI Command Modes

The CIPS CLI is similar to the Cisco ASA and IOS CLIs. It has a configuration command mode that you enter by invoking the **configure terminal** command. Example 12-4 demonstrates how to enter into global configuration mode.

Example 12-4 *Entering Configuration Mode*

```
NewYorkSSM# configure terminal
NewYorkSSM(config)#
```

The **(config)#** prompt is displayed after you invoke the **configure terminal** command.

As in Cisco IOS and ASA, you can display the help for a specific command by typing a question mark (?) after the command. You can also type a question mark to view the valid keywords that complete the command. There are certain commands that generate user interactive prompts. An example of this is the **setup** command, which is covered in the following section.

Initializing the AIP-SSM

Before the AIP-SSM can communicate with any management station and start analyzing data from the network, you must first configure basic settings with the **setup** command. The AIP-SSM first displays the current configuration and then generates user interactive prompts that guide you to complete the initial settings.

Note The default input is displayed inside brackets, [ ]. To accept the default input, press **Enter**.

Example 12-5 includes the output of the **setup** command.

Example 12-5 *Configuring Initial Settings with the* **setup** *Command*

```
NewYorkSSM# setup
     —- System Configuration Dialog —-
At any point you may enter a question mark '?' for help.
User ctrl-c to abort configuration dialog at any prompt.
Default settings are in square brackets '[]'.
Current Configuration:
service host
network-settings
host-ip 127.0.0.1
host-name sensor
telnet-option enabled
ftp-timeout 300
login-banner-text
exit
time-zone-settings
offset -420
standard-time-zone-name GMT-07:00
exit
summertime-option recurring
offset 60
summertime-zone-name PDT
start-summertime
month april
week-of-month first
day-of-week sunday
time-of-day 02:00:00
exit
end-summertime
month october
week-of-month last
day-of-week sunday
time-of-day 02:00:00
exit
exit
ntp-option disabled
exit
service web-server
port 443
exit
Current time: Tue Aug 25 03:24:09 2009
Setup Configuration last modified: Tue Aug 25 03:11:23 2009
```

```
Continue with configuration dialog?[yes]: yes
Enter host name[sensor]: NewYorkSSM
Enter IP interface[10.1.9.201/24,10.1.9.1]: 192.168.10.28/24,192.168.10.1
Enter telnet-server status[disabled]:enable
Enter web-server port[443]:
Modify current access list?[no]: yes
Current access list entries:
Delete:
Permit: 192.168.10.0/24
Modify system clock settings?[no]: yes
  Use NTP?[no]: yes
    NTP Key ID[]: 1
    NTP Key Value[]: cisco
    NTP Server IP Address[]:192.168.10.123    NTP Key ID[1]:
  Modify summer time settings?[no]:
  Modify system timezone?[no]:
Modify virtual sensor "vs0" configuration?[no]: yes
Current interface configuration
  Command control: GigabitEthernet0/0
  Unused:
    GigabitEthernet0/1
  Monitored:
    None
Add Monitored interfaces?[no]: yes
Interface[]:
```

Follow these steps after the AIP-SSM prompt asks whether you would like to continue with the configuration dialog:

Step 1. The configuration dialog asks you to enter the hostname to be assigned to the AIP-SSM. The default hostname is *sensor*. Enter the new hostname (case sensitive) as follows:

```
Enter host name[sensor]: NewYorkSSM
```

Step 2. You are asked to enter the IP address and default gateway for the management interface of the AIP-SSM. The default IP address is 10.1.9.201 and the default gateway is 10.1.9.1. Enter the IP address and gateway configuration in the following format:

<ip address>/<mask-bits>,<gateway>

The IP address 192.168.10.28 with a 24-bit mask and gateway of 192.168.10.1 is entered in the following example:

```
Enter IP interface[10.1.9.201/24,10.1.9.1]:
192.168.10.28/24,192.168.10.1
```

Step 3. Telnet services are disabled by default. The AIP-SSM allows you to enable Telnet services at this point:

```
Enter telnet-server status[disabled]:enable
```

Note that the Telnet protocol is not a secure protocol. SSH should be used instead of Telnet.

Step 4. The default web server port is TCP port 443 (because it is the default for most web servers that support SSL/TLS). The configuration dialog enables you to change the port at this point:

```
Enter web-server port[443]:
```

The default port is selected in this example.

Step 5. The configuration dialog prompts you to modify the current access list. Enter **yes** to add or delete hosts or networks that will be allowed to communicate with the AIP-SSM.

```
Modify current access list?[no]: yes
Current access list entries:
Delete:
Permit: 192.168.10.0/24
```

The 192.168.10.0/24 network is added to the list in this example.

Step 6. After adding or deleting entries to your access list, the configuration dialog prompts you to change the clock settings. In the following example, NTP is enabled:

```
Modify system clock settings?[no]: yes
Use NTP?[no]: yes
    NTP Key ID[]: 1
    NTP Key Value[]: cisco
    NTP Server IP Address[]: 192.168.10.123
```

The NTP key ID is set to **1**, the key is **cisco**, and the NTP server address is **192.168.10.123**.

Step 7. You can also modify daylight savings time settings. The default is recurring, which automatically adjusts the time:

```
Modify summer time settings?[no]: yes
```

```
    Recurring, Date or Disable?[Recurring]:
    Start Month[march]:
    Start Week[second]:
    Start Day[sunday]:
    Start Time[02:00:00]:
    End Month[november]:
    End Week[first]:
    End Day[sunday]:
    End Time[02:00:00]:
    DST Zone[GMT-04:00]:GMT-05:00
    Offset[60]:
```

Step 8. The configuration dialog asks you to specify the time zone to be displayed when standard time is in effect:

```
Modify system timezone?[no]: yes
    Timezone[CST]: EST
    UTC Offset[-300]:
```

Step 9. The last step is to modify the monitored interface. In case of the AIP-SSM, the only interface used for monitoring is the internal Gigabit Ethernet interface:

```
Modify virtual sensor "vs0" configuration?[no]: yes
Current interface configuration
  Command control: GigabitEthernet0/0
  Unused:
    GigabitEthernet0/1
  Monitored:
    None
Add Monitored interfaces?[no]: yes
```

Step 10. The AIP-SSM displays a summary of the configuration entered:

```
The following configuration was entered.
service host
network-settings
host-ip 192.168.10.28/24,192.168.10.1
host-name NewYorkSSM
telnet-option enabled
access-list 192.168.10.0/24
ftp-timeout 300
no login-banner-text
exit
time-zone-settings
offset -420
standard-time-zone-name GMT-05:00
exit
```

```
summertime-option recurring
offset 60
summertime-zone-name PDT
start-summertime
month april
week-of-month first
day-of-week sunday
time-of-day 02:00:00
exit
end-summertime
month october
week-of-month last
day-of-week sunday
time-of-day 02:00:00
exit
exit
ntp-option enabled
 exit
service web-server
port 443
service analysis-engine
virtual-sensor vs0
physical-interface FastEthernet2/3
exit
exit
exit
[0] Go to the command prompt without saving this config.
[1] Return back to the setup without saving this config.
[2] Save this configuration and exit setup.
Enter your selection[2]:
```

From the menu, you can select any of the available options:

- Go to the command prompt without saving the configuration.
- Return back to the setup without saving the configuration.
- Save the configuration and exit setup.

Select option 2 if you are satisfied with the configuration and you want to save it in the system.

You can use the **Startup Wizard** in ASDM 6.x or later to set up or to modify an AIP-SSM that has already been configured. However, it cannot be used for initializing a new (not configured) AIP-SSM. You must use the **setup** command to initialize a new AIP-SSM. To set up or modify the AIP-SSM through ASDM, navigate to **Configuration > IPS > Sensor Setup > Startup Wizard** and click **Launch Startup Wizard.** The **Startup Wizard** leads you through similar steps, followed by the **setup** CLI command. It enables you to configure basic settings, configure interfaces, create virtual sensors, create policies, assign policies and interfaces to the virtual sensor, and save your changes to the AIP-SSM.

User Administration

Different types of users can be configured in the AIP-SSM with different roles associated with them. This section covers the AIP-SSM user administration.

User Account Roles and Levels

Each AIP-SSM user account has a role associated to it. A total of four roles can be assigned to a specific account:

- Administrator
- Operator
- Viewer
- Service

Administrator Account

The administrator account has the highest privilege level. Users with this role are able to do the following:

- Add users
- Assign passwords
- Control all interfaces on the AIP-SSM
- Configure IP addressing
- Add and delete hosts allowed to connect to the AIP-SSM
- Tune signatures
- Perform all virtual sensor configurations
- Configure shunning

Operator Account

The operator account has the second highest privilege level. These users can view the configuration and statistics. They can also perform some administrative tasks such as modifying their own passwords, tuning signatures, and configuring shunning.

Viewer Account

Users with viewer privileges can view events and some configuration files. They can also change their own passwords.

IPS monitoring applications require viewer access only to perform their monitoring operations. However, if the application is used to perform administrative tasks, a higher privilege account is needed.

Note The viewer account has the lowest of the privilege levels.

Service Account

The service account does not have direct access to the AIP-SSM CLI. It has access to a bash shell, which enables it to perform specific administrative tasks on the AIP-SSM. This account is not enabled by default.

Note Only one service account can be configured in the AIP-SSM and any other device running CIPS software. The service account should be created only at the request of the Cisco Technical Assistance Center (TAC).

Adding and Deleting Users

This section guides you on how to create and delete users on the AIP-SSM. It also shows you how to assign different privilege levels to users, depending on their roles.

Complete the following steps to add a user using ASDM:

Step 1. Log in to ASDM, navigate to **Configuration > IPS > Sensor Setup > Users**, and click on **Add**. The **Add User** dialog box shown in Figure 12-6 is displayed.

Step 2. Enter the username in the **Username** field; **viewuser** is the username used in this example.

Step 3. Select the user role in the **User Role** pull-down menu. You can select from **Administrator**, **Operator**, **Service**, and **Viewer**. The user in this example is configured with **Viewer** privileges.

Step 4. Enter and confirm the password for the new user under the Password section.

Step 5. Click **OK**.

Step 6. Click **Apply** to apply the configuration changes.

Step 7. Click **Save** to save the configuration.

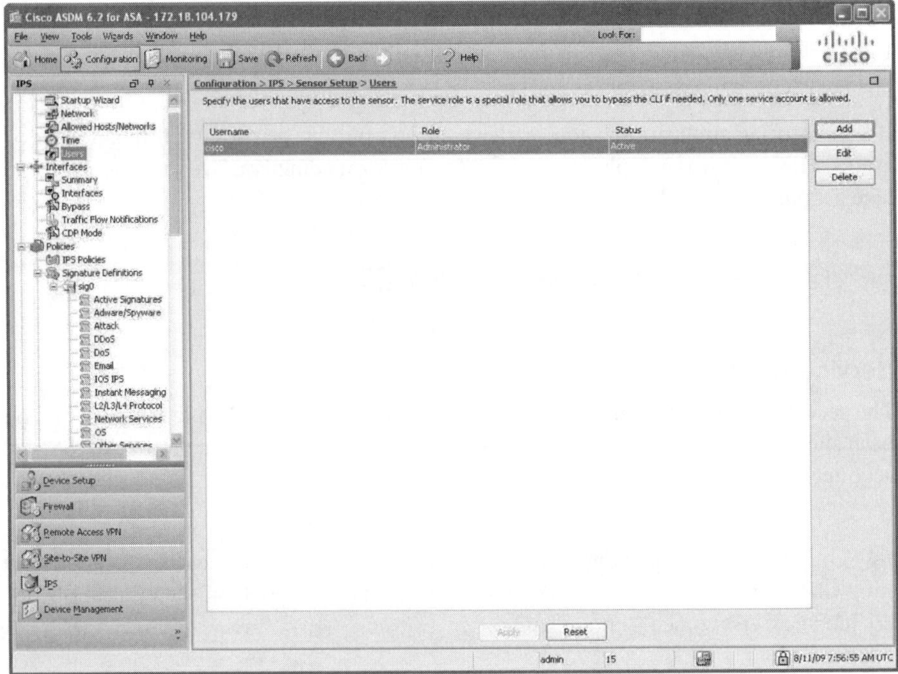

Figure 12-6 *Adding Users*

Alternatively, you can add users on the AIP-SSM via the CLI by using the **username** command. The following is the command syntax:

```
username name [password password] [privilege privilege]
```

Example 12-6 demonstrates how to create the service account, called **service** with a password of **0plm(OKN**.

Example 12-6 *Creating the Service Account Using the CLI*

```
NewYorkSSM# configure terminal
NewYorkSSM(config)# username service password 0plm(OKN privilege service
NewYorkSSM(config)# exit
```

Example 12-7 demonstrates how two accounts are created and assigned operator and viewer roles, respectively.

Example 12-7 *Creating Other Accounts Using the CLI*

```
NewYorkSSM# configure terminal
NewYorkSSM(config)# username opuser password 23798yfdf privilege operator
NewYorkSSM(config)# username viewuser password 93#&*shg privilege viewer
```

A user called **opuser** is created and assigned operator role privileges, and a user called **viewuser** is created and assigned viewer privileges.

Note Usernames must begin with an alphanumeric character and can be 1 to 64 characters in length. The minimum password length is 6 characters, and passwords can be up to 32 characters in length. All characters except spaces and the question mark (?) are allowed to be used in passwords.

Deleting Users

To delete users in the AIP-SSM through ASDM navigate to **Configuration > IPS > Sensor Setup > Users**, select the user to be deleted, and click the **Delete** button. If using the CLI, use the **no username** ***username*** command. Example 12-8 demonstrates how the **opuser** is deleted from the AIP-SSM.

Example 12-8 *Deleting a User via the CLI*

```
NewYorkSSM# configure terminal
NewYorkSSM(config)# no username opuser
```

Changing Passwords

To change a user's password in the AIP-SSM through ASDM, navigate to **Configuration > IPS > Sensor Setup > Users**, select the user, and click the **Edit** button. Select the **Change the Password to Access the Sensor** button and enter the new password.

Using the CLI, you can change your own or other user passwords by using the **password** command. To change the password for another user, you must be logged in through an account with administrator privileges. Example 12-9 demonstrates how the AIP-SSM administrator changes the password for user **viewuser.**

Example 12-9 *Changing* viewuser's *Password*

```
NewYorkSSM# configure terminal
NewYorkSSM(config)# password viewuser
Enter New Login Password: ******
Re-enter New Login Password: ******
```

Example 12-10 demonstrates how you can change your own password by just invoking the **password** command from configuration mode.

Example 12-10 *Changing Your Own Password*

```
NewYorkSSM# configure terminal
NewYorkSSM(config)# password
Enter old login password : ********
```

```
Enter New Login Password: ******
Re-enter New Login Password: ******
```

AIP-SSM Maintenance

This section includes information on administrative maintenance tasks on the AIP-SSM. These tasks include the following:

- Adding trusted hosts to connect to the AIP-SSM
- Upgrading the CIPS software and signatures via the CLI and ASDM
- Displaying software version and configuration information
- Backing up the AIP-SSM configuration
- Displaying and clearing events

Adding Trusted Hosts

For a device to be able to connect to the AIP-SSM for management and monitoring purposes, it needs to be added to the trusted host list. To use ASDM to add trusted hosts that will be able to communicate with the AIP-SSM, navigate to **Configuration > IPS > Sensor Setup > Allowed Hosts/Networks** and click on **Add** to add the new hosts or networks. If using the CLI, complete the following steps:

Step 1. Enter configuration mode and invoke the **service host** command. You will be placed into host configuration mode.

```
NewYorkSSM# configure terminal
NewYorkSSM (config)# service host
NewYorkSSM (config-hos)#
```

Step 2. Invoke the **network-settings** command to start adding entries to the ACL for hosts or networks allowed to connect to the AIP-SSM:

```
NewYorkSSM (config-hos)# network-settings
NewYorkSSM (config-hos-net)# access-list 192.168.10.123/32
NewYorkSSM (config-hos-net)# exit
NewYorkSSM (config-hos)# exit
Apply Changes:?[yes]: yes
NewYorkSSM (config)#
```

In this example, a host with IP address 192.168.10.123 is added to the ACL.

After you exit from both configuration modes, the AIP-SSM prompts you to apply the changes to the configuration. Enter **yes** if the configuration parameters are correct.

SSH Known Host List

For any any SSH server to communicate with the AIP-SSM, you must first add it into the SSH known host list. To add an SSH known host key through ASDM, navigate to **Configuration > IPS > Sensor Management > SSH > Known Host Keys** and click on **Add** to add the SSH host key.

If using the CLI, the **ssh host-key** command can be used to add a host to the AIP-SSM SSH known host list. Example 12-11 shows how a host with IP address 192.168.10.33 is added to the NewYork SSM.

Example 12-11 *Adding an Entry to the SSH Known Host List*

```
NewYorkSSM# configure terminal
NewYorkSSM(config)# ssh host-key 192.168.10.33
Would you like to add this to the known hosts table for this
host?[yes] yes
```

The AIP-SSM asks the administrator to confirm the addition of the SSH host entry. Type **yes** or press **Enter** to confirm. The SSH host must be accessible when this command is issued.

TLS Known Host List

The CIPS software enables you to restrict what systems are able to establish a TLS/SSL session to the AIP-SSM.

To use ASDM to add a TLS trusted host to the AIP-SSM, navigate to **Configuration > IPS > Sensor Management > Certificates > Trusted Hosts** and click **Add** to add the new host. If using the CLI, use the **tls trusted-host** command. Example 12-12 demonstrates how to add a TLS host configured with IP address 192.168.10.34. The AIP-SSM does an SSL/TLS exchange with the specified host to obtain its SSL/TLS certificate.

Example 12-12 *Adding a TLS Known Host*

```
NewYorkSSM# configure terminal
NewYorkSSM(config)# tls trusted-host ip-address 192.168.10.34
```

Upgrading the CIPS Software and Signatures

You can apply the CIPS software service packs and signature updates using any of the following supported protocols:

- File Transfer Protocol (FTP)
- Hypertext Transfer Protocol (HTTP)
- Hypertext Transfer Protocol Secure (HTTPS)

- Secure Copy Protocol (SCP)

> **Note** If HTTPS/SSL is used, a trusted TLS host entry must be added for the server from which you will retrieve the service pack or signature update file.

You can perform one-time upgrades or schedule recurring automatic upgrades.

One-Time Upgrades

To use ASDM to upgrade the AIP-SSM, navigate to **Configuration > IPS > Sensor Management > Update Sensor**. The screen shown in Figure 12-7 is displayed.

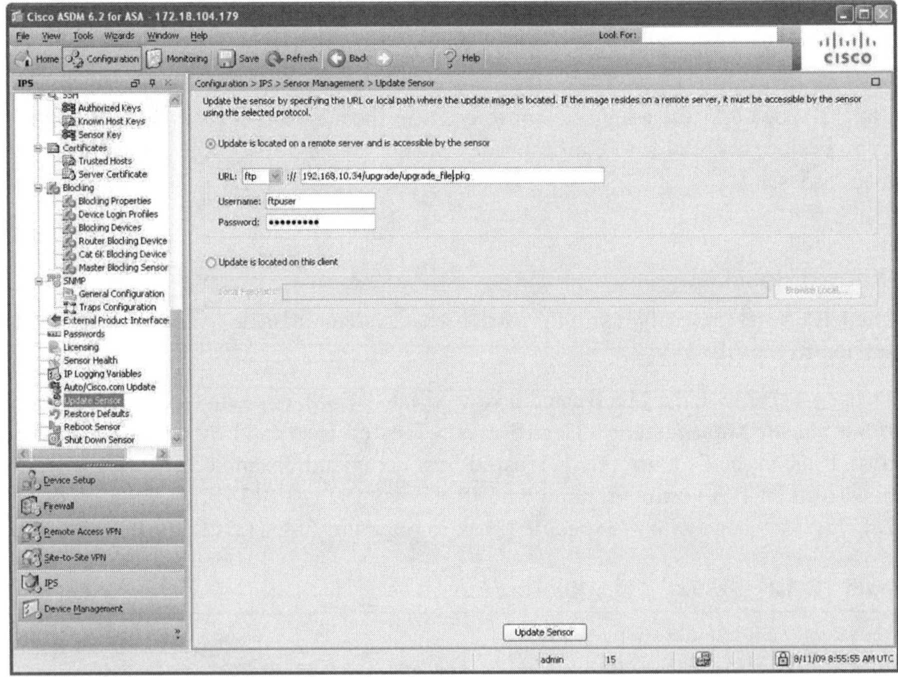

Figure 12-7 *Upgrading the AIP-SSM Through ASDM*

In the example illustrated in Figure 12-7, the FTP protocol is used. The FTP URL is ftp://192.168.10.34/upgrade/upgrade_file.pkg, and the FTP username is **ftpuser**.

If using the CLI, the **upgrade** command can be used to apply service packs and signature updates to the AIP-SSM. The following is the command syntax:

```
upgrade source-url
```

The *source-url* is the location where the AIP-SSM retrieves the upgrade file.

The following is the URL syntax if FTP is used:

ftp:[[//username @]location]/relativeDirectory/filename

or

ftp:[[//username@]location]//absoluteDirectory/filename

The syntax for HTTP is as follows:

http:[[//username@]location]/directory]/filename

The syntax for HTTPS is as follows:

https:[[//username@]location]/directory]/filename

The syntax for SCP is as follows:

scp:[[//username@]location]/relativepath]/filename

or

scp:[[//username@]location]/absolutepath]/filename

You are prompted to enter the user's password when invoking the previously discussed commands. An absolute path is created whenever a link uses the full URL of an object or page. For instance, https://myaipssm.com/ is an absolute path. In contrast, the relative path points to a file or directory in relation to the present file or directory (folder).

Tip If you enter just the **upgrade** command followed by a protocol prefix (**ftp:**, **http:**, **https:**, or **scp:**), the CLI prompts you for all the required information.

In Example 12-13, a signature update is retrieved from the HTTP server that was previously entered into the TLS trusted list (192.168.10.34). A user called httpsuser is being used for authentication purposes. After invoking the command, the AIP-SSM prompts you to enter the password for the HTTPS server user.

Example 12-13 *Applying Signature Updates*

```
NewYorkSSM# configure terminal
NewYorkSSM(config)# upgrade https://httpsuser@192.168.10.34/upgrade/sigupdate.pkg
Enter password: *****
```

Scheduled Upgrades

As a best practice, you may want to configure automatic service pack upgrades or signature updates. This eases administration and provides a mechanism to make sure that your AIP-SSM is running updated signatures.

Note Cisco offers a service where customers can subscribe to obtain IPS signatures shortly after security threats and vulnerabilities are announced. For more information, visit http://www.cisco.com/security.

Automatic updates do not work with Windows FTP servers configured with DOS-style paths. Make sure the server configuration has the UNIX-style path option enabled rather than DOS-style paths.

In the example illustrated in Figure 12-8, the goal is to configure the AIP-SSM module in the NewYork ASA appliance to automatically retrieve signature updates every Monday, Wednesday, and Friday at 1:00 a.m.

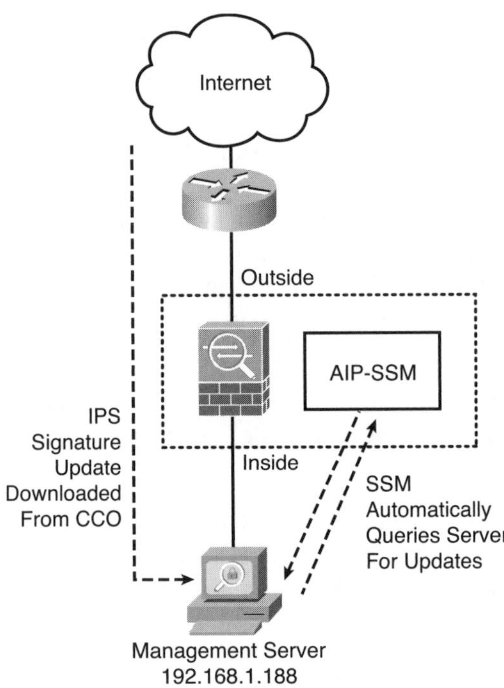

Figure 12-8 *Scheduled Upgrades*

Take the following steps on each device to achieve this goal when using ASDM:

Step 1. Log in to ASDM and navigate to **Configuration > IPS > Sensor Management > Auto/Cisco.com Update.** The screen shown in Figure 12-9 is displayed.

Step 2. Select the **Enable Auto Update from a Remote Server** option.

Step 3. Enter the IP address of the remote server in the IP Address field. The server's IP address in this example is **192.168.1.188**.

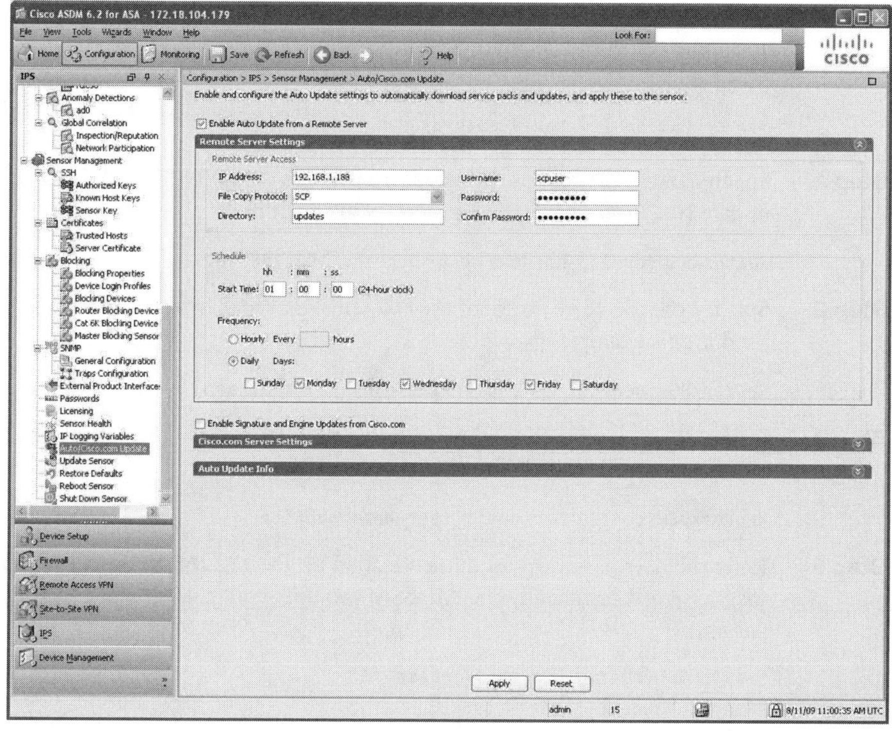

Figure 12-9 *Scheduling Upgrades Using ASDM*

Step 3. Select the protocol to be used using the **File Copy Protocol** pull-down menu. The SCP protocol is used in this example.

Step 4. Enter the directory where the updates will be stored in the remote server, using the **Directory** field. The directory in this example is called **updates**.

Step 5. Enter the username and password of the remote server user, using the **Username** and **Password** fields respectively. The username in this example is **scpuser**.

Step 6. Configure the start time and frequency for the automatic updates under the **Schedule** section. In this example, the AIP-SSM module in the NewYork ASA appliance has been set to automatically retrieve signature updates every Monday, Wednesday, and Friday at 1:00 a.m.

Step 7. Click **Apply** to apply the configuration changes.

Step 8. Click **Save** to save the configuration.

Take the following steps on each device to achieve this goal when using the CLI:

Step 1. The IPS signature update from Cisco.com is downloaded and saved on the management server. To enable automatic upgrades and configure auto-upgrade settings, go into service host configuration mode and enable the auto-upgrade option as follows:

```
NewYorkSSM(config)# service host
NewYorkSSM(config-hos)# auto-upgrade user-server
```

Step 2. Specify the IP address of the server from which the AIP-SSM will retrieve the update file. In this case, the server is 192.168.1.188:

```
NewYorkSSM(config-hos-ena)# ip-address 192.168.10.188
```

Step 3. Specify the file copy protocol used to download files from the server. SCP is used in this example:

```
NewYorkSSM(config-hos-ena)# file-copy-protocol scp
```

Step 4. Define the username for authentication on the 192.168.10.188 server. The user in this example is called scpuser:

```
NewYorkSSM(config-hos-ena)# user-name scpuser
```

Step 5. Enter the user password for authentication on the 192.168.10.188 server with the **password** command. The AIP-SSM prompts you to enter and confirm the password:

```
NewYorkSSM(config-hos-ena)# password
Enter password[]: *****
Re-enter password: *****
```

Step 6. Specify the directory where upgrade files are located on the server. A leading forward slash (/) indicates an absolute path. The directory in this example is called **updates** and the update file is called sigupdatefile.pkg:

```
NewYorkSSM(config-hos-ena)# directory updates/
```

Step 7. You can configure two types of scheduled updates:

- **Calendar based**—Specify what days and times of the week the AIP-SSM is to attempt the updates.
- **Periodic**—Configure the time that the first automatic upgrade should occur, and how long the AIP-SSM will wait between automatic upgrades.

In this example, the AIP-SSM will automatically retrieve signature updates every Monday, Wednesday, and Friday at 1:00 a.m.:

```
NewYorkSSM(config-hos-ena)# schedule-option calendar-schedule
NewYorkSSM (config-hos-ena-cal)# times-of-day 01:00:00
NewYorkSSM (config-hos-ena-cal)# days-of-week Monday
NewYorkSSM (config-hos-ena-cal)# days-of-week Wednesday
NewYorkSSM (config-hos-ena-cal)# days-of-week Friday
NewYorkSSM (config-hos-ena-cal)# exit
```

Step 8. Use the **show settings** command to view and confirm all the settings entered:

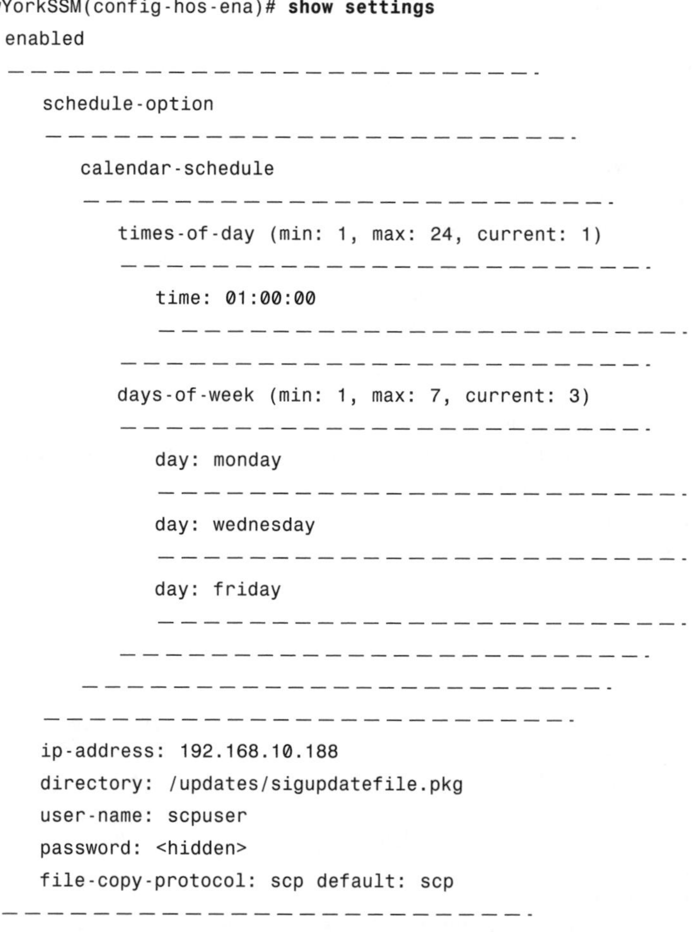

```
NewYorkSSM(config-hos-ena)# show settings
   enabled
   -----------------------------------------------
      schedule-option
      -----------------------------------------------
         calendar-schedule
         -----------------------------------------------
            times-of-day (min: 1, max: 24, current: 1)
            -----------------------------------------------
               time: 01:00:00
               -----------------------------------------------
            -----------------------------------------------
            days-of-week (min: 1, max: 7, current: 3)
            -----------------------------------------------
               day: monday
               -----------------------------------------------
               day: wednesday
               -----------------------------------------------
               day: friday
               -----------------------------------------------
            -----------------------------------------------
         -----------------------------------------------
      -----------------------------------------------
      ip-address: 192.168.10.188
      directory: /updates/sigupdatefile.pkg
      user-name: scpuser
      password: <hidden>
      file-copy-protocol: scp default: scp
   -----------------------------------------------
```

Step 9. Exit configuration mode. You will be asked to apply the changes. Enter **yes** if the information is correct.

```
NewYorkSSM(config-hos-ena)# exit
NewYorkSSM(config-hos-aut)# exit
NewYorkSSM(config-hos)# exit
Apply Changes:?[yes]: yes
```

Displaying Software Version and Configuration Information

You can use the **show version** command to display the version of the CIPS software, signature packages, and IPS processes running on the AIP-SSM. Example 12-14 shows the output of the **show version** command at the NewYorkSSM.

Example 12-14 *Output of AIP-SSM show version Command*

```
NewYorkSSM# show version
sensor# show version
Application Partition:
Cisco Intrusion Prevention System, Version 7.0(1)E3
Host:
    Realm Keys            key1.0
Signature Definition:
    Signature Update     S388.0                        2009-03-25
    Virus Update          V1.4                          2007-03-02
OS Version:               2.4.30-IDS-smp-bigphys
Platform:                 ASA-SSM-20
Serial Number:            JAF10370413
No license present
Sensor up-time is 20:35.
Using 1022148608 out of 2093604864 bytes of available memory (48% usage)
system is using 16.5M out of 38.5M bytes of available disk space (43% usage)
application-data is using 43.9M out of 166.8M bytes of available disk space
(28%usage)
boot is using 40.6M out of 68.6M bytes of available disk space (62% usage)
application-log is using 123.5M out of 513.0M bytes of available disk space (24%
usage)
MainApp             B-BEAU_2009_APR_18_08_00_7_0_1    (Release)    2009-04-
18T08:05:25-0500    Running
AnalysisEngine      B-BEAU_2009_APR_18_08_00_7_0_1    (Release)    2009-04-
18T08:05:25-0500    Running
CollaborationApp    B-BEAU_2009_APR_18_08_00_7_0_1    (Release)    2009-04-
18T08:05:25-0500    Running
CLI                 B-BEAU_2009_APR_18_08_00_7_0_1    (Release)    2009-04-
18T08:05:25-0500
Upgrade History:
  IPS-K9-7.0-1-E3   08:00:00 UTC Sat Apr 18 2009
Recovery Partition Version 1.1 - 7.0(1)E3
Host Certificate Valid from: 09-Aug-2009 to 10-Aug-2011
```

The first shaded line in Example 12-14 shows the CIPS software version running on the AIP-SSM. The second shaded line shows that the AIP-SSM has been up for 20 hours and 35 minutes. The third shaded line shows information about previous upgrades and updates to this AIP-SSM. Other information such as disk and memory utilization is also displayed.

To display the software version when using ASDM, navigate to **Home** and select the **Intrusion Prevention** tab. This screen provides information about the state of the sensor according to the gadgets that you choose to display. Each gadget displays the local host time. The gadgets contain the following information:

- **Sensor Information**—Including the version, IP address, device type, and other information.
- **Sensor Health**—Includes high-level sensor and network security health information.
- **Licensing**—Includes the status of the license key, signature updates, and signature engine updates.
- **Interface Status**—Shows information about the management and sensing interfaces.
- **Network Security**—Displays alert counts and average and maximum threat and risk ratings.
- **Top Applications**—Shows the top ten applications the AIP-SMM has discovered.
- **CPU, Memory, & Load**—Shows the sensor load, CPU, memory, and disk usage for the AIP-SSM.

You can use the **show configuration** command to display the current configuration on the AIP-SSM, as shown in Example 12-15.

Example 12-15 *Output of AIP-SSM* **show configuration** *Command*

```
NewYorkSSM# show configuration
! ----------------
! Version 5.0(1)
! Current configuration last modified Tue Feb 08 15:54:43 2005
! ----------------
service analysis-engine
exit
! ----------------
service authentication
exit
! ----------------
service event-action-rules rules0
exit
! ----------------
service host
network-settings
host-ip 172.23.62.92/24,172.23.62.1
host-name NewYorkSSM
telnet-option enabled
access-list 192.168.10.123/32
exit
time-zone-settings
```

```
offset -420
standard-time-zone-name GMT-07:00
exit
summertime-option recurring
summertime-zone-name PDT
exit
auto-upgrade-option enabled
schedule-option calendar-schedule
times-of-day 01:00:00
days-of-week monday
days-of-week wednesday
days-of-week friday
exit
ip-address 192.168.10.188
directory /updates/sigupdatefile.pkg
user-name scpuser
password cisco
file-copy-protocol scp
exit
exit
! ----------------
service interface
exit
! ----------------
service logger
exit
! ----------------
service network-access
general
never-block-hosts 10.0.0.1
exit
user-profiles a
exit
exit
! ----------------
service notification
snmp-agent-port 165
exit
! ----------------
service signature-definition sig0
exit
! ----------------
service ssh-known-hosts
exit
```

```
! ----------------
service trusted-certificates
exit
! ----------------
service web-server
enable-tls true
port 443
exit
```

Backing Up Your Configuration

It is recommended that you back up your configuration on a regular basis. You can back up your configuration to the local Flash on the AIP-SSM or to a remote server.

Use the **copy current-config backup-config** command to make a backup of the current configuration to a file (called **backup-config**) locally stored on the AIP-SSM. You can merge the backup configuration file with the current configuration file or overwrite the current configuration file with the backup configuration file. In Example 12-16, the AIP-SSM merges the backup configuration into the current configuration.

Example 12-16 *Merging the Backup Configuration*

```
NewYorkSSM# copy backup-config current-config
```

In Example 12-17, the AIP-SSM overwrites the backup configuration file into the current configuration file.

Example 12-17 *Overwriting the Backup Configuration into Current AIP-SSM Configuration*

```
NewYorkSSM# copy /erase backup-config current-config
```

As a best practice, you should back up your configuration file to an external server. In the following example, SecureMe's NewYork AIP-SSM copies a backup of its configuration file to FTP server 192.168.10.159.

Example 12-18 shows the command entered on the AIP-SSM.

Example 12-18 *Backing Up the Configuration to an FTP Server*

```
NewYorkSSM# copy current-config ftp://192.168.10.159
User: ftpuser
File name: NewYorkSSM_Config
Password: ********
```

The configuration is successfully copied to a file named **NewYorkSSM_Config** on the FTP server **192.168.10.159**. The AIP-SSM prompts the administrator to enter the FTP user, filename, and password.

Displaying and Clearing Events

The **show events** command enables you to view the events stored in the AIP-SSM's local event log. After this command has been invoked, all the events are displayed as a live feed (to exit, press **Ctrl-C**). Example 12-19 lists all the available options for the **show events** command.

Example 12-19 show events *Command Options*

```
NewYorkSSM#  show events ?
<cr>
alert           Display local system alerts.
error           Display error events.
hh:mm[:ss]      Display start time.
log             Display log events.
nac             Display NAC shun events.
past            Display events starting in the past specified time.
status          Display status events.
|               Output modifiers.
```

In Example 12-20, the AIP-SSM displays past events since 8:00 a.m.

Example 12-20 *Displaying Past Events*

```
NewYorkSSM# show events past 08:00:00
evStatus: eventId=1104988000052754141 vendor=Cisco
  originator:
    hostId: NewYorkSSM
    appName: cidwebserver
    appInstanceId: 276
  time: 2009/09/09 18:54:56 2009/09/09 11:54:56 GMT-09:00
  controlTransaction: command=getEventServerStatistics successful=true
    description: Control transaction response.
    requestor:
      user: cisco
      application:
        hostId: 127.0.1.1
        appName: -cidcli
        appInstanceId: 13200
evStatus: eventId=1104988000052754142 vendor=Cisco
```

```
originator:
  hostId: NewYorkSSM
  appName: mainApp
  appInstanceId: 276
time: 2009/09/09 18:54:56 2009/09/09 11:54:56 GMT-09:00
controlTransaction: command=getEventStoreStatistics successful=true
  description: Control transaction response.
  requestor:
    user: cisco
    application:
      hostId: 127.0.1.1
      appName: -cidcli
      appInstanceId: 13200
```

To show IPS events using ASDM, navigate to **Monitoring > IPS > Sensor Monitoring > Events**, as shown in Figure 12-10.

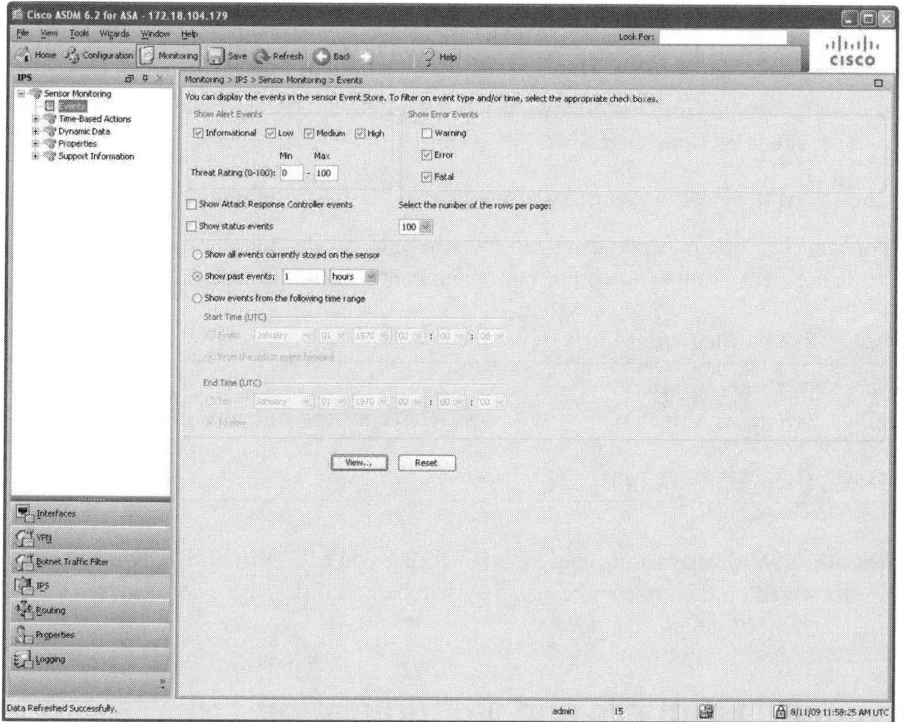

Figure 12-10 *Displaying IPS Events Through ASDM*

The following are the fields displayed in Figure 12-10:

- **Show Alert Events**—Enables you to configure the level of alert to be displayed (informational, low, medium, or high). By default, all levels are enabled.
- **Threat Rating (0-100)**—Used to configure the range (minimum and maximum levels) of the threat rating value.
- **Show Error Events**—Used to configure the type of errors to be displayed (warning, error, or fatal). By default, all levels are enabled.
- **Show Attack Response Controller Events**—This was formerly known as Network Access Controller events. This option is disabled by default.
- **Show Status Events**—Used to show status events. This option is disabled by default.
- **Select the Number of the Rows per Page**—Enables you to configure how many rows of IPS events are to be displayed per page. The valid range is 100 to 500 and the default is 100.
- **Show All Events Currently Stored on the Sensor**—Used to retrieve all events stored on the AIP-SSM.
- **Show Past Events**—Enables you to configure a specified number of hours or minutes within which you can view past events.
- **Show Events from the Following Time Range**—Used to retrieves events from within the specified time range.

Click **View** to view the events based on the previously configured options.

You can clear events stored locally in the AIP-SSM by clicking the **Reset** button or by using the **clear events** CLI command, as demonstrated in Example 12-21.

Example 12-21 *Clearing Events*

```
NewYorkSSM# clear events
Warning: Executing this command will remove all events currently stored in the
event store.
Continue with clear? []: yes
```

The AIP-SSM displays a warning message asking you to confirm the removal of all the events stored on the system because they will be lost if they have not been retrieved by a management or monitoring device.

Advanced Features and Configuration

This section covers advanced configuration topics and features on the AIP-SSM CIPS software. These topics include the following:

- Custom signatures

- IP logging
- Shunning
- Cisco Security Agent integration
- Anomaly detection

Custom Signatures

The capability to create custom signatures provides you with more flexibility in identifying security threats and network misconduct in a very effective fashion. To create custom signatures, you must know what exactly you want to detect in your network. This section demonstrates how to create a TCP custom signature.

Figure 12-11 illustrates our first example.

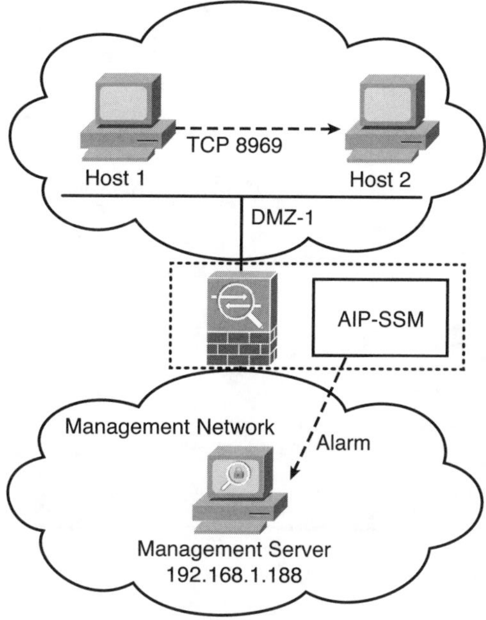

Figure 12-11 *Custom Signatures Example*

In this example, the security administrator knows that a new vulnerability exists whereby a machine can compromise other hosts and install malicious software while creating a TCP connection on port 8969. Unfortunately, this port is used by other critical applications in the network. The idea is to create a custom signature to detect this behavior, generate an alarm, and report it to a management station from hosts that are not supposed to send any traffic on TCP port 8969. In Figure 12-11, a custom signature on the AIP-SSM triggers an alarm if Host 1 attempts to establish a connection to Host 2 over TCP port 8969. Take the following steps to accomplish this task with ASDM:

Step 1. Log in to ASDM and navigate to **Configuration > IPS > Policies > Signature Definitions > sig0 > All Signatures.**

Step 2. Click **Add** to add a new signature. The dialog box shown in Figure 12-12 is displayed.

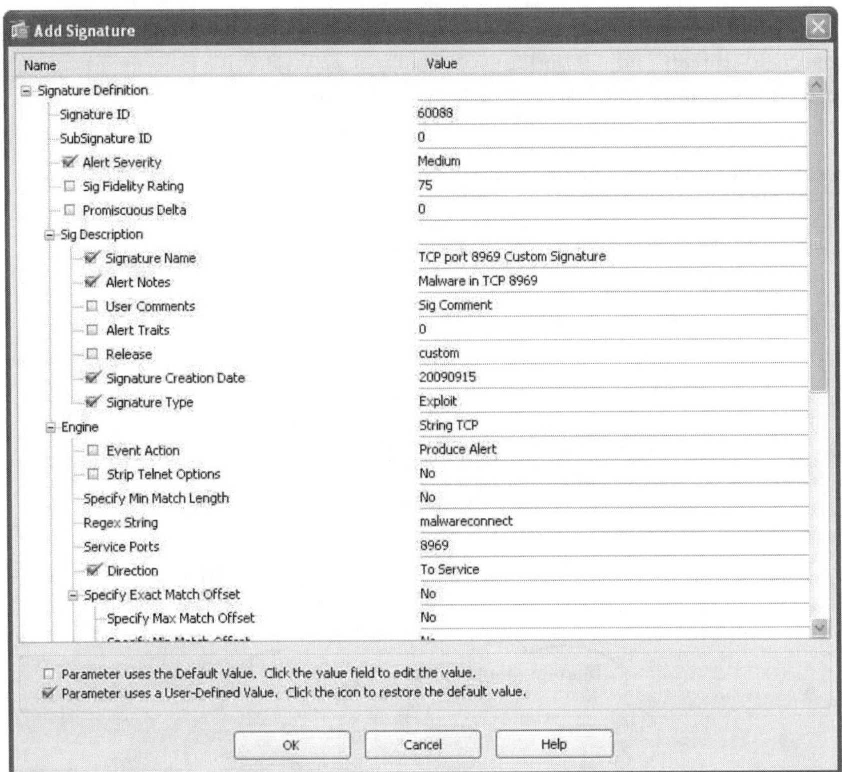

Figure 12-12 *Add Signature Dialog Box*

Step 3. Custom signature identifier values are in the range of 60000 to 65000. In this example, the signature identifier is **60088**.

Step 4. The **SubSignature ID** identifies a more granular version of a broad signature. The value can be anything from 0 to 255 (the number 0 is used in this example).

Step 5. The **Alert Severity** can be **High, Informational, Medium,** or **Low.** In this example, the **Alert Severity** is set to **Medium.**

Step 6. The **Sig Fidelity Rating** is used to define how well this signature might perform in the absence of specific knowledge of the target. The value is 0 to 100. In this example, the default value (75) is used.

Step 7. The **Promiscuous Delta** is used to define the seriousness of the alert. This example uses the default value (0).

Step 8. Enter the name for the new custom signature under the **Signature Name** field. The signature name in this example is **TCP port 8969 Custom Signature**.

Step 9. The **Alert Notes** field enables you to enter a note to be included within an alert produced by this signature. In this example, the alert note configured is **Malware in TCP 8969**.

Step 10. The **User Comments** field enables you to add custom comments about this signature.

Step 11. The **Release** field shows the software release in which the signature first appeared, in this case, the word **custom** is displayed for a custom signature.

Step 12. The **Event Action** field enables you to configure the actions the sensor takes when it responds to events. In this case, the default action is configured (**Produce Alert**).

Step 13. Enter the regular expression string under the **Regex String** field. In this example, the signature is configured to match the **malwareconnect** string.

Step 14. Enter the service ports under the **Service Ports** field. In this example, port 8969 is used.

Step 15. The **Direction** field enables you to configure the direction in which the packet will be inspected. In this example, the direction is **To Service**.

Step 16. Click **OK** to add the new signature.

The following are the steps necessary to add this custom signature with the CIPS CLI:

Step 1. Select the signature engine and signature identifier. Log in with a user that has administrator privileges and enter into signature definition submode:

```
NewYorkSSM# configure terminal
NewYorkSSM(config)# service signature-definition sig0
NewYorkSSM(config-sig)# signatures 60088 0
```

The signature ID for the new custom signature is 60088. The subsignature ID is 0 because we will have only one signature ID for this example.

Step 2. Enter into signature description submode and define a name for the new signature:

```
NewYorkSSM(config-sig-sig)# sig-description
NewYorkSSM(config-sig-sig-sig)# sig-name TCP port 8969 Custom
Signature
NewYorkSSM(config-sig-sig-sig)# exit
```

The new signature name is TCP port 8969 Custom Signature.

Step 3. Define the service port under the string-tcp engine configuration, as well as the direction of the connection, as follows:

```
NewYorkSSM(config-sig-sig)# engine string-tcp
NewYorkSSM(config-sig-sig-str)# service-ports 8969
NewYorkSSM(config-sig-sig-str)# direction to-service
```

The direction is configured with the to-service option. If you select this option, the AIP-SSM inspects connections from all clients to the server listening on port 8969.

Step 4. Enter the regular expression (regex) string to search for in the TCP packet:

```
NewYorkSSM(config-sig-sig-str)# regex-string malwareconnect
NewYorkSSM(config-sig-sig-str)# exit
```

In this case, the offending host sends a known stream to its victim (malwareconnect). After this is detected, the AIP-SSM generates an alarm and alert the administrator.

Step 5. To verify the settings, enter the **show settings** command under the **signature definition** submode for the new custom signature (60088):

```
NewYorkSSM(config-sig-sig)# show settings
   sig-id: 60088
   subsig-id: 0
   -----------------------------------------------
      alert-severity: medium default: medium
      sig-fidelity-rating: 75 <defaulted>
      promisc-delta: 0 <defaulted>
      sig-description
      -----------------------------------------------
         sig-name: TCP port 8969 Custom Signature default: My Sig
         sig-string-info: Malware in TCP 8969 default: My Sig Info
         sig-comment: Sig Comment <defaulted>
         alert-traits: 0 <defaulted>
         release: custom <defaulted>
         sig-creation-date: 20090915 default: 20000101
         sig-type: Exploit default: Other
      -----------------------------------------------
      engine
      -----------------------------------------------
         string-tcp
         -----------------------------------------------
            event-action: produce-alert <defaulted>
            strip-telnet-options: false <defaulted>
            specify-min-match-length
            -----------------------------------------------
```

```
            no
            -----------------------------.
            -----------------------------.
        -----------------------------.
        regex-string: malwareconnect
        service-ports: 8969
        direction: to-service default: to-service
        specify-exact-match-offset
        -----------------------------.
            no
            -----------------------------.
                specify-max-match-offset
                -----------------------------.
                    no
                    -----------------------------.
                    -----------------------------.
                -----------------------------.
                specify-min-match-offset
                -----------------------------.
                    no
                    -----------------------------.
                    -----------------------------.
                -----------------------------.
            -----------------------------.
        -----------------------------.
        swap-attacker-victim: false <defaulted>
    -----------------------------.
-----------------------------.
event-counter
-----------------------------.
    event-count: 1 <defaulted>
    event-count-key: Axxx <defaulted>
    specify-alert-interval
    -----------------------------.
        no
        -----------------------------.
        -----------------------------.
    -----------------------------.
-----------------------------.
alert-frequency
-----------------------------.
    summary-mode
    -----------------------------.
        summarize
        -----------------------------.
```

```
                summary-interval: 15 <defaulted>
                summary-key: Axxx <defaulted>
                specify-global-summary-threshold
                -----------------------------------------------
                   no
                   -----------------------------------------------
                   -----------------------------------------------
                -----------------------------------------------
             -----------------------------------------------
          -----------------------------------------------
       -----------------------------------------------
       status
       -----------------------------------------------
          enabled: true <defaulted>
          retired: false <defaulted>
          obsoletes (min: 0, max: 65535, current: 0)
          -----------------------------------------------
          -----------------------------------------------
       -----------------------------------------------
       vulnerable-os: general-os <defaulted>
       specify-mars-category
       -----------------------------------------------
          yes
          -----------------------------------------------
             mars-category: Info/Misc <defaulted>
          -----------------------------------------------
```

Note This process also applies to UDP and ICMP custom signatures. The parameters depend on the specific protocol services and ports.

IP Logging

The IP Logging feature enables the AIP-SSM to capture IP packet data if an attack or security threat is seen. This section demonstrates how to configure IP Logging to help perform deep analysis of a security threat on the network.

Note IP Logging can affect performance on the AIP-SSM. You can limit the size of log files so that performance is not degraded. As an alternative, you may transfer the data to a dedicated management server.

The AIP-SSM can also be configured to capture all IP traffic from a specific host on the network. You can also specify the following:

- The duration during which the IP traffic should be logged
- The number of packets to be logged
- The maximum number of bytes to be logged

Note The AIP-SSM stops logging packets if any of these parameters is met.

Automatic Logging

The goal in the following example is to configure the AIP-SSM to automatically log IP packets for attacker or victim traffic if a signature is triggered. The AIP-SSM logs the packets until any of the following criteria are met:

- No more than 250 packets
- No more than 300 seconds of logging
- No more than 81920 bytes of data

To accomplish this goal, complete the following steps:

Step 1. Log in to the AIP-SSM and enter into signature IP log configuration submode:

```
NewYorkSSM# configure terminal
NewYorkSSM(config)# service signature-definition sig0
NewYorkSSM(config-sig)# ip-log
```

Step 2. Configure the AIP-SSM to only log 250 packets, using the ip-log-packets subcommand:

```
NewYorkSSM(config-sig-ip)# ip-log-packets 250
```

Step 3. Specify the duration during which you want the AIP-SSM to log packets:

```
NewYorkSSM(config-sig-ip)# ip-log-time 45
```

Step 4. Specify the number of bytes to be logged:

```
NewYorkSSM(config-sig-ip)# ip-log-bytes 81920
```

Step 5. Invoke the **show settings** command to verify the parameters entered:

```
NewYorkSSM(config-sig-ip)# show settings
   ip-log
   -----------------------------------------------
      ip-log-packets: 250 default: 0
      ip-log-time: 45 default: 30
```

```
ip-log-bytes: 81920 default: 0
-------------------------------------------------
NewYorkSSM(config-sig-ip)#
cyanide(config-sig-ip)# exit
cyanide(config-sig)# exit
Apply Changes?[yes]: yes
```

The shaded lines show the parameters entered and the default values.

Manual Logging of Specific Host Traffic

In the example illustrated in Figure 12-13, the goal is to capture all packets from a host with IP address 10.10.10.21. The security administrator was informed that other hosts in the network are seeing unusual packets from this host.

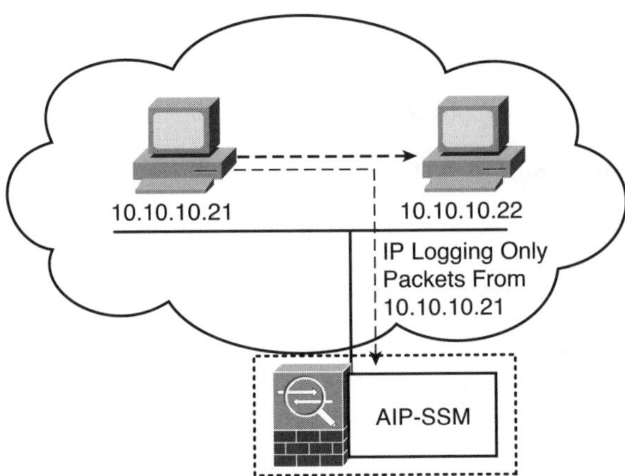

Figure 12-13 *Manual Logging Example*

The administrator uses the **iplog** command to configure manual IP Logging to log IP packets only from and to 10.10.10.21 during a three-minute period, as demonstrated in Example 12-22.

Example 12-22 *Configuring Manual IP Logging*

```
NewYorkSSM# iplog vs0 10.10.10.21 duration 3
Logging started for virtual sensor vs0, IP address 10.10.10.21, Log ID 1
Warning: IP Logging will affect system performance.
NewYorkSSM#
```

Notice the warning the AIP-SSM gives the administrator about the performance impact of the IP Logging feature.

The following is the **iplog** command syntax and all the available parameters:

```
iplog name ip-address [duration minutes] [packets numPackets] [bytes numBytes]
```

You can monitor the status of the packets logged by using the **iplog-status** command, as demonstrated in Example 12-23.

Example 12-23 *IP Logging Status*

```
NewYorkSSM# iplog-status
Log ID:                1
IP Address 1:         10.10.10.21
Virtual sensor:       vs0
Status:                added
Event ID:              0
Bytes Captured:       3693
Packets Captured:     3
NewYorkSSM#
```

To stop logging packets, use the **no iplog** command. This does not delete any captured packets from the system.

After capturing the respective IP packets, you can copy the IP log files to an FTP or SCP server. This enables you to examine those files with different sniffing tools, such as tcp-dump or Wireshark. Use the **copy iplog** command to copy the IP log files. The following is the command syntax:

```
copy iplog log-id destination-url
```

In Example 12-24, the IP log file that was previously captured is copied to an FTP server with IP address 192.168.10.44.

Example 12-24 *IP Logging Status*

```
NewYorkSSM# copy iplog 1 ftp://user1@192.168.10.44/iplog1
```

The IP Log ID displayed in the **iplog-status** command output is copied to the FTP server 192.168.10.44 and saved as a file named iplog1 by user1 (username on the FTP server).

Configuring Blocking (Shunning)

This section demonstrates how you can configure the AIP-SSM to interact with Cisco IOS routers, switches, PIX firewalls, and Cisco ASA appliances to block (shun) attacking IP addresses. It is important that you analyze your network topology to understand which attacking IP addresses should be blocked by the AIP-SSM and which IP addresses should never be blocked.

The AIP-SSM and other Cisco IPS sensors can interact with Cisco IOS routers and Catalyst switches. The AIP-SSM can apply ACLs in Cisco IOS routers or VACLs in Catalyst switches to permit or deny their interfaces or VLANs. The Cisco PIX Firewall does not use ACLs or VACLs; it uses the **shun** command to perform this operation.

You can configure the AIP-SSM to be able to block itself with the **allow-sensor-block [true | false]** command in the service network-access submode. However, this action is not recommended because it causes all packets sent and received by the blocking devices to be dropped.

In the example illustrated in Figure 12-14, the AIP-SSM is configured to interact with a Cisco IOS router (10.10.12.254) that provides extranet connectivity on a dedicated link to a partner connection.

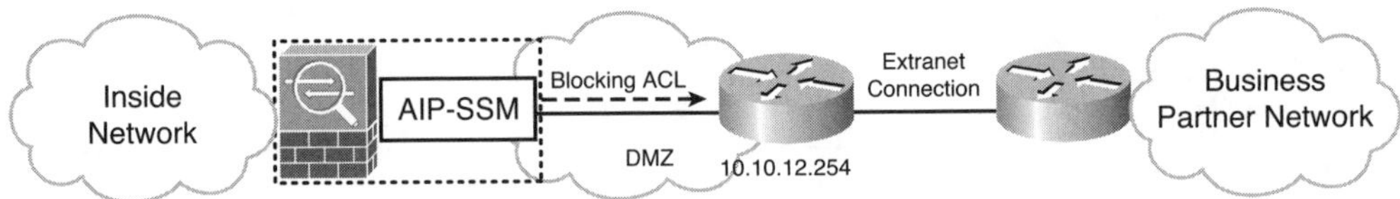

Figure 12-14 *Blocking (Shunning) Example*

The following steps demonstrate how to configure the AIP-SSM:

Step 1. Configured a user profile called myprofile. Within this profile is stored the information that will be sent to the router for the AIP-SSM to be able to log in and manage it.

```
NewYorkSSM# configure terminal
NewYorkSSM(config)# service network-access
NewYorkSSM(config-net)# user-profiles myprofile
NewYorkSSM(config-net-use)# username admin
NewYorkSSM(config-net-use)# password
Enter password[]: ********
Re-enter password ********
NewYorkSSM(config-net-use)# enable-password
Enter enable-password[]: ********
Re-enter enable-password ********
NewYorkSSM(config-net-use)# exit
```

The username in this example is admin. You must also enter the **router enable** password.

Step 2. After configuring the user profile, enter the IP address of the router, as follows:

```
NewYorkSSM(config-net)# router-devices 10.10.12.254
```

Step 3. The previously configured user profile (myprofile) is associated to the NAC configuration:

```
NewYorkSSM(config-net-rou)# profile-name myprofile
```

Step 4. Specify the protocol the AIP-SSM is to use to communicate with the router:

```
NewYorkSSM(config-net-rou)# communication ssh-3des
```

SSH using the 3DES encryption algorithm is selected. You can use Telnet, SSH-DES, or SSH-3DES. The default is SSH-3DES.

> **Note** If you select DES or 3DES, you must add the router to the trusted SSH hosts in the AIP-SSM with the ssh host-key command.

Step 5. Optionally, you can specify the AIP-SSM NAT address (if the module is behind a NAT device) with the **nat-address <nat_address>** subcommand. NAT is not used in this example.

Step 6. Set the router's interface name and direction in which the ACL will be applied (inbound or outbound):

```
NewYorkSSM(config-net-rou)# block-interfaces ethernet0 in
```

The ACL will be applied inbound to the **ethernet0** interface on the router.

Step 7. Optionally, you can add a preblock ACL. This is generally used for permitting the traffic that the AIP-SSM should never block. A preblock ACL named preACL is configured in this example:

```
NewYorkSSM(config-net-rou-blo)# pre-acl-name preACL
```

Step 8. You can also (optionally) add a post-block ACL. This is mainly used to block or permit additional traffic on the same interface or direction.

```
NewYorkSSM(config-net-rou-blo)# post-acl-name postACL
```

Step 9. Exit service network access submode and apply the changes:

```
NewYorkSSM(config-net-rou-blo)# exit
NewYorkSSM(config-net-rou)# exit
NewYorkSSM(config-net)# exit
Apply Changes:?[yes]: yes
NewYorkSSM(config)# exit
```

You can also configure the AIP-SSM to not block specific IP addresses or networks. In Example 12-25, the host with IP address 192.168.10.1 and the network 192.168.10.0/24 will never be blocked.

Example 12-25 *Avoiding Blocking Critical Devices and Networks*

```
NewYorkSSM# configure terminal
NewYorkSSM(config)# service network-access
NewYorkSSM(config-net)# general
NewYorkSSM(config-net-gen)# never-block-hosts 192.168.10.1
NewYorkSSM(config-net-gen)# never-block-networks 192.168.10.0/24
```

To allow the AIP-SSM to save the router's configuration after sending the respective commands, use the procedure demonstrated in Example 12-26.

Example 12-26 *Enabling the AIP-SSM to Write Configuration to NVRAM*

```
NewYorkSSM# configure terminal
NewYorkSSM(config)# service network-access
NewYorkSSM(config-net)# general
NewYorkSSM(config-net-gen)# enable-nvram-write true
```

The default value of the maximum number of devices or networks that can be blocked in the AIP-SSM is 250. However, you can use the **max-block-entries** command, as demonstrated in Example 12-27, to set how many blocks are maintained simultaneously. The range is from 0 to 65535.

Example 12-27 *Maximum Block Entries*

```
NewYorkSSM# configure terminal
NewYorkSSM(config)# service network-access
NewYorkSSM(config-net)# general
NewYorkSSM(config-net-gen)# block-max-entries 500
```

The maximum number of block entries in Example 12-27 is 500.

> **Note** You should implement blocking/shunning very carefully because it can disrupt legitimate services within your network caused by false positives. This is why the tuning process is so important. Attackers can launch a DoS attack if they know about your shunning configuration. These DoS attacks can be orchestrated spoofing legitimate source addresses, consequently causing disruption of legitimate hosts and services.

Cisco Security Agent Integration

The Cisco Security Agent (CSA) solution provides numerous capabilities used to enforce security policies on end-user machines. This section covers the integration and configuration of CSA with the AIP-SSM.

The CSA solution has two components:

- Agents that reside on and protect endpoints
- Management Console (MC) used to manage the agents

The CSA agents send CSA MC host posture information based on the configured security policies. Subsequently, the CSA MC maintains a list of IP addresses that it has determined should be quarantined from the network. The CSA MC can be configured to send two types of events to the AIP-SSM or any Cisco IPS sensor:

- Host posture events
- Quarantined IP address events

Host posture events provide the following information:

- Unique host ID assigned by CSA MC
- CSA agent status
- Host system hostname
- Set of IP addresses enabled on the host
- CSA software version
- CSA polling status
- CSA test mode status
- NAC posture

Note The host posture events are called *imported OS identifications* in IPS and AIP-SSM.

The quarantined host events provide the following information:

- IP address
- Reason for the quarantine
- Protocol associated with a rule violation (TCP, UDP, or ICMP)
- Indicator of whether a rule-based violation was associated with an established session or a UDP packet.

Note The collection of quarantined host events is called the *watch list* in IPS and AIP-SSM.

SSL/TLS is used for communications between CSA MC and the AIP-SSM. The AIP-SSM initiates the SSL/TLS transactions with the CSA MC; however, this communication is mutually authenticated.

Note The CSA MC must be added as a trusted host within the AIP-SSM. Instructions on how to add a trusted host in AIP-SSM were covered earlier in this chapter.

The following are several key points to remember when integrating CSA into the AIP-SSM:

- The AIP-SSM can store only a certain number of host records. If this number exceeds 10,000, subsequent records are dropped. If the 10,000 limit is reached and then the number drops to below 9900, new records are no longer dropped.
- Hosts can change an IP address because of DHCP lease expiration or movement in a wireless network and then appear as another host record. The AIP-SSM presumes the most recent host posture event to be the most accurate. IP address conflicts are also a known issue.
- A network can include overlapping IP address ranges in different VLANs, but host postures do not include VLAN ID information.
- The CSA MC event server allows up to ten open SDEE subscriptions by default; however, this value is configurable. On the other hand, you must have an administrative account to open SDEE subscriptions.
- The CSA data is not virtualized and is treated globally by the AIP-SSM.

Complete the following steps to configure the AIP-SSM to process CSA events:

Step 1. Log in to ASDM and navigate to **Configuration > IPS > Sensor Management > External Product Interfaces.**

Step 2. Click **Add** to add the CSA MC. The **Add External Product Interface** dialog box shown in Figure 12-15 is displayed.

Step 3. Enter the CSA MC IP address in the **External Product's IP Address** field. The IP address of the CSA MC in this example is **192.168.10.155**.

Step 4. Click the **Enable Receipt of Information** check box to enable the AIP-SSM to receive information from CSA MC.

Step 5. Enter the SDEE URL and port under the Communication Settings section. You must configure the URL based on the software version of the CSA MC with which the IPS is communicating as follows:

- CSA MC version 5.0 uses **/csamc50/sdee-server.**
- CSA MC version 5.1 uses **/csamc51/sdee-server.**
- CSA MC version 5.2 and higher uses **/csamc/sdee-server** (which is the default value).

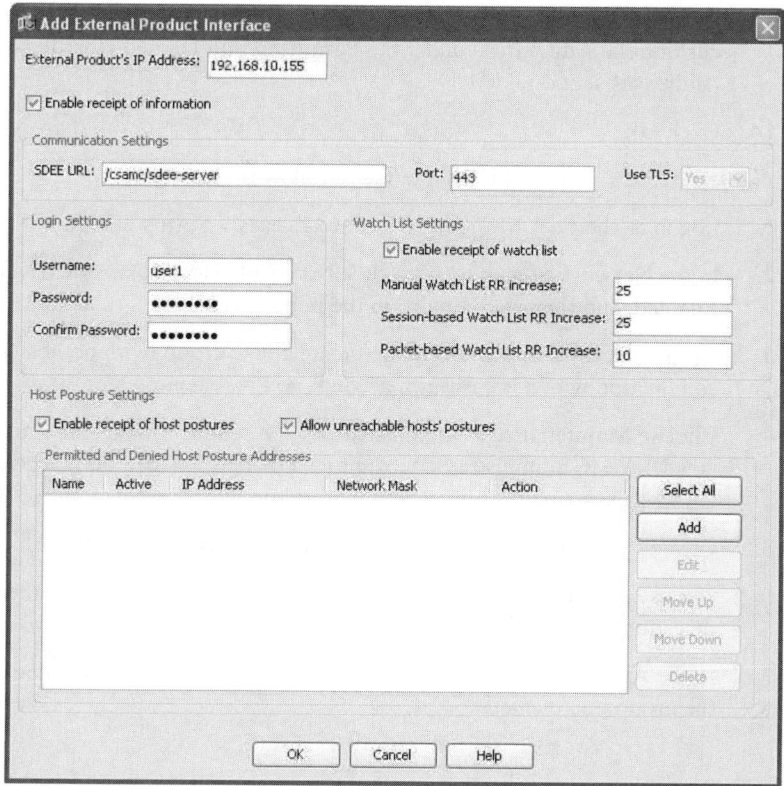

Figure 12-15 *Adding the CSA MC*

Step 6. Enter the credentials required to log in to CSA MC under the **Login Settings** section.

Step 7. Click the **Enable Receipt of Watch List** check box to enable the receipt of the watch list information CSA MC.

Step 8. Enter the manual watch list risk rating (RR) in the **Manual Watch List RR Increase** field. The default value (25) is used in this example.

Step 9. The **Session RR Increase** field enables you to increase the percentage of the session-based watch list RR. The default value (**25**) is used in this example.

Step 10. The **Packet RR Increase** field enables you increase the percentage of the packet-based watch list RR. The default value (**10**) is used in this example.

Step 11. Click the **Enable Receipt of Host Postures** check box to enable the receipt of the host posture information.

Step 12. Check the **Allow Unreachable Hosts' Postures** check box to allow the receipt of host posture information for hosts that are not reachable by the CSA MC.

Step 13. Enter the addresses of hosts that will be explicitly permitted or denied by clicking the **Add** button under the **Permitted and Denied Host Posture Addresses** section.

Step 14. Click **OK**.

To configure CSA MC to support IPS interfaces, follow these steps:

Step 1. Log in to the CSA MC and navigate to **Events > Status Summary**.

Step 2. In the **Network Status** section, click **No** beside **Host History Collection Enabled**, and then click **Enable** in the popup window.

Step 3. Navigate to **Systems > Groups** to create a new group (with no hosts) to use in conjunction with administrator account you will next create.

Step 4. Choose **Maintenance > Administrators > Account Management** to create a new CSA MC administrator account to provide IPS (AIP-SSM) access to the CSA MC system.

Step 5. Create a new administrator account with the role of **Monitor**.

Step 6. Choose **Maintenance > Administrators > Access Control** to further limit this administrator account.

Step 7. In the **Access Control** window, select the administrator you created and select the group you created.

Anomaly Detection

The Cisco IPS solution includes limited anomaly detection (AD) capabilities. The AD component of the AIP-SSM allows it to be less dependent on signature updates for protection against worms and scanners, such as Code Red, SQL Slammer, Conficker, and others. The AD component lets the AIP-SSM learn normal activity and send alerts or take dynamic response actions for behavior that deviates from what it has learned as normal behavior. This section covers the configuration of the AD component.

When the AIP-SSM is configured for AD, it initially conducts a learning process and then derives a set of policy thresholds that best fit the normal network. This initial learning mode is done for the default period of 24 hours. It is assumed that during this 24-hour period no attack is being carried out. AD creates an initial network traffic baseline, known as a knowledge base (KB).

Note The default interval value for periodic schedule is 24 hours and the default action is rotate, meaning that a new KB is saved and loaded, and then replaces the initial KB after 24 hours.

After the learning mode, the AD should remain in "detect" mode for 24 hours a day, 7 days a week. AD goes into "inactive" mode when the AD feature is disabled in the AIP-

SSM.

Complete the following steps to configure AD in the AIP-SSM when using ASDM:

Step 1. Log in to ASDM and navigate to **Configuration > IPS > Policies > Anomaly Detection.**

In the **Anomaly Detections** pane, you can add, clone, or delete an AD policy. The default AD policy is **ad0**. When you add a policy, a control transaction is sent to the sensor to create the new policy instance. In this example, the default AD policy is used.

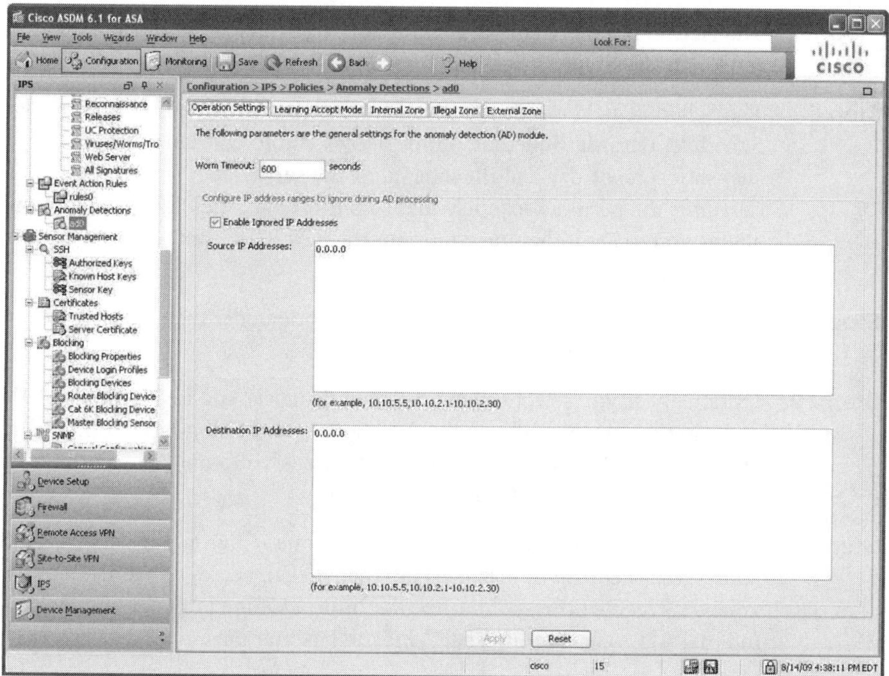

Figure 12-16 *Configuring Anomaly Detection*

Step 2. Select **ad0**. The screen shown in Figure 12-16 is displayed.

Step 3. On the **Operation Settings** tab, set the worm detection timeout in the **Worm Timeout** field. The range is 120 to 10,000,000 seconds. The default value of 600 seconds is used in this example. After this timeout, the scanner threshold returns to the configured value. You can also configure source and destination IP addresses that you want the sensor to ignore when AD is gathering information for a KB. AD does not track these source and destination IP addresses and the KB thresholds are not affected by these IP addresses.

Step 4. Configure IP address ranges to ignore during AD processing. Click the **Enable Ignored IP Addresses** check box to enable the list of ignored IP addresses entered in the **Source IP Addresses** and **Destination IP Addresses** fields respectively.

Step 5. Click the **Learning Accept Mode** tab to configure whether you want the sensor to create a new KB after a specified time interval. You can configure whether the KB is created and loaded (Rotate) or saved (Save Only). You can schedule how often and when the KB is loaded or saved.

Step 6. Click the **Automatically Accept Learning Knowledge Base** check box to enable the AIP-SSM to automatically update the KB.

Step 7. The **Action** pull-down menu enables you to specify whether to rotate or save the KB. If **Save Only** is selected, the new KB is created.

Step 8. The Schedule field enables you to choose **Calendar Schedule** or **Periodic Schedule. Periodic Schedule** option allows you to configure the first learning snapshot time of day and the interval of the subsequent snapshots. The default is the periodic schedule in 24-hour format. The **Start Time** option allows you to enter the time you want the new KB to start. The valid format is hh:mm:ss.

Step 9. Enter how long AD should be in learning mode under the **Learning Interval** field (in hours). The default value is 24 hours.

Step 10. Optionally, if you select **Calendar Schedule**, click **Add** under **Times of Day** and enter the times of day in the **Add Start Time** dialog box. Additionally, check the check boxes of the days of the week you want AD to be in learning mode under the **Days of the Week** section.

Step 11. AD uses the concept of network zones. A zone is a group of destination IP addresses. There are three zones: internal, illegal, and external. Each of these zones has its own threshold. Click the **Internal Zone** tab to configure the internal AD zone. The **Internal Zone** tab has four tabs:

- **General**—Used to enable the internal zone and specify its subnets.
- **TCP Protocol**—Used to enable TCP protocol and configure your own thresholds and histograms.
- **UDP Protocol**—Used to enable UDP protocol and configure your own thresholds and histograms.
- **Other Protocols**—Used to enable other protocols and your own thresholds and histograms.

Step 12. The illegal zone should represent IP address ranges that should never be seen in normal traffic. An example is unallocated IP addresses or part of your internal IP address range that is not being used. Click the **Illegal Zone** tab to configure the illegal AD zone. The **Illegal Zone** tab has four tabs that enable you to configure the same parameters as the ones in the **Internal Zone**:

- **General**—Used to enable the illegal zone and specify which subnets it contains.
- **TCP Protocol**—Used to enable TCP-based protocols and configure your own thresholds and histograms.
- **UDP Protocol**—Used to enable UDP-based protocols and configure your own thresholds and histograms.
- **Other Protocols**—Used to enable other protocols and your own thresholds and histograms.

Step 13. Click on the **External Zone** to configure the external AD zone. The **External Zone** tab has three other tabs:

- **TCP Protocol**—Used to enable TCP protocol and configure your own thresholds and histograms.
- **UDP Protocol**—Used to enable UDP protocol and configure your own thresholds and histograms.
- **Other Protocols**—Used to enable other protocols and your own thresholds and histograms.

Step 14. Click **Apply** to apply the configuration changes.

Step 15. Click **Save** to save the configuration.

The AIP-SSM Traffic Anomaly signature engine has nine AD signatures. Each signature has two sub-signatures: one for the scanner and the other for the worm-infected host. When an anomaly is detected, the AIP-SSM triggers an alert for these signatures.

> **Note** All the AD signatures are enabled by default. Additionally, their alert severity is set to high by default.

The following are the supported actions for AD signatures:

- Produce alert
- Deny attacker inline (if the AIP-SSM is configured in inline mode).
- Log attacker packets
- Deny attacker service pair inline
- Request SNMP trap
- Request block host

Cisco ASA Botnet Detection

Cisco ASA software release 8.2 introduced the Botnet Traffic Filter feature. This feature leverages IronPort technology to identify potential botnet traffic through the ASA. A botnet is a group of Internet robots (bots) that run malicious software often operated by different criminal entities. Although this is not an IPS feature, it is often referred to as an intrusion prevention feature. This section covers the configuration of the Cisco ASA Botnet Traffic Filter feature.

The Cisco ASA Botnet Traffic Filter feature has three major categories:

- Dynamic and Administrator Blacklist Data
- DNS Snooping
- Traffic Classification

The Botnet Traffic Filter feature does not automatically block botnet-related traffic. An administrator must manually configure ACLs to block malicious traffic.

Dynamic and Administrator Blacklist Data

The Cisco ASA Botnet Traffic Filter feature uses a dynamic database that is downloaded from an IronPort server accessible on the Internet. This database contains domain names and IP addresses for known malware and botnet sites. Complete the following steps to enable the Botnet Traffic Filter feature and configure the dynamic database and administrator black list data:

Step 1. Log in to ASDM and navigate to **Configuration > Firewall > Botnet Traffic Filter > Botnet Database**. The screen shown in Figure 12-17 is displayed.

Step 2. Check the **Enable Botnet Updater Client** check box to enable the Cisco ASA to fetch the latest database from the Cisco (Ironport) server.

Step 3. Check the **Use Botnet Data Dynamically Downloaded from Updater Server** check box to enable dynamic updates.

Step 4. The **Fetch Botnet Database** button is for testing purposes only. It is used to download and verify the dynamic database. However, it does not store the entries in running memory.

Step 5. To purge the botnet database, click the **Purge Botnet Database** button.

Step 6. Click **Apply** to apply the configuration changes.

You can also manually configure domain names or IP addresses to blacklist or whitelist. To configure a blacklist or whitelist, complete the following steps:

Step 1. Navigate to **Configuration > Firewall > Botnet Traffic Filter > Black and White List** pane. The screen shown in Figure 12-18 is displayed.

Step 2. Click **Add** for the **Whitelist** or **Blacklist**.

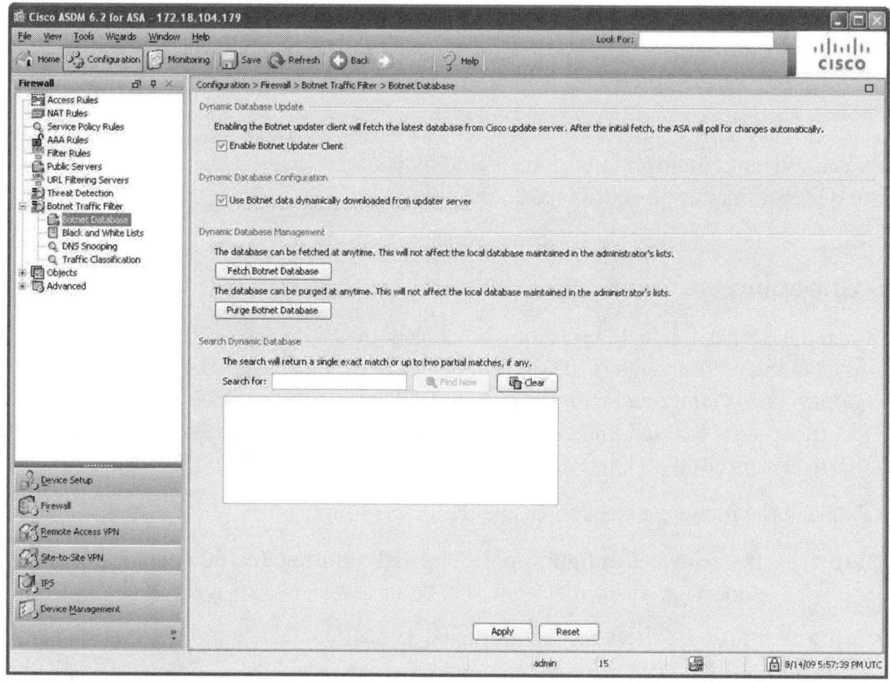

Figure 12-17 *Configuring the Botnet Database*

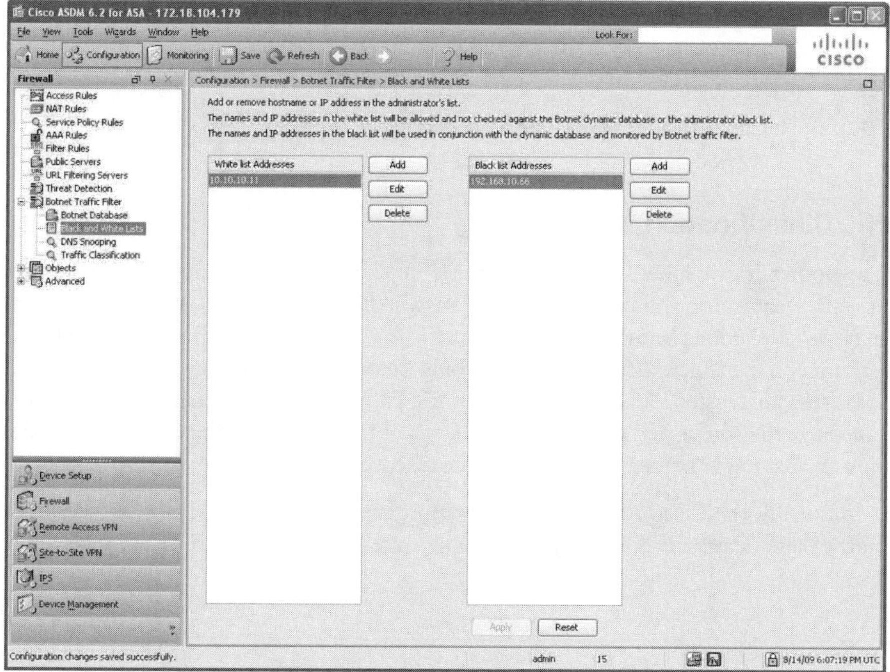

Figure 12-18 *Configuring a Black and White List*

Step 3. Enter the hostname or the IP Address when the dialog box appears. In this example, the **10.10.10.11** host is added to the white list and the **192.168.10.66** host is added to the black list.

> **Tip** You can enter multiple entries separated by commas, spaces, lines, or semi-colons. Up to 1000 entries can be configured for each type.

DNS Snooping

When the Botnet Traffic Filter feature is enabled, the Cisco ASA compares DNS A-records and CNAME records against the domain names in the database. This is known as DNS snooping and is integrated with the current DNS inspection available on the ASA. When DNS snooping is enabled, the Cisco ASA builds a DNS reverse cache (DNSRC) for all the DNS replies received on interfaces where DNS snooping is enabled.

Complete the following steps to enable the DNS snooping:

Step 1. Navigate to **Configuration > Firewall > Botnet Traffic Filter > DNS Snooping.** The screen shown in Figure 12-19 is displayed.

Step 2. Check the **DNS Snooping Enabled** check box to enable DNS snooping to an existing DNS inspection map. In this example, DNS snooping is enabled in the **my-dns-map** inspection map. Chapter 6, "Authentication, Authorization, and Accounting (AAA) Services" covers DNS inspection configuration in detail. The **my-dns-map** is the DNS inspection map configured in the example in Chapter 7. DNS snooping should be configured only on interfaces that are expected to receive external DNS queries.

Step 3. Click **Apply** to apply the configuration changes.

Traffic Classification

The Botnet Traffic Filter feature allows the administrator to configure different policies to specify what traffic will be inspected or "classified." Additionally, it makes it possible to exclude certain interfaces to not inspect traffic for botnet activity. For instance, an administrator could enable traffic classification only on the outside interface because all other interfaces are trusted. When the Botnet Traffic Filtering feature is enabled, the Cisco ASA compares the source and destination addresses of traffic that is subject to the classification against the IP addresses that have been discovered for the various lists available.

Additionally, the Cisco ASA can log and report any related events. The Cisco ASA botnet traffic classification is done only for a connection received on the first interface where

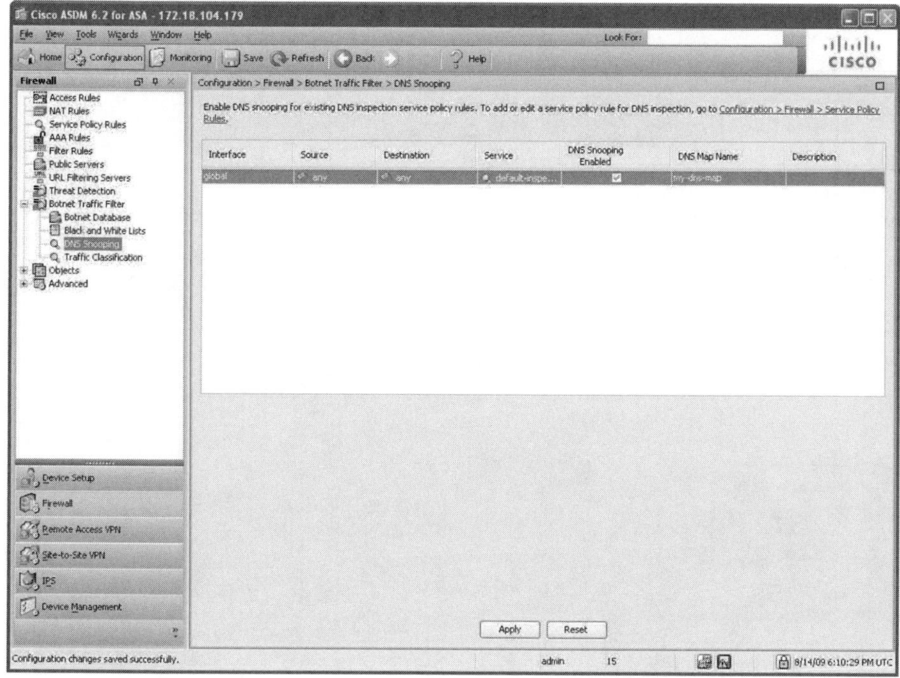

Figure 12-19 *Configuring DNS Snooping*

the feature is enabled. Complete the following steps to configure Traffic Classification and Reporting on the Cisco ASA:

Step 1. Navigate to **Configuration > Firewall > Botnet Traffic Filter > Traffic Classification.** The screen shown in Figure 12-20 is displayed.

Step 2. Check the **Traffic Classified** check box for each interface on which Traffic Classification should be enabled. Alternatively, you can configure Traffic Classification globally, applying it to all interfaces, This is done by checking the **Traffic Classified** box for **Global (All Interfaces)**, as shown in Figure 12-20.

Step 3. (Optional) You can add or edit access control lists (ACLs) to configure more granular parameters to specify what traffic should be classified. For instance, you can create an ACL to only inspect TCP port 80 from a specific network. To add or edit an ACL, click the **Manage ACL** option to bring up the **ACL Manager** and add the new ACL.

Step 4. Click **Apply** to apply the configuration changes.

Example 12-28 shows the equivalent CLI command for the previous ASDM configuration steps.

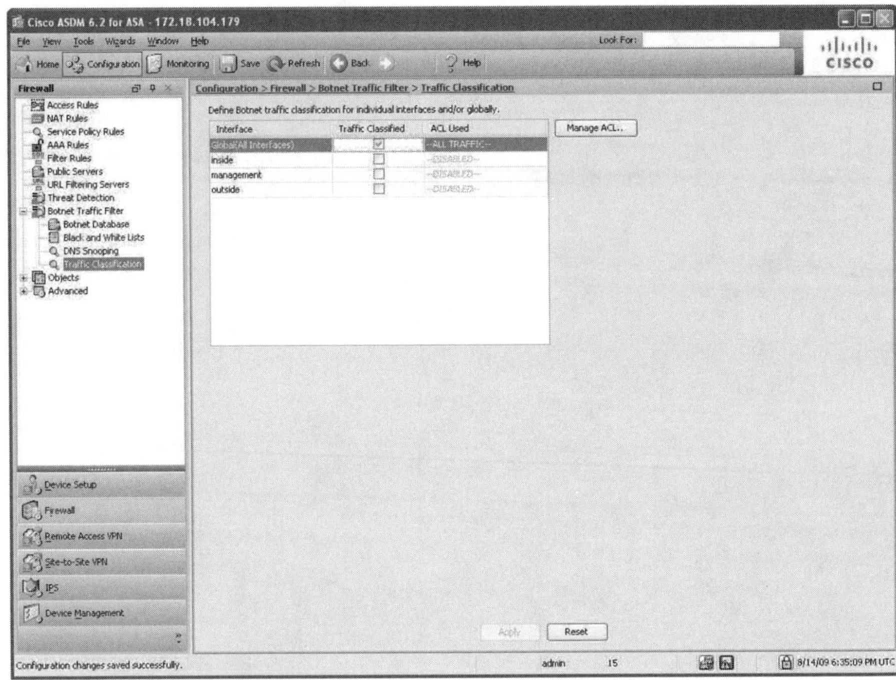

Figure 12-20 *Configuring Traffic Classification*

Example 12-28 Configuring Botnet Traffic Filter Through the CLI

```
NewYork(config)# dynamic-filter updater-client enable
NewYork(config)# dynamic-filter use-database
NewYork(config)# dynamic-filter enable
NewYork(config)# dynamic-filter whitelist
NewYork(config-llist)# address 10.10.10.11 255.255.255.255
NewYork(config-llist)# dynamic-filter blacklist
NewYork(config-llist)#  address 192.168.10.66 255.255.255.255
NewYork(config-llist)# policy-map global_policy
NewYork(config-pmap)# class inspection_default
NewYork(config-pmap-c)# inspect dns my-dns-map dynamic-filter-snoop
```

Summary

Cisco ASA, in conjunction with the AIP-SSM modules, delivers a new generation of highly accurate and intelligent inline prevention services. This provides security administrators an Adaptive Threat Defense (ATD) across their business networks and applications. This chapter provided an overview of the Cisco IPS software architecture that runs in the AIP-SSM to provide IPS services. It included an introduction to the CLI, user administration, and maintenance tasks, and explained in depth advanced configuration tasks such as custom signatures, blocking, CSA integration, and anomaly detection. Additionally, the Cisco ASA Botnet Traffic Filter feature was covered in detail.

Chapter 13

Tuning and Monitoring IPS

This chapter covers the following topics:

- IPS Tuning
- Monitoring and tuning the AIP-SSM using CS-MARS
- Displaying and clearing statistics

In Chapter 12, you learned how to configure the AIP-SSM module. You also learned that the AIP-SSM comes with a preset number of signatures enabled. These signatures are suitable in most cases; however, it is important that you tune your AIP-SSM when you first deploy them and then tune them again periodically. Failing to do so could result in numerous false positive events (false alarms), which could cause you to overlook real security incidents. The initial tuning will probably take more time than any subsequent tuning. This chapter covers instructions on how to tune and monitor the AIP-SSM.

IPS Tuning

Tuning is the process by which you configure the AIP-SSM appropriately to decrease the number of false positives and false negatives. Figure 13-1 shows the guidelines to be followed when deploying and tuning IPS devices.

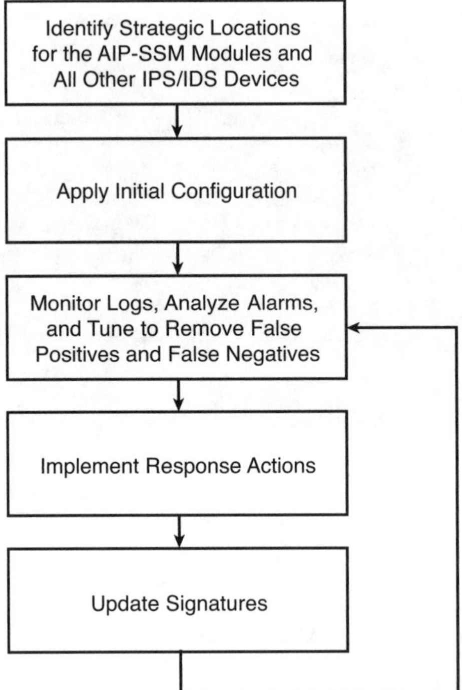

Figure 13-1 *IPS Deployment and Tuning Process*

> **Note** The process outlined in Figure 13-1 is based on the guidelines and recommendations of the Cisco SAFE architecture (http://www.cisco.com/go/safe).

The following are the IPS deployment and tuning steps outlined in Figure 13-1:

Step 1. Identify strategic locations for all IPS devices and identify how they will be configured. For example, you should consider performance, scalability, and what traffic you are trying to monitor. The Cisco SAFE blueprint recommends that you place IPS devices behind firewalls and any traffic-filtering devices. Traffic is filtered and only traffic destined for the internal devices is processed by the IDS/IPS device. This reduces the device workload and increases performance. This can be easily accomplished with Cisco ASA and AIP-SSM module.

Step 2. Apply the initial configuration, as covered in Chapter 12, "Configuring and Troubleshooting Intrusion Prevention System."

Step 3. Monitor and analyze the IPS logs and identify what alarms are being triggered because of malicious activity versus normal network activity. Disable alarms that are creating false positives, as discussed later in this section.

The initial monitoring period can last several days to generate sufficient logs and create a baseline of network activity.

You can also deploy a threat-analysis system to help validate the alarms' significance, impact, and appropriate response. Cisco Threat Response (CTR) and Cisco MARS provide an automated, real-time analysis of IPS alarms to eliminate false positives.

Step 4. Implement the most adequate response actions, such as TCP resets, drop, shunning, and IP logging. Steps on how to configure IPS response actions were covered in Chapter 12.

Step 5. Continuously update the IPS signatures. Automatic signature updates are recommended for ease of management and scalability.

You can change a signature's status by using the **status** subcommand in signature definition submode. With the use of this command, you can disable or retire a specific signature, as described in the following sections.

Disabling IPS Signatures

If a signature is just disabled, it is still processed by the signature engine and configuration list, but does not generate any logs. The following steps demonstrate how to disable a specific signature on the AIP-SSM CLI:

Step 1. Log in to the CLI and enter into signature configuration submode:

```
NewYorkSSM# configure terminal
NewYorkSSM(config)# service signature-definition sig0
```

Step 2. Select the signature to be disabled:

```
NewYorkSSM(config-sig)# signatures 20961 0
```

Signature 20961 is selected in this example.

Step 3. Change the status of the selected signature:

```
NewYorkSSM(config-sig-sig)# status
NewYorkSSM(config-sig-sig-sta)# enabled false
```

Step 4. You can verify the settings by invoking the **show settings** command:

```
NewYorkSSM(config-sig-sig-sta)# show settings
   status
```

```
 -----------------------------
    enabled: false default: false
    retired: false <defaulted>
 -----------------------------
```

Step 5. Exit signature configuration submode and apply the changes to the configuration:

```
NewYorkSSM(config-sig-sig-sta)# exit
NewYorkSSM(config-sig-sig)# exit
NewYorkSSM(config-sig)# exit
Apply Changes:?[yes]:yes
```

To disable a specific signature using the Adaptive Security Device Manager (ASDM), navigate to **Configuration > IPS > Policies > Signature Definitions > sig0 > All Signatures**, search for the specific signature, and uncheck the **Enabled** check box.

Retiring IPS Signatures

When a signature is retired, it is removed from the engine but remains in the signature configuration list. This signature can later be activated. However, when you reactivate a retired signature, the AIP-SSM needs to rebuild the signature list for that engine, which could delay signature processing. This process could take several minutes.

The following steps demonstrate how to retire a specific signature on the AIP-SSM:

Step 1. Log in to the CLI and enter into signature definition submode:

```
NewYorkSSM# configure terminal
NewYorkSSM(config)# service signature-definition sig0
```

Step 2. Select the signature to be retired:

```
NewYorkSSM(config-sig)# signatures 23456 0
```

Signature 23456 is selected in this example.

Step 3. Change the status of the selected signature and retire the signature:

```
NewYorkSSM(config-sig-sig)# status
NewYorkSSM(config-sig-sig-sta)# retired true
```

Step 4. You can verify the settings by invoking the **show settings** command:

```
NewYorkSSM(config-sig-sig-sta)# show settings
   status
   -----------------------------
      enabled: false default: false
      retired: true default: false
   -----------------------------
```

Step 5. Exit signature configuration submode and apply the changes to the configuration:

```
NewYorkSSM(config-sig-sig-sta)# exit
NewYorkSSM(config-sig-sig)# exit
NewYorkSSM(config-sig)# exit
Apply Changes:?[yes]:yes
```

To retire a specific signature using the Adaptive Security Device Manager (ASDM), navigate to **Configuration > IPS > Policies > Signature Definitions > sig0 > All Signatures**, search for the specific signature, and check the **Retired** check box under the **Status** section.

Monitoring and Tuning the AIP-SSM Using CS-MARS

CS-MARS enables you to identify, classify, validate, and mitigate security threats. In Chapter 12, you learned different mechanisms that give you visibility of the network and its devices, such as NetFlow, SYSLOGs, and SNMP. The analysis and manipulation of the data provided by these features can be a time-consuming process and, in some environments, may even be impossible because of staff requirements.

CS-MARS supports the correlation of events from numerous networking devices from different vendors. The supported devices and technologies include the following:

- Cisco IOS routers and switches
- Cisco ASA
- Cisco PIX
- NetFlow
- Cisco Security Agent
- Cisco Secure ACS
- Cisco IDS/IPS (including the AIP-SSM)
- Third-party firewalls such as Checkpoint and Netscreen
- Third-party antivirus software
- Third-party IDS/IPS systems such as Snort
- Operating system (Windows and UNIX/Linux) events
- Application-specific events

Note A complete of list of supported devices can be found at http://www.cisco.com/en/US/products/ps6241/products_device_support_tables_list.html.

For a complete list of available CS-MARS models, go to http://www.cisco.com/go/mars.

Adding the AIP-SSM in CS-MARS

Complete the following steps to add and configure an AIP-SSM in CS-MARS:

Step 1. Log in to the CS-MARS web management console with administrative rights and click **Admin > System Setup > Security and Monitor Devices > Add.**

Step 2. Select **Cisco IPS 5.x** from the **Device Type** list to add the AIP-SSM.

Step 3. Enter the hostname of the AIP-SSM in the **Device Name** field. The **Device Name** value must be identical to the hostname configured in the AIP-SSM.

Step 4. Enter the AIP-SSM IP address in the **Access IP** field.

Step 5. Enter the administrative AIP-SSM IP address in the **Reporting IP** field.

Step 6. Enter the username associated with the AIP-SSM administrative account that will be used to access the AIP-SSM in the **Login** field, as well as the password in the **Password** field.

Step 7. Enter the TCP port used by the AIP-SSM in the **Port** field. The default HTTPS port is 443.

Step 8. Optionally, to pull the IP logs from the sensor, select **Yes** in the **Pull IP Logs** box.

Note You can manually define the networks to be monitored by using the **Define a Network** radio button and entering the corresponding network address and network mask values.

Step 9. Click **Test Connectivity** to verify the configuration and connectivity to the AIP-SSM.

Step 10. Click **Submit** to submit the configuration changes.

Note You must add the CS-MARS as a trusted host in the AIP-SSM. Adding a trusted host in the AIP-SSM was covered in Chapter 12.

Tuning the AIP-SSM Using CS-MARS

The following steps include an example of how an administrator uses the CS-MARS to initially tune the AIP-SSM:

Step 1. Log in to the CS-MARS via the web interface.

Step 2. Click the **Query/Reports** tab.

Step 3. Select the **Activity: All–Top Event Types (Peak View)** option from the second pull-down menu under the **Load Report as On-Demand Query with Filter** section.

Step 4. Click the **Edit** button to select the time interval for the query and enter **1 day** under the **Filter by Time** section to trigger the CS-MARS to display the top event types in the past 24 hours.

Step 5. Click **Apply and Submit Inline** in the next screen to obtain the report. In this example, the administrator notices more than 1480 events that are the same (ARP Reply-to-Broadcast) have been detected in the past 24 hours.

Step 6. Click the event to obtain more information and read the following from the CS-MARS details screen: "This signature detects an ARP Reply packet where the destination MAC address in the ARP payload is a layer 2 broadcast address. This is not normal traffic and can indicate an ARP poisoning attack."

Step 7. Click **q** by the event and select **Source IP Address Ranking** under the **Result Format** section to investigate the source.

Step 8. The administrator notices that only one device (10.10.10.254 in this example) is triggering these events. After further investigation, he discovers that this is the normal behavior of an application that is running on that machine and marks this incident as a **False Positive** in CS-MARS.

Step 9. The administrator notices that these events are not shown anymore in CS-MARS; however, they are still shown if the **show events** command is used in the CLI of the IPS sensors. When you mark an incident/event/session in CS-MARS as a False Positive, it does not disable or tune this signature in the actual IPS device. The events are still sent to the CS-MARS from the IPS devices; however, CS-MARS does not process these events. If you do not want the IPS sensor to send or process the events, you must tune or disable the signature on the IPS device. You can tune signatures based on source and destination. For example, in this case, you can tune the IPS signature not to alert you if the host with the IP address 10.10.10.254 sends this type of packet. However, you can configure the IPS signature to alert you if any other device generates this type of traffic.

Displaying and Clearing Statistics

The CLI enables you to collect statistics about different IPS services, components, and applications. The **show statistics** command is used to display such information. Example 13-1 shows the **show statistics** command options.

Example 13-1 show statistics *Command Options*

```
NewYorkSSM# show statistics ?
analysis-engine         Display analysis engine statistics.
authentication          Display authentication statistics.
denied-attackers        Display denied attacker statistics.
event-server            Display event server statistics.
event-store             Display event store statistics.
host                    Display host statistics.
logger                  Display logger statistics.
network-access          Display network access controller statistics.
notification            Display notification statistics.
sdee-server             Display SDEE server statistics.
transaction-server      Display transaction server statistics.
transaction-source      Display transaction source statistics.
virtual-sensor          Display virtual sensor statistics.
web-server              Display web werver statistics.
```

The **show statistics analysis-engine** command displays traffic statistics and health information about the AIP-SSM analysis engine. Example 13-2 includes the output of this command.

Example 13-2 show statistics analysis-engine *Command Output*

```
NewYorkSSM# show statistics analysis-engine
Analysis Engine Statistics
   Number of seconds since service started = 1665921
   Measure of the level of current resource utilization = 0
   Measure of the level of maximum resource utilization = 0
   The rate of TCP connections tracked per second = 0
   The rate of packets per second = 0
   The rate of bytes per second = 0
   Receiver Statistics
      Total number of packets processed since reset = 0
      Total number of IP packets processed since reset = 0
   Transmitter Statistics
      Total number of packets transmitted = 0
      Total number of packets denied = 0
      Total number of packets reset = 0
```

```
  Fragment Reassembly Unit Statistics
     Number of fragments currently in FRU = 0
     Number of datagrams currently in FRU = 0
  TCP Stream Reassembly Unit Statistics
     TCP streams currently in the embryonic state = 0
     TCP streams currently in the established state = 0
     TCP streams currently in the closing state = 0
     TCP streams currently in the system = 0
     TCP Packets currently queued for reassembly = 0
  The Signature Database Statistics.
     Total nodes active = 0
     TCP nodes keyed on both IP addresses and both ports = 0
     UDP nodes keyed on both IP addresses and both ports = 0
     IP nodes keyed on both IP addresses = 0
  Statistics for Signature Events
     Number of SigEvents since reset = 0
  Statistics for Actions executed on a SigEvent
     Number of Alerts written to the IdsEventStore = 0
```

You can use the **show statistics authentication** command to display statistics on failed and total authentication attempts to the AIP-SSM module. Example 13-3 shows the output of this command.

Example 13-3 show statistics authentication *Command Output*

```
NewYorkSSM# show statistics authentication
General
   totalAuthenticationAttempts = 144
   failedAuthenticationAttempts = 9
```

Example 13-3 shows 9 failed authentication attempts out of 144 total attempts.

Example 13-4 includes the output of the **show statistics event-server** command. This command is used to display the number of open and blocked connections o the AIP-SSM from event management stations.

Example 13-4 show statistics event-server *Command Output*

```
NewYorkSSM# show statistics event-server
General
   openSubscriptions = 10
   blockedSubscriptions = 0
Subscriptions
```

The show **statistics event-store** command gives you more useful information. It displays detailed information about the event store. Example 13-5 includes the output of this command.

Example 13-5 show statistics event-store *Command Output*

```
NewYorkSSM# show statistics event-store
Event store statistics
   General information about the event store
      The current number of open subscriptions = 10
      The number of events lost by subscriptions and queries = 0
      The number of queries issued = 0
      The number of times the event store circular buffer has wrapped = 0
   Number of events of each type currently stored
      Debug events = 0
      Status events = 59
      Log transaction events = 0
      Shun request events = 0
      Error events, warning = 1
      Error events, error = 8
      Error events, fatal = 0
      Alert events, informational = 2
      Alert events, low = 0
      Alert events, medium = 0
      Alert events, high = 0
```

Another command that is very useful for troubleshooting is the **show statistics host** command. It includes network and link statistics, health of the AIP-SSM module (for example, CPU and memory utilization), and other administrative items such as NTP and auto-update statistics. Example 13-6 includes the output of this command.

Example 13-6 show statistics host *Command Output*

```
NewYorkSSM# show statistics host
General Statistics
   Last Change To Host Config (UTC) = 03:00:39  Tue Feb 15 2005
   Command Control Port Device = GigabitEthernet0/0
Network Statistics
   ge0_0      Link encap:Ethernet  HWaddr 00:0B:FC:F8:01:2C
              inet addr:172.23.62.92  Bcast:172.23.62.255  Mask:255.255.255.0
              UP BROADCAST RUNNING MULTICAST  MTU:1500  Metric:1
              RX packets:3758776 errors:0 dropped:0 overruns:0 frame:0
              TX packets:272436 errors:0 dropped:0 overruns:0 carrier:0
              collisions:0 txqueuelen:1000
              RX bytes:471408183 (449.5 MiB)  TX bytes:183240697 (174.7 MiB)
```

```
              Base address:0xbc00 Memory:f8200000-f8220000
NTP Statistics
   status = Not applicable
Memory Usage
   usedBytes = 500649984
   freeBytes = 1484054528
   totalBytes = 1984704512
Swap Usage
   Used Bytes = 0
   Free Bytes = 0
   Total Bytes = 0
Summertime Statistics
   start = 03:00:00 PDT Sun Apr 03 2005
   end = 01:00:00 GMT-08:00 Sun Oct 30 2005
CPU Statistics
   Usage over last 5 seconds = 0
   Usage over last minute = 0
   Usage over last 5 minutes = 0
Memory Statistics
   Memory usage (bytes) = 500559872
   Memory free (bytes) = 1484144640
Auto Update Statistics
   lastDirectoryReadAttempt = 01:03:09 GMT-08:00 Mon Feb 14 2005
     Read directory: scp://scpuser@192.168.10.188//updates/sigupdatefile.pkg/
     Error: Failed attempt to get directory listing from remote auto update server:
          ssh: connect to host 192.168.10.188 port 22: Connection timed out
   lastDownloadAttempt = N/A
   lastInstallAttempt = N/A
   nextAttempt = 01:00:00 GMT-08:00 Wed Feb 16 2005
```

In the shaded lines in Example 13-6, you can see that the AIP-SSM attempted to connect to the server with IP address 192.168.10.188 over SSH (TCP port 22) without success. The connection timed out because of network connectivity problems.

To display IP logger statistics, use the **show statistics logger** command. The output of this command is included in Example 13-7.

Example 13-7 show statistics logger *Command Output*

```
NewYorkSSM# show statistics logger
The number of Log interprocessor FIFO overruns = 0
The number of syslog messages received = 331
The number of <evError> events written to the event store by severity
   Fatal Severity = 0
   Error Severity = 78
```

```
    Warning Severity = 358
    TOTAL = 436
The number of log messages written to the message log by severity
    Fatal Severity = 0
    Error Severity = 78
    Warning Severity = 27
    Timing Severity = 0
    Debug Severity = 0
    Unknown Severity = 62
    TOTAL = 167
```

Summary

This chapter introduced the importance of carefully tuning the AIP-SSM to minimize the risk of false positives and false negatives. It covered the tuning process in detail, as well as how to use the CLI, ASDM, and CS-MARS to tune IPS signatures. At the end, high-level monitoring and statistical commands were covered to enhance learning.

Chapter 14

Configuring Cisco Content Security and Control Security Services Module

This chapter covers the following topics:

- Initial CSC SSM setup
- Configuring CSC SSM web-based features
- Configuring CSC SSM mail-based features
- Configuring CSC SSM File Transfer Protocol

The Content Security and Control Security Services Module (CSC SSM) provides mechanisms to detect and take action on viruses, worms, Trojans, and other security threats. It supports the inspection of SMTP, POP3, HTTP, and FTP network traffic. However, it does not support HTTPS. The CSC SSM provides the capability of blocking compressed or very large files that exceed specified parameters. Additionally, it can detect and remove spyware, adware, and other malware.

The following additional features are available if the Plus level of the CSC SSM license is purchased:

- Protecting against spam and phishing fraud (SMTP and POP3 traffic).
- Content filtering to allow or prohibit email traffic containing configurable keywords.
- URL blocking based on configurable parameters.
- Filtering of web traffic according to predefined categories that you allow or disallow, such as adult or mature content, games, chat or instant messaging, or gambling sites.
- Filtering of FTP files according to predefined rules.

This chapter covers the setup, integration, features, and configuration of the CSC SSM.

Initial CSC SSM Setup

Complete the following steps to perform the initial setup and configuration of the CSC SSM.

Step 1. Log in to the Adaptive Security Device Manager (ASDM) and navigate to **Configuration > Trend Micro Content Security > CSC Setup > Wizard Setup** and click on the **Launch Setup Wizard** button. The dialog box shown in Figure 14-1 is displayed.

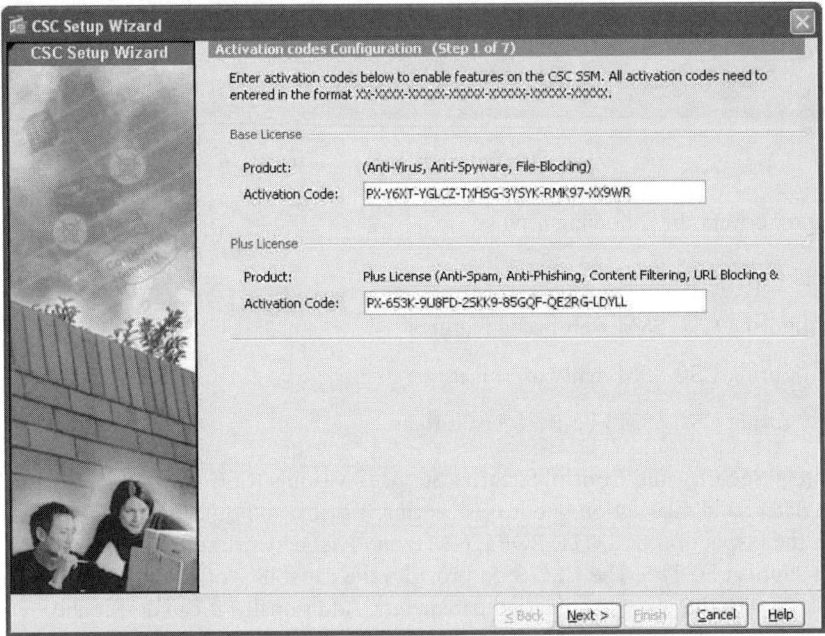

Figure 14-1 *CSC SSM Setup Wizard—License Activation*

Step 2. The first step during the initial configuration is to install the CSC SSM license on the device. Enter the activation code for the Base License to enable anti-virus, anti-spyware, and file-blocking capabilities on the device, as shown in Figure 14-1. If you have purchased the Plus license, enter the Plus License Activation code. If not, this field is blank. The Plus license includes anti-spam, anti-phishing, content filtering, URL blocking and filtering, and web reputation.

Step 3. Click **Next**. The IP Configuration screen shown in Figure 14-2 is displayed.

Step 4. The CSC SSM has a management interface that is used for configuration and monitoring. As a best practice, it is recommended that you configure this interface in your management network. Enter the IP address, mask, and gateway information for the management interface of the CSC SSM under the **Management Interface** section. In this example, the IP address of the

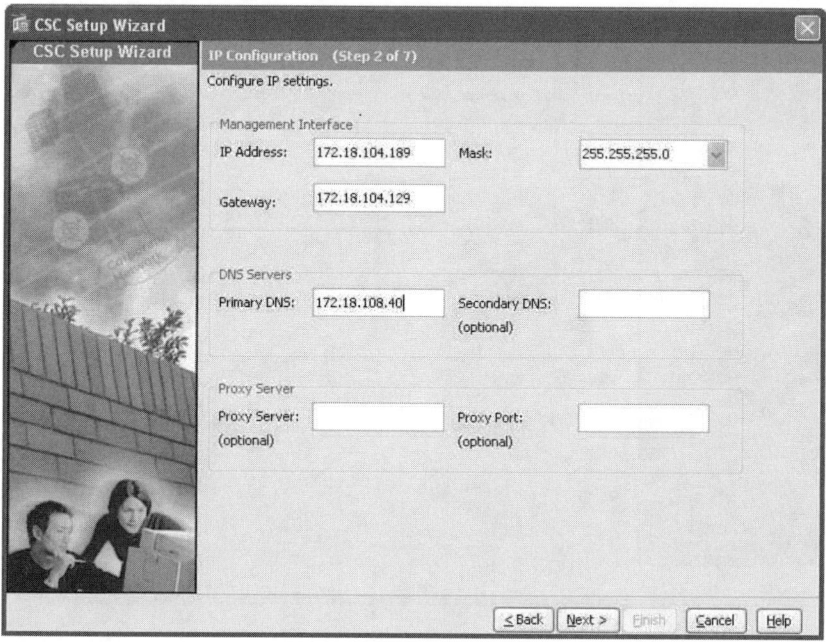

Figure 14-2 *CSC SSM Setup Wizard—IP Address Configuration*

management interface is **172.18.104.189**, with a subnet mask of **255.255.255.0**. The gateway is **172.18.104.129**.

Step 5. Enter the primary and secondary DNS server IP addresses under the **DNS Servers** section.

Step 6. If a proxy server is used within your network, enter the IP address and port under the **Proxy Server** section.

Step 7. Click **Next.** The Host Configuration screen shown in Figure 14-3 is displayed.

Step 8. The screen shown in Figure 14-3 enables you to enter the hostname for the CSC SSM and the name of the domain in which the CSC SSM resides under the **Host and Domain Names** section. The hostname used in this example is **NY-CSC-SSM** and the domain name is **securemeinc.com.**

Step 9. Enter the domain name for incoming email under the **Incoming E-mail Domain Name** section. The domain name **securemeinc.com** is used in this example.

Step 10. Enter the email address of the domain administrator, the IP address of the email server, and the port number used by the email server under the **Notification Settings** section. The administrator email used in this example is **administrator@securemeinc.com**, the email server IP address is **172.18.104.123**, and the port used is **25**.

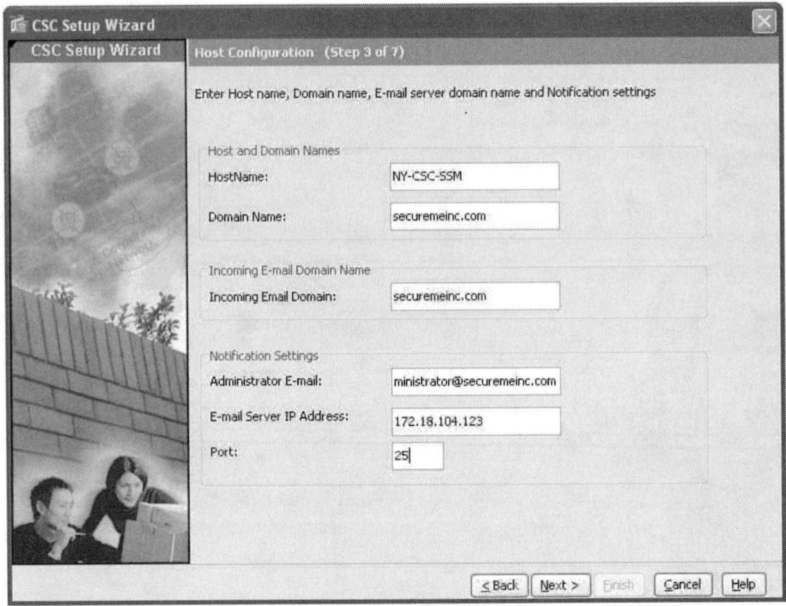

Figure 14-3 *CSC SSM Setup Wizard—Host Configuration*

Step 11. Click **Next**. The Management Access Configuration screen shown in Figure 14-4 is displayed.

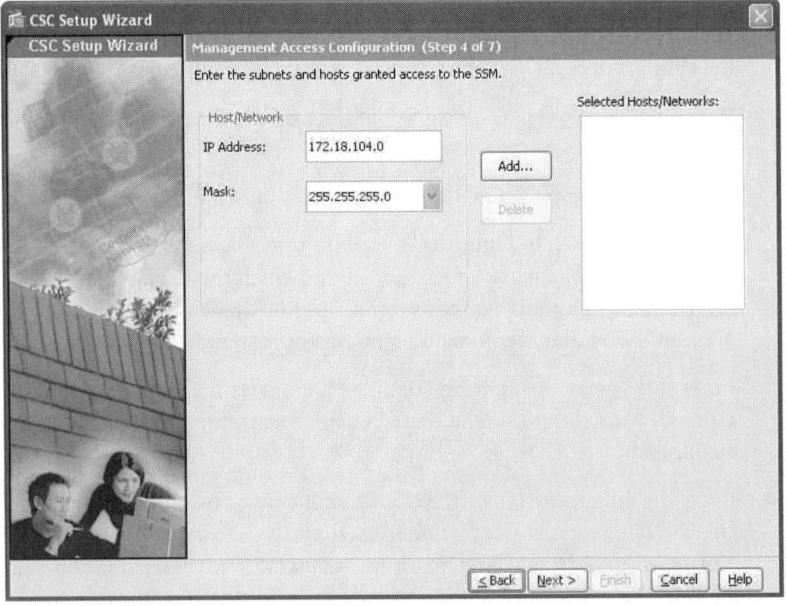

Figure 14-4 *CSC SSM Setup Wizard—Management Access Configuration*

Step 12. Enter the IP addresses for the hosts or networks that are allowed to connect to the CSC SSM for management purposes under the **Host/Network** section. After you have defined the specific hosts/networks, click **Add** to add it to the **Selected Hosts/Networks** table.

Step 13. Click **Next**. The Password Configuration screen shown in Figure 14-5 is displayed.

Step 14. The dialog box illustrated in Figure 14-5 enables you to change the password required for management access to the CSC SSM. After you have changed the administrative password, click **Next**. The Traffic Selection for CSC Scan screen shown in Figure 14-6 is displayed.

Step 15. The dialog box illustrated in Figure 14-6 enables you to define what traffic will be inspected by CSC SSM. Click **Add** to specify the interface, source, and destination of network traffic for the CSC SSM to scan, and the specific service/protocol. In this example, all traffic is inspected by all interfaces (globally).

Step 16. Click **Next**.

Step 17. A summary of all the settings that you have made with the CSC Setup Wizard is displayed. Click **Finish** to complete the CSC Setup Wizard and save the configuration.

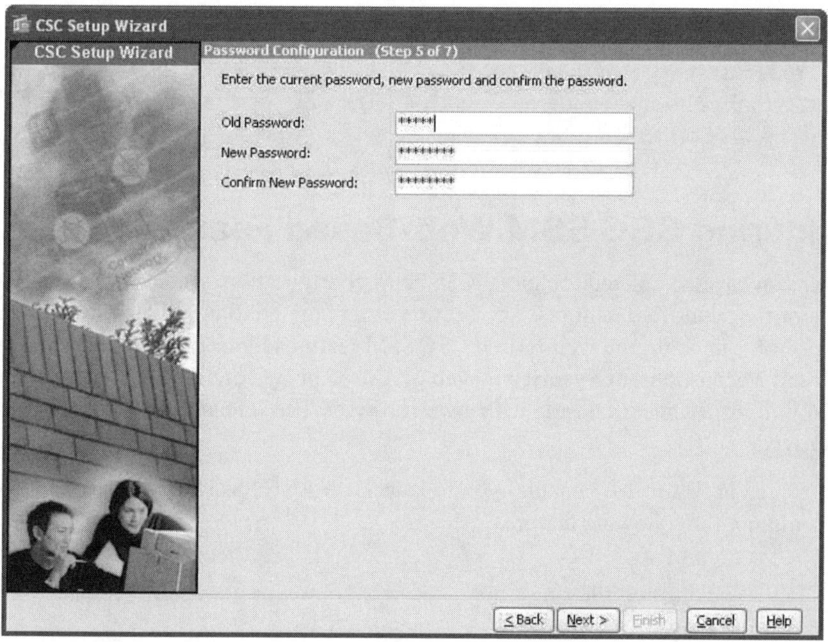

Figure 14-5 *CSC SSM Setup Wizard—Password Configuration*

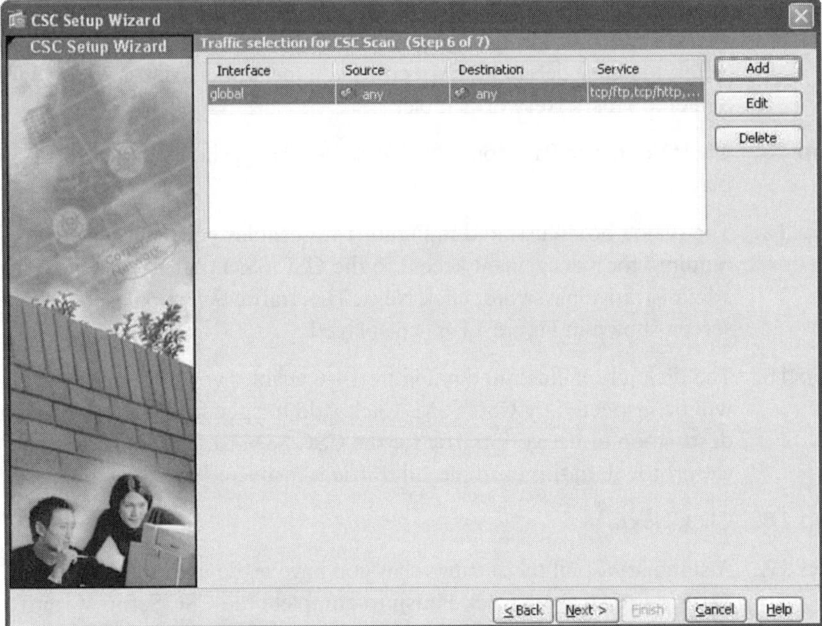

Figure 14-6 *CSC SSM Setup Wizard—Traffic Selection for CSC Scan*

Note You must verify that the Cisco ASA's clock has been set correctly because the CSC SSM synchronizes its clock with the Cisco ASA. The CSC SSM may experience problems if the time is not correct.

Configuring CSC SSM Web-Based Features

After you have completed the initial CSC SSM configuration, you can start configuring each of the supported features. This section covers the configuration of web-related features. You can configure web-related CSC SSM features by navigating to **Configuration > Trend Micro Content Security > Web** in ASDM or by connecting directly to the CSC SSM web management console with a web browser. The screen shown in Figure 14-7 is displayed.

The screen in Figure 14-7 enables you to launch the CSC SSM web management console to configure the following features:

- URL blocking and filtering
- File blocking
- HTTP scanning

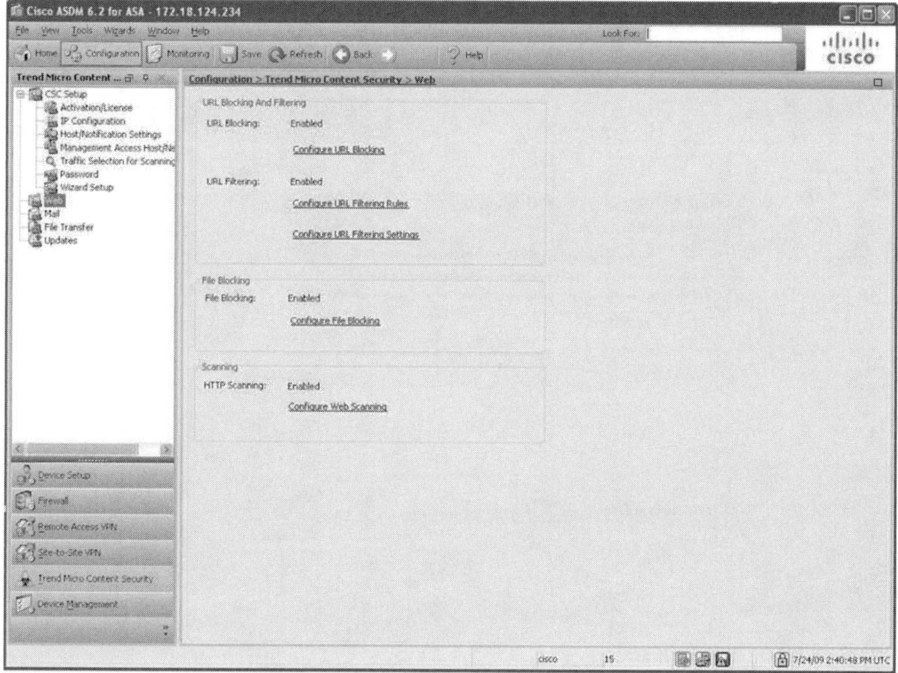

Figure 14-7 *CSC SSM URL Blocking and Filtering*

URL Blocking and Filtering

When you navigate to **Configuration > Trend Micro Content Security > Web** in ASDM, the URL Blocking section shows whether or not URL blocking is enabled on the CSC SSM. To configure URL blocking, click **Configure URL Blocking** to open the CSC SSM web management console.

Complete the following steps to configure URL blocking:

Step 1. After you click on **Configure URL Blocking** in ASDM, log in to the Trend Micro InterScan web management console. Navigate to **Web (HTTP) > URL Blocking.** The screen shown in Figure 14-8 is displayed.

Step 2. Under the **Via Local List** tab, you can enable or disable URL blocking. In this example, URL blocking is already enabled.

Step 3. The CSC SSM has a policy framework based on user and group identity to apply URL filtering and blocking policies to specific groups or individual users. Check the **Include User Group Policies** check box to enable URL blocking by users or groups.

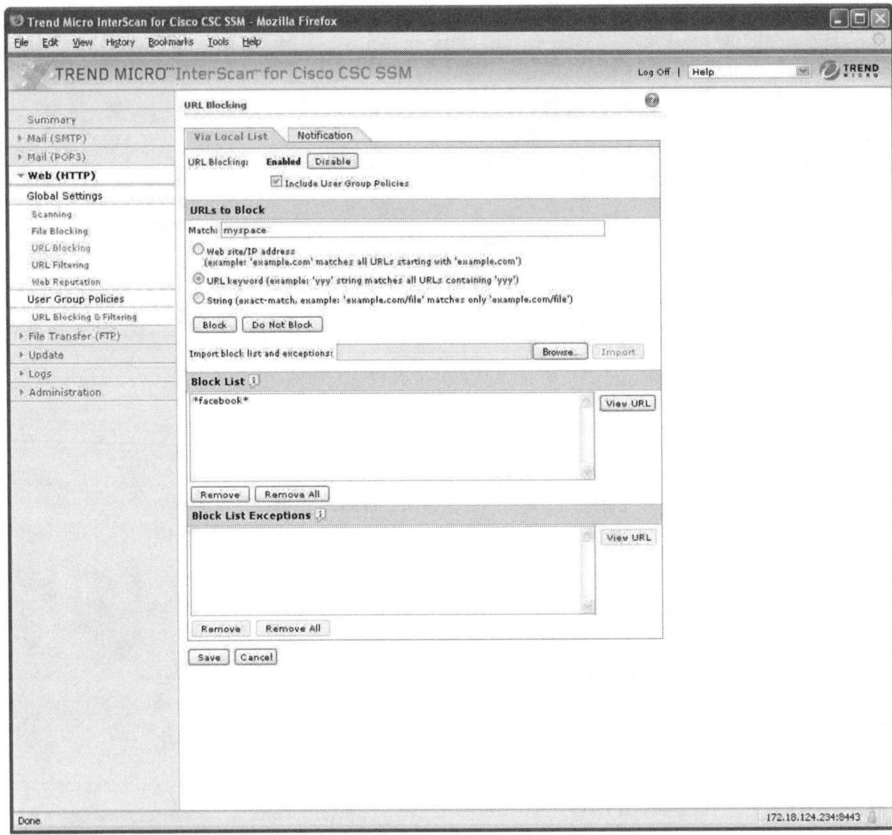

Figure 14-8 *Configuring URL Blocking*

Step 4. The URLs to Block section enables you to define a particular website name or IP address to be blocked. You can also define a URL keyword to include sites within a specific keyword. In this example, the keywords **facebook** and **myspace** are used to block these social networking sites. When you define these keywords the CSC SSM blocks all associated sites and folders such as the following:

- www.facebook.com
- example.facebook.com
- facebook.com/example
- www.myspace.com
- wxample.myspace.com
- myspace.com/example

Note After entering the website, URL keyword, or string under the **Match** field, click the **Block** button to add it to the **Block List** or the **Do Not Block** button to add it to the **Block List Exceptions**. Entries remain as blocked or exceptions until you remove them.

Alternatively, you can also use a string to block a site matching an exact match of that string. Note that you must configure the correct domain name within the URL. For instance, in this example, www.example.com/facebook will not be blocked.

Similarly, you can enter specific URLs, keywords, or strings and click the **Do Not Block** button to define blocking exceptions.

Step 5. You can also create a block and exception list in a text file and import it to the CSC SSM. The text file must have the title **URL Blocking Import File** followed by **[block]** and **[allow]** entries, as shown in the following example:

```
URL Blocking Import File
[block]
*facebook*
*myspace*
[allow]
*cisco.com*
```

Step 6. Click **Save** to save the configuration.

Note The **Notification** tab allows you to create a notification message to be displayed to the user when an attempt to access a blocked URL via HTTP is detected.

File Blocking

When you navigate to **Configuration > Trend Micro Content Security > Web** in ASDM, the File Blocking section shows whether or not file blocking is enabled on the CSC SSM. To configure file blocking, click **Configure File Blocking** to open the CSC SSM web management console and configure file blocking.

Complete the following steps to configure file blocking.

Step 1. After you click on **Configure File Blocking** in ASDM, log in to the Trend Micro InterScan web management console. Navigate to **Web (HTTP) > File Blocking**. The screen shown in Figure 14-9 is displayed.

Step 2. Check the types of files to be blocked by file type group. Unchecked groups of file types that will not be blocked. The following file types are predefined:

- Audio/Video (.avi, .cda, .m2a, .mov, .mp3, .mpeg, .mpg, .ra, .rm, .ram, .wav, .wma)

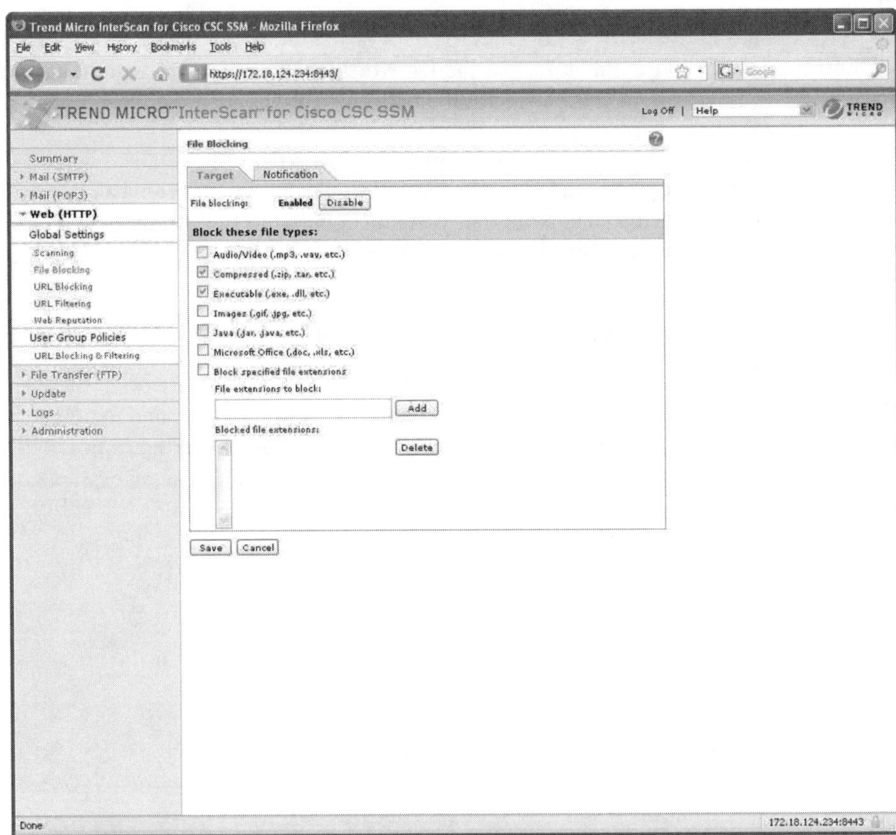

Figure 14-9 *Configuring Web File Blocking*

- Compressed (.zip, .tar, .arj)
- Executable (.exe, .dll, .vbs)
- Images (.bmp, .gif, .jpg, .png, .svg)
- Java (.jar, .java)
- Microsoft Office (.csv, .doc, .pdf, .ppt, .rtf, .txt, .wpd, .xls)

Step 3. Optionally, check **Block Specified File Extensions** to add file types that are not listed in the group file types.

Step 4. Click **Save** to save the configuration.

> **Note** The **Notification** tab enables you to create a notification message to be displayed to the user when an attempt to access a blocked file type is detected.

HTTP Scanning

When you navigate to **Configuration > Trend Micro Content Security > Web** in ASDM, the Scanning section shows whether or not HTTP scanning is enabled on the CSC SSM. To configure HTTP scanning, click **Configure Web Scanning** to open the CSC SSM web management console and configure HTTP scanning.

Complete the following steps to configure HTTP Scanning:

Step 1. After you click on **Configure HTTP Scanning** in ASDM, log in to the Trend Micro InterScan web management console. Navigate to **Web (HTTP) > Scanning.** The screen shown in Figure 14-10 is displayed.

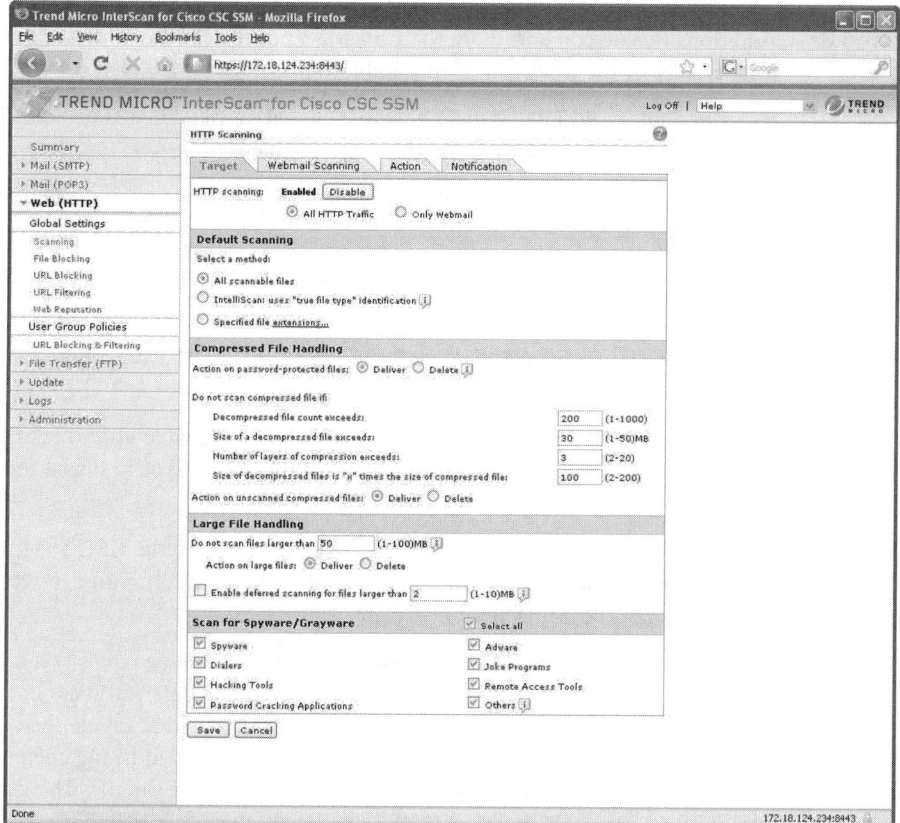

Figure 14-10 *Configuring HTTP Scanning*

Step 2. Make sure that HTTP Scanning is enabled. However, the **Disable** button allows the administrator to disable HTTP scanning if it is not needed.

Step 3. Select **All HTTP Traffic** to scan all HTTP traffic (the default setting), or select **Only Webmail** to scan only traffic matching the scanning parameters.

Step 4. Select the method used to scan the file types under the Default Scanning section. The following are the available scanning methods:

- **All scannable files**—Scans all files regardless of the file type. This is the default setting.
- **IntelliScan**—Used to scan only files identified by Trend Micro, using true file type identification.
- **Specified file extensions**—Enables you to specify file types to be scanned.

Step 5. In the Compressed File Handling section, you can define how to handle password-protected files that cannot be scanned.

Step 6. Additionally, you can configure the CSC SSM not to scan a compressed file if it meets any of the following configurable parameters:

- **Decompressed File Count Exceeds**—Specify a file count threshold. The value can be from 1 to 1000 (the default value is 500).
- **Size of a Decompressed File Exceeds**—The value can be from 1 to 50 MB (the default value is 30 MB).
- **Number of Layers of Compression Exceeds**—The value can be from 2 to 20 (the default value is 3).
- **Size of Decompressed Files Is "x" Times the Size of Compressed File**—The value can be from 2 to 200 (the default value is 100).

Step 7. The **Action on Unscanned Compressed Files** buttons enable you to configure the CSC SSM to deliver an unscanned compressed file or to delete the file.

Step 8. The **Large File Handling** section enables you to configure the CSC SSM not to scan files that are larger than a specific value. Additionally, you can set the action on large files to **Deliver** or **Delete**.

Step 9. The **Enable Deferred Scanning for Files Larger Than** field enables you to specify a file size (in megabytes) to be processed using deferred scanning. Deferred scanning is a way to scan a large file for threats that divide the file into multiple chunks. The first part of the file is downloaded to the client; this is while the CSC SSM still scanning subsequent chunks of the file. The values can be from 1 to 10 megabytes (MB). The default value is 2 MB.

Step 10. Select the type of spyware or grayware you would like the CSC SSM to detect under the **Scan for Spyware/Grayware** section. The available options are as follows

- Spyware
- Dialers

- Hacking Tools
- Password Cracking Applications
- Adware
- Joke Programs
- Remote Access Tools
- Others

When the **Others** option is used, the CSC SSM may detect several commercial products. However, some of these programs can also be used with malicious intent or are unwanted applications in the network environment.

Step 11. Click **Save** to save the configuration.

Configuring CSC SSM Mail-Based Features

The CSC SSM supports both SMTP and POP3 threat detection and filtering. This section covers the configuration of the mail-based features supported by the CSC SSM.

SMTP Scanning

The CSC SSM supports the scanning of incoming and outgoing SMTP messages. This section covers the configuration of both.

Configuring SMTP Incoming Scanning

When you navigate to **Configuration > Trend Micro Content Security > Mail** in ASDM, the Scanning section under the **SMTP** tab shows whether or not scanning of incoming SMTP messages is enabled on the CSC SSM. To configure incoming SMTP scanning, click the **Configure Incoming Scan** hyperlink to open the CSC SSM web management console and configure incoming SMTP scanning.

Complete the following steps to configure incoming SMTP scanning.

Step 1. After you click on **Configure Incoming Scan** in ASDM, log in to the Trend Micro InterScan web management console. Navigate to **Mail (SMTP) > Scanning > Incoming.** The screen shown in Figure 14-11 is displayed.

Notice that the screen displayed in Figure 14-11 is very similar to the screen used to configure HTTP Scanning.

Step 2. Make sure that **SMTP Incoming Message Scan** is enabled. However, the **Disable** button allows the administrator to disable SMTP message scanning if it is not needed.

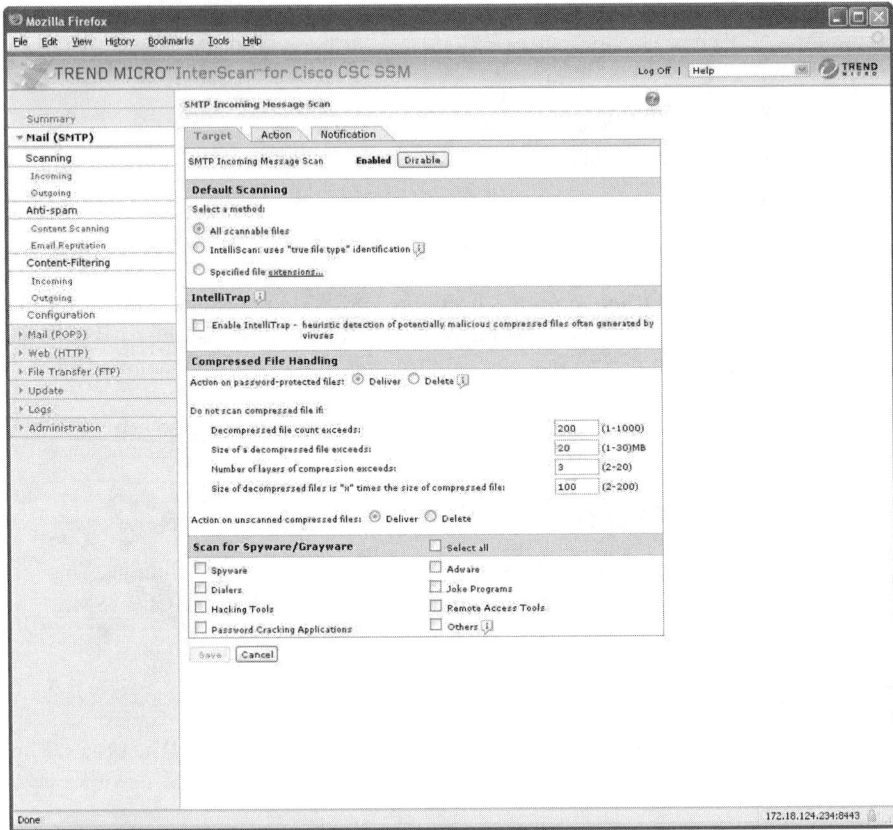

Figure 14-11 *Configuring Incoming SMTP Scanning*

Step 3. Select the method used to scan the file types under the Default Scanning section. The following are the available scanning methods:

- **All scannable files**—Scans all files regardless of the file type. This is the default setting.
- **IntelliScan: Uses "True File Type" Identification**—Used to scan only files identified by Trend Micro using true file type identification.
- **Specified File Extensions**—Allows you to specify file types to be scanned.

Step 4. Select **Enable IntelliTrap** to enable the IntelliTrap CSC SSM feature used to detect potentially malicious code in real-time compressed executable email attachments.

Step 5. The Compressed File Handling section enables you to define how to handle password-protected files that cannot be scanned.

Step 6. Additionally, you can configure the CSC SSM not to scan a compressed file if it meets any of the following configurable parameters:

- **Decompressed File Count Exceeds**—Specify a file count threshold. The value can be from 1 to 1000 (the default value is 500).
- **Size of a Decompressed File Exceeds**—The value can be from 1 to 50 MB (the default value is 30 MB).
- **Number of Layers of Compression Exceeds**—The value can be from 2 to 20 (the default value is 3).
- **Size of Decompressed Files Is "x" Times the Size of Compressed File**—The value can be from 2 to 200 (the default value is 100).

Step 7. The **Action on Unscanned Compressed Files** buttons allow you to configure the CSC SSM to deliver an unscanned compressed file or to delete the file.

Step 8. In the Large File Handling section (not shown in Figure 14-11) you can configure the CSC SSM to not scan files that are larger than a specific value. Additionally, you can set the action on large files to **Deliver** or **Delete**.

Step 9. The **Enable Deferred Scanning for Files Larger Than** field (not shown in Figure 14-11) enables you to specify a file size (in megabytes) to be processed by deferred scanning. Deferred scanning is a way to scan a large file for threats that divide the file into multiple chunks. The first part of the file is downloaded to the client; this happens while the CSC SSM is still scanning subsequent chunks of the file. The values can be from 1 to 10 megabytes (MB). The default value is 2 MB.

Step 10. Select the type of spyware or grayware you would like the CSC SSM to detect under the Scan for Spyware/Grayware section. The available options are the following:

- Spyware
- Dialers
- Hacking Tools
- Password Cracking Applications
- Adware
- Joke Programs
- Remote Access Tools
- Others

When the **Others** option is used, the CSC SSM may detect several commercial products and other "hacking tools". However, some of these programs can also be used with malicious intent or are unwanted applications on the network environment.

Step 11. The **Action** tab displays a set of options that enable you to specify what action is taken when a malware or spyware has been detected in an incoming SMTP message. The least risky option is to clean the message and the most risky choice is to deliver the message anyway.

Step 12. The **Notification** tab displays a set of options that enable you to define who will be notified when a security risk has been detected. An inline notification message that would appear in all incoming email can also be composed. The settings on the **Notifications** tab are optional. A default message appears in each message text box; however, you can change this to any message that best fits your environment and security policies.

Step 13. Click **Save** to save the configuration.

Configuring SMTP Outgoing Scanning

When you navigate to **Configuration > Trend Micro Content Security > Mail** in ASDM, the Scanning section under the **SMTP** tab shows whether or not scanning of outgoing SMTP messages is enabled on the CSC SSM. To configure outgoing SMTP scanning, click the **Configure Outgoing Scan** hyperlink to open the CSC SSM web management console and configure outgoing SMTP scanning. The configuration steps for configuring outgoing messages are exactly the same as the ones described for scanning incoming SMTP messages. In this instance, navigate to **Mail (SMTP) > Scanning > Outgoing.**

SMTP Anti-Spam

The CSC SSM supports the detection and blocking of spam email messages. When configuring the SMTP anti-spam feature, you can configure Content Scanning or Email Reputation. The following sections cover the configuration of both features.

Configuring SMTP Anti-Spam Content Scanning

When you navigate to **Configuration > Trend Micro Content Security > Mail** in ASDM, the Anti-spam section under the **SMTP** tab shows whether or not Anti-spam Content Scanning is enabled on the CSC SSM. To configure Anti-spam Content Scanning, click the **Configure Anti-spam (Content Scanning)** hyperlink to open the CSC SSM web management console.

Complete the following steps to configure Anti-spam Content Scanning:

Step 1. After you click on **Configure Anti-spam (Content Scanning)** in ASDM, log in to the Trend Micro InterScan web management console. Navigate to **Mail (SMTP) > Anti-spam > Content Scanning.** The screen shown in Figure 14-12 is displayed.

Step 2. Make sure that SMTP Anti-spam is enabled. To disable it, click on the **Disable** button.

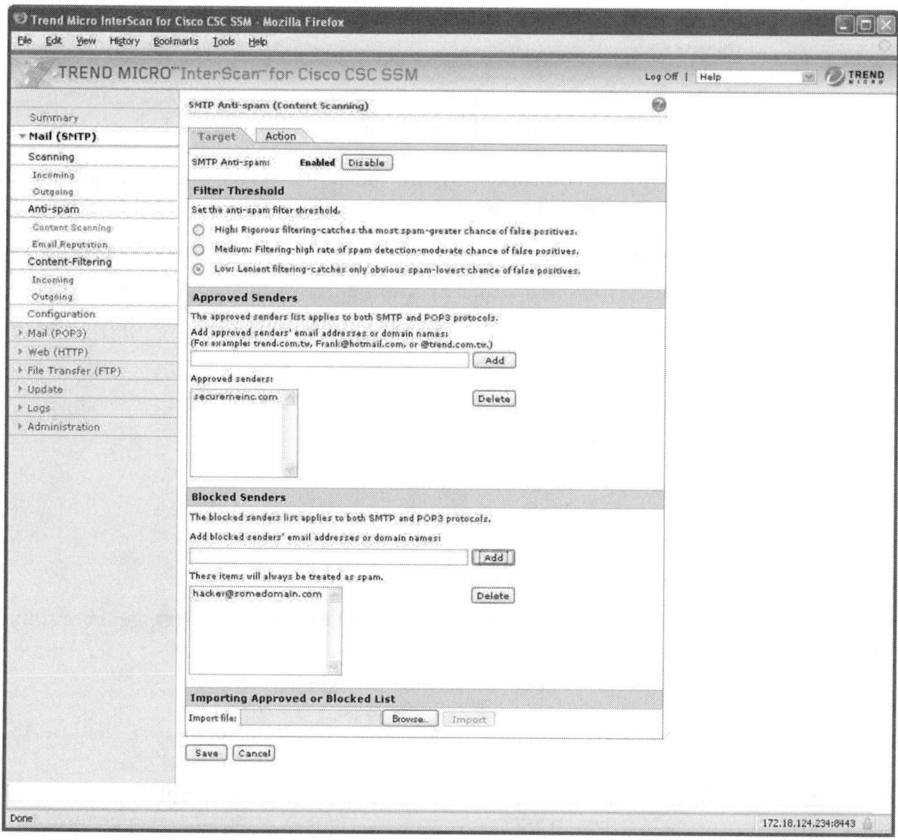

Figure 14-12 *Configuring Anti-Spam Content Scanning*

Step 3. The Filter Threshold section enables you to configure one of three levels of spam settings (**High**, **Medium**, and **Low**). The most restrictive is the **High** option. Use this setting carefully because it also has a greater chance of false positives. The least restrictive option is **Low**, which is the default. When the **Low** option is selected, the CSC SSM blocks the most commonly known spam mail; however, it may allow some spam to enter your network. It is always recommended to start with the **Low** setting and increase it later as needed. This minimizes the implementation impact within your organization.

Step 4. In the Approved Senders section, you can define specific email addresses or domain names that are always allowed to send email. The CSC SSM does not scan messages from these addresses and domain names for spam purposes. This applies to both SMTP and POP3 traffic. In this example, the domain name **securemeinc.com** is entered.

Step 5. The Blocked Senders section enables you to define specific email addresses or domain names that are automatically classified as spam. In this example, the email address **hacker@somedomain.com** is automatically classified as a spam originator.

Step 6. The Importing Approved or Blocked List section enables you to import a preformatted file that can include a list with approved or blocked senders.

Step 7. In the **Action** tab, you can configure the action taken when an SMTP message is classified as spam. The available actions are as follows

- **Stamp Message**—An identifier is placed in the subject field of all messages identified as spam. This can be the word "spam" or any other identifier that better suits your security policy and requirements. This is the default action.
- **Delete Message**—This is used to delete the offending message before it reaches the recipient.

Click **Save** to save the configuration.

Configuring SMTP Anti-Spam Email Reputation

Email Reputation is a Trend Micro feature set that enables you to leverage a combination of Real-time Blacklist (RBL+) and Quick IP Lookup (QIL) technologies to determine whether an email message is spam or a legitimate message.

When you navigate to **Configuration > Trend Micro Content Security > Mail** in ASDM, the Anti-spam section under the **SMTP** tab shows whether or not Anti-spam Email Reputation is enabled on the CSC SSM. To configure Anti-spam Email Reputation, click the **Configure Anti-spam (Email Reputation)** hyperlink to open the CSC SSM web management console.

Complete the following steps to configure Anti-spam Email Reputation:

Step 1. After you click on **Configure Anti-spam (Email Reputation)** in ASDM, log in to the Trend Micro InterScan web management console. Navigate to **Mail (SMTP) > Anti-spam > Email Reputation.** The screen shown in Figure 14-13 is displayed.

Step 2. Make sure that SMTP Anti-spam (Email Reputation) is enabled. However, the **Disable** button allows the administrator to disable SMTP antispam scanning if it is unnecessary.

Step 3. The Email Reputation feature is available only if you have purchased the Plus license. Select the service level that applies to you under the **Set Service Level** section. Two options are available (**Standard** and **Advanced**). The Standard level uses a reputation database that includes numerous well-known spam sources.. To obtain more information about the standard service level offering, go to http://us.trendmicro.com/go/ers/standard.

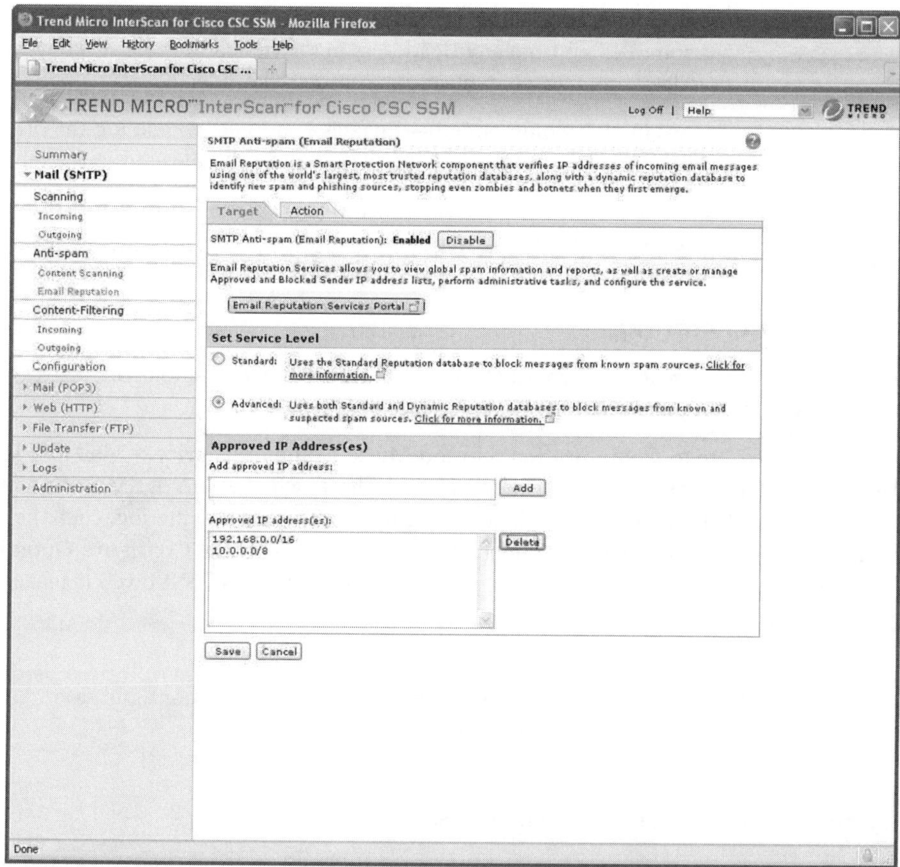

Figure 14-13 *Configuring Anti-Spam Email Reputation*

The advanced service level combines entries from the standard reputation database with a dynamic real-time reputation database that includes anti-spam technology provided by Trend Micro.

Step 4. In the Approved IP Address(es) section, you can configure exceptions to the Email Reputation checking. In this example, the 192.168.0.0/16 and 10.0.0.0/8 networks are added to the approved list.

Step 5. The **Action** tab enables you to define the action to be taken when a host matches the Standard and Advanced service level databases entries within an incoming SMTP message. You can select the following actions:

- **Intelligent Action**—Permanently denies connection to email from any IP address in the standard or advanced reputation database. The CSC SSM sends a "Mail-blocked" message to the sender, although this message is configurable. This is the default action.

- **Close Connection with No Error Message**—Permanently denies connection to email from any IP address in the standard or advanced reputation database with no explanation sent to the sender.
- **Bypass (Not Recommended)**—Enables you to detect and log the offending IP address; however, the offending message is delivered to the recipient.

Step 6. Click **Save** to save the configuration.

SMTP Content Filtering

Content filtering is a feature where the CSC SSM intercepts and prohibits the delivery of email messages that contain offensive or restricted content.

When you navigate to **Configuration > Trend Micro Content Security > Mail** in ASDM, the Content Filtering section under the **SMTP** tab shows whether or not SMTP Content Filtering is enabled on the CSC SSM. To configure SMTP Content Filtering, click the **Configure Incoming Filtering** (for incoming email messages) or the **Configure Outgoing Filtering** (for outgoing email messages) hyperlink to open the CSC SSM web management console.

Note The incoming and outgoing filtering sections contain the same configuration parameters. The only difference is the direction of the email messages.

Complete the following steps to configure SMTP Content Filtering.

Step 1. After you click the **Configure Incoming Filtering** or the **Configure Outgoing Filtering** hyperlink in ASDM, log in to the Trend Micro InterScan web management console. Navigate to **Mail (SMTP) > Content-Filtering** and select either **Incoming** or **Outgoing.**

Step 2. Make sure that SMTP Incoming Content Filter is enabled. To disable it, click on the **Disable** button.

Step 3. In the **Message Size** section, you can filter incoming messages of a certain size (in kilobytes (KB) or megabytes (MB)). If nothing is configured, the CSC SSM does not filter incoming messages based on a specific size.

Step 4. The **Message Subject and Body** section enables you to define words within the subject or body of an email message to be filtered.

Step 5. The Message Attachment section enables you to define words within a filename of an email message attachment. You can also configure wildcards with an asterisk [*]. For example, to match any attachment that has the word *confidential* within its filename, use ***confidential***.

Additionally, you can also filter attachments based on the file type. The following file types are predefined:

- Audio/Video (.avi, .cda, .m2a, .mov, .mp3, .mpeg, .mpg, .ra, .rm, .ram, .wav, .wma)
- Compressed (.zip, .tar, .arj)
- Executable (.exe, .dll, .vbs)
- Images (.bmp, .gif, .jpg, .png, .svg)
- Java (.jar, .java)
- Microsoft Office (.csv, .doc, .pdf, .ppt, .rtf, .txt, .wpd, .xls)

Step 6. The **Actions** tab enables you to define the action taken when a violation has been detected in an incoming email message or attachment.

Step 7. The **Notifications** tab enables you to define different notification messages sent to an administrator, the sender, or the recipient when a violation has been detected in an incoming email message or attachment.

Step 8. Click **Save** to save the configuration.

POP3 Support

The CSC SSM also supports the POP3 email protocol. The following POP3 features are supported:

- POP3 Scanning
- Anti-spam
- Content Filtering

These features are configured exactly the same way that the previous SMTP features were configured. The only difference is that there is no concept of incoming vs. outgoing in POP3 (that is, all messages are incoming).

Configuring CSC SSM File Transfer Protocol (FTP)

The CSC SSM supports the scanning and blocking of files being transferred via FTP. The following sections describe how to configure FTP scanning and file blocking.

Configuring FTP Scanning

When you navigate to **Configuration > Trend Micro Content Security > File Transfer** in ASDM, the File Scanning section shows whether or not scanning of files transferred via the FTP protocol is enabled on the CSC SSM. To configure FTP scanning, click the **Configure File Scanning** hyperlink to open the CSC SSM web management console.

Complete the following steps to configure FTP scanning:

Step 1. After you click on **Configure File Scanning** in ASDM, log in to the Trend Micro InterScan web management console. Navigate to **File Transfer (FTP) > Scanning.** The screen shown in Figure 14-14 is displayed.

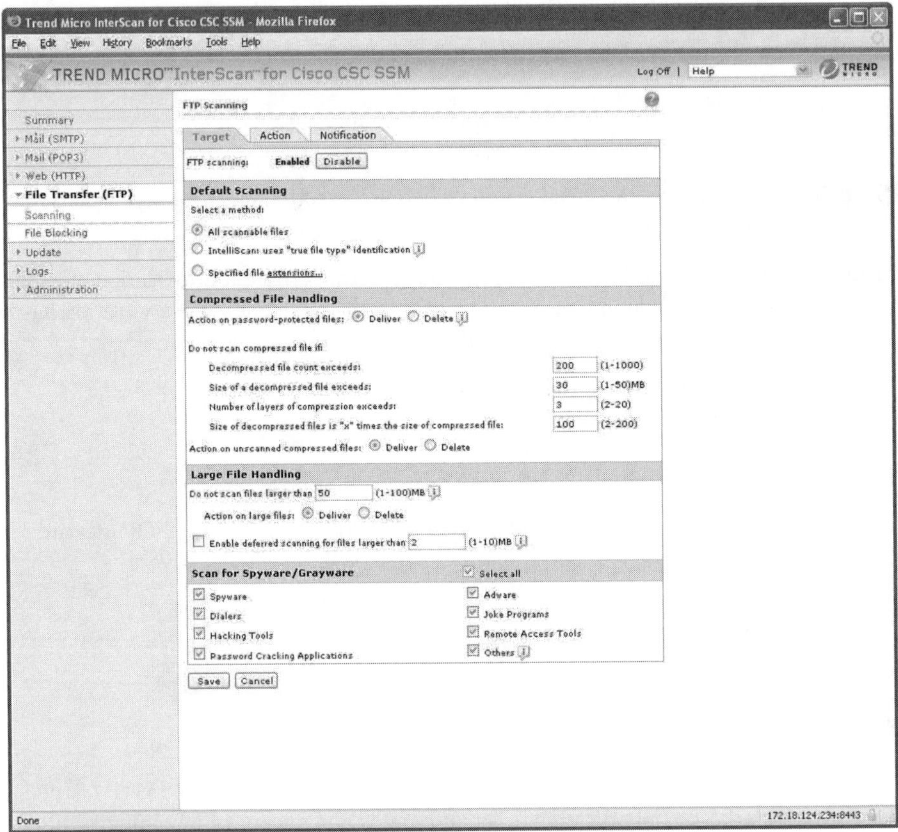

Figure 14-14 *Configuring FTP Scanning*

Notice that the screen displayed in Figure 14-14 is very similar to the screen used to configure HTTP and SMTP Scanning.

Step 2. Make sure that FTP Scanning is enabled. To disable it, click on the **Disable** button.

Step 3. Select the method used to scan the file types under the Default Scanning section. The following are the available scanning methods:

- **All Scannable Files—**Scans all files regardless of the file type. This is the default setting.
- **IntelliScan: Use "True File Type" Identification—**Used to scan only files identified by Trend Micro via true file type identification.

- **Specified File Extensions**—Enables you to specify file types to be scanned.

Step 4. The Compressed File Handling section enables you to define how to handle password-protected files that cannot be scanned.

Step 5. Additionally, you can configure the CSC SSM not to scan a compressed file if it meets any of the following configurable parameters:

- **Decompressed File Count Exceeds**—Specify a file count threshold. The value can be from 1 to 1000 (the default value is 500).
- **Size of a Decompressed File Exceeds**—The value can be from 1 to 50 MB (the default value is 30 MB).
- **Number of Layers of Compression Exceeds**—The value can be from 2 to 20 (the default value is 3).
- **Size of Decompressed Files Is "x" Times the Size of Compressed File**—The value can be from 2 to 200 (the default value is 100).

Step 6. The **Action on Unscanned Compressed Files** buttons enable you to configure the CSC SSM to deliver an unscanned compressed file or to delete the file.

Step 7. The **Large File Handling** section enables you to configure the CSC SSM to not scan files that are larger than a specific value. Additionally, you can set the action on large files to **Deliver** or **Delete**.

Step 8. The **Enable Deferred Scanning for Files Larger Than** field enables you to specify a file size (in megabytes) to be processed using deferred scanning. Deferred scanning is a way to scan a large file for threats that divide the file into multiple chunks. The first part of the file is downloaded to the client; this happens while the CSC SSM is still scanning subsequent chunks of the file. The values can be from 1 to 10 megabytes (MB). The default value is 2 MB.

Step 9. Select the type of spyware or grayware you would like the CSC SSM to detect under the Scan for Spyware/Grayware section. The available options are as follows:

- Spyware
- Dialers
- Hacking Tools
- Password Cracking Applications
- Adware
- Joke Programs
- Remote Access Tools
- Others

When the **Others** option is used, the CSC SSM may detect several commercial products. However, some of these programs can also be used with malicious intent or are unwanted applications on the network environment.

Step 10. The **Action** tab displays a set of options that enable you to specify what action is taken when a malware or spyware has been detected in an incoming FTP file. The least risky choice is to clean the file and the most risky choice is to allow the file anyway.

Step 11. The **Notification** tab displays a set of options that enable you to define who will be notified when a security risk has been detected. The settings on the **Notifications** tab are optional. A default message appears in each message text box; however, you can change this to any message that best fits your environment and security policies.

Step 12. Click **Save** to save the configuration.

FTP File Blocking

When you navigate to **Configuration > Trend Micro Content Security > File Transfer** in ASDM, the File Blocking section shows whether or not FTP file blocking is enabled on the CSC SSM. To configure FTP file blocking, click **Configure File Blocking** to open the CSC SSM web management console.

Complete the following steps to configure FTP File blocking:

Step 1. After you click on **Configure File Blocking** in ASDM, log in to the Trend Micro InterScan web management console. Navigate to **File Transfer (FTP) > File Blocking.** The screen shown in Figure 14-15 is displayed.

Notice that the screen displayed in Figure 14-15 is very similar to the screen used to configure HTTP File Blocking.

Step 2. Make sure that File Blocking is enabled. To disable it, click on the **Disable** button.

Step 3. Check the types of files to be blocked by file type group. Unchecked groups of file types will not be blocked. The following file types are predefined:

- Audio/Video (.avi, .cda, .m2a, .mov, .mp3, .mpeg, .mpg, .ra, .rm, .ram, .wav, .wma)
- Compressed (.zip, .tar, .arj)
- Executable (.exe, .dll, .vbs)
- Images (.bmp, .gif, .jpg, .png, .svg)
- Java (.jar, .java)
- Microsoft Office (.csv, .doc, .pdf, .ppt, .rtf, .txt, .wpd, .xls)

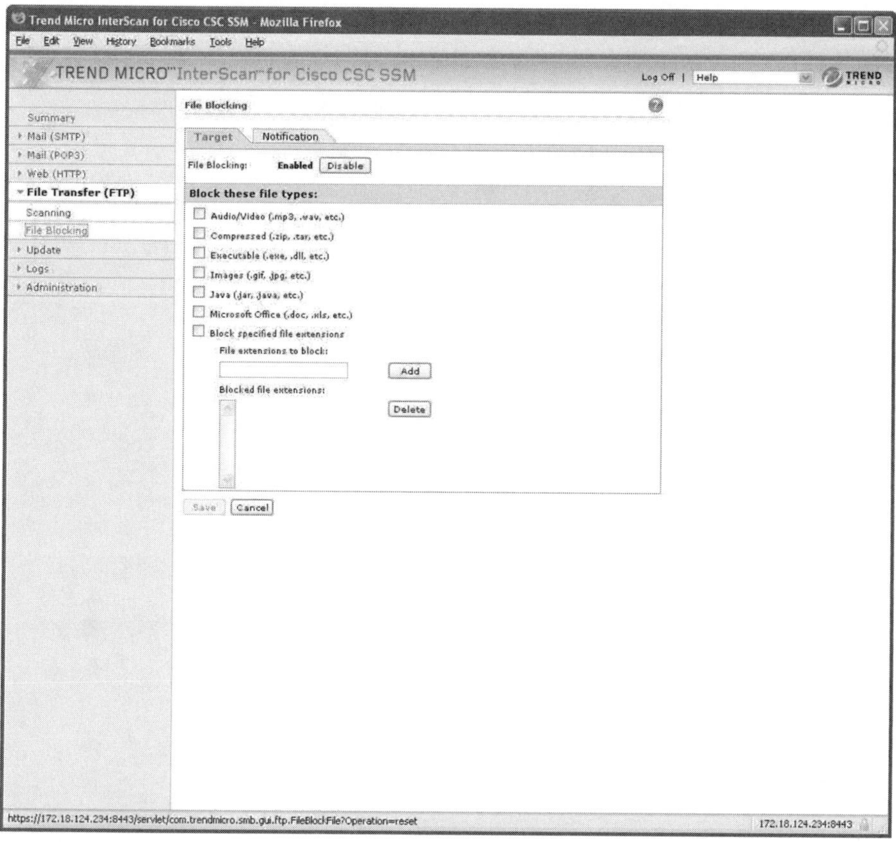

Figure 14-15 *Configuring FTP File Blocking*

Step 4. Optionally, check **Block Specified File Extensions** to add file types that are not listed in the group file types.

Step 5. The **Notification** tab enables you to create a notification message to be displayed to the user when an attempt to access a blocked file type is detected.

Step 6. Click **Save** to save the configuration.

Summary

The CSC SSM provides a framework to help you detect and take action on viruses, worms, Trojans, and other security threats. It supports the inspection of SMTP, POP3, HTTP, and FTP network traffic. This chapter provided step-by-step instructions on how to configure HTTP scanning, file blocking, URL blocking, URL filtering, and web reputation features. The configuration of SMTP and POP3 email features was also covered in detail, as well as the configuration of FTP scanning and file blocking.

Chapter 15

Monitoring and Troubleshooting the Cisco Content Security and Control Security Services Module

This chapter covers the following topics:

- Monitoring the CSC SSM
- Troubleshooting the CSC SSM

In Chapter 14, you learned how to configure the Content Security and Control Security Services Module (CSC SSM). This chapter covers the monitoring and troubleshooting of the CSC SSM, as well as other administrative tasks.

Monitoring the CSC SSM

The Adaptive Security Device Manager (ASDM) enables you to view CSC SSM high-level device information by selecting the **Content Security** tab within the ASDM Home screen. The Content Security tab is illustrated in Figure 15-1.

The Content Security tab provides the following details:

- **Model**—In this example the CSC SSM model is ASA-SSM-CSC-10.
- **Mgmt IP**—This is the IP address of the management interface (192.168.3.2 is used in this example).
- **Version**—Displays the CSC SSM software version. The CSC SSM is running version 6.3.1172.0 in this example.
- **Daily Node #**—Number of devices for which the CSC SSM provided services within the last 24 hours (this number is updated every day at midnight).
- **Last Update**—The date of the last software update downloaded from Trend Micro.
- **Base License**—Displays the base license expiration date.
- **Plus License**—Displays the plus license expiration date (if the plus license has been purchased).

■ **Licensed Nodes**—Displays the maximum number of devices that are supported by the license installed in the system.

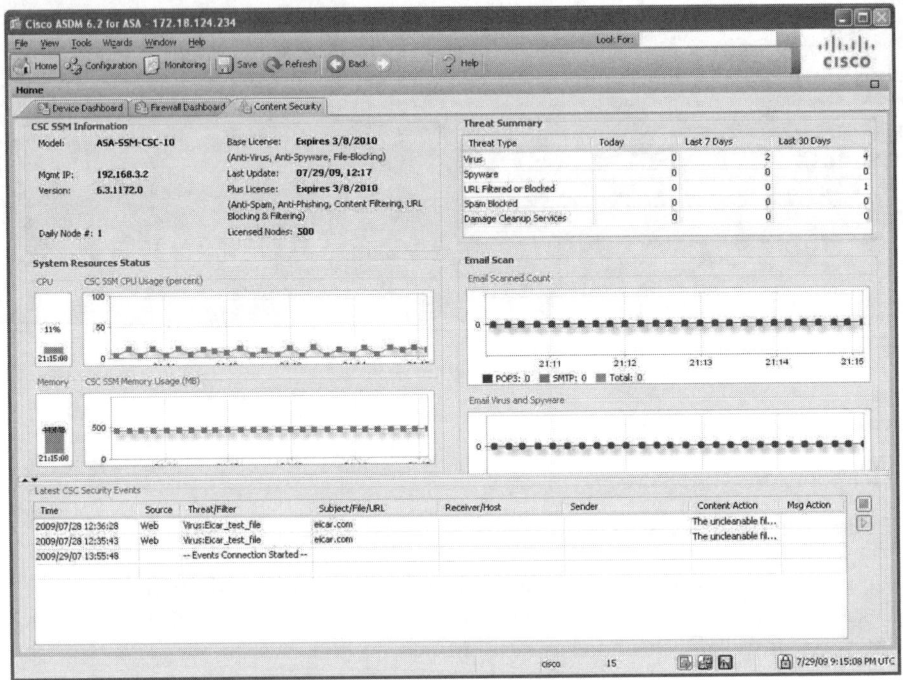

Figure 15-1 *ASDM CSC SSM Device Information*

■ **System Resources Status**—Displays CSC SSM CPU and memory utilization statistics.

■ **Threat Summary**—Displays virus, spyware, URL blocked, URL filtered, and spam statistics for the present day, last 7 days, and last 30 days.

■ **Email Scan**—Displays a graph illustrating statistics of scanned emails and the email viruses and spyware detected.

■ **Latest CSC Security Events**—Displays (in real time) security event messages generated by the CSC SSM.

The information included in the Content Security provides a high-level overview of the traffic and events in the CSC SSM. The following sections describe more advanced CSC SSM monitoring features and techniques.

Detailed Live Event Monitoring

You can access a more detailed report of real-time CSC SSM security events in ASDM by navigating to **Monitoring > Trend Micro Content Security > Live Security Events.** The Buffer Limit field shows the maximum number of log messages that will be stored in the buffer. The default is 1000; however, the buffer limit can be any number from 100 to 2000.

To view live security events messages that are received from the CSC SSM, click **View** and complete the following steps:

Step 1. After you click on **View**, the **Live Log** dialog box is displayed.

The Live Log dialog box has the following display-only columns:

- **Time**—The time an event occurred.
- **Source**—The IP address or host of the source that triggered such event.
- **Threat/Filter**—The type of threat or URL filtering event that triggered the event.
- **Subject/File/URL**—The subject of emails that include a threat, the names of FTP files that contain a threat, or blocked/filtered URLs.
- **Receiver/Host**—The email address or host recipient of malicious emails.
- **Sender**—The sender of emails that include a threat.
- **Content Action**—The action taken upon the content of a message.
- **Msg Action**—The action taken on a message.

Step 2. You can filter messages by using the **Filter By** drop-down list. The following options are available:

- **Show All**—Displays all messages.
- **Filter by Text**—Allows you to filter messages based on text that you enter.

Step 3. Click **Filter** to filter event messages based on the selected criteria.

Step 4. You can also search event messages by using the **Find** field and clicking **Find Messages.**

Step 5. Click **Pause** to pause the scrolling of live events.

Step 6. Click **Save** to save the log to a text file.

Step 7. Click **Clear Display** to clear the list of events.

Configuring Syslog

Similar to any other networking device, the memory space on the CSC SSM is limited; therefore, it is recommended that you configure the CSC SSM to send security event messages to a syslog server. Complete the following steps to configure the CSC SSM to send security event messages to a syslog server:

Step 1. Log in to the Trend Micro InterScan for CSC SSM web management console and navigate to **Logs > Settings.** The screen shown in Figure 15-2 is displayed.

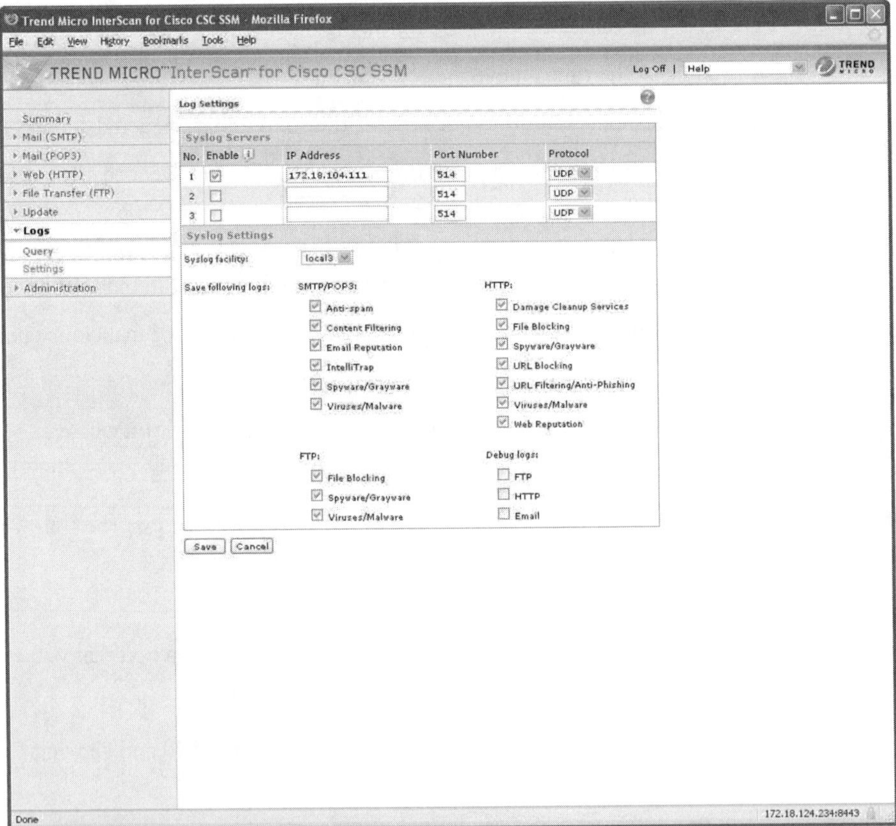

Figure 15-2 *Configuring Syslog*

Step 2. Check the **Enable** check box for each syslog server to be configured. In this example, the syslog server IP address is 172.18.104.111.

Step 3. Configure the port number that is used to communicate to the syslog server under the Port Number column. The default port (**514**) is configured in this example.

Step 4. Select the protocol to be used under the Protocol pull-down menu. The UDP protocol is used in this example.

Step 5. Select the syslog facility under the Syslog facility pull-down menu (**local3** is used in this example). The syslog facility is an identifier in the range local0 to local7 for the purpose of identifying the CSC SSM when sending messages to the syslog server.

Step 6. Select the features for which you want events to be sent to the syslog server under the **Save Following Logs** section.

Note Debug logs generate very detailed information about traffic and other events in the CSC SSM. It is recommended that you enable debug logs only when troubleshooting a specific problem and not during normal operation. Debug logs are covered later in this chapter.

Step 7. Click **Save** to save the configuration.

Note For detailed information about the CSC SSM-related system log messages, refer to the Cisco Content Security and Control SSM Administrator Guide at the following link:

http://www.cisco.com/en/US/products/ps6120/products_installation_and_configuration_guides_list.html.

Troubleshooting the CSC SSM

This section covers several tips and methodologies that can be used to troubleshoot CSC SSM problems.

Re-Imaging the CSC SSM

In very rare occasions, you may encounter a problem where you need to install the CSC SSM software via the Cisco ASA command-line interface (CLI). This may be because of a software corruption or hardware replacement after a failure. Complete the following steps to install the CSC SSM software via the Cisco ASA CLI:

Step 1. Enter the **hw-module module 1 recover configure** command, as shown in the following example:

```
NewYork# hw-module module 1 recover configure
Image URL [tftp://0.0.0.0/]: tftp://172.18.108.26/csc-software.bin
Port IP Address [0.0.0.0]: 172.18.104.123
VLAN ID [0]: 10
Gateway IP Address [0.0.0.0]: 172.18.104.1
```

Step 2. Enter the TFTP server URL at the **Image URL [tftp://0.0.0.0/]:** prompt. The URL used in this example is **tftp://172.18.108.26/csc-software.bin.**

Step 3. Enter the IP address to be assigned to the CSC SSM management interface at the **Port IP Address [0.0.0.0]:** prompt (**172.18.104.123** is used in this example).

Step 4. Enter the VLAN ID at the **VLAN ID [0]:** prompt. VLAN **10** is used in this example.

Step 5. Enter the IP address of the gateway at the **Gateway IP Address [0.0.0.0]:** prompt. **172.18.104.1** is the gateway IP address in this example.

Step 6. Use the **hw-module module 1 recover boot** command to start the software recovery, as shown in the following example:

```
NewYork# hw-module module 1 recover boot
The module in slot 1 will be recovered.  This may
erase all configuration and all data on that device and
attempt to download a new image for it.
Recover module in slot 1? [confirm]
Recover issued for module in slot 1
```

Step 7. After about a minute, the CSC SSM goes into the ROMMON mode, and prints messages similar to the following

```
Slot-1 224>!!!!!!!!!!!!!!!!!!!!!!!!!!!!!!!!!!!!!!!!!!!!!!!!!!!!!!!!!!!!!
<output truncated>
```

Step 8. The software is downloaded from the TFTP server and installed into the CSC SSM.

Step 9. To verify that the installation is successful, use the Cisco ASA **show module** command, as shown in the following example:

```
NewYork# show module
Mod Card Type                                    Model
Serial No.
--- -------------------------------------------- ------------------ -
-----
  0 ASA 5520 Adaptive Security Appliance         ASA5520
JMX0944K06P
  1 ASA 5500 Series Content Security Services Mo ASA-SSM-CSC-10
JAB101900KH
Mod MAC Address Range                 Hw Version   Fw Version   Sw
Version
--- --------------------------------- ------------ ------------ ---
-----
  0 0013.c480.c98e to 0013.c480.c992  1.0          1.0(10)0     8.2(1)
  1 0016.c79f.8276 to 0016.c79f.8276  1.0          1.0(10)0     CSC
SSM 6.3.1172.0
```

```
Mod SSM Application Name           Status           SSM Application
Version
--- ------------------------------ ---------------- ------------------
-----
  1 CSC SSM                          Up               6.3.1172.0
Mod Status                 Data Plane Status     Compatibility
--- ------------------ --------------------- -------------
  0 Up Sys                 Not Applicable
1 Up                     Up
```

In this example, the Cisco ASA has a CSC SSM model ASA-SSM-CSC-10 installed. The output of this command also shows the software version of the CSC SSM. The software version installed in the CSC SSM in this example is **6.3.1172.0**. The CSC SSM status is displayed at the end of the output of the **show module** command. The **show module 1 details** command displays more detailed information, as shown in the following example:

```
NewYork# show module 1 details
Getting details from the Service Module, please wait...
ASA 5500 Series Content Security Services Module-10
Model:                ASA-SSM-CSC-10
Hardware version:    1.0
Serial Number:       JAB101900KH
Firmware version:    1.0(10)0
Software version:    CSC SSM 6.3.1172.0
MAC Address Range:   0016.c79f.8276 to 0016.c79f.8276
App. name:           CSC SSM
App. Status:         Up
App. Status Desc:    CSC SSM scan services are available
App. version:        6.3.1172.0
Data plane Status:   Up
Status:              Up
HTTP Service:        Up
Mail Service:        Up
FTP  Service:        Up
Activated:           Yes
Mgmt IP addr:        172.18.104.123
Mgmt web port:       8443
Peer IP addr:        <not enabled>
```

Troubleshooting CSC SSM Software Installations The following are some troubleshooting tips that can help you if you encounter problems during the CSC SSM software installation:

- Make sure that the TFTP server you are using supports the transfer of files larger than 60 megabytes (MB).
- Verify that the size of the CSC SSM software image in your TFTP server is correct. You can also perform an MD5 checksum to see whether it matches the checksum published with the image at Cisco.com.
- If your TFTP server is in the same IP subnet as the CSC SSM, the gateway IP address must be set to 0.0.0.0.
- If not in the same subnet, make sure that UDP port 69 is not being blocked by any router or firewall between the CSC SSM and your TFTP server.
- Verify the image path is correct in correlation to the location on the TFTP server, and that the directory and file are readable to all users.
- Retry the download and installation after following the previous tips. If the installation is not successful a second time, contact the Cisco Technical Assistance Center (TAC) for further troubleshooting assistance.
- The **hw-module module 1 recover stop** command can be used to stop the recovery action and the downloading of the recovery image. After this command is invoked, the CSC SSM boots from the original image. You must enter this command within 30 to 45 seconds after starting recovery, using the **hw-module module boot** command. If you issue the **stop** command after this period, it might cause unexpected results, such as the SSM becoming unresponsive.

Password Recovery

There are two passwords used to manage the CSC SSM: the ASDM/Web interface password and the root account password. The default entry for both passwords is the word cisco.

Caution Use the root account only under the supervision of Cisco TAC. Unauthorized modifications made through the root account are not supported and require that the device be reimaged to guarantee correct operation.

If you have lost the root account password, but still have the ASDM/Web interface/CLI password, you can continue to manage the CSC SSM via the web interface. On the other hand, if all passwords are lost, the CSC SSM must be reimaged, unless you have configured the password-reset policy to **Allowed.**

Complete the following steps to change the password-reset policy:

Step 1. Use the **session** *<module number>* command from the Cisco ASA CLI to access the CSC SSM CLI menu, as shown in the following example:

```
NewYork# session 1
Opening command session with slot 1.
Connected to slot 1. Escape character sequence is 'CTRL-^X'.
login: administrator
Password:
Last login: Thu Jul 30 10:40:17 on pts/0
***NOTICE***
This product contains cryptographic features and is subject to United
States and local country laws governing import, export, transfer and
use. Delivery of Cisco cryptographic products does not imply third-
party authority to import, export, distribute or use encryption.
Importers, exporters, distributors and
users are responsible for compliance with U.S. and local country
laws. By using this product you agree to comply with applicable laws
and regulations. If you are unable to comply with U.S. and local laws,
return this product immediately.
A summary of U.S. laws governing Cisco cryptographic products may be
found at:
http://www.cisco.com/wwl/export/crypto/tool/stqrg.html
If you require further assistance please contact us by sending email to
export@cisco.com.
     Trend Micro InterScan for Cisco CSC SSM Setup Main Menu
---------------------------------------------------------------------.
1. Network Settings
2. Date/Time Settings
3. Product Information
4. Service Status
5. Password Management
6. Restore Factory Default Settings
7. Troubleshooting Tools
8. Reset Management Port Access Control List
9. Ping
10. Exit ...
Enter a number from [1-10]: 5
```

Log in with administrator credentials to access the Trend Micro InterScan for Cisco CSC SSM Setup Main Menu.

Step 2. Select **Password Management** (number 5). The following menu is displayed:

```
                    Password Management
-------------------------------------------------------
1. Change Password
2. Modify Password-reset Policy
3. Return to Main Menu
Enter a number from [1-3]: 2
```

Step 3. To modify the password reset policy, select **Modify Password-reset Policy** (number 2). The **Modify Password-reset Policy** options are displayed, as shown in the following example:

```
                 Modify Password-reset Policy
-------------------------------------------------------
Current CSC SSM password-reset policy: Allowed
"Allowed" allows the Adaptive Security Device Manager (ASDM)
to reset the CSC SSM password without verifying the old password.
"Denied" does not allow the ASDM to reset the CSC SSM password
without re-imaging and re-activating the CSC SSM.
Do you want to modify the CSC SSM password-reset policy now? [y¦n] y
Updated CSC SSM password-reset policy: Denied
```

In this example, the current CSC SSM password-reset policy is already set to **Allowed**; to change to Denied type **y** at the **Do You Want to Modify the CSC SSM Password-Reset Policy Now? [y|n]** prompt. Leaving the password-reset policy to Allowed compromises the security of the CSC SSM because you can reset the CSC SSM password through the ASDM without verifying the old password. Under this setting, you can reset the password, even if the current password has been lost.

Configuration Backup

Backing up your configuration is a best practice that you should always follow. The CSC SSM allows you to back up your configuration to a file. The following information is saved when you back up your configuration:

- Selected scanning method for SMTP, POP3, HTTP, and FTP protocols and the actions to take when a threat is detected
- Compressed and large file handling
- Whether you want to scan for spyware and other malicious software

- Anti-spam filter threshold settings
- Approved and blocked senders
- Message size limitations
- Content filtering criteria
- Email reputation and Web reputation (filter level, and action)
- File blocking rules
- URL blocking and filtering criteria
- Scheduled update settings
- Proxy settings
- Syslog settings
- Connection settings
- Device failover settings
- Notification settings
- System time settings
- System patch status
- Licensing information and status
- Domain Controller Agent and Domain Controller Server information
- User and group information

Complete the following steps to back up your configuration:

Step 1. Log in to the Trend Micro InterScan for CSC SSM web management console and navigate to **Administration > Configuration Backup**.

Step 2. To back up the configuration, click the **Export** button under the Export InterScan SSM Settings into the Configuration File section. After you click the **Export** button, the configuration parameters are built into a compressed file. The default name of the configuration file is **config.tgz**; however, you can rename this file to any other filename while keeping the .tgz extension.

Note To import the backup configuration file, log in to the Trend Micro InterScan for CSC SSM web management console and navigate to **Administration > Configuration Backup**. Then click the **Browse** button under the **Import InterScan SSM Configuration File** section. A standard file browsing dialog box opens, which enables you to search for and select the configuration file to be imported. When you locate the file in the dialog box, click **Open**. Then click **Import**.

Upgrading the CSC SSM Software

Follow these steps to upgrade the Trend Micro InterScan for Cisco CSC SSM as new software becomes available:

Step 1. Download the new image to your local workstation.

Step 2. Log in to the Trend Micro InterScan for CSC SSM web management console and navigate to **Administration > Product Upgrade**.

Step 3. Click **Browse** to locate the upgrade files on your local drive. A standard file browsing dialog box opens, which enables you to search for and select the configuration file to be imported. When you locate the file in the dialog box, click **Open** and then click **Upload**.

Note The Installed Patches table shows the last version updates that have taken place in the system.

CLI Troubleshooting Tools

Earlier in this chapter, in the "Password Recovery" section, you learned how to log in to the CSC SSM CLI, using the Cisco ASA **session** command. The CSC SSM CLI has several troubleshooting tools that can be useful when trying to determine the root cause of certain problems you may encounter. When you log in to the CSC SSM CLI and select **Troubleshooting Tools** from the Trend Micro InterScan for Cisco CSC SSM Setup Main Menu, the options shown in Example 15-1 are displayed.

Example 15-1 *CSC SSM CLI Troubleshooting Tools*

```
                        Troubleshooting Tools
-----------------------------------------.


1. Enable Root Account
2. Show System Information
3. Gather Logs
4. Gather Packet Trace
5. Modify Upload Settings
6. Modify Management Port Console Access Settings
7. Return to Main Menu
```

To enable the root account, select **Enable Root Account** (number 1).

Caution Use the root account only under the supervision of Cisco TAC. Unauthorized modifications made through the root account are not supported and require that the device be reimaged to guarantee correct operation.

Select **Show System Information** (number 2) to display detailed system information, as shown in Example 15-2.

Example 15-2 *Troubleshooting Tools—Show System Information*

```
         Troubleshooting Tools - Show System Information
-------------------------------------------------------------
1. Show System Information on Screen
2. Upload System Information
3. Return to Troubleshooting Tools Menu
Enter a number [1-3]: 1
++++++++++++++++++++++
Thu Jul 30 18:22:16 UTC 2009 (0)
System is : Up
#@ Product Information
Trend Micro InterScan for Cisco CSC SSM
Version: 6.3.1172.0
Upgrade History: 6.2.1599.4 6.2.1599.5 6.2.1599.6 6.3.1172.0
Engineering Build:
SSM Model: SSM-10
SSM S/N: JAB101900KH
#@ Scan Engine and Pattern Information
Virus Scan Engine: 8.7.1004 (Updated: 2009-07-03 15:10:07)
Virus Pattern: 6.333.00 (Updated: 2009-07-30 18:17:17)
Spyware/Grayware Pattern: 0.807.00 (Updated: 2009-07-30 01:32:59)
AntiSpam Engine: 5.6.1016 (Updated: 2009-07-03 15:10:45)
AntiSpam Rule: 16796 (Updated: 2009-07-30 13:17:14)
IntelliTrap Pattern: 0.119.00 (Updated: 2009-07-08 09:10:11)
IntelliTrap Exception Pattern: 0.455.00 (Updated: 2009-07-28 04:17:13)
#@ License Information
Product:Base License
License profile host info check OK.
Version:Standard
Activation Code:PX-6ULS-LE8LQ-FQBMU-SM9VC-9KX3P-S5XDB
Seats:000500
Status:Activated
Expiration date:3/8/2010
Product:Plus License
License profile host info check OK.
Version:Standard
Activation Code:PX-YNDT-GZ2BE-FLJ8R-KLDXN-7MP9V-D5ENE
Status:Activated
Expiration date:3/8/2010
Daily Node Count: 0
Current Node Count: 0
```

```
#@ Kernel Information
Linux csc 2.6.17.8 #2 PREEMPT Sun Feb 1 08:37:18 PST 2009 i686 unknown
ASDP Driver 1.1(0) is UP:
         Total Connection Records: 159623
         Connection Records in Use: 0
         Free Connection Records: 159623
#@ Disk Information
Filesystem           1k-blocks      Used Available Use% Mounted on
/dev/hda2               227927    165353     50806  76% /mnt/rw
/dev/hda2               227927    165353     50806  76% /dev
/dev/hda2               227927    165353     50806  76% /etc
/dev/hda2               227927    165353     50806  76% /home
/dev/hda2               227927    165353     50806  76% /lib/modules
/dev/hda2               227927    165353     50806  76% /opt
none                    256000        80    255920   0% /opt/trend/isvw/temp
none                     50176       340     49836   1% /opt/trend/isvw/log
none                      4096         0      4096   0%
<...output truncated for brevity>
none                    126902         1    126901   0% /coredump
none                    126902        71    126831   0% /var
/dev/boot                 3776        25      3751   1% /boot
none                    126902       100    126802   0% /tmp
# Detail file listing:
#@ File Descriptor Information
file: 733        0        98926
inode: 9216        0
#@ Memory Information
# Detail (meminfo):
MemTotal:       1015216 kB
MemFree:         405016 kB
Buffers:          14256 kB
Cached:          231848 kB
SwapCached:           0 kB
Active:          459132 kB
Inactive:        118044 kB
HighTotal:       131072 kB
HighFree:           260 kB
LowTotal:        884144 kB
LowFree:         404756 kB
SwapTotal:            0 kB
SwapFree:             0 kB
Dirty:              360 kB
Writeback:            0 kB
Mapped:          359276 kB
```

```
Slab:            25528 kB
CommitLimit:    507608 kB
Committed_AS:  2004468 kB
PageTables:       3684 kB
VmallocTotal:   114680 kB
VmallocUsed:      1812 kB
VmallocChunk:   112736 kB
HugePages_Total:     0
HugePages_Free:      0
HugePages_Rsvd:      0
Hugepagesize:     4096 kB
# Reported to ASDM:
mem_unknown=61440
mem_cached=231848
mem_total=1015216
mem_est_free=546792
mem_buffers=14256
mem_free=405700
mem_used=468424
mem_tmpfs=43572
#@ Process Information
top - 18:22:20 up 26 days, 22:52,  2 users,  load average: 1.28, 1.40, 1.11
Tasks: 122 total,   3 running,  67 sleeping,   0 stopped,  52 zombie
Cpu(s):  1.2%us,  1.0%sy,  0.0%ni, 97.0%id,  0.7%wa,  0.0%hi,  0.0%si,  0.0%st
Mem:   1015216k total,  610200k used,  405016k free,   14256k buffers
Swap:        0k total,        0k used,        0k free,  231848k cached

  PID USER      PR  NI  VIRT  RES  SHR S %CPU %MEM    TIME+  COMMAND
26796 root      25   0  2380  516  432 R 96.6  0.1  16:34.06 more
  692 root      18   0  1988  876  652 R  2.0  0.1   0:00.01 top
    1 root      16   0  2364  520  444 S  0.0  0.1   0:37.10 init
    2 root      34  19     0    0    0 S  0.0  0.0   0:08.14 ksoftirqd/0
    3 root      10  -5     0    0    0 S  0.0  0.0   0:00.00 events/0
    4 root      10  -5     0    0    0 S  0.0  0.0   0:00.01 khelper
    5 root      11  -5     0    0    0 S  0.0  0.0   0:00.00 kthread
    7 root      10  -5     0    0    0 S  0.0  0.0   0:00.29 kblockd/0
    8 root      20  -5     0    0    0 S  0.0  0.0   0:00.00 kseriod
<...output truncated for brevity>
#@ Hardware Information
SSM-IPS10-K9
field 0x00 type 0x0040 CONTROLLER TYPE 1177
field 0x01 type 0x0041 HW REV 1.0
field 0x02 type 0x00CB PID ASA-SSM-CSC-10
field 0x03 type 0x0089 VID V01
```

```
field 0x04 type 0x0087 TOP 68 LEVEL PN 68-2731-01
field 0x05 type 0x0082 PCB 73 LEVEL PN 73-8935-05
field 0x06 type 0x0042 PCB REV 68.48
field 0x07 type 0x00C1 PCB SN JAB101900KH
field 0x08 type 0x00C2 CHASSIS SN JAB101900KH
field 0x09 type 0x0088 NEW DEVIATION NUM 0001455A
field 0x0A type 0x00C4 MFG TEST INFO 0000000000000000
field 0x0B type 0x0081 RMA NUM 00000000
field 0x0C type 0x0004 RMA HIST INFO 00
field 0x0D type 0x00C6 CLEI CODES
field 0x0E type 0x00DA DESC ASA 5500 Series Content Security Services Module-10
field 0x0F type 0x00C3 CHASSIS MAC ADDR 00:16:C7:9F:82:76
field 0x10 type 0x0043 MAC ADDR_BLK SZ 1
field 0x11 type 0x008C UNKNOWN TYPE 01000A00

#@ Ethernet Interface Information
cisco_asd Link encap:UNSPEC  HWaddr 00-00-00-00-00-00-00-00-00-00-00-00-00-00-00-00
          UP  MTU:1496  Metric:1
          RX packets:0 errors:0 dropped:0 overruns:0 frame:0
          TX packets:0 errors:0 dropped:0 overruns:0 carrier:0
          collisions:0 txqueuelen:0
          RX bytes:0 (0.0 B)  TX bytes:0 (0.0 B)
dummy0    Link encap:Ethernet  HWaddr 2E:F8:E2:3F:A0:E4
          BROADCAST NOARP  MTU:1500  Metric:1
          RX packets:0 errors:0 dropped:0 overruns:0 frame:0
          TX packets:0 errors:0 dropped:0 overruns:0 carrier:0
          collisions:0 txqueuelen:0
          RX bytes:0 (0.0 B)  TX bytes:0 (0.0 B)
eth0      Link encap:Ethernet  HWaddr 00:00:00:02:00:02
          UP BROADCAST RUNNING MULTICAST  MTU:1796  Metric:1
          RX packets:8703200 errors:0 dropped:0 overruns:0 frame:0
          TX packets:8693833 errors:0 dropped:0 overruns:0 carrier:0
          collisions:0 txqueuelen:1000
          RX bytes:558685567 (532.8 MiB)  TX bytes:558052663 (532.2 MiB)
          Base address:0xcc00 Memory:f8100000-f8120000
eth1      Link encap:Ethernet  HWaddr 00:16:C7:9F:82:76
          inet addr:192.168.3.2  Bcast:192.168.3.255  Mask:255.255.255.0
          UP BROADCAST RUNNING MULTICAST  MTU:1500  Metric:1
          RX packets:1098863 errors:0 dropped:0 overruns:0 frame:0
          TX packets:1501524 errors:0 dropped:0 overruns:0 carrier:0
          collisions:0 txqueuelen:1000
          RX bytes:425545954 (405.8 MiB)  TX bytes:1426235681 (1.3 GiB)
          Base address:0xbc00 Memory:f8200000-f8220000
eth2      Link encap:Ethernet  HWaddr 00:00:00:02:00:01
```

```
          inet addr:127.0.2.1  Bcast:127.0.255.255  Mask:255.255.0.0
          UP BROADCAST RUNNING MULTICAST  MTU:1500  Metric:1
          RX packets:3495967 errors:0 dropped:0 overruns:0 frame:0
          TX packets:1177211 errors:0 dropped:0 overruns:0 carrier:0
          collisions:0 txqueuelen:1000
          RX bytes:245153743 (233.7 MiB)  TX bytes:105737798 (100.8 MiB)
          Interrupt:169 Memory:f8300000-f8300fff
lo        Link encap:Local Loopback
          inet addr:127.0.0.1  Mask:255.255.255.255
          UP LOOPBACK RUNNING  MTU:16436  Metric:1
          RX packets:5458845 errors:0 dropped:0 overruns:0 frame:0
          TX packets:5458845 errors:0 dropped:0 overruns:0 carrier:0
          collisions:0 txqueuelen:0
          RX bytes:575949009 (549.2 MiB)  TX bytes:575949009 (549.2 MiB)
#@ Connection Information
sockets: used 68
TCP: inuse 23 orphan 0 tw 32 alloc 24 mem 3
UDP: inuse 3
RAW: inuse 0
FRAG: inuse 0 memory 0
Active Internet connections (only servers)
Proto Recv-Q Send-Q Local Address               Foreign Address             State
tcp        0      0 0.0.0.0:20000               0.0.0.0:*                   LISTEN
tcp        0      0 127.0.0.1:5060              0.0.0.0:*                   LISTEN
tcp        0      0 127.0.0.1:8005              0.0.0.0:*                   LISTEN
tcp        0      0 0.0.0.0:8009                0.0.0.0:*                   LISTEN
tcp        0      0 0.0.0.0:110                 0.0.0.0:*                   LISTEN
tcp        0      0 0.0.0.0:80                  0.0.0.0:*                   LISTEN
tcp        0      0 0.0.0.0:1812                0.0.0.0:*                   LISTEN
tcp        0      0 0.0.0.0:21                  0.0.0.0:*                   LISTEN
tcp        0      0 0.0.0.0:65014               0.0.0.0:*                   LISTEN
tcp        0      0 0.0.0.0:22                  0.0.0.0:*                   LISTEN
tcp        0      0 0.0.0.0:23                  0.0.0.0:*                   LISTEN
tcp        0      0 0.0.0.0:8888                0.0.0.0:*                   LISTEN
tcp        0      0 0.0.0.0:7000                0.0.0.0:*                   LISTEN
tcp        0      0 0.0.0.0:25                  0.0.0.0:*                   LISTEN
tcp        0      0 0.0.0.0:8443                0.0.0.0:*                   LISTEN
udp        0      0 127.0.0.1:10011             0.0.0.0:*
udp        0      0 127.0.0.1:33770             0.0.0.0:*
Active UNIX domain sockets (only servers)
Proto RefCnt Flags       Type       State         I-Node Path
unix  2      [ ACC ]     STREAM     LISTENING     5279775 /var/run/isv
unix  2      [ ACC ]     STREAM     LISTENING     5279777
/var/run/isvw/sssmtp.sock
```

```
unix  2      [ ACC ]     STREAM     LISTENING     5279791 /var/run/isvw/sspt-
nupdt.sock
unix  2      [ ACC ]     STREAM     LISTENING     5279778
/var/run/isvw/sspop3.sock
unix  2      [ ACC ]     STREAM     LISTENING     5279779
/var/run/isvw/ssfiletype.sock
unix  2      [ ACC ]     STREAM     LISTENING     1143198 /var/run/urlf.sock
unix  2      [ ACC ]     STREAM     LISTENING     1144281 /var/run/log.sock
unix  2      [ ACC ]     STREAM     LISTENING     1144283 /var/run/log.sock2
unix  2      [ ACC ]     STREAM     LISTENING     4794071 /dev/log
Active Internet connections (w/o servers)
Proto Recv-Q Send-Q Local Address           Foreign Address         State
tcp        0      0 127.0.2.1:23            127.0.1.1:1036          ESTABLISHED
tcp        1      0 127.0.0.1:54795         127.0.0.1:5060          CLOSE_WAIT
tcp        0      0 127.0.2.1:7000          127.0.1.1:1025          ESTABLISHED
tcp        0      0 192.168.3.2:8888        192.168.3.2:59750       ESTABLISHED
tcp       24      0 192.168.3.2:8443        10.116.126.242:3896     CLOSE_WAIT
tcp        0      0 192.168.3.2:59750       192.168.3.2:8888        ESTABLISHED
<...output truncated for brevity>
Active Internet connections (w/o servers)
Proto Recv-Q Send-Q Local Address           Foreign Address         State
udp        0      0 127.0.0.1:33771         127.0.0.1:33770         ESTABLISHED
#@ Routing Table
Kernel IP routing table
Destination     Gateway         Genmask         Flags   MSS Window  irtt Iface
192.168.3.0     0.0.0.0         255.255.255.0   U         0 0          0 eth1
127.0.0.0       0.0.0.0         255.255.0.0     U         0 0          0 eth2
0.0.0.0         192.168.3.1     0.0.0.0         UG        0 0          0 eth1
#@ Routing Cache
ian_src  out_hit out_slow_tot out_slow_mc  gc_total gc_ignored gc_goal_miss
gc_dst_overflow in_hlist_search out_hlist_search
000036b4  003451d3 00001f6a 00000000 00000000 00000000 00000000 00000000  00142878
0000ad4e 00000000 00000000 00000000 00000000 00000000 00000008 00003c3d
#@ Failover Status
Failover is disabled
#@ Procfs Status
This is only available in export mode due to the amount of info.
+++++++++++++++++++++
Press Enter to continue ...
```

The output of the Show System Information in Example 15-2 displays detailed system information, such as the following:

- General product information
- Scan engine and pattern information

- License information
- Kernel details
- System disk details
- Detailed file listing
- Detailed memory usage and information
- Detailed system process information
- Hardware details
- Ethernet interface information
- Connection information
- Routing table
- Routing cache
- Failover status

The output of Show System Information can also be compiled into a text file. This output or file can be very useful while troubleshooting problems with the assistance of the Cisco TAC.

To gather and create a temporary file with all log entries in the CSC SSM, select **Gather Logs** under the Troubleshooting Tools menu, as shown in Example 15-3.

Example 15-3 *Troubleshooting Tools—Gather Logs*

```
                         Troubleshooting Tools
--------------------------------------------------------------------------.
1. Enable Root Account
2. Show System Information
3. Gather Logs
4. Gather Packet Trace
5. Modify Upload Settings
6. Modify Management Port Console Access Settings
7. Return to Main Menu
Enter a number from [1-7]: 3
                Troubleshooting Tools - Gather Logs
--------------------------------------------------------------------------.
Gather logs now? [y¦n] y
Gathering logs ...
Creating temporary file CSCSSM-LOG-20090730-184337.tar.gz
Uploading temporary file CSCSSM-LOG-20090730-184337.tar.gz
Uploading file ...
```

In Example 15-3, a temporary file named **CSCSSM-LOG-20090730-184337.tar.gz** is created and uploaded to a preconfigured FTP or TFTP server. To configure the FTP or TFTP server information, select **Modify Upload Settings.** Your FTP or TFTP server must be set up to enable uploading. When you enter **5** (**Modify Upload Settings**), the following prompts appear:

```
Troubleshooting Tools - Upload Settings
---------------------------------------
Choose a protocol [1=FTP 2=TFTP]: (default:1) 2
Enter TFTP server IP: (default:10.2.42.134)
Enter TFTP server port: (default:69)
Saving Upload Settings: OK
Press Enter to continue...
```

Respond to the prompts to configure the upload settings. The settings are saved for future use. When you are finished, enter 7, **Return to Main Menu.**

> **Note** The **Gather Packet Trace** function is now obsolete. Please use the **capture** command in the Cisco ASA CLI for the **asa_dataplane** interface. The configuration of the capture command is covered is Chapter 3, "System Maintenance."

To modify management port console access settings, select the **Modify Management Port Console Access Settings** option. The output of the Troubleshooting Tools—Management Port Console Access Settings menu is shown in Example 15-4.

Example 15-4 *Troubleshooting Tools—Management Port Console Access Settings*

```
Troubleshooting Tools - Management Port Console Access Settings
---------------------------------------
Current Telnet Access : Disabled
Current SSH Access    : Disabled
Modify Telnet Setting [1=Enable 2=Disable]: (default:2) 2
Modify SSH Setting [1=Enable 2=Disable]: (default:2) 1
Saving Management Port Console Access Settings: OK
Press Enter to continue ...
```

Select **1** to enable the respective management protocol, at each prompt, or **2** to disable it.

Summary

This chapter covered information about monitoring your CSC SSM to enable you to detect and take action on viruses, worms, Trojans, and other security threats. Additionally, different troubleshooting tips and administrative tasks were covered.

Chapter 16

Site-to-Site IPSec VPNs

This chapter covers the following topics:

- Preconfiguration checklist
- Configuration steps
- Advanced features
- Optional features
- Deployment scenarios
- Monitoring and troubleshooting

Corporations continuously expand their operations by adding remote offices. These offices need network connectivity back to the corporate network for data transfer and resource access. Network administrators must evaluate the security policies of an enterprise to develop secure channels to connect all remote offices. This includes selecting not only the proper network hardware platforms but also the appropriate WAN technology to interconnect the branch and small offices. Some point-to-point WAN technologies include Frame Relay, Integrated Services Digital Network (ISDN), and Asynchronous Transfer Mode (ATM). Though these technologies do provide connectivity between locations, they are not very cost effective. Corporations look for ways to cut costs for increased profitability.

Network professionals can reduce the high maintenance cost of point-to-point WAN links by using the IPSec VPN tunnel in site-to-site mode. They can use broadband connections, including digital subscriber line (DSL) or cable modem, to achieve Internet connectivity at a considerably cheaper rate, and then they can deploy IPSec VPN on top of that to connect the remote locations to the central site. This enables them to accomplish the following goals in a cost-effective manner:

- Internet access for clear-text traffic
- Intranet connectivity over a secure VPN tunnel

This chapter focuses on configuring, deploying, monitoring, and troubleshooting site-to-site IPSec tunnels on the Cisco Adaptive Security Appliances. It discusses a preconfiguration checklist, configuration steps, and different design scenarios. This chapter also discusses how to monitor the IPSec site-to-site tunnel to make sure that the traffic is flowing flawlessly. If the IPSec VPN is having connectivity issues, the chapter provides extensive troubleshooting help later in this chapter.

Preconfiguration Checklist

As discussed in the VPN section of Chapter 1, "Introduction to Security Technologies," IPSec can use Internet Key Exchange (IKE) for key management and tunnel negotiation. IKE uses a combination of different Phase 1 and Phase 2 attributes that are negotiated between the peers. If any one of the attributes is misconfigured, the IPSec tunnel fails to establish. It is therefore highly recommended that security professionals understand the importance of a preconfiguration checklist and discuss it with other network administrators in case the far end of the VPN tunnel is managed by a different organization.

Table 16-1 lists all the possible values of Phase 1 attributes that are supported by Cisco ASA. It also includes the default values for each attribute. Highlighting the options and parameters that will be configured on the other end of the VPN tunnel is recommended.

Table 16-1 *ISAKMP Attributes*

Attribute	Possible Value	Default Value
Encryption	DES 56-bit 3DES 168-bit* AES 128-bit AES 192-bit AES 256-bit	3DES 168-bit or DES 56-bit, if 3DES feature is not active
Hashing	MD5 or SHA-1	SHA-1
Authentication method	Preshared keys RSA signature Crack**	Preshared keys
DH group	Group 1 768-bit field Group 2 1024-bit field Group 5 1536-bit field Group 7 ECC 163-bit field***	Group 2 1024-bit field
Lifetime	120 seconds - unlimited	86,400 seconds

*For 3DES and AES encryption, you must have a VPN-3DES-AES feature set–enabled license key.

** Crack (Challenge/Response for Authenticated Cryptographic Keys) is an IKE Challenge/Response mechanism for Authenticated Cryptographic Keys protocol for mobile IPSec-enabled clients. Using CRACK, you can avoid the deployment of PKI on the client and only the VPN server needs a certificate.

*** Cisco ASA has deprecated support for DH group 7 in version 8.2 or higher.

In addition to the IKE parameters, the two IPSec devices also negotiate the mode of operation. Cisco ASA uses main mode as the default mode for the site-to-site tunnels, but it can use aggressive mode if set up accordingly. After discussing Phase 1 attributes, it is important to highlight Phase 2 attributes for the IPsec VPN connection. The Phase 2 security associations (SAs) are used to encrypt and decrypt the actual data traffic. These SAs are also referred as the IPSec SAs. Table 16-2 lists all the possible Phase 2 attributes and their default values, offered by Cisco ASA.

After you determine what Phase 1 and Phase 2 attributes to use, you are ready to configure the site-to-site tunnel.

Table 16-2 *IPSec Attributes*

Attribute	Possible Value	Default Value
Encryption	None DES 56-bit 3DES 168-bit* AES 128-bit AES 192-bit AES 256-bit	3DES 168-bit or DES 56-bit, if 3DES feature is not active
Hashing	MD5, SHA-1 or None	None
Network information	IP protocol, Network/Subnet information and/or port number	No default parameter
Lifetime	120–2,147,483,647 seconds 10–2,147,483,647 KB	28,800 seconds 4,608,000 KB
Mode	Tunnel or transport	Tunnel
PFS group	None Group 1 768-bit DH prime modulus Group 2 1024-bit DH prime modulus Group 5 1536-bit DH prime modulus Group 7 ECC 163-bit field**	None

* For 3DES and AES encryption, you must have a VPN-3DES-AES feature set–enabled license key.

** Cisco ASA has deprecated support for DH group 7 in version 8.2 or higher.

Note Advanced Encryption Standard (AES) is a relatively new standard developed by two Belgian cryptographers—Joan Daemen and Vincent Rijmen. AES is expected to replace the aging Data Encryption Standard (DES), which is commonly implemented by the IPSec vendors.

It is a best practice to use AES encryption over DES for enhanced security. Make sure that both IPSec devices support AES before implementing it.

Configuration Steps

There are many ways to set up a static site-to-site tunnel through Cisco ASDM. We emphasize a configuration method that gives you the most control and flexibility in defining a secure connection. This method uses seven configuration steps for successfully defining a site-to-site IPSec tunnel:

Step 1. Enable ISAKMP.

Step 2. Create ISAKMP policy.

Step 3. Set the tunnel type.

Step 4. Define the IPSec policy.

Step 5. Configure the crypto map.

Step 6. Configure traffic filtering (optional).

Step 7. Bypass NAT (optional).

The alternative configuration methods present simple configuration steps; however, they do not offer a lot of control when you need to define specific attributes. The alternative configuration methods are also discussed later in this chapter.

Figure 16-1 illustrates a network topology for SecureMe, Inc. It has two locations: one in Chicago and one in New York. We use the security appliance in Chicago to demonstrate how a site-to-site tunnel can be configured.

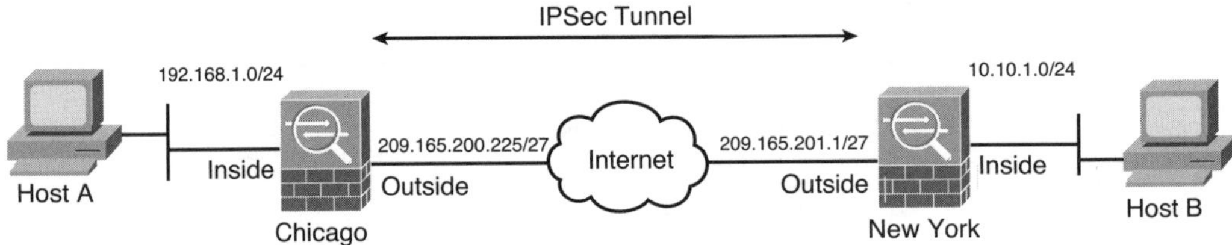

Figure 16-1 *IPSec Topology for SecureMe Inc.*

Step 1: Enable ISAKMP

IKE Phase 1 configuration starts by enabling ISAKMP on the interface that terminates the VPN tunnels. Typically, it is enabled on the Internet-facing or the outside interface. If ISAKMP is not enabled on an interface, then the security appliance does not listen for the ISAKMP traffic (UDP port 500) on that interface. So even if you have a fully configured IPSec tunnel and ISAKMP is not enabled on the outside interface, the security appliance does not respond to a tunnel initialization request.

Navigate to **Configuration > Site-to-Site VPN > Connection Profiles** and select the **Allow Access** option next to the interface where you want to terminate the sessions, typically the outside interface. To push this configuration to the security appliance, click the **Apply** button in ASDM.

> **Note** When ASDM delivers the commands to enable ISAKMP on an interface, it also pushes down two ISAKMP policies (policy number 5 and 10) that are preconfigured in ASDM. ISAKMP policies are discussed in the next section

Example 16-1 illustrates the command line interface (CLI) output if you want to enable ISAKMP on the outside interface.

Example 16-1 *Enabling ISAKMP on the Outside Interface*

```
Chicago(config)# crypto isakmp enable outside
```

> **Note** IPSec VPN functionality is not available if the Cisco ASA is virtualized. If site-to-site tunnels are required, then the Cisco ASA has to be set up in single mode. This functionality is being considered for future software releases.
>
> There are certain limitations on Cisco ASA's VPN feature if transparent firewall mode is enabled. Review Chapter 9, "Transparent Firewalls," for additional details.

Step 2: Create the ISAKMP Policy

After you enable ISAKMP on the interface, create a Phase 1 policy that matches the other end of the VPN connection. Phase 1 policy negotiates the encryption and other parameters that are useful in authenticating the remote peer as well as establishing a secure channel for both VPN peers to use for communication.

To configure a new ISAKMP policy in the security appliance, navigate to **Configuration > Site-to-Site VPN > Advanced > IKE Policies** and click **Add.** ASDM launches a new window where you can specify the following attributes:

- **Priority**—A number between 1 and 65535. By default, ASDM has priority number 5 and 10 preconfigured. If multiple ISAKMP policies are configured, the Cisco ASA checks the ISAKMP policy with the lowest priority number first. If there is no match, it checks the policy with the next priority number, and so on until all policies have been evaluated. A priority value of 1 is evaluated first, and a priority value of 65535 is evaluated in the last.

- **Encryption**—Select the appropriate encryption type from the drop-down list. Refer to Table 16-1 for all the supported encryption types. Cisco ASA employs a dedicated hardware encryption accelerator to process IKE requests. It is recommended that you select AES 256-bit encryption because the performance impact is pretty much the same as using a weaker encryption algorithm such as DES.
- **Hash**—Select the appropriate hash type from the drop-down list. A hashing algorithm provides data integrity by verifying that the packet has not been changed in transit. You have the option to use SHA-1 or MD5. It is recommended to use SHA-1 because it provides better security than MD5.
- **Authentication**—Select the appropriate authentication type from the drop-down list. The authentication mechanism establishes the identity of the remote IPSec peer. You can use Preshared keys for authenticating a small number of IPSec peers, whereas RSA signatures are useful if you are authenticating a large number of peers. Chapter 18 discusses RSA signatures in detail.
- **D-H Group**—Select the appropriate D-H group from the drop-down list. D-H group is used to derive a shared secret to be used by the two VPN devices.
- **Lifetime**—Specify the lifetime within which a new set of ISAKMP keys can be renegotiated. You can specify a finite lifetime between 120 and 2147483647 seconds. You can also select unlimited lifetime in case the remote peer does not propose a lifetime. Cisco recommends that you use the default lifetime of 86400 seconds for IKE rekeys.

Figure 16-2 shows that an ISAKMP policy of priority 1 is being added. The encryption method is AES-256, the hashing algorithm is SHA, the authentication mechanism is preshared keys, the D-H group is 2, and the lifetime of 86400 seconds is specified.

> **Note** If the VPN-3DES-AES feature is not enabled, the security appliance allows DES encryption for only the ISAKMP and IPSec policies.

If you prefer the CLI, use the **crypto isakmp policy** command to define a new policy. Example 16-2 illustrates how to configure an ISAKMP policy for AES-256 encryption, SHA hashing, DH group 2, and preshared keys for authentication with 86,400 seconds as the lifetime.

Example 16-2 *Creating an ISAKMP Policy*

```
Chicago(config)# crypto isakmp policy 1
Chicago(config-isakmp-policy)# authentication pre-share
```

```
Chicago(config-isakmp-policy)# encryption aes-256
Chicago(config-isakmp-policy)# hash sha
Chicago(config-isakmp-policy)# group 2
Chicago(config-isakmp-policy)# lifetime 86400
```

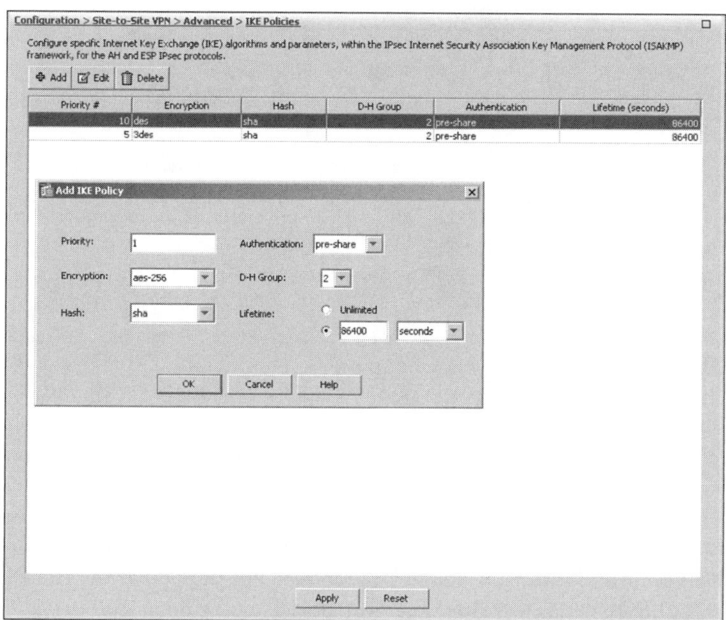

Figure 16-2 *Defining IKE Policy via ASDM*

> **Note** If one of the ISAKMP attributes is not configured, the security appliance adds that attribute with its default value. To remove an ISAKMP policy, use the **clear config crypto isakmp policy** command, followed by the policy number to be removed.

Step 3: Set Up the Tunnel Groups

A tunnel group, also known as *connection profile*, defines a site-to-site or a remote-access tunnel and is used to map the attributes that are assigned to a specific IPSec peer. The remote-access connection profile is used to terminate all types of remote access VPN tunnels such as IPSec, L2TP over IPSec, and SSL VPN. Remote-access VPNs are discussed in Chapters 17, 19, and 20.

You can configure a tunnel group by choosing **Configuration > Site-to-Site VPN > Advanced > Tunnel Groups.** Click **Add** to specify a new tunnel group name. As shown in Figure 16-3, a tunnel group called **209.165.201.1** has been added.

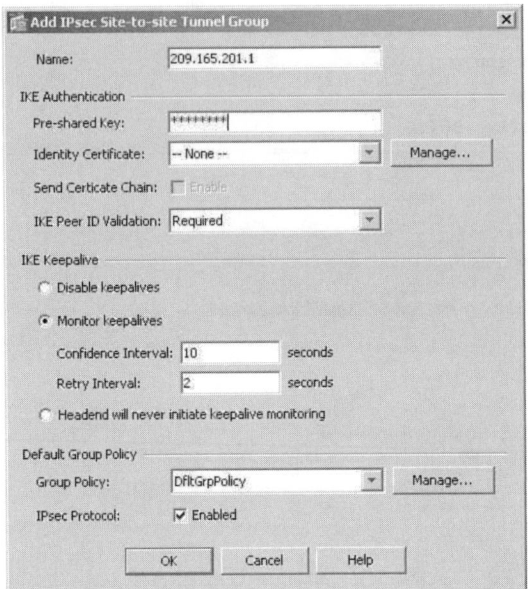

Figure 16-3 *Configuration of a Tunnel Group*

For the site-to-site IPSec tunnels, the IP address of the remote VPN device is used as the tunnel group name. For an IPSec device whose IP address is not defined as the tunnel group, the security appliance tries to map the remote device to the default site-to-site group called **DefaultL2LGroup**, given that the preshared key between the two devices matches. DefaultL2LGroup is shown in the ASDM configuration, but if you look at the configuration via CLI, it does not appear unless a default attribute within that tunnel group is modified.

Note The concept of a tunnel group is taken from the VPN 3000 Series Concentrators.

If your ISAKMP policy uses preshared keys as the authentication method, a preshared key must be configured under the tunnel group. It is recommended that you configure a long alphanumeric key with special characters. It will be hard to decode a complex preshared key even if someone tries to break it by using brute force. In Figure 16-3, a preshared key of **C!$cOK3y** (obfuscated) is set up for the **209.165.201.1** tunnel group.

Example 16-3 illustrates how to configure a site-to-site tunnel group on Cisco ASA if the peer's public IP address is **209.165.201.1**. You define the preshared key under the ipsec-attributes of the tunnel group by using the **pre-shared-key** command.

Example 16-3 *Tunnel Group Definition*

```
Chicago(config)# tunnel-group 209.165.201.1 type ipsec-l2l
Chicago(config)# tunnel-group 209.165.201.1 ipsec-attributes
Chicago(config-tunnel-ipsec)# pre-shared-key C!$c0K3y
```

Tip The security appliance obfuscates the preshared key in the configuration for security reasons. If you really want to view the key, copy the running configuration to the flash and then view that configuration by using the **more** command, as follows:

```
Chicago# show running | inc pre-shared-key
 pre-shared-key *
Chicago# copy running-config disk0:/config.cfg
Source filename [running-config]?
Destination filename [config.cfg]?
Cryptochecksum: 546a2d4a 5b6b8ede a4a709aa 0738da96

9198 bytes copied in 3.440 secs (3066 bytes/sec)
Chicago# more disk0:/config.cfg | inc pre-shared-key
 pre-shared-key C!$c0K3y
```

Step 4: Define the IPSec Policy

An IPSec transform set specifies what type of encryption and hashing to use for the data packets after a secure connection has been established. This provides data authentication, confidentially, and integrity. The IPSec transform set is negotiated during Quick Mode, discussed in Chapter 1. To configure a new transform set through ASDM, navigate to **Configuration > Site-to-Site VPN > Advanced > IPsec Transform Sets** and click **Add.** A new window opens, enabling you to configure the following attributes:

- **Set Name**—Specify the name for this transform set. This name has local significance and is not transmitted during IPSec tunnel negotiations.
- **Encryption**—Select the appropriate encryption type from the drop-down list. Refer to Table 16-2 for all the supported encryption types. Cisco ASA employs a dedicated hardware encryption accelerator to process data encryption and hashing. It is recommended that you select AES 256-bit encryption because the performance impact is pretty much the same as using a weaker encryption algorithm such as DES.
- **Hash**—Select the appropriate hash type from the drop-down list. A hashing algorithm provides data integrity by verifying that the packet has not been changed in transit. You have the option to use SHA-1, MD5, or None. It is recommended to use SHA-1 because it provides better security than MD5.

- **Mode**—Select the appropriate encapsulation mode from the drop-down list. You have the option to use transport or tunnel mode. Transport is used to encrypt and authenticate the data packets that are originated by the VPN peers. Tunnel mode is used to encrypt and authenticate the IP packets when they are originated by the hosts connected behind the VPN device. In a typical site-to-site IPsec connection, tunnel mode is always used.

In Figure 16-4, a new transform set called **NY-AES256SHA** is being defined. It is set up to use AES-256 encryption and SHA hashing for data packets. The encapsulation mode is defined as tunnel.

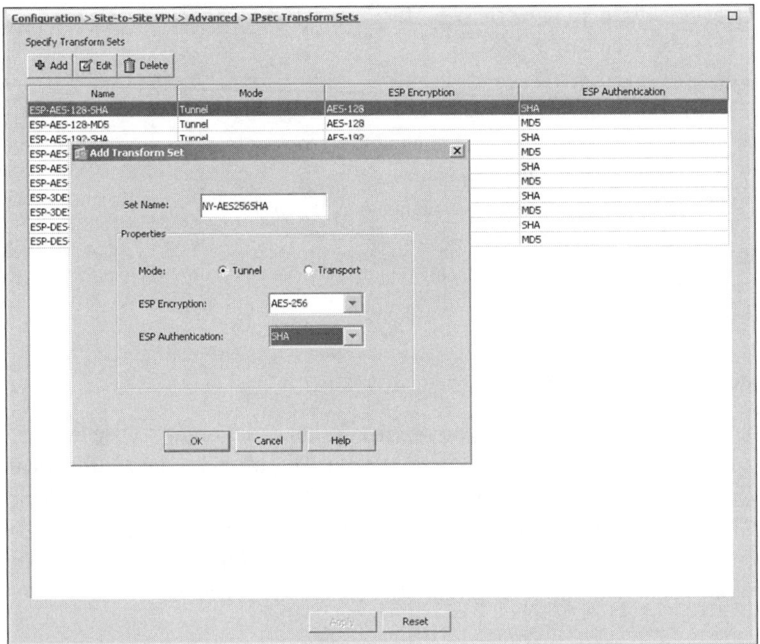

Figure 16-4 *Configuring IPSec Transform Set*

Note Cisco ASA supports only ESP as the encapsulation protocol. Support for AH currently is not planned.

Example 16-4 shows how an IPSec transform set can be configured through the CLI.

Example 16-4 *Transform Set Configuration*

```
Chicago(config)# crypto ipsec transform-set NY-AES256SHA esp-aes-256 esp-sha-hmac
```

Note Cisco ASDM has ten predefined IPSec transform sets. You do not have to define a new transform set if you want to use a predefined transform set.

Step 5: Create a Crypto Map

After you have configured both Phase 1 and Phase 2 policies, create a crypto map so that these policies can be applied to a static site-to-site IPsec connection. A crypto map instance is considered complete when it has the following three parameters:

- At least one transform set
- At least one VPN peer
- An encryption ACL

Crypto map uses a priority number (or sequence number) to define an IPSec instance. Each IPSec instance defines a VPN connection to a specific peer. You can have multiple IPSec tunnels destined to different peers. If the security appliance terminates an IPSec tunnel from another VPN peer, a second VPN tunnel can be defined, using the existing crypto map name with a different priority number. Each priority number uniquely identifies a site-to-site tunnel. However, the security appliance evaluates the site-to-site tunnel with the lowest priority number first.

Note Cisco ASA does not support manual keying for IPSec tunnels. Manual keying is vulnerable to security flaws because the VPN peers always use the same encryption and authentication keys.

To define a new crypto map, navigate to **Configuration** > **Site-to-Site VPN > Advanced > Crypto Maps**, click **Add** to specify a new map. A new window is launched, enabling you to configure the following attributes:

- **Interface**—You must select an interface that terminates the IPSec site-to-site tunnel. As mentioned earlier, it is usually the Internet-facing interface. You can apply only one crypto map per interface. If there is a need to configure multiple site-to-site tunnels, you must use the same crypto map with different priority numbers. Please consult deployment scenario 2, "Fully Meshed Topology with RRI," later in this chapter for an example of multiple crypto map priority numbers.
- **Policy Type**—If the remote IPSec peer has a static IP address, select **Static** from the drop-down menu. For a remote static peer, the local security appliance can initiate as well as respond to an IPSec tunnel request. A "dynamic" policy type is useful if the remote peer receives a dynamic IP address on its outside interface. In this scenario, where the peer is marked as dynamic, it is the peer's responsibility to initiate the VPN connection; it cannot be initiated by the hub.

- **Priority**—You must specify the priority number for this site-to-site connection. If multiple site-to-site connections are defined for a particular crypto map, Cisco ASA checks the connection with the lowest priority number first. A priority value of 1 is evaluated first; priority value of 65535 is evaluated last.
- **Transform Sets**—Select a predefined transform set from the drop-down menu. You can select multiple transform sets. In this case, the security appliance sends all the configured transform sets to its peer if it is initiating the connection. If the security appliance is responding to a VPN connection from the peer, it matches the received transform sets with the locally configured transform sets and chooses one to utilize for the VPN connection. You can add up to 11 transform sets here.
- **Connection Type**—If you want either VPN peers to initiate an IPSec tunnel, select Bidirectional from the drop-down menu. For the other option, refer to the "Connection Type" section under "Modifying Default Parameters" later in this chapter.
- **IP Address of Peer to Be Added**—Specify the IP address of the remote VPN peer. Typically, it is the public IP address of the remote VPN device.
- **Enable Perfect Forward Secrecy**—If you want to enable perfect forward secrecy (PFS), enable this option and specify the Diffie-Hellman group you want to use. For more information on PFS, consult it under the "Advanced Features" section later in this chapter.

In Figure 16-5, a new crypto map is being defined with a priority number of **10**. This crypto map is marked as **static**, and the **outside** interface is designated as the VPN termination point. The IPSec transform set, defined in the previous step, is mapped to this map, whereas the remote VPN peer's public IP address is **209.165.201.1**. If the security appliance needs to initiate a tunnel, it will contact the remote VPN peer, using this IP address.

As mentioned earlier, a crypto map is not complete until you define an ACL for the interesting traffic that needs to be encrypted. When a packet enters the security appliance, it gets routed based on the destination IP address. When it leaves the interface, which is set up for a site-to-site tunnel, the encryption engine intercepts that packet and matches it against the encryption access control entries (ACE) to determine whether it needs to be encrypted. If a match is found, the packet is encrypted and then sent out to the remote VPN peer.

An ACL can be as simple as permitting all IP traffic from one network to another or as complicated as permitting traffic originating from a unique source IP address on a particular port destined to a specific port on the destination address.

Note The IPSec connection between Cisco ASA and other vendors may or may not work because Cisco adheres to IPSec industry standards and other vendors may have their own implementation of the standards.

Additionally, deploying complicated crypto ACLs, using TCP or UDP ports, is not recommended. Many IPSec vendors do not support port-level encryption ACLs.

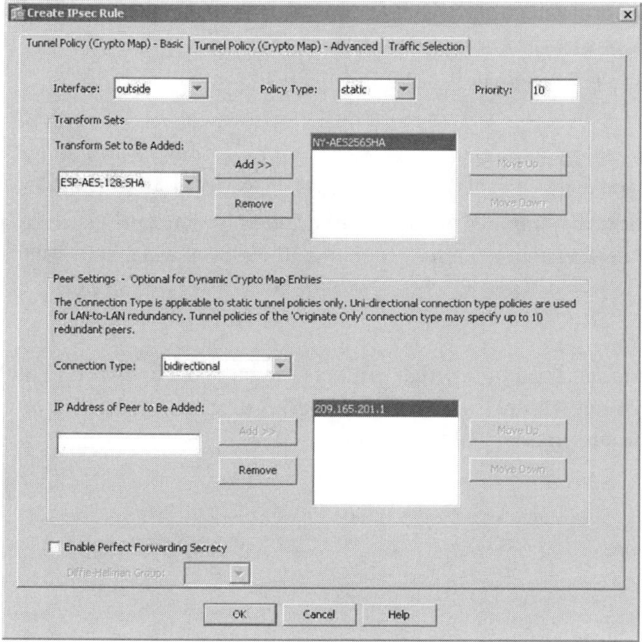

Figure 16-5 *Defining a New Crypto Map*

To create a new encryption ACL, select the **Traffic Selection** tab in the crypto map window, to specify the private networks that you want to encrypt. The required attributes in an encryption ACL are as follows:

- **Action**—Select the action, either **Protect** or **Do Not Protect**, for the traffic matching this ACE. If traffic is protected, the ASA encrypts it.
- **Source**—Specify the source host IP, network, and object-group. This is the private host or network address of the security appliance.
- **Destination**—Specify the destination host IP, network, object-group. This is the private host or network address of the remote VPN peer.
- **Service**—Specify the destination service name such as TCP, UDP, SMTP, HTTP. In a site-to-site IPSec VPN tunnel, the destination service typically includes all IP services.

Note For more details on the arguments used in an access control entry, consult Table 4-2 in Chapter 4, "Controlling Network Access."

Encryption ACLs also perform a security check for the inbound encrypted traffic. If a clear-text packet matches one of the encryption ACEs, the security appliance drops that packet and generates a syslog message indicating this incident.

Note Each ACE creates two unidirectional IPSec SAs. If you have 100 entries in your ACL, then the ASA creates 200 IPSec SAs. Using host-based encryption ACEs is not recommended because that results in a number of ACEs and eventually double the number of SAs. The security appliance uses system resources to maintain the SAs, which may affect overall performance.

Figure 16-6 shows a traffic selection policy that protects (or encrypts in this case) all IP traffic from 192.168.1.0/24 network to 10.10.1.0/24 subnet. A description of **ACL to encrypt traffic from Chicago to NY** is added as well.

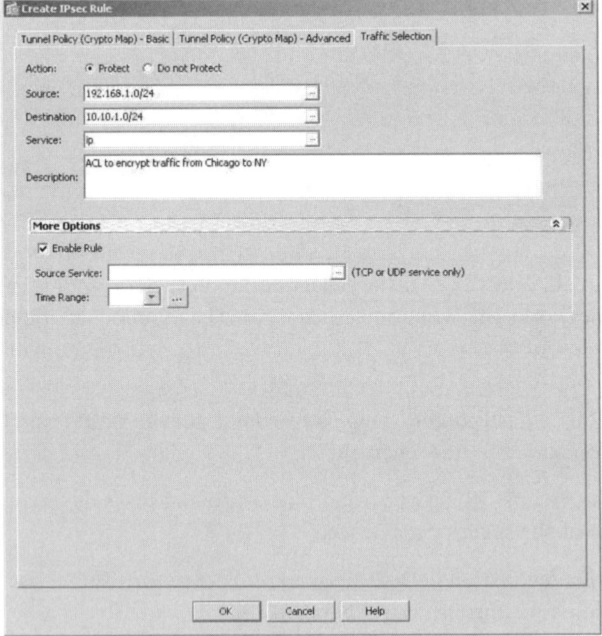

Figure 16-6 *Defining an Encryption ACL Within Crypto Map*

After a crypto map has been added to ASDM, you may add another ACE to this crypto map by clicking the pull-down **Add** list and selecting **Insert Traffic Selection After** option. ASDM launches another window where you can select the private networks to be included in the encryption ACL.

Example 16-5 shows the Chicago ASA is set up to protect all IP traffic sourced from **192.168.1.0** with a mask of **255.255.255.0** and destined to **10.10.1.0** with a mask of **255.255.255.0**. The ACL name is **outside_cryptomap_10**.

Example 16-5 *Crypto Map Configuration*

```
Chicago# configure terminal
Chicago(config)# access-list outside_cryptomap_10 remark ACL to encrypt traffic
  from Chicago to NY
Chicago(config)# access-list outside_cryptomap_10 extended permit ip 192.168.1.0
  255.255.255.0 10.10.1.0 255.255.255.0
Chicago(config)# crypto map outside_map 10 match address outside_cryptomap_10
Chicago(config)# crypto map outside_map 10 set peer 209.165.201.1
Chicago(config)# crypto map outside_map 10 set transform-set NY-AES256SHA
Chicago(config)# crypto map outside_map interface outside
```

The security appliance does not allow IP traffic from the remote private network to connect directly to the ASA's inside interface. Many enterprises prefer to manage the security appliance using its inside interface from the management network using the VPN connection. You can configure this feature by using the **management-access** command, discussed later in this chapter.

Step 6: Configure Traffic Filtering (Optional)

Like a traditional firewall, the Cisco ASA can protect the trusted (inside) network by blocking new inbound connections from the outside, unless the ACL explicitly permits these connections. However, by default, the security appliance allows all inbound connections from the remote VPN network to the inside network without an ACL explicitly allowing them. What that means is that even if the inbound ACL on the outside interface denies the decrypted traffic to pass through, the security appliance still allows it.

This default behavior can be changed if you want the outside interface ACL to inspect the IPSec protected traffic. In Figure 16-7, if Host B is allowed to send traffic only to Host A on TCP port 23, you must

Step 1. Define an inbound ACE on the Chicago ASA outside interface ACL

Step 2. Disable the vpn sysopt feature that allows new inbound connections initiated from over the VPN to bypass all access list checks.

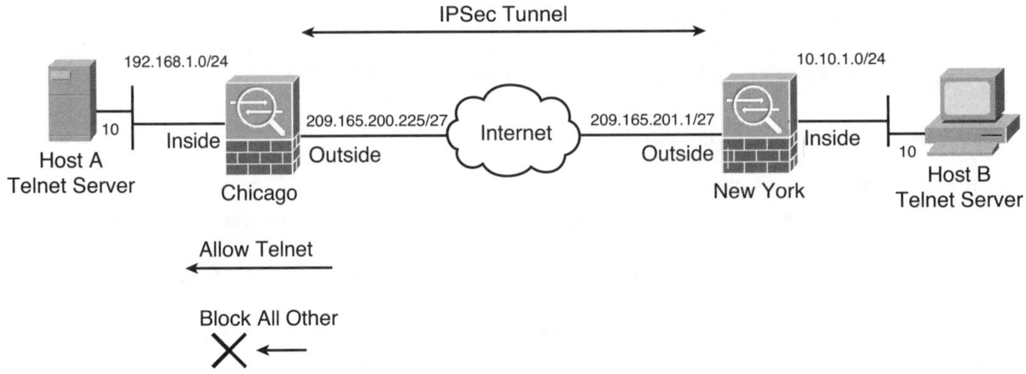

Figure 16-7 *Filtering Traffic Across a VPN Tunnel*

This way, the inbound VPN traffic on port 23 from Host B to Host A is inspected by the interface ACL and then allowed in.

The CLI configuration is illustrated in Example 16-6. The outside ACL allows traffic from a remote host 10.10.1.10 to go to a local host 192.168.1.10 on TCP port 23. The **no sysopt connection permit-vpn** command enables the security appliance to subject all new inbound connections through the firewall to the configured interface access lists.

Example 16-6 *Access List to Allow Decrypted Traffic to Pass Through the ASA*

```
Chicago(config)# access-list outside_acl extended permit tcp host 10.10.1.10 host
  192.168.1.10 eq 23
Chicago(config)# access-group outside_acl in interface outside
Chicago(config)# no sysopt connection permit-vpn
```

Note The **sysopt connection permit-vpn** command is a global command. It is enabled by default and allows the security appliance to bypass the ACL check for all the VPN tunnels, including remote access IPSec as well as SSL VPN tunnels. You can still control traffic by defining authorization access lists on group policies and user policies.

Using ASDM, disable vpn sysopt by navigating to **Configuration > Site-to-Site VPN > Advanced > System Options** and deselecting the Enable Inbound IPSec Sessions to Bypass Interface Access-Lists option.

Step 7: Bypass NAT (Optional)

In most cases, you do not want to change the IP addresses for the traffic going over the tunnel. If NAT is configured on the security appliance to change the source or destination IP addresses for non-VPN traffic, you can set up the NAT exempt rules to bypass address translation for traffic destined over the VPN tunnels, as discussed in Chapter 4.

To bypass address translation, you must identify traffic that needs to go over the VPN tunnel and then apply the NAT exemption rule. Using ASDM, navigate to **Configuration > Firewall > NAT Rules > Add**, select **Add NAT Exempt Rule** and specify the following information:

- **Action**—Select the Exempt radio button.
- **Interface**—Select the inside interface or the interface that you are protecting with the VPN tunnel.
- **Source**—Specify the local protected network/subnet information.
- **Destination**—Specify the remote protected network/subnet information.
- **NAT Exempt Direction**—Select NAT Exempt Outbound Traffic from Interface Inside to Lower Security Interfaces.
- **Description**—Specify a brief description.

Figure 16-8 shows a NAT exempt policy for the traffic originated from 192.168.1.0/24 to 10.10.1.0/24 on the inside interface.

Example 16-8 shows the CLI version of the NAT Exempt Policy for IPSec Encryption. The ACL is called **inside_nat0_outbound.**

Example 16-8 *Access List to Bypass NAT*

```
Chicago(config)# access-list inside_nat0_outbound remark NAT Exempt Policy for
  IPSec Encryption
Chicago(config)# access-list inside_nat0_outbound extended permit ip 192.168.1.0
  255.255.255.0 10.10.1.0 255.255.255.0
Chicago(config)# nat (inside) 0 access-list inside_nat0_outbound
```

Note If you do not define a NAT exemption policy and NAT is done for VPN traffic, then the crypto ACL should match the post-NAT (or global) IP addresses.

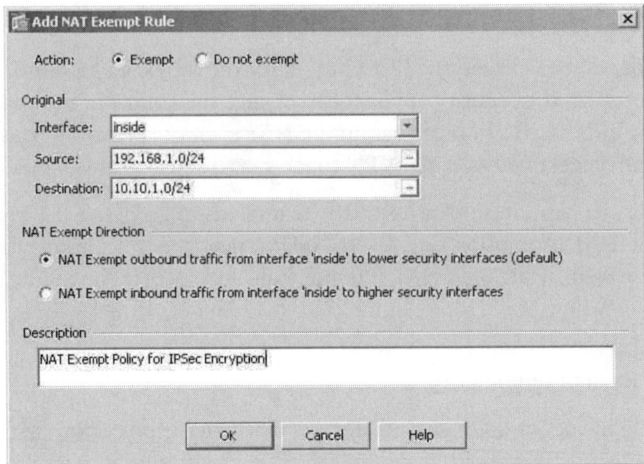

Figure 16-8 *NAT Exempt Policy to Bypass NAT for IPSec Tunnel*

Alternate Configuration Methods Through ASDM

There are two additional methods by which you can define the site-to-site tunnels. These alternate methods are available if you configure the security appliance through ASDM. They include:

- IPSec Wizard
- Connection Profiles

Defining Site-to-Site Tunnel Through IPSec VPN Wizard

The simplest and easiest way to define a new site-to-site connection is by following the IPSec VPN wizard. You can launch the wizard by clicking **Wizards** in the toolbar and then selecting **IPSec VPN Wizard.** ASDM launches the VPN Wizard with the option to choose a VPN tunnel type. Follow these steps to successfully define the site-to-site tunnel:

Step 1. Select **Site-to-Site** radio button.

Because the remote peer of the site-to-site VPN tunnel resides toward the appliance's outside interface, select **outside** from the drop-down menu in the VPN Tunnel Interface field. Make sure that the Enable Inbound IPsec Sessions to Bypass Interface Access option is enabled to bypass ACL check for the decrypted traffic. Click **Next** to move to the Remote Site Peer window.

Step 2. Specify Peer Information.

In the next window, the VPN wizard prompts you to specify peer information, such as its public IP address and ISAKMP authentication method. Using Figure 16-1 for illustration purposes, the public IP address of the appliance in New York is **209.165.201.1**. Use this IP address in the **Peer IP Address** field. The Tunnel Group Name is also auto-populated with the same IP address. Under **Pre-shared Key as the Authentication Method**, specify **C!$cOK3y.** Click **Next** to move to the IKE Policy window.

Step 3. Select the IKE policy.

Select the appropriate IKE policy for this peer. Use **AES-256** for encryption, **SHA** for authentication, and **DH group 5** for key generation to match the configuration with the remote peer. Click **Next** to move to the IPSec Encryption and Authentication window.

Step 4. Set up the IPSec transform set.

You configure the IPSec transform set by selecting an encryption and authentication algorithm. Use **AES-256** for encryption and **SHA** for hash authentication to match with the configuration of the remote IPSec peer. Do not enable perfect forwarding secrecy (PFS). Click **Next** to move to the Local and Remote Hosts and Networks window.

Step 5. Identify local and remote networks.

Select the hosts/subnets or networks to be used as the local and remote proxies during the IPSec negotiation. The appliance recognizes all the local and remote networks, if their routes are in the routing table. You can click the **...** button to see a list of the local networks. Optionally, you may manually add an address in the IP Address field with the appropriate subnet mask. For the local network, specify **192.168.1.0/24**, and for the remote network, specify **10.10.1.0/24.** Leave the Exempt ASA Side Host/Network from Address Translation box checked to bypass address translation. Click **Next to** verify your configuration. If all parameters look accurate, click **Finish** to complete the VPN Wizard.

Defining a Site-to-Site Tunnel Through Connection Profile

You can also define a Site-to-Site tunnel by adding a new connection profile. First navigate to **Configuration > Site-to-Site VPN > Connection Profiles** and enable **Allow Access** on the outside interface under the Access Interfaces option. Click **Add** under **Connection Profiles** to define a new Site-to-Site tunnel. ASDM opens a new window where you can specify the following attributes:

- **Peer IP Address**—Specify the public IP address of the remote VPN device. In most Site-to-Site implementation, you a static IP addresses assigned to the remote VPN device. If this is the case, then make sure that the Static box is checked. If the remote

VPN peer receives its IP address dynamically, then uncheck the Static box. The Peer IP address box is grayed out if Static box is unchecked.

- **Connection Name**—If the static box is checked and you have an IP address defined in the Peer IP Address box, then by default the connection name is the same as the peer IP address box in the static box. If the static box is not enabled, then you can specify a name for this connection in this box.
- **Interface**—Select the interface that terminates the IPSec tunnel. In most cases, this is the outside interface of the security appliance.
- **Pre-shared key**—Pre-shared keys remain the most commonly used IKE authentication method in the IPSec Site-to-Site tunnels. If you prefer to use preshared keys as the authentication method, specify a key in this box.
- **Identity Certificate**—If you would rather use certificates as the IKE authentication method, select an identity certificate from the drop-down menu. Chapter 18,"Public Key Infrastructure (PKI)," covers PKI and certificates in detail.
- **Local Network**—Select the local network you want to protect by this site-to-site tunnel.
- **Remote Network**—Select the remote network you want to protect by this site-to-site tunnel.
- **IKE Proposal**—By default, ASDM selects all the configured IKE proposals in this box. You can manage (edit, add or remove) IKE proposals by clicking the **Manage** button.
- **IPsec Proposal**—By default, ASDM shows and selects all the IPSec transform sets. You can select one or more transform sets for an IPSec connection.

After you have all the information specified, click **OK** to push the configuration to the security appliance. As shown in Figure 16-9, the peer's IP address is **209.165.201.1** and the connection is terminated on the **outside** interface. A preshared key of **C!$cOK3y** is defined as the IKE authentication method. The local network is **192.168.1.0/24**, and the remote network of **10.10.1.0/24** is also defined. The IKE and IPSec proposals are **pre-share-aes-256-sha** and **NY-AES256SHA**, respectively.

Advanced Features

Cisco ASA provides many advanced features to suit your site-to-site VPN implementations. These features include the following:

- OSPF updates over IPSec
- Reverse route injection
- NAT Traversal (NAT-T)
- Tunnel default gateway
- Management Access
- Perfect Forward Secrecy (PFS)

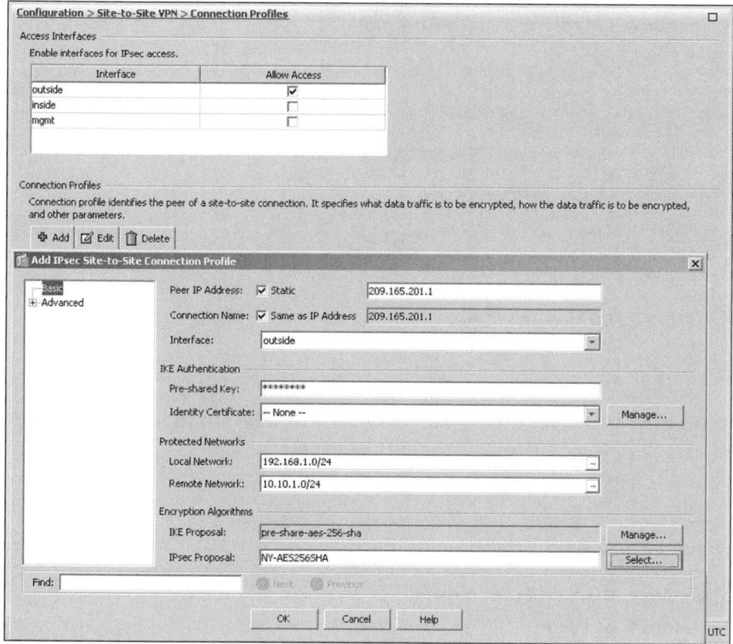

Figure 16-9 *Site-2-Site IPSec Definition via Connection Profile*

OSPF Updates over IPSec

As discussed in Chapter 5, "IP Routing," Open Shortest Path First (OSPF) uses the multicast methodology to communicate with its neighbors. IPSec, on the other hand, does not allow encapsulation of the multicast traffic. Cisco ASA solves this problem by enabling you to statically define the neighbors so that unicast OSPF packets can be sent to the remote VPN peer. Refer to Chapter 5 for in-depth coverage of the OSPF neighbor feature.

To enable the security appliance to send the OSPF routing updates over a site-to-site IPsec tunnel, follow these steps:

Step 1. Designate the outside interface (or any IPSec terminating interface) as a non-broadcasting interface. Navigate to **Configuration > Device Setup > Routing > OSPF > Interface > Properties** tab, select the **outside** interface, click **Edit** and uncheck the **Broadcast** option.

Step 2. Statically add the remote VPN device as an OSPF neighbor. Browse to **Configuration > Device Setup > Routing > OSPF > Static Neighbor > Add** and select the OSPF process you are using in your network. Specify your IPSec peer's public address and select the VPN terminating interface. Figure 16-10 illustrates a remote VPN ASA (**209.165.201.1**) being added as a static OSPF neighbor for OSPF process **100**. The OSPF neighbor is located toward the **outside** interface.

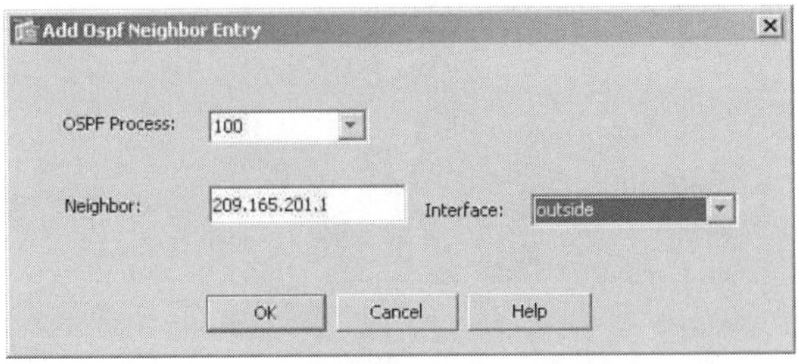

Figure 16-10 *OSPF Updates over IPSec*

Example 16-9 shows how to set up the outside interface as a nonbroadcast media and specify the remote VPN peer as the OSPF neighbor on the outside interface.

Example 16-9 *OSPF Updates over IPSec*

```
Chicago(config)# interface GigabitEthernet0/0
Chicago(config-if)# nameif outside
Chicago(config-if)# security-level 0
Chicago(config-if)# ip address 209.165.200.225 255.255.255.224
Chicago(config-if)# ospf network point-to-point non-broadcast
Chicago(config)# router ospf 100
Chicago(config-router)# network 209.165.200.225 255.255.255.255 area 0
Chicago(config-router)# neighbor 209.165.201.1 interface outside
```

Note The OSPF Update over IPSec feature works only between two Cisco security appliances.

Reverse Route Injection

Reverse route injection (RRI) is a way to distribute remote network information into the local network with the help of a routing protocol. With RRI, the Cisco ASA automatically adds static routes about the remote private networks across the tunnel to its routing table and then announces these routes to its neighbors on the local private network, using OSPF. Figure 16-11 shows an IPSec topology that uses OSPF to propagate the remote private network information into the local LAN of the Chicago ASA.

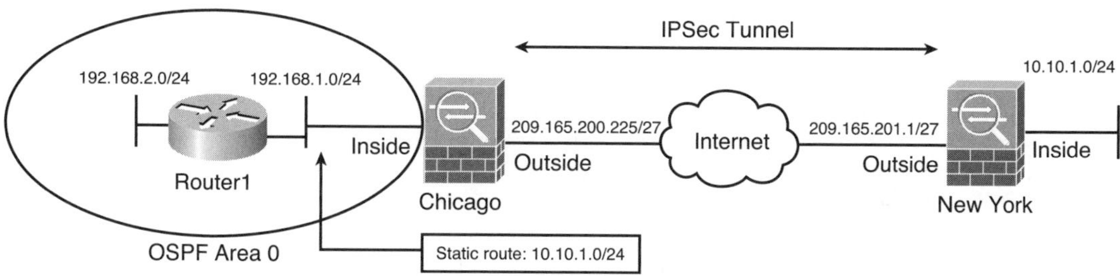

Figure 16-11 *Example of RRI in the ASA*

To configure RRI through ASDM, modify the crypto map properties by navigating to **Configuration > Site-to-Site VPN > Advanced > Crypto Maps**. Select your previously configured crypto map, edit its properties, and then select **Enable Reverse Route Injection** under the **Tunnel Policy (Crypto Map)-Advanced** tab.

Example 16-10 illustrates a crypto map called **outside_cryptomap_10**, set up to use RRI.

Example 16-10 *Configuration of Reverse Route Injection*

```
Chicago(config)# crypto map outside_cryptomap_10 10 set reverse-route
```

To check whether the ASA is adding the remote network information in its routing table, type **show route**, as illustrated in Example 16-11.

Example 16-11 *Routing Table on the ASA*

```
Chicago# show route
S     0.0.0.0 0.0.0.0 [1/0] via 209.165.200.226, outside
C     192.168.1.0 255.255.255.0 is directly connected, inside
C     209.165.200.224.0 255.255.255.224 is directly connected, outside
S     10.10.1.0 255.255.255.0 [1/0] via 209.165.200.226, outside
```

If you see the static route for the remote private network in the routing table, advertise the static route to the OSPF peers. You can do that within ASDM by browsing to

Configuration > Device Setup > Routing > OSPF > Redistribution > Add, selecting the OSPF process you are using, choosing **Static** under the Protocol option, and then selecting the **Use Subnets** option. Example 16-12 illustrates the same steps using the CLI.

Example 16-12 *OSPF Configuration on the ASA*

```
Chicago(config)# router ospf 100
Chicago(config-router)# redistribute static subnets
```

The internal router (Router1) will receive this route and install it in its routing table, as demonstrated in Example 16-13.

Example 16-13 *Routing Table on Internal Router*

```
Router1# show ip route
C     192.168.1.0/24 is directly connected, Ethernet0
C     192.168.2.0/24 is directly connected, FastEthernet0
O E2 10.10.1.0/24 [110/20] via 192.168.1.1, 00:00:03, Ethernet0
```

NAT Traversal

Traditionally, the IPSec tunnels fail to pass traffic if there is a PAT device between the peers. By default, IPSec devices use the ESP protocol, which does not have any Layer 4 information and therefore the PAT device ends up dropping the IPSec packet.

Note Consult Chapter 1 for more information on ESP through PAT implementations.

To remedy this problem, Cisco drafted an IETF standard called NAT Traversal (NAT-T) to encapsulate the ESP packets into a UDP port connection on port 4500 so that any intermediate PAT device would have no trouble translating the encrypted packets. NAT-T is dynamically negotiated if the following two conditions are met:

- Both VPN peers are NAT-T-capable
- There is a NAT or PAT device between the peers

If both conditions are met, VPN peers start their communication using ISAKMP (UDP port 500), and as soon as a NAT or PAT device is detected, switch to UDP port 4500 to complete the rest of their negotiations.

NAT-T is globally enabled on the security appliance by default. In many cases, the NAT/PAT devices time out the NAT-T encrypted connection on UDP port 4500 entries if there is no active traffic passing through them. NAT-T keepalives are used so that the security appliance can send periodic keepalive messages to prevent the entries from timing out on the intermediary devices. You can specify a NAT-T keepalive range between 10 and 3600 seconds with a default keepalive timeout of 20 seconds.

If NAT-T is not enabled for some reason, you can enable it by navigating to **Configuration > Site-to-Site VPN > Advanced > IKE Parameters** and then checking the **Enable IPSec over NAT-T** option. If NAT-T is globally enabled, and you do not want one of the peers to negotiate it, you can navigate to **Configuration > Site-to-Site VPN > Advanced > Crypto Maps**. Select your previously configured crypto map, edit its properties, and then disable the **Enable NAT-T** option under the **Tunnel Policy (Crypto Map)-Advanced** tab.

Example 16-14 illustrates how NAT-T is globally enabled with keepalives sent every 30 seconds in the CLI. It also illustrates how NAT-T can be disabled for a particular VPN peer that uses sequence number 10.

Example 16-14 *Disabling NAT-T for a Peer*

```
Chicago(config)# crypto isakmp nat-traversal 30
Chicago(config)# crypto map outside_map 10 set nat-t-disable
```

Tunnel Default Gateway

A Layer 3 device typically has a default gateway that it uses to route packets when the destination address is not found in its routing table. Tunnel default gateway, a concept first introduced in the VPN3000 concentrators, is used to route the packets if they reach the security appliance over an IPSec tunnel and if their destination IP address is not found in the routing table. The tunneled traffic can be either remote access or site-to-site VPN traffic. The tunnel default gateway next-hop address is generally the IP address of the inside router, Router1 (illustrated in Figure 16-11), or any Layer 3 device.

The tunnel default gateway feature is important if you do not want to define routes to your internal networks on the Cisco ASA and you rather want the tunneled traffic to be sent to the internal router for routing.

To set up a tunnel default gateway, navigate to **Configuration > Device Setup > Routing > Static Routes > Add**. A new window appears where you can add a default route with the gateway IP being the next-hop IP address of the inside route (Router1). Make sure that you enable the **Tunneled** radio button, as shown in Figure 16-12.

If you prefer to use the CLI, make sure that you add the keyword **tunneled** to the statically configured default route. Example 16-15 shows the configuration of the appliance with the tunnel default gateway specified as 192.168.1.2, located on the inside interface.

Example 16-15 *Tunnel Default Gateway Configuration*

```
Chicago(config)# route inside 0.0.0.0 0.0.0.0 192.168.1.2 tunneled
```

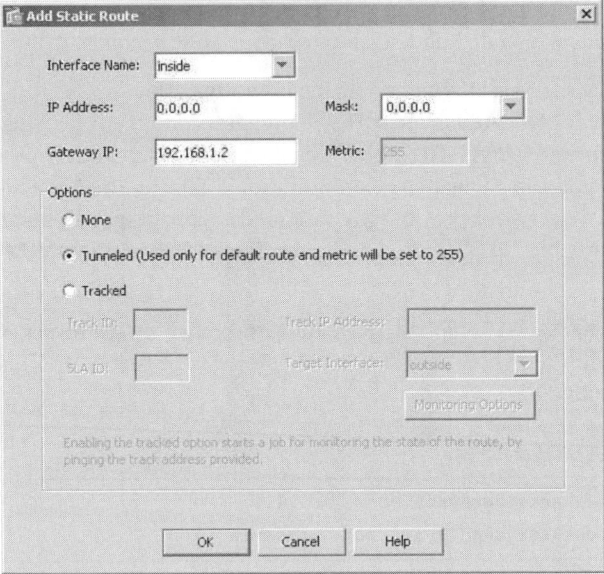

Figure 16-12 *Defining a Tunnel Default Gateway*

Note Before you implement the default route tunneled option, you must understand the current restrictions:

- You cannot enable unicast RPF on the egress interface of tunneled route.
- You cannot enable TCP intercept on the egress interface of the tunneled route.
- Many VoIP inspection engines (such as H.323, GTP, MGCP, RTSP, SIP, SKINNY), the DNS inspect engine, and the DCE RPC inspection engine ignore the tunneled route.
- You can define only one default route with the tunneled option.

Management Access

As briefly mentioned earlier in the chapter, Cisco ASA does not allow the remote private network to manage the security appliance if

- The traffic traverses over a VPN tunnel.
- The traffic accesses the inside (or any interface other than the interface through which the VPN traffic entered the firewall) of the security appliance.

This is true even if the inside interface's IP address is included in the encryption ACL. Many enterprises want to monitor the status of the inside interface over the tunnel to check the appliance's health. To solve this, enable the "Management Access" feature on the inside interface of the appliance. With this feature turned on, remote devices can use management applications such as SNMP polls, ASDM, Telnet, SSH, ping, HTTPS requests access, syslog messages, and NTP requests.

Enable the feature by browsing to **Configuration > Device Management > Management Access > Management Interface** and selecting the inside (or any other) interface from the drop-down menu. You can also enable this feature through the CLI by using the **management-access** command followed by the name of the interface. In Example 16-16, the **inside** interface is being set up for management access.

Example 16-16 *Management Access on the Inside Interface*

```
Chicago(config)# management-access inside
```

Note You can make only one interface the management access interface.

Perfect Forward Secrecy

Perfect Forward Secrecy (PFS) is a cryptographic technique where the newly generated keys are unrelated to any previously generated key. With PFS enabled, the security appliance generates a new set of keys that are used during the IPSec Phase 2 negotiations. Without PFS, the Cisco ASA uses Phase 1 keys in the Phase 2 negotiations. The Cisco ASA uses Diffie-Hellman group 1, 2, and 5 for PFS to generate the keys. Diffie-Hellman group 1 uses a 768-bit modulus size to generate the keys, whereas group 2 uses 1024 bits and group 5 uses a 1536-bits modulus size. Group 5 is the most secure technique but requires more processing overhead.

To configure PFS through ASDM, browse to **Configuration > Site-to-Site VPN > Advanced > Crypto Maps**. Select your previously configured crypto map, edit its properties, and then enable the **Enable Perfect Forwarding Secrecy** option. Specify a Diffie-Hellman group you want to use for this tunnel. As shown in Figure 16-13, a DH group 5 is used for the PFS option in the crypto map.

Example 16-17 illustrates how to enable PFS group 5 for a peer that uses sequence number 10, using the CLI.

Example 16-17 *Configuring PFS Group 5 for a Peer*

```
Chicago(config)# crypto map outside_map 10 set pfs group5
```

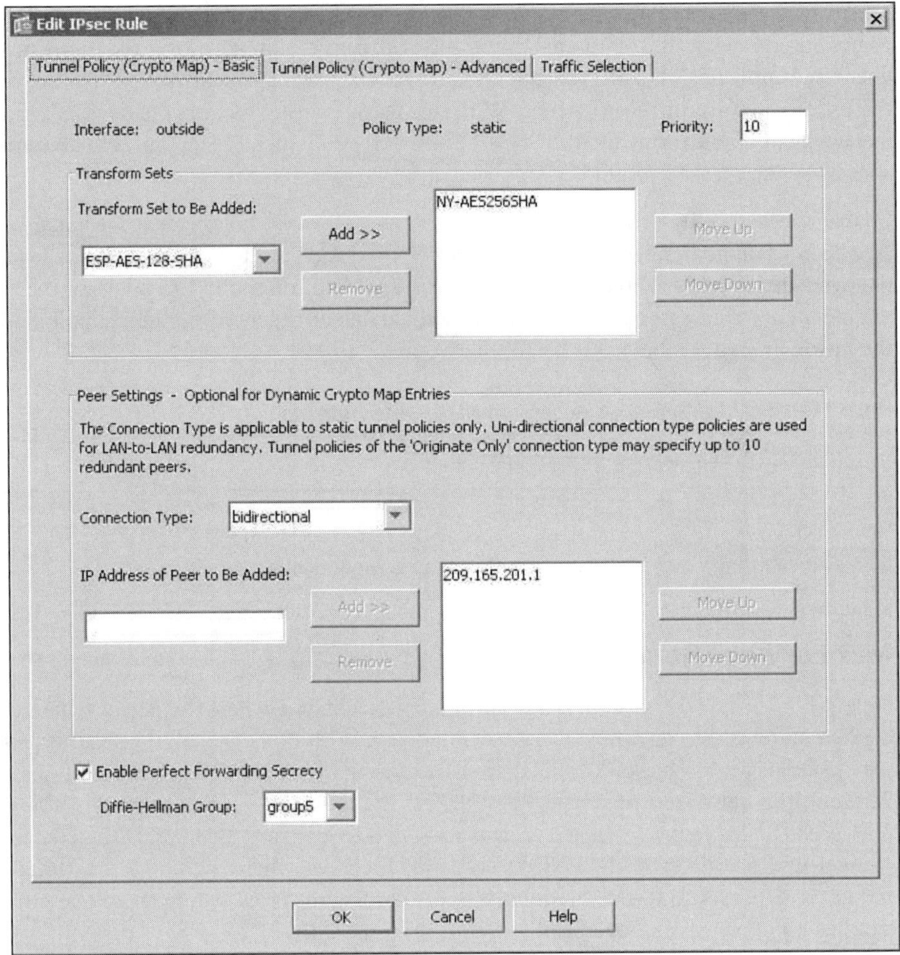

Figure 16-13 *Enabling PFS for a Tunnel*

Modifying Default Parameters

In addition to the advanced features discussed in the preceding section, you can optionally tweak many default parameters to optimize the site-to-site connections. This section discusses these parameters:

- Security association lifetimes
- Phase 1 mode
- Connection type
- ISAKMP keepalives
- IPSec and packet fragmentation

Security Association Lifetimes

IPSec security association lifetimes specify when the IPSec peers should renegotiate a new pair of data encryption keys. If you do not specify the IPSec security association lifetimes, the Cisco ASA uses the default values of 28,800 seconds or 4,275,000 KB. Like NAT-T, the IPSec security association lifetimes can be set either globally or per crypto map instance. ASDM, however, does not allow you to configure the global values of security association lifetimes. You must use the CLI to modify the global default values.

To modify the default IPSec SA lifetimes for a specific crypto map instance, navigate to **Configuration > Site-to-Site VPN > Advanced > Crypto Maps.** Select your previously configured crypto map, edit its properties, and then specify the new values of the IPSec SA lifetime under the **Tunnel Policy (Crypto Map)-Advanced** tab. You may want to set lifetime values shorter, such as 4 hours, so that your data encryption keys are negotiated more often. It is useful in those scenarios where you are transferring very confidential and crucial data and you want to regenerate new keys often. You can also modify the IPSec SA volume lifetime in kilobytes so that it negotiates new keys when a specific amount of data has been encrypted by the current keys.

Figure 16-14 illustrates how to modify the IPSec SA lifetime. The current encryption key will expire in either 14,400 seconds (4 hours) or 2,500,000 kilobytes, whichever comes first.

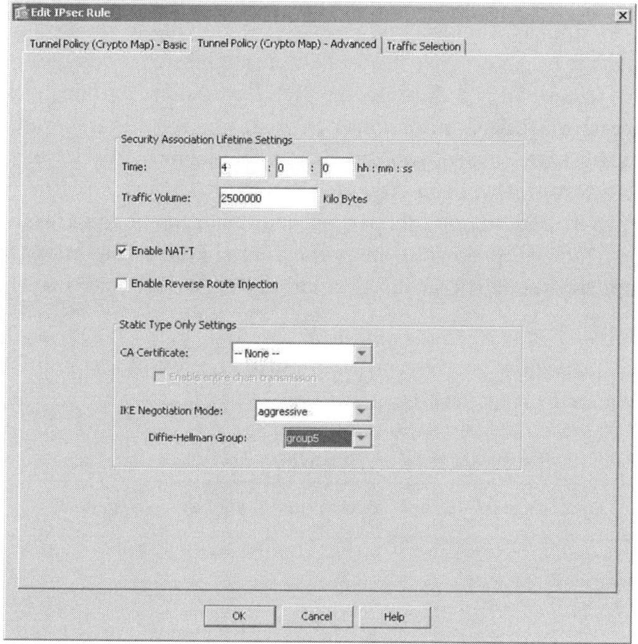

Figure 16-14 *Changing IPSec SA Timeout*

Example 16-18 illustrates, using the CLI, how to set the IPSec SA to expire in either 14,400 seconds (4 hours) or 2,500,000 kilobytes, whichever comes first.

Example 16-18 *Configuring PFS Group 5 for a Peer*

```
Chicago(config)# crypto map outside_map 10 set security-association lifetime kilo
  bytes 2500000 seconds 14400
```

Lifetime in seconds can vary between 120 and 2,147,483,647, and lifetime in kilobytes can range from 10 to 2,147,483,647 KB. To configure IPSec SA lifetime globally, use the following CLI syntax:

```
crypto ipsec  security-association lifetime
```

After you specify both security-association lifetime values (in kilobytes and seconds), they appear as separate CLI commands in the configuration.

Phase 1 Mode

ISAKMP implementation in Cisco ASA, by default, uses main mode for Phase 1 negotiations. If the remote VPN peer initiates a site-to-site tunnel using aggressive mode, the security appliance responds back to the tunnel request in aggressive mode. Aggressive mode has some security weaknesses, so it is recommended to use main mode where possible. This is why the security appliance allows you to disable it globally if you do not want to accept connections that use aggressive mode. Disable aggressive mode by browsing to **Configuration > Site-to-Site VPN > Advanced > IKE Parameters** and unchecking the **Disable Inbound Aggressive Mode Connections** option. If you would rather initiate Phase 1 negotiations using aggressive mode, you can change the default behavior by navigating to **Configuration > Site-to-Site VPN > Advanced > Crypto Maps**, selecting your previously configured crypto map, editing its properties, and then selecting **aggressive** under the **IKE Negotiation Mode** drop-down menu in the **Tunnel Policy (Crypto Map)-Advanced** tab. You must specify the Diffie-Hellman group to be used for initiating the aggressive mode request.

Figure 16-14 and Example 16-19 show you how you can use aggressive mode with DH group 5 to initiate IKE requests.

Example 16-19 *Enabling Aggressive Mode for Crypto Map*

```
Chicago(config)# crypto map outside_map 10 set phase1-mode aggressive group5
```

Connection Type

The Cisco ASA in the site-to-site tunnel can respond to as well as initiate a VPN connection. This bidirectional default behavior can be changed to answer-only or originate-only mode. For example, if you want to limit the security appliance to just initiate IKE tunnels and never respond to a tunnel request, you can set the connection type to **originate-only.** This way, if the remote VPN peer tries to initiate the connection, the local appliance will not honor the request. Similarly, if you want the security appliance to accept IKE tunnels only from the peer, then you can set the connection type to **answer-only.**

Note If you need to specify multiple peers in your crypto map sequence number for redundancy, you must set your connection type to **originate-only** mode.

You can change the connection type by navigating to **Configuration > Site-to-Site VPN > Advanced > Crypto Maps**, selecting your previously configured crypto map, editing its properties, selecting the **Tunnel Policy (Crypto Map) - Basic** tab and then changing the **Connection Type** to either **originate-only** or **answer-only.** Figure 16-15 illustrates that Chicago ASA's connection type is set up as **originate-only** for the peer **209.165.201.1.**

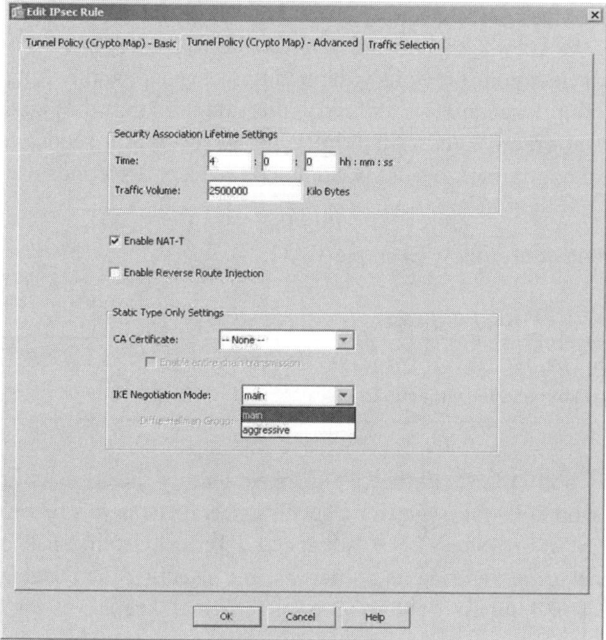

Figure 16-15 *Changing Connection Type*

Example 16-20 illustrates Chicago ASA's connection type as set up, using the CLI, as **originate-only** for a peer that uses sequence number 10.

Example 16-20 *Configuring Connection Type to Originate-Only for a Peer*

```
Chicago(config)# crypto map outside_map 10 set connection-type originate-only
```

ISAKMP Keepalives

The ISAKMP keepalives feature is a way to determine whether the remote VPN peer is still reachable or there are any lingering SAs (SAs that do not get cleared properly). By default, Cisco ASA starts sending Dead Peer Detection (DPD) packets after it stops receiving encrypted traffic over the tunnel from the peer. If it does not hear from its peer for 10 seconds (confidence interval), it sends out a DPD R_U_THERE packet. It keeps sending the R_U_THERE packets every 2 seconds (the retry interval). If it does not receive R_U_THERE_ACK for four consecutive DPDs polling periods, the security appliance deletes the corresponding ISAKMP and IPSec SAs.

You can also tweak the keepalive parameters to suit your needs. If you have an unreliable connection to the remote VPN peer, you may want to increase the keepalive timer so that it does not timeout the SAs because of connection issues. To change the default IKE keepalive values through ASDM, browse to **Configuration > Site-to-Site VPN > Advanced > Tunnel Groups**, select your previously defined tunnel group, and edit its properties. Specify the new confidence interval and retry interval in seconds. In Figure 16-16, if the Cisco ASA does not receive encrypted traffic for 30 seconds, it sends out the first DPD packet. It is also configured to send periodic DPDs every 3 seconds if it fails to get an ACK.

To change the IKE keepalive timeout, follow Example 16-22.

Example 16-22 *Changing ISAKMP Keepalives*

```
Chicago(config)# tunnel-group 209.165.201.1 ipsec-attributes
Chicago(config-ipsec)# isakmp keepalive threshold 30 retry 3
```

Some non-Cisco vendors may not understand the DPD packets sent by the security appliance. If you do not want to send DPD messages for a specific peer, disable this feature by navigating to **Configuration > Site-to-Site VPN > Advanced > Tunnel Groups**, selecting your previously defined tunnel group, editing its properties, and selecting the **Disable Keepalives** option. Example 16-23 illustrates how to disable ISAKMP keepalives for peer 209.165.201.1.

Example 16-23 *Disabling ISAKMP Keepalives*

```
Chicago(config)# tunnel-group 209.165.201.1 ipsec-attributes
Chicago(config-ipsec)# isakmp keepalive disable
```

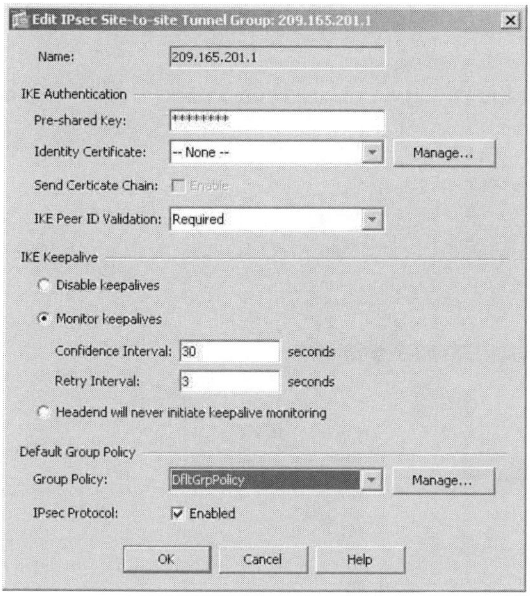

Figure 16-16 *Changing IKE Keepalive Timeout*

IPSec and Packet Fragmentation

The outbound maximum transmission unit (MTU) of an Ethernet interface is typically 1500 bytes. As discussed in Chapter 1, IPSec appends headers when it encrypts the data packets. Therefore, when an original packet is the same size or larger than the outbound interface's MTU, then the packet must be fragmented so that IPSec can successfully add its headers. Most of the VPN devices perform fragmentation after encryption. Therefore, the other end of the VPN tunnel is responsible for defragmenting and decrypting the packet. The problem with this approach is that packet reassembly is typically done at the processer level, which utilizes extra CPU cycles for this additional task. If the packets are fragmented before they are encrypted, then the other side of the tunnel is responsible only for decrypting the packets, and the destination host will be responsible for defragmenting them. Thus you save the CPU overhead of defragmentation on the security appliance by delegating this task to the end hosts.

The Cisco security appliance, by default, allows fragmentation to occur before packets are encrypted. However, if the do-not-fragment (DF) bit is set on the packets, the security appliance retains the DF-bit and the original packet does not get fragmented. Therefore, if large packets with the DF-bit set try to pass through the security appliance, they are dropped. This may be something you do not want in your network.

To change the default behavior, browse to **Configuration > Site-to-Site VPN > Advanced > IPsec Prefragmentation Policies**, select the VPN terminating interface (usually the outside interface), edit the attribute values, and select **Clear** under the "DF Bit Setting Policy."

Figure 16-17 illustrates how to clear the DF-bit on the encrypted packets egressing the outside interface over the VPN tunnel.

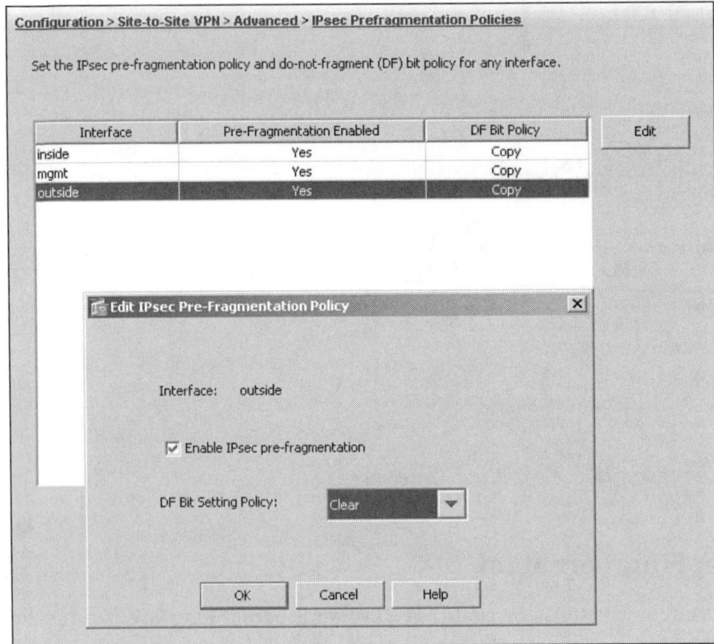

Figure 16-17 *Clearing DF-Bit for IPSec Packets*

Example 16-24 illustrates how to clear the DF-bit for the packets going over the IPsec tunnel. It also shows how to enable fragmentation before encryption if this behavior was changed earlier.

Example 16-24 *Clearing the DF-Bit for IPSec packets*

```
Chicago(config)# crypto ipsec df-bit clear-df outside
Chicago(config)# crypto ipsec fragmentation before-encryption outside
```

Deployment Scenarios

The ASA VPN solution can be deployed in many different ways. This section covers two of these deployment scenarios:

- Single site-to-site tunnel configuration using NAT-T
- Fully meshed topology with RRI

Note The deployment scenarios discussed in this section should be used solely to reinforce learning. They should be used for reference purposes only.

Single Site-to-Site Tunnel Configuration Using NAT-T

Figure 16-18 shows a network topology of SecureMe, which has deployed two Cisco ASAs—one at the hub site in Chicago, and the other at its New York location. The New York ASA is connected to the Internet via a broadband connection that is set up to perform PAT for the traffic passing through it. Because the PAT device does not allow passing of the non-TCP and non-UDP traffic, the security appliances are set up for NAT-T. During the ISAKMP negotiations, the security appliances will detect that a PAT device exists between them, therefore forcing the traffic to be encapsulated into UDP port 4500. These security appliances are set up to send NAT-T keepalives every 50 seconds to keep the connection entries active. The administrator wants to implement the strongest available encryption and hashing algorithm for a secure connection.

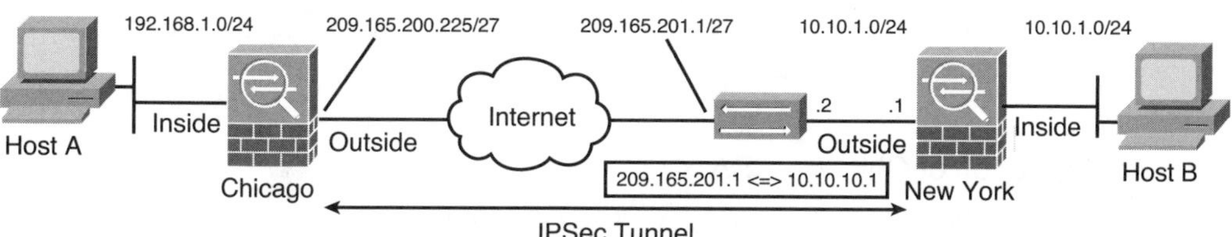

Figure 16-18 *SecureMe Network Using NAT-T*

Configuration Steps Through ASDM

The relevant configuration through ASDM is discussed below. These configuration steps assume that you have IP connectivity from the ASDM client to the management IP address of the security appliances. 172.18.82.64 is the management IP address of the Chicago ASA, and 172.18.101.164 is the IP address of the New York ASA. Because all devices need to have identical encryption and hashing policies, the following configurations steps are common on both devices:

Step 1. To enable IKE processing on the outside interface, navigate to **Configuration > Site-to-Site VPN > Connection Profile** and select the **Allow Access** option under the **Outside** access interface.

Step 2. Create an IKE Phase 1 policy by navigating to **Configuration > Site-to-Site VPN > Advanced > IKE Policies > Add** and specifying the following attributes:

- Priority: **1**
- Authentication: **pre-share**

- Encryption: **AES-256**
- D-H Group: **5**
- Hashing: **SHA**
- Lifetime: **86400** seconds. Click **OK** when you are finished.

Step 3. Create an IPSec transform set by navigating to **Configuration > Site-to-Site VPN > Advanced > IPSec Transform Sets > Add** and specifying the following attributes:

- Set Name: **AES-SHA**
- Mode: **Tunnel**
- ESP Encryption: **AES-256**
- ESP Authentication: **SHA.** Click **OK** when you are finished.

Make sure that the Enable Inbound IPSec Sessions to Bypass Interface Access Lists. Group Policy and Per-User Authorization Access Lists Still Apply to the Traffic option is enabled under **Configuration > Site-to-Site VPN > Advanced > System Options.** It is required to bypass traffic filtering of the encrypted traffic through the interface ACL checks.

Configuration of Chicago ASA

Step 1. Define a Tunnel Group by navigating to **Configuration > Site-to-Site VPN > Advanced > Tunnel Group > Add** and specifying the following attributes:

- Name: **209.165.201.1**
- Preshared Key: **C1$c0123**
- Make sure that **IPSec Protocol** check box is enabled. Leave all other options to their default values and click **OK** when you are finished.

Step 2. Navigate to **Configuration > Site-to-Site VPN > Advanced > IKE Parameters** and select the **Enable IPsec over NAT-T** option. The NAT Keepalive should be **50** seconds to meet SecureMe requirements.

Step 3. Next, navigate to **Configuration > Site-to-Site VPN > Advanced > Crypto Maps > Add**, click the **Tunnel Policy (Crypto Map)- Basic** tab, and specify the following attributes:

- Interface: **outside**
- Policy Type: **Static**
- Priority: **1**
- Transform Set to be Added: **AES-SHA** and click **Add>>.**

- Connection Type: **bidirectional**
- IP Address of Peer to be Added: **209.165.201.1** and click **Add>>.**

Step 4. To specify the interesting traffic for encryption, click the **Traffic Selection** tab of the crypto map properties and define the following attributes:

- Action: **Protect**
- Source: **192.168.1.0/24**
- Destination: **10.10.1.0/24**
- Service: **IP**
- Description: **To Encrypt Traffic from 192.168.1.0/24 to 10.10.1.0/24.** Click **OK** when you are finished.

Step 5. If NAT-Control<$IASDM (Adaptive Security Device Manager);site-to-site IPSec VPN deployments;single site-to-site tunnel configuration via NAT Traversal> is enabled, navigate to **Configuration > Firewall > NAT Rules > Add > Add NAT Exempt Rule** and define the following attributes:

- Action: **Exempt**
- Interface: **inside**
- Source: **192.168.1.0/24**
- Destination: **10.10.1.0/24**
- NAT Exempt Direction: **NAT Exempt outbound traffic from interface 'inside' to lower security interfaces (default).**
- Description: **To Bypass NAT from 192.168.1.0/24 to 10.10.1.0/24.** Click **OK** when you are finished.

Configuration of New York ASA

Step 1. Define a Tunnel Group by navigating to **Configuration > Site-to-Site VPN > Advanced > Tunnel Group > Add** and specifying the following attributes:

- Name: **209.165.200.225**
- Preshared Key: **C1$c0123**
- Make sure that the **IPSec Protocol** check box is enabled, leave all other options at their default values, and click **OK** when you are finished.

Step 2. Navigate to **Configuration > Site-to-Site VPN > Advanced > IKE Parameters** and select the **Enable IPsec over NAT-T** option. The NAT Keepalive should be **50** seconds to meet SecureMe requirements.

Step 3. Next, navigate to **Configuration > Site-to-Site VPN > Advanced > Crypto Maps > Add**, click the **Tunnel Policy (Crypto Map)- Basic** tab, and specify the following attributes:

- Interface: **outside**
- Policy Type: **Static**
- Priority: **1**
- Transform Set to be Added: **AES-SHA and click Add>>.**
- Connection Type: **bidirectional**
- IP Address of Peer to be Added: **209.165.200.225** and click **Add>>**

Step 4. To specify the interesting traffic for encryption, click the **Traffic Selection** tab of the crypto map properties and define the following attributes:

- Action: **Protect**
- Source: **10.10.1.0/24**
- Destination: **192.168.1.0/24**
- Service: **IP**
- Description: **To Encrypt Traffic from 10.10.1.0/24 to 192.168.1.0/24.** Click **OK** when you are finished.

Step 5. If NAT-Control is enabled, navigate to **Configuration > Firewall > NAT Rules > Add > Add NAT Exempt Rule** and define the following attributes:

- Action: **Exempt**
- Interface: **inside**
- Source: **10.10.1.0/24**
- Destination: **192.168.1.0/24**
- NAT Exempt Direction: **NAT Exempt outbound traffic from interface 'inside' to lower security interfaces (default).**
- Description: **To Bypass NAT from 10.10.1.0/24 to 192.168.1.0/24.** Click **OK** when you are finished.

Configuration Steps Through CLI

Example 16-25 shows the relevant configuration to achieve the goals listed earlier.

Example 16-25 *ASA's Relevant Configuration for Site-to-Site IPSec Tunnel*

```
Chicago ASA:
Chicago# show running
!
hostname Chicago
! outside interface configuration
interface GigabitEthernet0/0
 nameif outside
 security-level 0
 ip address 209.165.200.225 255.255.255.224
! inside interface configuration
interface GigabitEthernet0/1
 nameif inside
 security-level 100
 ip address 192.168.1.1 255.255.255.0
! Management interface configuration
interface Management0/0
 nameif mgmt
 security-level 100
 ip address 172.18.82.64 255.255.255.0
! NAT Exempt Access-list to bypass traffic from 192.168.1.0/24 to 10.10.1.0/24
access-list inside_nat0_outbound remark To Bypass NAT from 192.168.1.0/24 to
10.10.1.0/24
access-list inside_nat0_outbound extended permit ip 192.168.1.0 255.255.255.0
10.10.1.0 255.255.255.0
nat (inside) 0 access-list inside_nat0_outbound
! Encryption Access-list to encrypt the traffic from 192.168.1.0/24 to
10.10.1.0/24
access-list outside_cryptomap_1 remark To Encrypt Traffic from 192.168.1.0/24 to
10.10.1.0/24
access-list outside_cryptomap_1 extended permit ip 192.168.1.0 255.255.255.0
10.10.1.0 255.255.255.0
!
route outside 0.0.0.0 0.0.0.0 209.165.200.231 1
!
http server enable
http 172.18.82.0 255.255.255.0 mgmt
! Transform set to specify encryption and hashing algorithm
crypto ipsec transform-set AES-SHA esp-aes-256 esp-sha-hmac
! Crypto map configuration
crypto map outside_map_1 match address outside_cryptomap_1
crypto map outside_map 1 set peer 209.165.201.1
crypto map outside_map 1 set transform-set AES-SHA
crypto map outside_map interface outside
! isakmp configuration
crypto isakmp enable outside
```

```
crypto isakmp policy 1
 authentication pre-share
 encryption aes-256
 hash sha
 group 5
 lifetime 86400
! NAT-T configuration
crypto isakmp nat-traversal 50
! L2L tunnel-group configuration
tunnel-group 209.165.201.1 type ipsec-l2l
tunnel-group 209.165.201.1 ipsec-attributes
 pre-shared-key C1$c0123
<some output removed for brevity>
```

New York ASA:

```
NewYork# show running
!
hostname NewYork
! outside interface configuration. The outside address is translated to
209.165.201.1 by PAT
interface GigabitEthernet0/0
 nameif outside
 security-level 0
 ip address 10.10.10.1 255.255.255.0
! inside interface configuration
interface GigabitEthernet0/1
 nameif inside
 security-level 100
 ip address 10.10.1.1 255.255.255.0
! Management interface configuration
interface Management0/0
 nameif mgmt
 security-level 100
 ip address 172.18.101.164 255.255.255.0
! NAT Exempt Access-list to bypass traffic from 10.10.1.0/24 to 192.168.1.0/24
access-list inside_nat0_outbound remark To Bypass NAT from 10.10.1.0/24 to
192.168.1.0/24
access-list inside_nat0_outbound extended permit ip 10.10.1.0 255.255.255.0
192.168.1.0 255.255.255.0
nat (inside) 0 access-list inside_nat0_outbound
! Encryption Access-list to encrypt the traffic from 10.10.1.0/24 to
192.168.1.0/24
access-list outside_cryptomap_1 remark To Encrypt Traffic from 10.10.1.0/24 to
192.168.1.0/24
```

```
access-list outside_cryptomap_1 extended permit ip 10.10.1.0 255.255.255.0
192.168.1.0 255.255.255.0
!
route outside 0.0.0.0 0.0.0.0 10.10.10.2 1
!
http server enable
http 172.18.101.0 255.255.255.0 mgmt
! Transform set to specify encryption and hashing algorithm
crypto ipsec transform-set AES-SHA esp-aes-256 esp-sha-hmac
! Crypto map configuration
crypto map outside_map 1 match address outside_cryptomap_1
crypto map outside_map 1 set peer 209.165.200.225
crypto map outside_map 1 set transform-set AES-SHA
crypto map outside_map_1 interface outside
! isakmp configuration
crypto isakmp enable outside
crypto isakmp policy 1
 authentication pre-share
 encryption aes-256
 hash sha
 group 5
 lifetime 86400
! NAT-T configuration
crypto isakmp nat-traversal 50
! L2L tunnel-group configuration
tunnel-group 209.165.200.225 type ipsec-l2l
tunnel-group 209.165.200.225 ipsec-attributes
 pre-shared-key C!$c0123
<some output removed for brevity>
```

Fully Meshed Topology with RRI

SecureMe is planning to add a new site, London, into its existing network. Figure 16-19 shows the new network topology. SecureMe wants to have a fully meshed topology so that each site will have two IPSec tunnels going to the respective IPSec peers. It also wants to use RRI to distribute remote network information into the local network of Chicago, using OSPF.

Configuration Steps Through ASDM

The relevant configuration through ASDM is discussed in the following steps. These configuration steps assume that you have IP connectivity from the ASDM client to the management IP address of the security appliances. The management IP address of the Chicago ASA is 172.18.82.64, the IP address of the New York ASA is 172.18.101.164, and the IP address of the London ASA is 172.18.200.64. Because all three devices need to have identical encryption and hashing policies, the following configurations steps are common across all devices.

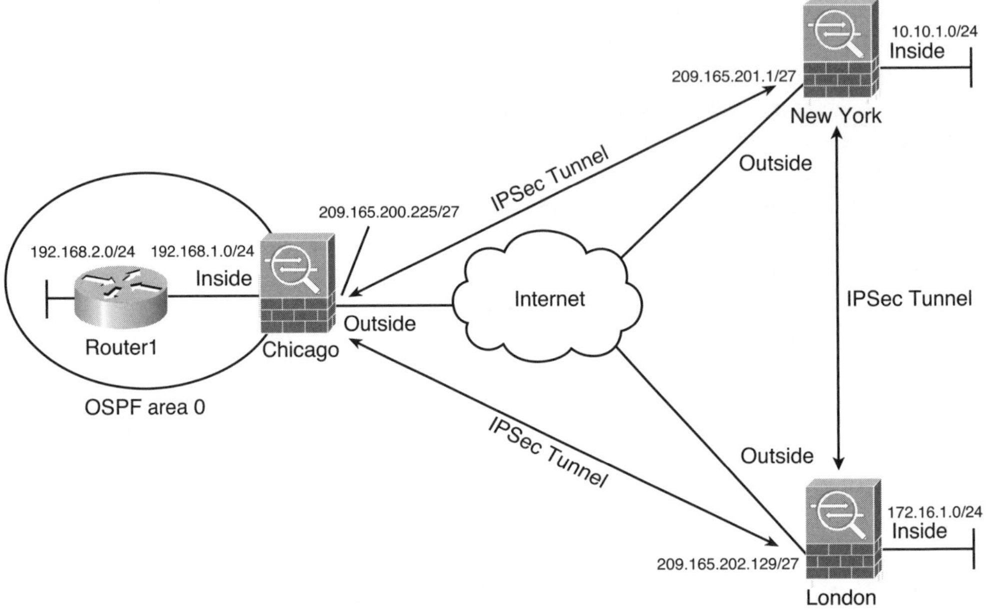

Figure 16-19 *SecureMe Network Using RRI in a Fully Meshed VPN*

Step 1. To enable IKE processing on the outside interface, navigate to **Configuration > Site-to-Site VPN > Connection Profile** and select the **Allow Access** option under the **Outside** access interface.

Step 2. Create an IKE Phase 1 policy by navigating to **Configuration > Site-to-Site VPN > Advanced > IKE Policies > Add** and specifying the following attributes:

- Priority: **1**
- Authentication: **pre-share**
- Encryption: **AES-256**
- D-H Group: **5**
- Hashing: **SHA**
- Lifetime: **86,400** seconds. Click **OK** when you are finished.

Step 3. Create an IPSec transform set by navigating to **Configuration > Site-to-Site VPN > Advanced > IPSec Transform Sets > Add** and specifying the following attributes:

- Set Name: **AES-SHA**
- Mode: **Tunnel**
- ESP Encryption: **AES-256**
- ESP Authentication: **SHA.** Click **OK** when you are finished.

Step 4. Make sure that the Enable Inbound IPSec Sessions to Bypass Interface Access Lists. Group Policy and Per-User Authorization Access Lists Still Apply to the Traffic option is enabled under **Configuration > Site-to-Site VPN > Advanced > System Options.** It is required to bypass traffic filtering of the encrypted traffic through the interface ACL checks.

Configuration of Chicago ASA

Step 1. Define a Tunnel Group for New York ASA by navigating to **Configuration > Site-to-Site VPN > Advanced > Tunnel Group > Add** and specifying the following attributes:

- Name: **209.165.201.1**
- Preshared Key: **C1$c0123**
- Make sure that the **IPSec Protocol** check box is enabled, leave all other options to their default values, and click **OK** when you are finished.

Step 3. Define a Tunnel Group for London ASA by navigating to **Configuration > Site-to-Site VPN > Advanced > Tunnel Group > Add** and specifying the following attributes:

- Name: **209.165.202.129**
- Preshared Key: **C1$c0123**
- Make sure that the **IPSec Protocol** check box is enabled, leave all other options to their default values, and click **OK** when you are finished.

Step 4. Next, add a crypto map for New York ASA. Navigate to **Configuration > Site-to-Site VPN > Advanced > Crypto Maps > Add**, click the **Tunnel Policy (Crypto Map)- Basic** tab, and specify the following attributes:

- Interface: **outside**
- Policy Type: **Static**
- Priority: **1**
- Transform Set to be Added: **AES-SHA** and click **Add>>.**
- Connection Type: **bidirectional**
- IP Address of Peer to be Added: **209.165.201.1** and click **Add>>.**

Step 5. To configure RRI, click the **Tunnel Policy (Crypto Map)-Advanced** tab and select **Enable Reverse Route Injection.**

Step 6. To specify the interesting traffic for encryption, click the **Traffic Selection** tab of the crypto map properties and define the following attributes:

- Action: **Protect**
- Source: **192.168.1.0/24**
- Destination: **10.10.1.0/24**
- Service: **IP**
- Description: **To Encrypt Traffic from 192.168.1.0/24 to 10.10.1.0/24.** Click **OK** when you are finished.

Step 7. Next, Add a crypto map for London ASA. Navigate to **Configuration > Site-to-Site VPN > Advanced > Crypto Maps > Add**, click the **Tunnel Policy (Crypto Map)- Basic** tab, and specify the following attributes:

- Interface: **outside**
- Policy Type: **Static**
- Priority: **2**
- Transform Set to be Added: **AES-SHA** and click **Add>>.**
- Connection Type: **bidirectional**
- IP Address of Peer to be Added: **209.165.202.129** and click **Add>>.**

Step 8. To configure RRI, click the **Tunnel Policy (Crypto Map)-Advanced** tab and select **Enable Reverse Route Injection.**

Step 9. To specify the interesting traffic for encryption, click the **Traffic Selection** tab of the crypto map properties and define the following attributes:

- Action: **Protect**
- Source: **192.168.1.0/24**
- Destination: **172.16.1.0/24**
- Service: **IP**
- Description: **To Encrypt Traffic from 192.168.1.0/24 to 172.16.1.0/24.** Click **OK** when you are finished.

Step 10. If NAT-Control is enabled, you must bypass address translation for the encrypted traffic. Navigate to **Configuration > Firewall > NAT Rules > Add**

> Add NAT Exempt Rule and define the following attributes for traffic going to New York ASA:

- Action: **Exempt**
- Interface: **inside**
- Source: **192.168.1.0/24**
- Destination: **10.10.1.0/24**
- NAT Exempt Direction: **NAT Exempt outbound traffic from interface 'Inside' to lower security interfaces (default).**
- Description: **To Bypass NAT from 192.168.1.0/24 to 10.10.1.0/24.** Click **OK** when you are finished.

Step 11. If NAT-Control is enabled, navigate to **Configuration > Firewall > NAT Rules > Add > Add NAT Exempt Rule** and define the following attributes for traffic going to London ASA:

- Action: **Exempt**
- Interface: **inside**
- Source: **192.168.1.0/24**
- Destination: **172.16.1.0/24**
- NAT Exempt Direction: **NAT Exempt outbound traffic from interface 'Inside' to lower security interfaces (default).**
- Description: **To Bypass NAT from 192.168.1.0/24 to 172.16.1.0/24.** Click **OK** when you are finished.

Step 12. Advertise the static route to the OSPF peers by browsing to **Configuration > Device Setup > Routing > OSPF > Redistribution > Add**, selecting the OSPF process you are using, choosing **Static** under the Protocol option, and then selecting the **Use Subnets** option.

Configuration of New York ASA

Step 1. Define a Tunnel Group for Chicago ASA by navigating to **Configuration > Site-to-Site VPN > Advanced > Tunnel Group > Add** and specifying the following attributes:

- Name: **209.165.200.225**
- Preshared Key: **C1$c0123**
- Make sure that the **IPSec Protocol** check box is enabled, leave all other options to their default values, and click **OK** when you are finished.

Step 2. Define a Tunnel Group for London ASA by navigating to **Configuration > Site-to-Site VPN > Advanced > Tunnel Group > Add** and specifying the following attributes:

- Name: **209.165.202.129**
- Preshared Key: **C1$c0123**
- Make sure that **IPSec Protocol** option is enabled and leave all other options to their default values and click **OK** when you are finished.

Step 3. Next, add a crypto map for Chicago ASA. Navigate to **Configuration > Site-to-Site VPN > Advanced > Crypto Maps > Add**, click the **Tunnel Policy (Crypto Map)- Basic** tab, and specify the following attributes:

- Interface: **outside**
- Policy Type: **Static**
- Priority: **1**
- Transform Set to be Added: **AES-SHA** and click **Add>>**
- Connection Type: **bidirectional**
- IP Address of Peer to be Added: **209.165.200.225** and click **Add>>**

Step 4. To specify the interesting traffic for encryption, click the **Traffic Selection** tab of the crypto map properties and define the following attributes:

- Action: **Protect**
- Source: **10.10.1.0/24**
- Destination: **192.168.1.0/24**
- Service: **IP**
- Description: **To Encrypt Traffic from 10.10.1.0/24 to 192.168.1.0/24**. Click **OK** when you are finished.

Step 5. Next, add a crypto map for London ASA. Navigate to **Configuration > Site-to-Site VPN > Advanced > Crypto Maps > Add**, click the **Tunnel Policy (Crypto Map)- Basic** tab, and specify the following attributes:

- Interface: **outside**
- Policy Type: **Static**
- Priority: **2**
- Transform Set to be Added: **AES-SHA** and click **Add>>**
- Connection Type: **bidirectional**
- IP Address of Peer to be Added: **209.165.202.129** and click **Add>>**

Step 6. To specify the interesting traffic for encryption, click the **Traffic Selection** tab of the crypto map properties and define the following attributes:

- Action: **Protect**
- Source: **10.10.1.0/24**
- Destination: **172.16.1.0/24**
- Service: **IP**
- Description: **To Encrypt Traffic from 10.10.1.0/24 to 172.16.1.0/24**. Click **OK** when you are finished.

Step 7. If NAT-Control is enabled, you must bypass address translation for the encrypted traffic. Navigate to **Configuration > Firewall > NAT Rules > Add > Add NAT Exempt Rule** and define the following attributes for traffic going to Chicago ASA:

- Action: **Exempt**
- Interface: **inside**
- Source: **10.10.1.0/24**
- Destination: **192.168.1.0/24**
- NAT Exempt Direction: **NAT Exempt outbound traffic from interface 'Inside' to lower security interfaces (default)**
- Description: **To Bypass NAT from 10.10.1.0/24 to 192.168.1.0/24**. Click **OK** when you are finished.

Step 8. If NAT-Control is enabled, navigate to **Configuration > Firewall > NAT Rules > Add > Add NAT Exempt Rule** and define the following attributes for traffic going to London ASA:

- Action: **Exempt**
- Interface: **inside**
- Source: **10.10.1.0/24**
- Destination: **172.16.1.0/24**
- NAT Exempt Direction: **NAT Exempt outbound traffic from interface 'Inside' to lower security interfaces (default)**
- Description: **To Bypass NAT from 192.168.1.0/24 to 172.16.1.0/24**. Click **OK** when you are finished.

Configuration of London ASA

Step 1. Define a Tunnel Group for New York ASA by navigating to **Configuration > Site-to-Site VPN > Advanced > Tunnel Group > Add** and specifying the following attributes:

- Name: **209.165.201.1**
- Preshared Key: **C1$c0123**
- Make sure that the **IPSec Protocol** checkbox is enabled and leave all other options to their default values and click **OK** when you are finished.

Step 2. Define a Tunnel Group for Chicago ASA by navigating to **Configuration > Site-to-Site VPN > Advanced > Tunnel Group > Add** and specifying the following attributes:

- Name: **209.165.200.225**
- Preshared Key: **C1$c0123**
- Make sure that the **IPSec Protocol** checkbox is enabled and leave all other options to their default values and click **OK** when you are finished.

Step 3. Next, add a crypto map for New York ASA. Navigate to **Configuration > Site-to-Site VPN > Advanced > Crypto Maps > Add**, click the **Tunnel Policy (Crypto Map)- Basic** tab, and specify the following attributes:

- Interface: **outside**
- Policy Type: **Static**
- Priority: **1**
- Transform Set to be Added: **AES-SHA** and click **Add>>**
- Connection Type: **bidirectional**
- IP Address of Peer to be Added: **209.165.201.1** and click **Add>>**

Step 4. To specify the interesting traffic for encryption, click the **Traffic Selection** tab of the crypto map properties and define the following attributes:

- Action: **Protect**
- Source: **172.16.1.0/24**
- Destination: **10.10.1.0/24**
- Service: **IP**
- Description: **To Encrypt Traffic from 172.16.1.0/24 to 10.10.1.0/24.** Click **OK** when you are finished.

Step 5. Next, add a crypto map for Chicago ASA. Navigate to **Configuration > Site-to-Site VPN > Advanced > Crypto Maps > Add**, click the **Tunnel Policy (Crypto Map)- Basic** tab, and specify the following attributes:

- Interface: **outside**
- Policy Type: **Static**
- Priority: **2**
- Transform Set to be Added: **AES-SHA and click Add>>**
- Connection Type: **bidirectional**
- IP Address of Peer to be Added: **209.165.200.225** and click **Add>>**

Step 6. To specify the interesting traffic for encryption, click the **Traffic Selection** tab of the crypto map properties and define the following attributes:

- Action: **Protect**
- Source: **172.16.1.0/24**
- Destination: **192.168.1.0/24**
- Service: **IP**
- Description: **To Encrypt Traffic from 172.16.1.0/24 to 192.168.1.0/24.** Click **OK** when you are finished.

Step 7. If NAT-Control is enabled, you must bypass address translation for the encrypted traffic. Navigate to **Configuration > Firewall > NAT Rules > Add > Add NAT Exempt Rule** and define the following attributes for traffic going to New York ASA:

- Action: **Exempt**
- Interface: **inside**
- Source: **172.16.1.0/24**
- Destination: **10.10.1.0/24**
- NAT Exempt Direction: **NAT Exempt outbound traffic from interface 'Inside' to lower security interfaces (default)**
- Description: **To Bypass NAT from 172.16.1.0/24 to 10.10.1.0/24.** Click **OK** when you are finished.

Step 8. If NAT-Control is enabled, navigate to **Configuration > Firewall > NAT Rules > Add > Add NAT Exempt Rule** and define the following attributes for traffic going to Chicago ASA:

- Action: **Exempt**
- Interface: **inside**

- Source: **172.16.1.0/24**
- Destination: **192.168.1.0/24**
- NAT Exempt Direction: **NAT Exempt outbound traffic from interface 'Inside' to lower security interfaces (default)**
- Description: **To Bypass NAT from 172.16.1.0/24 to 192.168.1.0/24**. Click **OK** when you are finished.

Configuration Steps Through CLI

Example 16-26 shows the relevant configuration of all the Cisco ASA devices set up in a fully meshed IPSec network. There are two crypto map instances—one for each peer configured on the security appliances.

Example 16-26 *Full Configuration of the Chicago, London, and Paris ASAs*

```
Chicago ASA:
Chicago# show running
!
hostname Chicago
! outside interface configuration
interface GigabitEthernet0/0
 nameif outside
 security-level 0
 ip address 209.165.200.225 255.255.255.224
! inside interface configuration
interface GigabitEthernet0/1
 nameif inside
 security-level 100
 ip address 192.168.1.1 255.255.255.0
! Management interface configuration
interface Management0/0
 nameif mgmt
 security-level 100
 ip address 172.18.82.64 255.255.255.0
! NAT Exempt Access-list to bypass traffic from 192.168.1.0/24 to 10.10.1.0/24
access-list inside_nat0_outbound remark To Bypass NAT from 192.168.1.0/24 to
10.10.1.0/24
access-list inside_nat0_outbound extended permit ip 192.168.1.0 255.255.255.0
10.10.1.0 255.255.255.0
! NAT Exempt Access-list to bypass traffic from 192.168.1.0/24 to 172.16.1.0/24
access-list inside_nat0_outbound remark To Bypass NAT from 192.168.1.0/24 to
172.16.1.0/24
access-list inside_nat0_outbound extended permit ip 192.168.1.0 255.255.255.0
172.16.1.0 255.255.255.0
! NAT inside 0 to bypass address translation
```

```
nat (inside) 0 access-list inside_nat0_outbound
! Encryption Access-list to encrypt the traffic from 192.168.1.0/24 to
10.10.1.0/24
access-list outside_cryptomap_1 remark To Encrypt Traffic from 192.168.1.0/24 to
10.10.1.0/24.
access-list outside_cryptomap_1 extended permit ip 192.168.1.0 255.255.255.0
10.10.1.0 255.255.255.0
! Encryption Access-list to encrypt the traffic from 192.168.1.0/24 to
172.16.1.0/24
access-list outside_cryptomap_2 remark To Encrypt Traffic from 192.168.1.0/24 to
172.16.1.0/24.
access-list outside_cryptomap_2 extended permit ip 192.168.1.0 255.255.255.0
172.16.1.0 255.255.255.0
!
route outside 0.0.0.0 0.0.0.0 209.165.200.227 1
! OSPF Process
router ospf 100
 area 0
 network 192.168.0.0 255.255.0.0 area 0 network
 redistribute static
!
http server enable
http 172.18.82.0 255.255.255.0 mgmt
! Transform set to specify encryption and hashing algorithm
crypto ipsec transform-set AES-SHA esp-aes-256 esp-sha-hmac
! Crypto map configuration for NewYork ASA

crypto map outside_map 1 match address outside_cryptomap_1
crypto map outside_map 1 set peer 209.165.201.1
crypto map outside_map 1 set transform-set AES-SHA
crypto map outside_map 1 set reverse-route
! Crypto map configuration for London ASA
crypto map outside_map 2 match address outside_cryptomap_2
crypto map outside_map 2 set peer 209.165.202.129
crypto map outside_map 2 set transform-set AES-SHA
crypto map outside_map 2 set reverse-route
crypto map outside_map interface outside
! isakmp configuration
crypto isakmp enable outside
crypto isakmp policy 1
 authentication pre-share
 encryption aes-256
 hash sha
 group 5
 lifetime 86400
! L2L tunnel-group configuration for New York ASA
```

```
tunnel-group 209.165.201.1 type ipsec-l2l
tunnel-group 209.165.201.1 ipsec-attributes
 pre-shared-key C!$c0123
! L2L tunnel-group configuration for London ASA
tunnel-group 209.165.202.129 type ipsec-l2l
tunnel-group 209.165.202.129 ipsec-attributes
 pre-shared-key C!$c0123
<some output removed for brevity>
```

```
New York ASA:
NewYork# show running
!
hostname NewYork
! outside interface configuration. The outside address is translated to
209.165.201.1 by PAT
interface GigabitEthernet0/0
 nameif outside
security-level 0
ip address 209.165.201.1 255.255.255.224
! inside interface configuration
interface GigabitEthernet0/1
 nameif inside
 security-level 100
 ip address 10.10.1.1 255.255.255.0
! Management interface configuration
interface Management0/0
 nameif mgmt
 security-level 100
 ip address 172.18.101.164 255.255.255.0
! NAT Exempt Access-list to bypass traffic from 10.10.1.0/24 to 192.168.1.0/24
access-list inside_nat0_outbound remark To Bypass NAT from 10.10.1.0/24 to
192.168.1.0/24
access-list inside_nat0_outbound extended permit ip 10.10.1.0 255.255.255.0
192.168.1.0 255.255.255.0
! NAT Exempt Access-list to bypass traffic from 10.10.1.0/24 to 172.16.1.0/24
access-list inside_nat0_outbound remark To Bypass NAT from 10.10.1.0/24 to
172.16.1.0/24
access-list inside_nat0_outbound extended permit ip 10.10.1.0 255.255.255.0
172.16.1.0 255.255.255.0
nat (inside) 0 access-list inside_nat0_outbound
! Encryption Access-list to encrypt the traffic from 10.10.1.0/24 to
192.168.1.0/24
access-list outside_cryptomap_1 remark To Encrypt Traffic from 10.10.1.0/24 to
192.168.1.0/24
```

```
access-list outside_cryptomap_1 extended permit ip 10.10.1.0 255.255.255.0
192.168.1.0 255.255.255.0
! Encryption Access-list to encrypt the traffic from 10.10.1.0/24 to 172.16.1.0/24
access-list outside_cryptomap_2 remark To Encrypt Traffic from 10.10.1.0/24 to
172.16.1.0/24
access-list outside_cryptomap_2 extended permit ip 10.10.1.0 255.255.255.0
172.16.1.0 255.255.255.0
!
route outside 0.0.0.0 0.0.0.0 209.165.201.2 1
!
!
http server enable
http 172.18.101.0 255.255.255.0 mgmt
! Transform set to specify encryption and hashing algorithm
crypto ipsec transform-set AES-SHA esp-aes-256 esp-sha-hmac
! Crypto map configuration for Chicago ASA
crypto map outside_map 1 match address outsidecryptomap1
crypto map outside_map 1 set peer 209.165.200.225
crypto map outside_map 1 set transform-set AES-SHA
! Crypto map configuration for London ASA
crypto map outside_map 2 match address outsidecryptomap2
crypto map outside_map 2 set peer 209.165.202.129
crypto map outside_map 2 set transform-set AES-SHA
crypto map outside_map interface outside
! isakmp configuration
crypto isakmp enable outside
crypto isakmp policy 1
 authentication pre-share
 encryption aes-256
 hash sha
 group 5
 lifetime 86400
! L2L tunnel-group configuration for Chicago ASA
tunnel-group 209.165.200.225 type ipsec-l2l
tunnel-group 209.165.200.225 ipsec-attributes
 pre-shared-key C!$c0123
! L2L tunnel-group configuration for London ASA
tunnel-group 209.165.202.129 type ipsec-l2l
tunnel-group 209.165.202.129 ipsec-attributes
 pre-shared-key C!$c0123
<some output removed for brevity>
```

```
London ASA:
London# show running
```

```
!
hostname London
! outside interface configuration
interface GigabitEthernet0/0
 nameif outside
 security-level 0
 ip address 209.165.202.129 255.255.255.0
! inside interface configuration
interface GigabitEthernet0/1
 nameif inside
 security-level 100
 ip address 172.16.1.1 255.255.255.0
! Management interface configuration
interface Management0/0
 nameif mgmt
 security-level 100
 ip address 172.18.200.64 255.255.255.0
! NAT Exempt Access-list to bypass traffic from 172.16.1.0/24 to 10.10.1.0/24
access-list inside_nat0_outbound remark To Bypass NAT from 172.16.1.0/24 to
10.10.1.0/24
access-list inside_nat0_outbound extended permit ip 172.16.1.0 255.255.255.0
10.10.1.0 255.255.255.0
! NAT Exempt Access-list to bypass traffic from 172.16.1.0/24 to 192.168.1.0/24
access-list inside_nat0_outbound remark To Bypass NAT from 172.16.1.0/24 to
192.168.1.0/24
access-list inside_nat0_outbound extended permit ip 172.16.1.0 255.255.255.0
192.168.1.0 255.255.255.0
! NAT inside 0 to bypass address translation
nat (inside) 0 access-list inside_nat0_outbound
! Encryption Access-list to encrypt the traffic from 172.16.1.0/24 to 10.10.1.0/24
access-list outside_cryptomap_1 remark To Encrypt Traffic from 172.16.1.0/24 to
10.10.1.0/24.
access-list outside_cryptomap_1 extended permit ip 172.16.1.0 255.255.255.0
10.10.1.0 255.255.255.0
! Encryption Access-list to encrypt the traffic from 172.16.1.0/24 to
192.168.1.0/24
access-list outside_cryptomap_2 remark To Encrypt Traffic from 172.16.1.0/24 to
192.168.1.0/24.
access-list outside_cryptomap_2 extended permit ip 172.16.1.0 255.255.255.0
192.168.1.0 255.255.255.0
!
route outside 0.0.0.0 0.0.0.0 209.165.202.130 1
!
!
http server enable
http 172.18.200.0 255.255.255.0 mgmt
```

```
! Transform set to specify encryption and hashing algorithm
crypto ipsec transform-set AES-SHA esp-aes-256 esp-sha-hmac
! Crypto map configuration for NewYork ASA
crypto map outside_map 1 match address outside_cryptomap_1
crypto map outside_map 1 set peer 209.165.201.1
crypto map outside_map 1 set transform-set AES-SHA
! Crypto map configuration for Chicago ASA
crypto map outside_map 2 match address outside_cryptomap_2
crypto map outside_map 2 set peer 209.165.200.225
crypto map outside_map 2 set transform-set AES-SHA
crypto map outside_map interface outside
! isakmp configuration
crypto isakmp enable outside
crypto isakmp policy 1
 authentication pre-share
 encryption aes-256
 hash sha
 group 5
 lifetime 86400
! L2L tunnel-group configuration for New York ASA
tunnel-group 209.165.201.1 type ipsec-l2l
tunnel-group 209.165.201.1 ipsec-attributes
 pre-shared-key C!$c0123
! L2L tunnel-group configuration for Chicago ASA
tunnel-group 209.165.200.225 type ipsec-l2l
tunnel-group 209.165.200.225 ipsec-attributes
 pre-shared-key C!$c0123
<some output removed for brevity>
```

Monitoring and Troubleshooting Site-to-Site IPSec VPNs

Cisco ASA comes with many **show** commands to check the health and status of the IPSec tunnels. For troubleshooting purposes, Cisco ASA also provides a rich set of **debug** commands to isolate the IPSec-related issues.

Monitoring Site-to-Site VPNs

To check the status of the IPSec tunnels, start by looking at Phase 1 SA state. Type **show crypto isakmp sa detail**, as demonstrated in Example 16-27. If the ISAKMP negotiations are successful, you should see the state as MM_ACTIVE. The example also displays the type of the IPSec tunnel and the negotiated Phase 1 policy.

Example 16-27 *Output of* **show crypto isakmp sa detail**

```
Chicago# show crypto isakmp sa detail

   Active SA: 1
    Rekey SA: 0 (A tunnel will report 1 Active and 1 Rekey SA during rekey)
Total IKE SA: 1

1   IKE Peer: 209.165.201.1
    Type    : L2L              Role     : responder
    Rekey   : no               State    : MM_ACTIVE
    Encrypt : aes-256          Hash     : SHA
    Auth    : preshared        Lifetime : 86400
    Lifetime Remaining: 86312
```

You can also check the status of the IPSec SA by using the **show crypto ipsec sa** command, as shown in Example 16-28. It displays the negotiated proxy identities (networks to be encrypted), along with the actual number of packets encrypted and decrypted by the IPSec engine.

Example 16-28 *Output of* **show crypto ipsec sa**

```
Chicago# show crypto ipsec sa
interface: outside
    Crypto map tag: outside_map0, seq num: 1, local addr: 209.165.200.225
      access-list outside_cryptomap_1 permit ip 192.168.1.0 255.255.255.0
10.10.1.0 255.255.255.0
      local ident (addr/mask/prot/port): (192.168.1.0/255.255.255.0/0/0)
      remote ident (addr/mask/prot/port): (10.10.1.0/255.255.255.0/0/0)
      current_peer: 209.165.201.1
      #pkts encaps: 4, #pkts encrypt: 4, #pkts digest: 4
      #pkts decaps: 4, #pkts decrypt: 4, #pkts verify: 4
      #pkts compressed: 0, #pkts decompressed: 0
      #pkts not compressed: 4, #pkts comp failed: 0, #pkts decomp failed: 0
      #pre-frag successes: 0, #pre-frag failures: 0, #fragments created: 0
      #PMTUs sent: 0, #PMTUs rcvd: 0, #decapsulated frgs needing reassembly: 0
      #send errors: 0, #recv errors: 0
      local crypto endpt.: 209.165.200.225, remote crypto endpt.: 209.165.201.1
      path mtu 1500, ipsec overhead 74, media mtu 1500
      current outbound spi: 550821BD
    inbound esp sas:
      spi: 0x4AACC730 (1252837168)
         transform: esp-aes esp-sha-hmac no compression
         in use settings ={L2L, Tunnel, }
         slot: 0, conn_id: 28672, crypto-map: outside_map0
         sa timing: remaining key lifetime (kB/sec): (179695/3441)
```

```
          IV size: 16 bytes
          replay detection support: Y
Anti replay bitmap:
         0x00000000 0x0000001F
    outbound esp sas:
      spi: 0x550821BD (1426596285)
          transform: esp-aes esp-sha-hmac no compression
          in use settings ={L2L, Tunnel, }
          slot: 0, conn_id: 28672, crypto-map: outside_map0
          sa timing: remaining key lifetime (kB/sec): (179695/3441)
          IV size: 16 bytes
          replay detection support: Y
Anti replay bitmap:
         0x00000000 0x00000001
```

All Cisco ASAs have an encryption accelerator installed. If you want to look at the counter information to monitor how many packets have gone through the card, you can type the **show crypto accelerator statistics** command, as demonstrated in Example 16-29.

Example 16-29 *Output of* show crypto accelerator statistics

```
Chicago# show crypto accelerator statistics
Crypto Accelerator Status
-------------.
[Capability]
   Supports hardware crypto: True
   Supports modular hardware crypto: False
   Max accelerators: 1
   Max crypto throughput: 225 Mbps
   Max crypto connections: 750
[Global Statistics]
   Number of active accelerators: 1
   Number of non-operational accelerators: 0
   Input packets: 298
   Input bytes: 163448
   Output packets: 36542
   Output error packets: 0
   Output bytes: 31455254
<output removed for brevity>

[Accelerator 1]
   Status: OK
   Status: OK
   Encryption hardware device : Cisco ASA-55x0 on-board accelerator (revision 0x
```

```
0)
                  Boot microcode    : CN1000-MC-BOOT-2.00
                  SSL/IKE microcode: CNLite-MC-SSLm-PLUS-2.03
                  IPSec microcode   : CNlite-MC-IPSECm-MAIN-2.04
   Slot: 1
   Active time: 725496 seconds
   Total crypto transforms: 39864
   Total dropped packets: 0
   [Input statistics]
      Input packets: 298
      Input bytes: 119240
      Input hashed packets: 35
      Input hashed bytes: 4340
      Decrypted packets: 298
      Decrypted bytes: 117560
   [Output statistics]
      Output packets: 36544
      Output bad packets: 0
      Output bytes: 31355856
      Output hashed packets: 22
      Output hashed bytes: 2992
      Encrypted packets: 36544
      Encrypted bytes: 31354624
   [Diffie-Hellman statistics]
      Keys generated: 78
      Secret keys derived: 14
<output removed for brevity>
```

To monitor the IPSec sessions through ASDM, navigate to **Monitoring > VPN > VPN Statistics > Sessions** and check how many active IPSec tunnels are established on the security appliance. The security appliance shows you all the active VPN sessions, including the remote-access connections. With the CLI, you can find similar information by using the **show vpn-sessiondb summary** command, as shown in Example 16-30.

Example 16-30 show vpn-sessiondb summary *Command Output*

```
Chicago# show vpn-sessiondb summary
Active Session Summary

Sessions:
                            Active : Cumulative : Peak Concurrent : Inactive
  IPsec LAN-to-LAN        :        1 :            1 :                     1
  Totals                  :        1 :            1
```

```
License Information:
  IPsec   :     750    Configured :     750    Active :       1    Load :    0%
  SSL VPN :       2    Configured :       2    Active :       0    Load :    0%
                              Active : Cumulative : Peak Concurrent
  IPsec               :            1 :            1 :             1
  Totals              :            1 :            1

Active NAC Sessions:
  No NAC sessions to display

Active VLAN Mapping Sessions:
  No VLAN Mapping sessions to display
```

Troubleshooting Site-to-Site VPNs

If the IPSec tunnel is not working, make sure that you have the proper **debug** turned on. The two most important **debug** commands to look at are the following:

```
debug crypto isakmp [debug level 1-255]
```

and

```
debug crypto ipsec [debug level 1-255]
```

By default, the debug level is set to 1. You can increase the debug level up to 255 to get detailed logs. However, in most cases, setting the logging level to 127 gives enough information to determine the root cause of an issue.

Refer to Figure 16-1 for an example of a site-to-site tunnel between the ASAs in Chicago and New York. The ISAKMP and IPSec negotiations are discussed on the security appliance in Chicago. The following debug commands are enabled on the security appliance:

```
Chicago# debug crypto isakmp 127
Chicago# debug crypto ipsec 127
```

Tip If you have hundreds of IPSec sessions established to a security appliance, enabling the **crypto isakmp** and **crypto ipsec** debugs can generate a lot of output.

In version 8.0 or higher, the crypto conditional debug feature was introduced, which enables a user to debug an IPSec tunnel based on predefined conditions such as the peer's IP address, SPI values, or even the connection ID. For example, if you want to look at the **crypto isakmp** and **crypto ipsec** debugs for peer 209.165.201.1, enable the following commands:

```
Debug crypto isakmp 127
Debug crypto ipsec 127
Debug crypto condition peer 209.165.201.1
```

As mentioned in Chapter 1, the tunnel negotiations begin with an exchange of ISAKMP proposals. If the proposal is acceptable, the ASA displays the **IKE SA Proposal Transform Acceptable** message, as shown in Example 16-31.

Example 16-31 *Debugs to Show ISAKMP Proposal Is Acceptable*

```
[IKEv1 DEBUG], IP = 209.165.201.1, processing SA payload
[IKEv1 DEBUG], IP = 209.165.201.1, Oakley proposal is acceptable
.....
[IKEv1 DEBUG], IP = 209.165.201.1, IKE SA Proposal # 1, Transform # 1 acceptable
Matches global IKE entry # 4
```

Note The VPN **debug** messages on the security appliance are very similar to the log messages generated on the VPN 3000 Series Concentrators.

During the ISAKMP SA negotiations, the security appliance matches the IP address of the VPN peer with the tunnel group. If it finds a match, it displays a "Connection landed on tunnel group" message, as shown in Example 16-32, and continues with the rest of the negotiations (shown as ...). The Cisco ASA displays a Phase 1 Completed message when the ISAKMP SA is successfully negotiated.

Example 16-32 *Debugs to Show Phase 1 Negotiations Are Completed*

```
[IKEv1]: IP = 209.165.201.1, Connection landed on tunnel_group 209.165.201.1
...
[IKEv1]: Group = 209.165.201.1, IP = 209.165.201.1, PHASE 1 COMPLETED
```

After completing Phase 1 negotiations, the security appliance maps the remote VPN peer to a static crypto map sequence number and checks the IPSec Phase 2 proposal sent by the remote VPN peers. If the received proxy identities and the IPSec Phase 2 proposals match on the security appliance, it displays an IPSec SA Proposal Transform Acceptable message, as demonstrated in Example 16-33.

Example 16-33 *Debugs to Show Proxy Identities and Phase 2 Proposals Are Accepted*

```
[IKEv1 DECODE]: ID_IPV4_ADDR_SUBNET ID received—10.10.1.0—255.255.255.0
[IKEv1]: Group = 209.165.201.1, IP = 209.165.201.1, Received remote IP Proxy Subnet
data in ID Payload: Address 10.10.1.0, Mask 255.255.255.0, Protocol 0, Port 0
[IKEv1 DEBUG]: Group = 209.165.201.1, IP = 209.165.201.1, Processing ID
[IKEv1 DECODE]: ID_IPV4_ADDR_SUBNET ID received—192.168.1.0—255.255.255.0
[IKEv1]: Group = 209.165.201.1, IP = 209.165.201.1, Received local IP Proxy Subnet
data in ID Payload:   Address 192.168.1.0, Mask 255.255.255.0, Protocol 0, Port 0
...
[IKEv1]: Group = 209.165.201.1, IP = 209.165.201.1, Static Crypto Map check,
checking map = IPSec_map, seq = 10...
```

```
[IKEv1]: Group = 209.165.201.1, IP = 209.165.201.1, Static Crypto Map check, map
outside_map0, seq = 1 is a successful match
[IKEv1]: Group = 209.165.201.1, IP = 209.165.201.1, IKE Remote Peer configured for
SA: outside_map0
[IKEv1]: Group = 209.165.201.1, IP = 209.165.201.1, processing IPSEC SA
[IKEv1 DEBUG]: Group = 209.165.201.1, IP = 209.165.201.1, IPSec SA Proposal # 1,
Transform # 1 acceptable  Matches global IPSec SA entry # 1
```

After accepting the transform set, both VPN devices agree on the inbound and outbound IPSec SAs, as shown in Example 16-34. After the IPSec SAs have been created, both VPN devices should be able to pass bidirectional traffic across the tunnel.

Example 16-34 *Debugs Showing IPSec SAs Are Activated*

```
 [IKEv1 DEBUG]: Group = 209.165.201.1, IP = 209.165.201.1, loading all IPSEC SAs
<some outpout removed for brevity>
[IKEv1]: Group = 209.165.201.1, IP = 209.165.201.1, Security negotiation complete
for LAN-to-LAN Group (209.165.201.1)  Responder, SPI = 0x65e271c7, Outbound SPI =
0x59346641
```

The following four scenarios discuss how to troubleshoot the common issues related to IPSec tunnels. The debug messages are shown if **debug crypto isakmp 127** is enabled on the security appliance.

ISAKMP Proposal Unacceptable

In this scenario, if the ISAKMP proposals are mismatched between the two VPN devices, the Cisco ASA appliance displays an All SA Proposals Found Unacceptable message after processing the first main mode packet, as shown in Example 16-35.

Example 16-35 *Debugs to Show Mismatched ISAKMP Policies*

```
[IKEv1 DEBUG]: IP = 209.165.201.1,, processing SA payload
[IKEv1]: IP = 209.165.201.1, IKE DECODE SENDING Message (msgid=0) with payloads :
HDR + NOTIFY (11) + NONE (0) total length : 96
[IKEv1 DEBUG]: IP = 209.165.201.1, All SA proposals found unacceptable
```

Mismatched Preshared Keys

If the preshared key is mismatched between the VPN devices, the Cisco ASA appliance displays an Error, Had Problems Decrypting Packet, Probably Due to Mismatched Pre-Shared Key message after processing the fourth main mode packet. This is shown in Example 16-36.

Example 16-36 *Debugs to Show Mismatched Preshared Keys*

```
[IKEv1]: Group = 209.165.201.1, IP = 209.165.201.1Received encrypted Oakley Main
Mode packet with invalid payloads, MessID = 0
[IKEv1]: IP = 209.165.201.1, IKE DECODE SENDING Message (msgid=0) with payloads :
HDR + NOTIFY (11) + NONE (0) total length : 104
IKEv1]: Group = 209.165.201.1, IP = 209.165.201.1, ERROR, had problems decrypting
packet, probably due to mismatched pre-shared key. Aborting
```

Incompatible IPSec Transform Set

The security appliance displays an All IPSec SA Proposals Found Unacceptable message if the IPSec transform set is mismatched between the VPN devices. In this case, the Phase 1 SA gets established and the VPN devices fail to negotiate the IPSec SA. The Cisco ASA checks the validity of the crypto map before rejecting the IPSec SA, as shown in Example 16-37.

Example 16-37 *Debugs When Incompatible IPSec Transform Set Is Used*

```
[IKEv1]: Group = 209.165.201.1, IP = 209.165.201.1, Static Crypto Map check,
checking map = IPSec_map, seq = 10...
[IKEv1]: Group = 209.165.201.1, IP = 209.165.201.1, Static Crypto Map check, map
IPSec_map, seq = 10 is a successful match
[IKEv1]: Group = 209.165.201.1, IP = 209.165.201.1, IKE Remote Peer configured for
SA: IPSec_map
[IKEv1]: Group = 209.165.201.1, IP = 209.165.201.1, processing IPSEC SA
[IKEv1]: Group = 209.165.201.1, IP = 209.165.201.1, All IPSec SA proposals found
unacceptable!
```

Mismatched Proxy Identities

If the encryption ACL on the security appliance does not match the encryption ACL offered by the other end of the VPN tunnel, the Cisco ASA rejects the IPSec SA and displays a No Matching crypto map Entry error with the associated local and remote subnets that the remote VPN device offered. In Example 16-38, the VPN peer 209.165.201.1 wants to negotiate IPSec SAs between 10.10.1.0 and 192.168.2.0, which the security appliance rejects because the received identities do not match the configured crypto ACL.

Example 16-38 *Debugs to Show Mismatched Proxy Identities*

```
[IKEv1]: Group = 209.165.201.1, IP = 209.165.201.1, Received remote IP Proxy Subnet
data in ID Payload:   Address 10.10.1.0, Mask 255.255.255.0, Protocol 0, Port 0
[IKEv1 DEBUG]: Group = 209.165.201.1, IP = 209.165.201.1, processing ID payload
[IKEv1 DECODE]: Group = 209.165.201.1, IP = 209.165.201.1, ID_IPV4_ADDR_SUBNET ID
received—192.168.2.0—255.255.255.0
[IKEv1]: Group = 209.165.201.1, IP = 209.165.201.1, Received local IP Proxy Subnet
data in ID Payload:   Address 192.168.2.0, Mask 255.255.255.0, Protocol 0, Port 0
<some output removed for brevity>
[IKEv1]: Group = 209.165.201.1, IP = 209.165.201.1, Static Crypto Map check, map =
outside_map0, seq = 1, ACL does not match proxy IDs src:10.10.1.0 dst:192.168.2.0
```

```
[IKEv1]: Group = 209.165.201.1, IP = 209.165.201.1, Rejecting IPSec tunnel: no
matching crypto map entry for remote proxy 10.10.1.0/255.255.255.0/0/0 local proxy
192.168.2.0/255.255.255.0/0/0 on interface outside
```

ISAKMP Captures

If you are troubleshooting an IPSec issues on the security appliance and prefer to see the detailed debug messages for the IPSec tunnel negotiations, you can enable the ISAKMP capture on the interface that terminates the VPN tunnel. After the captures are enabled, the security appliance captures the interesting packets and stores them in the buffer. You can view the captures packets by using the **show capture** command. In Example 16-39, an ISAKMP capture, called **IPSecCapture**, is enabled on the outside interface. After enabling the capture, try to establish the VPN tunnel by sending interesting traffic over the tunnel. Last, issue the **show capture IPSecCapture decode** command to view the log messages.

Example 16-39 *Enable ISAKMP Captures*

```
Chicago# capture IPSecCapture type isakmp interface outside
Chicago# show capture IPSecCapture decode

18 packets captured

   1: 02:43:17.1043700 209.165.201.1.500 > 209.165.200.225.500:  udp 76
      ISAKMP Header
        Initiator COOKIE: 8d d9 c8 9f 04 a1 0b 20
        Responder COOKIE: ac 4c 69 16 8e d0 4e 9f
        Next Payload: Hash
        Version: 1.0
        Exchange Type: Informational
        Flags: (Encryption)
        MessageID: 56EE3A19
        Length: 76

   2: 02:43:17.1043700 209.165.201.1.500 > 209.165.200.225.500:  udp 76
      ISAKMP Header
        Initiator COOKIE: 8d d9 c8 9f 04 a1 0b 20
        Responder COOKIE: ac 4c 69 16 8e d0 4e 9f
        Next Payload: Hash
        Version: 1.0
        Exchange Type: Informational
        Flags: (none)
        MessageID: 56EE3A19
        Length: 76
        Payload Hash
```

```
    Next Payload: Delete
    Reserved: 00
    Payload Length: 24
    Data:
      59 16 3f a0 2c ef 3c 07 4a fe bc 26 58 aa 5f 65
      04 55 f3 46
  Payload Delete
    Next Payload: None
    Reserved: 00
    Payload Length: 16
    DOI: IPsec
    Protocol-ID: PROTO_IPSEC_ESP
    Spi Size: 4
    # of SPIs: 1
    SPI (Hex dump): fe 8d fc 4d
  Extra data: 00 00 00 00 00 00 00 00
```

Summary

Every day, more and more organizations are deploying IPSec site-to-site tunnels to cut costs on traditional WAN links. It is the responsibility of the security professional to design and implement an IPSec solution that will fit the needs of an organization. If the other end of the IPSec VPN tunnel is managed by a different security professional, make sure that you consult with him before configuring the ISAKMP and IPSec attributes in the ASA. This chapter discussed the configuration necessary to implement the site-to-site tunnels and discussed two deployment scenarios. If you implement the solution, and the IPSec tunnel is not working as expected, use the appropriate **show** commands and monitor the status of the SAs. You can also turn on the ISAKMP and IPSec **debug** commands to help troubleshoot the issue.

Chapter 17

IPSec Remote-Access VPNs

This chapter covers the following topics:

- Cisco IPSec Remote Access VPN solution
- Advanced Cisco IPSec VPN features
- L2TP Over IPSec Remote Access VPN solution
- Deployment scenarios
- Monitoring and troubleshooting

Remote-access VPN services provide a way to connect home and mobile users to the corporate network. Until a decade ago, the only way to provide this service was through dialup connections using analog modems. Corporations had to maintain a huge pool of modems and access servers to accommodate remote users. Additionally, they were billed for providing toll-free and long-distance phone services. With the rapid growth of Internet technologies, more and more dialup mobile users are migrating to broadband DSL and cable-modem connections. As a result, corporations moved these dialup users to remote-access VPNs for faster communication.

There are many remote-access VPN protocols available to provide secure network access. The commonly used ones include the following:

- Point-to-Point Tunneling Protocol (PPTP)
- Layer 2 Tunneling Protocol (L2TP)
- Layer 2 Forwarding (L2F) Protocol
- IPSec
- L2TP over IPSec
- SSL VPN

The Cisco ASA supports the native IPSec and L2TP over IPSec to provide VPN services in a secure manner. Table 17-1 lists major differences between them. The Cisco IPSec Remote Access solution uses Cisco VPN clients while L2TP over IPSec uses the built-in VPN client on Microsoft operating systems.

Both Native IPSec and L2TP over IPSec VPN solutions are discussed in this chapter.

Cisco IPSec Remote Access VPN Solution

With the Cisco IPSec solution, Cisco ASA allows mobile and home users to establish a VPN tunnel by using Cisco software and Cisco hardware VPN clients. During Phase 1 IKE tunnel negotiations, the Cisco VPN client uses aggressive mode if preshared keys are used and uses main mode when public key infrastructure (PKI) is used. After bringing up the ISAKMP SA for secure communication, Cisco ASA prompts the user to specify the user credentials. In this phase, also known as *X-Auth* or *extended authentication*, the security appliance validates the user against the configured authentication database. If the user authentication is successful, Cisco ASA sends a successful authentication message back to the client. After X-Auth, the Cisco VPN client requests configuration parameters such as the IP address and the DNS and WINS server IP addresses, to name a few. During this phase, known as *mode-config*, the security appliance sends the configured parameters back to the client. The final step for a successful VPN tunnel is the negotiation of Phase 2 parameters, as illustrated in Figure 17-1. After completing the tunnel negotiations, the client can send or receive traffic over the secured connection.

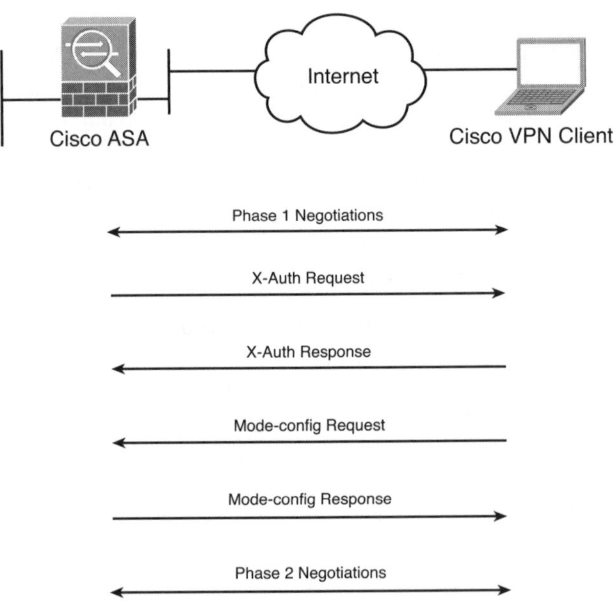

Figure 17-1 *Tunnel Negotiations for Cisco VPN Client*

Table 17-1 *Contrasting Native IPSec and L2TP over IPSec*

Feature	Cisco IPSec	L2TP over IPSec
VPN Client	Must install the Cisco VPN client 3.x or higher on endpoints.	Is pre-installed on most Windows operating systems
Transport	Uses IP protocol 50 ESP for transport.	Uses UDP port 1701 for data encapsulation. The L2TP packets are then encapsulated in ESP.
Encapsulation	Uses IPSec for data encryption and encapsulation.	Uses L2TP for data encapsulation and then IPSec for data encryption.
Authentication	Provides group- and user-level authentication.	Provides user-level authentication, using PPP authentication protocols.
Operating Systems	Supported on Windows, Linux, Mac OS X, and Solaris.	Supported on all Windows platforms and some Linux distributions.

> **Note** It is recommended to use main mode for IKE authentication, which requires RSA signatures because of the known vulnerabilities in aggressive mode.

IPSec Remote-Access Configuration Steps

Figure 17-2 illustrates SecureMe's Chicago hub office, which is to be configured for the Cisco remote-access VPN solution. This topology will be used to show the following configuration steps required to establish a successful VPN tunnel. Many of these steps are identical to the steps discussed in Chapter 16, "Site-to-Site IPSec VPNs." At the end of each configuration step, we show the equivalent CLI in case you prefer to configure the security appliances through the command line.

Step 1. Enable ISAKMP.

Step 2. Create ISAKMP policy.

Step 3. Set up tunnel and group policies.

Step 4. Define IPSec policy.

Step 5. Configure user authentication.

Step 6. Assign an IP addresss.

Step 7. Create a crypto map.

Step 8. Configure traffic filtering (Optional).

Step 9. Bypass NAT (Optional).

Step 10. Set up split tunneling (Optional).

Step 11. Define DNS and WINS addresses (Optional).

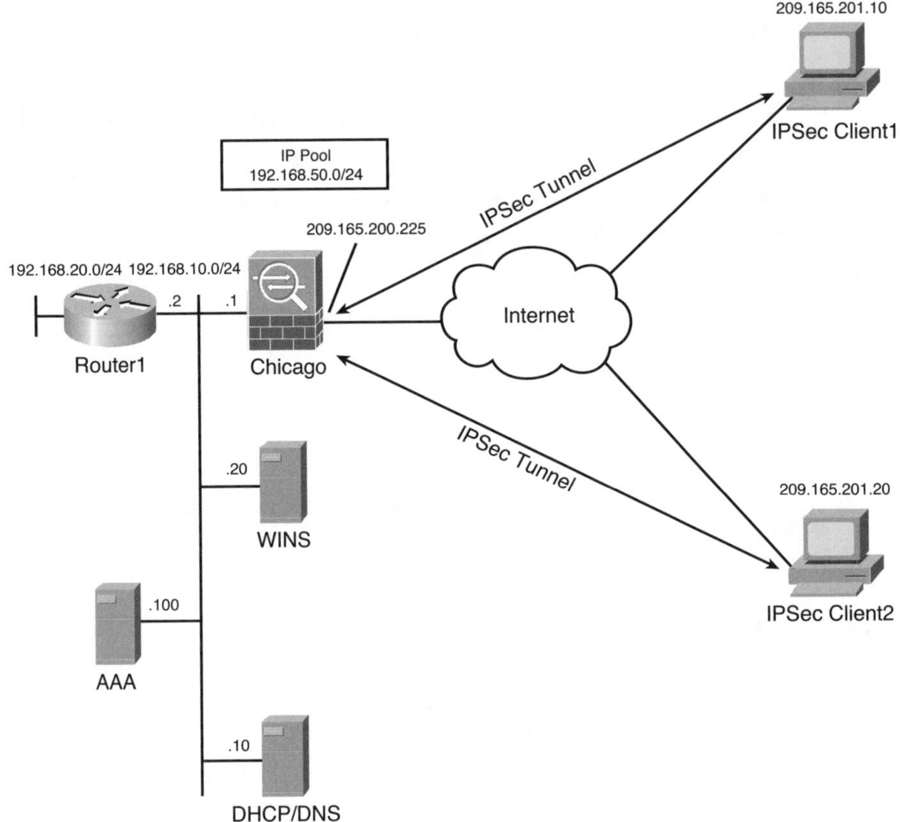

Figure 17-2 *Remote-Access Network Topology for SecureMe*

Step 1: Enable ISAKMP

IKE Phase 1 configuration starts by enabling ISAKMP on the interface that terminates the VPN tunnels. Typically, it is enabled on the Internet-facing or the outside interface. If ISAKMP is not enabled on an interface, the security appliance does not listen for the ISAKMP traffic on that interface. If you have a fully configured IPSec tunnel and ISAKMP is not enabled on the outside interface, the security appliance does not respond to a tunnel initialization request.

To enable ISAKMP on an interface, navigate to **Configuration > Remote Access VPN > Network (Client) Access > IPSec Connection Profiles** and select the **Allow Access** option next to the interface where you want to terminate the sessions. To terminate the IPSec sessions on the outside interface, select the **Allow Access** option next to the

outside interface. To push this configuration to the security appliance, click the **Apply** button in ASDM.

> **Note** When ASDM delivers the commands to enable ISAKMP on an interface, it also configures a number parameters, including
>
> - Two ISAKMP policies (policy numbers 5 and 10). They are discussed in the next section.
> - Ten IPSec Policies. They are discussed in the "Define the IPSec Policy" section.
> - A dynamic and a static crypto map. The static crypto map is applied to the VPN terminating interface. The crypto maps are discussed in the "Create a Crypto Map" section.

Example 17-1 shows the command line interface (CLI) output if you want to enable ISAKMP on the **outside** interface.

Example 17-1 *Enabling ISAKMP on the Outside Interface*

```
Chicago# configure terminal
Chicago(config)# crypto isakmp enable outside
```

> **Tip** IPSec VPN functionality is not available if the Cisco ASA is virtualized, discussed in Chapter 8, "Virtualization,".

Step 2: Create the ISAKMP Policy

After you enable ISAKMP on the interface, the next step is to create a Phase 1 policy that matches a policy on the VPN client. Phase 1 policy negotiates the encryption and other parameters that are useful in authenticating the remote peer as well as establishing a secure channel over which the VPN client and the security appliance entities can communicate.

To configure a new ISAKMP policy in the security appliance, navigate to **Configuration > Remote Access VPN > Network (Client) Access > Advanced > IPSec > IKE Policies** and click **Add.** ASDM launches a new window where you can specify the following attributes:

- **Priority—**A number between 1 and 65535. By default, ASDM has priority number 5 and 10 preconfigured. If multiple ISAKMP policies are configured, the Cisco ASA checks the ISAKMP policy with the lowest number first. If there is no match, it checks the policy with the next priority number, and so on until all policies have been evaluated. A priority value of 1 is evaluated first, and a priority value of 65535 is evaluated last.

- **Encryption**—Select the appropriate encryption type from the drop-down list. Cisco ASA employs a dedicated hardware encryption accelerator to process IKE requests. It is recommended that you select AES 256-bit encryption because the performance impact is pretty much the same as using a weaker encryption algorithm such as DES.
- **Hash**—Select the appropriate hash type, either MD5 or SHA, from the drop-down list. A hashing algorithm provides data integrity by verifying that the packet has not been changed in transit. It is recommended to use SHA because it provides better security than MD5.
- **Authentication**—Select the appropriate authentication type from the drop-down list. The authentication mechanism establishes the identity of the remote IPSec peer. You can use Preshared Keys, CRACK, or RSA. Chapter 18 discusses RSA signatures in detail.
- **D-H Group**—Select the appropriate D-H group from the drop-down list. D-H group is used to derive a shared secret to be used by the two VPN devices. The Cisco IPSec clients by default offer D-H group 2 and 5 when proposing IKE policies.
- **Lifetime**—Specify the lifetime after which a new set of ISAKMP keys are negotiated. You can specify a finite lifetime between 120 and 2,147,483,647 seconds. You can also select unlimited lifetime in case the remote peer does not propose a lifetime. Cisco recommends that you use the default lifetime of 86400 seconds for IKE rekeys.

Figure 17-3 shows that an ISAKMP policy of priority 1 is being added. The encryption method is **AES-256**, the hashing algorithm is **SHA**, the authentication mechanism is **preshared** keys, the D-H group is **2**, and the lifetime of **86400** seconds is specified.

> **Note** If the VPN-3DES-AES feature is not enabled, the security appliance allows DES encryption only for the ISAKMP and IPSec policies.

If you prefer the CLI, use the **crypto isakmp policy** command to define a new policy. Example 17-2 illustrates how to configure an ISAKMP policy for **AES-256** encryption, **SHA** hashing, DH **group 2**, and **preshared** keys for authentication, with **86,400** seconds as the lifetime.

Example 17-2 *Creating an ISAKMP Policy*

```
Chicago# configure terminal
Chicago(config)# crypto isakmp policy 1
Chicago(config-isakmp-policy)# authentication pre-share
Chicago(config-isakmp-policy)# encryption aes-256
Chicago(config-isakmp-policy)# hash sha
Chicago(config-isakmp-policy)# group 2
Chicago(config-isakmp-policy)# lifetime 86400
```

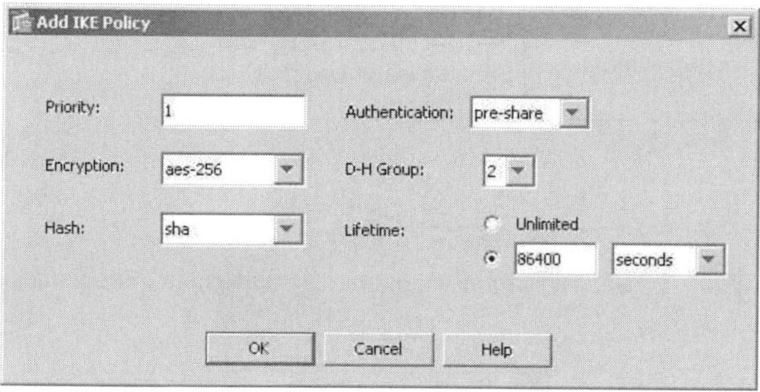

Figure 17-3 *Defining IKE Policy via ASDM*

Step 3: Set Up Tunnel and Group Policies

Cisco ASA uses an inheritance model when it pushes network and security policies to the end-user sessions. Using this model, you can configure policies at the following three locations:

- Under default group policy
- Under user's assigned group policy
- Under specific user's policy

In the inheritance model, a user inherits the attributes and policies from the user policy, which inherits its attributes and policies from the user group-policy, which in turn inherits its attributes and policies from the default group-policy, as illustrated in Figure 17-4. A user, ciscouser, receives a traffic ACL and an IP address from the user policy, the domain name from the user group policy, and IP Compression along with the number of simultaneous logins from the default group policy.

After these policies are defined, they must be bound to a tunnel group where users terminate their sessions. This way, a user who establishes his VPN session to a tunnel group inherits all the policies mapped to that tunnel. The tunnel group defines a VPN connection profile, of which each user is a member.

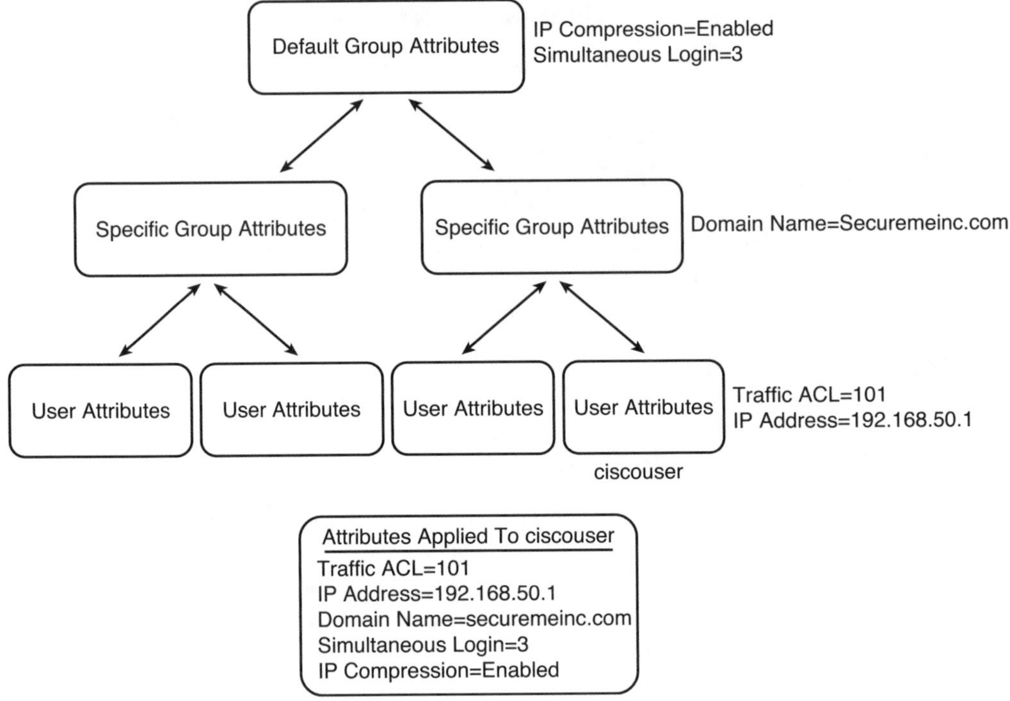

Figure 17-4 *ASA Attributes and Policies Inheritance Model*

Configuring Group Policies

You configure the user group and default group policies by choosing **Configuration > Remote Access VPN > Network (Client) Access > Group Policies.** Click **Add** to add a new group policy. As shown in Figure 17-5, a user group policy called **IPSecGroupPolicy** has been added. This group policy allows only IPSec tunnels to be established and strictly rejects all the other tunneling protocols. If you would rather assign attributes to the default group policy, modify DfltGrpPolicy (System Default). Any attribute that is modified here is propagated to any user group policy that inherits that attribute. A group policy name other than DfltGrpPolicy is treated as a user group policy.

> **Note** DfltGrpPolicy is a special group name that gets created by default and is used solely for the default group policy.

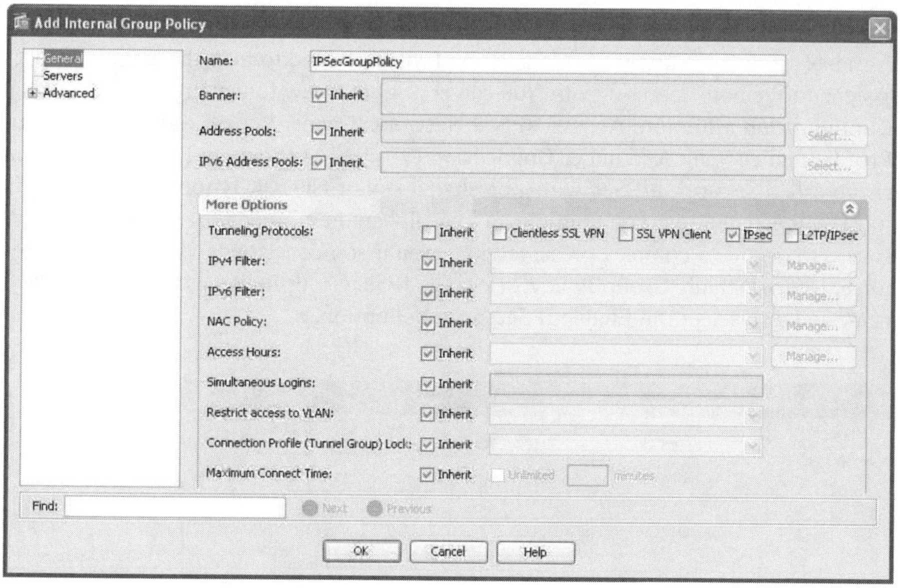

Figure 17-5 *User Group Policy Configuration*

The user, group, and default group polices can be applied to clientless, AnyConnect, and IPSec-based remote access VPN tunnels. The IPSec-specific attributes are discussed in detail in the next few sections of this chapter.

Note You can configure a user policy by choosing **Configuration > Remote Access VPN > AAA/Local Users > Local Users.**

Example 17-3 illustrates how to define a user group policy called **IPSecGroupPolicy**. This policy allows only the IPSec tunnels to be terminated on the group.

Example 17-3 *Tunnel Group Definition*

```
Chicago(config)# group-policy IPSecGroupPolicy internal
Chicago(config)# group-policy IPSecGroupPolicy attributes
Chicago(config-group-policy)# vpn-tunnel-protocol IPSec
```

Configuring a Tunnel Group

A tunnel group, also known as Connection Profile, is used to map the attributes that are assigned to remote access clients. You can configure a new tunnel group by choosing **Configuration > Remote Access VPN > Network (Client) Access > IPSec Connection Profiles** and clicking **Add** under **Connection Profiles.** As shown in Figure 17-6, a tunnel group called **SecureMeIPSec** with a preshared key of **C!$c0K3y** (obfuscated) is defined. It is recommended that you configure a long alphanumeric key with special characters. It is hard to decode a complex preshared key even if someone tries to break it by brute force. Under **Default Group Policy**, select the **IPSecGroupPolicy** as the group policy" name and also select the **Enable IPSec protocol** option.

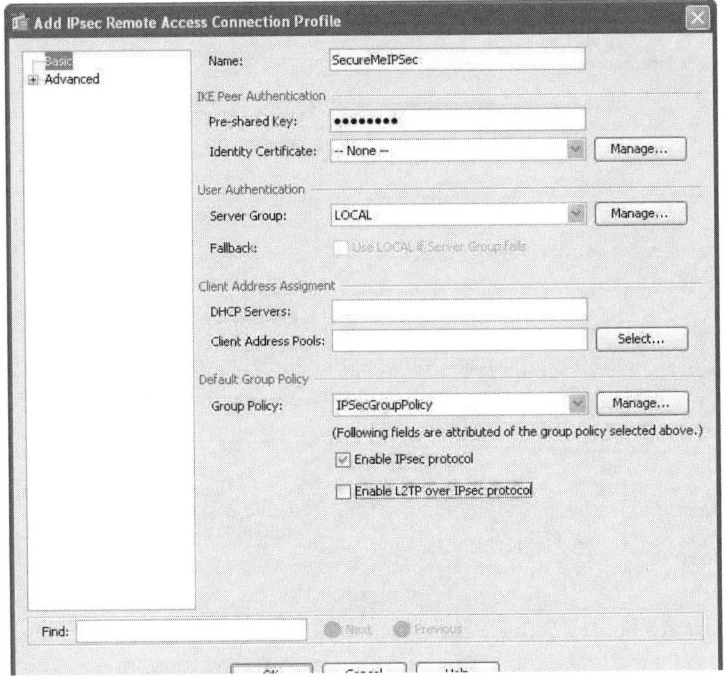

Figure 17-6 *Configuration of a Tunnel Group*

> **Note** The concept of *tunnel group* is taken from the VPN 3000 Series Concentrators.

Example 17-4 illustrates how to configure a remote-access tunnel group of **SecureMeIPSec**. The preshared key is defined under the **ipsec-attributes** of the tunnel group, using the **pre-shared-key** command.

Example 17-4 *Tunnel Group Definition*

```
Chicago(config)# tunnel-group SecureMeIPSec type remote-access
```

```
Chicago(config)# tunnel-group SecureMeIPSec general-attributes
Chicago(config-tunnel-general)# default-group-policy IPSecGroupPolicy
Chicago(config-tunnel-general)# tunnel-group SecureMeIPSec ipsec-attributes
Chicago(config-tunnel-ipsec)# pre-shared-key C!$c0K3y
```

Step 4: Define the IPSec Policy

An IPSec transform set specifies what type of encryption and hashing to use for the data packets after a secure connection has been established. This provides data authentication, confidentiality, and integrity. The IPSec transform set is negotiated during Quick Mode. To configure a new transform set through ASDM, navigate to **Configuration > Remote Access VPN > Network (Client) Access > Advanced > IPSec > IPSec Transform Sets** and click **Add**. A new window opens, allowing you to configure the following attributes:

- **Set Name**—Specify the name for this transform set. This name has local significance and is not transmitted during IPSec tunnel negotiations.
- **ESP Encryption**—Select the appropriate encryption type from the drop-down list. It is recommended that you select AES 256-bit encryption because the performance impact is pretty much the same as using a weaker encryption algorithm such as DES.
- **ESP Authentication**—Select the appropriate hash type—SHA, MD5, or none—from the drop-down list. A hashing algorithm provides data integrity by verifying that the packet has not been changed in transit. It is recommended to use SHA because it provides better security than MD5.
- **Mode**—Select the appropriate encapsulation mode from the bullet list. You have the option to use either transport or tunnel mode. Transport is used to encrypt and authenticate the data packets that are originated by the VPN peers. Tunnel mode is used to encrypt and authenticate the IP packets when they are originated by the hosts connected behind the VPN device. In a remote-access connection, tunnel mode is always used.

Note Cisco ASDM has ten predefined IPSec transform sets. You do not have to define a new transform set if you want to use a predefined transform set.

In Figure 17-7, a new transform set called **RA-AES256SHA** is being defined. It is set up to use **AES-256** encryption and **SHA** hashing for data packets. The encapsulation mode is defined as **tunnel**, the default mode.

Example 17-5 shows how an IPSec transform set can be configured through the CLI.

Example 17-5 *Transform-Set Configuration*

```
Chicago(config)# crypto ipsec transform-set RA-AES256SHA esp-aes-256 esp-sha-hmac
```

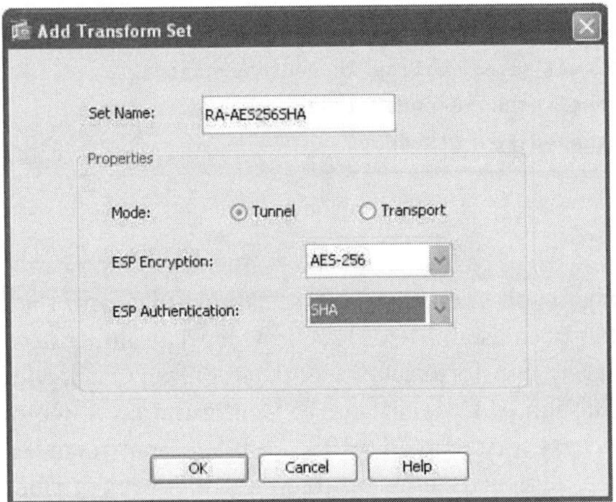

Figure 17-7 *Configuring IPSec Transform Set*

Step 5: Configure User Authentication

Cisco ASA supports a number of authentication servers, such as RADIUS, NT domain, Kerberos, SDI, LDAP, digital certificates, smart cards, and local databases. For small organizations, a local database can be set up for user authentication. For medium to large remoteaccess IPSec VPN deployments, it is highly recommended that you use an external authentication server, such as RADIUS or Kerberos, as the user authentication database. If you are deploying remote-access IPSec VPN for a few users, you can use the local database. You define users by choosing **Configuration** > **Remote Access VPN** > **AAA/Local Users** > **Local Users > Add.** As shown in Example 17-6, two accounts, **ciscouser** and **adminuser**, are configured for user authentication. The **ciscouser** account, with a password of **C1$c0123**, will be used for IPSec user authentication, whereas **adminuser**, with a password of **@d1m123**, will be used to manage the security appliance.

Example 17-6 *Local User Accounts*

```
Chicago(config)# username ciscouser password C1$c0123
Chicago(config)# username adminuser password @dmin123
```

Many enterprises either use a RADIUS server or Kerberos to leverage their existing active directory infrastructure for user authentication. Before configuring an external authentication server on Cisco ASA, you must specify authentication, authorization, and accounting (AAA) server groups by choosing **Configuration** > **Remote Access VPN** > **AAA/Local Users> AAA Server Groups > Add.** Specify a server group name that can be referenced by the other AAA processes. Select an authentication protocol for this server group name. For example, if you plan to use a RADIUS server for authentication, select **RADIUS** from the drop-down menu. This option ensures that the security appliance requests the appropriate information from the end users and forwards it to the RADIUS server for authentication and verification.

After enabling RADIUS processing, define a list of the RADIUS servers. The Cisco security appliance checks their availability on a round-robin basis. If the first server is not reachable, it tries the second server, and so on. If a server is available, the security appliance keeps using that server until it fails to receive a response. In this case, it checks the availability of the next server. It is highly recommended that you set up more than one RADIUS server in case the first server is not reachable. You can define a RADIUS server entry by navigating to **Configuration** > **Remote Access VPN** > **AAA/Local Users> AAA Server Groups**, selecting the correct AAA server Group, and clicking **Add** under Servers in the Selected Group. You can specify the IP address of the RADIUS server as well as the interface closest to the server. The security appliance authenticates itself to the RADIUS server by using a shared secret key. The security appliance, for security reasons, never sends this shared secret key over the network.

Figure 17-8 shows the Cisco ASA configured with an AAA server under the server group called **Radius**. The server is located toward the **inside** interface at **192.168.1.100** and uses a server secret key of **C1$c0123** (obfuscated).

Note You can optionally modify the authentication and accounting port numbers if your RADIUS server does not use the default ports. The security appliance uses UDP ports 1645 and 1646 as defaults for authentication and accounting, respectively. Most of the RADIUS servers use ports 1812 and 1813 as authentication and accounting ports, respectively.

After defining the authentication servers, you have to bind them to the IPSec process under a tunnel group. Figure 17-9 illustrates that the newly created **Radius** AAA server group is mapped to the **SecureMeIPSec** tunnel group.

Tip For large VPN deployments (both IPSec and SSL VPNs), you can even control user access and policy mapping from an external authentication server. You should pass the user group policy name as a RADIUS or LDAP attribute to the security appliance. By doing so, you guarantee that a user will always get the same policy, regardless of the tunnel group name to which he connects. If you are using RADIUS as the authentication and authorization server, you can specify the user group policy name as attribute 25 (class attribute). Append the keyword **OU=** as the value of the class attribute. For example, if you define a user group policy called engineering group, you can enable attribute **25** and specify **OU=engineering** as its value.

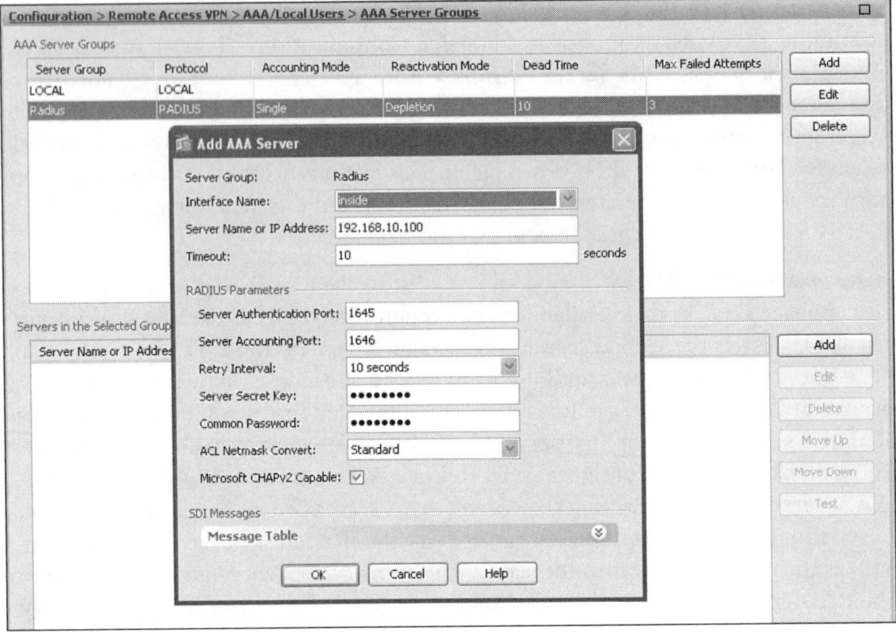

Figure 17-8 *Defining a RADIUS Server for Authentication*

Example 17-7 shows how a radius server can be defined. The radius group name is **Radius** and it is located toward the **inside** interface at **192.168.10.100**. The shared secret is **C1$c0123.**

Example 17-7 *Defining RADIUS for IPSec Authentication*

```
Chicago(config)# aaa-server Radius protocol radius
Chicago(config)# aaa-server Radius (inside) host 192.168.10.100
Chicago(config-aaa-server-host)# key C1$c0123
Chicago(config-aaa-server-host)# exit
Chicago(config) tunnel-group SecureMeIPSec general-attributes
Chicago(config-tunnel-general)# authentication-server-group Radius
```

For configuration of external servers, consult Chapter 6, "Authentication, Authorization, and Accounting (AAA) Services."

Step 6: Assign an IP Address

During the tunnel negotiations, an IP address is assigned to the VPN adapter of the IPSec VPN Client. The client uses this IP address to access resources on the protected side of the tunnel. Cisco ASA supports three different methods to assign an IP address back to the client:

- Local address pool
- DHCP server
- RADIUS server

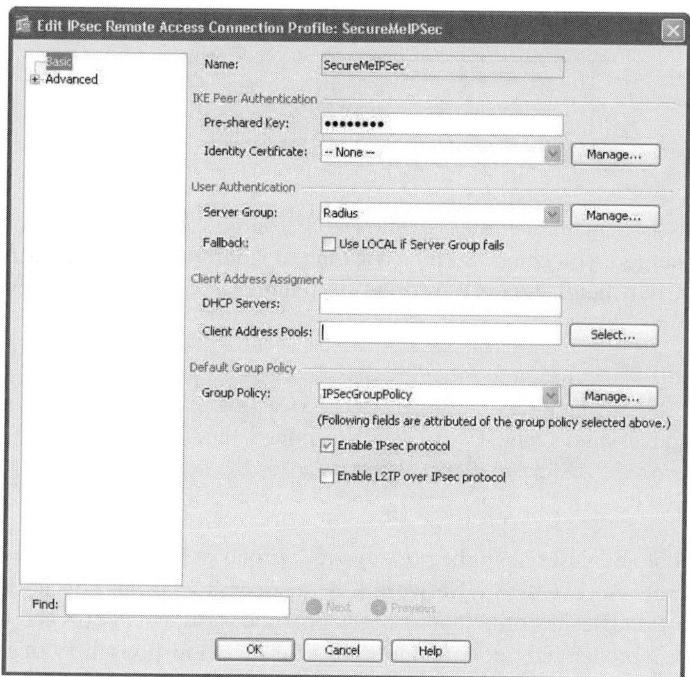

Figure 17-9 *Mapping a RADIUS Server to a Tunnel Group*

Many organizations prefer assigning an IP address from the local pool of addresses for flexibility. You can assign the IP address by configuring an address pool and then linking the pool to a group policy. You can either create a new pool of addresses or select a pre-configured address pool. You define a new pool of addresses by choosing **Configuration > Remote Access VPN > Network (Client) Access > Address Assignment > Address Pools.** Click **Add** and configure the following attributes, as illustrated in Figure 17-10:

- **Name**—An alphanumeric name to be assigned to this pool. A pool name of **IPPool** is assigned.
- **Starting IP Address**—The first IP address to be assigned to a client. A starting IP address of **192.168.50.1** is assigned.
- **Ending IP Address**—The last IP address to be assigned to a client. A starting IP address of **192.168.50.254** is assigned.
- **Subnet mask**—The associated subnet mask for this pool of addresses. A subnet mask of **255.255.255.0** is configured.

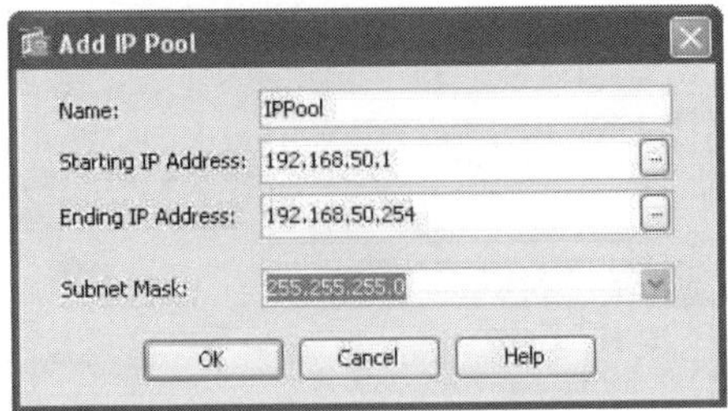

Figure 17-10 *Defining an Address Pool Through ASDM*

By default, all address assignment methods are allowed. If you want to disable a specific address assignment method, you can do so by navigating to **Configuration** > **Remote Access VPN** > **Network (Client) Access** > **Address Assignment** > **Assignment Policy.**

Note If all three methods are configured for address assignment, Cisco ASA prefers RADIUS over DHCP and internal address pools. If Cisco ASA is not able to get an address from the RADIUS server, it contacts the DHCP server for address allocation. If that method fails as well, Cisco ASA checks the local address pool as the last resort.

After defining a pool of addresses, map the pool to a user group policy. Choose **Configuration** > **Remote Access VPN** > **Network (Client) Access > Group Policies > IPSecGroupPolicy > Edit.** Deselect the **Inherit** check box under **Address Pools** and then click **Select** to choose a predefined pool of addresses. A new window pops up with all the preconfigured address pools. Select the address pool you want to use and click **Assign** to map the pool to this policy. In Figure 17-11, the **IPPool** is assigned to **IPSecGroupPolicy**. Click **OK** when finished.

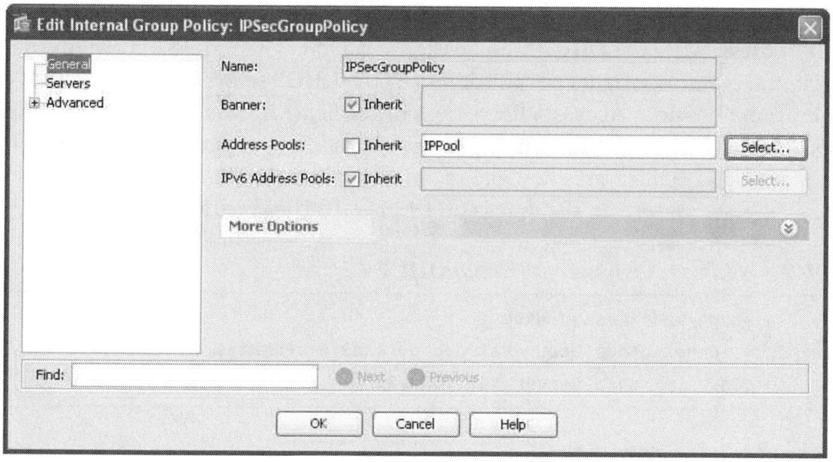

Figure 17-11 *Mapping an Address Pool to a Group Policy*

> **Note** A static IP address can be assigned to a user under the user policy. The VPN user receives the same IP address, regardless of the number of times that use connects to the Cisco ASA.

Example 17-8 shows how to assign an address from a pool called **IPPool**, which is mapped to a group policy called **IPSecGroupPolicy**.

Example 17-8 *Defining Pool of Addresses*

```
Chicago(config)# ip local pool IPPool 192.168.50.1-192.168.50.254 mask
  255.255.255.0
Chicago(config) group-policy IPSecGroupPolicy attributes
Chicago(config-group-policy)# address-pools value IPPool
```

> **Tip** You can also link a pool of addresses to the tunnel group. However, if a pool is mapped to a group policy and a different pool is mapped to a tunnel-group, then the security appliance prefers the pool mapped to the group policy.

For ease of management, the security appliance can contact a DHCP server when allocating an IP address. After the DHCP server assigns an address, Cisco ASA forwards that IP address to the client. Configure the IP address of the DHCP server by navigating to **Configuration > Remote Access VPN > Network (Client) Access > IPSec Connection Profiles > SecureMeIPSec > Edit** and specifying an address under the **DHCP Servers** option. Example 17-9 illustrates how the security appliance in Chicago can be configured to use a DHCP server with an IP address of **192.168.10.10** for address assignment.

Example 17-9 *Address Assignment from a DHCP Server*

```
Chicago(config)# vpn-addr-assign dhcp
Chicago(config)# tunnel-group SecureMeIPSec general-attributes
Chicago(config-general)# dhcp-server 192.168.10.10
```

Step 7: Create a Crypto Map

VPN clients often get dynamic IP addresses from their ISPs. In a crypto map, which requires a static IP address for the VPN peer, there is no way to map those dynamic IP addresses. Cisco ASA solves this problem by allowing configuration of a dynamic crypto map. When you enable ISAKMP on an interface, Cisco ASDM preconfigures a dynamic crypto map for you. If you want to change any parameters, you can navigate to **Configuration > Remote Access VPN > Network (Client) Access > Advanced > IPSec > Crypto Maps**, select the dynamic crypto map—that has a priority of 65535—and click **Edit**. Example 17-10 demonstrates the configuration of the Cisco ASA to use the defined transform set **ESP-AES-256-SHA** with the default dynamic crypto map. The dynamic crypto map name is **SYSTEM_DEFAULT_CRYPTO_MAP** and it is configured with a sequence number of **65535**. Assigning a transform set to a dynamic crypto map is a required configuration step.

Example 17-10 *Defining Dynamic Crypto Map*

```
Chicago(config)# crypto dynamic-map SYSTEM_DEFAULT_CRYPTO_MAP 65535 set transform-
  set ESP-AES-256-SHA
```

You can optionally configure many IPSec attributes in the dynamic crypto map. They include disabling NAT-T, configuring PFS, and reverse-route injection (RRI), and setting security association (SA) lifetimes. Chapter 16 covers these attributes.

When a dynamic map is defined via Cisco ASDM, it also creates a crypto map entry, which eventually gets applied to the interface terminating the IPSec tunnels. Example 17-11 shows the crypto map configuration when a dynamic map called SYSTEM_DEFAULT_CRYPTO_MAP is linked to a static map called **outside_map**.

Example 17-11 *Defining Static Crypto Map*

```
Chicago(config)# crypto map outside_map 65535 ipsec-isakmp dynamic
  SYSTEM_DEFAULT_CRYPTO_MAP
```

The crypto map can have both static and dynamic crypto map entries, discussed later in the deployment section Load Balancing with Cisco IPSec Clients and Site-to-Site Integration.

The Cisco ASA limits you to apply one crypto map per interface. If there is a need to configure multiple VPN tunnels, use the same crypto map name with a different sequence number. However, the security appliance evaluates a VPN tunnel with the lowest sequence number first.

The next step in setting up a remote-access tunnel is to bind the crypto map to an interface. When ISAKMP is enabled on an interface, Cisco ASDM applies the crypto map on the interface dynamically. If you are configuring the IPSec tunnels via the CLI, use the **crypto map** command followed by the name of the crypto map and the interface terminating the tunnels. In Example 17-12, the crypto map, **outside_map**, is applied to the **outside** interface of the Chicago ASA.

Example 17-12 *Applying a Crypto Map to the Outside Interface*

```
Chicago(config)# crypto map outside_map interface outside
```

Step 8: Configure Traffic Filtering (Optional)

Like a traditional firewall, the Cisco ASA protects the trusted network from outside traffic, unless the access control lists (ACL) explicitly permit traffic to pass through it. However, by default, the security appliance allows all IPSec traffic to pass through the interface ACLs. For example, even if the outside interface ACL does not permit the decrypted traffic to pass through, the security appliance trusts the remote private network and permits the decrypted packets to pass through.

You can change this default behavior, if you want the outside interface ACL to inspect the IPSec protected traffic, by navigating to **Configuration > Remote Access VPN > Network (Client) Access > Advanced > IPSec > System Options** and deselecting the **Enable Inbound IPSec Sessions to Bypass Interface Access-Lists** option. If you prefer to use the CLI, issue the **no sysopt connection permit-vpn** command and define appropriate ACLs to allow VPN traffic to pass through. Example 17-13 shows that only the Telnet traffic from the VPN pool of addresses (192.168.50.0/24) to an inside host located at 192.168.10.10 is allowed to pass through the security appliance.

Example 17-13 *Disabling Sysopt and Configuring ACLs*

```
Chicago(config)# no sysopt connection permit-vpn
Chicago(config)# access-list outside_acl extended permit tcp 192.168.50.0
  255.255.255.0 host 192.168.10.10 eq 23
Chicago(config)# access-group outside_acl in interface outside
```

If you do not want to disable the **sysopt connection permit-vpn** and still want to filter VPN traffic for a specific user or group policy, you can define an access list to allow or deny specific traffic and map that access list to a user or group policy. Using ASDM, choosing **Configuration > Remote Access VPN > Network (Client) Access > Group Policies > IPSecGroupPolicy > Edit > General > More Options**, deselect the **Inherit** box for the **IPv4 Filter** option, and select an ACL from the drop-down menu.

Example 17-14 shows that only the Telnet traffic from the VPN pool of addresses (**192.168.50.0/24**) to an inside host located at **192.168.10.10** is allowed to pass through the **IPSecGroupPolicy.**

Example 17-14 *Disabling Sysopt and Configuring ACLs*

```
Chicago(config)# access-list FilterTelnet extended permit tcp 192.168.50.0
  255.255.255.0 192.168.10.10 255.255.255.0 eq telnet
Chicago(config)# group-policy IPSecGroupPolicy attributes
Chicago(config-group)# vpn-filter value FilterTelnet
```

Step 9: Bypass NAT (Optional)

In most cases, you do not want to change the IP addresses for the traffic going over the tunnel. If NAT is configured on the security appliance to change the source or destination IP addresses, you can set up the NAT exemption rules to bypass address translation, as discussed in Chapter 4, "Controlling Network Access," and in Chapter 16.

Step 10: Set Up Split Tunneling (Optional)

After the tunnel is up, the default behavior of the Cisco IPSec VPN Client is to encrypt traffic to all destination IP addresses. This means that if an IPSec user wants to browse to http://www.cisco.com over the Internet, as illustrated in Figure 17-12, the packets get encrypted and are sent to Cisco ASA. After decrypting them, the security appliance looks at its routing table and forwards the packet to the appropriate next-hop IP address in clear text. These steps are reversed when traffic returns from the web server and is destined to the SSL VPN client.

This behavior might not always be desirable for the following two reasons:

- Traffic destined to the nonsecure networks traverses over the Internet twice: once encrypted and once in clear text.
- Cisco ASA handles extra VPN traffic destined to the nonsecure subnet. The security appliance analyzes all traffic leaving and coming from the Internet and that impacts overall device performance.

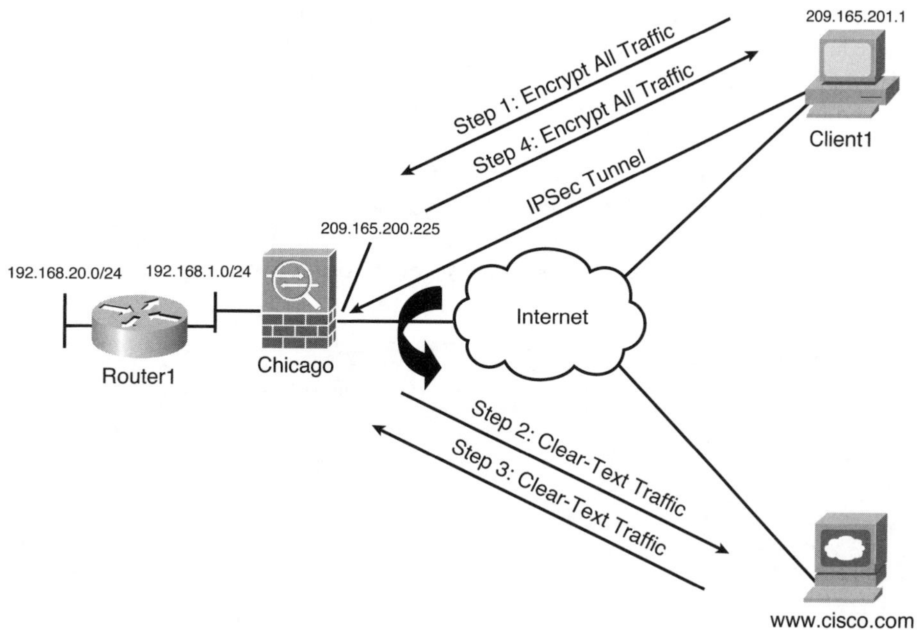

Figure 17-12 *Traffic with No Split Tunneling*

With split tunneling, the security appliance can notify the IPSec VPN client about the secured subnets. The VPN client, using the secured routes, encrypts only those packets that are destined for the networks behind the security appliance.

> **Caution** With split tunneling, the remote computer is susceptible to hackers, who can potentially take control over the computer and direct traffic over the tunnel. To mitigate this behavior, a personal firewall is highly recommended on the IPSec VPN clients' workstations.

The security appliance provides three modes for split tunneling:

- Tunnel all traffic (no split tunneling)
- Tunnel specific networks (split tunneling)
- Tunnel all but specific networks (exclude split tunneling)

In the Tunnel All but Specific Networks options, Cisco ASA tunnels all traffic except for a list of networks that require clear-text access. This feature is useful if users require clear-text access to their local LAN and an encrypted tunnel for all other traffic.

Split tunneling can be configured under a user, user group policy, or default group policy. Choose **Configuration > Remote Access VPN > Network (Client) Access > Group**

Policies > IPSecGroupPolicy > Edit > Advanced > Split Tunneling. Under **Policy** and **Network List**, deselect the **Inherit** check box. Select **Tunnel Network List Below** from the **Policy** drop-down menu. Additionally, select a network list from the drop-down menu of **Network List.** If you would rather define a new network list, click the **Manage** option. Cisco ASDM launches the ACL Manager and prompts you to define a new list. Under the **Standard ACL** tab, click **Add** to add an ACL. In Figure 17-13, a new ACL, called **SplitTunnelList** has been added. Select the newly defined list, click **Add** again under the **Standard ACL**, and add an ACE. An ACE entry for 192.168.10.0/24 has been added with a description of **List to Allow Access to Inside Network.**

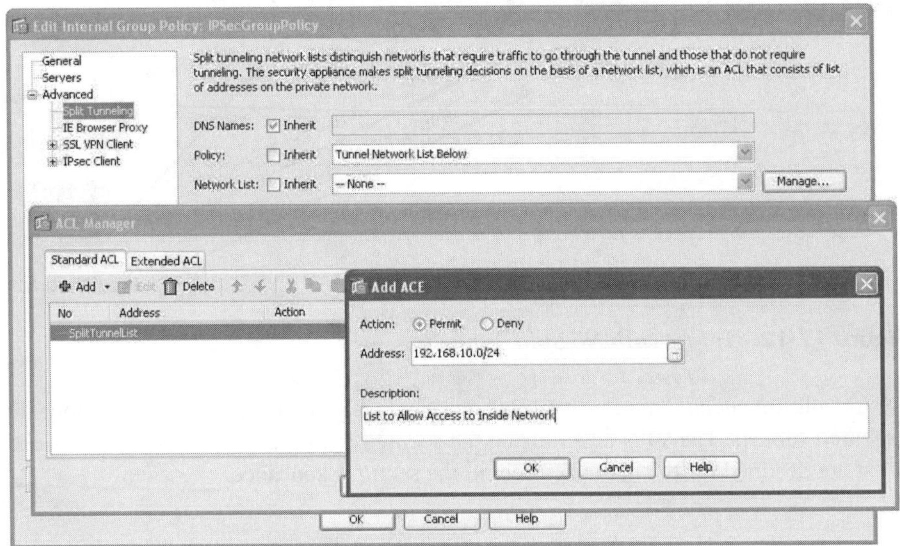

Figure 17-13 *Split Tunneling Configuration*

Example 17-14 *Split Tunnel Configuration*

```
Chicago(config)# access-list SplitTunnelList standard permit 192.168.10.0
  255.255.255.0
Chicago(config)# access-list SplitTunnelList remark List to Allow Access to
  Inside Network
Chicago(config)# group-policy IPSecGroupPolicy attributes
Chicago(config-group-policy)# split-tunnel-policy tunnelspecified
Chicago(config-group-policy)# split-tunnel-network-list value SplitTunnelList
```

Step 11: Assign DNS and WINS (Optional)

For the IPSec VPN clients, you can assign DNS and WINS server IP addresses so that they can browse and access internal sites after their tunnel has established. You can configure these attributes by choosing **Configuration > Remote Access VPN > Network (Client) Access > Group Policies > IPSecGroupPolicy > Edit > Servers** and deselecting the Inherit box for DNS Servers, WINS Servers, and Default Gateway. To add multiple DNS or WINS servers, use a comma (,) to separate the entries. In Figure 17-14, the primary DNS server is defined as **192.168.10.10**, and the secondary DNS server is **192.168.10.20**. The primary WINS server is **192.168.10.20**, and the secondary WINS server is **192.168.10.10**. The default domain name to be pushed to the IPSec VPN Client is **securemeinc.com**.

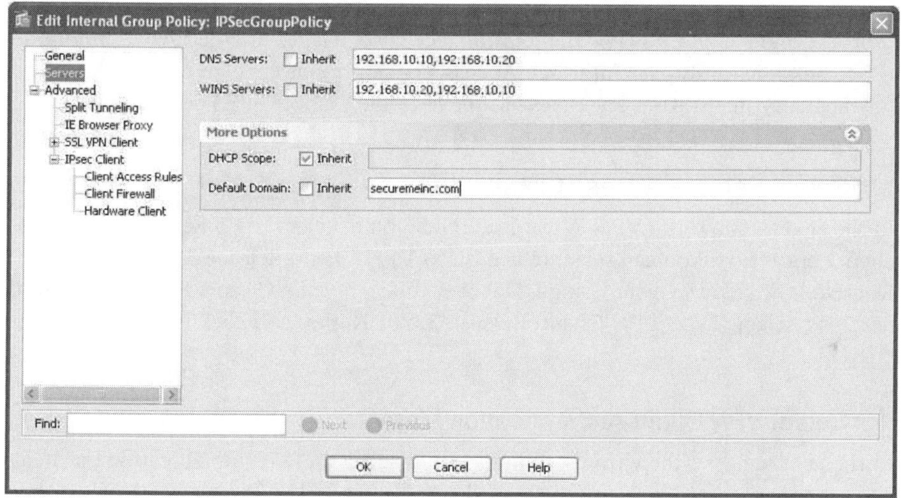

Figure 17-14 *Defining DNS and WINS Servers for IPSec VPN Clients*

Example 17-15 shows the CLI equivalent of Figure 17-14.

Example 17-15 *Defining DNS and WINS Servers for IPSec VPN Clients*

```
Chicago(config)# group-policy IPSecGroupPolicy attributes
Chicago(config-group-policy)# wins-server value 192.168.10.20 192.168.10.10
Chicago(config-group-policy)# dns-server value 192.168.10.10 192.168.10.20
Chicago(config-group-policy)# default-domain value securemeinc.com
```

Alternate Configuration Method through ASDM

The simplest and easiest way to define a new IPSec remote access connection is by clicking **Wizards** in the toolbar and then selecting **IPSec VPN Wizard.** ASDM launches the VPN Wizard with the option to choose a VPN tunnel type. Follow these steps to successfully define a remote-access IPSec tunnel.

Step 1: Select Tunnel Type

After the IPSec Wizard is launched, the very first thing the ASDM wizard prompts you is to specify the tunnel type. You can either select site-to-site or remote-access tunnels. Select **Remote Access** as the VPN tunnel type.

The wizard also prompts you to specify the interface that will be terminating the IPSec tunnels. If your VPN terminating interface is the outside interface, select **outside** from the drop-down menu in the **VPN Tunnel Interface** field. Make sure the **Enable Inbound IPSec Sessions to Bypass Interface Access Lists** option is enabled to bypass ACL check for the decrypted traffic. Click **Next** to move to the Remote Site Peer window.

Step 2: Select Remote Access Client

In the next window, the VPN Wizard prompts you to select the IPSec remote-access client connection. You can select either Cisco VPN Client, Release 3.x or Higher or Microsoft Windows Client Using L2TP over IPSec. For the Cisco VPN client-based connections, select **Cisco VPN Client, Release 3.x or Higher** and click **Next.**

Step 3: Select VPN Client Authentication Method

In the next window, the wizard prompts you to select an IKE authentication mechanism such as the preshared keys or preinstalled certificates. Select **Pre-shared Keys** as the authentication method and specify **C!$c0K3y.** ASDM also prompts you to specify the tunnel group name. Specify **SecureMeIPSec** as the group name. Click **Next** to move to the user authentication window.

Step 4: Specify User Authentication Method

In the next window, the wizard prompts you to select a user authentication mechanism such as the local database or an external server. If you want to use an external server, such as RADIUS, select **Authenticate Using an AAA Server Group** and select a predefined server group name. If a server is not defined, click **New** to define a new external authentication server. If you would rather use the local database, select **Authenticate Using the Local User Database.** After you click **Next,** ASDM prompts you to add any additional users that you want to declare. If you do not want to add any additional local users, click Next to specify a pool of addresses to be assigned to the VPN clients.

Step 5: Specify an Address Pool

The Cisco ASDM Wizard, in the next window, prompts you to select a predefined pool of addresses under the **Pool Name** drop-down menu. If a pool of addresses is not currently defined, you can click **New** and specify a pool name of **IPPool**, a start address of **192.168.50.1**, an end address of **192.168.50.254**, and a mask of **255.255.255.0** for the new pool of addresses. Click **Next to continue.**

Step 6: Specify Attributes Pushed to Clients

After defining the pool of addresses, the Cisco ASDM Wizard prompts you to specify mode-config attributes such as the primary and secondary DNS and WINS server and a default domain name. All these parameters are optional and sent to the VPN client during tunnel negotiations. Specify **192.168.10.10** and **192.168.10.20** as the DNS addresses and **192.168.10.20** and **192.168.10.10** as the WINS addresses. Also specify a domain name of **securemeinc.com.** Click **Next** to specify an IKE policy.

Step 7: Select the IKE Policy

Select the appropriate IKE policy for this peer. Use **AES-256** for encryption, **SHA** for authentication, and **DH group 5** for key generation to match the configuration with the remote peer. Click **Next** to move to the IPSec Settings window.

Step 8: Select the IPSec Settings

In the next window, the wizard prompts you to specify some of the optional IPSec parameters such as address translation bypass mechanism, split-tunneling, and perfect forwarding secrecy (PFS). Select the appropriate IKE policy for this peer. If you do not specify any networks in the selected Network/Host list, then the security appliance bypasses addresses translation for the traffic from all internal networks to the pool of addresses. If you specify a specific network, then traffic from that network to the pool of VPN traffic will be bypassed for address translation.

You can also enable split tunneling so that the selected networks and hosts are pushed to the VPN split-tunneling policy. The VPN clients send only encrypted data to the selected networks and hosts, and all other data from the VPN clients is sent out in clear text. To enable split-tunneling, select the **Enable Split Tunneling** option after selecting the networks/host in the list.

The IPSec Wizard also enables you to enable PFS with the appropriate D-H group type. PFS is discussed in Chapter 16 in more detail.

Step 9: Verify the Configuration

The VPN wizard shows you a summary of all the features and configurations you have set. After you have verified the configuration, click **Finish** to push the configuration to the security appliance.

Cisco VPN Client Configuration

The Cisco VPN Client, also known as the Cisco Easy VPN Client, initiates the IPSec tunnel to the security appliance. If the configuration and user credentials are valid, the tunnel is established and traffic is processed over it. The Cisco VPN clients come in two different types, which are discussed in the sections that follow:

- Software-based VPN clients
- Hardware-based VPN clients

Software-Based VPN Clients

The software-based VPN client runs on a variety of operating systems, such as Windows, Solaris, Linux, and Mac OS/X. It can be downloaded from Cisco.com free of charge as long as the Cisco ASA is under a valid service contract.

Before you configure the Cisco VPN client, it needs to be installed on the host machine. Please refer to http://www.cisco.com/go/vpnclient for the installation instructions. Cisco ASA supports version 3.x or higher VPN clients.

Note The installation of Cisco VPN Client requires administrative privileges on the workstation.

In Windows-based operating systems, you launch the **VPN client** by running the VPN client executable found under **Start > Program > Cisco Systems VPN Client** after it is installed. The operating system runs the executable and displays the VPN Client utility.

The configuration of a Windows-based VPN client requires five parameters:

- Name of the connection entry
- Public IP address of the Cisco ASA
- Group name to which the VPN client will be connecting
- Group preshared key
- Tunnel encapsulation

You can configure these parameters on the Cisco VPN client by clicking the **New** icon. The Cisco VPN client shows a different window in which you can enter the necessary information. In Figure 17-15, the user has specified the Connection Entry as **Chicago ASA.** You can name this entry any way you like because it is locally significant and is not forwarded to the security appliance. You can optionally enter the description for this connection entry. In this example, the connection description is **Connection to Chicago ASA.** The VPN client requires you to input the IP address or the hostname of the security appliance. Because the public IP address of the security appliance in Chicago is **209.165.200.225**, the VPN client is set up to use this address. The group name that the

VPN client is configured to use is **SecureMeIPSec**, and the group password is **C!$cOK3y**, displayed as asterisks. The group password on the client is the preshared key configured on the security appliance.

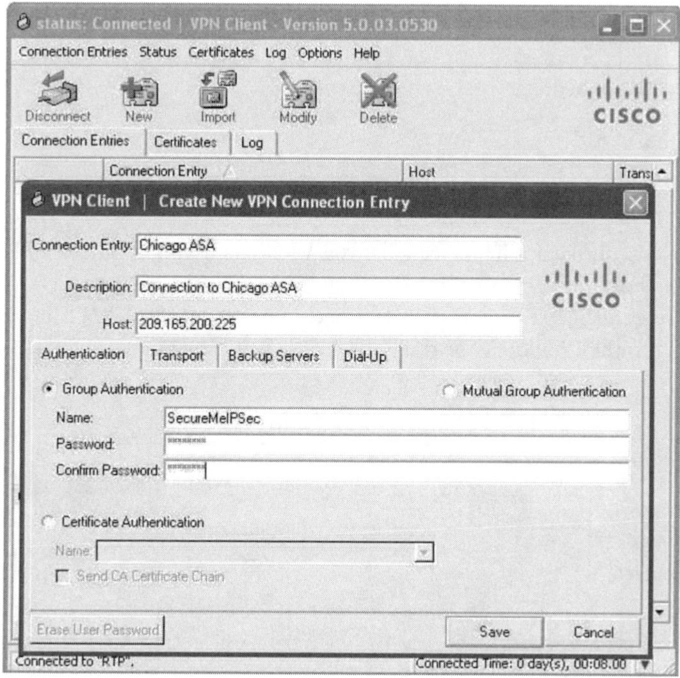

Figure 17-15 *VPN Client Configuration*

You can specify what type of data encapsulation the Cisco VPN client should be using. This is set up under the Transport tab. If IPSec over UDP or NAT-T is the encapsulation mode, then check the **Enable Transparent Tunneling** box with **IPSec over UDP (NAT/PAT)** as the selected option. If IPSec over TCP is the required encapsulation, then select **IPSec over TCP** and specify the appropriate port number.

Note The security appliance must to be set up for transparent tunneling as well. Consult the upcoming section "Transparent Tunneling" for a detailed explanation and configuration.

Note If the Enable Transparent Tunneling box in the Transport tab is disabled, the VPN client uses only the native IPSec encapsulation mode, using ESP.

After configuring the VPN client, the user can click the **Connect** icon to establish the connection to the security appliance.

Hardware-Based VPN Clients

The Cisco hardware-based VPN clients can also provide the remote-access IPSec functionality by using the dedicated Cisco hardware devices. Easy VPN is supported on the following platforms:

- Cisco IOS router
- Cisco PIX Firewall
- Cisco ASA 5505
- Cisco VPN 3002 hardware client

A Cisco 5505 security appliance can act as a VPN client and initiate a VPN tunnel on behalf of the hosts residing on the private subnet, as shown in Figure 17-16. When the 5005 ASA receives interesting traffic destined to pass over the VPN tunnel, it initiates an IPSec tunnel to the IP address of the headend security appliance.

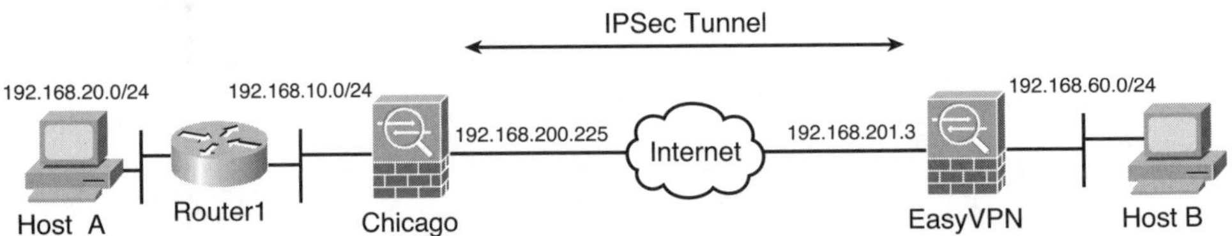

Figure 17-16 *Cisco ASA-Based Easy VPN Client Connecting to Headend Cisco ASA*

Two connection modes are supported by the hardware-based Easy VPN devices:

- **Client mode**—Also called the Port Address Translation (PAT) mode. It isolates all hosts on the private side of the hardware VPN client from those on the corporate network. The hardware-based Easy VPN client translates all traffic initiated by the hosts on the private side to a single-source IP address before sending it over the tunnel. This source IP address is assigned to the client by the security appliance during the mode-config exchange. The client translates the original source IP address by assigning a random source port. The client keeps and maintains a port translation table to identify where to send responses on the private network. Using the client mode, the hosts on the private network can initiate traffic destined to the corporate network. However, the hosts on the corporate network cannot initiate traffic back to the private network of the Easy VPN client.
- **Network Extension Mode (NEM)**—Acts similarly to a site-to-site tunnel in that hosts behind the corporate network can initiate traffic destined to the network behind the Easy VPN client, and vice versa. Thus, hosts on either side know each other by their actual addresses. The major difference between the site-to-site and NEM VPN tunnels is that when you use NEM VPN tunnels, the IPSec connection has to be initiated by

the Easy VPN client. Using NEM, there is no need for the security appliance to assign an IP address to the client. Therefore, the client does not participate in PAT for traffic destined over the VPN tunnel.

The Easy VPN configuration on the Cisco ASA 5505 requires the use of **vpnclient** commands. In Example 17-16, EasyVPN is configured on a 5505 to connect to the headend ASA's public IP address of **209.165.200.225**. The group name that the EasyVPN client is using is **SecureMeIPSec**, with the group password of **C!$cOK3y**. The administrator has set up **network-extension-mode** for this connection. For X-Auth, a username of **ciscouser** with a password of **C1$c0123** is being configured.

Example 17-16 *Cisco 5505 Easy VPN Client Configuration*

```
interface Vlan1
 nameif inside
 security-level 100
 ip address 192.168.60.1 255.255.255.0
!
interface Vlan2
 nameif outside
 security-level 0
 ip address 209.165.201.3  255.255.255.0
!
interface Ethernet0/0
 switchport access vlan 2
! Address Translation rules for the inside hosts to connect to the Internet
global (outside) 1 interface
nat (inside) 1  192.168.60.0 255.255.255.0
!—- Specify the IP address of the VPN server.
vpnclient server 209.168.200.225
!—- This example uses network extension mode.
vpnclient mode network-extension-mode
!—- Specify the group name and the pre-shared key.
vpnclient vpngroup SecureMeIPSec password C!$c0K3y
!—- Specify the authentication username and password.
vpnclient username ciscouser password C1$c0123
!—- In order to enable the device as hardware vpnclient, use this command.
vpnclient enable
```

Note For Cisco PIX, IOS and VPN 3002 Hardware Client installation and configuration documents, refer to the following links.

PIX Easy VPN Client:

http://www.cisco.com/en/US/docs/security/pix/pix63/configuration/guide/pixclnt.html

IOS Easy VPN Client:

http://www.cisco.com/go/easyvpn

VPN 3002 Hardware Client:

http://www.cisco.com/univercd/cc/td/doc/product/vpn/vpn3002/4-1/referenc/tunnel.htm

Advanced Cisco IPSec VPN Features

Cisco ASA provides many advanced features to suit your remote-access VPN implementations, including the following:

- Tunnel Default Gateway
- Transparent tunneling
- IPSec hairpinning
- VPN load-balancing
- Client auto-update
- Client firewalling
- Easy VPN features

Tunnel Default Gateway

A Layer 3 device typically has a default gateway that it uses to route packets when the destination address is not found in its routing table. Tunnel default gateway is used to route packets if they reach the security appliance over an IPSec tunnel and if their destination IP address is not found in the routing table. The tunneled traffic can be either remote access or site-to-site VPN traffic. The tunnel default gateway next-hop address is generally the IP address of the inside router, or any Layer 3 device.

The tunnel default gateway feature is important if you do not want to define routes for your internal networks on the Cisco ASA, and instead you want all tunneled traffic to be sent to the internal router for routing.

To set up a tunnel default gateway, navigate to **Configuration > Device Setup > Routing > Static Routes > Add.** A new window appears where you can add a default route with the gateway IP being the next-hop IP address of the inside router (Router1). Make sure that you select the **Tunneled** radio button, as shown in Figure 17-17.

If you prefer to use the CLI, make sure that you add the keyword **tunneled** to the statically configured default route. Example 17-17 shows the configuration of the appliance with the tunnel default gateway specified as 192.168.10.2, located on the inside interface.

Example 17-17 *Tunnel Default Gateway Configuration*

```
Chicago(config)# route inside 0.0.0.0 0.0.0.0 192.168.10.2 tunneled
```

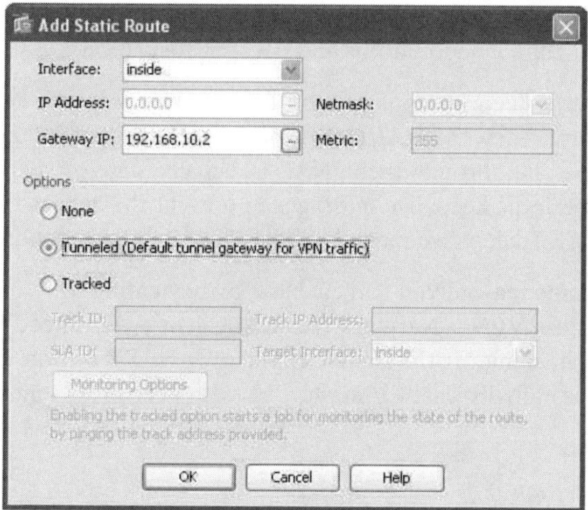

Figure 17-17 *Defining a Tunnel Default Gateway*

Transparent Tunneling

In many network topologies, the VPN clients reside behind a NAT/PAT device that inspects the Layer 4 port information for address translation. Because IPSec uses ESP (IP protocol 50), which does not have Layer 4 information, the PAT device is usually incapable of translating the encrypted packets going over the VPN tunnel. To remedy this problem, Cisco ASA offers three solutions:

- NAT Traversal (NAT-T)
- IPSec over UDP
- IPSec over TCP

NAT Traversal

NAT-T, RFC 3947, is a feature that encapsulates the ESP packets into UDP port 4500 packets. NAT-T is dynamically negotiated if the following two conditions are met:

- Both VPN devices are NAT-T-capable
- A NAT or PAT device exists between VPN peers

If both conditions are true, the VPN client tries to connect to the security appliance, using UDP port 500 for IKE negotiations. As soon as the VPN peers discover that they are NAT-T-capable and a NAT/PAT device resides between them, they switch over to UDP port 4500 for the rest of tunnel negotiations and data encapsulation.

NAT-T is globally enabled on the security appliance by default, with a default keepalive timeout of 20 seconds. In many cases, the NAT/PAT devices time out the UDP port 4500 entries if no active traffic is passing through them. NAT-T keepalives are used so that the security appliance can send periodic keepalive messages to prevent the entries from timing out. You can specify a NAT-T keepalive range between 10 and 3600 seconds.

If NAT-T is not enabled for some reason, you can enable it by navigating to **Configuration > Remote Access VPN > Network (Access) Client > Advanced > IPSec > IKE Parameters** and then checking off the **Enable IPSec over NAT-T** option. Example 17-18 illustrates how NAT-T is globally enabled in the CLI, with keepalives sent to every 30 seconds.

Example 17-18 *Enabling NAT-T Globally*

```
Chicago(config)# crypto isakmp nat-traversal 30
```

Note NAT-T is supported on Cisco VPN clients running version 3.6 or higher.

IPSec over UDP

IPSec over UDP, similar to NAT-T, is used to encapsulate the ESP packets using a UDP wrapper. This is useful in scenarios where the VPN clients do not support NAT-T and are behind a firewall that does not allow ESP packets to pass through. In IPSec over UDP, the IKE negotiations still use UDP port 500. During the negotiations, Cisco ASA informs the VPN client to use IPSec over UDP for data transport. Additionally, Cisco ASA updates the VPN client about the UDP port it should use.

You can enable IPSec over UDP in a user group policy by navigating to **Configuration > Remote Access VPN > Network (Client) Access > Group Policies > IPSecGroupPolicy > Edit > Advanced > IPSec Client** and deselecting the **inherit** option for the **IPSec Over UDP** and **IPSec Over UDP Port** parameters. Select **Enable** for **IPSec over UDP** and port **10000** for **IPSec Over UDP Port.**

Example 17-19 shows how Cisco ASA can be set up in the CLI to use IPSec over UDP for the remote-access group **IPSecGroupPolicy**. Cisco ASA pushes UDP port **10000** as the data encapsulation port to the VPN client.

Example 17-19 *IPSec over UDP Configuration*

```
Chicago(config)# group-policy IPSecGroupPolicy attributes
Chicago(config-group-policy)# ipsec-udp enable
Chicago(config-group-policy)# ipsec-udp-port 10000
```

IPSec over TCP

IPSec over TCP is an important feature used in scenarios where

- UDP port 500 is blocked, resulting in incomplete IKE negotiations.
- ESP (IP protocol 50) is not allowed to pass, and as a result encrypted traffic does not traverse.
- The network administrator prefers to use a connection-oriented protocol.

With IPSec over TCP, the security appliance negotiates the VPN tunnel, using TCP as the protocol over a preconfigured port. When the tunnel is up, both VPN devices (Cisco ASA and the VPN client) pass traffic through the same connection. You can enable it by navigating to **Configuration > Remote Access VPN > Network (Access) Client > Advanced > IPSec > IKE Parameters**, then selecting the **Enable IPSec over TCP** option, and then specifying a port number. Example 17-20 illustrates how to configure IPSec over TCP on Cisco ASA. The administrator of the security device prefers to use TCP port **10000** for tunnel setup and data transport. Cisco ASA allows up to ten TCP ports to be used for this feature.

Example 17-20 *IPSec over TCP Configuration*

```
Chicago(config)# isakmp ipsec-over-tcp port 10000
```

To verify whether the VPN clients are using IPSec over TCP, you can use the **show crypto ipsec sa | include settings** command, as demonstrated in Example 17-21. The **In Use Settings** option indicates that the particular VPN connection is a remote-access tunnel using TCP encapsulation.

Example 17-21 *Verifying VPN Client Use of IPSec over TCP*

```
Chicago(config)# show crypto ipsec sa | include settings
        in use settings ={RA, Tunnel,  TCP-Encaps, }
        in use settings ={RA, Tunnel,  TCP-Encaps, }
```

IPSec Hairpinning

Cisco ASA, by default, does not allow a packet to leave the same interface on which it was originally received. Cisco ASA supports receiving the IPSec traffic from one VPN tunnel and then redirecting it into a different VPN tunnel, if both tunnels terminate on the same interface. This feature is known as *IPSec hairpinning*. Using this feature, you can implement a true hub-and-spoke scenario, as shown in Figure 17-18.

If Client1 needs to send traffic to Client2, it sends all traffic to the hub Cisco ASA. The hub Cisco ASA, after checking the routing table for the destination address, sends traffic to Client2 over the other VPN tunnel, and vice versa. However, this feature requires both remote VPN devices to be a part of the same crypto map and the crypto map must be applied to the same interface.

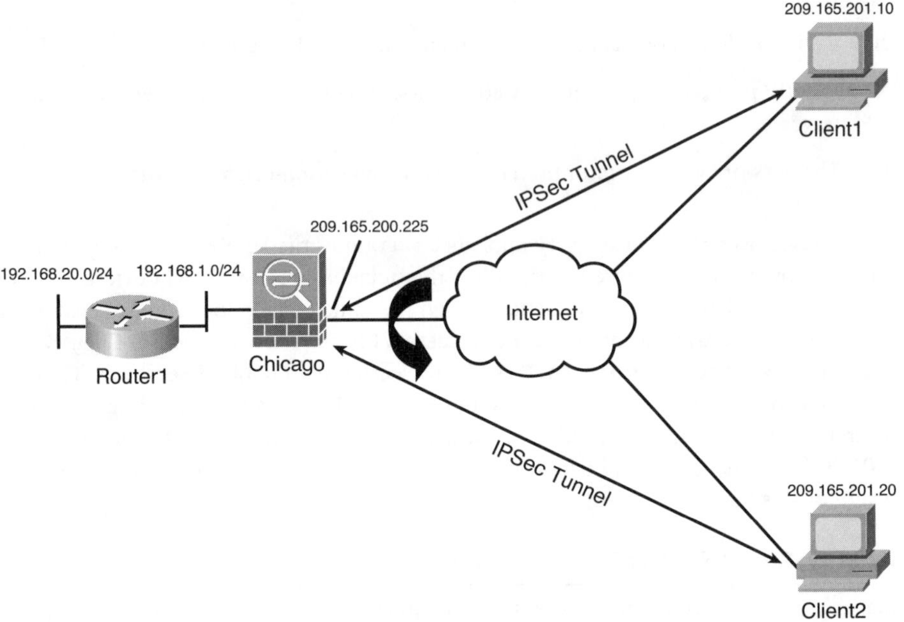

Figure 17-18 *IPSec Hairpinning*

You can enable IPSec hairpinning by navigating to **Configuration > Device Setup > Interfaces** and selecting the **Enable Traffic Between Two or More Hosts Connected to the Same Interface** option. Using the CLI, you can use the global **same-security-traffic permit intra-interface** command to permit VPN traffic to leave the same physical interface when traffic needs to go over the other VPN tunnel.

Cisco ASA also supports receiving traffic from an IPSec client and then redirecting it to the Internet in clear text. This feature, also known as *Client U-turn,* is useful if you

- Are not using split-tunneling and all traffic is sent to the security appliance.
- Want to provide Internet access to your IPSec clients.
- Do not want return traffic from the Internet that is destined to the VPN clients to enter the inside network of your organization.

Cisco ASA applies firewall rules (ACL checking, packet inspection, NAT, IDS, URL filtering) before sending traffic out to the same interface for both IPSec hairpinning and Client U-turn. As shown in Example 17-22, if the pool of addresses is 192.168.50.0/24, then you must configure the NAT and global commands to allow the VPN client traffic to access the Internet. Additionally, both **global** and **nat** commands must be attached to the same interface.

Example 17-22 *Allowing VPN Clients for Internet Access*

```
Chicago(config)# same-security-traffic permit intra-interface
Chicago(config)# ip local pool IPPool 192.168.50.1-192.168.50.254
Chicago(config)# global (outside) 1 209.165.200.230
Chicago(config)# nat (outside) 1 192.168.50.0 255.255.255.0
```

VPN Load Balancing

VPN load balancing is a way to distribute remote-access IPSec and SSL VPN connections across multiple security appliances. When two or more Cisco ASA devices are deployed in load balancing, they form a virtual cluster, with one of the security appliances acting as the cluster master. All Cisco ASA devices in the cluster are configured with a virtual IP address, and the cluster master takes ownership of that IP address, as illustrated in Figure 17-19.

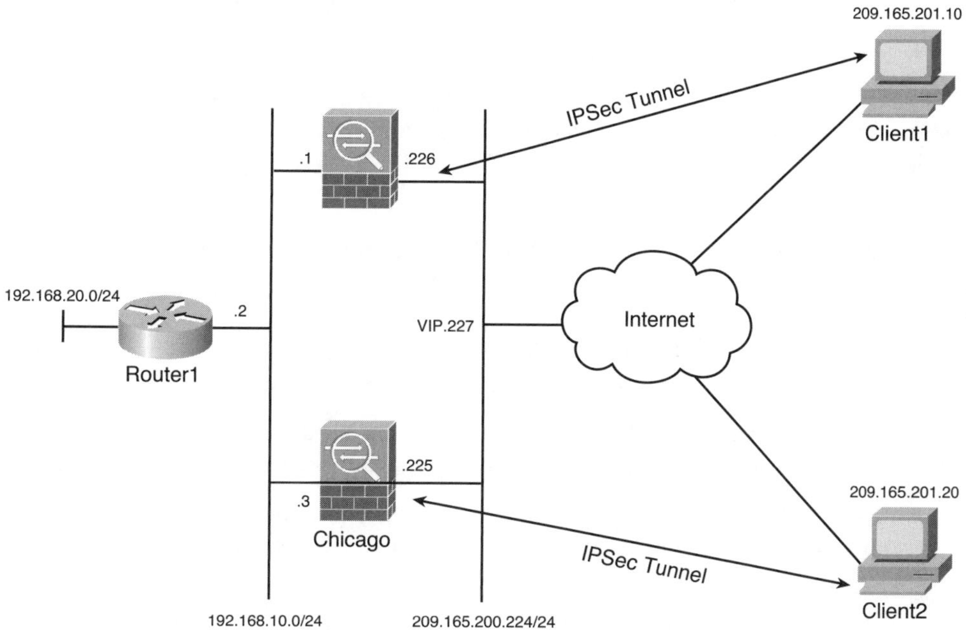

Figure 17-19 *VPN Load-Balancing*

The VPN clients use this IP address to initiate the tunnel request. The master appliance, after receiving the request, looks at the load-balance database and determines which security appliance has the least load. The master appliance sends a redirect message back to the client with the IP address of the security appliance to which the client should connect. After receiving the IP address of the Cisco ASA, the client initiates a new request to the Cisco ASA and goes through the IKE negotiations.

Note The Cisco ASA load-balancing feature is fully compatible with the load-balancing feature on the VPN3000 concentrators. This is useful if you are migrating from an existing VPN 3000 deployment to a Cisco ASA environment and want to use both devices for a period of time.

The load-balancing feature is supported on the following remote access client types:

- Cisco AnyConnect VPN Client (Release 2.0 or higher)
- Cisco IPSec VPN Client (Release 3.0 and later)
- Cisco ASA 5505 Security Appliance as an Easy VPN client
- Cisco VPN 3002 Hardware Client (Release 3.5 or later)
- Cisco PIX 501/506E as an Easy VPN client
- IOS Easy VPN Client devices, such as 831/871 supporting IKE-redirect
- Clientless SSL VPN

Note Load balancing is not supported on L2TP over IPSec tunnels and IPSec site-to-site tunnels.

To set up VPN load balancing, navigate to **Configuration > Remote Access VPN > Load Balancing** and configure the following attributes:

- **Participate in Load Balancing Cluster**—Enable this box if you want this security appliance to participate in load balancing the remote-access sessions.
- **Cluster IP Address**—The cluster IP address is the virtual IP address of the load-balancing cluster that the remote-access clients use to establish their initial connections.
- **UDP Port**—Specify a port that is used by the security appliance to send and receive the load-balancing information. By default, it uses UDP port 9023.
- **Enable IPSec Encryption**—Enable this box if you want the Cisco ASAs to optionally secure their communication when they exchange load-balancing information.
- **IPSec Shared Secret**—Specify a shared secret to be used by the load-balancing process to encrypt communication. If there is a mismatch in the key, the security appliance fails to join the cluster.
- **Public Interface**—Specify the interface that terminates the IPSec tunnels. By default, it is the outside interface.
- **Private Interface**—Specify the interface that connects to the internal network. By default, it is the inside interface. You must enable ISAKMP processing on the inside interface if you choose to encrypt load-balancing information.

- **NAT Assigned IP address**—If the Cisco ASA devices sit behind a NAT device, then you can configure the security appliance's translated IP address as the NAT assigned IP address.
- **Priority**—You can set the appropriate priority to indicate the likelihood of a Cisco ASA device becoming the cluster master, either during bootup or when the existing cluster master fails to respond. The default priority of Cisco ASA devices is determined based on the model number. Table 17-2 lists all the default priorities of the Cisco ASA devices.

Table 17-2 *Appliances and the Default Load-Balancing Priorities*

Cisco ASA Model	Default Priority
ASA 5510	2
ASA 5520	5
ASA 5540	7
ASA 5550	8
ASA 5580	10

If two Cisco ASA devices with the same priority are powered up simultaneously, then the security appliance with the lowest IP address becomes the cluster master. Otherwise, the security appliance with the highest priority assumes the role of master cluster.

If the cluster master fails to respond during operation, the secondary appliance with the highest priority becomes the new cluster master. You can specify a priority between 1 and 10. When the original master appliance comes online, it does not preempt to regain control

Note Cisco ASA 5510 supports the VPN load-balancing feature if you are running version 8.0(2) or higher with the Security Plus license.

In Figure 17-20 a security appliance is configured to participate in VPN load balancing. The cluster IP address is **209.165.200.227**, whereas the IPSec shared secret is **C1$c0123**. The device priority is **6**.

If you prefer to configure VPN load balancing via the CLI, Example 17-23 shows the relevant configuration.

Example 17-23 *VPN Load-Balancing Configuration with Encryption*

```
Chicago(config)# vpn load-balancing
Chicago(config-load-balancing)# priority 6
Chicago(config-load-balancing)# cluster key C1$c0123
Chicago(config-load-balancing)# cluster ip address 209.165.200.227
Chicago(config-load-balancing)# cluster encryption
Chicago(config-load-balancing)# participate
```

Note VPN load balancing requires you to enable ISAKMP on all the interfaces participating in load balancing. If you enable load balancing but ISAKMP is not enabled on an interface, you receive the following error message.

```
Chicago(config-load-balancing)# participate
ERROR: Need to enable isakmp on interface inside to use encryption.
```

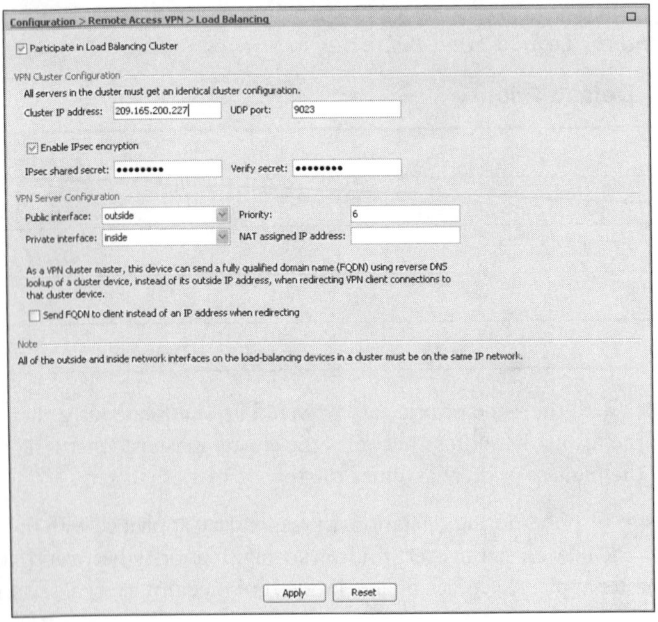

Figure 17-20 *Configuring VPN Load Balancing*

Client Firewalling

The Cisco VPN client has an integrated personal firewall that protects a machine from the Internet by inspecting packets both inbound and outbound. When you have the firewall option enabled on the VPN client, the client provides extra security if the VPN tunnel-group to which the user is connecting has split tunneling enabled. In this way, the VPN client firewall denies packets received from the unprotected networks, resulting in more secure corporate networks. Cisco ASA supports two different scenarios for client firewalling, discussed in the sections that follow.

Note Only Windows VPN clients support the client firewalling feature.

Personal Firewall Check

The Cisco VPN client can check to see whether the firewall service on the machine is running by sending periodic keepalives, also known as *Are you there (AYT)* messages, to the specified VPN client firewall. If the firewall service on the client machine is not running, the VPN client fails to establish the secured connection. Additionally, if the VPN tunnel is up and the user manually turns off the firewall service, the keepalives time out and the Cisco VPN client drops the connection.

You can configure the client firewall option under **Configuration > Remote Access VPN > Network (Client) Access > Group Policies > IPSecGroupPolicy > Edit > Advanced > IPSec Client > Client Firewall**. Uncheck the **Inherit from default group policy** box and select a firewall type. An administrator can set up Cisco ASA for three firewall check types:

- **No Firewall**—The personal firewall check is disabled. This mode is useful if non-Windows clients are connecting to a group.
- **Firewall Optional**—Cisco ASA checks to see whether the firewall services on the VPN client are running. If they are disabled, Cisco ASA still allows the VPN connection to come up. This mode is useful if Windows and non-Windows clients connect to a group.
- **Firewall Required**—If the firewall service is not running, Cisco ASA does not allow the VPN tunnel to be established. This mode is recommended if only Windows clients connect to a group.

For optional (**opt**) and required (**req**) modes, Cisco ASA provides a list of currently supported personal firewalls, including the built-in Cisco Integrated Client Firewall. As shown in Figure 17-21, Cisco Security Agent (CSA) is selected as a required firewall before the VPN sessions are allowed to connect. If the VPN clients don't have this firewall running, Cisco ASA stops the tunnels from getting established.

Note You can define a customized firewall, if you know the vendor ID and product ID, by using the Custom Firewall option.

Central Protection Policy

When split tunneling is employed, Cisco ASA can additionally send security policies in the form of ACLs to the client machine and restrict its clear-text traffic capabilities. This deployment scenario, known as *Centralized Protection Policy (CPP)* or *policy pushed*, uses ACLs that can be pushed to the client firewall. This feature is extremely useful if you want your remote users to browse a limited set of IP addresses when they are sending traffic in clear-text and want to filter out all other traffic.

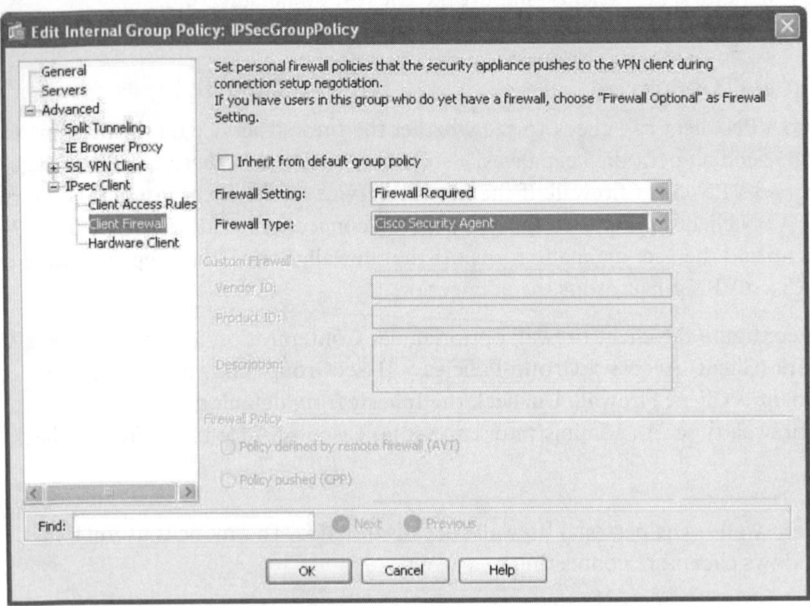

Figure 17-21 *Configuring Client Firewall Check*

Note CPP is supported in only those Windows VPN clients that have the integrated stateful firewall functionality. Microsoft Windows 2003 and Windows Vista do not support this feature.

To define a CPP, navigate to **Configuration > Remote Access VPN > Network (Client) Access > Group Policies > IPSecGroupPolicy > Edit > Advanced > IPSec Client > Client Firewall.** Uncheck **Inherit from default group policy** and select **Firewall Required** as the **Firewall Setting.** Also select **Cisco Integrated Client Firewall (CIC)** as the Firewall Type. Under Firewall Policy, make sure that **Policy Pushed (CPP)** is selected. ASDM enables you to select an inbound and an outbound policy to be applied to the user connections. If you do not have an ACL defined, click the Manage button and a new window pops up where you can specify the ACLs to be pushed to the user connections.

As shown in Figure 17-22, ASDM requires that the VPN client use the Cisco Integrated Client Firewall (CIC). Cisco ASA also restricts the client machine to send and receive traffic based on the configured inbound ACL, named **FW-IN**, and the outbound ACL, named

FW-OUT. These ACLs allow IP traffic only from 192.168.100.0/24 (Target network) to 192.168.50.0/24 (VPN Pool of addresses) and vice versa.

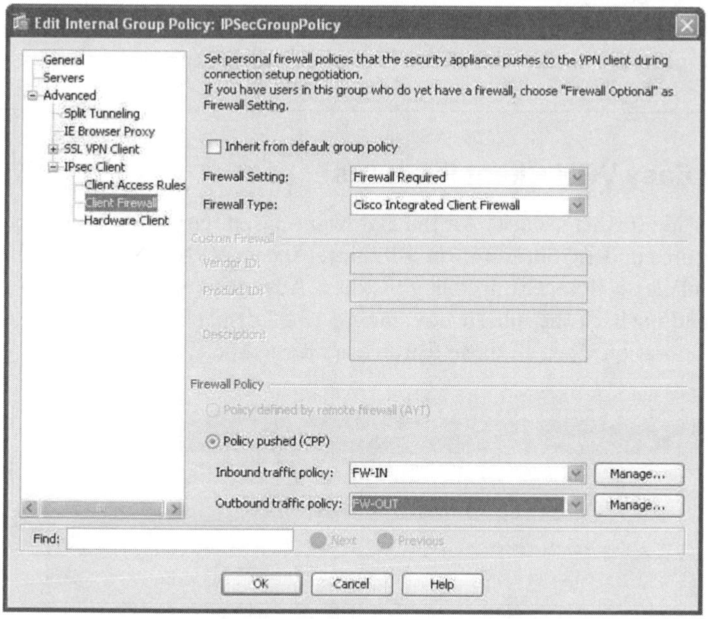

Figure 17-22 *Configuring Centralized Protection Policy*

> **Note** The CIC ACLs are defined from the VPN client's perspective. That means the outbound ACL should have the pool of addresses as the source and the target network as the destination. Similarly, the inbound ACL should have the target network as the source and the pool of addresses as the destination.
>
> If you are defining ACLs at the protocol level, make sure that you allow DNS queries and the responses in the policies. For example, if the DNS server resides at 192.168.101.1, then allow port 53 for the DNS server's IP address in your ACLs.

You can define an identical policy as Figure 17-22 via the CLI, as shown in Example 17-24.

Example 17-24 *Configuration of Central Protection Policy*

```
Chicago(config)# access-list FW-IN extended permit ip 192.168.100.0 255.255.255.0
  192.168.50.0 255.255.255.0
Chicago(config)# access-list FW-IN extended permit udp host 192.168.101.1 eq 53
  192.168.50.0 255.255.255.0
```

```
Chicago(config)# access-list FW-OUT extended permit ip 192.168.50.0 255.255.255.0
  192.168.100.0 255.255.255.0
Chicago(config)# access-list FW-OUT extended permit udp 192.168.50.0 255.255.255.0
  host 192.168.101.1 eq 53
Chicago(config)# group-policy IPSecGroupPolicy attributes
Chicago(config-group-policy)# client-firewall req cisco-integrated acl-in FW-IN
  acl-out FW-OUT
```

Hardware-Based Easy VPN Client Features

Cisco ASA can provide further security for the Hardware-Based Easy VPN client if you enable specific features under **Configuration > Remote Access VPN > Network (Client) Access > Group Policies > IPSecGroupPolicy > Edit > Advanced > IPSec Client > Hardware Client** and uncheck the **Inherit** box. Figure 17-23 displays these features and shows ASDM configuration when all these features are turned on.

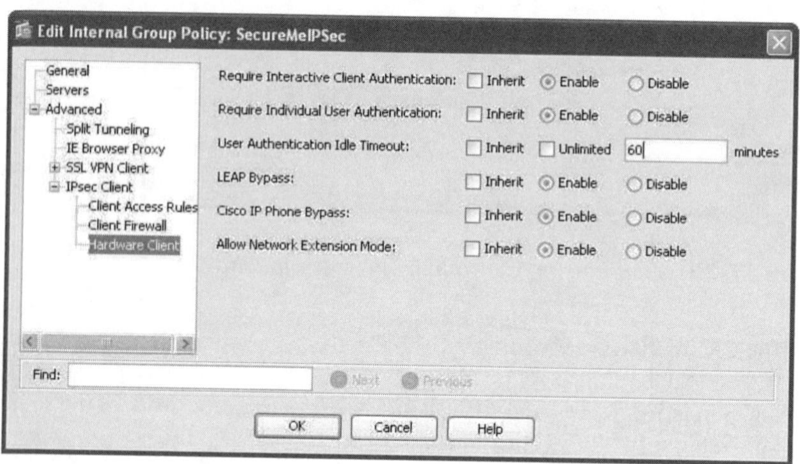

Figure 17-23 *Configuring Hardware-Based Easy VPN Features*

Interactive Client Authentication

Cisco ASA can use the interactive hardware client authentication feature, also known as *secure unit authentication*, which ensures that the Hardware-Based Easy VPN client provides user credentials every time the tunnel is negotiated. That way, the security appliance does not allow user passwords to be saved on the Hardware-Based Easy VPN client, which provides additional security. If the user password is saved on the Hardware-Based

Easy VPN client, Cisco ASA pushes down a policy during mode-config to delete the saved password from the Hardware-Based Easy VPN client configuration. Select the **Require Interactive Client Authentication** option to enable this feature. Example 17-25 shows configuration to set up Cisco ASA for interactive hardware client authentication for the **IPSecGroupPolicy** group.

Example 17-25 *Configuration of Interactive Client Authentication*

```
Chicago(config)# group-policy IPSecGroupPolicy attributes
Chicago(config-group-policy)# secure-unit-authentication enable
```

Individual User Authentication

Using the Individual User Authentication feature, Cisco ASA secures the VPN tunnel by making sure that users behind the Hardware-Based Easy VPN Client are authenticated before they can access corporate resources. To be able to pass traffic over the tunnel, a user behind the Hardware-Based Easy VPN client must launch a web browser and present valid user credentials. The Hardware-Based Easy VPN client forwards the user information to the Cisco ASA, which in turn uses the configured authentication method to validate the user information.

Tip The user does not have to manually point the web browser to the IP address of the Hardware-Based Easy VPN client. Instead, users can try to browse to any server behind the security appliance, and the Hardware-Based Easy VPN client redirect them for user credentials.

Select the **Require Individual User Authentication** to enable this feature. Example 17-26 shows the Cisco ASA configuration for Individual User Authentication for the **IPSecGroupPolicy** group.

Example 17-26 *Configuration of Individual User Authentication*

```
Chicago(config)# group-policy IPSecGroupPolicy attributes
Chicago(config-group-policy)# user-authentication enable
```

You can also specify the idle-time period if there is no activity over a user's connection. When the idle-time period expires, Cisco ASA terminates that particular connection. Specify the timeout in minutes or as unlimited under the **User Authentication Idle Timeout** option. In Example 17-27, group IPSecGroupPolicy is configured to time out inactive users after 60 minutes.

Example 17-27 *Configuration of Individual User Idle Timeout*

```
Chicago(config)# group-policy IPSecGroupPolicy attributes
Chicago(config-group-policy)# user-authentication-idle-timeout 60
```

Note User authentication is done based on the source IP address of the clients.

LEAP Bypass

LEAP bypass is a feature in the security appliance that allows Lightweight Extensible Authentication Protocol (LEAP) packets to go over the VPN tunnel when individual hardware client authentication is configured. You can enable LEAP bypass by selecting the **LEAP Bypass** option. Example 17-29 shows the Cisco ASA configuration for LEAP bypass for the **IPSecGroupPolicy** group.

Example 17-29 *Configuration of Cisco Aironet LEAP Bypass*

```
Chicago(config)# group-policy IPSecGroupPolicy attributes
Chicago(config-group-policy)# leap-bypass enable
```

Note This feature works only with Cisco Aironet access points using LEAP for authentication. It does not work if interactive hardware client authentication is enabled.

Cisco IP Phone Bypass

When individual hardware client authentication is enabled, Cisco ASA tries to authenticate Cisco IP Phones if they send traffic to go over the tunnel. You can set up the security appliance to bypass authentication for Cisco IP Phones by enabling the **Cisco IP Phone Bypass** option. In Example 17-28, this feature is enabled for **IPSecGroupPolicy** group policy.

Example 17-28 *Configuration of Cisco IP Phone Bypass*

```
Chicago(config)# group-policy IPSecGroupPolicy attributes
Chicago(config-group-policy)# ip-phone-bypass enable
```

Note For this feature to work, make sure that the Hardware-Based Easy VPN client is using network extension mode.

Hardware Client Network Extension Mode

You have the option to configure a group policy to disable network extension mode (NEM) on Cisco ASA. When you use this option, the Hardware-Based Easy VPN clients are restricted to using client/PAT mode for VPN tunnels. If they try to use NEM, Cisco ASA blocks the tunnel from being established. You can enable NEM by selecting **Allow Network Extension Mode.** Example 17-30 shows the Cisco ASA configuration to allow NEM for the **IPSecGroupPolicy** group.

Example 17-30 *Configuration to Allow NEM*

```
Chicago(config)# group-policy IPSecGroupPolicy attributes
Chicago(config-group-policy)# nem enable
```

L2TP Over IPSec Remote Access VPN Solution

Organizations that prefer to use a built-in remote access client in the Windows-based operating systems can use L2TP. However, L2TP fails to provide strong data confidentiality. Therefore, most of the L2TP implementations use IPSec to provide data security. This methodology is commonly referred to as L2TP over IPSec and is documented in RFC 3193.

In an L2TP over IPSec implementation, the client workstation and the security appliance go through seven steps, as depicted in Figure 17-24.

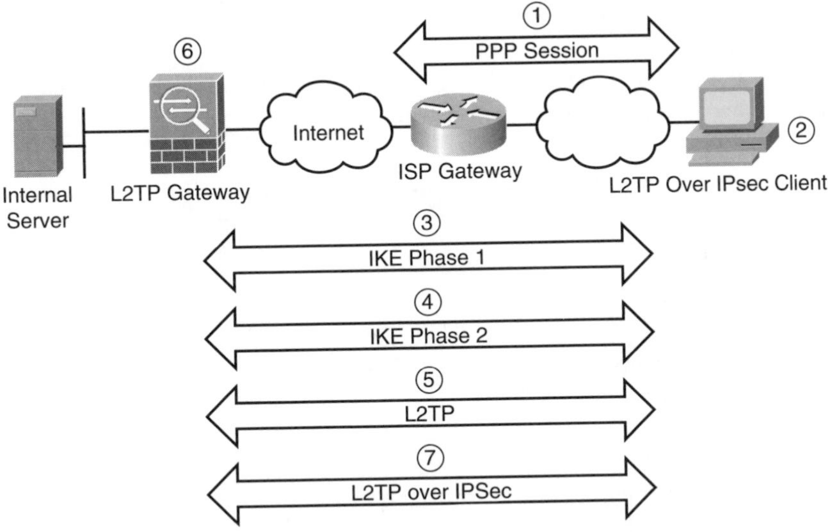

Figure 17-24 *L2TP over IPSec Negotiations*

Step 1. The user establishes a PPP session to the service provider access router and receives a dynamic public IP address. This step is optional if the workstation already has an IP address and can send traffic to the Internet.

Step 2. The user launches the L2TP client that is configured to use IPSec for data security.

Step 3. The client workstation initiates a session and negotiates a secure channel for exchanging keys (Phase 1 negotiations of IPSec).

Step 4. After successfully establishing Phase 1, the client establishes two secure channels for data encryption and authentication (Phase 2 negotiations of IPSec).

The data channels are set up to encrypt L2TP traffic that is destined to UDP port 1701.

Step 5. After IPSec is established, the client initiates an L2TP session within IPSec.

Step 6. The user-specified authentication credentials are used to validate the L2TP session. Any PPP or L2TP attributes are negotiated after the user has been successfully authenticated.

Step 7. After the L2TP session is established, the user workstation sends data traffic that is encapsulated within L2TP. The L2TP packets are encrypted by IPSec and then sent out to the other end of the tunnel over the Internet.

> **Note** If you have a firewall between the L2TP over an IPSec client and the home gateway, you need to allow IP protocol 50 (ESP) and UDP port 500 to pass through. L2TP packets (UDP port 1701) are encapsulated within ESP. Some L2TP over IPSec vendors allow NAT transparency (NAT-T) by encapsulating traffic into UDP port 4500.

Figure 17-25 shows an L2TP over IPSec packet format after all the headers and encapsulations have been added to the original packet.

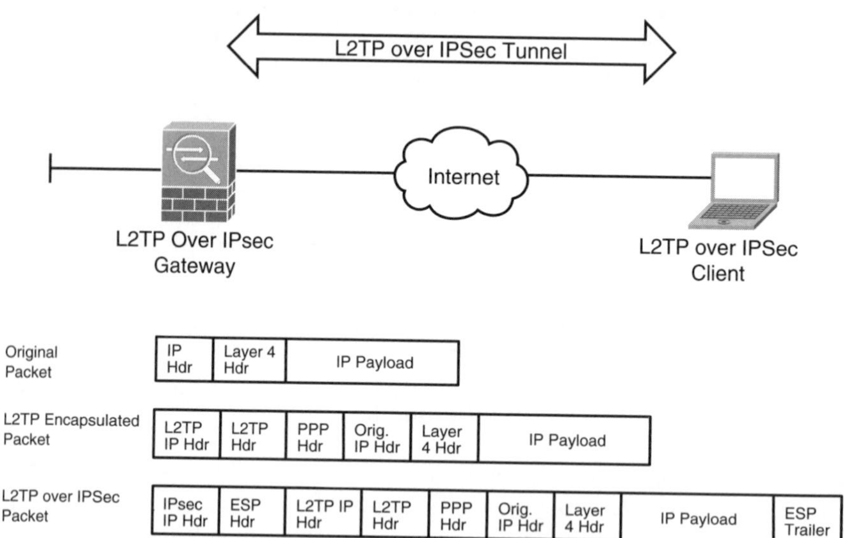

Figure 17-25 *L2TP over IPSec Packet Format*

> **Note** You can have multiple L2TP over IPSec clients behind a PAT device terminate their session on the security appliance using NAT-T. For more information about NAT-T on Windows platforms, refer to the Microsoft knowledge base article number 926179: http://support.microsoft.com/kb/926179

L2TP over IPSec Remote-Access Configuration Steps

Figure 17-26 illustrates SecureMe's Chicago hub office to be configured for the L2TP over IPSec solution. This topology will be used to show the following configuration steps required to establish a successful tunnel. The best way to successfully establish an IPSec remote-access tunnel is through the use of the ASDM wizard. Many of these steps are identical to the steps discussed earlier in the chapter under the Cisco IPSec VPN client configuration section.

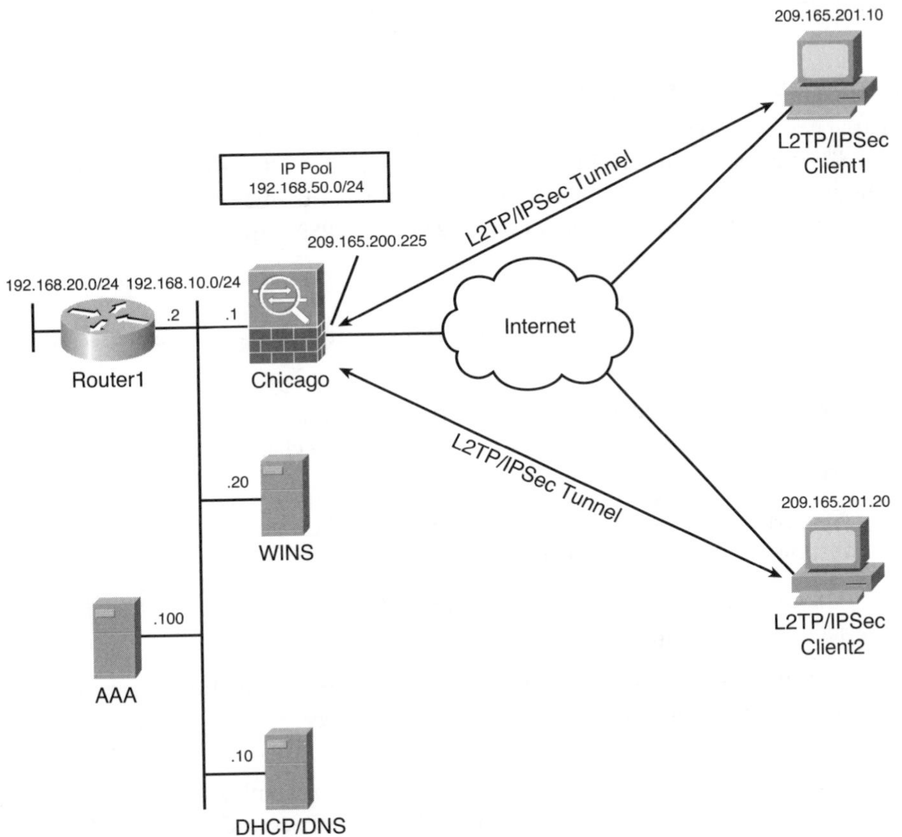

Figure 17-26 *L2TP over IPSec Network Topology*

Launch the IPSec VPN wizard by clicking **Wizards** in the toolbar and then selecting **IPSec VPN Wizard.** ASDM launches the VPN Wizard with the option to choose a VPN tunnel type. Follow the steps in the following sections to successfully define a L2TP over IPSec remote access tunnel.

Step 1: Select Tunnel Type

After the IPSec wizard is launched, the very first thing the ASDM wizard prompts you to do is to specify the tunnel type. You can either select site-2-site or remote-access tunnels. Select **Remote Access** as the VPN tunnel type.

The wizard also prompts you to specify the interface that will be terminating the IPSec tunnels. If your VPN terminating interface is the outside interface, select **outside** from the drop-down menu in the VPN Tunnel Interface field. Make sure that **Enable Inbound IPSec Sessions to Bypass Interface Access** option is enabled to bypass ACL check for the decrypted traffic. Click **Next** to move to the Remote Site Peer window.

Step 2: Select Remote Access Client

In the next window, the VPN Wizard prompts you to select the IPSec remote-access client connection. You can either select Cisco VPN Client, Release 3.x or Higher or select Microsoft Windows Client Using L2TP over IPSec. For the L2TP over IPSec connections, select **Microsoft Windows Client Using L2TP over IPSec**. Specify a PPP authentication protocol. Cisco ASA supports:

- PAP— It is the most unsecure form of authentication because it sends username and password in cleartext.
- CHAP— It is considered more secure than PAP because the username is sent in cleartext but the password is sent as a response to a challenge by the server. The data, however, is sent in cleartext.
- MS-CHAP— It is an enhanced version of CHAP in which the client sends a response in MD4 hash to a challenge by the server.
- MS-CHAP2— It offers additional security enhancements over MS-CHAP version 1, such as mutual authentication between peers.
- EAP-Proxy— It allows the security appliance to proxy the PPP authentication process to an external RADIUS authentication server.

You can choose one or more authentication protocols. An authentication protocol is negotiated based on what is offered by the L2TP over IPSec client. Select **MS-CHAP** and **MS-CHAP2** as the authentication protocols. Click **Next**.

Step 3: Select VPN Client Authentication Method

In the next window, the wizard prompts you to select an IKE authentication mechanism such as the preshared keys or pre-installed certificates. Select **Pre-shared Keys** as the authentication method and specify **C!$cOK3y**. Click **Next** to move to the user authentication window.

Step 4: Specify User Authentication Method

In the next window, the wizard prompts you to select a user authentication mechanism such as the local database or an external server. If you want to use an external server, such as RADIUS, select **Authenticate Using an AAA Server Group** and select a predefined server group name. If a server is not defined, you can click **New** and define a new external authentication server. If you would rather use the local database, select **Authenticate Using the Local User Database.** After you click **Next**, ASDM prompts you to add any additional users that you want to declare. If you do not want to add any additional local users, click **Next.**

Step 5: Specify an Address Pool

In the next window, the Cisco ASDM Wizard prompts you to select a predefined pool of addresses under the Pool Name drop-down menu. If a pool of addresses is not currently defined, you can click **New** and specify a start address of **192.168.50.1** and an end address of **192.168.50.254** for the new pool of addresses. Click **Next.**

Step 6: Specify Attributes Pushed to Clients

After defining the pool of addresses, the Cisco ASDM Wizard prompts you to specify mode-config attributes such as the primary and secondary DNS and WINS server and a default domain name. All these parameters are optional and sent to the VPN client during L2TP tunnel negotiations. Specify **192.168.10.10** as the DNS address and **192.168.10.20** as the WINS address. Define **securemeinc.com** as the default domain name. Click **Next to specify an IKE policy.**

Step 7: Select the IKE Policy

Select the appropriate IKE policy for this peer. Use **AES-256** for encryption, **SHA** for authentication, and **DH group 5** for key generation to match the configuration with the remote peer. Click **Next** to move to the IPSec Settings window.

Step 8: Select the IPSec Settings

In the next window, the wizard prompts you to specify some of the optional IPSec parameters such as address translation bypass mechanism, split-tunneling, and perfect forwarding secrecy (PFS). Select the appropriate IKE policy for this peer. If you do not specify any networks in the selected Network/Host list, then the security appliance bypasses addresses translation for the traffic from all internal networks to the pool of addresses. If you specify a specific network, then traffic from that network to the pool of VPN traffic will be bypassed for address translation.

Step 9: Verify the Configuration

The VPN Wizard shows you a summary of all the features and configuration you have done. After you have verified the configuration, click **Finish** to push the configuration to the security appliance.

Windows L2TP over IPSec Client Configuration

On Windows devices such as Windows XP, you can configure the basic L2TP over IPSec parameters by following these steps:

Step 1. Create a new connection by navigating to **Start > Settings > Control Panel > Network Connections.** Under Network Tasks left panel, click **Create a New Connection.** Windows launches the New Connection Wizard. Click **Next** to define a new connection entry.

Step 2. Select **Connect to the Network at My Workplace** and click **Next.**

Step 3. Under **Network Connection**, select **Virtual Private Network Connection** and click **Next.**

Step 4. Specify a name for this connection, such as **L2TPIPSecCorp**, and click **Next.**

Step 5. If the Public Network window comes up, select **Do Not Dial the Initial Connection.**

Step 6. Specify the public IP address, such as 209.165.200.225, of the security appliance. Click **Next** to continue.

Step 7. If the Smart Cards window is provided, select **Do Not Use My Smart Card.** Click **Next** to continue.

Step 8. Under Connection Availability, specify whether you want to use this connection for everyone or only for the user who is currently logged in to the Windows workstation. Click **Next** and then **Finish** to complete the connection setup.

Step 9. Windows launches the newly defined connection entry. Choose the **Properties** option and go to the **Security** tab. Under the **Data Encryption** drop-down menu, select **Require Encryption (Disconnect if Server Declines)**. Select an authentication protocol by clicking **Advanced** and then **Settings.** Choose the **MS-CHAP** and **MS-CHAP2** protocols as shown in Figure 17-27. Click **OK** when you are finished.

Step 10. Click the Click IPSec Settings, check **Use Pre-shared Key for Authentication**, and type in the preshared key to set the preshared key. As shown in Figure 17-27, a preshared key of **C1@c0K3y** is used. Click **OK** after specifying a key.

Step 11. Click the **Networking** tab and select **L2TP IPSec VPN** under the **Type of VPN** drop-down menu. Click **OK** to complete this configuration.

Step 12. Specify a username and password and then click **Connect** to start an L2TP over IPSec connection to the security appliance.

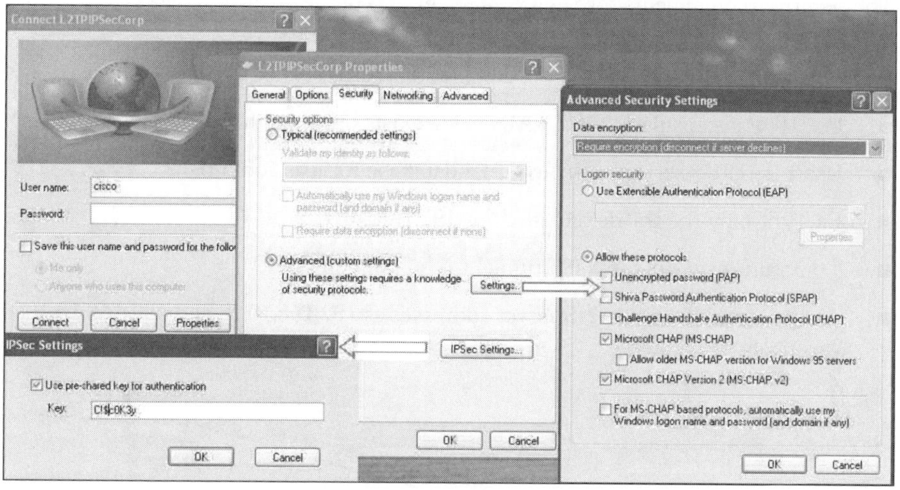

Figure 17-27 *Windows XP L2TP over IPSec Configuration*

Tip For more information on how to fine-tune L2TP over IPSec policies on the Windows endpoints, please refer to the Microsoft's knowledge article 240262 at http://support.microsoft.com/default.aspx?scid=kb;EN-US;q240262

Deployment Scenarios

The ASA VPN solution can be deployed in many different ways. In this section, we cover two design scenarios for ease of understanding:

- Load balancing with Cisco IPSec clients and site-to-site integration
- L2TP over IPSec with traffic hairpinning

Note The design scenarios discussed in this section should be used solely to reinforce learning. They should be used for reference purposes only.

Load Balancing of Cisco IPSec Clients and Site-to-Site Integration

SecureMe's headquarters office in Chicago wants to deploy Cisco ASA to be used for remote-access VPN tunnels that will support about 20,000 users. However, SecureMe wants to make sure that users do not overburden the system and therefore wants to use two security appliances in load-balancing mode. SecureMe also wants to terminate a site-to-site tunnel on one of the security appliances. Figure 17-28 shows SecureMe's network topology in Chicago.

The security requirements for SecureMe's Chicago office are as follows:

- Load balance Cisco IPSec VPN connections across two Cisco ASA devices.
- Use UDP encapsulation if a NAT device exists between the VPN devices.
- Use a RADIUS server as the external database for user lookup.
- Encrypt only the traffic destined for 192.168.0.0/16.
- Configure a site-to-site VPN tunnel to the London ASA.
- Assign the DNS and WINS server addresses as 192.168.10.10 and 192.168.10.20, respectively.

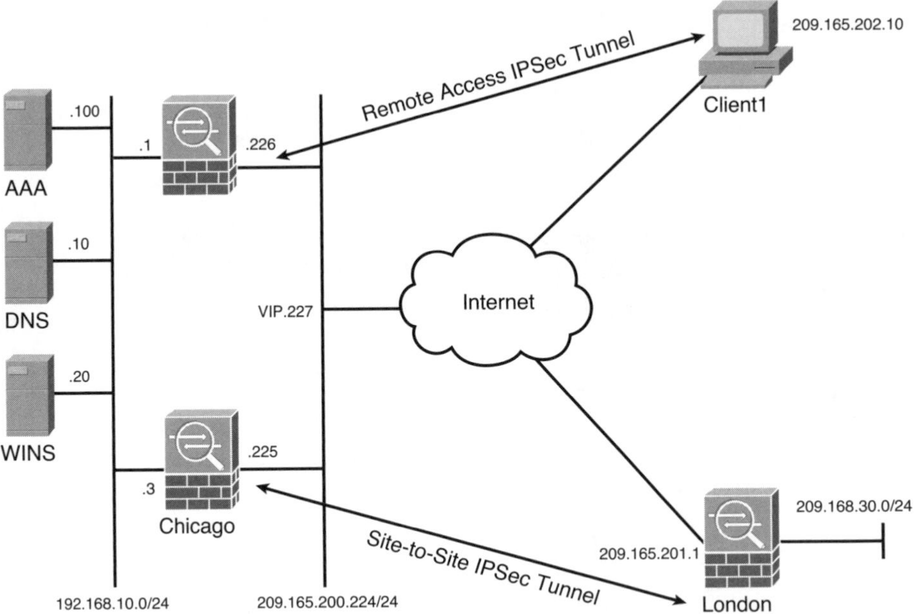

Figure 17-28 *SecureMe's Remote-Access Topology in Chicago*

To meet these requirements, split tunneling is proposed for the Cisco VPN client so that traffic destined to 192.168.0.0/16 is encrypted. NAT-T, which is enabled by default, is to be used for UDP encapsulation.

Configuration Steps Through ASDM

The relevant configuration through ASDM is discussed below. These configuration steps assume that you have IP connectivity from the ASDM client to the management IP address of the security appliances. The management IP address of the Chicago ASA is 172.18.82.64:

Step 1. Launch the IPSec VPN Wizard by clicking **Wizards** in the toolbar and then selecting **IPSec VPN Wizard.** ASDM launches the VPN Wizard with the option to choose a VPN tunnel type. Select **Remote Access** as the VPN tunnel type and select **outside** from the drop-down menu in the VPN Tunnel Interface field. Make sure that **Enable Inbound IPSec Sessions to Bypass Interface Access** option is enabled to bypass ACL check for the decrypted traffic. Click **Next.**

Step 2. In the next window, select **Cisco VPN Client, Release 3.x or higher** and click **Next.**

Step 3. Select **Pre-shared Keys** as the authentication method and specify **C!$c0K3y.** Under **Tunnel Group**, specify **SecureMeIPSec** as the tunnel name. Click **Next.**

Step 4. In the next window, the wizard prompts you to select a user authentication mechanism. Use an external server such as RADIUS by selecting **Authenticate Using an AAA Server Group.** If a server is not defined, you can click **New** and define a new external authentication server group called **Radius**, located toward the **inside** interface at **192.168.10.100** with a shared secret of **C1$c0123.**

Step 5. If a pool of addresses is not currently defined, you can click **New** and specify a name of **IPPool** with the start address of **192.168.32.1** and the end address of **192.168.64.254** with a mask of **255.255.224.0.** Click **Next.**

Step 6. Configure the DNS and WINS server addresses of **192.168.10.10** and **192.168.10.20** respectively. Define **securemeinc.com** as the default domain name. Click **Next to specify an IKE policy.**

Step 7. Select an IKE policy that uses **AES-256** for encryption, **SHA** for authentication, and **DH group 5** for key generation. Click **Next.**

Step 8. In the next IPSec policy window, select the **inside** interface and specify **192.168.0.0/16** as **Address** and then click **Add.** Select **Enable Split Tunneling to Let Remote Users** to turn on split-tunneling. Uncheck the **Enable Perfect Forwarding Secrecy (PFS)** box. Click **Next** to continue.

Step 9. The VPN Wizard shows you a summary of all the features and configurations you have set. After you have verified the configuration, click **Finish** to push the configuration to the security appliance.

Step 10. Before you configure load-balancing, enable ISAKMP on the private (inside) interface so that the load-balancing packets can be encrypted. Navigate to

Configuration > Remote Access VPN > Network (Client) Access > IPSec Connection Profiles and select the **Allow Access** option for the **inside** interface.

Step 11. Next, configure load balancing by navigating to **Configuration > Remote Access VPN > Load Balancing.** Define the following attributes to enable load-balancing:

- Participate in Load Balancing Cluster: **Checked**
- Cluster IP address: **209.165.200.227**
- UDP Port: **9023**
- Enable IPSec Encryption: **Checked**
- IPSec shared secret: **C1$c0123**
- Public Interface: **Outside**
- Private Interface: **Inside**
- Priority: **9**

Step 12. Launch the IPSec VPN Wizard again by clicking **Wizards** in the toolbar and then selecting **IPSec VPN Wizard.** ASDM launches the VPN Wizard with the option to choose a VPN tunnel type. Select **Site-to-Site** as the VPN tunnel type and select **outside** from the drop-down menu in the **VPN Tunnel Interface** field. Make sure that the **Enable Inbound IPSec Sessions to Bypass Interface Access** option is enabled to bypass ACL check for the decrypted traffic. Click **Next.**

Step 13. In the next window, specify **209.165.201.1** as the **Peer IP Address.** Select **Pre-shared Key** as the authentication protocol and specify **C!Sc0K3y** as the preshared key. Click **Next.**

Step 14. Select an IKE policy that uses **AES-256** for encryption, **SHA** for authentication, and **DH group 5** for key generation. Click **Next.**

Step 15. Select an IPSec rule policy that uses **AES-256** for encryption, **SHA** for authentication. Disable **PFS** and click **Next.**

Step 16. In the next Host and Network policy window, select action **Protect** and then **192.168.10.0/24** as Local Networks and **192.168.30.0/24** as the Remote Networks. Select **Exempt ASA Side Host/Network from Address Translation** on the **inside** interface. Click **Next** to continue.

Step 17. The VPN Wizard shows you a summary of all the features and configurations you have set. After you have verified the configuration, click **Finish** to push the configuration to the security appliance.

Configuration Steps using CLI

Example 17-31 shows the complete configuration of SecureMe's Cisco ASA in Chicago to meet the design requirements.

Example 17-31 *Configuration to Load balance Cisco IPSec Clients with Site-to-Site*

```
Chicago# show running-config
ASA Version 8.2(1)
! ip address on the outside interface
interface GigabitEthernet0/0
 nameif outside
 security-level 0
 ip address 209.165.200.225 255.255.255.0
! ip address on the inside interface
interface GigabitEthernet0/1
 nameif inside
 security-level 100
 ip address 192.168.10.1 255.255.255.0
! ip address on the mgmt interface
interface Management0/0
 nameif mgmt
 security-level 100
 ip address 172.18.82.64 255.255.255.0
 management-only
!
hostname Chicago
domain-name securemeinc.com
! Access-list entries to bypass NAT for the traffic going from Chicago to London
access-list inside_nat0_outbound extended permit ip 192.168.10.0 255.255.255.0
192.168.30.0 255.255.255.0
! Access-list entries to bypass NAT for the traffic going from Chicago to
  RA_clients
access-list inside_nat0_outbound extended permit ip 192.168.0.0 255.255.0.0
192.168.32.0 255.255.224.0
! Encryption Access-list to encrypt the traffic from Chicago to London
access-list outside_1_cryptomap extended permit ip 192.168.10.0 255.255.255.0
192.168.30.0 255.255.255.0
! ACL for Split-Tunneling
access-list SecureMeIPSec_splitTunnelAcl standard permit 192.168.0.0 255.255.0.0
! IP Pool used to assign IP address to the VPN client
ip local pool IPPool 192.168.32.1-192.168.64.254 mask 255.255.224.0
! NAT ACL is bound to NAT 0 statement to bypass address translation
nat (inside) 0 access-list inside_nat0_outbound
! Radius configuration to enable user authentication
aaa-server Radius protocol radius
aaa-server Radius (inside) host 192.168.10.100
```

```
 key C1$c0123
! Configuration of ASDM for Appliance management
http server enable
http 0.0.0.0 0.0.0.0 mgmt
! Transform set to specify encryption and hashing algorithm
crypto ipsec transform-set ESP-AES-256-MD5 esp-aes-256 esp-md5-hmac
crypto ipsec transform-set ESP-DES-SHA esp-des esp-sha-hmac
crypto ipsec transform-set ESP-DES-MD5 esp-des esp-md5-hmac
crypto ipsec transform-set ESP-AES-192-MD5 esp-aes-192 esp-md5-hmac
crypto ipsec transform-set ESP-3DES-MD5 esp-3des esp-md5-hmac
crypto ipsec transform-set ESP-AES-256-SHA esp-aes-256 esp-sha-hmac
crypto ipsec transform-set ESP-AES-128-SHA esp-aes esp-sha-hmac
crypto ipsec transform-set ESP-AES-192-SHA esp-aes-192 esp-sha-hmac
crypto ipsec transform-set ESP-AES-128-MD5 esp-aes esp-md5-hmac
crypto ipsec transform-set ESP-3DES-SHA esp-3des esp-sha-hmac
! Dynamic crypto-map for Remote-Access Clients and Static Crypto map for London ASA
crypto dynamic-map SYSTEM_DEFAULT_CRYPTO_MAP 65535 set transform-set ESP-AES-128-
SHA ESP-AES-128-MD5 ESP-AES-192-SHA ESP-AES-192-MD5 ESP-AES-256-SHA ESP-AES-256-
MD5 ESP-3DES-SHA ESP-3DES-MD5 ESP-DES-SHA ESP-DES-MD5
crypto map outside_map 1 match address outside_1_cryptomap
crypto map outside_map 1 set peer 209.165.201.1
crypto map outside_map 1 set transform-set ESP-AES-256-SHA
crypto map outside_map 65535 ipsec-isakmp dynamic SYSTEM_DEFAULT_CRYPTO_MAP
crypto map outside_map interface outside
! isakmp configuration- Enabled on the outside interface
isakmp enable outside
! isakmp configuration- Enabled on the inside interface for VPN LB
isakmp enable inside
! isakmp policy configuration
 crypto isakmp enable outside
crypto isakmp enable inside
crypto isakmp policy 10
 authentication pre-share
 encryption aes-256
 hash sha
 group 5
 lifetime 86400
! NAT-T is enabled by default, so no additional configuration is required
! tunnel-group configuration for VPN client. The group-name is SecureMeIPSec
group-policy SecureMeIPSec internal
group-policy SecureMeIPSec attributes
 wins-server value 192.168.10.20
 dns-server value 192.168.10.10
 domain-name securemeinc.com
 vpn-tunnel-protocol IPSec
```

```
 split-tunnel-policy tunnelspecified
 split-tunnel-network-list value SecureMeIPSec_splitTunnelAcl
tunnel-group SecureMeIPSec type remote-access
tunnel-group SecureMeIPSec general-attributes
 address-pool IPPool
 authentication-server-group Radius
 default-group-policy SecureMeIPSec
tunnel-group SecureMeIPSec ipsec-attributes
 pre-shared-key *
! L2L tunnel-group configuration for London
tunnel-group 209.165.201.1 type ipsec-l2l
tunnel-group 209.165.201.1 ipsec-attributes
 pre-shared-key *
! VPN Load-balancing. The virtual IP address is  209.165.200.227. Encryption is
  enabled with using C1$c0123 as the key
vpn load-balancing
 priority 9
 cluster key C1$c0123
 cluster ip address 209.165.200.227
 cluster encryption
```

L2TP over IPSec with Traffic Hairpinning

SecureMe has recently installed a new Cisco ASA in its Chicago office to provide VPN access to its remote and home users. Figure 17-29 shows SecureMe's network topology in Chicago.

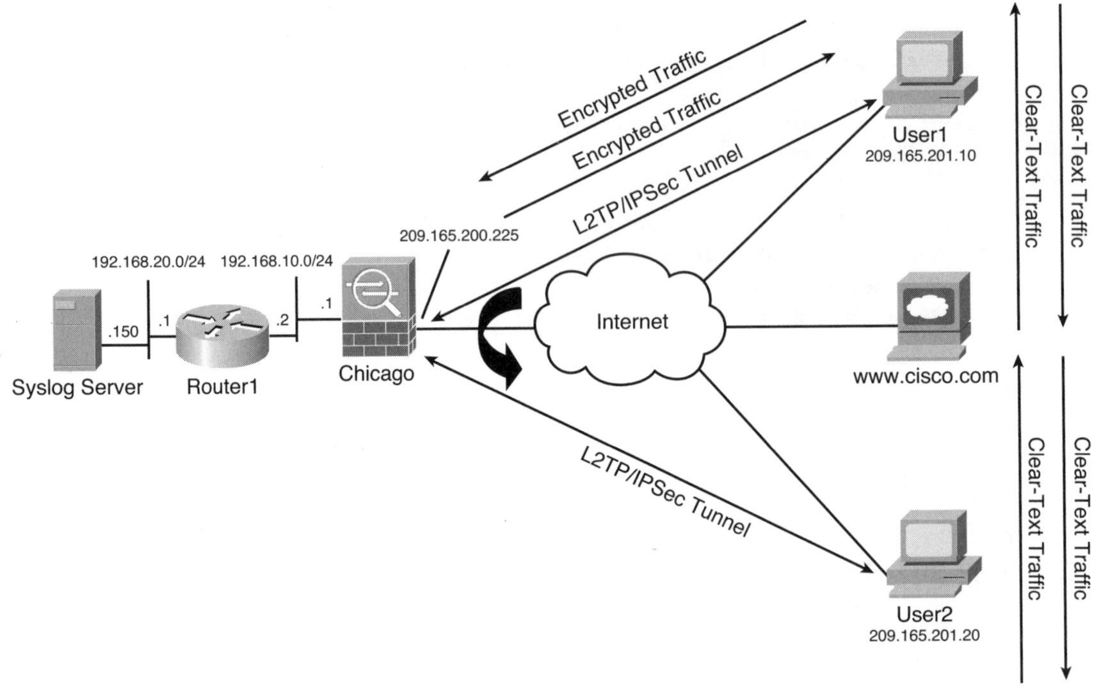

Figure 17-29 *SecureMe's Remote-Access Topology for L2TP over IPSec*

The security requirements for SecureMe are as follows:

- Encrypt all traffic leaving the remote-access clients. Don't install any IPSec Clients on the workstations.
- Allow VPN clients to communicate with each other.
- Allow VPN clients to access the Internet.
- Use local database for user authentication.
- Log all the system-generated syslog messages to a server.

To meet these requirements, SecureMe has decided to use L2TP over IPSec and the IPSec hairpinning feature. Access to the Internet will be provided by translating the VPN pool of addresses to the public IP address of the security appliance.

Configuration Steps Through ASDM

The relevant configuration through ASDM is described here. These configuration steps assume that you have IP connectivity from the ASDM client to the management IP address of the security appliances. The management IP address of the Chicago ASA is 172.18.82.64.

Step 1. Launch the IPSec VPN Wizard by clicking **Wizards** in the toolbar and then selecting **IPSec VPN Wizard.** ASDM launches the VPN Wizard with the option to choose a VPN tunnel type. Select **Remote Access** as the VPN tunnel type and select **outside** from the drop-down menu in the VPN Tunnel Interface field. Make sure that the **Enable Inbound IPSec Sessions to Bypass Interface Access** option is enabled to bypass ACL check for the decrypted traffic. Click **Next.**

Step 2. In the next window, select **Microsoft Windows Client using L2TP over IPSec.** Specify **MS-CHAP-V1** and **MS-CHAP-V2** as the PPP authentication protocols. Click **Next.**

Step 3. Select **Pre-shared Keys** as the authentication method and specify **C!$cOK3y.** Click **Next.**

Step 4. In the next window, select **Authenticate Using the Local User Database.** After you click **Next, ASDM prompts you to add any additional users that you want to declare.**

Step 5. If a pool of addresses is not currently defined, you can click **New** and specify a name of **IPPool** with the start address of **192.168.50.1** and the end address of **192.168.50.100** for the new pool of addresses. Select **255.255.255.0** as the subnet mask. Click **Next.**

Step 6. Configure the DNS and WINS server addresses of **192.168.10.10** and **192.168.10.20** respectively. Define **securemeinc.com** as the default domain name. Click **Next to specify an IKE policy.**

Step 7. Select an IKE policy that uses **AES-256** for encryption, **SHA** for authentication, and **DH group 5** for key generation. Click **Next.**

Step 8. In the next IPSec Settings window, you do not specify any networks in the selected Network/Host list. Uncheck the **Enable Perfect Forwarding Secrecy (PFS)** box. Click **Next** to continue.

Step 9. The VPN Wizard shows you a summary of all the features and configurations you have set. After you have verified the configuration, click **Finish** to push the configuration to the security appliance.

Step 10. To allow traffic hairpinning, navigate to **Configuration > Device Setup > Interfaces** and select **Enable Traffic Between Two or More Hosts Connected to the Same Interface.**

Step 11. Create a NAT rule to translate the 192.168.50.0/24 (pool of addresses) to the outside IP address of Cisco ASA. Navigate to **Configuration > Firewall > NAT Rules > Add > Add Dynamic Rules**, click the **Manage** button, and then click **Add** under **Manage Global Pool.** Specify the following attributes to define the outside interface as the translated address:

- Interface: **Outside**

- Pool ID: **1**
- Port Address Translated (PAT) Using IP address of the Interface: **Selected** and added under **Addresses Pool.** Click **OK** when you are finished.

Step 12. Navigate to **Configuration > Firewall > NAT Rules > Add > Add Dynamic NAT Rule** and define the following attributes for traffic going to Chicago ASA:

Original Interface: **Outside**

Source: **192.168.50.0/24**

Translated: Select **Pool ID 1**, defined in the previous step

Step 13. Navigate to **Configuration > Device Management > NAT Rules > Logging > Syslog Server** and click **Add.** Specify the following under

Interface: **inside**

IP Address: **192.168.20.150**

Protocol: **UDP**, Port: **514.** Click **OK** when done.

Step 14. Navigate to **Configuration > Device Management > Logging > Logging Filters**, select **Syslog Servers**, and click **Edit.** Under **Filter on severity**, choose **Informational** from the drop-down menu.

Step 15. Navigate to **Configuration > Device Management > Logging > Syslog Setup.** Select **Include Timestamps in Syslogs** to add timestamps when syslogs are generated.

Configuration Steps Through CLI

Example 17-32 shows the relevant configuration to achieve the goals listed earlier.

Example 17-32 *Configuring L2TP over IPSec with Traffic Hairpinning*

```
Chicago# show running-config
ASA Version 8.2(1)
! ip address on the outside interface
interface GigabitEthernet0/0
 nameif outside
 security-level 0
ip address 209.165.200.225 255.255.255.0
! ip address on the inside interface
interface GigabitEthernet0/1
 nameif inside
 security-level 100
 ip address 192.168.10.1 255.255.255.0
! ip address on the Management interface
interface Management0/0
```

```
 nameif mgmt
 security-level 100
 ip address 172.18.82.64 255.255.255.0
 management-only
!
hostname Chicago
domain-name securemeinc.com
! To Allow IPSec hairpinning on the same interface
same-security-traffic permit intra-interface
! Enable logging to send syslog messages to 192.168.20.150
logging enable
logging timestamp
logging host inside 192.168.20.150
logging trap informational
! IP Pool used to assign IP address to the L2TP/IPSec client
ip local pool IPPool 192.168.50.1-192.168.50.100 mask 255.255.255.0
! Translate 192.168.50.0/24 to a Internet routable address
global (outside) 1 interface
nat (outside) 1 192.168.50.0 255.255.255.0
! NAT rule to bypass address translation
access-list inside_nat0_outbound extended permit ip any 192.168.50.0 255.255.255.0
nat (inside) 0 access-list inside_nat0_outbound
! IPSec Transform set definition
crypto ipsec transform-set TRANS_ESP_3DES_SHA esp-3des esp-sha-hmac
crypto ipsec transform-set TRANS_ESP_3DES_SHA mode transport
crypto ipsec transform-set ESP-AES-256-MD5 esp-aes-256 esp-md5-hmac
crypto ipsec transform-set ESP-DES-SHA esp-des esp-sha-hmac
crypto ipsec transform-set ESP-3DES-SHA esp-3des esp-sha-hmac
crypto ipsec transform-set ESP-DES-MD5 esp-des esp-md5-hmac
crypto ipsec transform-set ESP-AES-192-MD5 esp-aes-192 esp-md5-hmac
crypto ipsec transform-set ESP-3DES-MD5 esp-3des esp-md5-hmac
crypto ipsec transform-set ESP-AES-256-SHA esp-aes-256 esp-sha-hmac
crypto ipsec transform-set ESP-AES-128-SHA esp-aes esp-sha-hmac
crypto ipsec transform-set ESP-AES-192-SHA esp-aes-192 esp-sha-hmac
crypto ipsec transform-set ESP-AES-128-MD5 esp-aes esp-md5-hmac
crypto ipsec security-association lifetime seconds 28800
crypto ipsec security-association lifetime kilobytes 4608000
! Dynamic and Static Crypto Map definition
crypto dynamic-map SYSTEM_DEFAULT_CRYPTO_MAP 65535 set transform-set ESP-AES-128
-SHA ESP-AES-128-MD5 ESP-AES-192-SHA ESP-AES-192-MD5 ESP-AES-256-SHA ESP-AES-256
-MD5 ESP-3DES-SHA ESP-3DES-MD5 ESP-DES-SHA ESP-DES-MD5
crypto map outside_map 65535 ipsec-isakmp dynamic SYSTEM_DEFAULT_CRYPTO_MAP
crypto map outside_map interface outside
! ISAKMP Policy definition
```

```
crypto isakmp enable outside
crypto isakmp policy 10
 authentication pre-share
 encryption aes-256
 hash sha
 group 5
 lifetime 86400
! Username for local Authentication
username cisco password YjgNYkzySWB2C.ut encrypted privilege 15
! Default Group-Policy definition
group-policy DefaultRAGroup internal
group-policy DefaultRAGroup attributes
 wins-server value 192.168.10.20
 dns-server value 192.168.10.10
 vpn-tunnel-protocol l2tp-ipsec
 default-domain value securemeinc.com
! Tunnel Group definition
tunnel-group DefaultRAGroup general-attributes
 address-pool IPPool
 default-group-policy DefaultRAGroup
tunnel-group DefaultRAGroup ipsec-attributes
 pre-shared-key *
tunnel-group DefaultRAGroup ppp-attributes
 no authentication chap
 authentication ms-chap-v2
```

Monitoring and Troubleshooting Cisco Remote-Access VPN

Cisco ASA comes with a number of **show** commands to check the health and status of the IPSec tunnels. For troubleshooting purposes, there is a rich set of **debug** commands to isolate the IPSec-related issues.

Monitoring Cisco Remote Access IPSec VPNs

To monitor the IPSec sessions through ASDM, navigate to **Monitoring > VPN > VPN Statistics > Sessions** and check how many active IPSec tunnels are established on the security appliance. The security appliance shows you all the active VPN sessions, including the clientless and AnyConnect SSL VPN client connections. As shown in Figure 17-30, an active IPSec connection is created by a user called **cisco**. The user computer's assigned IP address is 192.168.60.1, and the negotiated encryption type is IKE IPSec AES128. The user is connected for almost 25 seconds. Should you prefer to get detailed information about a user's connection, select that specific user session and then click the **Details** button.

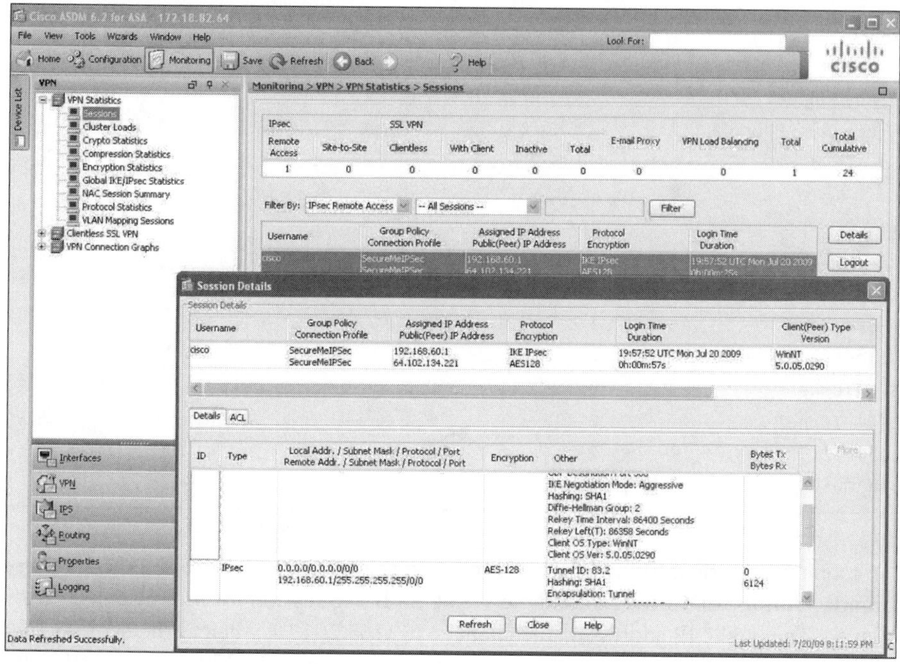

Figure 17-30 *Monitoring IPSec Sessions Through ASDM*

Using the CLI, you can find similar information by using the **show vpn-sessiondb detail** command, as shown in Example 17-33.

Example 17-33 **show vpn-sessiondb detail** *Command Output*

```
Chicago# show vpn-sessiondb detail
Active Session Summary
Sessions:
                              Active : Cumulative : Peak Concurrent : Inactive
  SSL VPN                 :        0 :                 6 :            1
    Clientless only       :        0 :                 0 :            0
    With client           :        0 :                 6 :            1 :        0
  Email Proxy             :        0 :                 0 :            0
  IPSec LAN-to-LAN        :        0 :                 0 :            0
  IPSec Remote Access     :        1 :                18 :            1
  VPN Load Balancing      :        0 :                 0 :            0
  Totals                  :        1 :                24

License Information:
  IPSec   :     750    Configured :    750    Active :      1    Load :    0%
  SSL VPN :       2    Configured :      2    Active :      0    Load :    0%
                             Active : Cumulative : Peak Concurrent
```

```
  IPSec                :          1 :          24 :                1
  SSL VPN              :          0 :           6 :                1
    AnyConnect Mobile :          0 :           0 :                0
    Linksys Phone      :          0 :           0 :                0
  Totals               :          1 :          30

Tunnels:
                     Active : Cumulative : Peak Concurrent
  IKE            :          1 :          18 :                1
  IPSec          :          1 :          18 :                1
  Clientless     :          0 :           6 :                1
  SSL-Tunnel     :          0 :           6 :                1
  DTLS-Tunnel    :          0 :           6 :                1
Totals           :          2 :          54
<Some Output removed for Brevity>
```

To monitor specific information about the remote users, you can use the **show vpn-sessiondb remote** command. In Example 17-34, an IPSec session for user **ciscouser** is displayed. The public IP address of the client is 209.165.201.10, whereas the negotiated address is 192.168.50.1. The security appliance has received 18,279 bytes of traffic while it has transmitted 19,876 bytes of data to the client. The security appliance has enforced policies from a user group called IPSecGroupPolicy. The user is connected for about 12 minutes and 20 seconds.

Example 17-34 show vpn-sessiondb remote *Command Output*

```
Chicago# show vpn-sessiondb remote
Session Type: IPSec
Username        : ciscouser                 Index        : 83
Assigned IP     : 192.168.50.1         Public IP     : 209.165.201.10
Protocol        : IKE IPSec
License         : IPSec
Encryption      : 3DES AES128          Hashing       : SHA1
Bytes Tx        : 19876                  Bytes Rx       : 18279
Group Policy    : IPSecGroupPolicy        Tunnel Group : SecureMeIPSec
Login Time      : 19:57:52 UTC Mon Jul 20 2009
Duration        : 0h:12m:20s
NAC Result      : Unknown
VLAN Mapping    : N/A                    VLAN          : none
```

If you want to see if the IPSec tunnels are working and passing traffic, start by looking at the status of Phase 1 SA. Type **show crypto isakmp sa detail**, as demonstrated in Example 17-35. If the ISAKMP negotiations are successful, you should see the state as **AM_ACTIVE**.

Example 17-35 **show crypto isakmp sa detail** *Command Output*

```
Chicago# show crypto isakmp sa detail
   Active SA: 1
    Rekey SA: 0 (A tunnel will report 1 Active and 1 Rekey SA during rekey)
Total IKE SA: 1

1   IKE Peer: 209.165.201.10
    Type      : user              Role      : responder
    Rekey     : no                State     : AM_ACTIVE
    Encrypt   : aes-256           Hash      : SHA
    Auth      : preshared         Lifetime  : 86400
    Lifetime Remaining: 86331
```

You can also check the status of the IPSec SA by using the **show crypto ipsec sa** command, as shown in Example 17-36. This command displays the negotiated proxy identities, along with the actual number of packets encrypted and decrypted by the IPSec engine.

Example 17-36 *Output of* **show crypto ipsec sa** *Command*

```
Chicago# show crypto ipsec sa
interface: outside
    Crypto map tag: outside_dyn_map, local addr: 209.165.200.225
      local ident (addr/mask/prot/port): (0.0.0.0/0.0.0.0/0/0)
      remote ident (addr/mask/prot/port): (192.168.50.60/255.255.255.255/0/0)
      current_peer: 209.165.201.10
      dynamic allocated peer ip: 192.168.50.60

      #pkts encaps: 10, #pkts encrypt: 10, #pkts digest: 10
      #pkts decaps: 10, #pkts decrypt: 10, #pkts verify: 10
      #pkts compressed: 0, #pkts decompressed: 0
      #pkts not compressed: 0, #pkts comp failed: 0, #pkts decomp failed: 0
      #send errors: 0, #recv errors: 0
```

You can check the status of a hardware encryption card with the **show crypto accelerator statistics** command. In Example 17-37, the important output from this command is shown, which displays the counter information, such as the number of packets going through the encryption card.

Example 17-37 **show crypto accelerator statistics** *Command Output*

```
Chicago# show crypto accelerator statistics
Crypto Accelerator Status
-------------------------
[Capability]
```

```
   Supports hardware crypto: True
   Supports modular hardware crypto: False
   Max accelerators: 1
   Max crypto throughput: 200 Mbps
   Max crypto connections: 750
[Global Statistics]
   Number of active accelerators: 1
   Number of non-operational accelerators: 0
   Input packets: 18
   Input bytes: 5424
   Output packets: 223
   Output error packets: 0
   Output bytes: 172405
[Accelerator 0]
   Status: Active
! Output omitted for brevity.
```

Cisco ASA can display global IKE and IPSec counter information, which is helpful in isolating VPN connection problems. Information such as the number of total requests, the number of total SAs created, and the number of failed requests is useful to determine the failure rate for IKE and IPSec SAs in the security appliance. As shown in Example 17-38, you can view this information by using the **show crypto protocol statistics ikev1** and **show crypto protocol statistics ipsec** command.

Example 17-38 *Output of* show crypto protocol statistics ikev1 *Command*

```
Chicago# show crypto protocol statistics ikev1
[IKEv1 statistics]
   Encrypt packet requests: 23
   Encapsulate packet requests: 23
   Decrypt packet requests: 23
   Decapsulate packet requests: 23
   HMAC calculation requests: 63
   SA creation requests: 3
   SA rekey requests: 0
   SA deletion requests: 1
   Next phase key allocation requests: 4
   Random number generation requests: 0
   Failed requests: 1
Chicago# show crypto protocol statistics ipsec
[IPSec statistics]
   Encrypt packet requests: 0
   Encapsulate packet requests: 0
   Decrypt packet requests: 0
```

```
Decapsulate packet requests: 0
HMAC calculation requests: 0
SA creation requests: 4
SA rekey requests: 0
SA deletion requests: 2
Next phase key allocation requests: 0
Random number generation requests: 0
Failed requests: 1
```

Troubleshooting Cisco IPSec VPN Clients

If the IPSec tunnel is not working for some reason, make sure that you have the proper **debug** command turned on. The following are the two most important to look at:

- **debug crypto isakmp** [*debug level 1-255*]
- **debug crypto ipsec** [*debug level 1-255*]

By default, the debug level is set to 1. You can increase the severity level up to 255 to get detailed logs. However, in most cases, setting this to 127 provides enough information to determine the root cause of an issue.

Refer to Figure 17-18 and look at the tunnel negotiation between the Cisco ASA and the VPN client located at 209.165.201.10. To enforce learning, the following debugs have been enabled:

- **debug crypto isakmp 127**
- **debug crypto ipsec 127**

As mentioned in Chapter 1, "Introduction to Security Technologies," the tunnel negotiations opens with an exchange of ISAKMP proposals. The security appliance shows the tunnel group, SecureMeIPSec in this case, to which the VPN client is trying to connect. If the proposal is acceptable, the Cisco ASA displays a message indicating that the IKE SA proposal is acceptable, as shown in Example 17-39.

Example 17-39 **debug** *Output to Show ISAKMP Proposal Is Acceptable*

```
Chicago# debug crypto isakmp 127
Chicago# debug crypto ipsec 127
[IKEv1 DEBUG]: Group = , IP = 209.165.201.10, processing SA payload
[IKEv1 DEBUG]: Group = , IP = 209.165.201.10, processing ke payload
[IKEv1 DEBUG]: Group = , IP = 209.165.201.10,processing VID payload,
<snip>
[IKEv1]: IP = 209.165.201.10, Connection landed on tunnel_group SecureMeIPSec
[IKEv1 DEBUG]: Group = SecureMeIPSec, IP = 209.165.201.10, processing IKE SA
```

```
[IKEv1 DEBUG]: Group = SecureMeIPSec, IP = 209.165.201.10, IKE SA Proposal # 1,
Transform # 10 acceptable  Matches global IKE entry # 1,
```

If the proposal is acceptable, the VPN devices try to discover whether they are NAT-T capable and if there is an address-translation device between them. If NAT-T is not negotiated or a NAT/PAT device is not detected, they display the **Remote End Is NOT Behind a NAT Device. This End Is NOT Behind a NAT Device** message, as shown in Example 17-40.

Example 17-40 debug *Output to Show NAT-T Discovery Process*

```
[IKEv1 DEBUG]: Group = SecureMeIPSec, IP = 209.165.201.10, processing NAT-
  Discovery payload
[IKEv1 DEBUG]: Group = SecureMeIPSec, IP = 209.165.201.10, computing NAT
  Discovery hash
[IKEv1 DEBUG]: Group = SecureMeIPSec, IP = 209.165.201.10, processing NAT-
  Discovery payload
[IKEv1]: Group = SecureMeIPSec, IP = 209.165.201.10, Automatic NAT Detection
  Status: Remote end is NOT behind a NAT device. This end is NOT behind a NAT device
```

After NAT-T negotiations, Cisco ASA prompts the user to specify user credentials. Upon successful user authentication, the security appliance displays a message indicating that the user (ciscouser in this example) is authenticated, as shown in Example 17-41.

Example 17-41 debug *Output to Show User Is Authenticated*

```
[IKEv1]: Group = SecureMeIPSec, Username = ciscouser, IP = 209.165.201.10, User
  (ciscouser) authenticated.,
[IKEv1 DEBUG]: Group = SecureMeIPSec, Username = ciscouser, IP = 209.165.201.10,
  constructing blank hash
[IKEv1 DEBUG]: Group = SecureMeIPSec, Username = ciscouser, IP = 209.165.201.10,
  constructing qm hash
```

The client requests **mode-config** attributes by sending a list of client-supported attributes, as shown in Example 17-42. Cisco ASA replies back with all its supported attributes and the appropriate information.

Example 17-42 debug *Output to Show Mode-Config Requests*

```
[IKEv1 DEBUG]Processing cfg Request attributes,
[IKEv1 DEBUG]MODE_CFG: Received request for IPV4 address!,
[IKEv1 DEBUG]MODE_CFG: Received request for IPV4 net mask!,
[IKEv1 DEBUG]MODE_CFG: Received request for DNS server address!,
[IKEv1 DEBUG]MODE_CFG: Received request for WINS server address!,
```

After pushing down the attributes, Cisco ASA displays the "PHASE 1 COMPLETED" message, indicating that the ISAKMP SA is successfully negotiated, as demonstrated in Example 17-43.

Example 17-43 debug *Output to Show Phase 1 Negotiations Are Completed*

```
[IKEv1]: Group = SecureMeIPSec, Username = ciscouser, IP = 209.165.201.10 PHASE 1
  COMPLETED,
<snip>
[IKEv1 DEBUG]: Group = SecureMeIPSec, Username = ciscouser, IP = 209.165.201.10
  Processing ID,
[IKEv1 DECODE]ID_IPV4_ADDR ID received 192.168.50.60,
[IKEv1]: Group = SecureMeIPSec, Username = ciscouser, IP = 209.165.201.10 Received
  remote Proxy Host data in ID Payload:  Address 192.168.50.60, Protocol 0, Port 0,
```

After completing Phase 1 negotiations, the VPN peers try to negotiate Phase 2 SAs by exchanging the proxy identities and the IPSec Phase 2 proposal. If they are acceptable, Cisco ASA displays a message indicating that the IPSec SA proposal is acceptable, as shown in Example 17-44.

Example 17-44 debug *Output to Show Proxy Identities and Phase 2 Proposal Are Accepted*

```
[IKEv1 DEBUG]: Group = SecureMeIPSec, Username = ciscouser, IP =
  209.165.201.10, IPSec SA Proposal # 12, Transform # 1 acceptable  Matches
  global IPSec SA entry # 10,
[IKEv1 DEBUG]: Group = SecureMeIPSec, Username = ciscouser, IP = 209.165.201.10 ,
  Transmitting Proxy Id:
  Remote host: 192.168.50.60  Protocol 0  Port 0
  Local subnet:  0.0.0.0  mask 0.0.0.0 Protocol 0  Port 0
```

After accepting the transform set values, both VPN devices agree on the inbound and outbound IPSec SAs, as shown in Example 17-45. After the IPSec SAs have been created, both VPN devices should be able to pass traffic bidirectionally across the tunnel.

Example 17-45 debug *Output to Show IPSec SAs Are Activated*

```
[IKEv1 DEBUG]: Group = SecureMeIPSec, Username = ciscouser, IP = 209.165.201.10 ,
  loading all IPSEC SAs
[IKEv1]: Group = SecureMeIPSec, Username = ciscouser, IP = 209.165.201.10 Security
  negotiation complete for User (ciscouser)  Responder, Inbound SPI = 0x00c6bc19,
  Outbound SPI = 0xa472f8c1,
[IKEv1]: Group = SecureMeIPSec, Username = ciscouser, IP = 209.165.201.10 Adding
  static route for client address: 192.168.50.60 ,
[IKEv1]: Group = SecureMeIPSec, Username = ciscouser, IP = 209.165.201.10 , PHASE
  2 COMPLETED (msgid=8732f056)
```

Summary

Using the remote-access methods available with Cisco ASA, security administrators can deploy Cisco ASA into almost any network topology. The Cisco IPSec VPN solution is available for remote users who want to access their enterprise network over a secure VPN connection as if they were directly connected to it. The L2TP over IPSec solution is available for those customers who do not wish to install any IPSec client software to the end machines. To reinforce learning, many different deployment scenarios were discussed, along with their configurations. This chapter covered extensive **show** and **debug** commands to assist in troubleshooting complicated remote-access IPSec VPN deployments.

Chapter 18

Public Key Infrastructure (PKI)

This chapter covers the following topics:

- Introduction to PKI
- Installing certificates
- The Local Certificate Authority
- Configuring IPSec site-to-site tunnels using certificates
- Configuring the Cisco ASA to accept remote-access VPN clients using certificates
- Troubleshooting PKI

PKI is usually defined as a set of standards and systems whose main purpose is to verify and authenticate the validity of each party involved in a network transaction. This chapter starts with an introduction to PKI and then shows you how to configure, enroll, and troubleshoot the Cisco ASA with digital certificates.

Introduction to PKI

PKI is a security architecture that provides a higher level of confidence for exchanging information over insecure networks. PKI is based on public key cryptography, a technology that was first created to encrypt and decrypt data involving two different types of keys: a public and a private key. A user gives a public key to other users, keeping the private key. Data that is encrypted with the public key can be decrypted only with the corresponding private key, and vice versa. Figure 18-1 illustrates how this works.

The following is the sequence in Figure 18-1:

Step 1. User A obtains User B's public key and uses it to encrypt a message destined for User B.

Step 2. User A sends the encrypted message over the unsecured network.

Step 3. User B receives the encrypted message and decrypts it using his own private key.

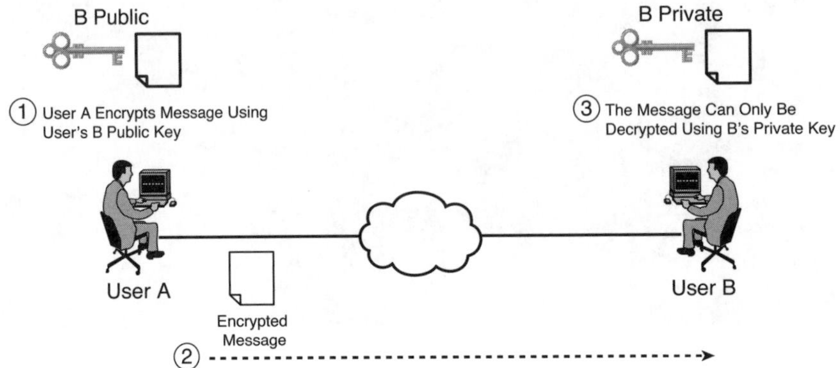

Figure 18-1 *Private and Public Keys*

The following are several key terms and concepts used in PKI:

- Certificates
- Certificate authority (CA)
- Certificate revocation list (CRL)
- Simple Certificate Enrollment Protocol (SCEP)

These terms and concepts are defined in the following sections

Certificates

Digital certificates are commonly used to authenticate and validate users and devices while simultaneously securing information exchanged over unsecured networks. Certificates can be issued for a user or a network device. Certificates securely bind the user's or device's public key along with other information that describe the user's or device's identity.

The certificate syntax and format are defined in the X.509 standard of the International Telecommunication Union-Telecommunication Standardization Sector (ITU-T). An X.509 certificate includes the public key and information about the user or device, information about the certificate itself, and optional issuer information. Generally, certificates contain the following information:

- The entity's public key
- The entity's identifier information, such as the name, email address, organization, and locality

- The validity period (the length of time that the certificate is considered valid)
- Issuer's information
- CRL distribution point

Digital certificates can be used in many implementations, such as IPSec and Secure Sockets Layer (SSL), secure email using Secure/Multipurpose Internet Mail Extensions (S/MIME), and many others. The same certificate might have different purposes. For example, a user certificate can be used for remote-access VPN, accessing application servers, and for S/MIME email authentication.

Note Cisco ASA supports digital certificates for remote-access and site-to-site IPSec VPN session authentication, as well as for WebVPN and SSL administrative sessions.

The CA that issues the certificate determines the implementations for each certificate. The usage of the certificate is configured on the CA (that is, SSL, IPSec, and so on).

Certificate Authority (CA)

A CA is a device or entity that can issue a certificate to a user or network device. Before any PKI operations can begin, the CA generates its own public and private key pair and creates a self-signed CA certificate. A fingerprint in the certificate is used by the end entity to authenticate the received CA certificate. The fingerprint is created by the result of a hash (MD5 or SHA-1) calculation on the whole CA certificate. The fingerprint value corresponds to the ultimate root certificate, in cases in which multiple levels of CA exist. Keep in mind that SHA-1 is more secure than MD5.

CAs can be configured in a hierarchy, as illustrated in Figure 18-2. The CA at the top of a certification hierarchy is usually referred as the *main root CA*.

In the example in Figure 18-2, the root CA server has two subordinate CAs: U.S. and Australia. The U.S. CA server also has two subordinates, New York and Los Angeles. Each CA server grants or denies certificate enrollment requests from its corresponding users and network devices (Cisco ASAs in this example).

A user or network device chooses the certificate issuer as a trusted root authority by accepting the issuer CA's self-signed certificate containing the issuer's public key. The certificate information from all trusted CAs within the hierarchy is often referred to as the *certificate chain of trust*.

The Cisco ASA has a local CA that integrates basic certificate deployment, providing revocation checking of issued certificates. The LOCAL CA user enrollment is supported by browser web page login.

Note The local CA functionality is discussed later in this chapter.

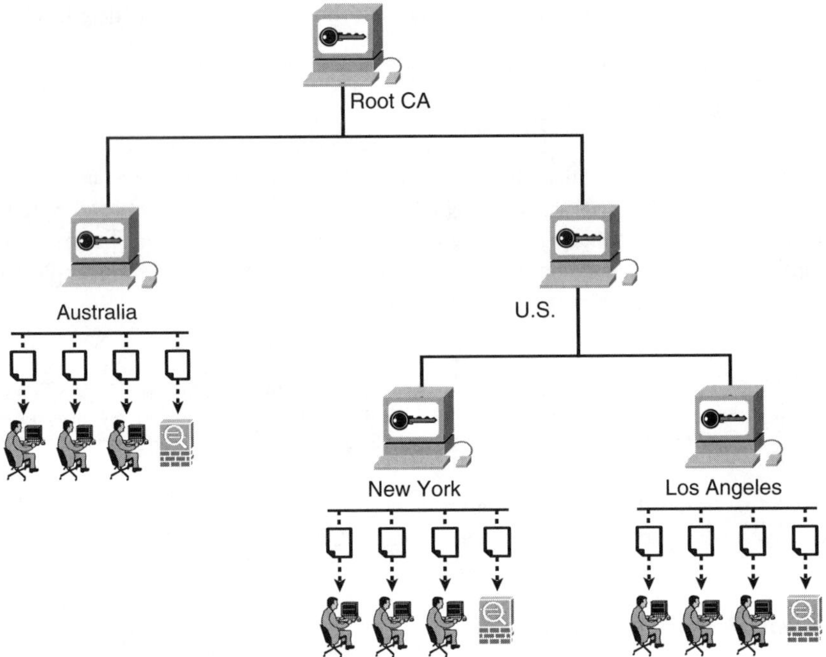

Figure 18-2 *Certification Hierarchy*

There are several CA vendors. The following are some of the CAs supported by Cisco ASA:

- Microsoft Windows 2000 and 2003 CA Server(s)
- VeriSign
- Baltimore UniCERT
- RSA Keon
- Entrust
- Cisco IOS router configured as a CA server

Several PKI implementations also include the use of registration authorities (RAs). An RA acts as an interface between the client (user or network device) and the CA server. An RA verifies and identifies all certificate requests and requests the CA to issue them. RAs can be configured within the same CA (server) or in a separate system. Microsoft CA server, RSA Keon, and Entrust are examples of PKI servers that utilize an RA.

A certificate is valid only for the period of time specified by the issuing CA. After a certificate expires, a new certificate must be requested. You can also revoke a specific user and device certificate. The inventory of serial numbers of revoked certificates is maintained on a certificate revocation list (CRL).

Certificate Revocation List

When you revoke a certificate, the CA publishes the serial number of the revoked certificate to the CRL. This CRL can be maintained on the same CA or a separate system. The CRL can be accessed by any entity trying to check the validity of any given certificate. LDAP and HTTP are the most commonly used protocols when publishing and obtaining a CRL. Storing CRLs in a separate system other than the CA server is often recommended for large environments, for better scalability and to avoid single points of failure.

Figure 18-3 illustrates how a certificate can be revoked on a CA and subsequently published to a CRL server.

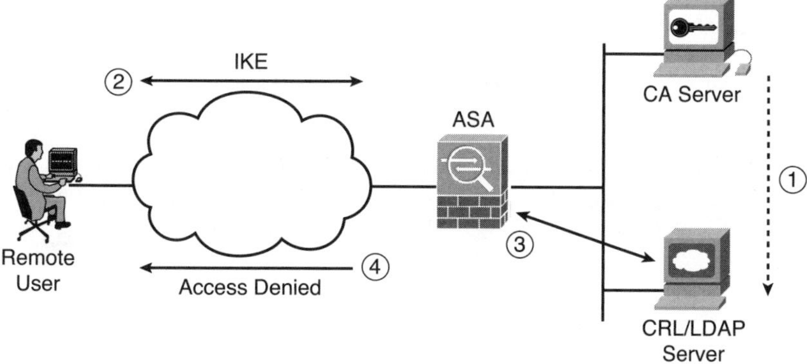

Figure 18-3 *Certificate Revocation and CRL Example*

The following is the sequence of events in Figure 18-3:

Step 1. The user certificate is revoked in the CA server. The CA server updates the CRL/LDAP server.

Step 2. The user attempts to establish an IPSec VPN connection to the Cisco ASA.

Step 3. The Cisco ASA is configured to query the CRL server. It downloads the CRL and finds the certificate serial number on the list of revoked certificates.

Step 4. The Cisco ASA denies access to the user and sends an IKE delete message.

You need to use CRLs for several reasons. Revoking a certificate is crucial if it might have been compromised or if the user might not have authority to use such certificate. For example, you should always revoke certificates when employees leave your organization.

Simple Certificate Enrollment Protocol

Simple Certificate Enrollment Protocol (SCEP) is a protocol developed by Cisco. SCEP provides secure issuance of certificates to users and network devices in a scalable manner. It uses HTTP for the transport mechanism for enrollment and uses LDAP or HTTP for CRL checking. SCEP supports the following operations:

- CA and RA public key distribution
- Certificate enrollment
- Certificate revocation
- Certificate query
- CRL query

Cisco ASA supports enrollment via SCEP and manually via a cut-and-paste method.

> **Tip** Using SCEP is recommended for better scalability. The manual cut-and-paste method is normally used when the CA server does not support SCEP or an HTTP connection is not possible.

Installing Certificates

Enrollment is the process of obtaining a certificate from a CA server. This section covers the necessary steps to configure and enroll a Cisco ASA to an external CA server.

Installing Certificates Through ASDM

You can install a certificate on the Cisco ASA through ASDM from an external CA by using the following methods:

- From a certificate file
- By copying and pasting the certificate in PEM format
- By using SCEP

The following sections demonstrate how to install CA and identity certificates by each of these supported certificate installation methods.

Installing a CA Certificate from a File

Complete the following steps to install a CA certificate from a file, using ASDM.

Step 1. Log in to ASDM and navigate to **Configuration > Device Management > Certificate Management > CA Certificates**. You can alternatively navigate to **Configuration > Remote Access VPN > Certificate Management > CA**; navigating to either of these locations within ASDM enables you to accomplish the same tasks.

Step 2. Click on **Add.**

Step 3. The **Install Certificate** dialog box illustrated in Figure 18-4 is displayed. By default ASDM names the trustpoint **ASDM_TrustPoint0.** The **0** at the end of the trustpoint name increments every time a new certificate is imported. You can also edit the name to the name of your preference. In this example the trustpoint name is left to the default value of **ASDM_TrustPoint0.**

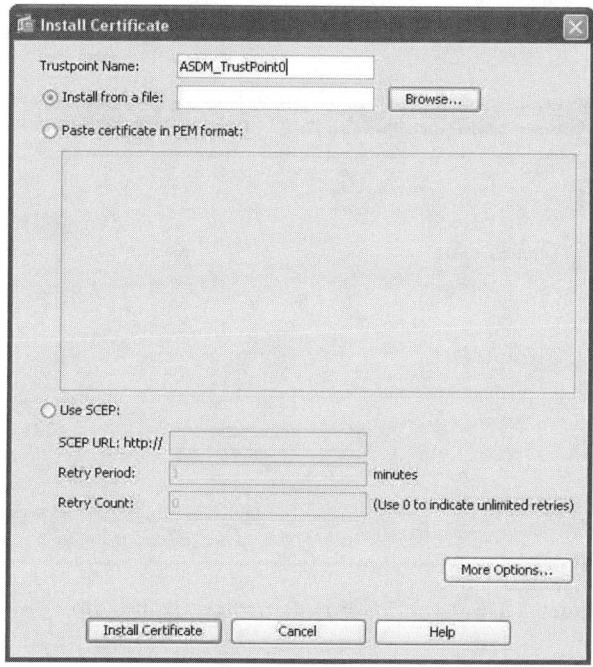

Figure 18-4 *Install Certificate Dialog Box*

Step 4. In this example the CA certificate is installed from a file. Select **Install from a File** and click on **Browse** to locate the certificate file in your local system.

Step 5. Click on **Install Certificate** to install the CA certificate.

Step 6. Click on **Apply** to apply the changes in ASDM.

Step 7. Click on **Save** to save the configuration on the Cisco ASA.

Installing an Identity Certificate from a File

Complete the following steps to install an identity certificate from a file, using ASDM.

Step 1. Log in to ASDM and navigate to **Configuration > Device Management > Certificate Management > Identity Certificates.** You can alternatively navigate to **Configuration > Remote Access VPN > Certificate Management > Identity Certificates;** navigating to either of these locations within ASDM enables you to accomplish the same tasks.

Step 2. Click on **Add.**

Step 3. The **Add Identity Certificate** dialog box illustrated in Figure 18-5 is displayed.

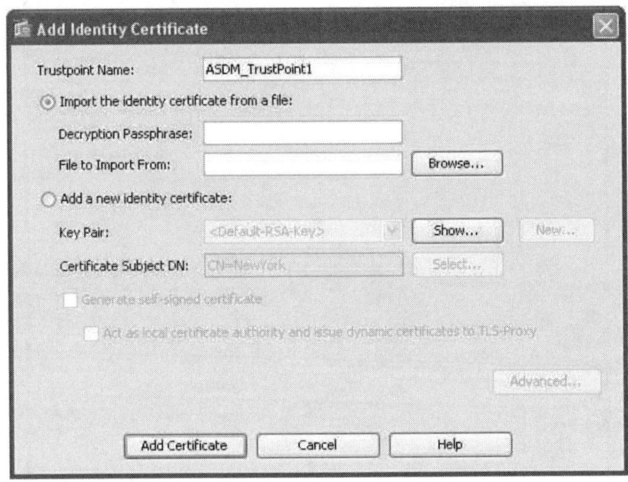

Figure 18-5 *Add Identity Certificate Dialog Box*

Step 4. In this example the CA certificate is installed from a file. Select **Import the Identity Certificate from a File** and click on **Browse** to locate the certificate file in your local system.

Step 5. If your certificate has a passphrase used for encryption, enter such passphrase under the **Decryption Passphrase** field.

Step 6. Click on **Add Certificate** to install the CA certificate.

Step 7. Click on **Apply** to apply the changes in ASDM.

Step 8. Click on **Save** to save the configuration on the Cisco ASA.

Installing a CA Certificate by the Copy and Paste Method

You can also install a CA certificate by pasting the PEM formatted file into ASDM. Complete the following steps to install a CA certificate by the copy-and-paste method, using ASDM.

Step 1. Log in to ASDM and navigate to **Configuration > Device Management > Certificate Management > CA Certificates.** You can alternatively navigate to **Configuration > Remote Access VPN > Certificate Management > CA Certificates**; navigating to either of these locations within ASDM enables you to accomplish the same tasks.

Step 2. Click on **Add.**

Step 3. The **Install Certificate** dialog box illustrated in Figure 18-6 is displayed. Select **Paste Certificate in PEM Format** and paste the CA certificate into the form field, as shown in Figure 18-6.

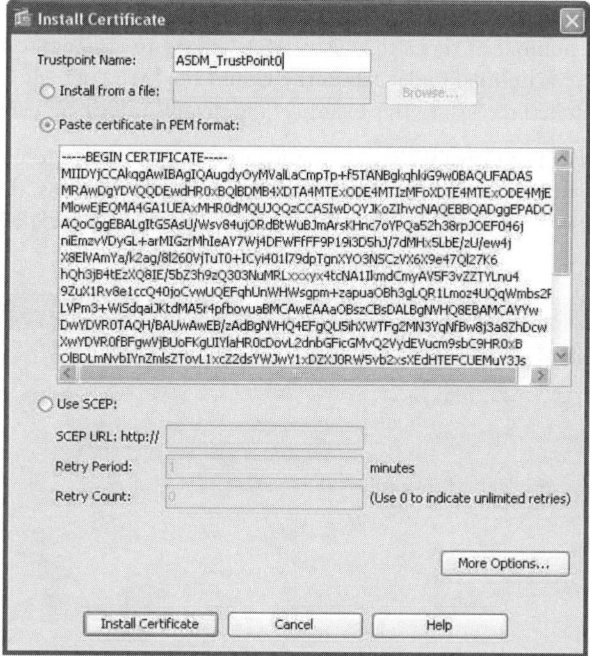

Figure 18-6 *Pasting a CA Certificate from a PEM-Formatted File*

Step 4. Click on **Install Certificate** to install the CA certificate.

Step 5. Click on **Apply** to apply the changes in ASDM.

Step 6. Click on **Save** to save the configuration on the Cisco ASA.

Installing a CA Certificate Using SCEP

Complete the following steps to install a CA certificate using SCEP via ASDM.

Step 1. Log in to ASDM and navigate to **Configuration > Device Management > Certificate Management > CA Certificates.** You can alternatively navigate to **Configuration > Remote Access VPN > Certificate Management > CA Certificates**; navigating to either of these locations within ASDM enables you to accomplish the same tasks.

Step 2. Click on **Add**.

Step 3. The **Install Certificate** dialog box is shown. Select **Use SCEP** to install the CA certificate using SCEP.

Step 4. Enter the CA server SCEP URL in the **SCEP URL** field.

Step 5. By default the retry period for the Cisco ASA to try to connect the CA server using SCEP is 1 minute. To define a different retry period, enter the value (in minutes) under the **Retry Period** field.

Step 6. The number of times the Cisco ASA will try to connect to the CA server via SCEP is defined under the **Retry Count** field. The default is 0, which indicates unlimited retries. In this example, the default values are used.

Step 7. You can optionally click on the **More Options** button to enter advanced configuration parameters. After you click on **More Options**, the Configuration Options for CA Certificate dialog box shown in Figure 18-7 is displayed.

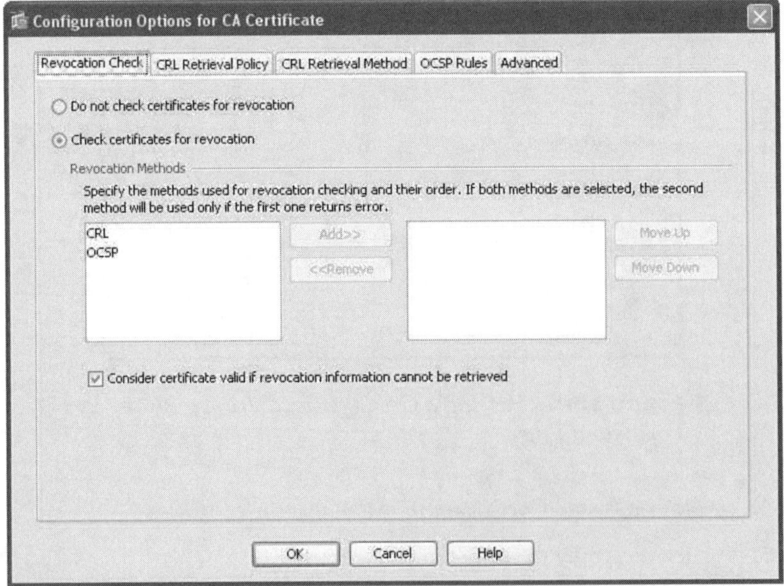

Figure 18-7 *Configuration Options for CA Certificate Dialog Box*

Step 8. Under the **Revocation Check** tab you can configure the Cisco ASA to check whether a certificate has been revoked or not, using CRL checking or OCSP. To have the Cisco ASA check whether a certificate has been revoked, select the **Check Certificate for Revocation** option, as shown in Figure 18-7.

Step 9. Specify the method used for revocation checking and the order on which each check will take place. The available methods are **CRL** and **OCSP**. Select the method and click on **Add.** If both methods are selected, the second method will be used only if the first one fails.

Step 10. As a fallback mechanism, you can configure the Cisco ASA to consider a certificate valid if revocation information cannot be retried, as shown in Figure 18-7.

Step 11. Under the **CRL Retrieval Policy** tab you can specify whether the CRL distribution point is used from the certificate issued or from a configured static URL, as shown in Figure 18-8. In this example, the default behavior is used; the **Use CRL Distribution Point from the Certificate Option** is selected.

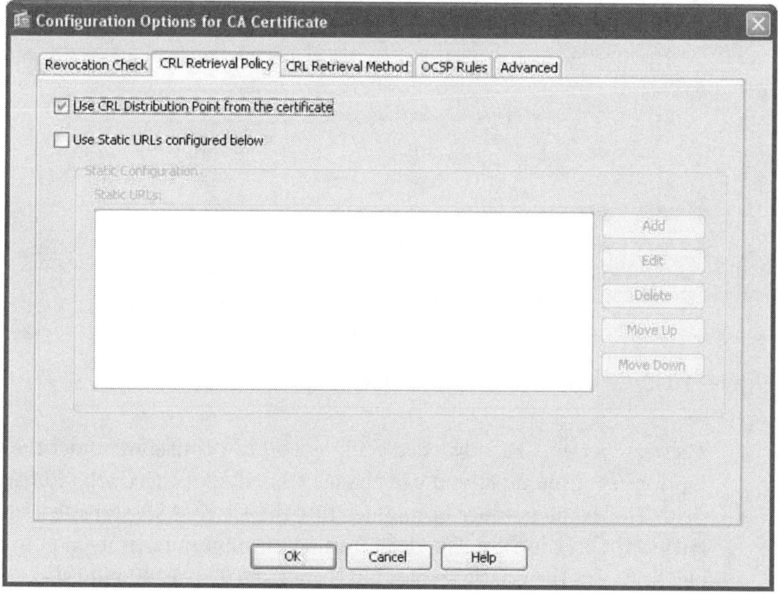

Figure 18-8 *CRL Retrieval Policy Tab*

Step 12. You can optionally use the **CRL Retrieval Method** tab to select the method to be used for CRL checking. You can configure the Lightweight Directory Access Protocol (LDAP), HTTP CRL retrieval, or SCEP. If you specify LDAP as the CRL retrieval option, TCP port 389 is used by the Cisco ASA by default. Additionally, if LDAP is selected, you must enter the username, password, and LDAP server IP address. The default TCP port 389 can also be changed based on your implementation requirements. In this example, HTTP is selected.

Step 13. In the OSCP Rules tab you can optionally configure OCSP rules for obtaining certificate revocation status. You must configure a certificate map before you configure OCSP rules. This certificate map matches user rules to specific fields in a certificate. In this example, OSPC is not used.

Step 14. The **Advanced** tab enables you to configure CRL and OCSP optional advanced parameters, as illustrated in Figure 18-9.

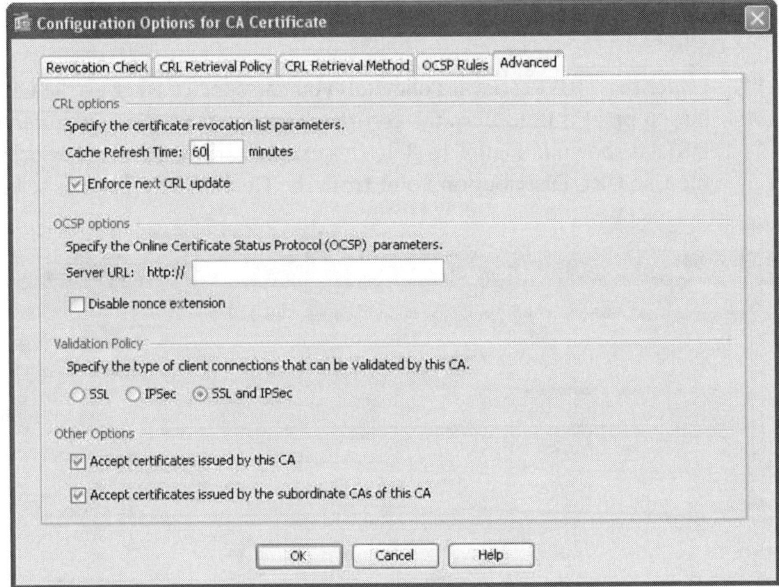

Figure 18-9 *Advanced CRL and OSCP Options*

There are a two CRL advanced options you can configure under the CRL Options section. First, you can change the value of the **Cache Refresh Time** field. This is the number of minutes that the Cisco ASA stores/caches retrieved CRLs locally. The default value of 60 minutes is used in this example; however, the configurable values are from 1 to 1440 minutes.

By default the Cisco ASA enforces CRL checking immediately after it is configured. To disable this, uncheck the **Enforce Next CRL Update** option.

Under the OCSP Options section, you can specify the URL for the OCSP server to be used for certificate status check. By default the OCSP request includes the nonce extension used to prevent replay attacks. However, you can disable the nonce extension if the OCSP server is configured to send replies that do not contain this matching nonce extension or if the server does not support it.

The Validation Policy section enables you to specify the type of VPN connections that will be validated. You can select SSL, IPSec, or both. The default option is to validate certificates for both SSL and IPSec connections.

Under the Other Options section you can configure the Cisco ASA to accept certificates granted by the configured CA and/or accept certificates issued by any subordinate CAs of this CA. Both options are enabled by default, as shown in Figure 18-9.

Step 15. Click **OK** to accept the configured values.

Step 16. Click on **Install Certificate** to install the CA certificate.

Step 17. Click on **Apply** to apply the changes in ASDM.

Step 18. Click on **Save** to save the configuration on the Cisco ASA.

Installing an Identity Certificate Using SCEP

Complete the following steps to install an identity certificate using SCEP via ASDM.

Step 1. Log in to ASDM and navigate to **Configuration > Device Management > Certificate Management > Identity Certificates.** You can alternatively navigate to **Configuration > Remote Access VPN > Certificate Management > Identity Certificates**; navigating to either of these locations within ASDM enables you to accomplish the same tasks.

Step 2. Click on **Add.**

Step 3. The **Install Certificate** dialog box shown in Figure 18-10 is displayed. Select **Add a New Identify Certificate.**

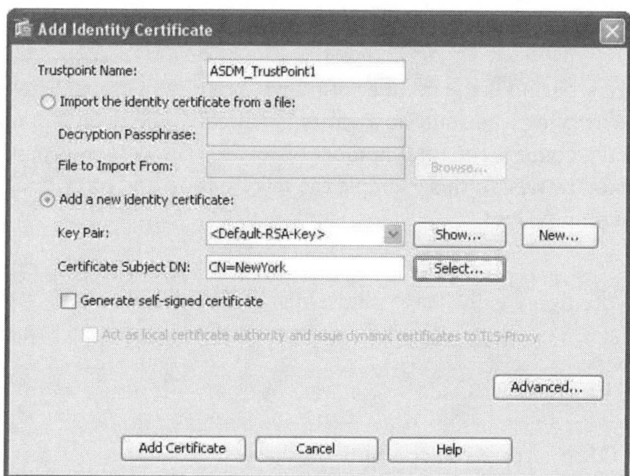

Figure 18-10 *Installing an Identity Certificate Using SCEP*

Step 4. Before starting the enrollment process, you must either select the default RSA key pair (generated by ASDM) or generate a new one. In this example, the default RSA key pair is used. To generate a new one, click on the **New** button. To show the current key pair, click the **Show** button.

Step 5. You can define the certificate distinguished name (DN) in the Identity certificate by clicking the **Select** button under the **Certificate Subject DN** section. The Certificate Subject DN panel is displayed.

Step 6. You can define several attributes; these include the following:

- CN = Common Name
- OU = Department
- O = Company Name
- C = Country
- ST = State/Province
- L = Location
- EA = Email Address

In this example, NewYork is defined as the CN.

Click **OK** after defining the DN attributes for the identity certificate.

Step 7. Click on the **Advanced** button to enter advanced enrollment parameters. The **Advanced Options** dialog box is displayed.

Step 8. Select the **Enrollment Mode** tab.

Step 9. In this example enrollment is done via SCEP. Select the **Request from CA** button to enroll via SCEP.

Step 10. Enter the URL of the CA server under the **Enrollment URL (SCEP)** field.

Step 11. The retry period is the number of minutes that the Cisco ASA will wait before retrying to install the identity certificate. The default is one minute. The retry count is the total number of retries. The default is 0, which indicates unlimited retries. In this example the retry period and retry count are left to their default values.

> **Note** You can also configure a challenge phrase that is registered with the CA during SCEP enrollment. The CA typically uses this phrase to authenticate a subsequent revocation request.

Step 12. Click **OK** to accept the configured values.

Step 13. Click on **Add Certificate** to send the identity certificate request to the CA server. The enrollment request has been sent to the CA server. To check the enrollment status, click on the **Refresh** button.

Step 14. After the identity certificate is issued and installed, you will see it listed under **Configuration > Remote Access VPN > Certificate Management > Identity Certificates** and under **Configuration > Device Management > Certificate Management > Identity Certificates.**

Step 15. Click on **Save** to save the configuration on the Cisco ASA.

Tip ASDM also enables you to enroll the Cisco ASA to an Entrust CA server. To enroll using an Entrust CA, navigate to **Configuration > Remote Access VPN > Certificate Management > Identity Certificates** and click the **Enroll ASA SSL VPN with Entrust** button. The **Generate Certificate Signing Request** dialog box appears, enabling you to configure and generate a certificate-signing request to send to Entrust. You can do the same thing by navigating to **Configuration > Device Management > Certificate Management > Identity Certificates.**

Installing Certificates Using the CLI

This section demonstrates how to install certificates using the CLI instead of ASDM.

Generating the RSA Key Pair in the CLI

Before starting the enrollment process via the CLI, you must generate the RSA key pair with the **crypto key generate rsa** command. To generate the keys, you must first configure a hostname and domain name. Example 18-1 demonstrates how to configure the Cisco ASA hostname and domain name and generate the RSA key pair.

Example 18-1 *Generating the RSA Key Pair*

```
ASA(config)# hostname NewYork
NewYork(config)# domain-name securemeinc.com
NewYork(config)# crypto key generate rsa modulus 1024
INFO: The name for the keys will be: <Default-RSA-Key>
Keypair generation process begin.
```

Note In Example 18-1, the name for the key pair is **<Default-RSA-Key>**. The **<Default-RSA-Key>** is replaced with a key pair label if configured, which you do by using the **label** keyword. If you attempt to create another key pair with the same label, the Cisco ASA displays an warning message.

Use the **crypto key zeroize rsa** command if an RSA key pair exists and a new pair needs to be regenerated. Example 18-2 demonstrates how to remove existing RSA key pairs.

Example 18-2 *Removing Existing RSA Key Pair*

```
NewYork(config)# crypto key zeroize rsa
WARNING: All RSA keys will be removed.
WARNING: All certs issued using these keys will also be removed.
Do you really want to remove these keys? [yes/no]: yes
```

To verify the generation of the RSA key pair, use the **show crypto key mypubkey rsa** command. Example 18-3 shows the output of this command.

Example 18-3 *Viewing RSA Key Pair Information*

```
NewYork# show crypto key mypubkey rsa
Key pair was generated at: 08:46:31 UTC Jun 10 2009
Key name: <Default-RSA-Key>
 Usage: General Purpose Key
 Modulus Size (bits): 1024
 Key Data:
  30819f30 0d06092a 864886f7 0d010101 05000381 8d003081 89028181 00f26be4
  08b00ac5 fb06adda 7c7a2ae6 26c136ce 990f5612 41d6fa09 79ef251f d229dcc0
  64bc15f8 1b3a4f1e 131f1765 866dfb3a bb8c3a59 f8605625 8e8ff0ca 90d291d0
  75c753c3 dd5f55f3 6d49d774 523b9d8b 78ad05b4 efd75793 88ac9646 7e8c8816
017d464d 4a817041 a559dc63 2532c657 cc12373a c7b733f1 a50bdb82 61020301 0001
```

Note The same RSA key pair is used for Secure Shell (SSH) connections to the security appliance.

Configuring a Trustpoint

The Cisco ASA certificate configuration commands are similar to Cisco IOS commands. The **crypto ca trustpoint** command declares the CA that your Cisco ASA should use and enables you to configure all the necessary certificate parameters. Invoking this command puts you in **ca-trustpoint** configuration mode, as shown in Example 18-4.

Example 18-4 *Configuring a Trustpoint*

```
NewYork# configure terminal
NewYork(config)# crypto ca trustpoint CISCO
NewYork(config-ca-trustpoint)#
```

Table 18-1 lists and describes all the trustpoint subcommands.

Table 18-1 *Enrollment Configuration Subcommands*

Subcommand	Description
accept-subordinates	Allows the Cisco ASA to accept subordinate CA certificates
crl	CRL options (explained later in this chapter)
default	Returns all enrollment parameters to their default values
Email	Used to enter the email address to be used in the enrollment request
enrollment	Enrollment parameters: **retry**—Polling retry count and period **self**—Enrollment generates a self-signed certificate **terminal**—Used for manual enrollment (cut-and-paste method) **url**—The URL of the CA server
fqdn	Includes fully qualified domain name
id-cert-issuer	Accepts ID certificates
id-usage	Specifies how the device identity represented by this trustpoint can be used
ip-address	Includes IP address
keypair	Specifies the key pair whose public key is to be certified
match	Used to match a certificate map
ocsp	Used to configure the following OCSP parameters: **disable-nonce**—Disable OCSP Nonce Extension **url**—OCSP server URL
password	Returns password
proxy-ldc-issuer	Used to configure an issuer for TLS proxy local dynamic certificates
revocation-check	Used to configure the following certificate revocation check parameters: **crl**—Used to enable revocation check by CRL **none**—Used to ignore revocation check **ocsp**—Used to enable revocation check by OCSP
serial-number	Includes serial number
subject-name	Subject name

Figure 18-11 illustrates a topology that is used in the next example. A Cisco ASA is configured to enroll via SCEP to the CA server 209.165.202.130.

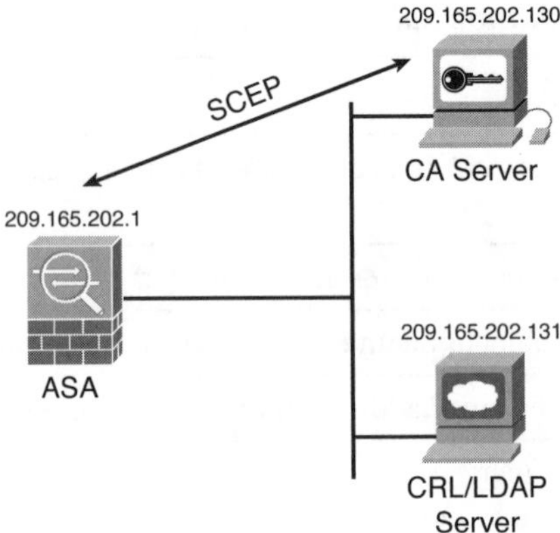

Figure 18-11 *Enrollment via SCEP Example*

Example 18-5 includes the Cisco ASA trustpoint configuration.

Example 18-5 *Configuring the ASA to Enroll via SCEP*

```
NewYork# configure terminal
NewYork(config)# crypto ca trustpoint CISCO
NewYork(configure-ca-trustpoint)# enrollment url
http://209.165.202.130/certsrv/mscep/mscep.dll
NewYork(configure-ca-trustpoint)# enrollment retry count 3
NewYork(configure-ca-trustpoint)# enrollment retry period 5
NewYork(configure-ca-trustpoint)# fqdn NewYork.securemeinc.com
NewYork(configure-ca-trustpoint)# exit
NewYork(config)# exit
NewYork#
```

In Example 18-5, the Cisco ASA is configured with a trustpoint named **CISCO.** The **enrollment url** subcommand is used to declare the location of the CA server.

> **Note** In this example, the CA server is a Microsoft Windows CA Server with SCEP services. The complete URL is http://209.165.202.130/certsrv/mscep/mscep.dll.
>
> The SCEP plug-in for Microsoft Windows can be downloaded from Microsoft's website at www.microsoft.com.

The Cisco ASA is configured to retry three times in case the certificate is not successfully obtained from the CA Server. It is also configured to wait five minutes between each request to the CA. The fully qualified domain name (FQDN) used in the enrollment request is configured to be NewYork.securemeinc.com.

In this example, the Cisco ASA enrolls with the CA to use certificates for IPSec authentication. The Cisco ASA needs to obtain the CA certificate and request an ID certificate from the CA server. To obtain the CA certificate, use the **crypto ca authenticate** command. Example 18-6 demonstrates how to use this command to retrieve the CA certificate from the CA server.

Example 18-6 *Obtaining the CA Certificate from the CA Server*

```
NewYork# configure terminal
NewYork(config)# crypto ca authenticate CISCO
INFO: Certificate has the following attributes:
Fingerprint:     3736ffc2 243ecf05 0c40f2fa 26820675
Do you accept this certificate? [yes/no]: yes
```

In Example 18-6, **CISCO** is the name of the previously configured trustpoint. After executing this command, the Cisco ASA establishes a TCP port 80 connection to the 209.165.202.130 CA server (via SCEP). While doing this transaction, the Cisco ASA prompts you to accept the certificate.

Note The Cisco ASA also retrieves RA certificates from the server if an RA is used.

After the CA certificate is obtained from the CA server, use the **crypto ca enroll** command to generate an identity certificate request to the 209.165.202.130 CA server. Example 18-7 demonstrates how to use this command to obtain the ID certificate.

Note The request is a PKCS#7 certificate request.

Example 18-7 *Obtaining the ID Certificate from the CA Server*

```
NewYork(config)# crypto ca enroll CISCO
%
% Start certificate enrollment ..
% Create a challenge password. You will need to verbally provide this
   password to the CA Administrator in order to revoke your certificate.
   For security reasons your password will not be saved in the configuration.
   Please make a note of it.
Password: ******
Re-enter password: ******
% The fully-qualified domain name in the certificate will be:
NewYork.securemeinc.com
% Include the router serial number in the subject name? [yes/no]: no
Request certificate from CA? [yes/no]: yes
% Certificate request sent to Certificate Authority
NewYork(config)# The certificate has been granted by CA!
```

The word **CISCO** is the name of the previously configured trustpoint. After invoking the **crypto ca enroll** command, the Cisco ASA asks for a password to be used for this certificate. The Cisco ASA displays the FQDN to be used in the certificate. The Cisco ASA asks whether you would like to include its serial number in the subject name of the certificate. This is not selected in this example. The serial number is not used by IKE, but it may be used by the CA server to authenticate certificates or to associate a certificate with a particular device. If you are in doubt, ask your CA administrator whether you need to include the serial number in your certificate request. In the shaded line, the Cisco ASA finally asks whether you would like to request the certificate from the CA. If your answer is **yes** and the subsequent request is successful, the message in the shaded line is shown, indicating a successful certificate enrollment.

Use the **show crypto ca certificates** command to verify and display the root/CA and ID certificate information. Example 18-8 shows the output of this command.

Example 18-8 *Output of the* show crypto ca certificates *command*

```
NewYork# show crypto ca certificates
Certificate
  Status: Available
  Certificate Serial Number: 1c91af4500000000000d
Certificate Usage: General Purpose
  Public Key Type: RSA (1024 bits)
Issuer Name:
    cn=SecuremeCAServer
    ou=ENGINEERING
    o=Secureme
    l=NewYork
    st=IL
    c=US
    ea=administrator@securemeinc.com
Subject Name:
    Name: NewYork.securemeinc.com
    Serial Number:
    hostname=NewYork.securemeinc.com
  CRL Distribution Point:
    http://NewYork-ca.securemeinc.com/CertEnroll/SecuremeCAServer.crl
  Validity Date:
    start date: 02:58:05 UTC May 2 2009
    end   date: 03:08:05 UTC May 2 2012
  Associated Trustpoints: CISCO
!
CA Certificate
```

```
  Status: Available
  Certificate Serial Number: 225b38e6471fcca649427934cf289071
Certificate Usage: Signature
  Public Key Type: RSA (2048 bits)
Issuer Name:
    cn=SecuremeCAServer
    ou= ENGINEERING
    o=Secureme
    l=NewYork
    st=IL
    c=US
    ea=administrator@securemeinc.com
Subject Name:
    cn=SecuremeCAServer
    ou=ENGINEERING
    o=Secureme
    l=NewYork
    st=IL
    c=US
    ea=administrator@securemeinc.com
  CRL Distribution Point:
    http://NewYork-ca.securemeinc.com/CertEnroll/SecuremeCAServer.crl
  Validity Date:
    start date: 20:15:19 UTC Jun 10 2009
    end   date: 20:23:42 UTC Jun 10 2012
  Associated Trustpoints: CISCO
NewYork#
```

The certificate information is shown in Example 18-8, which includes the following:

- The status of each certificate
- The certificate usage
- The issuer distinguished name (DN) information (i.e., organization, organizational unit, locality, etc.)
- CRL distribution point (CDP)
- The validity period of each certificate
- The trustpoint associated to the certificate

This command is very useful for troubleshooting and verification purposes.

Manual (Cut-and-Paste) Enrollment via the CLI

The manual, or cut-and-paste, enrollment method is mostly used in any of the following circumstances:

- The CA server does not support SCEP.
- There is no IP connectivity between the Cisco ASA and the CA server.
- TCP port 80 is blocked between the Cisco ASA and the CA server.

The configuration of the Cisco ASA for manual enrollment is very similar to its configuration for the SCEP enrollment process. However, the **enrollment terminal** subcommand is used instead of the **enrollment url** subcommand. Example 18-9 shows the trustpoint configuration for manual enrollment.

Example 18-9 *Configuring the Cisco ASA for Manual Enrollment*

```
NewYork# configure terminal
NewYork(config)# crypto ca trustpoint MANUAL
NewYork(configure-ca-trustpoint)# enrollment terminal
NewYork(configure-ca-trustpoint)# exit
NewYork(config)# exit
NewYork#
```

The name of the trustpoint in Example 18-9 is **MANUAL.** The **enrollment terminal** subcommand is used to specify manual enrollment.

The administrator retrieves (copies and pastes) the certificate from the CA server. Use the **crypto ca authenticate** command to import the CA certificate. Example 18-10 demonstrates how to import the CA certificate to the Cisco ASA manually.

Example 18-10 *Importing the CA Certificate Manually*

```
NewYork(config)# crypto ca authenticate MANUAL
Enter the base 64 encoded CA certificate.
End with the word "quit" on a line by itself ---BEGIN CERTIFICATE---
MIIC0jCCAnygAwIBAgIQIls45kcfzKZJQnk0zyiQcTANBgkqhkiG9w0BAQUFADCB
hjEeMBwGCSqGSIb3DQEJARYPamF6aWJAY2lzY28uY29tMQswCQYDVQQGEwJVUzEL
MAkGA1UECBMCTkMxDDAKBgNVBAcTA1JUUDEWMBQGA1UEChMNQ2lzY28gU3lzdGVt
czEMMAoGA1UECxMDVEFDMRYwFAYDVQQDEw1KYXppYkNBU2VydmVyMB4XDTA0MDYy
NTIwMTUxOVoXDTA3MDYyNTIwMjM0MlowgYYxHjAcBgkqhkiG9w0BCQEWD2phemli
QGNpc2NvLmNvbTELMAkGA1UEBhMCVVMxCzAJBgNVBAgTAk5DMQwwCgYDVQQHEwNS
VFAxFjAUBgNVBAoTDUNpc2NvIFN5c3RlbXMxDDAKBgNVBAsTA1RBQzEWMBQGA1UE
AxMNSmF6aWJDQVNlcnZlcjBcMA0GCSqGSIb3DQEBAQUAA0sAMEgCQQDnCRVLNn2L
wgair5gaw9bGFoWG2bS9G4LPl2/lTDffk9yD3h7/R3bBLIcSwy3nt1V5/brUtGFR
CoVV2XQ4RZEtAgMBAAGjgcMwgcAwCwYDVR0PBAQDAgHGMA8GA1UdEwEB/wQFMAMB
```

```
Af8wHQYDVR0OBBYEFKTqtaUJ6Pm9Pc/0IRc/EklKnT9TMG8GA1UdHwRoMGYwMKAu
oCyGKmh0dHA6Ly90ZWNoaWUvQ2VydEVucm9sbC9KYXppYkNBU2VydmVyLmNybDAy
oDCgLoYsZmlsZTovL1xcdGVjaGllXENlcnRFbnJvbGxcSmF6aWJDQVNlcnZlci5j
cmwwEAYJKwYBBAGCNxUBBAMCAQAwDQYJKoZIhvcNAQEFBQADQQCw4XI7Ocff7MIc
LlAEyrhrTn3c2yqTbWZ61O/QGaC4LdfyEDMeA0HvpkbB2GGJSj1AZocRCtB33GLi
QkiMpjnK
```


```
—-END CERTIFICATE—-
quit
INFO: Certificate has the following attributes:
Fingerprint:      82a0095e 2584ced6 b66ed6a8 e48a5ad1
Do you accept this certificate? [yes/no]: yes
Trustpoint CA certificate accepted.
% Certificate successfully imported
```

As shown in Example 18-10, the CA certificate is manually imported to the Cisco ASA by the cut-and-paste method. Enter a blank line or the word **quit** after pasting the Base64-encoded CA certificate to the Cisco ASA to exit the CA configuration screen. If the certificate is recognized, the Cisco ASA asks you whether you would like to accept the certificate; enter **yes.** The Certificate Successfully Imported message is displayed if the CA certificate import is successful.

To generate the ID certificate request, use the **crypto ca enroll** command. Example 18-11 demonstrates how to generate the certificate request.

Example 18-11 *Generating the ID Certificate Request*

```
NewYork(config)# crypto ca enroll MANUAL
% Start certificate enrollment ..
% The fully-qualified domain name in the certificate will be:
NewYork.securemeinc.com
% Include the device serial number in the subject name? [yes/no]: noDisplay
Certificate Request to terminal? [yes/no]: yes
Certificate Request follows:
```


```
MIIBpDCCAQ0CAQAwLTErMA4GA1UEBRMHNDZmZjUxODAZBgkqhkiG9w0BCQIWDE5Z
LmNpc2NvLmNvbTCBnzANBgkqhkiG9w0BAQEFAAOBjQAwgYkCgYEA1n+8nczm8ut1
X5PVngaA1470A1Us3YWRvOYcfwj/tosNRoJ/lY2tVQMnZ+aKlai2+PcZfyP2u2Ar
cadRwkwY0KfKrt5f7LAKrhmHyavNT0rRXBxEMPbtvWuacghmaNXAiRGNpNOHpQjB
QCth9fw7s+anAkXZlfd2ZzAu1Y60s6cCAwEAAaA3MDUGCSqGSIb3DQEJDjEoMCYw
CwYDVR0PBAQDAgWgMBcGA1UdEQQQMA6CDE5ZLmNpc2NvLmNvbTANBgkqhkiG9w0B
AQQFAAOBgQDGcYSC8VGy+ekUNkDayW1g+TQL4lYldLmT9xXUADAQqmGhyA8A36d0
VtZlNc2pXHaMPKkqxMEPMcJVdZ+o6JpiIFHPpYNiQGFUQZoHGcZveEbMVor93/KM
IChEgs4x98fCuJoiQ2RQr452bsWNyEmeLcDqczMSUXFucSLMm0XDNg==
```


```
—-End - This line not part of the certificate request—-
Redisplay enrollment request? [yes/no]: no
NewYork(config)#
```

Example 18-11 shows how the certificate request is generated. Copy and paste the certificate request to your CA server and generate the new ID certificate for the Cisco ASA.

Tip Make sure not to copy and paste the second highlighted line in Example 18-11. The certificate request will be malformed if this is included.

Note Obtain a Base64-encoded certificate from your CA server. You cannot copy and paste a Distinguished Encoding Rules (DER) encoded certificate.

The Cisco ASA gives you the option to redisplay the certificate request if needed (as shown in Example 18-11).

After the ID certificate is approved by the CA server, use the **crypto ca import** command to import the Base64-encoded ID certificate. Example 18-12 demonstrates how to import the ID certificate.

Example 18-12 *Manually Importing the ID Certificate*

```
NewYork(config)# crypto ca import MANUAL certificate
% The fully-qualified domain name in the certificate will be:
NewYork.securemeinc.com
Enter the base 64 encoded certificate.
End with the word "quit" on a line by itself
——-BEGIN CERTIFICATE——-
```

```
MIIECDCCA7KgAwIBAgIKHJGvRQAAAAAADTANBgkqhkiG9w0BAQUFADCBhjEeMBwG
CSqGSIb3DQEJARYPamF6aWJAY2lzY28uY29tMQswCQYDVQQGEwJVUzELMAkGA1UE
CBMCTkMxDDAKBgNVBAcTA1JUUDEWMBQGA1UEChMNQ2lzY28gU3lzdGVtczEMMAoG
A1UECxMDVEFDMRYwFAYDVQQDEw1KYXppYkNBU2VydmVyMB4XDTA0MDkwMjAyNTgw
NVoXDTA1MDkwMjAzMDgwNVowLzEQMA4GA1UEBRMHNDZmZjUxODEbMBkGCSqGSIb3
DQEJAhMMTlkuY2lzY28uY29tMIGfMA0GCSqGSIb3DQEBAQUAA4GNADCBiQKBgQDW
f7ydzOby63Vfk9WeBoDXjvQDVSzdhZG85hx/CP+2iw1Ggn+Vja1VAydn5oqVqLb4
9xl/I/a7YCtxp1HCTBjQp8qu3l/ssAquGYfJq81PStFcHEQw9u29a5pyCGZo1cCJ
EY2k04elCMFAK2H1/Duz5qcCRdmV93ZnMC7VjrSzpwIDAQABo4ICEjCCAg4wCwYD
VR0PBAQDAgWgMBcGA1UdEQQQMA6CDE5ZLmNpc2NvLmNvbTAdBgNVHQ4EFgQUxMvq
7pWbd8bye1PKnXTKYO3A5JQwgcIGA1UdIwSBujCBt4AUpOq1pQno+b09z/QhFz8S
SUqdP1OhgYykgYkwgYYxHjAcBgkqhkiG9w0BCQEWD2phemliQGNpc2NvLmNvbTEL
MAkGA1UEBhMCVVMxCzAJBgNVBAgTAk5DMQwwCgYDVQQHEwNSVFAxFjAUBgNVBAoT
DUNpc2NvIFN5c3RlbXMxDDAKBgNVBAsTA1RBQzEWMBQGA1UEAxMNSmF6aWJDQVNl
cnZlcoIQIls45kcfzKZJQnk0zyiQcTBvBgNVHR8EaDBmMDCgLqAshipodHRwOi8v
dGVjaGllL0NlcnRFbnJvbGwvSmF6aWJDQVNlcnZlci5jcmwwMqAwoC6GLGZpbGU6
Ly9cXHRlY2hpZVxDZXJ0RW5yb2xsXEphemliQ0FTZXJ2ZXIuY3JsMIGQBggrBgEF
BQcBAQSBgzCBgDA9BggrBgEFBQcwAoYxaHR0cDovL3RlY2hpZS9DZXJ0RW5yb2xs
L3RlY2hpZV9KYXppYkNBU2VydmVyLmNydDA/BggrBgEFBQcwAoYzZmlsZTovL1xc
```

```
dGVjaGllXENlcnRFbnJvbGxcdGVjaGllX0phemliQ0FTZXJ2ZXIuY3J0MA0GCSqG
SIb3DQEBBQUAA0EAQ1+WBtysPhOAhTKLYemj8X1TpGrqtUl3mCyNH5OXppfYjSGu
SGzFQHtnqURciJBtay9RNnMpZmZYpfOHzmeFmQ==
---END CERTIFICATE---
quit
INFO: Certificate successfully imported
NewYork(config)#
```

The Base64-encoded ID certificate is successfully imported to the Cisco ASA.

Configuring CRL Options via the CLI

This section teaches you how to configure CRL checking on the Cisco ASA. You can configure the Cisco ASA to do any of the following:

- Not require CRL checking
- Optionally accept the peer's certificate if the security appliance is not able to retrieve the CRL
- Require CRL checking

To bypass CRL checking, use the **crl nocheck** trustpoint subcommand.

> **Tip** Bypassing CRL checking is insecure and therefore is not recommended.

The **crl optional** subcommand enables the Cisco ASA to optionally accept its peer's certificate if the required CRL is not available.

Use the **crl required** subcommand to force the Cisco ASA to perform CRL checking. The CRL server must be reachable and available for a peer certificate to be validated. After this command is enabled, you must configure the CRL parameters. To configure the CRL options, use the **crl configure** trustpoint subcommand. After invoking this command, you are placed in the **ca-crl** prompt, as shown in Example 18-13.

Example 18-13 *The* **crl configure** *Subcommand*

```
NewYork(config)# crypto ca trustpoint CISCO
NewYork(configure-ca-trustpoint)# crl required
NewYork(configure-ca-trustpoint)# crl configure
NewYork(config-ca-crl)#
```

Table 18-2 lists all the CRL configuration options.

Table 18-2 crl configure *Configuration Options*

Subcommand	Description
cache-time	Used to configure the refresh time (in minutes) for the CRL cache. The range is from 1 to 1440 minutes. The default value is 60 minutes.
default	Returns all the options to the default value.
enforcenext update	Used to define how to handle the **NextUpdate** CRL field. If this option is configured, CRLs are required to have a **NextUpdate** field that has not yet lapsed.
ldap-defaults	Used to define the default LDAP server and port to use if the distribution point extension of the certificate being checked is missing these values.
ldap-dn	Used to configure the Login DN and password used to access the CRL database.
policy	Used to configure the CRL retrieval policy. The following options are available: **both**—The Cisco ASA uses the CRL distribution points from the certificate being checked, or else uses static distribution points. **cdp**—The Cisco ASA uses the CRL distribution points from the certificate being checked. **static**—The Cisco ASA uses statically configured URLs.
protocol	The protocol used for CRL retrieval. The options are **http**, **ldap**, and **scep.**
url	A static URL for the site from which CRLs may be retrieved. You can specify up to five URLs. An index value is used to determine the rank of the configured URL.

Example 18-14 demonstrates how to configure CRL checking and the use of several of the previous options.

Example 18-14 *CRL Checking Example*

```
crypto ca trustpoint CISCO
 crl required
 enrollment retry count 3
 enrollment url http://209.165.202.130:80/certsrv/mscep/mscep.dll
 fqdn NewYork.securemeinc.com
 crl configure
  policy static
  url 1 ldap://NewYork-crl1.securemeinc.com/CRL/CRL.crl
  url 2 ldap://NewYork-crl2.securemeinc.com/CRL/CRL.crl
  url 3 ldap://NewYork-crl3.securemeinc.com/CRL/CRL.crl
```

In Example 18-14, a Cisco ASA is configured to require CRL checking with the **crl required** trustpoint subcommand. The Cisco ASA has three CRL servers statically defined. LDAP is used as the transport protocol.

> **Note** Make sure to configure a domain name server on the Cisco ASA when using FQDN for CRL distribution points. Use the **dns name-server** *ip-address* command to specify the domain name server to be used.

The Cisco ASA first tries the CRL server named NewYork-crl1.securemeinc.com. Subsequently, it tries NewYork-crl2.securemeinc.com and NewYork-crl3.securemeinc.com, in that order, as shown in Figure 18-12.

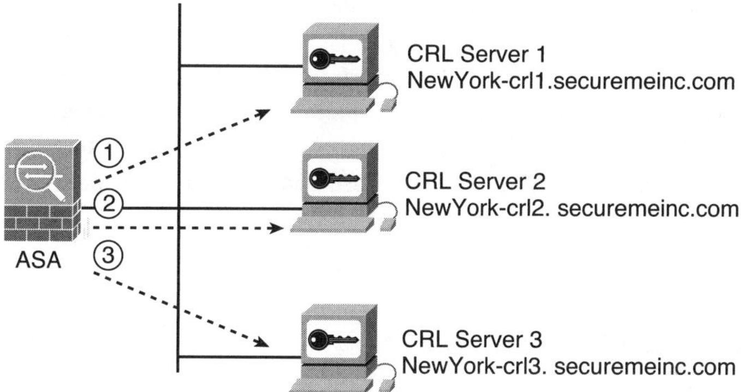

Figure 18-12 *CRL Checking Example*

You can manually request the retrieval of the CRL by using the **crypto ca crl request** command. Example 18-15 demonstrates how to manually retrieve the CRL.

Example 18-15 *CRL Manual Retrieval via the CLI*

```
NewYork(config)# crypto ca crl request CISCO
CRL received
```

The CRL is received successfully. To view the CRL, use the **show crypto ca crls** command, as demonstrated in Example 18-16.

Example 18-16 *Output of the* **show crypto ca crls** *Command*

```
NewYork# show crypto ca crls
CRL Issuer Name:
cn=SecuremeCAServer,ou=ENGINEERING,o=Secureme,l=NewYork,st=IL,c=US,ea=administra-
tor@securemeinc.com
```

```
LastUpdate: 14:18:11 UTC Sep 10 2009
NextUpdate: 02:38:11 UTC Sep 18 2009
Retrieved from CRL Distribution Point:
  http://NewYork-crl1.securemeinc.com/CertEnroll/SecuremeCAServer.crl
Size (bytes): 1095
```

The first and second shaded lines in Example 18-16 show when the last CRL update took place and when the next one will be. The third shaded line shows the URL of the CRL distribution point.

The Local Certificate Authority

The Cisco ASA offers basic certificate authority functionality to issue digital certificates, as well as to do basic revocation checking of issued certificates. This feature is often referred to as the *Local Certificate Authority* (Local CA). The certificates issued by the Cisco ASA's local CA are for both browser- and client-based SSL VPN connections. When the local CA is configured and enabled on the Cisco ASA, users can enroll for a certificate by visiting a specified browser-based enrollment webpage. This section demonstrates how to configure and enable the Cisco ASA's local CA, using ASDM and the CLI.

Configuring the Local CA Through ASDM

Complete the following steps to configure the local CA through ASDM.

Step 1. Log in to ASDM and navigate to **Configuration > Remote Access VPN > Certificate Management > Local Certificate Authority > CA Server**. The screen shown in Figure 18-13 is displayed.

Step 2. Click on **Create Certificate Authority Server** to configure the local CA.

Step 3. Select **Enable** to enable the local CA.

Step 4. You can enter a passphrase to secure the Local CA server from unauthorized or accidental shutdown under the **Passphrase** field.

Step 5. Enter the issuer name used for the CA certificate to be generated by the Cisco ASA's local CA under the **Issuer Name** field. In this example, **CN = NewYorkCA** is used.

Step 6. Select the key modulus size used for the CA server certificate under the **CA Server Key Size** pull-down menu. The configurable values are from 512 to 2048. In this example, the default size of **1024** is used.

Step 7. Select the key modulus size used for the client certificates under the **Client Key Size** pull-down menu. The configurable values are from 512 to 2048. In this example, the default size of **1024** is used.

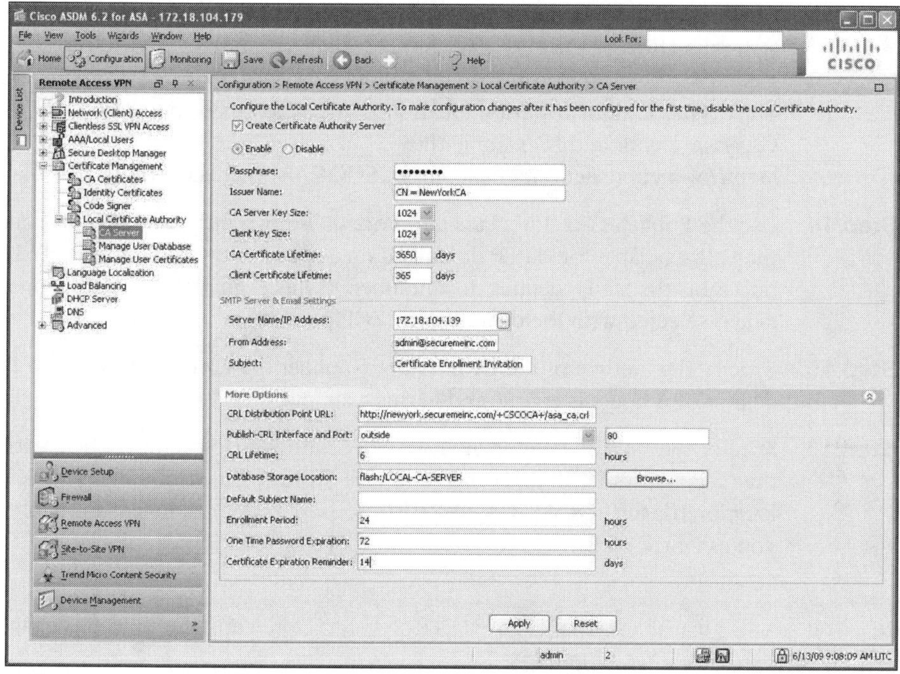

Figure 18-13 *Configuring the Local CA Using ASDM*

Step 8. Enter the validity period (lifetime) for the local CA certificate (in days) under the **CA Certificate Lifetime** field. In this example, the default value of **3650** days is used.

Step 9. Enter the validity period (lifetime) for all client certificates that will be issued by the local CA (in days) under the **Client Certificate Lifetime** field. In this example, the default value of **365** days is used.

Step 10. The Cisco ASA uses the Simple Mail Transfer Protocol (SMTP) to send emails that deliver one-time passwords for an enrollment invitation to users. Enter the IP address or server name of the SMTP server in your network under the **Server Name/IP Address** field under the **SMTP Server & Email Settings** section. In this example, the IP address of the SMTP server is **172.18.104.139**.

Step 11. Enter the email address that will be used when the emails are sent to the users under the **From Address** field. This is typically an administrator's address or group, depending on your policies. In this example, the email address used is **admin@securemeinc.com**.

Step 12. Enter the subject used in the enrollment email to be sent to the users under the **Subject** field. In this example, the default subject (**Certificate Enrollment Invitation**) is used.

Step 13. Click on **More Options** to enter advanced local CA configuration options. Enter the URL for the CRL distribution point within the Cisco ASA to be included within each certificate under the **CRL Distribution Point URL** field. The default CRL distribution location is http://hostname.domain/+CSCO-CA+/asa_ca.crl. In this example the **http://newyork.securemeinc.com/+CSCOCA+/asa_ca.crl** URL is used.

Step 14. Use the **Publish-CRL Interface and Port** pull-down menu and field to make the CRL available for HTTP download on a specific interface or port. TCP port 80 is the HTTP default port number. In this example the **outside** interface is selected with the default port (TCP port 80).

Step 15. Specify the lifetime of the CRL (in hours) under the **CRL Lifetime** field. The default of **6** hours is configured in this example.

Step 16. Specify the storage area for the Local CA configuration and data files within the Cisco ASA's flash under the **Database Storage Location** field. The default location (**flash:/LOCAL-CA-SERVER**) is used in this example. Alternatively, you can click on **Browse** to search for a specific location.

Note You can also use an external CIFS or FTP server to store certificates. In this example, the local flash is used for simplicity.

Step 17. Optionally, you can configure a default subject name to append to a username on issued certificates under the **Default Subject Name** field. This is left blank in this example.

Step 18. Enter the number of hours a user has to enroll and retrieve a user certificate under the **Enrollment Period** field. In this example the default enrollment period of 24 hours is used.

Step 19. The One Time Password Expiration field enables you to configure the validity period for the one-time password emailed to the user. In this example the default enrollment period of 72 hours is used.

Step 20. Enter the number of days before expiration reminders are sent to the users that have not completed the enrollment under the **Certificate Expiration Reminder** field. In this example the default enrollment period of 14 days is used.

Step 21. Click on **Apply** to apply the changes in ASDM.

Step 22. Click on **Save** to save the configuration on the Cisco ASA.

Configuring the Local CA Using the CLI

Use the **crypto ca server** command to configure the local CA using the CLI, as shown in Example 18-17.

Example 18-17 *Configuring the Local CA Using the CLI*

```
NewYork(config)# crypto ca server
NewYork(config-ca-server)# cdp-url
http://newyork.securemeinc.com/+CSCOCA+/asa_ca.crl
NewYork(config-ca-server)# issuer-name CN = NewYorkCA
NewYork(config-ca-server)# smtp from-address admin@securemeinc.com
NewYork(config-ca-server)# publish-crl outside 80
```

Example 18-17 shows the values used in the previous examples when configuring the local CA via ASDM. The **cdp-url** subcommand is used to specify the CRL distribution point URL. The **issuer-name** subcommand is used to specify the issuer name information to be used in the CA certificate. The **smtp from-address** subcommand is used to define the **from** email address used in the emails sent to users during the enrollment process. The **publish-crl** subcommand is used to specify the interface and port where the CRL distribution point is accessed.

To specify the SMTP server to be used by the Cisco ASA, use the **smtp-server** global configuration command, as shown in Example 18-18.

Example 18-18 *Configuring the SMTP Server*

```
NewYork(config)# smtp-server 172.18.104.139
```

The **lifetime ca-certificate** command can be used to specify the lifetime for the Local CA certificate. Example 18-19 shows the values used in the previous example when configuring the local CA, using ASDM.

Example 18-19 *Configuring Certificate Lifetimes*

```
NewYork(config)# crypto ca server
NewYork(config-ca-server)# lifetime ca-certificate 3650
NewYork(config-ca-server)# lifetime certificate 365
```

The **keysize** command specifies the size of the public and private keys generated at user-certificate enrollment. The **keysize server** command is used to configure the size of the local CA's own key-pair.

Note As previously mentioned, the default key size for both the server and user certificates is 1024. When these values are configured, these commands are not shown in the configuration. For both the **keysize** command and the **keysize server** command, the options are 512, 768, 1024, and 2048 bits.

To enable the local CA server, issue the **no shutdown** subcommand, as shown in Example 18-20.

Example 18-20 *Enabling the Local CA*

```
NewYork(config)# crypto ca server
NewYork(config-ca-server)#no shutdown
% Some server settings cannot be changed after CA certificate generation.
% Please enter a passphrase to protect the private key
% or press return to exit
```

After the local CA is enabled, the Cisco ASA generates its CA certificate chain and it is displayed in the configuration, as shown in Example 18-21.

Example 18-21 *Local CA Certificate Chain*

```
crypto ca certificate chain LOCAL-CA-SERVER
 certificate ca 01
    30820203 3082016c a0030201 02020101 300d0609 2a864886 f70d0101 04050030
    15311330 11060355 0403130a 204e6577 596f726b 4341301e 170d3039 30363133
    30393139 34355a17 0d313230 36313230 39313934 355a3015 31133011 06035504
    03130a20 4e657759 6f726b43 4130819f 300d0609 2a864886 f70d0101 01050003
    818d0030 81890281 8100db2d 324a8481 e9554044 af1064d3 ce6faa28 2a1bd2b8
    9e5348b2 e4ca4003 7e5a5a79 b9b12e3a 0c6578af a94e99fb 2ffa21ba 77da04f8
    6194d3bf 83aad420 a0d762a1 67738aa3 a35f3d68 827f9edf fe403e70 2c486d1c
    c021ee73 c6d8fafe 1f357861 400ec2b5 0261b083 ed664177 35d62e1e 37edc24d
    ed6b91d8 0da04aeb fb750203 010001a3 63306130 0f060355 1d130101 ff040530
    030101ff 300e0603 551d0f01 01ff0404 03020186 301f0603 551d2304 18301680
    14ef32a1 a35889c2 4cf22c13 32d47619 0c693dac e3301d06 03551d0e 04160414
    ef32a1a3 5889c24c f22c1332 d476190c 693dace3 300d0609 2a864886 f70d0101
    04050003 818100a0 8e1c6e8d 625385fc 91ca4918 dc531473 00a9c122 d3afc256
    afe56fd7 a58d71ab e70ee0a5 c6beaa3c 4f045911 e68696bc 6b6f2857 cadf0ad2
    f59f187d 167dca1e 7b03c86f 37ee13b8 b0d074b2 e94dd26b 9f3362a8 d5ff7355
    b8183677 c3530edb 1504c1f9 af3c13c5 59faf495 ea7a3bfe c79b3ead ad4175b5
    1f54962a 016822
  quit
```

The **show crypto ca server** command can be used to verify that the local CA server is enabled and to show other statistics, as shown in Example 18-22.

Example 18-22 *Output of the* **show crypto ca server** *Command*

```
NewYork# show crypto ca server
Certificate Server LOCAL-CA-SERVER:
    Status: enabled
    State: enabled
    Server's configuration is locked  (enter "shutdown" to unlock it)
    Issuer name: CN = NewYorkCA
    CA certificate fingerprint/thumbprint: (MD5)
        ab1174ad fe12d6ef e8b7551c e6eb9e06
    CA certificate fingerprint/thumbprint: (SHA1)
        6752c25c 94aeeedf d57add2e 6f4b1630 2cef182d
    Last certificate issued serial number: 0x1
    CA certificate expiration timer: 09:19:45 UTC Jun 12 2012
    CRL NextUpdate timer: 15:19:45 UTC Jun 13 2009
    Current primary storage dir: flash:/LOCAL-CA-SERVER/

    Auto-Rollover configured, overlap period 30 days
    Autorollover timer: 09:19:45 UTC May 13 2012
```

The **show crypto ca server certificate** command can be used to display the base-64 encoded local CA certificate, as shown in Example 18-23.

Example 18-23 *Output of the* **show crypto ca server certificate** *Command*

```
NewYork# show crypto ca server certificate
Current Local CA Certificate (Base64 encoded):
——-BEGIN CERTIFICATE——-
MIICAzCCAWygAwIBAgIBATANBgkqhkiG9w0BAQQFADAVMRMwEQYDVQQDEwogTmV3
WW9ya0NBMB4XDTA5MDYxMzA5MTk0NVoXDTEyMDYxMjA5MTk0NVowFTETMBEGA1UE
AxMKIE5ld1lvcmtDQTCBnzANBgkqhkiG9w0BAQEFAAOBjQAwgYkCgYEA2y0ySoSB
6VVARK8QZNPOb6ooKhvSuJ5TSLLkykADflpaebmxLjoMZXivqU6Z+y/6Ibp32gT4
YZTTv4Oq1CCg12KhZ3OKo6NfPWiCf57f/kA+cCxIbRzAIe5zxtj6/h81eGFADsK1
AmGwg+1mQXc11i4eN+3CTe1rkdgNoErr+3UCAwEAAaNjMGEwDwYDVR0TAQH/BAUw
AwEB/zAOBgNVHQ8BAf8EBAMCAYYwHwYDVR0jBBgwFoAU7zKho1iJwkzyLBMy1HYZ
DGk9rOMwHQYDVR0OBBYEFO8yoaNYicJM8iwTMtR2GQxpPazjMA0GCSqGSIb3DQEB
BAUAA4GBAKCOHG6NYlOF/JHKSRjcUxRzAKnBItOvwlav5W/XpY1xq+cO4KXGvqo8
TwRZEeaGlrxrbyhXyt8K0vWfGH0WfcoeewPIbzfuE7iw0HSy6U3Sa58zYqjV/3NV
uBg2d8NTDtsVBMH5rzwTxVn69JXqejv+x5s+ra1BdbUfVJYqAWgi
——-END CERTIFICATE——-
```

Enrolling Local CA Users Through ASDM

All users to be enrolled within the local CA must be added manually to the Cisco ASA's local CA server user database. Complete the following steps to enroll local CA users through ASDM.

Step 1. Log in to ASDM and navigate to **Configuration > Remote Access VPN > Certificate Management > Local Certificate Authority > Manage User Database.**

Step 2. Click on **Add** to add a user. The screen shown in Figure 18-14 is displayed.

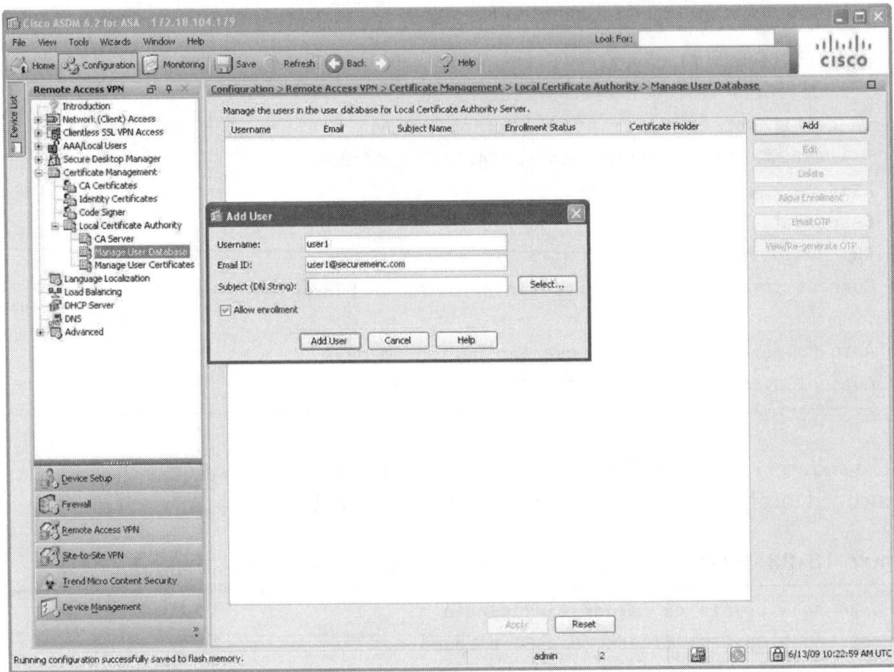

Figure 18-14 *Adding Local CA Users Through ASDM*

Step 3. Enter the username for the new user under the **Username** field. The username **user1** is used in this example.

Step 4. Enter the user's email address under the **Email ID** field. In this example, the certificate enrollment invitation email is sent to **user1@securemeinc.com.**

Step 5. Enter the certificate DN information under the **Subject (DN String)** field. Click the **Select** button to select and configure the available DN attributes. The **Certificate Subject DN** dialog box is displayed, as illustrated in Figure 18-15. Figure 18-15 shows all available DN attributes that can be configured.

Step 6. Click **OK** after you configure the appropriate DN attributes.

Step 7. Make sure that the **Allow Enrollment** check box is selected to allow this user to obtain the certificate from the local CA.

Step 8. Click **Add User** to add the new user.

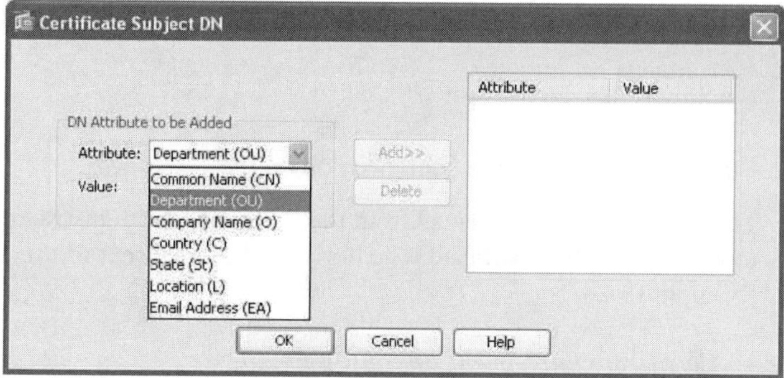

Figure 18-15 *Certificate Subject DN Dialog Box*

Step 9. The user is now shown under the **Manage User Database** screen, as shown in Figure 18-16.

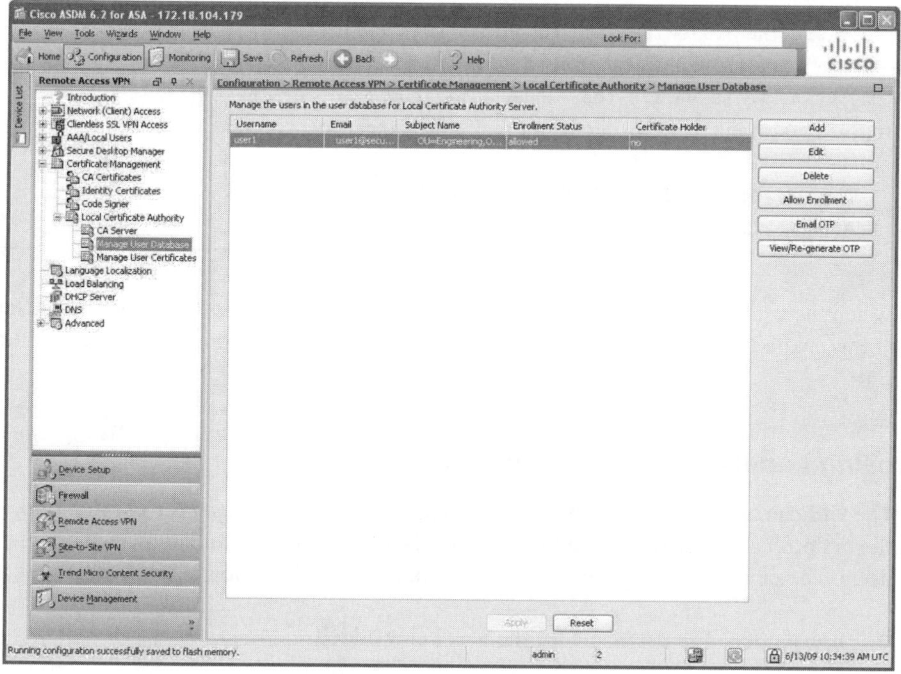

Figure 18-16 *Manage User Database Screen*

Step 10. Click the **Email OTP** button to send the certificate enrollment invite email to the user, along with the one-time password.

Note You can view or re-generate the one-time password by clicking the **View/Re-generate OTP** button.

Step 11. Click on **Save** to save the configuration on the Cisco ASA.

The user will receive an email from the Cisco ASA with instructions on how to obtain the new certificate. The body of the email sent to user1 is shown in Example 18-24.

Example 18-24 *Certificate Enrollment Invitation Email*

```
You have been granted access to enroll for a certificate.
The credentials below can be used to obtain your certificate.
   Username: user1
   One-time Password: 52FCE582EF0F38BF
   Enrollment is allowed until: 10:34:54 UTC Tue Jun 16 2009
NOTE: The one-time password is also used as the passphrase to unlock the
certificate file.
Please visit the following site to obtain your certificate:
https://NewYorkCA.securemeinc.com/+CSCOCA+/enroll.html
You may be asked to verify the fingerprint/thumbprint of the CA certificate
during installation of the certificates. The fingerprint/thumbprint
should be:
     MD5: AB1174AD FE12D6EF E8B7551C E6EB9E06
    SHA1: 6752C25C 94AEEEDF D57ADD2E 6F4B1630 2CEF182D
```

When the user visits the specified URL, the user is asked to enter the credentials included in this email. If authentication is successful, the user is allowed to install the new certificate.

Enrolling Local CA Users Through the CLI

The CLI can also be used to add local CA users. The **crypto ca server user-db add** and the **crypto ca server user-db allow** commands are used to add and allow new local CA users. The **crypto ca server user-db add** command has the following options:

- **username**—The username for the user being added.
- **dn**—The distinguished name information
- **email**—The user's email address, where OTPs and notices are to be sent.

Example 18-25 shows how user1 is added to the local CA database.

Example 18-25 *Adding New Local CA Users Through the CLI*

```
NewYork(config)# crypto ca server user-db add user1 dn
OU=Engineering,O=SecureMeInc email user1@securemeinc.com
NewYork(config)# crypto ca server user-db allow user1
```

In Example 18-25, user1 is added to the local CA user database. The Organization Unit (OU) within the DN is set to **Engineering** and the Organization (O) is **SecureMeInc.** User1's email address is **user1@securemeinc.com** and is entered with the **email** keyword. The **crypto ca server user-db allow user1** command is used to allow user1 to enroll with the Cisco ASA.

To send the enrollment invitation email to the new user, use the **crypto ca server user-db email-otp <username>** command, as follows:

```
NewYork# crypto ca server user-db email-otp user1
```

The user receives an email from the Cisco ASA with instructions on how to obtain the new certificate.

Use the **show crypto ca server user-db** ***username*** command to display the information about a specific user, as shown in Example 18-26.

Example 18-26 *Output of the* **show crypto ca server user-db username user1** *Command*

```
NewYork# show crypto ca server user-db username user1
username: user1
email:    user1@securemeinc.com
dn:       OU=Engineering,O=SecureMeInc
allowed:  10:34:54 UTC Tue Jun 16 2009
notified: 1 times
enrollment status: Allowed to Enroll
```

Note The **show crypto ca server user-db** (without the **username** keyword) displays all users within the local CA user database.

Note You can also use the **show crypto ca server user-db enrolled** command to display all users that have successfully enrolled with the local CA. The **show crypto ca server user-db allowed** command lists all users in the user enrollment database that are currently allowed to enroll. The **show crypto ca server user-db expired** command displays all users holding expired certificates. The **show crypto ca server user-db on-hold** command shows all users that do not hold a certificate and are not currently allowed to enroll.

Configuring IPSec Site-to-Site Tunnels Using Certificates

Chapter 16, "Site-to-Site IPSec VPNs," illustrated how to configure an IPSec site-to-site tunnel using preshared keys. This section illustrates how to use digital certificates to configure an IPSec site-to-site tunnel between two Cisco ASAs.

In the following examples, a branch office in London needs to create an IPSec site-to-site tunnel to the New York office. Figure 18-17 illustrates a high-level network topology of SecureMe's implementation.

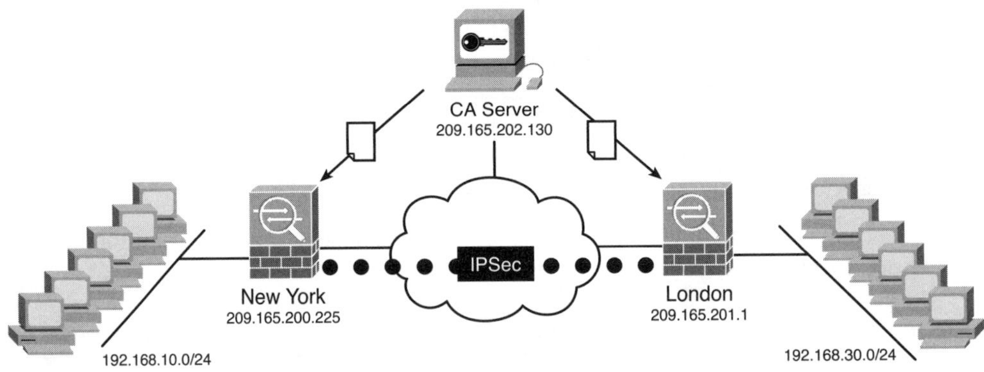

Figure 18-17 *IPSec Site-to-Site Tunnel, Using Certificates*

The Cisco ASAs in both locations successfully enroll with the CA server and build the IPSec site-to-site tunnel, using its corresponding certificates for authentication.

Example 18-27 includes New York's ASA trustpoint configuration.

Example 18-27 *New York ASA Trustpoint Configuration*

```
crypto ca trustpoint NewYork
 enrollment retry period 5
 enrollment retry count 5
 enrollment url http://209.165.202.130/certsrv/mscep/mscep.dll
 fqdn NewYork.securemeinc.com
 subject-name O=secureme, OU=NewYork
```

Note To add the identity certificate through ASDM, navigate to **Configuration > Site-to-Site VPN > Certificate Management** and follow the steps outlined in the previous sections of this chapter.

The Cisco ASA is configured to enroll and obtain a certificate from the CA server 209.165.202.130. The certificate distinguished name information contains **O=secureme** and **OU=NewYork** in this example. The O represents the organization name and OU represents the organizational unit.

Example 18-28 demonstrates how the ISAKMP policy is configured in NewYork's Cisco ASA. The **isakmp identity auto** command is configured in this example. Usually, the IP address identity is used for preshared key authentication. The keyword **hostname** is generally used for certificate-based connections. The **auto** keyword automatically determines the ISAKMP identity. This is recommended if you have a combination of some IPSec tunnels that use preshared keys and others that use certificates for authentication.

Example 18-28 *ISAKMP Policy Configuration*

```
isakmp identity auto
isakmp enable outside
crypto isakmp policy 1
 authentication rsa-sig
 encryption aes-256
 hash sha
 group 2
 lifetime 86400
```

The shaded line in Example 18-28 shows that the Cisco ASA is configured for RSA signature authentication.

Example 18-29 includes NewYork's ASA crypto map configuration.

Example 18-29 *Crypto Map Configuration*

```
access-list 100 extended permit ip 192.168.10.0 255.255.255.0 192.168.30.0
  255.255.255.0
crypto ipsec transform-set myset esp-aes-256 esp-sha-hmac
crypto map NewYork 10 match address 100
crypto map NewYork 10 set peer 209.165.201.1
crypto map NewYork 10 set transform-set myset
crypto map NewYork 10 set trustpoint NewYork
crypto map NewYork interface outside
```

The crypto map configuration is similar to the configuration examples in Chapter 16. The shaded line in Example 18-29 associates the crypto map with the trustpoint that defines the certificate used while the IPSec connection is negotiated.

Example 18-30 includes the tunnel group configuration for NewYork's ASA.

Example 18-30 *Tunnel Group Configuration*

```
tunnel-group 209.165.201.1 type ipsec-l2l
tunnel-group 209.165.201.1 ipsec-attributes
  peer-id-validate cert
!used to validate the identity of the peer using the peer's certificate
  chain
! Enables sending certificate chain
  trust-point NewYork
! used to configure the name of the trustpoint that identifies the
! certificate to be used for this tunnel
```

Note the differences in the configuration in Example 18-30 in comparison to the configuration of an IPSec site-to-site tunnel that uses preshared keys. The **peer-id-validate cert** command is used to validate the identity of the IPSec peer, using its certificate. The **chain** command enables the Cisco ASA to send the complete certificate chain to its peer. The **trust-point** command associates the trustpoint that identifies the certificate to be used for this tunnel.

To configure a site-to-site tunnel to use digital certificate through ASDM, complete the following steps.

Step 1. Navigate to **Configuration > Site-to-Site VPN > Advanced > Tunnel Groups.**

Step 2. In this example, an existing tunnel will be edited. Select the site-to-site tunnel group and click **Edit.**

Step 3. The **Edit IPsec Site-to-site Tunnel Group** dialog box is displayed. Under the **IKE Authentication** section select the respective identity certificate by using the **Identity Certificate** pull-down menu and select **Send Certificate Chain.**

Step 4. Click **OK.**

Step 5. Click **Apply** to apply the configuration changes.

Step 6. Click **Save** to save the configuration on the Cisco ASA.

Example 18-31 shows London's Cisco ASA site-to-site IPSec configuration.

Example 18-31 *London's ASA Site-to-Site IPSec Configuration*

```
access-list 100 extended permit ip 192.168.30.0 255.255.255.0 192.168.10.0
  255.255.255.0
crypto ipsec transform-set myset esp-aes-256 esp-sha-hmac
! crypto transform-set and crypto map configuration matching the IPSec Policies
! from its peer
crypto map London 10 match address 100
crypto map London 10 set peer 209.165.200.225
```

```
crypto map London 10 set transform-set myset
crypto map London 10 set trustpoint London
! The trustpoint configured below is applied to the crypto map.
crypto map London interface outside
crypto ca trustpoint London
 enrollment retry period 5
 enrollment retry count 3
 enrollment url http://209.165.202.130/certsrv/mscep/mscep.dll
 fqdn London.securemeinc.com
 subject-name O=secureme, OU=London
! The certificate subject name information is defined
 crl configure
crypto ca certificate map 1
! The following is the certificate information appended to the configuration
! after enrollment
crypto ca certificate chain London
 certificate 02
    30820210 308201ba a0030201 02020102 300d0609 2a864886 f70d0101 04050030
    3e311430 12060355 040b130b 454e4749 4e454552 494e4731 16301406 0355040a
    130d4369 73636f20 53797374 656d7331 0e300c06 03550403 1305696f 73636130
    1e170d30 34303931 30313332 3230375a 170d3035 30393130 31333232 30375a30
    56311030 0e060355 040b1307 41746c61 6e746131 10300e06 0355040a 13074765
    6f726769 61313030 0e060355 04051307 34343436 37303830 1e06092a 864886f7
    0d010902 16114174 6c616e74 612e6369 73636f2e 636f6d30 5c300d06 092a8648
    86f70d01 01010500 034b0030 48024100 be06c890 637c426c 5c1e431e c6247567
    c0b7c279 86f87c1f 5c01a305 cdaf699a 84dd872d 7b45b0ba 4bf7f28c 2097fe6f
    5f07926a 9bfcdc03 0a383e9f 4b32d0b3 02030100 01a3818a 30818730 39060355
    1d1f0432 3030302e a02ca02a 86286874 74703a2f 2f63726c 73657276 65722e63
    6973636f 2e636f6d 2f43524c 2f636973 636f2e63 726c301c 0603551d 11041530
    13821141 746c616e 74612e63 6973636f 2e636f6d 300b0603 551d0f04 04030205
    a0301f06 03551d23 04183016 80142ff7 332973b2 4d6ddb0d 711bd3fb b033359a
    6981300d 06092a86 4886f70d 01010405 00034100 abe66626 4d58e0d6 25fa809d
    c30bfaed 4cae7ef3 e4f6a120 206ba892 faa81224 1497ea80 f9e28bf6 4a73037f
    570c7e19 f56a05ca a6942805 508e9b37 61dac8c3
  quit
 certificate ca 01
    308201d0 3082017a a0030201 02020101 300d0609 2a864886 f70d0101 04050030
    3e311430 12060355 040b130b 454e4749 4e454552 494e4731 16301406 0355040a
    130d4369 73636f20 53797374 656d7331 0e300c06 03550403 1305696f 73636130
    1e170d30 34303931 30313332 3035365a 170d3037 30393130 31333230 35365a30
    3e311430 12060355 040b130b 454e4749 4e454552 494e4731 16301406 0355040a
    130d4369 73636f20 53797374 656d7331 0e300c06 03550403 1305696f 73636130
    5c300d06 092a8648 86f70d01 01010500 034b0030 48024100 dc7d0b35 1bfa7577
    99cbab8b 69c32a44 47ecd0ae 7cb13fc0 808e7520 9d5e6132 1bc4565a 1ede26a4
```

```
    fc01650e 240aa737 824e07c3 c92f9796 5dd10ac7 4e1a5b75 02030100 01a36330
    61300f06 03551d13 0101ff04 05300301 01ff300e 0603551d 0f0101ff 04040302
    0186301d 0603551d 0e041604 142ff733 2973b24d 6ddb0d71 1bd3fbb0 33359a69
    81301f06 03551d23 04183016 80142ff7 332973b2 4d6ddb0d 711bd3fb b033359a
    6981300d 06092a86 4886f70d 01010405 00034100 7982764a c82daaf0 ed3b0a6e
    25df09b2 4caa7ce8 b27098f1 982085bc 0fda9bcf 86dedda6 84c30abc 48c43fc8
    692386ad 595e2b1e aafd3388 9d711b3c 6314cb5e
  quit
! ISAKMP identity is set to auto
isakmp identity auto
isakmp enable outside
! ISAKMP authentication is set to rsa-sig
crypto isakmp policy 1
 authentication rsa-sig
 encryption aes-256
 hash sha
 group 2
 lifetime 86400! Tunnel group configuration for the site-to-site tunnel
tunnel-group 209.165.200.225 type ipsec-l2l
tunnel-group 209.165.200.225 ipsec-attributes
! The ASA will validate the identity of the peer, using the peer's certificate
peer-id-validate cert
! The chain subcommand enables the ASA to send the complete certificate chain
! the previously configured trust point is applied to the tunnel group
trust-point London
```

The shaded lines in Example 18-31 explain the relevant configuration parameters in London's ASA.

Configuring the Cisco ASA to Accept Remote-Access IPSec VPN Clients Using Certificates

This section demonstrates how to configure the Cisco ASA to terminate Cisco VPN client IPSec connections using certificates. The steps to configure remote-access VPNs using preshared keys are covered in Chapter 17. Figure 18-18 illustrates the topology and components used in the following example.

In Figure 18-18, remote-access users using the Cisco VPN Client connect to the Cisco ASA to access the corporate internal resources in New York. The clients and the Cisco ASA obtain certificates from the CA server 209.165.202.130. The steps necessary to enroll the Cisco ASA to the CA server are the same as those demonstrated previously in this chapter. The following subsection demonstrates how to enroll the Cisco VPN with the CA server.

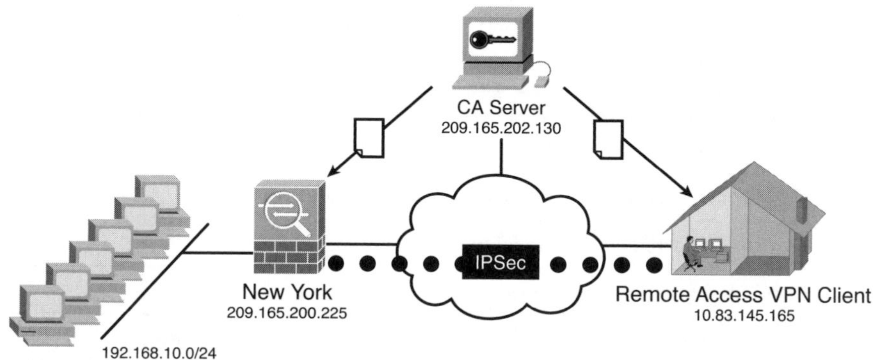

Figure 18-18 *Remote Access IPSec VPN Using Certificates*

Enrolling the Cisco VPN Client

The Cisco VPN client is capable of enrolling to a CA server via either SCEP or manual (file-based) enrollment. Click the **Certificates** tab on the VPN Client to configure the enrollment parameters. Figure 18-19 shows the Certificates tab of the Cisco VPN client.

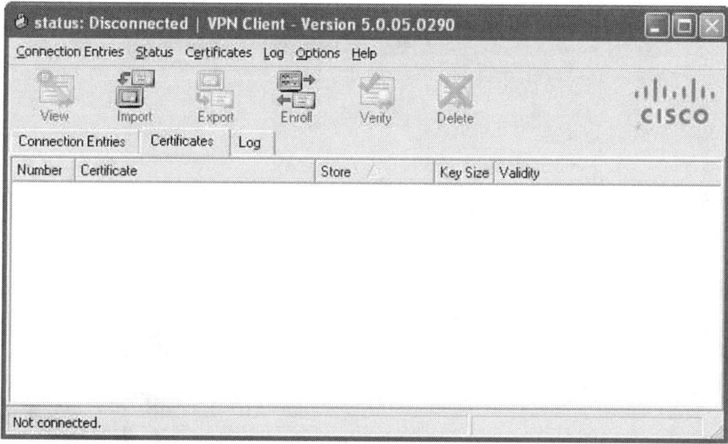

Figure 18-19 *Cisco VPN Client Certificate Configuration Options*

> **Note** The Certificates tab and toolbar are only viewable in advanced mode. Running the VPN client in simple mode does not show these options. To change from simple mode to advanced mode, choose **Options > Advanced Mode.**

The Cisco VPN Client toolbar displays the tasks you can execute from the Certificates tab. Table 18-3 lists all the toolbar options and their usage.

Table 18-3 *Cisco VPN Client Certificates Tab Toolbar Options*

Option	Description
View	Shows the details of a selected certificate. Information includes validity period, issuer information, and distinguished name information such as CN, OU, O, etc.
Import	Used to import a certificate from a file or certificate store.
Export	Used to export a selected certificate.
Enroll	Used to begin an enrollment process.
Verify	Used to check whether the selected certificate is valid (not expired).
Delete	Deletes the selected certificate or certificate request.

SCEP provides an easy mechanism to enroll the Cisco VPN Client. The following are the necessary steps to enroll the Cisco VPN Client via SCEP.

Step 1. Click the **Enroll** button on the toolbar. The VPN Client Certificate Enrollment window is displayed, as shown in Figure 18-20.

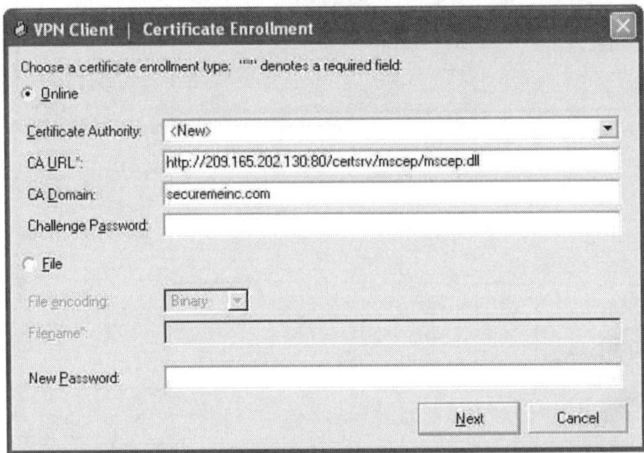

Figure 18-20 *Cisco VPN Client Certificates Enrollment Window*

Step 2. Select **Online** as the certificate enrollment type.

Step 3. Enter the CA URL, domain, and challenge password (if applicable) and click **Next**. Various CA servers require the user to provide a password during enrollment. The Cisco VPN client enables you to enter the password in the Challenge Password field. This password is provided by the CA administrator. The New Password option is used for the password that protects this certificate. If your connection entry requires certificate authentication, you must enter this password each time you connect.

Step 4. The VPN Client Certificate Enrollment information form is displayed, as shown in Figure 18-21.

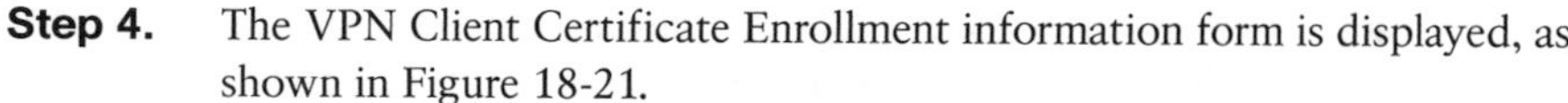

Figure 18-21 *Cisco VPN Client Certificates Enrollment Form*

This form enables you to enter the information to be included in the certificate request. After you enter the necessary information, click **Enroll** to send the certificate enrollment request to the CA server via SCEP. The following are the parameters you can specify on the certificate request:

- **Name [CN]**—The unique common name (CN) for the user certificate. This can be the name of a user, system, or other entity. This field is required. The CN of **RemoteUser** is used in this example.
- **Department [OU]**—Usually the name of the department to which the user belongs. **SALES** is used in this example.

> **Note** By default, the Cisco ASA matches the OU with the VPN group name. Other DN fields can also be used for this purpose.

- Company [O]—The name of the company or organization to which the user belongs. **securemeinc** is used in this example.
- **State [ST]**—The name of the state. New York (**NY**) is used in this example.

  Country [C]—A two-letter country code. **US** is used in this example.

  Email [E]—User's email address. **remoteuser@securemeinc.com** is used in this example.
- **IP Address**—The IP address of the user's system. It is recommended that you do not use this field if the system's IP address will change (for example, if DHCP is used).

- **Domain**—The domain name to which the user's system belongs. This example uses **securemeinc.com**.

Step 5. The Cisco VPN Client sends the enrollment request to the CA server. After the certificate is granted, the Cisco VPN Client stores it on the Cisco certificate store.

Configuring the Cisco ASA

Complete the following steps after you have enrolled the Cisco ASA to the CA server. Example 18-32 shows the ISAKMP policy configuration of the Cisco ASA.

Example 18-32 *ISAKMP Policy for Remote-Access VPN*

```
isakmp identity hostname
isakmp enable outside
crypto isakmp policy 1
 authentication rsa-sig
 encryption aes-256
 hash sha
 group 2
 lifetime 86400
```

The shaded line in Example 18-32 shows how the ISAKMP authentication type is set to **rsa-sig** for certificate authentication.

Example 18-33 shows the crypto map configuration to dynamically terminate remote-access VPN client connections.

Example 18-33 *Dynamic Crypto Map Configuration for Remote-Access VPN*

```
crypto ipsec transform-set NewYorktrans esp-3des esp-sha-hmac
crypto dynamic-map dynmap 10 set transform-set NewYorktrans
crypto map NewYorkmap 65525 ipsec-isakmp dynamic dynmap
crypto map NewYorkmap interface outside
```

The commands in Example 18-33 are the same as those covered in Chapter 17 while using preshared keys. Example 18-34 demonstrates the VPN tunnel-group configuration parameters.

Example 18-34 *Tunnel-Group Configuration for Remote-Access VPN*

```
tunnel-group SALES type ipsec-ra
tunnel-group SALES general-attributes
 address-pool ippool
 authentication-server-group LOCAL
```

```
tunnel-group SALES ipsec-attributes
 peer-id-validate cert
 trust-point NewYork
```

The first shaded line in Example 18-34 makes the Cisco ASA validate the identity of the VPN client by using the peer's certificate. The second shaded line associates the group with the configured trustpoint.

The name of the VPN group in Example 18-34 is **SALES**. This matches the OU value from the client's certificate. By default, the Cisco ASA binds the client connection to a specific group, using the OU value. However, you can use any DN certificate information to associate the client to a respective group. This is similar to the Cisco VPN 3000 Concentrator certificate DN-matching feature.

To configure remote access IPsec VPN connections to use digital certificate using ASDM, complete the following steps.

Step 1. Navigate to **Configuration > Remote Access VPN > Network (Client) Access > IPsec Connection Profiles.**

Step 2. In this example, an existing tunnel is edited. Select the applicable connection profile (tunnel group) and click **Edit**.

Step 3. The **Edit IPsec Remote Access Connection Profile** dialog box is displayed. Under the **IKE Peer Authentication** section select the respective identity certificate in the **Identity Certificate** pull-down menu.

Step 4. Click **OK**.

Step 5. Click **Apply** to apply the configuration changes.

Step 6. Click **Save** to save the configuration on the Cisco ASA.

To configure the Cisco ASA to associate a VPN client connection using the peer's certificate DN information, you can use the **tunnel-group-map** command in combination with a certificate map. Example 18-35 demonstrates how to configure the Cisco ASA to associate any VPN clients on which its certificate has an email address containing **securemeinc.com** to the VPN group named **SALES**.

Example 18-35 *DN Matching Example*

```
crypto ca certificate map 10
! A certificate map is created with a sequence number of 10
 subject-name attr ea co securemeinc.com
! The Cisco ASA is configured to match the email address (ea) of the client's
! certificate. Any certificates that contain securemeinc.com in the email
! address field will be associated to the specified group.
```

```
tunnel-group-map enable rules
! A tunnel-group-map is enabled to match the previously defined rules.
tunnel-group-map 10 SALES
!The certificate map 10 is associated to the VPN group SALES.
```

The following are all the available DN attributes:

- **c**—Country
- **cn**—Common name
- **dc**—Domain component
- **dnq**—DN qualifier
- **ea**—Email address
- **genq**—Generational qualifier
- **gn**—Given name
- **i**—Initials
- **ip**—IP address
- **l**—Locality
- **n**—Name
- **o**—Organization name
- **ou**—Organizational unit
- **ser**—Serial number
- **sn**—Surname
- **sp**—State/province
- **t**—Title
- **uid**—User ID
- **uname**—Unstructured name

The following are the operands that can be used with the **subject-name** subcommand under the certificate map:

- **co**—Contains
- **eq**—Equal to
- **nc**—Does not contain
- **ne**—Not equal to

Troubleshooting PKI

Several troubleshooting commands and techniques are used to troubleshoot PKI on the Cisco ASA.

Time and Date Mismatch

One of the most common problems experienced when first implementing PKI is time and date mismatch. The certificate validity period is the time period during which a certificate is valid. Incorrect time settings in the Cisco ASA, its peers, or the CA can cause the IKE negotiation to fail.

> **Tip** It is suggested that you configure Network Time Protocol (NTP) on the Cisco ASA and the CA server to avoid this problem.

Example 18-36 includes an excerpt of the output of **debug crypto isakmp 127** and **debug crypto ca** while a Cisco ASA had incorrect clock settings.

Example 18-36 *Output of* **debug crypto isakmp 127** *and* **debug crypto ca** *with Incorrect Clock Settings*

```
Oct 07 11:33:16 [IKEv1 DEBUG], Group = , IP = 209.165.201.1
    processing cert payload
Oct 07 11:33:16 [IKEv1 DEBUG], Group = , IP = 209.165.201.1,
    processing cert request payload
Oct 07 11:33:16 [IKEv1 DEBUG], Group = , IP = 209.165.201.1 processing
    RSA signature,
Oct 07 11:33:16 [IKEv1 DEBUG], Group = , IP = 209.165.201.1, computing hash
Oct 07 11:33:16 [IKEv1 DECODE]0000: 8D01E129 F25F46B3 C3CA9D4E
    55571486      ...)._F....NUW..
0010: BDA26964 FA025484 03C271EB 43A7E69C      ..id..T...q.C...
0020: 2A9AD9FA 49E523B1 94AC4874 E352B13B      *...I.#...Ht.R.;
0030: 07354EA9 DB81F8E2 62276185 1A5EF2FC      .5N.....b'a..^..
0040: 7436999D A6E54E96 AB5A5023 23BD1613      t6....N..ZP##...
0050: A2CB28F6 C817A665 9140C932 21EA5AAC      ..(....e.@.2!.Z.
0060: 33D1A3C9 CC8B1B7F 792D3A63 3C220A25      3.......y-:c<".%
0070: 7B3ACB97 1CC09506 879D40B7 41E28A20      {:........@.A..
Oct 07 11:33:16 [IKEv1 DEBUG], Group = , IP = 209.165.201.1,
    Processing Notify payload
Oct 07 11:33:16 [IKEv1], IP = 209.165.201.1Trying to find group
    via cert rules...,
Tunnel Group Match on map sequence # 10.
Group name is SALES
Oct 07 11:33:16 [IKEv1], IP = 209.165.201.1, Connection landed on
```

```
    tunnel_group SALES
CRYPTO_PKI: looking for cert in handle=375b290, digest=
92 3c f9 ac b2 65 e3 fe 49 5a dc b8 64 d4 cd 9e    ¦  .<...e..IZ..d...
CRYPTO_PKI: Cert record not found, returning E_NOT_FOUND
CRYPTO_PKI: crypto_pki_get_cert_record_by_subject()
CRYPTO_PKI: Found a subject match
CRYPTO_PKI(make trustedCerts list)Oct 07 11:33:16 [IKEv1], Group = SALES,
    IP = 209.165.201.1 Peer Certificate authentication failed,
Oct 07 11:33:16 [IKEv1 DEBUG], Group = SALES, IP = 209.165.201.1 IKE MM
    Responder FSM error history (struct &0x49cc114)
<state>, <event>:
MM_BLD_MSG6, EV_UPDATE_CERT
MM_BLD_MSG6, EV_UPDATE_CERT
MM_BLD_MSG6, EV_UPDATE_CERT
MM_BLD_MSG6, EV_UPDATE_CERT,
Oct 07 11:33:16 [IKEv1 DEBUG], Group = SALES, IP = 209.165.201.1 ,
    IKE SA MM:ce9697e1 terminating:

flags 0x0105c002, refcnt 0, tuncnt 0
Oct 07 11:33:16 [IKEv1 DEBUG], sending delete/delete with reason message
Oct 07 11:33:16 [IKEv1 DEBUG], Group = SALES, IP = 209.165.201.1 ,
    constructing blank hash
Oct 07 11:33:16 [IKEv1 DEBUG], constructing IKE delete payload
continues
Oct 07 11:33:16 [IKEv1 DEBUG], Group = SALES, IP = 209.165.201.1,
    constructing qm hash
Oct 07 11:33:16 [IKEv1],
IP:( 209.165.201.1), IKE DECODE
 SENDING Message (msgid=7bd21f5e) with payloads :
HDR + HASH (8) + DELETE (12)
total length : 80
```

To check the validity period of the installed certificates, use the **show crypto ca certificates** command.

Example 18-37 includes the **show crypto ca certificates** and **show clock** commands output, showing the date mismatch.

Example 18-37 *Output of* show crypto ca certificates *and* show clock *Commands*

```
NewYork# show crypto ca certificates
Certificate
  Status: Available
  Certificate Serial Number: 1c91af4500000000000d
  Certificate Usage: General Purpose
```

```
  Issuer:
    cn=SecuremeCAServer
    ou=ENGINEERING
    o=Secureme
    l=NewYork
    st=IL
    c=US
    ea=adminsitrator@securemeinc.com
  Subject Name
    Name: NewYork.securemeinc.com
    Serial Number: 46ff518
    hostname=NewYork.securemeinc.com
    serialNumber=46ff518
  CRL Distribution Point:
    http://NewYork-ca.ssecuremeinc.com/CertEnroll/SecuremeCAServer.crl
  Validity Date:
    start date: 02:58:05 UTC Sep 2 2009
    end   date: 03:08:05 UTC Sep 2 2011
  Associated Trustpoints: NewYork
!
CA Certificate
  Status: Available
  Certificate Serial Number: 225b38e6471fcca649427934cf289071
  Certificate Usage: Signature
  Issuer:
    cn=SecuremeCAServer
    ou= ENGINEERING
    o=Secureme
    l=NewYork
    st=IL
    c=US
    ea=administrator@securemeinc.com
  Subject:
    cn=SecuremeCAServer
    ou=ENGINEERING
    o=Secureme
    l=NewYork
    st=IL
    c=US
    ea= administrator@securemeinc.com
  CRL Distribution Point:
    http://NewYork-ca/CertEnroll/SecuremeCAServer.crl
  Validity Date:
    start date: 20:15:19 UTC Jun 25 2009
```

```
    end   date: 20:23:42 UTC Jun 25 2011
  Associated Trustpoints: NewYork
NewYork# show clock
11:50:27.165 UTC Thu Oct 7 2012
```

The **clock set** command is used to correct the time and date settings problem.

SCEP Enrollment Problems

SCEP uses TCP port 80 for its communications. Make sure that TCP port 80 is not blocked anywhere when enrolling the Cisco ASA. The following **debug** commands are useful when troubleshooting certificate enrollment problems on the Cisco ASA:

- **debug crypto ca transactions**
- **debug crypto ca messages**

Example 18-38 includes the output of these **debug** commands when the Cisco ASA attempts to enroll but the CA server never responds because of communication problems.

Example 18-38 *Output of* **debug crypto ca transactions** *and* **debug crypto ca messages**

```
crypto_ca_get_ca_certificate(48b4884, 1850fa0)
crypto_pki_req(48b4884, 11, ...)
Crypto CA thread wakes up!
CRYPTO_PKI: Sending CA Certificate Request:
GET /cgi-bin/pkiclient.exe?operation=GetCACert&message=NewYork HTTP/1.0
CRYPTO_PKI: status = 65535: failed to send out the pki message
CRYPTO_PKI: transaction GetCACert completed Crypto CA thread sleeps!
```

The error messages in Example 18-38 are displayed if the Cisco ASA is not able to communicate with the CA server because of any communication problems, such as routing problems, blocked ports, and so on.

Time and date settings are also crucial during enrollment. Example 18-39 shows an unsuccessful enrollment request when the incorrect time and date settings were set in the Cisco ASA. The **debug crypto ca transactions** and **debug crypto ca messages** commands are enabled.

Example 18-39 *Errors Due to Incorrect Time and Date Settings During Enrollment*

```
NewYork(config)# crypto ca enroll NewYork
%
% Start certificate enrollment ..
% Create a challenge password. You will need to verbally provide this
```

```
   password to the CA Administrator in order to revoke your certificate.
   For security reasons your password will not be saved in the configuration.
   Please make a note of it.
Password:
Re-enter password:
% The subject name in the certificate will be: O=secureme, OU=NewYork
% The fully-qualified domain name in the certificate will be:
NewYork.securemeinc.com
% Include the router serial number in the subject name? [yes/no]: no
Request certificate from CA? [yes/no]: yes
% Certificate request sent to Certificate Authority
NewYork(config)#
Certificate is not valid yet.
The current certificate enrollment session is cancelled.
```

The shaded lines in Example 18-39 show that the certificate enrollment request failed because the certificate received is not valid yet. The start date in the certificate validity period was later than the current date in the Cisco ASA.

CRL Retrieval Problems

During IKE Phase 1 negotiation, if CRL checking is required, the ASA verifies the revocation status of the peer certificate. CRLs exist on external servers maintained by CAs. To verify the revocation status, the Cisco ASA retrieves the CRL by using one of the available CRL distribution points and checks the peer certificate serial number against the list of serial numbers in the CRL. The Cisco ASA can use LDAP or HTTP (SCEP) for CRL checking. LDAP uses TCP port 389. Make sure that the necessary ports are not blocked by any device between the Cisco ASA and the CRL distribution point.

Use the **show crypto ca crls** command to view the CRL information on the Cisco ASA, as previously shown in Example 18-16.

If you chose a CRL retrieval policy that uses static distribution points, you must enter at least one (and not more than five) valid URLs. This enables you to configure backup CRL distribution points to maximize availability.

Summary

This chapter provided an introduction to PKI and then progressed into detailed configuration and enrollment topics. To use digital certificates for authentication, you must first enroll with a CA and obtain and install a CA certificate on the Cisco ASA. Next, you must enroll and install an identity certificate from the same CA. This chapter showed how to enroll and install digital certificates on the Cisco ASA via SCEP or manually with the cut-and-paste method.

The Cisco ASA's local CA integrates a basic certificate authority functionality to deploy certificates and provides secure revocation checking of issued certificates. In this chapter you learned how to configure the local CA through ASDM, as well as in the CLI.

Additionally, this chapter also provided detailed configuration steps an administrator can follow to configure the Cisco ASA to use digital certificates to authenticate site-to-site and remote-access IPSec VPN sessions. Several troubleshooting tips and techniques were included at the end of the chapter.

Chapter 19

Clientless Remote-Access SSL VPNs

This chapter covers the following topics:

- SSL VPN design considerations
- SSL VPN prerequisites
- Pre-SSL VPN configuration guide
- Clientless SSL VPN configuration guide
- Cisco Secure Desktop
- Host Scan
- Dynamic access policies
- Deployment scenarios
- Monitoring and troubleshooting

Secure Socket Layer (SSL) Virtual Private Network (VPN) is the rapidly evolving VPN technology that complements the existing IPsec remote-access VPN deployments. As discussed in Chapter 1, the actual data encryption and decryption occur at the application layer, usually by a browser in the clientless SSL VPN tunnels. Consequently, you do not need to install additional software or hardware clients to enable SSL VPN in your network infrastructure. Furthermore, if you want to provide full network access to your remote users, you can leverage the full tunnel mode functionality of the SSL VPN tunnels, discussed in Chapter 20. Most customers prefer using the full tunnel mode option because a VPN client can be automatically pushed to a user after a successful authentication.

The SSL VPN implementation on Cisco ASAs provides the most robust feature set in the industry. In the current software release, Cisco ASA supports all three flavors of SSL VPN. They include:

- **Clientless**—In the clientless mode, the remote client needs only an SSL enabled browser to access resources on the private network of the security appliances. SSL clients can access internal resources such as HTTP, HTTPS, or even Windows file shares over the SSL tunnel.
- **Thin client**—In the thin client mode, the remote client needs to install a small Java-based applet to establish a secure connection to the TCP-based internal resources. SSL clients can access internal resources such as HTTP, HTTPS, SSH, and Telnet servers.
- **Full Tunnel**—In the full tunnel client mode, the remote client needs to install a SSL VPN client first that can give full access to the internal private over a SSL tunnel. Using the full tunnel client mode, remote machines can send all IP unicast traffic such as TCP-, UDP-, or even ICMP-based traffic. SSL clients can access internal resources such as HTTP, HTTPS, DNS, SSH, and Telnet servers.

In many recent Cisco documents, clientless and thin client solutions are grouped under one umbrella and classified as clientless SSL VPN. This chapter focuses on both clientless and thin client solutions in the security appliances. Chapter 20 discusses the full tunnel solution that uses the Cisco AnyConnect VPN Client. Many enterprises use the clientless SSL VPN solution to provide limited access to the contractors who need access to a few applications.

SSL VPN Design Considerations

Before you implement the SSL VPN services in Cisco ASA, you must analyze your current environment and determine which features and modes might be useful in your implementation. You have the option to install a Cisco IPSec VPN client, Cisco AnyConnect VPN client, or go with the clientless SSL VPN functionality. Table 19-1 lists the major differences between the Cisco VPN client solution and the clientless SSL VPN solution. Clientless SSL VPN is an obvious choice for someone who wants to check email from a hotel or an Internet café without having to install and configure a Cisco VPN client.

If you choose SSL VPN as your remote-access VPN solution, you must take into account these SSL VPN design considerations:

User Connectivity

Before designing and implementing the SSL VPN solution for your corporate network, you need to determine whether your users connect to your corporate network from public shared computers, such as workstations made available to guests in a hotel or computers in an Internet kiosk. In this case, using a clientless SSL VPN is the preferred solution to access the protected resources.

Table 19-1 *Contrasting Cisco VPN Client and SSL VPN*

Feature	Cisco VPN Client	Clientless SSL VPN
VPN Client	Uses Cisco VPN Client software for complete network access.	Uses a standard web browser to access limited corporate network resources. Eliminates the need for separate client software.
Management	You must install and configure Cisco VPN client.	You do not need to install a VPN client. No configuration is required on the client machine.
Encryption	Uses a variety of encryption and hashing algorithms.	Uses SSL encryption native to web browsers.
Connectivity	Establishes seamless connection to network.	Supports application connectivity through browser portal.
Applications	Encapsulates all IP protocols, including TCP, UDP, and ICMP.	Supports limited TCP-based client/server applications.

ASA Feature Set

A Cisco security appliance can run various features such as IPsec VPN tunnels, routing engines, firewalls, and data inspection engines. Enabling the SSL VPN feature can add further load if your existing appliance is already running a number of features. You must check the CPU, memory, and buffer utilization before enabling SSL VPN.

Infrastructure Planning

Because SSL VPN provides network access to remote users, you have to consider the placement of the VPN termination devices. Before implementing the SSL VPN feature, ask the following questions:

- Should the Cisco ASA be placed behind another firewall? If so, what ports should be opened in that firewall?
- Should the decrypted traffic be passed through another set of firewalls? If so, what ports should be allowed in those firewalls?

Implementation Scope

Network security administrators need to determine the size of the SSL VPN deployment, especially the number of concurrent users that will connect to gain network access. If one Cisco ASA is not enough to support the required number of users, the use of ASA clustering or load balancing must be considered to accommodate all the potential remote users.

Note The security appliances support load-balancing the clientless SSL VPN sessions. Because the SSL VPN load-balancing configuration is identical to the remote-access IPSec load-balancing configuration, consult Chapter 17 for a sample load-balancing configuration

Table 19-2 lists the secure appliances and the number of supported simultaneous SSL VPN users for each platform.

Table 19-2 *ASA Platforms and Supported Concurrent SSL VPN Users*

Security Appliance	Maximum VPN Throughput	Maximum Supported Concurrent Users
5505	100 Mbps	25
5510	170 Mbps	250
5520	225 Mbps	750
5540	325 Mbps	2500
5550	425 Mbps	5000
5580-20	1 Gbps	10,000
5580-40	1 Gbps	10,000

*The VPN throughput is calculated when 3DES/AES encryption is used for VPN tunnels.

Note Cisco uses SSL VPN and WebVPN interchangeably.

SSL VPN Prerequisites

You must meet a number of prerequisites before you can start implementing an SSL VPN in your enterprise. They are discussed in the following sections.

SSL VPN Licenses

The SSL VPN functionality on the ASAs requires that you have appropriate licenses. For example, if your environment is going to have 75 SSL VPN users, you can buy the SSL VPN license that can accommodate up to 100 potential users. Table 19-3 lists the available licenses and their respective part numbers. Note that an SSL VPN license file for 10 users is supported on all platforms because all security appliances can support ten users. However, a 10,000-user license can be installed only on ASA 5580. Similarly, a 750-user license can be installed on ASA 5520, ASA 5540, ASA 5550, and ASA 5580.

Table 19-3 *Available Licenses for ASAs*

SSL VPN User Requirement	License Part Number
10 Users	ASA5500-SSL-10=
25 Users	ASA5500-SSL-25=
50 Users	ASA5500-SSL-50=
100 Users	ASA5500-SSL-100=
250 Users	ASA5500-SSL-250=
500 Users	ASA5500-SSL-500=
750 Users	ASA5500-SSL-750=
1000 Users	ASA5500-SSL-1000=
2500 Users	ASA5500-SSL-2500=
5000 Users	ASA5500-SSL-5000=
10,000 Users	ASA5500-SSL-10K=

Cisco Systems provides a two-user complimentary license on all supported ASA devices. You do not have to purchase licenses if you want to test SSL VPN features in a lab environment where the user count is not going to exceed 2.

Note The minimum version of code to run an SSL VPN is 7.0. In the first release of the ASA, Cisco supported the clientless and thin client modes. The full tunnel SSL VPN client support was added in version 7.1. However, it is highly recommended that you use version 8.0 or higher of the software to utilize all the SSL VPN features discussed in this chapter. This chapter focuses strictly on version 8.2(1) because of the SSL VPN enhancements that were added in this version of code.

In 8.x versions, you can purchase an additional license to implement the Advanced Endpoint Assessment feature. This feature enables the ASA to scan a remote workstation for active antivirus, antispyware, and personal firewalls and to try to update the noncompliant computers to meet the requirements of an enterprise's security policy. This feature is discussed in the Host Scan section of this chapter in more detail. The part number for this license is ASA-ADV-END-SEC.

Starting with Cisco ASA version 8.2, Cisco has introduced specific licenses to be used in the SSL VPN environment. They include:

- AnyConnect Premium

- AnyConnect Essentials
- AnyConnect Mobile
- Shared Premium Licensing

AnyConnect Premium

The AnyConnect Premium license is designed for those customers who want to deploy both clientless as well as the AnyConnect SSL VPN tunnels in a single Cisco ASA. The AnyConnect Premium license supports advanced SSL VPN features such as Cisco Secure Desktop (CSD) and Host Scanning.

AnyConnect Essentials

The AnyConnect Essentials license is designed for those customers who want to deploy solely full tunnel AnyConnect clients. The AnyConnect Essentials license does not support advanced SSL VPN features such as Cisco Secure Desktop (CSD), Host Scanning, and or clientless SSL VPN tunnels. It is a great option for those customers who are in the process of migrating from the Cisco IPSec VPN solution to a Cisco AnyConnect solution or require support for Windows 64-bit operating systems.

After you install the AnyConnect Essential license, you must use the **anyconnect-essential** command in the webvpn subconfiguration menu to enable AnyConnect Essential on the security appliance.

AnyConnect Mobile

For customers who want to extend the AnyConnect SSL VPN functionality to mobile endpoints such as Treo, iPAQ, and Axim, they can purchase the AnyConnect Mobile license. This is an add-on license to the AnyConnect Essential or SSL VPN premium license. The mobile endpoints need to be running Windows Mobile 5.0, 6.0, or 6.1. For a complete list of supported VPN devices, consult http://www.cisco.com/en/US/docs/security/asa/compatibility/vpn-platforms-82.html.

Shared Premium Licensing

Shared Licenses are designed for those customers who want to purchase the SSL VPN licenses in bulk and then share them among a number of Cisco ASAs on an as-needed basis. The pool of licenses is maintained by a master license server. The SSL VPN terminating security appliances are known as the participants. When participants need SSL VPN licenses, they send a request to the master server. The server, depending on license availability, grants licenses to the participants in small chunks.

By using this model, customers can benefit from operational flexibility and investment protection because they can add devices to their deployments without needing to purchase specific SSL VPN licenses for each device. In this licensing structure, the SSL user count is what is shared among the participating firewalls.

Table 19-4 provides detailed information on the different license types and the supported SSL VPN features.

Table 19-4 *License Types and Supported SSL VPN Features*

License Type	AnyConnect Essentials	AnyConnect Mobile	Premium Single	Premium Shared
AnyConnect VPN Client	Yes	Yes	Yes	Yes
Cisco Secure Desktop	Not Supported	Yes	Yes	Yes
Clientless SSL VPN	Not Supported	Not Supported	Yes	Yes
Smartphones AnyConnect	Yes, but is an add-on to the AnyConnect Essentials, Premium single, or Premuim shared license	Yes, but is an add-on to the AnyConnect Essentials, Premium single, or Premuim shared license	Yes, but AnyConnect Mobile License is also needed	Yes, but AnyConnect Mobile License is also needed

Note All license keys, except for Shared Premium license, are associated per device. That means you cannot share a license among multiple Cisco ASAs, even if they are in high-availability or clustered environments. Customers who want to deploy the security appliances in high-availability areas can purchase the SSL/IPsec VPN Edition bundle with a specific license size.

If using the Shared Premium license in an Active/Standby failover scenario, the active security appliance requests the license from the license server. The standby appliance does not need any licenses.

VPN Flex Licenses

Cisco Systems also provides its customers an emergency or business continuity license called *VPN Flex* license. Using the SSL VPN Flex Licenses on the security appliances, customers can temporarily increase (burst) the number of SSL licenses on a box for up to 60 days. This license is extremely useful in those circumstances when a large number of employees cannot come to the office in emergency situations such as extreme weather conditions and they end up working from home through the SSL VPN tunnels. In this case, the security appliance administrator can apply a VPN flex license for a week and revert back to the permanent license when the extreme conditions end.

Client Operating System and Browser and Software Requirements

The SSL VPN functionality on Cisco security appliances is supported on a number of client operating systems and on a number of browsers. The supported platforms are discussed next.

- **Compatible browser—**You must use an SSL-enabled browser such as Microsoft Internet Explorer, Firefox, Opera, Safari, Mozilla, Netscape, or Pocket Internet Explorer (PIE). Table 19-5 provides a list of operating systems and the supported Internet browsers.

Note Cisco has certified HP iPaq H4150 Pocket PC 2003 running Windows CE 4.20.0 build 14053 with Pocket Internet Explorer. The ROM version is 1.10.03ENG with a 07/16/2004 ROM date. Cisco has also certified HP iPaq hx2495b running Windows CE 5.0.5.1.1702. You do not need to configure anything special on the security appliance to make mobile devices to work.

- **Sun JRE—**The browser must be enabled with Java Runtime Environment (JRE) version 1.4.1.x or higher for SSL VPN features such as port forwarding and smart tunnels.
- **ActiveX—**SSL VPN also uses ActiveX for Internet Explorer on Microsoft-based operating systems. ActiveX is used by smart tunnels and Cisco Secure Desktop.
- **Web folder—**Microsoft hotfix 892211 must be installed on Windows operating systems for web folders to be accessible in the clientless SSL VPN mode.

Note Browser cookies must be enabled if you want to access applications through port forwarding or smart tunnels.

Table 19-5 *Supported Operating Systems and Internet Browsers*

Operating System	Supported Browser
Windows XP	Internet Explorer version 6.0 and 7.0 Firefox version 1.5, through 3.0
Windows Vista (both 32- and 64-bit platforms)	Internet Explorer version 7.0 Firefox version 2.0
Apple iPhone	Safari
Pocket PC 2003 & Windows CE 4.20.0 Windows Mobile 5.0.5.1.465	Pocket Internet Explorer
Macintosh OS X 10.4 and 10.5	Safari version 2.0–3.1.1 Firefox version 2.0 and 2.1
Linux	Firefox version 1.5 through 3.0

Infrastructure Requirements

The infrastructure requirements for SSL VPNs include, but are not limited to, the following options:

- **ASA placement**—If you are installing a new security appliance, determine the location that best fits your requirements. If you plan to place it behind an existing corporate firewall, make sure that you allow appropriate SSL VPN ports to pass through the firewall.
- **User account**—Before SSL VPN tunnels are established, users must authenticate themselves to either the local database or to an external authentication server. The supported external servers include RADIUS (including Password Expiry using MSCHAPv2 to NT LAN Manager), RADIUS one-time password (OTP), RSA SecurID, Active Directory/Kerberos, and Generic Lightweight Directory Access Protocol (LDAP). Make sure that SSL VPN users have accounts and appropriate access. LDAP password expiration is available for Microsoft and Sun LDAP.
- **Administrative privileges**—Administrative privileges on the local workstation are required for all connections with port forwarding if you want to use host mapping.

Pre-SSL VPN Configuration Guide

After analyzing the deployment consideration and selecting the SSL VPN as the remote-access VPN solution, you must follow the configuration steps described in this section to properly set up the SSL VPN so that it can be enabled on a Cisco security appliance. These tasks include the following:

- Enroll digital certificates (recommended)
- Set up tunnel and group policies
- Set up user authentication

Enroll Digital Certificates (Recommended)

Enrollment is the process of obtaining a certificate from a certificate authority (CA). Even though the security appliance can generate self-signed certificates, using an external CA is highly recommended. The enrollment process can be broken into three steps, as described in the following sections.

Step 1: Obtaining a CA Certificate

Obtain a CA/root certificate before requesting an identity certificate from the CA server. Make sure that you have received a CA certificate from the server in the Base64 format. After you have the CA certificate, you can use ASDM to navigate to **Configuration > Device Management > Certificate Management > CA Certificates > Add**. Specify a Trustpoint Name, select the **Install from a File** option, browse your local directory where the CA certificate resides, and click **Install Certificate** to install the CA certificate in the security appliance. As shown in Figure 19-1, a trustpoint called **SecureMeSSLCert** is defined. The name of the CA certificate file is **certnewroot.cer.** After you click **Install Certificate**, the security appliance should acknowledge that the certificate was installed successfully.

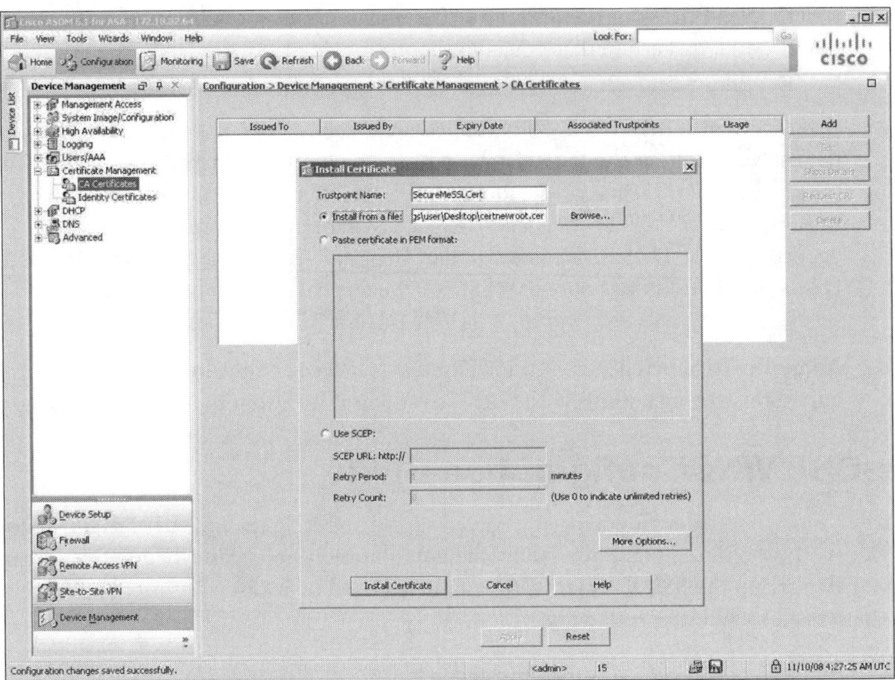

Figure 19-1 *Importing CA Certificate*

If you prefer to use the Cisco ASA CLI, define a trustpoint and then use the **crypto ca authenticate** command to import the CA certificate, as shown in Example 19-1.

Example 19-1 *Importing the CA Certificate Manually*

```
Chicago(config)# crypto ca trustpoint SecureMeSSLCert
Chicago(config-ca-trustpoint)# enrollment terminal
Chicago(config)# crypto ca authenticate SecureMeSSLCert
Enter the base 64 encoded CA certificate.
End with the word "quit" on a line by itself
---BEGIN CERTIFICATE---
MIIC0jCCAnygAwIBAgIQIls45kcfzKZJQnk0zyiQcTANBgkqhkiG9w0BAQUFADCB
hjEeMBwGCSqGSIb3DQEJARYPamF6aWJAY2lzY28uY29tMQswCQYDVGEwJVUzEL
MAkGA1UECBMCTkMxDDAKBgNVBAcTA1JUUDEWMBQGA1UEChMNQ2lzY28gU3lzdGVt
czEMMAoGA1UECxMDVEFDMRYwFAYDVDEw1KYXppYkNBU2VydmVyMB4XDTA0MDYy
```

```
---END CERTIFICATE---
quit
INFO: Certificate has the following attributes:
Fingerprint:     82a0095e 2584ced6 b66ed6a8 e48a5ad1
Do you accept this certificate? [yes/no]: yes
Trustpoint CA certificate accepted.
% Certificate successfully imported
```

Step 2: Request a Certificate

Before requesting an identity certificate, you must generate the RSA key pair through ASDM or through the CLI. If you already have the RSA keys generated that you want to use for SSL encryption, you can skip creating new ones. If you want to create new keys, navigate to **Configuration > Device Management > Certificate Management > Identity Certificates** and click **Add.** Specify the same Trustpoint Name that you defined in step 1, select the **Add a New Identity Certificate** option, and click **New.** Specify a key pair name, select its usage as **General Purpose** and click **Generate Now** to generate a new RSA key pair. As shown in Figure 19-2, a new RSA pair called **SecureMeSSLRSA** is being generated for SecureMeSSLCert Trustpoint. If a key pair already exists, you can use it rather than create a new one.

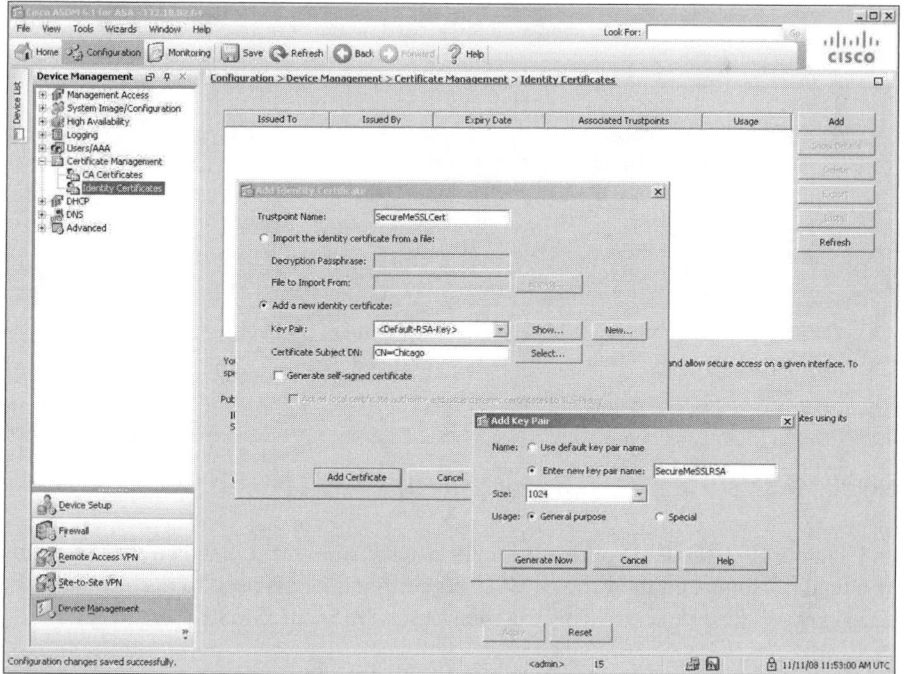

Figure 19-2 *Generating RSA Keys and Requesting an ID Certificate*

Note After generating a request for the identity certificate via ASDM, you may receive the following error message. You can ignore the error message and continue with the rest of the configuration steps:

[ERROR] enrollment terminal

Trustpoint enrollment configuration cannot be changed for an authenticated trustpoint.

After generating the RSA keys, request an identity certificate to be used for SSL VPN. When you click **Add Certificate,** Cisco ASDM enables you to specify where to save the CSR file that is generated by the ASA to request a certificate from the CA server. As illustrated in Figure 19-3, the trustpoint name is **SecureMeSSLCert** and it is using the **SecureMeSSLRSA** key pair. The name in the CSR file is **SecureMe.CSR** and it is located in the user's Desktop folder.

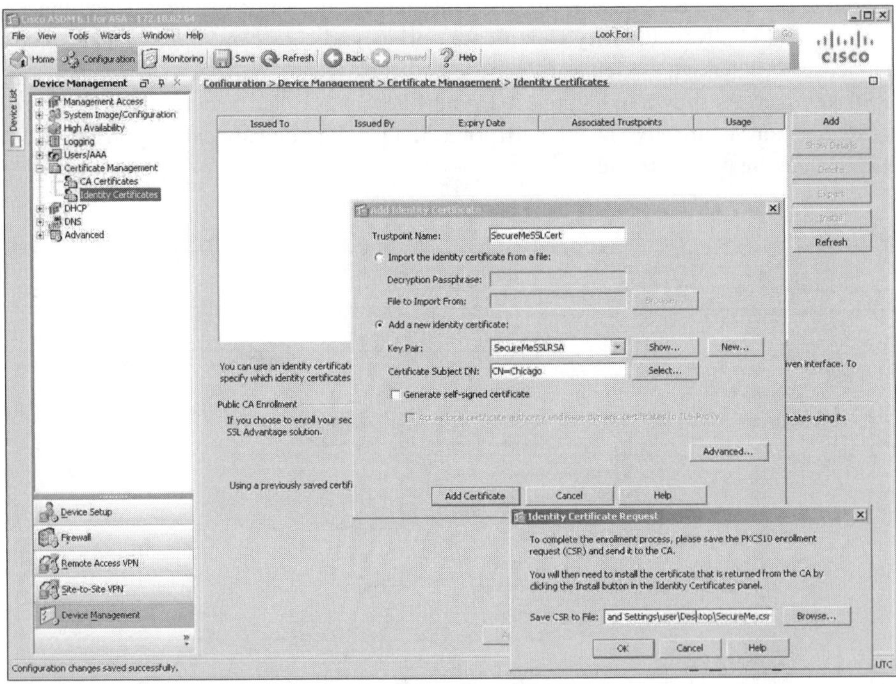

Figure 19-3 *Name and Location of CSR File*

In Example 19-2, the CLI configuration for manual enrollment is shown. The **enrollment terminal** subcommand in SecureMeSSLCert configuration is used to declare manual enrollment of the CA server. This trustpoint uses the **SecureMeSSLCert** RSA key.

Example 19-2 *Configuring Cisco ASA for Manual Enrollment*

```
Chicago# configure terminal
```

```
Chicago(config)# domain-name securemeinc.com
Chicago(config)# crypto key generate rsa label SecureMeSSLRSA
The name for the keys will be: Chicago.securemeinc.com

% The key modulus size is 1024 bits
% Generating 1024 bit RSA keys, keys will be non-exportable...[OK]
Chicago(config)# crypto ca trustpoint SecureMeSSLCert
Chicago(ca-trustpoint)# keypair SecureMeSSLRSA
Chicago(ca-trustpoint)# id-usage ssl-ipsec
Chicago(ca-trustpoint)# no fqdn
Chicago(ca-trustpoint)# subject-name CN=Chicago
Chicago(ca-trustpoint)# enrollment terminal
Chicago(ca-trustpoint)# crypto ca enroll SecureMeSSLCert
```

After you submit a certificate request, the certificate should be in a pending state until the CA administrator approves it. You can navigate to **Configuration > Device Management > Certificate Management > Identity Certificates** to check its status. After the identity certificate is approved, you can select the pending certificate request and click **Install.** A new window pops up where you can paste your approved certificate in Base64 encoding. Click **Install Certificate** to install the identity certificate in the appliance, as shown in Figure 19-4.

Using the CLI, after the identity certificate is approved by the CA server administrator, use the **crypto ca import** command to import the Base64-encoded ID certificate. Example 19-3 demonstrates how to import the ID certificate.

Example 19-3 *Manually Importing the ID Certificate*

```
Chicago(config)# crypto ca import SecureMeSSLCert certificate
% The fully-qualified domain name in the certificate will be:
Chicago.securemeinc.com
Enter the base 64 encoded certificate.
End with the word "quit" on a line by itself
——-BEGIN CERTIFICATE——-
MIIECDCCA7KgAwIBAgIKHJGvRQAAAAAADTANBgkqhkiG9w0BAQUFADCBhjEeMBwG
CSqGSIb3DQEJARYPamF6aWJAY2lzY28uY29tMQswCQYDVGEwJVUzELMAkGA1UE
CBMCTkMxDDAKBgNVBAcTA1JUUDEWMBQGA1UEChMNQ2lzY28gU3lzdGVtczEMMAoG
A1UECxMDVEFDMRYwFAYDVDEw1KYXppYkNBU2VydmVyMB4XDTA0MDkwMjAyNTgw
NVoXDTA1MDkwMjAzMDgwNVowLzEQMA4GA1UEBRMHNDZmZjUxODEbMBkGCSqGSIb3
SGzFQHtnqURciJBtay9RNnMpZmZYpfOHzmeFmQ==
——-END CERTIFICATE——-
Chicago(config)#
```

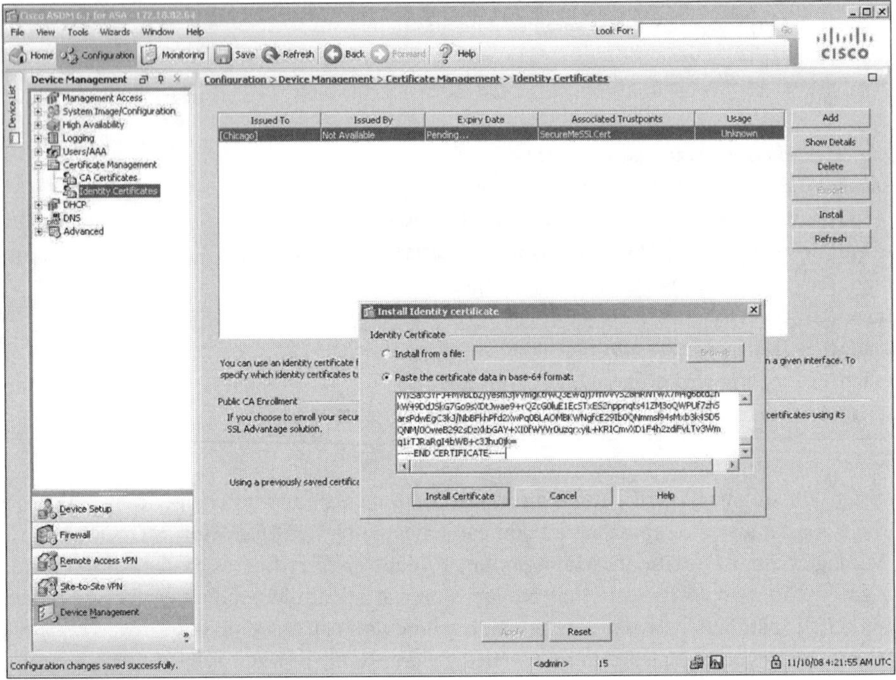

Figure 19-4 *Installing Identity Certificate in the Security Appliance*

> **Note** The same RSA key pair can be used for Secure Shell (SSH) connections to the security appliances.

Step 3: Apply Identity Certificate for SSL VPN Connections

After the certificate is imported, navigate to **Configuration > Device Management > Advanced > SSL Settings**, select the ` interface or the interface where you want to terminate the SSL VPN connections, click **Edit**, and select the newly installed certificate from the **Primary Enrolled Certificate** drop-down option menu as shown in Figure 19-5.

Using the CLI, issue the **ssl trust-point SecureMeSSLCert outside** command to activate the imported certificate on the outside interface to terminate the SSL sessions, as shown in Example 19-4.

Example 19-4 *Activating the Identity Certificate on the Outside Interface*

```
Chicago(config)# ssl trust-point SecureMeSSLCert outside
```

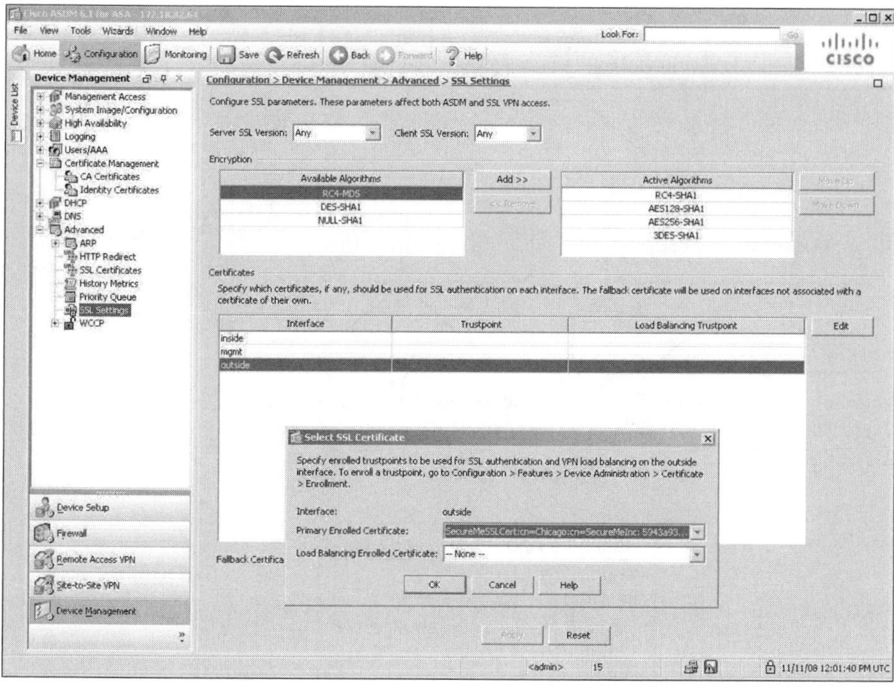

Figure 19-5 *Mapping Identity Certificate to an Interface*

Set Up Tunnel and Group Policies

As discussed in Chapter 17, Cisco ASA uses an inheritance model when it pushes network and security policies to the end-user sessions. Using this model, you can configure policies at the following three locations:

- Under default group policy
- Under user's assigned group policy
- Under specific user's policy

In the inheritance model, a user inherits the attributes and policies from the user policy, which inherits its attributes and policies from the user group policy, which in turn inherits its attributes and policies from the default group policy, as illustrated in Figure 19-6. In this example, a user with ID "sslvpnuser" receives a traffic access control list (ACL) and an assigned IP address from the user policy, the domain name from the user group policy, and Windows Internet Naming Server (WINS) information along with the number of simultaneous logins from the default group policy.

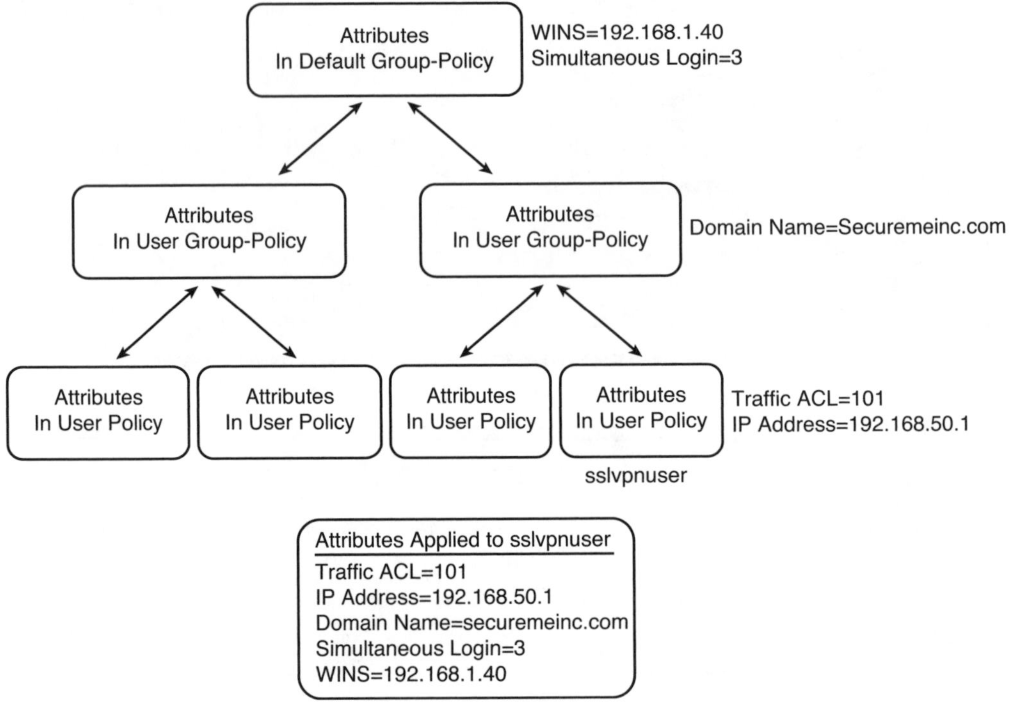

Figure 19-6 *ASA Attributes and Policies Inheritance Model*

> **Note** DfltGrpPolicy is a special group name, used solely for the default group policy.

After these policies are defined, they must be bound to a tunnel group where users terminate their sessions. This way, a user who establishes his VPN session to a tunnel group inherits all the policies mapped to that tunnel. The tunnel group defines a VPN connection profile, of which each user is a member.

Configure Group Policies

You configure the user group and default group policies by choosing **Configuration > Remote Access VPN > Clientless SSL VPN Access** or **Network (Client) Access** > **Group Policies.** Click **Add** to add a new group policy. As shown in Figure 19-7, a user group policy, called **ClientlessGroupPolicy**, has been added. This group policy allows only clientless SSL VPN tunnels to be established and strictly rejects all the other tunneling protocols. If you would rather assign attributes to a default group policy, you can modify DfltGrpPolicy (System Default). Any attribute that is modified under DfltGrpPolicy is propagated to any user group policy that inherits that attribute. A group policy name other than DfltGrpPolicy is treated as a user group policy.

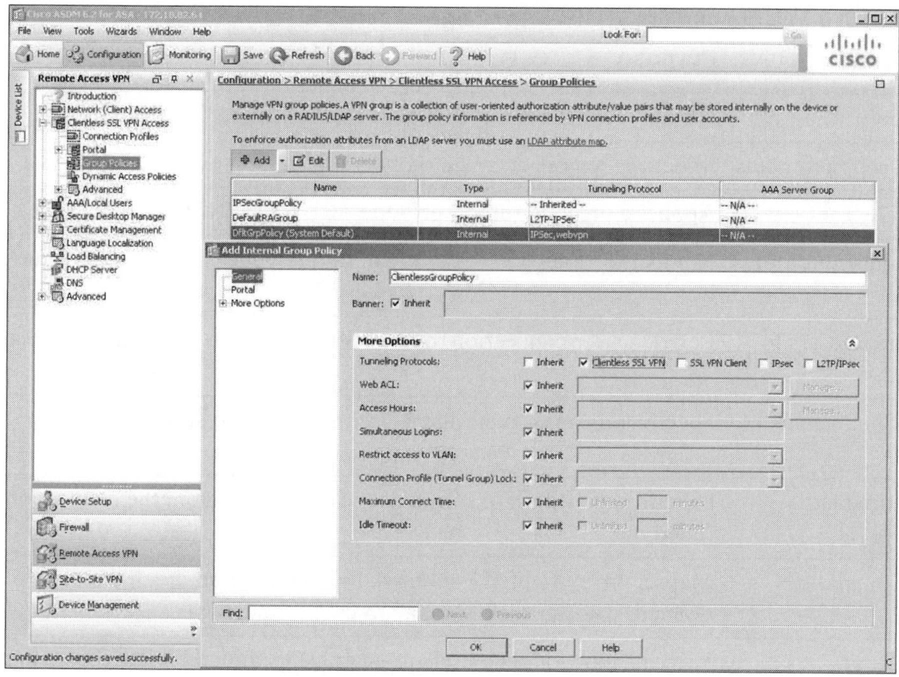

Figure 19-7 *User Group Policy Configuration*

> **Note** The default and user group policies are set up to allow both Cisco IPsec VPN and SSL VPN tunnels. If you want to restrict a policy to solely use SSL VPN, use either clientless SSL VPN or SSL VPN client options under Tunneling Protocols, as illustrated in Figure 19-7.

Example 19-5 illustrates how to define a user group policy called **ClientlessGroupPolicy**. This policy allows only the clientless tunnels to be terminated on the group.

Example 19-5 *Group-Policy Definition*

```
Chicago(config)# group-policy ClientlessGroupPolicy internal
Chicago(config)# group-policy ClientlessGroupPolicy attributes
Chicago(config-group-policy)# vpn-tunnel-protocol webvpn
```

Table 19-6 lists all the SSL VPN attributes that can be mapped to a user group and default group policies. The attributes with an asterisk (*) can also be configured under a user policy.

The user, group, and default group polices can be applied to clientless, AnyConnect, and IPsec-based remote-access VPN tunnels. The Clientless SSL VPN–specific attributes are discussed in detail in the next few sections of this chapter.

Table 19-6 *Configurable SSL VPN Attributes*

Attribute	Purpose
Banner	Creates a banner that is displayed to user connections.
Tunneling protocols	Select the remote-access protocols that users are allowed to access.
Web ACL	Applies a preconfigured web-type ACL for traffic filtering.
Simultaneous logins	Number of times a user can log in to the security appliance concurrently.
Restrict access to VLAN	Restricts user connection to a specific VLAN on the security appliance.
Maximum connect time	Specifies the maximum time a user is allowed to stay connected.
Idle timeout	Specifies the length of time a user can be idle before the connection is timed out.
Bookmark list	Maps a preconfigured bookmark list to the group. If a list is not defined, you can click **Manage** to create a new one.
URL entry	You can allow or deny users to enter URLs directly into the user portal page.
File server entry	Allows or denies users to enter the file server names.
File server browsing	Allows or denies file browsing on the Common Internet File System (CIFS) shares.
Hidden share access	Allows or denies access to hidden shares on a CIFS server.
Port-forwarding list	Applies a port-forwarding list to a group.
Smart tunnel	Applies a smart tunnel list to a group.
ActiveX relay	Allows or denies users to launch Microsoft Office components.
HTTP proxy	Configures an external HTTP proxy server.
HTTP compression	Configures HTTP compression.
Portal customization	Applies a preconfigured user portal list to a group policy.
Homepage URL (optional)	Configures a URL of the web page you want to configure for a user session.
Access deny message	Displays a message to clientless users who log in to the security appliance but do not have SSL VPN privileges.
Post login setting	Prompts the user on whether to download the AnyConnect client.

Table 19-6 *Configurable SSL VPN Attributes*

Attribute	Purpose
Default post login selection	Specifies the default login selection if a user does not make a selection in the specified time.
Single sign-on server	Specifies the single sign-on server address.
User storage location	Specifies the location where personalized user information is stored.
Storage key	Specifies the string to provide user access to the storage location.
Storage objects	Specifies object-like cookies, credentials, or both that the server uses in association with the user.
Transaction size	Specifies the volume limit in kilobytes to time out a session when the limit is reached. The transaction larger than the specified limit resets the session timeout clock.

Note You can configure a user policy by choosing **Configuration > Remote Access VPN > AAA/Local Users > Local Users.**

Configure a Tunnel Group

You can configure a tunnel group, also known as a connection profile, by choosing **Configuration > Remote Access VPN > Clientless SSL VPN Access > Connection Profiles.** Click **Add** to add a new tunnel group. As shown in Figure 19-8, a tunnel group called **SecureMeClientlessTunnel** has been added. If you configure your internal websites using the fully qualified domain name (FQDN), you must configure a Domain Name System (DNS) server on the security appliance to resolve the hostnames. Specify the DNS server address to **Servers** under the DNS option. In Figure 19-8, a DNS server of **192.168.1.10** is configured with a domain name of **securemeinc.com**. After defining a tunnel group name, you can bind a user group policy to a tunnel group. After a user is connected, the attributes and policies defined under the group policy are applied to the user. A user group policy of **ClientlessGroupPolicy** is linked to this tunnel group.

Note If you do not define the IP address of the DNS server, you receive the following message:

"There is no DNS server defined, so you cannot access any URL with FQDN from the portal. Are you sure about this?"

You can choose to ignore this message if your security appliance is not going to resolve any FQDNs

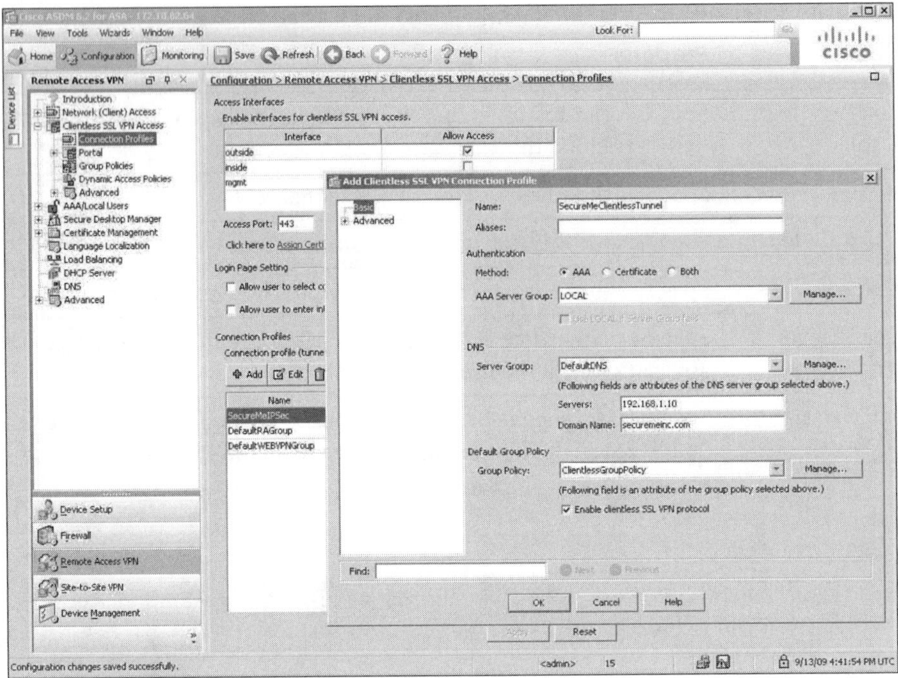

Figure 19-8 *Configuration of a Tunnel Group*

Example 19-6 illustrates how to configure a remote-access tunnel group of **SecureMeClientlessTunnel**. The previously defined group policy, **ClientlessGroupPolicy,** is added to the tunnel group.

Example 19-6 *Tunnel Group Definition*

```
Chicago(config)# tunnel-group SecureMeClientlessTunnel type remote-access
Chicago(config)# tunnel-group SecureMeClientlessTunnel general-attributes
Chicago(config-tunnel-general)# default-group-policy ClientlessGroupPolicy
Chicago(config-tunnel-general)# exit
Chicago(config)# dns server-group DefaultDNS
Chicago(config-dns-server-group)# domain-name securemeinc.com
Chicago(config-dns-server-group)# name-server 192.168.1.10
```

After configuring a Connection Profile, you can define a URL that users can use to connect to this tunnel group. This is useful if you want to create a specific URL for each connection profile you create and distribute the URL accordingly so that users do not have to decide to which connection profile they should connect.

Define a specific URL by modifying the connection profile and then clicking the **Advanced > SSL VPN** option. Under **Group URL**, click **Add** and specify a URL. For the SecureMeClientlessTunnel connection profile,

https://sslvpn.securemeinc.com/SecureMeClientless is the group URL. Verify that the **Enable** check box is selected. Click **OK** to exit. When users need to connect via SSL VPN, they can use this URL to connect specifically to this tunnel group.

Example 19-7 illustrates how to specify a group-url of **https://sslvpn.securemeinc.com/SecureMeClientless** for **SecureMeClientlessTunnel.**

Example 19-7 *Tunnel Group Definition*

```
Chicago(config)# tunnel-group SecureMeClientlessTunnel webvpn-attributes
Chicago(config-tunnel-webvpn)# group-url
https://sslvpn.securemeinc.com/SecureMeClientless enable
```

Set Up User Authentication

Cisco ASA supports a number of authentication servers, such as RADIUS, NT domain, Kerberos, SDI, LDAP, digital certificates, smart cards, and local databases. For small organizations, a local database can be set up for user authentication. For medium to large SSL VPN deployments, it is highly recommended that you use an external authentication server, such as RADIUS or Kerberos, as the user authentication database. If you are deploying the SSL VPN feature for a few users, you can use the local database. You define the users by choosing **Configuration > Remote Access VPN > AAA/Local Users > Local Users.** As shown in Figure 19-9, two accounts, **sslvpnuser** and **adminuser**, are configured for user authentication. The **sslvpnuser** account, with a password of **C1$c0123** (obfuscated), will be used for SSL VPN user authentication, whereas **adminuser**, with a password of **@d1m123** (obfuscated), will be used to manage the security appliance.

As shown in Example 19-8, two accounts, **sslvpnuser** and **adminuser**, are configured for user authentication.

Example 19-8 *Local User Accounts*

```
Chicago(config)# username ciscouser password C1$c0123
Chicago(config)# username adminuser password @dmin123
```

Many enterprises use either a RADIUS server or Kerberos to leverage their existing active directory infrastructure for user authentication. Before configuring an authentication server on Cisco ASA, you must specify authentication, authorization, and accounting (AAA) server groups by choosing **Configuration > Remote Access VPN > AAA/Local Users> AAA Server Groups > Add.** Specify a server group name that can be referenced by the other AAA processes. Select an authentication protocol for this server group name. For example, if you plan to use a RADIUS server for authentication, select **RADIUS** from the drop-down menu. This option ensures that the security appliance requests the appropriate information from the end users and forwards it to the RADIUS server for authentication and verification.

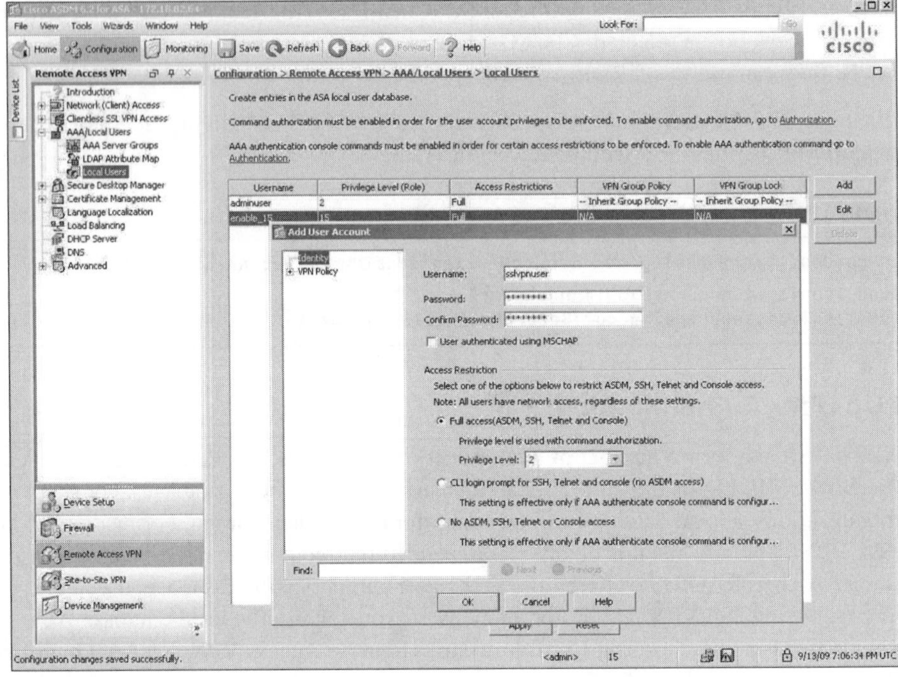

Figure 19-9 *Local Database*

After enabling RADIUS processing, define a list of the RADIUS servers. The Cisco security appliance checks their availability on a round-robin basis. If the first server is not reachable, it tries the second server, and so on. If a server is available, the security appliance keeps using that server until it fails to receive a response. In this case, it checks the availability of the next server. It is highly recommended that you set up more than one RADIUS server, in case the first server is not reachable. You can define a RADIUS server entry by navigating to **Configuration > Remote Access VPN > AAA/Local Users> AAA Server Groups** and clicking **Add** under **Servers in the Selected Group.** You must specify the IP address of the RADIUS server, as well as the interface closest to the server. The security appliance authenticates itself to the RADIUS server by using a shared secret key.

Note User passwords are sent as encrypted values from the Cisco ASA to the RADIUS server. This protects this critical information from an intruder. The security appliance hashes the password, using the shared secret that is defined on the security appliance and the RADIUS server.

Figure 19-10 shows the Cisco ASA configured with an AAA server under the server group called **Radius.** The server is located toward the **inside** interface at **192.168.1.20.** The server secret key is **c1$0123** (obfuscated).

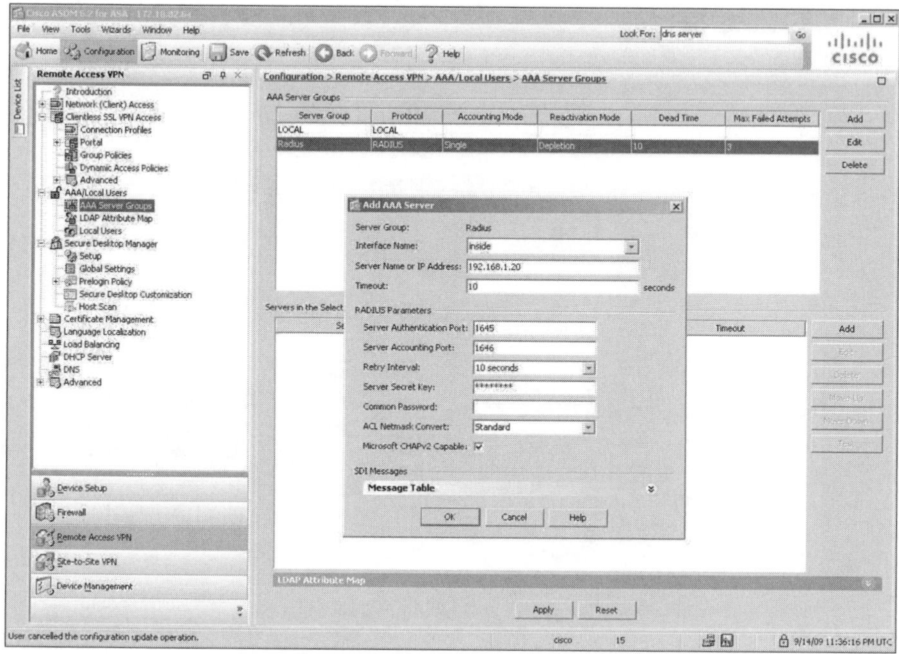

Figure 19-10 *Defining a RADIUS Server for Authentication*

> **Note** You can optionally modify the authentication and accounting port numbers if your RADIUS server does not use the default ports. The security appliance uses UDP ports 1645 and 1646 as defaults for authentication and accounting, respectively. Most of the RADIUS servers use the official IANA assigned ports 1812 and 1813 as authentication and accounting ports, respectively.

After defining the authentication server group, you have to bind it to the SSL VPN process under a tunnel group. Figure 19-11 illustrates that the newly created "Radius" AAA server group is mapped to the **SecureMeClientlessTunnel** tunnel group.

Example 19-9 shows how a radius server can be defined. The radius group-name is **Radius** and it is located toward the **inside** interface at **192.168.1.20**. The shared secret is **C1$c0123**. The radius server is linked to **SecureMeClientlessTunnel**.

Example 19-9 *Defining RADIUS for IPSec Authentication*

```
Chicago(config)# aaa-server Radius protocol radius
Chicago(config)# aaa-server Radius (inside) host 192.168.1.20
Chicago(config-aaa-server-host)# key C1$c0123
Chicago(config-aaa-server-host)# exit
Chicago(config) tunnel-group SecureMeClientlessTunnel general-attributes
Chicago(config-tunnel-general)# authentication-server-group Radius
```

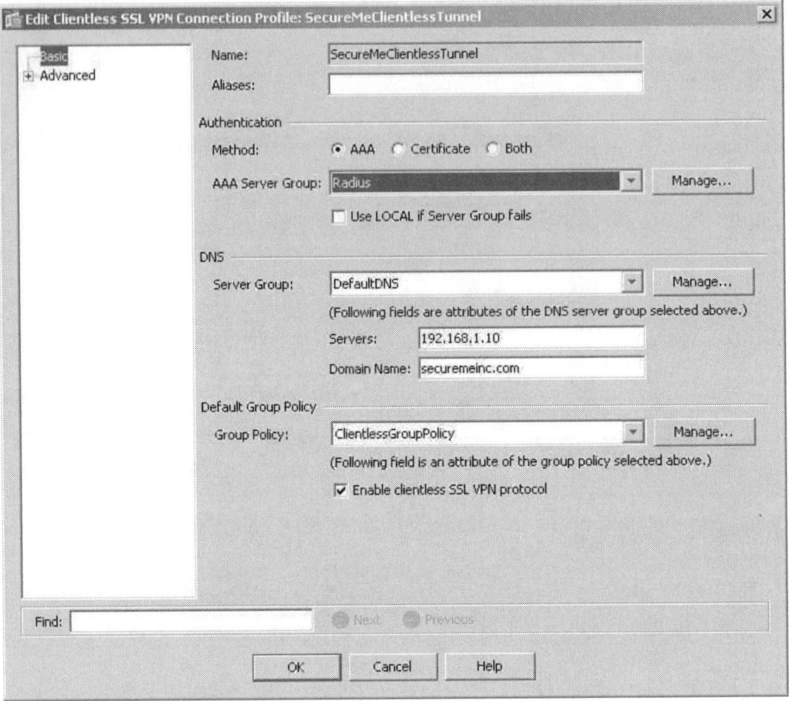

Figure 19-11 *Mapping a RADIUS Server to a Tunnel Group*

> **Tip** For large VPN deployments (both IPsec and SSL VPNs), you can even control user access and policy mapping from an external authentication server. You should pass the user group policy name as a RADIUS or LDAP attribute to the security appliance. By doing so, you guarantee that a user will always get the same policy, regardless of the tunnel group name to which he connects. If you are using RADIUS as the authentication and authorization server, you can specify the user group policy name as attribute 25 (class attribute). Append the keyword **OU=** as the value of the class attribute. For example, if you define a user group policy called engineering group, you can enable attribute 25 and specify **OU=engineering** as its value.

Note Starting from 8.2(1), the security appliance supports the double authentication feature where a user must provide two separate sets of login credentials at the login page. For example, you can choose to authenticate users on a primary authentication server such as Active Directory as well as on a secondary authentication server such as RADIUS. When both authentications succeed, the user is allowed to establish the SSL VPN tunnel. The secondary authentication server is specified under the Connection Profile settings.

Clientless SSL VPN Configuration Guide

The clientless configuration of SSL VPN describes the mandatory steps for enabling SSL VPNs and setting up the user interface for clientless SSL VPN users. The following sections focus on the clientless users who want to access internal corporate resources but do not have an SSL VPN client loaded on their workstations. These users typically access protected resources from shared workstations or even from the hotels or Internet cafes. The clientless configuration on Cisco ASA can be broken down into the following subsections:

- Enable Clientless SSL VPN on an interface
- Configure SSL VPN portal customization
- Configure bookmarks
- Configure web-type ACLs
- Configure application access
- Configure client-server plug-ins

Figure 19-12 is used throughout these sections to demonstrate how to set up Cisco ASA for clientless users. As shown in this figure, the security appliance is set up to accept the SSL VPN connections from the hosts on the Internet. On the private network of the security appliance, we have a number of servers.

Table 19-7 provides a description of those servers used in this setup.

Table 19-7 *Description and Location of Servers*

Server	Location	Purpose
CA server	192.168.1.30	To issue CA and ID certificates
WINS server	192.168.1.40	To resolve NetBIOS names with IP addresses
DNS server	192.168.1.10	To resolve hostnames with IP addresses
RADIUS server	192.168.1.20	To authenticate users
Web server	192.168.1.100	To host internal websites
File server	192.168.1.101	To host and present files and folders to SSL VPN users
Terminal server/SSH server	192.168.1.102	To provide terminal and SSH services to SSL VPN users

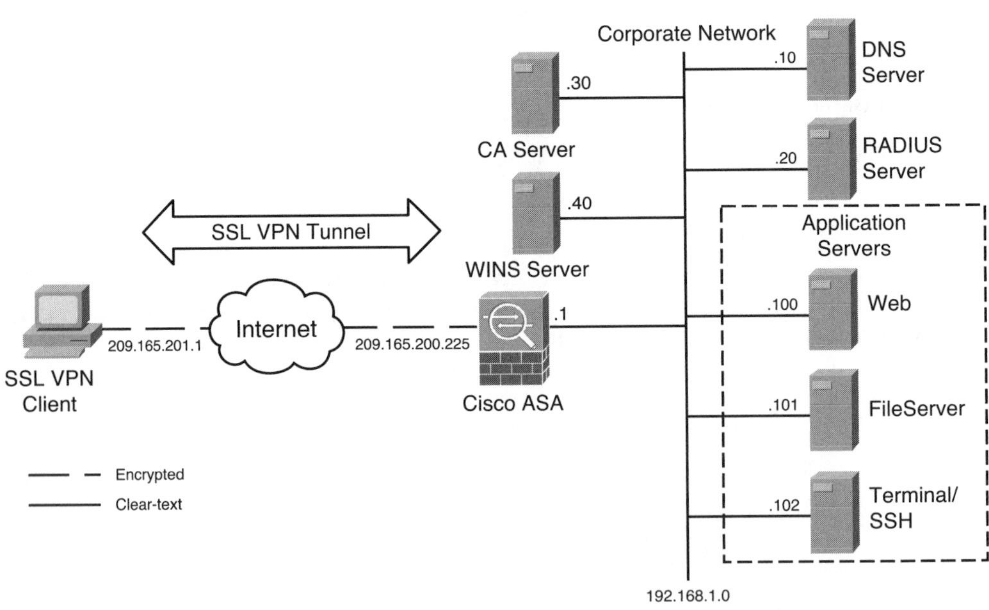

Figure 19-12 *SSL VPN Network Topology*

Enable Clientless SSL VPN on an Interface

The first step in setting up a clientless SSL VPN on the security appliances is to enable an SSL VPN on the interface that will terminate the user session. If an SSL VPN is not enabled on the interface, Cisco ASA does not accept any connections, even if SSL VPN is globally enabled.

To enable an SSL VPN on an interface through ASDM, choose **Configuration > Remote Access VPN > Clientless SSL VPN Access > Connection Profiles** and select the **Allow Access** check box next to the interface on which you want to enable SSL VPN. As shown in Figure 19-8, an SSL VPN is enabled on the **outside** interface, using the default port 443. Click **Apply** to send the appropriate command from ASDM to the security appliance.

Example 19-10 shows that SSL VPN functionality is enabled on the **outside** interface

Example 19-10 *Enabling SSL VPN on the Outside Interface*

```
Chicago(config)# webvpn
Chicago(config-webvpn)# enable outside
```

After SSL VPN is enabled on an interface, the security appliance is ready to accept the connections. However, you still need to go through other configuration steps to successfully accept user connections and to allow traffic to pass through.

Configure SSL VPN Portal Customization

Figure 19-13 shows the default SSL VPN page when a connection is initiated from a web browser. The title of the page is SSL VPN Service and the Cisco Systems logo is displayed in the upper-left corner of the web page. The initial page prompts the user for user authentication credentials.

You can customize the initial SSL VPN login page based on your organization's security policies. Cisco ASA also enables you to customize the user web portal by offering a number of options to choose from. The security appliance enables you to upload images and unique XML data to fully customize the login page. In version 8.0 and higher software, you can even customize the initial login page based on the user group membership.

> **Note** Portal customization can only be achieved through ASDM. You cannot modify the configuration through the CLI.

Using portal customization, you can design and present the SSL VPN page in any way you like. ASA allows you to design the default login page as well as the login page for a group of users. For example, if you want contractors to access a few applications, you can customize a web portal to include those applications and then map that portal to the

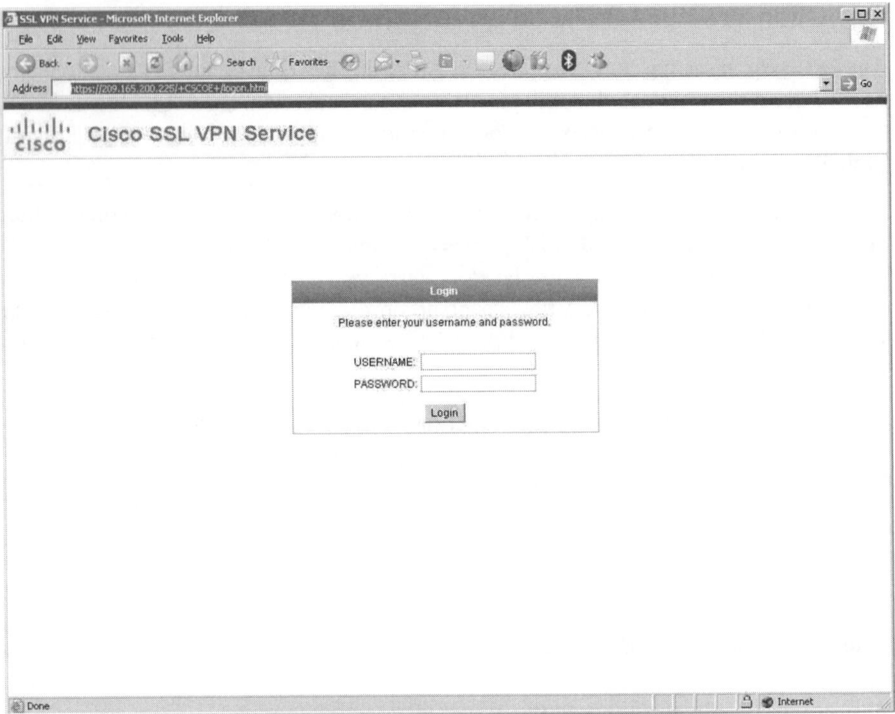

Figure 19-13 *Default SSL VPN Login Page*

group policy that contractors use. This way, when a user who belongs to the contractor group policy tries to log in, he sees only applications that are listed in his portal.

> **Note** Portal customization can use dynamic content through the use of a JavaScript include file, <script src="/+CSCOE+/custom.js"></script>. This file is useful if you want use the functions defined for an SSL VPN session to create your own web page.
>
> If you want to use customization through XML, Cisco ASA contains a customization template. You should export the template to a workstation and modify its content. You can import the customized content into the security appliance as a new customized object. XML customization is outside the scope of this book.

You configure the user portal customization by choosing **Configuration > Remote Access VPN > Clientless SSL VPN Access > Portal > Customization**. You can either modify the **DfltCustomization** object or define a new customized portal. If you want to create a new portal, click **Add** and specify the new object name. After the new object is created, you can select it and click **Edit** to modify its properties. Throughout this book, we use a new object called SecureMePortal. Cisco ASA launches a new browser window where you can customize the following three portal pages when a clientless user connects to a Cisco ASA:

- Logon page
- Portal page
- Logout page

Logon Page

You can change the appearance of the logon page for clientless SSL VPN users. You can either customize the default logon page that affects all users or customize a tunnel-specific page that affects users who connect to that tunnel group.

At a high-level architecture, the login portal customization is broken into four elements, discussed in the following sections and illustrated in Figure 19-14.

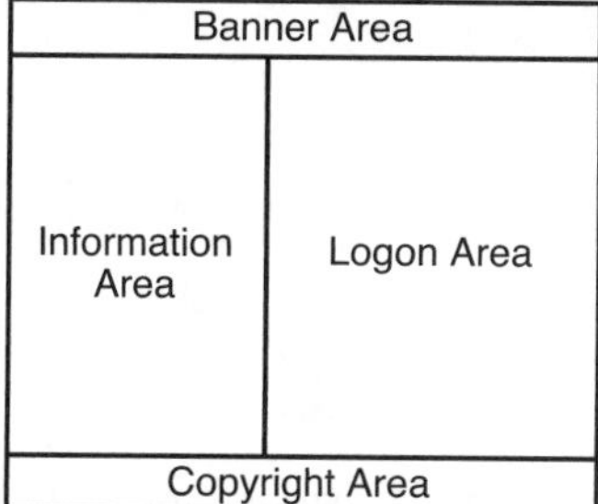

Figure 19-14 *SSL VPN Logon Page Customization*

Banner Area

The banner area acts as a page title, and thus customers can define their own text for a web page. For example, if you want to present "SecureMe SSL VPN Service" as the title of the logon page, you can define it under the title panel of the customization editor. This element of a web page can be hidden or displayed to the end users by an SSL VPN administrator. You can customize the banner based on your needs. For example, you can change the font and size of the banner text, add or change your company's logo, and position the text and logo on the page. In Figure 19-15, the administrator defines **SecureMe SSL VPN Service** as the page's title. An image called **securemeinc-sml.jpg** has been set as the logo URL, the font color is set to #000000 (black), and the background color is set to #ffffff (white). The administrator has enabled a gradient that is used to gradually change the background color.

Note If you want to upload customized images or files, choose **Configuration > Remote Access VPN > Clientless SSL VPN Access > Portal > Web Contents** and upload the files. An example is shown in the "Full Customization of a Logon Page" section later in this chapter.

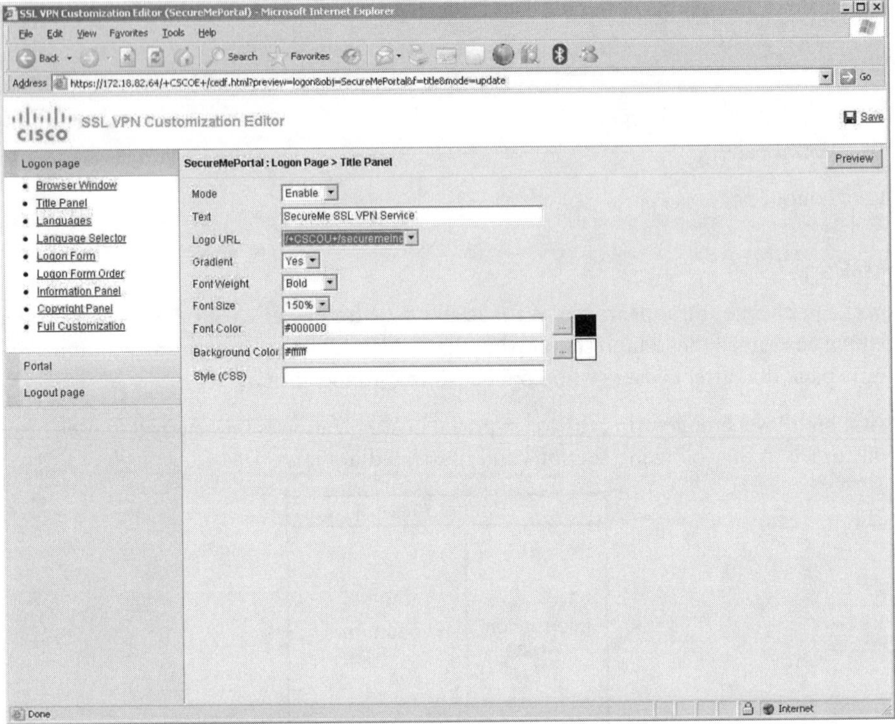

Figure 19-15 *Logon Page Banner Customization*

You can click the **Preview** button to preview the portal you have designed. This is a great way to test your configuration without actually pushing it to the security appliance and then testing it using the clientless SSL VPN tunnel. Click **Save** to save these settings.

Note You cannot preview a portal page if you choose Full Customization or upload an XML file.

Logon Area

The logon area, also known as the logon form, prompts the user to input his or her user credentials. You can customize the title, the logon message, the username and password prompts, and the color and font of the text. You can even choose whether you want users to select a group that they want to use for their authentication. In Figure 19-16, the Cisco ASA administrator has configured the logon form to meet SecureMe's policies. The title of the logon box is changed to **SecureMe Logon Box** and the message within the logon box is **Please Enter Your User Credentials.** The text in the username and password prompts is **Username:** and **Password:** respectively. The text in the secondary username and secondary password prompts is **Secondary Username:** and **Secondary Password:** respectively. The Hide Internal Password prompt is enabled while the text in the group selector prompt is **Group:**. The text within the login button is Click here to Login." The text color of the logon box title is **#ffffff** (white), whereas the background color in the title is **#666666** (gray). The font color of the text inside the logon box is **#000000** (black), and the background color of the logon form is **#ffffff** (white).

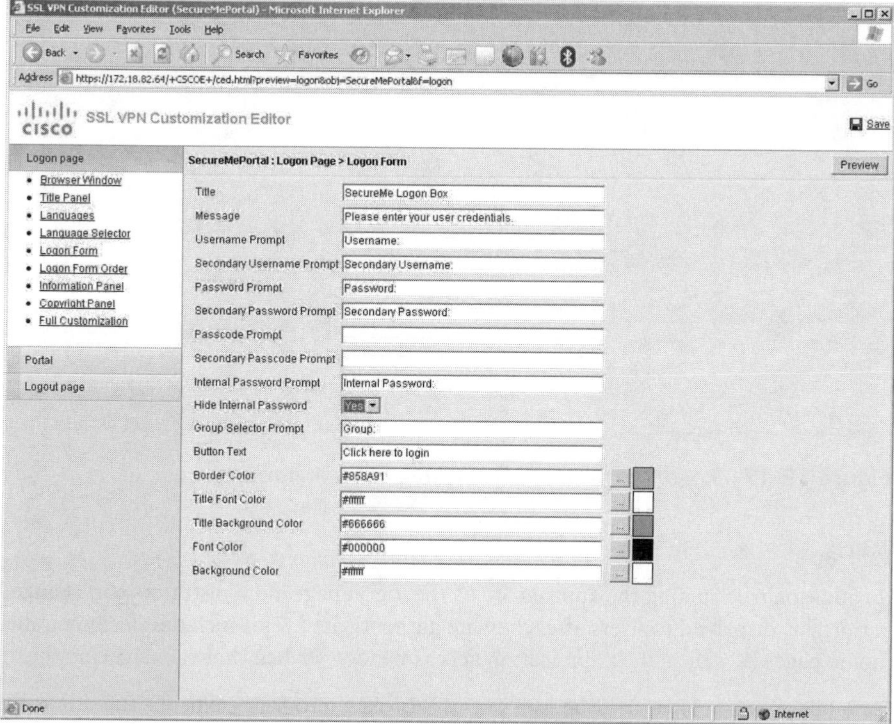

Figure 19-16 *Logon Form Customization*

Information Area

The information area shows any text and image that you want to display on the logon page. You can specify whether you want to display the information area to the left or the right side of the logon form. The Cisco ASA administrator can choose to enable or disable this element under the Information Panel option. In Figure 19-17, the information panel is disabled by the administrator.

Copyright Area

If you want to display the copyrighted information on the logon page, you can specify it in the Copyright area. Most customers use this area to display a logon warning or important information regarding user logons.

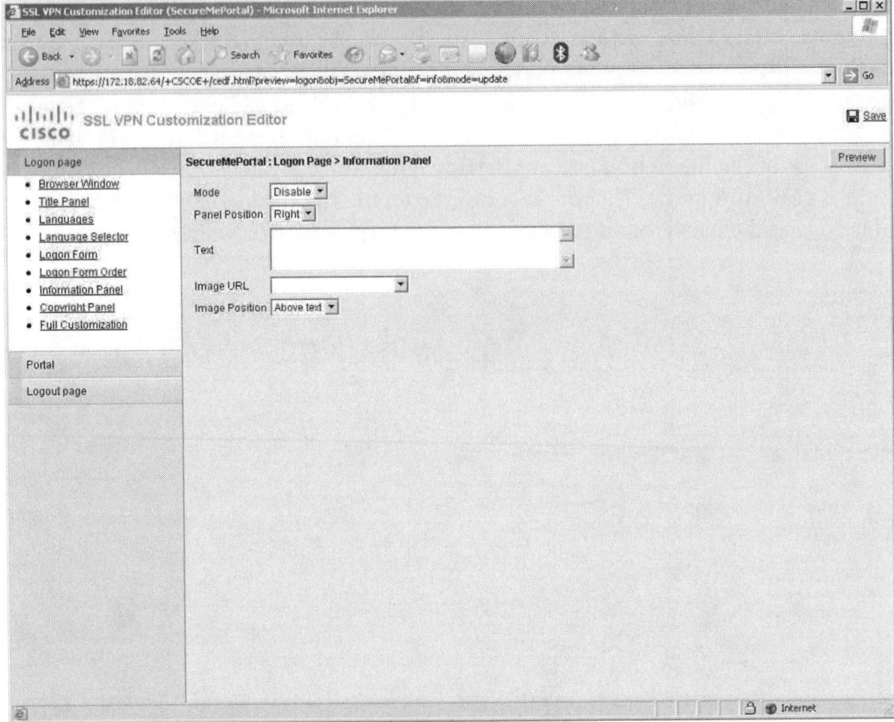

Figure 19-17 *Logon Page Information Area Customization*

Portal Page

In addition to changing the appearance of the logon page, administrators can change how a portal is displayed to users after they are authenticated. This includes designing their home pages as well as their application access windows when they launch an application.

At a high-level architecture, the web portal is broken into four elements: the title panel, toolbar, navigation pane, and content area. These elements are discussed next and are illustrated in Figure 19-18.

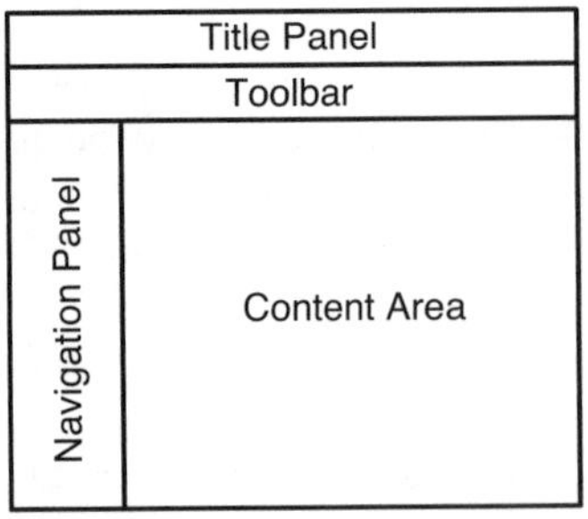

Title Panel
Toolbar
Navigation Panel
Content Area

Figure 19-18 *SSL VPN User Web Portal Customization*

Title Panel

The title panel designs the title frame on the user portal after the user is logged in. An administrator can choose to hide or display the title panel by disabling or enabling the Mode option. If you choose to display the title panel when a user logs into the security appliance via SSL VPN tunnel, you can specify the title text and logo and customize the font size and colors of the frame. For example, you can present "**SecureMe SSL VPN Service**" as the title and load SecureMe's company logo as the title image, as shown in Figure 19-19. The font color is **#800000** (maroon), and the background color is **#ffffff** (white). The font size is set to 150 percent of the regular font size.

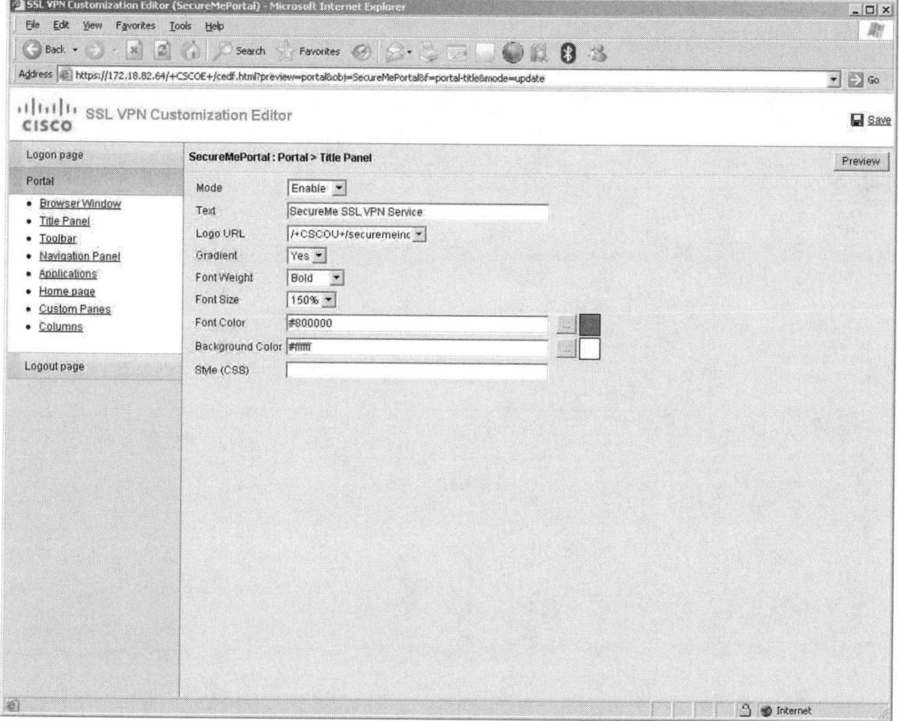

Figure 19-19 *SSL VPN Web Portal Title Panel Customization*

Toolbar

The toolbar is used to define user prompts such as the URL box and logout. You can also define browser button text here. An administrator can hide the toolbar from the user portal for additional security by disabling the Mode option.

Navigation Panel

The navigation panel, if enabled, can list all applications that you want SSL VPN users to access. In the navigational panel, select **Enabled** for the mode and click **Save** to save the settings. After it is saved, click **Applications** and define all the applications that appear vertically in the left pane after a user logs in to the portal. An administrator can choose to enable or hide an application, or move an application up or down the list. As illustrated in Figure 19-20, the administrator has enabled the following applications:

- Home
- Web applications
- Browse networks
- AnyConnect
- Application access
- Telnet/SSH servers

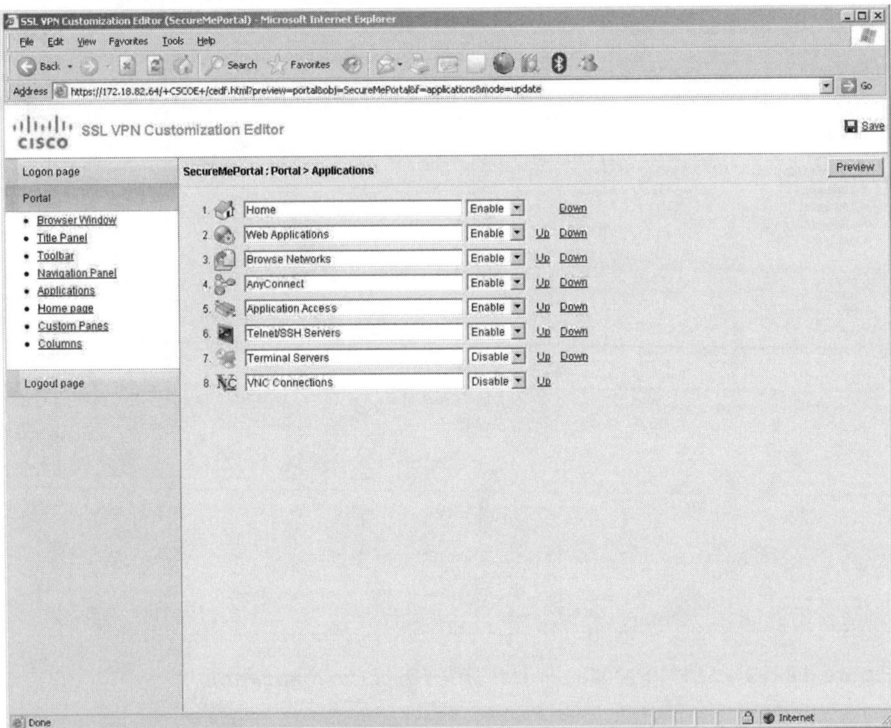

Figure 19-20 *SSL VPN Web Portal Application Customization*

Content Area

The content area shows content for each application. An administrator can choose to split the content area, shown as Content Pane in ASDM, into multiple frames of text, HTML, RSS feeds, or image panes. You can even define an initial web-page URL in case you want SSL VPN users to see important notifications when their connections are established.

Logout Page

Cisco ASA even allows you to customize the logout page. You can define the logout message and provide an option for whether users can be allowed to log back in. You can pick the color of the title font and title background, and the font and background colors of the logout page. In Figure 19-21, the administrator has added the logout message "**Please clear your browser's cache, delete any downloaded files, and close all open browsers before you sign out.**" The login button is not allowed, and thus the user needs to specify the SSL VPN server IP address in the browser to start a new session. The text color of the logout box title is **#ffffff** (white), and the background color of the title is **#666666** (gray). The font color of the text inside the logout box is **#000000** (black), and the background color of the logout form is **#ffffff** (white).

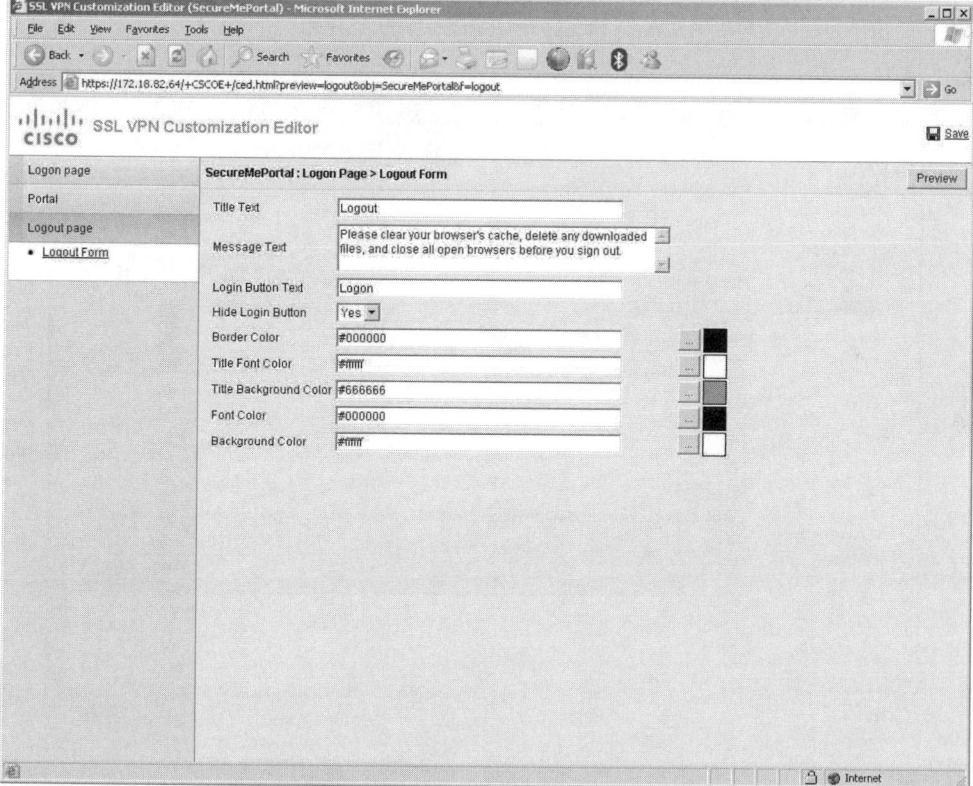

Figure 19-21 *SSL VPN Logout Page Customization*

Portal Customization and User Group

When you are finished customizing the login, portal, and logout pages, these customized objects can then be applied to the appropriate user connection profile. The following sections discuss two scenarios.

Customized Login Page and User Connection Profile

After customizing the login page, display it to the users who log in to the security appliances. You have two ways to display the login page to the user:

- **DefaultWEBVPNGroup connection profile—**If you want your customized login page to be displayed to all users who access the security appliance using its FQDN (fully qualified domain name) or the IP address, apply the customized object under the DefaultWEBVPNGroup connection profile by choosing **Configuration > Remote Access VPN > Clientless SSL VPN Access > Connection Profiles.** Select **DefaultWEBVPNGroup** and click **Edit** to modify its contents. Cisco ASDM launches a new window. Choose **Advanced > Clientless SSL VPN** and select **SecureMePortal** under Portal Page Customization, as shown in Figure 19-22. Click **OK** when finished. The clientless SSL VPN users can access the customized login portal by navigating to https://*<FQDNofASA>* or https://*<IPAddressOfASA>*.

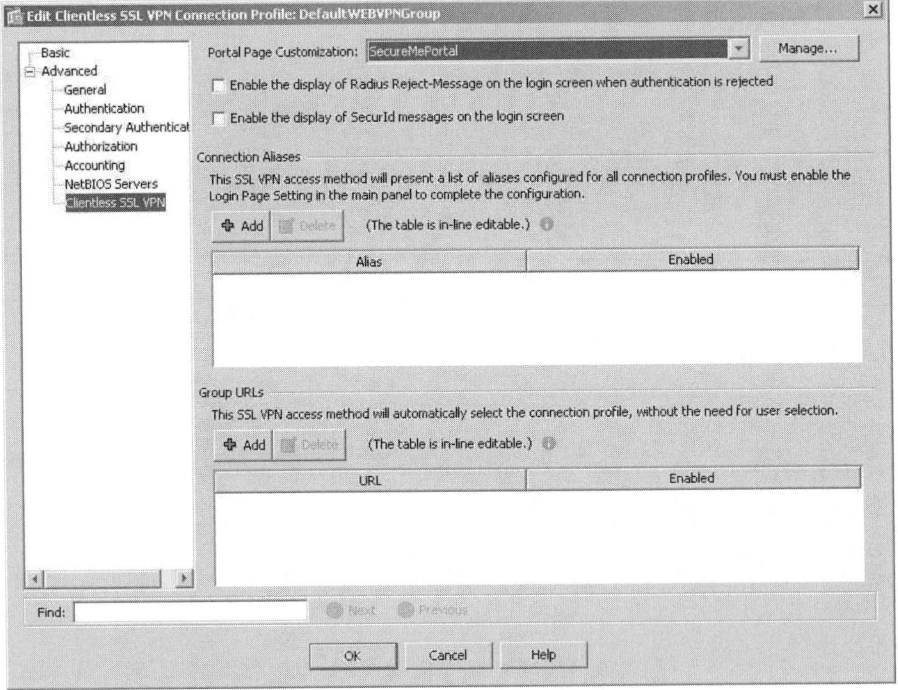

Figure 19-22 *Mapping of a Customized Portal to a Default Tunnel Group*

The CLI equivalent of Figure 19-22 is as follows:

```
Chicago(config)# tunnel-group DefaultWEBVPNGroup webvpn-attributes
Chicago(config-tunnel-webvpn)# customization SecureMePortal
```

- **User connection profile—**You can also present the customized login page to a user by applying the object under a user connection profile. However, the customized login page is displayed only if the user accesses a specific login URL that is set up by the administrator. To apply a customized login page to a user connection profile, choose **Configuration > Remote Access VPN > Clientless SSL VPN Access > Connection Profiles.** Select a user connection profile or create a new one. In this scenario, we use a connection profile called SecureMeClientlessTunnel for the clientless SSL VPN session. Select the profile and click **Edit** to modify its settings. Cisco ASDM launches a new window. Under **Aliases**, specify a name that users will use to connect to the security appliance. In Figure 19-23, SecureMeClientless is configured as the alias. After setting up the alias, the next step is to map the preconfigured customized object to this connection profile. Choose **Advanced > Clientless SSL VPN** and select **SecureMePortal** under **Portal Page Customization**. Click **OK** when finished. The clientless SSL VPN users can access the customized login portal by navigating to https://*<FQDNofASA>*/ SecureMeClientless or https://*<IPAddressOf ASA>*/SecureMeClientless.

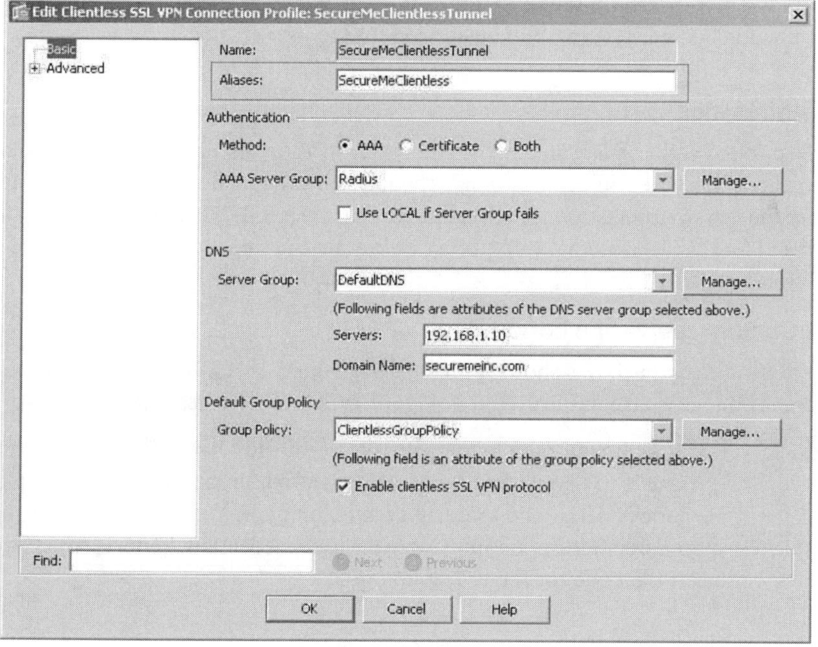

Figure 19-23 *Connection Profile Alias*

The CLI equivalent of Figure 19-23 is as follows:

```
Chicago(config)# tunnel-group SecureMeClientlessTunnel webvpn-attributes
Chicago(config-tunnel-webvpn)# group-alias SecureMeClientless enable
```

Customized Portal Page and User Connection Profile

When a user first connects to the security appliance, the logon portal is presented based on how the SSL VPN connection is established. For example, if a user selects a logon group after a successful user authentication, a user portal is shown based on what customization object is mapped to that user connection profile. You have the following three ways to display the customized portal page to a user:

- **Default Login without Group Selection**—When a user accesses the login page and authenticates himself without selecting a group to log in to, he is presented with the user portal page that is mapped to the DefaultWEBVPNGroup Connection Profile.
- **Default Login with Group Selection**—When a user accesses the login page and authenticates himself after selecting a login group, he is presented with the user portal page that is mapped to that specific user connection profile.
- **User Connection Profile Login**—When a user logs in to the system using the group-specific URL, he is presented with the user portal page that is mapped to that specific user connection profile. For example, if a user accesses the security appliance by entering **https://sslvpn.securemeinc.com/SecureMeClientless**, a web portal that is defined in SecureMePortal will be applied for the user session.

Full Customization

As mentioned earlier, you can use the full customization feature available in Cisco ASA running version 8.*x*. You can customize the logon, portal, and logout pages. Customers prefer the full customization functionality so that their SSL VPN portal has the same look and feel as their internal web portal. Below are the steps for customizing the logon and web portals.

Full Customization of a Logon Page

The default logon page was shown previously in Figure 19-13. If you would rather have a customized logon page as illustrated in Figure 19-24, follow these steps:

Step 1. Begin with your own logon page. If you already have HTML code, you can leverage it to define the logon customization. In the following example, a simple code is developed to design the logon page. You can see that we have left space after "Please log in using your user credentials." This is where we will insert the code for the user logon box.

```
<head>
<title>SecureMe SSL VPN Portal</title>
</head>
<body lang=EN-US style='tab-interval:.5in'><div class=Section1>
<span style='mso-fareast-font-family:"Times New Roman"; mso-no-
proof:yes'><img width=85 height=93 id="_x0000_i1025"
src="Doc1_files/image003.jpg"></span><b style='mso-bidi-font-
weight:normal'><span style='font-size:30.0pt;mso-fareast-font-
family:"Times New Roman"'>Welcome to SecureMe SSL VPN Logon
```

```
Page<u1:p></u1:p></span></b><span style='mso-fareast-font-family:"Times
New Roman"'><o:p></o:p></span></p>
<br><br><br><br>
<b><span style='font-size:16.0pt'>Please Login using your user creden-
tials</b></p>
<br><br><br>
<!—Insert Logon Dialogue Box code here>
<br><br><br>
<b><style='mso-bidi-font-weight:normal'><i style='mso-bidi-font-
style:normal'><u>Unauthorized users will be prosecuted according to
the Federal and State Laws</u></i></b></p>
</div>
</body>
</html>
```

Figure 19-24 *Customized Logon Page*

Step 2. Replace any reference to the images with the keyword **/+CSCOU+/**. When you upload an image to the security appliance, it is stored in the /+CSCOU+/ directory, which resides on the local flash. Thus, when you instruct the security appliance to load an image, it checks the content in that directory. The snippet of the modified code is highlighted in gray.

```
<span style='mso-fareast-font-family:"Times New Roman"; mso-no-
proof:yes'><img width=85 height=93 id="_x0000_i1025"
src="/+CSCOU+/image003.jpg"></span><b style='mso-bidi-font-weight:nor-
mal'><span style='font-size:30.0pt;mso-fareast-font-family:"Times New
Roman"'>Welcome to SecureMe SSL VPN Logon
Page<u1:p></u1:p></span></b><span style='mso-fareast-font-family:"Times
New Roman"'><o:p></o:p></span></p>
```

Step 3. Before saving the HTML code, you need to insert the logon box. In the following example, we inserted the logon dialog box by replacing <!—Insert Logon Dialog Box code here>.

```
<br><br><br>
<body
onload="csco_ShowLoginForm('lform');csco_ShowLanguageSelector('selec-
tor')" bgcolor="white">
<table><tr><td colspan=3 height=20 align=left>
<div id="selector" style="width"300px"></div></td></tr>
<tr><td align=middle valign=middle> <div id=lform> Loading credentials
</div></td></tr></table>
<br><br><br>
```

Step 4. Save the HTML code as an include file so that the security appliance can add the appropriate JavaScript to support the login box. In this example, we named this file logonscript.inc.

Step 5. Import the appropriate images and logon script into the security appliance. Choose **Configuration > Remote Access VPN > Clientless SSL VPN Access > Portal > Web Contents** and upload the **logonscript.inc** and **image003.jpg** files from the local workstation to the flash of the security appliance. Make sure that you select "**No. For example, use this option to make the content available to logon or portal page**" for the "Require Authentication to Access Its Content" option.

Step 6. After uploading the web content, choose **Configuration > Remote Access VPN > Clientless SSL VPN Access > Portal > Customization**, select the portal page you are customizing, and click **Edit**. The portal customization browser window opens. Click **Logon Page > Full Customization** and change the mode to **Enable**. Select **/+CSCOU+/logonscript.inc** under **HTML Content URL**.

Step 7. Associate the customized object to a tunnel group to which the user can connect.

Note You can upload images and logos in the JPEG, GIF, and PNG formats.

Full Customization of a User Portal Page

If you want to customize the user web portal, you can use the following steps to provide full customization. These steps are similar to the steps described for the logon page customization. The default user web portal is shown in Figure 19-25.

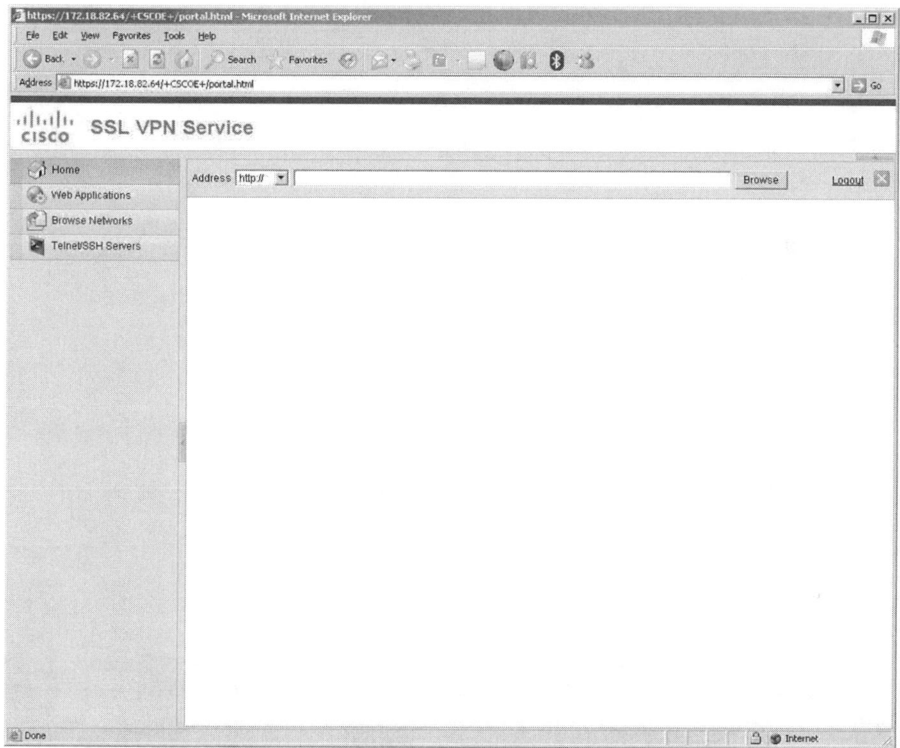

Figure 19-25 *Default User Web Portal Page*

Step 1. Choose **Configuration > Remote Access VPN > Clientless SSL VPN Access > Portal > Customization** and edit the **SecureMePortal** object under **Portal > Custom Panes.**

Step 2. Under **Type HTML**, make sure that the mode is set to **Enable** and then specify a title for the web link. In Figure 19-26, a title of "Cisco Systems Webpage" is added. Under URL, add the URL that you want users to see. In the previous example, the link to the Cisco System web page, **http://www.cisco.com**, is shown.

Step 3. Under **Type RSS**, make sure that the mode is set to **Enable** and then specify a title of the RSS feed link. In Figure 19-27, a title of "Internal Company News" is added. Under URL, specify the link to the RSS feed. In the previous example, an RSS feed file resides at **http://192.168.1.100/SecureMe.xml**. Click **Save** to save these changes.

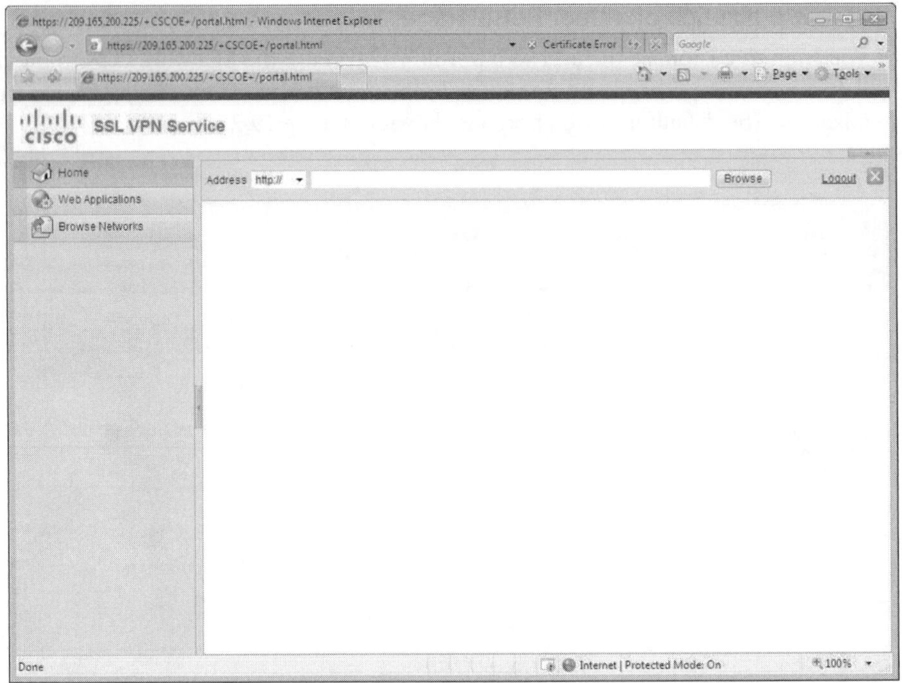

Figure 19-26 *User Web Portal Full Customization*

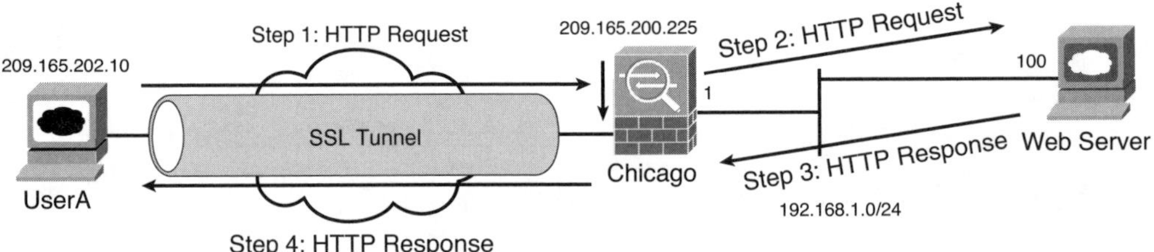

Figure 19-27 *HTTP Requests Through ASA*

Step 4. Associate the customized object to a tunnel group to which the user can connect. If you already have the object mapped to a tunnel group, you do not need to link it again.

Configure Bookmarks

Using a clientless SSL VPN, remote users can browse their internal websites, file server shares, and Outlook Web Access (OWA) servers. Cisco ASA achieves this functionality by terminating the SSL tunnels on its outside interface and then rewriting the content before sending it to the internal server. For example, if a user tries to access an internal website, the user's HTTPS connection is terminated to the outside interface. The ASA then forwards the HTTP or HTTPS request to the internal web server. The response from the web server is then encapsulated into HTTPS and forwarded to the client. This process is illustrated in Figure 19-27. The following sequence of events takes place when UserA tries to connect to a web server located at 192.168.1.100:

Step 1. UserA initiates an HTTP request to the web server, located on the other side of the SSL VPN tunnel. The user request is encapsulated into the SSL tunnel and is then forwarded to the security appliance.

Step 2. Cisco ASA de-encapsulates the traffic and initiates a connection to the server on behalf of the web client.

Step 3. The response from the server is sent to the security appliance.

Step 4. The security appliance, in turn, encapsulates and sends it to UserA.

Note If you frequently use Java and ActiveX coding in a web page, Cisco ASA might not be able to rewrite web pages that embed the contents. You can enable the smart tunnel option within bookmarks to tunnel HTTP traffic directly to the web server.

The security appliance does not allow SSL VPN communication with websites that present expired certificates during session negotiations.

You can define bookmarks for the internal servers. A user, after logging in, can see those bookmarks and browse the content of the servers by clicking them. Bookmarks are links to commonly used websites to which your clientless SSL VPN users connect. Furthermore, by defining all the websites or servers to which you want to allow access, you can deny users access to any other site or server. This is one way to restrict their access to the internal network after establishing the VPN tunnel.

You can configure bookmarks by choosing **Configuration > Remote Access VPN > Clientless SSL VPN Access > Portal > Bookmarks > Add.** You can specify a bookmark list name that is then mapped to a user or group policy. After specifying a list name, you can click **Add** to specify a URL heading that appears on the main portal page after a successful user authentication. Under Bookmarks, you can add many different types of application servers, including the following:

- Websites (HTTP and HTTPS)
- File servers (CIFS)

- FTP
- SSH/Telnet
- Remote Desktop Protocol (RDP)
- Virtual Network Computing (VNC)

Note You will not see an option for VNC, RDP, or SSH/Telnet if you do not import their plug-ins first. Consult the section "Configure Client-Server Plug-ins," later in this chapter, for details.

Configure Websites

After adding a bookmark list, you can add a bookmark entry for the internal web servers to which you want the clientless users to have access. In Figure 19-28, a bookmark list name of **InternalServers** has been added. Because it is a new list, the administrator has added a bookmark title of **InternalWebServer** with a URL value of **http://intranet.securemeinc.com.** Under advanced options, a subtitle of **"This is the internal web portal for SecureMe Inc. Employees"** is added with a thumbnail of the **securemeinc-sml.png** icon. The administrator has enabled the smart tunnel option to tunnel HTTP traffic directly to the web server.

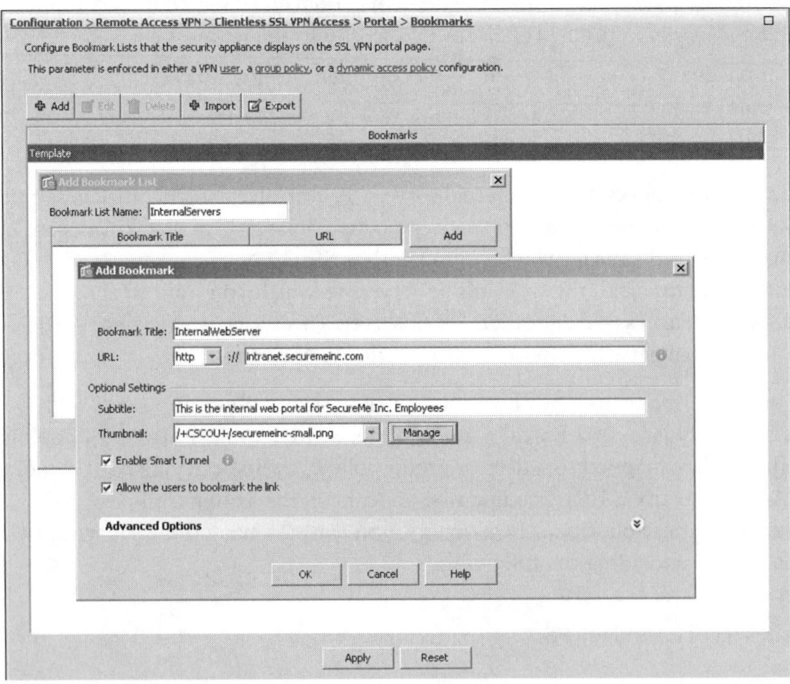

Figure 19-28 *Website Bookmark Configuration*

Note In the current implementation, you must use ASDM to define bookmarks.

Note If you configure your internal websites using the fully qualified domain name (FQDN), you must configure a Domain Name System (DNS) server on the security appliance to resolve the hostnames. You configure the DNS server by choosing **Configuration > Device Management > DNS > DNS Client** and clicking **Add** to add DNS servers under DNS Server Group.

Caution The clientless SSL VPN does not ensure that the communication from the client is secure to all the websites it is accessing. For example, if an external website is accessed by a user, and the traffic is proxied by the security appliance, the connection from the security appliance to the external web server is not encrypted.

Configure File Servers

In addition to the web servers, you can also define a bookmark list of the file servers that the clientless users can access. Cisco ASA supports network file sharing using the Common Internet File System (CIFS), a file system that uses the original IBM and Microsoft networking protocols. Through CIFS, users can access their file shares located on the file servers. Users can download, upload, delete, or rename the files under the shared directories, but only if the file system permissions allow them to perform those actions. They can even create subdirectories, assuming that they are allowed to do so.

Note You must install Microsoft hotfix 892211 on Windows operating systems to access web folders in the clientless SSL VPN mode.

The configuration of CIFS requires the use of a NetBIOS Name Server (NBNS), also known as Windows Internet Naming Server (WINS). When a clientless user queries to browse the network, the security appliance contacts the WINS and acquires the list of available domains, workgroups, and workstations. Use the following steps to successfully configure Windows file server for clientless SSL VPN users:

Step 1. In ASDM, specify a NetBIOS server by choosing **Configuration > Remote Access VPN > Clientless SSL VPN Access > Connection Profile > SecureMeClientlessTunnel > Edit > Advanced > NetBIOS Servers > Add.** Specify the IP address of the NBNS server for CIFS name resolution. The "Master Browser" option specifies that the configured NBNS server acts as the master browser in addition to being a WINS server. The Timeout value instructs an appliance to wait for the configured number of seconds (default is 2 seconds) before sending another query to the next server. The Retry option is used to specify the number of times the security appliance has to go through the list of the configured NBNS servers. The default number of retries is 2, and it can range from 0 to 10. In Figure 19-29, a NetBIOS server located at 192.168.1.40 is added. The Master Browser option is also enabled.

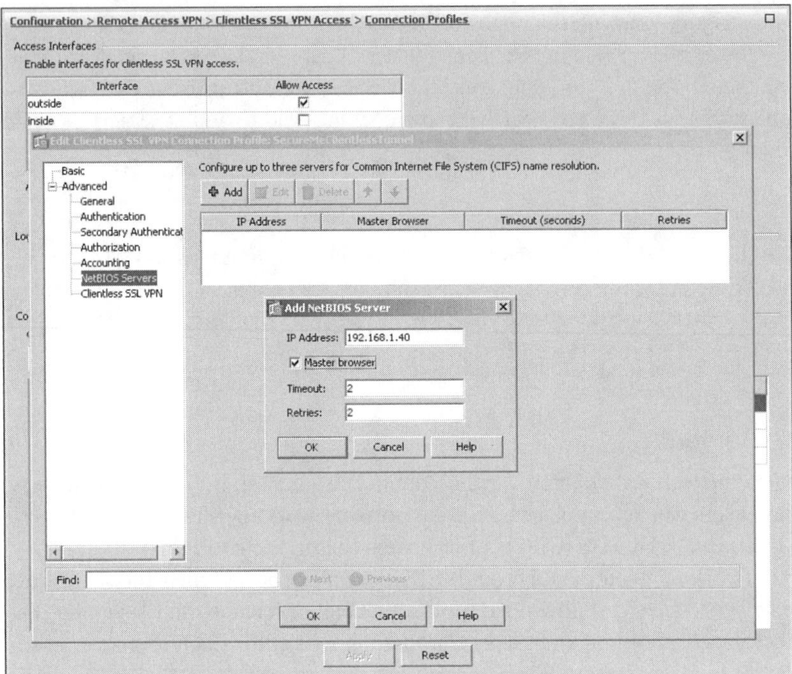

Figure 19-29 *WINS Server Definition*

Example 19-11 defines a new NBNS server located at 192.168.1.40.

Example 19-11 Defining a WINS Server

```
Chicago(config)# tunnel-group SecureMeClientlessTunnel webvpn-attributes
Chicago(config-tunnel-webvpn)# nbns-server 192.168.1.40 master timeout 2 retry 2
```

Step 2. Define a bookmark for the file server by choosing **Configuration > Remote Access VPN > Clientless SSL VPN Access > Portal > Bookmarks > InternalServers > Edit > Add.** Specify a bookmark title of **InternalFileServer**, select **cifs** as the URL value, and add the IP address of the file server. In Figure 19-30, a **cifs** file server that is located at **192.168.1.101** is added. The administrator has added "This is the internal FileServer for SecureMe Inc." as the description for this file server.

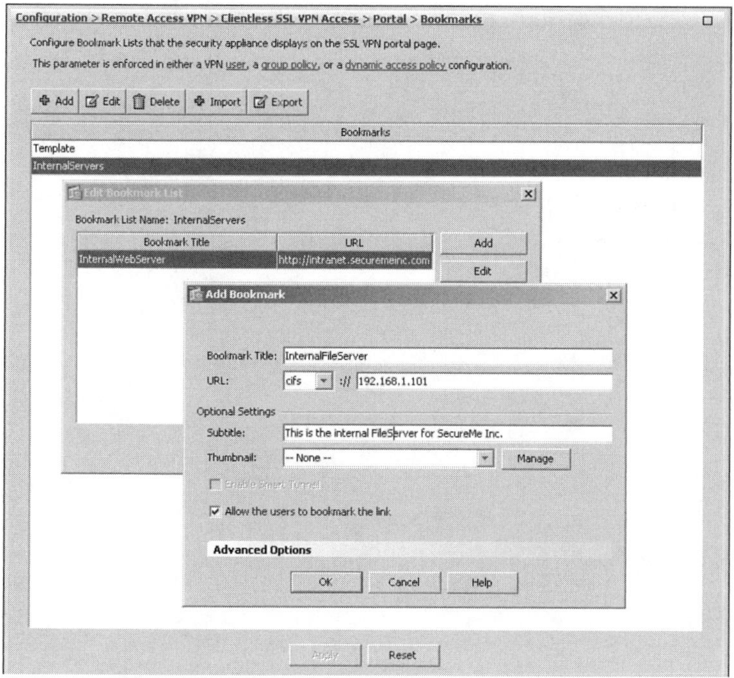

Figure 19-30 *File Server Definition*

Apply a Bookmark List to a Group Policy

You can apply the bookmark list to a user or group policy. As shown in Figure 19-31, choose **Configuration > Remote Access VPN > Clientless SSL VPN Access > Group Policies > ClientlessGroupPolicy > Edit > Portal**, deselect the **Inherit** box, and then choose **InternalServers** under **Bookmark List.**

Single Sign-on

Optionally, you can add a single sign-on (SSO) server to ensure that clientless users do not get prompted again to enter their user credentials when they try to access Windows-based shares. In SSO, the security appliance acts as a proxy between the clientless SSL VPN user and the authentication server. The security appliance uses users' cached credentials (an authentication cookie) when the user tries to access secure websites or shares within the private network. If you use NT LAN Manager (NTLM) authentication in your environment, you can define SSO attributes under user or group policies. As shown in Figure 19-32, SSO is enabled for all clientless SSL VPN users that send authentication requests to the servers in the 192.168.1.0 subnet, using NTLM authentication.

Example 19-12 shows the equivalent CLI configuration of Figure 19-32.

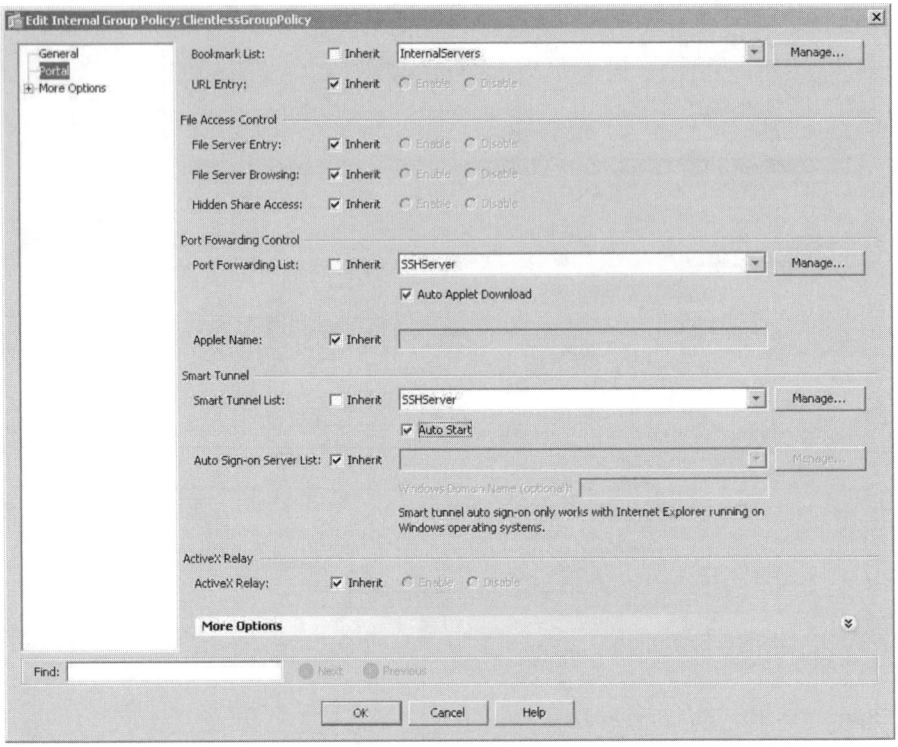

Figure 19-31 *Bookmark to Policy Group Mapping*

Example 19-12 *Single Sign-on Definition via the CLI*

```
Chicago(config)# group-policy ClientlessGroupPolicy attributes
Chicago(config-group-policy)# webvpn
Chicago(config-group-webvpn)# auto-signon allow ip 192.168.1.0 255.255.255.0 auth-
type ntlm
```

Cisco ASA, in addition to NTLM, supports many other authentication methods. They include basic HTTP, SSO authentication using SiteMinder, SAML browser post profile, and using the HTTP Form protocol.

Configure Web-Type ACLs

Cisco ASA enables network administrators to further their clientless SSL VPN security by configuring web-type access control lists (ACL) to manage access to web, Telnet, SSH, citrix, FTP, file and email servers, or all types of traffic. These ACLs affect only the clientless SSL VPN traffic and are processed in sequential order until a match is found. If an ACL is defined but no match exists, the default behavior on the security appliance is to drop the packets. On the other hand, if no web-type ACL is defined, Cisco ASA allows all traffic to pass through it.

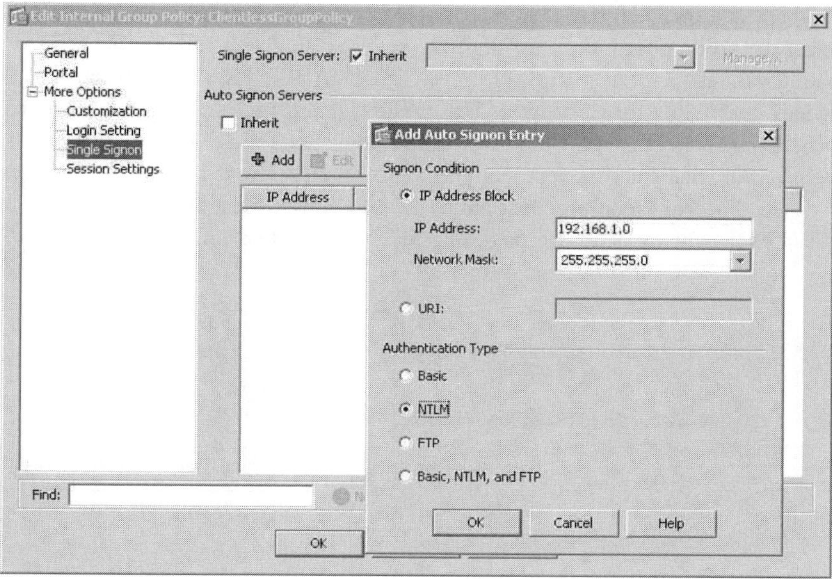

Figure 19-32 *Single Sign-on Server Definition*

Moreover, this robust SSL VPN feature allows these ACLs to be downloaded from a Cisco Secure Access Control Server (CS-ACS) through the use of vendor-specific attributes (VSA). This allows central control and management of user access into the corporate network because ACL definitions are offloaded to an ACS server.

Tip Using CS-ACS, you can configure a web-type ACL by specifying the webvpn:inacl# prefix in the downloadable ACLs, where # indicates the sequence number of an access control entry (ACE).

You configure a web-type ACL by choosing **Configuration > Remote Access VPN > Clientless SSL VPN Access > Advanced > Web ACLs.** Click **Add** and select **Add ACL** to define a new web-type ACL. Specify a web ACL name and click **OK.** Select the newly created ACL name, click **Add** again, and select **Add ACE.** You have two options to add a web-type ACL:

- **Filter on URL**—A URL-based web ACL is used to filter out SSL VPN packets if they contain a URL such as http://internal.securemeinc.com.
- **Filter on address and service**—An address- and service-based web ACL is used to filter out SSL VPN packets if they use TCP encapsulation based on the IP address and a Layer 4 port number.

If you prefer to add a URL-based entry to filter out SSL VPN traffic, select **Filter on URL** and select the protocol you want to filter. The security appliance allows you to filter based on CIFS, citrix, citrixs, FTP, HTTP, HTTPS, IMAP4, NFS, POP3, smart tunnel, SMTP, SSH, and Telnet for all types of URLs. Next, specify the URL or a wildcard to filter traffic. For example, if you want the security appliance to restrict web traffic destined to internal.securemeinc.com, select **Deny** as the "Action," choose **http** as the filter protocol, and select **internal.securemeinc.com** as the URL entry. This is illustrated in Figure 19-33. Click **OK** when you are finished. The ACL name is **Restrict.**

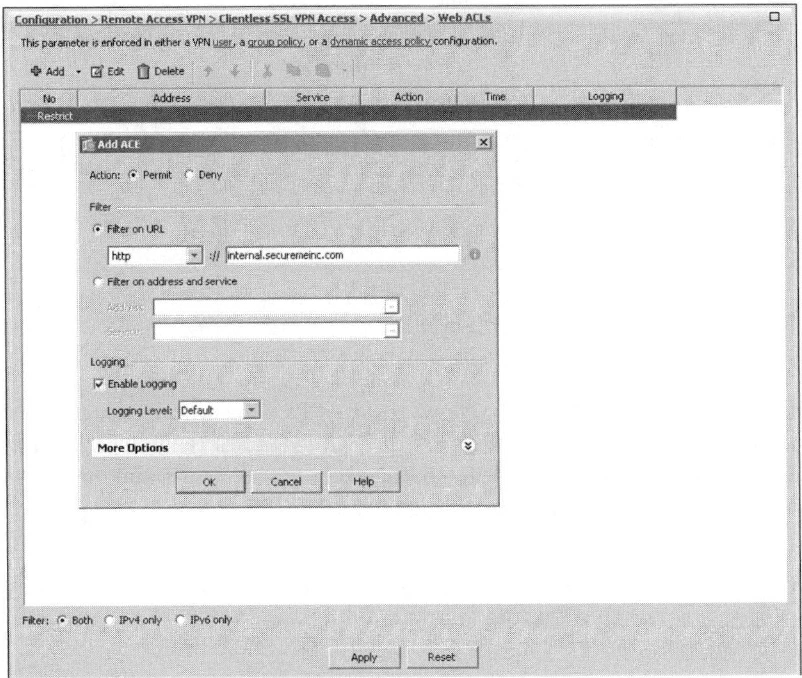

Figure 19-33 *Defining Web-Type ACLs*

Note You must import the VNC, SSH/Telnet, and RDP plug-ins to be able to filter those protocols via a web-type ACL. SSL VPN plug-ins are discussed later in this chapter.

If you want to include all URLs that are not explicitly matched in the ACL, you can include an asterisk (*) as a wildcard. For example, to block POP3 email access and allow all other protocols, take the following actions:

- Add an ACE and deny POP3 for the protocol and add * as a wildcard URL entry.
- Add another ACE and permit **any** for the protocol type.

If you would rather permit or block TCP traffic that is destined to particular addresses on specific ports, choose the **Filter on Address and Service** option. For example, to block all clientless traffic destined to 192.168.0.0/16 on port 23, select **Deny** as the "Action", specify **192.168.0.0/16** under "Address", and choose **23** under "Service". Click **OK** when you are finished.

Tip When you define a deny ACE, make sure that you configure another ACE to permit all other clientless SSL VPN traffic because there is an implicit deny at the end of each ACL.

After a web ACL is configured, link it to a default user group or user policy. Choose **Configuration > Remote Access VPN > Clientless SSL VPN Access > Group Policies > ClientlessGroupPolicy > Edit > General > More Options**, deselect the Web ACL **Inherit** check box and choose **Restrict** from the Web ACL drop-down menu.

Example 19-13 shows that a web-type ACL called **Restrict** being configured to allow **http://internal.securemeinc.com.** This ACL is then applied to **ClientlessGroupPolicy**.

Example 19-13 *Defining a Web-Type ACL*

```
Chicago(config)# access-list Restrict webtype permit url http://internal.secure-
meinc.com
Chicago(config)# group-policy ClientlessGroupPolicy attributes
Chicago(config-group-policy)# webvpn
Chicago(config-group-webvpn)# filter value Restrict
```

Caution Web ACLs do not block a user from accessing the resources outside the SSL VPN tunnel. For example, if a user opens another tab with a web browser and accesses a different site, that traffic is not sent to the ASA, and therefore the security policies configured on the ASA will have no effect.

Configure Application Access

Cisco ASA allows clientless SSL VPN users to access applications that reside on the protected network. Application access supports only applications that use TCP ports such as SSH, Outlook, and Remote Desktop. In version 8.0 or higher, Cisco ASA allows the following two methods to configure application access:

- Port forwarding
- Smart tunnels

Configure Port Forwarding

Using port forwarding, the clientless SSL VPN users can access corporate resources over the known and fixed TCP ports such as Telnet, SSH, Terminal Services, SMTP, and so on. The port-forwarding feature requires you to install Sun Microsystems' Java Runtime Environment (JRE) and configure applications on the end user's PC. If users are establishing the SSL VPN tunnel from public computers, such as Internet kiosks or web cafes, they might not be able to use this feature because JRE installation requires administrative rights on the client computer.

> **Note** Port forwarding is supported only on the 32-bit-based operating systems such as Windows 7, Vista, XP, and Windows 2000.

To use port forwarding, the authenticated user selects Application Access from the navigation pane and clicks the **Start Applications** button. The port-forwarding Java applet is downloaded and then executed on the user's computer. This applet starts listening on the locally configured ports, and when traffic is destined to those ports, the applet makes an HTTP POST request to the port-forwarding URL such as https://ASA-IP-Address/tcp/remoteserver/remoteport.

> **Note** To customize the Application Access name in the navigation pane, choose **Configuration > Remote Access VPN > Clientless SSL VPN Access > Group Policies > ClientlessGroupPolicy > Edit > Portal**, deselect the **Inherit** check box under "Applet Name," and specify the customized text that you want to display in the navigation pane.

When port forwarding is in use, the HOSTS file on the client computer is modified to resolve the hostname using one of the loopback addresses. Cisco ASA uses an available address in the range from 127.0.0.2 to 127.0.0.254. This requires the logged-in user to have admin rights so that the HOSTS file can be modified. In case the HOSTS file cannot be modified, the host listens on 127.0.0.1 and the configured local port. When the session is terminated, the application port mapping is restored to the default.

> **Note** Certain security applications such as Cisco Security Agent (CSA) detect the modifications of the HOST and other files. You might be asked to acknowledge these modifications.
>
> Smart tunnels, port forwarding, and plug-ins are not supported on Microsoft Windows Mobile.

Configuration of port forwarding on a security appliance is a two-step process:

Step 1. Define port-forwarding lists.

Step 2. Map port-forwarding lists to a group policy.

Step 1: Define Port-Forwarding Lists

You must define a list of servers and their respective applications that you want clientless SSL VPN users to access. You define a port-forwarding list by choosing **Configuration > Remote Access VPN > Clientless SSL VPN Access > Portal > Port Forwarding > Add.** Specify a name for the new port-forwarding list. This list name has local significance, and it is eventually used to map the port-forwarding attributes to a group policy, discussed in the next step. To define a specific application to be used for port forwarding, click **Add** and specify the following attributes:

- **Local TCP Port**—You should use a local port between 1024 and 65535 to avoid conflicts with the existing network services.
- **Remote Server**—The IP address of the server hosting the application.
- **Remote TCP Port**—The application port number, such as 22 for SSH service.
- **Description**—A description to identify this list.

As shown in Figure 19-34, a port-forwarding list called **SSHServer** is defined. A server, located at **192.168.1.102** and listening on port **22**, is added in this list. The administrator has configured it to use a local port of **1100** for this connection and has added a description of "Access to Internal Terminal/SSH Server."

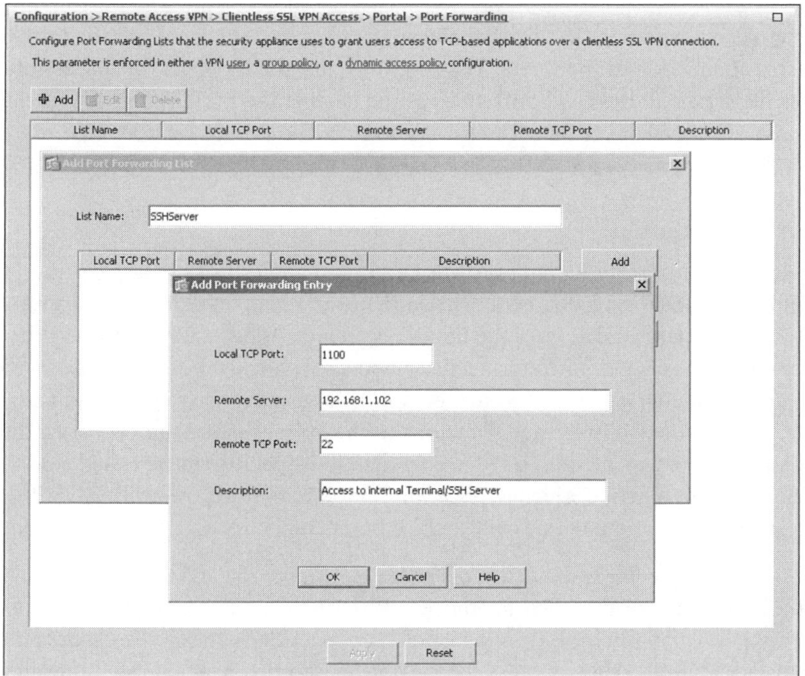

Figure 19-34 *Defining Port-Forwarding List*

Step 2: Map Port Forwarding Lists to a Group Policy

The port-forwarding list, defined in Step 1, is then mapped to a user or group policy. Choose **Configuration > Remote Access VPN > Clientless SSL VPN Access > Group Policies > ClientlessGroupPolicy > Edit > Portal** and select the list on the **Port Forwarding List** drop-down menu. Additionally, select the **Auto Applet Download** option to automatically install and start the applet as soon as the clientless SSL VPN user establishes a connection to the security appliance. As shown in Figure 19-31, a port-forwarding list of **SSHServer** is selected.

Example 19-14 shows that a port forwarding list **SSHServer** is being defined to tunnel traffic to an SSH server located at **192.168.1.102** if the traffic is destined to the loopback address of the host on port **1100.** This port forwarding list is then applied to **ClientlessGroupPolicy**

Example 19-14 *Defining Port-Forwarding via CLI*

```
Chicago(config)# webvpn
Chicago(config-webvpn)# port-forward SSHServer 1100 192.168.1.102 22 Access to
internal Terminal/SSH Server
Chicago(config-webvpn)# group-policy ClientlessGroupPolicy attributes
Chicago(config-group-policy)# webvpn
Chicago(config-group-webvpn)# port-forward auto-start SSHServer
```

After the applet is loaded on the client, the user launches an SSH client such as Putty.exe to establish a connection to the server. The user must use the loopback IP address of 127.0.0.1 as the server address and port 1100 as the destination port. This redirects the connection over the SSL VPN tunnel to the server at 192.168.1.102 on port 22.

Configure Smart Tunnels

As discussed earlier, port forwarding provides access to applications that use static TCP ports. It modifies the HOSTS files on a host so that traffic can be redirected to a forwarder that encapsulates traffic over the SSL VPN tunnel. Additionally, with port forwarding, the Cisco ASA administrator needs to know to which addresses and ports the SSL VPN users will connect, and requires the SSL VPN users to have admin rights to modify the HOSTS file. To overcome some of the challenges related to port forwarding, Cisco ASA presents a new method to tunnel application–specific traffic called *smart tunnels*. Smart tunnels define which application can be forwarded over the SSL VPN tunnel, whereas port forwarding defines which TCP ports can be forwarded over the tunnel.

Smart tunnels do not require administrators to pre-configure the addresses of the servers running the application or the ports for those applications. In fact, smart tunnels work at the application layer by establishing a Winsock 2 connection between the client and the server. It loads a stub into each process for the application that needs to be tunneled and then intercepts socket calls through the security appliance. Thus, the principal benefit of smart tunnels over port forwarding is that users do not need to have administrative rights to use this feature.

Smart tunnels provide better performance than port forwarding and the user experience is simpler because they don't need to configure their applications for a loopback address and for a specific local port.

Note Smart tunnels require browsers with ActiveX, Java, or JavaScript support. Only 32-bit-based operating systems such as Windows Vista, XP, 2000, and MAC OS 10.4 and 10.5 are supported.

Like port forwarding, smart tunnel configuration is also a two-step process:

Step 1. Define a smart tunnel list.

Step 2. Map a smart tunnel list to a group policy

Step 1: Define a Smart Tunnel List

You must define a list of the applications that you want clientless SSL VPN users to access. You define a smart tunnel list by choosing **Configuration > Remote Access VPN > Clientless SSL VPN Access > Portal > Smart Tunnels > Add.** Specify a name for the new smart tunnel list. This list name has only local significance, and it is eventually used to map the smart tunnel attributes to a group policy, discussed in the next step. To define a specific application to be used for smart tunneling, click **Add** and specify the following attributes:

- **Application ID**—Name or ID of the application to be tunneled. The application ID has only local significance.
- OS—Select the host operating system where this application will be launched.
- **Process name or full path**—Name of the process to be tunneled. For example, if you want the SSH traffic to be tunneled through Putty, specify putty.exe as the process name.
- **Hash (optional)**—The hash is used only to provide additional security so that a user cannot change the filename and gain access to other resources over the tunnel.

As shown in Figure 19-35, a smart tunnel list called **SSHServer** is defined. The application ID is **Putty**, and the process name is **putty.exe**.

Note The process name should be in the system path. If the application is not in the system path, the smart tunnel will not be able to forward traffic. In such a case, define the full application path under Process Name.

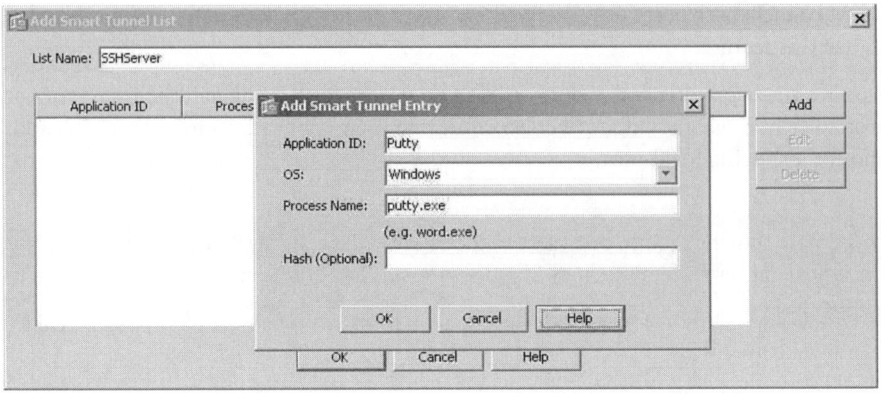

Figure 19-35 *Defining a Smart Tunnel List*

Step 2: Map a Smart Tunnel List to a Group Policy

The smart tunnel list, defined in Step 1, is then mapped to a user or group policy. Choose **Configuration > Remote Access VPN > Clientless SSL VPN Access > Group Policies > ClientlessGroupPolicy > Edit > Portal**, deselect the **Inherit** check box of the **Smart Tunnel List**, and choose the **SSHServer** list from the drop-down menu as illustrated in Figure 19-31. Additionally, select the **Auto Start** option to automatically install and start the applet as soon as the clientless SSL VPN user connects to the security appliance

Example 19-15 shows that a smart tunnel list called **SSHServer** is being defined to tunnel traffic for **putty.exe** application. This port forwarding list is then applied to **ClientlessGroupPolicy.**

Example 19-15 *Defining Smart Tunnel via the CLI*

```
Chicago(config)# webvpn
Chicago(config-webvpn)# smart-tunnel list SSHServer Putty putty.exe platform windows
Chicago(config-webvpn)# group-policy ClientlessGroupPolicy attributes
Chicago(config-group-policy)# webvpn
Chicago(config-group-webvpn)# smart-tunnel auto-start SSHServer
```

After the applet is loaded on the client, the user launches an SSH client such as Putty.exe to establish a connection to any server that offers SSH service.

Note Smart tunnel and port-forwarding sessions are not failover enabled. Users must start a new SSL VPN session if a failover occurs.

Configure Client-Server Plug-ins

For known applications, such as VNC, Remote Desktop, Telnet, and SSH, you can allow the clientless SSL VPN users to connect to the protected network when they use the supported applications. This way, when a clientless SSL VPN user is authenticated, the user can choose to launch an application plug-in such as VNC and connect to an internal server running the VNC application. Cisco provides the client-server plug-ins for VNCs, Remote Desktop, and SSH/Telnet. These plug-ins can be downloaded from Cisco's website and are packaged in the .jar file format. After the plug-ins are uploaded and activated on the security appliance, they can be defined as a URL similar to HTTP:// and cifs:// under a user web portal. For example, for Remote Desktop, an SSL VPN user selects rdp:// and specifies the IP address of the server to which it connects. If you want to use a plug-in not provided by Cisco Systems, you can contact third parties to develop the .jar file for their applications.

Before you use the client-server plug-ins, you must understand the following restrictions:

- If you have a proxy server between the SSL VPN client and the security appliance, the plug-ins do not work.
- The plug-ins support single sign-on (SSO). You must install the plug-in, add a bookmark entry to display a link to the server, and specify SSO support when adding the bookmark.
- You must have guest privilege mode at a minimum to use the plug-ins

Tip Some of the client-server plug-ins can be obtained from the following websites:

http://javassh.org

http://properjavardp.sourceforge.net

http://www.ultravnc.com

You must import the .jar files into the security appliance before you can activate a specific application for this feature. Choose **Configuration > Remote Access VPN > Clientless SSL VPN Access > Portal > Client-Server Plug-ins > Import** and select the plug-in name from the drop-down menu. You can select to import the plug-in from a workstation, from the local flash of the security appliance, or from a remote server using FTP. After you select the file you want to import, click **Import Now**. This should upload the file into the security appliance. In Figure 19-36, the **ssh-plugin.jar** file is being uploaded from a local workstation to be used for SSH and Telnet sessions.

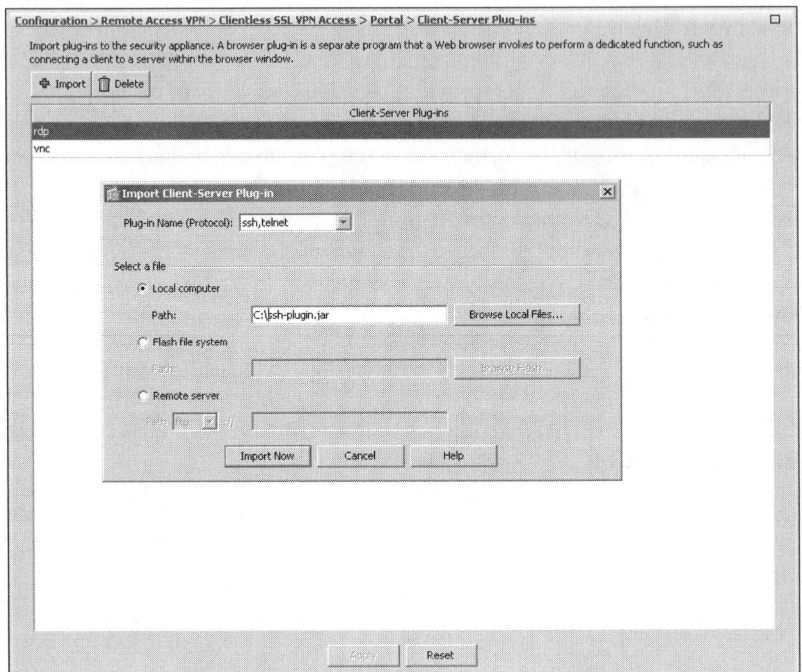

Figure 19-36 *Importing Client-Server Plug-ins*

After a plug-in has been uploaded, the authenticated clientless SSL VPN users can select the appropriate protocol from the Address drop-down menu.

Note In the current implementation, you must use ASDM to import client-server plug-ins.

Cisco Secure Desktop

Cisco Secure Desktop (CSD) provides a secure desktop environment to remote users after validating a number of security parameters on the client workstation. The purpose of CSD is to minimize the risk posed by the remote workstations. CSD collects the necessary information from those workstations. If the received information matches the preconfigured criteria, the security appliance can create a secure environment and optionally apply certain policies and restrictions on the user session. When this happens, users who want to access corporate resources from a hotel workstation or even from an Internet cafe can create a secure vault from which corporate resources can be accessed through a clientless tunnel or even for AnyConnect clients. When the user is finished using the public workstation, the vault can be destroyed to ensure that data cannot be accessed by a different user. CSD removes cookies, temporary files, browser history, and even any downloaded content when the secure vault is destroyed.

CSD is designed to help system administrators to enforce security policies for remote users. When a user tries to connect to the SSL VPN gateway, a client component is downloaded and installed on the client workstation. This client component scans the computer and gathers information such as the operating system, installed service pack, antivirus version, and installed personal firewall. This information is sent to the security appliance and then matched against predefined criteria. If the user's computer meets the criteria, the user is given appropriate access to the internal resources. If the criteria are not met, users are granted either limited or no access. For example, an administrator might require that all remote computers must have Windows XP with Service Pack 3 installed. If remote computers meet this condition, they are matched against a profile and then allowed to launch Secure Desktop or Cache Cleaner. If dynamic access policy (DAP) is used, then appropriate actions such as network restrictions can be applied to the user sessions.

Note Cache Cleaner is discussed in the next section, and DAP is discussed later in the chapter.

You can configure a number of parameters and group them together to define a specific location. When a remote host is scanned and the received information matches the criteria, the host is assigned that location. CSD supports five attributes to identify the location of an SSL VPN client. For example, you can define a range of IP addresses and a specific registry key, group them together, and declare them a location called "Work." When clients connect from this address range and have that registry key, they are given access based on the defined policies. The supported attributes include the following:

- Issuer or distinguish name in a certificate
- IP address of the client
- Presence of a file
- Presence of a registry key
- Operating system version (including Windows, Mac, and Linux)

CSD uses the proven industry standards such as Triple Data Encryption Standard (3DES) and Rivest Cipher 4 (RC4) to ensure security of the vault. If the logged-in user has administrative privileges, CSD uses the 3DES encryption algorithm, and if the user has lesser privileges, it uses RC4 to encrypt the data.

CSD Components

CSD consists of three components, discussed in the next sections.

Secure Desktop Manager

Secure Desktop Manager is a GUI-based application that allows administrators to define policies and locations for remote users. It currently supports two modules: Secure Desktop and Cache Cleaner. Secure Desktop Manager can be used only within ASDM to configure CSD properties, and thus you cannot use the CLI to configure it.

Secure Desktop

Secure Desktop, also known as Secure Session, is a module that creates an encrypted vault in the client computer and enables users to securely access local resources or even allows users to establish SSL VPN sessions. Files created in this vault are encrypted and cannot be accessed by the applications outside this secure desktop. The vault can be configured so that after a user disconnects a session, the vault can be destroyed.

By using Secure Desktop, users are given appropriate access to the corporate network after their system information, such as operating system and service pack, is detected. It can also detect whether the client workstation has any keystroke-logging applications installed before granting access. This system detection is transparent to the end user because CSD collects this information without any user intervention.

Cache Cleaner

Cache Cleaner securely removes local browser data such as web pages, history information, and cached user credentials when the SSL VPN session is over. Cache Cleaner is supported on the Windows operating systems as well as the Linux and MAC OS X systems.

When Cache Cleaner is launched on a client computer, it closes any existing browser windows and initiates the Cache Cleaner process. It monitors the browser data, and when the user logs out of the SSL VPN session, it closes the browser and cleans the cache associated with the SSL VPN session.

Note Cache Cleaner and Secure Desktop do not protect your computer from downloaded attachments after CSD is set up on the end user systems. Therefore they do not guarantee full system cleanup.

Cache Cleaner monitors only one browser application per SSL VPN session. If the initial session was established through Internet Explorer (IE), only IE-specific browser data is cleaned after the user session is terminated. If the user launches Firefox after Cache Cleaner has already started, the Firefox browser data is not wiped out after the user terminates a session.

CSD Requirements

Before you deploy CSD into a production environment, analyze your current system and network architecture to make sure that they meet the minimum versions of supported operating systems and Internet browsers.

Supported Operating Systems

When this book was written, Secure Desktop was supported only in the Windows environment. The supported Windows platforms include:

- Windows Vista 32-bit (x86) Service Pack 1
- Windows XP, including options with no service pack, Service Pack 1 through Service Pack 3
- Windows 2000, including options with no service pack, Service Pack 1, Service Pack 2, Service Pack 3, and Service Pack 4.

Windows XP and Vista 64-bit, MAC OS X 32-bit and 64-bit, and Linux-based operating system (both 32 and 64-bit) users can use Cache Cleaner on remote clients. You can also choose to use Cache Cleaner for Windows Vista, XP, and 2000 operating systems.

Mac OS X 10.4 and 10.5 and 32-bit Linux are listed as supported for host scan and prelogin assessment as well in CSD 3.2.1.

User Privileges

You do not have to be a system administrator to install CSD on a client machine. CSD can be installed on a host machine, using one of the following four methods.

- **ActiveX**—Requires administrative privileges
- **Microsoft Java VM**—Requires power user privileges
- **Sun Java VM**—Does not require power-user or administrative privileges
- **Executable**—Requires user to have executables rights.

Supported Internet Browsers

You can use the following browsers to manage, use, configure, and administer the currently released version of CSD. When this book was written, the released version of CSD was 3.4.2048.

- Internet Explorer version 6.0 Service Pack 1 and version 7.0
- Safari 2.0 and 3.1.1 on Mac OS X

- Mozilla 1.7.*x*
- Mozilla Firefox 1.5, 2.0 and 3.0

Internet Browser Settings

You must configure the appropriate security settings in your Internet browser before CSD can be installed through ActiveX, Java, or a binary executable. For example, in Internet Explorer, use the guidelines discussed in Table 19-8. You configure these settings by choosing **Tools > Internet Options > Security tab > Internet > Custom Level.**

Table 19-8 *Internet Browser Settings*

Attribute	Setting
ActiveX controls and plug-ins > Download signed ActiveX controls	Enable
ActiveX controls and plug-ins > Run ActiveX controls and plug-ins	Enable
Downloads > File download	Enable
Scripting > Active scripting	Enable
Scripting > Scripting of Java applets	Enable
Microsoft VM > Java permissions	High, medium, or low safety

CSD Architecture

CSD not only checks certain attributes on the client computer to ensure its compliance, but also enhances data security by providing an encrypted vault to authorized users. When a user wants to establish an SSL VPN session and CSD is enabled, the client and the gateway go through a number of steps, discussed here and illustrated in Figure 19-37.

Step 1. A user tries to request the SSL VPN login page by pointing his or her browser to the gateway IP address.

Step 2. The user session is redirected to a different web page (/start.html) because a secure desktop session has not been created. The gateway tries to install the Secure Desktop client component on the user's workstation using ActiveX, Java, or Executable mode.

Step 3. After installing the client component, the system is scanned and necessary information is collected from the client workstation. This information is forwarded to the gateway.

Step 4. The collected information is matched against the policies that are defined in Secure Desktop Manager and are stored in data.xml.

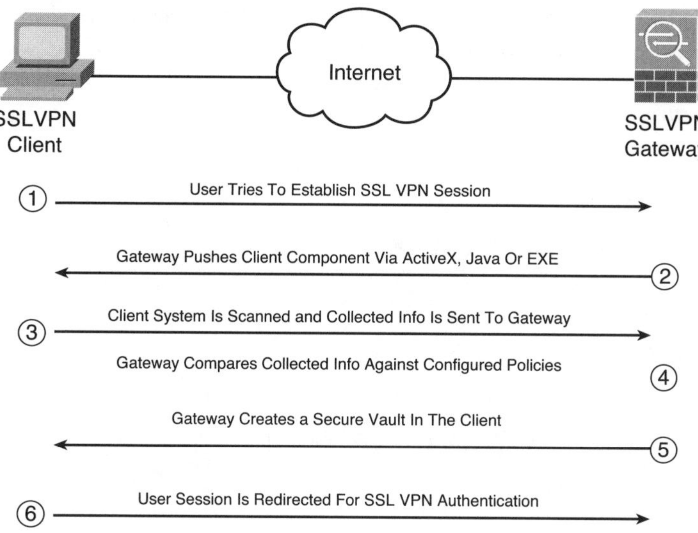

Figure 19-37 *CSD System Architecture*

Step 5. A secure desktop cookie is written on the client computer and the secure vault is created on the hard disk. The web session is redirected to the SSL VPN user login page.

Step 6. The user presents authentication credentials, and if authentication is successful, the clientless SSL VPN session (or even the AnyConnect client) is created.

The data.xml file contains CSD-specific configuration information, including:

- Location information
- Criteria for SSL VPN features

Configuring CSD

The configuration of CSD is broken into two steps:

Step 1. Load the CSD package

Step 2. Define Prelogin Sequences

Step 1: Load the CSD Package

You must load the CSD package in the local flash of the security appliance. If you are not sure whether you have CSD installed in your security appliance, choose **Tools > File Management** and look at the contents of the local flash. If you do not see a securedesktop-asa-3.x.xxx-k9.pkg file or a csd.x.x.xxx.pkg file, upload the file from the local flash of the management host to the flash of the security appliance. After the CSD file is uploaded, choose **Configuration > Remote Access VPN > Secure Desktop Manager > Setup** and click **Browse Flash** to select the CSD file. In Figure 19-38, a **csd_3.4.2048.pkg** file is selected from the flash. After the file is selected, select the **Enable Secure Desktop** option.

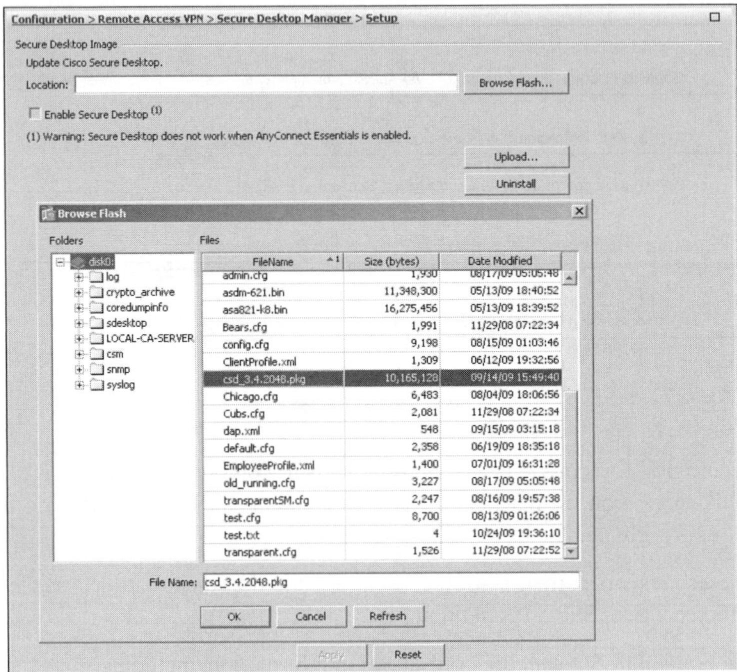

Figure 19-38 *Installing the CSD Package*

In Example 19-16, a CSD image called **csd_3.4.2048** is loaded from the local flash. CSD is also enabled globally in the security appliance.

Example 19-16 *Loading CSD*

```
Chicago(config)# webvpn
Chicago(config-webvpn)# csd image disk0:/csd_3.4.2048.pkg
Chicago(config-webvpn)# csd enable
```

> **Note** Starting from 8.2(1), the security appliance enables you to customize the Secure Desktop windows displayed to remote users. This includes changing the Secure Desktop background, text color, Cache Cleaner, and Keystroke Logger, to name a few options.

Step 2: Defining Prelogin Sequences

To configure CSD parameters, choose **Configuration > Remote Access VPN > Secure Desktop Manager > Prelogin Policy**. You can define a prelogin sequence that CSD will use to identify a host and match it to an appropriate profile. If the client's computer matches a certain profile, CSD can either create a Secure Desktop or launch Cache Cleaner. Configure Secure Desktop Manager and define the profiles and the respective policies for the SSL VPN users as follows:

- Define prelogin policies
- Assign CSD policy
- Identify keystroke loggers
- Define Secure Desktop general attributes
- Apply Secure Desktop restrictions
- Define Cache Cleaner policies
- Define Secure Desktop settings

Define Prelogin Policies

In the supported Windows, OS X, and Linux-based operating systems, you can define the potential locations from which the client computers might be connecting. For example, if your users connect from the office network, a home office network, and Internet cafes, you can define a location for each setup and give appropriate access to your users. For users connecting from the office network, you can classify those hosts fairly securely and allow a less restrictive environment. For users connecting from their home office, you can classify them as somewhat secure and apply more restrictive policies. For users connecting from Internet cafes, you can classify them as least secure and apply the most restrictive policies.

Note In the current implementation, you must use ASDM to configure CSD.

Throughout this chapter, we use three prelogin locations to build configurations. They include:

- **OfficeCorpOwned—**This location is defined for those workstations that establish an SSL VPN tunnel from the corporate-owned IP addresses. Additionally, the workstation must have a unique registry setting to identify it as a corporate-owned computer. If workstations match this profile, Secure Desktop or Cache Cleaner will not be launched.

Note Starting from 8.2(1), you can disable CSD for a particular Connection Profile. This option is useful if you want to allow AnyConnect clients to connect to a Connection Profile but you do not want to launch CSD for their corporate machines.

- **HomeCorpOwned**—This location is defined for those Windows computers that are corporate-owned but are employed by users who establish an SSL VPN tunnel from their home offices; these addresses do not match the corporate-owned address range. The workstations are classified as corporate owned by their unique registry settings. If workstations match this profile, Secure Desktop is launched.
- **InternetCafe**—This location is defined for those computers that do not match any of the previous profiles. Cache Cleaner is launched.

To define these profiles, choose **Configuration > Remote Access VPN > Secure Desktop Manager > Prelogin Policy**. You can define prelogin locations by having the workstations meet a number of criteria. CSD supports the following five ways to identify a host:

- **Certificates**—If your client workstations use unique computers, you can use the subject and the issuer names to match a specific profile. The subject and issuer names contain a number of subordinate fields such as common name (CN), organization (O), organizational unit (OU), and country (C). You can use one of the subordinate fields in the subject and issuer names to identify computers that match a specific profile. A registry check is applicable only for Windows-based operating systems.

Note To identify computers based on certificates, specify the values of the subordinate fields. For example, to identify computers based on organizational unit (OU), simply specify the value of OU but do not list "OU" in the names.

- **IP address range**—If you know the IP address space of client computers, use this feature to identify computers that match a profile. You can define one or multiple address spaces to identify computers.

Note If the client computer has multiple IP addresses, CSD uses the first identified IP address to match against a profile.

- **File setting**—You can use the location of a file to identify computers. This feature is useful if, for example, you want to identify a specific file to determine whether computers are corporate owned.
- **Registry setting**—You can use a registry key to identify computers. This feature is useful if you want to identify a specific registry location to determine whether computers are corporate owned. A registry check is applicable only for Windows-based operating systems.
- **Operating system version**—The host assessment provides the version of operating systems running on the remote workstation. The operating system check is for Windows 9*x*, 2000, XP, Vista, Mac OS X, and Linux. Secure Desktop is allowed only

for Windows Vista, XP and 2000 operating systems. For other operating systems including Windows, Cache Cleaner is supported.

> **Note** If you specify more than one registry key or file location, CSD applies an OR logical operation. For example, if you define the location of a registry key and define the location of a file, only one of the locations must be present for a host to be identified.

To configure a prelogin location, choose **Configuration > Remote Access VPN > Secure Desktop Manager > Prelogin Policy**, click the (+) icon, and select the appropriate check from the drop-down menu. As illustrated in Figure 19-39, a registry check is being done. If **HKEY_LOCAL_MACHINE\SOFTWARE\McAfee\VirusScan** exists, CSD continues on and performs other checks. If a workstation does not have this registry key, it is classified as “InternetCafe”.

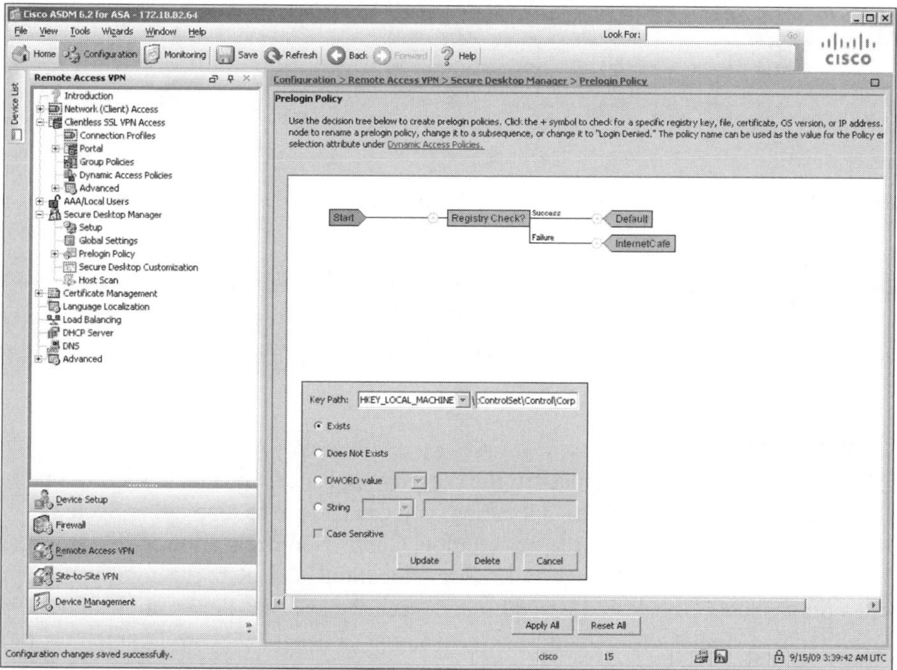

Figure 19-39 *Defining a Registry Check*

The workstations that have the registry setting are further assessed for additional checks. In Figure 19-40, workstations are checked for their IP addresses. If they are in the **192.168.1.0/24** subnet, they are identified as “OfficeCorpOwned” workstations. If they are not, they are identified as “HomeCorpOwned” workstations.

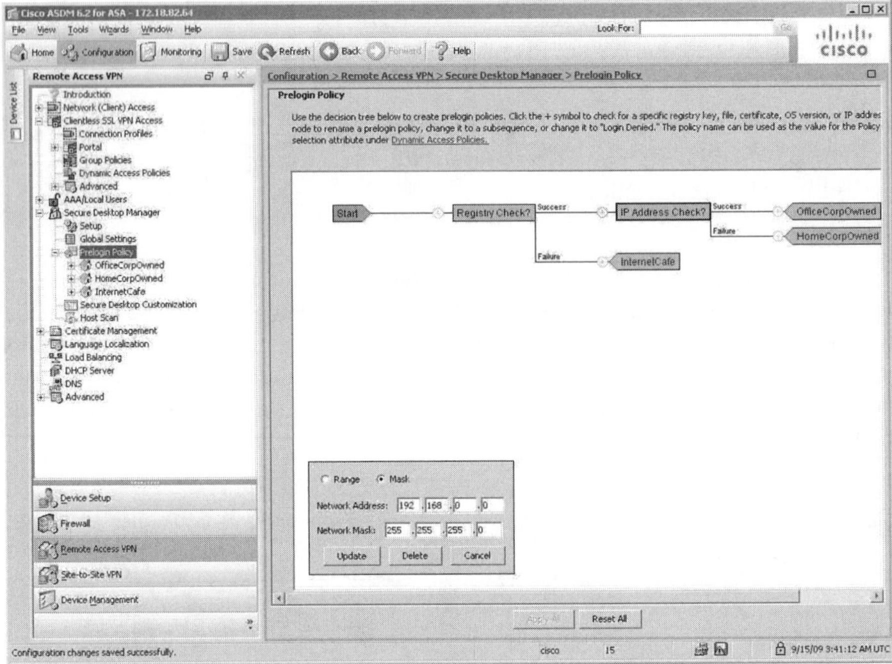

Figure 19-40 *Defining an IP Range Check*

Note If you want to identify a computer by locating a specific file in the system and ensuring the integrity of the file, you can find its checksum. To assist you with calculating the correct checksum of a file, CSD provides the crc32.exe application.

Assign CSD Policy

When a computer tries to connect to the security appliance, CSD matches it to one of the predefined locations. For each location, you can choose to load either Secure Desktop or Cache Cleaner on the workstation. Choose **Configuration > Remote Access VPN > Secure Desktop Manager > [Prelogin location]** and select the appropriate option. The option should be selected based on your security policies. For example, if a user is identified as a HomeCorpOwned workstation, you can enable Secure Desktop for those computers, as shown in Figure 19-41.

Identify Keystroke Loggers and Host Emulators

The robust implementation of CSD enables you to detect certain software-based keystroke loggers in a workstation and take appropriate actions before allowing a user's computer to create a secure environment. Keystroke loggers usually capture keystrokes without informing the legitimate user of the computer. These applications then send the captured information to a server, generally owned by hackers. If, for example, you have a keystroke logger installed on your computer and you are doing online banking, the

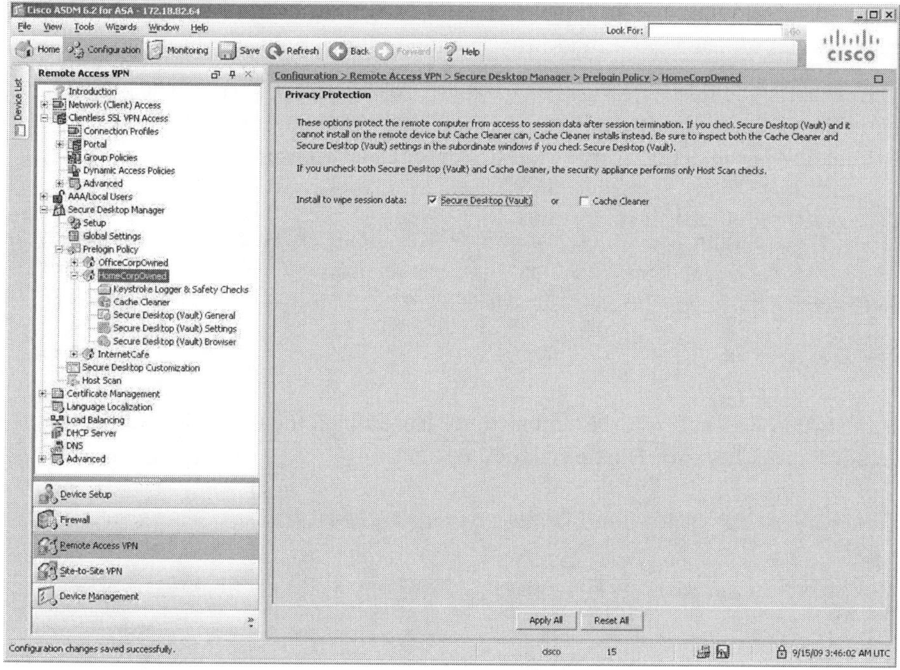

Figure 19-41 *Assigning a CSD Policy*

keystroke logger can potentially capture your user credentials and pass that information to a hacker, who can misuse your personal information for his or her advantage.

You can also detect host emulations to check whether a remote workstation is running any virtualization software. If the **Always Deny Access If Running Within Emulation** option is selected, remote workstations running emulation are not allowed to connect through the SSL VPN tunnel. If the **Always Deny Access If Running Within Emulation** option is not selected but host emulation detection is enabled, CSD prompts users to decide whether they want to continue with the SSL VPN session.

> **Note** Keystroke loggers are detected only when users have administrative rights to their workstations.

To prevent user computers that have a keystroke logger installed from establishing an SSL VPN tunnel, select **Keystroke Logger & Safety Checks** under the name of the location and enable the **Check for Keystroke Loggers** option. With this option enabled, the system scans and detects a keystroke-logging application on the workstation. If one is detected, the system prompts the user to identify the application as safe. However, if you do not trust user discretion, you can enable **Force Admin Control on List of Safe Modules** and manually identify which keystroke loggers are safe. Applications, such as

Corel PaintShop Pro, usually capture keystrokes to allow users to modify data easily. In that case, an administrator can identify PaintShop Pro as a safe application.

CSD enables you to define a list of safe keystroke-logger application. Click **Add** and then enter the module's path. After an application is added, it appears under List of Safe Modules. You can define as many keystroke-logging applications as you want.

> **Note** If Force Admin Control on List of Safe Modules is enabled, contents under List of Safe Modules are defined, and then you disable Force Admin Control on List of Safe Modules, CSD still keeps the content under List of Safe Modules. It simply deactivates the defined values.

As shown in Figure 19-42, the administrator has enabled the **Check for Keystroke Loggers** and **Check for Host Emulation** options.

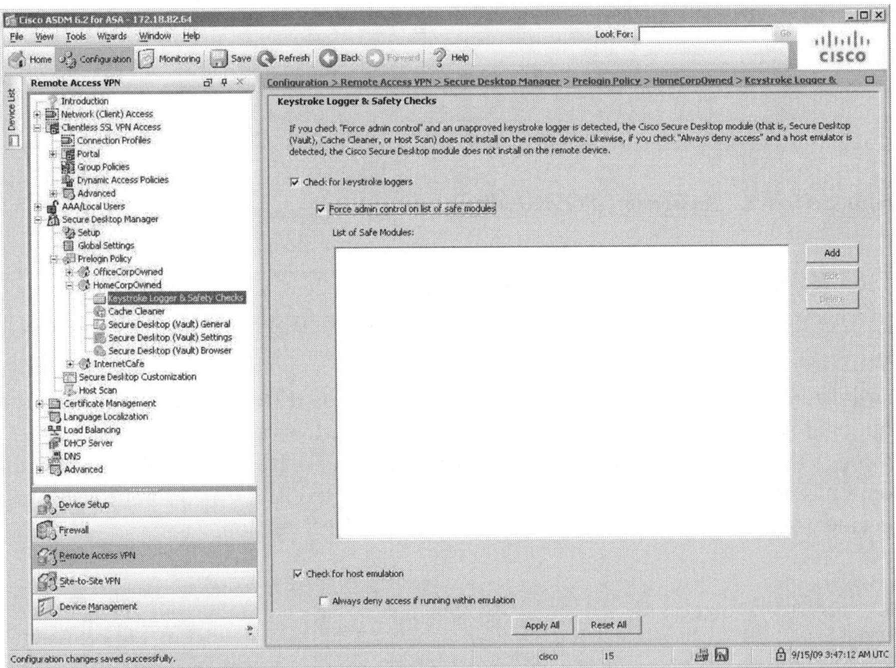

Figure 19-42 *Example of a Keystroke-Logging Application*

Define Secure Desktop (Vault) General Attributes

In CSD, you can set up general attributes that are applied to all SSL VPN sessions within a predefined location. For example, you may enable a feature to allow users to switch between Secure Desktop and Local Desktop. The supported Secure Desktop general attributes include:

- **Enable Switching Between Secure Desktop (Vault) and Local Desktop**—With this option enabled, the user has an option to switch back and forth between Secure Desktop and Local Desktop. In many cases, when an application is launched within Secure Desktop, it sends a notification or user prompt to the Local Desktop. Hence, you should enable this option if you need to switch to Local Desktop to respond to a prompt or query.
- **Enable Vault Reuse (User Chooses a Password)**—This option is useful if, for example, users use the same desktop computer in their office and home. Knowing that their computers are fairly secure at home, you can let them use the same vault that they had used before. This vault is protected by a password that can be up to 127 characters long. In CSD version 3.3, you can enable one of the two options under Enable Vault Reuse. The Suggest Application Uninstall upon Secure Desktop (Vault) Closing option prompts and recommends the user to uninstall Secure Session when it closes. On the other hand, the Force Application Uninstall upon Secure Desktop (Vault) Closing option uninstalls Secure Desktop on the remote workstation when users close it.
- **Enable Secure Desktop (Vault) Inactivity Timeout**—When this option is enabled, the system automatically closes the secure vault after a specified duration of inactivity. This option is useful for sessions that are left behind without the application having been properly closed. You should enable this option for those locations that are not secure, such as Internet cafes or untrusted host computers. If users are allowed to access critical or sensitive applications over the SSL VPN tunnel, you can configure a lower timeout value such as 5 minutes. If users access insensitive data, you can set a higher timeout such as 30 minutes.
- **Open Following Web Page After Secure Desktop (Vault) Closes**—As the name suggests, this option requires you to input a URL that you want to launch after Secure Desktop disconnects on a user computer. This option is useful if you want to redirect user web sessions to a website that lists a company's policies for SSL VPN usage.
- **Secure Delete**—When Secure Desktop is terminated, CSD converts all data to binary 0s. It then changes all vault space to binary 1s and eventually randomizes data to 0s and 1s. This entire process is considered one pass. You can change the default setting (from 3) to run this process multiple times. After it goes through all the configured passes, it eventually deletes the allocated space that was being used by Secure Desktop.
- **Launch the Following Application After Installation**—You can configure CSD to launch an application after Secure Desktop has been installed. This is useful if you require users to work on a specific application when they connect through an SSL VPN session. The application must reside in the Program Files folder in Windows-based operating systems.

As shown in Figure 19-43, the administrator has defined Secure Desktop General Attributes for the "HomeCorpOwned" Windows location. Users are allowed to switch desktops. The secure delete is set for five passes and the inactivity timeout for five minutes with audio alert.

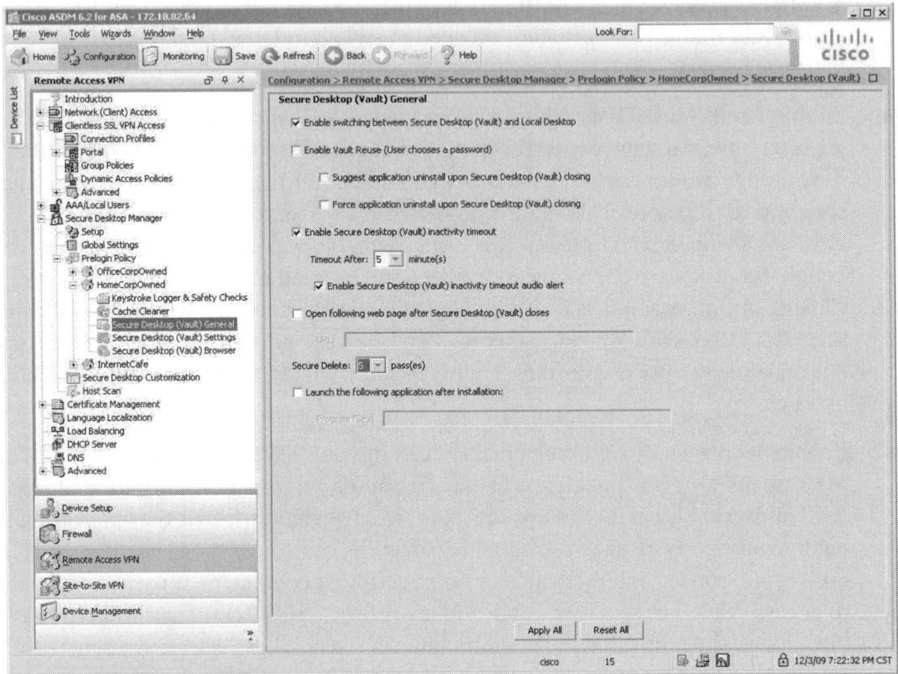

Figure 19-43 *Defining Secure Desktop General Attributes*

Apply Secure Desktop Restrictions

In addition to the global parameters that can be configured (discussed in the preceding section), you can apply certain restrictions to Secure Desktop to further enhance the level of security for SSL VPN sessions. These restrictions are defined in Secure Desktop (Vault) Settings under a predefined location. These restrictions include the following:

- **Restrict Application Usage to the Web Browser Only, with the Following Exceptions**—This option restricts the user to launch a browser other than the browser that originally initiated Secure Desktop. Choosing this option limits the user's ability to use other applications, but increases the level of security. For example, if a user launches Secure Desktop using Internet Explorer, he is denied the ability to launch a different browser, such as Firefox, from within Secure Desktop. This option enhances security on the system because features such as Cache Cleaner do not clean the cache if a different browser is launched. In CSD version 3.2.1 or higher, the Secure Desktop Manager inserts a text box so that you can also select a preconfigured application that can run on Secure Session. If the application you want to allow is not on the preconfigured list, you can type the name of the executable files into the text box.

Caution If your users access internal pages through Java and you apply application restrictions, make sure you allow the following entries to the browser list:

c:\program

java.exe

jp2launcher.exe

- **Disable Access to Network Drives and Network Folders**—With this option, a user is denied access to network folders and drives. This even includes printers and any network shares that use Server Message Block (SMB) protocols. You should enable this restriction for those locations that are the least secure so that unauthorized or illegitimate users do not access protected network shares or resources. Because CSD does not clean up files that are written to mapped network drives, it is strongly recommended that you enable this option.
- **Disable Access to Removable Drives and Removable Folders**—When this option is enabled, users are denied access to their portable drives such as thumb or external hard drives with the Secure Desktop environment. This restriction is recommended so that users cannot copy sensitive data on a portable drive when accessing data from insecure Windows locations.
- **Do Not Encrypt Files on Removable Drives**—With this option enabled, users cannot save encrypted files on portable drives. This option is grayed out if Disable Access to "Removable Drives and Removable Folders" is enabled.
- **Disable Registry Modification**—To restrict users from modifying the system registry within Secure Desktop, enable this option.
- **Disable Command Prompt Access**—If unauthorized users get access to a system running Secure Desktop, they can launch command-line-based attacks to corporate resources. You should deny users command-prompt access within Secure Desktop to prevent such scenarios.
- **Disable Printing**—If an illegitimate user gains access to a Secure Desktop environment, the user can print sensitive data such as software code on a local printer. You should prevent users in the least secure Windows locations from being able to print.
- **Allow Email Applications to Work Transparently**—With this option enabled, users can access their emails while requiring Secure Desktop to erase the deleted emails when the session terminates. The supported email clients include Microsoft Outlook Express, Microsoft Outlook, and Eudora Lotus Notes. This option allows users to save email attachments to the My Documents folder, which can be accessed from Secure Desktop and from the Local Desktop.

In Figure 19-44, the CSD administrator has enabled all restrictions for the "HomeCorpOwned" predefined location. Additionally, **Microsoft Word (winword.exe)** is selected as an exception for a Secure Desktop session.

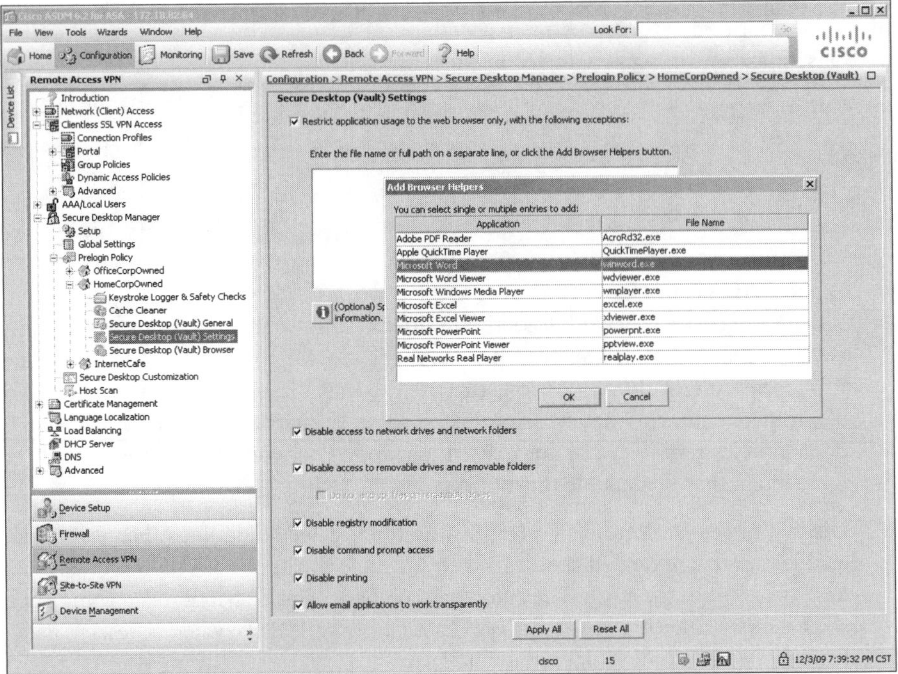

Figure 19-44 *Enabling Secure Desktop Restrictions*

Define Cache Cleaner Policies

As discussed earlier in this chapter, Cache Cleaner securely removes local browser data such as web pages, history information, and cached user credentials. When Cache Cleaner is launched on a client computer, it closes any existing browser windows, monitors browser data after a new browser window is launched. When the user logs out of the SSL VPN session, it closes the browser and cleans the cache associated with the SSL VPN session. Cache Cleaner can be enabled or disabled when you select a predefined location as shown in Figure 19-41.

Cache Cleaner can be launched for any location, if enabled. Table 19-9 lists the options available when Cache Cleaner is enabled for a Windows location.

Table 19-9 *Available Cache Cleaner Options*

Available Option	Description
Launch Hidden URL After Installation	After Cache Cleaner is installed, you might want the system to access a hidden URL. This way you can track the users and know whether they have successfully installed Cache Cleaner. This is recommended if you want to know how many users use Cache Cleaner.
Show Success Message at the End of Successful Installation (Windows only)	With this option, users are shown a message that Cache Cleaner has been successfully installed. This is recommended so that users know that the cache-cleaning process has started on their computers.
Launch Cleanup upon Timeout Based on Inactivity	To start the cache cleanup process after users have been idle for a while, you can enable this option and specify the timeout value in minutes. If this option is enabled, the default timeout value is 5 minutes.
Launch Cleanup upon Closing of All Browser Instances or SSL VPN Connection	This option is useful if you want to start the Cache Cleaner after users close all their browser windows.
Disable Cancel button	If this option is enabled, the remote user is prevented from cancelling the deletion of the cache.
Clean the Whole Cache in Addition to the Current Session Cache (IE Only)	If this option is enabled, Cache Cleaner removes the entire Internet Explorer (IE) cache, including the data and files that were generated before CSD was launched.
Secure Delete	When Secure Desktop is terminated, CSD converts all cached data to binary 0s. It then changes all cached data to 1s and eventually randomizes all data to 0s and 1s. This entire process is considered one pass. You can change this default setting to run multiple times. After it goes through all the configured passes, it eventually deletes the allocated space that was being used by Secure Desktop.

In Figure 19-45, the administrator has enabled Launch Hidden URL After Installation and added a hidden URL of **http://www.securemeinc.com/cachecleaner.html** for the HomeCorpOwned location. All users that match this profile will be shown a message that the Cache Cleaner process has successfully started. If user sessions are inactive for 10 minutes or if users close all browser windows, the Cache Cleaner process starts. Cache Cleaner also removes the entire IE cache.

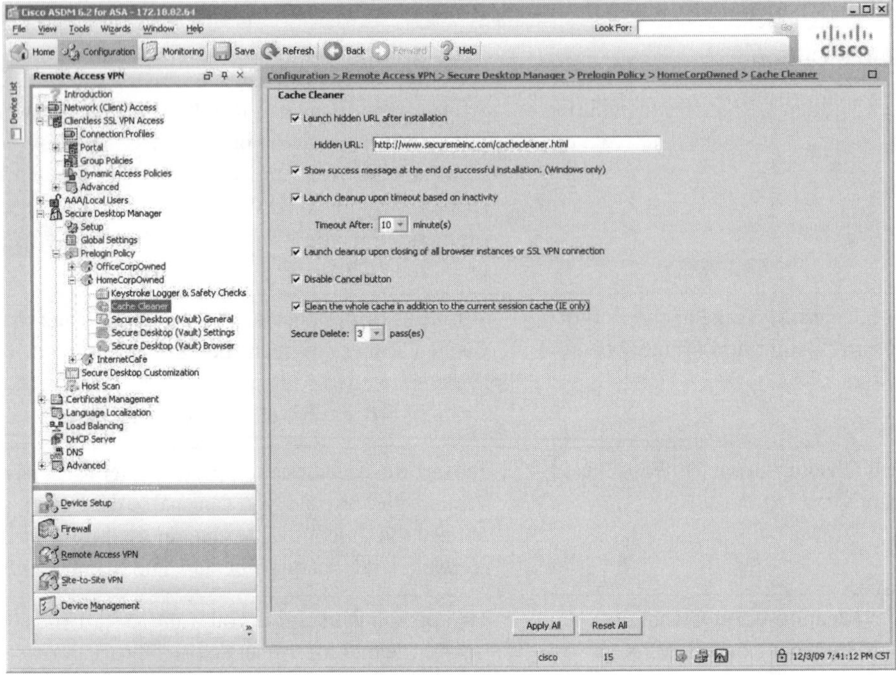

Figure 19-45 *Defining Cache Cleaner Policies*

Define Secure Desktop (Vault) Browser Settings

Using Secure Desktop, you can present users with a predefined list of browser bookmarks. These bookmarks are generally the most common URLs (or favorite sites) that users connect to after their SSL VPN session is established. These bookmarks are defined under the Secure Desktop (Vault) Browser of a Windows location. You can customize these bookmarks under folders, or if just a few bookmarks exist, define them under the parent folder.

Host Scan

Host Scan is a modular component of CSD. It is installed on the end host before the user logs in to the security appliance over an SSL VPN tunnel. If CSD is in use, Host Scan can collect some important endpoint attributes and pass them to other processes such as DAP for appropriate action. Host Scan can scan an end host for information that you want to collect, such as registry entries, filenames, and process names. Host Scan functionality can be greatly enhanced if an advanced Endpoint Assessment license is used, which can collect information regarding antivirus and antispyware applications, firewalls, operating systems, and associated updates.

Host Scan, in CSD version 3.4.2048, is currently supported in

- Microsoft Windows Vista (32- and 64-bit) with Service Pack 1

- Microsoft Windows XP (32-bit) with Service Pack 2 and 3, and Microsoft Windows XP (64-bit) with Service Pack 2
- Microsoft Windows 2000 with Service Pack 4
- Mac OS X 10.4 and 10.5 (32- and 64-bit)
- Linux (32- and 64-bit biarch) systems. Successfully tested Redhat Enterprise 3 and 4, Fedora Core 4 and later, and Ubuntu

> **Note** Host Scan functionality occurs after CSD goes through the prelogin assessment and before DAP enforces its policies.

Host Scan Modules

Host Scan currently supports three modules:

- Basic Host Scan
- Endpoint Assessment
- Advanced Endpoint Assessment

Basic Host Scan

Basic Host Scan can be used to identify the following information on a remote computer:

- Operating systems and their respective service packs
- Specific process names (in Windows operating systems only)
- Specific filenames (in Windows operating systems only)
- Registry keys (in Windows operating systems only)

You can use basic Host Scan to determine whether a remote workstation matches a specific user profile by checking information such as its operating system, registry, files, or even an actively running process. When the basic Host Scan is run on a computer, it sends the operating system, service pack information, and any checks that you configure within CSD to the security appliance.

Endpoint Assessment

Endpoint Assessment scans a remote computer for a large collection of firewall, antivirus, and antispyware software, as well as their associated signatures and definition updates. The collected information is then forwarded to the security appliance so that a specific action can be taken and enforced by dynamic access policy (DAP). You do not need to purchase any specific licenses to configure a security appliance to check for the presence of personal firewalls, antivirus software, and antispyware applications.

Advanced Endpoint Assessment

Advanced Endpoint Assessment is a licensed feature that enables you to update noncompliant computers to meet the requirements of an enterprise's security policy. For example, if a remote user, running an older version of an antivirus definition, logs in to a security appliance, the Advanced Endpoint Assessment feature can attempt to update the definition on the remote workstation. The Advanced Endpoint Assessment is independent of the basic Host Scan and Endpoint Assessment, which were discussed earlier.

Advance Endpoint Assessment benefits you by forcing the following actions:

- Turn on an antivirus or antispyware application scan functionality if it is disabled or if it is stopped.
- Update the signature definition files for the antivirus or antispyware applications if they have not been updated for a configurable number of days.
- Apply a number of configured rules to the supported personal firewalls.

Configuring Host Scan

You can configure Host Scan by choosing **Configuration > Remote Access VPN > Secure Desktop Manager > Host Scan.**

> **Note** In the current implementation, you must use ASDM to configure Host Scan.

Set Up Basic Host Scan

To configure CSD to scan a remote computer for basic information, click **Add** under Basic Host Scan and select the type of basic scan you would like to configure. As mentioned in the previous section, a basic Host Scan can identify registry keys, active processes, and files located on the remote workstation. For example, if you want CSD to scan a registry key from the workstation and based on that information you want to apply appropriate action by DAP, add Registry Scan under Basic Host Scan. The system prompts you to configure the following attributes:

- **Endpoint ID**—Specify a meaningful name or unique string that you can later use under DAP to check the endpoint attributes. This endpoint ID is case sensitive. You can, for example, use Corp-Registry as an endpoint ID.
- **Entry Path menu**—Select the initial path of the registry key from the drop-down menu. For example, if the registry key you want to scan resides at HKEY_LOCAL_MACHINE\SYSTEM\CurrentControlSet\Control\Corp, select HKEY_LOCAL_MACHINE from the drop-down menu.
- **Entry Path field**—Specify the complete name of the registry key, except for the initial directory path that you provided on the Entry Path menu. For example, if the registry key you want to scan resides at HKEY_LOCAL_MACHINE\SYSTEM\CurrentControlSet\Control\Corp, specify

SYSTEM\CurrentControlSet\Control\Corp as the Entry Path field, as shown in Figure 19-46. Click **OK** when you are finished defining the attributes.

Similarly, you can add a basic Host Scan for active processes and files residing on the remote workstation. To add a process scan, click **Add** and select **Process Scan**. To add a file scan, click **Add** and select **File Scan**. Refer to Table 19-10 for information on configuring file and process scans for a basic Host Scan.

Table 19-10 *Basic Host Scan Configuration*

Scan Type	Endpoint ID	Scan Setting	Example
File scan	A unique ID such as Corp-File-Check	Specify the complete path and filename, such as C:\Program Files\SecureMe\ID.hid, under File Path.	Endpoint-ID: Corp-File-Check File path: C:\Program Files\SecureMe\ID.hid
Process scan	A unique ID such as Corp-Process-Check	Specify the process name that you want to scan, such as mcshield.exe, under Process Name.	Endpoint-ID: Corp-Process-Check Process name: mcshield.exe

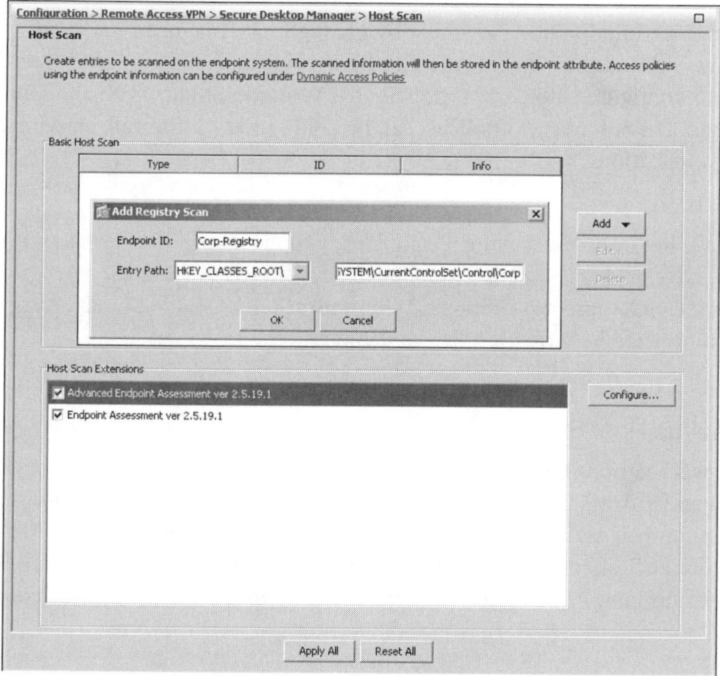

Figure 19-46 *Defining a Registry Key Scan*

Enable Endpoint Host Scan

Enable Endpoint Assessment by choosing **Configuration > Remote Access VPN > Secure Desktop Manager > Host Scan** and then selecting the **Endpoint Assessment ver w.x.y.z** check box, where w.x.y.z is the version of Endpoint Host Scan you are using. Figure 19-46 illustrates Endpoint Assessment as being enabled and running version 2.5.19.1. After it is enabled, the Endpoint Assessment can scan for antivirus, personal firewall, and antispyware applications and updates.

After a user's workstation passes through prelogin assessment, CSD scans the remote computer, using the endpoint assessments–defined checks, and forwards the results to the DAP engine for further action. These scan results are used as a condition for the completion of a clientless SSL VPN connection (or even a Cisco AnyConnect connection).

Set Up an Advanced Endpoint Host Scan

You must install the Advanced Endpoint Assessment license before you can use the Advanced Endpoint Host Scan feature. If a license is already installed, navigate to **Configuration > Remote Access VPN > Secure Desktop Manager > Host Scan** and then select the **Advanced Endpoint Assessment ver w.x.y.z** check box, where w.x.y.z is the version of Advanced Endpoint Host Scan you are using. After it is enabled, you can update remote hosts that are noncompliant so that they can meet the configured security requirements.

Configure the Advanced Endpoint Assessment by highlighting **Advanced Endpoint Assessment ver w.x.y.z** and then clicking the **Configure** button. A new window opens that enables you to configure enforcement policies for Windows, Mac OS X, and Linux-based workstations. The enforcement policies can be configured for firewall, antivirus, and antispyware applications.

Note If this option is not available on your Cisco ASA, you must acquire a new activation key that has the advanced assessment feature enabled from Cisco Systems. After you have the new key, you can activate it by choosing **Configuration > Device Management > System Image/Configuration > Activation Key** and entering the new key.

Configure Antivirus Host Scan

To check remote workstations for antivirus compliance and to update noncompliant computers, click **Add** under AntiVirus. A new window opens with a list of all the supported antivirus vendors and their antivirus products. Select the antivirus vendor and product that you use in your environment from the list and click **OK** when finished. You can enable a number of options, if your antivirus application supports them. They include the following:

- **Force File System Protection**—To make sure that the remote workstations scan any received files against the antivirus process, enable this option. If the received file contains a virus, the antivirus software should detect the virus and file access is blocked.

- **Force Virus Definitions Update**—To force the remote workstations to check for a virus definition update, enable this option. This option is beneficial if you do not want workstations running older antivirus definitions to connect to your network. If this option is enabled, you must specify the age in days that triggered the last update.

Configure Firewall Host Scan

To check remote workstations for personal firewall compliance, click **Add** under Personal Firewall. A new window opens with a list of all the supported firewall vendors and their respective products. Select the firewall vendor and product that you use in your environment from the list and click **OK** when finished. You can also configure a firewall action if your firewall application supports it. This option is useful if you want to make sure that the remote workstation has an active firewall process running. Select **Force Enable** or **Force Disable** from the drop-down menu. Certain firewalls also support configuring specific rules. For example, you can configure a Microsoft Windows Vista firewall to allow or block certain applications from processing traffic on specific ports.

Configure AntiSpyware Host Scan

To set up the security appliance to scan the remote workstation for antispyware, click **Add** under AntiSpyware. You can check remote workstations for antispyware compliance and update noncompliant computers. A new window opens with a list of all supported antispyware vendors and their respective products. Select the antispyware vendor and product that you use in your environment from the list and click **OK** when finished. Similar to the antivirus scan option, you can also force the remote workstations to check for antispyware definition updates. This way, you can restrict workstations from connecting to your network if they are running older antispyware definitions. To enable this option, select **Force Spyware Definitions Update** and specify the age in days that triggered the last update.

In Figure 19-47, the administrator is setting up the Advanced Endpoint Assessment. He has enabled McAfee VirusScan Enterprise 8.*x* for an antivirus check and Cisco Security Agent 5.*x* for a personal firewall check.

Dynamic Access Policies

In remote-access setups, such as SSL VPN, it is becoming extremely difficult to correctly identify users' environments. A remote user may establish an SSL VPN tunnel from his corporate-owned workstation in the morning, connect to the corporate resources from an Internet café in the afternoon and then connect to the same corporate resources from home in the evening. Moreover, if you are managing a remote-access solution, it is challenging to map appropriate user authorization attributes based on their connection type. To provide a solution to these issues, Cisco introduced *dynamic access policies* (DAP).

DAP is defined as the collection of access control attributes that is specific to a user's session. These policies are generated dynamically after user authorization attributes have been evaluated, such as the tunnel type to which the user is connecting and the appropriate action, such as access lists or filters is determined. After a DAP policy is generated, it is applied to the user's session to allow or deny access to internal resources.

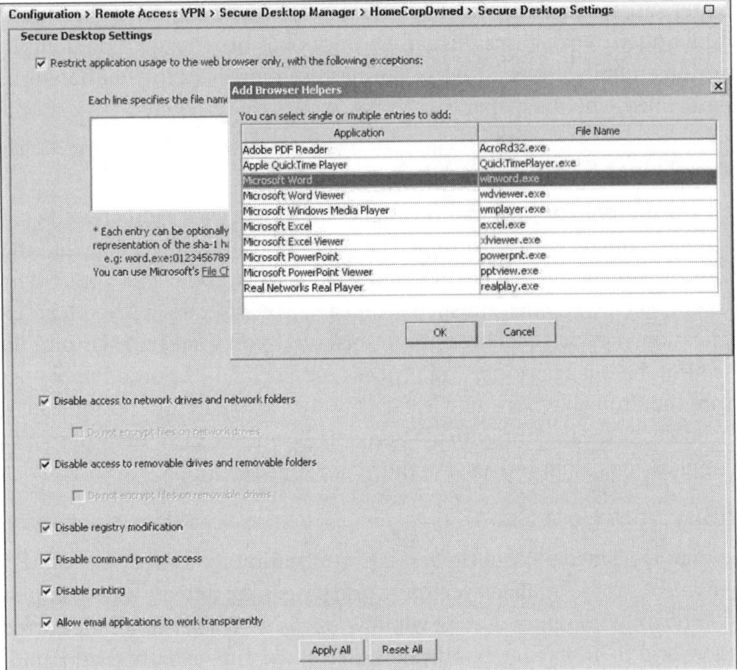

Figure 19-47 *Setting Up Advanced Endpoint Assessment*

For example, consider a user who connects to the security appliance from two different machines for the SSL VPN tunnel. When he connects from his corporate laptop and is running Cisco Security Agent (CSA) as the firewall, he is given full access to the network via the AnyConnect client. However, if he connects from his home machine, he is only given access to a limited number of servers over the clientless SSL VPN tunnel.

Note DAP also supports a number of other security appliance features such as IPsec and Cut-through-Proxy.

DAP Architecture

As mentioned earlier, DAP analyzes the posture assessment result of a host and applies dynamically generated access policies when a user session is established. It is designed to complement the authentication, authorization, and accounting (AAA) services by aggregating the locally defined attributes with the received attributes from the AAA server. In the case of an authorization attribute conflict, the locally defined attribute is selected. Therefore, it is possible to generate DAP authorization attributes by aggregating multiple DAP records from the AAA server and the posture assessment information for a user session.

DAP supports a number of posture assessment methods to collect endpoint security attributes. They include the following:

- **Cisco Secure Desktop**—CSD collects the file information, registry key values, running processes information, operating system information, and policy information from an end workstation.
- **Cisco NAC**—For Network Admission Control deployments, you can use the posture assessment string passed by the CS-ACS server.
- **Host Scan**—Host Scan is a modular component of CSD. It provides information such as antivirus, antispyware, and personal firewall software information about an end host.

The posture assessment information from end hosts can be complemented by the authorization attributes from the AAA server, such as RADIUS or LDAP.

DAP architecture consists of the following components:

- DAP records
- DAP selection configuration file
- DAP selection rules

DAP Records

The DAP records (DAPR) contain access policy attributes, such as user connection type and user membership, and the selection criteria. These records are defined locally on the security appliances. The selection criteria determine what DAP records should be selected during a tunnel negotiation.

DAP Configuration File

DAP stores its configuration in an XML file (DAP.XML) that is located in the flash of a security appliance. This file contains all the selection criteria for each DAPR.

DAP Selection Rules

The selection rules are simply the Boolean conditions that identify what DAPRs should be selected when a session gets negotiated. These selection rules reside in the DAP configuration file.

DAP Sequence of Events

When a user tries to establish an SSL VPN tunnel (whether clientless or AnyConnect) to the security appliance and DAP is enabled, the following sequence of events occurs:

Step 1. The user negotiates an SSL VPN tunnel and is presented with a login page.

Step 2. The security appliance collects user credentials and passes them to an authentication server.

Step 3. If the user credentials are valid, the user is authenticated and the security appliance receives authorization attributes from the authentication server.

Step 4. The posture assessment process is invoked by the appropriate process, such as Cisco Secure Desktop (CSD).

Step 5. Based on the assessment results, the DAP access policy attributes are requested for the user session. The DAP records are selected based on the assessment results collected in the previous step.

Note DAP is supported in a single routed mode security appliance.

Configuring DAP

When a user tries to establish a connection, DAP can analyze the posture assessment result of a remote host and apply access policies that are dynamically generated. A user connection might match multiple DAP records. For example, you can have a DAP record that scans only the remote workstations for a registry key. You can have another DAP record that checks the remote computer for an active process. If a remote workstation has the registry key and the process is active as well, that workstation matches against both DAP records. In this case, the security appliance combines both records dynamically and applies an aggregated access policy to a user connection.

The security appliance has a default DAP record called DfltAccessPolicy. This DAP record cannot be deleted and can contain only access policy attributes. It does not allow you to define any AAA or endpoint selection attributes. It is applied to all sessions that do not match any configured DAP records. By default, the DfltAccessPolicy does not restrict a session and allows traffic to pass through without imposing any access policies.

Note The default behavior of DfltAccessPolicy is identical to pre-DAP-supported security appliance versions (pre 8.0), where no policy enforcement existed on user sessions.

Configure DAP by choosing either of the following navigation paths:

- **Configuration > Remote Access VPN > Network (Client) Access > Dynamic Access Policies**
- **Configuration > Remote Access VPN > Clientless SSL VPN Access > Dynamic Access Policies**

Create a new DAP record by clicking **Add.** ASDM opens a new window, where you can specify a name for this policy. The security appliance also enables you to specify a priority for this record. The priority is used to logically order the DAP records in case a user session matches multiple DAP records. The higher the number of a DAP record, the higher the priority.

For each DAP record, specify selection criteria and configure appropriate actions. For ease of understanding, DAP configuration is divided into the following three subconfiguration options:

- Select AAA attributes
- Select endpoint attributes
- Define access policies

Select an AAA Attributes

Because DAP complements the AAA process, the security appliance can select DAP records based on AAA authorization attributes that it receives from the following storages:

- Cisco
- LDAP
- RADIUS

Table 19-11 defines the attributes that you can select within ASDM.

Table 19-11 *Supported AAA Attributes*

Attribute Type	Supported Attribute	Maximum Length	Attribute Description
Cisco	username	128	Authenticated username.
Cisco	Group Policy	64	Group policy that is applied to user connections. This group policy can be locally defined or can be sent to the appliance via the Class attribute (IETF attribute 25).
Cisco	ipaddress	Not Applicable	Assigned framed IP address.
Cisco	connection Profile	64	Tunnel group name to which the user connects.
LDAP	memberOf	128	LDAP attribute value.
RADIUS	RADIUS attribute ID	128	RADIUS attribute value.

Note You can leverage the advanced option under DAP policy construction by using Lua, which is a lightweight, fast, and powerful scripting language. For more information about Lua, refer to http://www.lua.org. To define AAA attributes under the advanced section, add the aaa and then the attribute type, followed by the attribute name. For example, if you want to define a Cisco username using Lua, you would specify it as **aaa.cisco.username.**

You can create one or multiple AAA attribute pairs to define a condition so that a specific DAP can be selected. In case you have more than one attribute pair defined, you can specify a logical operation (any, all, or none). For example, if you want users who connect to a tunnel group of **employees** or users who are members of a group **fullaccess** to be a part of the same DAP policy, select **User Has ANY of the Following AAA Attribute Values.** If you want users to match all conditions before a DAP policy can be selected, choose **User Has ALL of the Following AAA Attribute Values.** Additionally, you can select **User Has NONE of the Following AAA Attribute Values** if you want to select a DAP action and the authenticated user does not match any defined conditions.

Using the LDAP attribute type, you can leverage the native LDAP response attributes. The **memberOf** attribute of Active Directory specifies the distinguished name (DN) string of a group record. Specifically, the common name (CN) in the DN string is considered for group mapping. For example, if you are using LDAP authorization and you want to select users who are members of a CN called Employees, add the following under AAA attribute:

AAA Attribute Type: LDAP

Attribute ID: memberOf

Value: "=" from the drop-down menu, and "Employees" as value

Note Using Lua, you can configure the LDAP memberOf as follows: **aaa.ldap.memberOf=Employees.**

Like LDAP, the RADIUS attribute type can also leverage the native RADIUS response attributes. These attributes are configured as attribute numbers and value pairs in the DAP record. For example, if you are using RADIUS authorization and you want to select users who belong to the **class** attribute of **Employees**, add the following under AAA attribute:

AAA Attribute Type: RADIUS

Attribute ID: 25

Value: "=" from the drop-down menu, and "Employees" as value

Note The attribute ID is always the attribute number; you cannot use the attribute name. Using Lua, you can configure the RADIUS class attribute as follows: **aaa.radius.25=Employees.**

In Figure 19-48, the SecureMe Inc. administrator is creating a new DAP entry called **Clientless-DAP.** The description **This Policy is applied to employees logging in through Clientless SSLVPN hosts** is being added. SecureMe prefers to apply this policy for users who connect to the security appliance tunnel group of **SecureMeClientlessTunnel** and are members of the LDAP directory group attribute of **Employees.**

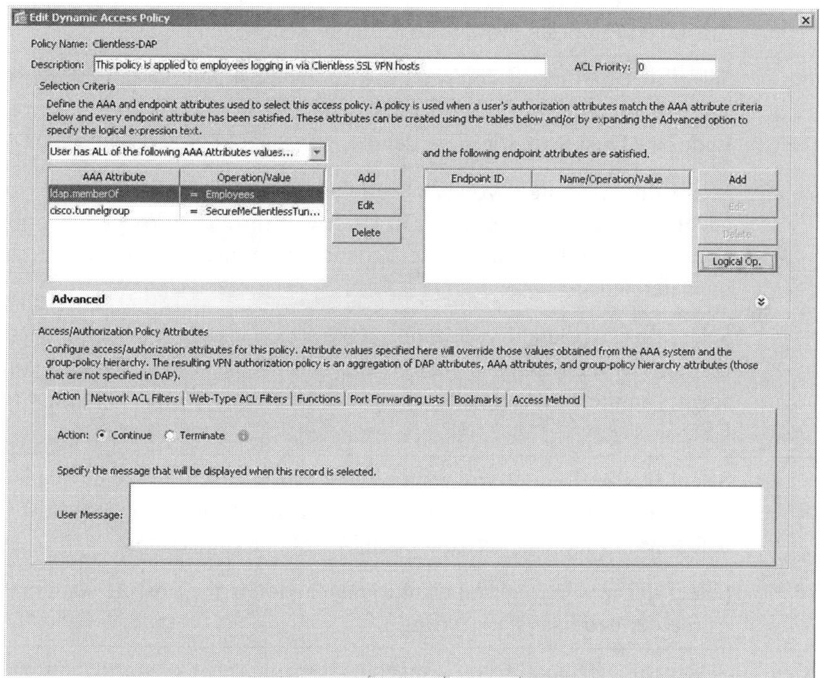

Figure 19-48 *Defining a AAA Attribute*

Selecting Endpoint Attributes

After defining the AAA attributes, you can optionally select the endpoint attributes. These attributes are collected by a number of sources, including Host Scans (basic, Endpoint, or Advanced Endpoint), Secure Desktop, and NAC. The AAA attributes are validated during user authentication, whereas the endpoint attributes are collected by the security appliance prior to user authentication. Table 19-12 presents all the available attributes that you can select and configure under endpoint attributes.

> **Note** When defining AAA attributes as well as endpoint attributes, DAP uses a logical **AND** operation between the two fields to determine a match.
>
> DAP also uses a logical **AND** operation among all the configured endpoint attribute categories (such as antispyware, antivirus, and file).
>
> DAP also uses a logical **OR** operation among all the endpoints of the same type. You can change this operation to a logical **AND** by clicking on the **Logical Op** button and selecting the **Match All** radio button for a particular type.

Table 19-12 *Available Endpoint Attributes*

Endpoint Attribute Type	Attribute Description
Anti-spyware	Select this attribute if you want to scan the host computer for antispyware. This option requires the use of CSD. Review the sections on Advanced Endpoint Host Scan for more details.
Anti-virus	Select this attribute if you want to scan the host computer for antivirus. This option requires the use of CSD. Review the sections on Advanced Endpoint Host Scan for more details.
Application	Select this attribute if you want to take action if the users connect from clientless, AnyConnect, IPsec, L2TP, or Cut-through-Proxy connections. You can even take action if users connect from methods other than the ones defined.
File	Select this attribute if you want to take action if the users' computers contain the file that you specify here. This uses endpoint IDs that you specify in the CSD's Host Scan option. This option requires the use of CSD.
Device	Select this attribute if you want to take action based on the device-level information from the host machine. You can take actions based hostname, MAC address, active version of CSD on the endhost.
NAC	Select this attribute if you want to take action if the posture state matches the defined user status string.
Operating system	Select this attribute if you want to take action if the operating system and the service pack of the end host match the configured operating system and service pack. This option requires the use of CSD.
Personal firewall	Select this attribute if you want to scan the host computer for a personal firewall. This option requires the use of CSD. Review the sections on Advanced Endpoint Host Scan for more details.
Policy	Select this attribute if you want to take action if the prelogin location of a user session matches the configured policy. This option requires the use of CSD.
Process	Select this attribute if you want to take action if the user's computer is running the process specified here. This uses endpoint IDs specified in CSD's Host Scan option. This option requires the use of CSD.
Registry	Select this attribute if you want to take action if the users' computers contain the registry entry specified here. This uses endpoint IDs specified in CSD's Host Scan option. This option requires the use of CSD.

In Figure 19-49, SecureMe Inc. is checking the prelogin location and operating system of the remote workstations. For this DAP record, the users' computers must meet the prelogin location of **OfficeCorpOwned**, and the operating system must match **Windows XP Service Pack 3**.

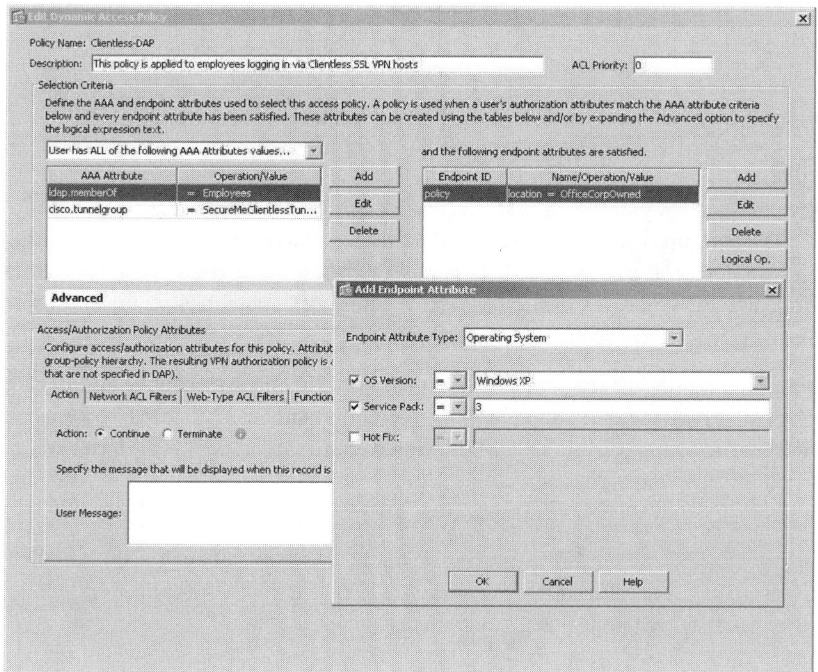

Figure 19-49 *Defining an Endpoint Attribute*

Defining Access Policies

After selecting the AAA and the endpoint attributes, the next step is to configure the policies that you want to apply to user sessions that match the attributes. You can configure VPN access attributes for a specific DAP record by using procedures outlined later in this chapter. For example, if a user's AAA and endpoint attributes match a DAP record, you can choose to allow that connection but apply certain ACLs to restrict user traffic. The DAP enforcements take precedence over other enforcement policies, whether those be AAA filters, user or group policies, or tunnel group attributes.

As an administrator, you can configure a limited set of attribute values for a DAP record. ASDM provides seven configuration tabs to configure such attribute values:

- Action
- Network ACL Filters

- Web-Type ACL Filters
- Functions
- Port Forwarding Lists
- Bookmarks
- Access Method

The configuration of these tabs is discussed in the following sections.

Action Tab

The Action tab enables you to select which action will be enforced for a single DAP record. If the configured AAA and endpoint attributes match the received information from a user session, you can choose to either allow or terminate the session for that DAP record. Additionally, you can show a message of up to 128 characters to a user. The message blinks three times to get the user's attention.

If multiple DAP records are selected for a user session, the most restrictive action is taken as the aggregated policy. For example, if a user session matches three DAP records, two of them have an action of Continue, and the third record has an action of Terminate, the collective policy terminates the user connection.

Tip The messages are shown in HTML format. That means you can even display a URL or links to users if they do not comply with policies so that they can take appropriate actions to remediate their workstations.

Network ACL Tab

The Network ACL tab enables you to apply traffic filters for the user session that match the DAP record. You can define traffic filters in the form of network ACLs. Each ACL can have either permit or deny statements, but not both. If an ACL has both permit and deny rules, DAP rejects it as a configuration error.

If a user session matches multiple DAP records, an aggregated ACL is applied on the user. The aggregated list considers a number of parameters, such as the priority of each DAP record as well as duplications of access control entries (ACE).

To configure a network ACL, click the Network ACL tab and select a preconfigured ACL from the drop-down menu. Click the **Add** button to move the selected ACLs to the right under Network ACLs. The Network ACL tab even enables you to define a new ACL or modify an existing ACL. Click the **Manage** button to manage ACLs. In Figure 19-50, **RestrictSSLVPN** is selected and applied to this DAP record.

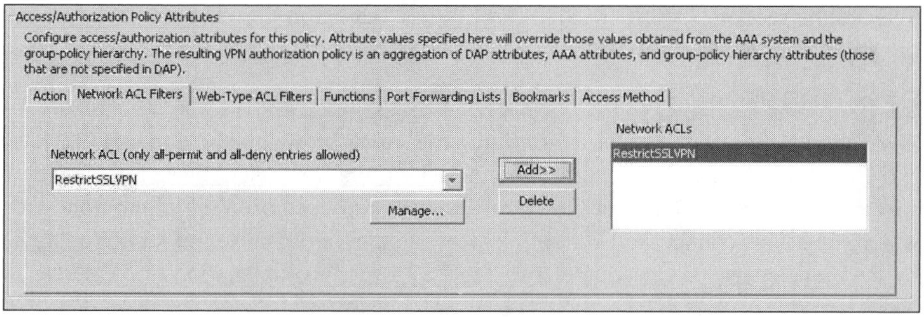

Figure 19-50 *Defining Network ACLs for DAP*

Web-Type ACL Tab

The Web-Type ACL tab, also known as the Application ACL tab, enables you to apply application-specific filters for a user session that matches a particular DAP record. You can define traffic filters in the form of network ACLs. Each ACL can have either permit or deny statements, but not both. If a web-type ACL has both permit and deny rules, DAP rejects it as a configuration error.

> **Note** If you happen to have an ACL entry that contains both permits and denies as access control entries, the command is rejected and the following message is displayed:
>
> "Unable to assign an access list with mixed deny and permit rules to a dynamic access policy."

If a user session matches multiple DAP records, an aggregated ACL is applied on the user. The aggregated list considers a number of parameters, such as the priority of each DAP record, as well as duplications of ACEs.

To configure a web-type ACL, click the **Web-Type ACL** tab and select a preconfigured ACL from the drop-down menu. Click the **Add** button to move the selected ACLs to the right under **Web-Type ACLs.** The Web-Type ACL tab even enables you to define a new ACL or modify an existing ACL. Click the **Manage** button to manage ACLs. In Figure 19-51, **RestrictApplication** is selected and applied to this DAP record.

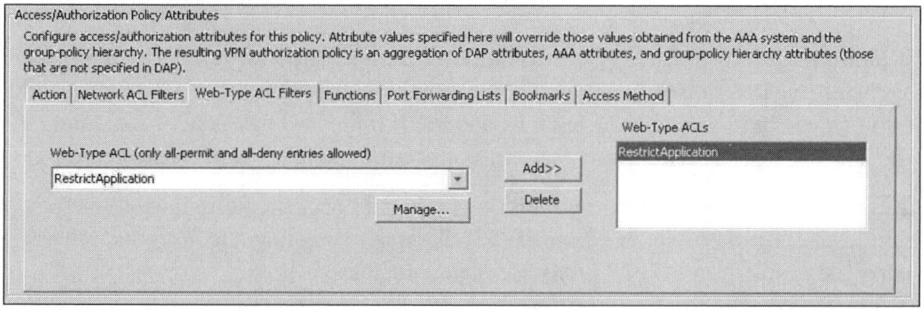

Figure 19-51 *Defining Web-Type ACLs for DAP*

Refer to the section "Configure Web-Type ACLs," earlier in this chapter, for information on how to manage web-type ACLs.

Functions Tab

The Functions tab enables you to configure file server browsing and entry, HTTP proxy, and URL entry. You can choose to allow or deny users from using these features for a specific DAP record. You can even choose to use the values from the group policy to which the user is connecting. For HTTP proxy, you have the option to launch an applet by DAP when a user connects. Refer to Table 19-13 for an explanation of file server browsing and entry, HTTP proxy, and URL entry features.

Table 19-13 *Description of Functions Tab Features*

Feature	Unchanged	Enable/Disable	Auto-Start
File server browsing	Applies values from a group policy to which the user is assigned	Allows or denies users from CIFS browsing for file servers	Not applicable
File server entry	Applies values from a group policy to which the user is assigned	Allows or denies user from entering file server paths and names on the portal page	Not applicable
HTTP proxy	Applies values from a group policy to which the user is assigned	Allows or denies user from using HTTP proxy	Allows DAP to automatically start applets; also enables HTTP proxy for a user session
URL entry	Applies values from a group policy to which the user is assigned	Allows or denies user from entering HTTP or HTTPS URLs on the portal page	Not applicable

Note You must enable WINS if you want to enable file browsing. Refer to the section "Configure File Servers," earlier in this chapter, for more details. If WINS is not defined, the security appliance uses the configured DNS server to resolve names.

If multiple DAP records are selected for a user session, the least restrictive action is taken as the aggregated policy. For example, if a user session matches three DAP records and two of them have an action of Disable, and the third record has an action of Auto-start, the collective policy auto-starts the user connection for that specific feature.

To configure functions, click the **Functions** tab and select the radio button for the option you would like to enable. In Figure 19-52, file server browsing and entry as well as URL entry are enabled, and HTTP proxy is set to auto-start.

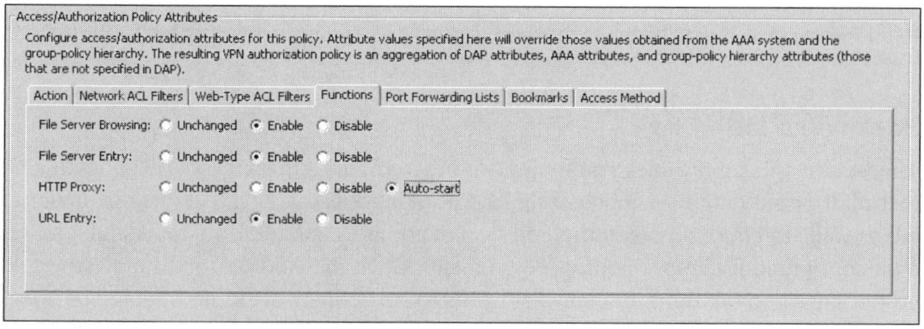

Figure 19-52 *Selection of User Functions*

Port Forwarding Lists Tab

The Port Forwarding Lists tab enables you to apply a preconfigured port-forwarding list to a DAP record. If you do not have a preconfigured port-forwarding list, you can define one under this tab. Because DAP enforces action and policies, you can deny users the use of a port-forwarding list even if the group policy to which the user is assigned allows it. Similarly, if a group policy does not have a port-forwarding list mapped to the group policy, you can choose to auto-start the selected list.

To choose a preconfigured port-forwarding list, click the Port Forwarding Lists tab and select a preconfigured list from the drop-down menu. Click the **Add** button to move the selected ACLs to the right. If a new list needs to be defined, click the **New** button. As illustrated in Figure 19-53, a port-forwarding list called **SSHServer** is selected and applied to this DAP record. The port forwarding **Auto-Start** option is also selected so that the DAP record automatically starts the port forwarding applets.

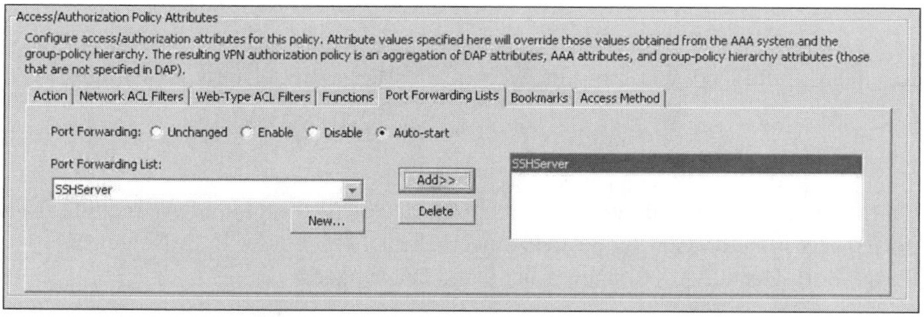

Figure 19-53 *Selecting a Port-Forwarding List*

If a user session matches multiple DAP records, an aggregated policy is applied on the user. The aggregated policy concatenates the attribute values from the selected DAP records and removes any duplicates values.

Note Refer to the section "Configure Port Forwarding," earlier in this chapter, to learn more.

Bookmarks Tab

The Bookmarks tab enables you to apply a preconfigured Bookmark (URL) list to a DAP record. If you do not have a preconfigured bookmark list, you can define one under this tab as well. To choose a preconfigured bookmark list, click the Bookmarks tab and select a preconfigured list from the drop-down menu. Click the **Add** button to move the selected bookmark to the right. If a new list needs to be defined, click the **Manage** button. As illustrated in Figure 19-54, bookmarks are enabled and a bookmark called **InternalServers** is selected and applied to this DAP record.

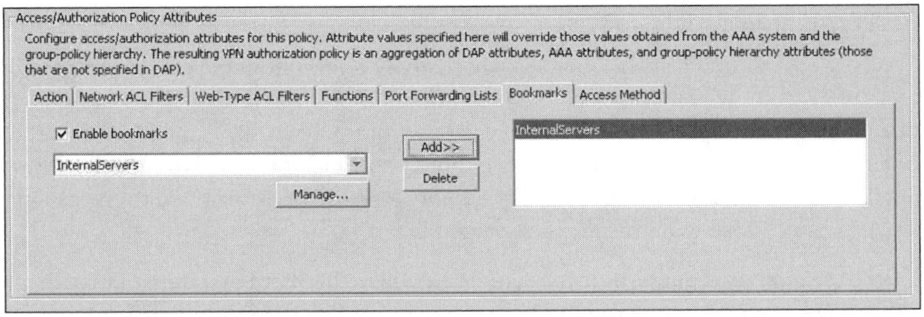

Figure 19-54 *Selecting a URL List*

If a user session matches multiple DAP records, an aggregated policy is applied on the user. The aggregated policy concatenates the attribute values from the selected DAP records and removes any duplicates values.

Note Refer to the section "Configure Websites" earlier in this chapter, to learn more.

Access Method Tab

On the Access Method tab you can specify an access method for a DAP record. The supported access methods include AnyConnect Client, Web-Portal, Both-Default-Web-Portal, Both-Default-AnyConnect Client, and Unchanged.

For example, if users match a DAP record but you do not want to give them AnyConnect Client functionality, select the Web-Portal option for that particular DAP record. If you select either the Both-Default-Web-Portal or Both-Default-AnyConnect Client, users who match the DAP record have access to both features and the default method is tried first. If you select Unchanged as the option, the user is allowed an access method based on the group policies that she acquires for her session. As shown in Figure 19-55, an access method of Web-Portal is selected and applied to a DAP record.

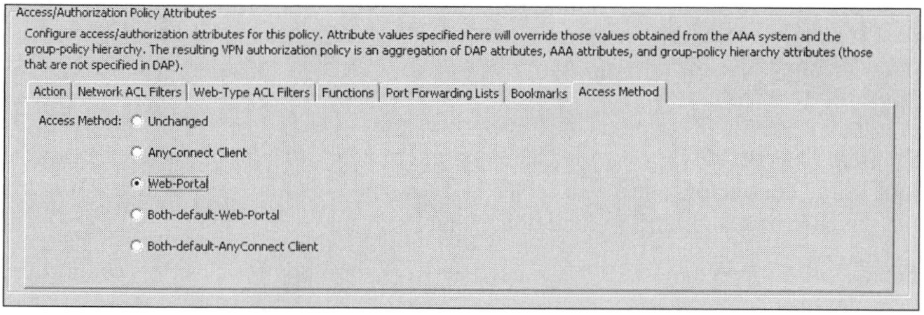

Figure 19-55 *Selecting an Access Method*

A user session can match multiple DAP records. In this case, the applied aggregated policy selects the least restrictive access method. For example, if a DAP record has Web-Portal as its access method, whereas another DAP record has Both-Default-AnyConnect Client, the user's access method is Both-Default-AnyConnect Client. However, if Both-Default-AnyConnect Client and Both-Default-Web-Portal are selected for a user session, the aggregates policy applies Both-Default-Web-Portal as the access method.

In Example 19-17, a DAP record called **Clientless-DAP** is being defined. This record allows "file browsing" and "file entry" and also sets HTTP proxy to auto-start. A port forwarding list, called **SSHServer**, and a bookmark list, called **InternalServers**, are applied to this DAP record. A Web-type ACL, called **RestrictApplication**, is also applied.

Example 19-17 *Defining a DAP Record*

```
Chicago(config)# dynamic-access-policy-record Clientless-DAP
Chicago(config-dynamic-access-policy-record)# description "This policy is applied
to employees logging in via Clientless SSL VPN hosts"
Chicago(config-dynamic-access-policy-record)# webvpn
Chicago(config-dap-webvpn)# file-browsing enable
Chicago(config-dap-webvpn)# file-entry  enable
Chicago(config-dap-webvpn)# http-proxy auto-start
Chicago(config-dap-webvpn)# url-entry enable
Chicago(config-dap-webvpn)# port-forward auto-start SSHServer
Chicago(config-dap-webvpn)# svc ask none default webvpn
Chicago(config-dap-webvpn)# url-list value InternalServers
Chicago(config-dap-webvpn)# appl-acl RestrictApplication
```

Deployment Scenarios

The Cisco SSL VPN solution is useful in deployments where remote and home users need access to corporate networks and administrators want to control their access based on a number of attributes. The SSL VPN solution can be deployed in many ways; however, this chapter covers one design scenario for ease of understanding.

Note The design scenario discussed in the following section should be used solely to reinforce learning. It is for reference purposes only.

SecureMe has decided to provide clientless functionality to a group of mobile contractors. These contractors use a web server for browsing, a terminal server, and a Windows file server to save and retrieve their documents.

Figure 19-56 shows SecureMe's proposed network topology for clientless connections.

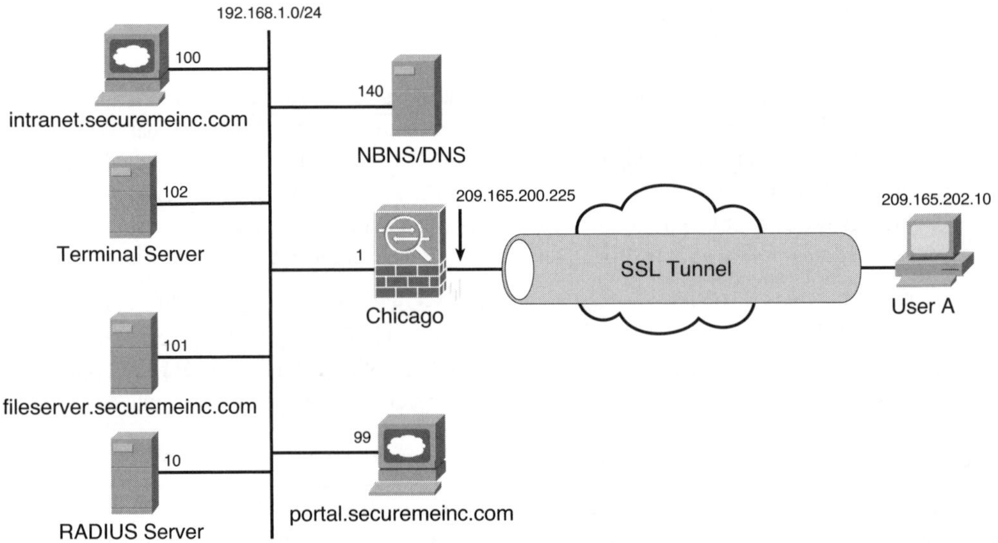

Figure 19-56 *SecureMe's Clientless Connection Topology with DAP*

The security requirements for SecureMe are as follows:

- Allow access to internal web server located at portal.securemeinc.com.
- Deny access to all other internal web servers including intranet.securemeinc.com.
- Allow access to a file server with an IP address of 192.168.1.101.
- Allow access to a terminal server with an IP address of 192.168.1.102.
- SecureMe uses RADIUS for user authentication and uses attribute 25 for role mapping within the enterprise.
- Contractors must have an active McAfee firewall (McAfee Personal Firewall version 8.*x*) running before access to SecureMe's network can be granted.
- Contractors should not be able to browse or specify any other web server in the SecureMe network.

To achieve SecureMe's requirements, the administrator has proposed that the security appliance be configured for clientless access. Bookmarks and smart tunnels will be configured to provide access to the internal web servers, CIFS servers, and terminal servers. The preconfigured RADIUS will be leveraged for user authentication. Attribute 25 will be used by DAP to assign specific policies based on user roles. Additionally, an endpoint assessment will be done to ensure that contractors have an active firewall running. If the security appliance receives attribute 25 with a value of **contractor** and endpoint assessment determines that the McAfee firewall is running, contractors will be allowed to connect through the web portal.

The following sections describe the steps to implement the proposed solution.

Step 1: Define Clientess Connections

Set up clientless connections for remote contractors as follows:

Step 1. Define bookmarks for the internal servers (web and CIFS) by choosing **Configuration > Remote Access VPN > Clientless SSL VPN Access > Portal > Bookmarks > Add.** Specify a bookmark list name called **Contractors-List** and then click **Add** to specify a bookmark title of **Internal-Web.** Select **http** under the **URL Value** drop-down menu, and configure a URL value of **portal.securemeinc.com.** Under **Advanced Options**, enable the **Smart Tunnel** option to tunnel HTTP traffic directly to the web server. Click **OK** when finished. Click **Add** to add another entry for the CIFS server. Under **Bookmark Title**, specify **Internal-FileServer** and select **cifs** from the **URL Value** drop-down menu. Configure a URL value of **fileserver.securemeinc.com.**

Step 2. Configure a web-type ACL by choosing **Configuration > Remote Access VPN > Clientless SSL VPN Access > Advanced > Web ACLs.** Click **Add**, select **Add ACL**, and define a list called **AllowWebServer.** Select the newly created ACL name, click **Add** again, select **Add ACE**, and select **Permit** as the **Action.** Choose **http** as the filter protocol and specify **portal.securemeinc.com** as the URL entry. The implicit deny at the end of a Web-type ACL will deny access to internal.securemeinc.com. Click **OK** when finished.

Step 3. Choose **Configuration > Remote Access VPN > Clientless SSL VPN Access > Portal > Smart Tunnels > Add** to define an entry for the terminal server. Specify a list name of **TerminalServer**, an **Application ID** of **Terminal**, and a **Process Name** of **mstsc.exe.**

Step 4. Define a group policy to link the bookmark and smart tunnel lists. Choose **Configuration > Remote Access VPN > Clientless SSL VPN Access > Group Policies > Add** and specify **ContractorGroupPolicy** as the policy name for the clientless users. Under **More Options**, deselect the **Inherit** check box for **Tunneling Protocols** and select **Clientless SSL VPN.** Click the **Portal** option in the left pane and deselect the **Inherit** check box for **Bookmark List.** Select **Contractor-List** from the drop-down list. Now, deselect the **Inherit**

check box for **Smart Tunnel List** and select **TerminalServer** from the drop-down list. Also enable **Auto Start** so that the smart tunnel is automatically initiated when the tunnel is established for a user. Click **OK** when finished.

Step 5. Choose **Configuration > Remote Access VPN > Clientless SSL VPN Access > Connection Profiles**, and under **Access Interfaces** select the **Allow Access** check box for the **outside** interface. Create a new tunnel group by clicking **Add** under **Connection Profiles.** Specify **SecureMeContractorTunnel** as the tunnel group name. Select **RADIUS** under **AAA Server Group** and select **ContractorGroupPolicy** under **Default Group Policy**. Specify **192.168.1.140** as the DNS server address and **securemeinc.com** as the domain name. Specify **SecureMeContractor** as the alias for this tunnel group.

Step 6. Because you are using bookmarks for the web and CIFS servers, you need to define a WINS and a DNS server. Go to **Configuration > Remote Access VPN > Clientless SSL VPN Access > Connection Profiles > SecureMeContractorTunnel** > **Edit** > **Advanced** > **NetBIOS Servers** option in the left pane. Click **Add**, specify **192.168.1.140** as the IP address of the NBNS server, and enable the **Master Browser** option. .

Step 7. Click the **Advanced** > **Clientless SSL VPN** option in the left pane. Under Group URL, click **Add** and specify **https://sslvpn.securemeinc.com/contractors.** Verify that the **Enable** check box is selected. Click **OK** to exit.

Step 2: Configure DAP

SecureMe wants to apply policy enforcements through DAP. Configure DAP by choosing **Configuration > Remote Access VPN > Clientless SSL VPN Access > Dynamic Access Policies.**

Step 1. Create a new DAP record by clicking **Add** and specifying the record name of **Contractors-DAP.** Under AAA attribute selection criteria, click **Add** and select **RADIUS** as the **AAA Attribute Type.** Under **Attribute ID,** specify **25** and select **Value** equal to **Contractors.** Insert another AAA attribute type of **Cisco,** select the **Connection Profile** check box, and specify **SecureMeContractorTunnel** as the **Tunnel Group** value. Select **User Has ALL of the Following AAA Attribute Types** as the **Selection Criteria.**

Step 2. Configure the endpoint attribute selection. Click **Add**, select **Personal Firewall** as the **Endpoint Attribute Type**, and select the **Exists** radio button. Under **Vendor**, select **McAfee, Inc.** and enable the **Product Description** and **Version** check boxes. Select **McAfee Personal Firewall** as the **Product Description** and **8.x** as the **Version.** Click **OK** when finished.

Step 3. Configure the **Access/Authorization Policy Attributes.** On the **Action** tab, choose **Continue.** Click the **Web-Type ACL** tab and select **AllowWebServer** from the drop-down menu. Click the **Add** button to move the selected ACLs to the right under **Web-Type ACLs.** Now select the **Functions** tab and choose **Enable** for **File Server Browsing.** Also choose **Disable** for **File Server Entry, HTTP Proxy,** and **URL Entry.**

Step 4. On the **Bookmarks** tab, click **Enable Bookmarks** and select **Contractors-List** from the drop-down menu. Click the **Add** button to move the selected list to the right. Finally, select **Web-Portal** as the **Access Method** on the **Access Method** tab. Click **OK** when finished.

You can now connect to the ASA by using the following URL in your browser: https://sslvpn.securemeinc.com/contractors.

Monitoring and Troubleshooting SSL VPN

The following sections discuss the monitoring and troubleshooting steps that are available to help you run the SSL VPN solution smoothly on a security appliance.

Monitoring SSL VPN

To monitor the WebVPN sessions, first check how many active SSL VPN tunnels are established on the security appliance. Check this by choosing **Monitoring > VPN > VPN Statistics > Sessions.** The security appliance shows all the active VPN sessions, including the clientless and full tunnel client connections. As shown in Figure 19-57, an active clientless connection is created by a user called sslvpnuser. The user computer's IP address is 209.165.200.230, and the negotiated encryption type is RC4. The security appliance has received 1,296,849 bytes of traffic, whereas it has transmitted 1,146,682 bytes of data to the client. The user is connected for just over a minute. Should you prefer to get detailed information about a user's connection, select that specific user session and then click the **Details** button.

To view the DAP policies that are configured on the security appliance in Lua, issue the **debug menu dap 2** command, as shown in Example 19-18. Two DAP records are configured: Clientless-DAP and Contractors-DAP.

Example 19-18 debug menu dap *Command*

```
Chicago# debug menu dap 2
DAP record [     Clientless-DAP   ]:
(EVAL(aaa.ldap.memberOf,"EQ","Employees","string") or EVAL(aaa.cisco.tunnel-
group,"EQ","SecureMeClientlessTunnel","string")) and ((EVAL(endpoint.os.ver-
sion,"EQ","Windows XP","string") and EVAL(endpoint.os.servicepack,"EQ","2","inte-
ger"))) and ((EVAL(endpoint.policy.location,"EQ","Corp-Owned","string")))

DAP record [     Contractors-DAP ]:
(EVAL(aaa.radius["25"],"EQ","Contractors","string") and EVAL(aaa.cisco.tunnel-
group,"EQ","SecureMeClientlessTunnel","string")) and
((EVAL(endpoint.fw.McAfeeFW.exists,"EQ","true","string") and
EVAL(endpoint.fw.McAfeeFW.description,"EQ","McAfee Desktop Firewall","string")))
Chicago#
```

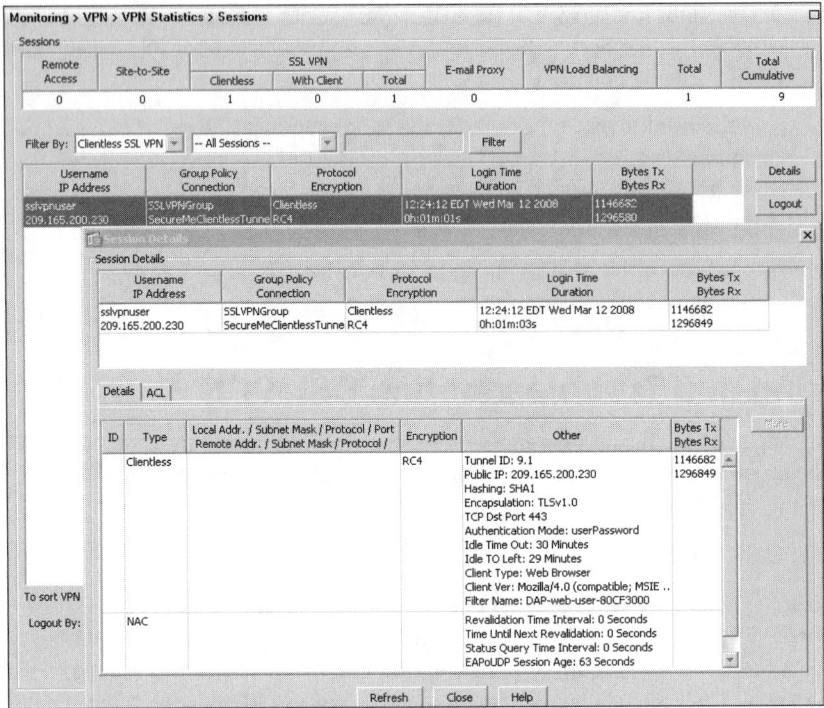

Figure 19-57 *Monitoring SSL VPN Sessions Through ASDM*

Additionally, if you want to monitor user sessions through syslogs, you can enable the **webvpn**, **svc**, **csd**, and **dap** classes. These classes are useful for understanding how users are getting authenticated, what information is being collected, and what type of attributes and policies are being applied on their sessions. As shown in Example 19-19, the administrator is collecting debug-level information for the **webvpn**, **svc**, **csd**, and **dap** classes. The syslog messages are being collected in the local buffer of the security appliance. Based on the syslog messages, an sslvpn user tries to connect to the SecureMeClientlessTunnel tunnel group. CSD determines that user's host machine connects from the Internet cafe location, and the security appliance applies a DAP called Contractors-DAP. The user session is successfully authenticated, and the user is allowed to connect through a clientless SSL VPN (WebVPN) tunnel.

Example 19-19 class *Syslog Commands*

```
Chicago(config)# logging enable
Chicago(config)# logging buffer-size 1048576
Chicago(config)# logging class webvpn buffered debugging
Chicago(config)# logging class svc buffered debugging
```

```
Chicago(config)# logging class csd buffered debugging
Chicago(config)# logging class dap buffered debugging
Chicago(config)# exit
Chicago# show log
Syslog logging: enabled
    Facility: 20
    Timestamp logging: disabled
    Standby logging: disabled
    Deny Conn when Queue Full: disabled
    Console logging: disabled
    Monitor logging: disabled
    Buffer logging:  level debugging, class webvpn svc csd dap,133 messages logged
    Trap logging: disabled
    History logging: disabled
    Device ID: disabled
    Mail logging: disabled
    ASDM logging: disabled
%ASA-7-734003: DAP: User sslvpnuser, Addr 209.165.200.230: Session Attribute
aaa.cisco.username = sslvpnuser
%ASA-7-734003: DAP: User sslvpnuser, Addr 209.165.200.230: Session Attribute
aaa.cisco.tunnelgroup = SecureMeClientlessTunnel
%ASA-7-734003: DAP: User sslvpnuser, Addr 209.165.200.230: Session Attribute end-
point.os.version = "Windows XP"
%ASA-7-734003: DAP: User sslvpnuser, Addr 209.165.200.230: Session Attribute end-
point.os.servicepack = "2"
%ASA-7-734003: DAP: User sslvpnuser, Addr 209.165.200.230: Session Attribute end-
point.policy.location = "InternetCafe"
%ASA-7-734003: DAP: User sslvpnuser, Addr 209.165.200.230: Session Attribute
endpoint.protection = "secure desktop"
<snip>
%ASA-7-734003: DAP: User sslvpnuser, Addr 209.165.200.230: Session Attribute end-
point.enforce = "success"
%ASA-6-734001: DAP: User sslvpnuser, Addr 209.165.200.230, Connection Clientless:
The following DAP records were selected for this connection: Contractors-DAP
 %ASA-6-716001: Group <ClientlessGroupPolicy> User <sslvpnuser> IP
<209.165.200.230> WebVPN session started.
%ASA-6-716038: Group <ClientlessGroupPolicy> User <sslvpnuser> IP
<209.165.200.230> Authentication: successful, Session Type: WebVPN.
```

Note The debug-level syslogs should be used if you are monitoring sessions in a lab environment. They should be used only for troubleshooting in the production environment and should be disabled when you have collected the necessary information.

Troubleshooting SSL VPN

Cisco ASA provides a number of troubleshooting and diagnostic commands for SSL VPNs. The following sections focus on three troubleshooting scenarios related to SSL VPN.

Troubleshooting SSL Negotiations

If you have a user who is not able to connect to the security appliance using SSL, follow these recommendations to isolate the SSL negotiation issues:

- Verify that the user's computer can ping the security appliance's outside IP address.
- If the user's workstation can ping the address, issue the **show running all | include ssl** command on the security appliance and verify that SSL encryption is configured.
- If SSL encryption is properly configured, use an external sniffer to verify whether the TCP three-way handshake is successful.

Troubleshooting Clientless Issues

The following sections provide guidelines on troubleshooting the three most commonly seen clientless issues

Issues with Websites

If you use clientless SSL VPN to provide connectivity to remote users and a user is having issues connecting to the websites through bookmarks, follow these recommendations to isolate the problem:

- Check whether the user is having connectivity issues with all configured websites. If so, check whether other applications, such as CIFS, port forwarding, or smart tunnels, are working well.
- If connectivity issues are limited to one web server, check whether one user or all users are having issues connecting to that website.
- Verify whether using smart tunnels for the configured website bookmark fixes the issue.
- If the issue is still not fixed, disable additional features such as CSD and DAP to see whether that fixes the issue.
- You can also try a different browser to isolate a browser-specific issue.
- As a last option, test connectivity to the server by using AnyConnect VPN Client to rule out other issues.

Issues with CIFS

You can provide CIFS services to the clientless users so that they can access their shared resources on the Windows file servers. If the clientless SSL VPN users have issues with multiple logons when they try to access the servers, you can configure a single sign-on and see whether that resolves the issue.

If users have issues connecting to the servers or have issues accessing their shared folders or files, you can try to access them by entering the server name and share through the address bar inside the web portal page. This helps in isolating issues with CIFS bookmarks.

In some cases, clientless SSL VPN users can receive a "Failed to retrieve domains" error message when they select Browse Entire Networks with the web portal page. You can resolve this issue by adding the WINS (NBNS) server under the correct tunnel group.

In the early 8.0 version of code, an issue exists when users periodically get an "Error contacting host" error message when they try to access servers through CIFS bookmarks or click the Browse Entire Network option. The only work-around at this time is to reboot the security appliance. This issue is identified as CSCsl94183 and is fixed in versions 8.0(4), 8.1(2), and later versions.

Note You can enable **debug ntdomain 255** and **debug webvpn cifs 255** to collect the appropriate information. A packet capture between the ASA and the CIFS server is also helpful. You can submit the debug output and capture to a Cisco TAC engineer for further analysis.

Troubleshooting CSD

If you have deployed CSD in your environment, users can sometimes experience slow processing when CSD is being loaded. This could be the result of the following issues:

- **Number of registry keys and values reads**—The more registry reads you have, the more time CSD needs to read and process entries.
- **Version of Java running**—Some versions of Java can process many more registry reads than some older versions.

You can help by clearing the SSL state on the Internet browser and by turning off the certificate revocation check. You can also use the latest version of CSD.

Troubleshooting DAP

The best way to troubleshoot DAP-related issues is to enable **debug dap trace**. For example, you can identify who is connecting to the security appliance, what tunnel group is being selected, what CSD prelogin location is chosen, what hotfixes the host is running, and what DAP record is being applied for that connection. As shown in Example 19-20, the username is sslvpnuser and the session is using the SecureMeClientlessTunnel tunnel group. The CSD prelogin location is determined as InternetCafe, and the security appliance assigns the Contractors-DAP policy for this user session.

Example 19-20 debug dap trace *Command*

```
Chicago# debug dap trace
DAP_TRACE: DAP_open: D44B80A8
DAP_TRACE: DAP_add_CSD: csd_token = [3463312075D26823695DDD52]
DAP_TRACE: Username: sslvpnuser, aaa.cisco.username = sslvpnuser
DAP_TRACE: Username: sslvpnuser, aaa.cisco.tunnelgroup = SecureMeClientlessTunnel
DAP_TRACE: dap_add_to_lua_tree:aaa["cisco"]["username"] = "sslvpnuser";
DAP_TRACE: dap_add_to_lua_tree:aaa["cisco"]["tunnelgroup"] =
"SecureMeClientlessTunnel";
DAP_TRACE: dap_add_to_lua_tree:endpoint["application"]["clienttype"] =
"Clientless";
DAP_TRACE: Username: sslvpnuser, dap_add_csd_data_to_lua:
endpoint.os.version = "Windows XP";
endpoint.os.servicepack = "2";
endpoint.policy.location = "InternetCafe";
endpoint.protection = "secure desktop";
endpoint.device.hostname = "home-pc";
endpoint.os.windows.hotfix["KB873339"] = "true";
endpoint.os.windows.hotfix["KB884016"] = "true";
<snip>
endpoint.fw["MSWindowsFW"].description = "Microsoft Windows Firewall";
endpoint.fw["MSWindowsFW"].version = "XP SP2+";
endpoint.fw["MSWindowsFW"].enabled = "failed";
endpoint.enforce = "success";
DAP_TRACE: Username: sslvpnuser, Selected DAPs: ,Contractors-DAP
DAP_TRACE: dap_request: memory usage = 40%
DAP_TRACE: dap_process_selected_daps: selected 1 records
DAP_TRACE: Username: sslvpnuser, dap_aggregate_attr: rec_count = 1
DAP_TRACE: Username: sslvpnuser, dap_comma_str_fcn: [Contractors-List] 16 128
DAP_TRACE: Username: sslvpnuser, DAP_close: D44B80A8
```

Summary

This chapter provided details about the SSL VPN functionality in Cisco ASA. Using the robust features available in Cisco ASA SSL VPN remote access, security administrators can deploy Cisco ASA in almost any network topology. This chapter discussed clientless SSL VPN client implementations. The chapter also focused on Cisco Secure Desktop (CSD) and offered guidance in setting up CSD features. The chapter discussed the Host Scan feature that is used to collect posture information about end workstations. The DAP feature and its usage were explained, and detailed configuration examples were also provided. To reinforce learning, we presented a deployment scenario along with its configuration. This chapter covered extensive **show** and **debug** commands to assist in troubleshooting complicated clientless SSL VPN deployments.

Chapter 20

Client-Based Remote-Access SSL VPNs

This chapter covers the following topics:

- SSL VPN deployment considerations
- SSL VPN prerequisites
- Pre-SSL VPN configuration guide
- AnyConnect VPN client configuration guide
- Deployment scenarios
- Monitoring and troubleshooting AnyConnect SSL VPNs

Chapter 19 discussed the implementation of SSL VPN on clientless workstations. However, the clientless implementation does not provide full network access to your remote users. If you want your users to have full network connectivity from their remote workstations, similar to what they would have with remote-access IPSec but by using SSL VPN, you can implement the full-tunnel-mode functionality on the Cisco ASA. Using the full tunnel client mode, remote machines can send all IP unicast traffic including TCP, UDP, or even ICMP-based packets. SSL clients can access internal resources via HTTP, HTTPS, SSH, or Telnet, to name a few.

Many enterprises are in the process of migrating from an existing IPSec-based deployment. Their main motivation is that the Cisco SSL VPN client is easy to deploy and maintain, has a smaller package size, requires no machine reboots during client install, and is easy to configure.

In the full tunnel mode, Cisco AnyConnect client can be pushed or installed on the remote workstations. Most customers prefer using the full tunnel mode option because a VPN client is automatically pushed to a user after a successful authentication. After it is installed, you can choose to keep the client installed permanently and thus reduce the connection time for the remote user.

SSL VPN Deployment Considerations

As discussed in Chapter 19, you have to analyze your current environment and determine which features and modes might be useful in your implementation before you implement the SSL VPN services in Cisco ASA. You have the option to install a Cisco IPSec VPN client, Cisco AnyConnect VPN client, or go with the clientless SSL VPN functionality. Table 20-1 lists the major differences between the Cisco VPN client solution and the Cisco AnyConnect SSL VPN client solution. Cisco AnyConnect SSL VPN is an obvious choice for someone who wants to give full network access to an enterprise's network, using SSL-based tunnels.

When you have determined AnyConnect SSL VPN as your choice of remote-access VPN solution, here are some of the SSL VPN design considerations that you must consider.

AnyConnect Licenses

Starting with Cisco ASA version 8.2, Cisco has introduced specific licenses to be used in the SSL VPN environment. They include

- AnyConnect Premium
- AnyConnect Essentials
- AnyConnect Mobile
- Shared Premium Licensing

AnyConnect Premium

The AnyConnect Premium license is designed for those customers who want to deploy both clientless as well as the AnyConnect SSL VPN tunnels in a single Cisco ASA. The AnyConnect Premium license supports advanced SSL VPN features such as Cisco Secure Desktop (CSD) and Host Scanning.

AnyConnect Essentials

The AnyConnect Essentials license is designed for those customers who want to deploy solely full tunnel AnyConnect clients. The AnyConnect Essentials license does not support advanced SSL VPN features such as Cisco Secure Desktop (CSD), Host Scanning, and or clientless SSL VPN tunnels. It is a great option for those customers who are in the process of migrating from a Cisco IPSec VPN solution to a Cisco AnyConnect solution or who require support for Windows 64-bit operating systems.

Even if you have the AnyConnect Essential license installed, you must use the **anyconnect-essential** command in the webvpn subconfiguration menu to enable AnyConnect Essential on the security appliance.

If you want to deploy both AnyConnect and clientless SSL VPNs, you must purchase the AnyConnect Premium license that also includes CSD.

Table 20-1 *Contrasting Cisco VPN Client and SSL VPN*

Feature	Cisco VPN Client	AnyConnect SSL VPN Client
VPN Client	Uses Cisco VPN Client software for complete network access.	Uses Cisco AnyConnect Client software for complete network access.
Management	You must install and configure Cisco VPN client.	You do not need have to install Cisco AnyConnect client. The client can be pushed to a user machine.
Encryption	Uses a variety of encryption and hashing algorithms.	Uses SSL RC4 encryption.
Operating Systems	Supported on Windows 7, Vista, XP, 2000, Tablet PC 2004/2005. Linux (Intel) 6.2 or later, Solaris 2.6 or higher, and Mac OS X 10.4 or later. X64-bit operating systems are not supported.	Supported on Windows 7, Vista, XP and 2000, Mac OS X (Version 10.4 or later), Red Hat Linux Version 9 or later, and Linux Intel 2.4 or 2.6 kernels. It is also supported on Windows XP and Vista 64-bit systems. Windows Mobile 5.0, 6.0, and 6.1 are supported.
License	License is available at no extra cost.	Must purchase either AnyConnect Essential or AnyConnect Premium License. Cisco SMARTnet customers can download the client for free but the license needs to be installed on the security appliance.

AnyConnect Mobile

For customers who want to extend the AnyConnect SSL VPN functionality to mobile endpoints such as Treo, iPAQ, and Axim, you can purchase the AnyConnect Mobile license. This is an add-on license to the AnyConnect Essential or SSL VPN Premium license. The mobile endpoints need to be running Windows Mobile 5.0, 6.0, or 6.1. For a complete list of supported VPN devices, consult http://www.cisco.com/en/US/docs/security/asa/compatibility/vpn-platforms-82.html.

Shared Premium Licensing

Shared Licenses are designed for those customers who want to purchase the SSL VPN licenses in bulk and then share them among a number of Cisco ASA on an as-needed basis. The pool of licenses is maintained by a master license server. The SSL VPN terminating security appliances are known as the *participants*. When a participant needs SSL VPN licenses, they send a request to the server. The server, depending on license availability, grants licenses to the participants in small chunks.

By using this model, customers can benefit from operational flexibility and investment protection because they can add devices to their deployments without having to purchase specific SSL VPN licenses for each device. In this licensing structure, the SSL user count is what is shared among the participating firewalls.

Table 20-2 provides detailed information on the different license types and the supported SSL VPN features.

Table 20-2 *License Types and Supported SSL VPN Features*

License Type	AnyConnect Essentials	AnyConnect Mobile	Premium Single	Premium Shared
AnyConnect VPN Client	Yes	Yes	Yes	Yes
Cisco Secure Desktop	Not Supported	Yes	Yes	Yes
Clientless SSL VPN	Not Supported	Not Supported	Yes	Yes
Smartphones AnyConnect	Yes, but is an add-on to the AnyConnect Essentials, Premium single, or Premuim shared license	Yes, but it is an add-on to the AnyConnect Essentials, Premium Single, or Premuim Shared license.	Yes, but also need AnyConnect Mobile license	Yes, but also need AnyConnect Mobile license

Note All license keys, except for the Shared Premium license, are associated per device. That means you cannot share a license among multiple Cisco ASAs, even if they are in high-availability or clustered environments. Customers who want to deploy the security appliances in high-availability areas can purchase the SSL/IPsec VPN Edition bundle with a specific license size.

If using the Shared Premium license in an Active/Standby failover scenario, the active security appliance requests the license from the license server. The standby appliance does not need any licenses.

VPN Flex Licenses

Cisco Systems also provides its customers an emergency or business continuity license called a *VPN flex* license. By using the SSL VPN flex licenses on the security appliances, customers can temporarily increase (burst) the number of SSL licenses on a box for up to 60 days. This license is extremely useful in those circumstances when a large number of employees cannot come to the office in emergency situations such as extreme weather conditions, and they end up working from home through the SSL VPN tunnels. In this case, the security appliance administrator can apply a VPN flex license for a week and revert back to the permanent license when the extreme conditions end.

Cisco ASA Design Considerations

Before you deploy AnyConnect SSL VPN, make sure that you understand the impact it has in your environment. Some of the design considerations are included in the following subsections.

ASA Feature Set

A Cisco security appliance can run various features such as IPsec VPN tunnels, routing engines, firewalls, and data inspection engines. Enabling the SSL VPN feature can add further load if your existing appliance is already running a number of features. You must check the CPU, memory, and buffer utilization before enabling SSL VPN.

Infrastructure Planning

Because SSL VPN provides network access to remote users, you have to consider the placement of the VPN termination devices. Before implementing the SSL VPN feature, ask the following questions:

- Should the Cisco ASA be placed behind another firewall? If so, what ports should be opened in that firewall?
- Should the decrypted traffic be passed through another set of firewalls? If so, what ports should be allowed in those firewalls?
- Are there any proxy servers between the client and the security appliances?

> **Note** If you have an HTTP 1.1 proxy server between the AnyConnect client and the server, your connection should succeed as long as the proxy server uses Basic and NTLM authentication. In the current implementation, Socks proxies are not supported.
>
> Additionally, if the proxy server runs only TCP, you cannot run DTLS. DTLS is discussed in the "Configuring DTLS" section of this chapter.

Implementation Scope

Network security administrators need to determine the size of the SSL VPN deployment, especially the number of concurrent users that will connect to gain network access. If one Cisco ASA is not enough to support the required number of users, the use of ASA clustering or load balancing must be considered to accommodate all the potential remote users.

Table 20-3 lists the secure appliances and the number of supported simultaneous AnyConnect SSL VPN users for each platform.

Table 20-3 *ASA Platforms and Supported Concurrent SSL VPN Users*

Security Appliance	Maximum VPN Throughput	Maximum Supported Concurrent Users
5505	100 Mbps	25
5510	170 Mbps	250
5520	225 Mbps	750
5540	325 Mbps	2500
5550	425 Mbps	5000
5580-20	1 Gbps	10,000
5580-40	1 Gbps	10,000

*The VPN throughput is calculated when 3DES/AES encryption is used for VPN tunnels.

Note You cannot apply Quality of Service (QoS) policies to the AnyConnect client connections.

SSL VPN Prerequisites

You must meet a number of prerequisites before you can start implementing an SSL VPN in your enterprise. They are discussed in the following sections.

Cisco Systems provides a two-user complementary license on all supported ASA devices. You do not have to purchase licenses if you want to test SSL VPN features in a lab environment where the user count is not going to exceed 2.

Note This chapter focuses strictly on version 8.2 because of the SSL VPN enhancements that were added in this version of code.

Client Operating System and Browser and Software Requirements

The SSL VPN functionality on Cisco security appliances is supported on a number of client operating systems and on a number of browsers. The supported platforms are discussed next.

Supported Operating Systems

The AnyConnect SSL VPNs are supported on the Windows-, Linux-, and Mac OS X-based systems. Table 20-4 provides a list of operating systems and the requirements for each operating system.

Table 20-4 *Supported Operating Systems*

Operating System Vendor	Supported Operating Systems	Operating Systems Requirements
Windows	Windows 7 (both 32- and 64-bit platforms) Windows Vista (both 32- and 64-bit platforms) with Service Pack 1* or 2 Windows XP SP2 or later Windows 2000 SP4	Pentium class processor or greater. x64 or x86 processors on Windows XP and Windows Vista. 5 MB hard disk space. RAM: • 128 MB for Windows 2000. • 256 MB for Windows XP • 512 MB for Windows Vista. Microsoft Installer, version 3.1.
Macintosh	Mac OS X 10.4 and later	50 MB hard disk space
Linux	Linux Kernel releases 2.4 and 2.6 on 32-bit architectures, and 64-bit architectures that support biarch • Ubuntu 7 and 8 (32-bit only) • Red Hat Enterprise Linux 3 or 4 • Fedora Core 4 through 9[1] • Slackware 11 or 12.1 • openSuSE 10 or SuSE 10.1	• 32 MB RAM • 20 MB hard disk space • Superuser privileges • libstdc++ users must have libstdc++ version 3.3.2 • Firefox 2.0 or later with libnss3.so • libcurl 7.10 or later • openssl 0.9.7a or later • java 1.5 or later • zlib or later • gtk 2.0.0, gdk 2.0.0, libpango 1.0 • iptables 1.2.7a or later • tun module supplied with kernel 2.4.21 or 2.6
Windows Mobile	Windows Mobile 6.1, 6.0 and 5.0 Professional and Classic for touch-screens only	

* For Vista SP1, you also need KB952876 installed.

> **Note** For Fedora 9, you must first install Sun Microsystems JRE 6 Update 5 or higher.
>
> The Linux platforms do not support web-based install.
>
> The current release of Cisco AnyConnect client does not support any virtualization software, such as VMWare or Parallels Desktop for Mac OS.

Compatible Browsers

You must use an SSL-enabled browser such as Microsoft Internet Explorer, Firefox, Opera, Safari, Mozilla, Netscape, or Pocket Internet Explorer (PIE) to download the AnyConnect client from the security appliance. For Windows-based workstations, use Internet Explorer 6.0+ or Firefox 2.0+, and enable ActiveX or install Sun JRE 1.5 or higher, with JRE 6 recommended.

Infrastructure Requirements

The infrastructure requirements for SSL VPNs include, but are not limited to, the following options:

- ASA placement
- User account
- Administrative privileges

ASA Placement

If you are installing a new security appliance, determine the location that best fits your requirements. If you plan to place it behind a firewall, make sure that you allow appropriate SSL VPN ports to pass through the firewall. In most cases, it is placed near the Internet edge.

User Account

Before SSL VPN tunnels are established, users must authenticate themselves to either the local database or to an external authentication server. The supported external servers include RADIUS (including Password Expiry using MSCHAPv2 to NT LAN Manager), RADIUS one-time password (OTP), RSA SecurID, Active Directory/Kerberos, and Generic Lightweight Directory Access Protocol (LDAP). Make sure that SSL VPN users have accounts and appropriate access. LDAP password expiration is available for Microsoft and Sun LDAP.

Administrative Privileges

AnyConnect VPN client requires administrative rights for the initial installations.

> **Note** Smartcard support is not available for Linux-based AnyConnect clients. They are, however, fully supported on Windows Vista, Windows XP with SP2 and Windows 2000 Professional with SP4, and Mac OS X 10.4 and higher.

Pre-SSL VPN Configuration Guide

After analyzing the deployment consideration and selecting the SSL VPN as your choice of remote-access VPN solution, you must configure the security appliance for the tasks listed in the following subsections even before you enable SSL VPN. These tasks include the following:

- Enrolling digital certificates (recommended)
- Setting up tunnel and group policies
- Setting up user authentication

Enrolling Digital Certificates (Recommended)

Enrollment is the process of obtaining a certificate from a certificate authority (CA). The certificate enrollment process for AnyConnect SSL VPN client is identical to the enrollment process discussed in Chapter 19 for clientless SSL VPN tunnels. If you have not gone through the process of enrolling SSL VPN certificates into a Cisco security appliance, please consult the "Enroll Digital Certificates" section in Chapter 19.

Setting Up Tunnel and Group Policies

As discussed in Chapter 19, Cisco ASA uses an inheritance model when it pushes network and security policies to the end-user sessions. Using this model, you can configure policies at the following three locations:

- Under default group policy
- Under user group policy
- Under user policy

In the inheritance model, a user inherits the attributes and policies from the user policy, which inherits its attributes and policies from the user group policy, which in turn inherits its attributes and policies from the default group policy.

Note "DfltGrpPolicy" is a special group name, used solely for the default group policy.

After defining these policies, you must bind them to a tunnel group where users terminate their sessions. This way, a user who establishes his VPN session to a tunnel group inherits all the policies mapped to that tunnel. The tunnel group defines a VPN connection profile, of which each user is a member.

Configuring Group Policies

You configure the user group and default group policies by choosing **Configuration > Remote Access VPN > Network (Client) Access > Group Policies.** Click **Add** to add a new group policy. As shown in Figure 20-1, a user group policy, called **AnyConnectGroupPolicy**, has been added. This group policy allows only clientless SSL VPN tunnels to be established and rejects all the other tunneling protocols. If you would rather assign attributes to default group policy, you can modify **DfltGrpPolicy** (System Default). Any attribute that is modified here is propagated to any user group policy that inherits that attribute. A group policy name other than **DfltGrpPolicy** is treated as a user group policy.

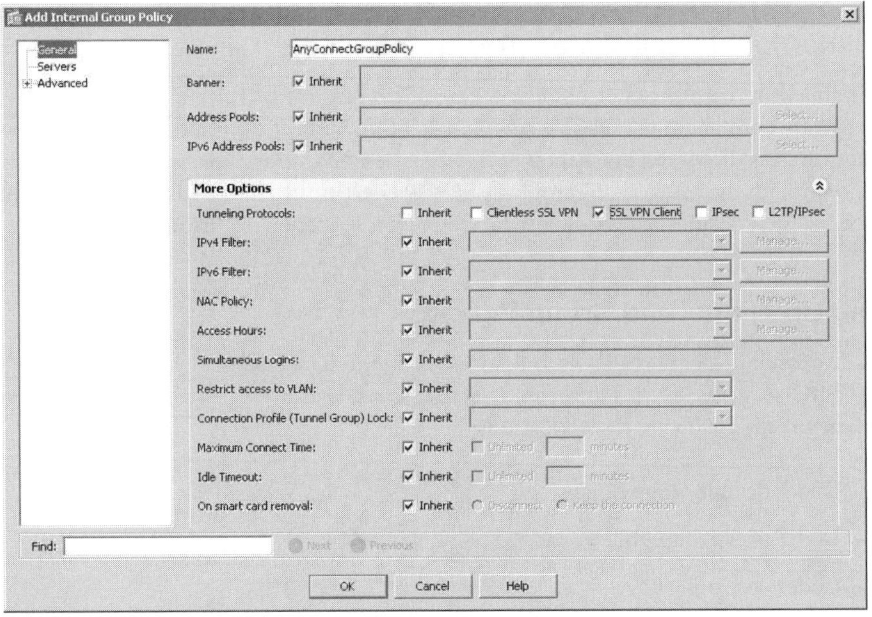

Figure 20-1 *User Group Policy Configuration*

Note The default and user group policies are set up to allow both Cisco IPsec VPN and SSL VPN tunnels. If you want to restrict a policy to use only SSL VPN, use either the Clientless SSL VPN or the SSL VPN Client options under Tunneling Protocols, as illustrated in Figure 20-1.

The user, group, and default group polices can be applied to clientless, AnyConnect, and IPsec-based remote-access VPN tunnels. The AnyConnect SSL VPN specific attributes are discussed in detail in the next few sections of this chapter.

Note You can configure a user policy by choosing **Configuration > Remote Access VPN > AAA/Local Users > Local Users.**

Example 20-1 illustrates how to define a user group policy called **AnyConnectGroupPolicy**. This policy allows only the IPSec tunnels to be terminated on the group.

Example 20-1 *Group Policy Definition*

```
Chicago(config)# group-policy AnyConnectGroupPolicy internal
Chicago(config)# group-policy AnyConnectGroupPolicy attributes
Chicago(config-group-policy)# vpn-tunnel-protocol svc
```

Configuring a Tunnel Group

You can configure a tunnel group, also known as connection profile, by choosing **Configuration > Remote Access VPN > Network (Client) Access > AnyConnect Connection Profiles** and clicking **Add**. As shown in Figure 20-2, a tunnel group called **SecureMeAnyConnect** has been added. After defining a tunnel group name, you can bind a user group policy to a tunnel group. After a user is connected, the attributes and policies defined under the group policy are applied to the user. A user group policy of **AnyConnectGroupPolicy** is linked to this tunnel group.

Example 20-2 illustrates how to configure a remote-access tunnel group of **SecureMeAnyConnect**. The previously defined group policy, **AnyConnectGroupPolicy**, is added to the tunnel group.

Example 20-2 *Tunnel Group Definition*

```
Chicago(config)# tunnel-group SecureMeAnyConnect type remote-access
Chicago(config)# tunnel-group SecureMeAnyConnect general-attributes
Chicago(config-tunnel-general)# default-group-policy AnyConnectGroupPolicy
```

After configuring a Connection Profile, you can define a specific URL that users can use to connect to this tunnel group. This is useful if you want to create a specific URL for each Connection Profile you create and distribute the URL accordingly so that users do not have to decide to which Connection Profile to connect.

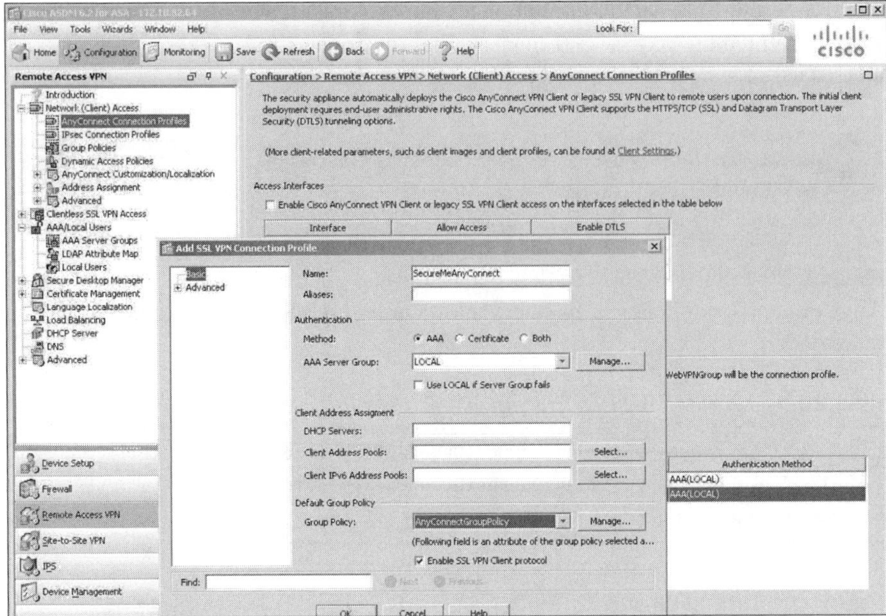

Figure 20-2 *Configuration of a Tunnel Group*

You can define a specific URL by modifying the Connection Profile and then clicking the **Advanced** > **SSL VPN** option. Under **Group URL**, click **Add** and specify a URL. For the SecureMeAnyConnect connection profile, specify **https://sslvpn.securemeinc.com/sslvpnclient** as the group URL. Verify that the **Enable** check box is selected. Click **OK** to exit. When users need to connect via SSL VPN, they can use this URL to connect specifically to this tunnel group.

Setting Up User Authentication

Cisco ASA supports a number of authentication servers, such as RADIUS, NT domain, Kerberos, SDI, LDAP, digital certificates, smart cards, and local databases. For small organizations, a local database can be set up for user authentication. For medium to large SSL VPN deployments, it is highly recommended that you use an external authentication server, such as RADIUS or Kerberos, as the user authentication database. If you are deploying the SSL VPN feature for a few users, you can use the local database. You define the users by choosing **Configuration** > **Remote Access VPN** > **AAA/Local User** > **Local Users.**

Many enterprises either use a RADIUS server or Kerberos to leverage their existing active directory infrastructure for user authentication. Before configuring an authentication server on Cisco ASA, you must specify authentication, authorization, and accounting (AAA) server groups by choosing **Configuration** > **Remote Access VPN** > **AAA/Local User > AAA Server Groups > Add.** Specify a server group name that can be referenced by the other AAA processes. Select an authentication protocol for this server group name. For example, if you plan to use a RADIUS server for authentication, select **RADIUS** from the drop-down menu. This option ensures that the security appliance requests the appropriate information from the end users and forwards it to the RADIUS server for authentication and verification.

After enabling RADIUS processing, define a list of the RADIUS servers. The Cisco security appliance checks their availability on a round-robin basis. If a server is available, the security appliance keeps using that server until it fails to receive a response. In this case, it checks the availability of the next server. It is highly recommended that you set up more than one RADIUS server, in case the first server is not reachable. You can define a RADIUS server entry by navigating to **Configuration** > **Remote Access VPN** > **AAA/Local User** > **AAA Server Groups** and clicking **Add** under **Servers in the Selected Group**. You can specify the IP address of the RADIUS server as well as the interface closest to the server. The security appliance authenticates itself to the RADIUS server by using a shared secret key. Figure 20-3 shows the Cisco ASA configured with an AAA server under the server group called Radius. The server is located toward the inside interface at **192.168.1.40**. The shared key is **C1$c0123** (obfuscated).

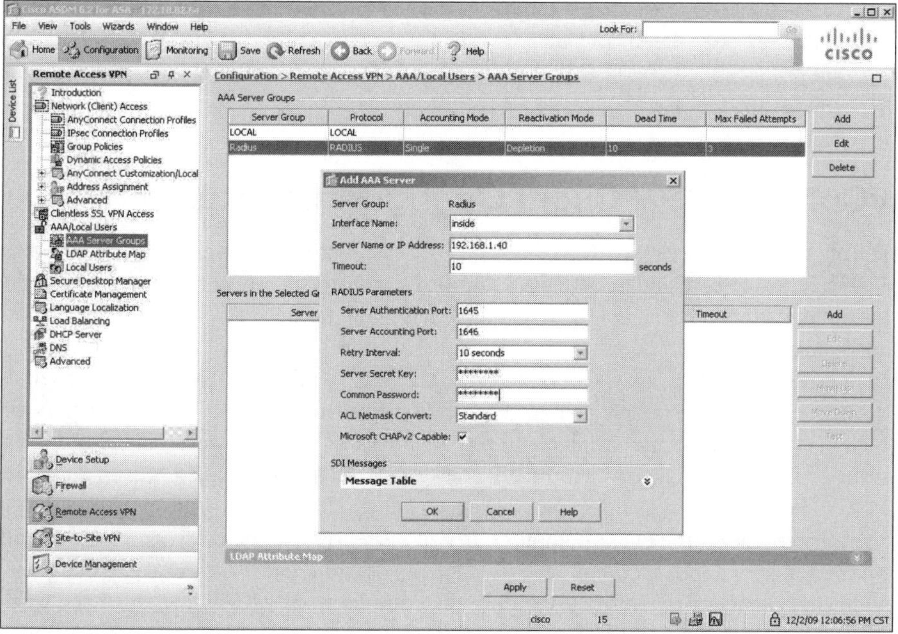

Figure 20-3 *Defining a RADIUS Server for Authentication*

After defining the authentication servers, bind them to the SSL VPN process under a tunnel group. Refer to Figure 20-2 to see that the newly created Radius AAA server group is mapped to the **SecureMeAnyConnect** tunnel group. Example 20-3 shows how a radius server can be defined. The radius group-name is **Radius** and it is located toward the

inside interface at **192.168.1.40**. The shared secret is **C1$c0123**. The radius server is added to **SecureMeAnyConnect**

Example 20-3 *Defining RADIUS for IPSec Authentication*

```
Chicago(config)# aaa-server Radius protocol radius
Chicago(config)# aaa-server Radius (inside) host 192.168.1.40
Chicago(config-aaa-server-host)# key C1$c0123
Chicago(config-aaa-server-host)# exit
Chicago(config) tunnel-group SecureMeAnyConnect general-attributes
Chicago(config-tunnel-general)# authentication-server-group Radius
```

Tip For large VPN deployments (both IPsec and SSL VPNs), you can even control user access and policy mapping from an external authentication server. You should pass the user group policy name as a RADIUS or LDAP attribute to the security appliance. By doing so, you guarantee that a user will always get the same policy, regardless of the tunnel group name to which he connects. If you are using RADIUS as the authentication and authorization server, you can specify the user group policy name as attribute 25 (class attribute). Append the keyword **OU=** as the value of the class attribute. For example, if you define a user group policy called engineering group, you can enable attribute 25 and specify **OU=engineering** as its value.

AnyConnect VPN Client Configuration Guide

During the early development period of SSL VPNs, network administrators needed a VPN client that had similar benefits of an IPsec remote-access VPN client, but required less administrative overhead than installing and maintaining the IPsec VPN client. To accommodate those requirements, the idea of a full tunnel SSL VPN client emerged. In the pre-version 8.0 releases, Cisco provided the SSL VPN Client (SVC). This is a self-downloading, self-installing, self-configuring, and self-uninstalling VPN that offers all benefits that are currently available in the Cisco IPsec client. However, in 8.0 or later versions of Cisco ASA, Cisco introduced a newer SSL VPN client called "Cisco AnyConnect VPN Client". The AnyConnect VPN clients leverage the SSL encryption engine that is already present on the client computer. If you currently use the pre-version 8.0 of code on the security appliances and have SVC clients deployed, test the AnyConnect version in a lab environment first before upgrading the code to version 8.0 or higher of the software. Table 20-5 discusses the differences between the SVC and AnyConnect VPN clients. If you decide that the AnyConnect VPN client will be beneficial in your environment, you can plan to upgrade your security appliance to version 8.*x* of the code.

Because versions 8.*x* of code support only AnyConnect VPN client, we discuss only AnyConnect in this chapter.

Table 20-5 *Contrasting SVC and AnyConnect*

Feature	SVC	AnyConnect
Operating system support	Supported in Windows XP and Windows 2000	Supported in Windows 7, Vista and XP (both 32- and 64-bit), Windows 2000, Mac OS X (version 10.4 or higher), and Red Hat Linux (version 9 or higher)
DTLS with SSL connections	Not supported	Fully supported
Package size	Approximately 400 KB	Approximately 1.2 MB
Administrative rights	Required to install and upgrade the package	Required to install the package initially; no administrative privileges are required subsequently
Platform support	Supported on VPN 3000, Cisco IOS routers, and Cisco ASA	Supported only on Cisco ASA and IOS routers
Start before login	Not supported	Supported on Windows 2000 and Windows XP systems
IPv6 support	Not supported	Supported on Windows XP SP2 and Windows Vista
Standalone connection	Requires SVC to be downloaded from Cisco ASA through a web browser	Can be installed as a standalone application or through a web browser

Note If you use 64-bit (x64) platforms, Cisco provides support only through the Cisco AnyConnect VPN Client. Cisco AnyConnect VPN Client supports Windows 7, XP as well as Windows Vista x64 platforms. Cisco currently does not have plans to provide support for 64-bit platforms for the Cisco IPsec VPN Client or even the Cisco SSL VPN Client (SVC).

AnyConnect VPN client can be installed on a user's computer using one of these two methods:

- **Web-enabled mode**—In this method, the client is downloaded to a user computer through a browser. The user opens a browser and references the IP address or the FQDN of Cisco ASA to establish an SSL VPN tunnel. The user is presented with the standard SSL VPN logon page and is prompted for credentials. If credentials are valid, users are allowed to log in, and if they are using Internet Explorer, they are prompted to download the client using ActiveX. Otherwise, they are prompted to start it manually through the AnyConnect link. If ActiveX fails, the browser tries to download the client through Java. If either ActiveX or Java is successful, the client is downloaded and installed. After it is installed, it tries to connect to the security appliance and establishes an SSL VPN tunnel.

Note If you are installing the AnyConnect client on Windows Vista and are running low-rights Internet Explorer, the installation will fail. To fix this issue, users *must* include the Secure Gateway to the Trusted Zone.

- **Standalone mode**—In this method, the client is downloaded as a standalone application from a file server or directly from the Cisco Systems website. The Microsoft Software Installer (MSI) is executed to install the client to the workstation. If the client is not preconfigured, the user needs to specify the IP address or FQDN of the security appliance, the tunnel group to connect to, the username, and the associated password.

Note If you receive the following message, you need to copy MSVCP60.dll and MSVCRT.dll into the system32 directory. Please consult the Microsoft's article KB259403 for more information.

"The required system DLL *filename* is not present on the system."

The configuration of AnyConnect VPN client is a two-step process:

Step 1. Loading the AnyConnect package

Step 2. Defining AnyConnect VPN client attributes

Note If you have Cisco Security Agent (CSA) installed on the AnyConnect VPN clients, you must import the new CSA policies on the workstations. CSA version 4.5 or higher ships with the AnyConnect policies that are attached to the Remote Desktops and Laptops group. You must select them to prevent the AnyConnect client from failing with CSA version 4.5 because these policies are not enabled by default.

Loading the AnyConnect Package

Before you define configuration policies for the AnyConnect VPN client, you have to load the AnyConnect VPN client package in the local flash of the security appliance. You can verify whether it is installed by choosing **Configuration** > **Remote Access VPN** > **Network (Client) Access** > **Advanced** > **SSL VPN** > **Client Setting.** If an AnyConnect VPN client image is not installed, you can click **Add** to:

- Browse through the local flash of the security appliance and select the AnyConnect file you want to use. As shown in Figure 20-4, **anyconnect-win-2.3.0254-k9.pkg** is being added from the local flash of the security appliance.
- Upload a file from the local computer to the local flash of Cisco ASA. You should check for the latest version of the AnyConnect package file at the Cisco website.

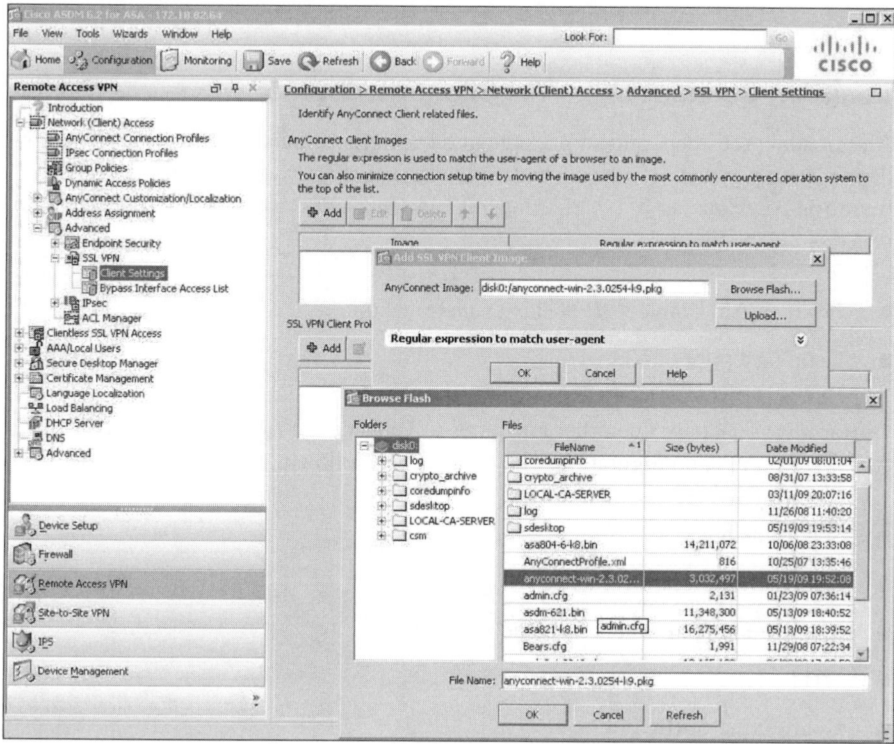

Figure 20-4 *Installing the AnyConnect VPN Client Package*

> **Note** You can upload multiple SSL VPN client packages. The order in which the files are listed reflects the order in which they are presented to a user to be downloaded.

> **Caution** Do not rename the package files that you download from the Cisco website. If you change the filename, the hash verification that includes the filename fails.

Example 20-4 shows an AnyConnect image, **anyconnect-win-2.3.0254-k9.pkg**, being installed in the security appliance.

Example 20-4 *Enabling AnyConnect SSL VPN*

```
Chicago(config)# webvpn
Chicago(config-webvpn)# svc image disk0:/anyconnect-win-2.3.0254-k9.pkg 1
```

Defining AnyConnect SSL VPN Client Attributes

After loading the AnyConnect package in the security appliance's configuration, you can define client parameters such as the IP address that client should receive via ASDM. Before an AnyConnect SSL VPN tunnel is functional, you have to configure the following two required attributes:

- Enabling AnyConnect VPN client functionality
- Defining a pool of addresses

Optionally, you can define other attributes to enhance the functionality of the AnyConnect VPN configuration. They include the following:

- Split tunneling
- DNS and WINS assignment
- Keeping SSL VPN client installed
- DTLS
- Configuring traffic filters
- Configuring a tunnel group

All these options are defined in the next sections.

Figure 20-5 is used throughout these sections to demonstrate how to set up Cisco ASA for AnyConnect users. As shown in this figure, the security appliance is set up to accept the SSL VPN connections from hosts on the Internet. On the private network of the security appliance are a number of servers.

Table 20-6 provides a description of the servers used in this setup.

Table 20-6 *Description and Location of Servers*

Server	Location	Purpose
CA server	192.168.1.30	To issue CA and ID certificates
WINS server	192.168.1.20	To resolve NetBIOS names with IP addresses
DNS server	192.168.1.10	To resolve hostnames with IP addresses
RADIUS server	192.168.1.40	To authenticate users
Web server	192.168.1.100	To host internal websites
File server	192.168.1.101	To host and present files and folders to SSL VPN users
Terminal server/SSH server	192.168.1.102	To provide terminal and SSH services to SSL VPN users

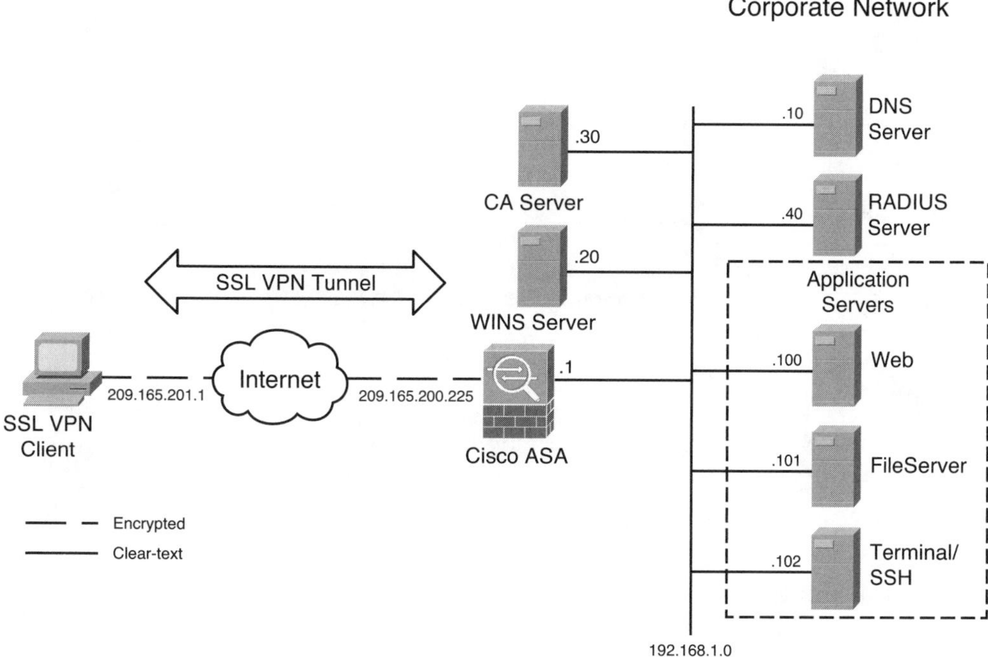

Figure 20-5 *SSL VPN Network Topology*

Enabling AnyConnect VPN Client Functionality

After the AnyConnect VPN client is loaded into flash, the next step is to enable the AnyConnect Client functionality on the interface that terminates the connection. You do so by selecting "Enable Cisco AnyConnect VPN Client or Legacy SSL VPN Client access on the interfaces selected in the table below" in **Configuration > Remote Access VPN > Network (Client) Access > AnyConnect Connection Profiles.** Select the **outside** interface if it is the interface that will terminate the SSL VPN connection. This is shown in Figure 20-6. Specify the SSL VPN port that the clients should be using to establish the VPN tunnel. By default, it is TCP port 443 and DTLS UDP port 443. DTLS is discussed later in this chapter.

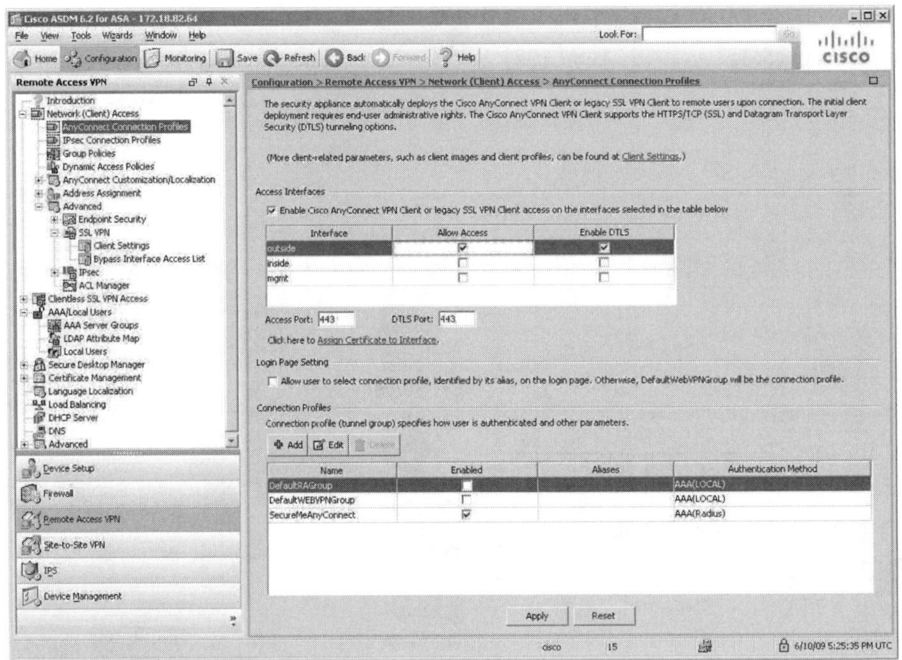

Figure 20-6 *Enabling AnyConnect VPN Client Functionality on an Interface*

Example 20-5 shows that AnyConnect functionality is enabled on the outside interface.

Example 20-5 *Enabling SSL VPN on the Outside Interface*

```
Chicago(config)# webvpn
Chicago(config-webvpn)# enable outside
```

The AnyConnect VPN client requires administrative privileges on the client computer when it is installed. When AnyConnect client is launched, no administrative privileges are required subsequently.

Defining a Pool of Addresses

During the SSL VPN tunnel negotiations, an IP address is assigned to the VPN adapter of the AnyConnect VPN client. The client uses this IP address to access resources on the protected side of the tunnel. Cisco ASA supports three different methods to assign an IP address back to the client:

- Local address pool
- DHCP server
- RADIUS server

Many organizations prefer assigning an IP address from the local pool of addresses for flexibility. You assign the IP address by configuring an address pool and then linking the pool to a policy group. You can either create a new pool of addresses or select a preconfigured address pool. You can define a new pool of addresses by choosing **Configuration** > **Remote Access VPN** > **Network (Client) Access** > **Address Assignment** > **Address Pools.** Click **Add** and configure the following attributes, as illustrated in Figure 20-7:

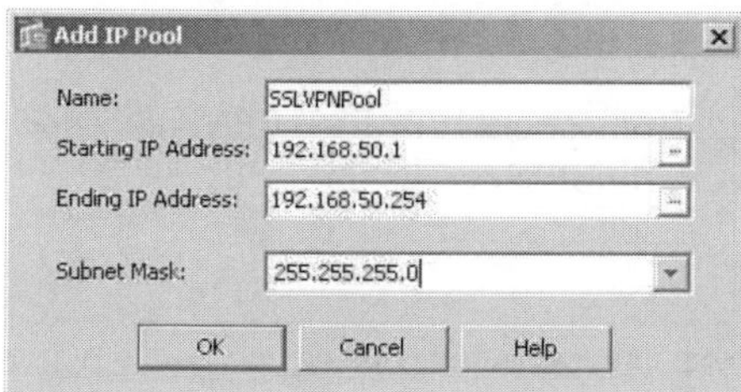

Figure 20-7 *Defining an Address Pool Using ASDM*

- **Name**—An alphanumeric name to be assigned to this pool. A pool name of SSLVPNPool is assigned.

- **Starting IP address**—The first IP address to be assigned to a client. A starting IP address of 192.168.50.1 is assigned.
- **Ending IP address**—The last IP address to be assigned to a client. A starting IP address of 192.168.50.254 is assigned.
- **Subnet mask**—The associated subnet mask for this pool of addresses. A subnet mask of 255.255.255.0 is configured.

By default, all address assignment methods are allowed. If you want to disable a specific address assignment method, you can do so by navigating to **Configuration** > **Remote Access VPN** > **Network (Client) Access** > **Address Assignment** > **Assignment Policy.**

Note If all three methods are configured for address assignment, Cisco ASA prefers RADIUS over DHCP and internal address pools. If Cisco ASA is not able to get an address from the RADIUS server, it contacts the DHCP server for address allocation. If that method fails as well, Cisco ASA checks the local address pool as the last resort.

After defining a pool of addresses, map the pool to a user group policy. Choose **Configuration** > **Remote Access VPN** > **Network (Client) Access > Group Policies > AnyConnectGroupPolicy > Edit.** Deselect the **Inherit** check box under **Address Pools** and then click **Select** to choose a predefined pool of addresses. A new window pops up with all the preconfigured address pools. Select the address pool you want to use and click **Assign** to map the pool to this policy. In Figure 20-8, the **SSLVPNPool** is assigned to **AnyConnectGroupPolicy**. Click **OK** when finished.

Example 20-6 shows how to assign an address from a pool called **SSLVPNPool**, which is mapped to a group policy called **AnyConnectGroupPolicy**.

Example 20-6 *Defining Pool of Addresses*

```
Chicago(config)# ip local pool SSLVPNPool 192.168.50.1-192.168.50.254 mask
255.255.255.0
Chicago(config) group-policy AnyConnectGroupPolicy attributes
Chicago(config-group-policy)# address-pools value SSLVPNPool
```

Tip You can also link a pool of addresses to the tunnel group. However, if a pool is mapped to a group policy and a different pool is mapped to a tunnel group, then the security appliance prefers the pool that is linked to the group policy.

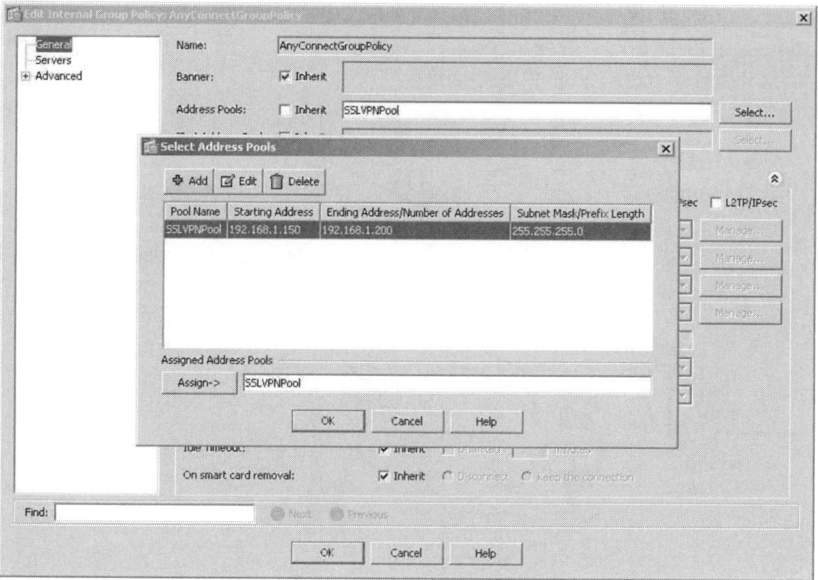

Figure 20-8 *Mapping an Address Pool to a Group Policy*

Advanced Full Tunnel Features

After setting up basic full tunnel client parameters, you can configure some of the advanced parameters to enhance the SSL VPN implementation in your network. Some of the important full tunnel features are discussed in the next sections:

- Split tunneling
- DNS and WINS assignment
- Keeping the SSL VPN client installed
- Configuring DTLS
- Configuring traffic filters

Split Tunneling

After the tunnel is established, the default behavior of the Cisco AnyConnect VPN client is to encrypt traffic to all the destination IP addresses. This means that if an SSL VPN user wants to browse to http://www.cisco.com over the Internet, as illustrated in Figure 20-9, the packets are encrypted and sent to Cisco ASA. After decrypting them, the security appliance looks at its routing table and forwards the packet to the appropriate next-hop IP address in clear text. These steps are reversed when traffic returns from the web server and is destined to the SSL VPN client.

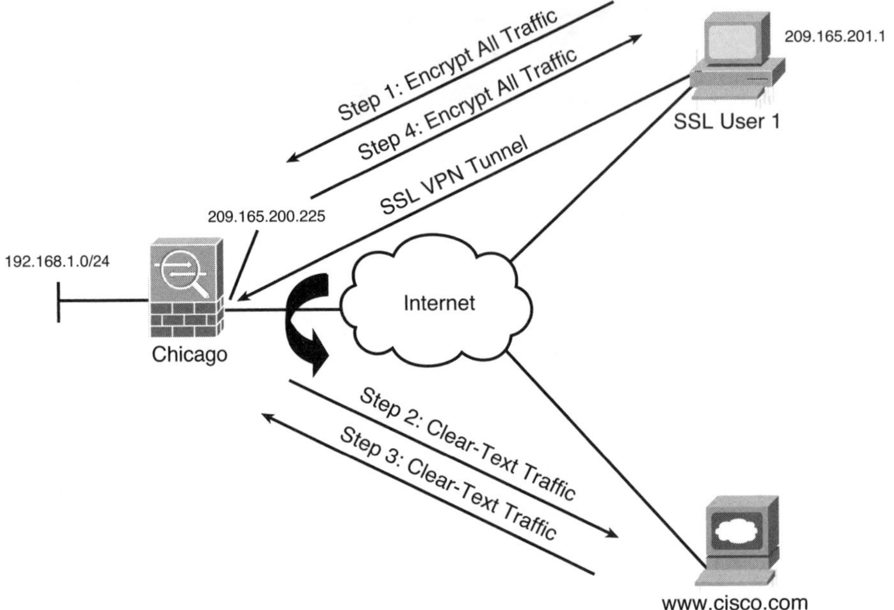

Figure 20-9 *Traffic with No Split Tunneling*

This behavior might not always be desirable for the following two reasons:

- Traffic destined to the non-secure networks traverses over the Internet twice: once encrypted and once in clear text.
- Cisco ASA handles extra VPN traffic destined to the nonsecure subnet. The security appliance analyzes all traffic leaving and coming from the Internet

With split tunneling, the security appliance can notify the AnyConnect VPN client about the secured subnets. The VPN client, using the secured routes, encrypts only those packets that are destined for the networks behind the security appliance.

Caution With split tunneling, the remote computer is susceptible to hackers, who can potentially take control over the computer and direct traffic over the tunnel. To mitigate this behavior, a personal firewall is highly recommended on the AnyConnect VPN clients workstations.

Split tunneling can be configured under a user, user group policy, or default group policy. Choose **Configuration > Remote Access VPN > Network (Client) Access > Group**

Policies > AnyConnectGroupPolicy > Edit > Advanced > Split Tunneling. Under **Policy** and **Network List**, deselect the **Inherit** check box. Select **Tunnel Network List Below** from the **Policy** drop-down menu. Additionally select a network list from the drop-down menu. If you would rather define a new network list, click the **Manage** option. Cisco ASDM launches the ACL Manager and prompts you to define a new list. Under the **Standard ACL** tab, click **Add** to add an ACL. In Figure 20-10, a new ACL, called **SplitTunnelList**, has been added. Select the newly defined list, click **Add** again under the **Standard ACL**, and add an ACE. In Figure 20-10, an ACE entry for **192.168.1.0/24** has been added with a description of **List to Allow Access to Inside Network.**

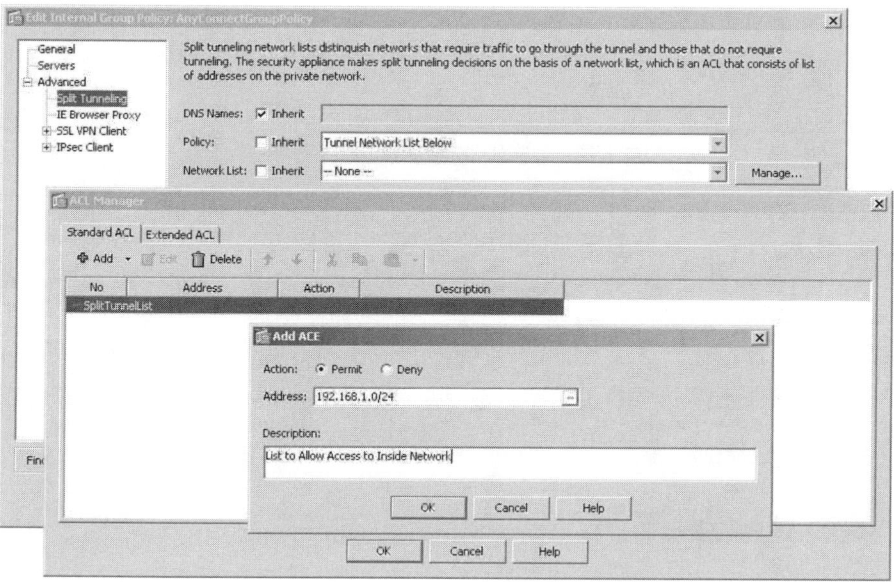

Figure 20-10 *Split Tunneling Configuration*

Example 20-7 shows the CLI equivalent of Figure 20-10.

Example 20-7 *Split Tunnel Configuration*

```
Chicago(config)# access-list SplitTunnelList standard permit 192.168.0.0
255.255.255.0
Chicago(config)# group-policy AnyConnectGroupPolicy attributes
Chicago(config-group-policy)# split-tunnel-policy tunnelspecified
Chicago(config-group-policy)# split-tunnel-network-list value SplitTunnelList
```

DNS and WINS Assignment

For the AnyConnect VPN clients, you can assign DNS and WINS server IP addresses so that they can browse and access internal sites after their SSL tunnel is established. You can configure these attributes by choosing **Configuration > Remote Access VPN > Network (Client) Access > Group Policies > AnyConnectGroupPolicy > Edit > Servers.** To add multiple DNS or WINS servers, use a comma (,) to separate the entries. In Figure 20-11, the primary DNS server is defined as **192.168.1.10** and the secondary DNS server is **192.168.1.20**. The primary WINS server is **192.168.1.20**, and the secondary WINS server is **192.168.1.10**. The default domain name to be pushed to the AnyConnect VPN client is **securemeinc.com.**

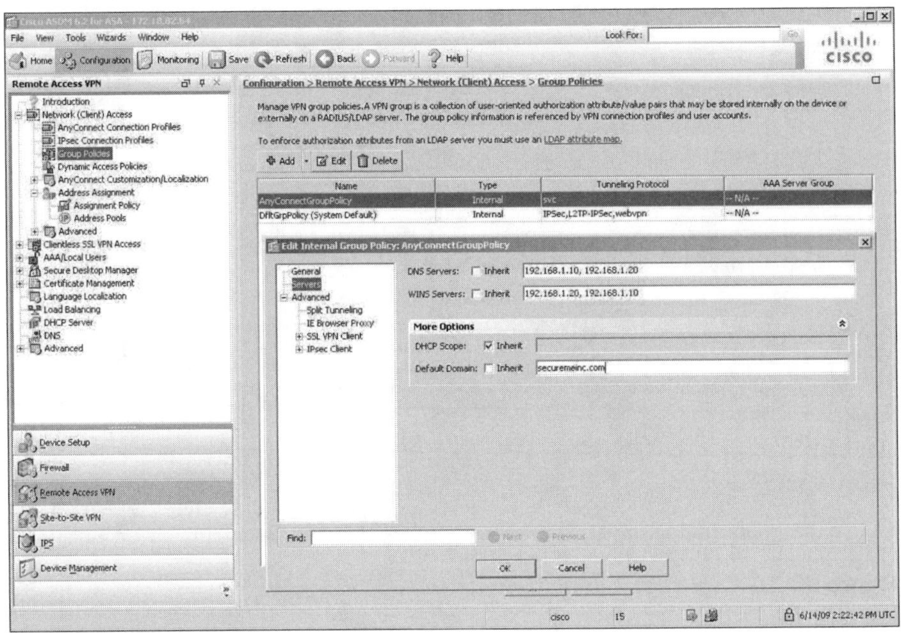

Figure 20-11 *Defining DNS and WINS Servers for AnyConnect VPN clients*

Example 20-8 shows the CLI equivalent of Figure 20-11.

Example 20-8 *Defining DNS and WINS Servers for IPSec VPN Clients*

```
Chicago(config)# group-policy AnyConnectGroupPolicy attributes
Chicago(config-group-policy)# dns-server value 192.168.1.10 192.168.1.20
Chicago(config-group-policy)# wins-server value 192.168.1.20 192.168.1.10
Chicago(config-group-policy)# default-domain value securemeinc.com
```

Keeping the SSL VPN Client Installed

After the AnyConnect client is successfully installed, the security appliance, by default, keeps the client installed on the computer, even if the tunnel is disconnected. You should keep this option enabled so that users do not need to go through the process of installing the client. Additionally, the initial AnyConnect Client installation requires administrative rights. If you do not allow your end users to have administrative privileges, keep the client installed on the workstation. If you want to uninstall the client after the user disconnects the SSL VPN tunnel, navigate to **Configuration > Remote Access VPN > Network (Client) Access > Group Policies > AnyConnectGroupPolicy > Edit > Advanced > SSL VPN Client**, deselect the **Keep Installer on Client System** option, and select **No.**

Example 20-9 shows how you can uninstall the client after the user disconnects the SSL VPN tunnel through the CLI.

Example 20-9 *Uninstalling AnyConnect Client After Session Disconnects*

```
Chicago(config)# group-policy AnyConnectGroupPolicy attributes
Chicago(config-group)# webvpn
Chicago(config-group-webvpn)# svc keep-installer none
```

Configuring DTLS

Datagram Transport Layer Security (DTLS), defined in RFC 4347, provides security and privacy for UDP packets. This allows UDP-based applications to send and receive traffic in a secure fashion without worrying about packet tampering and message forgery. Thus, applications that do not want to be associated with the delays associated with TCP but still want to communicate securely can use DTLS.

Cisco AnyConnect Client supports both SSL as well as DTLS transport protocols. DTLS is enabled, by default, on the security appliance. If it is enabled and UDP is blocked or filtered, communication between the client and the security appliance reverts to the SSL protocol.

You can disable or re-enable DTLS by choosing **Configuration > Remote Access VPN > Network (Client) Access > Group Policies > AnyConnectGroupPolicy > Edit > Advanced > SSL VPN Client**, deselecting the **Inherit** box for the **Datagram TLS** option, and selecting **Enable** or **Disable.**

Note If the security appliance is set up to use RC4-MD5 encryption, the AnyConnect client fails to establish a DTLS tunnel. You can use any other encryption type.

Example 20-10 shows how you to disable DTLS for the **AnyConnectGroupPolicy** group policy, using the CLI.

Example 20-10 *Uninstalling AnyConnect Client After Session Disconnects*

```
Chicago(config)# group-policy AnyConnectGroupPolicy attributes
Chicago(config-group)# webvpn
Chicago(config-group-webvpn)# svc dtls none
```

Configuring Traffic Filters

In its default firewall role, the Cisco ASA allows decrypted traffic to pass through. This is extremely useful if you trust all your remote AnyConnect VPN clients. Cisco ASA permits all decrypted SSL VPN packets to pass through it without inspecting them against the configured ACL.

You can change this default behavior if you want the outside interface ACL to inspect the IPSec-protected traffic by navigating to **Configuration > Remote Access VPN > Network (Client) Access > Advanced > SSL VPN > Bypass Interface Access List** and deselecting the **Enable Inbound IPSec Sessions to Bypass Interface Access-Lists** option. If you prefer to use the CLI, issue the **no sysopt connection permit-vpn** command and define appropriate ACLs to allow VPN traffic to pass through. Example 20-11 shows that only the Telnet traffic from the VPN pool of addresses (192.168.50.0/24) to an inside host located at 192.168.1.10 is allowed to pass through the security appliance.

Example 20-11 *Disabling Sysopt and Configuring ACLs*

```
Chicago(config)# no sysopt connection permit-vpn
Chicago(config)# access-list outside_acl extended permit tcp 192.168.50.0
255.255.255.0 host 192.168.1.10 eq 23
Chicago(config)# access-group outside_acl in interface outside
```

If you do not want to disable the **sysopt connection permit-vpn** and still want to filter VPN traffic for a specific user or group policy, you can define an access list to allow or deny specific traffic and map that access list to a user or group policy.

If you prefer to use ASDM, choose **Configuration** > **Remote Access VPN** > **Network (Client) Access** > **Group Policies** > **AnyConnectGroupPolicy** > **Edit** > **General** > **More Options**, deselect the **Inherit** box for the **IPv4 Filter** option, and select an ACL from the drop-down menu.

Example 20-12 shows that only the Telnet traffic from the VPN pool of addresses (**192.168.50.0/24**) to an inside host located at **192.168.1.10** is allowed to pass through the **AnyConnectGroupPolicy**.

Example 20-12 *Filtering SSL VPN Traffic*

```
Chicago(config)# access-list FilterTelnet extended permit tcp 192.168.50.0
255.255.255.0 host 192.168.1.10 eq telnet
Chicago(config)# group-policy AnyConnectGroupPolicy attributes
Chicago(config-group)# vpn-filter value FilterTelnet
```

AnyConnect Client Configuration

The AnyConnect client must be configured so that it can be connected to the correct security appliance. You do so by defining a client profile and then loading the profile on the client machine.

Creating AnyConnect Client Profile

These configuration settings are stored in the form of user profiles that are automatically delivered to a client machine during connection setup. Some of the things you want to define in the user profile include the following:

- The hostname or the IP address of the security appliance
- Any backup security appliances
- The tunnel group name to which you want to connect
- The username that you want to use for authentication

A user profile is stored locally on the AnyConnect client in an XML file. The name of the file is AnyConnectProfile.xml, and it can be found at the following locations, depending on the operating system.

For Windows-based clients, excluding Vista:

C:\Documents and Settings\All Users\Application Data\Cisco\Cisco AnyConnect VPN Client\Profile

For Windows Vista–based clients:

C:\ProgramData\Cisco\Cisco AnyConnect VPN Client\Profile

For MAC OS X and Linux, the path is as follows

/opt/cisco/vpn/profile

There are two ways to create/modify the AnyConnectProfile.xml file:

- Manual Method
- Profile Editor

Manual Method

Using the manual method, you can create or modify the AnyConnectProfile.xml file by using any XML Editor such as XML Notepad or Arbortext. Example 20-13 shows the output of an AnyConnectProfile.xml file. The IP address of the headend security appliance is defined as 209.165.200.225 and the remote users are allowed to log in to the workstations to launch the AnyConnect client.

Note When the AnyConnect client is installed, it also copies a profile template named as AnyConnectProfile.tmpl. You can use this template to create the AnyConnectProfile.xml file.

Example 20-13 *Output of AnyConnectProfile.xml File*

```
<?xml version="1.0" encoding="UTF-8"?>
<AnyConnectProfile xmlns="http://schemas.xmlsoap.org/encoding/"
xmlns:xsi="http://www.w3.org/2001/XMLSchema-instance"
xsi:schemaLocation="http://schemas.xmlsoap.org/encoding/ AnyConnectProfile.xsd">
     <ClientInitialization>
          <UseStartBeforeLogon UserControllable="true">false</UseStartBeforeLogon>
          <ShowPreConnectMessage>false</ShowPreConnectMessage>
          <LocalLanAccess UserControllable="true">true</LocalLanAccess>
          <AutoReconnect UserControllable="false">true
               <AutoReconnectBehavior
UserControllable="false">DisconnectOnSuspend</AutoReconnectBehavior>
          </AutoReconnect>
          <AutoUpdate UserControllable="false">true</AutoUpdate>
          <WindowsLogonEnforcement>SingleLocalLogon</WindowsLogonEnforcement>
          <WindowsVPNEstablishment>AllowRemoteUsers</WindowsVPNEstablishment>
     </ClientInitialization>
     <ServerList>
          <HostEntry>
               <HostName>209.165.200.225</HostName>
          </HostEntry>
     </ServerList>
</AnyConnectProfile>
```

Note In AnyConnect version 2.3, Cisco introduced the support to allow remote users to log in to a workstation via Windows Remote Desktop. You can now create a VPN connection to a secure gateway from within the Remote Desktop (RDP) session. However, this feature requires that you enable split tunneling on the security appliance.

Profile Editor

A better approach is to use the Profile Editor. It is a Java-based application, developed by Cisco Systems, that enables you to create and modify the Cisco AnyConnect Profile. You can download this file from Cisco.com by searching for AnyConnectProfileEditor. In Figure 20-12, a profile editor is being used to define a new profile. This file must be saved with the .xml extension.

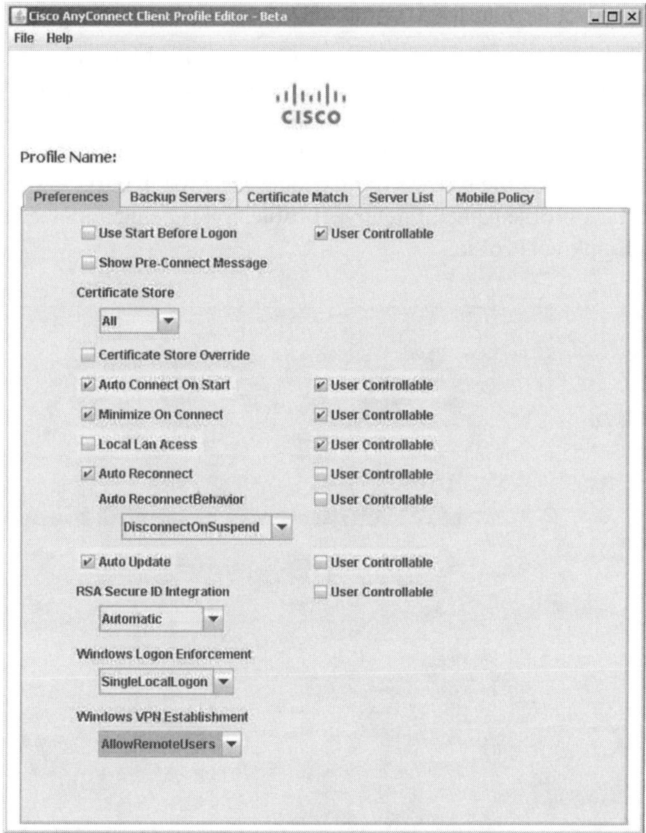

Figure 20-12 *AnyConnect Profile Editor*

> **Tip** A number of tools can be used to validate the output of an XML file. If you create or modify an AnyConnect profile and want to verify the syntax of your XML file, you can validate the file by going to http://tools.decisionsoft.com/schemaValidate/.
>
> This site prompts you to upload you XML profile (AnyConnectProfile.xml) and the schema (AnyConnectProfile.xsd) and produce a report with any found errors. The AnyConnect profile schema file is located in the same directory as the AnyConnectProfile.xml file.

> **Note** For a complete list of all the parameters that can be enabled through Profile Editor, consult the AnyConnect Client Administrator Guide and refer to section "Sample AnyConnect Profile and XML Schema":
>
> http://www.cisco.com/en/US/partner/products/ps8411/prod_maintenance_guides_list.html

Loading AnyConnect Profile into Cisco ASA

After a profile has been created, the next step is to import it into the security appliance and apply it to the users. Navigate to **Configuration** > **Remote Access VPN** > **Network (Client) Access** > **Advanced** > **SSL VPN > Client Settings** and select **Add** under **SSL VPN Client Profiles.** Click **Upload** and select the XML file from your computer. Specify a profile name and start the process of uploading the XML file to the security appliance. In Figure 20-13, a profile named **EmployeeProfile.xml** is being imported into the security appliance as **EmployeeProfile.**

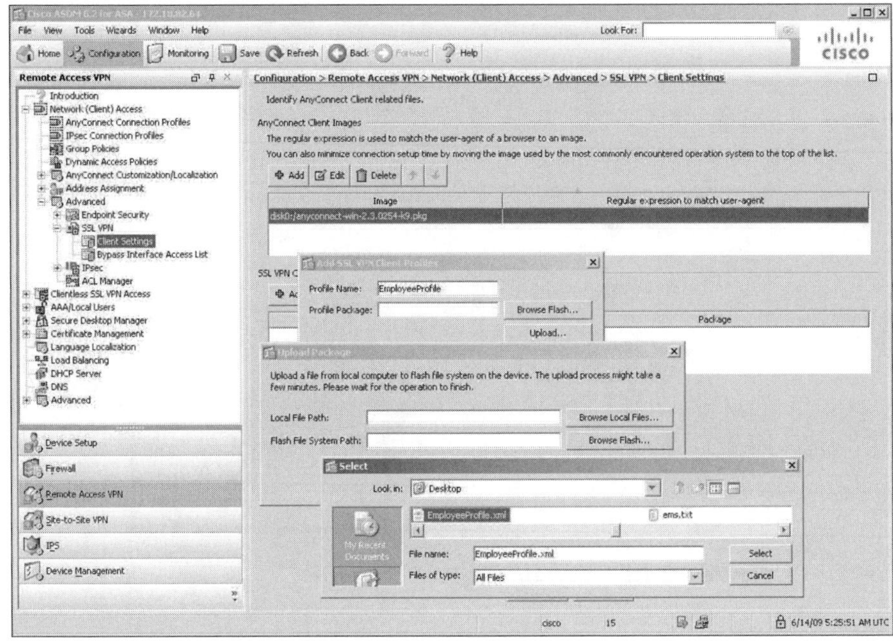

Figure 20-13 *AnyConnect Profile Editor*

After loading the client profile to the security appliance, the next step is to apply the profile to the appropriate group policy. This way, any user connecting to the tunnel group that has the group policy with the profile mapped can receive the updated client policy. Navigate to **Configuration** > **Remote Access VPN** > **Network (Client) Access > Group Policies > AnyConnectGroupPolicy** > **Edit** > **Advanced** > **SSL VPN Client,** deselect the **Inherit** check box next to **Client Profile to Download**, and select **EmployeeProfile** that was defined earlier.

Example 20-14 shows a client profile called **EmployeeProfile** is loaded from the local flash. It is being applied to a group policy called **AnyConnectGroupPolicy.**

Example 20-14 *Loading and Applying Client Profile*

```
Chicago(config)# webvpn
```

```
Chicago(config-webvpn)# svc profiles EmployeeProfile disk0:/EmployeeProfile.xml
Chicago(config-webvpn)# exit
Chicago(config)# group-policy AnyConnectGroupPolicy attributes
Chicago(config-group)# webvpn
Chicago(config-group-webvpn)# svc profiles value EmployeeProfile
```

Connecting from AnyConnect Client

As mentioned earlier in this chapter, there are two ways (web-enabled and standalone) to install the AnyConnect Client to a computer. In the web-enabled mode, the VPN client is downloaded from the security appliance. After it is downloaded, the client connects to the security appliance. For our configuration example, use the web-enabled mode to connect to the appliance, launch a web browser, and navigate to https://sslvpn.securemeinc.com/sslvpnclient.

In standalone mode, the client is downloaded as a standalone application. If the client is not preconfigured, the user needs to specify the IP address or FQDN of the security appliance, the tunnel group to connect to, the username, and the associated password.

Deployment Scenario of AnyConnect Client

The Cisco SSL VPN solution is useful in deployments where remote and home users need access to corporate networks and administrators want to control their access based on a number of attributes. The SSL VPN solution can be deployed in many ways; however, we discuss one design scenario for ease of understanding

Note The design scenario discussed in this chapter should be used solely to reinforce learning.

SecureMe has recently learned about the SSL VPN functionality in Cisco ASA and wants to deploy it for a number of remote employees in Chicago. These employees need full access to the internal network without restriction to complete their tasks if they meet criteria defined by the administrator.

Figure 20-14 shows SecureMe's network topology for AnyConnect Client.

SecureMe's security requirements are as follows:

- Allow full access to the internal network when a user machine is deemed a corporate asset.
- Use a RADIUS server as the external database for user lookup.
- Apply appropriate policies on users based on their user authentication.
- Encrypt all traffic from the client to the security appliance.
- Provide Internet access to remote users via the security appliance.

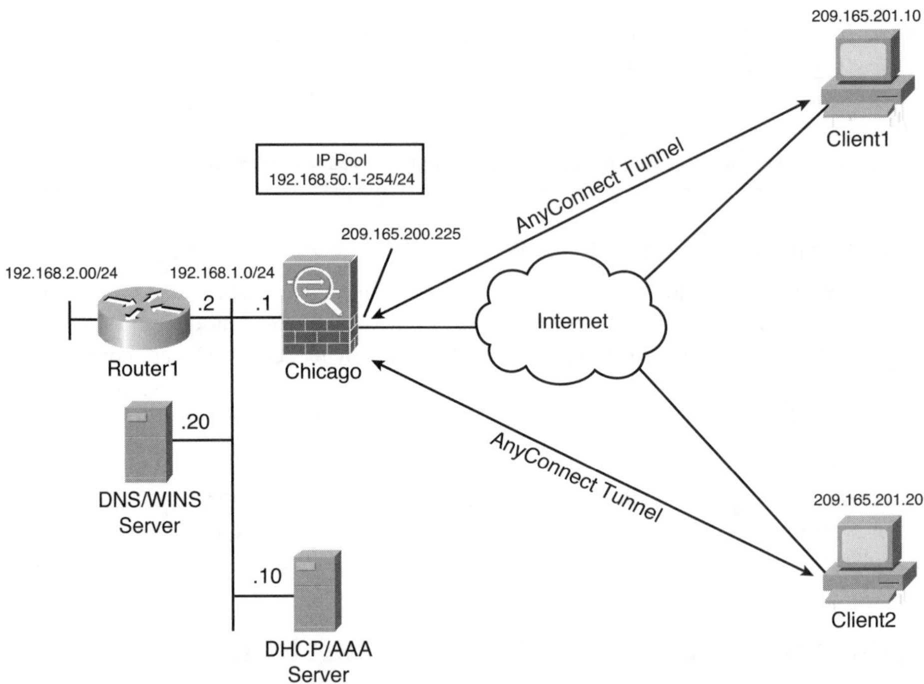

Figure 20-14 *SecureMe's SSL VPN for AnyConnect Clients*

To achieve SecureMe's requirements, the administrator has proposed that the security appliance use CSD and collect information from the remote workstation. If workstations have a registry key of HKLM\SYSTEM\CurrentControlSet\Control\Corp and their IP addresses do not fall within the corporate network range, they are declared "CorpOwnedHomeMachine". Users will be prompted for credentials, and those credentials will be checked against the RADIUS database. If users are successfully authenticated, they will be allowed to establish an SSL VPN tunnel through the AnyConnect Client. After an AnyConnect Client is loaded on the workstation, it should remain installed. On the security appliance, address translation rules need to be configured to provide Internet access to the AnyConnect VPN users.

The steps to implement the proposed solution are as follows:

Step 1. Set up CSD for registry check

Step 2. Set up RADIUS for authentication

Step 3. Configure AnyConnect SSL VPN

Step 4. Enable address translation for internet access

The following sections cover these steps in detail.

Step 1: Set Up CSD For Registry Check

The first step in achieving the listed goals is to create a secure environment for remote users. You do so by following these steps:

Step 1. Choose **Configuration > Remote Access VPN > Secure Desktop Manager > Setup**, click **Browse Flash** to select the CSD file you want to use, and select **Enable Secure Desktop.**

Step 2. Choose **Configuration** > **Remote Access VPN** > **Secure Desktop Manager** > **Prelogin Policy** and define a prelogin sequence based on registry key and IP address range. Create a new Windows location called **CorpOwnedHomeMachines** that has a registry key check of **HKLM\SYSTEM\CurrentControlSet\Control\Corp** and an address check where the address should not fall in the **209.165.200.224/27** subnet.

Step 3. Choose **Configuration** > **Remote Access VPN** > **Secure Desktop Manager** > **CorpOwnedHomeMachines** and deselect the **Secure Desktop** and the **Cache Cleaner** option.

Step 2: Set Up RADIUS for Authentication

The second step is to set up a RADIUS server for user authentication. Do so by following these guidelines:

Step 1. Choose **Configuration** > **Remote Access VPN** > **AAA/Local Users** > **AAA Server Groups** > **Add.** Specify the server group called **RADIUS** and select **RADIUS** from the drop-down menu. Click **OK** when finished.

Step 2. Click the newly created server group, and under **Servers in the Selected Groups**, click **Add.** Under **Interface Name**, select **inside** from the drop-down menu and specify **192.168.1.10** as the IP address of the RADIUS server. Configure a **Server Secret Key** of **SecureMe123** and click **OK** when finished.

Step 3: Configure AnyConnect SSL VPN

The third step needed to meet the listed requirements is to configure AnyConnect VPN client on the security appliance for remote users. Follow these guidelines to achieve the goals:

Step 1. Choose **Configuration** > **Remote Access VPN** > **Network (Client) Access** > **Advanced** > **SSL VPN** > **Client Settings** > **Add.** Click **Browse Files**, select a **AnyConnect VPN client**, and click **OK.**

Step 2. After loading the AnyConnect Client, enable full tunnel client functionality on the outside interface. This is achieved by selecting the **Enable Cisco AnyConnect VPN Client or Legacy SSL VPN Client Access on the Interfaces Selected in the Table Below** option under **Configuration** > **Remote Access VPN** > **Network (Client) Access** > **AnyConnect Connection Profiles**

on the **outside** interface. Make sure that the **Allow Access** check box is selected for the outside interface. Also select the **Enable DTLS** option.

Step 3. Choose **Configuration > Remote Access VPN > Network (Client) Access > Address Assignment > Address Pools > Add.** Under **Name**, specify **SSLVPNPool** and configure **192.168.50.1** through **192.168.50.254** as the pool of addresses and a mask of **255.255.255.0.**

Step 4. Choose **Configuration > Remote Access VPN > Network (Client) Access > Group Policies > Add.** Specify **AnyConnectGroupPolicy** as the group policy name. Under **Address Pools**, deselect the **Inherit** check box and select **SSLVPNPool.**

Step 5. Click the option for **Advanced > Split Tunneling** in the left pane. Under **Policy**, deselect the **Inherit** check box and select **Tunnel All Networks.**

Step 6. Click the **Servers** option in the left pane and configure **192.168.1.20** as the WINS and DNS server addresses.

Step 7. Click the **Advanced > SSL VPN Client** option in the left pane and make sure that **Keep Installer on Client System** option is enabled and set to **Yes.** Click **OK** when you are finished.

Step 8. Create a new tunnel group by choosing **Configuration > Remote Access VPN > Network (Client) Access > AnyConnect Connection Profiles.** Under **Connection Profiles**, click **Add** and specify **SecureMeAnyConnect** as the tunnel group name. Select **RADIUS** under **AAA Server Group** and select **AnyConnectGroupPolicy** under **Default Group Policy.** Make sure that the **SSL VPN Client Protocol** check box is selected.

Step 9. Click the **Advanced > SSL VPN** option in the left pane. Under **Group URL**, click **Add** and specify **https://sslvpn.securemeinc.com/sslvpnclient. Verify that the** Enable **check box is selected. Click** OK **to exit.**

Step 4: Enable Address Translation for Internet Access

The final step is to define address translation. The AnyConnect clients send all encrypted data to the security appliance. For the AnyConnect clients to access the Internet, you must define address translation rules for the pool of addresses handed out to the clients. You do so by following these guidelines:

Step 1. Choose **Configuration > Device Setup > Interfaces** and select **Enable Traffic Between Two or More Hosts Connected to the Same Interface.**

Step 2. Choose **Configuration > Firewall > NAT Rules > Add > Add Dynamic NAT Rules.** Under the Translated section, click **Manage > Add** and configure the following policy for the Global Address Pool:

- **Interface: outside**
- **Pool ID: 1**

- **IP Address to Add: Port Address Translation (PAT)**, using IP address of the interface. Click **Add>>** and then **OK** when done.

Step 3. Configure the following **NAT Access Rule** under the **Original** section:

- **Interface: outside**
- **Source: 192.168.50.0/24**
- **Translated Global Pool ID: 1**. Click **OK** when done.

You can now connect to the ASA, using the following URL in your browser: https://sslvpn.securemeinc.com/sslvpnclient.

Monitoring and Troubleshooting AnyConnect SSL VPNs

The following sections discuss the monitoring and troubleshooting steps that are available to help you in running the SSL VPN solution smoothly on a security appliance.

Monitoring SSL VPN

To monitor the WebVPN sessions, first check how many active SSL VPN tunnels are established on the security appliance. You can do this by choosing **Monitoring** > **VPN** > **VPN Statistics** > **Sessions**. The security appliance shows you all the active VPN sessions, including the clientless and full tunnel client connections. As shown in Figure 20-15, an active AnyConnect connection is created by a user called cisco. The user computer's assigned IP address is 192.168.1.151, and the negotiated encryption type is RC4. The security appliance has received 15,923 bytes of traffic, whereas it has transmitted 655 bytes of data to the client. The user is connected for almost seven minutes. Should you prefer to get detailed information about a user's connection, select that specific user session and then click the **Details** button.

Troubleshooting SSL VPN

Cisco ASA provides a number of troubleshooting and diagnostic commands for SSL VPNs. The following sections focus on two troubleshooting scenarios related to SSL VPN.

Troubleshooting SSL Negotiations

If you have a user who is not able to connect to the security appliance using SSL, you can follow these steps to isolate the SSL negotiation issues:

Step 1. Verify that the user's computer can ping the security appliance's outside IP address.

Step 2. If the user's workstation can ping the address, issue the **show running all | include ssl** command on the security appliance and verify that SSL encryption is configured.

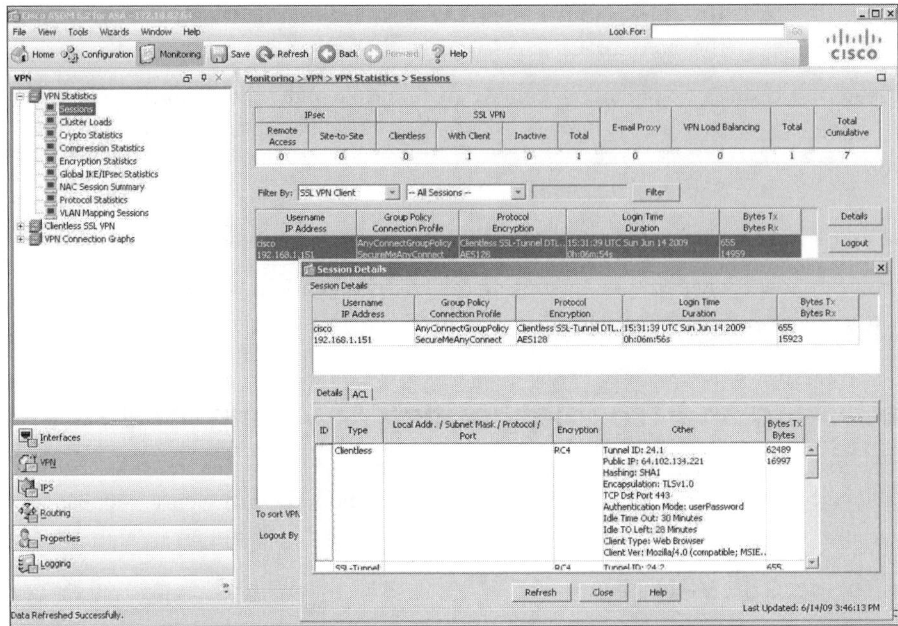

Figure 20-15 *Monitoring SSL VPN Sessions Through ASDM*

Step 3. If SSL encryption is properly configured, use an external sniffer to verify whether the TCP three-way handshake is successful.

> **Note** AnyConnect clients will fail to establish connection if the security appliances are configured to accept connection with SSL Server version v3. You must use TLSv1 for AnyConnect clients. Navigate **to Configuration > Remote Access VPN > Advanced > SSL Settings** to specify the SSL encryption type and version that you want to use.

Troubleshooting AnyConnect Client Issues

The following sections provide guidelines on troubleshooting the commonly seen AnyConnect VPN client issues and cover troubleshooting two issues.

Initial Connectivity Issues

If you are using AnyConnect VPN client in your environment and a user is having initial connectivity issues, enable **debug webvpn svc** on the security appliance and analyze the debug messages. You can fix most of the configuration-specific issues easily by looking at the error messages. For example, if your security appliance is not configured to assign an IP address, you receive a "No assigned address" error message in the debugs. This is highlighted in Example 20-15.

Example 20-15 debug webvpn svc *Command*

```
Chicago# debug webvpn svc
CSTP state = HEADER_PROCESSING
http_parse_cstp_method()
...input: 'CONNECT /CSCOSSLC/tunnel HTTP/1.1'
webvpn_cstp_parse_request_field()
...input: 'Host: 209.165.200.225'
<snip>
Processing CSTP header line: 'X-DTLS-CipherSuite: AES256-SHA:AES128-SHA:DES-CBC3-
SHA:DES-CBC-SHA'
Validating address: 0.0.0.0
CSTP state = WAIT_FOR_ADDRESS
webvpn_cstp_accept_address: 0.0.0.0/0.0.0.0
webvpn_cstp_accept_address: no address?!?
CSTP state = HAVE_ADDRESS
No assigned address
webvpn_cstp_send_error: 503 Service Unavailable
CSTP state = ERROR
```

Optionally, you can enable an SVC-specific syslog on the security appliance and look at the messages. For example, if the security appliance does not assign an IP address to an AnyConnect client, you should see the "No address available for SVC connection" message, as shown in Example 20-16.

Example 20-16 *SVC Logging*

```
Chicago(config)# logging on
Chicago(config)# logging class svc buffered debugging
Chicago(config)# exit
Chicago# show logging
%ASA-3-722020: TunnelGroup <SSLVPNTunnel> GroupPolicy <AnyConnectGroupPolicy> User
<sslvpnuser> IP <209.165.200.230> No address available for SVC connection
```

Additionally, you can look at the AnyConnect VPN client logs in Windows Event Viewer. Choose **Start > Settings > Control Panel > Administrative Tools > Event Viewer > Cisco AnyConnect VPN client** and review the logs. If an address is not being assigned, you should see an error message.

Traffic-Specific Issues

If you are able to connect but fail to successfully send traffic over the SSL VPN tunnel, look at the traffic statistics on the client to verify that traffic is being received and transmitted by the client. As illustrated in Figure 20-16, the client has encrypted 6886 bytes and decrypted 1529 bytes. Therefore, as far as the client is concerned, it is transmitting and receiving traffic.

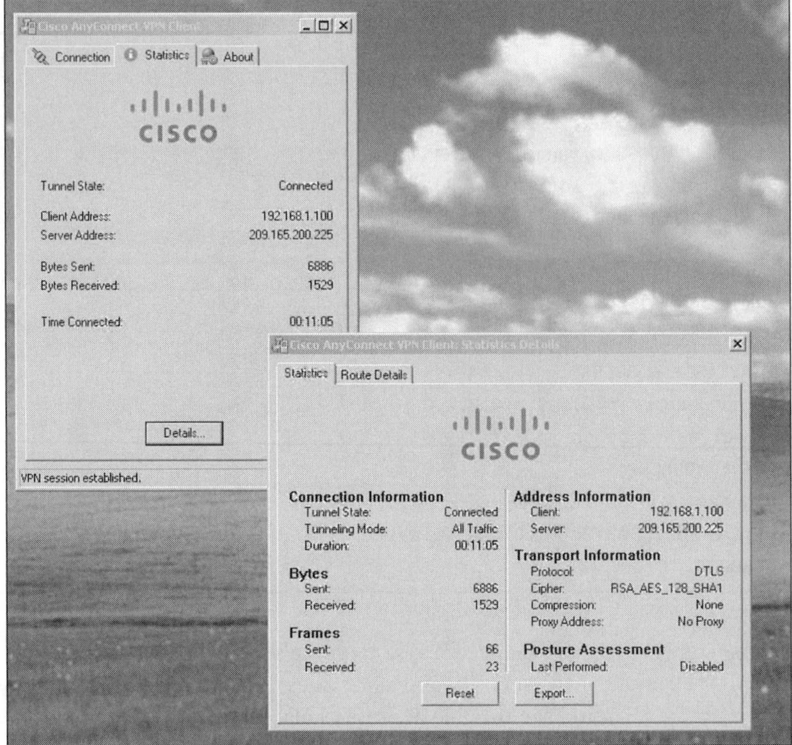

Figure 20-16 *Monitoring SSL VPN Traffic Statistics on AnyConnect VPN Client*

Next, check the security appliance for received and transmitted traffic, as shown previously in Figure 20-15. If the security appliance applies a filter, the filter name is shown and you can look at the ACL entries to check whether your traffic is being dropped.

Note If you are using a MAC AnyConnect VPN client, the logs are stored at /var/log/system.log.

If you are troubleshooting AnyConnect VPN client issues, the logs are stored at ~/Library/Logs/CrashReporter/Cisco AnyConnect VPN Client.crash.log.

Summary

This chapter provided details about the AnyConnect SSL VPN functionality in Cisco ASA. Using the robust features available in Cisco ASA SSL VPN remote access, security administrators can deploy Cisco ASA in almost any network topology. The chapter also focused on using the AnyConnect profile editor to show how a client profile can be defined. To reinforce learning, a deployment scenario was presented, along with configurations. This chapter covered extensive **show** and **debug** commands to assist in troubleshooting complicated AnyConnect VPN deployments.

Index

SYMBOLS

A

B

C

D

E

F

G

H

I

J - K

L

M

N

O

P

Q

R

S

T

U

V

W

X - Y - Z

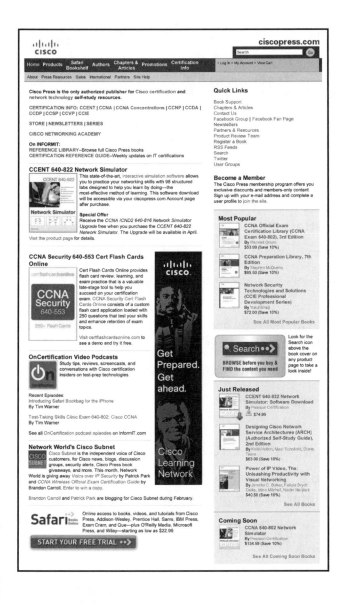

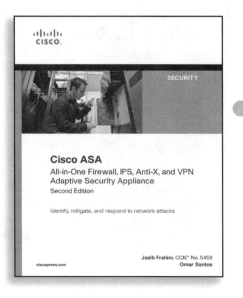

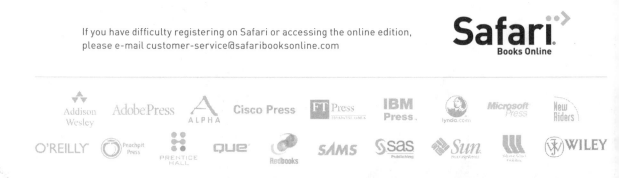